THE HANDBOOK OF NATIONAL LEGISLATURES

Where is the power? Students of politics have pondered this question, and social scientists have scrutinized formal political institutions and the distribution of power among agencies of the government and the state. But we still lack a rich bank of data measuring the power of specific governmental agencies, particularly national legislatures.

This book assesses the strength of the national legislature of every country in the world with a population of at least a half-million inhabitants. The Legislative Powers Survey (LPS) is a list of thirty-two items that gauges the legislature's sway over the executive, its institutional autonomy, its authority in specific areas, and its institutional capacity. Data were generated by means of a vast international survey of experts, extensive study of secondary sources, and painstaking analysis of constitutions and other relevant documents. Individual country chapters provide answers to each of the thirty-two survey items, supplemented by expert commentary and relevant excerpts from constitutions.

M. Steven Fish is Professor of Political Science at the University of California, Berkeley. He is author of *Democracy Derailed in Russia: The Failure of Open Politics* (2005), which was the recipient of the Best Book Award of 2006 presented by the Comparative Democratization Section of the American Political Science Association. He is also author of *Democracy from Scratch: Opposition and Regime in the New Russian Revolution* (1995) and a coauthor of *Postcommunism and the Theory of Democracy* (2001). His articles have appeared in *World Politics, Comparative Political Studies, Journal of Democracy, Post-Soviet Affairs,* and other journals. He served as a Senior Fulbright Fellow and Visiting Professor at Airlangga University, Surabaya, Indonesia, in 2007 and at the European University at St. Petersburg, St. Petersburg, Russia, in 2000–1. In 2005 he was the recipient of the Distinguished Social Sciences Teaching Award of the College of Letters and Science, University of California, Berkeley.

Matthew Kroenig is Assistant Professor in the Department of Government and the Edmund A. Walsh School of Foreign Service at Georgetown University. His articles have appeared in *Security Studies, Foreign Policy, Democratization,* and other journals. He has held fellowships from the National Science Foundation, the Belfer Center for Science and International Affairs at Harvard University, the Center for International Security and Cooperation at Stanford University, and the Institute on Global Conflict and Cooperation at the University of California. He has also served as a strategist on the policy-planning staff in the Office of the Secretary of Defense, where he was the principal author of the first-ever U.S. government-wide strategy for deterring terrorist networks. For his work he received the Office of the Secretary of Defense's Award for Outstanding Achievement.

For our parents,
Michael Fish and Cherrie Robinson
and
Mark Kroenig and Barb Kroenig

The Handbook of National Legislatures

A GLOBAL SURVEY

M. Steven Fish

University of California, Berkeley

Matthew Kroenig

Georgetown University

CAMBRIDGE
UNIVERSITY PRESS

CAMBRIDGE UNIVERSITY PRESS
Cambridge, New York, Melbourne, Madrid, Cape Town,
Singapore, São Paulo, Delhi, Tokyo, Mexico City

Cambridge University Press
32 Avenue of the Americas, New York, NY 10013-2473, USA

www.cambridge.org
Information on this title: www.cambridge.org/9781107602472

© M. Steven Fish and Matthew Kroenig 2009

First published 2009
First paperback edition 2011

A catalog record for this publication is available from the British Library.

Library of Congress Cataloging in Publication Data

Fish, M. Steven (Michael Steven), 1962–
The handbook of national legislatures : a global survey / M. Steven Fish and
Matthew Kroenig.
    p.   cm.
Includes bibliographical references and index.
ISBN 978-0-521-51466-8 (hardback)
1. Legislative bodies – Handbooks, manuals, etc. I. Kroenig, Matthew. II. Title.
JF511.F57 2008
328.03–dc22   2008010769

ISBN   978-0-521-51466-8 Hardback
ISBN   978-1-107-60247-2 Paperback

CONTENTS

1 Introduction

This book is the product of a lot of curiosity and a bit of dissatisfaction. The curiosity focuses on a matter that interests anyone who studies politics: Where is the power? The dissatisfaction arises from the shortage of information that addresses that question in a global framework. We are particularly interested in where *official* power – that is, the power vested in the government and the organs of state – resides. In our research on a variety of topics, each of us – one a student of comparative politics, the other a specialist in international relations – consistently encounters a shortage of information. In our many conversations with colleagues both inside and outside the academy, we have come to realize that demand for information on where power resides exceeds supply. For millennia, students of politics have analyzed power, and for at least a century, social scientists have scrutinized formal political institutions and the distribution of power among agencies of government and the state. But we still do not have a rich bank of data measuring the power of this or that agency, and information on legislatures is in especially short supply. For many countries one is hard-pressed to find any relevant information at all. In recent decades, pioneering scholars, particularly in political science, have taken up the challenge of studying legislatures outside the advanced industrialized countries. Still, writings on legislatures in many parts of the world remain negligible, even if the quality of available studies is often high. As we found as we scoured the scholarly literature, articles on the newly resurrected Scottish parliament, which was established in 1999 to handle matters that the parliament of the United Kingdom devolved to it, outnumber articles on the legislatures of all African countries combined.

We therefore set out to assess the powers of the central representative institution of national politics, and to do so for all countries of the world. We knew – and at the end of our efforts are even more acutely aware – that measuring the powers of legislatures perfectly is a vain hope. We nevertheless decided that an attempt to measure those powers, even if the results were imperfect, promised to generate useful data, which is the aim of this volume.

We expect that this information will be of interest primarily to social scientists, but we hope that government officials, political activists, journalists, staffers in nongovernmental organizations, businesspeople, lawyers, and indeed anyone interested in politics will find it useful as well.

This study is not the first to attempt to measure the powers of legislatures, but it encompasses a richer array of dimensions of power and includes a larger number of countries than the handful of other available studies. To the best of our knowledge, moreover, no work on the powers of any other official bodies – presidencies, judiciaries, militaries, particular ministries, or other agencies – provides the depth or breadth of coverage that the present work furnishes on legislatures.[1]

Our main tool is the Legislative Powers Survey (LPS). The LPS is a list of thirty-two items that gauge thirty-two separate indicators of the legislature's strength. We administered the LPS as a survey to country experts. We complemented the survey findings with our own analysis of national constitutions and other relevant sources. We then used the LPS as the basis for generating a Parliamentary Powers Index (PPI). The PPI, which ranges from zero (least powerful) to one (most powerful), is a score that reflects a legislature's aggregate strength.

The present chapter, an introduction to the study, places our effort in the context of contemporary writings on constitutional systems, examines the survey on which our study is based, discusses each item in the survey, presents the index that was created using the survey, explains how constitutional excerpts are adduced, and ruminates on how the study might be used. It closes by

---

[1] For other efforts to measure the powers of official bodies, see, for example, Matthew Soberg Shugart and John M. Carey, *Presidents and Assemblies: Constitutional Design and Electoral Dynamics* (Cambridge: Cambridge University Press, 1992); Timothy Frye, "A Politics of Institutional Choice: Post-Communist Presidencies," *Comparative Political Studies* 30, 5 (October 1997), pp. 523–52; and André Krouwel, "Measuring Presidentialism and Parliamentarism: An Application to Central and East European Countries," *Acta Politica* 38, 4 (2003), pp. 333–64.

acknowledging the assistance of those who have made a special contribution to the project. Chapter 2, which forms the heart of the book, presents the country studies. There is one study on each country. Each begins with a brief narrative overview, followed by the results of the survey. The answer to each item in the survey for the country is provided. Along with each answer, we include commentary as well as the relevant excerpt from the country's constitution where appropriate. Chapter 3 furnishes lists of the data generated by the survey. Chapter 4 presents a list of the experts who participated in the survey. The book concludes with a bibliography, which, while extensive, is incomplete. We could not provide a comprehensive list of relevant works, but merely listed those that we found especially useful in creating the present volume.

CONVENTIONAL CATEGORIES OF CONSTITUTIONAL SYSTEMS

The tripartite classification of parliamentary, semipresidential, and presidential systems, as well as the expanded typology of parliamentary, premier-presidential, president-parliamentary, and presidential systems, has long guided scholars. Yet these typologies have obvious limitations. They produce categorical rather than ordinal data, which limits their usefulness for empirical analysis. Furthermore, classifying countries is often problematic. Scholars agree that if elements of the legislature form the government, the prime minister exercises considerable executive power and answers to the legislature, and there is no president or one who is elected by the legislature, the system is parliamentary. Yet that is where easy agreement ends. Some analysts hold that any system in which the president is elected directly cannot be classified as parliamentary, but should be considered semipresidential (or presidential), even if the president has only ceremonial functions. Others, embracing Maurice Duverger's classic conceptualization of semipresidentialism, hold that the president must have substantial power for the system to qualify as semipresidential (or presidential); otherwise it is parliamentary.[2] Thus, some scholars consider Ireland's system semipresidential; others say it is parliamentary. Some classify Bulgaria's system as semipresidential; others say it is parliamentary.

Analysts also differ over the boundary between semipresidential and presidential systems.

Duverger considered a system semipresidential if the president is directly elected and has considerable power but there is also a prime minister who is accountable to the legislature. Yet in some countries that formally meet these requirements, the legislature's instruments for controlling the government are paltry. In such cases some scholars see semipresidentialism, whereas others see presidentialism. Kazakhstan and Russia are examples.

In sum, the conventional distinctions among constitutional systems do not fully specify where power resides. And where power resides is what matters for real-life politics and government.

The data presented in this volume suggest that even within each of the major types of constitutional systems there is wide variation in the capacity of legislatures. The Parliamentary Powers Index scores show that in some parliamentary systems, the legislature is, in fact, very powerful. In Germany and Macedonia, it is the main stage of national politics. In other parliamentary systems, the legislature is strong but nevertheless shares substantial power with extra-parliamentary agencies, be they monarchs, militaries, presidents, dominant prime ministers, Governors General, or someone else. Australia and Thailand (even before the latter country's 2006 coup) are examples. These countries' scores on the PPI are markedly lower than those of Germany and Macedonia. In still other countries with parliamentary systems, despite formal provisions for parliamentarism, the legislature is subordinated to a prime minister whose power depends less on parliament than on a hegemonic party, the military, or some other extra-parliamentary agency. Ethiopia and Malaysia fit this description.

Great variation in the actual powers of the legislature is also – indeed, especially – found among semipresidential systems. Some semipresidential systems have weak legislatures, as in Russia and Kazakhstan. Others have commanding legislatures and highly constrained presidents, as in Austria and Mongolia. Some countries with semipresidential systems fall in between, meaning that the legislature has substantial but not vast power, as in France and Taiwan.

Variation in the legislature's powers is also conspicuous among presidential systems. Some countries have an overpowering presidency and a marginal legislature, as in Belarus, Kenya, and Uzbekistan. Some include a legislature that is not a commanding force but that is still influential, for example, Honduras, Indonesia, and Namibia. Yet other presidential systems, such as those of Georgia and South Korea, include still more potent

---

[2] Maurice Duverger, "A New Political System: Semi-Presidential Government," *European Journal of Political Research* 8, 1 (June 1980), pp. 165–87.

legislatures. The data presented in this volume show that the national legislatures of Nicaragua, Ukraine, the United States, and Uruguay, with their presidential systems, are as potent or nearly as potent as their counterparts in Australia, Jamaica, Japan, and South Africa, which have parliamentary systems.

THE LEGISLATIVE POWERS SURVEY

We realized that if we wanted to gauge how much power is actually lodged in the legislature, we would have to grapple with issues that are not always encoded in law. For example, after engaging in preliminary canvassing of experts and parliamentarians, and relying on simple common sense, we decided that whether or not legislators have support staff might affect the legislature's institutional capacity. Yet this matter is rarely addressed in constitutions; often it is not addressed in any law at all. A second example is found in the question of whether or not the legislature has a substantial voice in the operation of the state-owned media. Influence over the media is a matter that is of consequence for the legislature's power, yet the law is often silent or ambiguous on this issue.

The inclusion of such matters in our assessments clarified for us the need to consult experts. The indispensability of expert opinion became more obvious when we realized that even some questions that seemed exceedingly straightforward are not always so simple to answer in practice.

Thus we embarked upon the long, trying, rewarding endeavor of administering the Legislature Powers Survey as a questionnaire to specialists who have expert knowledge of specific countries. The questionnaire consisted of the thirty-two items (which we also call "questions" here) used in this volume with the following introductory material:[3]

---

[3] As we compiled and examined the completed questionnaires and other sources, we realized that our wording of three of the items had not reflected precisely what we were trying to assess, and we slightly modified the wording of the item in the final product. The first of those items is number 7, which was originally stated as "The legislature's approval is required to confirm the appointment of individual ministers; or the legislature itself appoints ministers." Here we deleted the word "individual" in the final analysis. The second item is number 9. Here, in its original formulation, the item read: "The legislature can vote no confidence in the government without jeopardizing its own term (that is, without the threat of dissolution)." We subsequently realized that we were concerned with the right to vote no confidence alone, and we deleted "without jeopardizing its own term (that is, without the threat of dissolution)." The third item is question 12. The item originally read: "Laws passed by the legislature are veto-proof

ITEMS FOR CONSTRUCTION OF AN INDEX MEASURING THE POWERS OF THE NATIONAL LEGISLATURE

EXPERT SURVEY

The authors have attempted to phrase each statement such that affirmation of the statement indicates greater rather than lesser power for the national legislature. Thus, affirmation of each statement (one could also think in terms of a "check mark" next to each statement) would produce a score of 32, indicating an all-powerful legislature. A very low score would indicate a weak legislature. Please simply place a plus sign just to the left of the number of the statement if it applies to the country you are evaluating. Please indicate the name of the country at the top of the survey, and please use a different copy of this survey for each country you evaluate. If you believe that the statement cannot be said to apply or not apply without some qualification, please write the basis for your qualification in on the survey.

We asked the experts to affirm or negate the statement made in each item. We realized that such an up-or-down answer may fail to capture complexity, and we invited the experts to provide comments on any item they wished. Many experts did write remarks, often extensive, in response to specific items. Their comments provided a trove of precious information that we tapped in preparing this book.

Aware that people make mistakes and that some items in the survey require judgment calls, we solicited answers from numerous specialists on each country. We set the goal of obtaining five completed questionnaires for each country. After launching the quest for experts, we saw the advantages of offering the survey in multiple languages, so we had it translated into Spanish and French.

The survey is very much the product of the Internet age: It would have been impossible before the advent of the World Wide Web, which we used to hunt for specialists. We sought experts primarily from academia, but we also raided the ranks of parliamentarians and parliamentary staffers, jurists, diplomats, and journalists. We also sought out leaders of think tanks, nongovernmental organizations, and international organizations. In most instances we sent the survey by e-mail, and received the completed survey back by e-mail.

or essentially veto-proof; that is, the executive lacks veto power, or has veto power but the veto can be overridden by a simple majority in the legislature." We found that an ambiguity between the common and technical meaning of simple majority caused confusion, and we deleted the word "simple." Furthermore, the order of the questions in the questionnaires differed a bit from what we present here as the final survey. As we assessed responses and prepared this volume, we saw that we could slightly improve the presentation for readers by changing the placement of a handful of items, which we did.

Occasionally a respondent mailed us a paper copy, or answered the survey in face-to-face meetings in which we posed the questions and received answers orally.

For some countries, everyone we asked to participate responded positively, and five requests yielded five completed surveys. But such magical moments were rare. Much more frequently, some of those we contacted declined, and our hunt for experts continued. Many people who declined kindly put us in touch with colleagues; we thus used experts to find other experts. We offered no compensation. People participated solely out of graciousness and dedication to advancing knowledge. Given our determination to secure at least five responses per country, and that we cover every country in the world that had a population of a half-million or more inhabitants as of 2000, our efforts stretched on for nearly half a decade. We began contacting experts in late 2002. In late 2006 we finally had all the responses we needed.

Yet we failed to get all the responses we wanted. Although we averaged over five responses per country for the world as a whole, for some countries no amount of canvassing would yield five completed surveys. Unsurprisingly, most of these countries do not have functioning legislatures, and their legislatures are rarely, if ever, the object of scholarly or public inquiry. In some of these countries, the state itself is falling apart or has already disintegrated; in some, the state is new and is still in formation; in still others, the political order does not include a place for a bona fide legislature. The countries for which we failed to obtain the desired five respondents are Bhutan, Chad, Comoros, Côte d'Ivoire, Cuba, Eritrea, Haiti, Iraq, Jamaica, North Korea, Laos, Liberia, Myanmar, Oman, Qatar, Saudi Arabia, Somalia, Sudan, Timor-Leste, and Vietnam. In these cases we did the best we could with the expertise available to us.

THE SURVEY ITEMS

The LPS, which the experts answered as a survey, consists of thirty-two items. The first nine items gauge the legislature's *influence over the executive*. They ask whether the legislature can oust the executive, have its own members serve in the government, question officials from the executive, investigate the executive, oversee the agencies of coercion, appoint the prime minister (if there is one), appoint or at least confirm ministers, elect the president (if there is one), and express no confidence in the government. Items 10–18 evaluate the legislature's *institutional autonomy*. They ask whether the legislature is immune from dissolution by

the executive, vested with exclusive lawmaking authority, free from the threat of an effective executive veto, free from the threat of judicial review, able to legislate on any issue, in charge of government expenditures, in control of its own finances, composed of members who are immune from arrest, and free from executive appointees. The third group of items, numbers 19–26, focuses on *specified powers*. Items in this category inquire about whether the legislature is vested with powers to change the constitution, authorize war, ratify treaties, grant amnesty, grant pardon, influence judicial appointments, appoint the head of the central bank, and influence the state-owned media. The final group, numbers 27–32, measures the legislature's *institutional capacity*. It assesses whether legislators meet regularly, have staff, are eligible for re-election, seek re-election, and number among their own a significant cohort of experienced colleagues.

Each survey item is dichotomous. If the legislature possesses the power in question, the item is scored in the affirmative. If the legislature lacks the power in question, the item is scored in the negative. The use of an identical, dichotomous scoring system for each question provides the benefits of consistency across the questions and allows for the aggregation of the individual items into the larger index. Of course, some of the items measured in this survey could be conceived of as having more than two categories. For example, question 7 asks whether "The legislature's approval is required to confirm the appointment of ministers; or the legislature itself appoints ministers." This item is scored in the affirmative if either of the above statements is true. Alternatively, this item could have been scored as having three separate categories (the legislature appoints, the legislature confirms, or the legislature has no appointment power) in rank order. This alternative scoring system might have provided greater precision, but would also have made it exceedingly difficult to present the data, to compare items to one another, and to aggregate the items into a broader index. We believe that the gain in the consistency of a yes/no answer to every question outweighs the potential loss of precision. To capture the varieties of power within any particular item, we note the range of categories that potentially exist for each item in the discussion of the items below and in the country chapters. In this way we hope to provide anyone interested in developing a more fine-grained measure of any specific item with the information necessary to do so.

Some of the items may appear to be strictly "applicable" only to parliamentary – or, alternatively, presidential or semipresidential – systems. Indeed, framing the survey items in language that makes sense in the context of every country in the world, across all conceivable types of constitutional systems, was challenging. Nevertheless, we believe that we have succeeded. By disregarding the distinction among types of systems and focusing instead on specific powers, moreover, we may have uncovered a blind spot in political science. Many scholars trained in the West are understandably accustomed to thinking in terms of the idealtypical systems represented by, say, the United Kingdom's Westminster model and the United States' presidential model, but such "pure types" are rare. Outside of Western Europe and North America it is difficult to find "pure" parliamentary, semipresidential, or presidential systems. As the present study reveals, many of the world's legislatures are, in a sense, hybrids. For example, many countries in Africa have a directly elected president and a prime minister accountable to parliament, as well as a mechanism for impeachment and a vote of no confidence. Moreover, one sometimes finds answers that are especially illuminating in cases in which at first glance there might appear to be a poor "fit" between the survey item and the country's constitutional system. For example, executive veto power (addressed in item 12) might seem irrelevant to parliamentary systems, where executive and legislative powers are fused. Why, after all, would the executive veto its own legislation? Yet some parliamentary systems have a president or a monarch who wields veto power. One even finds an example of parliamentarism in which the executive has what we consider an effective veto, meaning that the veto can be overridden only by a supermajority in the legislature. In Thailand a two-thirds majority vote is required to override the monarch's veto. Furthermore, questions on the appointment of the prime minister (item 6) and the executive's dissolution powers (item 10) might seem to be irrelevant to presidential systems. In the classic paradigm of presidentialism, such as one finds in the United States, there is no prime minister, and the legislature has a fixed term. But numerous countries with presidential systems actually also have a prime minister and/or provisions for presidential dissolution of the legislature. The presidential systems of Armenia, Belarus, Burkina Faso, and Mali, for example, all have prime ministers, and the legislatures in each lack fixed terms and are subject to dissolution by the president.

In sum, in many polities legislatures hold a grab bag of powers rather than neat sets of prerogatives typically associated with a distinct type of constitutional system. Thus, the notion that any given item in the survey is relevant only for a certain type of constitutional system is unsound.

Below we list the items and further explicate how we answered them.

1. The legislature alone, without the involvement of any other agencies, can impeach the president or replace the prime minister.

Can the legislature control executive power by unseating, or threatening to unseat, the executive? The answer focuses on the legislature's power over the leading executive in the system. The item includes the phrase "impeach the president *or* replace the prime minister" (emphasis added). We word the item the way we do in order to make it applicable to either presidential or parliamentary systems. The potentially ambiguous wording of the item may create the impression that the answer is affirmative if either one of the two is true. This is not the case; what we mean to gauge is whether the legislature can change *the most powerful executive in the system,* be he or she the president, prime minister, or someone else. In monarchies we treat the monarch as the executive of concern if he or she rules. If he or she reigns but does not rule, some other actor (typically the prime minister) is the executive of concern. Fortunately, the difference between monarchs who rule and those who merely reign is usually quite obvious, and determining whether the prime minister or the monarch is the predominant executive is unproblematic. In most systems that are commonly identified as parliamentary, the leading executive is the prime minister, and the legislature may dispatch him or her without the involvement of other agencies. For these countries the item is answered in the affirmative. In several countries whose constitutions are often classified as parliamentary, the prime minister is a de facto dictator whose power rests on his or her independent control of the agencies of coercion, rather than on parliament per se. In such cases it is impossible to imagine the prime minister being replaced by the parliament alone. In this event the answer is negative. In presidential and most semipresidential systems in which acts of the legislature alone can dislodge the president, the answer is affirmative. In those in which the participation of a high court, the public voting in a referendum, or some other actor is also required, the answer is negative. The only grounds for ambiguity arise in a handful of semipresidential systems in which both the prime minister and the president clearly wield substantial authority. In most of these cases we base the answer on whether the legislature can impeach the president rather than on whether it can replace the prime minister, although in several semipresidential systems the prime minister is clearly the dominant executive, and in these cases the answer is based on parliament's sway over the prime minister. Where feasible and appropriate, we include information on the legislature's power over several executives (e.g., the president and the prime minister, the Governor General and the prime minister, the prime minister and the monarch). In all such cases, in the discursive portion of the answer we address *first* the executive of concern for answering the item, and only then the other executive. Thus, if the king merely reigns and the prime minister is the executive of concern, we first mention whether or not the legislature can dismiss the prime minister, and only then – if at all – what the legislature may do with the monarch. If, on the other hand, the royal palace really rules and the prime minister is its servant, we mention the crown first and then – if at all – the prime minister. A caveat is in order: We present the constitutional excerpts in the order in which they appear in the constitution. Thus, sometimes the portion of the constitution that deals with the executive of central concern appears first in the constitutional excerpts, and sometimes it appears second or, in rare cases, not at all.

2. Ministers may serve simultaneously as members of the legislature.

May legislators staff the cabinet themselves? We are aware that there is a debate over whether the recruitment of ministers from the legislature bolsters the legislature's power.[4] We agree with Max Weber's contention, explicated in his polemic in favor of parliamentary government in Germany, that the legislature is more powerful if parliamentarians head the ministries. In systems in which the ministers come from the ranks of the legislature's members, the legislature is fully the fount of executive as well as legislative power. In such systems the results of elections for the legislature largely determine the partisan composition of the executive. Furthermore, the legislature may have more consistent influence over the government's operations where the ministers are themselves working parliamentarians, and members of parliament are the ministers' colleagues. Where ministers are recruited from outside the legislature or where they may be drawn from it but must resign their seats upon receiving a ministerial post, the ministers work at a distance from the legislature, and their

jobs are only indirectly, or not at all, dependent upon the will and composition of the legislature.[5] An affirmative answer is therefore an indication of a stronger rather than a weaker legislature. The answer to this item is affirmative if a person may simultaneously serve as a member of the legislature and a member of the cabinet or government. The answer is negative if a person may not so serve. It is also negative if a parliamentarian may serve as a minister but forfeits his or her voting rights in the legislature upon assuming a ministerial position. Such an institution, sometimes called a "sleeping mandate," effectively withdraws the minister from the legislative setting and separates the government from the legislature.

3. The legislature has powers of summons over executive branch officials and hearings with executive branch officials testifying before the legislature or its committees are regularly held.

Can the legislature question the executive and force it to explain its policies? For the item to be answered in the affirmative, the legislature must be capable in practice of calling officials from the executive to testify, and it must exercise that right. Usually legislatures that enjoy the power in practice also enjoy it on paper. But even if the right is not encoded in law, the answer is affirmative if the practice exists. The item is also answered in the affirmative if the polity has the practice of "question time," in which ministers must regularly answer queries posed by legislators. In constitutional jargon, *interpellate* is often used to mean "question," and that august verb occurs often in discussion of this item. The item is answered in the negative if the legislature does not regularly question executive branch officials. In some cases the constitution provides the power of summons, but the power exists only on paper, and the legislature rarely or never actually gets to exercise its formal rights. In such an instance the item is answered in the negative.

4. The legislature can conduct independent investigation of the chief executive and the agencies of the executive.

Can the legislature probe the executive? This item states that the legislature can, not just may, investigate the executive, meaning that the legislature has the ability to do so. One would not

---

[4] Geoffrey Smith and Nelson W. Polsby, *British Government and Its Discontents* (New York: Basic Books, 1981); and Thomas Poguntke and Paul Webb, eds., *The Presidentialization of Politics: A Comparative Study of Modern Democracies* (Oxford: Oxford University Press, 2007).

[5] Max Weber, "Parliament and Government in a Reconstructed Germany," in Max Weber, *Economy and Society*, vol. 2 (Berkeley: University of California Press, 1978), pp. 1381–1469.

necessarily expect investigations, even where they are possible, to be as frequent as ordinary hearings with executive branch officials. Thus, unlike in item 3, in which we stipulate that hearings must be held regularly to elicit an affirmative answer, we do not stipulate in item 4 that investigations must be held regularly. If investigation is merely possible, the answer is affirmative. Yet the executive must really have grounds to fear parliamentary scrutiny for the item to be affirmed. Moreover, the chief executive must be subject to investigation; the mere right to probe a subordinate agency in the executive branch is not enough to merit an affirmative answer. If the legislature cannot investigate the chief executive, the answer is negative.

5. The legislature has effective powers of oversight over the agencies of coercion (the military, organs of law enforcement, intelligence services, and the secret police).

Can the legislature monitor the state's coercive agencies? If the police, military, and intelligence agencies report directly to the legislature, or the legislature has the ability to oversee these agencies with, for example, powers to question, investigate, regulate, and fund these agencies, the answer is affirmative. If, on the other hand, the agencies of coercion are under the exclusive control of the executive branch and there is little or no legislative oversight of their operations, the answer is negative. Even in some cases in which the legislature has such power on paper, it does not have it in practice. We are concerned with whether the legislature really has such authority, which is reflected in the wording "effective powers of oversight." Obviously, deciding on what counts as "effective" requires a judgment call. In actual practice in the contemporary world, legislatures' ability to control the agencies of coercion is rarely extensive, even in systems with powerful parliaments. But here, as with other items in this survey, everything is relative. In some countries legislatures do at least have some powers of oversight, and in others they do not. In the event of uncertainty or lack of consensus, we corroborated experts' judgments with extensive research of our own in press and secondary sources.

6. The legislature appoints the prime minister.

Does the legislature appoint the head of the government? Where the legislature itself elects the prime minister, the answer is affirmative. If the head of state (usually a president, Governor General, or monarch) is charged with appointing the prime minister, but is obliged to select the candidate who enjoys the support of parliament, the answer is also affirmative. In such cases the head of state typically selects the leader of the party or coalition that won parliamentary elections or the candidate who enjoys majority support in parliament (or who at least can form a government). Here the composition of the legislature predetermines the decision, and the president's, Governor General's, or monarch's right of appointment of the prime minister is largely a formality. The item is therefore scored as affirmative. In other cases the president, Governor General, or monarch selects the prime minister, and the decision does not depend on the will of the legislature. Here extra-parliamentary appointment power is not a mere formality, and the answer is therefore negative. To receive an affirmative answer, the country must have a prime minister; countries that lack a prime ministerial post (or its equivalent) receive a negative answer on this item.

7. The legislature's approval is required to confirm the appointment of ministers; or the legislature itself appoints ministers.

Does the legislature influence the composition of the cabinet? If the legislature makes the ministerial appointments, the answer is affirmative. The answer is also affirmative if the prime minister appoints the ministers but the cabinet must subsequently be confirmed by a vote of the legislature in order to assume office. Further, the answer is affirmative if the president (or monarch) appoints the ministers and the legislature's approval is needed to confirm the appointments. The answer is negative if the executive appoints the ministers and the appointments do not require the legislature's approval.

8. The country lacks a presidency entirely or there is a presidency, but the president is elected by the legislature.

Does the legislature select the president – or need it not even contend with one? If there is no president, the answer is affirmative. If there is a president but he or she is elected by the legislature, the answer is affirmative. The answer is negative if there is a directly elected president.

9. The legislature can vote no confidence in the government.

Can legislators express their opposition to the government with a vote of no confidence? If it is possible to vote no confidence (sometimes referred to as a "motion of censure"), the answer is affirmative; if not, it is negative. In some countries the legislature has the ability to vote no confidence in individual ministers, but not in the government as a whole. This provision allows the legislature to express displeasure with a specific minister, but renders it virtually impossible for the legislature to remove the entire government. If the legislature may vote no confidence in, or censure, individual ministers but not the government as a whole, the answer is negative.

10. The legislature is immune from dissolution by the executive.

Is the legislature's term fixed even in the event of executive displeasure? If the legislature is free from the danger of dissolution, the answer is affirmative. The answer is also affirmative if the legislature can vote to dissolve itself but is still immune from dissolution by the executive. There is wide variation across countries in the conditions under which the executive can dissolve the legislature. In some countries powerful presidents can dissolve the legislature at will. In other countries the executive can dissolve the legislature only under narrowly specified conditions, such as immediately following multiple votes of no confidence in the government by the same legislature. Even in situations in which the conditions for dissolution are constrained and partly in the control of the legislature, however, the legislature is still potentially subject to dissolution, and the legislature's powers are constrained. If the executive may dissolve the legislature, under any conditions, the answer is negative.

11. Any executive initiative on legislation requires ratification or approval by the legislature before it takes effect; that is, the executive lacks decree power.

Does the legislature have a monopoly on lawmaking authority? If the legislature is in fact a participant in the making of all laws, the answer is affirmative. If the executive can make laws by decree, the legislature in practice shares lawmaking power with the executive, and the answer is negative. Regulatory decrees and executive orders to implement laws do not count as decrees as we define them here. If the executive can issue regulatory decrees or executive orders but not decrees that have the force of law, we do not regard the executive as having decree power, and the answer to the item is affirmative. The answer is also affirmative if the legislature has the right – but is not compelled – to delegate temporary decree powers to the executive in some specified areas of authority. Furthermore, the answer is affirmative if decree powers are limited to emergencies; we do not consider emergency powers to be genuine decree powers unless they are regularly and habitually abused. If the executive may make laws without the prior permission of the legislature in nonemergency situations, the answer is negative. Executive decree power takes a variety of forms. In the most constrained case, the executive may issue decrees, but their force automatically lapses after some specified interval if the legislature does not approve them. In a less limited scenario, the legislature's active approval is not needed, but the legislature still enjoys the right to annul decrees if it so desires. Here the executive's decrees stand unless the legislature rescinds them. The most robust decree power is found where the executive's decrees enjoy the force of law regardless of the legislature's will; here the legislature does not have the right to rescind. All these varieties of executive lawmaking authority count as decree power; if any is present, the answer to the item is negative.

12. Laws passed by the legislature are veto-proof or essentially veto-proof; that is, the executive lacks veto power, or has veto power but the veto can be overridden by a majority in the legislature.

Can the legislature make laws without great concern for executive defiance? If a bill automatically becomes law once the legislature passes it, the executive lacks veto power, and the answer is affirmative. The answer is also affirmative if the executive has a veto but the legislature can override it with a majority vote. Such a veto may signal executive disapproval and may retard the passage of legislation, but it is not normally a weighty check on the legislature. If a supermajority is required to override, the veto has teeth. In this event the legislature can override the veto only by mustering a larger majority than was necessary to pass the legislation to begin with, and the answer therefore is negative. The threshold for override where a supermajority is required is typically two-thirds, although in some cases it is three-fifths or four-fifths.

A word is in order about our conception of "majority": We mean either a vote of 50 percent plus one of present members (sometimes referred to as a "simple majority") or a vote of 50 percent plus one of total members (sometimes called an "absolute majority"). There may be a significant practical difference between these thresholds, especially in situations of chronically high absenteeism among legislators. But in either case, that is, if the legislature can override an executive veto with a simple majority or an absolute majority, we score the answer as affirmative. The distinction that determines the answer to the item is between the need for a mere majority (either of present members or of all members) override, on the one hand, and a supermajority override, on the other.

13. The legislature's laws are supreme and not subject to judicial review.

Are the legislature's laws the final word? This item is scored as affirmative if the legislature's laws cannot be rejected by the judiciary. If the judiciary has the right to rule on the constitutionality of laws and void those it determines to be unconstitutional, the item is scored as negative. If the legislature does not itself pass laws, as is the case in, for example, some of the advisory bodies in the Gulf States, it cannot be said that "the legislature's laws are supreme," and the answer is also negative.

14. The legislature has the right to initiate bills in all policy jurisdictions; the executive lacks gatekeeping authority.

May the legislature make laws in any area it wishes? This answer is affirmative if the legislature may discuss and pass laws in any domain. In some countries the right to introduce legislation in some areas is reserved for the executive. Common areas in which the executive can engage in such "gatekeeping" over the legislative process are the domains of law on taxation, public expenditures, and government debt. In such cases the executive is said to have gatekeeping authority, and the answer to the item is negative. In some countries the right to introduce the budget is reserved for the executive. Such power is fairly common and is not considered an instance of executive gatekeeping for the purposes of this survey. If this is the only power reserved for the executive, the answer is still affirmative. Yet, if once the budget is passed, the legislature alone cannot introduce measures that alter revenues or expenditures, executive control over budgetary matters extends beyond the mere right to introduce the budget. Such a restriction may have wide ramifications for the legislature's right to legislate. In this event the answer is negative. In federal systems in which some powers are reserved for subnational units, the answer is affirmative provided that the legislature may initiate legislation in all policy areas that are under the jurisdiction of the national government.

In all events, the answers on this item depend on whether the legislature *can* initiate bills in all policy jurisdictions rather than on whether legislation *usually does originate* with the legislature. In many countries legislation normally originates with the government, and the role of the legislature as a whole is often limited in practice to accepting or rejecting such initiatives. If the leading party or coalition of parties that make up the government is usually the source of legislation, and it is difficult for rank-and-file members to introduce bills that have a good chance of passage without the government's backing, one might say that the executive holds informal gatekeeping authority. In fact, this is the way legislative politics normally works in parliamentary systems. But such informal power does not count as gatekeeping authority here. The answer to the item is affirmative so long as the legislature *can* initiate bills in all policy jurisdictions.

15. Expenditure of funds appropriated by the legislature is mandatory; the executive lacks the power to impound funds appropriated by the legislature.

Must the government spend the money the legislature appropriates? If the legislature's appropriations must be spent in the manner that the legislature specifies, the answer is affirmative. If the legislature appropriates funds but the executive can then block, redirect, or otherwise manipulate their actual expenditure, the executive is often said to have "impoundment power." An executive who can impound funds has substantial – if hidden and unofficial – budgetary authority. Impoundment power is rarely specified in constitutions, but in practice is present in some systems with powerful executives. If the executive can impound funds or otherwise substantially manipulate the expenditures that the legislature authorizes, the item is scored as negative.

16. The legislature controls the resources that finance its own internal operation and provide for the perquisites of its own members.

Does the legislature enjoy financial autonomy? A legislature that controls its own resources enjoys an important measure of autonomy from the executive. In the event, the answer is affirmative. An executive who controls the resources that fund the legislature's operation (such as those that provide for the legislators' perks) may use that leverage to influence legislators' behavior. If the executive has such authority, the item is scored as negative.

17. Members of the legislature are immune from arrest and/or criminal prosecution.

Are legislators free from fear of punishment? Immunity enables legislators to work without worrying that the executive will use the organs of law enforcement to punish them. If legislators are immune, the answer is affirmative. In almost every country legislators who are caught *flagrante delicto* (meaning in the act of a crime) may be apprehended. If this is the only exception to legislative immunity, we still score the item in the affirmative. So too is the item affirmed if legislators enjoy immunity but the legislature, and only the legislature, has the power to lift it. In such cases the legislature as an institution can still shield its own members from executive abuse. If legislators lack any type of immunity from arrest and prosecution, the item is negated. Where legislators have immunity but it can be revoked by an agency other than the legislature itself, the item is also scored as negative. Where only official parliamentary business is covered by immunity, where legislators are immune only while they are in, or traveling to and from, the grounds of the legislature, or where legislators are immune only when the legislature is in session, the item is scored as negative as well. In such cases a force external to the legislature may still use arrest or the threat of it to intimidate legislators. The item is also scored as negative if legislators enjoy immunity on paper but are habitually persecuted anyway in defiance of the law.

18. All members of the legislature are elected; the executive lacks the power to appoint any members of the legislature.

Is the legislature free of executive appointees? If the legislature contains no executive appointees, the answer is affirmative. The answer is also affirmative if the executive appoints members of an upper chamber, provided that the upper chamber is largely ceremonial and possesses little or no real legislative power. The answer is affirmative as well if the executive may appoint a mere handful of members, which we define as no more than 2 percent of total members, or if the executive may appoint some members but these appointees lack voting rights. In the latter two cases, executives enjoy the right to make appointments, but these appointments are symbolic – and usually honorific – and do not appreciably shape the legislature's composition. For example, in Italy the president can appoint up to five "Senators for life" from the "social, scientific, artistic, and literary fields."

At any given time, there are only a handful of appointed members in the Italian Senate. On the other hand, in Afghanistan the president appoints one-third of the members of the upper house of the legislature. The 2 percent cutoff point distinguishes between countries in which the executive has symbolic, but politically insignificant, appointment powers and countries in which the executive shapes the composition of the legislature through political appointments. There is nothing magic in the 2 percent cutoff we impose, but we do find a natural break in the data between this very low number of appointees, such as one finds in Italy (as well as in, for example, India), and the substantially higher number of appointees one finds in Afghanistan (as well as in, for example, Kazakhstan). If the executive may appoint a substantial number (more than 2 percent) of total members and if these members have voting rights, the answer is negative.

19. The legislature alone, without the involvement of any other agencies, can change the Constitution.

Can the legislature by itself change the fundamental law? The right to alter the constitution carries the power to reshape political life and the political regime. If the legislature can do so alone, the answer is affirmative. The legislature need not be the only actor that can change the constitution in order for the answer to be affirmative. If some other actor can do so, the answer is still affirmative, provided that the legislature also has such power. If the legislature does not play a part, or if it does play a role but a referendum, court ruling, or executive assent is also necessary, the answer is negative. In some countries the legislature has the power to amend parts of the constitution, but other parts of the constitution can be changed only by referendum or some other means. If the legislature can alter the majority of the constitution's provisions, the answer is affirmative. If the legislature is barred from changing a large and highly substantial portion of the fundamental document, the answer is negative.

20. The legislature's approval is necessary for the declaration of war.

Is action by the legislature needed to declare war? The right to declare war, or at least to confirm or reject the declaration of war, is crucial to the legislature's influence on the country's security and external relations. If action by the legislature is needed to declare war, the answer is affirmative; if not, it is negative. In many countries the legislature's approval is necessary to declare war, although the president or monarch has the right to declare war without consulting the legislature in the event of invasion or the immediate threat thereof. If the legislature's approval is normally needed, even if the executive can declare war without the legislature's approval in the case of an attack or imminent attack, the answer is still affirmative. If the executive's scope for unilateral action is wider, the answer is negative. For example, if the executive may declare war without the legislature's approval under "special circumstances" or other such vaguely specified conditions, the answer is negative. The need for retroactive approval by the legislature is not sufficient to merit an affirmative answer unless the executive's war-declaration powers are limited to the case of foreign attack. Some countries lack a formal provision for the declaration of war, but instead have a procedure for declaring a state of defense, siege, emergency, martial law, or other such extraordinary circumstance. In these cases we analyze the power to declare such an extraordinary condition.

21. The legislature's approval is necessary to ratify treaties with foreign countries.

Is action by the legislature needed to ratify treaties? The right to accept or reject treaties negotiated by the government is central to the legislature's influence on foreign policy and international relations. If the legislature's approval is necessary to ratify treaties, the answer is affirmative; if not, it is negative. In some cases the legislature's approval is necessary to enact some, but not other, types of treaties. If the need for the legislature's ratification is not limited to insubstantial agreements, the item is answered in the affirmative.

22. The legislature has the power to grant amnesty.

May the legislature grant amnesty? The power to grant amnesty carries the potential to influence the administration of justice on a large scale. If the legislature can grant amnesty, the answer is affirmative; if not, it is negative. If, according to the constitution, the legislature has the power to grant amnesty, but in practice it would be unthinkable for the legislature to grant amnesty without the executive's approval, the answer is also negative.

Amnesty and pardon are sometimes confused. According to common usage, amnesty applies to political offenses and pardon to nonpolitical criminal offenses. In another usage, amnesty applies to a class of people and pardon to individuals. There is considerable overlap between these two usages, since political crimes, such as taking part in human rights abuses or participating in an insurgency, are usually committed by a class of people and nonpolitical criminal offenses by people as individuals. Conceptions of amnesty and pardon vary somewhat from country to country.

23. The legislature has the power of pardon.

May the legislature grant pardon? If so, the answer is affirmative; if not, it is negative. If, according to the constitution, the legislature has the power of pardon, but in practice it would be unthinkable for the legislature to grant pardon without the executive's approval, the answer is also negative. See also comments on item 22.

24. The legislature reviews and has the right to reject appointments to the judiciary; or the legislature itself appoints members of the judiciary.

Does the legislature have a hand in the appointment of members of the judiciary? The right to influence the composition of the judiciary carries the potential to affect the legal system and the administration of justice. Where the legislature appoints members to the judiciary or the legislature's approval has a role in judicial appointments, the answer is affirmative. Where it lacks a role in either appointment or confirmation, the answer is negative. The threshold for an affirmative answer here is not high. Purely token responsibility, such as the right to appoint or confirm only a single member of the judiciary, is not sufficient for an affirmative answer, but if the legislature has responsibilities that extend beyond a single appointment, the answer is affirmative. We focus on appointments to national-level courts, often referred to as the Supreme Court, the High Court, and/or the Constitutional Court. Although constitutional courts are sometimes separate from the judiciary proper, we consider them part of the judiciary for the purposes of this item. Thus, if the legislature is involved in appointments to a constitutional court, the answer is affirmative.

25. The chairman of the central bank is appointed by the legislature.

Does the legislature appoint the chief of the central bank? This power may afford clout over administration of the economy. If the legislature appoints, the answer is affirmative; if not, it is negative. In some countries there is no dedicated chairman of the central bank, and responsibility for running the central bank rests with a cabinet minister, often the minister of finance. In these countries, if the legislature appoints the minister that heads the central bank, the answer is affirmative. If not, the answer is negative. In countries that lack a national central bank because they are members of a multinational monetary authority, the answer is negative.

26. The legislature has a substantial voice in the operation of the state-owned media.

Does the legislature influence the state-owned media? A say in the provision of public information is a say in shaping public opinion, as well as an opportunity to counterbalance the dominance of the executive that often prevails in the state-owned media. If the legislature itself governs state-owned media, or the legislature appoints members to the body that governs state-owned media, the answer is affirmative. If legal provisions guarantee parliamentarians the right to supervise (or, perhaps in the eyes of critics, interfere in) the operation of the public media, the answer is also affirmative. If the legislature lacks these means of obtaining a voice in the operation of the state-owned media, the answer is negative.

27. The legislature is regularly in session.

Is the legislature regularly in session? A body that meets frequently will normally have greater ability to exercise its authority than one that does not. In the wording of the item, we do not set a threshold for what counts as "regularly" in session. Our intention is to assess whether the legislature's sessions are lengthy enough to enable it to handle the load of a responsible, working assembly. As we conducted our research, we came to understand that six months per year was a meaningful threshold dividing legislatures that are regularly in session and those that are not, and we use it as the basis for answering the item. The answer is affirmative if the legislature is in session for six months or more, and negative if it is in session for less than six months.

28. Each legislator has a personal secretary.

Does each member of the legislature have a secretary? This item and item 29 gauge whether mem-

bers of the legislature have help with their work. Students of the U.S. Congress are accustomed to thinking of a seat in the legislature as including a personal staff of dozens as well as access to armies of committee staff. Such a circumstance, however, is rare in the global context. In most countries legislators are happy to have even a handful of assistants. The availability of staff may influence legislators' effectiveness, and legislators' effectiveness may affect the legislature's capacity. If each member has a secretary to assist him or her, the item is affirmed; if not, it is negated.

29. Each legislator has at least one non-secretarial staff member with policy expertise.

Does each member of the legislature have at least one staffer who helps with policy matters? Having such a person tends to boost legislators' effectiveness and bolster the legislature's capacity. The answers to this item and, less commonly, item 28 are not always straightforward. In some places funds are available to hire staff, but members are not obliged to use them for a staffer with policy expertise. In some countries members have access to staff employed by committees or party groups, and members may draw on the expertise of what amount to common pool personnel resources. Sometimes committee chairs or other prominent members have staff but other members do not. We score the answer as affirmative if each member effectively has use of at least one person with policy expertise, whether that staffer is employed by the member's office, a committee, or a party. If each member does not have such a resource, the answer is negative.

30. Legislators are eligible for re-election without any restriction.

Are legislators free from the restrictions of term limits? A legislative body in which politicians can make careers will be more likely to attract brighter talent than one in which members may spend only one or several terms before moving on to other jobs. More talented legislators make for a stronger legislature. Furthermore, politicians who are committed to a career – or at least an open-ended stint – in the legislature are more likely to be devoted to the institution and jealous of its prerogatives. If legislators need not fear term limits, the answer is affirmative; if there are term limits, the answer is negative. This item refers to term limits (or their absence). It does not deal with informal or political obstacles to re-election such as might be encountered by an opponent of the government or one who has lost the support of his or her party.

31. A seat in the legislature is an attractive enough position that legislators are generally interested in and seek re-election.

Do legislators sincerely hope to keep their jobs? In most countries, a seat in the legislature is a prestigious position that attracts qualified talent. In some countries, however, a seat in the legislature is not highly esteemed and is seen as a mere stepping stone to another, more attractive position. More highly valued jobs attract and retain better political talent, and the rate at which legislators seek re-election is higher when they value their positions. Members may value their positions for perks rather than power. But legislators who do not value their jobs enough to desire re-election find that both power and perks are in short supply. If, according to the judgment of our country experts, legislators are normally interested in keeping their jobs, the answer is positive; if not, it is negative.

32. The re-election of incumbent legislators is common enough that at any given time the legislature contains a significant number of highly experienced members.

Does the legislature have a cohort of members who know the ropes? The presence of a sizable group of long-serving members tends to bolster the legislature's capacity. Legislators may, of course, be experienced without being qualified or effective. Still, the sum total of expertise in the assembly on policy matters, legislative procedure, and how to resist executive encroachment depends in part on how much experience members have. If, in the judgment of our country experts, the legislature includes a significant number of experienced members, the answer is affirmative; if not, it is negative. If multiple elections for the legislature have not been held, re-election cannot be common, and if the legislature is relatively new, it cannot, by definition, contain highly experienced members. In countries with very young legislatures and legislatures for which there have not been multiple rounds of elections, the answer is also negative.

THE PARLIAMENTARY POWERS INDEX

We determined the answer to each item for each country by studying the expert consultants' completed questionnaires, the constitution, and relevant press and secondary sources. In general, the experts' answers were consistent with what one finds in constitutions and other published sources. Sometimes constitutions did not provide many clues. Items 15, 26, 28, 29, 31, and 32 were usually not addressed in constitutions; items 3, 5, 16, and 27 were sometimes addressed but often were not. For these items we had to rely especially heavily on our experts.

Sometimes practice regularly and blatantly contravenes legal formalities, as the experts often noted in their responses. In such instances we favored practice in answering the item. Where such a discrepancy between the law and practice exists, we note it in our discussion of the answer to the item. In the relatively rare instances in which constitutions were silent or inconclusive and the experts were split, we undertook further research, including further consultation with experts, before answering the item.

To arrive at the Parliamentary Powers Index for each country, we divide the total number of affirmative answers by the total number of items in the survey. This procedure is simple and cannot provide anything more than a rough guide to the power of the legislature.

Assigning equal weight to each item obviously has its costs. Yet weighting the items would involve difficult and arbitrary distinctions. We are aware that each item cannot be equally important. But the importance of an item may vary from country to country and from time to time. Several examples may illustrate the point. In a polity that has a long history of protection for rights and few opportunities for politicians to trump up charges in order to punish or intimidate foes, whether or not parliamentarians enjoy immunity from prosecution (item 17) may have little practical effect on the legislature's institutional autonomy. But in a country that lacks long-standing protections for rights and that has an executive who may be tempted to sic law enforcement agencies on recalcitrant legislators, immunity from prosecution may be a precious protection that strengthens the legislature. In countries where a dictatorial executive controls the parliament through a hegemonic party, whether the executive has effective veto power (item 12) may be of little consequence. But if political life is competitive, whether the executive has a veto may be highly consequential. In a polity that has little recent history of violent civil conflict, the right to grant amnesty (item 22) may be of little moment. But if a country has a recent history of human rights abuses, coup attempts, or insurgency, amnesty may be a burning issue. Who is vested with the right to grant it may be a matter of utmost importance. The weight of an item might also vary from time to time within a country. For example, veto power (item 12) might be of greater importance when the president and the legislature are rivals than when a single party or coalition controls both the presidency and the legislature.

Some weighting of issues is built into the survey itself. Items 1–9 focus on the legislature's influence on executive power, 10–18 inquire about the institutional autonomy of the legislature, 19–26 address an array of specific powers, and 27–32 measure the legislature's institutional capacity. Thus, 9/32 of the survey is about sway over the executive, 9/32 about autonomy, 8/32 about specific powers, and 6/32 about capacity.

The answers to the survey items and the overall country scores reflect the state of affairs in 2006 and 2007, when we wrote this book. The answers to the survey items may, of course, change over time. Coding the answers to every item for every country was in itself a challenge; we were unable to record how the answers to each item may have changed within each country throughout history. We did our best, however, to note any major changes that have occurred in recent years. At the beginning of each country chapter, we list the date of the legislature's founding and discuss the most notable changes that affect items in the survey. This information should help readers who are interested in, for example, how a legislature's powers have changed over time or whether specific powers granted to the legislature have had the time to be tested in practice. We intend to update the present work with subsequent editions to capture future changes.

One of the authors (Fish) has published an article and a book, both on the postcommunist region, which tapped some of the preliminary data drawn from the present project.[6] Some of the data presented in those publications differ from those furnished in this volume. One reason is the author used the survey in part to assess conditions at an earlier point in time (namely, the late 1980s through the mid-1990s), and some of the scores have changed since the earlier period. Furthermore, we have more systematically analyzed the findings over the last few years, slightly altered three of the survey items and preliminary

assessments that Fish drew upon, and arrived at more complete and precise data.

The data presented in this volume supersede anything related to this project published earlier. The data and information presented here, and not in any earlier publications, provide our final, corrected assessments.

Given that we cover the whole world, including many legislatures about which up-to-date, detailed information is exceedingly hard to obtain, we cannot exclude the possibility that we have overlooked a relevant change here and there. Nor can we rule out the possibility of errors more generally. We have endeavored to obtain the best quality information available, relying upon nearly 800 consultants as well as our own analysis of constitutions, the press, and the secondary literature. But the data we present here may contain some inaccuracies. We cover 158 countries, including many whose legislatures have been the subject of little or no attention in social science. At thirty-two items for each country, there are 5,056 answers. The number of countries covered and the considerable detail we present on each probably make error unavoidable. We prize our experts' evaluations, and we take satisfaction in having secured a large number of responses from such distinguished analysts. At the same time, years of poring over constitutions, books, articles, press sources, and completed surveys have sensitized us to the possibility of mistakes and differences of interpretation. Even some items that one might expect to elicit straightforward affirmative-or-negative answers are often complicated in practice.

Indeed, in a work that aims to create data that are comparable across an enormous variety of cases, some ambiguity is unavoidable even on basic matters. The identity of the "national legislature" is generally unproblematic, although formal distinctions among the meanings of "parliament," "legislature," "congress," and "assembly" are often blurred in practice, and we do not attempt to draw distinctions among these terms. We use them interchangeably here. Such nomenclature is not problematic. Each country included in this study has a body that is universally recognized as the national legislature, although several countries, most notably the monarchies of the Persian Gulf region, have advisory councils that serve the monarch rather than legislatures in the traditional sense.

But in some cases the identity of even such a basic agency as "the executive" is not self-evident. In presidential or semipresidential systems the matter is usually straightforward. In some constitutional monarchies, however, the prime minister

---

[6] M. Steven Fish, *Democracy Derailed in Russia: The Failure of Open Politics* (New York: Cambridge University Press, 2005), and "Stronger Legislatures, Stronger Democracy," *Journal of Democracy* 17, 1 (January 2006), pp. 5–20.

is the most powerful executive, but the monarch is the head of state and has some relevant functions. In some former British colonies the Governor General has substantial authority. We identify the relevant executive in cases where his or her identity might be ambiguous.

Try though we do to overcome ambiguities, our efforts can be only imperfect. Answering the same questions for cases that span the entire world, as we do here, always involves complications, but, we hope, it also provides the benefits of addressing a single, unified set of questions in a truly global setting.

In the studies that follow, many countries rank where one would expect. No one will be surprised to see that Italy and Israel have strong legislatures whereas Zambia and Egypt do not. But there are some surprises. The legislatures of Fiji, with its parliamentary system, and France, with its semipresidential one, score lower on the PPI than many might expect. In some other countries, the numbers suggest that the legislature might be a sleeping (or a quiet) giant. For example, although presidents and militaries often overshadow parliaments in writings on Bangladesh, Colombia, El Salvador, Indonesia, South Korea, Panama, and Peru, the legislature in each of these countries has clout. In some countries that have legislatures that receive little attention, the legislature may not be a giant, even a sleeping one, but it nevertheless has some capacity. The legislatures of, for example, Azerbaijan, China, Iran, and Kuwait stand closer to the sidelines than to the center of national politics, but they are not entirely devoid of power. They differ notably from their counterparts in, say, Algeria, Belarus, and Cameroon, which are indeed impotent. This state of affairs potentially holds relevance for present-day politics and government, as well as for legislatures' potential to assert themselves in the future.

THE USE OF CONSTITUTIONS

Throughout the country studies presented in chapter 2, we adduce relevant passages from constitutions in the answer to each survey item where such passages exist.[7] We always present the constitutional excerpts in the order in which they appear in the constitution. If the excerpt seems to contradict the answer to the survey item, we note the reason for the discrepancy, which usually is a gap between the letter of the law and actual practice. Even where such a gap exists, we cite the relevant passage from the constitution, so in some places the constitutional excerpt will appear to contradict the answer. As noted above, where the law is a dead letter, we go with practice in our answers.

Instances of disparity between the law and actual practice are not uncommon, but as the reader will see, neither are they the norm. Indeed, we were surprised at the regularity with which the law – at least roughly – matches practice. We expected at the onset of the project to find a plethora of instances in which the law formally vests in the legislature a power that the legislature lacks in actual practice. In fact, we found that where legislatures lack power in practice, they usually lack it on paper as well – even if the constitution's language strains to present a semblance of modernity and democracy.

We draw on several sources for translations of constitutions that were not penned in English. For each country except Comoros, an adequate English translation was readily available. Here and there, even in the best translations, one often finds awkward moments in the prose. We left these passages as they are. Where we found a misspelling or where the clarity of the prose was compromised by the accidental omission of a preposition, we corrected the inaccuracy; we saw little to be gained from leaving mistakes in place and inserting "*sic.*" We never made any substantive alterations.

Whether the constitution was originally penned in English or another language, in the excerpts one encounters bits of jargon that may be unfamiliar. *Interpellate* appears frequently, especially in entries under item 3 in the survey. It means to interrogate a government official about policy, action, or personal behavior. It is a fancy word for the verb "to question." *Puisne* is mainly a British term that means "lower" or "of lesser rank" and is found here mostly in reference to judges in excerpts from constitutions cited under item 24. *Prorogue* means to discontinue a session of a legislature and occasionally appears in reference to executive powers to dissolve parliament. *Flagrante delicto* means "caught in the act." This phrase appears frequently in passages under item 17, which addresses legislators' immunity from arrest and/or prosecution. In many cases in which legislators enjoy immunity, an exception is made for *flagrante delicto*. In effect this rule means that legislators may be apprehended if, and only if, they are caught red-handed.

---

[7] We relied upon two sources for constitutions: "Constitutions of the Countries of the World," from Oceana Law (available online at www.oceanalaw.com); and "International Constitutional Law," available online at http://www.oefre.unibe.ch/law/icl/index.html.

USE OF THE DATA

The survey presented here is richer than anything done to date on the powers of national legislatures. As such, it undoubtedly will elicit objections. Some scholars will see the inclusion of this or that item as unjustified. They might view the survey as too lengthy and involved and wish it were more compact and included only the items they regard as most significant. Others may wish that some items were weighed more heavily than others in the creation of the PPI. Some scholars will think that the survey overlooked this or that important question; they may want to add items of their own.

Analysts who wish to use only parts of the survey or to add items of their own, perhaps to construct their own indexes, are, of course, free to do so. We hope that publishing the answer to every item for every country will facilitate the work of other scholars.

The data may be of use not only to those who desire a comparative measure of legislatures' overall powers, but also to those who seek particular pieces of information. Any one item or group of items may be extracted and treated as a set of data. For example, the reader who seeks information on where legislators enjoy immunity from prosecution and where they do not may refer to item 17. The reader interested in legislatures' institutional autonomy more generally may focus on items 10–18 or some subset of these items.

The data may help advance understanding of how particular facets of the legislature's power affect this or that outcome. For example, what aspect of the legislature's power has the greatest effect on political stability or civil war? Employing some indicator for political stability and treating it as the dependent variable, the analyst may use particular items or groups of items from the LPS as independent variables and test their influence. One might also assess how the legislature's sway over the executive affects the economy. Here one could draw on the first nine items of the LPS and test their effect on economic growth, macroeconomic stability, or some other indicator of economic performance. Partisans of democratization might use the data to assess whether strengthening legislatures is a better or worse investment than other endeavors. If the overall strength of the legislature is a good predictor of the success of democratization, bolstering legislatures is a good investment. If it is not a good predictor, perhaps training civil servants or funding independent media is a better use of resources. Or perhaps one or another of the legislature's powers – or some combination of

powers – is important for democratization, whereas other powers are of little consequence.

The value of the PPI to future research is not limited to students of comparative politics. International relations scholars could potentially use the PPI to study urgent questions in their own field. Scholars may wish to assess the effect of legislative power on international conflict. Are countries with powerful legislatures more or less likely to go to war? Could the findings of the "democratic peace" literature really be masking an underlying "parliamentary peace"? Scholars could also test the relationship between the PPI and trade openness: Are countries with powerful legislatures more or less open to international trade?

Alternatively, the data presented here might be treated as a dependent variable. What determines cross-national variation in the PPI? How, if at all, do economic development, historical experience, or other factors influence the powers of national legislatures in comparative perspective? Scholars could perform descriptive analyses of the PPI data. How and why do legislatures' powers vary across world regions? What accounts for gaps, where they are found, between the formal powers of the legislature and powers exercised by the legislature in practice?

We do not expect that the data presented here will supplant the traditional distinctions among parliamentary, semipresidential, and presidential systems; indeed, we use these categories ourselves and do not regard them as obsolete. But we do hope that the present study will help overcome the limitations of the conventional categories. At the very least, the information we present may facilitate a more differentiated understanding of legislative bodies around the world.

DEBTS AND ACKNOWLEDGMENTS

Our greatest and most obvious debt is to the experts who participated in the survey that underpins the data presented in this book. The experts are really our coauthors, although at nearly 800 strong, they cannot be named as such on the book's cover. Each expert completed the survey for one or more countries, and many provided discursive commentary as well. We drew on these enormously helpful comments while composing the country studies that follow. Many consultants endured a stream of entreaties for completed surveys, requests for further information, and (undoubtedly often irritating) follow-up questions that arose out of our curiosity and desire to investigate this or that piece of data further. The consultants for each country are noted in the appropriate country studies, and chapter 4 provides a comprehensive list.

All our consultants went above the call of duty. All lent their valuable expertise gratis; we provided no compensation. Some colleagues in one way or another – or in numerous ways – went even farther above the call of duty. They offered comments on the survey in its early stages of development, completed the survey for more than one country, and/or both completed a survey themselves and helped us locate other experts to participate in the survey as well. On this score we would like especially to recognize Şener Aktürk, Leslie Anderson, Elisabete Azevedo, Robin Brooks, Jean-Pierre Cabestan, John Carey, Ernesto Castaneda, Irina Chernykh, John Clark, Harold Crouch, Robert Elgie, Alain Faupin, Jan Fidrmuc, Natalia Ajenjo Fresno, Venelin Ganev, Theocharis Grigoriadis, Anna Grzymała-Busse, Carlos Guevara Mann, Jonathan Hartlyn, Michael Herb, Percy Hintzen, Barrie Hofmann, Maiah Jaskoski, Niraja Gopal Jayal, David Kang, Mujeeb Khan, Andrej Krickovic, David Leonard, Peter Lewis, Staffan Lindberg, Pauline Jones Luong, Ellen Lust-Okar, Eleanor Marchant, Edward McMahon, Andreas Mehler, Amer Mohsen, Fatima Mojaddedi, Conor O'Dwyer, Gérard Roland, Mark Rosenberg, Abdoulaye Saine, Aqil Shah, Nicholas Shaxson, William Stanley, L. Sumati, Lucan Way, Richard Weisfelder, and Alan Zuckerman.

We are also indebted to the colleagues who did not complete the survey themselves but who helped us locate experts who did complete it. They include Farda Asadov, Gloria Atiba-Davies, Owolabi Bjälkander, Marie-Ange Bunga, Fernando Coronil, Elizabeth Côté, Irene Csokay, Brittany Danisch, Sinclair Dinnen, Juris Dreifelds, Ulf Engel, Peter Fiamor, Kenneth Greene, Barbara Groeblinghoff, Danica Fink Hafner, Mark Hallerberg, Aileen Hanel, Franz Heimer, Luz Maria Helguero, Terry Hoverter, Donald Kaniaru, David Karol, Darlene Laule, Manfred Lohmann, Chris Lovelace, Vicki Luker, Christian Lund, Stjepan Malović, Rytis Martikonis, Cathie Jo Martin, Shelley McConnell, Wilfredo Mendez, Katy Mudge, Turi Munthe, Emma Murphy, Dorina Nastase, Collins Odote, René Otayek, Wynie Pankani, A. J. Panos, Claire Perez, Melissa Phillips, Jacqueline Pomeroy, Kourtney Pompi, Jon Quah, Sergio Rivas, Roland Roblain, Kristen Sample, Peter Sanchez, David Scott, Erwin Schweisshelm, Ulrich Storck, Paul Sutton, Ilona Tip, Balefi Tsie, Nicole Velasco, Rachel Wax, Mui Teng Yap, and Peter Zinoman.

So too are we grateful to colleagues who did not complete the survey themselves but who reviewed drafts for certain countries and/or offered comments on country conditions. The input of these colleagues saved us from numerous errors. We would like especially to acknowledge Neven Andelić, Betsy Carter, Kathleen Collins, Jonathan Harder, David Karol, William Liddle, Stephen McGinness, Rachel Neild, Magda Stepanyan, Robert Templer, and Jakub Wrzesniewski.

In a work such as the present book, where we identify the contributing consultants at every step along the way, more than the usual absolution of helpful colleagues for shortcomings in the final product is in order. In no case should the appearance of an expert's name be taken to suggest that that expert concurred with the specifics of the information that we present. In some instances an expert's answers on specific items were overridden by other experts, by our own scoring rules and research, and/or by a recent turn of events. The final decisions on the answers to each of the survey items for each country were exclusively our own. We alone are responsible for any errors.

We have benefited from the talents of gifted research assistants, including Pilar Gonzales and Nonna Gorilovskaya. Among our research assistants, we owe a special debt of gratitude to Neva Tassan and Stephen Lee, who became full partners in the project during the last two years of its execution. Neva's expertise in law and her painstaking research in secondary sources and Stephen's work on constitutions were essential to bringing the volume to fruition.

For the Spanish translation of the survey we are indebted to Maricio Benitez; for the French version, to Ivan Ascher.

For valuable financial support, we are grateful to the Institute for International Studies, the Institute on Global Conflict and Cooperation, the Institute of Governmental Studies, the Committee on Research, the Institute of Slavic, East European, and Eurasian Studies, and the Department of Political Science, all of the University of California, Berkeley. We are also indebted to the Center for International Security and Cooperation at Stanford University, the Belfer Center for Science and International Affairs at Harvard University, and the National Science Foundation.

We dedicate this book to our parents, Michael Fish and Cherrie Robinson, and Mark Kroenig and Barb Kroenig, with love and gratitude.

NATIONAL ASSEMBLY OF AFGHANISTAN (*JIRGA*)

Expert consultants: Ahmad Behzad, Pietro Calogero, Shahnaz Hemmati, Mohammad Isaqzadeh, Qayyum Kochai, Fatima Mojaddedi, Michael Schoiswohl, Roshanak Wardak

Score: .38

Influence over executive (2/9)		Institutional autonomy (4/9)		Specified powers (3/8)		Institutional capacity (3/6)	
1. replace		10. no dissolution	X	19. amendments		27. sessions	X
2. serve as ministers		11. no decree		20. war	X	28. secretary	X
3. interpellate		12. no veto		21. treaties	X	29. staff	
4. investigate	X	13. no review		22. amnesty		30. no term limits	X
5. oversee police		14. no gatekeeping		23. pardon		31. seek re-election	
6. appoint PM		15. no impoundment	X	24. judiciary	X	32. experience	
7. appoint ministers	X	16. control resources	X	25. central bank			
8. lack president		17. immunity	X	26. media			
9. no confidence		18. all elected					

The National Assembly (*Jirga*) of Afghanistan was established in 2003 following the United States–led invasion and overthrow of the Taliban government. The bicameral Assembly consists of a lower house, the House of Representatives (*Wolesi Jirga*), and an upper house, the House of Elders (*Meshrano Jirga*). Afghanistan held presidential elections in 2004 and legislative elections in 2005. Constitutional government is still young, and it is too early to say with any certainty how the legislature will function.

The constitution grants the Assembly a bit of control over the executive, in the form of the right to establish a special commission of investigation and to confirm or reject the president's choice of ministers. Otherwise, the legislature lacks sway over the executive. The legislature also lacks a great deal of institutional autonomy. The constitution grants the president a number of powers that circumscribe the legislature's institutional autonomy; for example, the executive has decree power and gatekeeping authority over financial bills. The president also appoints one-third of the members of the legislature's upper house. The Assembly has several specific powers; its assent is needed for declarations of war, the ratification of foreign treaties, and the confirmation of some presidential appointments to the judiciary. It is too early to assess the Assembly's institutional capacity, although the constitution's provisions for regular sessions lasting nine months each year, the presence of secretarial staff for members of the Assembly, and the absence of term limits indicate the presence of some institutional capacity.

SURVEY

1. The legislature alone, without the involvement of any other agencies, can impeach the president or replace the prime minister.

No. Presidential impeachment requires the involvement of a special court.

> Article 69
> (2) Accusations of crime against humanity, national treason or crime can be leveled against the President by one-third of the members of the House of Representatives.
> (3) If two-thirds of the House of Representatives votes for charges to be brought forth, the House of Representatives shall convene a Grand Council within one month.
> (4) If the Grand Council approves the accusation by a two-thirds majority of votes the President is then dismissed, and the case is referred to a special court.
> (5) The special court is composed of three members of the House of Representatives and three members of the Supreme Court appointed by the Grand Council and the Chair of the Senate.
> (6) The lawsuit is conducted by a person appointed by the Grand Council.

2. Ministers may serve simultaneously as members of the legislature.

No. Legislators are prohibited from serving simultaneously in ministerial positions.

> Article 73
> (2) If a member of the National Assembly is appointed as a minister, he loses his membership in the National Assembly, and is replaced by another person in accordance with the provisions of law.

3. The legislature has powers of summons over executive branch officials and hearings with executive branch officials testifying before the legislature or its committees are regularly held.

No. Formally, the legislature can interpellate officials from the executive, but the practice of doing so has not been established.

> Article 92
> (1) House of Representatives based on a proposal by one-tenth of all members, can interpellate each of the Ministers.

> Article 93
> (1) Any commission of both Houses of the National Assembly can question each of the Ministers about specific topics.
> (2) The person questioned can provide verbal or written response.

4. The legislature can conduct independent investigation of the chief executive and the agencies of the executive.

Yes. According to the constitution, the legislature can establish a special commission to investigate the executive. How effectively this power will be used remains to be seen.

> Article 89
> (1) The House of Representatives has the authority to set up a special commission if one-third of its members put forward a proposal to inquire about and study government actions.
> (2) The composition and procedure of this commission shall be specified by the internal regulations of the House of Representatives.

5. The legislature has effective powers of oversight over the agencies of coercion (the military, organs of law enforcement, intelligence services, and the secret police).

No. The constitution lacks provisions granting the legislature powers of oversight over the agencies of coercion, and there is not yet sufficient evidence to conclude that the legislature enjoys these powers in practice.

6. The legislature appoints the prime minister.

No. There is no prime minister.

7. The legislature's approval is required to confirm the appointment of ministers; or the legislature itself appoints ministers.

Yes. The legislature's approval is necessary to confirm the president's ministerial appointments.

> Article 71
> (1) The government consists of the ministers who work under the Chairmanship of the President.
> (2) Ministers are appointed by the President and shall be introduced for approval to the National Assembly.

8. The country lacks a presidency entirely or there is a presidency, but the president is elected by the legislature.

No. The president is directly elected.

> Article 61
> (1) The President is elected by receiving more than 50% of the votes cast through free, general, secret, and direct voting.

9. The legislature can vote no confidence in the government.

No. The legislature may vote no confidence in individual ministers, but not in the government as a whole.

Article 92

(1) House of Representatives based on a proposal by one-tenth of all members, can interpellate each of the Ministers.

(2) If the responses given are not satisfactory, House of Representatives shall consider the issue of vote of no confidence.

(3) Vote of no confidence on a Minister should be explicit, direct, and on the basis of well founded reasons.

(4) This vote should be approved by a majority of all members of the House of Representatives.

10. The legislature is immune from dissolution by the executive.

Yes. The legislature is immune from dissolution.

11. Any executive initiative on legislation requires ratification or approval by the legislature before it takes effect; that is, the executive lacks decree power.

No. The executive can issue decrees when the legislature is in recess. The decrees lapse if they are not subsequently approved by the legislature.

Article 79

(1) In cases of recess of the House of Representatives, the government can adopt legislation in an emergency situation on matters other than those related to budget and financial affairs.

(2) The legislative decrees become laws after they are signed by the President.

(3) The legislative decrees should be submitted to the National Assembly in the course of thirty days beginning from the first session of the National Assembly.

(4) In case of rejection by the National Assembly, the legislations become void.

12. Laws passed by the legislature are veto-proof or essentially veto-proof; that is, the executive lacks veto power, or has veto power but the veto can be overridden by a majority in the legislature.

No. A two-thirds majority in the House of Representatives is needed to override a presidential veto.

Article 94

(2) In case the President does not agree to what the National Assembly approves, he or she can send the document back with justifiable reasons to the House of Representatives within fifteen days of its submission.

(3) With the passage of this period or in case the House of Representatives approves a particular case again with a majority of two-thirds votes, the bill is considered endorsed and enforced.

13. The legislature's laws are supreme and not subject to judicial review.

No. The Supreme Court can review the constitutionality of laws.

Article 121

The Supreme Court upon request of the Government or the Courts can review compliance with the Constitution of laws, legislative decrees, international treaties, and international conventions, and interpret them, in accordance with the law.

14. The legislature has the right to initiate bills in all policy jurisdictions; the executive lacks gatekeeping authority.

No. The legislature is prohibited from introducing legislation related to financial affairs.

Article 96

Proposals for budget and financial affairs are initiated only by the government.

15. Expenditure of funds appropriated by the legislature is mandatory; the executive lacks the power to impound funds appropriated by the legislature.

Yes. The constitution does not formally grant the executive impoundment power, and there is not yet sufficient evidence to conclude that the president exercises impoundment power in practice.

16. The legislature controls the resources that finance its own internal operation and provide for the perquisites of its own members.

Yes. The constitution establishes some basis for financial autonomy for the legislature.

Article 155

For . . . members of the National Assembly . . . appropriate salaries shall be paid in accordance with the provisions of law.

17. Members of the legislature are immune from arrest and/or criminal prosecution.

Yes. Legislators are immune with the common exception for cases of *flagrante delicto*, here expressed as "evident crime."

Article 101

No member of the National Assembly is legally prosecuted due to expressing his views while performing his duty.

Article 102

(1) When a member of the National Assembly is accused of a crime, the law enforcement authority informs the house, of which the accused is member, about the case, and the accused member can be prosecuted.

(2) In case of an evident crime, the law enforcement authority can legally pursue and arrest the accused without the permission of the house, which the accused is a member of.

(3) In both cases, when legal prosecution requires detention of the accused, law enforcement authorities are obligated to inform the respective house, about the case immediately.

(4) If the accusation takes place when the assembly is in recess, the permission of arrest is obtained from the administrative board of the respective house and the decision of this board is presented to the first session of the aforementioned house for a decision.

18. All members of the legislature are elected; the executive lacks the power to appoint any members of the legislature.

No. The president appoints one-third of the members of the House of Elders. All members of the House of Representatives are elected.

> Article 83
> (1) Members of the House of Representatives are elected by the people through free, general, secret, and direct elections.

> Article 84
> (1) Members of the Senate are elected and appointed as follows:
> (4) The President from among experts and experienced personalities – including two representatives from the disabled and impaired and two representatives from the Kochis – appoints the remaining one-third of the members for a period of five years.
> (5) The president appoints 50% of these people from among women.

19. The legislature alone, without the involvement of any other agencies, can change the Constitution.

No. The constitution can be amended only by a Grand Council made up of members of the legislature and chairpersons of provincial and district councils.

> Article 111
> Grand Council is convened in the following situations:
> – To amend the provisions of this Constitution.

20. The legislature's approval is necessary for the declaration of war.

Yes. The legislature's approval is necessary for presidential war declarations.

> Article 64
> [The president can issue a] declaration of war and cease-fire with the approval of the National Assembly.

21. The legislature's approval is necessary to ratify treaties with foreign countries.

Yes. The legislature's approval is necessary to ratify international treaties.

> Article 90
> The National Assembly has the following powers:
> – Ratification of international treaties and agreements, or abrogation of the membership of Afghanistan to them.

22. The legislature has the power to grant amnesty.

No. Pardon and amnesty are not treated separately, and the legislature lacks the power to grant amnesty. See item 23.

23. The legislature has the power of pardon.

No. The president has the power to grant pardon.

> Article 64
> The powers and duties of the President are as follows:
> – Reducing and pardoning penalties in accordance with law.

24. The legislature reviews and has the right to reject appointments to the judiciary; or the legislature itself appoints members of the judiciary.

Yes. The House of Representatives' approval is needed to confirm the president's appointments to the Supreme Court.

> Article 117
> (1) The Supreme Court is composed of nine members who are appointed by the President for a period of ten years with the approval of the House of Representatives.

25. The chairman of the central bank is appointed by the legislature.

No. The president appoints the director of the Central Bank.

> Article 64
> The powers and duties of the President are as follows:
> – Appointing . . . the Director of the Central Bank . . . with the approval of the House of Representatives.

26. The legislature has a substantial voice in the operation of the state-owned media.

No. According to the constitution, the media will be regulated by law. In practice, the National Assembly has yet to gain a substantial voice in the operation of the public media.

> Article 34
> (4) Directives related to printing house, radio, television, press, and other mass media, will be regulated by the law.

27. The legislature is regularly in session.

Yes. The legislature meets in ordinary session for about nine months each year.

> Article 107
> (1) The National Assembly convenes two ordinary sessions each year.
> (2) The term of the National Assembly in each year is nine months.

28. Each legislator has a personal secretary.

Yes.

29. Each legislator has at least one non-secretarial staff member with policy expertise.

No.

30. Legislators are eligible for re-election without any restriction.

Yes. There are no restrictions on re-election.

31. A seat in the legislature is an attractive enough position that legislators are generally interested in and seek re-election.

No. It is too early to tell. There has only been one election for the National Assembly and thus inadequate opportunity to observe how legislators may behave with regard to re-election.

32. The re-election of incumbent legislators is common enough that at any given time the legislature contains a significant number of highly experienced members.

No. About a quarter of the members of the legislature had formal political experience prior to their election in 2005. The fledgling legislature includes some prominent actors, including warlords, heads of clan networks, and leaders from the era of communist rule during the 1980s. But Afghanistan has had only a single parliamentary election, in 2005, and the legislature does not yet have a significant number of experienced members.

ASSEMBLY OF ALBANIA (*KUVENDI*)

Expert consultants: Jennifer L. Butz, Elda Hysenllari, Altin Ilirjani, Remzi Lani, Artur Nura, Shinasi A. Rama

Score: .75

Influence over executive (8/9)		Institutional autonomy (7/9)		Specified powers (5/8)		Institutional capacity (4/6)	
1. replace	X	10. no dissolution		19. amendments	X	27. sessions	X
2. serve as ministers	X	11. no decree	X	20. war	X	28. secretary	
3. interpellate	X	12. no veto	X	21. treaties	X	29. staff	
4. investigate	X	13. no review		22. amnesty	X	30. no term limits	X
5. oversee police		14. no gatekeeping	X	23. pardon		31. seek re-election	X
6. appoint PM	X	15. no impoundment	X	24. judiciary	X	32. experience	X
7. appoint ministers	X	16. control resources	X	25. central bank			
8. lack president	X	17. immunity	X	26. media			
9. no confidence	X	18. all elected	X				

The Assembly (*Kuvendi*) of Albania was established in its present form in Albania's 1998 constitution. Albania was ruled by a communist-party dictatorship from the end of World War II until the early 1990s. In 1991 an interim constitution, the "Law on Major Constitutional Provisions," revoked the communist-era constitution and established a system for more open politics. The 1998 constitution made changes to the interim constitutional document that strengthened the legislature's hand. The 1998 document formalizes the legislature's role in choosing the prime minister. Previously the power was reserved for the president, but the 1998 constitution stipulates that the president is required to nominate a candidate with majority support in parliament. The new constitution also narrows the conditions under which the president may exercise decree power, from "urgent cases" in the 1991 document to the more precise "during the state of war" in the 1998 version.

Yet the 1998 constitution also weakened the legislature in several ways. Prior to 1998, the legislature had the authority to interpret the constitution and the constitutionality of laws; since 1998 the Constitutional Court has exercised this power. The 1998 document also removed language granting the legislature control over official media.

The legislature's oversight powers over the executive increased in 2002 with the establishment of a new parliamentary committee to investigate the property holdings of government officials.

The legislature's overall level of power is very high. It exercises a good deal of control over the executive. It has substantial institutional autonomy and enjoys several enumerated powers. Its institutional capacity is limited by the lack of parliamentary staff.

SURVEY

1. The legislature alone, without the involvement of any other agencies, can impeach the president or replace the prime minister.

Yes. The legislature can replace the prime minister with a vote of no confidence. Presidential impeachment requires the involvement of the Constitutional Court. Prior to the 1998 constitutional changes, the parliament acting alone could remove the president from office.

> Article 93
> (2) The President of the Republic may be discharged for serious violations of the Constitution. In these cases, a proposal for the discharge of the President may be made by not less than one fourth of the members of the Assembly and shall be supported by not less than two thirds of all its members.
> (3) The decision of the Assembly is sent to the Constitutional Court, which, when it verifies the guilt of the President of the Republic, declares his discharge from office.

> Article 108
> (1) If a motion of confidence presented by the Prime Minister is refused by a majority of all the members of the Assembly, the Assembly elects another Prime Minister within 15 days.

2. Ministers may serve simultaneously as members of the legislature.

Yes. Legislators may serve simultaneously in ministerial positions.

> Article 70
> (2) A deputy may be a member of the Council of Ministers.

3. The legislature has powers of summons over executive branch officials and hearings with executive branch officials testifying before the legislature or its committees are regularly held.

Yes. The legislature regularly interpellates officials from the executive.

> Article 80
> (1) The Prime Minister and any other member of the Council of Ministers is obligated to answer interpellances and questions of the deputies within three weeks.

4. The legislature can conduct independent investigation of the chief executive and the agencies of the executive.

Yes. The legislature can establish committees to investigate the executive.

> Article 77
> (2) The Assembly has the right, and with the request of one-fourth of its members is obliged, to designate investigatory committees to examine a particular issue.

5. The legislature has effective powers of oversight over the agencies of coercion (the military, organs of law enforcement, intelligence services, and the secret police).

No. The legislature lacks effective powers of oversight over the agencies of coercion.

6. The legislature appoints the prime minister.

Yes. Since 1998, the president has been required to name as prime minister the candidate with majority support in the parliament. Before the 1998 constitutional revision, the president could select his or her own choice for prime minister.

> Article 99
> (1) The President of the Republic, at the beginning of a legislature, as well as in every case of vacancy, names as Prime Minister the candidate presented by the party or coalition of parties that have the majority of seats in the Assembly.

7. The legislature's approval is required to confirm the appointment of ministers; or the legislature itself appoints ministers.

Yes. The president appoints ministers on the recommendation of the prime minister, and the parliament's approval is necessary to confirm the appointments. In practice, moreover, the president allocates ministerial portfolios as instructed by the leading parliamentary groups.

Article 102

(1) A minister is appointed and dismissed by the President of the Republic, on the proposal of the Prime Minister, within 7 days.

(2) The decree is approved within 10 days by the Assembly.

8. The country lacks a presidency entirely or there is a presidency, but the president is elected by the legislature.

Yes. The legislature elects the president.

Article 90

(2) The President of the Republic is elected by secret vote and without debate by the Assembly by a majority of three-fifths of all its members.

9. The legislature can vote no confidence in the government.

Yes. The legislature can vote no confidence in the government.

Article 108

(1) If a motion of confidence presented by the Prime Minister is refused by a majority of all the members of the Assembly, the Assembly elects another Prime Minister within 15 days.

10. The legislature is immune from dissolution by the executive.

No. The president can dissolve the legislature.

Article 90

(7) If even in the fifth voting (for president) neither of the two candidates has received the required majority, the Assembly dissolves and within 60 days new general elections take place.

Article 100

(1) If the Prime Minister named is not approved, the Assembly elects a new Prime Minister within 15 days from the voting.

(2) If the election does not take place within this time period, the Assembly within the next 7 days does a new election of the Prime Minister.

(3) If the one elected receives the votes of a majority of all the members of the Assembly, the President of the Republic shall appoint him within seven days.

(4) When this majority is not achieved, the President of the Republic dissolves the Assembly within seven days.

11. Any executive initiative on legislation requires ratification or approval by the legislature before it takes effect; that is, the executive lacks decree power.

Yes. The executive lacks decree power. During a state of war, however, the president may issue acts that have the force of law. The prime minister also can issue decrees that have the force of law during

periods of emergency. The decrees lapse if they are not subsequently approved by the legislature.

Article 167

When the Assembly cannot be assembled during the state of war, the President of the Republic, with the proposal of the Council of Ministers, has the right to issue acts that have the force of the law, which have to be approved by the Assembly in its first meeting.

Article 28

19. [The president] issues decrees of individual character and decisions, and in urgent cases issues even decrees of normative character, which are submitted for approval to the People's Assembly in its nearest session.

12. Laws passed by the legislature are veto-proof or essentially veto-proof; that is, the executive lacks veto power, or has veto power but the veto can be overridden by a majority in the legislature.

Yes. The legislature can override a presidential veto by a majority vote of its total membership.

Article 85

(1) The President of the Republic has the right to return a law for review only once.

(2) The decree of the President for the review of a law loses its effect when a majority of all the members of the Assembly vote against it.

13. The legislature's laws are supreme and not subject to judicial review.

No. Since 1998 the Constitutional Court has had the power to review the constitutionality of laws. Prior to 1998 the legislature itself was responsible for interpreting the constitution.

Article 168

(1) The Constitutional Court guarantees respect for the Constitution and makes final interpretations of it.

(2) The Constitutional Court is subject only to the Constitution.

14. The legislature has the right to initiate bills in all policy jurisdictions; the executive lacks gatekeeping authority.

Yes. The legislature can initiate bills in all policy jurisdictions.

15. Expenditure of funds appropriated by the legislature is mandatory; the executive lacks the power to impound funds appropriated by the legislature.

Yes. The executive lacks the power to impound funds appropriated by the legislature.

16. The legislature controls the resources that finance its own internal operation and provide for the perquisites of its own members.

Yes. The legislature enjoys financial autonomy.

17. Members of the legislature are immune from arrest and/or criminal prosecution.

Yes. Legislators are immune with the common exception for cases of *flagrante delicto,* here expressed as "caught during or immediately after the commission of a serious crime."

> Article 73
> (1) A deputy does not bear responsibility for opinions expressed in the Assembly and votes given. This provision is not applicable in the case of defamation.
> (2) A deputy may not be detained or arrested without the authorization of the Assembly.
> (3) He may be detained or arrested in the act without authorization only when he is caught during or immediately after the commission of a serious crime. In these cases, the General Prosecutor immediately notifies the Assembly, which when it determines that the proceeding is out of place, shall decide to lift the measure.

18. All members of the legislature are elected; the executive lacks the power to appoint any members of the legislature.

Yes. All members of the legislature are elected.

> Article 64
> (2) 100 deputies are elected directly in single-member electoral zones with approximately the same number of voters.
> (3) Supplemental mandates are given to the parties or coalition of parties from their multi-name lists in proportion to the votes won by the respective candidates on the national scale in the first round.

19. The legislature alone, without the involvement of any other agencies, can change the Constitution.

Yes. The Assembly can change the constitution with a two-thirds majority vote. Still, there is some ambiguity concerning whether a popular referendum is, or should be, needed to approve constitutional changes made by parliament. The issue is currently under discussion in Albania.

> Article 178
> (1) Initiative for revision of the Constitution may be undertaken by not less than one-fifth of the members of the Assembly.
> (4) The draft law is approved by not less than two-thirds of all members of the Assembly.
> (7) The President of the Republic does not have the right to return for review the law approved by the Assembly for revision of the Constitution.

20. The legislature's approval is necessary for the declaration of war.

Yes. The legislature itself declares war with the common exception for cases of foreign invasion. In cases of armed aggression against the country, the president, on the recommendation of the Council of Ministers, can declare war without the legislature's approval.

> Article 162
> (1) In case of armed aggression against the Republic of Albania, the President of the Republic upon request of the Council of Ministers can declare the state of war.
> (2) In case of external threat, or when a common defense obligation derives from an international agreement, the Assembly, upon proposal of the President of the Republic, declares the state of war, decides the state of general or partial mobilization or demobilization.

21. The legislature's approval is necessary to ratify treaties with foreign countries.

Yes. The legislature's approval is necessary to ratify international treaties on most major issues.

> Article 124
> (1) The ratification and denunciation of international agreements by the Republic of Albania is done by law in cases that have to do with:
>   a) territory, peace, alliance, political and military issues;
>   b) freedoms, human rights and obligations of citizens as are provided in the Constitution;
>   c) membership of the Republic of Albania in international organizations;
>   d) the undertaking of financial obligations by the Republic of Albania;
>   e) the approval, amendment, supplementing or repeal of laws.
> (2) The Assembly may, with a majority of all its members, ratify other international agreements that are not contemplated in Paragraph (1) of this article.
> (3) The Prime Minister notifies the Assembly whenever the Council of Ministers is going to sign an international agreement that is not ratified by law.
> (4) The principles and procedures for ratification and denunciation of international agreements are provided by law.

22. The legislature has the power to grant amnesty.

Yes. The legislature can grant amnesty by a three-fifths majority vote. The Council of the Assembly, a body within the Assembly that consists of the speaker, deputy speakers, and leaders of parliamentary groups, typically convenes in advance of a vote to ensure that the required supermajority is in place.

Article 81
(2) The following are approved by the majority specified in article 87:
  h) the law on amnesty.

Article 87
(1) The Council of the Assembly:
  a) reviews preliminarily draft laws contemplated in Article 81 (2) of the Constitution.

23. The legislature has the power of pardon.

No. The president has the power of pardon.

Article 95
b) [The president] exercises the right of pardon according to the law.

24. The legislature reviews and has the right to reject appointments to the judiciary; or the legislature itself appoints members of the judiciary.

Yes. The Assembly's consent is required for the president's judicial appointments.

Article 128
(1) The Chairman and the members of the High Court are appointed by the President of the Republic with the consent of the Assembly.
(3) Other judges are appointed by the President of the Republic upon the proposal of the High Council of Justice.

Article 169
(1) The Constitutional Court is composed of 9 members, which are appointed by the President of the Republic with the consent of Assembly.
(4) The Chairman of the Constitutional Court is appointed from the ranks of the members by the President of the Republic with the consent of the Assembly for a 3 year term.

25. The chairman of the central bank is appointed by the legislature.

No. The president appoints the governor of the Bank of Albania with the approval of the legislature.

Article 152
(2) The Bank of Albania is directed by its Board, which is chaired by the Governor. The Governor is elected by the Assembly for 7 years, upon proposal of the President of the Republic.

26. The legislature has a substantial voice in the operation of the state-owned media.

No. The legislature lacks a substantial voice in the operation of the state-owned media. The 1991 constitution granted the legislature control over official media. This provision, however, was stripped from the 1998 constitution.

27. The legislature is regularly in session.

Yes. The legislature regularly meets in ordinary session.

Article 74
(1) The Assembly conducts its annual work in two sessions. The first session begins on the third Monday of January and the second session on the first Monday of September.

28. Each legislator has a personal secretary.

No.

29. Each legislator has at least one non-secretarial staff member with policy expertise.

No.

30. Legislators are eligible for re-election without any restriction.

Yes. There are no restrictions on re-election.

31. A seat in the legislature is an attractive enough position that legislators are generally interested in and seek re-election.

Yes.

32. The re-election of incumbent legislators is common enough that at any given time the legislature contains a significant number of highly experienced members.

Yes. Albania's most recent rounds of parliamentary elections were held in 1997, 2001, and 2005. Turnover in 2001 was not high, but was considerably higher in 2005; half of all deputies entering parliament in 2005 were new members. Still, about one-sixth of all members have been re-elected at least twice and have served since 1997, giving a legislature a significant, albeit not large, cohort of highly experienced members.

PARLIAMENT OF ALGERIA (*BARLAMAN*)

Expert consultants: Abdallah Bedaida, Youcef Bouandel, Lazhar Chine, E. G. H. Joffé, Robert Mortimer, Robert Peri, Megan Reif

Score: .25

Influence over executive (1/9)	Institutional autonomy (2/9)		Specified powers (1/8)		Institutional capacity (4/6)	
1. replace	10. no dissolution		19. amendments		27. sessions	X
2. serve as ministers	11. no decree		20. war		28. secretary	
3. interpellate	12. no veto		21. treaties	X	29. staff	
4. investigate	13. no review		22. amnesty		30. no term limits	X
5. oversee police	14. no gatekeeping	X	23. pardon		31. seek re-election	X
6. appoint PM	15. no impoundment	X	24. judiciary		32. experience	X
7. appoint ministers	16. control resources		25. central bank			
8. lack president	17. immunity		26. media			
9. no confidence	X	18. all elected				

In 1976, with the military's support, a new constitution was approved that established the unicameral National People's Assembly (*Al-Majlis Ech-Chaabi Al-Watani*) and granted sweeping powers to the president. A 1996 amendment added an upper house to the legislature, the Council of the Nation, to create a bicameral Parliament (*Barlaman*) of Algeria.

The 1976 constitution was revised in 1986, 1989, and 1996. The 1989 reforms liberalized the political system to some degree, but the 1996 amendments, along with creating the Council of the Nation, aggrandized the already overwhelming powers of the president. After an Islamist party won the first round of parliamentary elections in 1991, the government annulled the elections, sparking a gruesome, protracted civil war. The violence has largely subsided, although the country officially remains in a state of emergency. Since 1996 the president has had the power to rule by decree when the legislature is in recess. Another amendment expanded presidential appointment power to include magistrates and the central bank governor.

The legislature has little power. It has very little influence over the executive, minimal institutional autonomy, and only one of the specified powers assessed in this survey. It has some institutional capacity deriving from the fact that a position in the legislature is still seen as attractive, the legislature is regularly in session, legislators may serve consecutive terms, and the legislature includes many long-serving members.

SURVEY

1. The legislature alone, without the involvement of any other agencies, can impeach the president or replace the prime minister.

No. The legislature cannot impeach the president. The legislature can replace the prime minister with a motion of censure.

> Article 136
> The motion of censure must be approved by a vote taken by a majority of two-thirds of the deputies. The vote cannot be held until three days after the introduction of the motion of censure.

> Article 137
> After the motion of censure is approved by the National People's Assembly, the Head of the Government must present the resignation of his government to the President of the Republic.

2. Ministers may serve simultaneously as members of the legislature.

No. Ministers are prohibited from serving simultaneously in the legislature.

3. The legislature has powers of summons over executive branch officials and hearings with executive branch officials testifying before the legislature or its committees are regularly held.

No. While the legislature enjoys the formal right to question the prime minister and government, this power is strictly limited to paper; it has no substance in practice.

Article 133
The members of the Parliament can interpellate the government on a question of current concern.
The commissions of the Parliament may hear the members of the Government.

Article 134
The members of the Parliament may address orally or in written form any question to any member of the government. The written question must receive a reply on the same form within a maximum period of thirty days.

4. The legislature can conduct independent investigation of the chief executive and the agencies of the executive.

No. According to the constitution, the legislature can establish commissions of inquiry. In practice, it is unthinkable that the legislature would investigate the president.

Article 161
Each of the two chambers may, at any time, establish within the framework of its powers a commission of inquiry on any matter of general interest.

5. The legislature has effective powers of oversight over the agencies of coercion (the military, organs of law enforcement, intelligence services, and the secret police).

No. The agencies of coercion report to the president and are not subject to legislative oversight.

6. The legislature appoints the prime minister.

No. The president appoints the prime minister.

Article 77
5. [The president] appoints the Head of the Government and puts an end to its function.

7. The legislature's approval is required to confirm the appointment of ministers; or the legislature itself appoints ministers.

No. The president appoints ministers, and the appointments do not require the legislature's approval.

Article 78
The President of the Republic appoints:
3. To designations determined in the Council of Ministers.

Article 79
The Head of the Government presents the members of the government, which he has chosen, to the President of the Republic for appointment.

8. The country lacks a presidency entirely or there is a presidency, but the president is elected by the legislature.

No. The president is directly elected.

Article 71
The President of the Republic is elected by universal, direct and secret suffrage.

9. The legislature can vote no confidence in the government.

Yes. The legislature can vote no confidence in the government.

Article 81
In case of non-approval of his program by the National People's Assembly, the Head of the Government presents the resignation of his government to the President of the Republic who appoints another Head of the Government in accord with the same provisions.

Article 84
The Head of the Government may demand a vote of confidence from the National People's Assembly. If the motion of confidence is not voted, the Head of the Government presents the resignation of his Government.

Article 136
The motion of censure must be approved by a vote taken by a majority of two-thirds of the deputies. The vote cannot be held until three days after the introduction of the motion of censure.

Article 137
After the motion of censure is approved by the National People's Assembly, the Head of the Government must present the resignation of his government to the President of the Republic.

10. The legislature is immune from dissolution by the executive.

No. The president can dissolve the legislature.

11. Any executive initiative on legislation requires ratification or approval by the legislature before it takes effect; that is, the executive lacks decree power.

No. The president can issue decrees that have the force of law when the legislature is not in session. The decrees lapse if they are not subsequently approved by both houses of the legislature.

Article 77
6. [The president] signs presidential decrees.

Article 85
4. [The head of government] signs executive decrees.

Article 124
In case of vacancy of the National People's Assembly or in periods of intersession of the Parliament, the President of the Republic can legislate by ordinance. The President of the Republic submits the texts which he has framed for the approval of each of the chambers of Parliament, at their next session. Ordinances not adopted by the Parliament are null. In case of a state of exception defined in Article 93 of the Constitution, the President of the Republic may legislate by ordinances. The ordinances are framed in the Council of Ministers.

12. Laws passed by the legislature are veto-proof or essentially veto-proof; that is, the executive lacks veto power, or has veto power but the veto can be overridden by a majority in the legislature.

No. A two-thirds majority vote of the total membership of the National People's Assembly is needed to override a presidential veto. Furthermore, in 1996 an upper house of parliament, the Council of the Nation, was established. A three-fourths majority vote in the upper house is required to pass legislation – not just to override a presidential veto, but to pass any legislation. Since the president appoints one-third of the members of the upper house, legislative proposals have little chance of becoming law without presidential backing. The arrangement has the effect of furnishing the president with an absolute veto.

Article 127
The President of the Republic can demand a second reading of a voted law, within thirty days following its adoption. In that case, a majority of two-thirds of the members of the National People's Assembly is required for the adoption of the law.

13. The legislature's laws are supreme and not subject to judicial review.

No. The Constitutional Council can review the constitutionality of laws.

Article 165
Aside from the other functions which are expressly conferred by other provisions of the Constitution, the Constitutional Council rules on the constitutionality of treaties, laws and negotiations, either by an opinion, if these are not rendered executory, or by a decision, in the opposite case.

14. The legislature has the right to initiate bills in all policy jurisdictions; the executive lacks gatekeeping authority.

Yes. The legislature can initiate bills in all policy jurisdictions.

15. Expenditure of funds appropriated by the legislature is mandatory; the executive lacks the power to impound funds appropriated by the legislature.

Yes. The executive lacks the power to impound funds appropriated by the legislature.

16. The legislature controls the resources that finance its own internal operation and provide for the perquisites of its own members.

No. The constitution grants the legislature control over its own operations, but in practice, the legislature is dependent on the president for the resources that finance its own operations.

Article 115
The organization and the functioning of the National People's Assembly and of the Council of the Nation, as well as the functional relations between the chambers of the Parliament and the Government are determined by an organic law. The budget of the two chambers, as well as the remuneration of the deputies and the members of the Council of the Nation are determined by the law. The National People's Assembly and the Council of the Nation elaborate and adopt their internal regulations.

17. Members of the legislature are immune from arrest and/or criminal prosecution.

No. Despite constitutional provisions to the contrary, legislators are subject to arrest. For example, legislators were arrested in 2004 and 2005 for participating in demonstrations in support of a candidate who opposed the president.

Article 109
Parliamentary immunity is granted to the deputies and to the members of the Council of the Nation during the term of their mandate. They may not be prosecuted, arrested, or in general be the object of civil or criminal action nor all forms of pressure, on account of opinions expressed, speeches delivered or votes cast in the exercise of their mandate.

Article 110
The prosecutions for a delinquent act against a deputy or a member of the Council of the Nation may not be initiated except by express renunciation of the concerned or upon authorization in each case by the National People's Assembly or the Council of the Nation which decides by a majority of its members the lifting of their immunity.

Article 111
In case of a flagrant offense or flagrant crime by the deputy or a member of the Council of the Nation, the arrest can proceed. The bureau of the National People's Assembly or the Council of the Nation must be informed immediately. The pertinent bureau may demand the suspension of the prosecutions and the release of the deputy or the member of the Council of the Nation. He is to be treated in conformity with the provisions of Article 110 above.

18. All members of the legislature are elected; the executive lacks the power to appoint any members of the legislature.

No. The president appoints one-third of the members of the upper house.

> Article 101
> One-third of the members of the Council of the Nation is designated by the President of the Republic among the personalities and national competencies in the scientific, cultural, professional, economic and social fields.

19. The legislature alone, without the involvement of any other agencies, can change the Constitution.

No. Constitutional amendments require approval in a popular referendum.

> Article 174
> A constitutional revision is decided upon on the initiative of the President of the Republic. It is voted on equal terms by the National People's Assembly and the Council of the Nation under the same conditions as a legislative text. It is submitted by referendum for the approval by the people in fifty days following its adoption. The constitutional revision, approved by the people, is promulgated by the President of the Republic.

> Article 177
> Three-fourths of the members of the two chambers of the Parliament, meeting in joint session, may propose a constitutional revision and present it to the President of the Republic, who can submit it in a referendum. If its approval is obtained, it is promulgated.

20. The legislature's approval is necessary for the declaration of war.

No. The president must consult with the legislature before declaring war, but the legislature's approval is not required.

> Article 95
> Having assembled the Council of Ministers, and heard the High Council of Security, and having consulted the President of the National People's Assembly and the President of the Council of the Nation, the President of the Republic declares war in case of effective or imminent aggression in conformity with the pertinent provisions of the Charter of the United Nations.

21. The legislature's approval is necessary to ratify treaties with foreign countries.

Yes. The legislature's approval is necessary to ratify international treaties on most major issues.

> Article 77
> 9. [The president] concludes and ratifies international treaties.

> Article 131
> Armistice accords, treaties of peace, of alliances and union, the treaties concerning the frontiers as well

as treaties concerning the status of person and those which involve expenditures not foreseen in the budget of the State are ratified by the President of the Republic after explicit approval by each of the two chambers of Parliament.

22. The legislature has the power to grant amnesty.

No. Amnesty and pardon are not treated separately, and the legislature lacks the power to grant amnesty. See item 23.

23. The legislature has the power of pardon.

No. The president has the power of pardon.

> Article 77
> 7. [The president] has the right of pardon, the reduction or the commutation of penalties.

> Article 156
> The High Council of the Judiciary provides preliminary consultative opinion to the President of the Republic concerning the exercise of the right of pardon.

24. The legislature reviews and has the right to reject appointments to the judiciary; or the legislature itself appoints members of the judiciary.

No. The president appoints members of the judiciary and judicial appointments do not require legislative approval. In 2000 the president undertook a major purge of the judiciary and replaced the vast majority of leading judges.

> Article 78
> The President of the Republic appoints... the Magistrates.

25. The chairman of the central bank is appointed by the legislature.

No. The president appoints the governor of the Bank of Algeria.

> Article 78
> The President of the Republic appoints... the Governor of the Bank of Algeria.

26. The legislature has a substantial voice in the operation of the state-owned media.

No. Public broadcasters are created and governed by presidential decree.

27. The legislature is regularly in session.

Yes. The legislature regularly meets in ordinary session.

> Article 118
> The Parliament meets in two ordinary sessions each year, each with a minimum duration of four months.

28. Each legislator has a personal secretary.

No. Each party has only two paid assistants. Nearly all deputies have full-time jobs other than their legislative responsibilities, many as lawyers or doctors, and some use external sources of income to hire parliamentary staff.

29. Each legislator has at least one non-secretarial staff member with policy expertise.

No. See item 28.

30. Legislators are eligible for re-election without any restriction.

Yes. There are no restrictions on re-election.

> Article 105
> The mandate of deputy and of the member of the Council of the Nation . . . is renewable.

31. A seat in the legislature is an attractive enough position that legislators are generally interested in and seek re-election.

Yes. A seat in the legislature comes with benefits, including pensions, diplomatic passports, a generous salary, housing benefits, free phone calls, and travel.

32. The re-election of incumbent legislators is common enough that at any given time the legislature contains a significant number of highly experienced members.

Yes. The re-election rate is high, although this state of affairs is due largely to the manipulation of election outcomes by the ruling party and the military.

NATIONAL ASSEMBLY OF ANGOLA (*ASSEMBLEIA NACIONAL*)

Expert consultants: Inge Amundsen, Hermenegildo Avelino, Armando Marques Guedes, André de Oliveira Sango, Nicholas Shaxson

Score: .44

Influence over executive (2/9)		Institutional autonomy (3/9)		Specified powers (6/8)		Institutional capacity (3/6)	
1. replace		10. no dissolution		19. amendments	X	27. sessions	X
2. serve as ministers		11. no decree		20. war	X	28. secretary	
3. interpellate	X	12. no veto		21. treaties	X	29. staff	
4. investigate		13. no review		22. amnesty	X	30. no term limits	X
5. oversee police		14. no gatekeeping		23. pardon	X	31. seek re-election	X
6. appoint PM		15. no impoundment	X	24. judiciary	X	32. experience	
7. appoint ministers		16. control resources		25. central bank			
8. lack president		17. immunity	X	26. media			
9. no confidence	X	18. all elected	X				

The unicameral National Assembly (*Assembleia Nacional*) of Angola was established in the 1991 constitution. From independence in 1975 until 1991, Angola was engulfed in civil war, and a passive People's Assembly existed as part of a single-party communist system. A respite in the fighting in the early 1990s led to the new constitution, the establishment of the National Assembly, and parliamentary elections in 1992. A quick return to civil war meant that many deputies elected in 1992 did not take their seats until 1997.

Despite these setbacks, the National Assembly is still operating on the basis of the 1992 elections. Since 2002 a more stable peace appears to have emerged, and the National Assembly has begun to exercise more of its formal powers. In January 2004 a new draft constitution was presented to the National Assembly. Preparations are under way for new elections. They may or may not lead to the adoption of the new constitution and the emergence of meaningful constitutional politics.

As presently constituted, the legislature has negligible control over the executive. It has some institutional autonomy. It derives much of its authority from specified powers; it holds six of the eight such powers assessed here. Its institutional capacity is modest.

SURVEY

1. The legislature alone, without the involvement of any other agencies, can impeach the president or replace the prime minister.

No. Presidential impeachment requires the involvement of the Supreme Court.

Article 65
(1) The President of the Republic shall not be responsible for acts carried out during the discharge of his duties, except in the case of bribery or treason.
(2) Proceedings shall be initiated by the National Assembly, on the proposal of one-fifth and a decision approved by a two-thirds majority of Members present, and the trial shall be conducted by the Supreme Court.
(3) Sentencing shall imply dismissal from the post and impossibility of standing as a candidate for another term of office.

2. Ministers may serve simultaneously as members of the legislature.

No. Legislators are prohibited from serving simultaneously in ministerial positions.

Article 82
(1) The term of office of a Member shall be incompatible with . . . a ministerial post.

3. The legislature has powers of summons over executive branch officials and hearings with executive branch officials testifying before the legislature or its committees are regularly held.

Yes. The legislature regularly interpellates officials from the executive.

Article 83
Members of the National Assembly shall have the right, in accordance with the Constitutional Law and the Regulations of the National Assembly, to question the Government or any of the members thereof, and to obtain from all public bodies and enterprises the cooperation needed to discharge their duties.

Article 99
(2) The Prime Minister and members of the Government shall appear before the Assembly plenum at meetings the regularity of which shall be set out in the Regulations of the National Assembly to reply to Members' questions and requests for clarification, made verbally or in writing.

4. The legislature can conduct independent investigation of the chief executive and the agencies of the executive.

No. According to the constitution, the legislature can establish commissions of inquiry to investigate the executive, but in practice, the legislature lacks investigatory powers.

Article 101
(1) Members of the National Assembly may constitute parliamentary commissions of inquiry to examine acts of the Government and administration.
(2) A commission of inquiry shall be requested by any Member and, on a mandatory basis, comprise one-fifth of Members present, and shall be limited to one per Member per legislative session.
(3) Parliamentary commissions of inquiry shall have the investigating powers of judicial bodies.

5. The legislature has effective powers of oversight over the agencies of coercion (the military, organs of law enforcement, intelligence services, and the secret police).

No. The agencies of coercion are responsible to the president and are not subject to legislative oversight.

6. The legislature appoints the prime minister.

No. The president appoints the prime minister.

Article 66
The President of the Republic shall have the following powers:
(a) To appoint the Prime Minister, after hearing the political parties represented in the National Assembly.

7. The legislature's approval is required to confirm the appointment of ministers; or the legislature itself appoints ministers.

No. The president appoints ministers, and the appointments do not require the legislature's approval.

Article 76
The Council of the Republic shall be presided over by the President of the Republic and shall be composed of the following members:
(a) The President of the National Assembly;
(b) The Prime Minister;
(c) The President of the Constitutional Court;
(d) The Attorney General;
(e) Former President of the Republic;
(f) The Presidents of Political Parties represented in the National Assembly;
(g) Ten citizens appointed by the President of the Republic.

8. The country lacks a presidency entirely or there is a presidency, but the president is elected by the legislature.

No. The president is directly elected.

> Article 57
> (1) The President of the Republic shall be elected by universal, direct, equal, secret and periodic suffrage by citizens resident in the national territory, in accordance with the law.

9. The legislature can vote no confidence in the government.

Yes. The legislature can vote no confidence in the government.

> Article 88
> The National Assembly shall:
> (n) Vote motions of confidence or no confidence in the Government.

10. The legislature is immune from dissolution by the executive.

No. The president can dissolve the legislature.

> Article 66
> (e) [The president has the power to] decree the dissolution of the National Assembly after consultation with the Prime Minister, the President of the National Assembly and the Council of the Republic.

11. Any executive initiative on legislation requires ratification or approval by the legislature before it takes effect; that is, the executive lacks decree power.

No. The president and the government issue decrees that have the force of law.

> Article 70
> After they have been signed by the Prime Minister, the President of the Republic shall sign Government decrees thirty days after receiving them and shall inform the Government of the reasons for refusing to sign them.
>
> Article 74
> In the exercise of his powers, the President of the Republic shall issue presidential decrees and dispatches that shall be published in the *Diário da República*.
>
> Article 88
> (l) The national assembly shall . . . ratify decrees.
>
> Article 114
> (3) In the discharge of their duties, the Prime Minister, Ministers and Secretaries of State shall issue executive decrees and dispatches that shall be published in the *Diário da República*.

12. Laws passed by the legislature are veto-proof or essentially veto-proof; that is, the executive lacks veto power, or has veto power but the veto can be overridden by a majority in the legislature.

No. A two-thirds majority vote is needed to override a presidential veto.

> Article 69
> (2) Within this period, the President of the Republic may request the National Assembly to consider the law or any of its provisions.
> (3) If after reconsideration a two-thirds majority of the Members of the National Assembly are in favor of approving the law, the President of Republic shall promulgate the law within fifteen days of receiving it.

13. The legislature's laws are supreme and not subject to judicial review.

No. The Constitutional Court can review the constitutionality of laws.

> Article 134
> The Constitutional Court shall in general administer justice on legal and constitutional matters, and shall:
> (a) Prevent unconstitutionality.
> (b) Consider whether laws, executive laws, ratified international treaties and any rules are unconstitutional.
> (c) Verify and consider non-compliance with the Constitutional Law owing to failure to take the requisite measures to make constitutional rules executable.
> (d) Consider appeals in respect of the constitutional nature of all decisions of other courts that refuse to apply any rule on the grounds that it is unconstitutional.
> (e) Consider appeals in respect of the constitutional nature of all decisions of other courts that apply a rule the constitutional nature of which has been evoked during the trial.

14. The legislature has the right to initiate bills in all policy jurisdictions; the executive lacks gatekeeping authority.

No. The legislature is prohibited from introducing legislation related to the "national plan," which involves a bundle of issues related to economic and social policies that extend well beyond purely budgetary matters.

> Article 88
> The National Assembly shall:
> (b) Approve laws on all matters, except those reserved by the Constitutional Law for the Government;
> (d) Approve, on the proposal of the Government, the National Plan and the General State Budget;
> (e) Approve, on the proposal of the Government, the reports on the execution of the National Plan and the General State Budget.
>
> Article 112
> In the discharge of its administration duties, the Government shall:
> (a) Draft and promote implementation of the country's economic and social development plan;

(b) Draft, approve and direct the execution of the State Budget.

15. Expenditure of funds appropriated by the legislature is mandatory; the executive lacks the power to impound funds appropriated by the legislature.

Yes. The executive does not impound funds authorized by the legislature, but this is partly because the executive operates a parallel budgetary structure beyond the legislature's control.

16. The legislature controls the resources that finance its own internal operation and provide for the perquisites of its own members.

No. The legislature is dependent on the executive for the resources that finance its own operations.

17. Members of the legislature are immune from arrest and/or criminal prosecution.

Yes. Legislators are immune with the common exception for cases of *flagrante delicto*.

> Article 84
> (1) No Member of the National Assembly shall be detained or arrested without authorization by the National Assembly or the Standing Commission thereof, unless caught in flagrante delicto committing a felony punishable by imprisonment.
> (2) Members shall not be held responsible for views they express in the discharge of their duties.

18. All members of the legislature are elected; the executive lacks the power to appoint any members of the legislature.

Yes. All members of the legislature are elected.

> Article 79
> (1) The National Assembly shall be composed of two hundred and twenty-three Members elected by universal, equal, direct, secret and periodic suffrage for a four-year term of office.

19. The legislature alone, without the involvement of any other agencies, can change the Constitution.

Yes. The legislature can change the constitution with a two-thirds majority vote.

> Article 88
> The National Assembly shall:
> (a) Amend the current Constitutional Law and approve the Constitution of the Republic of Angola.

> Article 92
> (1) The National Assembly shall, in the exercise of its powers, issue laws for the constitutional amendment of the Constitution of the Republic of Angola, organic laws, laws, motions and resolutions.

(2) Acts provided for in Article 88 (a) shall take the form of a law on constitutional amendment or amendment of the Constitution of the Republic of Angola.

> Article 158
> (1) The National Assembly may review the Constitutional Law and approve the Constitution of the Republic of Angola on the decision of two-thirds of Members present.
> (2) No less than ten Members or the President of the Republic may propose amendment of the Constitution.
> (3) The Constitutional Law may be amended at any time.
> (4) The National Assembly shall determine the manner of proposing the drafting of the Constitution of the Republic of Angola.
> (5) The President of the Republic shall not refuse to promulgate the Law Amending the Constitution of the Republic of Angola adopted in accordance with the first paragraph of the present article.

20. The legislature's approval is necessary for the declaration of war.

Yes. The legislature's approval is necessary for presidential war declarations.

> Article 66
> [The president has the power] to declare war and make peace, after hearing the Government and following authorization by the National Assembly.

21. The legislature's approval is necessary to ratify treaties with foreign countries.

Yes. The legislature's approval is necessary to ratify international treaties on most major issues.

> Article 88
> The National Assembly shall:
> (k) approve international treaties on matters within its absolute legislative powers, as well as treaties on peace, Angola's participation in international organizations, the rectification of borders, friendship, defense, military matters and any others submitted to it by the Government.

> Article 110
> In the discharge of the political duties, the Government shall:
> (c) Negotiate and conclude international treaties and approve treaties that do not fall within the sole competence of the National Assembly or have not been submitted thereto.

22. The legislature has the power to grant amnesty.

Yes. The legislature has the power to grant amnesty.

> Article 88
> The national assembly shall:
> (h) Grant amnesties and general pardons.

23. The legislature has the power of pardon.

Yes. The legislature has the power of pardon.

> Article 88
> The national assembly shall:
> (h) Grant amnesties and general pardons.

24. The legislature reviews and has the right to reject appointments to the judiciary; or the legislature itself appoints members of the judiciary.

Yes. The legislature makes appointments to the High Council of the Judicial Bench and the Constitutional Court.

> Article 132
> (2) The High Council of the Judicial Bench shall be presided over by the President of the Supreme Court and shall be composed of the following:
> (b) Five lawyers nominated by the National Assembly.

> Article 135
> (1) The Constitutional Court shall be composed of seven judges, nominated from among lawyers and judges as follows:
> (b) Three judges elected by the National Assembly by a two-thirds majority of Members present.

25. The chairman of the central bank is appointed by the legislature.

No. The president, on the recommendation of the prime minister, appoints the governor of the National Bank of Angola.

> Article 66
> The President of the Republic shall have the following powers:
> (b) To appoint and dismiss...the Governor of the National Bank of Angola, on the proposal of the Prime Minister.

26. The legislature has a substantial voice in the operation of the state-owned media.

No. The executive controls the state-owned media.

27. The legislature is regularly in session.

Yes. The legislature is in session for about eight months each year.

> Article 96
> (3) The normal period in which the National Assembly shall function shall be eight months and shall start on 15 October, without prejudice to intervals provided for in the Regulations of the National Assembly and suspensions determined by a two-thirds majority of Members present.

28. Each legislator has a personal secretary.

No. Party groups provide legislative staff, but on average there is less than one staff person for each legislator.

29. Each legislator has at least one non-secretarial staff member with policy expertise.

No. See item 28.

30. Legislators are eligible for re-election without any restriction.

Yes. There are no restrictions on re-election.

31. A seat in the legislature is an attractive enough position that legislators are generally interested in and seek re-election.

Yes. A spot in the legislature provides a steady job in a very poor country.

32. The re-election of incumbent legislators is common enough that at any given time the legislature contains a significant number of highly experienced members.

No. The opportunity for re-election has not occurred under the extant constitutional order. Legislative elections last occurred in 1992 immediately before the political process collapsed into civil war. New elections are now scheduled for September 2008.

ARGENTINE NATIONAL CONGRESS (*CONGRESO*)

Expert consultants: Leslie E. Anderson, Natalia Ferretti, Gretchen Helmke, Mark P. Jones, Ana M. Mustapic, Aníbal S. Pérez-Liñán, Erik Wibbels, Rodrigo Zarazaga

Score: .50

Influence over executive (3/9)		Institutional autonomy (5/9)		Specified powers (4/8)		Institutional capacity (4/6)	
1. replace	X	10. no dissolution	X	19. amendments		27. sessions	X
2. serve as ministers		11. no decree		20. war	X	28. secretary	X
3. interpellate	X	12. no veto		21. treaties	X	29. staff	X
4. investigate	X	13. no review		22. amnesty	X	30. no term limits	X
5. oversee police		14. no gatekeeping	X	23. pardon		31. seek re-election	
6. appoint PM		15. no impoundment		24. judiciary	X	32. experience	
7. appoint ministers		16. control resources	X	25. central bank			
8. lack president		17. immunity	X	26. media			
9. no confidence		18. all elected	X				

Argentina's present constitution, adopted in 1853, established the bicameral Argentine National Congress (*Congreso*). In the subsequent century and a half the legislature has endured periods of marginalization, first due to civil violence in the late nineteenth century and later as a result of military rule in the second half of the twentieth century. In 1949 constitutional amendments augmented presidential power and enabled Juan Domingo Perón to be re-elected president, but by 1956 Peron's amendments were rescinded, and the 1853 constitution was reinstated by the successor government. Congress was suspended from 1966 to 1973 and completely dissolved by a military junta in 1976. A return to civilian rule in 1983 once again granted the legislature independent decision-making power.

Although Congress has the exclusive right to create laws, over the course of the twentieth century Argentine presidents have sometimes invoked "emergency powers" allowing them to rule by decree. This de facto presidential decree power was recognized by the Supreme Court in 1990 and formally institutionalized by a constitutional amendment in 1994.

Another constitutional amendment was passed in 1994 with the aim of rebalancing the playing field between Argentina's historically powerful executive and the other branches of government. A separate executive branch position, the Chief of the Ministerial Cabinet, was created in order to make the executive branch more accountable to Congress. The Chief of the Ministerial Cabinet is appointed and can be dismissed by the president, but can also be removed by a vote of censure from Congress. To date, however, this official has served as little more than an assistant to the president.

Overall, Congress has a moderate level of power. It enjoys some influence over the executive and some institutional autonomy. It holds several enumerated powers. It has some institutional capacity, but that capacity is limited by the relatively diminutive number of experienced legislators.

SURVEY

1. The legislature alone, without the involvement of any other agencies, can impeach the president or replace the prime minister.

Yes. The House of Deputies can impeach the president by a two-thirds majority vote of its present members. The proceedings then move to the Senate for a public trial. Even though the trial is presided over by the Chief Justice of the Supreme Court, the president can be declared guilty by a two-thirds majority vote of the Senate's present members. Argentina lacks a prime minister. The Chief of the Ministerial Cabinet can be removed by the legislature, although to date the holder of this office has functioned as a mere assistant to the president.

Section 53
Only the House of Deputies has the power to impeach before the Senate the President... in such cases of responsibility as are brought against them for misconduct or crimes committed in the fulfillment of their duties; or for ordinary crimes, after having known about them and after the decision to bring an action had been voted by a majority of two-thirds of its members present.

Section 59
The Senate is empowered to judge in public trial those impeached by the House of Deputies, its members being on oath for the case. When the President of the Nation is impeached, the Senate shall be presided by the Chief Justice of the Supreme Court. No person shall be declared guilty without the majority of two-thirds of the members present.

Section 101
The Chief of the Ministerial Cabinet... may be interpellated for the purpose of considering a vote of censure, by the vote of the absolute majority of all the members of either House, and he may be removed by the vote of the absolute majority of the members of each House.

2. Ministers may serve simultaneously as members of the legislature.

No. Ministers are prohibited from serving simultaneously in the legislature.

Section 105
Ministers shall be neither senators nor deputies without resigning their offices as ministers.

3. The legislature has powers of summons over executive branch officials and hearings with executive branch officials testifying before the legislature or its committees are regularly held.

Yes. The legislature has summons power, and hearings are regularly held.

Section 101
The Chief of the Ministerial Cabinet shall attend Congress at least once a month, alternating between each House, to report on the progress of the government.

Section 71
Either House shall summon the Ministers of the Executive Power to receive such explanations or reports as it may deem necessary.

4. The legislature can conduct independent investigation of the chief executive and the agencies of the executive.

Yes. The legislature can investigate the executive.

5. The legislature has effective powers of oversight over the agencies of coercion (the military, organs of law enforcement, intelligence services, and the secret police).

No. The legislature lacks effective powers of oversight over these agencies.

6. The legislature appoints the prime minister.

No. There is no prime minister. The Chief of the Ministerial Cabinet holds a title that may sound like that of a prime minister, but the holder of this office in practice is little more than a spokesperson for and assistant to the president.

Section 99
7. [The president] appoints and removes... the Chief of the Ministerial Cabinet.

7. The legislature's approval is required to confirm the appointment of ministers; or the legislature itself appoints ministers.

No. The president appoints ministers, and the appointments do not require the legislature's approval.

Section 99
7. [The president] appoints and removes... the Ministers.

8. The country lacks a presidency entirely or there is a presidency, but the president is elected by the legislature.

No. The president is directly elected.

Section 94
The President and Vice-President of the Nation shall be directly elected by the people, by second ballot, according to this Constitution.

9. The legislature can vote no confidence in the government.

No. The legislature cannot vote no confidence in the government, although since 1994 the legislature has had the power to censure and remove the Chief of the Ministerial Cabinet.

Section 101
The Chief of the Ministerial Cabinet... may be interpellated for the purpose of considering a vote of censure, by the vote of the absolute majority of all the members of either House, and he may be removed by the vote of the absolute majority of the members of each House.

10. The legislature is immune from dissolution by the executive.

Yes. The legislature is immune from dissolution.

11. Any executive initiative on legislation requires ratification or approval by the legislature before it takes effect; that is, the executive lacks decree power.

No. The president issue decrees that have the force of law in "exceptional circumstances." The 1853 constitution allowed presidents to rule by decree as an emergency power. In 1990 the Supreme

Court accepted the legality of decree-laws in normal political circumstances, and this power was formally recognized in the constitution in 1994. The constitution stated that the decrees would have to go to the legislature for approval within ten days to become effective. It also mandated that within a year from the signing of the new constitution the legislature issue a law regulating the decree procedures. After a long delay, in 2006 Congress enacted a law that regulates decree procedures, and it established a sixteen-member congressional commission that scrutinizes decrees. Presidential decree power is the subject of extensive debate in Argentina. The threshold that constitutes the "exceptional circumstances" that justify the president's making what are known as "necessity and urgency decrees" is at the center of the controversy. Between 1853 and the end of the 1980s, the threshold was high; only twenty-five decrees were issued during this time. But President Carlos Menem changed the norm radically by issuing some 260 decrees during his decade in power, which spanned the 1990s. Menem's successors have followed his example; on average, they issued more than one decree per week between 2000 and 2006. Some activists and scholars in Argentina recently have challenged the legal justification for such action, asserting that in the vast majority of cases conditions do not meet the test of "exceptional circumstances" that allow for presidential decree.

Section 99
Only when due to exceptional circumstances the ordinary procedures foreseen by this Constitution for the enactment of laws are impossible to be followed, and when rules are not referred to criminal issues, taxation, electoral matters, or the system of political parties, [the president] shall issue decrees on grounds of necessity and urgency, which shall be decided by a general agreement of ministers who shall countersign them together with the Chief of the Ministerial Cabinet. Within the term of ten days, the Chief of the Ministerial Cabinet shall personally submit the decision to the consideration of the Joint Standing Committee of Congress, which shall be composed according to the proportion of the political representation of the parties in each House. Within the term of ten days, this committee shall submit its report to the plenary meeting of each House for its specific consideration and it shall be immediately discussed by both Houses. A special law enacted with the absolute majority of all the members of each House shall regulate the procedure and scope of Congress participation.

12. Laws passed by the legislature are veto-proof or essentially veto-proof; that is, the executive lacks veto power, or has veto power but the veto can be overridden by a majority in the legislature.

No. A two-thirds majority vote in both houses is required to override a presidential veto.

Section 83
If a bill is totally or partially rejected by the Executive Power, it shall return with the objections to the originating House; the latter shall reconsider it and if it is confirmed by a majority of two-thirds of the votes, it shall be sent again to the revising House. If both Houses approve it by such majority, the bill becomes a law and is sent to the Executive Power for promulgation.

13. The legislature's laws are supreme and not subject to judicial review.

No. The Supreme Court can review the constitutionality of laws.

14. The legislature has the right to initiate bills in all policy jurisdictions; the executive lacks gatekeeping authority.

Yes. The legislature can initiate bills in all policy jurisdictions.

15. Expenditure of funds appropriated by the legislature is mandatory; the executive lacks the power to impound funds appropriated by the legislature.

No. The legislature must approve the general budget, but the president is in full control of the operations of the public sector. In August 2006 Congress enacted laws that allowed the Chief of the Ministerial Cabinet to make changes in the budget at the will of the executive. This act of interbranch delegation enhanced the president's already formidable control over the public purse.

16. The legislature controls the resources that finance its own internal operation and provide for the perquisites of its own members.

Yes. The legislature enjoys financial autonomy, including control over members' remuneration.

Section 74
The senators and deputies shall receive remuneration for their services, to be ascertained by law, and paid out of the Treasury of the Nation.

17. Members of the legislature are immune from arrest and/or criminal prosecution.

Yes. Legislators are immune with the common exception for cases of *flagrante delicto*.

Section 68
No member of Congress shall be accused, judicially examined, or disturbed for opinions expressed or speeches delivered by him while holding office as legislator.

Section 69
No senator or deputy shall be arrested as from the day of his election until the expiration of his term, except when flagrantly surprised committing a crime

deserving capital punishment or other infamous or serious punishment, in which case a summary report of the facts shall be submitted to the corresponding House.

Section 70
When a written complaint is filed before the ordinary courts against any senator or deputy, once examined if there is enough evidence in a public trial, each House may, with the concurrence of two-thirds of the votes, suspend the accused party from his office and place him under the jurisdiction of the competent court to be judged.

18. All members of the legislature are elected; the executive lacks the power to appoint any members of the legislature.

Yes. All members of Congress are elected.

Section 45
The House of Deputies shall be composed of representatives directly elected by the people of the provinces, of the City of Buenos Aires, and of the Capital City in case of its moving, which for this purpose are considered as constituencies of a single state, and by simple plurality of votes.

Section 54
The Senate shall be composed of three senators for each province, and three for the City of Buenos Aires, jointly and directly elected, corresponding two seats to the political party obtaining the majority of votes, and the other seat to the political party following in number of votes.

19. The legislature alone, without the involvement of any other agencies, can change the Constitution.

No. Constitutional amendments require the establishment of a special assembly for the purpose. The legislature calls for the special assembly and specifies the aspects of the constitution that the special assembly is permitted to discuss and change.

Section 30
The Constitution may be totally or partially amended. The necessity of reform must be declared by Congress with the vote of at least two-thirds of the members; but it shall not be carried out except by an Assembly summoned to that effect.

20. The legislature's approval is necessary for the declaration of war.

Yes. The legislature's approval is necessary for presidential war declarations.

Section 75
Congress is empowered:
25. To authorize the Executive Power to declare war or make peace.

Section 99
15. [The president] declares war and orders reprisals with the consent and approval of Congress.

21. The legislature's approval is necessary to ratify treaties with foreign countries.

Yes. The legislature's approval is necessary to ratify international treaties.

Section 75
Congress is empowered:
22. To approve or reject treaties concluded with other nations and international organizations, and concordats with the Holy See.

22. The legislature has the power to grant amnesty.

Yes. A general amnesty may be passed only through congressional legislation.

23. The legislature has the power of pardon.

No. The president has the power of pardon.

Section 99
5. [The president] may grant pardons or commute punishments for crimes subject to federal jurisdiction, after the report of the corresponding court, except in cases of impeachment by the House of Deputies.

24. The legislature reviews and has the right to reject appointments to the judiciary; or the legislature itself appoints members of the judiciary.

Yes. The Senate's consent is required for the president's judicial appointments.

Section 99
4. [The president] appoints the justices of the Supreme Court with the consent of the Senate by two-thirds of its members present, in a public meeting convoked to this effect.
He appoints the other judges of the lower federal courts according to a binding proposal consisting of a list of three candidates submitted by the Council of Magistracy, with the consent of the Senate in a public meeting, in which the qualifications of the candidates shall be taken into account.

25. The chairman of the central bank is appointed by the legislature.

No. The president appoints the governor of the Central Bank of Argentina with the Senate's approval.

26. The legislature has a substantial voice in the operation of the state-owned media.

No. The legislature lacks a substantial voice in the operation of the public media.

27. The legislature is regularly in session.

Yes. Congress is in regular session for about nine months each year.

Section 63
Both Houses shall assemble, on their own account, every year in ordinary legislative session from March 1 until November 30. The President of the Nation may convoke to extraordinary legislative session or extend the ordinary one.

28. Each legislator has a personal secretary.

Yes. Legislators are given a staffing budget.

29. Each legislator has at least one non-secretarial staff member with policy expertise.

Yes. See item 28.

30. Legislators are eligible for re-election without any restriction.

Yes. There are no restrictions on re-election.

Section 50
Deputies shall hold office for a term of four years and may be re-elected.

Section 56
Senators shall hold office for a term of six years and may be indefinitely re-elected.

31. A seat in the legislature is an attractive enough position that legislators are generally interested in and seek re-election.

No. Most legislators cannot obtain access to the ballot because it is controlled by party leaders. Parties are reluctant to renominate incumbents in the lower chamber, so only about one-quarter of sitting legislators are included in lists for re-election, and not all of these are re-elected. Congress often is not an attractive place for rising stars. The best and brightest frequently prefer to seek positions in the provincial or national executive branches or to win the mayoralty of a major city.

32. The re-election of incumbent legislators is common enough that at any given time the legislature contains a significant number of highly experienced members.

No. See item 31.

ARMENIAN NATIONAL ASSEMBLY (*AZGAYIN ZHOGHOV*)

Expert consultants: Artur Atanesyan, Alexander Markarov, Boris Navasardian, Ellie Valentine, Darren Wagner

Score: .56

Influence over executive (3/9)		Institutional autonomy (5/9)		Specified powers (6/8)		Institutional capacity (4/6)	
1. replace		10. no dissolution		19. amendments		27. sessions	X
2. serve as ministers		11. no decree		20. war	X	28. secretary	
3. interpellate	X	12. no veto	X	21. treaties	X	29. staff	
4. investigate		13. no review		22. amnesty	X	30. no term limits	X
5. oversee police	X	14. no gatekeeping	X	23. pardon		31. seek re-election	X
6. appoint PM		15. no impoundment	X	24. judiciary	X	32. experience	X
7. appoint ministers		16. control resources	X	25. central bank	X		
8. lack president		17. immunity		26. media	X		
9. no confidence	X	18. all elected	X				

In 1995 the Armenian National Assembly (*Azgayin Zhoghov*) was formally established in Armenia's first constitution following the collapse of the Soviet Union. The fledgling body endured tragedy in October 1999, when armed gunmen stormed the parliament building and assassinated the prime minister and six other members of parliament with the alleged purpose of inciting a popular revolt.

A referendum on constitutional amendments was rejected by voters in February 2003. The sweeping changes would have altered over three-fourths of the constitution's articles. The amendments were advertised as an effort to redistribute powers from the presidency to the other branches of government. Critics argued that the reforms would have actually further enhanced already-formidable presidential power.

The Assembly enjoys some control over the executive by dint of its powers of oversight, although electoral manipulation by sitting presidents has reduced the legislature's ability to challenge the executive branch. The legislature's institutional autonomy is limited by the president's powers of dissolution and decree, though the legislature can override a presidential veto with a majority vote. The legislature enjoys numerous specified powers and has some institutional capacity.

SURVEY

1. The legislature alone, without the involvement of any other agencies, can impeach the president or replace the prime minister.

No. Presidential impeachment requires action by the Constitutional Court.

Article 57
The President may be removed from office for state treason or other high crimes. In order to request a determination on questions pertaining to the removal of the President of the Republic from office, the National Assembly must appeal to the Constitutional Court by a resolution adopted by the majority of the deputies. A decision to remove the President of the Republic from office must be reached by the National Assembly by a minimum two thirds majority vote of the total number of deputies, based on the determination of the Constitutional Court.

Article 100
The Constitutional Court, in accordance with the law:
5) shall determine whether there are grounds for the removal of the President of the Republic.

2. Ministers may serve simultaneously as members of the legislature.

No. Legislators are prohibited from serving simultaneously in ministerial positions.

Article 65
A Deputy may not hold any other public office.

3. The legislature has powers of summons over executive branch officials and hearings with executive branch officials testifying before the legislature or its committees are regularly held.

Yes. Ministers are questioned in biweekly question-and-answer sessions and can be called to committee hearings.

Article 80
Deputies are entitled to ask questions to the Government. For one sitting each week during the regular sessions of the Assembly, the Prime Minister and the members of the Government shall answer questions raised by the Deputies. The National Assembly shall not pass any resolutions in conjunction with the questions raised by the Deputies.

4. The legislature can conduct independent investigation of the chief executive and the agencies of the executive.

No. The legislature cannot investigate the executive.

5. The legislature has effective powers of oversight over the agencies of coercion (the military, organs of law enforcement, intelligence services, and the secret police).

Yes. The legislature has effective powers of oversight over the agencies of coercion.

6. The legislature appoints the prime minister.

No. The president appoints the prime minister.

Article 55
4) [The president] shall appoint and remove the Prime Minister.

7. The legislature's approval is required to confirm the appointment of ministers; or the legislature itself appoints ministers.

No. The president appoints ministers, and the appointments do not require the legislature's approval.

Article 55
4) The President shall appoint and remove the members of the Government upon the recommendation of the Prime Minister.

8. The country lacks a presidency entirely or there is a presidency, but the president is elected by the legislature.

No. The president is directly elected.

Article 50
The President of the Republic shall be elected by the citizens of the Republic of Armenia for a five year term of office.

9. The legislature can vote no confidence in the government.

Yes. The legislature can vote no confidence in the government.

Article 55
The President of the Republic:
4) In the event that the National Assembly adopts a vote of no confidence against the Government, the

President shall, within twenty-one days accept the resignation of the Government, appoint a Prime Minister and form a Government.

Article 74

Within twenty days of the formation of a newly elected National Assembly or of its own formation, the Government shall present its program to the National Assembly for its approval, thus raising the question of a vote of confidence before the National Assembly . . . If a vote of no confidence is passed, the Prime Minister shall submit the resignation of the Government to the President of the Republic.

Article 84

The National Assembly may adopt a vote of no confidence toward the Government by a majority vote of the total number of Deputies.

10. The legislature is immune from dissolution by the executive.

No. The president can dissolve the legislature.

Article 55

The President of the Republic:
3) may dissolve the National Assembly and designate special elections after consultations with the President of the National Assembly and the Prime Minister.

Article 63

The National Assembly may be dissolved in accordance with the Constitution.

11. Any executive initiative on legislation requires ratification or approval by the legislature before it takes effect; that is, the executive lacks decree power.

No. The president issues decrees that have the force of law. The legislature can also delegate temporary decree power to the president on specific issue areas.

Article 56

The President of the Republic may issue orders and decrees which shall be executed throughout the Republic. The orders and decrees of the President of the Republic shall not contravene the Constitution and the laws.

Article 78

In order to ensure the legislative basis of the Government's program, the National Assembly may authorize the Government to adopt resolutions that have the effect of law that do not contravene any laws in force during a period specified by the National Assembly. Such resolutions must be signed by the President of the Republic.

12. Laws passed by the legislature are veto-proof or essentially veto-proof; that is, the executive lacks veto power, or has veto power but the veto can be overridden by a majority in the legislature.

Yes. The legislature can override a presidential veto by a majority vote of its total membership.

Article 72

The National Assembly shall deliberate on a priority basis any law which has been remanded by the President.

Should the National Assembly decline to accept the recommendations and objections presented by the President of the Republic, it shall pass the remanded law, again with a majority vote of the number of Deputies.

13. The legislature's laws are supreme and not subject to judicial review.

No. The Constitutional Court can review the constitutionality of laws.

Article 100

The Constitutional Court, in accordance with the law:
1) shall decide on whether the laws, the resolutions of the National Assembly, the orders and decrees of the President of the Republic and the resolutions of Government are in conformity with the Constitution.

14. The legislature has the right to initiate bills in all policy jurisdictions; the executive lacks gatekeeping authority.

Yes. The legislature can initiate bills in all policy jurisdictions.

15. Expenditure of funds appropriated by the legislature is mandatory; the executive lacks the power to impound funds appropriated by the legislature.

Yes. The executive lacks the power to impound funds appropriated by the legislature.

16. The legislature controls the resources that finance its own internal operation and provide for the perquisites of its own members.

Yes. The legislature enjoys financial autonomy.

Article 79

The President of the National Assembly shall chair the sittings, manage its material and financial resources, and shall ensure its normal functioning.

17. Members of the legislature are immune from arrest and/or criminal prosecution.

No. Despite constitutional provisions to the contrary, legislators are subject to arrest. For example, during a 2004 nationwide public vote of confidence in the president, some opposition legislators were arrested and alleged to have been beaten by police.

Article 66

A Deputy shall not be prosecuted or held liable for actions arising from the performance of his or her status, or for the expression of his or her opinions expressed in the National Assembly, provided these are not slanderous or defamatory. A Deputy may not be arrested and subjected to administrative or criminal prosecution through judicial proceedings without the consent of the National Assembly.

18. All members of the legislature are elected; the executive lacks the power to appoint any members of the legislature.

Yes. All members of the legislature are elected.

> Article 68
> Regular elections to the National Assembly shall be held within sixty days prior to the expiration of the term of the current Assembly. Procedures for elections to the National Assembly shall be prescribed by law.

19. The legislature alone, without the involvement of any other agencies, can change the Constitution.

No. Constitutional amendments require approval in a popular referendum.

> Article 111
> The Constitution shall be adopted or amended by referendum which may be initiated by the President of the Republic or the National Assembly.

20. The legislature's approval is necessary for the declaration of war.

Yes. The legislature declares war on the recommendation of the president.

> Article 55
> 13) [The president] shall decide on the use of the armed forces. In the event of an armed attack against or of an immediate anger to the Republic, or a declaration of war by the National Assembly, the President shall declare a state of martial law and may call for a general or partial mobilization.

> Article 81
> Upon the recommendation of the President of the Republic, the National Assembly:
> 3) may declare war.

21. The legislature's approval is necessary to ratify treaties with foreign countries.

Yes. The legislature's approval is necessary to ratify international treaties.

> Article 55
> 7) [The president] shall ... sign international treaties that are ratified by the National Assembly.

> Article 81
> Upon the recommendation of the President of the Republic, the National Assembly:
> 2) shall ratify or revoke the international treaties signed by the Republic of Armenia.

22. The legislature has the power to grant amnesty.

Yes. The legislature has the power to grant amnesty.

> Article 81
> Upon the recommendation of the President of the Republic, the National Assembly:
> 1) may declare an amnesty.

23. The legislature has the power of pardon.

No. The president has the power of pardon.

> Article 55
> 17) [The president] may grant pardons to convicted individuals.

24. The legislature reviews and has the right to reject appointments to the judiciary; or the legislature itself appoints members of the judiciary.

Yes. The Assembly appoints five of nine members of the Constitutional Court.

> Article 99
> The Constitutional Court shall be composed of nine members, five of whom shall be appointed by the National Assembly and four by the President of the Republic.

25. The chairman of the central bank is appointed by the legislature.

Yes. The Assembly, on the recommendation of the president, appoints the chairman of the Central Bank of Armenia.

> Article 83
> The National Assembly:
> 1) shall appoint the Chairman of the Central Bank upon the recommendation of the President of the Republic.

26. The legislature has a substantial voice in the operation of the state-owned media.

Yes. The legislature has a voice in the operation of the state-owned newspaper, *Hayastani Hanrapetutyun* (Republic of Armenia).

27. The legislature is regularly in session.

Yes. The legislature is in regular session for about seven months each year.

> Article 69
> The regular sessions of the National Assembly shall convene twice per year from the second Monday of September to the second Wednesday of December and from the first Monday of February to the second Wednesday of June.

28. Each legislator has a personal secretary.

No. Legislators are allowed voluntary staff, but on average there is less than one staff person for each legislator. There are about one or two secretaries and two to four experts for each standing commission of the parliament. Each standing commission contains roughly twenty legislators.

29. Each legislator has at least one non-secretarial staff member with policy expertise.

No. See item 28.

30. Legislators are eligible for re-election without any restriction.

Yes. There are no restrictions on re-election.

31. A seat in the legislature is an attractive enough position that legislators are generally interested in and seek re-election.

Yes.

32. The re-election of incumbent legislators is common enough that at any given time the legislature contains a significant number of highly experienced members.

Yes. Re-election of incumbent legislators is common. The total number of experienced legislators has been decreasing, however, because of the reduction in the size of the Armenian parliament from 190 members before 1995 to 131 members after 1995.

PARLIAMENT OF AUSTRALIA

Expert consultants: John Chesterman, Peter Hallahan, Jeremy Moon, Andrew Parkin, Bruce Stone, David Sullivan

Score: .63

Influence over executive (8/9)		Institutional autonomy (6/9)		Specified powers (0/8)		Institutional capacity (6/6)	
1. replace	X	10. no dissolution		19. amendments		27. sessions	X
2. serve as ministers	X	11. no decree	X	20. war		28. secretary	X
3. interpellate	X	12. no veto	X	21. treaties		29. staff	X
4. investigate	X	13. no review		22. amnesty		30. no term limits	X
5. oversee police	X	14. no gatekeeping	X	23. pardon		31. seek re-election	X
6. appoint PM	X	15. no impoundment	X	24. judiciary		32. experience	X
7. appoint ministers		16. control resources	X	25. central bank			
8. lack president	X	17. immunity		26. media			
9. no confidence	X	18. all elected	X				

The Parliament of Australia in its present form was established with the constitution of 1900, but it was not until 1942 and the Statute of Westminster that Australia received effective independence from Great Britain. Complete legal separation occurred only with the Australia Act of 1986, which abolished all remaining provisions that allowed appeals from Australian courts to be heard in London.

The Australian constitution is a thin document with a substantial portion devoted to rules for electing legislators. Many of the institutions specified in other constitutions, if discussed at all in the Australian constitution, are mentioned only to stipulate that their features are to be "determined by law." The lacunae in the Australian constitution are filled by a century of conventions, precedents, and custom.

Australia operates a Westminster-style system. The basic Westminster structure is complicated by the position of the Governor General. Australia's official head of state is still the Queen of England, and Australia's functional head of state remains the "queen's representative" in Australia, the Governor General, who is appointed by the queen on the recommendation of the Australian prime minister. The Australian parliament shares some executive powers with the Governor General.

Australia's most unusual constitutional feature is the double dissolution mechanism (Section 57)

for resolving a deadlock between the two houses of the bicameral legislature. This provision allows for the dissolution of both houses if the Senate twice rejects a bill passed by the House of Representatives.

In general, parliament enjoys a high level of control over executive power and substantial institutional autonomy. Remarkably, however, it holds none of the specified powers and prerogatives assessed in this survey. It has formidable institutional capacity.

SURVEY

1. The legislature alone, without the involvement of any other agencies, can impeach the president or replace the prime minister.

Yes. The legislature can remove the prime minister with a vote of no confidence.

2. Ministers may serve simultaneously as members of the legislature.

Yes. Ministers are required to serve simultaneously in the legislature.

> Section 64
> No minister of state shall hold office for a longer period than three months unless he is or becomes a senator or a member of the House of Representatives.

3. The legislature has powers of summons over executive branch officials and hearings with executive branch officials testifying before the legislature or its committees are regularly held.

Yes. The legislature regularly questions officials of the executive. Summons power is particularly evident in the annual round of public hearings held by Senate committees considering the proposed expenditure of public funds.

4. The legislature can conduct independent investigation of the chief executive and the agencies of the executive.

Yes. The legislature can investigate the executive.

5. The legislature has effective powers of oversight over the agencies of coercion (the military, organs of law enforcement, intelligence services, and the secret police).

Yes. The legislature and a statutory body, the Auditory General, have effective powers of oversight over the agencies of coercion.

6. The legislature appoints the prime minister.

Yes. The prime minister is formally appointed by the Governor General, but the Governor General by convention must appoint the parliamentary leader of the party, or coalition of parties, that has the support of the House of Representatives.

7. The legislature's approval is required to confirm the appointment of ministers; or the legislature itself appoints ministers.

No. Ministers are appointed by the Governor General on the recommendation of the prime minister, and the appointments do not require the legislature's approval.

> Section 62
> There shall be a Federal Executive Council to advise the Governor-General in the government of the Commonwealth, and the members of the Council shall be chosen and summoned by the Governor-General and sworn as Executive Councillors, and shall hold office during his pleasure.

> Section 67
> Until the Parliament otherwise provides, the appointment and removal of all other officers of the Executive Government of the Commonwealth shall be vested in the Governor-General in Council.

8. The country lacks a presidency entirely or there is a presidency, but the president is elected by the legislature.

Yes. The country lacks a presidency. The Governor General is the head of state.

9. The legislature can vote no confidence in the government.

Yes. No confidence votes, while rare, are possible. In February 2003 the Senate passed its first-ever vote of no confidence in a serving leader against Prime Minister John Howard over his handling of the Iraq crisis.

10. The legislature is immune from dissolution by the executive.

No. The Governor General can dissolve the legislature. Australia's peculiar "double dissolution" mechanism also allows the Governor General to dissolve both houses of parliament to break legislative deadlock. Double dissolution is an option if the House of Representatives passes the same bill twice and has it rejected by the Senate both times.

> Section 5
> (1) The Governor-General may ... in like manner dissolve the House of Representatives.

> Section 28
> Every House of Representatives shall continue for three years from the first meeting of the House, and no longer, but may be sooner dissolved by the Governor-General.

Section 57

(1) If the House of Representatives passes any proposed law, and the Senate rejects or fails to pass it, or passes it with amendments to which the House of Representatives will not agree, and if after an interval of three months the House of Representatives, in the same or the next session, again passes the proposed law with or without any amendments which have been made, suggested, or agreed to by the Senate, and the Senate rejects or fails to pass it, or passes it with amendments to which the House of Representatives will not agree, the Governor-General may dissolve the Senate and the House of Representatives simultaneously. But such dissolution shall not take place within six months before the date of the expiry of the House of Representatives.

11. Any executive initiative on legislation requires ratification or approval by the legislature before it takes effect; that is, the executive lacks decree power.

Yes. The executive lacks decree power.

12. Laws passed by the legislature are veto-proof or essentially veto-proof; that is, the executive lacks veto power, or has veto power but the veto can be overridden by a majority in the legislature.

Yes. In practice, there is no executive veto in Australia. Formally, the Governor General and the queen have veto power, in that they may withhold their assent from a law. In practice, however, it would be unthinkable for them to exercise this power.

Section 58

(1) When a proposed law passed by both Houses of the Parliament is presented to the Governor-General for the Queen's assent, he shall declare, according to his discretion, but subject to this Constitution, that he assents in the Queen's name or that he withholds assent, or that he reserves the law for the Queen's pleasure.

(2) The Governor-General may return to the house in which it originated any proposed law so presented to him, and may transmit therewith any amendments which he may recommend, and the Houses may deal with the recommendation.

Section 59

The Queen may disallow any law within one year from the Governor-General's assent, and such disallowance on being made known by the Governor-General by speech or message to each of the Houses of the Parliament, or by Proclamation, shall annul the law from the day when the disallowance is so made known.

Section 60

A proposed law reserved for the Queen's pleasure shall not have any force unless and until within two years from the day on which it was presented to the Governor-General for the Queen's assent the Governor-General makes known, by speech or message to each of the Houses of the Parliament, or by Proclamation, that it has received the Queen's assent.

13. The legislature's laws are supreme and not subject to judicial review.

No. Laws can be challenged in the High Court.

14. The legislature has the right to initiate bills in all policy jurisdictions; the executive lacks gatekeeping authority.

Yes. The legislature can initiate bills in all policy jurisdictions under the jurisdiction of the national government.

15. Expenditure of funds appropriated by the legislature is mandatory; the executive lacks the power to impound funds appropriated by the legislature.

Yes. Once legislation appropriating funds is passed, the funds must be spent for the purposes specified, although specified purposes are often fairly broad.

16. The legislature controls the resources that finance its own internal operation and provide for the perquisites of its own members.

Yes. The legislature enjoys financial autonomy.

17. Members of the legislature are immune from arrest and/or criminal prosecution.

No. Legislative immunity extends to official parliamentary business only. Legislators are subject to arrest for common crimes.

Section 49

The powers, privileges, and immunities of the Senate and of the House of Representatives, and of the members and the committees of each House, shall be such as are declared by the Parliament, and until declared shall be those of the Commons House of Parliament of the United Kingdom, and of its members and committees, at the establishment of the Commonwealth.

18. All members of the legislature are elected; the executive lacks the power to appoint any members of the legislature.

Yes. All members of the legislature are elected.

Section 7

The Senate shall be composed of senators for each State, directly chosen by the people of the State.

Section 24

The House of Representatives shall be composed of members directly chosen by the people of the Commonwealth.

19. The legislature alone, without the involvement of any other agencies, can change the Constitution.

No. Constitutional amendments require approval in a popular referendum.

Section 128
This Constitution shall not be altered except in the following manner:
(1) The proposed law for the alteration thereof must be passed by an absolute majority of each House of the Parliament, and not less than two nor more than six months after its passage through both Houses the proposed law shall be submitted in each State and Territory to the electors qualified to vote for the election of members of the House of Representatives.
(2) But if either House passes any such proposed law by an absolute majority, and the other House rejects or fails to pass it, or passes it with any amendment to which the first-mentioned House will not agree, and if after an interval of three months the first-mentioned House in the same or the next session again passes the proposed law by an absolute majority with or without any amendment which has been made or agreed to by the other House, and such other House rejects or fails to pass it or passes it with any amendment to which the first-mentioned House will not agree, the Governor-General may submit the proposed law as last proposed by the first-mentioned House, and either with or without any amendments subsequently agreed to by both Houses, to the electors in each State and Territory qualified to vote for the election of the House of Representatives.
(4) And if in a majority of the States a majority of the electors voting approve the proposed law, and if a majority of all the electors voting also approve the proposed law, it shall be presented to the Governor-General for the Queen's assent.

20. The legislature's approval is necessary for the declaration of war.

No. The government can declare war without the legislature's approval.

21. The legislature's approval is necessary to ratify treaties with foreign countries.

No. The government can conclude international treaties without the legislature's approval. A parliamentary committee was established in the mid-1990s to vet international treaties before they are signed, but its role is purely advisory.

22. The legislature has the power to grant amnesty.

No. The government has the power to grant amnesty.

23. The legislature has the power of pardon.

No. The government has the power of pardon.

24. The legislature reviews and has the right to reject appointments to the judiciary; or the legislature itself appoints members of the judiciary.

No. Members of the judiciary are appointed by the Governor General, and the legislature's approval is not required.

Section 72
The Justices of the High Court and of the other courts created by the Parliament –
(i) Shall be appointed by the Governor-General.

25. The chairman of the central bank is appointed by the legislature.

No. The treasurer, a cabinet minister whose functions in some respects resemble those associated with a minister of finance, appoints the governor of the Reserve Bank of Australia.

26. The legislature has a substantial voice in the operation of the state-owned media.

No. The legislature lacks a substantial voice in the operation of the public media.

27. The legislature is regularly in session.

Yes. The legislature's ordinary sessions are spread over nine months each year, which keeps the legislature in regular working session. It merits note, however, that sittings are spread quite thinly over this time.

28. Each legislator has a personal secretary.

Yes. Each legislator has a personal secretary. Most legislators have someone who manages appointments and travel as well an office manager.

29. Each legislator has at least one non-secretarial staff member with policy expertise.

Yes.

30. Legislators are eligible for re-election without any restriction.

Yes. There are no restrictions on re-election.

31. A seat in the legislature is an attractive enough position that legislators are generally interested in and seek re-election.

Yes.

32. The re-election of incumbent legislators is common enough that at any given time the legislature contains a significant number of highly experienced members.

Yes. Re-election rates are sufficiently high to produce a significant number of highly experienced members.

AUSTRIAN PARLIAMENT (*PARLAMENT*)

Expert consultants: David Campbell, Ursula Dorfinger, Christian Hütterer, Wolfgang C. Müller, Hubert Sickinger, Leo Stollwitzer, Peter Ulram

Score: .72

Influence over executive (5/9)		Institutional autonomy (7/9)		Specified powers (6/8)		Institutional capacity (5/6)	
1. replace		10. no dissolution		19. amendments	X	27. sessions	X
2. serve as ministers	X	11. no decree	X	20. war	X	28. secretary	X
3. interpellate	X	12. no veto	X	21. treaties	X	29. staff	
4. investigate	X	13. no review		22. amnesty	X	30. no term limits	X
5. oversee police	X	14. no gatekeeping	X	23. pardon		31. seek re-election	X
6. appoint PM		15. no impoundment	X	24. judiciary	X	32. experience	X
7. appoint ministers		16. control resources	X	25. central bank			
8. lack president		17. immunity	X	26. media	X		
9. no confidence	X	18. all elected	X				

The Austrian Parliament (*Parlament*) was established in the 1920 constitution. The Austrian Parliament consists of the popularly elected National Council (*Nationalrat*) and the Federal Council (*Bundesrat*), whose members are elected by the state legislatures. A constitutional amendment in 1929 provided for direct presidential elections. The amendment also gave the president the power to appoint the chancellor and, on the chancellor's recommendation, to appoint the government. Prior to 1929 the legislature elected the president, the chancellor, and the government.

The constitution was suspended during 1934–45 in the face of two consecutive domestic authoritarian rulers and the *Anschluss* that brought Austria under the control of Nazi Germany. In 1945 the 1920 constitution, complete with the 1929 amendments, was reinstated, thereby establishing a semipresidential system for postwar Austria.

Parliament enjoys a broad scope of authority. Although it plays a limited role in the formation of the government, it wields effective oversight powers and can remove individual ministers or the government as a whole with a vote of no confidence. The National Council is subject to dissolution by the president and its laws are subject to judicial review, but otherwise it enjoys full institutional autonomy. The executive has no gatekeeping or decree power. The legislature also enjoys substantial powers and prerogatives and has a high level of institutional capacity.

SURVEY

1. The legislature alone, without the involvement of any other agencies, can impeach the president or replace the prime minister.

No. Presidential impeachment requires the involvement of the Constitutional Court. The National Council can replace the prime minister (chancellor) with a vote of no confidence.

Article 74
(1) If the National Council passes an explicit vote of no confidence in the Federal Government or individual members thereof, the Federal Government or the Federal Minister concerned shall be removed from office.

2. Ministers may serve simultaneously as members of the legislature.

Yes. According to law, ministers may also serve in the legislature. For the past three decades, however, no minister has served simultaneously in the legislature.

Article 70
(2) Only persons eligible for the National Council can be appointed Federal Chancellor, Vice-Chancellor, or Federal Minister; members of the Federal Government need not belong to the National Council.

3. The legislature has powers of summons over executive branch officials and hearings with executive branch officials testifying before the legislature or its committees are regularly held.

Yes. The legislature regularly interpellates officials from the executive.

Article 52
(1) The National Council and the Federal Council are entitled to examine the administration of affairs by the Federal Government, to interrogate its members about all subjects of its execution, and to demand all relevant information as well as to ventilate in resolutions their wishes about exercise of the executive power.
(2) Every member of the National Council and the Federal Council is entitled during the sessions of the National Council and the Federal Council to address brief oral questions to members of the Federal Government.
(3) The detailed regulations respecting the right of interrogation will be settled by the federal law on the National Council's Standing Orders as well as in the Federal Council's Standing Orders.

4. The legislature can conduct independent investigation of the chief executive and the agencies of the executive.

Yes. The legislature can establish committees of inquiry to investigate the executive.

Article 53
(1) The National Council can, by resolution, set up committees of inquiry.
(3) The courts and all other authorities are obliged to comply with the request of these committees to take evidence; all public departments must on demand produce their files.

5. The legislature has effective powers of oversight over the agencies of coercion (the military, organs of law enforcement, intelligence services, and the secret police).

Yes. Legislative committees have effective powers of oversight over the agencies of coercion.

6. The legislature appoints the prime minister.

No. The president appoints the chancellor. The president generally chooses, but is not required, to appoint the candidate who enjoys the support of the National Council.

Article 70
(1) The Federal Chancellor and, on his recommendation, the other members of the Federal Government are appointed by the Federal President.

7. The legislature's approval is required to confirm the appointment of ministers; or the legislature itself appoints ministers.

No. The president appoints the ministers on the recommendation of the chancellor, and the appointments do not require the legislature's approval.

Article 70
(1) The Federal Chancellor and, on his recommendation, the other members of the Federal Government are appointed by the Federal President.

8. The country lacks a presidency entirely or there is a presidency, but the president is elected by the legislature.

No. The president is directly elected.

Article 60
(1) The Federal President is elected by the nation on the basis of equal, direct, secret, and personal suffrage.

9. The legislature can vote no confidence in the government.

Yes. The legislature can vote no confidence in the government.

Article 74
(1) If the National Council passes an explicit vote of no confidence in the Federal Government or individual members thereof, the Federal Government or the Federal Minister concerned shall be removed from office.

10. The legislature is immune from dissolution by the executive.

No. The president can dissolve the National Council, although he or she may not do so twice for the same reason.

Article 29
(1) The Federal President can dissolve the National Council, but he may avail himself of this prerogative only once for the same reason.

11. Any executive initiative on legislation requires ratification or approval by the legislature before it takes effect; that is, the executive lacks decree power.

Yes. The executive lacks decree power.

12. Laws passed by the legislature are veto-proof or essentially veto-proof; that is, the executive lacks veto power, or has veto power but the veto can be overridden by a majority in the legislature.

Yes. The executive lacks veto power.

13. The legislature's laws are supreme and not subject to judicial review.

No. The Constitutional Court can review the constitutionality of laws.

Article 140
(1) The Constitutional Court pronounces on application by the Administrative Court, the Supreme Court, or a competent appellate court whether a Federal or State law is unconstitutional, but ex officio in so far as the Court would have to apply such a law in a pending suit. It pronounces . . . on application by a State Government or by one third of the National Council's members whether Federal laws are unconstitutional.

14. The legislature has the right to initiate bills in all policy jurisdictions; the executive lacks gatekeeping authority.

Yes. The legislature can initiate bills in all policy jurisdictions.

15. Expenditure of funds appropriated by the legislature is mandatory; the executive lacks the power to impound funds appropriated by the legislature.

Yes. The executive lacks the power to impound funds appropriated by the legislature.

16. The legislature controls the resources that finance its own internal operation and provide for the perquisites of its own members.

Yes. The legislature enjoys financial autonomy.

17. Members of the legislature are immune from arrest and/or criminal prosecution.

Yes. Members of the National Council are immune with the common exception for cases of *flagrante delicto*. The immunity of members of the Federal Council is determined by the laws of the state they represent.

Article 57
(1) The members of the National Council may never be made responsible for votes cast in the exercise of their function and only by the National Council on the grounds of oral or written utterances made in the course of their function.
(2) The members of the National Council may, on the ground of a criminal offence – except for apprehension in flagrante delicto – be arrested only with the consent of the National Council. Searches of the home of National Council members likewise require the National Council's consent.
(3) Other legal action on the ground of a criminal offence may be taken against members of the National Council without the National Council's consent only if it is manifestly not connected to the political activity of the member in question. The authority

concerned must seek a ruling by the National Council on the existence of such a connection if the member in question or a third of the members belonging to the Standing Committee entrusted with these matters so demands. Every act of legal process shall in the case of such a demand immediately cease or be discontinued.

Article 58
The members of the Federal Council enjoy for the whole duration of their tenure of office the immunity of the members of the State Parliament which has delegated them.

18. All members of the legislature are elected; the executive lacks the power to appoint any members of the legislature.

Yes. All members of the legislature are elected.

Article 26
(1) The National Council is elected by the nation in accordance with the principles of proportional representation on the basis of equal, direct, secret, and personal suffrage.

Article 35
(1) The members of the Federal Council and their substitutes are elected by the State Parliaments for the duration of their respective legislative periods in accordance with the principle of proportional representation.

19. The legislature alone, without the involvement of any other agencies, can change the Constitution.

Yes. The National Council can change the constitution with a two-thirds majority vote. A "total revision" of the constitution, however, requires approval in a popular referendum.

Article 44
(1) Constitutional laws or constitutional provisions contained in simple laws can be passed by the National Council only in the presence of at least half the members and by a two thirds majority of the votes cast, they shall be explicitly specified as such.
(2) Any total revision of the Federal Constitution shall . . . be submitted to a referendum by the entire nation, whereas any partial revision requires this only if one third of the members of the National Council or the Federal Council so demands.

20. The legislature's approval is necessary for the declaration of war.

Yes. The legislature declares war.

Article 38
The National Council and the Federal Council meet, together building the Federal Assembly, in public session at the seat of the National Council for the affirmation of the Federal President as well as for the adoption of a resolution on a declaration of war.

Article 40
(2) The resolutions of the Federal Assembly upon a declaration of war shall be officially published by the Federal Chancellor.

21. The legislature's approval is necessary to ratify treaties with foreign countries.

Yes. The legislature's approval is necessary to ratify international treaties.

Article 50
(1) Political treaties, and others in so far as their contents modify or complement existent laws, may only be concluded with the sanction of the National Council.

22. The legislature has the power to grant amnesty.

Yes. The legislature can make laws that grant amnesty.

Article 93
[Amnesties] for acts punishable by the courts are extended by federal law.

23. The legislature has the power of pardon.

No. The president has the power of pardon.

Article 65
(2) Furthermore, the following powers – notwithstanding the powers assigned to him by other provisions of this Constitution – are vested in the President:
c) in individual cases to pardon persons sentenced without further resources of appeal, to mitigate and commute sentences pronounced by the courts, as an act of grace to annul sentences and to grant remission from their legal consequences, and moreover to quash criminal proceedings in actions subject to prosecution ex officio.

24. The legislature reviews and has the right to reject appointments to the judiciary; or the legislature itself appoints members of the judiciary.

Yes. Nine of the twenty members of the Constitutional Court are appointed by the president from a slate of candidates that the legislature presents.

Article 147
(2) The President, the Vice-President, six additional members, and three substitute members [of the Constitutional Court] are appointed by the Federal President on the recommendation of the Federal Government... The remaining six members and three substitute members are appointed by the Federal President on the basis of recommendations listing three candidates for each vacancy, the National Council submitting those for three members and two

substitute members and the Federal Council those for three members and one substitute member.

25. The chairman of the central bank is appointed by the legislature.

No. The president appoints the head of the Austrian National Bank.

26. The legislature has a substantial voice in the operation of the state-owned media.

Yes. The operation of the state-owned television and radio network is regulated by law, and some members of the media supervisory committee are appointed by the legislature.

27. The legislature is regularly in session.

Yes. The legislature regularly meets in ordinary session.

Article 28
(1) The Federal President convokes the National Council each year for an Ordinary session which shall not begin before 15 September and not last longer than 15 July the following year.

28. Each legislator has a personal secretary.

Yes. Members of parliament are allocated funds for personal secretarial staff and have access to staff provided by their parties.

29. Each legislator has at least one non-secretarial staff member with policy expertise.

No. Legislators have access to staff with policy expertise. See item 28. On average, however, there is less than one staff member with policy expertise for each legislator.

30. Legislators are eligible for re-election without any restriction.

Yes. There are no restrictions on re-election.

31. A seat in the legislature is an attractive enough position that legislators are generally interested in and seek re-election.

Yes.

32. The re-election of incumbent legislators is common enough that at any given time the legislature contains a significant number of highly experienced members.

Yes. Re-election rates are sufficiently high to produce a significant number of highly experienced members.

PARLIAMENT OF AZERBAIJAN (*MILLI MAJLIS*)

Expert consultants: Shain Abbasov, Intigam Aliyev, Gorkhmaz Askerov, Akbar Noman, Fuad Suleymanov

Score: .44

Influence over executive (1/9)		Institutional autonomy (5/9)		Specified powers (4/8)		Institutional capacity (4/6)	
1. replace		10. no dissolution	X	19. amendments		27. sessions	X
2. serve as ministers		11. no decree		20. war	X	28. secretary	
3. interpellate		12. no veto		21. treaties	X	29. staff	
4. investigate		13. no review		22. amnesty	X	30. no term limits	X
5. oversee police		14. no gatekeeping	X	23. pardon		31. seek re-election	X
6. appoint PM		15. no impoundment	X	24. judiciary	X	32. experience	X
7. appoint ministers		16. control resources		25. central bank			
8. lack president		17. immunity	X	26. media			
9. no confidence	X	18. all elected	X				

The Parliament (*Milli Majlis*) of Azerbaijan was formally established in Azerbaijan's 1992 constitution, following the collapse of the Soviet Union. Due to post-independence instability, which included a military coup, the first post-Soviet parliamentary elections were not held until 1995.

In July 2002 the legislature amended the constitution in a bid to reign in the powers of the executive branch. One change formally required the cabinet to provide parliament with an annual report of the previous year's dealings. Another amendment empowered parliament to question individual cabinet ministers and to vote no confidence in the government. In practice, however, parliament has not yet exercised these powers and exerts little oversight over the executive branch. In fact, the legislature exerts practically no sway over the executive. Legislative autonomy is eroded by constitutional provisions that grant the president decree powers. The legislature does enjoy some prerogatives. Declaration of war, international treaties, and appointments to the judiciary all require the legislature's approval. The legislature also enjoys a fair amount of institutional capacity. Legislators are interested in re-election, and parliament contains a significant number of experienced members.

SURVEY

1. The legislature alone, without the involvement of any other agencies, can impeach the president or replace the prime minister.

No. Impeachment of the president requires the involvement of the Constitutional Court.

Article 95
(1) The following questions fall under the competence of the Parliament [*Milli Majlis*] of the Azerbaijan Republic:
12. dismissal of the President of the Azerbaijan Republic by way of impeachment based on recommendation of Constitutional Court of the Azerbaijan Republic.

Article 107
(1) In case of grave crime done by the President of the Azerbaijan Republic the question of dismissal of the President may be submitted to the Parliament of the Azerbaijan Republic on initiative of Constitutional Court of the Azerbaijan Republic based on conclusions of Supreme Court of the Azerbaijan Republic presented within 30 days.
(2) The President of the Azerbaijan Republic may be dismissed from his post by decree of the Parliament of the Azerbaijan Republic taken by majority of 95 votes of deputies. This decree is signed by the Chairman of Constitutional Court of the Azerbaijan Republic. If Constitutional Court of the Azerbaijan Republic fails to sign said decree within one week it shall not come into force.

2. Ministers may serve simultaneously as members of the legislature.

No. Legislators are prohibited from serving simultaneously in ministerial positions.

Article 89
(1) The deputy of the Parliament of the Azerbaijan Republic looses his/her mandate in the following cases:
   3. on taking position in state bodies.

3. The legislature has powers of summons over executive branch officials and hearings with executive branch officials testifying before the legislature or its committees are regularly held.

No. Parliament does not regularly question ministers.

4. The legislature can conduct independent investigation of the chief executive and the agencies of the executive.

No. A 2002 amendment granted parliament the legal right to investigate the executive, but no investigations have occurred, and there is little evidence to suggest that they could occur.

5. The legislature has effective powers of oversight over the agencies of coercion (the military, organs of law enforcement, intelligence services, and the secret police).

No. The agencies of coercion report directly to the president and are not subject to legislative oversight.

6. The legislature appoints the prime minister.

No. The president appoints the prime minister and submits the candidate to the parliament for approval. If the parliament rejects three consecutive candidates for the position of prime minister, the president can appoint the prime minister of his or her choice.

Article 118
(1) Prime-minister of Azerbaijan Republic is appointed by the President of the Azerbaijan Republic on consent of the Parliament of the Azerbaijan Republic.
(3) The Parliament of the Azerbaijan Republic takes decision concerning the candidate to the post of Prime-minister of the Azerbaijan Republic not later than within one week from the day when such candidature has been proposed. Should said procedure be violated, or candidatures proposed by the President of the Azerbaijan Republic for the post of Prime-minister of the Azerbaijan Republic be rejected three times, then the President of the Azerbaijan Republic may appoint Prime-minister of the Azerbaijan Republic without consent of the Parliament of the Azerbaijan Republic.

7. The legislature's approval is required to confirm the appointment of ministers; or the legislature itself appoints ministers.

No. The president appoints ministers, and the appointments do not require the legislature's approval.

Article 109
The President of the Azerbaijan Republic:
5. appoints and dismisses members of Cabinet of Ministers of the Azerbaijan Republic.

8. The country lacks a presidency entirely or there is a presidency, but the president is elected by the legislature.

No. The president is directly elected.

Article 101
(1) The President of the Azerbaijan Republic is elected for a 5-year term by way of general, direct and equal elections, with free, personal and secret ballot.

9. The legislature can vote no confidence in the government.

Yes. The legislature can vote no confidence in the government.

Article 95
(1) The following questions fall under the competence of the Parliament [*Milli Majlis*] of the Azerbaijan Republic
   14. taking decision regarding a vote of confidence in the Cabinet of Ministers of the Azerbaijan Republic.

10. The legislature is immune from dissolution by the executive.

Yes. The legislature is immune from dissolution.

11. Any executive initiative on legislation requires ratification or approval by the legislature before it takes effect; that is, the executive lacks decree power.

No. The president can issue decrees that have the force of law as long as the decrees do not contravene the constitution or laws.

Article 113
Acts of the President of the Azerbaijan Republic
(1) Establishing general procedures the President of the Azerbaijan Republic issues decrees, as per all other questions – he issues orders.
(2) If not specified otherwise in decrees and orders of the President of the Azerbaijan Republic they become valid from the day of their publication.

Article 149
(4) Decrees of the President of the Azerbaijan Republic should not contradict the Constitution and laws of the Azerbaijan Republic. Use and implementation of published decrees is obligatory for all citizens, executive power bodies, legal entities.

(5) Decrees of Cabinet of Ministers of the Azerbaijan Republic should not contradict the Constitution, laws of the Azerbaijan Republic and decrees of the President of the Azerbaijan Republic. Use and implementation of published decrees of the Cabinet of Ministers is obligatory for citizens, central and local executive power bodies, legal entities.

12. Laws passed by the legislature are veto-proof or essentially veto-proof; that is, the executive lacks veto power, or has veto power but the veto can be overridden by a majority in the legislature.

No. A supermajority vote in the legislature is required to override a presidential veto.

Article 110
(1) If the President of the Azerbaijan Republic has objections against a law he may return it to the Parliament of the Azerbaijan Republic within specified term without signing, together with his comments.
(2) If the Parliament of the Azerbaijan Republic accepts by majority of 95 votes laws that have been accepted previously by majority of 83 votes, and by majority of 83 votes the laws that have been accepted previously by majority of 63 votes, said laws come into force after repeated voting.

13. The legislature's laws are supreme and not subject to judicial review.

No. The Constitutional Court can review the constitutionality of laws.

Article 130
(3) Constitutional Court of the Azerbaijan Republic... takes decisions regarding the following:
correspondence of laws of the Azerbaijan Republic... [and] decrees of the Parliament of the Azerbaijan Republic... to [the] Constitution of the Azerbaijan Republic.
(4) Constitutional Court of the Azerbaijan Republic gives interpretation of the Constitution and laws of the Azerbaijan Republic based on inquiries of the President of the Azerbaijan Republic, the Parliament of the Azerbaijan Republic, Cabinet of Ministers of the Azerbaijan Republic, Supreme Court of the Azerbaijan Republic, Procurator's Office of the Azerbaijan Republic and Ali Majlis of Nakhichevan Autonomous Republic.

14. The legislature has the right to initiate bills in all policy jurisdictions; the executive lacks gatekeeping authority.

Yes. The legislature can initiate bills in all policy jurisdictions.

15. Expenditure of funds appropriated by the legislature is mandatory; the executive lacks the power to impound funds appropriated by the legislature.

Yes. The executive lacks the power to impound funds appropriated by the legislature.

16. The legislature controls the resources that finance its own internal operation and provide for the perquisites of its own members.

No. The legislature is dependent on the executive for the resources that finance its own operations.

17. Members of the legislature are immune from arrest and/or criminal prosecution.

Yes. Legislators are immune with the common exception for cases of *flagrante delicto*, here expressed as "caught in the act of crime."

Article 90
(1) A deputy of the Parliament of the Azerbaijan Republic enjoys immunity during the whole term of his powers. Except cases when the deputy may be caught in the act of crime, the deputy of the Parliament of the Azerbaijan Republic may not be called to criminal responsibility during the whole term of his/her authority, arrested, disciplinary measures may not be applied to him by law court, he may not be searched. The deputy of the Parliament of the Azerbaijan Republic may be arrested only if he/she has been caught at a place of crime. In such case the body which detained the deputy of the Parliament of the Azerbaijan Republic must immediately notify General Procurator of the Azerbaijan Republic about the fact.
(2) Immunity of deputy of the Parliament of the Azerbaijan Republic might be stopped only by decision of the Parliament of the Azerbaijan Republic based on application of General Procurator of the Azerbaijan Republic.

18. All members of the legislature are elected; the executive lacks the power to appoint any members of the legislature.

Yes. All members of the legislature are elected.

Article 83
Deputies of the Parliament of the Azerbaijan Republic are elected based on majority and proportional voting systems and general, equal and direct elections by way of free, individual and secret voting.

19. The legislature alone, without the involvement of any other agencies, can change the Constitution.

No. Constitutional amendments require the president's approval.

Article 110
(2) Should the President of the Azerbaijan Republic fail to sign Constitutional laws they will not come into force.

Article 156
(1) Amendments to the Constitution of the Azerbaijan Republic are taken in the form of Constitutional laws in the Parliament of the Azerbaijan Republic, by majority of 95 votes.
(2) Constitutional laws on amendments to Constitution of the Azerbaijan Republic are put to the vote in the Parliament of the Azerbaijan Republic twice. The

second voting shall be held 6 months after the first one.

(3) Constitutional laws on amendments to Constitution of the Azerbaijan Republic are submitted to the President of the Azerbaijan Republic for signing in an order envisaged in the present Constitution for laws, both after the first and after the second voting.

(4) Constitutional laws and amendments to the Constitution of the Azerbaijan Republic become valid after they have been signed by the President of the Azerbaijan Republic after the second voting.

(5) Constitutional laws on amendments are integral part of Constitution of the Azerbaijan Republic and should not contradict main text of Constitution of the Azerbaijan Republic.

20. The legislature's approval is necessary for the declaration of war.

Yes. The legislature's approval is necessary for presidential war declarations.

Article 95
(1) The following questions fall under the competence of the Parliament of the Azerbaijan Republic:
17. based on request of the President of the Azerbaijan Republic giving consent for announcement of war and conclusion of peace treaty.

Article 109
The President of the Azerbaijan Republic:
30. on consent of the Parliament of the Azerbaijan Republic announces a war and concludes peace agreements.

21. The legislature's approval is necessary to ratify treaties with foreign countries.

Yes. The legislature's approval is necessary to ratify international treaties.

Article 94
(1) The Parliament of the Azerbaijan Republic establishes general rules concerning the following matters:
22. ratification and denunciation of international treaties.

Article 95
(1) The following questions fall under the competence of the Parliament of the Azerbaijan Republic:
4. ratification and denunciation of international agreements.

Article 109
The President of the Azerbaijan Republic:
17. presents interstate agreements to the Parliament of the Azerbaijan Republic for ratification and denunciation.

22. The legislature has the power to grant amnesty.

Yes. The legislature has the power to grant amnesty.

Article 95
(1) The following questions fall under the competence of the Parliament of the Azerbaijan Republic:
6. Amnesty.

23. The legislature has the power of pardon.

No. The president has the power of pardon.

Article 109
The President of the Azerbaijan Republic:
22. grants pardon.

24. The legislature reviews and has the right to reject appointments to the judiciary; or the legislature itself appoints members of the judiciary.

Yes. The legislature appoints members of the Constitutional Court, the Economic Court, and the Supreme Court, upon recommendation by the president.

Article 95
(1) The following questions fall under the competence of the Parliament of the Azerbaijan Republic:
10. based on recommendation by the President of the Azerbaijan Republic appointment of judges of Constitutional Court of the Azerbaijan Republic, Supreme Court of the Azerbaijan Republic and Economic Court of the Azerbaijan Republic.

Article 109
The President of the Azerbaijan Republic:
9. submits proposals to the Parliament of the Azerbaijan Republic about appointment of judges of Constitutional Court of the Azerbaijan Republic, Supreme Court of the Azerbaijan Republic and Economic Court of the Azerbaijan Republic.

Article 130
(1) Constitutional Court of the Azerbaijan Republic consists of 9 judges.
(2) Judges of Constitutional Court of the Azerbaijan Republic are appointed by the Parliament of the Azerbaijan Republic on recommendation by the President of the Azerbaijan Republic.

Article 131
(2) Judges of Supreme Court of the Azerbaijan Republic are appointed by the Parliament of the Azerbaijan Republic on recommendation of the President of the Azerbaijan Republic.

25. The chairman of the central bank is appointed by the legislature.

No. Formally, the legislature, on the recommendation of the president, appoints the board of the National Bank of Azerbaijan, but in practice, the appointment power rests wholly with the president.

Article 95
(1) The following questions fall under the competence of the Parliament of the Azerbaijan Republic:
15. based on recommendation by the President of the Azerbaijan Republic appointment and dismissal of members of Administration Board of National Bank of the Azerbaijan Republic.

Article 109
The President of the Azerbaijan Republic:
10. submits recommendations to the Parliament of the Azerbaijan Republic about appointment and dismissal of members of Administration Board of National Bank of the Azerbaijan Republic.

26. The legislature has a substantial voice in the operation of the state-owned media.

No. The executive branch controls the public media.

27. The legislature is regularly in session.

Yes. The legislature is in session for about seven months each year.

Article 88
(1) Every year two sessions of the Parliament [*Milli Majlis*] of the Azerbaijan Republic are held.
Spring session begins on 1 February and continues until 31 May.
Autumn session begins on 30 September and continues until 30 December.

28. Each legislator has a personal secretary.

No. Some, but not all, legislators have personal staff.

29. Each legislator has at least one non-secretarial staff member with policy expertise.

No. See item 28.

30. Legislators are eligible for re-election without any restriction.

Yes. There are no restrictions on re-election.

31. A seat in the legislature is an attractive enough position that legislators are generally interested in and seek re-election.

Yes.

32. The re-election of incumbent legislators is common enough that at any given time the legislature contains a significant number of highly experienced members.

Yes. Re-election rates are sufficiently high to produce a significant number of highly experienced members.

NATIONAL ASSEMBLY OF BAHRAIN (*MAJLIS AS-SHURA*)

Expert consultants: Colin S. Cavell, Camille Edmond, Michael Herb, Abd al-Hadi Khalaf, Laurence Louër, Jean-François Seznec

Score: .19

Influence over executive (2/9)		Institutional autonomy (0/9)	Specified powers (0/8)	Institutional capacity (4/6)	
1. replace		10. no dissolution	19. amendments	27. sessions	X
2. serve as ministers		11. no decree	20. war	28. secretary	X
3. interpellate	X	12. no veto	21. treaties	29. staff	
4. investigate		13. no review	22. amnesty	30. no term limits	X
5. oversee police		14. no gatekeeping	23. pardon	31. seek re-election	X
6. appoint PM		15. no impoundment	24. judiciary	32. experience	
7. appoint ministers		16. control resources	25. central bank		
8. lack president	X	17. immunity	26. media		
9. no confidence		18. all elected			

The National Assembly (*Majlis as-Shura*) of Bahrain was established in 1973 in Bahrain's first post-independence constitution. The unicameral assembly was dissolved by the monarch in 1975, and the al-Kahlifa family ruled without the National Assembly for over a quarter century. In 2002 a new constitution reestablished the National Assembly as a bicameral body comprising an upper house, the Consultative Council, and a lower house, the Chamber of Deputies.

Bahrain's new constitution, while resurrecting the National Assembly, did little to breathe life back into it. Although the legislature has become a forum for political contestation, particularly following the 2006 elections, royal dominance remains entrenched. The king is the official head of the executive, legislative, and judicial branches, and his dominance over legislation is nearly complete. The king can legislate by decree and alone chooses the prime minister and the government. The executive enjoys absolute gatekeeping authority; the legislature cannot even introduce a bill in the Assembly without first securing formal permission from the government. The entire upper house is also appointed by the king, and because the approval of both houses is required to pass legislation, legislation opposed by the king has virtually no chance of becoming law.

The National Assembly does enjoy a few scattered powers. For example, the Chamber of Deputies can interrogate ministers, and has done so. Any institutional independence, however, is stifled by the constant threat of dissolution, a power that the king can exercise at will.

SURVEY

1. The legislature alone, without the involvement of any other agencies, can impeach the president or replace the prime minister.

No. The legislature cannot impeach the monarch, nor can it replace the prime minister without action by the king.

Article 67
a. The subject of confidence in the Prime Minister shall not be raised in the Chamber of Deputies.
b. If, two-thirds of members of the Chamber of Deputies consider it not possible to cooperate with the Prime Minister, the matter will be referred to the National Assembly to consider it.
c. The National Assembly cannot issue its decision on the lack of possibility of cooperating with the Prime Minister prior to seven days from the date the matter was referred to it.
d. If the National Assembly decides by a majority of two thirds of its members that it is not possible to cooperate with the Prime Minister, the matter is submitted to the King for a decision, either by relieving the Prime Minister of his post and appointing a new Government, or by dissolving the Chamber of Deputies.

2. Ministers may serve simultaneously as members of the legislature.

No. Ministers are prohibited from serving simultaneously in the legislature.

Article 48
b. While in charge of his Ministry, a Minister may not assume any other public office.

Article 97
Membership of the Consultative Council and Chamber of Deputies may not be combined, nor may membership of either chamber be combined with the assumption of public office.
Other cases of non-combination shall be prescribed by law.

3. The legislature has powers of summons over executive branch officials and hearings with executive branch officials testifying before the legislature or its committees are regularly held.

Yes. The legislature regularly interpellates officials from the executive.

Article 65
(1) Upon an application signed by at least five members of the Chamber of Deputies, any Minister may be questioned on matters coming within his sphere of competence.

Article 91
(1) Any member of the Consultative Council or the Chamber of Deputies may direct written questions at Ministers to clarify matters coming within their sphere of competence, and only the questioner may comment once on the reply. If the Minister adds anything new, the member shall be further entitled to comment.

4. The legislature can conduct independent investigation of the chief executive and the agencies of the executive.

No. The legislature cannot investigate the king, although investigations of some executive agencies have been conducted.

Article 69
(1) The Chamber of Deputies may at any time form commissions of inquiry or delegate one or more of its members to investigate any matter coming within the powers of the Chamber stated in the Constitution, and the commission or member is to present the findings of the inquiry not later than four months from the date of commencement of the inquiry.
(2) Ministers and all State employees are to provide such testimony, documents and statements as are asked of them.

5. The legislature has effective powers of oversight over the agencies of coercion (the military, organs of law enforcement, intelligence services, and the secret police).

No. The agencies of coercion report directly to the monarch and are not subject to legislative oversight.

6. The legislature appoints the prime minister.

No. The king appoints the prime minister.

> Article 33
> d. The King appoints and dismisses the Prime Minister by Royal Order, and appoints and dismisses Ministers by Royal Decree as proposed by the Prime Minister.

7. The legislature's approval is required to confirm the appointment of ministers; or the legislature itself appoints ministers.

No. The king appoints ministers on the recommendation of the prime minister, and the appointments do not require the legislature's approval.

> Article 33
> d. The King appoints and dismisses the Prime Minister by Royal Order, and appoints and dismisses Ministers by Royal Decree as proposed by the Prime Minister.

8. The country lacks a presidency entirely or there is a presidency, but the president is elected by the legislature.

Yes. The country lacks a presidency. The king is the chief executive.

9. The legislature can vote no confidence in the government.

No. The legislature cannot vote no confidence in the government. It can notify the king that it is unable to cooperate with the prime minister, and the king can decide to remove the prime minister or dissolve the legislature.

> Article 67
> d. If the National Assembly decides by a majority of two thirds of its members that it is not possible to cooperate with the Prime Minister, the matter is submitted to the King for a decision, either by relieving the Prime Minister of his post and appointing a new Government, or by dissolving the Chamber of Deputies.

10. The legislature is immune from dissolution by the executive.

No. The king can dissolve the Chamber of Deputies.

> Article 42
> c. The King is entitled to dissolve the Chamber of Deputies by a Decree that states the reasons for the dissolution. The Chamber cannot be dissolved for the same reasons once again.

11. Any executive initiative on legislation requires ratification or approval by the legislature before it takes effect; that is, the executive lacks decree power.

No. The king can issue decree-laws when the legislature is in recess. The decrees lapse if they are not subsequently approved by the Chamber of Deputies.

> Article 38
> (1) If between the convening of both the Consultative Council and the Chamber of Deputies sessions, or during the period in which the National Assembly is in recess, any event should occur that requires expediting the adoption of measures that brook no delay, the King may issue relevant Decrees that have the force of law, provided they do not contravene the Constitution.
> (2) Such Decrees must be referred to both the Consultative Council and the Chamber of Deputies within one month from their promulgation if the two chambers are in session, or within a month of the first meeting of each of the two new chambers in the event of dissolution or if the legislative term had ended. If the Decrees are not so referred, their legal force shall abate retrospectively without a need to issue a relevant ruling. If they are referred to the two chambers but are not confirmed by them their legal force shall also abate retrospectively.

12. Laws passed by the legislature are veto-proof or essentially veto-proof; that is, the executive lacks veto power, or has veto power but the veto can be overridden by a majority in the legislature.

No. A two-thirds majority vote is needed to override the king's veto.

> Article 35
> c. With due regard for the provisions pertaining to amendment of the Constitution, if within the interval prescribed in the preceding clause the King returns to the Consultative Council and the Chamber of Deputies for reconsideration the draft of any law by way of a Decree in justification, he shall state whether it should be reconsidered in that same session or the next.
> d. If the Consultative Council and the Chamber of Deputies, or the National Assembly, re-approve the draft by a majority of two-thirds of their members, the King shall ratify it, and shall promulgate it within one month of its approval for the second time.

13. The legislature's laws are supreme and not subject to judicial review.

No. The Constitutional Court can review the constitutionality of laws.

> Article 106
> (1) A Constitutional Court shall be established... The court's area of competence is to watch over the constitutionality of laws and statutes.

14. The legislature has the right to initiate bills in all policy jurisdictions; the executive lacks gatekeeping authority.

No. The government has complete gatekeeping authority. The National Assembly is prohibited from pursuing lawmaking at all, except with the permission of the government.

Article 81
The Prime Minister shall present bills to the Chamber of Deputies, which is entitled to pass, amend or reject the bill.

Article 92
a. Any member of the two chambers is entitled to propose laws. Each proposal shall be referred to the relevant committee in the chamber in which the proposal was made for an opinion. If the chamber sees fit to accept the proposal, it shall refer it to the Government to formulate it . . . as a draft law and present it to the Chamber of Deputies during the same or succeeding period.

15. Expenditure of funds appropriated by the legislature is mandatory; the executive lacks the power to impound funds appropriated by the legislature.

No. In practice, the king is firmly in charge of all expenditures.

16. The legislature controls the resources that finance its own internal operation and provide for the perquisites of its own members.

No. The legislature is dependent on the executive for the resources that finance its own operations.

17. Members of the legislature are immune from arrest and/or criminal prosecution.

No. Legislators can be prosecuted for the expression of any opinion that is "prejudicial to the fundamentals of the religion or the unity of the nation, or the mandatory respect for the King, or is defamatory of the personal life of any person."

Article 89
b. No member of the Consultative Council or the Chamber of Deputies shall be called to account for expressing his opinions or ideas in the Council or its committees unless the opinion expressed is prejudicial to the fundamentals of the religion or the unity of the nation, or the mandatory respect for the King, or is defamatory of the personal life of any person.
c. Other than in a case of flagrant delicto, it shall be impermissible during the convening period for any detention, investigation, search, arrest or custodial procedures or any other penal action to be taken against a member except with the permission of the chamber of which he is a member. Outside the convening period, permission must be sought from the President of the relevant chamber.

18. All members of the legislature are elected; the executive lacks the power to appoint any members of the legislature.

No. The Consultative Council is entirely appointed by the king.

Article 52
The Consultative Council is composed of forty members appointed by Royal Order.

Article 56
The Chamber of Deputies comprises forty members elected by direct, secret general ballot in accordance with the provisions of the law.

19. The legislature alone, without the involvement of any other agencies, can change the Constitution.

No. Constitutional amendments require the king's approval.

Article 120
a. For any provision of this Constitution to be amended the amendment must be approved by a two-thirds majority of the members of whom both the Consultative Council and Chamber of Deputies are composed, and the amendment must be approved by the King.

20. The legislature's approval is necessary for the declaration of war.

No. The king can declare war without the legislature's approval.

Article 36
a. Aggressive war is forbidden. A defensive war is declared by a Decree which shall be presented to the National Assembly immediately upon its declaration, for a decision on the conduct of the war.

21. The legislature's approval is necessary to ratify treaties with foreign countries.

No. The king concludes treaties by decree. Treaties that require promulgation by law can also be decreed by the king. See item 11.

Article 37
(1) The King shall conclude treaties by Decree, and shall communicate them to the Consultative Council and the Chamber of Deputies forthwith accompanied by the appropriate statement. A treaty shall have the force of law once it has been concluded and ratified and published in the Official Gazette.
(2) However, peace treaties and treaties of alliance, treaties relating to State territory, natural resources, rights of sovereignty, the public and private rights of citizens, treaties pertaining to commerce, shipping and residence, and treaties which involve the State Exchequer in non-budget expenditure or which entail amendment of the laws of Bahrain, must be promulgated by law to be valid.

22. The legislature has the power to grant amnesty.

No. Formally, a total amnesty may be granted only by law. In practice, only the king has the power to grant amnesty.

Article 41
The King may abate or commute a sentence by Decree. A total amnesty may be granted only by law, and shall apply to offences committed before the amnesty was proposed.

23. The legislature has the power of pardon.

No. The king has the power of pardon (commute a sentence).

Article 41
The King may abate or commute a sentence by Decree. A total amnesty may be granted only by law, and shall apply to offences committed before the amnesty was proposed.

24. The legislature reviews and has the right to reject appointments to the judiciary; or the legislature itself appoints members of the judiciary.

No. The king appoints judges, and judicial appointments do not require the legislature's approval.

Article 33
h. The King chairs the Higher Judicial Council. The King appoints judges by Royal Orders, as proposed by the Higher Judicial Council.

25. The chairman of the central bank is appointed by the legislature.

No. The king appoints the head of the Central Bank of Bahrain.

26. The legislature has a substantial voice in the operation of the state-owned media.

No. The legislature lacks a substantial voice in the operation of the public media.

27. The legislature is regularly in session.

Yes. The legislature meets for at least seven months each year.

Article 72
The normal convening period for both the Consultative Council and the Chamber of Deputies shall last for at least seven months, and this convening period may not be closed before the budget is approved.

28. Each legislator has a personal secretary.

Yes. Each legislator receives funds for office staff.

29. Each legislator has at least one non-secretarial staff member with policy expertise.

No. Each legislator receives funds for office staff, but generally these funds are not large enough to cover policy staff as well as secretaries.

30. Legislators are eligible for re-election without any restriction.

Yes. There are no restrictions on re-election.

31. A seat in the legislature is an attractive enough position that legislators are generally interested in and seek re-election.

Yes.

32. The re-election of incumbent legislators is common enough that at any given time the legislature contains a significant number of highly experienced members.

No. In 2002 the National Assembly convened for the first time in twenty-five years; none of the legislators is highly experienced.

BANGLADESH PARLIAMENT (*JATIYA SANGSAD*)

Expert consultants: Q. K. Ahmad, Jamshed S. A. Choudhury, Sabine Mietzner, Atiur Rehman, Nadia Shafiullah

Score: .59

Influence over executive (8/9)		Institutional autonomy (4/9)		Specified powers (3/8)		Institutional capacity (4/6)	
1. replace	X	10. no dissolution		19. amendments	X	27. sessions	X
2. serve as ministers	X	11. no decree		20. war	X	28. secretary	
3. interpellate	X	12. no veto	X	21. treaties	X	29. staff	
4. investigate	X	13. no review	X	22. amnesty		30. no term limits	X
5. oversee police	X	14. no gatekeeping		23. pardon		31. seek re-election	X
6. appoint PM	X	15. no impoundment		24. judiciary		32. experience	X
7. appoint ministers		16. control resources	X	25. central bank			
8. lack president	X	17. immunity		26. media			
9. no confidence	X	18. all elected	X				

The Bangladesh Parliament (*Jatiya Sangsad*) was established in 1972 in the country's first post-independence constitution following separation from Pakistan. The unicameral parliament was in existence for only three years before it was dissolved and the government was overthrown in a military coup. Sweeping constitutional changes in 1975 transformed the country from a parliamentary to a presidential system. Legislative elections were held in 1978, but more instability followed. Civilian rule again gave way to a coup in 1981 and the imposition of martial law in 1985. In 1991 Bangladesh experienced a return to civilian rule and constitutional changes that restored a Westminster-style parliamentary system. Parliamentary elections scheduled for early 2007 were postponed after weeks of protests and violence in which opposition groups claimed that the polls were rigged in the government's favor. The elections originally were rescheduled for April 2007, but that date was subsequently pushed back by an emergency military-backed government, which as of this writing promises new elections by the end of 2008.

The parliament, at least during times when it is allowed to function normally, enjoys substantial power, including broad oversight authority over the executive branch. Furthermore, the Bangladesh Parliament is one of a few legislatures in the world whose laws are supreme and not subject to judicial review.

Still, the presence of a strong presidency distinguishes Bangladesh from a typical Westminster-style system. For example, the president has some gatekeeping authority and may rule by decree when parliament is not in session, circumscribing the legislature's institutional autonomy. The legislature possesses a few enumerated powers and has a moderate amount of institutional capacity.

SURVEY

1. The legislature alone, without the involvement of any other agencies, can impeach the president or replace the prime minister.

Yes. The legislature can impeach the president by a two-thirds majority vote of its total membership and can replace the prime minister by a majority vote of its total membership.

Article 52
(1) The President may be impeached on a charge of violating this Constitution or of grave misconduct, preferred by a notice of motion signed by a majority of the total number of members of the Parliament.
(2) The Conduct of the President may be referred by Parliament to any court, tribunal or body appointed or designated by Parliament for the investigation of a charge under this article.

(3) The President shall have the right to appear and to be represented during the consideration of the charge.
(4) If after the consideration of the charge a resolution is passed by Parliament by votes of not less than two-thirds of the total number of members declaring that the charge has been substantiated, the President shall vacate his office on the date on which the resolution is passed.

Article 57
(2) If the Prime Minister ceases to retain the support of a majority of the members of Parliament, he shall either resign his office or... the President shall, if he is satisfied that no other member of Parliament commands the support of the majority of the members of Parliament, dissolve Parliament accordingly.

2. Ministers may serve simultaneously as members of the legislature.

Yes. At least 90 percent of the ministers must be chosen from parliament.

Article 56
(2) The appointments of the Prime Minister and other Ministers and of the Ministers of State and Deputy Ministers, shall be made by the President: Provided that not less than nine-tenths of their number shall be appointed from among members of Parliament and not more than one-tenth of their number may be chosen from among persons qualified for election as members of Parliament.

3. The legislature has powers of summons over executive branch officials and hearings with executive branch officials testifying before the legislature or its committees are regularly held.

Yes. The legislature regularly interpellates officials from the executive.

Article 76
(2) In addition to the committees referred to in clause (1), Parliament shall appoint other standing committees, and a committee so appointed may, subject to this Constitution and to any other law
(c) in relation to any matter referred to it by Parliament as a matter of public importance, investigate or inquire into the activities or administration of a Ministry and may require it to furnish, through an authorized representative, relevant information and to answer questions, orally or in writing.

4. The legislature can conduct independent investigation of the chief executive and the agencies of the executive.

Yes. The legislature can investigate the executive.

5. The legislature has effective powers of oversight over the agencies of coercion (the military, organs of law enforcement, intelligence services, and the secret police).

Yes. The legislature has effective powers of oversight over the agencies of coercion.

6. The legislature appoints the prime minister.

Yes. The president is obliged to appoint as prime minister the member of parliament who commands majority support in the parliament.

Article 56
(3) The President shall appoint as Prime Minister the member of Parliament who appears to him to command the support of the majority of the members of Parliament.

7. The legislature's approval is required to confirm the appointment of ministers; or the legislature itself appoints ministers.

No. Ministers are appointed by the president on the recommendation of the prime minister, and the appointments do not require the legislature's approval.

Article 56
(1) There shall be Prime Minister, and such other Ministers, Ministers of State and Deputy Ministers as may be determined by the Prime Minister.
(2) The appointments of the... Ministers and of the Ministers of State and Deputy Ministers, shall be made by the President.

8. The country lacks a presidency entirely or there is a presidency, but the president is elected by the legislature.

Yes. The legislature elects the president.

Article 48
(1) There shall be a President of Bangladesh who shall be elected by members of Parliament in accordance with law.

9. The legislature can vote no confidence in the government.

Yes. The legislature can vote no confidence in the government.

Article 57
(2) If the Prime Minister ceases to retain the support of a majority of the members of Parliament, he shall either resign his office or... the President shall, if he is satisfied that no other member of Parliament commands the support of the majority of the members of Parliament, dissolve Parliament accordingly.

Article 58
(4) If the Prime Minister resigns from or ceases to hold office each of the other Ministers shall be deemed also to have resigned from office but shall, subject to the provisions of the Chapter, continue to hold office until his successor has entered upon office.

10. The legislature is immune from dissolution by the executive.

No. The president can dissolve the legislature. See item 9.

11. Any executive initiative on legislation requires ratification or approval by the legislature before it takes effect; that is, the executive lacks decree power.

No. The president can issue decree-laws when parliament is not in session. The decrees lapse if they are not subsequently approved by the legislature.

Article 93
(1) At any time when Parliament stands dissolved or is not in session, if the President is satisfied that circumstances exist which render immediate action necessary, he may make and promulgate such Ordinances as the circumstances appear to him to require, and any Ordinance so made shall, as from its promulgation have the like force of law as an Act of Parliament:
(2) An Ordinance made under clause (1) shall be laid before Parliament at its first meeting following the promulgation of the Ordinance and shall, unless it is earlier repealed, cease to have effect at the expiration of thirty days after it is so laid or, if a resolution disapproving of the Ordinance is passed by Parliament before such expiration, upon the passing of the resolution.

12. Laws passed by the legislature are veto-proof or essentially veto-proof; that is, the executive lacks veto power, or has veto power but the veto can be overridden by a majority in the legislature.

Yes. The legislature can override a presidential veto by a majority vote of its present members.

Article 80
(3) The President, within fifteen days after a Bill is presented to him shall assent to the Bill or, in the case of a Bill other than a money Bill may return it to parliament with a message requesting that the Bill or any particular provisions thereof by reconsidered.
(4) If the President so returns the Bill Parliament shall consider it together with the President's message, and if the Bill is again passed by Parliament with or without amendments, it shall be presented to the President for his assent.

13. The legislature's laws are supreme and not subject to judicial review.

Yes. The legislature's laws are supreme as the constitution does not empower the judiciary to engage in review of legislation.

14. The legislature has the right to initiate bills in all policy jurisdictions; the executive lacks gatekeeping authority.

No. The legislature is prohibited from introducing legislation related to taxation, public expenditures, and government debt.

Article 82
(1) In this Part "Money Bill" means a Bill containing only provisions dealing with all or any of the following matters –
(a) the imposition, regulation, alteration, remission or repeal of any tax;
(b) the borrowing of money or the giving of any guarantee by the Government, or the amendment of any law relating to the financial obligations of the Government;
(c) the custody of the Consolidated Fund, the payment of money into, or the issue or appropriation of moneys from, the Fund;
(d) the imposition of a charge upon the Consolidated Fund, or the alteration or abolition of any such charge;
(e) the receipt of moneys on account of the Consolidated Fund or the Public Account of the Republic, or the custody or issue of such moneys, or the audit of the accounts of the Government;
(f) any subordinate matter incidental to any of the matters specified in the foregoing sub-clauses.

Article 82
No Money Bill, or any Bill which involves expenditure from public moneys, shall be introduced into Parliament except on the recommendation of the President.

15. Expenditure of funds appropriated by the legislature is mandatory; the executive lacks the power to impound funds appropriated by the legislature.

No. The president can impound funds appropriated by the legislature.

16. The legislature controls the resources that finance its own internal operation and provide for the perquisites of its own members.

Yes. The legislature enjoys financial autonomy, including control over members' allowances.

Article 68
Members of Parliament shall be entitled to such allowances and privileges as may be determined by Act of Parliament or, until so determined, by order made by the President.

17. Members of the legislature are immune from arrest and/or criminal prosecution.

No. Legislative immunity extends to official parliamentary business only. Legislators are subject to arrest for common crimes.

Article 78
(3) A member of Parliament shall not be liable to proceedings in any court in respect of anything said, or any vote given, by him in Parliament or in any committed thereof.
(4) A person shall not be liable to proceedings in any court in respect of the publication by or under the

authority of Parliament of any report, paper, vote or proceeding.

18. All members of the legislature are elected; the executive lacks the power to appoint any members of the legislature.

Yes. All members of the legislature are elected.

> Article 65
> (2) Parliament shall consist of three hundred members to be elected in accordance with law from single territorial constituencies by direct election.

19. The legislature alone, without the involvement of any other agencies, can change the Constitution.

Yes. The legislature can amend the constitution with a two-thirds majority vote. Select articles of the constitution, including those related to fundamental principles and the constitutional amendment process itself, require approval in a popular referendum.

> Article 142
> (1) Notwithstanding anything contained in this Constitution –
> (a) any provision thereof may by amended by way of addition, alteration, substitution or by Act of Parliament:
> Provided that –
> (ii) no such Bill shall be presented to the President for assent unless it is passed by the votes of not less than two-thirds of the total number of members of Parliament.
> (1A) Notwithstanding anything contained in clause (1), when a Bill, passed as a aforesaid, which provides for the amendment of the Preamble or any provisions of articles 8, 48, 56, 94, 95 or this article, is presented to the President for assent, the President, shall within the period of seven days, after the Bill is presented to him, cause to be referred to a referendum the question whether the Bill should or should not be assented to.

20. The legislature's approval is necessary for the declaration of war.

Yes. The legislature's approval is necessary for the declaration of war.

> Article 63
> (1) War shall not be declared and the Republic shall not participate in any war except with the assent of Parliament.

21. The legislature's approval is necessary to ratify treaties with foreign countries.

Yes. The legislature's approval is necessary to ratify international treaties.

> Article 145A
> All treaties with foreign countries shall be submitted to the President, who shall cause them to be laid before Parliament.

22. The legislature has the power to grant amnesty.

No. Pardon and amnesty are not treated separately, and the legislature lacks the power to grant amnesty. See item 23.

23. The legislature has the power of pardon.

No. The president has the power to grant pardon.

> Article 49
> The President shall have power to grant pardons, reprieves and respites and to remit, suspend or commute any sentence passed by any court, tribunal or other authority.

24. The legislature reviews and has the right to reject appointments to the judiciary; or the legislature itself appoints members of the judiciary.

No. The president makes appointments to the judiciary, and the appointments do not require the legislature's approval.

> Article 95
> (1) The Chief Justice and other Judges shall be appointed by the President.
>
> Article 98
> Notwithstanding the provisions of article 94, if the President is satisfied that the number of the Judge of a division of the Supreme Court should be for the time being increased, the President may appoint one or more duly qualified person to be Additional Judges of that division.

25. The chairman of the central bank is appointed by the legislature.

No. The president appoints the governor of the Bangladesh Bank.

26. The legislature has a substantial voice in the operation of the state-owned media.

No. The legislature lacks a substantial voice in the operation of the public media.

27. The legislature is regularly in session.

Yes. Parliament determines its own schedule and is regularly in session.

> Article 72
> (5) The sittings of Parliament shall be held at such times and places as Parliament may, by its rules of procedure or otherwise determine.

28. Each legislator has a personal secretary.

No.

29. Each legislator has at least one non-secretarial staff member with policy expertise.

No.

30. Legislators are eligible for re-election without any restriction.

Yes. There are no restrictions on re-election.

31. A seat in the legislature is an attractive enough position that legislators are generally interested in and seek re-election.

Yes.

32. The re-election of incumbent legislators is common enough that at any given time the legislature contains a significant number of highly experienced members.

Yes. Re-election rates are sufficiently high to produce a significant number of highly experienced members.

NATIONAL ASSEMBLY OF BELARUS (*NATSIONALNOE SOBRANIE*)

Expert consultants: Arkady Cherepansky, Elena A. Korosteleva-Polglase, Yury Likhtarovich, Alexander Lukashuk, David R. Marples, Rodger Potocki, Alaksandar Salajka, Lucan A. Way

Score: .25

Influence over executive (2/9)		Institutional autonomy (0/9)		Specified powers (3/8)		Institutional capacity (3/6)	
1. replace		10. no dissolution		19. amendments		27. sessions	X
2. serve as ministers	X	11. no decree		20. war	X	28. secretary	
3. interpellate		12. no veto		21. treaties		29. staff	
4. investigate		13. no review		22. amnesty	X	30. no term limits	X
5. oversee police		14. no gatekeeping		23. pardon		31. seek re-election	X
6. appoint PM		15. no impoundment		24. judiciary	X	32. experience	
7. appoint ministers		16. control resources		25. central bank			
8. lack president		17. immunity		26. media			
9. no confidence	X	18. all elected					

The National Assembly (*Natsionalnoe Sobranie*) of Belarus was established in a 1996 constitutional amendment. The National Assembly is a bicameral legislature with a directly elected House of Representatives (*Palata Predstavitelei*) and an upper house, the Council of the Republic (*Sovet Respubliki*), made up of elected representatives and presidential appointees.

The amendments that created the National Assembly reshaped Belarus's first post-Soviet constitution, which was adopted in 1994. They replaced the previous legislature, the unicameral Supreme Council, with the National Assembly and greatly enhanced presidential power.

While the president was, in practice, the preeminent force in Belarusian politics between 1994 and 1996, the constitutional amendments of 1996 encoded presidential dominance. The 1996 amendments gave the president the power to appoint some members of parliament; previously the legislature had been entirely elected. Whereas the 1994 constitution provided the legislature with broad appointment powers, the new system gives the president free reign to appoint ministers without legislative approval. The legislature's previous independence in lawmaking was also circumscribed by changes that provide the president with some gatekeeping authority. Furthermore, under the 1994 constitution the legislature was immune from dissolution; the revised system grants the president dissolution powers.

The parliament is left with precious little power, although it retains the authority to grant amnesty, appoint some members of the Constitutional Court, and declare war.

SURVEY

1. The legislature alone, without the involvement of any other agencies, can impeach the president or replace the prime minister.

No. Formally, the parliament, acting alone, can impeach the president. In practice, presidential impeachment is unthinkable.

Article 88
The President may be removed from office for acts of state treason and other grave crimes. The decision to file a charge against the President shall be supported by a majority of the whole House of Representatives on behalf of no less than one-third of the number of deputies. The investigation of the charge shall be exercised by the Council of the Republic. The President shall be deemed to be removed from office if the decision is adopted by no less than two-thirds of the full composition of the Council of the Republic, and no less than two-thirds of the full House of Representatives...Where the President is removed in connection with the commission of a crime, the case shall be examined on the merits of the charge by the Supreme Court.

Article 97
The House of Representatives shall:
9) be entitled with a majority of the full composition of the House of Representatives to forward charges of treason or of some other grave crime against the President; on the basis of the decision of the Council of the Republic and with no less than a two-thirds majority of the full composition of the House take the decision to remove the President from office.

Article 98
The Council of the Republic shall:
7) consider charges of treason or of some other grave crime forwarded by the House of Representatives against the President and take decision on its investigation. Given the presence of substantial evidence take the decision to remove the President from office with no less than two-thirds of the full composition of the House.

2. Ministers may serve simultaneously as members of the legislature.

Yes. Deputies in the House of Representatives may serve simultaneously as ministers; members of the Council of the Republic, however, are prohibited from serving simultaneously as ministers.

Article 92
A deputy of the House of Representatives may simultaneously be member of the Government...A member of the Council of the Republic may not be simultaneously a member of the Government.

3. The legislature has powers of summons over executive branch officials and hearings with executive branch officials testifying before the legislature or its committees are regularly held.

No. Formally, the government is required to hold a monthly question time. At other times the legislature may submit inquires to the government, and the government is required to respond within twenty days. In practice, even this limited degree of oversight is not exercised.

Article 103
One sitting monthly shall be reserved for question time to the Government for the deputies of the Houses of Representatives and members of the Council of the Republic. A deputy of the House of Representatives or member of the Council of the Republic shall have the right to make an inquiry to the Prime minister or members of the Government and the heads of state bodies which are formed or elected by Parliament. The inquiry shall be included in the agenda of the chamber. The answer to the inquiry shall be given within twenty days of the current session to the order determined by the chamber of the Parliament.

4. The legislature can conduct independent investigation of the chief executive and the agencies of the executive.

No. The legislature cannot investigate the executive. Prior to the 1996 amendments, the legislature had the formal power to set up investigatory commissions.

5. The legislature has effective powers of oversight over the agencies of coercion (the military, organs of law enforcement, intelligence services, and the secret police).

No. The agencies of coercion are controlled by the president and are not subject to legislative oversight.

6. The legislature appoints the prime minister.

No. The president appoints the prime minister. The appointment requires the approval of the House of Representatives.

Article 84
The President of the Republic of Belarus shall:
6) appoint the Prime minister of the Republic of Belarus with the consent of the House of Representatives.

Article 106
The Prime minister shall be appointed by the President of the Republic of Belarus with the consent of the House of Representatives.

7. The legislature's approval is required to confirm the appointment of ministers; or the legislature itself appoints ministers.

No. The president appoints ministers and the appointments do not require the legislature's approval. Prior to the 1996 amendments, ministerial appointments, at least formally, required the legislature's approval.

> Article 84
> The President of the Republic of Belarus shall:
> 7) appoint and dismiss the deputy Prime ministers, ministers and other members of the Government.

8. The country lacks a presidency entirely or there is a presidency, but the president is elected by the legislature.

No. The president is directly elected.

> Article 81
> The President shall be elected directly by the people of the Republic of Belarus for a term of office of five years by universal, free, equal, direct and secret ballot.

9. The legislature can vote no confidence in the government.

Yes. The legislature can vote no confidence in the government.

> Article 97
> The House of Representatives shall:
> 5) consider the report of the Prime minister on the policy of the Government and approve or reject it; a second rejection by the House of the policy of the Government shall be deemed as an expression of non-confidence to the Government;
> 6) consider on the initiative of the Prime minister a call for a vote of confidence;
> 7) on the initiative of no less than one-third of the full composition of the House of Representatives express a non-confidence vote to the Government.

> Article 106
> The Prime minister may request from the House of Representatives a vote of confidence with regard to the governmental Programme or any other issue submitted to the House. If a non-confidence vote is passed by the House of Representatives, the President shall be entitled to accept the resignation of the Government, or dissolve the House of Representatives within ten days, and call on holding new elections. If the resignation of the Government is rejected the latter shall continue to discharge its duties.

10. The legislature is immune from dissolution by the executive.

No. The president can dissolve the legislature. Prior to the 1996 amendments, the legislature was immune from dissolution.

> Article 94
> The powers of the House of Representatives may be terminated prematurely where no confidence is expressed or a non-confidence vote is expressed to the Government, or where the House fails twice to give its consent for the appointment of the Prime Minister. The powers of the House of Representatives or the Council of the

Republic may be prematurely terminated in accordance with the conclusion of the Constitutional Court due to systematic and gross violation of the Constitution by the chambers of the Parliament.

11. Any executive initiative on legislation requires ratification or approval by the legislature before it takes effect; that is, the executive lacks decree power.

No. The president issues decrees that have the force of law. The president's decree powers are extraordinarily robust: Decrees remain in force unless they are rejected by a two-thirds majority vote of both chambers of parliament.

> Article 101
> In instances of necessity the President may personally initiate or to the proposal of the Government may issue temporary decrees which have the power of law. If such decrees are issued on the initiative of the Government, they shall be signed by the Prime minister. Temporary decrees shall be submitted for further approval within three days of their adoption to the House of Representatives, and then to the Council of the Republic. These decrees shall be valid if they are not rejected by a majority of no fewer than two-thirds of votes of the full composition of both chambers.

12. Laws passed by the legislature are veto-proof or essentially veto-proof; that is, the executive lacks veto power, or has veto power but the veto can be overridden by a majority in the legislature.

No. A two-thirds majority vote in both houses is required to override a presidential veto.

> Article 100
> If the President does not agree with the text of the bill, he shall return it together with his objections to the House of Representatives, which shall consider it with the President's objections within thirty days. If the bill has been adopted by the House of Representatives by no less than two-thirds of its full composition, it together with the President's objections and within five days shall be submitted to the Council of the Republic, which shall consider it for a second hearing within twenty days. The bill shall be deemed to have been approved if no less than two-thirds of the full composition of the Council of the Republic has voted for it. The bill, after the House of Representatives and the Council of the Republic have overrun the President's objections, shall be signed by the President within five days. The bill shall become a law even if it is not signed by the President within the assigned time.

13. The legislature's laws are supreme and not subject to judicial review.

No. The Constitutional Court can review the constitutionality of laws.

> Article 116
> The Constitutional Court ... shall produce a ruling on: the conformity of laws ... to the Constitution.

14. The legislature has the right to initiate bills in all policy jurisdictions; the executive lacks gatekeeping authority.

No. The legislature is prohibited from introducing legislation related to the reduction of state resources, the increase of public expenditures, or constitutional amendments. Prior to 1996 the legislature had the right to initiate bills in all policy jurisdictions.

Article 99
Draft laws the adoption of which may reduce state resources, or increase expenditures may be introduced in the House of Representatives only with the consent of the President or to his assignment by the Government.

Article 138
The issue of amending and supplementing the Constitution shall be considered by the chambers of the Parliament on the initiative of the President or of no fewer than 150,000 citizens of the Republic of Belarus who are eligible to vote.

15. Expenditure of funds appropriated by the legislature is mandatory; the executive lacks the power to impound funds appropriated by the legislature.

No. The president can impound funds appropriated by the legislature.

16. The legislature controls the resources that finance its own internal operation and provide for the perquisites of its own members.

No. The legislature is dependent on the executive for the resources that finance its own operations.

17. Members of the legislature are immune from arrest and/or criminal prosecution.

No. By law, legislators are immune except for cases of slander and insult. In practice, this exception has been used to persecute members of parliament. For example, in 2004 two opposition leaders were charged with "public slander" against the president and sentenced to two years in a labor camp.

Article 102
The deputies of the House of Representatives and members of the Council of the Republic shall enjoy immunity in the expression of their views and execution of their powers. This shall not refer to charges of slander and insult. During the period they exercise their powers the deputies and the members of Council of the Republic may be arrested or deprived of personal liberty in other manner only with the prior consent of the appropriate chamber with the exception of instances of high treason, or some other grave crime, as well as detention at the site where the crime was committed. A criminal case involving a deputy of the House of Representatives

or a member of the Council of the Republic shall be tried by the Supreme Court.

18. All members of the legislature are elected; the executive lacks the power to appoint any members of the legislature.

No. Eight members of the Council of the Republic are appointed by the president. Prior to the 1996 amendment all members of the legislature were elected.

Article 91
The election of deputies to the House of Representatives shall be carried out in accordance with the law on the basis of universal, equal, free, direct electoral suffrage and by secret ballot... Eight members of the Council of the Republic shall be appointed by the President of the Republic of Belarus.

19. The legislature alone, without the involvement of any other agencies, can change the Constitution.

No. Constitutional amendments can only be initiated by the president or the citizenry. Prior to 1996 the legislature alone could change the constitution.

Article 138
The issue of amending and supplementing the Constitution shall be considered by the chambers of the Parliament on the initiative of the President or of no fewer than 150,000 citizens of the Republic of Belarus who are eligible to vote.

20. The legislature's approval is necessary for the declaration of war.

Yes. The constitution grants the House of Representatives the formal power to declare war. There is not a sufficient evidentiary basis on which to conclude that this provision does not hold in practice.

Article 97
The House of Representatives shall:
2) consider draft laws, including the guidelines of the domestic and foreign policy of the Republic of Belarus; declaration of war and conclusion of peace.

21. The legislature's approval is necessary to ratify treaties with foreign countries.

No. In practice, the president concludes international treaties. According to the constitution, the legislature's approval is necessary to ratify international treaties, but the president generally refuses to submit international agreements to parliament.

Article 97
The House of Representatives shall:

2) consider draft laws, including the guidelines of the domestic and foreign policy of the Republic of Belarus; ratification and denunciation of interstate treaties.

22. The legislature has the power to grant amnesty.

Yes. The legislature has the power to grant amnesty.

Article 97
The House of Representatives shall:
2) consider draft laws, including the guidelines of the domestic and foreign policy of the Republic of Belarus; issues of criminal responsibility and amnesty.

23. The legislature has the power of pardon.

No. The president has the power of pardon.

Article 84
The President of the Republic of Belarus shall:
19) grant pardons to convicted citizens.

24. The legislature reviews and has the right to reject appointments to the judiciary; or the legislature itself appoints members of the judiciary.

Yes. The Council of the Republic appoints six of the twelve judges on the Constitutional Court and must approve the president's appointment for chairperson of the Constitutional Court.

Article 98
The Council of the Republic shall:
2) give its consent for the appointment by the President of the Chairperson of the Constitutional Court, Chairperson and judges of the Supreme Court, the Chairperson and judges of the Supreme Economic Court, the Chairperson of the Central Commission on Elections and National Referenda, the Procurator-General, the Chairperson and members of the National Bank;
3) elect six judges of the Constitutional Court.

Article 116
Six Judges of the Constitutional Court shall be appointed by the President of the Republic of Belarus and six elected by the Council of the Republic. The Chairperson of the Constitutional Court shall be appointed by the President with the consent of the Council of the Republic. The term of the members of the Constitutional Court shall be 11 years, and the permissible age limit shall be 70 years.

25. The chairman of the central bank is appointed by the legislature.

No. The president appoints the chairman of the National Bank of Belarus with the approval of the legislature.

Article 84
The President of the Republic of Belarus shall:
9) appoint with the consent of the Council of the Republic . . . the Chairperson and members of the Governing Board of the National Bank.

26. The legislature has a substantial voice in the operation of the state-owned media.

No. The president controls the public media.

27. The legislature is regularly in session.

Yes. The legislature meets for a maximum of 170 days each year. In practice, including special sessions, the legislature meets for more than six months each year.

Article 95
The chambers shall hold their regular sessions twice a year. The first session shall open on October 2; its duration may not exceed 80 days. The second session shall open on April 2 and its duration may not exceed 90 days.

28. Each legislator has a personal secretary.

No.

29. Each legislator has at least one non-secretarial staff member with policy expertise.

No.

30. Legislators are eligible for re-election without any restriction.

Yes. There are no restrictions on re-election.

31. A seat in the legislature is an attractive enough position that legislators are generally interested in and seek re-election.

Yes.

32. The re-election of incumbent legislators is common enough that at any given time the legislature contains a significant number of highly experienced members.

No. During the 1990s the president intervened aggressively in the legislature's affairs, pushing through constitutional changes that reshaped the legislature and enabled him to rid the body of his political opponents. The president's actions, combined with the relative youth of the post-Soviet legislature, have left the National Assembly short of highly experienced legislators.

FEDERAL PARLIAMENT OF BELGIUM (*FEDERALE PARLEMENT VAN BELGIË/ PARLEMENT FÉDÉRAL DA LA BELGIQUE*)

Expert consultants: Sam Depauw, Kris Deschouwer, Koen Muylle, Gérard Roland, Marc Swyngedouw

Score: .75

Influence over executive (8/9)		Institutional autonomy (6/9)		Specified powers (5/8)		Institutional capacity (5/6)	
1. replace	X	10. no dissolution		19. amendments	X	27. sessions	X
2. serve as ministers		11. no decree	X	20. war		28. secretary	X
3. interpellate	X	12. no veto	X	21. treaties	X	29. staff	
4. investigate	X	13. no review		22. amnesty	X	30. no term limits	X
5. oversee police	X	14. no gatekeeping	X	23. pardon		31. seek re-election	X
6. appoint PM	X	15. no impoundment	X	24. judiciary	X	32. experience	X
7. appoint ministers	X	16. control resources	X	25. central bank			
8. lack president	X	17. immunity		26. media	X		
9. no confidence	X	18. all elected	X				

The Federal Parliament (*Federale Parlement/ Parlement fédéral*) of Belgium was established in the constitution of 1831. The bicameral legislature consists of a directly elected House of Representatives (*Kamer van Volksvertegenwoordigers/Chambre des représentants*) and a Senate (*Senaat/Sénat*), whose members are partly elected and partly appointed by local representative bodies. The constitution was amended in 1893, 1920, 1970, 1980, 1988, and 1993. The amendments expanded suffrage and devolved power to linguistic communities, but did not greatly alter the powers of parliament.

The legislature enjoys considerable clout. It has effective control over the executive. Parliament chooses the prime minister, interpellates and investigates the government, and can remove the government with a vote of no confidence. The legislature's own institutional operations are largely autonomous. The legislature can introduce legislation in any policy jurisdiction, its laws are vetoproof, and it is largely immune from dissolution by the king. It is also vested with a number of specified powers and equipped with significant institutional capacity.

SURVEY

1. The legislature alone, without the involvement of any other agencies, can impeach the president or replace the prime minister.

Yes. The legislature can replace the prime minister with a vote of no confidence.

Article 96
(2) The Federal Government offers its resignation to the King if the House of Representatives, by an absolute majority of its members, adopts a motion of disapproval, proposing to the King the nomination of a successor to the Prime Minister, or proposes to the King the nomination of a successor to the Prime Minister within three days of the rejection of a motion of confidence. The King names the proposed successor as Prime Minister, who takes office the moment the new federal Government is sworn in.

2. Ministers may serve simultaneously as members of the legislature.

No. Legislators are prohibited from serving simultaneously in a ministerial position.

Article 50
Any member of one of the two Houses, appointed by the King as a minister and who accepts this nomination, ceases to sit in the House and takes up his mandate again when the King has put an end to his functions as a minister.

3. The legislature has powers of summons over executive branch officials and hearings with executive branch officials testifying before the legislature or its committees are regularly held.

Yes. Ministers regularly attend the meetings of parliament and answer questions.

Article 100
(2) The House of Representatives may demand the presence of ministers.

4. The legislature can conduct independent investigation of the chief executive and the agencies of the executive.

Yes. The legislature can investigate the executive.

Article 56
Each House has the right to hold an enquiry.

5. The legislature has effective powers of oversight over the agencies of coercion (the military, organs of law enforcement, intelligence services, and the secret police).

Yes. Legislative committees have effective powers of oversight over the agencies of coercion.

6. The legislature appoints the prime minister.

Yes. The king appoints as prime minister the candidate who enjoys the support of the House of Representatives.

Article 96
(1) The King appoints and dismisses his ministers.
(2) The Federal Government offers its resignation to the King if the House of Representatives, by an absolute majority of its members, adopts a motion of disapproval, proposing to the King the nomination of a successor to the Prime Minister, or proposes to the King the nomination of a successor to the Prime Minister within three days of the rejection of a motion of confidence. The King names the proposed successor as Prime Minister, who takes office the moment the new federal Government is sworn in.

7. The legislature's approval is required to confirm the appointment of ministers; or the legislature itself appoints ministers.

Yes. The king appoints ministers on the recommendation of the prime minister and with the approval of the legislature. The law does not explicitly stipulate that the government must receive

a vote of confidence before entering office, but by custom the crown and the prime minister are required to obtain such a vote from the legislature.

Article 96
(1) The King appoints and dismisses his ministers.

8. The country lacks a presidency entirely or there is a presidency, but the president is elected by the legislature.

Yes. The country lacks a presidency.

9. The legislature can vote no confidence in the government.

Yes. The legislature can vote no confidence in the government.

Article 46
(1) The King has only the right to dissolve the House of Representatives if the latter, with the absolute majority of its members:
1) either rejects a motion of confidence in the federal Government and does not propose to the King, within three days from the day of the rejection of the motion, the nomination of a successor to the Prime Minister;
2) or adopts a motion of disapproval with regard to the federal Government and does not simultaneously propose to the King the nomination of a successor to the Prime Minister.

Article 96
(2) The Federal Government offers its resignation to the King if the House of Representatives, by an absolute majority of its members, adopts a motion of disapproval, proposing to the King the nomination of a successor to the Prime Minister, or proposes to the King the nomination of a successor to the Prime Minister within three days of the rejection of a motion of confidence. The King names the proposed successor as Prime Minister, who takes office the moment the new federal Government is sworn in.

10. The legislature is immune from dissolution by the executive.

No. The king can dissolve the legislature.

Article 46
(1) The King has only the right to dissolve the House of Representatives if the latter, with the absolute majority of its members:
1) either rejects a motion of confidence in the federal Government and does not propose to the King, within three days from the day of the rejection of the motion, the nomination of a successor to the Prime Minister;
2) or adopts a motion of disapproval with regard to the federal Government and does not simultaneously propose to the King the nomination of a successor to the Prime Minister.

(4) The dissolution of the House of Representatives entails the dissolution of the Senate.

Article 195
(1) The federal legislative power has the right to declare a warranted constitutional revision of those matters which it determines.
(2) Following such a declaration, the two Houses are dissolved by full right.

11. Any executive initiative on legislation requires ratification or approval by the legislature before it takes effect; that is, the executive lacks decree power.

Yes. The king and the prime minister lack decree power. The legislature can, and on occasion has, passed legislation authorizing the government to rule temporarily by decree. For example, such decree power was authorized in the 1980s to grapple with an economic recession.

12. Laws passed by the legislature are veto-proof or essentially veto-proof; that is, the executive lacks veto power, or has veto power but the veto can be overridden by a majority in the legislature.

Yes. In theory, the king could refuse assent to a law passed by the legislature. In practice, however, the king almost always promulgates laws. When he has refused to do so, his objections have been ignored. For example, in 1990, when the king refused to assent to legislation legalizing abortion, the government promulgated the measure itself, and it became law.

13. The legislature's laws are supreme and not subject to judicial review.

No. The Court of Arbitration can review the constitutionality of laws.

Article 142
(1) There is, for all of Belgium, a Court of Arbitration, the composition, competencies, and functioning of which are established by law.
(2) This court statutes by means of ruling on:
3) the violation through a law, a decree, or through a ruling ... of constitutional articles determined by law.

14. The legislature has the right to initiate bills in all policy jurisdictions; the executive lacks gatekeeping authority.

Yes. The legislature can initiate bills in all policy jurisdictions.

15. Expenditure of funds appropriated by the legislature is mandatory; the executive lacks the power to impound funds appropriated by the legislature.

Yes. The executive lacks the power to impound funds appropriated by the legislature.

16. The legislature controls the resources that finance its own internal operation and provide for the perquisites of its own members.

Yes. The legislature enjoys financial autonomy. Each chamber of parliament provides for its own financial needs in the state budget. The perquisites of members of the House of Representatives are also encoded in the constitution.

Article 60
Each House determines, by its regulations, the way in which it exercises its duties.

Article 66
(1) Each member of the House of Representatives benefits from an annual indemnity of twelve thousand francs.
(2) He also has the right to free travel on all the means of communication operated or contracted out by the State.
(3) The law determines the means of transport that the representatives can use free of charge apart from those mentioned above.
(4) An annual indemnity to be deducted from the allocation destined to cover the expenditure of the House of Representatives can be attributed to the President of this assembly.
(5) The House determines the amount of the deductions that can be applied to the indemnity by way of a contribution to the pension funds that it judges necessary to establish.

Article 71
(1) Senators do not receive a salary.

17. Members of the legislature are immune from arrest and/or criminal prosecution.

No. Legislators are immune only while the legislature is in session.

Article 58
No member of either of the two Houses can be prosecuted or pursued with regard to opinions and votes given by him in the exercise of his duties.

Article 59
(1) No member of either of the two Houses can, during the duration of a session, be arrested or prosecuted for repression, except with the authorization of the House of which he is a member, except in cases of *flagrante delicto*.
(2) No imprisonment for debt can be undertaken against a member of either of the two Houses during a session, except with the same authorization.
(3) The detention of or a lawsuit against a member of either of the two Houses is suspended during a session and for its entire duration, if the House so requires.

18. All members of the legislature are elected; the executive lacks the power to appoint any members of the legislature.

Yes. The government and the crown lack the right to appoint members of the legislature, although members of the royal family in the line of succession are guaranteed a seat in the Senate. Members of the House of Representatives are directly elected, and members of the Senate are either elected or appointed by local representative bodies.

Article 61
(1) The members of the House of Representatives are elected directly by citizens who have completed the age of eighteen and who do not fall within the categories of exclusion stipulated by law.

Article 67
(1) Without prejudice to Article 72, the Senate is made up of seventy-one senators, of whom:
1) twenty-five senators elected in conformity with Article 61, by the Dutch electoral college;
2) fifteen senators elected in conformity with Article 61, by the French electoral college;
3) ten senators appointed by and within the Council of the Flemish Community, named the Flemish Council;
4) ten senators appointed by and within the Council of the French Community;
5) one senator appointed by and within the Council of the German-speaking Community;
6) six senators appointed by the senators referred to in 1) and 3);
7) four senators appointed by the senators referred to in 2) and 4).

19. The legislature alone, without the involvement of any other agencies, can change the Constitution.

Yes. The legislature can change the constitution through a complicated procedure. The sitting legislature can propose a constitutional amendment, and then, following an election, the subsequent legislature can approve the change with a two-thirds majority vote.

Article 195
(1) The federal legislative power has the right to declare a warranted constitutional revision of those matters which it determines.
(2) Following such a declaration, the two Houses are dissolved by full right.
(3) Two new Houses are then convened, in keeping with the terms of Article 46.
(4) These Houses statute, of common accord with the King, on those points submitted for revision.
(5) In this case, the Houses may debate only provided that two-thirds of the members composing each House are present; and no change may be adopted unless voted upon by a two-thirds majority.

20. The legislature's approval is necessary for the declaration of war.

No. The king declares war on the recommendation of the government, and war declarations do not require the legislature's approval.

Article 167
(1.2) The King commands the armed forces, and determines the state of war and the cessation of hostilities. He notifies the Houses as soon as State interests and security permit and he adds those messages deemed appropriate.

21. The legislature's approval is necessary to ratify treaties with foreign countries.

Yes. The legislature's approval is necessary to ratify international treaties.

Article 167
(1.3) Territorial transfers, exchanges, and additions may take place only by virtue of a law.
(2) The King concludes treaties...These treaties may take effect only following approval of the Houses.

22. The legislature has the power to grant amnesty.

Yes. Amnesty can be granted through legislation only.

23. The legislature has the power of pardon.

No. The king has the power of pardon.

Article 110
The King has the right to annul or to reduce sentences pronounced by judges, except for that which is statuted relative to ministers and members of Community and Regional Governments.

24. The legislature reviews and has the right to reject appointments to the judiciary; or the legislature itself appoints members of the judiciary.

Yes. The constitution does not specify rules for the composition of the Court of Arbitration (Constitutional Court). According to Article 32 of the Special Court of Arbitration Act, the Senate proposes a slate of nominees, whose appointment is then formalized by the king.

Article 142
(1) There is, for all of Belgium, a Court of Arbitration, the composition, competencies, and functioning of which are established by law.

25. The chairman of the central bank is appointed by the legislature.

No. The king, acting on the behest of the government, appoints the governor of the National Bank of Belgium.

26. The legislature has a substantial voice in the operation of the state-owned media.

Yes. Parliamentary group appoints some members of the state media board.

27. The legislature is regularly in session.

Yes. The legislature is in session for about ten months each year, from the beginning of October until the end of July.

> Article 44
> (1) The Houses meet by right each year on the second Tuesday of October, unless they have been called together prior to this by the King.
> (2) The Houses must meet each year for at least forty days.

28. Each legislator has a personal secretary.

Yes. Each member of parliament receives the resources to hire one staff person. The legislator can choose to hire a personal secretary or a staff member with policy expertise.

29. Each legislator has at least one non-secretarial staff member with policy expertise.

No. See item 28.

30. Legislators are eligible for re-election without any restriction.

Yes. There are no restrictions on re-election.

31. A seat in the legislature is an attractive enough position that legislators are generally interested in and seek re-election.

Yes.

32. The re-election of incumbent legislators is common enough that at any given time the legislature contains a significant number of highly experienced members.

Yes. Re-election rates are sufficiently high to produce a significant number of highly experienced members.

NATIONAL ASSEMBLY OF BENIN (*ASSEMBLÉE NATIONALE*)

Expert consultants: John R. Heilbrunn, Bruce A. Magnusson, Cédric Mayrargue, Linda Trudel, Leonard Wantchekon

Score: .56

Influence over executive (2/9)		Institutional autonomy (8/9)		Specified powers (4/8)		Institutional capacity (4/6)	
1. replace		10. no dissolution	X	19. amendments	X	27. sessions	X
2. serve as ministers		11. no decree	X	20. war		28. secretary	
3. interpellate	X	12. no veto	X	21. treaties	X	29. staff	
4. investigate	X	13. no review		22. amnesty	X	30. no term limits	X
5. oversee police		14. no gatekeeping	X	23. pardon		31. seek re-election	X
6. appoint PM		15. no impoundment	X	24. judiciary	X	32. experience	X
7. appoint ministers		16. control resources	X	25. central bank			
8. lack president		17. immunity	X	26. media			
9. no confidence		18. all elected	X				

The National Assembly (*Assemblée nationale*) of Benin was established in the constitution of 1990. Benin achieved independence in 1960 and was ruled by one military leader after another in a series of coups d'état. Major Mathieu Kérékou seized power in 1972 and managed to stay in power until 1990. Kérékou adopted communism as an ideological mantle and established a powerless legislature, the National Revolutionary Assembly. In 1990, in the midst of domestic unrest, Kérékou assented to a national conference that opened the way for multiparty politics and the 1990 constitution, which remains in effect today.

The National Assembly has considerable power, although its capabilities are unevenly distributed. It has precious little control over the executive. Yet while the legislature has little ability to influence executive power, it has a great deal of institutional autonomy. Among other sources of autonomy, it is immune from dissolution by the executive, it can initiate bills in all policy jurisdictions, and its laws are virtually veto-proof. The legislature also enjoys a number of powers and prerogatives.

Partly as a result of economic underdevelopment, the institutional capacity of the legislature is restricted. Legislators' salaries are very low, and a lack of funds for support personnel means that legislators must operate without staff.

SURVEY

1. The legislature alone, without the involvement of any other agencies, can impeach the president or replace the prime minister.

No. Presidential impeachment requires action by the Constitutional Court.

> Article 76
> There shall be an insult to the National Assembly when, to questions posed by the National Assembly concerning governmental activity, the President of the Republic shall not furnish any response within a period of thirty days.

> Article 77
> After this deadline, the President of the National Assembly shall submit this grave shortcoming to the Constitutional Court for constitutional action. The Constitutional Court shall decide within three days. The President of the Republic shall be required to furnish the responses to the National Assembly within the shortest period of time, and in all cases before the end of the current session.
> At the expiration of this period, if there has been no follow-up given by the President of the Republic to the decision of the Court, the President of the Republic shall be impeached before the High Court of Justice for insult to the National Assembly.

2. Ministers may serve simultaneously as members of the legislature.

No. Legislators are prohibited from serving simultaneously in ministerial positions.

> Article 92
> Any Deputy appointed to a ministerial post shall automatically lose his parliamentary mandate.

3. The legislature has powers of summons over executive branch officials and hearings with executive branch officials testifying before the legislature or its committees are regularly held.

Yes. The legislature regularly interpellates officials from the executive.

> Article 71
> The President of the Republic or any member of his Government in the exercise of his governmental office may be interpellated by the National Assembly.
> The President of the Republic shall respond to these interpellations in the presence of the National Assembly in person or by one of his ministers that he shall especially delegate.

4. The legislature can conduct independent investigation of the chief executive and the agencies of the executive.

Yes. The legislature can investigate the executive.

> Article 113
> The Government shall be obliged to furnish to the National Assembly all explanations which shall be demanded of it concerning its management and its activities.
> The means of information and of control of the National Assembly on governmental action shall be:
> – The interpellation in accordance with Article 71;
> – The written question;
> – The oral question with or without debate, and not followed by a vote;
> – The parliamentary committee of inquiry.
> These means shall be exercised under the conditions determined by the Rules of Procedure of the National Assembly.

5. The legislature has effective powers of oversight over the agencies of coercion (the military, organs of law enforcement, intelligence services, and the secret police).

No. The agencies of coercion report directly to the president and are not subject to legislative oversight.

6. The legislature appoints the prime minister.

No. Benin does not have a prime minister.

7. The legislature's approval is required to confirm the appointment of ministers; or the legislature itself appoints ministers.

No. The president appoints ministers after seeking the opinion of the National Assembly, but ministerial appointments do not require the legislature's approval.

Article 54
The President of the Republic...shall appoint, after an advisory opinion of the National Assembly, the members of the Government.

8. The country lacks a presidency entirely or there is a presidency, but the president is elected by the legislature.

No. The president is directly elected.

Article 42
The President of the Republic shall be elected by direct universal suffrage for a mandate of five years, renewable only one time.

9. The legislature can vote no confidence in the government.

No. The legislature cannot vote no confidence in the government.

10. The legislature is immune from dissolution by the executive.

Yes. The legislature is immune from dissolution.

11. Any executive initiative on legislation requires ratification or approval by the legislature before it takes effect; that is, the executive lacks decree power.

Yes. The executive lacks decree power. The president can exercise degree power only when specifically authorized to do so by the legislature.

Article 102
The Government may, for the execution of its program, request the National Assembly to vote a statute authorizing it to issue by edict, during a limited period of time, measures which are normally in the domain of the statute. This authorization may be granted only by a two-thirds majority of the members of the National Assembly.

12. Laws passed by the legislature are veto-proof or essentially veto-proof; that is, the executive lacks veto power, or has veto power but the veto can be overridden by a majority in the legislature.

Yes. The legislature can override a presidential veto by a majority vote of its total membership.

Article 57
The President of the Republic shall be able...to demand of the National Assembly a second deliberation of the law or of certain of its articles. This second deliberation may not be refused... The vote for this second deliberation shall be acquired by the absolute majority of members composing the National Assembly. If, after this last vote, the President of the Republic shall refuse to promulgate the law, the Constitutional Court upon a submission by the President of the National Assembly shall declare the law enforceable if it is in accordance with the Constitution.

13. The legislature's laws are supreme and not subject to judicial review.

No. The Constitutional Court can review the constitutionality of laws.

Article 114
The Constitutional Court...shall be the judge of the constitutionality of the law.

14. The legislature has the right to initiate bills in all policy jurisdictions; the executive lacks gatekeeping authority.

Yes. The legislature can initiate bills in all policy jurisdictions.

15. Expenditure of funds appropriated by the legislature is mandatory; the executive lacks the power to impound funds appropriated by the legislature.

Yes. The executive cannot impound funds appropriated by the legislature. On occasion the president has, however, increased the state's budgetary appropriations.

16. The legislature controls the resources that finance its own internal operation and provide for the perquisites of its own members.

Yes. The legislature enjoys financial autonomy, including control over members' salaries.

Article 91
Deputies shall collect the parliamentary salaries which shall be fixed by law.

17. Members of the legislature are immune from arrest and/or criminal prosecution.

Yes. Members of the legislature are immune with the common exception for cases of *flagrante delicto*.

Article 90
The members of the National Assembly shall enjoy parliamentary immunity. As a consequence, no Deputy may be followed, searched, arrested, detained or judged for opinions or votes issued by him during the exercise of his duties. A Deputy may, during the duration of the sessions, be followed or arrested in a criminal or correctional matter only with the authorization of the National Assembly except in the case of a flagrant offense. A Deputy outside of the session may be arrested only with the authorization of the Office of the National Assembly, except in the case of a flagrant offense, of authorized legal actions or of final conviction.

18. All members of the legislature are elected; the executive lacks the power to appoint any members of the legislature.

Yes. All members of the legislature are elected.

Article 80
The Deputies shall be elected by direct universal suffrage.

19. The legislature alone, without the involvement of any other agencies, can change the Constitution.

Yes. The legislature can change the constitution with a four-fifths majority vote.

Article 154
The initiative for the revision of the Constitution shall belong concurrently to the President of the Republic, after a decision taken in the Council of Ministers, and to the members of the National Assembly. In order to be taken into consideration, the draft or proposal of revision must be voted by a three-fourths majority of the members composing the National Assembly.

Article 155
The revision shall be agreed to only after having been approved by referendum, unless the draft or the proposal involved shall have been approved by a four-fifths majority of the members composing the Assembly.

20. The legislature's approval is necessary for the declaration of war.

No. The president can declare war without the legislature's approval under "exceptional circumstances."

Article 101
Declaration of war shall be authorized by the National Assembly.
When, following exceptional circumstances, the National Assembly cannot sit expediently, the decision of a declaration of war shall be taken before the Council of Ministers by the President of the Republic who shall immediately inform the nation of it.

21. The legislature's approval is necessary to ratify treaties with foreign countries.

Yes. The legislature's approval is necessary to ratify international treaties on most major issues.

Article 145
Peace treaties, treaties or agreements relating to international organization, those which involve the finances of the State, those which modify the internal laws of the State, those which allow transfer, exchange or addition of territory may be ratified only in accordance with a law.

22. The legislature has the power to grant amnesty.

Yes. The legislature may grant amnesty through legislation.

Article 97
The law shall be passed by the National Assembly by a simple majority.

Article 98
Under the domain of the law are the rules concerning . . . amnesty.

23. The legislature has the power of pardon.

No. The president has the power of pardon.

Article 60
The President of the Republic shall have the power of pardon.

24. The legislature reviews and has the right to reject appointments to the judiciary; or the legislature itself appoints members of the judiciary.

Yes. The Office of the National Assembly, which is composed of the president of the National Assembly and his or her staff, appoints four of the seven members of the Constitutional Court.

Article 115
The Constitutional Court shall be composed of seven members, four of whom shall be appointed by the Office of the National Assembly and three by the President of the Republic for a term of five years renewable only one time.

25. The chairman of the central bank is appointed by the legislature.

No. Benin is a member of the Central Bank of West African States, whose governor is selected by the member states.

26. The legislature has a substantial voice in the operation of the state-owned media.

No. The president appoints the head of the High Commission of Audio-Visuals and Communications, the body that oversees the public media. The legislature has little say in the commission's operation.

Article 56
The President of the Republic . . . after advice from the President of the National Assembly . . . shall appoint the President of the High Authority of Audio-Visuals and Communications.

27. The legislature is regularly in session.

Yes. Since the adoption of the constitution in 1990, the National Assembly has met each year for sessions that total six months, with occasional extra sessions as well.

Article 87
The Assembly shall convene in its own right in two special sessions per year.
The first session shall open during the first fortnight of the month of April.

The second session shall open during the second fortnight of the month of October.
Each of the sessions may not exceed three months.

28. Each legislator has a personal secretary.

No.

29. Each legislator has at least one non-secretarial staff member with policy expertise.

No.

30. Legislators are eligible for re-election without any restriction.

Yes. There are no restrictions on re-election.

> Article 80
> The Deputies shall be elected by direct universal suffrage... They may be re-elected.

31. A seat in the legislature is an attractive enough position that legislators are generally interested in and seek re-election.

Yes. A seat in the legislature is attractive despite a general problem of underemployment and low pay.

32. The re-election of incumbent legislators is common enough that at any given time the legislature contains a significant number of highly experienced members.

Yes. Party leaders invariably return to the legislature, and, along with other experienced incumbents, they form a core of experienced legislators.

NATIONAL ASSEMBLY OF BHUTAN (*TSHOGDU*)

No expert consultants

Score: .22

Influence over executive (4/9)		Institutional autonomy (2/9)		Specified powers (0/8)	Institutional capacity (1/6)	
1. replace		10. no dissolution	X	19. amendments	27. sessions	
2. serve as ministers	X	11. no decree		20. war	28. secretary	
3. interpellate	X	12. no veto		21. treaties	29. staff	
4. investigate		13. no review		22. amnesty	30. no term limits	X
5. oversee police		14. no gatekeeping	X	23. pardon	31. seek re-election	
6. appoint PM		15. no impoundment		24. judiciary	32. experience	
7. appoint ministers	X	16. control resources		25. central bank		
8. lack president	X	17. immunity		26. media		
9. no confidence		18. all elected				

The National Assembly (*Tshogdu*) of Bhutan was established by a 1953 royal order. For fifteen years the legislature served as a mere advisory body, but in 1968 the king amended the royal order to empower the legislative branch. The king rolled back his own absolute veto power and granted the Assembly the power to override his veto with a two-thirds majority vote. The reforms of 1968 also gave parliament responsibility for confirming the king's appointments to the government and gave parliament a vote of no confidence in the king. The power to vote no confidence was abolished in 1973, only to be reintroduced in another round of reforms in 1998. The 1998 reforms also gave the legislature the power to elect the government, known as the Council of Ministers, although in practice nominations still originate with the king, and transferred the head of government role from the king to the chairman of the Council of Ministers.

Even after these reforms, the Assembly's powers remain diminutive. The Assembly does have some power over the executive: Its members serve in government, it can question government officials, and its confirmation is needed for the king's ministerial appointments. Its institutional autonomy, however, is sharply circumscribed by, among other factors, the king's powers of decree, veto, and impoundment. The king's right to appoint roughly a quarter of the Assembly's members further compromises the legislature's autonomy. The legislature has none of the enumerated powers assessed in this survey. Finally, it has negligible institutional capacity: members lack staff, and the Assembly lacks a sizable cohort of experienced lawmakers.

The country's first full constitution currently awaits approval in a nationwide referendum. The new constitution proposes a ceremonial monarchy and invests executive powers in a government chosen by the National Assembly. Elections for the new National Assembly took place in March 2008, although the new constitution has not yet been adopted and the monarch has not yet transferred power to the legislature.

SURVEY

1. The legislature alone, without the involvement of any other agencies, can impeach the president or replace the prime minister.

No. From 1968 to 1973, and since 1998, the National Assembly has had the formal power to remove the king with a vote of no confidence. In practice, a vote of no confidence in the king is almost inconceivable.

2. Ministers may serve simultaneously as members of the legislature.

Yes. Ministers are chosen from, and required to serve simultaneously in, the National Assembly.

3. The legislature has powers of summons over executive branch officials and hearings with executive branch officials testifying before the legislature or its committees are regularly held.

Yes. The National Assembly regularly interpellates officials from the executive.

4. The legislature can conduct independent investigation of the chief executive and the agencies of the executive.

No. The legislature cannot investigate the executive.

5. The legislature has effective powers of oversight over the agencies of coercion (the military, organs of law enforcement, intelligence services, and the secret police).

No. The agencies of coercion report to the king and are not effectively overseen by the legislature. Although the king transferred the head-of-government function to the Council of Ministers, he still holds ultimate authority on security issues.

6. The legislature appoints the prime minister.

No. The head of government is elected for a one-year term by the Council of Ministers itself. The position rotates every year to a different member of the Council of Ministers.

7. The legislature's approval is required to confirm the appointment of ministers; or the legislature itself appoints ministers.

Yes. The National Assembly's approval is required to confirm the king's ministerial appointments. In 1998 the formal power to nominate and appoint ministers was transferred to the National Assembly, but in practice, the nominations still originate with the king.

8. The country lacks a presidency entirely or there is a presidency, but the president is elected by the legislature.

Yes. The country lacks a presidency.

9. The legislature can vote no confidence in the government.

No. The legislature can vote no confidence in individual ministers, but not in the government as a whole.

10. The legislature is immune from dissolution by the executive.

Yes. The legislature is immune from dissolution.

11. Any executive initiative on legislation requires ratification or approval by the legislature before it takes effect; that is, the executive lacks decree power.

No. The king issues decrees that have the force of law.

12. Laws passed by the legislature are veto-proof or essentially veto-proof; that is, the executive lacks veto power, or has veto power but the veto can be overridden by a majority in the legislature.

No. Prior to 1968 the king had absolute veto power. Since 1968 a two-thirds majority is required to override the king's vetoes. The king can also reverse legislation that, in his opinion, does not conform to the country's legal code.

13. The legislature's laws are supreme and not subject to judicial review.

No. Both the High Court and the king can reverse legislation that in their opinion does not conform to the principles of the legal code.

14. The legislature has the right to initiate bills in all policy jurisdictions; the executive lacks gatekeeping authority.

Yes. The legislature can initiate bills in all policy jurisdictions.

15. Expenditure of funds appropriated by the legislature is mandatory; the executive lacks the power to impound funds appropriated by the legislature.

No. The king can impound funds appropriated by the legislature.

16. The legislature controls the resources that finance its own internal operation and provide for the perquisites of its own members.

No. The legislature is dependent on the king for the resources that finance its own operations.

17. Members of the legislature are immune from arrest and/or criminal prosecution.

No. Legislators are subject to arrest and criminal prosecution. Legislators who contravene the rules and regulations set down for the conduct of Assembly members are to be punished with a fine or a three-month prison sentence.

18. All members of the legislature are elected; the executive lacks the power to appoint any members of the legislature.

No. Prior to March 2008 thirty-seven members of the 154-member legislature were appointed by the king, and twelve members were appointed by a religious body representing monks. Since March 2008 the king appoints five of the eighty members of parliament.

19. The legislature alone, without the involvement of any other agencies, can change the Constitution.

No. To date, all amendments to the fundamental law have been made by royal decree.

20. The legislature's approval is necessary for the declaration of war.

No. The king retains authority on security matters and can declare war without the legislature's approval.

21. The legislature's approval is necessary to ratify treaties with foreign countries.

No. The king can conclude international treaties without the legislature's approval.

22. The legislature has the power to grant amnesty.

No. The king has the power to grant amnesty.

23. The legislature has the power of pardon.

No. The king has the power of pardon.

24. The legislature reviews and has the right to reject appointments to the judiciary; or the legislature itself appoints members of the judiciary.

No. A single member of the five members of the High Court is elected by the National Assembly. The rest are appointed by the king, and the appointments do not require the legislature's approval.

25. The chairman of the central bank is appointed by the legislature.

No. The Royal Monetary Authority of Bhutan is led by the finance minister, who is, like the other cabinet members, appointed by the king with the legislature's approval.

26. The legislature has a substantial voice in the operation of the state-owned media.

No. The king controls the public media.

27. The legislature is regularly in session.

No. Each year, the legislature convenes for two ordinary sessions, each lasting about four weeks.

28. Each legislator has a personal secretary.

No. Legislators do not have personal secretaries, although there have been recent discussions about the possible creation of an independent legislative staff.

29. Each legislator has at least one non-secretarial staff member with policy expertise.

No. See item 28.

30. Legislators are eligible for re-election without any restriction.

Yes. There are no restrictions on re-election.

31. A seat in the legislature is an attractive enough position that legislators are generally interested in and seek re-election.

No. The country has only held one round of elections, so Council members have not had the opportunity to seek re-election.

32. The re-election of incumbent legislators is common enough that at any given time the legislature

contains a significant number of highly experienced members.

No. The level of experience remains low among lawmakers in Bhutan. Even longtime legislators are only now gaining real lawmaking experience as the National Assembly begins to acquire more legislative power.

BOLIVIAN NATIONAL CONGRESS (*CONGRESO NACIONAL*)

Expert consultants: Gloria Ardaya, Alvaro Galvez, Fabrice E. Lehoucq, René Mayorga, Maggy Morales, Gabriel Negretto, María T. Zegada

Score: .44

Influence over executive (2/9)		Institutional autonomy (5/9)		Specified powers (5/8)		Institutional capacity (2/6)	
1. replace		10. no dissolution	X	19. amendments		27. sessions	
2. serve as ministers		11. no decree	X	20. war	X	28. secretary	
3. interpellate	X	12. no veto		21. treaties	X	29. staff	
4. investigate	X	13. no review		22. amnesty	X	30. no term limits	X
5. oversee police		14. no gatekeeping		23. pardon	X	31. seek re-election	X
6. appoint PM		15. no impoundment	X	24. judiciary	X	32. experience	
7. appoint ministers		16. control resources	X	25. central bank			
8. lack president		17. immunity		26. media			
9. no confidence		18. all elected	X				

The Bolivian National Congress (*Congreso Nacional*) was established in the 1826 constitution. The constitution called for a tricameral Congress with an upper house whose members served for life. From 1826 to 1880 a series of strongmen governed Bolivia, and each brought a new constitutional order. Constitutions were promulgated in 1839, 1843, 1851, 1861, 1868, and 1871.

In 1880 a more enduring constitution and a bicameral legislature, formed from a House of Deputies (*Cámara de Diputados*) and a House of Senators (*Cámara de Senadores*), were introduced. Constitutional reforms in 1938, 1944, 1947, and 1961 brought some substantial changes in a number of areas but did not formally reshape Congress's power.

Bolivia's present constitution and bicameral legislature were unveiled in 1967, but because of a military coup and subsequent military rule, the new legal system did not come into force until civilian political control returned in the 1980s. According to the constitution, the president is directly elected, but in the event that no candidate wins an absolute majority of the popular vote, Congress chooses the president. In 1985 and 2002 presidents were chosen in a congressional runoff.

Amendments in 1994 established a constitutional tribunal to review the constitutionality of laws. Prior to 1994 laws were not subject to judicial review.

Another round of statutes in 2002 further altered the legislature's powers. Prior to 2002 only Congress could decide to lift a legislator's immunity. Since 2002 immunity can be lifted by the Supreme Court of Justice upon the request of the attorney general. Another change requires a popular referendum to change the constitution. Before 2002 the legislature acting alone had the power to amend the constitution.

Generally speaking, Congress's control over the executive is highly circumscribed, although it does have some oversight authority. Congress has a moderate amount of institutional autonomy. It enjoys some enumerated powers and modest institutional capacity.

At the time of this writing, a Constituent Assembly is in session and in the process of drawing up a new fundamental law. The new document is expected to increase indigenous rights and state control over the economy. It may also change the role of the legislature. Some supporters of President Evo Morales seek to increase executive power at the expense of Congress. Still, how the new constitution may alter the powers of the legislature, and when and whether the new document will be adopted, remain to be seen.

SURVEY

1. The legislature alone, without the involvement of any other agencies, can impeach the president or replace the prime minister.

No. Presidential impeachment requires action by the Supreme Court.

Article 68
The chambers shall meet in joint session of Congress for the following purposes:
11. To authorize the trial of the President and Vice President of the Republic.

Article 118
I. The powers of the Supreme Court are:
5. To decide charges of responsibility against the President and the Vice President of the Republic... for crimes committed in exercising their functions, at the request of the Attorney General of the Republic, upon previous authorization of the National Congress, juridically founded and granted by a two-thirds vote of its total members, in which case the indictment is the responsibility of the Penal Chamber; if this is pronounced for impeachment, the decision shall be substantiated by the other Chambers without further appeal.

2. Ministers may serve simultaneously as members of the legislature.

No. Legislators are prohibited from serving simultaneously in ministerial positions.

Article 49
Any Senator or Deputy may be... designated Minister of State... but he shall be suspended from his legislative functions for the time that he holds such position.

3. The legislature has powers of summons over executive branch officials and hearings with executive branch officials testifying before the legislature or its committees are regularly held.

Yes. The legislature regularly interpellates officials from the executive.

Article 70
I. At the initiative of any Parliamentarian, the Chambers may request verbal or written information from the Ministers of State for legislative purposes, for inspection or scrutiny.
II. At the initiative of any Parliamentarian, either Chamber may interpellate the Ministers of State, individually or collectively.

4. The legislature can conduct independent investigation of the chief executive and the agencies of the executive.

Yes. The legislature can investigate the executive.

Article 67
The following are the functions of each Chamber:
6. To undertake such investigations as are necessary in conformity with its constitutional function, for which it may appoint committees from among its members in order to facilitate this task.

Article 70
I. At the initiative of any Parliamentarian, the Chambers may... propose investigations concerning all subjects of national interest.

5. The legislature has effective powers of oversight over the agencies of coercion (the military, organs of law enforcement, intelligence services, and the secret police).

No. The agencies of coercion report to the president and are not subject to legislative oversight.

Article 210
I. The Armed Forces are subordinate to the President of the Republic and receive their orders from him on administrative matters, through the Minister of Defense; and on technical matters, through the Commander-in-Chief.

Article 216
The forces of the National Police are subordinate to the President of the Republic through the Minister of Government.

6. The legislature appoints the prime minister.

No. The country lacks a prime minister.

7. The legislature's approval is required to confirm the appointment of ministers; or the legislature itself appoints ministers.

No. The president appoints ministers, and the appointments do not require the legislature's approval.

Article 99
A decree of the President of the Republic shall be sufficient for [ministers'] appointment or removal.

8. The country lacks a presidency entirely or there is a presidency, but the president is elected by the legislature.

No. The president is directly elected. If no candidate wins an absolute majority of the popular vote, however, the president is elected by Congress. In 1985 and 2002 presidents were elected in a congressional runoff.

> Article 86
> The President of the Republic shall be elected by direct suffrage.

> Article 90
> I. If, in the general elections, none of the slates for President and Vice President of the Republic has obtained an absolute majority of valid votes, Congress shall elect them by an absolute majority of valid votes, through oral roll call voting, from between the two lists which had obtained the greatest number of valid votes.

9. The legislature can vote no confidence in the government.

No. The legislature cannot vote no confidence in the government. It can, however, censure individual ministers, although censure does not necessarily result in the removal of the minister in question.

> Article 70
> II. At the initiative of any Parliamentarian, either Chamber may . . . censure [ministers'] acts by an absolute majority of votes of National Representatives present.
> III. The purpose of censure is to modify the impugned policies and procedures; [censure] implies the resignation of the censured Minister or Ministers, which may be accepted or rejected by the President of the Republic.

10. The legislature is immune from dissolution by the executive.

Yes. The legislature is immune from dissolution.

11. Any executive initiative on legislation requires ratification or approval by the legislature before it takes effect; that is, the executive lacks decree power.

Yes. The executive lacks decree power. Only in a state of siege does the president have limited decree authority. In an emergency the president can decree that taxes will be collected ahead of schedule.

12. Laws passed by the legislature are veto-proof or essentially veto-proof; that is, the executive lacks veto power, or has veto power but the veto can be overridden by a majority in the legislature.

No. A two-thirds majority vote is needed to override a presidential veto.

> Article 77
> I. The objections of the executive shall be addressed to the chamber of origin.
> II. If both chambers, by a majority of two-thirds of the members present, find the objections to be unfounded, the President of the Republic shall promulgate it as law within a further period of ten days.

13. The legislature's laws are supreme and not subject to judicial review.

No. The Constitutional Tribunal can review the constitutionality of laws.

> Article 116
> IV. Control over constitutionality is exercised by the Constitutional Tribunal.

> Article 119
> I. The Constitutional Tribunal is the highest controlling organ of constitutionality.

> Article 120
> The Constitutional Tribunal shall have the power to [decide]:
> 1. In one instance, matters of pure right against the unconstitutionality of laws, decrees and any kind of non-judicial resolution.

14. The legislature has the right to initiate bills in all policy jurisdictions; the executive lacks gatekeeping authority.

No. The legislature is prohibited from introducing legislation related to taxation or development plans.

> Article 59
> The following are the functions of the legislative power:
> 2. Upon the initiative of the executive power, to impose taxes of any nature or kind, abolish existing ones, and determine their national, departmental, or university character, as well as to fix fiscal expenditures.
> 3. To fix the expenditures of the public administration for each financial period, after submission of the draft budget by the executive power.
> 4. To consider the development plans which the executive power submits for its consideration.

> Article 96
> The powers and duties of the President of the Republic are:
> 7. To submit to the legislative power, within the first thirty regular sessions, the national and departmental budgets for the succeeding financial period.
> 8. To present to the legislative power development plans not covered by ordinary budgets on the subject or in time for action.

15. Expenditure of funds appropriated by the legislature is mandatory; the executive lacks the power to impound funds appropriated by the legislature.

Yes. The executive lacks the power to impound funds appropriated by the legislature.

16. The legislature controls the resources that finance its own internal operation and provide for the perquisites of its own members.

Yes. The legislature enjoys financial autonomy, including control over members' perquisites.

Article 67
The following are the functions of each Chamber:
5. To fix the per diem to be received by the lawmakers; order payment of its budgets; appoint and remove its administrative personnel; and attend to all matters relating to its internal economy and procedure.

17. Members of the legislature are immune from arrest and/or criminal prosecution.

No. Legislators are immune, but legislative immunity may be lifted through a combined action of the Supreme Court of Justice and the Attorney General.

Article 51
Deputies and Senators are inviolable at all times for the opinions expressed by them in the discharge of their duties.

Article 52
No Senator or Deputy shall be accused or prosecuted in any criminal matter nor deprived of his freedom from the day of election continuously until the end of his term in office, without the prior authorization of the Supreme Court of Justice through the vote of two-thirds of its members, and at the request of the Attorney General of the Republic, except in the case of a flagrant crime.

18. All members of the legislature are elected; the executive lacks the power to appoint any members of the legislature.

Yes. All members of the legislature are elected.

Article 60
IV. Deputies are elected by universal, direct, secret vote.

Article 63
The Senate is composed of three Senators for each department, elected by universal and direct suffrage.

19. The legislature alone, without the involvement of any other agencies, can change the Constitution.

No. Constitutional amendments require approval in a popular referendum.

Article 231
I. In the first meetings of the legislative session of a new constitutional term the matter shall be taken up in

the chamber that proposed the amendment and, if it is approved by two-thirds of the votes it shall be sent to the other chamber for review, where it must also receive a two-thirds vote.
II. All other procedures shall be the same as is provided in the Constitution for relations between the two chambers.
III. The Chambers shall deliberate and vote on the Amendment, ensuring its consistency with the provisions established by its enabling Law.
IV. Within the fifteen days following the enactment of the Amendment Law, the National Congress shall convene a Constitutional Referendum so that the citizenry may approve or reject the Constitutional amendment; such event shall take place within the ninety days following the convocation, and its organization shall be supervised by the National Electoral Court.

Article 232
An amendment to the constitution is approved by a simple majority of the favorable votes cast in a Constitutional Referendum and shall be forwarded to the Executive for its promulgation, and the President of the Republic shall not have the power to review or veto it.

20. The legislature's approval is necessary for the declaration of war.

Yes. The legislature's approval is necessary for the declaration of war.

Article 59
The following are the functions of the legislative power:
15. To permit the transit of foreign troops through the territory of the Republic, fixing the time they will be allowed to remain therein.
16. To authorize national troops to leave the territory of the Republic, fixing the time of their absence.

Article 68
The chambers shall meet in joint session of Congress for the following purposes:
7. To decide on a declaration of war on petition of the executive.

21. The legislature's approval is necessary to ratify treaties with foreign countries.

Yes. The legislature's approval is necessary to ratify international treaties.

Article 59
The following are the functions of the legislative power:
12. To approve international treaties, concordats and conventions.

22. The legislature has the power to grant amnesty.

Yes. The legislature and president both have the power to grant amnesty.

Article 59
The following are the functions of the legislative power:

19. To decree amnesties for political offenses and grant pardons after receiving a report from the Supreme Court of Justice.

Article 96
The powers and duties of the President of the Republic are:
13. To grant amnesties for political offenses, without prejudice to those that may be granted by the legislative power.

23. The legislature has the power of pardon.

Yes. The legislature has the power of pardon.

Article 59
The following are the functions of the legislative power:
19. To decree amnesties for political offenses and grant pardons after receiving a report from the Supreme Court of Justice.

24. The legislature reviews and has the right to reject appointments to the judiciary; or the legislature itself appoints members of the judiciary.

Yes. The legislature appoints the members of the Supreme Court of Justice and the Constitutional Tribunal.

Article 59
The following are the functions of the legislative power:
20. To appoint, in a session of the Congress, the Ministers of the Supreme Court of Justice [and] the Magistrates of the Constitutional Tribunal...by the two-thirds vote of its members.

Article 68
The chambers shall meet in joint session of Congress for the following purposes:
12. To appoint the Ministers of the Supreme Court of Justice, the Magistrates of the Constitutional Tribunal.

Article 117
IV. The President and the Ministers [of the Supreme Court of Justice] shall be elected by the National Congress, by the votes of two-thirds of the totality of its members, from recommendations proposed by the Council of the Judicature.

Article 119
II. The President and Magistrates of the Constitutional Tribunal are appointed by the National Congress by the votes of two-thirds of the totality of its members.

25. The chairman of the central bank is appointed by the legislature.

No. The president appoints the president of the Central Bank of Bolivia.

26. The legislature has a substantial voice in the operation of the state-owned media.

No. The legislature lacks a substantial voice in the operation of the public media.

27. The legislature is regularly in session.

No. The full legislature meets for a maximum of only four months each year. A broad "congressional committee" meets when the legislature is not in session.

Article 46
II. Congress shall meet in ordinary session every year in the capital of the Republic on the sixth day of August, even when it has not been convoked. The sessions shall last ninety working days, which may be extended to one hundred twenty days, either by the will of Congress itself or upon request of the executive power.

Article 82
I. During the adjournment of the chambers a Congressional Committee shall function composed of nine Senators and eighteen Deputies, who, with their respective alternates, shall be elected by each chamber in a way that insofar as possible will reflect the territorial composition of Congress.

28. Each legislator has a personal secretary.

No.

29. Each legislator has at least one non-secretarial staff member with policy expertise.

No.

30. Legislators are eligible for re-election without any restriction.

Yes. There are no restrictions on re-election.

Article 57
Senators and Deputies may be reelected.

31. A seat in the legislature is an attractive enough position that legislators are generally interested in and seek re-election.

Yes.

32. The re-election of incumbent legislators is common enough that at any given time the legislature contains a significant number of highly experienced members.

No. Since 1994, the turnover rate has been quite high, resulting in a legislature that lacks a sizable cohort of highly experienced members.

PARLIAMENTARY ASSEMBLY OF BOSNIA AND HERZEGOVINA (*PARLAMENTARNA SKUPŠTINA*)

Expert consultants: Zijad Hasić, Dragica Hinić, Adem Huskić, Adnan Huskić, Tamara Musić

Score: .63

Influence over executive (5/9)		Institutional autonomy (6/9)		Specified powers (6/8)		Institutional capacity (3/6)	
1. replace		10. no dissolution		19. amendments	X	27. sessions	X
2. serve as ministers		11. no decree	X	20. war	X	28. secretary	
3. interpellate	X	12. no veto	X	21. treaties	X	29. staff	
4. investigate	X	13. no review		22. amnesty	X	30. no term limits	X
5. oversee police	X	14. no gatekeeping	X	23. pardon	X	31. seek re-election	X
6. appoint PM		15. no impoundment	X	24. judiciary	X	32. experience	
7. appoint ministers	X	16. control resources	X	25. central bank			
8. lack president		17. immunity		26. media			
9. no confidence	X	18. all elected	X				

The Parliamentary Assembly (*Parlamentarna skupština*) of Bosnia and Herzegovina was established in the 1995 constitution. The document was drawn up as part of the Dayton Peace Accords, which ended the war that ravaged the country following the disintegration of Yugoslavia. The constitution calls for a bicameral legislature comprising a lower chamber, the House of Representatives (*Predstavnički dom*), and an upper chamber, the House of Peoples (*Dom naroda*). The constitution includes a three-person presidency, guaranteeing representation for Bosniacs, Croats, and Serbs.

The legislature has substantial authority. It has a moderate amount of power over the executive, institutional autonomy, and institutional capacity. Much of the Assembly's power derives from specified powers and prerogatives, which include the powers to change the constitution, approve presidential declarations of war, approve international treaties, grant amnesties and pardons, and appoint members of the judiciary.

SURVEY

1. The legislature alone, without the involvement of any other agencies, can impeach the president or replace the prime minister.

No. The legislature cannot impeach the members of the presidency. It can remove the prime minister (chair of the Council of Ministers) with a vote of no confidence.

Article V
4. c. The Council of Ministers shall resign if at any time there is a vote of no-confidence by the Parliamentary Assembly.

2. Ministers may serve simultaneously as members of the legislature.

No. Ministers are prohibited from serving simultaneously in the legislature.

3. The legislature has powers of summons over executive branch officials and hearings with executive branch officials testifying before the legislature or its committees are regularly held.

Yes. The legislature regularly interpellates officials from the executive.

Article V
4. a. Together the Chair and the Ministers shall constitute the Council of Ministers, with responsibility for carrying out the policies and decisions of Bosnia and Herzegovina in the fields referred to in Article III(1), (4), and (5) and reporting to the Parliamentary Assembly (including, at least annually, on expenditures by Bosnia and Herzegovina).

4. The legislature can conduct independent investigation of the chief executive and the agencies of the executive.

Yes. The legislature can investigate the executive.

5. The legislature has effective powers of oversight over the agencies of coercion (the military, organs of law enforcement, intelligence services, and the secret police).

Yes. The legislature has effective powers of oversight over the agencies of coercion.

6. The legislature appoints the prime minister.

No. The prime minister (chair of the Council of Ministers) is appointed by the presidency.

> Article V
> 4. The Presidency shall nominate the Chair of the Council of Ministers, who shall take office upon the approval of the House of Representatives. The Chair shall nominate a Foreign Minister, a Minister for Foreign Trade, and other Ministers as may be appropriate, who shall take office upon the approval of the House of Representatives.

7. The legislature's approval is required to confirm the appointment of ministers; or the legislature itself appoints ministers.

Yes. The legislature's approval is required to confirm ministerial appointments.

> Article V
> 4. The Chair [of the Council of Ministers] shall nominate a Foreign Minister, a Minister for Foreign Trade, and other Ministers as may be appropriate, who shall take office upon the approval of the House of Representatives.

8. The country lacks a presidency entirely or there is a presidency, but the president is elected by the legislature.

No. Each member of the three-person presidency is directly elected.

> Article V
> The Presidency of Bosnia and Herzegovina shall consist of three Members: one Bosniac and one Croat, each directly elected from the territory of the Federation, and one Serb directly elected from the territory of the Republika Srpska.

9. The legislature can vote no confidence in the government.

Yes. The legislature can vote no confidence in the government.

> Article V
> Section 4. c. The Council of Ministers shall resign if at any time there is a vote of no-confidence by the Parliamentary Assembly.

10. The legislature is immune from dissolution by the executive.

No. The presidency can dissolve the House of Peoples.

> Article IV
> 3g. The House of Peoples may be dissolved by the Presidency or by the House itself, provided that the House's decision to dissolve is approved by a majority that includes the majority of Delegates from at least two of the Bosniac, Croat, or Serb peoples. The House of Peoples elected in the first elections after the entry into force of this Constitution may not, however, be dissolved.

11. Any executive initiative on legislation requires ratification or approval by the legislature before it takes effect; that is, the executive lacks decree power.

Yes. The executive lacks decree power.

12. Laws passed by the legislature are veto-proof or essentially veto-proof; that is, the executive lacks veto power, or has veto power but the veto can be overridden by a majority in the legislature.

Yes. The presidency lacks veto power.

13. The legislature's laws are supreme and not subject to judicial review.

No. The Constitutional Court can review the constitutionality of laws.

> Article VI
> 3. The Constitutional Court shall uphold this Constitution.
> a. The Constitutional Court shall have exclusive jurisdiction to decide any dispute that arises under this Constitution between the Entities or between Bosnia and Herzegovina and an Entity or Entities, or between institutions of Bosnia and Herzegovina, including but not limited to . . . whether any provision of an Entity's constitution or law is consistent with this Constitution.

14. The legislature has the right to initiate bills in all policy jurisdictions; the executive lacks gatekeeping authority.

Yes. The legislature can initiate bills in all policy jurisdictions.

15. Expenditure of funds appropriated by the legislature is mandatory; the executive lacks the power to impound funds appropriated by the legislature.

Yes. The executive lacks the power to impound funds appropriated by the legislature.

16. The legislature controls the resources that finance its own internal operation and provide for the perquisites of its own members.

Yes. The legislature enjoys financial autonomy.

Article IV

4. The Parliamentary Assembly shall have responsibility for:

b. Deciding upon the sources and amounts of revenues for the operations of the institutions of Bosnia and Herzegovina and international obligations of Bosnia and Herzegovina.

17. Members of the legislature are immune from arrest and/or criminal prosecution.

No. Legislative immunity extends to official parliamentary business only. Legislators are subject to arrest for common crimes.

Article IV

3j. Delegates and Members shall not be held criminally or civilly liable for any acts carried out within the scope of their duties in the Parliamentary Assembly.

18. All members of the legislature are elected; the executive lacks the power to appoint any members of the legislature.

Yes. All members of the legislature are elected.

Article IV

1. House of Peoples. The House of Peoples shall comprise 15 Delegates, two-thirds from the Federation (including five Croats and five Bosniacs) and one-third from the Republika Srpska (five Serbs).

a. The designated Croat and Bosniac Delegates from the Federation shall be selected, respectively, by the Croat and Bosniac Delegates to the House of Peoples of the Federation. Delegates from the Republika Srpska shall be selected by the National Assembly of the Republika Srpska.

b. Nine members of the House of Peoples shall comprise a quorum, provided that at least three Bosniac, three Croat, and three Serb Delegates are present.

2. House of Representatives. The House of Representatives shall comprise 42 Members, two-thirds elected from the territory of the Federation, one-third from the territory of the Republika Srpska.

19. The legislature alone, without the involvement of any other agencies, can change the Constitution.

Yes. The House of Representatives can change the constitution with a two-thirds majority vote.

Article X

1. Amendment Procedure. This Constitution may be amended by a decision of the Parliamentary Assembly, including a two-thirds majority of those present and voting in the House of Representatives.

20. The legislature's approval is necessary for the declaration of war.

Yes. Formally, the constitution mentions the use of armed force only to proscribe civil war. In practice,

the legislature's approval would be necessary for the declaration of war.

Article V

5a. Each member of the Presidency shall, by virtue of the office, have civilian command authority over armed forces. Neither Entity shall threaten or use force against the other Entity, and under no circumstances shall any armed forces of either Entity enter into or stay within the territory of the other Entity without the consent of the government of the latter and of the Presidency of Bosnia and Herzegovina.

21. The legislature's approval is necessary to ratify treaties with foreign countries.

Yes. The legislature's approval is necessary to ratify international treaties.

Article IV

4. The Parliamentary Assembly shall have responsibility for:

d. Deciding whether to consent to the ratification of treaties.

Article V

3. The Presidency shall have responsibility for:

d. Negotiating, denouncing, and, with the consent of the Parliamentary Assembly, ratifying treaties of Bosnia and Herzegovina.

22. The legislature has the power to grant amnesty.

Yes. The legislature can grant amnesty through legislation.

23. The legislature has the power of pardon.

Yes. The legislature can grant pardons through legislation.

24. The legislature reviews and has the right to reject appointments to the judiciary; or the legislature itself appoints members of the judiciary.

Yes. The legislature appoints six of the nine members of the Constitutional Court.

Article VI

1. The Constitutional Court of Bosnia and Herzegovina shall have nine members.

a. Four members shall be selected by the House of Representatives of the Federation, and two members by the Assembly of the Republika Srpska. The remaining three members shall be selected by the President of the European Court of Human Rights after consultation with the Presidency.

25. The chairman of the central bank is appointed by the legislature.

No. The presidency appoints the members of the Governing Board of the Central Bank of Bosnia and Herzegovina. The Board appoints the governor from among its members.

Article VII

2. The first Governing Board of the Central Bank shall consist of a Governor appointed by the International Monetary Fund, after consultation with the Presidency.
3. Thereafter, the Governing Board of the Central Bank of Bosnia and Herzegovina shall consist of five persons appointed by the Presidency for a term of six years. The Board shall appoint, from among its members, a Governor for a term of six years.

26. The legislature has a substantial voice in the operation of the state-owned media.

No. The legislature lacks a substantial voice in the operation of the public media.

27. The legislature is regularly in session.

Yes. The legislature regularly meets in ordinary session.

28. Each legislator has a personal secretary.

No.

29. Each legislator has at least one non-secretarial staff member with policy expertise.

No.

30. Legislators are eligible for re-election without any restriction.

Yes. There are no restrictions on re-election.

31. A seat in the legislature is an attractive enough position that legislators are generally interested in and seek re-election.

Yes.

32. The re-election of incumbent legislators is common enough that at any given time the legislature contains a significant number of highly experienced members.

No. Electoral politics is relatively new and turbulence in parliamentary elections quite high, resulting in a paucity of highly experienced legislators.

NATIONAL ASSEMBLY OF BOTSWANA

Expert consultants: Matthias Basedau, John Holm, Zibani Maundeni, Jack D. Parson, Abdi Ismail Samatar

Score: .44

Influence over executive (5/9)		Institutional autonomy (3/9)		Specified powers (2/8)		Institutional capacity (4/6)	
1. replace	X	10. no dissolution		19. amendments	X	27. sessions	X
2. serve as ministers	X	11. no decree	X	20. war		28. secretary	
3. interpellate	X	12. no veto	X	21. treaties		29. staff	
4. investigate		13. no review		22. amnesty	X	30. no term limits	X
5. oversee police		14. no gatekeeping		23. pardon		31. seek re-election	X
6. appoint PM		15. no impoundment		24. judiciary		32. experience	X
7. appoint ministers		16. control resources	X	25. central bank			
8. lack president	X	17. immunity		26. media			
9. no confidence	X	18. all elected					

The National Assembly of Botswana was established in 1966 following independence from Great Britain. Botswana's constitution establishes a unicameral legislature that elects the president. The institutional structure of the legislature has remained largely unchanged since its inception. Ten constitutional amendments have resulted in minor changes in the size of parliament, length of presidential terms, and electoral rules.

The National Assembly exercises some influence over the executive branch. The legislature elects the president. Legislative influence over the executive is further advanced by the provision that eighteen of the sixty-one members of the Assembly also serve as ministers in government.

The legislature's institutional autonomy, how-ever, is circumscribed by competing presidential powers. The president appoints some members of the National Assembly, can dissolve the legislature at will, and enjoys gatekeeping authority. The Assembly enjoys only two of the eight enumerated powers included in this survey, and it has a moderate measure of institutional capacity.

SURVEY

1. The legislature alone, without the involvement of any other agencies, can impeach the president or replace the prime minister.

Yes. The legislature can remove the president with a vote of no confidence.

Article 32
(8) An Elected Member of the National Assembly may...move...that the President does not enjoy the support of the majority of the Elected Members of the Assembly...If it appears as a result of the voting on that question that the President does not enjoy the support of a majority of the Elected Members of the Assembly, the office of President shall become vacant.
(9) Any Elected Member of the Assembly may give notice to the President that he intends to move in the Assembly a motion under the last foregoing subsection and notwithstanding any other provision of this Constitution the President shall not after receipt of any such notice be empowered to dissolve Parliament before the conclusion of the sitting of the Assembly mentioned in the last foregoing subsection.

2. Ministers may serve simultaneously as members of the legislature.

Yes. Ministers are selected from, and required to serve simultaneously in, the legislature.

Article 42
(3) Appointments to the office of Minister or Assistant Minister shall be made by the President from among Members of the National Assembly.

3. The legislature has powers of summons over executive branch officials and hearings with executive branch officials testifying before the legislature or its committees are regularly held.

Yes. The legislature regularly questions officials of the executive.

4. The legislature can conduct independent investigation of the chief executive and the agencies of the executive.

No. The Ombudsman Act of 1995 gave the legislature the power to call for an independent

investigation of the executive, but it is the president or the ministers who appoint the investigatory body and at the conclusion of the investigation decide whether to make the report public.

5. The legislature has effective powers of oversight over the agencies of coercion (the military, organs of law enforcement, intelligence services, and the secret police).

No. The agencies of coercion report directly to the president and, despite a constitutional provision to the contrary, are not subject to legislative oversight.

Article 48
(1) The supreme command of the armed forces of the Republic shall vest in the President and he shall hold the office of Commander in Chief.
(4) Parliament may regulate the exercise of the powers conferred by or under this section.

6. The legislature appoints the prime minister.

No. The country lacks a prime minister.

7. The legislature's approval is required to confirm the appointment of ministers; or the legislature itself appoints ministers.

No. The president appoints ministers, and the appointments do not require the legislature's approval.

Article 42
(3) Appointments to the office of Minister or Assistant Minister shall be made by the President from among Members of the National Assembly.

8. The country lacks a presidency entirely or there is a presidency, but the president is elected by the legislature.

Yes. The legislature elects the president.

Article 32
(1) Whenever Parliament is dissolved an election shall be held to the office of President in such manner as is prescribed by this section and, subject thereto, by or under an Act of Parliament.
(3) (a) a person nominated as a Parliamentary candidate may, at the time of his nomination and subject to the provisions of paragraph (b), declare in such manner as may be prescribed by or under an Act of Parliament which of the candidates in the election of President he supports.
(d) the returning officer shall declare to be elected as President any candidate for whom support has been declared in accordance with paragraph (a) above by not less than such number of persons elected as Members of the National Assembly in the Parliamentary election as corresponds to more than half the total number of seats for Elected Members in the Assembly, and if there

is no such person the returning officer shall declare that no candidate has been elected.

9. The legislature can vote no confidence in the government.

Yes. The legislature can vote no confidence in the government.

> Article 92
> If the National Assembly at any time passes a resolution supported by a majority of all the Members of the Assembly who are entitled to vote declaring that it has no confidence in the Government of Botswana, Parliament shall stand dissolved on the fourth day following the day on which such resolution was passed, unless the President earlier resigns his office or dissolves Parliament.

10. The legislature is immune from dissolution by the executive.

No. The president can dissolve the legislature.

> Article 91
> (2) Subject to the provisions of this Constitution, the President may at any time dissolve Parliament.

11. Any executive initiative on legislation requires ratification or approval by the legislature before it takes effect; that is, the executive lacks decree power.

Yes. The executive lacks decree power.

12. Laws passed by the legislature are veto-proof or essentially veto-proof; that is, the executive lacks veto power, or has veto power but the veto can be overridden by a majority in the legislature.

Yes. The legislature can override a presidential veto by a majority vote.

> Article 87
> (2) When a Bill is presented to the President for assent he shall either assent or withhold his assent.
> (3) Where the President withholds his assent to a Bill, the Bill shall be returned to the National Assembly.
> (4) If where the President withholds his assent to a Bill the Assembly resolves within six months of the Bill being returned to it that the Bill should again be presented for assent, the President shall assent to the Bill within twenty-one days of its being again presented to him, unless he sooner dissolves Parliament.

13. The legislature's laws are supreme and not subject to judicial review.

No. The High Court can review the constitutionality of laws.

> Article 105
> (1) Where any question as to the interpretation of this Constitution arises in any proceedings in any subordinate court and the court is of the opinion that the question involves a substantial question of law, the

court may, and shall if any party to the proceedings so requests, refer the question to the High Court.
> (2) Where any question is referred to the High Court in pursuance of this section, the High Court shall give its decision upon the question and the court in which the question arose shall, subject to any appeal, dispose of the case in accordance with that decision.

> Article 106
> An appeal shall lie as of right to the Court of Appeal from any decision of the High Court which involves the interpretation of this Constitution, other than a decision of the High Court under section 69 (1) of this Constitution:
> Provided that no appeal shall lie from a determination of the High Court under this section dismissing an application on the ground that it is frivolous or vexatious.

14. The legislature has the right to initiate bills in all policy jurisdictions; the executive lacks gatekeeping authority.

No. The legislature is prohibited from introducing legislation related to taxation, public expenditures, or government debt.

> Article 88
> (1) Except upon the recommendation of the President, which recommendation may be signified by the Vice-President or a Minister, the National Assembly shall not –
> (a) proceed upon any Bill (including any amendment to a Bill) that, in the opinion of the person presiding, makes provision for any of the following purposes –
> (i) for the imposition of taxation or the alteration of taxation otherwise than by reduction;
> (ii) for the imposition of any charge upon the revenues or other funds of Botswana or the alteration of any such charge otherwise than by reduction;
> (iii) for the payment, issue or withdrawal from any public fund of Botswana of any moneys not charged thereon or any increase in the amount of such payment, issue or withdrawal; or
> (iv) for the composition or remission of any debt to the Government of Botswana;
> (b) proceed upon any motion (including any amendment to a motion) the effect of which, in the opinion of the person presiding, would be to make provision for any of those purposes.
> (2) The National Assembly shall not proceed upon any Bill (including any amendment to a Bill) that, in the opinion of the person presiding, would, if enacted, alter any of the provisions of this Constitution or affect –
> (a) the designation, recognition, removal of powers of Chiefs, Sub-Chiefs or Headmen;
> (b) the organization, powers or administration of African Courts;
> (c) African customary law, or the ascertainment or recording of African customary law; or
> (d) tribal organization or tribal property, unless –

(i) a copy of the Bill has been referred to the House of Chiefs after it has been introduced in the National Assembly; and
(ii) a period of thirty days has elapsed from the date when the copy of the Bill was referred to the House of Chiefs.

15. Expenditure of funds appropriated by the legislature is mandatory; the executive lacks the power to impound funds appropriated by the legislature.

No. The president can refuse to spend funds that have been authorized by the legislature.

16. The legislature controls the resources that finance its own internal operation and provide for the perquisites of its own members.

Yes. The legislature enjoys financial autonomy.

17. Members of the legislature are immune from arrest and/or criminal prosecution.

No. Legislators are subject to arrest and prosecution and if convicted of charges are required to give up their seat in the legislature.

Article 68
(1) The seat of an Elected Member or a Specially Elected Member of the National Assembly shall become vacant –
(2) (a) If circumstances such as are referred to in paragraph (c) of the preceding subsection arise in relation to a Member of the Assembly by virtue of the fact that he is … sentenced to … imprisonment, or convicted of an election offence and it is open to the Member to appeal against the decision (either with the leave of the court or other authority or without such leave), he shall forthwith cease to perform his functions as a Member of the Assembly.

18. All members of the legislature are elected; the executive lacks the power to appoint any members of the legislature.

No. The president appoints four "special elected members" to the thirty-eight-member National Assembly.

Article 58
(2) The National Assembly shall consist of –
(a) thirty-four Elected Members who shall be elected in accordance with the provisions of this Constitution and subject thereto in accordance with the provisions of any Act of Parliament;
(b) four Special Elected Members who shall be elected in accordance with the provisions of the Schedule to this Constitution and subject thereto in accordance with the provisions of any Act of Parliament; and
(c) the Attorney-General.
Article 74
(2) The Attorney-General shall have no vote.

19. The legislature alone, without the involvement of any other agencies, can change the Constitution.

Yes. The legislature can change the constitution through the normal legislative process. Amendments to selected articles of the constitution require either a two-thirds majority vote in the Assembly or approval in a popular referendum.

Article 89
(1) Subject to the provisions of this section Parliament may alter this Constitution.
(3) In so far as it alters any of the provisions of –
(a) Chapter II; sections 30 to 44 inclusive, 47 to 51 inclusive, and 56; sections 77 to 79 inclusive and section 85; Chapter VII; or sections 117 to 120 inclusive and section 127 in its application to any of the provisions mentioned in this paragraph;
(b) sections 57, 63 to 67 inclusive, 86 to 89 inclusive, 90 (2) and (3), 91 (2), (3), (4) and (5), and 92; Chapter VI; and section 127 in its application to any of the provisions mentioned in this paragraph, a Bill for an Act of Parliament under this section shall not be passed by the National Assembly unless –
(i) the final voting on the Bill in the Assembly takes place not less than three months after the previous voting thereon in the Assembly; and
(ii) at such final voting the Bill is supported by the votes of not less than two-thirds of all the Members of the Assembly.
(4) In so far as it alters any of the provisions mentioned in subsection (3) (b) of this section no Bill shall be presented to the President for his assent unless after its passage by the Assembly it has been submitted to the electors qualified to vote in the election of the Elected Members of the National Assembly, and, on a vote taken in such manner as Parliament may prescribe, the majority of the electors voting have approved the Bill.

20. The legislature's approval is necessary for the declaration of war.

No. The president can declare war without the legislature's approval.

Article 48
(2) The powers conferred on the President by subsection (1) of this section shall include –
(a) the power to determine the operational use of the armed forces.

21. The legislature's approval is necessary to ratify treaties with foreign countries.

No. International treaties do not require the legislature's approval.

22. The legislature has the power to grant amnesty.

Yes. The legislature can grant amnesty through law.

23. The legislature has the power of pardon.

No. The president has the power of pardon.

> Article 53
> The President may –
> (a) grant to any person convicted of any offence a pardon, either free or subject to lawful conditions.

24. The legislature reviews and has the right to reject appointments to the judiciary; or the legislature itself appoints members of the judiciary.

No. The judges of the High Court and the Court of Appeal are appointed by the president, and the appointments do not require the legislature's approval.

> Article 96
> (1) The Chief Justice [of the High Court] shall be appointed by the President.
> (2) The puisne judges [of the High Court] shall be appointed by the President, acting in accordance with the advice of the Judicial Service Commission.

> Article 100
> (1) The President of the Court of Appeal shall, unless that office is held *ex-officio* by the Chief Justice, be appointed by the President.
> (2) The Justices of Appeal, if any, shall be appointed by the President, acting in accordance with the advice of the Judicial Service Commission.

25. The chairman of the central bank is appointed by the legislature.

No. The president appoints the governor of the Bank of Botswana.

26. The legislature has a substantial voice in the operation of the state-owned media.

No. The legislature lacks a substantial voice in the operation of the public media.

27. The legislature is regularly in session.

Yes. The legislature regularly meets in ordinary session.

> Article 90
> (1) Each session of Parliament shall be held at such place within Botswana and shall commence at such time as the President may appoint.
> (2) There shall be a session of Parliament at least once in every year so that a period of six months shall not intervene between the last sitting of Parliament in one session and the first sitting thereof in the next session.

28. Each legislator has a personal secretary.

No.

29. Each legislator has at least one non-secretarial staff member with policy expertise.

No.

30. Legislators are eligible for re-election without any restriction.

Yes. There are no restrictions on re-election.

31. A seat in the legislature is an attractive enough position that legislators are generally interested in and seek re-election.

Yes.

32. The re-election of incumbent legislators is common enough that at any given time the legislature contains a significant number of highly experienced members.

Yes. Re-election rates are sufficiently high to produce a significant number of highly experienced members.

NATIONAL CONGRESS OF BRAZIL (*CONGRESSO NACIONAL*)

Expert consultants: Scott W. Desposato, Zachary Elkins, Bolívar Lamounier, Fernando Limongi, David Samuels, Wendy M. Sinek, Kurt Weyland

Score: .56

Influence over executive (3/9)		Institutional autonomy (4/9)		Specified powers (5/8)		Institutional capacity (6/6)	
1. replace	X	10. no dissolution	X	19. amendments	X	27. sessions	X
2. serve as ministers		11. no decree		20. war	X	28. secretary	X
3. interpellate	X	12. no veto	X	21. treaties	X	29. staff	X
4. investigate	X	13. no review		22. amnesty	X	30. no term limits	X
5. oversee police		14. no gatekeeping		23. pardon		31. seek re-election	X
6. appoint PM		15. no impoundment		24. judiciary	X	32. experience	X
7. appoint ministers		16. control resources	X	25. central bank			
8. lack president		17. immunity		26. media			
9. no confidence		18. all elected	X				

The National Congress (*Congresso Nacional*) of Brazil originated in the 1891 constitution. The U.S. system provided the model for Brazil's constitution, which established a bicameral legislature consisting of a lower house, the Chamber of Deputies (*Câmara dos Deputados*), and an upper house, the Federal Senate (*Senado Federal*). Constitutional revisions in 1934, 1937, and 1946 did not fundamentally alter the legislature's formal power. In 1964 a military government swept to power, bringing with it a constitution, enacted in 1967, that sidelined the legislature. Following the end of military rule in 1985, a new constitution, adopted in 1988, restored the institutional order much as it had existed prior to the authoritarian interregnum.

Congress wields significant authority. It has some ability to influence the executive branch. It summons and questions executive branch officials, can set up investigatory commissions, and can impeach the president. Congress's institutional autonomy is sharply limited. Congress shares lawmaking power with the president, who can make decrees, although the latter lapse after thirty days if they are not subsequently approved by Congress. The president also enjoys gatekeeping authority. Furthermore, a legal change in 2001 revoked the immunity from prosecution that legislators enjoyed prior to 2001. Since 2001 legislators may be arrested and prosecuted for crimes not directly

related to their legislative duty. The legislature has numerous specified powers. Congress's power is most solid in the area of institutional capacity. Legislators are provided with secretarial and policy staff, there are no restrictions on re-election, and the legislature contains a body of highly experienced members.

SURVEY

1. The legislature alone, without the involvement of any other agencies, can impeach the president or replace the prime minister.

Yes. The legislature acting alone can impeach the president for criminal "malversion." It exercised this power in 1992, when it impeached Fernando Collor de Mello and swore in his vice president, Itamar Franco, to serve out the remained of Collor's term. The involvement of the Supreme Court is required to impeach the president for common criminal offenses.

Article 86
If charges against the President of the Republic are admitted by two thirds of the House of Representatives, he is submitted for trial before the Federal Supreme Court for common criminal offenses or before the Federal Senate for criminal malversion.

2. Ministers may serve simultaneously as members of the legislature.

No. Legislators who serve in government have a sleeping mandate, meaning that they may join the government but forfeit their voting rights in the legislature during their government service. They may return to the legislature when their government service ends.

Article 54
Representatives and Senators shall not be the holder of more than one public elective position or office.

Article 56
(0) A Representative or Senator does not lose his or her office if:
I. he or she is vested in an office of Minister of State.
(1) The alternate is called in cases of vacancy, of investiture in the functions set forth in this article, or of leave of absence exceeding one hundred and twenty days.

3. The legislature has powers of summons over executive branch officials and hearings with executive branch officials testifying before the legislature or its committees are regularly held.

Yes. The legislature regularly exercises its power to summon and question executive branch officials.

Article 49
It is exclusively incumbent upon Congress:
X. to supervise and control, directly or through the Federal Senate and/or the House of Representatives, the acts of the Executive.

Article 50
(0) The House of Representatives or the Federal Senate, as well as any of their Committees, may call upon a Minister of State to personally render information on a predetermined matter, and his absence without adequate justification shall constitute a criminal malversion.
(2) The Presiding Board of the House of Representatives and of the Federal Senate may forward written requests for information to the Ministers of State, and refusal or noncompliance with such request within a period of thirty days, as well as the rendering of false information, shall constitute a criminal malversion.

4. The legislature can conduct independent investigation of the chief executive and the agencies of the executive.

Yes. The legislature can investigate the executive. Such investigations, or the threat of them, have recently become highly salient factors in Brazilian politics. For example, in 2004 opposition leaders called for a congressional investigation after Waldomiro Diniz, the president's liaison to Congress, was caught on videotape soliciting campaign contributions from one of the kingpins of an illegal lottery game in exchange for political favors. Although a full investigation was never completed, the threat of it contributed to the rapid dismissal of Diniz. When a vote-buying scandal erupted in 2005, a congressional investigation commission formed and successfully pushed for the indictment

of many top officials, including the president's chief of staff and the minister of finance.

Article 58
(3) Parliamentary investigation committees, which shall have the investigation powers inherent to the judicial authorities, in addition to other powers set forth in their respective regulations, are created by the House of Representatives and by the Federal Senate, jointly or severally, at the request of one third of its members, for investigation of a certain fact and for a certain period of time, and their conclusions shall, if necessary, be forwarded to the Attorney General's Office to determine the civil or criminal liability of the offenders.

5. The legislature has effective powers of oversight over the agencies of coercion (the military, organs of law enforcement, intelligence services, and the secret police).

No. The agencies of coercion report directly to the president and are not subject to legislative oversight.

6. The legislature appoints the prime minister.

No. The country lacks a prime minister.

7. The legislature's approval is required to confirm the appointment of ministers; or the legislature itself appoints ministers.

No. The president appoints ministers, and the appointments do not require the legislature's approval.

Article 84
(0) It is incumbent exclusively upon the President of the Republic:
I. to appoint and dismiss the Ministers of State.

8. The country lacks a presidency entirely or there is a presidency, but the president is elected by the legislature.

No. The president is directly elected.

Article 77
(0) Election of the President and of the Vice President of the Republic takes place simultaneously, ninety days before the end of the current presidential term of office.
(2) The candidate who, being registered by a political party, obtains an absolute majority of votes, not counting blank or void votes, is considered to be elected as President.

9. The legislature can vote no confidence in the government.

No. The legislature cannot vote no confidence in the government.

10. The legislature is immune from dissolution by the executive.

Yes. The legislature is immune from dissolution.

Article 44
(1) Each legislature has a duration of four years.

11. Any executive initiative on legislation requires ratification or approval by the legislature before it takes effect; that is, the executive lacks decree power.

No. The president regularly issues decrees that have the force of law. Decrees lapse after thirty days if Congress does not approve them. Congress can also delegate to the president temporary decree power over limited issue areas.

Article 62
(0) In relevant and urgent cases, the President of the Republic may adopt provisional measures with the force of law and shall submit such measures to Congress immediately. If Congress is in recess, an extraordinary session shall be called within five days.
(1) Provisional measures lose their effectiveness as from the date of their issuance if they are not converted into law within a period of thirty days as from their publication, and Congress regulates the legal relations arising therefrom.

Article 68
(0) Delegated laws are drawn up by the President of the Republic who requests delegation from Congress.
(1) Acts subject to the exclusive authority of Congress, those subject to the exclusive authority of the House of Representatives or of the Federal Senate, matters reserved for supplemental laws, and legislation on the following shall not be delegated.
(2) Delegation to the President of the Republic is granted by resolution of Congress, which specifies its contents and the terms for performance thereof.

12. Laws passed by the legislature are veto-proof or essentially veto-proof; that is, the executive lacks veto power, or has veto power but the veto can be overridden by a majority in the legislature.

Yes. The legislature can override a presidential veto by a majority vote of the total membership in both houses.

Article 66
(0) The Chamber of Congress in which voting was concluded sends the bill of law to the President of the Republic, who sanctions it if he consents thereto.
(1) If the President of the Republic deems all or part of the bill to be unconstitutional or contrary to public interests, he shall veto it fully or partially within fifteen business days as from the date of receipt and advise the President of the Federal Senate of the reasons for the veto within forty-eight hours.
(4) A veto examines in a joint session within thirty days of receipt thereof, and may only be rejected by an absolute majority of the Representatives and Senators by secret ballot.

13. The legislature's laws are supreme and not subject to judicial review.

No. The Supreme Court can review the constitutionality of laws.

Article 97
The courts may declare the unconstitutionality of a law or of a normative act of the Government only by an absolute majority of their members or of the members of the respective special body.

Article 102
(0) The Federal Supreme Court is responsible, mainly, for safeguarding the Constitution and it is incumbent upon it:
I. to process and adjudicate, originally:
    a) direct actions of unconstitutionality of a federal or state law or normative act, and declaratory actions of constitutionality of a federal law or normative act.

14. The legislature has the right to initiate bills in all policy jurisdictions; the executive lacks gatekeeping authority.

No. The legislature is prohibited from introducing legislation related to many issue areas, including taxation.

Article 61
(1) The initiative of the following laws is incumbent solely upon the President of the Republic:
    I. laws which determine or modify the number of troops in the Armed Forces;
    II. laws which deal with:
        a) creation of public offices, functions, or positions in the direct administration and in autonomous government entities, or increase in the compensation thereof;
        b) administrative and judicial organization, tax, and budgetary matters, public services, and administrative personnel of the Territories;
        c) Government employees of the Republic and Territories, their legal treatment, appointment to offices, tenure and retirement of civil servants, retirement, and transfer of servicemen to inactivity;
        d) organization of the Attorney General's Office and of the Public Defender's Office of the Republic, as well as general rules for the organization of the Attorney General's Office and of the Public Defender's Office of the States, the Federal District and the Territories;
        e) creation, structuring, and duties of the Ministries and government administration agencies.

15. Expenditure of funds appropriated by the legislature is mandatory; the executive lacks the power to impound funds appropriated by the legislature.

No. The president is not required to spend the funds authorized in the budget.

16. The legislature controls the resources that finance its own internal operation and provide for the perquisites of its own members.

Yes. The legislature enjoys financial autonomy.

Article 49
It is exclusively incumbent upon Congress:

VII. to establish identical compensation for Federal Representatives and Senators.

Article 51
It is exclusively incumbent upon the House of Representatives:
III. to prepare its internal regulations;
IV. to provide for its organization, operation, police, creation, transformation, or extinction of offices, positions, and functions of its services and establishment of the respective compensation, observing the guidelines established in the budget directives law.

Article 52
(0) It is incumbent exclusively upon the Federal Senate
XII. to draw up its internal regulations;
XIII. to provide for its organization, operation, police, creation, transformation, or extinction of offices, positions, and functions of its services and to determine the respective compensation, with due regard for the guidelines established in the budget directives law.

17. Members of the legislature are immune from arrest and/or criminal prosecution.

No. Legislative immunity extends to official parliamentary business only. Legislators are subject to arrest for common crimes. Prior to 2001 legislators enjoyed complete immunity.

18. All members of the legislature are elected; the executive lacks the power to appoint any members of the legislature.

Yes. All members of the legislature are elected.

Article 45
(0) The House of Representatives is formed by representatives of the people, elected by the proportional system in each State, in each Territory and in the Federal District.

Article 46
(0) The Federal Senate is composed of members representing the States and the Federal District, elected by majority vote.

19. The legislature alone, without the involvement of any other agencies, can change the Constitution.

Yes. The legislature can change the constitution in multiple readings with a three-fifths majority vote.

Article 60
(0) The Constitution may be amended on the proposal of:
I. at least one third of the members of the House of Representatives or of the Federal Senate;
II. the President of the Republic;
III. more than one half of the Legislative Assemblies of the units of the Federation, each of which expresses itself by a simple majority of its members.
(2) The proposal is discussed and voted in each Chamber of Congress, in two rounds, and it is considered approved if it obtains three-fifths of the votes of the respective members in both rounds.

20. The legislature's approval is necessary for the declaration of war.

Yes. The legislature's approval is necessary for presidential war declarations.

Article 49
It is exclusively incumbent upon Congress:
II. to authorize the President of the Republic to declare war.

21. The legislature's approval is necessary to ratify treaties with foreign countries.

Yes. The legislature's approval is necessary to ratify international treaties.

Article 49
It is exclusively incumbent upon Congress:
I. to resolve conclusively on international acts, agreements, or treaties which involve charges or commitments against the national patrimony.

22. The legislature has the power to grant amnesty.

Yes. The legislature has the power to grant amnesty.

Article 48
It is incumbent upon Congress . . . to provide for all the matters within the jurisdiction of the Republic and especially on:
VIII. granting of amnesty.

23. The legislature has the power of pardon.

No. The president has the power of pardon.

Article 84
XII. [The president has the power] to grant pardons and reduce sentences.

24. The legislature reviews and has the right to reject appointments to the judiciary; or the legislature itself appoints members of the judiciary.

Yes. The Senate's confirmation is required for the president's appointments to the Supreme Court and to the Superior Court of Justice.

Article 84
(0) It is incumbent exclusively upon the President of the Republic:
XIV. to appoint, after approval by the Federal Senate, the Justices of the Federal Supreme Court and of the Superior Courts.

Article 101
(0) The Federal Supreme Court is formed by eleven Justices, chosen among citizens over thirty-five years and under sixty-five years of age, with notorious legal knowledge and unblemished reputation.
(1) The Justices of the Federal Supreme Court shall be appointed by the President of the Republic, after the choice is approved by the absolute majority of the Federal Senate.
Article 104
(0) The Superior Court of Justice is formed by at least thirty-three Justices.

(1) The Justices of the Superior Court of Justice are appointed by the President of the Republic...after approval of the choice by the Federal Senate.

25. The chairman of the central bank is appointed by the legislature.

No. The president appoints the president of the Central Bank of Brazil.

> Article 84
> (0) It is incumbent exclusively upon the President of the Republic:
> XIV. to appoint, after approval by the Federal Senate...the president and directors of the Central Bank.

26. The legislature has a substantial voice in the operation of the state-owned media.

No. The legislature lacks a substantial voice in the operation of the public media.

27. The legislature is regularly in session.

Yes. The legislature is in session for about eight months each year.

> Article 57
> (0) Congress meets each year in the Federal Capital, from February 15th to June 30th and from August 1st to December 15th.

28. Each legislator has a personal secretary.

Yes.

29. Each legislator has at least one non-secretarial staff member with policy expertise.

Yes.

30. Legislators are eligible for re-election without any restriction.

Yes. There are no restrictions on re-election.

31. A seat in the legislature is an attractive enough position that legislators are generally interested in and seek re-election.

Yes. Legislators generally seek re-election, although many former legislators opt to pursue positions in the executive branch.

32. The re-election of incumbent legislators is common enough that at any given time the legislature contains a significant number of highly experienced members.

Yes. The re-election rate since 1988 has been about 50 percent. There is a relatively stable group of highly experienced legislative leaders.

NATIONAL ASSEMBLY OF BULGARIA (*NARODNO SABRANIE*)

Expert consultants: Robin S. Brooks, Georgi Ganev, Venelin I. Ganev, Yonko Grozev, Georgi Karasimeonov, Albert P. Melone

Score: .78

Influence over executive (7/9)		Institutional autonomy (7/9)		Specified powers (7/8)		Institutional capacity (4/6)	
1. replace	X	10. no dissolution		19. amendments	X	27. sessions	X
2. serve as ministers		11. no decree	X	20. war	X	28. secretary	
3. interpellate	X	12. no veto	X	21. treaties	X	29. staff	
4. investigate	X	13. no review		22. amnesty	X	30. no term limits	X
5. oversee police	X	14. no gatekeeping	X	23. pardon		31. seek re-election	X
6. appoint PM	X	15. no impoundment	X	24. judiciary	X	32. experience	X
7. appoint ministers	X	16. control resources	X	25. central bank	X		
8. lack president		17. immunity	X	26. media	X		
9. no confidence	X	18. all elected	X				

The National Assembly (*Narodno Sabranie*) of Bulgaria traces its roots to Bulgaria's Turnovo Constitution of 1878. The Turnovo system, which provided for a National Assembly, served as the fundamental law in Bulgaria for the subsequent seven decades. Following Soviet occupation in World

War II, Bulgaria adopted a Soviet-type constitution and created a 400-member unicameral National Assembly. A constitutional change in 1971 explicitly recognized the Bulgarian Communist Party as the country's primary source of political power.

In 1990 Bulgaria's communist-era parliament began drafting a new constitution. In 1991, as the Soviet-style regime passed into history, a new constitution came into effect. It provides the National Assembly with considerable clout. The Assembly exercises considerable influence over the executive. It chooses the prime minister and the cabinet, interpellates and investigates ministers, and can remove the government with a vote of no confidence. The Assembly's institutional autonomy is well protected. It can override the president's veto with a majority vote and initiate bills in all policy jurisdictions. It enjoys a monopoly on lawmaking authority. The legislature is also endowed with many individually specified powers and prerogatives. It has a moderate level of institutional capacity.

A constitutional amendment in 2003 reformed the judiciary in order to meet European Union standards. The amendment did not affect legislative power.

SURVEY

1. The legislature alone, without the involvement of any other agencies, can impeach the president or replace the prime minister.

Yes. The legislature can replace the prime minister with a vote of no confidence. Presidential impeachment requires action by the Constitutional Court.

Article 89
(1) A motion of no confidence in the in the Council of Ministers shall require a seconding by one-fifth or more of the Members of the National Assembly. To be passed, the motion shall require a majority of more than half of the votes of all National Assembly Members.
(2) Should the National Assembly vote no confidence in the Prime Minister or the Council of Ministers, the Prime Minister shall hand in his government's resignation.

Article 103
(1) The President and Vice President shall not be held liable for actions committed in the performance of their duties, except for high treason, or a violation of the Constitution.
(2) An impeachment shall require a motion from no fewer than one-fourth of all Members of the National Assembly and shall stand if supported by more than two-thirds of the Members.

(3) An impeachment against the President or Vice President shall be tried by the Constitutional Court within a month following the lodging of the impeachment. Should the Constitutional Court convict the President or Vice President of high treason, or of a violation of the Constitution, the President's or Vice President's prerogatives shall be suspended.

2. Ministers may serve simultaneously as members of the legislature.

No. Legislators who serve in government have a sleeping mandate, meaning that they may join the government but forfeit their voting rights in the legislature during their government service. They may return to the legislature when their government service ends.

Article 68
(2) A Member of the National Assembly elected as a minister shall cease to serve as a Member during his term of office as a minister. During that period, he shall be substituted in the National Assembly in a manner established by law.

3. The legislature has powers of summons over executive branch officials and hearings with executive branch officials testifying before the legislature or its committees are regularly held.

Yes. Ministers field questions from the opposition every week during question time. The legislature also interpellates ministers.

Article 83
(2) The National Assembly and the parliamentary committees shall be free to order ministers to attend their sessions and respond to questions.

Article 90
(1) Members of the National Assembly shall have the right to address questions and interpellations to the Council of Ministers and to individual ministers, who shall be obligated to respond.

4. The legislature can conduct independent investigation of the chief executive and the agencies of the executive.

Yes. The legislature can establish committees to investigate the executive.

Article 79
(1) The National Assembly shall elect permanent and ad hoc committees from among its Members.
(2) The permanent committees shall aid the work of the National Assembly and shall exercise parliamentary control on its behalf.
(3) Ad hoc committees shall be elected to conduct inquiries and investigations.

5. The legislature has effective powers of oversight over the agencies of coercion (the military, organs of law enforcement, intelligence services, and the secret police).

Yes. Legislative committees have effective powers of oversight over the agencies of the coercion.

6. The legislature appoints the prime minister.

Yes. The president nominates the prime minister, but he or she is required to pick the candidate who enjoys the support of parliament.

Article 84
The National Assembly shall:
6) elect and dismiss the Prime Minister.

Article 99
(1) Following consultations with the parliamentary groups, the President shall appoint the Prime Minister candidate nominated by the party holding the highest number of seats in the National Assembly to form a government.
(2) Should the Prime Minister candidate fail to form a government within seven days, the President shall entrust this task to a Prime Minister candidate nominated by the second largest parliamentary group.
(3) Should the new Prime Minister candidate also fail to form a government within the period established by the preceding paragraph, the President shall entrust the task to a Prime Minister candidate nominated by one of the minor parliamentary groups.
(4) Should the consultations prove successful, the President shall ask the National Assembly to elect the Prime Minister candidate.

7. The legislature's approval is required to confirm the appointment of ministers; or the legislature itself appoints ministers.

Yes. The legislature appoints ministers on the recommendation of the prime minister.

Article 84
The National Assembly shall:
6) elect and dismiss the Prime Minister and, on his motion, the members of the Council of Ministers.

8. The country lacks a presidency entirely or there is a presidency, but the president is elected by the legislature.

No. The president is directly elected.

Article 93
(1) The President is elected directly by the voters for a period of five years by a procedure established by law.

9. The legislature can vote no confidence in the government.

Yes. The legislature can vote no confidence in the government.

Article 89
(1) A motion of no confidence in the in the Council of Ministers shall require a seconding by one-fifth or more

of the Members of the National Assembly. To be passed, the motion shall require a majority of more than half of the votes of all National Assembly Members.
(2) Should the National Assembly vote no confidence in the Prime Minister or the Council of Ministers, the Prime Minister shall hand in his government's resignation.

Article 112
(1) The Council of Ministers is free to ask for the National Assembly's vote of confidence in its overall policy, its program declaration, or on a specific issue. A resolution shall require a majority of more than half of the votes of the National Assembly Members present.
(2) Should the Council of Ministers fail to receive the requested vote of confidence, the Prime Minister shall hand in the government's resignation.

10. The legislature is immune from dissolution by the executive.

No. The president can dissolve the legislature.

Article 99
(1) Following consultations with the parliamentary groups, the President shall appoint the Prime Minister candidate nominated by the party holding the highest number of seats in the National Assembly to form a government.
(2) Should the Prime Minister candidate fail to form a government within seven days, the President shall entrust this task to a Prime Minister candidate nominated by the second largest parliamentary group.
(3) Should the new Prime Minister candidate also fail to form a government within the period established by the preceding paragraph, the President shall entrust the task to a Prime Minister candidate nominated by one of the minor parliamentary groups.
(4) Should the consultations prove successful, the President shall ask the National Assembly to elect the Prime Minister candidate.
(5) Absent an agreement on the formation of a government, the President shall appoint a caretaker government, dissolve the National Assembly and schedule new elections.

11. Any executive initiative on legislation requires ratification or approval by the legislature before it takes effect; that is, the executive lacks decree power.

Yes. The executive lacks decree power.

12. Laws passed by the legislature are veto-proof or essentially veto-proof; that is, the executive lacks veto power, or has veto power but the veto can be overridden by a majority in the legislature.

Yes. The legislature can override a presidential veto by a majority vote of its total membership.

Article 101
(1) Within the term established by Article 88 (3), the President is free to return a bill together with his

motives to the National Assembly for further debate, which shall not be denied.

(2) The new passage of such a bill shall require a majority of more than half of all Members of the National Assembly.

(3) Following a new passage of the bill by the National Assembly, the President shall promulgate it within seven days following its receipt.

13. The legislature's laws are supreme and not subject to judicial review.

No. The Constitutional Court can review the constitutionality of laws.

Article 149
(1) The Constitutional Court shall:
1) provide binding interpretations of the Constitution;
2) rule on challenges to the constitutionality of the laws and other acts passed by the National Assembly and the acts of the President.

14. The legislature has the right to initiate bills in all policy jurisdictions; the executive lacks gatekeeping authority.

Yes. The legislature can initiate bills in all policy jurisdictions.

15. Expenditure of funds appropriated by the legislature is mandatory; the executive lacks the power to impound funds appropriated by the legislature.

Yes. The executive lacks the power to impound funds appropriated by the legislature.

16. The legislature controls the resources that finance its own internal operation and provide for the perquisites of its own members.

Yes. The legislature enjoys financial autonomy, including control over members' perquisites.

Article 71
The National Assembly shall establish the emoluments of its Members.

Article 73
The National Assembly is organized and shall act in accordance with the Constitution and its own internal rules.

17. Members of the legislature are immune from arrest and/or criminal prosecution.

Yes. Legislators are immune with the common exception for cases of *flagrante delicto*, here expressed as "detained in the course of committing a grave crime." In 2006 a new provision was adopted stipulating that a criminal investigation against a member of parliament may proceed even in the absence of a warrant from the National Assembly or its chairman if the legislator in question agrees in writing to waive his or her right to

compel the investigative bodies to seek such a warrant. The measure was adopted in the context of pressure from the European Union to combat corruption. It actually does little to compromise the principle of parliamentary immunity, which is well entrenched in Bulgaria.

Article 70
A Member of the National Assembly is immune from detention or criminal prosecution except for the perpetration of a grave crime, when a warrant from the National Assembly or, in between its session, from the Chairman of the National Assembly, is required. No warrant shall be required when a Member is detained in the course of committing a grave crime; the National Assembly or, in between its session, the Chairman of the National Assembly, shall be notified forthwith.

18. All members of the legislature are elected; the executive lacks the power to appoint any members of the legislature.

Yes. All members of the legislature are elected.

Article 64
(1) The National Assembly is elected for a term of four years.

19. The legislature alone, without the involvement of any other agencies, can change the Constitution.

Yes. The legislature can change the constitution with a three-fourths majority vote. If the proposed amendment receives less than three-fourths, but greater than two-thirds of the votes, it can be passed by a two-thirds majority vote between two and five months later.

Article 153
The National Assembly is free to amend all provisions of the Constitution except those within the prerogatives of the Grand National Assembly.

Article 154
(1) The initiative to introduce a constitutional amendment bill shall belong to one-fourth of the Members of the National Assembly and to the President.
(2) An amendment bill shall be debated by the National Assembly not earlier than one month and not later than three months from the date on which it is introduced.

Article 155
(1) A constitutional amendment shall require a majority of three-fourths of the votes of all Members of the National Assembly in three ballots on three different days.
(2) A bill which has received less than three-fourths but more than two-thirds of the votes of all Members shall be eligible for reintroduction after not fewer than two months and not more than five months. To be passed at this new reading, the bill shall require a majority of two-thirds of the votes of all Members.

20. The legislature's approval is necessary for the declaration of war.

Yes. The legislature's approval is necessary for presidential war declarations with the common exception for cases of foreign invasion. In cases of armed attack against the country, the president can declare war and then seek retroactive legislative approval.

Article 84
The National Assembly shall:
10) resolve on the declaration of war and conclusion of peace.

Article 100
(5) The President shall proclaim a state of war in the case of an armed attack against Bulgaria or whenever urgent actions are required by virtue of an international commitment, or shall proclaim martial law or any other state of emergency whenever the National Assembly is not in session and cannot be convened. The National Assembly shall then be convened forthwith to endorse the decision.

21. The legislature's approval is necessary to ratify treaties with foreign countries.

Yes. The legislature's approval is necessary to ratify international treaties on most major issues.

Article 85
(1) The National Assembly shall ratify or denounce by law all international instruments which:
1) are of a political or military nature;
2) concern the Republic of Bulgaria's participation in international organizations;
3) envisage corrections to the borders of the Republic of Bulgaria;
4) contain obligations for the treasury;
5) envisage the state's participation in international arbitration or legal proceedings;
6) concern fundamental human rights;
7) affect the action of the law or require new legislation in order to be enforced;
8) expressly require ratification.
(2) Treaties ratified by the National Assembly may be amended or denounced only by their built-in procedure or in accordance with the universally acknowledged norms of international law.
(3) The conclusion of an international treaty requiring an amendment to the Constitution shall be preceded by the passage of such an amendment.

22. The legislature has the power to grant amnesty.

Yes. The legislature has the power to grant amnesty.

Article 84
The National Assembly shall:
13) grant amnesty.

23. The legislature has the power of pardon.

No. The president has the power of pardon.

Article 98
The President of the Republic shall:
11) exercise the right to pardon.

24. The legislature reviews and has the right to reject appointments to the judiciary; or the legislature itself appoints members of the judiciary.

Yes. The legislature appoints one-third of the members of the Constitutional Court and eleven of the twenty-five members of the Supreme Judicial Council.

Article 130
(3) Eleven of the [25] members of the Supreme Judicial Council shall be elected by the National Assembly, and eleven shall be elected by the bodies of the judicial branch.

Article 147
(1) The Constitutional Court shall consist of 12 justices, one-third of whom shall be elected by the National Assembly, one-third shall be appointed by the President, and one-third shall be elected by a joint meeting of the justices of the Supreme Court of Cassation and the Supreme Administrative Court.

25. The chairman of the central bank is appointed by the legislature.

Yes. The legislature appoints the governor of the Bulgarian National Bank.

Article 84
The National Assembly shall:
8) elect and dismiss the Governor of the Bulgarian National Bank.

26. The legislature has a substantial voice in the operation of the state-owned media.

Yes. The legislature appoints the members of the body that oversees the public media.

27. The legislature is regularly in session.

Yes. The legislature regularly meets in ordinary session.

Article 74
The National Assembly is a permanently acting body. It is free to determine its recesses.

28. Each legislator has a personal secretary.

No. Each parliamentary group has a small pool of secretaries, but on average there is less than one staff person for each legislator.

29. Each legislator has at least one non-secretarial staff member with policy expertise.

No. Some, but not all, legislators have staff members with policy expertise. See item 28.

30. Legislators are eligible for re-election without any restriction.

Yes. There are no restrictions on re-election.

31. A seat in the legislature is an attractive enough position that legislators are generally interested in and seek re-election.

Yes.

32. The re-election of incumbent legislators is common enough that at any given time the legislature contains a significant number of highly experienced members.

Yes. Despite considerable electoral volatility, parliament has a core group of highly experienced legislators.

NATIONAL ASSEMBLY OF BURKINA FASO (*ASSEMBLÉE NATIONALE*)

Expert consultants: Sten Hagberg, Ernest Harsch, Augustin Loada, Moussa Michel Tapsoba, Harold Tarver

Score: .53

Influence over executive (3/9)		Institutional autonomy (5/9)		Specified powers (5/8)		Institutional capacity (4/6)	
1. replace		10. no dissolution		19. amendments	X	27. sessions	X
2. serve as ministers		11. no decree		20. war	X	28. secretary	
3. interpellate	X	12. no veto	X	21. treaties	X	29. staff	
4. investigate	X	13. no review		22. amnesty		30. no term limits	X
5. oversee police		14. no gatekeeping	X	23. pardon		31. seek re-election	X
6. appoint PM		15. no impoundment		24. judiciary	X	32. experience	X
7. appoint ministers		16. control resources	X	25. central bank			
8. lack president		17. immunity	X	26. media	X		
9. no confidence	X	18. all elected	X				

The National Assembly (*Assmeblée nationale*) of Burkina Faso was established in the 1960 constitution. The legislature was in an almost constant state of suspension from 1966 to 1990 due to political instability and military coups. During this period legislation was passed almost exclusively by executive decree.

In 1991 Burkina Faso enacted a new constitution that established the groundwork for a functioning bicameral legislature. A constitutional amendment in 1997 increased the duration of the legislature's two annual sessions from sixty to ninety days each. Another amendment in 2002 dissolved the upper house, the Chamber of Representatives, reshaping the legislature into a unicameral National Assembly.

The legislature's influence over the executive is highly circumscribed. It cannot remove the president from office, its members cannot serve as ministers, and it does not make or approve the president's appointments for prime minister or government. The legislature can, however, interpellate, investigate, and censure the government. The legislature's autonomy is limited by the president's authority to issue decrees and dissolve the legislature. The strength of the legislature is bolstered by a number of specified powers and prerogatives and a moderate degree of institutional capacity.

SURVEY

1. The legislature alone, without the involvement of any other agencies, can impeach the president or replace the prime minister.

No. Presidential impeachment requires the involvement of the High Court of Justice.

Article 138
The High Court of Justice is competent to examine the acts committed by the President of Faso in the exercise of his functions and constituting high treason, of violating the Constitution or misappropriation of public funds.

Article 139
The impeachment of the President of Faso is voted by a majority of four-fifths of the voices of the Deputies composing the Assembly. That of the members of the Government is voted by a majority of two-thirds of the voices of the Deputies composing the Assembly.

Article 140
The High Court of Justice is bound by the definition of crimes and misdemeanors and by the determination of punishments resulting from the penal laws in force at the time when the acts had been committed.

2. Ministers may serve simultaneously as members of the legislature.

No. Ministers are prohibited from serving simultaneously in the legislature.

Article 70
The functions of the members of the Government are incompatible with the exercise of any parliamentary mandate.

3. The legislature has powers of summons over executive branch officials and hearings with executive branch officials testifying before the legislature or its committees are regularly held.

Yes. Ministers address the legislature's questions in a weekly question time.

Article 111
During the sessions, one sitting per week is reserved to the questions of the Deputies and the responses of the Government. The Assembly can address to the Government written or oral question, with or without debate.

4. The legislature can conduct independent investigation of the chief executive and the agencies of the executive.

Yes. The legislature can establish commissions of inquiry to investigate the executive.

Article 113
The Government is held to furnish to the Assembly all explications which are demanded of it concerning the management and concerning its acts.
The Assembly may constitute commissions of inquiry.

5. The legislature has effective powers of oversight over the agencies of coercion (the military, organs of law enforcement, intelligence services, and the secret police).

No. The agencies of coercion report directly to the president and are not subject to legislative oversight.

6. The legislature appoints the prime minister.

No. The president appoints the prime minister.

Article 46
The President of Faso appoints the Prime Minister and terminates his functions, either on the presentation by him of his resignation, or on his own authority in the superior interest of the Nation.

7. The legislature's approval is required to confirm the appointment of ministers; or the legislature itself appoints ministers.

No. The president appoints ministers on the proposal of the prime minister, and ministerial appointments do not require the legislature's approval.

Article 46
On the proposal of the Prime Minister, [the president] appoints the other members of the Government and terminates their functions.

8. The country lacks a presidency entirely or there is a presidency, but the president is elected by the legislature.

No. The president is directly elected.

Article 37
The President of Faso is elected for seven years by universal, direct, equal and secret suffrage. He is re-eligible.

9. The legislature can vote no confidence in the government.

Yes. The legislature can remove the prime minister with a motion of censure or a vote of no confidence.

Article 115
The National Assembly can present a motion of censure with respect to the Government. The motion of censure is signed by at least one-third of the Deputies of the Assembly. To be adopted, it must be voted by an absolute majority of the members composing the Assembly.

Article 116
The Prime Minister can, after deliberation of the Council of Ministers, engage before the National Assembly the responsibility of the Government on a program or on a declaration of general policy.
The confidence is refused to the Government if the text presented does not receive the absolute majority of the voices of the members composing the Assembly. The vote on the question of confidence cannot intervene less than forty-eight hours after the presentation of the text.

The Prime Minister can, after deliberation of the Council of Ministers, engage the responsibility of the Government before the Assembly on the vote of a text. In this case, this text is considered adopted except if a motion of censure, presented within the twenty-four hours which follow, is voted within the conditions specified in the lines below.

Article 117
If the motion of censure is voted or the confidence is refused, the President of Faso terminates, within a time period of eight days, the functions of the Prime Minster.

10. The legislature is immune from dissolution by the executive.

No. The president can dissolve the legislature.

Article 50
The President of Faso can, after consultation with the Prime Minister and the President of the Chamber of Representatives, pronounce the dissolution of the National Assembly.

11. Any executive initiative on legislation requires ratification or approval by the legislature before it takes effect; that is, the executive lacks decree power.

No. The president issues decrees that have the force of law.

Article 100
The simple decree is an act signed by the President of Faso or by the Prime Minister and countersigned by the competent member or members of the Government. The decree in the Council of Ministers is an act signed by the President of Faso and by the Prime Minister after advice of the Council of Ministers: it is countersigned by him or the competent members of the Government.

12. Laws passed by the legislature are veto-proof or essentially veto-proof; that is, the executive lacks veto power, or has veto power but the veto can be overridden by a majority in the legislature.

Yes. The legislature can override presidential vetoes by a majority vote.

Article 48
The President of Faso can, during the time period of promulgation, demand a second reading of the law or of certain of its articles.

13. The legislature's laws are supreme and not subject to judicial review.

No. The Supreme Court can review the constitutionality of laws.

Article 97
[The law] is voted by an absolute majority [of the National Assembly] and promulgated after declaration

of its conformity with the Constitution by the Supreme Court.

Article 152
The control of the constitutionality of the laws is assured by the Constitutional Chamber of the Supreme Court.

14. The legislature has the right to initiate bills in all policy jurisdictions; the executive lacks gatekeeping authority.

Yes. The legislature can initiate bills in all policy jurisdictions.

15. Expenditure of funds appropriated by the legislature is mandatory; the executive lacks the power to impound funds appropriated by the legislature.

No. The president can impound funds appropriated by the legislature.

16. The legislature controls the resources that finance its own internal operation and provide for the perquisites of its own members.

Yes. The legislature enjoys financial autonomy.

Article 93
The Assembly enjoys financial autonomy. Its President [of the Assembly] manages the credits which are allotted to it for its functioning. The President [of the Assembly] is responsible for this management before the Assembly; it can overrule him by an absolute majority for incompetence in his management.

17. Members of the legislature are immune from arrest and/or criminal prosecution.

Yes. Legislators are immune with the common exception for cases of *flagrante delicto*.

Article 95
No Deputy can be pursued, investigated, arrested, detained or judged because of the opinions or votes made by him during the exercise or on the occasion of the exercise of his functions.

Article 96
Except in the case of flagrante delicto, any Deputy can only be pursued or arrested in a correctional or criminal matter with the authorization of at least one-third of the members of the Assembly during the sessions or of the Bureau of the Assembly outside of the sessions.

18. All members of the legislature are elected; the executive lacks the power to appoint any members of the legislature.

Yes. All members of the legislature are elected.

Article 80
The Deputies are elected by direct, equal and secret universal suffrage. The Representatives are elected by indirect suffrage.

19. The legislature alone, without the involvement of any other agencies, can change the Constitution.

Yes. The legislature can change the constitution with a three-fourths majority vote.

Article 161
The initiative of the revision of the Constitution belongs concurrently:
– to the President of Faso;
– to the majority of the members of the National Assembly;
– to the people when a faction of at least thirty thousand persons having the right to vote, introduces before the National Assembly a petition constituting a proposal drafted and signed.

Article 163
The draft of revision is, in all cases, submitted preliminarily to the evaluation of the National Assembly, after the advice of the Chamber of Representatives.

Article 164
The draft of the text is then submitted to referendum. It is considered to have been adopted when it has obtained a majority of the votes cast...However, the draft of revision is adopted without recourse to referendum if it is approved by the majority of three-quarters of the members of the National Assembly.

20. The legislature's approval is necessary for the declaration of war.

Yes. The legislature's approval is necessary for the declaration of war.

Article 106
The declaration of war and the sending of troops abroad are authorized by the Assembly.

21. The legislature's approval is necessary to ratify treaties with foreign countries.

Yes. The legislature's approval is necessary to ratify international treaties on most major issues.

Article 149
Peace treaties, treaties of commerce, treaties which engage the finances of the State, those that modify the provisions of legislative nature, and those that are relative to the state of persons, can only be ratified or approved by virtue of a law. They can only take effect after having been ratified or approved.

22. The legislature has the power to grant amnesty.

No. The president has the power to grant amnesty.

Article 54
The President of Faso...proposes the laws of amnesty.

23. The legislature has the power of pardon.

No. The president has the power of pardon.

Article 54
The President of Faso exercises the right of pardon.

24. The legislature reviews and has the right to reject appointments to the judiciary; or the legislature itself appoints members of the judiciary.

Yes. The legislature elects the deputies of the High Court of Justice and three of the nine members of the Constitutional Chamber of the Supreme Court.

Article 137
There is instituted a High Court of Justice. The High Court of Justice is composed of the Deputies that the National Assembly elects after each general renewal.

Article 153
The Constitutional Chamber consists of, in addition to the President of the Supreme Court, three magistrates appointed by the President of Faso on the proposal of the Minister of Justice, three persons appointed by the President of Faso, three persons appointed by the President of the National Assembly.

25. The chairman of the central bank is appointed by the legislature.

No. Burkina Faso is a member of the Central Bank of West African States, whose governor is selected by the member states.

26. The legislature has a substantial voice in the operation of the state-owned media.

Yes. The legislature has a substantial voice in the operation of the public media.

27. The legislature is regularly in session.

Yes. The legislature meets for two ninety-day sessions every year.

Article 87
The Assembly meets of right every year in two ordinary sessions. The duration of each will not exceed ninety days. The first session opens the first Wednesday of March and the second the last Wednesday of September.

28. Each legislator has a personal secretary.

No.

29. Each legislator has at least one non-secretarial staff member with policy expertise.

No.

30. Legislators are eligible for re-election without any restriction.

Yes. There are no restrictions on re-election.

31. A seat in the legislature is an attractive enough position that legislators are generally interested in and seek re-election.

Yes.

32. The re-election of incumbent legislators is common enough that at any given time the legislature contains a significant number of highly experienced members.

Yes. Re-election rates are sufficiently high to produce a significant number of highly experienced members.

PARLIAMENT OF BURUNDI (*PARLEMENT*)

Expert consultants: Caty Clement, Alain Faupin, Jimmy MacClure, Edward McMahon, Louis-Marie Nindorera, Peter R. Sampson, Christophe Sebudandi

Score: .41

Influence over executive (3/9)		Institutional autonomy (4/9)		Specified powers (3/8)		Institutional capacity (3/6)	
1. replace		10. no dissolution		19. amendments		27. sessions	X
2. serve as ministers		11. no decree		20. war		28. secretary	
3. interpellate		12. no veto		21. treaties	X	29. staff	
4. investigate		13. no review		22. amnesty	X	30. no term limits	X
5. oversee police		14. no gatekeeping	X	23. pardon		31. seek re-election	X
6. appoint PM		15. no impoundment	X	24. judiciary	X	32. experience	
7. appoint ministers	X	16. control resources		25. central bank			
8. lack president	X	17. immunity	X	26. media			
9. no confidence	X	18. all elected	X				

The Parliament (*Parlement*) of Burundi was established in the 1992 constitution. Until the first multiparty elections in 1993, legislative power had often rested in the hands of executives who ruled by decree.

Throughout the 1990s implementation of the constitution was hampered by ethnic violence, high-level political assassinations, and political instability. In 2005 a new constitution was approved in a popular referendum and parliamentary elections were held.

The 2005 constitution calls for a bicameral parliament composed of a lower house, the National Assembly (*Inama NshingmateKa*), and an upper house, the Senate (*Sénat*). It is too early to say with any certainty how the legislature will function. By most appearances, the parliament's powers are modest but not entirely insignificant. The legislature has minimal influence over the executive, and presidential powers circumscribe the legislature's own autonomy.

SURVEY

1. The legislature alone, without the involvement of any other agencies, can impeach the president or replace the prime minister.

No. Presidential impeachment requires the involvement of the General Office of Prosecutors and the High Court of Justice.

Article 116
The President of the Republic may be removed from office for grave negligence, grave abuse or corruption by a resolution adopted by two-thirds of the members of the National Assembly and the Senate in joint session.

Article 117
The President of the Republic may only be impeached by the National Assembly and the Senate convened in Congress and deciding, in a secret vote, with a two-thirds majority of their members. The investigation may only be conducted by a team of at least three magistrates from the General Office of Prosecutors led by the General Prosecutor of the Republic.

Article 163
The two chambers of Parliament convene in Congress in order to:
2) Impeach the President in case of high treason by a resolution adopted by two-thirds of the members of the National Assembly and the Senate.

Article 234
The High Court of Justice is competent to try the President of the Republic for high treason.

2. Ministers may serve simultaneously as members of the legislature.

No. Legislators who serve in government have a sleeping mandate, meaning that they may join the government but forfeit their voting rights in the legislature during their government service. They may return to the legislature when their government service ends.

Article 137
The functions of [a] member of the Government are incompatible with the exercise of every [other] professional activity and the exercise of a parliamentary mandate.

Article 155
A deputy or senator who is appointed to the Government or any other public function incompatible with the parliamentary mandate and who accepts the appointment immediately ceases to hold a seat in the National Assembly or the Senate and is replaced by his proxy. The deputy or senator falling under one of the incompatibilities mentioned in the preceding paragraph resumes his functions as soon as the incompatibility has been removed and as long as the mandate to which he has been elected is still running.

3. The legislature has powers of summons over executive branch officials and hearings with executive branch officials testifying before the legislature or its committees are regularly held.

No. According to the constitution, the legislature may question officials from the executive, although in practice such hearings are rarely held.

Article 202
The National Assembly and the Senate may keep themselves informed of the action of the Government by way of oral or written questions addressed to the members of the Government.
During the session periods, at least one session per week is reserved by priority to the questions by the deputies and senators and to the answers by the Government. The Government is held to provide the National Assembly and the Senate with all explanations which are requested from it concerning its administration or its acts.

4. The legislature can conduct independent investigation of the chief executive and the agencies of the executive.

No. Formally, the legislature can establish committees to investigate the executive, although in practice it lacks this power.

Article 204
The National Assembly and the Senate have the right to constitute parliamentary committees charged with the investigation of specific matters of governmental action.

5. The legislature has effective powers of oversight over the agencies of coercion (the military, organs of law enforcement, intelligence services, and the secret police).

No. Despite constitutional provisions to the contrary, the legislature lacks effective powers of oversight over the agencies of coercion.

Article 242
The maintenance of national security and national defense are subject to the authority of the Government and the control of Parliament.

Article 243
The defense and security forces must account for their actions and work in absolute transparency.
Parliamentary committees charged with the task of controlling the work of the defense and security forces are established in accordance with the laws in force and following the rules of procedure of Parliament.

6. The legislature appoints the prime minister.

No. There is no prime minister.

7. The legislature's approval is required to confirm the appointment of ministers; or the legislature itself appoints ministers.

Yes. The president appoints the ministers but is obligated to do so on a basis proportional to party representation in the National Assembly.

Article 108
The President of the Republic, in consultation with the two Vice-Presidents, appoints the members of the Government and terminates their functions.

Article 129
The members [of government] come from different political parties which have received more than five percent of the vote and which so desire [to join the Government]. These parties have the right to a percentage, rounded up, of the total number of Ministries, which corresponds to the percentage of seats which they hold in the National Assembly.

8. The country lacks a presidency entirely or there is a presidency, but the president is elected by the legislature.

Yes. In 2005 the president was elected by the legislature. The constitution, however, provides for direct presidential elections in the future, the next to be held in 2010. The most recent presidential election prior to 2005 was held in 1993, when the president was elected directly.

Article 96
The President of the Republic is by direct universal suffrage for elected for a term of five years, and may be re-elected once.

9. The legislature can vote no confidence in the government.

Yes. The legislature can pass a motion of censure against the government.

Article 203
The National Assembly may present a motion of censure against the Government with a majority of two-thirds of its members. It may be dissolved by the head of state.

10. The legislature is immune from dissolution by the executive.

No. The president can dissolve the legislature.

Article 203
The National Assembly may present a motion of censure against the Government with a majority of two-thirds of its members. It may be dissolved by the head of state.

11. Any executive initiative on legislation requires ratification or approval by the legislature before it takes effect; that is, the executive lacks decree power.

No. According to the constitution, the executive may rule by decree only when authorized to do so by the legislature. In practice, the president often issues decrees that have the force of law.

Article 195
The Government may, for the execution of its program, request from Parliament the authorization to adopt by decree-law, for a limited time, the measures which are normally of the domain of the statutory law. Such decree-laws must be ratified by Parliament in the course of the following session. The ratification takes place by a single vote on the whole text of the law.
In the absence of a law of ratification, such decrees become lapsed; the lapse is stated by the Constitutional Court, if necessary.

12. Laws passed by the legislature are veto-proof or essentially veto-proof; that is, the executive lacks veto power, or has veto power but the veto can be overridden by a majority in the legislature.

No. A three-fourths majority vote in both houses is required to override a presidential veto.

Article 197
The laws adopted by Parliament are promulgated by the President of the Republic...unless he requests a second reading... After a second reading, the same text may not be promulgated unless it has been voted by a majority of three-quarters of the deputies and three-quarters (3/4) of the senators.

13. The legislature's laws are supreme and not subject to judicial review.

No. The Constitutional Court can review the constitutionality of laws.

Article 228
The Constitutional Court is competent to...decide on the constitutionality of laws and regulatory acts adopted in matters other than those falling within the domain of the statutory law.

14. The legislature has the right to initiate bills in all policy jurisdictions; the executive lacks gatekeeping authority.

Yes. The legislature can initiate bills in all policy jurisdictions.

15. Expenditure of funds appropriated by the legislature is mandatory; the executive lacks the power to impound funds appropriated by the legislature.

Yes. The executive lacks the power to impound funds appropriated by the legislature.

16. The legislature controls the resources that finance its own internal operation and provide for the perquisites of its own members.

No. Legislators' salaries are determined by law, but the legislature is dependent on the executive for the resources that finance its own operations.

Article 153
An organic law establishes the rules on allowances and benefits of the deputies and senators as well as rules on incompatibilities.

17. Members of the legislature are immune from arrest and/or criminal prosecution.

Yes. Legislators are immune with the common exception for cases of *flagrante delicto*.

Article 150
The deputies and senators may not be prosecuted, searched, arrested, detained or judged for opinions or

votes delivered during the parliamentary sessions. During sessions, deputies and senators may be prosecuted only with the authorization of the Executive Committee of the National Assembly or the Executive Committee of the Senate, except in case of *flagrante delicto*. When not in session, the deputies and senators may be arrested only with the authorization of the Executive Committee of the National Assembly for the deputies or the Executive Committee of the Senate for the senators, except in the cases of *flagrante delicto,* of previously-authorized prosecution or of final sentence.

18. All members of the legislature are elected; the executive lacks the power to appoint any members of the legislature.

Yes. All members of the legislature are elected, although former heads of state are guaranteed seats in the Senate.

Article 180
The Senate is composed of:
1) Two delegates from each province, elected by an electoral college composed of members of the local councils of the relevant province, coming from different ethnic communities and elected in distinct electoral procedures;
2) Three persons from the Twa ethnic group;
3) The former heads of State.

Article 164
The National Assembly is composed of at least hundred deputies . . . elected by direct universal suffrage for a term of five years, and of three deputies of the Twa ethnic group who are co-opted in accordance with the electoral code.

19. The legislature alone, without the involvement of any other agencies, can change the Constitution.

No. Constitutional amendments can be initiated only by the president.

Article 297
The right to initiate a revision of the Constitution belongs concurrently to the President of the Republic after consultation with the Government, the National Assembly or the Senate deciding respectively with an absolute majority of the members which compose them.

Article 298
The President of the Republic may submit a draft amendment of the Constitution to a referendum.

Article 299
No amendment procedure shall be accepted if it undermines national unity, the cohesion of the Burundian people, the secular character of the State, reconciliation, democracy or the territorial integrity of the Republic.

Article 300
The bill or proposal of amendment is adopted by a four-fifths majority of the members composing the National Assembly and two-thirds of the members of the Senate.

20. The legislature's approval is necessary for the declaration of war.

No. The president is required to consult with the legislature before declaring war, but the legislature's approval is not necessary.

Article 110
The President of the Republic is the Commander-in-Chief of the defense and security forces. He declares war and signs the armistice after consultation with the Government, with the Executive Committees of the National Assembly and the Senate and with the National Council of Security.

21. The legislature's approval is necessary to ratify treaties with foreign countries.

Yes. The legislature's approval is necessary to ratify international treaties on most major issues.

Article 158
The National Assembly adopts the law.

Article 289
The President of the Republic exercises the superior direction in international negotiations. He signs and ratifies the treaties and international agreements.

Article 290
The peace and commerce treaties, treaties relating to international organization, treaties which engage the finances of the State, [and] those that modify provisions of a legislative nature as well as those relating to the status of persons may be ratified only by virtue of a law.

22. The legislature has the power to grant amnesty.

Yes. The legislature may make laws granting amnesty. It exercised this power in an important case in 2006 and 2007. In 2006 it voted provisional immunity for political crimes committed between 1962 and 2006. It followed this act by releasing rebels from the Forces for National Liberation (FNL), a Hutu insurgent group. The legislature adopted the measure in an effort to bring the FNL, the last holdout from Burundi's long civil war, to accept the terms of a ceasefire agreement.

Article 158
The National Assembly adopts the law.

Article 159
[The following] are of the domain of the statutory law . . . amnesty.

23. The legislature has the power of pardon.

No. The president has the power of pardon.

Article 113
The President of the Republic has the right to grant pardon which he exercises after consultation with the two Vice-Presidents of the Republic and upon the advice of the Superior Council of the Magistrature.

24. The legislature reviews and has the right to reject appointments to the judiciary; or the legislature itself appoints members of the judiciary.

Yes. The Senate's approval is required for the president's appointments to the Supreme Court, the Constitutional Court, and other judicial positions.

> Article 187
> The Senate has the following powers:
> 9) To approve appointments only of the following positions:
> e) the members of the Superior Council of the Magistrature;
> f) the members of the Supreme Court;
> g) the members of the Constitutional Court;
> i) the President of the Court of Appeal and the President of the Administrative Court;
> j) the General Prosecutor at the Court of Appeal;
> k) the presidents of the upper courts, the Court of Commerce and the Labor Court.

> Article 215
> All appointments to judicial functions referred to in Article 187(9), except those to the Constitutional Court, are made by the President of the Republic on a proposal by the Minister responsible for the justice sector, upon advice by the Superior Council of the Magistrature and confirmation by the Senate.

> Article 218
> The members of the Superior Council of Magistrature are appointed by the President of the Republic after approval by the Senate.

> Article 222
> The judges of the Supreme Court are appointed by the President of the Republic upon proposal by the Minister responsible for the justice sector, upon advice of the Superior Council of the Magistrature and with the approval of the Senate.

> Article 226
> The Constitutional Court is composed of seven members. They are appointed by the President of the Republic after approval by the Senate. They have a nonrenewable term of office of six years.

25. The chairman of the central bank is appointed by the legislature.

No. The president appoints the governor of the Central Bank of Burundi.

26. The legislature has a substantial voice in the operation of the state-owned media.

No. The legislature lacks a substantial voice in the operation of the public media.

27. The legislature is regularly in session.

Yes. The legislature is in session for at least nine months each year.

> Article 174
> The National Assembly convenes every year for three ordinary session periods of three months each. The first session period starts on the first Monday of February, the second on the first Monday of June and the third on the first Monday of October.

> Article 185
> The Senate convenes every year for three ordinary session periods of three months each and at the same time as the National Assembly.

28. Each legislator has a personal secretary.

No.

29. Each legislator has at least one non-secretarial staff member with policy expertise.

No.

30. Legislators are eligible for re-election without any restriction.

Yes. There are no restrictions on re-election.

31. A seat in the legislature is an attractive enough position that legislators are generally interested in and seek re-election.

Yes.

32. The re-election of incumbent legislators is common enough that at any given time the legislature contains a significant number of highly experienced members.

No. The legislature is a young institution, and members have not yet acquired substantial experience.

NATIONAL ASSEMBLY OF CAMBODIA (*RADHSPHEA*)

Expert consultants: Ron Abney, Dominic Cardy, Neam Koy, Mong Hay Lao, Nimmith Men, Saumura Rainsy, Sophoan Rath, Sovandara Yin

Score: .59

Influence over executive (5/9)		Institutional autonomy (5/9)		Specified powers (5/8)		Institutional capacity (4/6)	
1. replace	X	10. no dissolution		19. amendments	X	27. sessions	X
2. serve as ministers		11. no decree		20. war	X	28. secretary	X
3. interpellate		12. no veto	X	21. treaties	X	29. staff	
4. investigate		13. no review		22. amnesty	X	30. no term limits	X
5. oversee police		14. no gatekeeping	X	23. pardon		31. seek re-election	X
6. appoint PM	X	15. no impoundment		24. judiciary	X	32. experience	
7. appoint ministers	X	16. control resources	X	25. central bank			
8. lack president	X	17. immunity	X	26. media			
9. no confidence	X	18. all elected	X				

The National Assembly (*Radhsphea*) of Cambodia was established in the 1947 constitution, which granted Cambodia autonomy within the French Union of Indochina. The country gained full independence in 1953. A 1970 constitution abolished the monarchy and created the Khmer Republic. In 1975 and 1976 Pol Pot and the Khmer Rouge seized power and, in a new constitution, created a powerless body named the People's Representative Assembly.

In 1981 Vietnam overthrew the Khmer Rouge and established a single-party communist government while retaining the People's Representative Assembly. According to the 1981 constitution, the legislature was "the highest organ of state power." In practice, the pro-Vietnamese Kampuchean People's Revolutionary Party ruled by decree.

Cambodia's current political order was defined in the country's 1993 constitution. The document, heavily influenced by the original 1947 constitution, rechristened the unicameral National Assembly. A coup in 1997 overthrew a democratically elected government and brought to power a dominant prime minister, Hun Sen, who continues to rule Cambodia with a strong hand. Constitutional

amendments in 1999 created a bicameral parliament by adding an upper house, the Senate.

The legislature enjoys some clout derived largely from formally specified prerogatives and some institutional capacity, but it is still largely subordinate to Hun Sen and his Cambodian People's Party (CPP). The legislature's control over, and autonomy from, Hun Sen are severely limited. For example, legislators are shielded from arrest or prosecution, but the legislature has voted to revoke its members' immunity for defaming the prime minister. The legislature has little ability to oversee the government, and its institutional autonomy is circumscribed by executive decree, dissolution, and impoundment powers.

SURVEY

1. The legislature alone, without the involvement of any other agencies, can impeach the president or replace the prime minister.

Yes. The legislature can remove the prime minister with a vote of no confidence. It merits note, however, that replacement of the current prime minister, Hun Sen, by the legislature, without action by agencies of coercion, would be highly unlikely. The legislature cannot remove the king.

Article 98
The National Assembly shall dismiss a member or members of the Royal Government or the whole Cabinet by the adoption of a motion of censure by 2/3 majority of the entire National Assembly.

2. Ministers may serve simultaneously as members of the legislature.

No. The constitution forbids ministers from serving simultaneously in the legislature, although some ministers appointed from the ranks of the National Assembly have refused to give up their seats while serving in government.

Article 79
The National Assembly mandate shall be incompatible with the holding of any active public function and of any membership in other institutions provided for in the Constitution, except when the assembly members is required to serve in the Royal Government.

3. The legislature has powers of summons over executive branch officials and hearings with executive branch officials testifying before the legislature or its committees are regularly held.

No. Formally, the legislature can question the government during weekly question time or in special hearings, but in practice, such hearings are rare. Even when they are held, opposition members are often excluded from participation.

Article 89
Upon the request by at least 1/10 of its members the National Assembly shall invite a high ranking official to clarify important special issues.

Article 96
The deputies have the right to put a motion against the Royal Government. The motion shall be submitted in writing through the Chairman of the National Assembly. The replies shall be given by one or several ministers depending on the matters related to the accountability of one or several ministers. If the case concerns the overall policy of the Royal Government, the Prime Minister shall reply in person. The explanations by the ministers or by the Prime Minister shall be given verbally or in writing. The explanations shall be provided within 7 days after the day when the question is received. In case of verbal reply, the Chairman of the National Assembly shall decide whether to hold an open debate or not. If there is no debate, the answer of the minister or the Prime Minister shall be considered final. If there is a debate, the questioner, other speakers, the ministers, or the Prime Minister may exchange views within the time-frame not exceeding one session. The National Assembly shall establish one day each

week for questions and answers. There shall be no vote during any session reserved for this purpose.

Article 97
The National Assembly commissions may invite any minister to clarify certain issues under his/her field of responsibility.

4. The legislature can conduct independent investigation of the chief executive and the agencies of the executive.

No. The legislature cannot investigate the executive.

5. The legislature has effective powers of oversight over the agencies of coercion (the military, organs of law enforcement, intelligence services, and the secret police).

No. The legislative committees exercise nominal oversight, but in practice this oversight is far from effective.

6. The legislature appoints the prime minister.

Yes. The king is required to appoint as prime minister the leader of the party or coalition of parties that enjoys the support of the legislature.

Article 19
The King shall appoint the Prime Minister and the Council of Ministers according to the procedures stipulated in Article 119.

Article 119
At the recommendation of the Chairman and with the agreement of both the Vice-Chairmen of the National Assembly, the King shall designate a dignitary from among the representatives of the winning party to form the Royal Government. This designated representative along with other members chosen from the political parties or represented in the National Assembly, then present themselves to the National Assembly to ask for a vote of confidence.
After the National Assembly has given its vote of confidence, the King shall issue a Royal Decree appointing the entire Council of Ministers.

7. The legislature's approval is required to confirm the appointment of ministers; or the legislature itself appoints ministers.

Yes. The legislature's approval is required to confirm ministerial appointments.

Article 119
At the recommendation of the Chairman and with the agreement of both the Vice-Chairmen of the National Assembly, the King shall designate a dignitary from among the representatives of the winning party to form the Royal Government. This designated representative along with other members chosen from the political parties or represented in the National Assembly, then

present themselves to the National Assembly to ask for a vote of confidence. After the National Assembly has given its vote of confidence, the King shall issue a Royal Decree appointing the entire Council of Ministers.

8. The country lacks a presidency entirely or there is a presidency, but the president is elected by the legislature.

Yes. The country lacks a presidency.

9. The legislature can vote no confidence in the government.

Yes. The legislature can vote no confidence in the government.

Article 90
The National Assembly shall pass a vote of confidence in the Royal Government by a two-third majority of all members of the entire National Assembly membership.

Article 98
The National Assembly shall dismiss a member or members of the Royal Government or the whole Cabinet by the adoption of a motion of censure by 2/3 majority of the entire National Assembly.

10. The legislature is immune from dissolution by the executive.

No. The king can dissolve the legislature.

Article 78:
The legislative term of the National Assembly shall be 5 years and terminates on the day when the new National Assembly convenes.
The National Assembly shall not be dissolved before the end of its term except when the Royal government is twice deposed within a period of twelve months. In this case, following a proposal from the Prime Minister and the approval of the Chairman of the National Assembly, the King shall dissolve the National Assembly.

11. Any executive initiative on legislation requires ratification or approval by the legislature before it takes effect; that is, the executive lacks decree power.

No. Despite constitutional provisions to the contrary, the prime minister issues decrees that have the force of law.

Article 90
The National Assembly is the only organ which has legislative power, and performs its duties as provided for in the constitution and laws.

12. Laws passed by the legislature are veto-proof or essentially veto-proof; that is, the executive lacks veto power, or has veto power but the veto can be overridden by a majority in the legislature.

Yes. The executive lacks veto power. Theoretically the king could refuse to assent to a bill, but this has never happened.

13. The legislature's laws are supreme and not subject to judicial review.

No. The Constitutional Court can review the constitutionality of laws.

Article 92
Laws adopted by the National Assembly which run counter to the principles of preserving national independence, sovereignty, territorial integrity, and affect the political unity or the administration of the nation shall be annulled. The Constitutional Council is the only organ which shall decide upon this annulment.

Article 136
The Constitutional Council shall have the duty to safeguard respect of the constitution, interpret the Constitution and laws adopted by the National Assembly and reviewed completely by the Senate.

Article 140
The King, The Prime Minister, The President of the National Assembly, 1/10 of the members of National Assembly, The President of the Senate, or 1/4 of the members of Senate may send draft laws adopted by National Assembly to the Constitutional Council for review before promulgation. The constitutional council shall decide within thirty days at the latest whether the above laws and internal rules of the National Assembly or the Senate are constitutional.

Article 141
After promulgation of any law, the King, the President of the Senate, the President of the National Assembly, the Prime Minister, 1/4 of members of Senate, 1/10 of members of National Assembly or the Courts may request the Constitutional Council to review the constitutionality of that law.
Khmer Citizens shall have the right to appeal against the constitutionality of any law through their representative or President of National Assembly or member of the Senate or President of the Senate as mentioned in the above articles.

Article 142
Provisions in any article ruled by the Constitutional Council as unconstitutional shall not be promulgated or implemented.

14. The legislature has the right to initiate bills in all policy jurisdictions; the executive lacks gatekeeping authority.

Yes. The legislature can initiate bills in all policy jurisdictions.

15. Expenditure of funds appropriated by the legislature is mandatory; the executive lacks the power to impound funds appropriated by the legislature.

No. The government can impound funds appropriated by the legislature.

16. The legislature controls the resources that finance its own internal operation and provide for the perquisites of its own members.

Yes. The legislature enjoys financial autonomy.

> Article 81
> The National Assembly shall have an autonomous budget to conduct its function.
> The deputies shall receive remuneration.

> Article 105
> The Senate shall have an autonomous budget to conduct its functions.
> Senators shall receive remuneration.

17. Members of the legislature are immune from arrest and/or criminal prosecution.

Yes. Legislators are immune with the common exception for cases of *flagrante delicto*. In 2005, however, legislators voted to strip immunity from three members of the Assembly for defaming the prime minister. In 2006 the legislature voted unanimously to restore these legislators' immunity.

> Article 80
> The deputies shall enjoy parliamentary immunity. No assembly member shall be prosecuted, detained or arrested because of opinions expressed during the exercise of his duties.
> The accusation, arrest, or detention of an assembly member shall be made only with the permission of the National Assembly or by the Standing Committee of the National Assembly between sessions, except in case of *flagrante delicto*. In that case, the competent authority shall immediately report to the National Assembly or to the Standing Committee for decision.
> The decision made by the Standing Committee of the National Assembly shall be submitted to the National Assembly at its next session for approval by a 2/3 majority vote of the assembly members. In any case, detention or prosecution of a deputy shall be suspended by a 3/4 majority vote of the National Assembly members.

> Article 104
> The Senator shall enjoy parliamentary immunity. No Senator shall be prosecuted, detained or arrested because of opinions expressed during the exercise of his or her duties. The accusation, arrest, or detention of a senator shall be made only with the permission of the Senate or by the Standing Committee of the Senate between sessions, except in the case of *flagrante delicto*. In that case the competent authority shall immediately report to the senate or to the Standing Committee for decision.

18. All members of the legislature are elected; the executive lacks the power to appoint any members of the legislature.

Yes. All members of the 120-person legislature are directly elected, with the exception of two senators who are elected by the National Assembly on the nomination of the king.

> Article 76
> The National Assembly consists of at least 120 members. The deputies shall be elected by a free, universal, equal, direct and secret ballot.
> The deputies may be re-elected.

> Article 100
> The king shall nominate two Senators.
> The Assembly shall elect two Senators by majority vote. Others shall be universally elected.

19. The legislature alone, without the involvement of any other agencies, can change the Constitution.

Yes. The legislature can change the constitution with a two-thirds majority vote.

> Article 151
> The initiative to review or to amend the Constitution shall be the prerogative of the King, the Prime Minister, [or] the Chairman of the National Assembly at the suggestion of 1/4 of all the assembly members. Revision or amendments shall be enacted by a Constitutional law passed by the National Assembly with a 2/3 majority vote.

20. The legislature's approval is necessary for the declaration of war.

Yes. The legislature's approval is necessary for royal war declarations.

> Article 24
> The King shall declare war after approval of the Assembly and the Senate.

> Article 90
> The National Assembly shall adopt the law on proclamation of war.

21. The legislature's approval is necessary to ratify treaties with foreign countries.

Yes. The legislature's approval is necessary to ratify international treaties.

> Article 26
> The King shall sign and ratify international treaties and conventions after a vote of approval by the National Assembly and the Senate.

> Article 90
> The National Assembly shall adopt or repeal treaties and International Convention.

22. The legislature has the power to grant amnesty.

Yes. Since 1999 the National Assembly and the king both have had the power to grant amnesty. Prior to 1999 the king alone had this power.

Article 27
The King shall have the right to grant partial or complete amnesty.

Article 90
The National Assembly shall adopt the law on the general amnesty.

23. The legislature has the power of pardon.

No. The king has the power of pardon.

24. The legislature reviews and has the right to reject appointments to the judiciary; or the legislature itself appoints members of the judiciary.

Yes. The National Assembly appoints three of the nine members of the Constitutional Council.

Article 137
The Constitutional Council shall consist of nine members with a nine-year mandate. 1/3 of the members of the Council shall be replaced every three years. 3 members shall be appointed by the King, 3 members by the National Assembly and 3 others by the Supreme Council of the Magistracy.

25. The chairman of the central bank is appointed by the legislature.

No. Formally, the legislature, on the recommendation of the Council of Ministers, appoints the governor of the National Bank of Cambodia, but in practice, the prime minister and the Council of Ministers are wholly responsible for the appointment.

26. The legislature has a substantial voice in the operation of the state-owned media.

No. The legislature lacks a substantial voice in the operation of the public media.

27. The legislature is regularly in session.

Yes. The legislature is in session for at least six months a year.

Article 83
The National Assembly shall hold its ordinary session twice a year.
Each session shall last at least three months. If there is a proposal from the King or the Prime Minister or at least 1/3 of the National Assembly members, the National Assembly Standing Committee shall call an extraordinary session of the National Assembly.

Article 107
The Senate shall hold its ordinary sessions twice a year. Each session shall last at least three months. If there is a proposal from the king or the prime Minister, or at least one-third of the senate, the Senate standing Committee shall call an extraordinary session of the Senate.

28. Each legislator has a personal secretary.

Yes.

29. Each legislator has at least one non-secretarial staff member with policy expertise.

No.

30. Legislators are eligible for re-election without any restriction.

Yes. There are no restrictions on re-election.

Article 76
The deputies may be re-elected.

31. A seat in the legislature is an attractive enough position that legislators are generally interested in and seek re-election.

Yes.

32. The re-election of incumbent legislators is common enough that at any given time the legislature contains a significant number of highly experienced members.

No. The first elections since 1970 were held in 1993 and resulted in a plurality of seats for a royalist party, which goes by its French acronym, FUNCINPEC. In 1997 Hun Sen, then serving as second prime minister, carried out a bloody military coup and deposed Prince Norodom Ranariddh, the leader of FUNCINPEC, who at the time was serving as first prime minister. Hun Sen subsequently took over as sole prime minister. In the 2003 parliamentary elections, Hun Sen's Cambodian People's Party (CPP), relying in part on the prime minister's control over the agencies of coercion, obtained a large plurality of votes and three-fifths of seats in the National Assembly. Under these conditions, turnover of legislators has been considerable, and opportunities for members of the fledging parliament to acquire substantial experience as legislators have been sharply restricted.

NATIONAL ASSEMBLY OF CAMEROON (*ASSEMBLÉE NATIONALE*)

Expert consultants: Robert Akoko, Jean-Germain Gros, Benedict Jua, Andreas Mehler, Immanuel Tatah Mentan, Francis B. Nyamnjoh

Score: .25

Influence over executive (1/9)	Institutional autonomy (3/9)		Specified powers (1/8)		Institutional capacity (3/6)	
1. replace	10. no dissolution		19. amendments		27. sessions	
2. serve as ministers	11. no decree		20. war		28. secretary	
3. interpellate	12. no veto	X	21. treaties	X	29. staff	
4. investigate	13. no review		22. amnesty		30. no term limits	X
5. oversee police	14. no gatekeeping	X	23. pardon		31. seek re-election	X
6. appoint PM	15. no impoundment		24. judiciary		32. experience	X
7. appoint ministers	16. control resources		25. central bank			
8. lack president	17. immunity	X	26. media			
9. no confidence	X	18. all elected				

The National Assembly (*Assemblée nationale*) of Cameroon was established along with a federal state in the country's 1961 constitution. The 1961 document set forth a unicameral legislature. A new constitution in 1972 provided for a unitary state structure but did not notably affect legislative power. In 1996 a constitutional amendment sought to create a bicameral legislature by adding an upper house of parliament, the Senate. At the time of this writing, the Senate had not yet been formed. The amendment gives the president the power to appoint three out of every ten members of the Senate. Prior to the 1996 amendments, all members of the legislature were elected.

The National Assembly is a feeble body. It has no significant ability to influence the executive branch. The president appoints the prime minister and ministers, and the legislature cannot effectively interpellate or investigate the government. Its own institutional autonomy is severely limited by the president's powers to appoint members of the legislature, dissolve the legislature, and rule by decree. Prerogatives specified in the constitution are reserved almost exclusively for the president. The legislature has modest institutional capacity.

SURVEY

1. The legislature alone, without the involvement of any other agencies, can impeach the president or replace the prime minister.

No. Presidential impeachment requires action by the Court of Impeachment. The legislature can vote no confidence in the government, forcing the resignation of the prime minister, but the president can simply reappoint the prime minister.

Article 34
(5) Where the National Assembly adopts a motion of censure or passes a vote of no confidence, the Prime Minister shall tender the resignation of the Government to the President of the Republic.
(6) The President of the Republic may re-appoint the Prime Minister and ask him to form a new Government.

Article 53
(1) The Court of Impeachment shall have jurisdiction, in respect of acts committed in the exercise of their functions, to try the President of the Republic for high treason and . . . for conspiracy against the security of the State.

2. Ministers may serve simultaneously as members of the legislature.

No. Ministers are prohibited from serving simultaneously in the legislature.

> Article 13
> The office of member of Government and any office ranking as such shall be incompatible with that of Member of Parliament.

3. The legislature has powers of summons over executive branch officials and hearings with executive branch officials testifying before the legislature or its committees are regularly held.

No. Although the legislature has the power of summons, this power is strictly limited to paper; it has no practical significance.

> Article 35
> (1) The Parliament shall control Government action through oral or written questions and by setting up committees of inquiry with specific terms of reference.
> (2) The Government shall, subject to the imperatives of national defence, the security of the State or the secrecy of criminal investigation, furnish any explanations and information to Parliament.
> (3) During each ordinary session, a special sitting shall be set aside each week for question time.

4. The legislature can conduct independent investigation of the chief executive and the agencies of the executive.

No. The legislature has some limited powers of investigation, but in practice, it must halt its investigation if the president so desires.

> Article 35
> (1) The Parliament shall control Government action through oral or written questions and by setting up committees of inquiry with specific terms of reference.

5. The legislature has effective powers of oversight over the agencies of coercion (the military, organs of law enforcement, intelligence services, and the secret police).

No. The agencies of coercion report directly to the president and are not subject to legislative oversight.

6. The legislature appoints the prime minister.

No. The president appoints the prime minister.

> Article 10
> (1) The President of the Republic shall appoint the Prime Minister and, on the proposal of the latter, the other members of Government.

7. The legislature's approval is required to confirm the appointment of ministers; or the legislature itself appoints ministers.

No. The president appoints ministers on the recommendation of the prime minister, and ministerial appointments do not require the legislature's confirmation.

> Article 10
> (1) The President of the Republic shall appoint the Prime Minister and, on the proposal of the latter, the other members of Government.

8. The country lacks a presidency entirely or there is a presidency, but the president is elected by the legislature.

No. The president is directly elected.

> Article 6
> (1) The President of the Republic shall be elected by a majority of the votes cast through direct, equal and secret universal suffrage.

9. The legislature can vote no confidence in the government.

Yes. The legislature can vote no confidence in the government.

> Article 34
> (5) Where the National Assembly adopts a motion of censure or passes a vote of no confidence, the Prime Minister shall tender the resignation of the Government to the President of the Republic.
> (6) The President of the Republic may re-appoint the Prime Minister and ask him to form a new Government.

10. The legislature is immune from dissolution by the executive.

No. The president can dissolve the legislature.

> Article 8
> (12) The President of the Republic may, if necessary and after consultation with the Government, the Bureaux of the National Assembly and the Senate, dissolve the National Assembly.

11. Any executive initiative on legislation requires ratification or approval by the legislature before it takes effect; that is, the executive lacks decree power.

No. Formally, the president may rule by decree only when delegated specific decree powers by the legislature. In practice, the president frequently issues decrees that have the force of law without prior legislative authorization.

> Article 28
> (1) Parliament may empower the President of the Republic to legislate by way of ordinance for a limited period and for given purposes.
> (2) Such ordinances shall enter into force on the date of their publication. They shall be tabled before the Bureaux of the National Assembly and the Senate for purposes of ratification within the time-limit laid down

by the enabling law. They shall be of a statutory nature as long as they have not been ratified.

(3) They shall remain in force as long as Parliament has not refused to ratify them.

12. Laws passed by the legislature are veto-proof or essentially veto-proof; that is, the executive lacks veto power, or has veto power but the veto can be over-ridden by a majority in the legislature.

Yes. The legislature can override a presidential veto by a majority vote of its total membership.

> Article 19
> (3) The President of the Republic may, before enacting any law, ask for a second reading. In such case, bills shall be passed by an absolute majority of the members of the National Assembly.

> Article 24
> (3) The President of the Republic may, before enacting a law, ask for a second reading.
> In such case, bills shall be passed by an absolute major-ity of the Senators.

13. The legislature's laws are supreme and not sub-ject to judicial review.

No. The Constitutional Court has the formal power to review the constitutionality of laws.

> Article 46
> The Constitutional Council shall have jurisdiction in matters pertaining to the Constitution. It shall rule on the constitutionality of laws. It shall be the organ regu-lating the functioning of the institutions.

14. The legislature has the right to initiate bills in all policy jurisdictions; the executive lacks gatekeeping authority.

Yes. The legislature can initiate bills in all policy jurisdictions.

15. Expenditure of funds appropriated by the legis-lature is mandatory; the executive lacks the power to impound funds appropriated by the legislature.

No. The president can impound funds appropri-ated by the legislature.

16. The legislature controls the resources that finance its own internal operation and provide for the perquisites of its own members.

No. The legislature is dependent on the executive for the resources that finance its own operations.

17. Members of the legislature are immune from arrest and/or criminal prosecution.

Yes. The constitution stipulates only that legisla-tive immunity will be determined by law. Accord-ing to practice and subsequent legislation, legisla-tors are immune from arrest unless immunity is lifted by the legislature. In October 2006 Edouard

Etondé Ekoto and André Booto'o á Ngon, promi-nent parliamentarians from the Cameroon Peo-ple's Democratic Movement, the country's dom-inant party and the main political organization headed by the president, Paul Biya, had their immunity lifted by the legislature as a first step toward criminal prosecution for corruption in their management of state enterprises. The case appar-ently confirmed both the existence of immunity from criminal prosecution and the necessity and ability of the legislature to lift it.

> Article 14
> (6) The conditions for the election of members of the National Assembly and of the Senate, as well as the immunities, ineligibilities, incompatibilities, allowances and privileges of the members of Parliament shall be determined by law.

18. All members of the legislature are elected; the executive lacks the power to appoint any members of the legislature.

No. The president appoints three out of every ten senators. It bears note that, although the Senate was established in a 1996 amendment, it has not yet been created. Prior to 1996 all members of the legislature were elected.

> Article 15
> (1) The National Assembly shall comprise 180 members elected by direct and secret universal suffrage for a five-year term of office.

> Article 20
> (2) Each region shall be represented in the Senate by 10 Senators of whom 7 shall be elected by indirect univer-sal suffrage on a regional basis and 3 appointed by the President of the Republic.

19. The legislature alone, without the involvement of any other agencies, can change the Constitution.

No. To date all constitutional amendments have been made by presidential decree. Formally, the legislature alone cannot change the constitution without the approval of the president. If the pres-ident objects to a constitutional amendment that has been passed by the legislature, he or she can choose to put the amendment to a popular refer-endum.

> Article 63
> (1) Amendments to the Constitution may be proposed either by the President of the Republic or by Parliament.
> (2) Any proposed amendment made by a member of Parliament shall be signed by at least one-third of the members of either House.
> (3) Parliament shall meet in congress when called upon to examine a draft or proposed amendment. The amendment shall be adopted by an absolute majority of

the members of Parliament. The President of the Republic may request a second reading; in which case the amendment shall be adopted by a two-third Majority of the members of Parliament.

(4) The President of the Republic may decide to submit any bill to amend the Constitution to a referendum; in which case the amendment shall be adopted by a simple majority of the votes cast.

20. The legislature's approval is necessary for the declaration of war.

No. The president can declare war without the legislature's approval.

21. The legislature's approval is necessary to ratify treaties with foreign countries.

Yes. The legislature's approval is necessary to ratify international treaties.

> Article 43
> The President of the Republic shall negotiate and ratify treaties and international agreements. Treaties and international agreements falling within the area of competence of the Legislative Power... shall be submitted to Parliament for authorization to ratify.

22. The legislature has the power to grant amnesty.

No. Pardon and amnesty are not treated separately, and the legislature lacks the power of pardon. See item 23.

23. The legislature has the power of pardon.

No. The president has the power of pardon (clemency).

> Article 8
> (7) [The president] shall exercise the right of clemency after consultation with the Higher Judicial Council.

24. The legislature reviews and has the right to reject appointments to the judiciary; or the legislature itself appoints members of the judiciary.

No. The president appoints the members of the Constitutional Council, and the appointments do not require the legislature's approval.

> Art. 51
> (2) Members of the Constitutional Council shall be appointed by the President of the Republic.

25. The chairman of the central bank is appointed by the legislature.

No. Cameroon belongs to the Bank of Central African States, whose governor is selected by the member countries.

26. The legislature has a substantial voice in the operation of the state-owned media.

No. The legislature lacks a substantial voice in the operation of the public media.

27. The legislature is regularly in session.

No. The legislature meets for three thirty-day sessions.

> Article 14
> (3) Both Houses of Parliament shall meet on the same dates:
> (a) in ordinary session during the months of June, November and March each year.
> (b) in extraordinary session, at the request of the President of the Republic or of one-third of the members of both Houses.

28. Each legislator has a personal secretary.

No.

29. Each legislator has at least one non-secretarial staff member with policy expertise.

No.

30. Legislators are eligible for re-election without any restriction.

Yes. There are no restrictions on re-election.

31. A seat in the legislature is an attractive enough position that legislators are generally interested in and seek re-election.

Yes.

32. The re-election of incumbent legislators is common enough that at any given time the legislature contains a significant number of highly experienced members.

Yes. The turnover rate is relatively low. The Cameroon People's Democratic Movement, the party of the president, Paul Biya, has dominated the legislature since the mid-1990s, obtaining overwhelming majorities in the 1997, 2002, and 2007 parliamentary elections. While the legislature contains a significant number of highly experienced members, it bears mention that the National Assembly's subordination to the president means that time spent in the legislature does not necessarily translate into significant member expertise in legislative work.

PARLIAMENT OF CANADA

Expert consultants: Charles Gonthier, Andrew Heard, Gregory S. Mahler, Christopher P. Manfredi, Richard Schultz, Kenneth Vigeant

Score: .72

Influence over executive (8/9)		Institutional autonomy (5/9)		Specified powers (4/8)		Institutional capacity (6/6)	
1. replace	X	10. no dissolution		19. amendments		27. sessions	X
2. serve as ministers	X	11. no decree	X	20. war	X	28. secretary	X
3. interpellate	X	12. no veto	X	21. treaties	X	29. staff	X
4. investigate	X	13. no review		22. amnesty	X	30. no term limits	X
5. oversee police	X	14. no gatekeeping	X	23. pardon	X	31. seek re-election	X
6. appoint PM	X	15. no impoundment	X	24. judiciary		32. experience	X
7. appoint ministers		16. control resources	X	25. central bank			
8. lack president	X	17. immunity		26. media			
9. no confidence	X	18. all elected	X				

The antecedents to Canadian parliamentary government can be traced back to 1791, when Britain split the North American possessions conquered from the French into the provinces of Upper Canada (later Ontario) and Lower Canada (later Quebec). Perhaps partly motivated by its experience with colonial discontent during the American Revolution as well as Canadian calls for "Responsible Government" (as local rule was then described), direct appointment of governing councils was replaced by a bicameral assembly for each province, with an elected Legislative Assembly and an appointed Legislative Council – although ultimate authority remained in Britain. The structure of colonial administration was reshuffled several times, and the two provinces, as well as their legislatures, were unified in 1840. In 1867 the British North America Act brought greater political unity to Canada, bringing several of the Maritime Provinces into Confederation, and designated the United Kingdom's parliament as Canada's highest legislative power. Legislation was subject to Britain's approval until the Statute of Westminster, enacted in 1931, which granted Canada formal independence. Complete legal separation from British legislative control was not achieved until the Canada Act of 1982.

Canada does not have a single constitution, but rather a number of conventions and constitutional acts. The bicameral legislature consists of the Senate and the House of Commons. The Senate is a fully appointed upper house. Although formally endowed with legislative powers, the Senate routinely approves legislation passed in the House of Commons. The Queen of England remains Canada's official head of state, although in practice this function is exercised by the Governor General. Most executive power rests with the prime minister and the cabinet.

Parliament is endowed with substantial powers. It has extensive control over the executive. While subject to dissolution, the legislature enjoys institutional autonomy. It does not share lawmaking authority with the executive, and its laws, in practice, are veto-proof. Parliament holds a number of specific powers and prerogatives and has a very high level of institutional capacity.

SURVEY

1. The legislature alone, without the involvement of any other agencies, can impeach the president or replace the prime minister.

Yes. The legislature can remove the prime minister with a vote of no confidence. The Governor

General can only be replaced by the queen on the advice of the prime minister.

2. Ministers may serve simultaneously as members of the legislature.

Yes. Ministers are selected from, and required to serve simultaneously in, the legislature.

3. The legislature has powers of summons over executive branch officials and hearings with executive branch officials testifying before the legislature or its committees are regularly held.

Yes. Parliamentary committees can compel cabinet members to testify with a majority vote. Committees often question ministry officials.

4. The legislature can conduct independent investigation of the chief executive and the agencies of the executive.

Yes. The legislature can investigate the executive.

5. The legislature has effective powers of oversight over the agencies of coercion (the military, organs of law enforcement, intelligence services, and the secret police).

Yes. Parliamentary committees have effective powers of oversight over the agencies of coercion.

6. The legislature appoints the prime minister.

Yes. The Governor General formally appoints the prime minister but must select the candidate who enjoys the support of the House of Commons.

7. The legislature's approval is required to confirm the appointment of ministers; or the legislature itself appoints ministers.

No. The Governor General appoints ministers on the recommendation of the prime minister, and the appointments do not require the legislature's approval.

Section 11
There shall be a Council to aid and advise in the Government of Canada, to be styled the Queen's Privy Council for Canada; and the Persons who are to be Members of that Council shall be from Time to Time chosen and summoned by the Governor General and sworn in as Privy Councillors, and Members thereof may be from Time to Time removed by the Governor General.

8. The country lacks a presidency entirely or there is a presidency, but the president is elected by the legislature.

Yes. The country lacks a presidency. The Governor General is the head of state.

Section 9
The Executive Government and Authority of and over Canada is hereby declared to continue and be vested in the Queen.

Section 10
The provisions of this act referring to the Governor General extend and apply to the Governor General for the Time being of Canada, or other the Chief Executive Officer or Administrator for the Time being carrying on the Government of Canada on behalf and in the Name of the Queen, by whatever Title he is designated.

9. The legislature can vote no confidence in the government.

Yes. The legislature can vote no confidence in the government.

10. The legislature is immune from dissolution by the executive.

No. The Governor General, on the recommendation of the prime minister, can dissolve the House of Commons.

11. Any executive initiative on legislation requires ratification or approval by the legislature before it takes effect; that is, the executive lacks decree power.

Yes. The executive lacks decree power.

12. Laws passed by the legislature are veto-proof or essentially veto-proof; that is, the executive lacks veto power, or has veto power but the veto can be overridden by a majority in the legislature.

Yes. Formally, the Governor General could refuse to give royal assent to legislation. This would amount to a veto power. In practice, it is unthinkable that the Governor General would withhold royal assent from legislation.

Section 55
Where a Bill passed by the Houses of Parliament is presented to the Governor General for the Queen's Assent, he shall declare, according to his Discretion, but subject to the provisions of this act and to Her Majesty's Instructions, either that he assents thereto in the Queen's name, or that he withholds the Queen's Assent, or that he reserves the Bill for the Signification of the Queen's Pleasure.

Section 57
A Bill reserved for the Signification of the Queen's Pleasure shall not have any Force unless and until, within Two Years from the Day on which it was presented to the Governor General for the Queen's Assent, the Governor General signifies, by Speech or Message to each of the Houses of the Parliament or by Proclamation, that it has received the Assent of the Queen in Council.

13. The legislature's laws are supreme and not subject to judicial review.

No. The Supreme Court can review the constitutionality of laws.

14. The legislature has the right to initiate bills in all policy jurisdictions; the executive lacks gatekeeping authority.

Yes. The legislature can initiate bills in all policy jurisdictions.

15. Expenditure of funds appropriated by the legislature is mandatory; the executive lacks the power to impound funds appropriated by the legislature.

Yes. The executive cannot withhold funds from a dedicated program without legislative approval.

16. The legislature controls the resources that finance its own internal operation and provide for the perquisites of its own members.

Yes. The legislature enjoys financial autonomy.

17. Members of the legislature are immune from arrest and/or criminal prosecution.

No. Legislative immunity extends to official parliamentary business only. Legislators are subject to arrest for common crimes.

Section 18
The privileges, immunities, and powers to be held, enjoyed, and exercised by the Senate and by the House of Commons, and by the Members thereof respectively, shall be such as are from time to time defined by Act of the Parliament of Canada, but so that any Act of the Parliament of Canada defining such privileges, immunities, and powers shall not confer any privileges, immunities, or powers exceeding those at the passing of such Act held, enjoyed, and exercised by the Commons House of Parliament of the United Kingdom of Great Britain and Ireland, and by the Members thereof.

18. All members of the legislature are elected; the executive lacks the power to appoint any members of the legislature.

No. All of the members of the Senate are appointed by the Governor General on the advice of the prime minister and the government. All members of the House of Commons are elected.

Section 24
The Governor General shall from Time to Time, in the Queen's Name, by Instrument under the Great Seal of Canada, summon qualified Persons to the Senate; and, subject to the provisions of this act, every Person so summoned shall become and be a Member of the Senate and a Senator.

Section 37
The House of Commons shall, subject to the provisions of this act, consist of two hundred and eighty-two members of whom ninety-five shall be elected for Ontario, seventy-five for Quebec, eleven for Nova Scotia, ten for

New Brunswick, fourteen for Manitoba, twenty-eight for British Columbia, four for Prince Edward Island, twenty-one for Alberta, fourteen for Saskatchewan, seven for Newfoundland, one for the Yukon Territory and two for the Northwest Territories.

19. The legislature alone, without the involvement of any other agencies, can change the Constitution.

No. Constitutional amendments require approval by the regional legislative assemblies in two-thirds of the provinces.

Section 38
(1) An amendment to the Constitution of Canada may be made by proclamation issued by the Governor General under the Great Seal of Canada where so authorized by
(a) resolutions of the Senate and the House of Commons; and
(b) resolutions of the legislative assemblies of at least two-thirds of the provinces.

20. The legislature's approval is necessary for the declaration of war.

Yes. A constitutional convention in place since 1939 requires the legislature's approval for declarations of war.

21. The legislature's approval is necessary to ratify treaties with foreign countries.

Yes. The executive can negotiate and ratify international treaties. The legislature must, however, approve treaties that would affect domestic legislation. Most treaties require separate legislative implementation.

Section 132
The Parliament and Government of Canada shall have all Powers necessary or Proper for performing the Obligations of Canada or of any Province thereof, as Part of the British Empire, towards Foreign Countries, arising under Treaties between the Empire and such Foreign Countries.

22. The legislature has the power to grant amnesty.

Yes. The legislature can grant amnesty through legislation.

23. The legislature has the power of pardon.

Yes. The legislature can grant a pardon through special legislation.

24. The legislature reviews and has the right to reject appointments to the judiciary; or the legislature itself appoints members of the judiciary.

No. The Governor General appoints members of the judiciary on the recommendation of the queen's Privy Council for Canada, a distinctive body that includes the prime minister, the cabinet, former Governors General, and a variety of other notables. The appointments do not require the legislature's approval.

Section 96
The Governor General shall appoint the Judges of the Superior, District, and County Courts in each Province, except those of the Courts of Probate in Nova Scotia and New Brunswick.

25. The chairman of the central bank is appointed by the legislature.

No. The prime minister appoints the governor of the Bank of Canada.

Section 91
It shall be lawful for the Queen, by and with the Advice and Consent of the Senate and House of Commons, to make laws for the Peace, Order, and good Government of Canada, in relation to all Matters not coming within the Classes of Subjects by this act assigned exclusively to the Legislatures of the Provinces... that is to say,
15) Banking, Incorporation of Banks, and the Issue of Paper Money.

26. The legislature has a substantial voice in the operation of the state-owned media.

No. The prime minister appoints the members of the board of directors of the Canadian Broadcasting Company.

27. The legislature is regularly in session.

Yes. The legislature is in session for between eight and nine months a year.

Section 5
There shall be a sitting of Parliament and of each legislature at least once every twelve months.

28. Each legislator has a personal secretary.

Yes.

29. Each legislator has at least one non-secretarial staff member with policy expertise.

Yes.

30. Legislators are eligible for re-election without any restriction.

Yes. There are no restrictions on re-election for members of the House of Commons. Senators hold their position until the age of seventy-five.

Section 29
(1) Subject to Subsection (2), a Senator shall, subject to the provisions of this act, hold his place in the Senate for life. (2) A Senator who is summoned to the Senate after the coming into force of this subsection shall, subject to this act, hold his place in the Senate until he attains the age of seventy-five years.

31. A seat in the legislature is an attractive enough position that legislators are generally interested in and seek re-election.

Yes.

32. The re-election of incumbent legislators is common enough that at any given time the legislature contains a significant number of highly experienced members.

Yes. Re-election rates in the House of Commons are sufficiently high to produce a significant number of highly experienced members.

NATIONAL ASSEMBLY OF THE CENTRAL AFRICAN REPUBLIC (*ASSEMBLÉE NATIONALE*)

Expert consultants: Stuart Crampton, Alain Faupin, Barrie Hofmann, Maxime-Faustin Mbringa-Takama, Andreas Mehler

Score: .34

Influence over executive (3/9)		Institutional autonomy (3/9)		Specified powers (3/8)		Institutional capacity (2/6)	
1. replace		10. no dissolution		19. amendments	X	27. sessions	
2. serve as ministers		11. no decree		20. war		28. secretary	
3. interpellate	X	12. no veto		21. treaties	X	29. staff	
4. investigate	X	13. no review		22. amnesty	X	30. no term limits	X
5. oversee police		14. no gatekeeping	X	23. pardon		31. seek re-election	X
6. appoint PM		15. no impoundment		24. judiciary		32. experience	
7. appoint ministers		16. control resources		25. central bank			
8. lack president		17. immunity	X	26. media			
9. no confidence	X	18. all elected	X				

The National Assembly (*Assemblée nationale*) of the Central African Republic was established in the 1959 constitution. The political order was overthrown in a 1965 military coup that brought Jean-Bedel Bokassa to power. Bokassa declared himself emperor and ruled until 1979, when he was overthrown with the help of French troops. The demise of Bokassa led to some political opening, which included a controversial presidential election in 1981 whose result was overturned in military coup just six months later, and a referendum that ratified a new constitution in 1986, which was followed by parliamentary elections in 1987. Reasonably open presidential elections were held in 1993. In 1994 the Central African Republic adopted a new constitution, but the experiment with open politics was turbulent and punctuated by civil unrest and coup attempts. In a 2003 military coup, François Bozizé seized power, declared himself president, and dissolved parliament. Under Bozizé, a new constitution was approved in 2004. The constitution did not differ markedly from its predecessor. The first legislative elections under the new system were held in the spring of 2005, and the legislature convened in the summer of 2005.

The National Assembly's role is not expansive. It can question and investigate the executive officials and remove the government with a vote of no confidence, but otherwise lacks influence over the executive. The president's powers of dissolution, decree, veto, gatekeeping, and impoundment restrict the legislature's institutional autonomy. The legislature is vested with some specified powers, including the right to amend the constitution. It has scant institutional capacity; members of the National Assembly lack staff, and the absence of a tradition of legislative institutions has prevented members from developing the expertise conducive to a proficient legislature.

SURVEY

1. The legislature alone, without the involvement of any other agencies, can impeach the president or replace the prime minister.

No. Presidential impeachment requires the involvement of the attorney general and the High Court of Justice. The legislature can remove the prime minister with a vote of no confidence.

Article 34
A vacancy of the Presidency of the Republic only occurs in the case of death, resignation, removal from office, conviction of the President or by his permanent incapacity to exercise his functions in conformity with the requirements of his post. In the case of conviction, the decision which pronounces [the conviction] is transmitted by the President of the jurisdiction concerned to the President of the Constitutional Court, who informs the President of the National Assembly by letter and the Nation by message.

Article 40

The Prime Minister, Head of Government, is responsible to the President of the Republic and to the National Assembly.

The Prime Minister may be dismissed, at any time, by the President of the Republic or following a censure motion adopted by the absolute majority of the members composing the National Assembly.

Article 41

After the appointment of the members of the Government, the Prime Minister, Head of Government, presents himself within a maximum period of sixty days before the National Assembly and explains his general policy program. In the case of non-observance of the sixty day time limit, Article 40 above applies. This program defines the main features of the action which the Government plans to carry out in the diverse sectors of national activity and particularly in the areas of economic, scientific, technical, technological, social, environmental, cultural and foreign policy. On this occasion, the Prime Minister, Head of Government, must ask the National Assembly for a vote of confidence. The confidence is granted or refused [to the Prime Minister] by the absolute majority of the members composing the National Assembly. The Prime Minister, Head of Government, may, after deliberation of the Council of Ministers, make the vote of a [legislative] text a matter of the Government's responsibility instead of the National Assembly's. In this case, the text is considered as adopted, unless a censure motion submitted within the following twenty-four hours is passed in the conditions established in Article 48 below.

Article 47

The National Assembly may involve the responsibility of the Government by voting a censure motion. The censure motion is remitted, signed, to the President of the National Assembly, who without delay notifies the Government of it. It obligatorily carries the title "MOTION OF CENSURE" and must be signed by one-third of the members composing the National Assembly.

The vote on the censure motion takes place within the forty-eight hours that follow its introduction. Voting takes place by secret ballot and with the absolute majority of the members composing the National Assembly.

Article 48

When the National Assembly adopts a motion of censure or when it disapproves the program or a declaration of general policy of the Government, the Prime Minister must submit without delay the resignation of his Government to the President of the Republic.

Article 96

The President of the Republic is responsible for the acts committed in the exercise of his functions only in the case of high treason.

Crimes of high treason are, in particular:

– the violation of the oath;

– politically-motivated homicides;

– business activities;

– any action which is contrary to the higher interests of the Nation.

The request for indictment is only admissible if it receives the signature of fifty percent of the members of the National Assembly.

The President of the Republic can only be indicted by the National Assembly with a two-thirds majority of the deputies voting in secret ballot.

The resolution of indictment, duly reasoned, is transmitted by the President of the National Assembly to the Attorney-General before the High Court of Justice.

However, with regard to the ordinary offenses committed by the Head of State before his election or term of office, he will be subject to prosecution before the competent tribunals only after the end of his term.

2. Ministers may serve simultaneously as members of the legislature.

No. Ministers are prohibited from serving simultaneously in the legislature.

Article 43

The functions of a member of Government are incompatible with those of a member of the National Assembly.

3. The legislature has powers of summons over executive branch officials and hearings with executive branch officials testifying before the legislature or its committees are regularly held.

Yes. The legislature regularly interpellates executive branch officials. For example, in 2006 several members of the Assembly, including the speaker, used their right to interrogate the executive to inveigh publicly against the government for massacres and insecurity in the northern part of the country.

Article 45

In matters relating to their departments, the Ministers are heard by the National Assembly on the occasion of oral and written questions submitted by members of Parliament.

Article 66

One session per week is reserved by priority for questions of the deputies and for the responses of the Government. The Ministers are required to respond to the questions at the latest in the following week.

Article 68

In addition to the motion of censure, the other instruments of control of the National Assembly with regard to the Government are:

– oral questions with or without debate;

– written questions;

– committee hearings;

– committees of inquiry and of control;

– questioning.

The law determines the conditions for the organization and functioning of the committees of inquiry as well as the powers of the committees of inquiry and control.

4. The legislature can conduct independent investigation of the chief executive and the agencies of the executive.

Yes. The legislature can establish committees of inquiry to investigate the executive.

> Article 68
> In addition to the motion of censure, the other instruments of control of the National Assembly with regard to the Government are:
> – oral questions with or without debate;
> – written questions;
> – committee hearings;
> – committees of inquiry and of control;
> – questioning.
> The law determines the conditions for the organization and functioning of the committees of inquiry as well as the powers of the committees of inquiry and control.

5. The legislature has effective powers of oversight over the agencies of coercion (the military, organs of law enforcement, intelligence services, and the secret police).

No. The legislature lacks effective powers of oversight over the agencies of coercion.

6. The legislature appoints the prime minister.

No. The president appoints the prime minister.

> Article 22
> The President ... appoints the Prime Minister, the Head of Government, and dismisses him. Upon the proposal of the Prime Minister, he appoints and dismisses the other members of the Government.

7. The legislature's approval is required to confirm the appointment of ministers; or the legislature itself appoints ministers.

No. The president appoints ministers, and the appointments do not require the legislature's approval.

> Article 22
> The President ... appoints the Prime Minister, the Head of Government, and dismisses him. Upon the proposal of the Prime Minister, he appoints and dismisses the other members of the Government.

8. The country lacks a presidency entirely or there is a presidency, but the president is elected by the legislature.

No. The president is directly elected.

> Article 21
> The Executive consists of the President of the Republic and the Government.
> The Central African People elects the PRESIDENT OF THE REPUBLIC by direct universal suffrage.

9. The legislature can vote no confidence in the government.

Yes. The legislature can vote no confidence in the government.

> Article 40
> The Prime Minister may be dismissed, at any time, by the President of the Republic or following a censure motion adopted by the absolute majority of the members composing the National Assembly.

> Article 41
> After the appointment of the members of the Government, the Prime Minister, Head of Government, presents himself within a maximum period of sixty days before the National Assembly and explains his general policy program. In the case of non-observance of the sixty day time limit, Article 40 above applies. This program defines the main features of the action which the Government plans to carry out in the diverse sectors of national activity and particularly in the areas of economic, scientific, technical, technological, social, environmental, cultural and foreign policy. On this occasion, the Prime Minister, Head of Government, must ask the National Assembly for a vote of confidence. The confidence is granted or refused [to the Prime Minister] by the absolute majority of the members composing the National Assembly. The Prime Minister, Head of Government, may, after deliberation of the Council of Ministers, make the vote of a [legislative] text a matter of the Government's responsibility instead of the National Assembly's. In this case, the text is considered as adopted, unless a censure motion submitted within the following twenty-four hours is passed in the conditions established in Article 48 below.

> Article 47
> The National Assembly may involve the responsibility of the Government by voting a censure motion. The censure motion is remitted, signed, to the President of the National Assembly, who without delay notifies the Government of it. It obligatorily carries the title "MOTION OF CENSURE" and must be signed by one-third of the members composing the National Assembly.
> The vote on the censure motion takes place within the forty-eight hours that follow its introduction. Voting takes place by secret ballot and with the absolute majority of the members composing the National Assembly.

> Article 48
> When the National Assembly adopts a motion of censure or when it disapproves the program or a declaration of general policy of the Government, the Prime Minister must submit without delay the resignation of his Government to the President of the Republic.

10. The legislature is immune from dissolution by the executive.

No. The president can dissolve the legislature.

> Article 33
> The President of the Republic may, after consultation with the Council of Ministers, the Bureau of the National Assembly and the President of the Constitutional Court, pronounce the dissolution of the National Assembly.

11. Any executive initiative on legislation requires ratification or approval by the legislature before it takes effect; that is, the executive lacks decree power.

No. The president issues decrees that have the force of law. According to the constitution, the president must obtain prior authorization from the National Assembly to issue decrees on specific issue areas, although in practice the president regularly issues decree-laws without prior legislative authorization.

Article 22
[The President] promulgates the laws, signs the ordinances and decrees.

Article 29
In exceptional circumstances, for a limited period and for the execution of a specific program, the President of the Republic may ask the National Assembly for authorization to take, by ordinance, measures which fall normally within the domain of statutory law. The ordinances are adopted in the Council of Ministers after the advice of the Constitutional Court. They enter into force upon their publication but become void if they have not been ratified on the expiration of the period fixed in the enabling law. After the expiration of this period, the ordinances, once they have been ratified, may no longer be modified except by statute, with regard to matters which fall within the legislative domain.

12. Laws passed by the legislature are veto-proof or essentially veto-proof; that is, the executive lacks veto power, or has veto power but the veto can be overridden by a majority in the legislature.

No. A two-thirds majority vote is required to override a presidential veto.

Article 27
The President of the Republic has the initiative of laws. He promulgates them in the fifteen days which follow the adoption of the final text by the National Assembly. This period is reduced to five days in the case of urgency declared by the National Assembly.
He may nevertheless, before the expiration of this period, ask the National Assembly for a new deliberation of the law or certain of its provisions. This request must be reasoned and the new deliberation may not be refused. It takes place obligatorily during the course of the same session. The adoption of the text submitted to this new deliberation in its original form may then only occur with a qualified two-thirds majority of the members of the National Assembly.

13. The legislature's laws are supreme and not subject to judicial review.

No. The Constitutional Court can review the constitutionality of laws.

Article 73
A Constitutional Court is established with the following functions:

– to monitor the regularity of electoral consultations, to examine and proclaim their results;
– to monitor the regularity of the referendum operations and to proclaim their results;
– to resolve electoral disputes;
– to resolve conflicts of competence between the executive power, the legislative power and the territorial collectivities.
Apart from these competences and those which are conferred upon it by Articles 25, 28, 29, 30, 31, 32, 33, 34, 65, 68 and 72, the Constitutional Court interprets the Constitution and rules on the constitutionality of ordinary and organic laws which have been promulgated or are ready to be promulgated, as well as on the rules of procedure of the National Assembly.

14. The legislature has the right to initiate bills in all policy jurisdictions; the executive lacks gatekeeping authority.

Yes. The legislature can initiate bills in all policy jurisdictions.

15. Expenditure of funds appropriated by the legislature is mandatory; the executive lacks the power to impound funds appropriated by the legislature.

No. The president can impound funds appropriated by the legislature.

16. The legislature controls the resources that finance its own internal operation and provide for the perquisites of its own members.

No. The legislature is dependent on the executive for the resources that finance its own operations.

17. Members of the legislature are immune from arrest and/or criminal prosecution.

Yes. Legislators are immune with the common exception for cases of *flagrante delicto.*

Article 52
The members of the National Assembly possess parliamentary immunity. As a consequence, no deputy may be pursued, investigated or arrested, detained or sentenced for reason of the views [expressed] or votes issued by him in the exercise of his functions. During the session, no deputy may be pursued or arrested in criminal matters without the authorization of the National Assembly, granted by secret vote with the absolute majority of the members composing the Assembly. Out of session, no deputy may be pursued or arrested without the authorization of the Bureau of the National Assembly. The authorization may be suspended if the National Assembly so decides by absolute majority. The deputy who has been caught *flagrante delicto* or is on the run after the perpetration of an offense or crime may be pursued and arrested without the authorization of the National Assembly or its Bureau. Except in cases in which his parliamentary

immunity is suspended, the pursuit of a deputy is postponed until the end of his term, if the National Assembly so requires, by a vote of the absolute majority of its members.

The deputy who has been the object of a final criminal conviction is removed from the list of the deputies of the National Assembly in the conditions established by an organic law.

18. All members of the legislature are elected; the executive lacks the power to appoint any members of the legislature.

Yes. All members of the legislature are elected.

Article 49
The Central African people elects by direct universal suffrage the citizens who compose PARLIAMENT and who carry the title of DEPUTY.

19. The legislature alone, without the involvement of any other agencies, can change the Constitution.

Yes. The legislature alone can change the constitution with a three-fourths majority vote. The Constitutional Court comments on proposed amendments, but its opinion is not binding.

Article 76
The draft amendments to the Constitution are submitted to the Constitutional Court for advice by the President of the Republic or the President of the National Assembly before they are submitted to the referendum or the vote of the National Assembly.

Article 106
The initiative of amending the Constitution belongs concurrently to the President of the Republic and the National Assembly deciding by a two-thirds majority of its members.

Article 107
The Constitution is amended when the draft amendment has been approved in the form submitted by a three-fourths majority of the members composing the National Assembly or has been adopted by referendum.

20. The legislature's approval is necessary for the declaration of war.

No. Formally, the legislature declares war. In practice, the president can declare war without the legislature's approval.

Article 59
Only the National Assembly has the power to authorize the declaration of war. It meets in special session for this purpose. The President of the Republic informs the Nation by message about it.

21. The legislature's approval is necessary to ratify treaties with foreign countries.

Yes. The legislature's approval is necessary to ratify international treaties on most major issues.

Article 22
[The President] negotiates and ratifies international treaties and agreements.

Article 69
The President of the Republic negotiates, signs, ratifies and denounces international treaties and agreements. The ratification or the denunciation may only intervene after authorization of Parliament, in particular where it concerns peace treaties, defense treaties, commercial treaties, treaties relating to the environment and natural resources or agreements relating to an international organization, [treaties] which have an impact upon the finances of the State, modify dispositions of a legislative nature, affect the status of persons and the Rights of Man or involve the cession, exchange or addition of territory.

22. The legislature has the power to grant amnesty.

Yes. The legislature has exclusive power to pass legislation that is "regulated by statute." This includes the power to grant amnesty.

Article 61
[The following] are regulated by statute:
(1) The rules concerning the following matters:
– amnesty.

23. The legislature has the power of pardon.

No. The president has the power of pardon.

Article 22
[The President] has the right of pardon.

24. The legislature reviews and has the right to reject appointments to the judiciary; or the legislature itself appoints members of the judiciary.

No. The legislature as a body does not appoint or approve appointments to the judiciary, although the president of the National Assembly appoints two of the nine members of the Constitutional Court.

Article 74
The Constitutional Court consists of nine members, at least three of whom are women; they carry the title of Counselor.

The non-renewable term of office of the Counselors is seven years.

The members of the Constitutional Court are designated as follows:
– two Magistrates, including one woman, who are elected by their peers;
– one Lawyer elected by his peers;
– two professors of law elected by their peers;
– two members, including one woman, appointed by the President of the Republic;
– two members, including one woman, appointed by the President of the National Assembly.

Article 94

A High Court of Justice is established as a non-permanent court.

It is composed of six magistrates and six deputies elected by secret ballot by their peers. The President of the High Court of Justice is elected from among the magistrates, and the Vice-President from among the deputies, in the same manner as specified above.

25. The chairman of the central bank is appointed by the legislature.

No. The Central African Republic belongs to the Bank of Central African States, whose governor is selected by the member countries.

26. The legislature has a substantial voice in the operation of the state-owned media.

No. The legislature lacks a substantial voice in the operation of the public media.

27. The legislature is regularly in session.

No. The legislature meets in ordinary session for less than six months each year.

Article 54

The National Assembly meets as of right in two ordinary sessions every year, with a maximum duration of ninety days each. The first session begins on the first of March, the second session on the first of October.

28. Each legislator has a personal secretary.

No.

29. Each legislator has at least one non-secretarial staff member with policy expertise.

No.

30. Legislators are eligible for re-election without any restriction.

Yes. There are no restrictions on re-election.

31. A seat in the legislature is an attractive enough position that legislators are generally interested in and seek re-election.

Yes. The legislative elections in 2005, for example, included over 900 candidates for 105 seats in the legislature.

32. The re-election of incumbent legislators is common enough that at any given time the legislature contains a significant number of highly experienced members.

No. Severe political turbulence has contributed to high turnover in the legislature and has prevented the emergence of a body of highly experienced members.

NATIONAL ASSEMBLY OF CHAD (*ASSEMBLÉE NATIONALE*)

Expert consultants: Alain Faupin, Barrie Hoffman

Score: .22

Influence over executive (1/9)		Institutional autonomy (2/9)		Specified powers (2/8)		Institutional capacity (2/6)	
1. replace		10. no dissolution		19. amendments		27. sessions	
2. serve as ministers		11. no decree		20. war	X	28. secretary	
3. interpellate		12. no veto		21. treaties	X	29. staff	
4. investigate		13. no review		22. amnesty		30. no term limits	X
5. oversee police		14. no gatekeeping	X	23. pardon		31. seek re-election	X
6. appoint PM		15. no impoundment		24. judiciary		32. experience	
7. appoint ministers		16. control resources		25. central bank			
8. lack president		17. immunity		26. media			
9. no confidence	X	18. all elected	X				

The National Assembly (*Assemblée nationale*) of Chad was established in the 1996 constitution. The document calls for a bicameral National Assembly, although the upper house, the Senate, has not yet been created. From independence in 1960 until the present, Chad has been plagued by internal violence, political instability, and foreign military intervention. Chad has had a succession of constitutions; in practice, however, the military or a hegemonic party has invariably ruled with little regard for the law.

A lull in the violence during the 1990s led to the adoption of the present constitution. Legislative elections were held in 1997 and 2002. War has returned to Chad in the form of an armed insurrection in the north that began in 1998 and cross-border unrest originating in neighboring Darfur, Sudan, that started in 2003. The wars and coups that plague Chad prevent the National Assembly from functioning as a working legislature.

SURVEY

1. The legislature alone, without the involvement of any other agencies, can impeach the president or replace the prime minister.

No. Presidential impeachment requires the involvement of the High Court of Justice.

> Article 180
> Impeachment of the President of the Republic and members of the Government is voted by secret ballot, by a majority of two-thirds of the members composing each of the two chambers of Parliament. The President of the Republic and the members of the Government are suspended in their functions in case of impeachment. In case of indictment, the President of the Republic is stripped of his powers and the ministers of their functions by the High Court of Justice.

2. Ministers may serve simultaneously as members of the legislature.

No. Ministers are prohibited from serving simultaneously in the legislature.

> Article 105
> The functions of a member of the Government are incompatible with the exercise of any parliamentary mandate.

3. The legislature has powers of summons over executive branch officials and hearings with executive branch officials testifying before the legislature or its committees are regularly held.

No. Formally, the constitution grants the legislature the power to interpellate officials from the executive, but in practice, this power is not exercised.

> Article 141
> One session every other week is reserved to the questions of the members of Parliament and to the answers by the Government.

> Article 145
> The Government must provide the Parliament all the explanations it demands concerning its management and concerning its activities.

The means of information and control of the Parliament on the action of Government are:
– interpellation;
– written question;
– oral question;
– the Commission of inquiry;
– the motion of censure;
– the hearing in Commissions.
These means are exercised according to conditions specified by the Internal Regulations of each chamber.

4. The legislature can conduct independent investigation of the chief executive and the agencies of the executive.

No. Formally, the legislature can establish commissions of inquiry to investigate the actions of the government. In practice, it would be unthinkable for the legislature to launch an investigation of the executive branch.

> Article 145
> The Government must provide the Parliament all the explanations it demands concerning its management and concerning its activities.
> The means of information and control of the Parliament on the action of Government are:
> – interpellation;
> – written question;
> – oral question;
> – the Commission of inquiry;
> – the motion of censure;
> – the hearing in Commissions.
> These means are exercised according to conditions specified by the Internal Regulations of each chamber.

5. The legislature has effective powers of oversight over the agencies of coercion (the military, organs of law enforcement, intelligence services, and the secret police).

No. The legislature lacks effective powers of oversight over the agencies of coercion.

6. The legislature appoints the prime minister.

No. The president appoints the prime minister.

> Article 79
> The President of the Republic appoints the Prime Minister.

7. The legislature's approval is required to confirm the appointment of ministers; or the legislature itself appoints ministers.

No. The president appoints ministers on the proposal of the prime minister, and ministerial appointments do not require the legislature's approval.

> Article 95
> The other members of the Government are appointed by the President of the Republic on the proposal of the Prime Minister.

8. The country lacks a presidency entirely or there is a presidency, but the president is elected by the legislature.

No. The president is directly elected.

> Article 61
> The President of the Republic is elected for a five-year mandate by direct universal suffrage.

9. The legislature can vote no confidence in the government.

Yes. The legislature can adopt a motion of censure against the government.

> Article 143
> When the National Assembly adopts a motion of censure or when it disapproves the program or a declaration of general policy of the Government, the Prime Minister must present the resignation of the Government to the President of the Republic.

10. The legislature is immune from dissolution by the executive.

No. The president can dissolve the legislature.

> Article 83
> When the regular functioning of the public powers is threatened by persistent crises between the executive power and the legislative power, or if the National Assembly, in the space of a year, overthrows the Government in two instances, the President of the Republic may, following consultation with the Prime Minister and the Presidents of the two Assemblies, declare the dissolution of the National Assembly.

11. Any executive initiative on legislation requires ratification or approval by the legislature before it takes effect; that is, the executive lacks decree power.

No. The government can issue decrees that have the force of law. Decrees, once passed into law, can be modified only by subsequent legislation.

> Article 129
> For the execution of its program, the Government may demand from the Parliament the authorization to take by ordinances, for a limited time, measures which are normally of the domain of the law. The ordinances are adopted in the Council of Ministers after consultation with the administrative chamber of the Supreme Court. They enter into force upon their publication and become lapsed if the bill of the law of ratification is not presented to the Parliament before the date established by the enabling law. At the expiration of the time limit mentioned in the first paragraph of this article, ordinances cannot be further modified except by the law, in matters which are of the legislative domain.

12. Laws passed by the legislature are veto-proof or essentially veto-proof; that is, the executive lacks veto power, or has veto power but the veto can be overridden by a majority in the legislature.

No. Formally, the legislature can override a presidential veto by a majority vote of its present members. In practice, laws do not pass without presidential approval.

> Article 81
> The President of the Republic ... may, before the expiration of this time limit, demand of Parliament a new deliberation of the law or certain of its articles.

13. The legislature's laws are supreme and not subject to judicial review.

No. The Constitutional Council can review the constitutionality of laws.

> Article 166
> The Constitutional Council is the judge of the constitutionality of laws, treaties and international agreements.

14. The legislature has the right to initiate bills in all policy jurisdictions; the executive lacks gatekeeping authority.

Yes. The legislature can initiate bills in all policy jurisdictions.

15. Expenditure of funds appropriated by the legislature is mandatory; the executive lacks the power to impound funds appropriated by the legislature.

No. The president controls the disbursement of funds.

16. The legislature controls the resources that finance its own internal operation and provide for the perquisites of its own members.

No. According to the constitution, the legislature provides for the perquisites of its members, but in practice, this provision is a dead letter. The legislature is dependent on the executive for the resources that finance its own operations.

> Article 113
> An organic law establishes the number of members of each Assembly, their allowances, their regime of ineligibilities and of incompatibilities.

17. Members of the legislature are immune from arrest and/or criminal prosecution.

No. Formally, legislators are immune with the common exception for cases of *flagrante delicto*, here expressed as "in the case of a flagrant offense." In practice, the president has the power to revoke legislators' immunity.

> Article 114
> The members of the Parliament enjoy parliamentary immunity. No member of Parliament may be prosecuted, sought, arrested, detained or judged for opinions or votes expressed by him in the exercise of his functions. No member of Parliament may, during session, be prosecuted or arrested in a criminal or correctional matter without the authorization of the Assembly to which

he belongs, except in the case of a flagrant offense. No member of Parliament may, in between sessions, be arrested without the authorization of the Bureau of his Assembly, except in the case of a flagrant offense, of authorized prosecution or of definitive condemnation. In case of crime or established offense, the immunity may be revoked by the Assembly to which the member of Parliament belongs during the sessions, or by the Bureau of the same Assembly between sessions. In case of flagrant offense, the Bureau of the Assembly to which the member of Parliament belongs is notified immediately of the arrest.

18. All members of the legislature are elected; the executive lacks the power to appoint any members of the legislature.

Yes. All members of the legislature are elected.

> Article 107
> The Deputies are elected by universal suffrage.

> Article 110
> The Senators are elected by indirect universal suffrage, by an electoral college composed of the regional, departmental, and municipal councilors.

19. The legislature alone, without the involvement of any other agencies, can change the Constitution.

No. Constitutional amendments require approval in a popular referendum. "Technical revisions" of the constitution, however, can be passed by a three-fifths majority vote in both houses of the legislature.

> Article 223
> The initiative of the revision belongs concurrently to the President of the Republic upon decision taken in the Council of Ministers and to the members of Parliament. To be taken into consideration, any draft or proposition of revision must be voted on, in identical terms, by a two-thirds majority of the members of the National Assembly and the Senate.

> Article 224
> The revision of the Constitution is approved by referendum. However, a technical revision may take place with the approval of a three-fifths majority of the members of the National Assembly and the Senate meeting in Congress.

20. The legislature's approval is necessary for the declaration of war.

Yes. The legislature's approval is necessary for the declaration of war.

> Article 127
> The declaration of war is authorized by the Parliament.

21. The legislature's approval is necessary to ratify treaties with foreign countries.

Yes. The legislature's approval is necessary to ratify international treaties on most major issues.

> Article 219
> The President of the Republic negotiates and ratifies the treaties. He is informed of all negotiations aiming to conclude any international agreement not submitted to ratification.

> Article 220
> Peace treaties, defense treaties, commercial treaties, treaties concerning the use of national territory or the exploitation of natural resources, agreements concerning international organization, those that involve State finances or those concerning the well-being of persons may be approved or ratified only upon the authorization of the Parliament. These treaties and agreements take effect only after being approved and ratified.

22. The legislature has the power to grant amnesty.

No. Formally, the legislature has the power to grant amnesty. In practice, amnesty is granted by the president.

> Article 125
> The law is passed by the Parliament.
> The law determines the rules concerning... amnesty.

23. The legislature has the power of pardon.

No. The president has the power of pardon.

> Article 89
> The President of the Republic exercises the right of pardon.

24. The legislature reviews and has the right to reject appointments to the judiciary; or the legislature itself appoints members of the judiciary.

No. The legislature as a body does not appoint or approve appointments to the judiciary, although the president of the National Assembly and the president of the Senate have some formal appointment powers. The Senate, although established on paper in the 1995 constitution, does not even exist in practice.

> Article 151
> The President of the Republic presides over the Superior Council of the Magistrature. The Minister of Justice is by right its First Vice President. The President of the Supreme Court is its second Vice President. The other members of the Superior Council of the Magistrature are elected by their peers, according to conditions specified by the law.

> Article 152
> The Superior Council of the Magistrature proposes the appointments and the promotions of the magistrates.

> Article 153
> The magistrates are appointed by a decree of the President of the Republic, upon affirmation of the Superior Council of the Magistrature.

Article 158

The President of the Supreme Court...is appointed by a decree of the President of the Republic upon consultation with the Presidents of the National Assembly and of the Senate.

The Counsellors are designated in the following fashion:

- eight chosen [from] among the high magistrates of the judicial order respectively:
- three by the President of the Republic;
- three by the President of the National Assembly;
- two by the President of the Senate.
- seven chosen [from] among the specialists of Administrative Law, Budgetary Law and [Law] of the Public Accounts, respectively:
- three by the President of the Republic;
- two by the President of the National Assembly;
- two by the President of the Senate.

Article 165

The Constitutional Council is composed of nine members including three magistrates and six jurists of the high level designated in the following manner:

- one magistrate and two jurists by the President of the Republic;
- one magistrate and two jurists by the President of the National Assembly;
- one magistrate and two jurists by the President of the Senate.

25. The chairman of the central bank is appointed by the legislature.

No. Chad belongs to the Bank of Central African States, whose governor is selected by the member countries.

26. The legislature has a substantial voice in the operation of the state-owned media.

No. The president appoints the members of the High Council of Communication, the body that oversees the state-owned media.

Article 184

The High Council of Communication is composed of nine members appointed by decree of the President of the Republic.

Article 186

The High Council of Communication:

- sees to the respect of ethical rules in matters of information and communication;
- guarantees the freedom of the press and pluralistic expression of opinions;

- regulates the relationship of communication between the public powers, the organs of information and the public;
- assures to the political parties equal access to the public media;
- guarantees to the associations equal access to the public media;
- gives technical advice, [and] recommendations on the questions concerning the domaine of information.

27. The legislature is regularly in session.

No. The legislature meets in two ordinary sessions, and neither session can exceed ninety days. In practice, civil turmoil prevents the legislature from meeting even this frequently.

Article 121

The Parliament meets of right in two ordinary sessions a year...The duration of each session cannot exceed ninety days.

28. Each legislator has a personal secretary.

No.

29. Each legislator has at least one non-secretarial staff member with policy expertise.

No.

30. Legislators are eligible for re-election without any restriction.

Yes. There are no restrictions on re-election.

Article 109

The mandate of Deputy is four years [and is] renewable.

Article 112

The duration of the mandate of the Senators is six years, renewable by thirds every other year.

31. A seat in the legislature is an attractive enough position that legislators are generally interested in and seek re-election.

Yes.

32. The re-election of incumbent legislators is common enough that at any given time the legislature contains a significant number of highly experienced members.

No. The legislature in Chad is relatively young and ineffectual. Legislators lack substantial expertise.

CONGRESS OF CHILE (*CONGRESO*)

Expert consultants: John M. Carey, Ernst Hillebrand, Maiah Jaskoski, Patricio D. Navia, Philip Oxhorn, Ricardo Israel Zipper

Score: .56

Influence over executive (3/9)		Institutional autonomy (4/9)		Specified powers (5/8)		Institutional capacity (6/6)	
1. replace	X	10. no dissolution	X	19. amendments		27. sessions	X
2. serve as ministers		11. no decree	X	20. war	X	28. secretary	X
3. interpellate	X	12. no veto		21. treaties	X	29. staff	X
4. investigate	X	13. no review		22. amnesty	X	30. no term limits	X
5. oversee police		14. no gatekeeping		23. pardon		31. seek re-election	X
6. appoint PM		15. no impoundment		24. judiciary	X	32. experience	X
7. appoint ministers		16. control resources	X	25. central bank			
8. lack president		17. immunity		26. media	X		
9. no confidence		18. all elected	X				

The Congress (*Congreso*) of Chile was established in the 1812 constitution upon independence from Spain. The bicameral Congress consists of a lower house, the Chamber of Deputies (*Cámara de Diputados*), and an upper house, the Senate (*Senado*). Chile adopted new constitutions in 1833 and 1925. In 1973 the military, led by General Augusto Pinochet, overthrew the government and disbanded Congress. Pinochet had himself appointed president and drew up a new constitution in 1980 that allowed the president arbitrarily to declare a state of emergency, appoint members of the Senate, and dissolve the Chamber of Deputies.

Pinochet's reign ended in 1990, following a 1988 plebiscite in which citizens voted for a return to civilian rule. In 1989, during the transition to civilian rule, the 1980 constitution fully came into force, accompanied by reforms that curtailed the president's powers to declare a state of emergency and eliminated the president's right to dissolve the Chamber of Deputies. Reforms in 2005 abolished the institution of appointed Senators and the automatic granting of membership of the Senate to former presidents.

The Congress of Chile is limited in its ability to influence the executive, although it can remove the president from office and has some powers of oversight. Its own institutional autonomy is circumscribed by presidential veto and gatekeeping powers. It enjoys a number of specified powers and prerogatives and a high level of institutional capacity.

SURVEY

1. The legislature alone, without the involvement of any other agencies, can impeach the president or replace the prime minister.

Yes. The Chamber of Deputies can accuse the president of acts that gravely compromise the honor and the security of the nation or that openly violate the constitutions or laws. The Senate can declare the president guilty and dismiss him or her from office by a two-thirds majority vote of its present members.

Article 52
The exclusive powers of the Chamber of Deputies are:
2. To declare whether or not accusations made by no less than ten or more than twenty of its members against the following persons have merit:
    a. The President of the Republic, for acts of his/her administration which have gravely compromised the honor and the security of the Nation, or have openly violated the Constitution or the laws. This accusation may be filed while the President is in office and within

six months following the expiration of his/her term. During the latter period he/she may not leave the Republic without the approval of the Chamber.

Article 53
The exclusive powers of the Senate are:
1. To decide on the accusations submitted to it by the Chamber of Deputies in accordance with the preceding article. The Senate shall act as jury and shall be limited to declare whether or not the accused is guilty of the offense, infraction or abuse of power imputed to him. The declaration of guilt must be pronounced by two-thirds of the senators in office when the accusation is brought against the President of the Republic, and by the majority of the senators in office in other cases. By the declaration of guilt, the accused shall be dismissed from his/her position and may not perform any public function, whether elective or not, until five years have passed. The official declared guilty shall be judged in accordance with the laws by a competent court in order to apply the penalty attached to the crime, if any, as well as in order to establish civil liability for the harm and damage caused to the State or to private individuals.

2. Ministers may serve simultaneously as members of the legislature.

No. Ministers are prohibited from serving simultaneously in the legislature.

3. The legislature has powers of summons over executive branch officials and hearings with executive branch officials testifying before the legislature or its committees are regularly held.

Yes. The legislature regularly summons executive branch officials for questioning.

Article 37
Without prejudice to the foregoing, the Ministers have to personally take part in the special sessions which are convened by the Chamber of Deputies or Senators in order to inform themselves on matters falling within the sphere of competences of the respective Secretaries of State which they agree to discuss.

Article 52
The exclusive powers of the Chamber of Deputies are:
1. To oversee the acts of the Government. In order to exercise this power, the Chamber may:
   a. with the vote of the majority of deputies present, adopt resolutions or submit observations which shall be transmitted in writing to the President of the Republic who must give a reasoned reply, through the competent Minister of State, within thirty days. Without prejudice to the foregoing, any deputy may, with the favorable vote of one-third of the Chamber members present, request specific documents from the Government. The President of the Republic shall give a reasoned reply, through the competent Minister of State, within the delay specified in the preceding paragraph. In no case shall the resolutions, observations or requests of documents

affect the political responsibility of the Ministers of State;
   b. summon a Minister of State, upon the application of at least one-third of the deputies in office, in order to question him/her on matters related to the exercise of his/her functions.

4. The legislature can conduct independent investigation of the chief executive and the agencies of the executive.

Yes. The Chamber of Deputies can establish special committees to investigate the executive.

Article 52
The exclusive powers of the Chamber of Deputies are:
c. establish special investigation committees upon the application of at least two-fifths of the deputies in office, with the objective to collect information in relation to specific Government actions. The investigation committees may, upon application of one-third of its members, issue summons and request documents. The Ministers of State, the other officials of the Administration and the staff of the companies run by the Government or of those in which the State holds a majority share, who are summoned by these committees shall be obliged to appear before them and to deliver the documents and the information which have been requested from them.

5. The legislature has effective powers of oversight over the agencies of coercion (the military, organs of law enforcement, intelligence services, and the secret police).

No. The legislature lacks effective powers of oversight over the agencies of coercion.

6. The legislature appoints the prime minister.

No. There is no prime minister.

7. The legislature's approval is required to confirm the appointment of ministers; or the legislature itself appoints ministers.

No. The president appoints ministers and the appointments do not require the legislature's approval.

Article 32
Special powers of the President of the Republic are:
7. To appoint and remove at will Ministers of State, Under-Secretaries, Superintendents and Governors.

8. The country lacks a presidency entirely or there is a presidency, but the president is elected by the legislature.

No. The president is directly elected.

Article 26
The President of the Republic shall be elected by direct ballot and by an absolute majority of the votes validly cast.

9. The legislature can vote no confidence in the government.

No. The legislature cannot vote no confidence in the government.

10. The legislature is immune from dissolution by the executive.

Yes. The legislature is immune from dissolution.

11. Any executive initiative on legislation requires ratification or approval by the legislature before it takes effect; that is, the executive lacks decree power.

Yes. The executive lacks decree power. The legislature can delegate temporary decree powers to the president in specific issue areas.

Article 32
Special powers of the President of the Republic are:
3. To dictate, subject to the prior authorization by Congress, decrees with the force of law on the matters determined by the Constitution.

Article 64
The President of the Republic may request authorization from the National Congress in order to issue provisions with the force of law during a period not exceeding more than one year on matters which fall within the domain of the law.

12. Laws passed by the legislature are veto-proof or essentially veto-proof; that is, the executive lacks veto power, or has veto power but the veto can be overridden by a majority in the legislature.

No. A two-thirds majority in both houses is needed to override a presidential veto.

Article 73
If the President of the Republic disapproves of the bill, it shall be returned to the Chamber of origin with the appropriate observations within a period of thirty days. In no case shall observations be admitted which do not have a direct relation with the central or fundamental ideas of the bill, unless they had been considered in the respective message. If the two Chambers approve the observations, the bill shall have the force of law and shall be returned to the President for its promulgation. If the two Chambers reject all or some of the observations, and persist with two-thirds of their members present with the whole or part of the draft approved by them, it shall be returned to the President for its promulgation.

13. The legislature's laws are supreme and not subject to judicial review.

No. The Constitutional Tribunal can review the constitutionality of laws.

Article 93
The powers of the Constitutional Tribunal are:
1. To control the constitutionality of laws interpreting a provision of the Constitution, of constitutional organic laws and of treaty rules relating to matters governed by them [the Constitution and the constitutional organic laws] before their promulgation.

14. The legislature has the right to initiate bills in all policy jurisdictions; the executive lacks gatekeeping authority.

No. The legislature is prohibited from introducing legislation related to the financial administration of the state, taxation, government loans, wages and pensions, or social security.

Article 65
The President of the Republic has the exclusive initiative for legal projects related to the alteration of the political or administrative division of the country or to the financial or budgetary administration of the State, including the amendments to the Budget Law.
Likewise, the President of the Republic shall also have the exclusive initiative for:
1. Imposing, suppressing, reducing or approving taxes of any type or nature, establishing exemptions or amending those in existence, and determining their form, proportionality or progression;
2. Creating new public services or remunerated jobs, whether they have a fiscal, semi-fiscal or autonomous character or the character of a State enterprise; suppressing them and determining their functions or attributes;
3. Contracting loans or carrying out any other operations that may compromise the credit or the financial responsibility of the State, of the semi-fiscal entities, autonomous agencies, of the regional governments or of the municipalities, and approving, reducing or amending obligations, interest, and other financial burdens of any nature established on behalf of the National Treasury or of the central organs or entities;
4. Fixing, modifying, granting or increasing wages, retirement payments, pensions, widows' pensions, rents and any other type of payments, loans or benefits to persons in service or in retirement and to the beneficiaries of the widows' and orphans' allowance of the Public Administration and of the other organizations and entities previously mentioned, as well as the fixing of minimum wages for workers of the private sector, the mandatory increase of their salaries and other economic benefits or the alteration of the bases which serve to determine them; all of this without prejudice to the provisions in the following numerals;
5. Establishing the norms and procedures of collective bargaining and determining the cases where bargaining is not allowed; and
6. Establishing or amending the rules on or regarding social security of both the public and the private sector.
The National Congress may only accept, reduce or reject the services, employments, payments, loans, benefits, expenditures and other initiatives on the matter that the President of the Republic proposes.

Article 67
The draft of the Budget Law must be presented by the President of the Republic to the National Congress at

least three months prior to the date on which it must start to be effective; and if the Congress does not pass it within sixty days from the date of its submission, the draft submitted by the President of the Republic shall become effective.

The National Congress may not increase nor diminish the estimation of revenues; it may only reduce the expenditures contained in the draft of the Budget Law, except those established by permanent law.

15. Expenditure of funds appropriated by the legislature is mandatory; the executive lacks the power to impound funds appropriated by the legislature.

No. The president can impound funds appropriated by the legislature.

16. The legislature controls the resources that finance its own internal operation and provide for the perquisites of its own members.

Yes. The legislature enjoys financial autonomy, including control over members' salaries.

Article 62
Deputies and senators shall receive as sole compensation a fee equal to the remuneration of a Minister of State including all the corresponding allowances.

17. Members of the legislature are immune from arrest and/or criminal prosecution.

No. Legislators are immune with the common exception for cases of *flagrante delicto,* but immunity can be revoked by the Court of Appeals.

Article 61
Deputies and senators are only inviolable with regard to the opinions they express and the votes they cast in performance of their duties in congressional sessions or committees. No deputy or senator, from the day of his/her election or from the taking of the oath, as the case may be, may be accused or deprived of his/her freedom except if he/she is caught in *flagrante delicto,* unless the Court of Appeals of the respective jurisdiction has previously authorized in plenary session the accusation, declaring that the case has merit. This decision may be appealed before the Supreme Court. In the case of a deputy or senator who is arrested on charges of a crime committed in *flagrante delicto,* he/she shall be brought immediately before the respective Court of Appeals with the corresponding summary information. The Court shall then proceed in accordance with the provisions of the aforementioned paragraphs. From the time it is declared by a firm resolution that the case has merit, the defendant deputy or senator shall be suspended from his/her position and submitted to the competent judge.

18. All members of the legislature are elected; the executive lacks the power to appoint any members of the legislature.

Yes. All members of the legislature are elected. Prior to 2005 nine senators were appointed; the president, the National Security Council, and the Supreme Court each made several appointments. Furthermore, former presidents who had completed a full term enjoyed status as senators-for-life. In 2005 the terms of the appointed members expired and the institution of appointed senators and senators-for-life was abolished. The Senate now consists of thirty-eight elected members.

Article 47
The Chamber of Deputies is composed of one hundred and twenty members elected by direct ballot in the electoral district established by the respective organic constitutional law.

Article 49
The Senate shall be composed of members elected by direct ballot in senatorial constituencies, with regard to the regions of the countries.

19. The legislature alone, without the involvement of any other agencies, can change the Constitution.

No. The legislature alone cannot change the constitution without the approval of the president. If the president objects to a constitutional amendment that has been passed by a two-thirds majority vote in Congress, he or she can choose to put the amendment to a popular referendum.

Article 127
Bills to amend the Constitution may be initiated by a message of the President of the Republic or by a motion of any member of the National Congress . . . In order to be approved, the reform bill shall require in each Chamber the consent of three-fifths of the deputies and senators in office. If the reform has an impact on Chapters I, III, VIII, XI, XII, or XV it shall need, in each Chamber, the approval of the two-thirds of the deputies and senators in office.

Article 128
The bill approved by both Chambers shall be submitted to the President of the Republic.

If the President of the Republic entirely rejects a reform bill approved by both Chambers and the latter insists upon the proposal in all its parts by two-thirds of the members in office of each Chamber, the President shall have to promulgate the proposal unless he/she consults the citizens through a plebiscite. If the President partially objects to the reform bill approved by both Chambers, the objections shall be understood to have been approved by a supporting vote of three-fifths or two-thirds of the members in office of each Chamber in conformity with the preceding article, and the bill shall be returned to the President for its promulgation. In case the Chambers do not approve all or some of the objections made by the President, no constitutional reform shall take place on the issues on which there is disagreement, unless two-thirds of the members in office of both Chambers insist upon the part of the bill approved by them. In the latter case, the part of the bill which has been the object of the insisting vote shall be returned to the President for its promulgation, unless the President consults the citizens through a plebiscite with respect to the matters in dispute.

Article 129
The convening of the plebiscite must take place within thirty days following the date on which both Chambers have insisted upon the proposal approved by them, and is decided by supreme decree fixing the date on which the plebiscite is to be held, which may not take place earlier than thirty days or later than sixty days after the publication of this decree. If this period expires and the President has not convoked a plebiscite, the proposal approved by Congress shall be promulgated. The decree of convocation shall contain, as the case may be, the proposal approved by the Plenary Congress and vetoed in total by the President of the Republic, or the parts of the bill on which the Congress has insisted [remain valid]. In the latter case, each of the issues on which there is disagreement shall be voted upon separately in the plebiscite. The Elections Tribunal shall communicate to the President of the Republic the result of the plebiscite and specify the text of the bill approved by the citizens which shall be promulgated as a constitutional reform within five days following this communication. Once the bill has been promulgated, and as of the date it enters into force, its provisions shall become a part of the Constitution and shall be regarded as incorporated therein.

20. The legislature's approval is necessary for the declaration of war.

Yes. The legislature's approval is necessary for presidential war declarations.

Article 32
Special powers of the President of the Republic are:
19. To declare war, after authorization by law and after having heard the National Security Council.

Article 63
Only the following are legislative matters:
15. Those that authorize the declaration of war upon the proposal of the President of the Republic.

21. The legislature's approval is necessary to ratify treaties with foreign countries.

Yes. The legislature's approval is necessary to ratify international treaties.

Article 32
Special powers of the President of the Republic are:
15. To . . . sign and ratify treaties deemed beneficial to the interest of the country, which must be submitted to the approval of Congress.

22. The legislature has the power to grant amnesty.

Yes. The legislature has the power to grant amnesty.

Article 63
Only the following are legislative matters:
16. Those that concede general pardons and amnesties.

23. The legislature has the power of pardon.

No. The power of pardon, or the revocation of punishment for individuals, rests with the president. Congress can legislate on "general pardons," which are normally understood in Chile as amnesties, meaning the revocation of punishment for groups of people.

Article 63
Only the following are legislative matters:
16. Those that concede general pardons and amnesties.

24. The legislature reviews and has the right to reject appointments to the judiciary; or the legislature itself appoints members of the judiciary.

Yes. The legislature appoints four of the ten members of the Constitutional Council.

Article 92
There shall be a Constitutional Tribunal composed of ten members appointed in the following manner:
a. Three members appointed by the President of the Republic;
b. Four members elected by the National Congress. Two members shall be appointed directly by the Senate, and two shall be proposed by the Chamber of Deputies for approval or rejection by the Senate. The appointments, or the proposal for appointment, take place by single ballot and require for their approval the favorable vote of two-thirds of the senators and deputies in office, as the case may be.

25. The chairman of the central bank is appointed by the legislature.

No. The president appoints the governor of the Central Bank of Chile.

26. The legislature has a substantial voice in the operation of the state-owned media.

Yes. The legislature has a substantial voice in the operation of the public media.

27. The legislature is regularly in session.

Yes. The legislature is in session for at least six months every year.

28. Each legislator has a personal secretary.

Yes.

29. Each legislator has at least one non-secretarial staff member with policy expertise.

Yes.

30. Legislators are eligible for re-election without any restriction.

Yes. There are no restrictions on re-election.

Article 51
Parliamentarians may be re-elected to their offices.

31. A seat in the legislature is an attractive enough position that legislators are generally interested in and seek re-election.
Yes.

32. The re-election of incumbent legislators is common enough that at any given time the legislature contains a significant number of highly experienced members.

Yes. Re-election rates are sufficiently high to produce a significant number of highly experienced members.

CHINESE NATIONAL PEOPLE'S CONGRESS (*QUANGUO RENMIN DAIBIAO DAHUI*)

Expert consultants: Jean-Pierre Cabestan, Michael Dowdle, Bruce Gilley, Kevin J. O'Brien, Dali L. Yang

Score: .34

Influence over executive (3/9)		Institutional autonomy (3/9)		Specified powers (2/8)		Institutional capacity (3/6)	
1. replace		10. no dissolution	X	19. amendments		27. sessions	
2. serve as ministers		11. no decree		20. war	X	28. secretary	
3. interpellate	X	12. no veto	X	21. treaties	X	29. staff	
4. investigate	X	13. no review		22. amnesty		30. no term limits	X
5. oversee police		14. no gatekeeping	X	23. pardon		31. seek re-election	X
6. appoint PM		15. no impoundment		24. judiciary		32. experience	X
7. appoint ministers	X	16. control resources		25. central bank			
8. lack president		17. immunity		26. media			
9. no confidence		18. all elected					

The Chinese National People's Congress (NPC) (*Quanguo Renmin Daibiao Dahui*) was established in 1954 in the first formal post-revolutionary constitution of the People's Republic of China. The NPC was formally vested with exclusive lawmaking powers, although in practice it remained impotent under Mao Zedong's centralized rule. Constitutional changes in 1975 and 1978 formalized NPC weakness, explicitly subordinating the legislature to the Chinese Communist Party (CCP) and abolishing the NPC's exclusive lawmaking authority.

In 1982 China drew up its most recent constitution, which formally reestablished the NPC as the "highest organ of national power." Still, China lacks a clear delineation of lawmaking authority, and the NPC shares legislative powers with the CCP and the State Council, an executive organ composed of the premier and ministers. China has a Soviet-type constitution and distribution of powers, meaning that the legislature has supreme lawmaking power on paper, but the party makes the major decisions itself and the legislature ratifies party decisions.

The legislature may, however, exert some influence. Although the CCP in practice remains China's supreme ruling body, and although the threat of the NPC voting down a bill or an appointment is slight, the NPC can embarrass the party by approving bills and appointments by less-than-overwhelming majorities, which it has done with increasing frequency in recent years.

In previous decades NPC membership was generally seen as a politically insignificant honorific bestowed on party cadres. In recent years, however, a position in the NPC, especially in the NPC's permanent organ, the Standing Committee, has been coveted by prominent politicians.

SURVEY

1. The legislature alone, without the involvement of any other agencies, can impeach the president or replace the prime minister.

No. According to law, the legislature does have the power of impeachment, but it has never been exercised, and such action is inconceivable without prior CCP instruction.

> Article 63
> The National People's Congress has the power to recall or remove from office the following persons:
> 1. the President and the Vice President of the People's Republic of China;
> 2. the Premier, Vice Premiers, State Councillors, Ministers in charge of ministries or commissions, and the Auditor General and the Secretary General of the State Council.

2. Ministers may serve simultaneously as members of the legislature.

No. Prior to the 1990s members of the NPC sometimes served simultaneously as ministers. Since the early 1990s the norm has changed, and members of the legislature do not now serve as ministers.

3. The legislature has powers of summons over executive branch officials and hearings with executive branch officials testifying before the legislature or its committees are regularly held.

Yes. The practice of summoning officials is gradually being institutionalized, and the legislature regularly questions officials from the executive. It bears note, however, that some ministers resist testifying before the NPC's committees by sending their deputy or refusing to show up. It remains difficult for the NPC to compel ministers to testify.

> Article 73
> Deputies to the National People's Congress during its sessions, and all those on its Standing Committee during its meetings, have the right to address questions, in accordance with procedures prescribed by law, to the State Council or the ministries and commissions under the State Council, which must answer the questions in a responsible manner.

4. The legislature can conduct independent investigation of the chief executive and the agencies of the executive.

Yes. The Standing Committee conducts investigations every year, writes reports, and sends the reports to the relevant agencies, although the end result is difficult to assess. The plenary session may also request investigations, although it cannot conduct them itself.

5. The legislature has effective powers of oversight over the agencies of coercion (the military, organs of law enforcement, intelligence services, and the secret police).

No. The Standing Committee has some ability to oversee the Ministry of Public Security, which handles regular police work. But neither the Standing Committee nor the plenary session of the legislature, despite the statement contained in Article 94, has oversight authority over the military or the intelligence services.

> Article 94
> The Chairman of the Central Military Commission is responsible to the National People's Congress and its Standing Committee.

6. The legislature appoints the prime minister.

No. The president appoints the premier of the State Council, and the NPC invariably approves the choice.

> Article 62
> The National People's Congress exercises the following functions and powers:
> 5. to decide on the choice of the Premier of the State Council upon nomination by the President of the People's Republic of China and to decide on the choice of the Vice Premiers.

> Article 80
> The President of the People's Republic of China, in pursuance of decisions of the National People's Congress and its Standing Committee, promulgates statutes, appoints and removes the Premier [and] Vice Premiers.

7. The legislature's approval is required to confirm the appointment of ministers; or the legislature itself appoints ministers.

Yes. The NPC must confirm the appointment of every individual minister. The constitution is ambivalent as to who makes the nomination, however. Article 62 states that the premier nominates ministers, but Article 80 suggests that the president may do the job. In practice the CCP picks the sole candidate for each position and submits the choice to the NPC for approval. The NPC can embarrass the party by approving appointments by less-than-overwhelming majorities, which it has done with increasing frequency in recent years. This potential for embarrassing the party encourages informal negotiation on appointment matters. There is reason to believe that the CCP now informally consults with NPC leaders before submitting nominations, which suggests the possibility of informal rejections prior to the official nomination stage. Although the NPC's role is still difficult to assess, it appears to be great enough to warrant an affirmative answer to this item.

> Article 62
> The National People's Congress exercises the following functions and powers:
> 5. to decide on the choice of the Premier of the State Council upon nomination by the President of the People's Republic of China, and to decide on the choice of the Vice Premiers, State Councillors, Ministers in charge of ministries or commissions, and the Auditor General and the Secretary General of the State Council upon nomination by the Premier.

> Article 80
> The President of the People's Republic of China, in pursuance of decisions of the National People's Congress and its Standing Committee, promulgates statutes, appoints and removes the Premier, Vice Premiers, State Councillors, Ministers in charge of ministries or commissions, and the Auditor General and the Secretary General of the State Council.

8. The country lacks a presidency entirely or there is a presidency, but the president is elected by the legislature.

No. The president of the People's Republic is formally elected by the NPC, but the election is strictly pro forma. The single candidate is selected by the CCP leadership.

> Article 62
> The National People's Congress exercises the following functions and powers:
> 4. to elect the President and the Vice President of the People's Republic of China.

> Article 79
> (1) The President and Vice President of the People's Republic of China are elected by the National People's Congress.

9. The legislature can vote no confidence in the government.

No. The legislature cannot vote no confidence in the government.

10. The legislature is immune from dissolution by the executive.

Yes. The NPC is elected every five years and cannot be dissolved before the end of the term.

11. Any executive initiative on legislation requires ratification or approval by the legislature before it takes effect; that is, the executive lacks decree power.

No. In practice, the party decrees laws. Some major initiatives, such as the Three Gorges Dam project, are submitted to the NPC for approval, although such action appears to be aimed primarily at enhancing the legitimacy of momentous and potentially controversial party decisions.

12. Laws passed by the legislature are veto-proof or essentially veto-proof; that is, the executive lacks veto power, or has veto power but the veto can be overridden by a majority in the legislature.

Yes. There is no provision for veto. It merits note, however, that bills are drawn up and approved by the CCP before being submitted to the legislature.

13. The legislature's laws are supreme and not subject to judicial review.

No. Formally, the Standing Committee of the NPC has the exclusive power to interpret the constitution, but in practice, the legislature's laws are not supreme because they are in no respect the handiwork of the National Assembly. Rather, they are the products of the CCP's decisions. The Supreme People's Court has occasionally floated the idea that it has the power to disregard NPC legislation that it considers unconstitutional. This is a controversial claim, however, and has never been acted upon. In practice, party supremacy trumps other provisions.

> Article 67
> The Standing Committee of the National People's Congress exercises the following functions and powers:
> 1. to interpret the Constitution and supervise its enforcement.

14. The legislature has the right to initiate bills in all policy jurisdictions; the executive lacks gatekeeping authority.

Yes. The legislature can initiate bills in all policy jurisdictions.

15. Expenditure of funds appropriated by the legislature is mandatory; the executive lacks the power to impound funds appropriated by the legislature.

No. The NPC's budgetary power was nonexistent until 1999, when a Working Committee on Budgetary Affairs under the Standing Committee was created in order to introduce some supervision, but this supervision remains strictly limited.

16. The legislature controls the resources that finance its own internal operation and provide for the perquisites of its own members.

No. There is little transparency about how the NPC is financed and the degree to which the NPC has financial autonomy. Delegates to the plenary sessions are not even paid; only Standing Committee members receive a salary. In practice, party organs control NPC funds.

17. Members of the legislature are immune from arrest and/or criminal prosecution.

No. By law legislators are immune, but the rule has no actual force. For example, in the late 1990s

Chen Kejie, then NPC vice president, was accused of corruption, expelled from the NPC, and executed.

Article 74
No deputy to the National People's Congress may be arrested or placed on criminal trial without the consent of the Presidium of the current session of the National People's Congress or, when the National People's Congress is not in session, without the consent of its Standing Committee.

18. All members of the legislature are elected; the executive lacks the power to appoint any members of the legislature.

No. Deputies are not directly elected by the people but are selected by the provincial CCP leadership, the central NPC leadership, and, most importantly, the central CCP leadership.

Article 59
(1) The National People's Congress is composed of deputies elected from the provinces, autonomous regions, municipalities directly under the Central Government, and the special administrative regions, and of deputies elected from the armed forces.
(2) Election of deputies to the National People's Congress is conducted by the Standing Committee of the National People's Congress.
(3) The number of deputies to the National People's Congress and the manner of their election are prescribed by law.

19. The legislature alone, without the involvement of any other agencies, can change the Constitution.

No. The NPC formally has the power to alter the constitution, but proposals to change the constitution, in practice, always begin and end with the CCP.

Article 62
The National People's Congress exercises the following functions and powers:
1. to amend the Constitution.

Article 64
(1) Amendments to the Constitution are to be proposed by the Standing Committee of the National People's Congress or by more than one-fifth of the deputies to the National People's Congress and adopted by a majority vote of more than two-thirds of all the deputies to the Congress.

20. The legislature's approval is necessary for the declaration of war.

Yes. Formally, the legislature's approval is necessary to declare war, and there is not sufficient evidence to conclude that this would not also be the case in practice. China has not declared war since the establishment of the present constitution in 1982.

Article 62
The National People's Congress exercises the following functions and powers:
14. to decide on questions of war and peace.

Article 80
The President of the People's Republic of China, in pursuance of decisions of the National People's Congress and its Standing Committee . . . proclaims a state of war; and issues mobilization orders.

21. The legislature's approval is necessary to ratify treaties with foreign countries.

Yes. The legislature's approval is necessary to ratify international treaties.

Article 67
The Standing Committee of the National People's Congress exercises the following functions and powers:
14. to decide on the ratification and abrogation of treaties and important agreements concluded with foreign states.

22. The legislature has the power to grant amnesty.

No. The legislature lacks the power to grant amnesty.

23. The legislature has the power of pardon.

No. The legislature lacks the power of pardon.

24. The legislature reviews and has the right to reject appointments to the judiciary; or the legislature itself appoints members of the judiciary.

No. The NPC formally appoints the members of the Supreme Court and the Supreme Procuratorate, but there is only one candidate for each position, someone who in all cases has been previously selected by the top CCP organs (the Politburo and Central Commission for Law and Politics). The NPC has never failed to approve a judge for one of these courts.

Article 62
The National People's Congress exercises the following functions and powers:
7. to elect the President of the Supreme People's Court.
Article 67
The Standing Committee of the National People's Congress exercises the following functions and powers:
11. to appoint and remove Vice Presidents and judges of the Supreme People's Court, members of its Judicial Committee, and the President of the Military Court at the suggestion of the President of the Supreme People's Court.

25. The chairman of the central bank is appointed by the legislature.

No. The CCP appoints the chairman of the People's Bank of China with the approval of the NPC.

26. The legislature has a substantial voice in the operation of the state-owned media.

No. The legislature lacks a substantial voice in the operation of the public media.

27. The legislature is regularly in session.

No. The plenary session meets only three weeks each year in one session in March. The Standing Committee is more powerful and assertive, but it meets only for 7–10 days every two months.

> Article 61
> (1) The National People's Congress meets in session once a year and is convened by its Standing Committee.

28. Each legislator has a personal secretary.

No. Only the chairman, the fifteen vice chairmen, some members of the Standing Committee, and the secretary general have secretaries.

29. Each legislator has at least one non-secretarial staff member with policy expertise.

No. See item 28.

30. Legislators are eligible for re-election without any restriction.

Yes. There are no restrictions on re-election.

31. A seat in the legislature is an attractive enough position that legislators are generally interested in and seek re-election.

Yes. In previous decades NPC membership was generally seen as a politically insignificant honorific bestowed upon party cadres. In recent years, however, a position in the NPC, especially in the NPC's permanent organ, the Standing Committee, has become coveted by talented politicians.

32. The re-election of incumbent legislators is common enough that at any given time the legislature contains a significant number of highly experienced members.

Yes. There is a sizable cohort of highly experienced members, especially in the Standing Committee.

CONGRESS OF COLOMBIA (*CONGRESO*)

Expert consultants: Ana Maria Bejarano, John Dugas, Erika Moreno, Eduardo Pizarro, Elizabeth Ungar, Rodrigo Uprimny

Score: .56

Influence over executive (3/9)		Institutional autonomy (4/9)		Specified powers (5/8)		Institutional capacity (6/6)	
1. replace	X	10. no dissolution	X	19. amendments	X	27. sessions	X
2. serve as ministers		11. no decree		20. war	X	28. secretary	X
3. interpellate	X	12. no veto	X	21. treaties	X	29. staff	X
4. investigate	X	13. no review		22. amnesty	X	30. no term limits	X
5. oversee police		14. no gatekeeping		23. pardon		31. seek re-election	X
6. appoint PM		15. no impoundment		24. judiciary	X	32. experience	X
7. appoint ministers		16. control resources	X	25. central bank			
8. lack president		17. immunity		26. media			
9. no confidence		18. all elected	X				

The Congress (*Congreso*) of Colombia traces its origins to the country's first constitution, adopted in 1821 upon independence from Spain. The bicameral legislature comprises the Senate (*Senado*) and the Chamber of Representatives (*Cámara de Representantes*). Colombian politics were plagued by outbreaks of mass violence in the first half of the twentieth century, the rise of a Marxist guerilla insurgency in the 1960s, competing right-wing paramilitary organizations that proliferated in the 1980s, and trafficking in illegal narcotics. In an environment of insecurity, Congress was overshadowed by presidents who frequently used emergency powers to bypass normal procedures and rule by decree.

A new constitution in 1991 scaled back the president's emergency powers. States of emergency, renamed "states of exception," still allow the president to rule by decree, although these periods cannot persist longer than ninety days without the Senate's approval. Congress also gained the power to censure members of the president's cabinet. The 1991 constitution prohibits members of Congress from serving as ministers. Prior to 1991 legislators could simultaneously serve in the government.

The legislature has some leverage over the executive. It can remove the president from office by itself and has some investigatory powers. Yet the president's powers to declare states of exception and rule by decree means that the legislature shares lawmaking authority with the executive. The Colombian Congress does enjoy, however, a number of explicitly delegated powers and has considerable institutional capacity.

SURVEY

1. The legislature alone, without the involvement of any other agencies, can impeach the president or replace the prime minister.

Yes. The Chamber of Representatives can charge the president with crimes, and the Senate can, by a two-thirds majority vote of its present members, remove the president from office. The president could then go before the Supreme Court for a criminal trial.

> Article 174
> It is the responsibility of the Senate to take cognizance of the charges brought by the Chamber of Representatives against the President of the Republic or whoever replaces him/her... In this case, the Senate will determine the validity of the charges concerning actions or omissions that have occurred in the discharge of their duties.

> Article 175
> The following rules will be observed in the decisions made by the Senate:
> 1. The accused is automatically suspended from his/her office whenever he/she admits publicly to a charge.
> 2. If the charge refers to crimes committed in the exercise of his/her functions or that he/she becomes unworthy to serve because of a misdemeanor, the Senate may only impose the sanction of discharge from office or the temporary or absolute suspension of political rights. However, the accused will be brought to trial before the Supreme Court of Justice if the evidence demonstrates that the individual to be responsible for an infraction and deserves other penalties.

> 3. If the charge refers to common crimes, the Senate will confine itself to declare whether or not there are grounds for further measures, and if so, it will place the accused at the disposal of the Supreme Court.
> 4. The Senate may commission a task force from among its own ranks for investigation, reserving for itself the decision and definitive sanction to be pronounced in a public session by at least two-thirds of the votes of the Senators present.

> Article 178
> The Chamber of Representatives will have the following special powers:
> 3. To charge before the Senate, when constitutional reasons may exist, the President of the Republic.

> Article 199
> The President of the Republic, during the period for which he/she is elected or whoever is entrusted with the presidency, may not be prosecuted or tried for crimes except following an indictment by the Chamber of Representatives and upon the declaration by the Senate that there are sufficient grounds for indictment/bill of particulars.

> Article 235
> The Supreme Court of Justice has the following powers:
> 2. To judge the President of the Republic or whoever replaces him/her and the senior officials covered by Article 174 for any punishable deed imputed to them, in accordance with Article 175, paragraphs 2 and 3.

2. Ministers may serve simultaneously as members of the legislature.

No. Legislators are prohibited from serving simultaneously in a ministerial position. Prior to 1991 legislators could serve in the cabinet.

> Article 128
> No one may hold more than one public position simultaneously or receive more than one salary originating from the Public Treasury, or from enterprises or institutions in which the State is a majority owner, except in cases expressly determined by the law.
> By Public Treasury, [it] is meant that of the nation, that of the territorial entities, and that of the decentralized entities.

3. The legislature has powers of summons over executive branch officials and hearings with executive branch officials testifying before the legislature or its committees are regularly held.

Yes. Congress regularly summons ministers for questioning.

> Article 135
> Each chamber [of Congress] will have the following powers:
> 3. Solicit from the government information that the chamber may need.
> 4. Determine the holding of sessions reserved on a priority basis to [address] the oral questions formulated

by the congressmen to the ministries and the answers thereof.

8. Summon and require the ministers to attend the sessions. The summons will have to be made not less than five days prior to a session and to take the form of a written questionnaire. In case that the ministers do not attend, without an excuse accepted by the respective chamber, the latter may propose a motion of censure. The ministers will have to be heard at the session for which they were summoned, without barring the discussion from continuing at subsequent sessions following a decision of the respective chamber.

4. The legislature can conduct independent investigation of the chief executive and the agencies of the executive.

Yes. The legislature can investigate the executive.

Article 137
Any permanent committee [of Congress] may summon any individual or legal entity to a special session to provide oral or written statements, which may be mandated under oath, on matters directly related to investigations pursued by the committee.

Article 178
The Chamber of Representatives will have the following special powers:
5. To request the assistance of other authorities for the conduct of investigations for which the Chamber is competent, and to commission the collection of evidence when the Chamber considers it appropriate.

5. The legislature has effective powers of oversight over the agencies of coercion (the military, organs of law enforcement, intelligence services, and the secret police).

No. The legislature lacks effective powers of oversight over the agencies of coercion.

6. The legislature appoints the prime minister.

No. There is no prime minister.

7. The legislature's approval is required to confirm the appointment of ministers; or the legislature itself appoints ministers.

No. The president appoints ministers, and the appointments do not require the legislature's approval.

Article 189
It is the responsibility of the President of the Republic, as the chief of state, head of the government, and supreme administrative authority to do the following:
1. Appoint and dismiss freely Cabinet ministers and directors of administrative departments.

8. The country lacks a presidency entirely or there is a presidency, but the president is elected by the legislature.

No. The president is directly elected.

Article 190
The President of the Republic will be elected for a period of four (4) years by one-half plus one of the ballots which, in a secret and direct manner, the citizens will cast on the date and following the procedures determined by the law.

9. The legislature can vote no confidence in the government.

No. The legislature may censure individual ministers but cannot vote no confidence in the government as a whole.

Article 135
Each chamber [of Congress] will have the following powers:
9. Propose a motion of censure with respect to ministers for matters related to functions for which they are responsible... Approval of the motion will mandate an absolute majority of the members of each house. Once the motion is approved, the minister will be relieved of his/her position. If it is rejected, no other motion of censure may be proposed concerning the same issue unless justified by new facts.

10. The legislature is immune from dissolution by the executive.

Yes. The legislature is immune from dissolution.

11. Any executive initiative on legislation requires ratification or approval by the legislature before it takes effect; that is, the executive lacks decree power.

No. The president, with the approval of his or her own government, can declare a state of emergency that allows him or her to issue decrees that have the force of law. Colombian presidents have often used this provision. The state of emergency can continue for ninety days without legislative approval. Congress can vote to repeal the laws that the president decrees.

Article 213
In the case of a serious disruption of the public order imminently threatening the institutional stability and security of the State, or the peaceful coexistence of the citizenry – and which cannot be met by the use of ordinary powers of the police authorities – the President of the Republic, with the approval of all the ministers, may declare a state of internal disturbance throughout the Republic or part of it for a period no longer than ninety days, extendable for two similar periods, the second of which requires the prior and favorable vote of the Senate of the Republic... The legislative decrees issued by the Government can suspend the laws incompatible with the state of disturbance and will no longer be in effect as soon as public order is declared to have been

restored. The Government may extend application [of those decrees for] up to ninety more days.

Article 214

The states of exception referred to in the previous articles will be subject to the following provisions:
1. The legislative decrees will be accompanied by the signature of the President of the Republic and all his/her ministers and may refer only to matters that have direct and specific connection with the situation as determined by the declaration of the state of exception.

Article 215

When events different from those provided for in Articles 212 and 213 occur that disrupt or threaten to disrupt in serious or imminent manner the economic, social, or ecological order of the country or which constitute a grave public calamity, the President, with the signature of all the ministers, may declare a state of emergency for periods up to thirty days in each case which, in all, may not exceed ninety days in a calendar year. By means of such a declaration, which will have to be validated, the President may, with the signature of all the ministers, issue decrees with the force of law, slated exclusively to check the crisis and halt the extension of its effects.

These decrees may refer to matters that have direct and specific connection with the state of emergency and may, in a provisional manner, establish new taxes or amend existing ones. In these latter cases, the measures will stop being in effect at the end of the subsequent fiscal year, except when Congress, during the subsequent year, should grant them permanent character.

In the decree declaring the state of emergency, the government will stipulate the deadline within which it would use its extraordinary powers in situations referred to in this article and will convene Congress if the latter should not be met within the 10 days following the expiration of the said deadline . . . During the year subsequent to the declaration of emergency, Congress may repeal, amend, or add to the decrees to which this article refers in areas that ordinarily fall under the Government's jurisdiction.

12. Laws passed by the legislature are veto-proof or essentially veto-proof; that is, the executive lacks veto power, or has veto power but the veto can be overridden by a majority in the legislature.

Yes. The legislature can override a presidential veto by a majority vote of its present members.

Article 165

Once a legislative bill is approved by both Chambers, it will be transmitted to the government for its approval. Should the government see no objections, it will approve the bill's promulgation as law; if it objects to it, the bill will be returned to the chamber in which it originated.

13. The legislature's laws are supreme and not subject to judicial review.

No. The Constitutional Court can review the constitutionality of laws.

Article 241

The safeguarding of the integrity and supremacy of the Constitution is entrusted to the Constitutional Court in the strict and precise terms of this article. For such a purpose, it will fulfill the following functions:
1. Decide on the petitions of unconstitutionality brought by citizens against measures amending the Constitution, no matter what their origin, exclusively for errors of procedure in their formation.
2. Decide, prior to a popular expression of opinion, on the constitutionality of the call for a referendum or a constituent assembly to amend the Constitution, exclusively for errors of procedure in their formation.
3. Decide on the constitutionality of referendums about laws and popular consultations and plebiscites of a national scope, in case of these last ones exclusively for errors of procedure in their convocation and implementation.
4. Decide on the petitions of unconstitutionality brought by citizens against the laws, both for their substantive content as well as for errors of procedure in their formation.
5. Decide on the petitions of unconstitutionality brought by citizens against decrees with the force of law issued by the government on the basis of Article 150, paragraph 10, and Article 341 of the Constitution for their substantive content as well as for errors of procedure in their formation.
7. Decide definitively on the constitutionality of the legislative decrees issued by the government on the basis of Articles 212, 213, and 215 of the Constitution.
10. Decide definitively on the feasibility of international treaties and the laws approving them. With such a purpose, the government will submit them to the Court within six days following the sanction of the law. Any citizen may intervene to defend or challenge their constitutionality. If the Court declares them constitutional, the Government may exchange said notes; in the contrary case the laws will not be ratified. When one or several provisions of a multilateral treaty are declared invalid by the Constitutional Court, the President of the Republic alone may declare consent, prescribing the pertinent exception.

14. The legislature has the right to initiate bills in all policy jurisdictions; the executive lacks gatekeeping authority.

No. The legislature is prohibited from introducing legislation related to the national development plan, government contracts and loans, the wages and benefits of public servants, or the central bank.

Article 150

It is the responsibility of Congress to enact laws. Through them, it exercises the following functions:
3. To approve the national development plan and public investments that must be undertaken or continued,

with the determination of the resources and appropriations which are authorized for their execution and the measures necessary to promote their implementation.

7. To determine the structure of the national administration and create, eliminate, or merge ministries, administrative departments, superintendencies, public establishments, and other entities at a national level, as well as to specify their objectives and organic structure; to regulate the creation and operation of regional autonomous corporations within a system of autonomy; and, similarly, to create or authorize the creation of industrial and commercial enterprises of the State and mixed economic societies.

9. To grant authorizations to the Government to enter into contracts, to negotiate loans, and to sell national assets. The Government will periodically inform Congress on the exercise of these authorizations.

11. To establish national revenues and to determine the expenditures of the administration.

19. To enact general rules that specify the objectives and criteria to which the Government must be subjected for the following purposes:

a) To organize public credit;

b) To regulate foreign trade and specify the international exchange system, in agreement with the functions which the Constitution assigns to the Board of Directors of the Bank of the Republic;

e) To establish the system of wage and benefits concerning public servants, members of the National Congress, and the Police Force; [and]

22. To issue laws concerning the Bank of the Republic and the functions that must be performed by its Board of Directors.

Article 154

The laws may originate in either of the chambers at the proposal of their respective members, the national government, the entities stipulated in Article 156, or through popular initiative in the cases provided for by the Constitution. However, the government may dictate or amend only those laws covered by paragraphs 3, 7, 9, 11, and 22 and by subparagraphs (a), (b), and (e) of paragraph 19 of Article 150; those which decree contributions to national revenues or transfers of same; those which authorize contributions or grants by the State to industrial or commercial enterprises; and those which decree exemptions from taxes, contributions, or national levies.

15. Expenditure of funds appropriated by the legislature is mandatory; the executive lacks the power to impound funds appropriated by the legislature.

No. The executive can impound funds appropriated by the legislature.

16. The legislature controls the resources that finance its own internal operation and provide for the perquisites of its own members.

Yes. The legislature enjoys financial autonomy. Members' salaries are protected by law.

Article 187

The remuneration of the members of Congress will be adjusted each year in proportion equal to the weighted average of the adjustments made in the remuneration of the public servants of the central administration on the basis of a certification that the Controller General of the Republic will issue for that purpose.

17. Members of the legislature are immune from arrest and/or criminal prosecution.

No. Legislators are immune, but immunity may be lifted by the Supreme Court of Justice.

Article 185

Members of Congress enjoy immunity for their opinions and the votes that they cast in the exercise of their office, without prejudice to the disciplinary rules included in the respective by-laws.

Article 186

For the offenses that members of Congress may commit, the Supreme Court of Justice is the sole authority that may order their detention. In case of *flagrante delicto*, members of Congress must be apprehended and placed immediately at the disposal of said court.

18. All members of the legislature are elected; the executive lacks the power to appoint any members of the legislature.

Yes. All members of the legislature are elected.

Article 132

Senators and representatives will be elected for a period of four years beginning on July 20 following the election.

19. The legislature alone, without the involvement of any other agencies, can change the Constitution.

Yes. The legislature can change the constitution through a complicated procedure. The sitting legislature can propose a constitutional amendment, and then, following an election, the subsequent legislature can approve the amendment.

Article 374

The Political Constitution may be reformed by Congress, a Constituent Assembly, or by the people through a referendum.

Article 375

The Government, ten members of the Congress, twenty percent of councilors or deputies, or citizens totaling at least five percent of the electoral rolls in force may introduce legislative bills. The bill will be discussed in two ordinary and consecutive session periods. After having been approved in the first period by a majority of those present, the bill will be published by the Government. In the second period, the approval will require the vote of the majority of the members of each

Chamber. In this second period only initiatives presented in the first period may be discussed.

Article 376
By means of a law approved by the members of both chambers, Congress may direct that the voters participating in the popular balloting decide if a Constituent Assembly should be called with the jurisdiction, term, and makeup as set forth by said law. It is understood that the people will convoke the Assembly, if they approve it by at least one-third of the electoral rolls.

Article 377
The constitutional reforms must be submitted to a referendum approved by Congress when referring to the rights recognized in Chapter I of Title II and to their guaranties, to the procedures of popular participation, or to Congress, if so requested, within the six months following the promulgation of the legislative act, by five percent of the citizens who make up the electoral rolls.

Article 378
Upon the initiative of the government or the citizens under the terms of Article 155, Congress, through the law which mandates the approval of the majority of the members of both Chambers, may submit to a referendum a bill of constitutional reform which the same Congress would include in the law. The referendum will be presented in such a manner that the voters may freely select from the agenda of the various items which they vote positively and which they vote negatively. The approval of constitutional reforms by means of a referendum mandates the affirmative vote of over one-half of the voters and that the number of these should exceed one-fourth of the total number of citizens included in the electoral rolls.

20. The legislature's approval is necessary for the declaration of war.

Yes. The Senate's approval is necessary for presidential war declarations with the common exception for cases of foreign invasion. The president can declare war to "repel foreign aggression" without prior congressional authorization.

Article 173
The following are the powers of the Senate:
5. To authorize the government to declare war on another state.

Article 189
It is the responsibility of the President of the Republic, as the chief of state, head of the government, and supreme administrative authority to do the following:
6. Declare war with the approval of the Senate or without such authorization to repel foreign aggression; and agree to and ratify peace treaties, regarding all of which matters the President will give an immediate account to Congress.

21. The legislature's approval is necessary to ratify treaties with foreign countries.

Yes. The legislature's approval is necessary to ratify international treaties.

Article 150
It is the responsibility of Congress to enact laws. Through them, it exercises the following functions:
16. To approve or reject treaties that the Government makes with other states or entities in international law.

Article 189
It is the responsibility of the President of the Republic, as the chief of state, head of the government, and supreme administrative authority to do the following:
2. Make international treaties or agreements with other states and international bodies to be submitted to the approval of Congress.

Article 224
In order to be valid, treaties must be approved by Congress.

22. The legislature has the power to grant amnesty.

Yes. The legislature has the power to grant amnesty.

Article 150
It is the responsibility of Congress to enact laws. Through them, it exercises the following functions:
17. To grant, by a two-thirds majority of the members of both Chambers or for grave reasons of public convenience, amnesties or general commutations for political crimes. In cases where the grantees are exempted from civil liability with respect to private individuals, the State must be obligated to make the proper compensations.

23. The legislature has the power of pardon.

No. The government has the power of pardon.

Article 201
It is the duty of the Government to do the following in relation with the Judiciary Branch:
2. Grant pardons.

24. The legislature reviews and has the right to reject appointments to the judiciary; or the legislature itself appoints members of the judiciary.

Yes. The Senate appoints the judges of the Constitutional Court from a list presented to it by the president, the Supreme Court, and the Council of State.

Article 173
The following are the powers of the Senate:
6. To elect the judges of the Constitutional Court.

Article 239
The judges of the Constitutional Court will be elected by the Senate of the Republic for single terms of eight years from lists presented to it by the President of the Republic, the Supreme Court of Justice, and the Council of State.

25. The chairman of the central bank is appointed by the legislature.

No. The president appoints the five members of the directorate of the Bank of the Republic who in turn select the governor.

26. The legislature has a substantial voice in the operation of the state-owned media.

No. An independent body oversees the operation of the public media, and the legislature does not have a substantial voice in its operation.

Article 77
Television will be regulated by an autonomous entity at the national level, subject to its own regime. The direction and execution of that entity's functions will be the responsibility of an Executive Board comprised of five members, who will appoint its director. Members of the Executive Board will serve for a fixed period. The national government will appoint two of them. Another member will be chosen from among the legal representatives of the regional television channels. The law will specify how the other members of the board are to be appointed and will regulate the organization and operation of the entity.

27. The legislature is regularly in session.

Yes. The legislature is in ordinary session for eight months each year.

Article 138
Of its own right, Congress will meet in ordinary sessions during two periods a year, which will constitute one legislative term. The first period of sessions will begin on July 20 and conclude on December 16; the second session will begin on March 16 and conclude on June 20.

28. Each legislator has a personal secretary.

Yes.

29. Each legislator has at least one non-secretarial staff member with policy expertise.

Yes.

30. Legislators are eligible for re-election without any restriction.

Yes. There are no restrictions on re-election.

31. A seat in the legislature is an attractive enough position that legislators are generally interested in and seek re-election.

Yes.

32. The re-election of incumbent legislators is common enough that at any given time the legislature contains a significant number of highly experienced members.

Yes. Re-election rates are sufficiently high to produce a significant number of highly experienced members.

ASSEMBLY OF COMOROS (*ASSEMBLÉE*)

Expert consultant: Edward McMahon

Score: .38

Influence over executive (1/9)	Institutional autonomy (5/9)		Specified powers (4/8)		Institutional capacity (2/6)	
1. replace	10. no dissolution		19. amendments		27. sessions	
2. serve as ministers	11. no decree	X	20. war	X	28. secretary	
3. interpellate	12. no veto	X	21. treaties	X	29. staff	
4. investigate	13. no review		22. amnesty	X	30. no term limits	X
5. oversee police	14. no gatekeeping		23. pardon		31. seek re-election	X
6. appoint PM	15. no impoundment	X	24. judiciary	X	32. experience	
7. appoint ministers	16. control resources		25. central bank			
8. lack president	17. immunity	X	26. media			
9. no confidence X	18. all elected	X				

The Assembly (*Assemblée*) of Comoros was established upon independence from France in 1975. The unicameral assembly contains thirty-three elected members. Since independence the country has been plagued by political instability resulting from military coups and secessionist demands made by breakaway islands. A new constitution in 2001 granted the islands greater autonomy but did not directly affect legislative power. The 2001 constitution is not yet available in English; the following constitutional excerpts are from the country's 1996 constitution.

The legislature has modest power. Its ability to influence the executive branch is slight, although it can vote no confidence in the government. The legislature has some institutional autonomy that is limited by executive dissolution and gatekeeping powers. The legislature can exercise some specified powers. Its institutional capacity is negligible.

SURVEY

1. The legislature alone, without the involvement of any other agencies, can impeach the president or replace the prime minister.

No. Presidential impeachment requires the involvement of the High Court of Justice. The prime minister can be removed with a motion of censure.

Article 24
The President of the Republic is penally responsible in case of treason or crime committed in the exercise or resulting from the exercise of his functions. However, the decision to prosecute, [and] the proposal to charge the President of the Republic, taken at the initiative of half the deputies, are voted by a majority of two-thirds of the members of the Federal Assembly, according to the procedure provided by the internal regulations of the said Assembly. Nonetheless, the charge may intervene only three days after the decision to prosecute has been taken. The charge is notified, within no more than eight days to the Procurator General of the High Council of the Republic sitting in the capacity of a High Court of Justice. This function is assured, should the occasion arise, by the Procurator General of the highest judicial jurisdiction. The High Council of the Republic, sitting as the High Court of Justice rules on the culpability of the President of the Republic. If the accused is found culpable, he is dismissed from his functions, without prejudice to the punishments of law incurred.

Article 28
Members of the Government may be collectively removed from office if the Federal Assembly questions their responsibility by the adoption of a motion of censure deposited by at least one-fourth of the deputies and voted by an absolute majority of the members who comprise the Assembly.

2. Ministers may serve simultaneously as members of the legislature.

No. Ministers are prohibited from serving simultaneously in the legislature.

Article 27
The functions of a member of the Government are incompatible with the exercise of the mandate of Deputy of the Federal Assembly.

3. The legislature has powers of summons over executive branch officials and hearings with executive branch officials testifying before the legislature or its committees are regularly held.

No. According to the constitution, the legislature can question officials from the executive, but in practice, this power is not effectively exercised.

Article 44
The Federal Assembly and its commissions by the intermediary of their respective presidents, may at their demand, obtain from the Government, its departments and all the authorities of the State, the information they require. The Federal Assembly and its commissions may require the presence of a member of the Government. The members of the Government have access to the sittings of the Federal Assembly and of its commissions and will be heard when they demand it. They may be accompanied by technicians to assist them. The members of the Government will equally be heard upon demand of the deputies, either in commissions or in plenary.

4. The legislature can conduct independent investigation of the chief executive and the agencies of the executive.

No. The legislature cannot investigate the executive.

5. The legislature has effective powers of oversight over the agencies of coercion (the military, organs of law enforcement, intelligence services, and the secret police).

No. The legislature lacks effective powers of oversight over the agencies of coercion.

6. The legislature appoints the prime minister.

No. The president appoints the prime minister.

Article 11
The President of the Republic appoints the Prime Minister. He terminates his functions.
On the proposal of the Prime Minister, he appoints the other members of the Government.

7. The legislature's approval is required to confirm the appointment of ministers; or the legislature itself appoints ministers.

No. The president appoints ministers on the recommendation of the prime minister, and the appointments do not require the legislature's approval.

Article 11
The President of the Republic appoints the Prime Minister. He terminates his functions.
On the proposal of the Prime Minister, he appoints the other members of the Government.

8. The country lacks a presidency entirely or there is a presidency, but the president is elected by the legislature.

No. The president is directly elected.

> Article 7
> The President of the Republic is elected by direct universal suffrage for a six-year term.

9. The legislature can vote no confidence in the government.

Yes. The legislature can vote no confidence in the government.

> Article 28
> Members of the Government may be collectively removed from office if the Federal Assembly questions their responsibility by the adoption of a motion of censure deposited by at least one-fourth of the deputies and voted by an absolute majority of the members who comprise the Assembly.

10. The legislature is immune from dissolution by the executive.

No. The president can dissolve the legislature.

> Article 19
> After written consultation with the Prime Minister and the presidents of the Federal Assembly and the High Council of the Republic, the President of the Republic can pronounce the dissolution of the Federal Assembly.

11. Any executive initiative on legislation requires ratification or approval by the legislature before it takes effect; that is, the executive lacks decree power.

Yes. The executive lacks decree power. The legislature can delegate temporary decree power to the government on specified issue areas.

> Article 14
> The President of the Republic signs the ordinances, decrees and acts deliberated in the Council of Ministers.

> Article 42
> The Government may, in order to execute its program, demand of the Federal Assembly authorization to take, by ordinances, for a limited period of time, measures that are normally of the domain of the law, except for matters concerning fundamental rights and public liberties.
> This legislative delegation is conferred through a law of habilitation. The ordinances are taken in the Council of Ministers following the advice of the High Council of the Republic. They come into effect upon their publication in the Official Journal, but become lapsed if the bill of law of ratification is not presented to the Federal Assembly before the date determined by the law of habilitation. At the expiration of the time period mentioned in the first paragraph, the ordinances may be

modified by law only. During that time, the Government may oppose the receivability of any proposal or amendment whose provisions concern those matters for which the habilitation has been given.

12. Laws passed by the legislature are veto-proof or essentially veto-proof; that is, the executive lacks veto power, or has veto power but the veto can be overridden by a majority in the legislature.

Yes. The executive lacks veto power.

13. The legislature's laws are supreme and not subject to judicial review.

No. The High Council of the Republic can review the constitutionality of laws.

> Article 53
> The High Council of the Republic, seized by the President of the Republic, the President of the Federal Assembly, the Prime Minister, the governors of the islands, the presidents of the councils of the islands, a third of the deputies of the Federal Assembly or the absolute majority of the council of an island, decides in case of disagreement, on the constitutionality of the laws, the ordinances, treaties or international agreements and any normative provision having the force of a law. The High Council of the Republic is seized, in this case, either before the promulgation of the laws or contested provisions, or within a time limit of one month following this promulgation.
> It decides within the time limit of a month. However, upon the demand of the President of the Republic, if there is urgency, this time limit may be reduced to eight days.
> In case of the seizing of the High Council of the Republic, the law or the contested provisions may neither be promulgated nor published, as long as the High Council has not decided.
> A provision that has been declared unconstitutional, may neither be promulgated and published, nor put into effect. The decisions of the High Council of the Republic are not susceptible to any recourse.

14. The legislature has the right to initiate bills in all policy jurisdictions; the executive lacks gatekeeping authority.

No. The legislature is prohibited from initiating legislation that would "cause a diminution of public resources."

> Article 37
> The initiative of laws and the right of amendment belong concurrently to the Government and the Federal Assembly.
> Bills of law are deliberated in the Council of Ministers. Proposals of law and amendment by the Deputies are not receivable when their adoption would cause a diminution of public resources, either by way of creating or increasing a public expense. If a proposal or an amendment does not appear to be within the domain

of the law or cannot be received because of the preceding provision, the Government has the authority to oppose the receivability.

15. Expenditure of funds appropriated by the legislature is mandatory; the executive lacks the power to impound funds appropriated by the legislature.

Yes. The executive lacks the power to impound funds appropriated by the legislature.

16. The legislature controls the resources that finance its own internal operation and provide for the perquisites of its own members.

No. The legislature is dependent on the executive for the resources that finance its own operations.

17. Members of the legislature are immune from arrest and/or criminal prosecution.

Yes. Legislators are immune with the common exception for cases of *flagrante delicto,* here expressed as a "flagrant offense."

Article 33
While a session is in progress, no deputy may be prosecuted, searched, arrested, detained or judged without the authorization of the Federal Assembly, except in the case of flagrant offence or crime. No deputy shall be prosecuted, searched, arrested, detained or judged because of his opinions or votes expressed in the exercise of his functions.

18. All members of the legislature are elected; the executive lacks the power to appoint any members of the legislature.

Yes. All members of the legislature are elected.

Article 32
The deputies of the Federal Assembly are elected for five years by direct suffrage.

19. The legislature alone, without the involvement of any other agencies, can change the Constitution.

No. Constitutional amendments require either the president's approval or approval in a popular referendum.

Article 68
The initiative to revise the Constitution belongs to the President of the Republic. However, a third of the members of the Federal Assembly may bring a proposal to the President of the Republic.
The bill or motion must be voted by the Federal Assembly with a majority of two-thirds of its members. Revision is definitive when it has been approved by referendum by a majority of votes throughout the Republic. The new Constitution takes effect upon proclamation of the results of the ballot by the High Council of the Republic. However, the President of the Republic may decide to promulgate, without submission to referendum, the bill or proposal that has been adopted by

the deputies and counselors of the islands convened in congress with a majority of two-thirds of the members which compose the congress. No procedure of revision may be engaged which carries affects to the integrity of the Republic or to the rights of the person.

20. The legislature's approval is necessary for the declaration of war.

Yes. The legislature declares war on the proposal of the government.

Article 45
The state of siege or the state of war is proclaimed by the Federal Assembly by the majority of two-thirds of its members, upon demand of the Government.

21. The legislature's approval is necessary to ratify treaties with foreign countries.

Yes. The legislature's approval is necessary to ratify international treaties.

Article 18
The President of the Republic negotiates and ratifies treaties. Peace treaties, treaties of commerce, treaties or agreements related to international organizations, those that engage the State Finances, those concerning the domain that the Constitution reserves to the law, those which are relative to the state of persons, may only be ratified or approved by virtue of a law.
The Federal Assembly is immediately informed of the conclusion of the other treaties and international agreements. Upon their publication, treaties and agreements that are regularly ratified or approved shall become part of the internal juridical order and have an authority superior to that of the law under reserve that each Agreement or Treaty is applied by the other party.

22. The legislature has the power to grant amnesty.

Yes. The legislature has the power to grant amnesty.

Article 39
The law is voted by the Federal Assembly.
The following matters are of the domain of the law:
– amnesty.

23. The legislature has the power of pardon.

No. The president has the power of pardon.

Article 21
The President of the Republic has the right of pardon.

24. The legislature reviews and has the right to reject appointments to the judiciary; or the legislature itself appoints members of the judiciary.

Yes. The legislature appoints three of the eight members of the High Council of the Republic.

Article 16
The Magistrates . . . are appointed by decree taken in the Council of Ministers.

Article 49
The High Council of the Republic sits in constitutional matters, in matters of control of the accounts, in the capacity as the High Court of Justice.
It is composed:
– of four members appointed by the President of the Republic;
– of three members elected by the Federal Assembly upon presentation by the President of the Federal Assembly
– of one member elected by the council of each island, upon presentation by the president of the council of the island.

25. The chairman of the central bank is appointed by the legislature.

No. The Council of Ministers appoints the governor of the Central Bank of Comoros.

Article 16
The Governor of the Central Bank... [is] appointed by decree taken in the Council of Ministers.

26. The legislature has a substantial voice in the operation of the state-owned media.

No. The legislature lacks a substantial voice in the operation of the public media.

27. The legislature is regularly in session.

No. The legislature is in session for only about five months each year.

Article 35
The Federal Assembly convenes, by right, each year in two ordinary sessions.

The first session starts the first Thursday of October and ends the last Thursday of December. The second session opens the last Thursday of April. Its duration cannot exceed three months.

28. Each legislator has a personal secretary.

No.

29. Each legislator has at least one non-secretarial staff member with policy expertise.

No.

30. Legislators are eligible for re-election without any restriction.

Yes. There are no restrictions on re-election.

31. A seat in the legislature is an attractive enough position that legislators are generally interested in and seek re-election.

Yes.

32. The re-election of incumbent legislators is common enough that at any given time the legislature contains a significant number of highly experienced members.

No. Violence and military interventions have hindered the formation of a body of highly experienced legislators in the Assembly. The country was ruled by the military from 1999 to 2002, and since then there has been only a single legislative election, in 2004.

PARLIAMENT OF CONGO-BRAZZAVILLE (REPUBLIC OF CONGO) (*PARLEMENT*)

Expert consultants: Rémy Bazenguissa-Ganga, John F. Clark, Max Fira, Ch. Didier Gondola, Cassie Knight

Score: .38

Influence over executive (1/9)		Institutional autonomy (6/9)		Specified powers (2/8)		Institutional capacity (3/6)	
1. replace		10. no dissolution	X	19. amendments		27. sessions	X
2. serve as ministers		11. no decree	X	20. war		28. secretary	
3. interpellate	X	12. no veto		21. treaties	X	29. staff	
4. investigate		13. no review		22. amnesty	X	30. no term limits	X
5. oversee police		14. no gatekeeping	X	23. pardon		31. seek re-election	X
6. appoint PM		15. no impoundment		24. judiciary		32. experience	
7. appoint ministers		16. control resources	X	25. central bank			
8. lack president		17. immunity	X	26. media			
9. no confidence		18. all elected	X				

The Parliament (*Parlement*) of Congo-Brazzaville (Republic of Congo) was established upon independence in the 1960 constitution. A one-party state was founded in the early years after independence, followed by military rule beginning in 1969. New constitutions were promulgated in 1969 and 1979. The first three decades of independence included experimentation with Marxism-Leninism as well as military rule. The legislature was, for the most part, marginalized during this time.

The end of the Cold War led to the abandonment of communist ideology and the adoption of a new constitution in 1992. During that same year, the country had relatively open elections for parliament and president. In 1993, however, the president dissolved the legislature, and another round of parliamentary elections was held. The 1993 elections were widely disputed and were followed by a decade that was punctuated by three rounds of civil war (in 1993–94, 1997, and 1998–99). A ceasefire paved the way for the adoption of the current constitution in 2002, which was followed by presidential and parliamentary elections. The constitution provides for a bicameral legislature consisting of a lower house, the National Assembly (*Assemblée nationale*), and an upper house, the Senate (*Sénat*). In the 2002 elections, the sitting president, Denis Sassou-Nguesso, was elected to a new seven-year term, and his Congolese Labor Party–United Democratic Forces coalition secured about two-thirds of seats in the National Assembly, thereby cementing Sassou-Nguesso's dominance of both the legislature and Congolese politics.

The 2002 constitution made a number of changes to the 1992 document that weakened the legislature. Prior to 2002 the legislature had the formal powers to interpellate ministers, conduct investigations of the government, and adopt a motion of censure against the government, but these powers were stripped from the 2002 document. The legislature also had enjoyed the formal power to appoint members of the judiciary, but the 2002 constitution gives the president this right. Furthermore, prior to 2002 the legislature's approval was necessary to approve presidential declarations of war. Since 2002 the president can, in "exceptional circumstances," declare war without consulting the legislature. Only one change instituted by the 2002 constitution strengthened the legislature: The 1992 constitution granted the president the power to dissolve the legislature, but the 2002 constitution provides the legislature with immunity from dissolution.

The result of the civil war, the constitutional changes, and the general situation in the politics of the country is a legislature that has very little control over the executive, some limited institutional autonomy, few specified powers, and some institutional capacity.

SURVEY

1. The legislature alone, without the involvement of any other agencies, can impeach the president or replace the prime minister.

No. Presidential impeachment requires action by the High Court of Justice.

Article 87
The personal responsibility of the President of the Republic cannot be invoked except in case of high treason. High treason is involved, if, in violation of the Constitution or the law, the President commits, deliberately, an act, contrary to the superior interests of the nation, which compromised gravely the national unity, social peace, social justice, the development of the country or carries grave danger to the human rights, the integrity of the territory, the independence and national sovereignty. The President of the Republic cannot be impeached except by the National Assembly based on a vote by secret ballot by a majority of two-thirds of its members.

Article 114
The National Assembly cannot dismiss the President of the Republic.

Article 153
The High Court of Justice is competent to judge the President of the Republic in case of high treason. The President of the Republic is arraigned under the conditions inferred to in paragraph 3 of Article 87.

2. Ministers may serve simultaneously as members of the legislature.

No. Legislators are prohibited from serving simultaneously in a ministerial position.

Article 75
The functions of a minister are incompatible with the exercise of any parliamentary mandate, any public employment, civil or military and any professional activity, with the exception of agricultural, cultural or teaching. They are equally incompatible with the position of a member of an organ of a local collectivity, an administrative council or of a directly committee of a public enterprise.

3. The legislature has powers of summons over executive branch officials and hearings with executive branch officials testifying before the legislature or its committees are regularly held.

Yes. The legislature was formally granted the power of summons in the 1992 constitution, but the power was deleted from the 2002 constitution. Still, the legislature regularly interpellates executive branch officials in practice.

4. The legislature can conduct independent investigation of the chief executive and the agencies of the executive.

No. The legislature had the power of investigation according to the 1992 constitution but lost it in the 2002 constitution. In practice, it cannot investigate the president and his or her cabinet.

5. The legislature has effective powers of oversight over the agencies of coercion (the military, organs of law enforcement, intelligence services, and the secret police).

No. The legislature lacks effective powers of oversight over the agencies of coercion.

6. The legislature appoints the prime minister.

No. There is no prime minister.

7. The legislature's approval is required to confirm the appointment of ministers; or the legislature itself appoints ministers.

No. The president appoints ministers, and the appointments do not require the legislature's approval.

Article 74
The President of the Republic appoints the ministers who shall be responsible to him. He puts an end to their functions. He determines by decree the attributions of each minister. He can delegate a part of his powers to a minister.

8. The country lacks a presidency entirely or there is a presidency, but the president is elected by the legislature.

No. The president is directly elected.

Article 57
The President of the Republic is elected for seven years by universal and direct suffrage. He is re-eligible one single time.

9. The legislature can vote no confidence in the government.

No. The legislature cannot vote no confidence in the government. Prior to the 2002 constitution, the legislature, at least formally, had the power to pass a motion of censure that would result in the government's resignation.

10. The legislature is immune from dissolution by the executive.

Yes. The legislature is immune from dissolution. Prior to the 2002 constitutional amendment, the president had the formal power to dissolve the legislature.

Article 114
The President of the Republic cannot dissolve the National Assembly and the National Assembly cannot dismiss the President of the Republic.

11. Any executive initiative on legislation requires ratification or approval by the legislature before it takes effect; that is, the executive lacks decree power.

Yes. The president lacks decree power. The legislature can delegate temporary decree power to the president on specified issue areas.

Article 132
The President of the Republic may, in order to expedite the execution of his program, demand of the Parliament to vote (on) a law authorizing the enactment by decree, during a limited time, the measures which are normally in the domain of the law. This authorization cannot be accorded except by simple majority of the members of Parliament. The demand must indicate the matter, in which the President of the Republic wishes to issue orders. The orders are taken in the Council of Ministers, after the advice of the Supreme Court. They come into force from the (moment) of their publication, but become null if the project of ratification is not filed in the Parliament before the date fixed by law of habilitation. When for unfounded reasons, the demand for habilitation is rejected, the President of the Republic may legislate by decree, after the advice of the Supreme Court. At the expiration of the time referred to in the first paragraph of this Article, the orders cannot be further modified except by the law, whose provisions are in the legislative domain.

12. Laws passed by the legislature are veto-proof or essentially veto-proof; that is, the executive lacks veto power, or has veto power but the veto can be overridden by a majority in the legislature.

No. A two-thirds majority vote in both houses is needed to override a presidential veto.

Article 83
The President of the Republic . . . can, before the expiration of his time limit, demand from Parliament a second deliberation of the law or certain Articles of it . . . The vote, for this second deliberation, requires a majority of two-thirds of the members of the National Assembly and the Senate reunited as Congress.

13. The legislature's laws are supreme and not subject to judicial review.

No. The Constitutional Court can review the constitutionality of laws.

Article 146
The Constitutional Court is charged with the control of the constitutionality of laws, treaties and international accords.

14. The legislature has the right to initiate bills in all policy jurisdictions; the executive lacks gatekeeping authority.

Yes. The legislature can initiate bills in all policy jurisdictions.

15. Expenditure of funds appropriated by the legislature is mandatory; the executive lacks the power to impound funds appropriated by the legislature.

No. The president can impound funds appropriated by the legislature.

16. The legislature controls the resources that finance its own internal operation and provide for the perquisites of its own members.

Yes. The legislature enjoys financial autonomy, including control over members' perquisites.

Article 91
The functions of deputy and senator give rise to the reimbursement of travel expenses and the payment of compensation for the sessions(s), whose rate and conditions of attribution are set by law.

17. Members of the legislature are immune from arrest and/or criminal prosecution.

Yes. Legislators are immune with the common exception for cases of *flagrante delicto,* here translated as "flagrant act."

Article 101
No member of Parliament may be pursued, investigated, detained or judged for opinions or votes cast by him in the exercise of his functions. No deputy, no senator may, during the sessions, be arrested or pursued without the authorization of the bureau of the National Assembly, except in a case of a flagrant act of authorized pursuit or a definitive sentence. No deputy, no senator may be pursued or arrested outside the session, without the authorization of the bureau of the chamber to which he belongs, except in the case of a flagrant act, authorized pursuits or definitive sentence.

18. All members of the legislature are elected; the executive lacks the power to appoint any members of the legislature.

Yes. All members of the legislature are elected.

Article 90
The members of the National Assembly carry the title of deputy. They are elected by universal direct suffrage . . . The members of the Senate carry the title of Senator. They are elected by indirect suffrage by the councils of local collectivities.

19. The legislature alone, without the involvement of any other agencies, can change the Constitution.

No. Constitutional amendments require approval in a popular referendum.

Article 187
When it emanates from the President of the Republic, the project of amendment is submitted directly to referendum, after the advice of conformity by the Constitutional Courts. When it emanates from the Parliament the project of amendment must be voted by two thirds of the members of the two chambers of Parliament united as Congress after the advice of conformity by the Constitutional Court. In the two cases the amendment is not definitive until after approval by referendum.

20. The legislature's approval is necessary for the declaration of war.

No. The president can declare war without the legislature's approval in "exceptional circumstances." Prior to 2001 the legislature's approval was required for the declaration of war.

Article 130
The declaration of war shall be authorized by the National Assembly. When, in the course of exceptional circumstances, the National Assembly cannot meet promptly, the decision on the declaration of war is taken in the Council of Ministers by the President of the Republic, following the advice of the High Council of the Nation. He (shall) immediately inform the Nation of it.

21. The legislature's approval is necessary to ratify treaties with foreign countries.

Yes. The legislature's approval is necessary to ratify international treaties on most major issues.

Article 179
The President of the Republic negotiates, signs and ratifies the treaties and international accords. The ratification can only take place after the authorization by the National Assembly, notably as it concerns peace treaties, defense treaties, commercial treaties, treaties relative to natural resources or accords relative to international organization, those which modify the provisions of a legislative nature, those which are relative to the status of persons, those that involve cession, exchange or addition of territory.

Article 180
The President of the Republic and the Parliament shall be informed of all negotiations tending to the conclusion of an international accord not submitted to ratification.

22. The legislature has the power to grant amnesty.

Yes. The legislature has the power to grant amnesty through law.

Article 110
The Parliament has the legislative initiative and alone passes the law.

Article 111
The (following) are in the domain of the law... amnesty.

23. The legislature has the power of pardon.

No. The president has the power of pardon.

Article 80
The President of the Republic exercises the right of pardon.

24. The legislature reviews and has the right to reject appointments to the judiciary; or the legislature itself appoints members of the judiciary.

No. The president appoints the members of the Supreme Court and the Constitutional Council, and the appointments do not require the legislature's approval. Prior to 2002 the legislature formally had the power to elect the members of the Supreme Court and half of the members of the High Court of Justice.

Article 141
The members of the Supreme Court and the magistrates of the other national jurisdictions are appointed by the President of the Republic on the proposal of the National Council of the Magistrature. The sitting magistrates are irremovable.

Article 144
The Constitutional Court is instituted. The Constitutional Court consists of nine members whose mandate of nine years is renewable. It is renewed by thirds every three years. Five members of the Constitutional Court are appointed by the President of the Republic. The other members are appointed by the President of the Republic by reason of two members on the proposal of the President of the National Assembly and two members on the proposal of the bureau of the Supreme Court from the members of this jurisdiction. The president of the Constitutional Court is appointed from among its members. He has the decisive vote in a case of an even division of votes.

25. The chairman of the central bank is appointed by the legislature.

No. Congo-Brazzaville belongs to the Bank of Central African States, whose governor is selected by the member countries.

26. The legislature has a substantial voice in the operation of the state-owned media.

No. The legislature lacks a substantial voice in the operation of the public media.

27. The legislature is regularly in session.

Yes. The legislature meets in ordinary session for at least 135 days every year. In practice, when the country is not at war, the legislature meets for at least six months each year.

Article 103
The Parliament meets by right in three ordinary sessions per year. The first session opens on March 2, the second on July 2, the third on October 15. Each session shall last forty five days or more. If March 2, July 2 or October 15 are holidays, the opening of the session shall take place on the first day that follows.

28. Each legislator has a personal secretary.

No.

29. Each legislator has at least one non-secretarial staff member with policy expertise.

No.

30. Legislators are eligible for re-election without any restriction.

Yes. There are no restrictions on re-election.

Article 92
The duration of the mandate of the deputy is five years. They are re-eligible.

31. A seat in the legislature is an attractive enough position that legislators are generally interested in and seek re-election.

Yes.

32. The re-election of incumbent legislators is common enough that at any given time the legislature contains a significant number of highly experienced members.

No. Mass violence and chaos brought to wrack the country's politics in the 1990s, and only since 2002 has Congo-Brazzaville had a legislature whose functioning was not interrupted by civil war. The current parliament, most recently renewed in 2007, does include some of Congo-Brazzaville's longtime political figures, but sufficient time has not passed since 2002 to make possible a parliament that contains many highly experienced members.

NATIONAL ASSEMBLY OF CONGO-KINSHASA (DEMOCRATIC REPUBLIC OF CONGO) (*ASSEMBLÉE NATIONALE*)

Expert consultants: Osita George Afoaku, Greg Basue Babu-Kazadi, Pascal Musulay Mukonde, Dennis Tull, Crawford Young

Score: .25

Influence over executive (1/9)		Institutional autonomy (3/9)		Specified powers (1/8)		Institutional capacity (3/6)	
1. replace		10. no dissolution		19. amendments		27. sessions	X
2. serve as ministers		11. no decree		20. war	X	28. secretary	
3. interpellate	X	12. no veto		21. treaties		29. staff	
4. investigate		13. no review		22. amnesty		30. no term limits	X
5. oversee police		14. no gatekeeping	X	23. pardon		31. seek re-election	X
6. appoint PM		15. no impoundment		24. judiciary		32. experience	
7. appoint ministers		16. control resources		25. central bank			
8. lack president		17. immunity	X	26. media			
9. no confidence		18. all elected	X				

The National Assembly (*Assemblée nationale*) of the Democratic Republic of Congo was established in 1960 upon independence from Belgium. It consisted of two chambers: the National Assembly (*Assemblée nationale*) and the Senate (*Sénat*). Shortly after independence, Joseph Mobutu seized power in a military coup, renamed the country Zaire, and declared himself president. During the period of Mobutu's rule, the parliament never exercised any of its lawful powers, and Mobutu ruled by decree, despite the efforts of would-be reformers in the early 1990s.

In 1997 anti-Mobutu rebels, with aid from Rwanda, Uganda, and other African countries, captured the capital, Kinshasa, and installed Laurent Kabila as president. After Kabila was assassinated in 2001, he was succeeded by his son, Joseph Kabila. In 2003 President Joseph Kabila signed an interim constitution, establishing a transitional government, and inaugurated an interim parliament.

The interim National Assembly adopted a new constitution that came into force in February 2006. Popular elections for the National Assembly and president, the country's first national elections since independence, were held in July 2006. The National Assembly was inaugurated in December 2006. It is too early to tell how the new National Assembly will function. If the past is any guide, the new body will remain essentially powerless.

SURVEY

1. The legislature alone, without the involvement of any other agencies, can impeach the president or replace the prime minister.

No. Presidential impeachment requires action by the Constitutional Court.

Article 164
The Constitutional Court is the criminal court for the President of the Republic . . . with regard to the offenses of high treason, contempt of Parliament, failings in matters of honor and integrity as well as insider crimes and all the other common law offenses committed in the exercise or on the occasion of the exercise of their functions.

Article 165
Without prejudice to the other provisions of the Constitution, high treason is established if the President of the Republic has deliberately violated the Constitution or if he or the Prime Ministers are identified authors, co-authors or accomplices of grave and specific human rights violations, or of the transfer of a part of the national territory. Failings in matters of honor and integrity are established particularly if the conduct of the President of the Republic or the Prime Minister is contrary to morality or if they are identified as authors, co-authors or accomplices of embezzlement of funds, corruption or unjustified enrichment. An insider crime of the President of the Republic or the Prime Minister is established if they conduct commercial operations with regard to immovable assets or goods on which they possess privileged information that they use for

their benefit before it is known by the public. The insider crime covers the purchase and the selling of shares based on information which would never be disclosed to the shareholders. Contempt of Parliament is established if the Prime Minister does not provide any response to questions asked by either of the Parliamentary Chambers concerning the activities of the Government within a time period of thirty days.

Article 166
The decision to prosecute and the bringing of charges against the President of the Republic and the Prime Minister are voted by a two-thirds majority of the members of Parliament assembled as Congress in accordance with the procedure provided for by the internal regulations.

Article 167
In case of a conviction, the President of the Republic and the Prime Minister are relieved of their functions. The termination of their functions is pronounced by the Constitutional Court.

2. Ministers may serve simultaneously as members of the legislature.

No. Legislators are prohibited from serving simultaneously in a ministerial position.

Article 108
The mandate of Deputy or Senator is incompatible with the following functions and mandates:
a) Government member.

3. The legislature has powers of summons over executive branch officials and hearings with executive branch officials testifying before the legislature or its committees are regularly held.

Yes. The new constitution grants the legislature the power to interpellate ministers, who regularly testify before the legislature.

Article 131
The members of the Government have access to the work of the National Assembly and the Senate as well as to that of their committees. If they are requested to do so, the members of the Government are obliged to be present at the meetings of the National Assembly and the Senate, to take the floor and to provide the members of Parliament with all the explanations on their activities on which they are asked.

Article 138
Without prejudice to the other provisions of this Constitution, the means of information and control of the National Assembly and the Senate with regard to the Government, the public companies, the public establishments and services are the following:
a) oral or written questions with or without discussion followed by a vote;
b) questions on current events;
c) interpellation;
d) investigation committee;

e) hearings before the commissions.

These means of control are used under the conditions prescribed by the internal regulations of each Chamber and give rise, as the case may be, to a motion of defiance or censure in accordance with Articles 146 and 147 of this Constitution.

4. The legislature can conduct independent investigation of the chief executive and the agencies of the executive.

No. In the past the legislature has lacked the power to investigate the executive. The new constitution would, at least formally, grant the legislature the power to conduct such investigations. It is difficult to imagine, whatever the constitution's formal provisions, the legislature conducting independent investigations of the president.

Article 138
Without prejudice to the other provisions of this Constitution, the means of information and control of the National Assembly and the Senate with regard to the Government, the public companies, the public establishments and services are the following:
a) oral or written questions with or without discussion followed by a vote;
b) questions on current events;
c) interpellation;
d) investigation committee;
e) hearings before the commissions.
These means of control are used under the conditions prescribed by the internal regulations of each Chamber and give rise, as the case may be, to a motion of defiance or censure in accordance with Articles 146 and 147 of this Constitution.

5. The legislature has effective powers of oversight over the agencies of coercion (the military, organs of law enforcement, intelligence services, and the secret police).

No. The agencies of coercion report to the president and are not subject to legislative oversight.

6. The legislature appoints the prime minister.

No. Traditionally the president has appointed the prime minister. According to the new constitution, the president must choose the prime minister from the ranks of the parliamentary majority. It remains to be seen whether this rule will be observed in practice.

Article 78
The President of the Republic appoints the Prime Minister from the ranks of the parliamentary majority after consultation of the latter.

7. The legislature's approval is required to confirm the appointment of ministers; or the legislature itself appoints ministers.

No. The president appoints ministers on the recommendation of the prime minister, and the appointments do not require the legislature's approval.

Article 78
The President of the Republic appoints the other members of the Government and terminates their functions upon proposal by the Prime Minister.

8. The country lacks a presidency entirely or there is a presidency, but the president is elected by the legislature.

No. The president is directly elected.

Article 70
The President of the Republic is elected by direct universal suffrage for a term of five years which is renewable only once.

9. The legislature can vote no confidence in the government.

No. In the recent past it was unthinkable that the legislature would vote no confidence in the government. The new constitution grants the legislature the formal power to adopt a motion of censure against the government that would result in the government's resignation. It is too early to tell if this provision will take effect.

Article 146
The Prime Minister may, after deliberation by the Council of Ministers, make the Government program, a general policy declaration or the vote of a text a matter of the Government's responsibility before the National Assembly. The National Assembly may challenge the responsibility of the Government or of a member of the Government by voting a motion of censure or defiance. The motion of censure against the Government is admissible only if it is signed by a quarter of the members of the National Assembly.

Article 147
If the National Assembly adopts a motion of censure, the Government is deemed to have resigned. In this case, the Prime Minister tenders the resignation of the Government to the President of the Republic within twenty-four hours.

10. The legislature is immune from dissolution by the executive.

No. The president can dissolve the National Assembly.

Article 148
In the case of a persisting crisis between the Government and the National Assembly, the President of the Republic may, after consultation of the Prime Minister and the Presidents of the National Assembly and the Senate, pronounce the dissolution of the National Assembly.

11. Any executive initiative on legislation requires ratification or approval by the legislature before it takes effect; that is, the executive lacks decree power.

No. The president issues decrees that have the force of law. In the new constitution, presidential decrees lapse if they are not subsequently approved by the legislature. The president acting alone also has the authority to declare a state of emergency, during which he or she may also issue decrees that have the force of law.

Article 129
The Government may, for the urgent execution of its action program, ask the National Assembly or the Senate for authorization, for a limited period, to take measures by "ordinance-laws" on specific matters that fall normally within the domain of statutory law. These ordinance-laws are deliberated on by the Council of Ministers. They come into force upon publication and lapse if the draft law for their ratification is not presented to Parliament before the latest date set by the enabling law. If Parliament does not ratify these ordinance-laws at the end of the period referred to in the first paragraph of this article, they automatically cease to produce legal effects. The ordinance-laws deliberated on by the Council of Ministers and ratified may not be amended in their provisions except by statutory law. The ordinance-laws cease automatically to produce any legal effects in case of the rejection of the law of ratification.

Article 144
In application of the provisions of Article 85 of this Constitution, the state of siege, like the state of emergency, is declared by the President of the Republic...The National Assembly and the Senate may by way of statute end at any moment the state of emergency or siege.

Article 145
In the case of a state of emergency or state of siege, the President of the Republic takes, by ordinances which have been deliberated by the Council of Ministers, the measures necessary to respond to the situation. Immediately after they have been signed, these ordinances are submitted to the Constitutional Court which suspends all its other work and declares whether or not they derogate from this Constitution.

12. Laws passed by the legislature are veto-proof or essentially veto-proof; that is, the executive lacks veto power, or has veto power but the veto can be overridden by a majority in the legislature.

No. In the past it would have been unthinkable for the legislature to override a presidential veto. According to the new constitution, the legislature can override a presidential veto by a majority vote of its total membership. It is too early to tell if this provision will take effect in practice.

Article 137
Within fifteen days from the date of transmission, the President of the Republic may ask the National Assembly or the Senate for a new deliberation of the law or of certain articles. This new deliberation may not be refused. The text submitted for second deliberation is adopted by the National Assembly and the Senate either in the original form or after amendment by the absolute majority of their members.

13. The legislature's laws are supreme and not subject to judicial review.

No. The Constitutional Court can review the constitutionality of laws.

Article 124
The statutory laws to which the Constitution confers the character of organic laws are adopted and amended by the absolute majority of members of each Chamber in the following conditions:
c) the organic laws may only be promulgated after the declaration of their conformity with the Constitution by the Constitutional Court within fifteen days after they have obligatorily been referred to the latter by the President of the Republic.

Article 139
Statutes may be referred to the Constitutional Court in order to obtain a declaration of non-conformity with the Constitution by the following authorities:
a) the President of the Republic, within fifteen days following the transmission to him of the law finally adopted;
b) the Government, within fifteen days following the transmission to it of the law finally adopted;
c) a number of Deputies and Senators equal to at least a tenth of the members of each Chamber, within a full fifteen days following its final adoption.
The statute may only be promulgated if it has been declared to be in accordance with the Constitution by the Constitutional Court, which rules within fifteen days after the matter has been referred to it. This deadline having lapsed, the statute is considered to be in conformity with the Constitution.

Article 160
The Constitutional Court is charged with the control of the constitutionality of laws and of measures having the force of law.

14. The legislature has the right to initiate bills in all policy jurisdictions; the executive lacks gatekeeping authority.

Yes. The legislature can initiate bills in all policy jurisdictions.

15. Expenditure of funds appropriated by the legislature is mandatory; the executive lacks the power to impound funds appropriated by the legislature.

No. The president can impound funds appropriated by the legislature.

16. The legislature controls the resources that finance its own internal operation and provide for the perquisites of its own members.

No. The legislature is dependent on the executive for the resources that finance its own operations, although the new constitution formally grants the legislature financial autonomy.

Article 100
Each Chamber [of Congress] enjoys administrative and financial autonomy and has its own allocation.

Article 109
The National Deputies and Senators . . . are entitled to an equitable indemnity which ensures their independence and their dignity. It is provided for in the Budget Law.

17. Members of the legislature are immune from arrest and/or criminal prosecution.

Yes. Legislators are immune with the common exception for cases of *flagrante delicto.*

Article 107
No member of Parliament may be prosecuted, searched, arrested, detained or judged for opinions or votes delivered in the exercise of his functions. Except in cases of flagrante delicto, a member of Parliament may be prosecuted or arrested during sessions only with the authorization of the National Assembly or the Senate, as the case may be. When not in session, a member of Parliament may only be arrested with the authorization of the Bureau of the National Assembly or the Bureau of the Senate for the Senators, except in cases of flagrante delicto, of previously authorized prosecution or of final sentence.

18. All members of the legislature are elected; the executive lacks the power to appoint any members of the legislature.

Yes. Since the legislative elections in 2006, all members of the legislature are elected. Members of the previous transitional legislature were appointed by various societal and political groups. According to the new constitution, former presidents will be guaranteed seats in the Senate, although no former presidents currently occupy a legislative seat.

Article 101
The members of the National Assembly are called National Deputies. They are elected by universal, direct and secret suffrage.

Article 104
Senators . . . are elected at the second level by the Provincial Assemblies. Each Senator is elected together with two proxies. The former elected Presidents of the Republic are by law Senators for life.

19. The legislature alone, without the involvement of any other agencies, can change the Constitution.

No. In practice, a constitutional amendment would be unthinkable without presidential support. Formally, the legislature can change the constitution with a three-fifths majority vote.

Article 218
The right to initiate a revision of the Constitution belongs concurrently to:
a) the President of the Republic;
b) the Government after deliberation by the Council of Ministers;
c) to either of the Chambers of Parliament upon initiative by half of its members;
d) to a fraction of the Congolese people, in the present case to 100.000 persons expressing themselves by way of petition addressed to either of the two Chambers.
Each of these initiatives is submitted to the National Assembly and the Senate which decide by absolute majority of each chamber on the substance of the project, proposal or petition for revision. The revision is only final if the project, proposal or petition is approved by referendum. However, the project, proposition or petition is not submitted to referendum if the National Assembly and the Senate meeting jointly as Congress approve it by a three-fifths majority of their members.

20. The legislature's approval is necessary for the declaration of war.

Yes. The president's war declarations require approval by both houses of the legislature.

Article 86
The President of the Republic declares war by an ordinance which has been deliberated on by the Council of Ministers after having heard the High Council for Defense and after approval of the measure by the National Assembly and the Senate in conformity with Article 144 of this Constitution.

Article 143
In accordance with the provisions of Article 86 of the Constitution, the President of the Republic declares war upon the decision of the Council of Ministers after hearing the High Council for Defense and after authorization by the two Chambers.

21. The legislature's approval is necessary to ratify treaties with foreign countries.

No. The president negotiates and ratifies international treaties. Many types of international treaties require approval by law, but given that the government can issue ordinance-laws (see item 11), the ratification of even these treaties does not necessarily require the legislature's approval in practice.

Article 213
The President of the Republic negotiates and ratifies international treaties and agreements.

The Government concludes international agreements not subject to ratification after deliberation by the Council of Ministers. It informs the National Assembly and the Senate about it.

Article 214

Peace treaties, trade agreements, treaties and agreements relating to international organizations and to the settlement of international conflicts, those which involve public finance, those which amend legislative provisions, those which relate to the status of individuals, or those which entail the exchange and addition of territory may only be approved or ratified by virtue of a law.

No transfer, exchange or addition of territory is valid without the approval of the Congolese people consulted by way of referendum.

22. The legislature has the power to grant amnesty.

No. In the past the president alone has had the power to grant amnesty. The new constitution endows the legislature with the power to grant amnesty through legislation, although it remains to be seen whether this power will be vested in the legislature in practice.

Article 122

Without prejudice to the other provisions of this Constitution, statutory law establishes the rules concerning:
i) amnesty and extradition.

23. The legislature has the power of pardon.

No. The president has the power of pardon.

Article 87

The President of the Republic exercises the right to pardon.

He may delay, commute or reduce sentences.

24. The legislature reviews and has the right to reject appointments to the judiciary; or the legislature itself appoints members of the judiciary.

No. The president appoints members of the judiciary, and the appointments do not require the legislature's approval.

Article 158

The Constitutional Court consists of nine members appointed by the President of the Republic.

25. The chairman of the central bank is appointed by the legislature.

No. The president appoints the head of the Congolese Central Bank.

26. The legislature has a substantial voice in the operation of the state-owned media.

No. The legislature lacks a substantial voice in the operation of the public media.

27. The legislature is regularly in session.

Yes. The National Assembly meets in ordinary session for six months each year.

Article 115

The National Assembly and the Senate hold by law each year two ordinary sessions:
a) the first starts on March 15 and closes on June 15;
b) the second starts on September 15 and closes on December 15.

28. Each legislator has a personal secretary.

No.

29. Each legislator has at least one non-secretarial staff member with policy expertise.

No.

30. Legislators are eligible for re-election without any restriction.

Yes. There are no restrictions on re-election.

Article 103

The National Deputy is elected for a term of five years. He may be re-elected.

Article 105

The Senator is elected for a term of five years. He may be re-elected.

31. A seat in the legislature is an attractive enough position that legislators are generally interested in and seek re-election.

Yes.

32. The re-election of incumbent legislators is common enough that at any given time the legislature contains a significant number of highly experienced members.

No. The National Assembly is a young institution, and legislators have not had time to develop significant expertise.

LEGISLATIVE ASSEMBLY OF COSTA RICA (*ASAMBLEA LEGISLATIVA*)

Expert consultants: Leslie E. Anderson, John M. Carey, Natalia Ajenjo Fresno, Otton Solís, Bruce M. Wilson

Score: .53

Influence over executive (3/9)		Institutional autonomy (6/9)		Specified powers (5/8)		Institutional capacity (3/6)	
1. replace		10. no dissolution	X	19. amendments	X	27. sessions	X
2. serve as ministers		11. no decree	X	20. war	X	28. secretary	X
3. interpellate	X	12. no veto		21. treaties	X	29. staff	X
4. investigate	X	13. no review		22. amnesty	X	30. no term limits	
5. oversee police	X	14. no gatekeeping	X	23. pardon		31. seek re-election	
6. appoint PM		15. no impoundment		24. judiciary	X	32. experience	
7. appoint ministers		16. control resources	X	25. central bank			
8. lack president		17. immunity	X	26. media			
9. no confidence		18. all elected	X				

The Legislative Assembly (*Asamblea Legislativa*) of Costa Rica traces its roots to the bodies that gathered following independence in 1821. Costa Rica's current constitution, which was adopted in 1949, provides the unicameral Legislative Assembly with some clout. It has oversight powers that give it some control over the executive. The legislature enjoys substantial institutional autonomy; the president lacks gatekeeping, decree, and dissolution powers. The Legislative Assembly also enjoys a number of exclusive powers and prerogatives, including the right to authorize war, approve international treaties, and grant amnesty.

The institutional capacity of Costa Rica's legislature is bolstered by the presence of staff for members. It is limited, however, by a prohibition on re-election of legislators, who are limited to a single consecutive term. Many aspiring politicians therefore view a seat in the legislature as a stepping stone to executive branch positions.

SURVEY

1. The legislature alone, without the involvement of any other agencies, can impeach the president or replace the prime minister.

No. Presidential impeachment requires action by the Supreme Court of Justice.

Article 121
The Legislative Assembly has exclusive powers to:
9. Admit or refuse any impeachment made against the person exercising the Presidency of the Republic... declaring by a vote of two thirds of the entire Assembly whether or not there are grounds for legal action against them, placing them, if there are, at the disposition of the Supreme Court of Justice for prosecution thereof.

2. Ministers may serve simultaneously as members of the legislature.

No. Ministers are prohibited from serving simultaneously in the legislature.

Article 109
The following may not be elected representatives or registered as candidates for that office:
2. Cabinet Ministers.

3. The legislature has powers of summons over executive branch officials and hearings with executive branch officials testifying before the legislature or its committees are regularly held.

Yes. The legislature regularly interpellates officials from the executive.

Article 121

In addition to other powers vested in it by this Constitution, the Legislative Assembly has exclusive powers to:

23. Appoint commissions from within its membership to investigate any matter entrusted to them by the Assembly and submit the appropriate report.

Such Commissions shall have free access to all official agencies to conduct their investigations and collect any data they may deem necessary. They may receive any kind of evidence and summon before them any person for purposes of interrogation;

24. Formulate questions to Cabinet Ministers and, in addition, by a vote of two thirds of the attending representatives, censure such officials if, in the opinion of the Assembly, they are guilty of illegal or unconstitutional acts or serious errors that have caused or may cause evident damages to the public interest.

4. The legislature can conduct independent investigation of the chief executive and the agencies of the executive.

Yes. The legislature can investigate the executive.

Article 121

In addition to other powers vested in it by this Constitution, the Legislative Assembly has exclusive powers to:

23. Appoint commissions from within its membership to investigate any matter entrusted to them by the Assembly and submit the appropriate report.

Such Commissions shall have free access to all official agencies to conduct their investigations and collect any data they may deem necessary. They may receive any kind of evidence and summon before them any person for purposes of interrogation.

24. Formulate questions to Cabinet Ministers and, in addition, by a vote of two thirds of the attending representatives, censure such officials if, in the opinion of the Assembly, they are guilty of illegal or unconstitutional acts or serious errors that have caused or may cause evident damages to the public interest.

5. The legislature has effective powers of oversight over the agencies of coercion (the military, organs of law enforcement, intelligence services, and the secret police).

Yes. Legislative committees have effective powers of oversight over the agencies of coercion.

6. The legislature appoints the prime minister.

No. There is no prime minister.

7. The legislature's approval is required to confirm the appointment of ministers; or the legislature itself appoints ministers.

No. The president appoints ministers, and the appointments do not require the legislature's approval.

Article 139

The following are the exclusive powers and duties of the occupant of the Presidency of the Republic:

1) To freely appoint and remove Cabinet Ministers.

8. The country lacks a presidency entirely or there is a presidency, but the president is elected by the legislature.

No. The president is directly elected.

Article 138

The President and Vice Presidents shall be elected simultaneously and by a majority vote that exceeds forty percent of the total number of validly cast votes.

9. The legislature can vote no confidence in the government.

No. The legislature can censure individual ministers, but it cannot vote no confidence in the government as a whole.

Article 121

In addition to other powers conferred by this constitution, the Legislative Assembly has exclusive power to:

24. Formulate questions to Cabinet Ministers and, in addition, by a vote of two thirds of the attending representatives, censure such officials if, in the opinion of the Assembly, they are guilty of illegal or unconstitutional acts or serious errors that have caused or may cause evident damages to the public interest.

10. The legislature is immune from dissolution by the executive.

Yes. The legislature is immune from dissolution.

11. Any executive initiative on legislation requires ratification or approval by the legislature before it takes effect; that is, the executive lacks decree power.

Yes. The executive lacks decree power.

12. Laws passed by the legislature are veto-proof or essentially veto-proof; that is, the executive lacks veto power, or has veto power but the veto can be overridden by a majority in the legislature.

No. A two-thirds majority vote in the Assembly is needed to override a presidential veto.

Article 127

When a bill of law is reconsidered by the Assembly with the observations of the Executive Branch, if the Assembly rejects them and the bill of law is again passed by a vote of two thirds of the total membership, it is thereby sanctioned and must be enforced as a law of the Republic.

13. The legislature's laws are supreme and not subject to judicial review.

No. The Supreme Court of Justice can review the constitutionality of laws. In 1989 a Constitutional

Chamber of the Supreme Court of Justice was created for this purpose.

Article 10
It shall be incumbent upon a specialized division of the Supreme Court of Justice to declare, by absolute majority of its members, the unconstitutionality of laws of whatever nature and of acts subject to Public Law. Not impugnable in this way are jurisdictional acts of the Judicial Power, declaration of election made by the Supreme Tribunal of Elections, and others determined by law.

14. The legislature has the right to initiate bills in all policy jurisdictions; the executive lacks gatekeeping authority.

Yes. The legislature can initiate bills in all policy jurisdictions.

15. Expenditure of funds appropriated by the legislature is mandatory; the executive lacks the power to impound funds appropriated by the legislature.

No. The executive can impound funds. The budget, once passed by the legislature, authorizes but does not oblige expenditures.

16. The legislature controls the resources that finance its own internal operation and provide for the perquisites of its own members.

Yes. The legislature enjoys financial autonomy, including control over members' compensation.

Article 113
The law shall fix the compensation of representatives as well as any technical and administrative assistance to be given to them.

17. Members of the legislature are immune from arrest and/or criminal prosecution.

Yes. Legislators are immune with the common exception for cases of *flagrante delicto*.

Article 110
A representative is not liable for any opinions expressed at the Assembly. During legislative sessions, he cannot be arrested on civil grounds, except by authorization of the Assembly or with the consent of the representative. From the time he is declared elected as representative or as an alternate representative, until expiration of his legal term in office, he may not be deprived of his freedom on criminal grounds, unless he has been previously suspended by the Assembly. Such immunity does not apply in case of flagrante delicto or when the representative waives it. Nevertheless, a representative who has been arrested for flagrante delicto will be released if the Assembly so orders.

18. All members of the legislature are elected; the executive lacks the power to appoint any members of the legislature.

Yes. All members of the legislature are elected.

Article 105
The power to legislate resides in the people, which delegate this power, by means of suffrage, to the Legislative Assembly. Such a power may not be waived or subject to limitations by any agreement or contract, either directly or indirectly, except in the case of treaties, in accordance with the principles of International Law.

Article 106
The deputies have this character for the nation and shall be elected by provinces.
The Assembly consists of fifty-seven deputies. Each time a general census of the population is taken, the Supreme Electoral Tribunal shall designate for the provinces their number of deputies in proportion to their population.

19. The legislature alone, without the involvement of any other agencies, can change the Constitution.

Yes. The legislature can change the constitution in multiple readings with a two-thirds majority vote. A complete rewrite of the constitution requires approval by a special Constituent Assembly.

Article 195
The Legislative Assembly may partially amend this Constitution complying strictly with the following provisions:
1. A proposal asking for the amendment of one or more articles must be submitted to the Assembly at regular sessions, signed by at least ten representatives;
2. The proposal shall be read three times at intervals of six days, to determine whether or not it shall be admitted for discussion;
3. If admitted, it shall be sent to a commission appointed by absolute majority of the Assembly, which has to render its opinion within a period of twenty business days;
4. Upon submission of this opinion, it shall be discussed in accordance with the procedure established for enactment of laws; said amendment shall be approved by a vote of no less than two thirds of the entire membership of the Assembly;
5. Once the amendment has been favorably voted, the Assembly shall prepare the appropriate bill of law through a commission, being an absolute majority enough for its approval;
6. Said bill of law shall be sent to the Executive Branch, which in turn shall send it with the Presidential Message to the Assembly at the start of the next regular legislative period, with his observations, or his recommendation;
7. The Legislative Assembly, at its first sessions, shall discuss the bill of law in three debates. If it is approved by a vote of no less than two thirds of the entire membership, it shall become a part of the Constitution and communicated to the Executive Branch for publication and observance thereof.

Article 196
A general amendment of this Constitution can only be made by a Constituent Assembly called for the purpose. A law calling such Assembly shall be passed by a vote of no less than two thirds of the total membership of the Legislative Assembly and does not require the approval of the Executive Branch.

20. The legislature's approval is necessary for the declaration of war.

Yes. The legislature's approval is necessary for the declaration of war.

Article 121
In addition to other powers vested in it by this Constitution, the Legislative Assembly has exclusive powers to:
6. Authorize the Executive Branch to declare a state of national defense and to reach peace agreements.

21. The legislature's approval is necessary to ratify treaties with foreign countries.

Yes. The legislature's approval is necessary to ratify international treaties.

Article 121
In addition to other powers vested in it by this Constitution, the Legislative Assembly has exclusive powers to:
4. Approve or disapprove international conventions, public treaties and concordats.
Public treaties and international conventions which confer or transfer certain powers to a community legal order for the purpose of achieving common regional objectives shall require the approval of the Legislative Assembly by a vote of not less than two-thirds of its entire membership.

22. The legislature has the power to grant amnesty.

Yes. The legislature has the power to grant amnesty.

Article 121
In addition to other powers vested in it by this Constitution, the Legislative Assembly has exclusive powers to:
21. By a vote of no less than two thirds of the entire membership, grant general amnesties and pardons for political crimes, except electoral offenses, for which there shall be no mercy.

23. The legislature has the power of pardon.

No. The president has the power of pardon.

24. The legislature reviews and has the right to reject appointments to the judiciary; or the legislature itself appoints members of the judiciary.

Yes. The legislature appoints the members of the Supreme Court of Justice.

Article 121
In addition to other powers vested in it by this Constitution, the Legislative Assembly has exclusive powers to:
3. Appoint the regular and alternate justices of the Supreme Court of Justice.

Article 157
The Supreme Court of Justice shall be composed of the number of Justices that may be considered necessary for a good service; they shall be elected by the Legislative Assembly, which shall make up the different Court Chambers established by law.

25. The chairman of the central bank is appointed by the legislature.

No. The president appoints the president of the Central Bank of Costa Rica.

26. The legislature has a substantial voice in the operation of the state-owned media.

No. The legislature lacks a substantial voice in the operation of the public media.

27. The legislature is regularly in session.

Yes. The legislature meets in ordinary session for six months each year.

Article 116
The Legislative Assembly shall meet each year on the first day of May, even if it has not been convoked, and its regular-session term shall last six months, divided into two periods: from the first day of May to the thirty-first day of July and from the first day of September to the thirtieth day of November.

28. Each legislator has a personal secretary.

Yes.

29. Each legislator has at least one non-secretarial staff member with policy expertise.

Yes.

30. Legislators are eligible for re-election without any restriction.

No. Consecutive re-election is forbidden. Legislators can run for re-election only after sitting out at least one term.

Article 107
Deputies shall hold office for four years and may not be reelected to a succeeding term.

31. A seat in the legislature is an attractive enough position that legislators are generally interested in and seek re-election.

No. Surveys show that most legislators want political careers, but the prohibition on consecutive re-election prevents most from seeking re-election, even after they become eligible for it.

32. The re-election of incumbent legislators is common enough that at any given time the legislature contains a significant number of highly experienced members.

No. The prohibition on consecutive re-election results in a low number of experienced members.

NATIONAL ASSEMBLY OF CÔTE D'IVOIRE (*ASSEMBLÉE NATIONALE*)

Expert consultants: Aghi Bahi, Abdoulaye Essy, Christof Hartmann, Eleanor Marchant

Score: .38

Influence over executive (1/9)	Institutional autonomy (5/9)		Specified powers (3/8)		Institutional capacity (3/6)	
1. replace	10. no dissolution	X	19. amendments		27. sessions	
2. serve as ministers	11. no decree		20. war	X	28. secretary	
3. interpellate X	12. no veto		21. treaties	X	29. staff	
4. investigate	13. no review		22. amnesty	X	30. no term limits	X
5. oversee police	14. no gatekeeping	X	23. pardon		31. seek re-election	X
6. appoint PM	15. no impoundment		24. judiciary		32. experience	X
7. appoint ministers	16. control resources	X	25. central bank			
8. lack president	17. immunity	X	26. media			
9. no confidence	18. all elected	X				

The National Assembly (*Assemblée nationale*) of Côte d'Ivoire was established in the 1960 constitution upon independence from France. For the next three decades, Côte d'Ivoire was ruled by its first president, Félix Houphouët-Boigny. In 1999 General Robert Guei seized power in a military coup and implemented a new constitution, which was approved by referendum in 2000. Increasing tensions between the government and the opposition erupted in an attempted coup and civil war in September 2002. Government and opposition forces subsequently agreed to a tenuous cease-fire held together by international peacekeeping troops.

The unicameral National Assembly, whose powers are defined in the 2000 constitution, is quite weak. It has little ability to influence the executive, and its own autonomy is circumscribed by, among other restrictions, presidential decree and veto powers. The legislature enjoys several powers and prerogatives. Until the civil strife that divides the country is resolved, the legislature will be unable to exercise even the modest powers that it formally enjoys.

SURVEY

1. The legislature alone, without the involvement of any other agencies, can impeach the president or replace the prime minister.

No. Presidential impeachment requires the involvement of the High Court of Justice, which is headed by the president of the Court of Cassation.

Article 108
The High Court of Justice is composed of Deputies that the National Assembly elects from within, at the first session of the legislature. It is presided over the by the President of the Court of Cassation. An organic law establishes the number of its members, its attributions

and the rules of its functioning as well as the procedure to be followed before it.

Article 109
The President of the Republic is not responsible for acts accomplished in the exercise of his functions and can only be brought before the High Court of Justice in the case of high treason.

Article 111
The impeachment of the President of the Republic and of the members of the Government is voted in secret ballot, by the National Assembly with a majority of 2/3 for the President of the Republic, and with an absolute majority for the members of the Government.

2. Ministers may serve simultaneously as members of the legislature.

No. Ministers are prohibited from serving simultaneously in the legislature.

Article 56
The functions of a member of the Government are incompatible with the exercise of any office and of any professional activity. A parliamentarian appointed member of the Government cannot sit in the National Assembly, for the duration of his ministerial functions.

3. The legislature has powers of summons over executive branch officials and hearings with executive branch officials testifying before the legislature or its committees are regularly held.

Yes. The legislature regularly interpellates officials from the executive.

Article 82
The means of information of the National Assembly concerning the governmental action are the oral question, the written question, [and] the commission of inquiry. During the term of the ordinary session, one meeting per month is reserved by priority to the questions of the Deputies and to the responses of the President of the Republic. The President of the Republic can delegate to the Head of Government and to the ministers the power to respond to the questions of the Deputies. In the circumstance, the National Assembly can take a resolution to make recommendations to the Government.

4. The legislature can conduct independent investigation of the chief executive and the agencies of the executive.

No. According to the constitution, the legislature can establish a commission of inquiry to investigate the executive, but in practice, it is unthinkable that the legislature would initiate an investigation of the president.

Article 82
The means of information of the National Assembly concerning the governmental action are the oral question, the written question, [and] the commission of inquiry. During the term of the ordinary session, one meeting per month is reserved by priority to the questions of the Deputies and to the responses of the President of the Republic. The President of the Republic can delegate to the Head of Government and to the ministers the power to respond to the questions of the Deputies. In the circumstance, the National Assembly can take a resolution to make recommendations to the Government.

5. The legislature has effective powers of oversight over the agencies of coercion (the military, organs of law enforcement, intelligence services, and the secret police).

No. The agencies of coercion report directly to the president and are not subject to legislative oversight.

6. The legislature appoints the prime minister.

No. The president appoints the prime minister.

Article 41
The President...appoints the Prime Minister, [the] Head of Government, who is responsible to him. He terminates his functions. The Prime Minister animates and coordinates the governmental action. On the proposal of the Prime Minister, the President of the Republic appoints the other members of the Government and determines their attributions. He terminates their functions under the same conditions.

7. The legislature's approval is required to confirm the appointment of ministers; or the legislature itself appoints ministers.

No. The president appoints ministers on the recommendation of the prime minister, and the appointments do not require the legislature's approval.

Article 41
On the proposal of the Prime Minister, the President of the Republic appoints the other members of the Government and determines their attributions.

8. The country lacks a presidency entirely or there is a presidency, but the president is elected by the legislature.

No. The president is directly elected.

Article 35
The President of the Republic is elected for five years by universal direct suffrage.

9. The legislature can vote no confidence in the government.

No. The legislature cannot vote no confidence in the government.

10. The legislature is immune from dissolution by the executive.

Yes. The legislature is immune from dissolution.

11. Any executive initiative on legislation requires ratification or approval by the legislature before it takes effect; that is, the executive lacks decree power.

No. The president can issue decrees that have the force of law. Presidential decrees remain in effect until explicitly modified by subsequent legislation. Furthermore, if the National Assembly does not approve the national budget within seventy days of its introduction, the president can pass the budget by decree.

Article 75
The President of the Republic can, for the execution of his program, demand of the National Assembly, the authorization to take by ordinance, for a limited time, the measures which are normally of the domain of the law. The ordinances are taken in the Council of Ministers after the possible advice of the Constitutional Council. They enter into force on their publication but, become lapsed if the bill of law of ratification is not deposited before the Parliament prior to the date established by the enabling law. After the expiration of the time limit mentioned in the first paragraph of this article, the ordinances can only be further modified by the law in their provisions which are of the legislative domain.

Article 80
The National Assembly is seized with the bill of the Law of Finance from the opening of the October session. The bill of the Law of Finance must provide the receipts necessary for the integral covering of expenses. The National Assembly votes the balanced budget. If the National Assembly has not decided within a time period of seventy days, the bill of law can be put into force by ordinance. The President of the Republic seizes, for ratification, the National Assembly convoked in extraordinary session, within a time limit of fifteen days. If the National Assembly has not voted the budget by the end of this extraordinary session, the budget is definitively established by ordinance. If the bill of the Law of Finance has not been deposited in a timely way to be promulgated before the beginning of the exercise, the President of the Republic demands [of] the National Assembly by urgency, the authorization to repeat the budget of the previous year by provisional twelfths.

12. Laws passed by the legislature are veto-proof or essentially veto-proof; that is, the executive lacks veto power, or has veto power but the veto can be overridden by a majority in the legislature.

No. A two-thirds majority vote in the National Assembly is needed to override a presidential veto.

Article 42
The President of the Republic can, before the expiration of this time period, demand of the National Assembly a second deliberation of the law or of certain of its articles. This second deliberation cannot be refused . . . The vote for this second deliberation is acquired by the majority of two-thirds of the members present of the National Assembly.

13. The legislature's laws are supreme and not subject to judicial review.

No. The Constitutional Council can review the constitutionality of laws.

Article 88
The Constitutional Council is [the] judge of the constitutionality of the law.

14. The legislature has the right to initiate bills in all policy jurisdictions; the executive lacks gatekeeping authority.

Yes. The legislature can initiate bills in all policy jurisdictions.

15. Expenditure of funds appropriated by the legislature is mandatory; the executive lacks the power to impound funds appropriated by the legislature.

No. The president can impound funds appropriated by the legislature.

16. The legislature controls the resources that finance its own internal operation and provide for the perquisites of its own members.

Yes. The legislature enjoys financial autonomy, including control over members' perquisites.

Article 69
The Deputies receive an indemnity, the amount of which is established by a law.

17. Members of the legislature are immune from arrest and/or criminal prosecution.

Yes. Legislators are immune with the common exception for cases of *flagrante delicto*.

Article 67
No Deputy can be prosecuted, investigated, arrested, detained or judged on the occasion of his opinions or of the votes made by him in the exercise of his functions.

Article 68
During the term of the sessions, no member of Parliament can be prosecuted or arrested in a criminal or correctional matter without the authorization of the National Assembly, except in a case of *flagrante delicto*. No Deputy can, out of session, be arrested without the authorization of the Bureau of the National Assembly except in cases of *flagrant delicto*, authorized prosecutions or definitive condemnations. The detention or the prosecution of a member of Parliament is suspended if the National Assembly requires it.

18. All members of the legislature are elected; the executive lacks the power to appoint any members of the legislature.

Yes. All members of the legislature are elected.

Article 58
The Parliament is composed of one sole chamber called the National Assembly having members carrying the title of Deputy. The Deputies are elected by universal direct suffrage.

19. The legislature alone, without the involvement of any other agencies, can change the Constitution.

No. Constitutional amendments require approval in a popular referendum.

Article 124
The initiative of the revision of the Constitution belongs concurrently to the President of the Republic and to the members of the National Assembly.

Article 125
To be taken into consideration, the bill or the proposal of revision must be voted by the National Assembly with the majority of 2/3 of its members effectively in [their] functions.

Article 126
The revision of the Constitution is only definitive after having been approved by referendum with the absolute majority of the suffrage expressed.

20. The legislature's approval is necessary for the declaration of war.

Yes. The legislature declares war.

Article 73
The declaration of war is authorized by the National Assembly.

21. The legislature's approval is necessary to ratify treaties with foreign countries.

Yes. The legislature's approval is necessary to ratify international treaties on most major issues.

Article 84
The President of the Republic negotiates and ratifies the treaties and international agreements.

Article 85
The peace Treaties, the Treaties and Agreements concerning international organization, [and] those that modify the internal laws of the State can only be ratified after passage of a law.

22. The legislature has the power to grant amnesty.

Yes. The legislature has the power to grant amnesty.

Article 71
The National Assembly holds the legislative power. It alone votes the law. The law establishes the rules

concerning . . . the determination of crimes and misdemeanors as well as the penalties which are applicable to them, the penal procedure, [and] amnesty.

23. The legislature has the power of pardon.

No. The president has the power of pardon.

Article 49
The President of the Republic has the right of pardon.

24. The legislature reviews and has the right to reject appointments to the judiciary; or the legislature itself appoints members of the judiciary.

No. By law, the legislature has a role in appointments to the High Court, the Constitutional Council, and the Superior Council of the Magistrature, but in practice, the legislature does not play a part in judicial appointments.

Article 89
The Constitutional Council is composed:
– of a President;
– of the former Presidents of the Republic, except [on] express renunciation on their part;
– of six councillors[,] of which three are designated by the President of the Republic and three by the President of the National Assembly.

Article 105
The Superior Council of the Magistrature comprehends:
– The President of the Court of Cassation, Vice President of right;
– The President of the Council of State;
– The President of the Court of Accounts;
– The Procurator General before the Court of Cassation;
– Six persons from outside of the Magistrature of which three principals and three substitutes are appointed in equal number by the President of the Republic and the President of the National Assembly;
– Three magistrates of the Bench of which two principals and one substitute and three magistrates of the Office of the Public Prosecutor of which two principals and one substitute, are designated by their peers. These magistrates cannot sit [if] they are affected by the deliberations of the Council.

Article 108
The High Court is composed of Deputies that the National Assembly elects from within, at the first session of the legislature. It is presided over the by the President of the Court of Cassation. An organic law establishes the number of its members, its attributions and the rules of its functioning as well as the procedure to be followed before it.

25. The chairman of the central bank is appointed by the legislature.

No. Côte d'Ivoire is a member of the Central Bank of West African States, whose governor is selected by the member states.

26. The legislature has a substantial voice in the operation of the state-owned media.

No. The legislature lacks a substantial voice in the operation of the public media.

27. The legislature is regularly in session.

No. The legislature is in session for less than five months a year.

> Article 62
> Each year, the Parliament meets of right in two ordinary sessions. The first session begins the last Wednesday of April; its duration cannot exceed three months. The second session begins the first Wednesday of October and ends the third Friday of December.

28. Each legislator has a personal secretary.

No.

29. Each legislator has at least one non-secretarial staff member with policy expertise.

No.

30. Legislators are eligible for re-election without any restriction.

Yes. There are no restrictions on re-election.

31. A seat in the legislature is an attractive enough position that legislators are generally interested in and seek re-election.

Yes.

32. The re-election of incumbent legislators is common enough that at any given time the legislature contains a significant number of highly experienced members.

Yes. Re-election rates are sufficiently high to produce a significant number of highly experienced members.

PARLIAMENT OF CROATIA (*SABOR*)

Expert consultants: Đorđe Gardašević, Nikola Jelić, Andrej Krickovic, Ivona Mendes, Vanja Škorić

Score: .78

Influence over executive (7/9)		Institutional autonomy (7/9)		Specified powers (7/8)		Institutional capacity (4/6)	
1. replace	X	10. no dissolution		19. amendments	X	27. sessions	X
2. serve as ministers		11. no decree	X	20. war	X	28. secretary	
3. interpellate	X	12. no veto	X	21. treaties	X	29. staff	
4. investigate	X	13. no review		22. amnesty	X	30. no term limits	X
5. oversee police	X	14. no gatekeeping	X	23. pardon		31. seek re-election	X
6. appoint PM	X	15. no impoundment	X	24. judiciary	X	32. experience	X
7. appoint ministers	X	16. control resources	X	25. central bank	X		
8. lack president		17. immunity	X	26. media	X		
9. no confidence	X	18. all elected	X				

The Parliament (*Sabor*) of Croatia traces its roots to representative bodies that convened in the late thirteenth century. The legislature was established in its current form in the country's 1990 constitution, which called for a bicameral assembly consisting of a lower house, the Chamber of Deputies (*Zastupnicki dom*), and an upper house, the Chamber of Counties (*Zupanjski dom*).

Constitutional amendments in 2000 shifted considerable power from the presidency to the parliament. The changes were characterized in Croatia and by some political scientists as the conversion of the Croatian political system from semipresidentialism to parliamentarism. Prior to 2000 the president had free reign to appoint the prime minister and the government. Since 2000 the president has been required to appoint a prime minister and government that enjoy majority support in the legislature. The 1990 constitution granted the president the power to appoint five members to the Chamber of Counties, but a constitutional amendment in 2000 eliminated the provision for appointed members. In March 2001 another constitutional amendment eliminated the Chamber of Counties altogether, creating a unicameral parliament.

The legislature is endowed with formidable authority. It influences the executive with powers of interpellation, investigation, and a vote of no confidence, among other powers. It does not share lawmaking powers with the president, who lacks decree, veto, and gatekeeping powers. The legislature is vested with a number of specified powers and prerogatives and has a substantial amount of institutional capacity.

SURVEY

1. The legislature alone, without the involvement of any other agencies, can impeach the president or replace the prime minister.

Yes. The legislature can remove the prime minister with a vote of no confidence. Presidential impeachment requires action by the Constitutional Court.

Article 105
(1) The President of the Republic shall be impeachable for any violation of the Constitution he has committed in the performance of his duties.
(2) Proceedings for the impeachment of the President of the Republic may be instituted by the Croatian Parliament by a two-thirds majority vote of all representatives.
(3) The impeachment of the President of the Republic shall be decided upon by the Constitutional Court of the Republic of Croatia by a two-thirds majority vote of all the judges.
(4) The Constitutional Court shall decide upon the impeachment of the President of the Republic during the term of 30 days form the day of the submission of the proposal to impeach the President of the Republic for violation of the Constitution.
(5) If the Constitutional Court of the Republic of Croatia sustains the impeachment, the duty of the President of the Republic shall cease by force of the Constitution.

Article 115
(1) At the proposal of at least one fifth of the members of the Croatian Parliament, a vote of confidence in the Prime Minster, in individual members of the Government, or in the Government as a whole, shall be put in motion.

(5) A no confidence decision shall be accepted if it has been voted for by the majority of the total number of members of the Croatian Parliament.
(7) If a vote of no confidence in the Prime Minister or in the Government as a whole is passed, the Prime Minister and the Government shall submit their resignation.

2. Ministers may serve simultaneously as members of the legislature.

No. According to the constitution, ministers may not perform any other public duty without the approval of the government. In practice, ministers do not serve simultaneously in the legislature.

Article 108
The Government of the Republic of Croatia consists of the Prime Minister, one or more Deputy Prime Ministers and Ministers.
Without the approval of the Government, the Prime Minister and members of the Government cannot perform any other public or professional duty.

3. The legislature has powers of summons over executive branch officials and hearings with executive branch officials testifying before the legislature or its committees are regularly held.

Yes. The legislature regularly interpellates officials from the executive.

Article 85
(1) Members of the Croatian Parliament shall have the right to ask the Government of the Republic of Croatia and individual ministers questions.
(2) At least one tenth of the representatives of the Croatian Parliament may submit an interpellation on the operation of the Government of the Republic of Croatia or some of its individual members.
(3) Questioning and interpellation shall be more specifically regulated by the Standing Rules.

4. The legislature can conduct independent investigation of the chief executive and the agencies of the executive.

Yes. The legislature can investigate the executive.

Article 91
The Croatian Sabor may form commissions of inquiry concerning any issue of public interest.
The commission of inquiry shall have a structure and scope in accord with law.
The President of the commission of inquiry is elected by a majority from its members.

5. The legislature has effective powers of oversight over the agencies of coercion (the military, organs of law enforcement, intelligence services, and the secret police).

Yes. Legislative committees have effective powers of oversight over the agencies of coercion.

6. The legislature appoints the prime minister.

Yes. The president is required to appoint as prime minister the candidate who enjoys majority support in parliament.

Article 97
The President of the Republic shall: confide the mandate to form the Government to the person who, upon the distribution of the seats in the Croatian Parliament and consultations held, enjoys confidence of the majority of its members.

7. The legislature's approval is required to confirm the appointment of ministers; or the legislature itself appoints ministers.

Yes. The legislature's approval is required to confirm ministerial appointments.

Article 109
(1) The person to whom the President of the Republic confides the mandate to form the Government shall propose its members.
(2) Immediately upon the formation of the Government, but not later than 30 days from the acceptance of the mandate, the mandatory shall present the Government and its program to the Croatian Parliament and demand a vote of confidence to be passed.
(3) The Government shall assume its duty if the vote of confidence is passed by a majority vote of all members of the Croatian Parliament.
(4) The Prime Minister and the members of the Government shall take a solemn oath before the Croatian Parliament. The text of the oath shall be determined by law.
(5) Upon the decision of the Croatian Parliament to express confidence to the Government of the Republic of Croatia, the ruling on the appointment of the Prime Minister shall be brought by the President of the Republic, with the counter signature of the President of the Croatian Parliament, and the ruling on the appointment of the members of the Government shall be brought by the Prime Minster with the counter signature of the President of the Croatian Parliament.

8. The country lacks a presidency entirely or there is a presidency, but the president is elected by the legislature.

No. The president is directly elected.

Article 94
(1) The President of the Republic shall be elected in direct elections by secret ballot, on the basis of universal and equal suffrage, for a term of five years.

9. The legislature can vote no confidence in the government.

Yes. The legislature can vote no confidence in the government.

Article 115
(1) At the proposal of at least one fifth of the members of the Croatian Parliament, a vote of confidence in the Prime Minster, in individual members of the Government, or in the Government as a whole, shall be put in motion.
(2) A vote of confidence in the Government may also be requested by the Prime Minister.
(5) A no confidence decision shall be accepted if it has been voted for by the majority of the total number of members of the Croatian Parliament.
(7) If a vote of no confidence in the Prime Minister or in the Government as a whole is passed, the Prime Minister and the Government shall submit their resignation. If the vote of confidence to a new mandatary and the members he proposes for the Government is not passed during the term of 30 days, the President of the Croatian Parliament shall notify thereof the President of the Republic of Croatia. After the notification is received the President of the Republic instantly issue a decision to dissolve the Croatian Parliament, and simultaneously call elections for the Croatian Parliament.

10. The legislature is immune from dissolution by the executive.

No. The president can dissolve the legislature.

Article 77
(1) The Croatian Parliament may be dissolved in order to call early elections if so decided by the majority of all the members.

(2) The President of the Republic may, in conformity with Article 103, dissolve the Croatian Parliament.

Article 103
(1) The President of the Republic, at the proposal of the Government and with the counter-signature of the Prime Minister, after consultations with the representatives of the clubs of parliamentary parties, dissolve the Croatian Parliament if, at the proposal of the Government, the Parliament has passed a vote of no confidence to the Government, or if it has failed to approve the state budget within 120 days from the date when it was proposed.

11. Any executive initiative on legislation requires ratification or approval by the legislature before it takes effect; that is, the executive lacks decree power.

Yes. The president and the government lack decree power. The legislature can delegate temporary decree power to the government on specified issue areas.

Article 87
(1) The Croatian Parliament may authorize the Government of the Republic of Croatia, for a maximum period of one year, to regulate by decrees certain issues within its competence, except those relating to the elaboration of the constitutionally defined human rights

and fundamental freedoms, national rights, the electoral system, the organization, authority and operation of government bodies and local self-government.

(2) Decrees based on statutory authority shall not have a retroactive effect.

(3) Decrees passed on the basis of statutory authority shall cease to be valid after the expiry of the period of one year from the date when such authority was granted, unless otherwise decided by the Croatian Parliament.

12. Laws passed by the legislature are veto-proof or essentially veto-proof; that is, the executive lacks veto power, or has veto power but the veto can be overridden by a majority in the legislature.

Yes. The president lacks veto power, although he may refer bills to the Constitutional Court to review their constitutionality.

Article 89
(1) Laws shall be promulgated by the President of the Republic within eight days from the date when they were passed in the Croatian Parliament.
(2) If the President of the Republic considers the promulgated law not in accordance with the Constitution, he may initiate proceedings to review the constitutionality of the law before the Constitutional Court of the Republic of Croatia.

13. The legislature's laws are supreme and not subject to judicial review.

No. The Constitutional Court can review the constitutionality of laws.

Article 128
The Constitutional Court of the Republic of Croatia shall . . . decide on the conformity of laws with the Constitution.

Article 130
(1) The Constitutional Court of the Republic of Croatia shall repeal a law if it finds it to be unconstitutional.
(2) The Constitutional Court of the Republic of Croatia shall repeal or annul any other regulation if it finds it to be unconstitutional or illegal.

14. The legislature has the right to initiate bills in all policy jurisdictions; the executive lacks gatekeeping authority.

Yes. The legislature can initiate bills in all policy jurisdictions.

15. Expenditure of funds appropriated by the legislature is mandatory; the executive lacks the power to impound funds appropriated by the legislature.

Yes. The executive lacks the power to impound funds appropriated by the legislature.

16. The legislature controls the resources that finance its own internal operation and provide for the perquisites of its own members.

Yes. The legislature enjoys financial autonomy, including control over members' remuneration.

Article 74
(2) Members of the Croatian Parliament shall receive a regular monetary remuneration and shall have other rights specified by law.

17. Members of the legislature are immune from arrest and/or criminal prosecution.

Yes. Legislators are immune with the exception of *flagrante delicto* for major crimes, here expressed as "caught in the act of committing a criminal offense which carries a penalty of imprisonment of more than five years."

Article 75
(1) Members of the Croatian Parliament shall enjoy immunity.
(2) No representative shall be prosecuted, detained or punished for an opinion expressed or vote cast in the Croatian Parliament.
(3) No representative shall be detained, nor shall criminal proceedings be instituted against him, without the consent of the Croatian Parliament.
(4) A representative may be detained without the consent of the Croatian Parliament only if he has been caught in the act of committing a criminal offence which carries a penalty of imprisonment of more than five years. In such a case, the President of the Croatian Parliament shall be notified thereof.
(5) If the Croatian Parliament is not in session, approval for the detention of a representative, or for the continuation of criminal proceedings against him, shall be given and his right to immunity decided by the credentials-and-immunity committee, such a decision being subject to subsequent confirmation by the Croatian Parliament.

18. All members of the legislature are elected; the executive lacks the power to appoint any members of the legislature.

Yes. All members of the legislature are elected.

Article 71
The Croatian Parliament shall have no less than 100 and no more than 160 members, elected on the basis of direct universal and equal suffrage by secret ballot.

19. The legislature alone, without the involvement of any other agencies, can change the Constitution.

Yes. The legislature can change the constitution with a two-thirds majority vote.

Article 80
The Croatian Parliament shall:

– decide on the enactment and amendment of the Constitution.

Article 142

(1) Amendments to the Constitution of the Republic of Croatia may be proposed by at least one- fifth of the members of the Croatian Parliament, the President of the Republic and the Government of the Republic of Croatia.

Article 143

(1) The Croatian Parliament shall decide by a majority vote of all representatives whether or not to start proceedings for the amendment of the Constitution.

(2) Draft amendments to the Constitution shall be determined by a majority vote of all the members of the Croatian Parliament.

Article 144

The decision to amend the Constitution shall be made by a two-thirds majority vote of all the members of the Croatian Parliament.

Article 145

Amendment of the Constitution shall be promulgated by the Croatian Parliament.

20. The legislature's approval is necessary for the declaration of war.

Yes. The legislature's approval is necessary for presidential war declarations with the common exception for cases of foreign invasion. The president can order the use of the armed forces without prior authorization in case of an "immediate threat to the independence, unity and existence of the state."

Article 99

(3) On the basis of the decision of the Croatian Parliament, the President of the Republic may declare war and conclude peace.

(4) In case of an immediate threat to the independence, unity and existence of the State, the President of the Republic may, with the counter signature of the Prime Minister, order the employment of the armed forces even if the state of war has not been declared.

21. The legislature's approval is necessary to ratify treaties with foreign countries.

Yes. The legislature must approve international treaties on most major issues.

Article 139

(1) International agreements which entail the passage of amendment of laws, international agreements of military and political nature, and international agreements which financially commit the Republic of Croatia shall be subject to ratification by the Croatian Parliament.

(2) International agreements which grant international organization or alliances powers derived from the Constitution of the Republic of Croatia, shall be subject to ratification by the Croatian Parliament by two-thirds majority vote of all representatives.

(3) The President of the Republic shall sign the documents of ratification, admittance, approval or acceptance of international agreements ratified by the Croatian Parliament in conformity with sections 1 and 2 of this Article.

(4) International agreements which are not subject of ratification by the Croatian Parliament are concluded by the President of the Republic at the proposal of the Government, or by the Government of the Republic of Croatia.

22. The legislature has the power to grant amnesty.

Yes. The legislature has the power to grant amnesty.

Article 80

The Croatian Parliament shall . . . grant amnesty for criminal offenses.

23. The legislature has the power of pardon.

No. The president has the power of pardon.

Article 97

The President of the Republic shall . . . grant pardons.

24. The legislature reviews and has the right to reject appointments to the judiciary; or the legislature itself appoints members of the judiciary.

Yes. The legislature elects the thirteen judges of the Constitutional Court and appoints, at the proposal of the president, the president of the Supreme Court.

Article 118

(1) The Supreme Court of the Republic of Croatia, as a highest court, shall secure uniform application of laws and equal justice to all.

(2) The President of the Supreme Court of the Republic of Croatia shall be appointed and relieved from duty by the Croatian Parliament at the proposal of the President of the Republic, with a prior opinion of the general session of the Supreme Court of the Republic of Croatia and of the authorized committee of the Croatian Parliament.

Article 125

(1) The Constitutional Court of the Republic of Croatia shall consist of thirteen judges elected by the Croatian Parliament for a term of eight years from among notable jurists, especially judges, public prosecutors, lawyers and university professors of law.

25. The chairman of the central bank is appointed by the legislature.

Yes. The legislature appoints the governor the Croatian National Bank.

26. The legislature has a substantial voice in the operation of the state-owned media.

Yes. The legislature has a substantial voice in the operation of the public media.

27. The legislature is regularly in session.

Yes. The legislature meets in ordinary session for nine months each year.

> Article 78
> (1) The Croatian Parliament shall be in regular session twice a year: the first period between January 15 and July 15, and the second period between September 15 and December 15.

28. Each legislator has a personal secretary.

No.

29. Each legislator has at least one non-secretarial staff member with policy expertise.

No.

30. Legislators are eligible for re-election without any restriction.

Yes. There are no restrictions on re-election.

31. A seat in the legislature is an attractive enough position that legislators are generally interested in and seek re-election.

Yes.

32. The re-election of incumbent legislators is common enough that at any given time the legislature contains a significant number of highly experienced members.

Yes. Re-election rates are sufficiently high to produce a significant number of highly experienced members.

NATIONAL ASSEMBLY OF PEOPLE'S POWER OF CUBA (*ASEMBLEA NACIONAL DEL PODER POPULAR*)

Expert consultant: Juan del Aguila

Score: .28

Influence over executive (2/9)		Institutional autonomy (4/9)		Specified powers (0/8)		Institutional capacity (3/6)	
1. replace		10. no dissolution	X	19. amendments		27. sessions	
2. serve as ministers	X	11. no decree		20. war		28. secretary	
3. interpellate	X	12. no veto	X	21. treaties		29. staff	
4. investigate		13. no review	X	22. amnesty		30. no term limits	X
5. oversee police		14. no gatekeeping	X	23. pardon		31. seek re-election	X
6. appoint PM		15. no impoundment		24. judiciary		32. experience	X
7. appoint ministers		16. control resources		25. central bank			
8. lack president		17. immunity		26. media			
9. no confidence		18. all elected					

The National Assembly of People's Power (*Asemblea Nacional del Poder Popular*) of Cuba was established in the 1976 constitution that codified the institutions of the then twenty-seven-year-old communist regime of Fidel Castro. The constitution provides for a popularly elected unicameral legislature that formally chooses the head of state and the head of government (the president of the Council of State), an executive organ that exercises legislative power when the legislature is not in session (the Council of State), and the government (the Council of Ministers). In practice, Fidel Castro, who has held the position of president of the Council of State since 1976, rules Cuba. When Castro fell ill in 2006, Raul Castro, Fidel's brother and the vice president of the Council of State, became acting president of the country. The Cuban Communist Party (CCP) is the island's sole legal political party.

The legislature has little meaningful power. It cannot choose or remove executive branch officials and has little oversight authority. Its institutional autonomy is limited by executive power to decree laws and the CCP's power to appoint legislators. It exercises none of the specified powers measured in this survey and has a bit of institutional capacity.

SURVEY

1. The legislature alone, without the involvement of any other agencies, can impeach the president or replace the prime minister.

No. The legislature cannot remove the chief executive, the president, from office.

2. Ministers may serve simultaneously as members of the legislature.

Yes. Members of the Council of State and the members of the Council of Ministers are selected from, and serve simultaneously in, the legislature.

Article 74
The National Assembly of People's Power elects, from among its deputies, the Council of State, which consists of one President, one First Vice President, five Vice Presidents, one Secretary and 23 other members.

Article 96
The Council of Ministers is composed of the Head of State and Government, as its President; the First Vice President; the Vice Presidents; the Ministers; the Secretary; and the other members that the law determines.

3. The legislature has powers of summons over executive branch officials and hearings with executive branch officials testifying before the legislature or its committees are regularly held.

Yes. The legislature regularly questions executive branch officials.

Article 86
The deputies to the National Assembly of People's Power have the right to make inquiries to the Council of State, the Council of Ministers or the members of either and to have these inquiries answered during the course of the same session or at the next session.

4. The legislature can conduct independent investigation of the chief executive and the agencies of the executive.

No. The legislature cannot investigate the executive.

5. The legislature has effective powers of oversight over the agencies of coercion (the military, organs of law enforcement, intelligence services, and the secret police).

No. The legislature lacks effective powers of oversight over the agencies of coercion.

6. The legislature appoints the prime minister.

No. There is no prime minister.

7. The legislature's approval is required to confirm the appointment of ministers; or the legislature itself appoints ministers.

No. Formally, the legislature elects the members of the Council of State and elects ministers on the recommendation of the president. In practice, the president chooses the members of the Council of State and ministers, and the appointments do not require the legislature's approval.

Article 74
The National Assembly of People's Power elects, from among its deputies, the Council of State, which consists of one President, one First Vice President, five Vice Presidents, one Secretary and 23 other members.

Article 75
The National Assembly of People's Power is invested with the following powers:
n) appointing, at the initiative of the President of the Council of State, the First Vice President, the Vice President and the other members of the Council of Ministers.

Article 93
The President of the Council of State is Head of Government and is invested with the power to:
d) propose to the National Assembly of People's Power, once elected by the latter, the members of the Council of Ministers.

8. The country lacks a presidency entirely or there is a presidency, but the president is elected by the legislature.

No. Formally, the legislature elects the president, but the election is strictly pro forma. Fidel Castro has held the position since its creation in 1976.

Article 74
The National Assembly of People's Power elects, from among its deputies, the Council of State, which consists of one President, one First Vice President, five Vice Presidents, one Secretary and 23 other members. The President of the Council of State is, at the same time, the Head of State and Head of Government.

Article 75
The National Assembly of People's Power is invested with the following powers:
n) appointing, at the initiative of the President of the Council of State, the First Vice President, the Vice President and the other members of the Council of Ministers.

9. The legislature can vote no confidence in the government.

No. The legislature cannot vote no confidence in the government.

10. The legislature is immune from dissolution by the executive.

Yes. The legislature is immune from dissolution.

> Article 72
> The National Assembly of People's Power is elected for a period of five years.

11. Any executive initiative on legislation requires ratification or approval by the legislature before it takes effect; that is, the executive lacks decree power.

No. The Council of State issues decrees with the force of law when the legislature is not in session.

> Article 90
> The Council of State is invested with the power to:
> c) issue decree-laws in the period between the sessions of the National Assembly of People's Power.

12. Laws passed by the legislature are veto-proof or essentially veto-proof; that is, the executive lacks veto power, or has veto power but the veto can be overridden by a majority in the legislature.

Yes. The legislature's laws are not subject to veto. It merits note, however, that laws are drawn up and approved by the CCP before being submitted to the legislature.

> Article 76
> All laws and resolutions of the National Assembly of People's Power, barring those in relation to reforms in the Constitution, are adopted by a simple majority vote.

> Article 77
> All laws approved by the National Assembly of People's Power go into effect on the date determined by those laws in each case.
> Laws, decree-laws, decrees and resolutions, regulations and other general provisions of the national organs of the State are published in the *Official Gazette* of the Republic.

13. The legislature's laws are supreme and not subject to judicial review.

Yes. The legislature's laws are not subject to judicial review. Formally, the legislature itself reviews the constitutionality of laws.

> Article 75
> The National Assembly of People's Power is invested with the following powers:
> c) deciding on the constitutionality of laws, decree-laws, decrees and all other general provisions.

14. The legislature has the right to initiate bills in all policy jurisdictions; the executive lacks gatekeeping authority.

Yes. The legislature can initiate bills in all policy jurisdictions.

15. Expenditure of funds appropriated by the legislature is mandatory; the executive lacks the power to impound funds appropriated by the legislature.

No. The Council of State can impound funds appropriated by the legislature.

16. The legislature controls the resources that finance its own internal operation and provide for the perquisites of its own members.

No. The legislature is dependent on the Council of State for the resources that finance its own operations.

17. Members of the legislature are immune from arrest and/or criminal prosecution.

No. Legislators can be arrested with the approval of the Council of State when the legislature is not in session.

> Article 83
> No deputy to the National Assembly of People's Power may be arrested or placed on trial without the authorization of the Assembly – or the Council of State if the Assembly is not in session – except in cases of flagrant offenses.

18. All members of the legislature are elected; the executive lacks the power to appoint any members of the legislature.

No. Formally, the legislature is elected, but in practice, there is but a single candidate for each seat, and the candidates are preselected by the CCP before the popular elections.

> Article 71
> The National Assembly of the People's Power is comprised of deputies elected through a free, direct, and secret ballot by the voters, in the proportion and according to the procedure that the law establishes.

19. The legislature alone, without the involvement of any other agencies, can change the Constitution.

No. Formally, the legislature can change the constitution with a two-thirds majority vote, but in practice, it would be unthinkable for the legislature to change the constitution without the government's direction.

> Article 75
> The National Assembly of People's Power is invested with the following powers:

a) deciding on reforms to the Constitution according to that [which is] established in Article 11.

Article 137
This Constitution can only be modified by the National Assembly of People's Power, by means of resolutions adopted by roll-call vote by a majority of no less than two-thirds of the total number of members; except [where the modification] regards the political, social and economic system, whose irrevocable character is established in Article 3 of Chapter I, and the prohibition against negotiations under aggression, threats or coercion by a foreign power as established in Article 11. If the modification has to do with the integration and authority of the National Assembly of the People's Power or its Council of State or involves any rights and duties contained in the Constitution, it shall also require the approval of the majority of citizens with the right to vote by means of a referendum called upon for this purpose by the Assembly itself.

20. The legislature's approval is necessary for the declaration of war.

No. Formally, the Council of State can declare war without the legislature's approval "in the event of aggression" when the legislature cannot be called to session, but in practice, war declarations do not require the legislature's approval.

Article 75
The National Assembly of People's Power is invested with the following powers:
i) declaring a state of war in the event of military aggression and approving peace treaties.

Article 90
The Council of State is invested with the power to:
f) decree general mobilizations whenever the defense of the country makes it necessary and assume the authority to declare war in the event of aggression or to approve peace treaties – duties which the Constitution assigns to the National Assembly of People's Power – when the Assembly is in recess and cannot be called to session with the necessary security and urgency.

21. The legislature's approval is necessary to ratify treaties with foreign countries.

No. The Council of Ministers approves and the Council of State ratifies international treaties, and treaties do not require the legislature's approval.

Article 90
The Council of State is invested with the power to:
m) ratify or denounce international treaties.

Article 98
The Council of Ministers is invested with the power to:
d) approve international treaties and submit them for ratification by the Council of State.

22. The legislature has the power to grant amnesty.

No. Formally, the legislature has the power to grant amnesty. In practice, it would be unthinkable for the legislature to grant amnesty without approval from the Council of State.

Article 75
The National Assembly of People's Power is invested with the following powers:
t) granting amnesty.

23. The legislature has the power of pardon.

No. The Council of State has the power of pardon.

Article 90
The Council of State is invested with the power to:
n) grant pardons.

24. The legislature reviews and has the right to reject appointments to the judiciary; or the legislature itself appoints members of the judiciary.

No. Formally, the legislature elects the judges of the Supreme Court, but in practice, justices are selected by the Council of State.

Article 75
The National Assembly of People's Power is invested with the following powers:
m) electing the President, Vice President and other judges of the People's Supreme Court.

25. The chairman of the central bank is appointed by the legislature.

No. The Council of State appoints the president of the Central Bank of Cuba.

26. The legislature has a substantial voice in the operation of the state-owned media.

No. The Council of State controls the state-owned media.

27. The legislature is regularly in session.

No. The legislature is in session for less than half the year.

Article 78
The National Assembly of People's Power holds two regular sessions a year and a special session when requested by one-third of the membership or when called by the Council of State.

28. Each legislator has a personal secretary.

No.

29. Each legislator has at least one non-secretarial staff member with policy expertise.

No.

30. Legislators are eligible for re-election without any restriction.

Yes. There are no restrictions on re-election.

31. A seat in the legislature is an attractive enough position that legislators are generally interested in and seek re-election.

Yes.

32. The re-election of incumbent legislators is common enough that at any given time the legislature contains a significant number of highly experienced members.

Yes. Re-election rates are sufficiently high to produce a significant number of highly experienced members. It should be noted that the de facto control of the legislature by the president and the CCP means that long experience of membership does not necessarily spell substantial experience in legislative work.

HOUSE OF REPRESENTATIVES OF CYPRUS (*VOULI ANTIPROSOPON*)

Expert consultants: Şener Aktürk, Angelos S. Gerontas, Theocharis Grigoriadis, Katerina Karakehagia, Demis Mavrellis

Score: .41

Influence over executive (1/9)		Institutional autonomy (4/9)		Specified powers (2/8)		Institutional capacity (6/6)	
1. replace		10. no dissolution	X	19. amendments	X	27. sessions	X
2. serve as ministers		11. no decree		20. war		28. secretary	X
3. interpellate	X	12. no veto		21. treaties	X	29. staff	X
4. investigate		13. no review		22. amnesty		30. no term limits	X
5. oversee police		14. no gatekeeping		23. pardon		31. seek re-election	X
6. appoint PM		15. no impoundment	X	24. judiciary		32. experience	X
7. appoint ministers		16. control resources	X	25. central bank			
8. lack president		17. immunity		26. media			
9. no confidence		18. all elected	X				

The House of Representatives (*Vouli Antiprosopon*) of Cyprus was founded in the 1960 constitution upon independence from Great Britain. The document called for a unicameral house that split seats between the country's two major ethnic groups, the Greeks and the Turks. In 1963 the Turks stopped participating in government and formed their own legislature, the Turkish Cypriot Legislative Assembly. Twenty years later, Northern Cyprus declared independence, although the move was never recognized by the international community. Negotiations over political reunification of the island began in 2002, but a solution acceptable to both sides has not yet been found.

The legislature's powers are circumscribed. The House can question executive branch officials but otherwise lacks influence over the executive. The House's institutional autonomy is limited by executive powers of decree, gatekeeping, and absolute veto over key issue areas. The legislature also lacks common powers and prerogatives, such as the power to make or approve judicial branch appointments. Yet the legislature does have considerable institutional capacity. Members have administrative and policy staff, and the legislature includes a significant number of highly experienced members.

SURVEY

1. The legislature alone, without the involvement of any other agencies, can impeach the president or replace the prime minister.

No. Presidential impeachment requires the involvement of the attorney general of the Republic and the High Court.

Article 45
The President or the Vice-President of the Republic may be prosecuted for high treason on a charge preferred by the Attorney-General and the Deputy Attorney-General of the Republic before the High Court upon a resolution of the House of Representatives carried by a secret ballot and a majority of three-fourths of the total number of Representatives: Provided that no such resolution shall be taken and no item shall be entered on the agenda or debated in the House of Representatives in connection therewith unless the proposal for such resolution is signed by at least one-fifth of the total number of Representatives. The President or the Vice-President of the Republic may be prosecuted for an offence involving dishonesty or moral turpitude upon a charge preferred by the Attorney-General and the Deputy Attorney-General of the Republic before the High Court with the leave of the President of the High Court. (1) The President or the Vice-President of the Republic upon being prosecuted under paragraph 2 or 3 of this Article shall be suspended from the performance of any of the functions of his office and thereupon the provisions of paragraph 2 of Article 36 shall apply. (2) The President or the Vice-President of the Republic on any such prosecution shall be tried by the High Court; on his conviction his office shall become vacant and on his acquittal he shall resume the performance of the functions of his office.

2. Ministers may serve simultaneously as members of the legislature.

No. Legislators are prohibited from serving simultaneously in ministerial positions.

Article 70
The office of a Representative shall be incompatible with that of a Minister.

3. The legislature has powers of summons over executive branch officials and hearings with executive branch officials testifying before the legislature or its committees are regularly held.

Yes. The legislature regularly questions executive branch officials.

4. The legislature can conduct independent investigation of the chief executive and the agencies of the executive.

No. The legislature cannot investigate the executive.

5. The legislature has effective powers of oversight over the agencies of coercion (the military, organs of law enforcement, intelligence services, and the secret police).

No. The legislature lacks effective powers of oversight over the agencies of coercion.

6. The legislature appoints the prime minister.

No. There is no prime minister.

7. The legislature's approval is required to confirm the appointment of ministers; or the legislature itself appoints ministers.

No. The president and vice president appoint the ministers, and confirmation by the legislature is not necessary.

Article 46
Ministers shall be designated respectively by the President and the Vice-President of the Republic who shall appoint them by an instrument signed by them both. The Ministers may be chosen from outside the House of Representatives.

Article 48
The executive power exercised by the President of the Republic consists of the following matters, that is to say:
(a) designation and termination of appointment of Greek Ministers.

8. The country lacks a presidency entirely or there is a presidency, but the president is elected by the legislature.

No. The president is directly elected.

Article 39
The election of the President and the Vice-President of the Republic shall be direct, by universal suffrage and secret ballot.

9. The legislature can vote no confidence in the government.

No. The legislature cannot vote no confidence in the government.

10. The legislature is immune from dissolution by the executive.

Yes. The legislature is immune from dissolution by the executive, although the House of Representatives can choose to dissolve itself.

Article 67
1. The House of Representatives may dissolve itself only by its own decision carried by an absolute majority including at least one third of the Representatives elected by the Turkish Community.

11. Any executive initiative on legislation requires ratification or approval by the legislature before it takes effect; that is, the executive lacks decree power.

No. The president issues decrees that have the force of law.

12. Laws passed by the legislature are veto-proof or essentially veto-proof; that is, the executive lacks veto power, or has veto power but the veto can be overridden by a majority in the legislature.

No. The president has absolute veto power over a broad range of issues, including foreign affairs, international treaties, and war. On other issues, parliament can override a presidential by a majority vote of its present members.

Article 50
1. The President and the Vice-President of the Republic, separately or conjointly, shall have the right of final veto on any law or decision of the House of Representatives or any part thereof concerning –
   (a) foreign affairs, except the participation of the Republic in international organisations and pacts of alliance in which the Kingdom of Greece and the Republic of Turkey both participate. For the purposes of this sub-paragraph "foreign affairs" includes –
      (i) the recognition of States, the establishment of diplomatic and consular relations with other countries and the interruption of such relations. The grant of acceptance to diplomatic representatives and of exequatur to consular representatives. The assignment of diplomatic representatives and of consular representatives, already in the diplomatic service, to posts abroad and the entrusting of functions abroad to special envoys already in the diplomatic service. The appointment and the assignment of persons, who are not already in the diplomatic service, to any posts abroad as diplomatic or consular representatives and the entrusting of functions abroad to persons, who are not already in the diplomatic service, as special envoys;
      (ii) the conclusion of international treaties, conventions and agreements;
      (iii) the declaration of war and the conclusion of peace;
      (iv) the protection abroad of the citizens of the Republic and of their interests;
      (v) the establishment, the status and the interests of aliens in the Republic;
      (vi) the acquisition of foreign nationality by citizens of the Republic and their acceptance of employment by, or their entering the service of, a foreign Government;
   (b) the following questions of defence: –
      (i) composition and size of the armed forces and credits for them;
      (ii) nomination of cadres and their promotions;
      (iii) importation of war materials and also explosives of all kinds;
      (iv) cession of bases and other facilities to allied countries;
   (c) the following questions of security: –
      (i) nominations of cadres and their promotions;
      (ii) distribution and stationing of forces;
      (iii) emergency measures and martial law;
      (iv) police laws.
It is specified that the right of veto under sub-paragraph (c) above shall cover all emergency measures or decisions, but not those which concern the normal functioning of the police and the gendarmerie.

2. The above right of veto may be exercised either against the whole of a law or decision or against any part thereof, and in the latter case such law or decision shall be returned to the House of Representatives for a decision whether the remaining part thereof will be submitted, under the relevant provisions of this Constitution, for promulgation.
3. The right of veto under this Article shall be exercised within the period for the promulgation of laws or decisions of the House of Representatives as in Article 52 provided.

Article 51
1. The President and the Vice-President of the Republic shall have the right, either separately or conjointly, to return any law or decision or any part thereof of the House of Representatives to the House for reconsideration.
2. On the adoption of the Budget by the House of Representatives the President and the Vice-President of the Republic, either separately or conjointly, may exercise his or their right to return it to the House of Representatives on the ground that in his or their judgement there is a discrimination.
4. If the House of Representatives persists in its decision the President and the Vice-President of the Republic shall, subject to the provisions of this Constitution, promulgate the law or decision or the Budget, as the case may be, within the time limit fixed for the promulgation of laws and decisions of the House of Representatives by publication of such law or decision or Budget in the official Gazette of the Republic.

13. The legislature's laws are supreme and not subject to judicial review.

No. The Supreme Constitutional Court can review the constitutionality of laws.

Article 140
3. In case the Supreme Constitutional Court is of the opinion that such law or decision or any provision thereof is repugnant to or inconsistent with any provision of this Constitution such law or decision or such provision thereof shall not be promulgated by the President and the Vice-President of the Republic.

14. The legislature has the right to initiate bills in all policy jurisdictions; the executive lacks gatekeeping authority.

No. The legislature is prohibited from introducing legislation that would increase government expenditures.

Article 80
1. The right to introduce Bills belongs to the Representatives and to the Ministers.
2. No Bill relating to an increase in budgetary expenditure can be introduced by any Representative.

15. Expenditure of funds appropriated by the legislature is mandatory; the executive lacks the power to impound funds appropriated by the legislature.

Yes. The executive cannot impound funds appropriated by the legislature.

16. The legislature controls the resources that finance its own internal operation and provide for the perquisites of its own members.

Yes. The legislature enjoys financial autonomy.

17. Members of the legislature are immune from arrest and/or criminal prosecution.

No. Legislators have immunity but it can be lifted by a decision of the High Court.

> Article 83
> 1. Representatives shall not be liable to civil or criminal proceedings in respect of any statement made or vote given by them in the House of Representatives.
> 2. A Representative cannot, without the leave of the High Court, be prosecuted, arrested or imprisoned so long as he continues to be a Representative. Such leave is not required in the case of an offence punishable with death or imprisonment for five years or more in case the offender is taken in the act. In such a case the High Court being notified forthwith by the competent authority decides whether it should grant or refuse leave for the continuation of the prosecution or detention so long as he continues to be a Representative.
> 3. If the High Court refuses to grant leave for the prosecution of a Representative, the period during which the Representative cannot thus be prosecuted shall not be reckoned for the purposes of any period of prescription for the offence in question.
> 4. If the High Court refuses to grant leave for the enforcement of a sentence of imprisonment imposed on a Representative by a competent court, the enforcement of such sentence shall be postponed until he ceases to be a Representative.

18. All members of the legislature are elected; the executive lacks the power to appoint any members of the legislature.

Yes. All members of the legislature are elected.

> Article 66
> 1. A general election for the House of Representatives shall be held on the second Sunday of the month immediately preceding the month in which the term of office of the outgoing House expires.

19. The legislature alone, without the involvement of any other agencies, can change the Constitution.

Yes. The legislature can change the constitution with a majority vote.

> Article 182
> 1. The Articles or parts of Articles of this Constitution set out in Annex III hereto which have been incorporated

from the Zurich Agreement dated 11th February, 1959, are the basic Articles of this Constitution and cannot, in any way, be amended, whether by way of variation, addition or repeal.
> 2. Subject to paragraph 1 of this Article any provision of this Constitution may be amended, whether by way of variation, addition or repeal, as provided in paragraph 3 of this Article.
> 3. Such amendment shall be made by a law passed by a majority vote comprising at least two-thirds of the total number of the Representatives belonging to the Greek Community and at least two-thirds of the total number of the Representatives belonging to the Turkish Community.

20. The legislature's approval is necessary for the declaration of war.

No. The president can declare war without the legislature's approval.

> Article 50
> 1. The President and the Vice-President of the Republic, separately or conjointly, shall have the right of final veto on any law or decision of the House of Representatives or any part thereof concerning –
> (iii) the declaration of war and the conclusion of peace.

21. The legislature's approval is necessary to ratify treaties with foreign countries.

Yes. The legislature's approval is necessary to ratify international treaties.

> Article 169
> Subject to the provisions of Article 50 and paragraph 3 of Article 57 –
> (1) every international agreement with a foreign State or any International Organisation relating to commercial matters, economic co-operation (including payments and credit) and modus vivendi shall be concluded under a decision of the Council of Ministers;
> (2) any other treaty, convention or international agreement shall be negotiated and signed under a decision of the Council of Ministers and shall only be operative and binding on the Republic when approved by a law made by the House of Representatives whereupon it shall be concluded;
> (3) treaties, conventions and agreements concluded in accordance with the foregoing provisions of this Article shall have, as from their publication in the official Gazette of the Republic, superior force to any municipal law on condition that such treaties, conventions and agreements are applied by the other party thereto.

22. The legislature has the power to grant amnesty.

No. Pardon and amnesty are not treated separately, and the legislature lacks the power to grant amnesty. See item 23.

23. The legislature has the power of pardon.

No. The president has the power of pardon (mercy).

Article 47
The executive power exercised by the President and the Vice-President of the Republic conjointly consists of the following matters that is to say:

(i) exercise of the prerogative of mercy in capital cases where the injured party and the convicted person are members of different Communities as in Article 53 provided; remission, suspension and commutation of sentences as in Article 53 provided.

Article 53
1. The President or the Vice-President of the Republic shall have the right to exercise the prerogative of mercy with regard to persons belonging to their respective Community who are condemned to death.

24. The legislature reviews and has the right to reject appointments to the judiciary; or the legislature itself appoints members of the judiciary.

No. The president appoints the judges of the Supreme Constitutional Court and the High Court, and the appointments do not require the legislature's approval.

Article 133
1. (1) There shall be a Supreme Constitutional Court of the Republic composed of a Greek, a Turk and a neutral judge. The neutral judge shall be the President of the Court.
(2) The President and the other judges of the Supreme Constitutional Court shall be appointed jointly by the President and the Vice-President of the Republic.

Article 153
1. (1) There shall be a High Court of Justice composed of two Greek judges, one Turkish judge and a neutral judge. The neutral judge shall be the President of the Court and shall have two votes.
(2) The President and the other judges of the High Court shall be appointed jointly by the President and the Vice-President of the Republic.

25. The chairman of the central bank is appointed by the legislature.

No. The president appoints the governor of the Central Bank of Cyprus (here called the Issuing Bank of the Republic).

Article 118
1. The President and the Vice-President of the Republic shall appoint jointly two fit and proper persons one to be the Governor and the other to be the Deputy-Governor of the Issuing Bank of the Republic.

26. The legislature has a substantial voice in the operation of the state-owned media.

No. The legislature lacks a substantial voice in the operation of the public media.

27. The legislature is regularly in session.

Yes. According to the constitution, the House of Representatives meets in ordinary session for three to six months each year. In practice, it is in session at least six months each year.

Article 74
2. The ordinary session of the House of Representatives shall last for a period of three to six months in each year, as the House of Representatives may determine.

28. Each legislator has a personal secretary.

Yes.

29. Each legislator has at least one non-secretarial staff member with policy expertise.

Yes.

30. Legislators are eligible for re-election without any restriction.

Yes. There are no restrictions on re-election.

31. A seat in the legislature is an attractive enough position that legislators are generally interested in and seek re-election.

Yes.

32. The re-election of incumbent legislators is common enough that at any given time the legislature contains a significant number of highly experienced members.

Yes. Re-election rates are sufficiently high to produce a significant number of highly experienced members.

PARLIAMENT OF THE CZECH REPUBLIC (*PARLAMENT*)

Expert consultants: Hilary Appel, Anna Grzymała-Busse, Jan Fidrmuc, Zdenka Mansfeldová, Conor O'Dwyer

Score: .81

Influence over executive (8/9)		Institutional autonomy (7/9)		Specified powers (5/8)		Institutional capacity (6/6)	
1. replace	X	10. no dissolution		19. amendments	X	27. sessions	X
2. serve as ministers	X	11. no decree	X	20. war	X	28. secretary	X
3. interpellate	X	12. no veto	X	21. treaties	X	29. staff	X
4. investigate	X	13. no review		22. amnesty		30. no term limits	X
5. oversee police	X	14. no gatekeeping	X	23. pardon		31. seek re-election	X
6. appoint PM		15. no impoundment	X	24. judiciary	X	32. experience	X
7. appoint ministers	X	16. control resources	X	25. central bank			
8. lack president	X	17. immunity	X	26. media	X		
9. no confidence	X	18. all elected	X				

The Parliament (*Parlament*) of the Czech Republic traces its origins to Czechoslovakia's 1920 constitution, which provided for a bicameral assembly consisting of a lower house, the Chamber of Deputies (*Poslanecká sněmovna*), and an upper house, the Senate (*Senát*). In 1948 a new constitution drawn up by the communist-party regime replaced the interwar parliament with a unicameral, and largely powerless, Soviet-type legislature. Following the collapse of the Soviet Union and the "velvet divorce" from Slovakia, the current constitution was established. The 1993 document is based broadly on the 1920 constitution of Czechoslovakia.

The legislature has broad powers. It controls the executive with powers to remove the prime minister, elect the president, and interpellate, investigate, and vote no confidence in the government. Further, its members may serve in government. It also enjoys extensive institutional autonomy. It does not share any significant lawmaking authority with the executive. It can be dissolved by the president, but only under specific conditions that are largely within the legislature's control. It also enjoys a number of specified powers and prerogatives and a high level of institutional capacity.

SURVEY

1. The legislature alone, without the involvement of any other agencies, can impeach the president or replace the prime minister.

Yes. The legislature can remove the prime minister with a vote of no confidence. Removing the president requires action by the Constitutional Court.

> Article 65
> (2) The President of the Republic can be prosecuted for high treason before the Constitutional Court on the basis of an indictment by the Senate. Punishment can be the loss of Presidential office and of the qualification to hold it again.

2. Ministers may serve simultaneously as members of the legislature.

Yes. Legislators may simultaneously serve in ministerial positions.

3. The legislature has powers of summons over executive branch officials and hearings with executive branch officials testifying before the legislature or its committees are regularly held.

Yes. The legislature regularly interpellates officials from the executive.

Article 38

(2) A member of the Government is obliged to attend personally a session of the Chamber of Deputies upon the basis of its resolution. This also applies to a session of a committee, commission, or investigatory commission, where, however, a member of the Government may have himself be represented by his deputy or any other member of the cabinet, if his or her personal presence is not expressly requested.

Article 53

(1) Every Deputy has the right to interpellate the Government or its members in matters falling under their jurisdiction.

(2) Interpellated members of Government shall be obliged to respond to the interpellation within a period of thirty days from the day of its notification.

4. The legislature can conduct independent investigation of the chief executive and the agencies of the executive.

Yes. The legislature can establish a commission to investigate the executive.

Article 30

(1) The Chamber of Deputies may set up an investigatory commission for the investigation of an affair of public interest if this is suggested by at last one fifth of deputies.

(2) Proceedings before the commission shall be determined by law.

Article 38

(2) A member of the Government is obliged to attend personally a session of the Chamber of Deputies upon the basis of its resolution. This also applies to a session of a committee, commission, or investigatory commission, where, however, a member of the Government may have himself be represented by his deputy or any other member of the cabinet, if his or her personal presence is not expressly requested.

5. The legislature has effective powers of oversight over the agencies of coercion (the military, organs of law enforcement, intelligence services, and the secret police).

Yes. Legislative committees have effective powers of oversight over the agencies of coercion.

6. The legislature appoints the prime minister.

No. The president appoints the prime minister (premier). It bears mention, however, that the leading coalition formed after elections names its own candidate as prime minister, and the president normally appoints this candidate as prime minister.

Article 62

The President of the Republic:

a) appoints and dismisses the Premier and other members of the Government.

7. The legislature's approval is required to confirm the appointment of ministers; or the legislature itself appoints ministers.

Yes. The legislature's approval is required to confirm ministerial appointments.

Article 62

The President of the Republic:

a) appoints and dismisses the Premier and other members of the Government.

Article 68

(2) The President of the Republic appoints the Premier and, on his suggestion, appoints other members of the Government and entrusts them with managing the ministries or other bodies.

(3) The Government shall appear before the Chamber of Deputies within thirty days of its appointment and request of it a vote of confidence.

(4) If the newly appointed Government fails to obtain the confidence of the Chamber of Deputies, the procedure advances in accordance with Paragraphs (2) and (3). If even the Government, appointed in this way, fails to obtain the confidence of the Chamber of Deputies, the President of the Republic shall appoint the Premier upon the suggestion of the Chairman of the Chamber of Deputies.

(5) In other cases, the President of the Republic appoints and dismisses, upon the suggestion of the Premier, other members of the cabinet and entrusts them with managing the ministries or other bodies.

8. The country lacks a presidency entirely or there is a presidency, but the president is elected by the legislature.

Yes. The legislature elects the president.

Article 54

(2) The President of the Republic is elected by Parliament at a joint session of both Chambers.

9. The legislature can vote no confidence in the government.

Yes. The legislature can vote no confidence in the government.

Article 72

(1) The Chamber of Deputies may pass a vote of no confidence in the Government.

(2) The Chamber of Deputies shall discuss a proposal for a vote of no confidence in the Government only if it is submitted in writing by no less than 50 deputies. Passing the proposal requires the consent of an absolute majority of all deputies.

Article 73

(1) The Premier offers his resignation to the President of the Republic. Other members of the Government offer their resignations to the President of the Republic through the Premier.

(2) The Government shall offer its resignation if the Chamber of Deputies rejects its request for a vote of confidence or if it passes a vote of no confidence in it. The Government shall always offer its resignation after the constituent session of a newly elected Chamber of Deputies.

(3) If the Government offers its resignation according to Paragraph (2), the President of the Republic shall accept it.

10. The legislature is immune from dissolution by the executive.

No. The president can dissolve the legislature.

Article 35
(1) The President of the Republic can dissolve the Chamber of Deputies if:
　a) the Chamber of Deputies passes a vote of non-confidence in a newly appointed Government whose Premier was appointed by the President of the Republic on the suggestion of the chairman of the Chamber of Deputies,
　b) the Chamber of Deputies fails to decide within three months on a Government bill with the discussion of which the Government links the question of confidence,
　c) a session of the Chamber of Deputies is adjourned for a longer period than admissible,
　d) the Chamber of Deputies has not reached a quorum for a period longer than three months, although its session was not adjourned and although it was repeatedly called to session during this period.
(2) The Chamber of Deputies cannot be dissolved three months before the expiration of its election term.

11. Any executive initiative on legislation requires ratification or approval by the legislature before it takes effect; that is, the executive lacks decree power.

Yes. The executive lacks decree power.

12. Laws passed by the legislature are veto-proof or essentially veto-proof; that is, the executive lacks veto power, or has veto power but the veto can be overridden by a majority in the legislature.

Yes. The Chamber of Deputies can override a presidential veto by a majority vote of its total membership.

Article 50
(1) The President of the Republic has the right to return an adopted law, except a constitutional law, giving explanation within fifteen days of the day of its advancement.
(2) The Chamber of Deputies shall vote on the rejected law once again. Draft amendments are inadmissible. If the Chamber of Deputies re-approves the returned law by an absolute majority of all deputies, the law is promulgated. Otherwise it is assumed that the law was not passed.

13. The legislature's laws are supreme and not subject to judicial review.

No. The Constitutional Court can review the constitutionality of laws.

Article 83
The Constitutional Court is a judicial body for the protection of constitutionality.

Article 87
(1) The Constitutional Court resolves:
　a) the nullification of laws or their individual provisions if they are in contradiction with a constitutional law or an international agreement under Article 10,
　b) the nullification of other legal regulations or their individual provisions if they are in contradiction with a constitutional law, legislation, or international agreement under Article 10.

14. The legislature has the right to initiate bills in all policy jurisdictions; the executive lacks gatekeeping authority.

Yes. The legislature can initiate bills in all policy jurisdictions.

15. Expenditure of funds appropriated by the legislature is mandatory; the executive lacks the power to impound funds appropriated by the legislature.

Yes. The government cannot impound funds appropriated by the legislature. A ministry can, however, spend up to 5 percent above the allocated amount according to the 1999 law on budgetary rules.

16. The legislature controls the resources that finance its own internal operation and provide for the perquisites of its own members.

Yes. The legislature enjoys financial autonomy.

17. Members of the legislature are immune from arrest and/or criminal prosecution.

Yes. Legislators are immune. Even in cases of *flagrante delicto*, legislators must be set free unless the respective chamber gives its consent to criminal prosecution.

Article 27
(1) A Deputy or a Senator may not be prosecuted for voting in the Chamber of Deputies or the Senate or their bodies.
(2) A Deputy or a Senator may not be prosecuted for statements made in the Chamber of Deputies or the Senate or their bodies. A Deputy or a Senator is only accountable to the disciplinary authority of the Chamber of which he or she is a member.
(3) A Deputy or a Senator shall be accountable for his or her misdemeanor only to the disciplinary authority

of the Chamber of which he or she is a member, unless determined otherwise by law.

(4) A Deputy or a Senator may not be criminally prosecuted without consent of the Chamber of which he or she is a member. If the respective Chamber declines its consent, criminal proceedings are rendered impossible forever.

(5) A Deputy or a Senator may be taken into custody only if caught while committing a criminal offence or immediately thereafter. The responsible body is obliged to immediately notify of the detention the Chairman of the Chamber of which the detainee is a member; if the Chamber's Chairman fails to give his or her consent to handing the detainee over to court within 24 hours of the detention, the responsible body is obliged to set him or her free. The Chamber shall decide with final authority about the admissibility of the prosecution at its first following session.

18. All members of the legislature are elected; the executive lacks the power to appoint any members of the legislature.

Yes. All members of the legislature are elected.

Article 18
(1) Elections to the Chamber of Deputies shall be held on the basis of universal, equal, and direct suffrage by secret ballot, according to the principles of proportional representation.
(2) Elections to the Senate shall take place on the basis of universal, equal, and direct suffrage by secret ballot, on the basis of the majority system.

19. The legislature alone, without the involvement of any other agencies, can change the Constitution.

Yes. The legislature can change the constitution through the normal legislative process.

Article 9
(1) The Constitution may be amended or altered solely by constitutional laws.
(2) Any change of fundamental attributes of the democratic law-observing state is inadmissible.
(3) Legal norms cannot be interpreted as warranting the removal or threatening of the foundations of the democratic state.

20. The legislature's approval is necessary for the declaration of war.

Yes. The approval of both chambers of parliament is necessary to declare war.

Article 39
(3) The passage of a resolution on the declaration of the state of war and a resolution approving the presence of foreign troops on the territory of the Czech Republic requires consent of an absolute majority of all deputies and of all Senators.

Article 43
(1) Parliament decides on a declaration of the state of war in the event that the Czech Republic is attacked or if it is necessary to meet international treaty obligations concerning joint defense against aggression.
(2) Armed forces can be sent outside the territory of the Czech Republic only with the consent of both Chambers.

21. The legislature's approval is necessary to ratify treaties with foreign countries.

Yes. The legislature's approval is necessary to ratify international treaties on most major issues.

Article 49
(1) International accords requiring consent from Parliament are passed by Parliament in the same way as draft laws.
(2) Accords on human rights and fundamental freedoms, political agreements, and economic agreements of a general nature, as well as agreements on the implementation of which a law must be passed, require consent from Parliament.

22. The legislature has the power to grant amnesty.

No. The president has the power to grant amnesty.

Article 63
(1) The President of the Republic further:
   j) has the right to grant amnesty.

23. The legislature has the power of pardon.

No. The president has the power of pardon.

Article 62
The President of the Republic:
g) pardons and mitigates penalties imposed by penal courts, orders that criminal proceedings be not opened, and if they have been, orders their discontinuation, and expunges previous sentences.

24. The legislature reviews and has the right to reject appointments to the judiciary; or the legislature itself appoints members of the judiciary.

Yes. The Senate's consent is required to approve the president's appointments to the Constitutional Court.

Article 84
(2) The judges of the Constitutional Court are appointed by the President of the Republic with the consent of the Senate.

25. The chairman of the central bank is appointed by the legislature.

No. The president appoints the members of the Czech National Bank.

Article 62
The President of the Republic:
k) appoints members of the Bank Council of the Czech National Bank.

26. The legislature has a substantial voice in the operation of the state-owned media.

Yes. The legislature has a substantial voice in the operation of the public media.

27. The legislature is regularly in session.

Yes. The legislature regularly meets in ordinary session.

> Article 34
> (1) The Chambers are continually in session. A session of the Chamber of Deputies is called by the President of the Republic so that it be started no later than the thirtieth day after the election day. If he fails to do so, the Chamber of Deputies shall meet on the thirtieth day after the election day.

28. Each legislator has a personal secretary.

Yes. Each legislator receives a monthly lump sum for personal policy and administrative staff. He or she also has access to parliamentary policy staff.

29. Each legislator has at least one non-secretarial staff member with policy expertise.

Yes. See item 28.

30. Legislators are eligible for re-election without any restriction.

Yes. There are no restrictions on re-election.

31. A seat in the legislature is an attractive enough position that legislators are generally interested in and seek re-election.

Yes.

32. The re-election of incumbent legislators is common enough that at any given time the legislature contains a significant number of highly experienced members.

Yes. Re-election rates are sufficiently high to produce a significant number of highly experienced members.

PARLIAMENT OF DENMARK (*FOLKETINGET*)

Expert consultants: Thomas Adelskov, Jakob From Høeg, Tim Knudsen, Asbjørn Skjæveland, Richard N. Swett

Score: .78

Influence over executive (8/9)		Institutional autonomy (7/9)		Specified powers (4/8)		Institutional capacity (6/6)	
1. replace	X	10. no dissolution		19. amendments		27. sessions	X
2. serve as ministers	X	11. no decree	X	20. war	X	28. secretary	X
3. interpellate	X	12. no veto	X	21. treaties	X	29. staff	X
4. investigate	X	13. no review		22. amnesty		30. no term limits	X
5. oversee police	X	14. no gatekeeping	X	23. pardon		31. seek re-election	X
6. appoint PM	X	15. no impoundment	X	24. judiciary	X	32. experience	X
7. appoint ministers		16. control resources	X	25. central bank			
8. lack president	X	17. immunity	X	26. media	X		
9. no confidence	X	18. all elected	X				

The Parliament (*Folketinget*) of Denmark was established in Denmark's 1849 constitution. This constitution called for a bicameral parliament (*Rigsdag*) that paired a lower house (*Folketinget*) with an upper house (*Landsting*). Constitutional amendments in 1853 and 1863 adjusted Denmark's territorial borders. In the late nineteenth century the Danish monarch wielded executive powers, but by 1901 the supremacy of the parliament was established, and the king began appointing ministers according to the wishes of the majority in parliament. The 1953 constitution encoded the monarch's ceremonial role and did away with the upper house of the legislature, leaving a unicameral parliament (*Folketinget*).

Today the legislature exercises substantial powers. It enjoys robust control over the executive. Among other powers, it chooses the prime minister, interpellates and investigates the government, and can remove the government with a vote of no confidence. It also enjoys considerable institutional autonomy. Its legislation is not subject to veto, and the executive lacks gatekeeping and decree powers. The legislature enjoys numerous specified powers and prerogatives and is equipped with strong institutional capacity.

SURVEY

1. The legislature alone, without the involvement of any other agencies, can impeach the president or replace the prime minister.

Yes. The legislature can replace the prime minister with a vote of no confidence.

> Section 15
> (1) A Minister shall not remain in office after the Parliament has passed a vote of no confidence in him.
> (2) Where the Parliament passes a vote of no confidence in the Prime Minister, he shall ask for the dismissal of the Ministry unless writs are to be issued for a general election. Where a vote of censure has been passed on a Ministry, or it has asked for its dismissal, it shall continue in office until a new Ministry has been appointed.

2. Ministers may serve simultaneously as members of the legislature.

Yes. Ministers may serve simultaneously in the legislature.

3. The legislature has powers of summons over executive branch officials and hearings with executive branch officials testifying before the legislature or its committees are regularly held.

Yes. The legislature questions ministers during weekly question time.

4. The legislature can conduct independent investigation of the chief executive and the agencies of the executive.

Yes. The legislature can establish committees to investigate the executive.

> Section 51
> The Parliament may appoint committees from among its Members to investigate matters of general importance. Such committees shall be entitled to demand written or oral information both from private citizens and from public authorities.

5. The legislature has effective powers of oversight over the agencies of coercion (the military, organs of law enforcement, intelligence services, and the secret police).

Yes. Legislative committees have effective powers of oversight over the agencies of coercion.

6. The legislature appoints the prime minister.

Yes. The king appoints the candidate for prime minister who enjoys the support of parliament. In case of doubt, the king seeks the advice from the parliamentary parties.

> Section 14
> The King shall appoint and dismiss the Prime Minister and the other Ministers.

7. The legislature's approval is required to confirm the appointment of ministers; or the legislature itself appoints ministers.

No. The king appoints ministers on the recommendation of the prime minister, and the appointments do not require the legislature's approval.

> Section 14
> The King shall appoint and dismiss the Prime Minister and the other Ministers.

8. The country lacks a presidency entirely or there is a presidency, but the president is elected by the legislature.

Yes. The country lacks a presidency. The king is the head of state.

> Section 3
> The executive power is vested in the King.

9. The legislature can vote no confidence in the government.

Yes. The legislature can vote no confidence in the government.

> Section 15
> (2) Where the Parliament passes a vote of no confidence in the Prime Minister, he shall ask for the dismissal of the Ministry unless writs are to be issued for a general election.

10. The legislature is immune from dissolution by the executive.

No. The king, on the request of the prime minister, can dissolve the legislature.

> Section 32
> (2) The King may at any time issue writs for a new election with the effect that the existing seats be vacated upon a new election.

11. Any executive initiative on legislation requires ratification or approval by the legislature before it takes effect; that is, the executive lacks decree power.

Yes. The executive lacks decree power.

12. Laws passed by the legislature are veto-proof or essentially veto-proof; that is, the executive lacks veto power, or has veto power but the veto can be overridden by a majority in the legislature.

Yes. Formally, the king can refuse to assent to a bill, but in practice, it is unthinkable that he would do so.

> Section 22
> A Bill passed by the Parliament shall become law if it receives the Royal Assent not later than thirty days after it was finally passed. The King shall order the promulgation of Statutes and shall see to it that they are carried into effect.

13. The legislature's laws are supreme and not subject to judicial review.

No. Laws are subject to judicial review. The Supreme Court has overruled but a single law passed by parliament in Denmark's history, however. In 1999, when a law regulating subsidies to independent schools contained explicit mention of a particular organization, the Supreme Court found the measure to be a breach of the principle of equality before the law. Until this decision in 1999, jurists disputed whether judicial review even existed in Denmark; the decision appears to have settled the question in the affirmative, meaning that the legislature's laws are not supreme and are subject to judicial review.

14. The legislature has the right to initiate bills in all policy jurisdictions; the executive lacks gatekeeping authority.

Yes. The legislature can initiate bills in all policy jurisdictions.

15. Expenditure of funds appropriated by the legislature is mandatory; the executive lacks the power to impound funds appropriated by the legislature.

Yes. The executive cannot impound funds appropriated by the legislature.

16. The legislature controls the resources that finance its own internal operation and provide for the perquisites of its own members.

Yes. The legislature enjoys financial autonomy. Members' salaries are protected by law.

> Section 58
> The Members of the Parliament shall be paid such remuneration as may be provided for in the Elections Act.

17. Members of the legislature are immune from arrest and/or criminal prosecution.

Yes. Legislators are immune with the common exception for cases of *flagrante delicto*.

> Section 57
> No Member of the Parliament shall be prosecuted or imprisoned in any manner whatsoever without the consent of the Parliament, unless he is caught in flagrante delicto. Outside the Parliament no Member shall be held liable for his utterance in the Parliament save by the consent of the Parliament.

18. All members of the legislature are elected; the executive lacks the power to appoint any members of the legislature.

Yes. All members of the legislature are elected.

> Section 31
> (1) The Members of the Parliament shall be elected by general and direct ballot.

19. The legislature alone, without the involvement of any other agencies, can change the Constitution.

No. Constitutional amendments require approval in a popular referendum.

> Section 88
> When the Parliament passes a Bill for the purposes of a new constitutional provision, and the Government wishes to proceed with the matter, writs shall be issued for the election of Members of a new Parliament. If the Bill is passed unamended by the Parliament assembling after the election, the Bill shall within six months after its final passing be submitted to the Electors for approval or rejection by direct voting. Rules for this voting shall be laid down by Statute. If a majority of the persons taking part in the voting, and at least 40 per cent of the Electorate has voted in favor of the Bill as passed by the Parliament, and if the Bill receives the Royal Assent it shall form an integral part of the Constitution Act.

20. The legislature's approval is necessary for the declaration of war.

Yes. The legislature's approval is required to authorize the use of military force with the common exception for cases of foreign invasion. When the use of force is necessary to defend the country against an armed attack, the legislature's approval may be sought retroactively.

> Section 19
> (2) Except for purposes of defence against an armed attack upon the Realm or Danish forces the King shall not use military force against any foreign state without the consent of the Parliament. Any measure which the King may take in pursuance of this provision shall immediately be submitted to the Parliament. If the Parliament is not in session it shall be convoked immediately.

21. The legislature's approval is necessary to ratify treaties with foreign countries.

Yes. The legislature's approval is necessary to ratify international treaties.

> Section 19
> (1) The King shall act on behalf of the Realm in international affairs. Provided that without the consent of the Parliament the King shall not undertake any act whereby the territory of the Realm will be increased or decrease, nor shall he enter into any obligation which for fulfillment requires the concurrence of the Parliament, or which otherwise is of major importance; nor shall the King, except with the consent of the Parliament, terminate any international treaty entered into with the consent of the Parliament.

22. The legislature has the power to grant amnesty.

No. The king has the power to grant amnesty.

> Section 24
> The King shall have the prerogative of mercy and of granting amnesty.

23. The legislature has the power of pardon.

No. The king has the power of pardon (mercy).

> Section 24
> The King shall have the prerogative of mercy and of granting amnesty.

24. The legislature reviews and has the right to reject appointments to the judiciary; or the legislature itself appoints members of the judiciary.

Yes. The parliament elects half of the members of the High Court of the Realm.

> Section 59
> (1) The High Court of the Realm shall consist of up to fifteen of the eldest – according to seniority of office – ordinary members of the highest court of justice of the Realm, and an equal number of members elected for six years by the Parliament according to proportional representation.

25. The chairman of the central bank is appointed by the legislature.

No. The king, on the recommendation of the government, appoints the governor of the National Bank of Denmark.

26. The legislature has a substantial voice in the operation of the state-owned media.

Yes. The legislature has a substantial voice in the operation of the public media.

27. The legislature is regularly in session.

Yes. The legislature regularly meets in ordinary session.

> Section 35
> (1) A newly elected Parliament shall assemble at twelve o'clock noon on the twelfth week-day after the day of election, unless the King has previously convoked a meeting of its Members.

> Section 36
> (1) The sessional year of the Parliament shall commence on the first Tuesday of October, and shall continue until the first Tuesday of October of the following year.
> (2) On the first day of the sessional year at twelve o'clock noon the Members shall assemble for a new session of the Parliament.

28. Each legislator has a personal secretary.

Yes.

29. Each legislator has at least one non-secretarial staff member with policy expertise.

Yes. Party groups provide staff members with policy expertise to legislators.

30. Legislators are eligible for re-election without any restriction.

Yes. There are no restrictions on re-election.

31. A seat in the legislature is an attractive enough position that legislators are generally interested in and seek re-election.

Yes.

32. The re-election of incumbent legislators is common enough that at any given time the legislature contains a significant number of highly experienced members.

Yes. Re-election rates are sufficiently high to produce a significant number of highly experienced members.

NATIONAL CONGRESS OF THE DOMINICAN REPUBLIC (*CONGRESO NACIONAL*)

Expert consultants: Flavio Dario Espinal, Guillermo Garcia, Pepijn Gerrits, Jonathan Hartlyn, Ricardo Sosa Montás

Score: .41

Influence over executive (2/9)		Institutional autonomy (4/9)		Specified powers (3/8)		Institutional capacity (4/6)	
1. replace	X	10. no dissolution	X	19. amendments	X	27. sessions	X
2. serve as ministers		11. no decree		20. war		28. secretary	
3. interpellate	X	12. no veto		21. treaties	X	29. staff	
4. investigate		13. no review		22. amnesty	X	30. no term limits	X
5. oversee police		14. no gatekeeping	X	23. pardon		31. seek re-election	X
6. appoint PM		15. no impoundment		24. judiciary		32. experience	X
7. appoint ministers		16. control resources		25. central bank			
8. lack president		17. immunity	X	26. media			
9. no confidence		18. all elected	X				

The National Congress (*Congreso Nacional*) of the Dominican Republic was established in the 1844 constitution upon independence from Haiti. The bicameral legislature consists of the Chamber of Deputies (*Cámara de Diputados*) and the Senate (*Senado*). Congress was essentially lifeless during 1930–61, under the military dictatorship of General Rafael Leónidas Trujillo Molina. The subjugation of the legislature was so complete that legislators would sometimes read the morning newspaper and find that they had "resigned" their seat in Congress.

In 1966 the current constitution was established, bringing a revitalized legislative branch. Constitutional amendments in 1994 and 2001 did not directly affect legislative powers.

Congress's powers, while more substantial than during periods of dictatorship, remain circumscribed. Congress is limited in its ability to influence the executive branch, although it can, acting alone, vote to remove the president from office. The legislature has some institutional autonomy. It can initiate bills in all policy jurisdictions, it cannot be dissolved by the president, and its members are immune from arrest. Congress also enjoys several specified powers and prerogatives and has some institutional capacity.

SURVEY

1. The legislature alone, without the involvement of any other agencies, can impeach the president or replace the prime minister.

Yes. Congress can impeach the president by a three-fourths majority vote of its total membership in each chamber.

Article 23
The following are powers of the Senate:
4. To try accusations presented by the Chamber of Deputies against public officials elected for a predetermined period for bad conduct or serious faults in the exercise of their functions. In response to accusations the Senate cannot impose penalties beyond removal from office. The person removed, however, shall remain subject, when appropriate, to indictment and trial according to the law.
The Senate cannot remove an official from office unless approved by a vote of at least three-fourths of its full membership.

Article 26
It is an exclusive function of the Chamber of Deputies to refer impeachments of public officials before the Senate in the cases specified in Article 23(5). The impeachment may not be ordered except by a vote of three-fourths of the total membership of the Chamber.

2. Ministers may serve simultaneously as members of the legislature.

No. Legislators are prohibited from serving simultaneously in ministerial positions.

Article 18
The offices of Senator and of Deputy are incompatible with any other office or position in the public administration.

3. The legislature has powers of summons over executive branch officials and hearings with executive branch officials testifying before the legislature or its committees are regularly held.

Yes. The legislature regularly interpellates officials from the executive.

Article 37
The following are powers of the Congress:
22. To interpellate the Secretaries of State and the Directors or Administrators of autonomous organs of the State, on matters within their competence, when agreed upon by two-thirds of the members present in the Chamber requesting it, upon demand of one or more of its members.

4. The legislature can conduct independent investigation of the chief executive and the agencies of the executive.

No. The legislature cannot investigate the executive.

5. The legislature has effective powers of oversight over the agencies of coercion (the military, organs of law enforcement, intelligence services, and the secret police).

No. The legislature lacks effective powers of oversight over the agencies of coercion.

6. The legislature appoints the prime minister.

No. There is no prime minister.

7. The legislature's approval is required to confirm the appointment of ministers; or the legislature itself appoints ministers.

No. The president appoints ministers, and the appointments do not require the legislature's approval.

Article 55
The President of the Republic is the head of the Public Administration and the supreme commander of all the armed forces of the Republic and of the police corps.
It belongs to the powers and duties of the President of the Republic:
1. To appoint the Secretaries and Undersecretaries of State and other public officials and employees whose appointment is not vested in any other power or

autonomous organ recognized by this Constitution or by the laws, to accept their resignations, and to remove them.

8. The country lacks a presidency entirely or there is a presidency, but the president is elected by the legislature.

No. The president is directly elected.

Article 49
The Executive Power is exercised by the President of the Republic, who shall be elected every four years by direct vote.

9. The legislature can vote no confidence in the government.

No. The legislature cannot vote no confidence in the government.

10. The legislature is immune from dissolution by the executive.

Yes. The legislature is immune from dissolution.

11. Any executive initiative on legislation requires ratification or approval by the legislature before it takes effect; that is, the executive lacks decree power.

No. The president issues decrees that have the force of law.

Article 55
The President of the Republic is the head of the Public Administration and the supreme commander of all the armed forces of the Republic and of the police corps.
It belongs to the powers and duties of the President of the Republic:
2. To issue regulations, decrees, and instructions whenever necessary.

12. Laws passed by the legislature are veto-proof or essentially veto-proof; that is, the executive lacks veto power, or has veto power but the veto can be overridden by a majority in the legislature.

No. A two-thirds majority vote is needed to override a presidential veto.

Article 41
Every bill approved by both Chambers shall be forwarded to the Executive Power. If the President has no objections, he shall promulgate it within eight days after receipt and cause it to be published within fifteen days after promulgation; if he has objections, he shall return it to the Chamber from which it came within eight days from the date on which it was sent to him, unless the matter has been declared urgent, in which case he shall return it within three days. The Chamber that has received his objections shall place them on the agenda of its next session and again discuss the bill. If, after this discussion, two-thirds of the total membership

of this Chamber again approve it, it shall be forwarded to the other Chamber, and if this Chamber approves it by a like majority, it shall definitively be considered a law. The President of the Republic shall be required to promulgate and publish the law within the periods indicated.

13. The legislature's laws are supreme and not subject to judicial review.

No. The Supreme Court of Justice can review the constitutionality of laws.

Article 67
The Supreme Court of Justice, without prejudice to other powers conferred exclusively to it by law:
1. To take cognizance the constitutionality of the laws.

14. The legislature has the right to initiate bills in all policy jurisdictions; the executive lacks gatekeeping authority.

Yes. The legislature can initiate bills in all policy jurisdictions.

15. Expenditure of funds appropriated by the legislature is mandatory; the executive lacks the power to impound funds appropriated by the legislature.

No. The president can impound funds appropriated by the legislature.

16. The legislature controls the resources that finance its own internal operation and provide for the perquisites of its own members.

No. The legislature is dependent on the executive for the resources that finance its operations.

17. Members of the legislature are immune from arrest and/or criminal prosecution.

Yes. Legislators enjoy immunity. Even in cases of *flagrante delicto*, here expressed as "apprehended in the moment of committing a crime," the legislature can demand the release of its members.

Article 31
The members of both Chambers shall enjoy the fullest penal immunity for the opinions they express in sessions.

Article 32
No Senator or Deputy may be deprived of his freedom during the legislative session without the authorization of the Chamber to which he belongs, except in the case of his being apprehended in the moment of committing a crime. In all cases the Senate or Chamber of Deputies, or, if they are not in session or there is no quorum, any member, may demand that a member who has been detained, arrested, imprisoned, or in any other way deprived of his liberty, be set free for the duration of the legislative session or any portion thereof. To

this end, the President of the Senate or of the Chamber of Deputies, or the Senator or Deputy, as the case may be, shall make such request to the Attorney General of the Republic; and if necessary, shall give the order for liberation directly, for which he may request the assistance of the public force, which must be given to him by every depositary thereof.

18. All members of the legislature are elected; the executive lacks the power to appoint any members of the legislature.

Yes. All members of the legislature are elected.

Article 17
The election of Senators and Deputies is by direct vote.

19. The legislature alone, without the involvement of any other agencies, can change the Constitution.

Yes. The legislature can change the constitution with a two-thirds majority vote.

Article 27
The Chambers shall meet together as a National Assembly in the cases indicated in the Constitution, and there must be present for this purpose more than one-half of the members of each Chamber.
Decisions shall be taken by absolute majority vote.

Article 116
This Constitution may be amended if the proposal of amendment is presented in the National Congress with the support of one-third of the members of either Chamber, or if it is submitted by the Executive Power.

Article 117
The need for amendment shall be declared through a law. This law, which may not be opposed by the Executive Power, shall order a meeting of the National Assembly, shall specify the purpose of the amendment, and shall indicate the articles of the Constitution that it will affect.

Article 118
To act on the proposed amendments, the National Assembly shall meet within fifteen days following publication of the law declaring the need for amendments, with the presence of more than half of the members of each of the Chambers. Once the National Assembly has voted and proclaimed the amendments, the Constitution shall be published in its entirety, incorporating the amended texts. As an exception to the provisions of Article 27, decisions shall be taken in this case by two-thirds of the votes.

20. The legislature's approval is necessary for the declaration of war.

No. There is no provision for the declaration of war. The president can declare a "state of siege" without the legislature's approval in "the event of the disturbance of the public peace" when Congress is not in session.

Article 37
The following are powers of the Congress:
7. To declare a state of siege, in the event of disturbance of the public peace or public disaster, and to suspend, wherever the foregoing exist, and for their duration, the human rights proclaimed in Article 8, paragraphs 2(b), (c), (d), (e), (f), and (g) and 3, 4, 6, 7, and 9.
8. In the event that national sovereignty is exposed to serious and imminent danger, Congress may declare a state of national emergency, suspending the exercise of individual rights, with the exception of the inviolability of life as affirmed in Article 8(1) of this Constitution. If Congress is not in session, the President of the Republic may take the same measure, and shall convoke Congress to inform it of the state of emergency and the measures he has taken.

Article 55
The President of the Republic is the head of the Public Administration and the supreme commander of all the armed forces of the Republic and of the police corps.
It belongs to the powers and duties of the President of the Republic:
7. In the event of a disturbance of the public peace if the National Congress is not in session, to declare a state of siege wherever the foregoing exists, and suspend the exercise of the rights which pursuant to Article 37(7) of this Constitution, Congress is permitted to suspend. He may also, in the event that the national sovereignty is in serious or imminent danger, declare a state of national emergency, with the effects and requisites indicated in paragraph (8) of that Article. In case of public disaster, he may also declare as disaster areas those in which damage has occurred, due to storms, earthquakes, floods, or any other phenomenon of nature, or as a consequence of epidemics.

21. The legislature's approval is necessary to ratify treaties with foreign countries.

Yes. The legislature's approval is necessary to ratify international treaties.

Article 37
The following are powers of the Congress:
14. To approve or reject international treaties and conventions concluded by the Executive Power.

Article 55
The President of the Republic is the head of the Public Administration and the supreme commander of all the armed forces of the Republic and of the police corps.
It belongs to the powers and duties of the President of the Republic:
6. To preside over all official acts of the Nation, to direct diplomatic negotiations and to conclude treaties with foreign nations or international organizations, which must be submitted to the approval of the Congress, without which they shall have no validity and shall not bind the Republic.

22. The legislature has the power to grant amnesty.

Yes. The legislature has the power to grant amnesty.

Article 37
The following are powers of the Congress:
21. To grant amnesty on political grounds.

23. The legislature has the power of pardon.

No. The president has the power of pardon.

Article 55
It belongs to the powers and duties of the President of the Republic:
27. To grant full or partial pardons, absolute or conditional, on February 27, August 16, and December 23 each year, in accordance with the law.

24. The legislature reviews and has the right to reject appointments to the judiciary; or the legislature itself appoints members of the judiciary.

No. The legislature as a body lacks the power to appoint or approve judicial branch appointments. The members of the Supreme Court of Justice are appointed by the National Council of the Magistrature, a body that is headed by the president and consists of the vice president, the attorney general, the president of the Supreme Court of Justice, a magistrate from the Supreme Court of Justice, and two representatives each from the Chamber of Deputies and the Senate.

Article 64
The Supreme Court of Justice shall consist of at least eleven judges; but it may sit, deliberate, and render judgments validly with a quorum determined by the law that regulates its organization.
Paragraph I The judges of the Supreme Court of Justice shall be designated by the National Council of the Magistrature, which shall be presided by the President of the Republic, and in his absence, by the Vice President of the Republic, and in the absence of both, by the Attorney General of the Republic. The other members shall be:
1. The President of the Senate and one Senator selected by the Senate that belongs to a party different than the party of the President of the Senate.
2. The President of the Chamber of Deputies and one Deputy selected by the Chamber of Deputies who belongs to a party different than the party of the President of the Chamber of Deputies.
3. The President of the Supreme Court of Justice.
4. A Magistrate of the Supreme Court of Justice chosen by this same body, who shall act as Secretary.

Article 68

There shall be at least nine Courts of Appeal throughout the Republic. The number of Judges to compose the courts, as well as the Judicial Districts corresponding to each Court, shall be determined by law.

Paragraph I. In electing the Judges of the Courts of Appeal, the Supreme Court of Justice shall specify which of them should occupy the presidency and shall designate a first and second substitute to replace the President in the event of default or impediment.

25. The chairman of the central bank is appointed by the legislature.

No. The president appoints the governor of the Central Bank of the Dominican Republic.

26. The legislature has a substantial voice in the operation of the state-owned media.

No. The legislature lacks a substantial voice in the operation of the public media.

27. The legislature is regularly in session.

Yes. The legislature is in regular session for at least six months each year.

Article 33

The Chambers shall meet regularly on February 27 and August 16 of each year, and each legislative session shall last ninety days, which may be extended for sixty days more.

28. Each legislator has a personal secretary.

No.

29. Each legislator has at least one non-secretarial staff member with policy expertise.

No.

30. Legislators are eligible for re-election without any restriction.

Yes. There are no restrictions on re-election.

31. A seat in the legislature is an attractive enough position that legislators are generally interested in and seek re-election.

Yes.

32. The re-election of incumbent legislators is common enough that at any given time the legislature contains a significant number of highly experienced members.

Yes. Despite a relatively low re-election rate, Congress retains a substantial core of highly experienced members.

NATIONAL CONGRESS OF ECUADOR (*CONGRESO NACIONAL*)

Expert consultants: Andrés Mejía Acosta, Marisa Kellam, Simón Pachano, Roberta L. Rice, Alison Vasconez

Score: .53

Influence over executive (3/9)		Institutional autonomy (4/9)		Specified powers (5/8)		Institutional capacity (5/6)	
1. replace	X	10. no dissolution	X	19. amendments	X	27. sessions	X
2. serve as ministers		11. no decree		20. war		28. secretary	X
3. interpellate	X	12. no veto		21. treaties	X	29. staff	
4. investigate	X	13. no review		22. amnesty	X	30. no term limits	X
5. oversee police		14. no gatekeeping		23. pardon	X	31. seek re-election	X
6. appoint PM		15. no impoundment		24. judiciary	X	32. experience	X
7. appoint ministers		16. control resources	X	25. central bank			
8. lack president		17. immunity	X	26. media			
9. no confidence		18. all elected	X				

The National Congress (*Congreso Nacional*) of Ecuador was established in the 1830 constitution. Since that time civilian rule has frequently been interrupted by military governments, the last of which lost power in 1979. Ecuador's formal institutional order has been turbulent and included eight new constitutions between 1845 and 1998.

The current 1998 constitution, compared to its 1978 predecessor, in some ways enhanced the powers of the unicameral Congress. The new constitution allows legislators to seek immediate re-election. Prior to 1998 legislators were required to sit out at least one term before returning to office. The new constitution also encoded a practice that had been implemented in 1996. Prior to 1996 Congress was required to be in session for only two months each year. The 1998 constitution inverted the calendar, requiring Congress to meet continually with only two months of annual vacation.

The legislature is endowed with substantial but not formidable power. It has some, but not a great deal of, influence over the executive. It can interpellate and investigate the government and impeach the president, but it lacks the powers to make or approve ministerial appointments. Nor can it vote no confidence in the government. The legislature's own institutional autonomy, moreover, is circumscribed by presidential veto, decree, and gatekeeping powers. The legislature is endowed with a substantial number of specific prerogatives, including the right to change the constitution alone and powers of amnesty and pardon. Due in large part to the above-mentioned changes of the mid- and late 1990s, which scrapped term limits and lengthened the legislature's calendar, Congress has considerable institutional capacity.

Ecuador's tradition of constitutional volatility endures. In 2006 Rafael Correa, a leftist committed to changing Ecuador's constitution, was elected president. In 2007 an overwhelming majority endorsed the idea of rewriting the constitution in a popular referendum, and an assembly was elected to pen the new document. The most contentious issues include a proposal to remove the anti-abortion provision from the fundamental law. Correa states that promoting political participation and inclusion and reducing the power of the country's traditional elites motivate his desire for constitutional change. How, if at all, a new constitution will affect the powers of the National Congress is not yet clear.

SURVEY

1. The legislature alone, without the involvement of any other agencies, can impeach the president or replace the prime minister.

Yes. Congress can impeach the president by a two-thirds majority vote of its total membership.

Article 130
The National Congress has the following duties and powers:
9. Proceed to a political trial, on the petition of at least one fourth of the members of the National Congress, of the President and Vice-President of the Republic ... during the exercise of their functions and until a year after their [functions] have ended. The President and Vice-President of the Republic may only be subject to a political trial for the commission of crimes against the security of the State or for crimes of extortion, bribery, peculation and illicit enrichment and their censure and removal can only be decided through a vote of two-thirds of the members of Congress. A criminal indictment is not necessary to start this process.
10. Authorize, with a vote of two-thirds of its members, the penal indictment of the President or Vice-President if the competent judge solicits it with good reason.

2. Ministers may serve simultaneously as members of the legislature.

No. Legislators are prohibited from serving simultaneously in ministerial positions.

Article 135
Deputies, while they act as such, cannot perform any other public or private function, nor dedicate themselves to their professional activities if they are incompatible with their status as a deputy.

3. The legislature has powers of summons over executive branch officials and hearings with executive branch officials testifying before the legislature or its committees are regularly held.

Yes. The legislature regularly interpellates officials from the executive.

Article 130
The National Congress has the following duties and powers:
8. Oversee the acts of the Executive Function and the Supreme Electoral Tribunal and solicit the information it considers necessary from public functionaries.

Article 179
The ministers of State have the following [powers or duties]:
3. To inform the National Congress on matters for which they are responsible each year and when it is required.

4. The legislature can conduct independent investigation of the chief executive and the agencies of the executive.

Yes. The legislature can establish commissions to investigate the executive.

Article 130
The National Congress has the following duties and powers:
16. Constitute the special permanent commissions.

5. The legislature has effective powers of oversight over the agencies of coercion (the military, organs of law enforcement, intelligence services, and the secret police).

No. The legislature lacks effective powers of oversight over the agencies of coercion.

6. The legislature appoints the prime minister.

No. There is no prime minister.

7. The legislature's approval is required to confirm the appointment of ministers; or the legislature itself appoints ministers.

No. The president appoints ministers, and ministerial appointments do not require the legislature's approval.

Article 171
The following are the powers and duties of the President of the Republic:
10. Freely name and remove the ministers of State . . . in conformity with the Constitution and the law.

Article 176
The ministers of State shall be freely appointed and removed by the President of the Republic.

8. The country lacks a presidency entirely or there is a presidency, but the president is elected by the legislature.

No. The president is directly elected.

Article 165
The President and the Vice-President, whose names shall be recorded on the same ballot, shall be elected by an absolute majority of votes cast in a universal, equal, direct and secret manner.

9. The legislature can vote no confidence in the government.

No. The legislature cannot vote no confidence in the government.

10. The legislature is immune from dissolution by the executive.

Yes. The legislature is immune from dissolution.

11. Any executive initiative on legislation requires ratification or approval by the legislature before it takes effect; that is, the executive lacks decree power.

No. If Congress does not act within thirty days on a bill that the president classifies as "economically urgent," the president can promulgate the bill as an executive decree. Congress can modify or revoke the decree through subsequent legislation.

Article 155
The President of the Republic may send bills classified as economically urgent to the National Congress. In this case, Congress must approve, modify or deny them within a maximum period of thirty days, counted from when they were received.

Article 156
If Congress does not approve, modify or deny the bill within the period indicated in the previous article, the President of the Republic shall promulgate it as an executive decree in the Official Register. The National Congress can, at any time, modify or derogate it according to the ordinary process foreseen in the Constitution.

Article 179
The ministers of State have the following [powers or duties]:
2. To sign, along with the President, the decrees issued on matters that concern their ministry.

12. Laws passed by the legislature are veto-proof or essentially veto-proof; that is, the executive lacks veto power, or has veto power but the veto can be overridden by a majority in the legislature.

No. A two-thirds majority vote in the legislature, following a one-year waiting period, is required to override a presidential veto. If the president only vetoes part of the bill, Congress must reconsider it within thirty days. A two-thirds majority vote in the legislature is also needed to override a partial veto.

Article 153
If the President of the Republic completely objects to the bill, Congress can only consider it again after one year from the date on which the objection was made. After this period has expired, Congress may ratify it in one sole debate with the vote of two-thirds of its members and shall immediately send it to the Official Register for its promulgation. If the objection was partial, Congress must consider it during a period of no longer than thirty days counted from the date the presidential objection was delivered and may, in one sole debate, yield to [the objection] and amend the bill, with the favorable vote of a majority of those attending the session. It may also ratify the initially approved bill with a vote of two-thirds of its members. In both cases, Congress shall send the bill to the Official Register for its promulgation. If Congress does not consider the objection during the indicated period, it shall be understood that it has yielded to it and the President of the Republic may arrange for the promulgation of the law in the Official Register.

13. The legislature's laws are supreme and not subject to judicial review.

No. The Constitutional Tribunal can review the constitutionality of laws.

Article 154
If the objection of the President of the Republic is based on the partial or total unconstitutionality of the bill, it shall be sent to the Constitutional Tribunal so that it can issue its judgment within a period of thirty days.

If the judgment confirms the total unconstitutionality of the bill it will be set aside. If it confirms its partial unconstitutionality, the National Congress shall make the necessary amendments so that the bill can then be passed on for the approval of the President of the Republic. If the Constitutional Tribunal judges that there is no unconstitutionality, Congress shall order its promulgation.

Article 276

The Constitutional Tribunal is responsible for [the following]:

1. To take cognizance of and resolve complaints of substantive or procedural unconstitutionality that are presented regarding organic or ordinary laws, decree-laws, decrees, ordinances, statutes, regulations and resolutions, emitted by organs of the institutions of the State, and totally or partially suspend their effect.

14. The legislature has the right to initiate bills in all policy jurisdictions; the executive lacks gatekeeping authority.

No. The legislature is prohibited from introducing bills related to taxation, public expenditures, and the political division of the country.

Article 147

Only the President of the Republic can present bills through which taxes are created, modified or suppressed, [or that] raise the public expenditure or modify the political-administrative division of the country.

15. Expenditure of funds appropriated by the legislature is mandatory; the executive lacks the power to impound funds appropriated by the legislature.

No. The president can impound funds appropriated by the legislature.

16. The legislature controls the resources that finance its own internal operation and provide for the perquisites of its own members.

Yes. The legislature enjoys financial autonomy.

17. Members of the legislature are immune from arrest and/or criminal prosecution.

Yes. Legislators are immune with the common exception for cases of *flagrante delicto*.

Article 137

Deputies are not civilly or penally responsible for the votes and opinions they emit in the exercise of their functions. Criminal charges cannot be initiated against them without the previous authorization of the National Congress, nor will they be deprived of their liberty, except in cases of flagrante delicto.

18. All members of the legislature are elected; the executive lacks the power to appoint any members of the legislature.

Yes. All members of the legislature are elected.

Article 126

The Legislative Function is exercised by the National Congress, located in Quito. Under exceptional circumstances it may meet in any other part of the national territory. It is integrated by two legislators elected for each province, and one more [legislator elected] for each three hundred thousand inhabitants or fraction thereof over one hundred and fifty thousand.

19. The legislature alone, without the involvement of any other agencies, can change the Constitution.

Yes. The legislature can change the constitution through a complicated procedure. After waiting one year after introducing and debating an amendment, Congress can make the change with a two-thirds majority vote.

Article 280

The Political Constitution may be reformed by the National Congress or through popular referendum.

Article 281

Proposals for the reform of the Constitution may be presented before the National Congress by a number of deputies equal to twenty percent of its members or a legislative block; the President of the Republic, the Supreme Court of Justice, the Constitutional Tribunal, or a number of persons in exercise of their political rights, whose names are recorded in the electoral registry, and who equal one percent of the persons recorded in it.

Article 282

The National Congress shall take cognizance of and discuss bills of constitutional reform, [and] follow the same procedure foreseen for the ratification of laws. The second debate, which requires the favorable vote of two-thirds of the total members of Congress, may not be carried out until one year after the realization of the first [debate].

Once the bill is approved, the National Congress shall remit it to the President of the Republic for its sanction or objection, in conformity with the dispositions of this Constitution.

Article 283

The President of the Republic, in cases of urgency, previously approved by the National Congress with a vote of the majority of its members, may submit the approval of constitutional reforms to popular referendum. In other cases, a referendum shall proceed when the National Congress has not taken cognizance of, approved or denied the reforms in a period of one hundred and twenty days counted from the expiration of the period of one year referred to in the previous article. In both events, concrete texts of constitutional reform shall be submitted for the consideration of the electorate, which, if approved, shall be immediately incorporated into the Constitution.

Article 284
In case of doubt over the scope of norms contained in this Constitution, the National Congress may interpret them in a generally obligatory manner. The same people or organisms that have the power to present bills to reform [the Constitution] shall have the initiative for the presentation of bills of constitutional interpretation, which shall be processed in the same way as the issuance of laws. Their approval shall require the favorable vote of two-thirds of the members of the National Congress.

20. The legislature's approval is necessary for the declaration of war.

No. There is no provision for the declaration of war. The president can, however, decree a state of emergency in the event of "imminent external aggression," "international war," or a "grave internal disturbance" without the authorization of Congress. Congress can subsequently revoke the decree.

Article 180
The President of the Republic shall decree a state of emergency in all or part of the national territory in case of imminent external aggression, international war, grave internal disturbance or natural catastrophes. The state of emergency can affect all or some of the activities of society.

Article 182
The President of the Republic shall notify the National Congress of the state of emergency within forty-eight hours after the publication of the corresponding decree. The National Congress may revoke the decree at any time if the circumstances justify it.
The decree of a state of emergency shall have effect for a maximum period of sixty days. If the reasons that motivated it persist, it may be renewed, [and] the National Congress shall be notified thereof.
When the reasons that motivated the state of emergency have disappeared, the President of the Republic shall decree its termination and, with the respective report, immediately notify the National Congress.

21. The legislature's approval is necessary to ratify treaties with foreign countries.

Yes. The legislature's approval is necessary to ratify international treaties.

Article 129
The National Congress has the following duties and powers:
7. Approve or reject international treaties, in the cases in which [the responsibility] corresponds to them.

Article 161
The National Congress shall approve or reject the following international treaties and agreements:
1. Those that refer to territorial or border matters.
2. Those that establish political or military alliances.
3. Those that bind the country to agreements of integration.

4. Those that attribute the exercise of powers derived from the Constitution or the law to international or supranational organisms.
5. Those which refer to the fundamental rights and duties of the people and the collective rights.
6. Those that contain a commitment to issue, modify or derogate any law.

Article 162
The ratification of treaties and agreements shall be made in one sole debate and with a conforming vote of the majority of Congress' members.
The judgment of the Constitutional Tribunal shall be previously solicited with respect to the conformity of the treaty or agreement with the Constitution.
A treaty or agreement that requires a constitutional reform may not be approved unless said reform is made beforehand.

22. The legislature has the power to grant amnesty.

Yes. Congress has the power to grant amnesty.

Article 130
The National Congress has the following duties and powers:
15. Concede general amnesties for political crimes and pardons for common crimes through the favorable vote of two-thirds of its members. In both cases, the decision shall be justified when humanitarian motives intercede. Pardons shall not be granted for crimes committed against the public administration and for the crimes mentioned in the third paragraph of number 2 of Art. 23.

23. The legislature has the power of pardon.

Yes. Both Congress and the president have the power of pardon.

Article 130
The National Congress has the following duties and powers:
15. Concede general amnesties for political crimes and pardons for common crimes through the favorable vote of two-thirds of its members. In both cases, the decision shall be justified when humanitarian motives intercede. Pardons shall not be granted for crimes committed against the public administration and for the crimes mentioned in the third paragraph of number 2 of Art. 23.

Article 171
The following are the powers and duties of the President of the Republic:
20. Pardon, decrease or commute sentences, in conformity with the law.

24. The legislature reviews and has the right to reject appointments to the judiciary; or the legislature itself appoints members of the judiciary.

Yes. The legislature appoints the members of the Constitutional Tribunal. Prior to 1997 the legislature also appointed members of the Supreme Court of Justice. Since 1997 the Supreme Court of Justice is independently appointed.

Article 130
The National Congress has the following duties and powers:
11. Appoint . . . the members of the managing boards of the Constitutional Tribunal.

Article 202
The magistrates of the Supreme Court of Justice shall not be subject to a fixed term in the exercise of their posts. They shall cease their functions for the reasons determined by the Constitution and the law. If a vacancy is produced, the plenary [session] of the Supreme Court of Justice shall designate the new magistrate with a favorable vote of two-thirds of its members, observing the criteria of professionalism and the judicial career, in conformity with the law.

Article 275
The Constitutional Tribunal, with national jurisdiction, shall maintain its seat in Quito. Nine board members, who shall have respective substitutes, shall integrate it . . . The National Congress shall designate them by the majority of its members, in the following manner:
Two, from lists of candidates sent by the President of the Republic.
Two, from lists of candidates presented by the Supreme Court of Justice which do not include any of its members.
Two, selected by the National Congress, who do not exhibit the characteristics of legislators.
One, from the list of candidates presented by the municipal mayors and the provincial prefects.
One, from the list of candidates presented by the legally recognized national workers headquarters and the national indigenous and peasant organizations.
One, from the list of candidates sent by the legally recognized Production Chambers.

25. The chairman of the central bank is appointed by the legislature.

No. The president of the Central Bank of Ecuador is elected by the bank's board of directors, who themselves are nominated by the president and confirmed by Congress.

Article 262
Five members proposed by the President of the Republic and confirmed by a majority of the members of the National Congress shall integrate the board of directors of the Central Bank. It shall exercise its functions for a period of six years, with partial renewal every three years. The National Congress shall make confirmations within ten days counted from the date on which it received the nomination of the candidates. If it does not do so within this period, the persons proposed by the President of the Republic will be understood to be confirmed. If Congress rejects any of the names or the entire list of nominations, the President of the Republic must propose new candidates. The members of the board of directors shall elect from amongst themselves [the Central Bank's] president, who shall carry out his functions for three years.

26. The legislature has a substantial voice in the operation of the state-owned media.

No. The legislature lacks a substantial voice in the operation of the public media.

27. The legislature is regularly in session.

Yes. Since 1996 the legislature meets in ordinary session for ten months each year. Prior to 1996 the legislature only met for two months of ordinary session each year.

Article 132
The National Congress meets in Quito, without the need for convocation, from January 5 of the year in which the President of the Republic takes possession of his post, and is in session in ordinary and permanent form, with two recesses of one month each every year. The sessions of Congress are public. Under exceptional circumstances, it can meet in a private session, subject to the law.

28. Each legislator has a personal secretary.

Yes.

29. Each legislator has at least one non-secretarial staff member with policy expertise.

No. Each legislator has at least two non-secretarial staff members, but few of them have policy expertise.

30. Legislators are eligible for re-election without any restriction.

Yes. Since 1998 there have been no restrictions on re-election. Prior to 1998 legislators were prohibited from seeking immediate re-election.

31. A seat in the legislature is an attractive enough position that legislators are generally interested in and seek re-election.

Yes.

32. The re-election of incumbent legislators is common enough that at any given time the legislature contains a significant number of highly experienced members.

Yes. More than half of the legislators have previous legislative experience, owing in part to the removal of the ban on consecutive re-elections in the 1998 constitution.

PEOPLE'S ASSEMBLY OF EGYPT (*MAJILIS AL-SHA'B*)

Expert consultants: Nathan J. Brown, Jason Brownlee, Tamir Moustafa, Samer Shehata, Joshua Stacher

Score: .28

Influence over executive (1/9)	Institutional autonomy (3/9)	Specified powers (1/8)	Institutional capacity (4/6)
1. replace	10. no dissolution	19. amendments	27. sessions X
2. serve as ministers X	11. no decree	20. war	28. secretary
3. interpellate	12. no veto	21. treaties X	29. staff
4. investigate	13. no review	22. amnesty	30. no term limits X
5. oversee police	14. no gatekeeping X	23. pardon	31. seek re-election X
6. appoint PM	15. no impoundment X	24. judiciary	32. experience X
7. appoint ministers	16. control resources X	25. central bank	
8. lack president	17. immunity	26. media	
9. no confidence	18. all elected		

The People's Assembly (*Majilis al-Sha'b*) of Egypt was established in the 1923 constitution. Egypt gained nominal independence under a constitutional monarchy in 1922, although the British continued to maintain forces of military occupation in Egypt for the next three decades. In 1952 Egypt obtained full independence from Great Britain, and the constitutional monarchy was overthrown in a military coup led by Colonel Gamel Abdel Nasser, who ruled without regard for the legislature until 1970.

The constitution that is currently in force was adopted in 1971. The bulk of legislative responsibility is formally invested in the lower house, the People's Assembly, while the upper house, the Advisory Council (*Majilis al-Shura*), which was established in 1980, plays a consultative role. In 2005 the constitution was amended to allow for the direct election of the president in competitive elections. Prior to 2005 a single presidential candidate was nominated by the legislature and approved in a popular referendum.

The powers of the People's Assembly are highly circumscribed. The legislature has scant ability to influence the executive branch. The legislature's own institutional autonomy is limited by presidential powers to decree legislation, appoint members of the legislature, veto legislation, and dissolve the legislature. Specified powers and prerogatives, such as the power to declare war, are almost all reserved for the president. The legislature has some institutional capacity.

SURVEY

1. The legislature alone, without the involvement of any other agencies, can impeach the president or replace the prime minister.

No. Presidential impeachment requires action by a special tribunal.

Article 85
Any charge against the President of high treason or of committing a criminal act shall be made upon a proposal by at least one-third of the members of the People's Assembly. No impeachment shall be issued except upon the approval of a majority of two-thirds of the Assembly members. The President shall be suspended from the exercise of his duty as from the issuance of the impeachment. The Vice-President shall take over the Presidency temporarily until the decision concerning the impeachment is taken. The President of the Republic shall be tried by a special tribunal set up by law. The law shall also organise the trial procedures and define the penalty.
If he is found guilty, he shall be relieved of his post, without prejudice to other penalties.

2. Ministers may serve simultaneously as members of the legislature.

Yes. Ministers may serve simultaneously in the legislature.

Article 134
The Prime Minister, his deputies, the Ministers and their deputies may become members of the People's Assembly.

3. The legislature has powers of summons over executive branch officials and hearings with executive branch officials testifying before the legislature or its committees are regularly held.

No. The legislature formally has the right to summon executive branch officials for questioning, but officials can and do often ignore such requests, and hearings are not regularly held.

Article 124
Every member of the People's Assembly shall be entitled to address questions to the Prime Minister or any of his deputies or the Ministers or their deputies concerning matters within their jurisdiction. The Prime Minister, his deputies, the Ministers and the persons they delegate on their behalf shall answer the questions put to them by members. The member may withdraw his question at any time; this same question may not be transformed into an interpellation in the same session.

Article 125
Every member of the People's Assembly shall be entitled to address Interpellations to the Prime Minister or his deputies or the Ministers or their deputies concerning matters within their jurisdiction.

4. The legislature can conduct independent investigation of the chief executive and the agencies of the executive.

No. Formally, ad hoc committees of the People's Assembly have the right to investigate the executive. In practice, such investigations never occur, and it is difficult to imagine that they could occur.

Article 131
The People's Assembly shall form an ad hoc committee or entrust any of its committees with the inspection of the activities of any of the administrative departments or the general establishments or any administrative or executive organ or any of the public projects, for the purpose of finding facts and informing the Assembly as to the actual financial or administrative or economic positions or for conducting investigations into a subject related to one of the said activities.
In the course of its work, such a committee shall be entitled to collect whatever evidence it deems necessary and to subpoena all those it needs. All executive and administrative bodies shall answer the demands of the committee and put under its disposal all the documents and evidence it asks for this purpose.

5. The legislature has effective powers of oversight over the agencies of coercion (the military, organs of law enforcement, intelligence services, and the secret police).

No. The legislature lacks effective powers of oversight over the agencies of coercion.

6. The legislature appoints the prime minister.

No. The president appoints the prime minister.

Article 141
The President of the Republic shall appoint the Prime Minister, his deputies, the Ministers and their deputies and relieve them of the posts.

7. The legislature's approval is required to confirm the appointment of ministers; or the legislature itself appoints ministers.

No. The president appoints the ministers, and the appointments do not require the legislature's approval.

Article 141
The President of the Republic shall appoint the Prime Minister, his deputies, the Ministers and their deputies and relieve them of the posts.

8. The country lacks a presidency entirely or there is a presidency, but the president is elected by the legislature.

No. Since 2005 the president is directly elected. Prior to 2005 the president was nominated by the legislature and elected in a popular referendum.

Article 76
The People's Assembly shall nominate the President of the Republic. The nomination shall be referred to the people for a plebiscite. The nomination to the post of President of the Republic shall be made in the People's Assembly upon the proposal of at least one third of its members. The candidate who wins two-thirds of the votes of the Assembly members shall be referred to the people for a plebiscite. If none of the candidates obtains the said majority the nomination process shall be repeated two days after the first vote. The candidate winning the votes with an absolute majority of the Assembly members shall be referred to the citizens for a plebiscite. The candidate shall be considered President of the Republic when he obtains an absolute majority of the votes cast in the plebiscite. If the candidate does not obtain this majority, the Assembly shall nominate another candidate and the same procedure shall be followed.

9. The legislature can vote no confidence in the government.

No. A legislative vote of no confidence requires approval in a popular referendum before it leads to the government's resignation.

Article 127
The People's Assembly shall determine the responsibility of the Prime Minister, on a proposal by one-tenth of its members . . . In the event that such responsibility is determined, the Assembly shall submit a report to the

President of the Republic including the elements of the subject, the conclusions reached on the matter and the reasons behind it. The President of the Republic may return such a report to the Assembly within ten days. If the Assembly ratifies it once again, the President of the Republic may put the subject of discord to a referendum. If the result of the referendum is in support of the government, the Assembly shall be considered dissolved, otherwise the President of the Republic shall accept the resignation of the council of Ministries.

Article 128
The Prime Minister shall submit his resignation to the President of the Republic if he is found responsible before the People's Assembly.

10. The legislature is immune from dissolution by the executive.

No. The president can dissolve the legislature after approval in a popular referendum.

Article 136
The President of the Republic shall not dissolve the People's Assembly unless it is necessary and after a referendum of the people. The President of the Republic shall issue a decision terminating the sessions of the Assembly and conducting a referendum within thirty days. If the total majority of the voters approve the dissolution of the Assembly, the President of the Republic shall issue the decision of dissolution.

11. Any executive initiative on legislation requires ratification or approval by the legislature before it takes effect; that is, the executive lacks decree power.

No. The president can issue decrees that have the force of law when the legislature is not in session. The decrees lapse if they are not subsequently approved by the legislature. The legislature can also delegate temporary decree power to the president on specified issue areas.

Article 108
The president of the Republic shall have the right, in case of necessity or in exceptional cases and on the authorisation of the People's Assembly upon the approval of a majority of two thirds of its members, to issue resolutions having the force of law. The authorisation must be for a limited period of time during which the subjects of the resolutions and the grounds upon which they are based, must be determined. The resolutions must be submitted to the People's Assembly in the first meeting after the end of the authorisation period.

Article 147
In case it becomes necessary, during the recess between the sessions of the People's Assembly, to take measures which cannot suffer delay, the President of the Republic shall issue decisions in their respect, which shall have the force of law. Such decisions must be submitted to the People's Assembly within fifteen days from their date of issuance if the Assembly is standing. In case of

dissolution or recess of the Assembly, they shall be submitted at its first meeting. In case they are not submitted, their force of law disappears with retroactive effect, without need for issuing a decision to this effect. If they are submitted and are not ratified, their force of law disappears with retroactive effect, unless the Assembly ratifies their validity in the previous period or settling their effects in another way.

12. Laws passed by the legislature are veto-proof or essentially veto-proof; that is, the executive lacks veto power, or has veto power but the veto can be overridden by a majority in the legislature.

No. A two-thirds majority vote in the legislature is needed to override a presidential veto.

Article 113
If the President of the Republic objects to a draft law ratified by the People's Assembly he shall refer it back to the Assembly within thirty days from the Assembly's communication of it. If the draft law is not referred back within this period, it is considered a law shall be promulgated. If it is referred back to the Assembly on the said date and approved once again by a majority of two-thirds of the members, it shall be considered a law and shall be promulgated.

13. The legislature's laws are supreme and not subject to judicial review.

No. The Supreme Constitutional Court can review the constitutionality of laws.

Article 175
The Supreme Constitutional Court alone shall undertake the judicial control in respect of the constitutionality of the laws and regulations, and shall undertake the explanation of the legislative texts, all of which in accordance with the manner prescribed by the law.

14. The legislature has the right to initiate bills in all policy jurisdictions; the executive lacks gatekeeping authority.

Yes. The legislature can initiate bills in all policy jurisdictions.

15. Expenditure of funds appropriated by the legislature is mandatory; the executive lacks the power to impound funds appropriated by the legislature.

Yes. The executive lacks the power to impound funds appropriated by the legislature.

16. The legislature controls the resources that finance its own internal operation and provide for the perquisites of its own members.

Yes. The legislature enjoys financial autonomy, including control over members' salaries.

Article 91
Members of the People's Assembly shall receive a remuneration determined by the law.

17. Members of the legislature are immune from arrest and/or criminal prosecution.

No. Formally, legislators are immune, but in practice, legislative immunity can be revoked. Members of parliament have been tried on corruption and embezzlement charges, and in recent years legislators have been arrested and beaten by security forces.

Article 98
Members of the People's Assembly shall not be censured for any opinions or thoughts expressed by them in the performance of their tasks in the Assembly or its committees.

Article 99
No member of the People's Assembly shall be subject to a criminal prosecution without the permission of the Assembly except in cases of flagrante delicto. If the Assembly is not in session, the permission of the President of the Assembly must be taken. The Assembly must be notified of the measures taken in its first subsequent session.

18. All members of the legislature are elected; the executive lacks the power to appoint any members of the legislature.

No. The President can appoint up to ten members of the People's Assembly, a body which contains at least 350 members.

Article 87
The law shall determine the constituencies into which the State shall be divided and the number of elected members of the People's Assembly must be at least 350 persons, of which one half at least must be workers and farmers elected by direct secret public balloting. The definition of the worker and the farmer shall be made by law. The President of the Republic may appoint a number of members not exceeding ten.

19. The legislature alone, without the involvement of any other agencies, can change the Constitution.

No. Constitutional amendments require approval in a popular referendum.

Article 189
The President of the Republic, as well as the People's Assembly, may request the amendment of one or more of the Constitution articles. The articles to be revised and the reasons justifying such amendment must be mentioned in the request for amendment. In case the request emanates from the People's Assembly, it should be signed by at least one third of the Assembly members. In all cases, the Assembly shall discuss the amendment in principle, and the decision in this respect shall be taken by the majority of its members. If the request is rejected, the amendment of the same particular articles may not be requested again before the expiration of one year from the date of such rejection. If the People's Assembly approves the principle of revision, the

articles requested to be mended shall be discussed after two months from the date of the said approval. If the modification is approved by two-thirds of the members of the Assembly, it must be referred to the people for a plebiscite.

20. The legislature's approval is necessary for the declaration of war.

No. Formally, the legislature's approval is necessary for the declaration of war. In practice, the president can declare war without the legislature's approval.

Article 150
The President of Republic shall be the Supreme Commander of the Armed Forces. He shall be the authority who declares war, after the approval of the People's Assembly.

21. The legislature's approval is necessary to ratify treaties with foreign countries.

Yes. The legislature's approval is necessary to ratify international treaties.

Article 151
The President of Republic shall conclude treaties and communicate them to the People's Assembly, accompanied with a suitable clarification. They shall have the force of law after their conclusion, ratification and publication according to the established procedure. However, peace treaties, alliance pacts, commercial and maritime and all the treaties involving modifications in the territory of the State, or having connection with the rights of sovereignty, or which lay upon the Treasury of the State certain charges not provided for in the budget, must acquire the approval of the People's Assembly.

22. The legislature has the power to grant amnesty.

No. Formally, a general amnesty can be granted by law. In practice, the president, and the president alone, has the power to grant amnesty.

Article 149
The President of Republic shall have the right of granting amnesty or commute a sentence. As for general amnesty, it can only be granted by virtue of a law.

23. The legislature has the power of pardon.

No. The president has the power of pardon, here expressed as the "right of granting amnesty or commute a sentence."

Article 149
The President of Republic shall have the right of granting amnesty or commute a sentence. As for general amnesty, it can only be granted by virtue of a law.

24. The legislature reviews and has the right to reject appointments to the judiciary; or the legislature itself appoints members of the judiciary.

No. According to the constitution, the conditions for appointment of members of the judiciary will be determined by law, which suggests a role for the legislature. In practice, the president makes judicial appointments, and the appointments do not require the legislature's approval.

> Article 167
> The law shall determine the judiciary organisations and their functions, organise the way of their formation, prescribe the conditions and measures for the appointment and transfer of their members.

25. The chairman of the central bank is appointed by the legislature.

No. The president appoints the chairman of the Central Bank of Egypt.

26. The legislature has a substantial voice in the operation of the state-owned media.

No. The state-owned media is run by the Minister of Information, who is subordinate to the president.

27. The legislature is regularly in session.

Yes. The legislature meets in ordinary session for at least seven months each year.

> Article 101
> The President of the Republic shall convoke the People's Assembly for its ordinary annual session before the second Thursday of November. If it is not convoked, the Assembly shall meet, by force of the Constitution, on the said day. The session of the ordinary meeting shall continue for at least seven months.

28. Each legislator has a personal secretary.

No.

29. Each legislator has at least one non-secretarial staff member with policy expertise.

No.

30. Legislators are eligible for re-election without any restriction.

Yes. There are no restrictions on re-election.

31. A seat in the legislature is an attractive enough position that legislators are generally interested in and seek re-election.

Yes.

32. The re-election of incumbent legislators is common enough that at any given time the legislature contains a significant number of highly experienced members.

Yes. The re-election rate is relatively high, resulting in a significant number of highly experienced members. Many of the longest serving members, however, come from the president's hegemonic ruling party or are domesticated opposition figures. The president's domination of the legislature means that long-serving members do not necessarily have experience in the business of legislating.

LEGISLATIVE ASSEMBLY OF EL SALVADOR (*ASAMBLEA LEGISLATIVA*)

Expert consultants: David Holiday, Gerardo Le Chevallier, Hugo Lopez, Margaret Popkin, William Stanley

Score: .59

Influence over executive (3/9)		Institutional autonomy (7/9)		Specified powers (6/8)		Institutional capacity (3/6)	
1. replace	X	10. no dissolution	X	19. amendments	X	27. sessions	
2. serve as ministers		11. no decree	X	20. war	X	28. secretary	
3. interpellate	X	12. no veto		21. treaties	X	29. staff	
4. investigate	X	13. no review		22. amnesty	X	30. no term limits	X
5. oversee police		14. no gatekeeping	X	23. pardon	X	31. seek re-election	X
6. appoint PM		15. no impoundment	X	24. judiciary	X	32. experience	X
7. appoint ministers		16. control resources	X	25. central bank			
8. lack president		17. immunity	X	26. media			
9. no confidence		18. all elected	X				

The Legislative Assembly (*Asamblea Legislativa*) of El Salvador was established in the 1841 constitution. Since then El Salvador has experienced much turbulence, going through fifteen constitutions. For most of the second half of the twentieth century, the legislature was sidelined by military rule and gruesome civil war. The current constitution was adopted in 1983 and calls for a unicameral assembly.

The legislature has significant powers, although its ability to influence the executive is not great. The Assembly cannot make or approve ministerial appointments or vote no confidence in the government. It does, however, have a fair degree of institutional autonomy. The executive lacks gatekeeping and decree powers. The legislature does, moreover, hold numerous specified powers and prerogatives, including the authority to appoint members of the judiciary and the power to change the constitution. Its institutional capacity is modest, due to lack of staff and a legislative calendar that keeps the Assembly in session for only about five-and-a-half months each year.

SURVEY

1. The legislature alone, without the involvement of any other agencies, can impeach the president or replace the prime minister.

Yes. The legislature can impeach the president.

Article 236

The President . . . shall answer to the Legislative Assembly for the official and common crimes [he] commit[s]. The Assembly, after hearing an accusing member and the accused official or special defender, as the case may be, shall declare whether or not there are grounds for a trial. In the former event, the case shall be sent to the Chamber of Second Instance specified by law, for a trial in first instance; and in the latter event, the case shall be dropped. The decisions rendered by the aforementioned Chamber shall be passed upon in second instance by one of the Divisions of the Supreme Court of Justice, and in cassation by the full court. Any person has the right to denounce the offenses with which this Article is concerned, and to appear as a party if he has the qualifications required by law.

Article 237

As soon as the Legislative Assembly or the Supreme Court of Justice declares that there are grounds for trial, the offender shall be suspended from the exercise of his functions and may not continue in his position for any reason whatsoever. If he does, he shall be guilty of the crime of prolonging of functions. If the sentence is condemnatory, he shall be dismissed from his position through the same act. If acquitted, he shall resume the exercise of his functions, if the position is one of those that is conferred for a determined time and the period of his election or appointment has not expired.

2. Ministers may serve simultaneously as members of the legislature.

No. Legislators who serve in government have a sleeping mandate, meaning that they may join the government but forfeit their voting rights in the legislature during their service in government. They may return to the legislature after their service in government ends.

Article 127
The following shall not be candidates for Deputies:
1. The Ministers and Vice Ministers of State.

Article 129
The Deputies in office shall not hold remunerated public positions during the time for which they have been elected, except those of a teaching or cultural character, and those related to the professional services of social assistance. Nevertheless, they may hold the positions of Ministers or Vice Ministers of State, Presidents of Official Autonomous Institutions, Heads of Diplomatic Missions, Consular [Missions] or carry out Special Diplomatic Missions. In these cases, they shall be reincorporated into the Assembly when their functions cease, if the period of their election is still in force.

3. The legislature has powers of summons over executive branch officials and hearings with executive branch officials testifying before the legislature or its committees are regularly held.

Yes. The legislature regularly interpellates officials from the executive.

Article 131
It corresponds to the Legislative Assembly:
34th. – To question Ministers.

4. The legislature can conduct independent investigation of the chief executive and the agencies of the executive.

Yes. The legislature can establish special commissions to investigate the executive.

Article 131
It corresponds to the Legislative Assembly:
32nd. – To name special commissions for the investigation of matters of national interest and to adopt the agreements or recommendations that are esteemed necessary based on the report of said commissions.

Article 132
All the public functionaries and employees, including those of Official Autonomous Institutions and the Members of the Armed Force, are under the obligation to collaborate with the special commissions of the Legislative Assembly; and the appearance and declaration of these as well as any other person required by the mentioned commissions shall be obligatory under the same summons that are observed in the judicial procedure. The conclusions of the special commissions of investigation of the Legislative Assembly shall not be obliging the tribunals, nor shall they affect the judicial proceedings or resolutions, without prejudice that the result be communicated to the General Office of the Attorney General of the Republic for the exercise of pertinent actions.

5. The legislature has effective powers of oversight over the agencies of coercion (the military, organs of law enforcement, intelligence services, and the secret police).

No. The agencies of coercion report to the president and are not subject to effective legislative oversight.

Article 213
The Armed Force forms a part of the Executive Organ and is subordinate to the authority of the President of the Republic in his capacity as Commander-General. Its structure, juridical regime, doctrine, composition, and functioning are defined by the law, the regulations and special provisions which the President of the Republic adopts.

6. The legislature appoints the prime minister.

No. There is no prime minister.

7. The legislature's approval is required to confirm the appointment of ministers; or the legislature itself appoints ministers.

No. The president appoints ministers, and the appointments do not require the legislature's approval.

Article 162
It corresponds to the President of the Republic to appoint, remove, accept the resignations of, and grant leave to, Ministers and Vice Ministers of State, as well as the Chief of Public Security and of the State Intelligence.

8. The country lacks a presidency entirely or there is a presidency, but the president is elected by the legislature.

No. The president is directly elected.

Article 151
To be elected President of the Republic it is required: to be a Salvadoran by birth, child of a Salvadoran father or mother; to be a layman, over thirty years of age, of well-known morality and instruction; to be in the exercise of the rights of citizenship, having been so for the six years preceding the election, and to be affiliated with one of the legally recognized political parties.

9. The legislature can vote no confidence in the government.

No. The legislature cannot vote no confidence in the government.

10. The legislature is immune from dissolution by the executive.

Yes. The legislature is immune from dissolution.

11. Any executive initiative on legislation requires ratification or approval by the legislature before it takes effect; that is, the executive lacks decree power.

Yes. The executive lacks decree power.

12. Laws passed by the legislature are veto-proof or essentially veto-proof; that is, the executive lacks veto power, or has veto power but the veto can be overridden by a majority in the legislature.

No. A two-thirds majority vote in the legislature is required to override a presidential veto.

> Article 137
> When the President of the Republic vetoes a bill of law, he shall return it to the Assembly within eight business days of receiving it, indicating the reasons on which his veto is founded; if within such term he has failed to return it, it shall be considered ratified and he shall order its publication as law. In the case of a veto, the Assembly shall reconsider the bill and if it should ratify it with at least two-thirds of the votes of elected Deputies, it shall send it again to the President of the Republic, and he shall sanction it and send it to be published.

13. The legislature's laws are supreme and not subject to judicial review.

No. The Supreme Court of Justice can review the constitutionality of laws.

> Article 138
> When a bill of law is returned because the President of the Republic considers it to be unconstitutional and the Legislative Organ ratifies it in the manner established in the preceding article, the President of the Republic shall present it to the Supreme Court of Justice within three business days, so that the latter may, after hearing the arguments of both sides, decide whether it is or is not constitutional, within fifteen business days at the latest. If the Court decides that the bill is constitutional, the President of the Republic shall be obligated to sanction it and to order its publication as law.

14. The legislature has the right to initiate bills in all policy jurisdictions; the executive lacks gatekeeping authority.

Yes. The legislature can initiate bills in all policy jurisdictions.

15. Expenditure of funds appropriated by the legislature is mandatory; the executive lacks the power to impound funds appropriated by the legislature.

Yes. The executive lacks the power to impound funds appropriated by the legislature.

16. The legislature controls the resources that finance its own internal operation and provide for the perquisites of its own members.

Yes. The legislature enjoys financial autonomy.

> Article 131
> It corresponds to the Legislative Assembly:
> 1st. – To determine its internal regulation;
> 10th. – To approve its budget and salary system, as well as its reforms, consulting previously with the President of the Republic on them, for the sole effect of guaranteeing that the necessary funds exist for their compliance. Once approved, said budget shall be incorporated into the Budget of Revenues and Expenditures of the Public Administration.

17. Members of the legislature are immune from arrest and/or criminal prosecution.

Yes. Legislators are immune. Even in cases of *flagrante delicto,* they can be released at the Assembly's behest.

> Article 125
> The Deputies represent the whole nation and are not bound by any imperative mandate. They are inviolable and shall not have responsibility at any time for the opinions or votes they emit.

> Article 130
> The Deputies shall cease in their position in the following cases:
> 1st. – When they are convicted for serious crimes in a definitive sentence;
> 2nd. – When they commit the prohibitions contained in Article 128 of this Constitution;
> 3rd. – When they resign without just cause qualified as such by the Assembly;
> In these cases, they shall remain unqualified to carry out any other public post during the period of their election.

> Article 238
> The Deputies may not be tried for serious offenses they commit from the day of their election until the end of the period for which they were elected, without the Legislative Assembly previously declaring that there are grounds for trial, in conformity with the procedure established in the preceding Article. For the less serious crimes and misdeeds they commit during the same period they may not be detained or imprisoned, nor called to testify until after the conclusion of the period of their election. If . . . a Deputy were to be caught in *flagrante delicto,* from the day of their election until the end of the period for which they were elected, they may be detained by any person or authority, who shall be obliged to place the case immediately at the disposition of the Assembly.

18. All members of the legislature are elected; the executive lacks the power to appoint any members of the legislature.

Yes. All members of the legislature are elected.

Article 121

The Legislative Assembly is a professional associated body composed of Deputies elected in the form prescribed by this Constitution, and to it fundamentally belongs the authority to legislate.

19. The legislature alone, without the involvement of any other agencies, can change the Constitution.

Yes. The legislature can change the constitution through a complicated procedure. The sitting legislature can propose an amendment, and then, following an election, the subsequent assembly can approve the amendment with a two-thirds majority vote.

Article 248

Reformation of this Constitution may be decided by the Legislative Assembly, with the vote of one-half plus one of the elected Deputies. For this amendment to be decreed, it must be ratified by the following Legislative Assembly by a vote of two-thirds of the elected Deputies. Thus ratified, the corresponding decree shall be issued and shall be published in the *Official Gazette*. Amendments may only be proposed by elected Deputies, by a number no less than ten.

Under no circumstances, may the articles of this Constitution, which refer to the form and system of government, to the territory of the Republic, and to the principle that a President cannot succeed himself, be amended.

20. The legislature's approval is necessary for the declaration of war.

Yes. The legislature declares war.

Article 131

It corresponds to the Legislative Assembly:
25th. – To declare war and ratify peace, on the basis of reports provided to it by the Executive Organ.

21. The legislature's approval is necessary to ratify treaties with foreign countries.

Yes. The legislature's approval is necessary to ratify international treaties.

Article 131

It corresponds to the Legislative Assembly:
7th. – To ratify the treaties or pacts made by the Executive with other States or international organisms, or to refuse their ratification.

Article 147

For the ratification of any treaty or pact for which any question related to the limits of the Republic are submitted to arbitration, a vote of at least three-quarters of the elected Deputies shall be necessary. Any treaty or agreement formalized by the Executive Organ referring to the national territory, shall also require a vote of at least three-quarters of the elected Deputies.

22. The legislature has the power to grant amnesty.

Yes. The legislature has the power to grant amnesty.

Article 131

It corresponds to the Legislative Assembly:
26th. – To grant amnesty for political or common crimes connected with these, or for common crimes committed by not less than twenty persons; and to grant pardons, upon favorable report of the Supreme Court of Justice.

23. The legislature has the power of pardon.

Yes. The legislature has the power of pardon.

Article 131

It corresponds to the Legislative Assembly:
26th. – To grant amnesty for political or common crimes connected with these, or for common crimes committed by not less than twenty persons; and to grant pardons, upon favorable report of the Supreme Court of Justice.

24. The legislature reviews and has the right to reject appointments to the judiciary; or the legislature itself appoints members of the judiciary.

Yes. The legislature elects the president and the members of the Supreme Court of Justice, the president and members of the Court of Accounts, and the members of the National Council of the Judiciary.

Article 131

It corresponds to the Legislative Assembly:
19th. – To elect in a public and registered vote the following functionaries: the President and Magistrates of the Supreme Court of Justice, the President and Magistrates of the Supreme Electoral Tribunal, the President and Magistrates of the Court of Accounts of the Republic . . . and Members of the National Council of the Judiciary.

Article 173

The Supreme Court of Justice shall be made up of the number of Magistrates determined by the law, who will be elected by the Legislative Assembly, and one of them shall be the President.

25. The chairman of the central bank is appointed by the legislature.

No. The president appoints the president of the Central Reserve Bank of El Salvador.

26. The legislature has a substantial voice in the operation of the state-owned media.

No. The legislature lacks a substantial voice in the operation of the public media.

27. The legislature is regularly in session.

No. The legislature meets in ordinary session from February 15th to May 15th and from October 15th to January 2nd each year. Its total time in session is less than six months each year.

28. Each legislator has a personal secretary.

No.

29. Each legislator has at least one non-secretarial staff member with policy expertise.

No.

30. Legislators are eligible for re-election without any restriction.

Yes. There are no restrictions on re-election.

> Article 124
> The members of the Assembly shall be renewed every three years and may be reelected.

31. A seat in the legislature is an attractive enough position that legislators are generally interested in and seek re-election.

Yes.

32. The re-election of incumbent legislators is common enough that at any given time the legislature contains a significant number of highly experienced members.

Yes. Re-election rates are sufficiently high to produce a significant number of highly experienced members.

NATIONAL ASSEMBLY OF ERITREA (*HAGERAWI BAITO*)

Expert consultants: Dan Connell, Edward McMahon

Score: .25

Influence over executive (2/9)		Institutional autonomy (3/9)		Specified powers (2/8)		Institutional capacity (1/6)	
1. replace		10. no dissolution		19. amendments		27. sessions	
2. serve as ministers	X	11. no decree	X	20. war	X	28. secretary	
3. interpellate		12. no veto	X	21. treaties	X	29. staff	
4. investigate		13. no review		22. amnesty		30. no term limits	X
5. oversee police		14. no gatekeeping	X	23. pardon		31. seek re-election	
6. appoint PM		15. no impoundment		24. judiciary		32. experience	
7. appoint ministers		16. control resources		25. central bank			
8. lack president	X	17. immunity		26. media			
9. no confidence		18. all elected					

The National Assembly (*Hagerawi Baito*) of Eritrea was established in 1993, following a thirty-year war for independence with Ethiopia. The Assembly was designed to meet as a transitional body until a constitution could be drafted and presidential and parliamentary elections could be held. Elections were scheduled for 2001 but were never carried out. The transitional legislature is still in place. A new constitution (excerpted in the survey below) was ratified in 1997, but has not yet been implemented, in part because of a revival of hostilities with Ethiopia.

The legislature has little power. Its sway over executive power is slight. It does have some institutional autonomy, because the president cannot issue decrees that have the force of law or veto the

Assembly's legislation. The bulk of specified powers and prerogatives are reserved for the president. The legislature's institutional capacity is extremely low.

SURVEY

1. The legislature alone, without the involvement of any other agencies, can impeach the president or replace the prime minister.

No. Formally, the legislature can impeach the president by a two-thirds majority vote of its total membership. In practice, it would be unthinkable for the legislature to impeach the president. For example, when legislators criticized the president in 2000, the president simply refused to call the body back into session until he had arrested his detractors and defused the dissent.

Article 32
(9) Pursuant to the provisions of Sub-Article 6(a) and (b) of Article 41 hereof, the National Assembly, by a vote of two-thirds majority of all its members, shall have the power to impeach and charge the President before the end of his term of office.

Article 41
(6) The President may be removed from office by two-thirds majority vote of all members of the National Assembly for the following reasons:
  a) violation of the Constitution or grave violation of the law;
  b) conducting himself in a manner which brings the authority or honour of the office of President into ridicule, contempt and disrepute;
  c) being incapable of performing the functions of his office by reason of physical or mental incapacity.

2. Ministers may serve simultaneously as members of the legislature.

Yes. Ministers may serve simultaneously in the legislature.

Article 46
(2) The President may select ministers from among members of the National Assembly or from among persons who are not members of the National Assembly.

3. The legislature has powers of summons over executive branch officials and hearings with executive branch officials testifying before the legislature or its committees are regularly held.

No. Formally, the legislature can interpellate ministers, but in practice, officials often refuse to attend legislative meetings.

Article 47
(2) The National Assembly or its committees may, through the Office of the President, summon any minister to appear before them to question him concerning the policies or operation of his ministry.

4. The legislature can conduct independent investigation of the chief executive and the agencies of the executive.

No. Formally, the legislature can establish investigatory committees, although in practice it cannot.

Article 37
(1) The National Assembly shall have a secretariat under the direction of its Chairman and committees for various fields of interest, as circumstance may dictate.
(2) The various committees established pursuant to the provisions of Sub-Article 1 of this Article shall have the power to call any person to appear before them to give evidence or to submit documents.

5. The legislature has effective powers of oversight over the agencies of coercion (the military, organs of law enforcement, intelligence services, and the secret police).

No. The agencies of coercion report to the president and are not subject to legislative oversight.

6. The legislature appoints the prime minister.

No. There is no prime minister.

7. The legislature's approval is required to confirm the appointment of ministers; or the legislature itself appoints ministers.

No. According to the – as of yet unimplemented – 1997 constitution, the legislature has responsibility for confirming the president's ministerial appointments. In practice, the president appoints ministers at will.

Article 32
(10) The National Assembly may approve the appointment of any person or persons pursuant to this Constitution.

Article 42
The President shall have the following powers and duties:
7. appoint with the approval of the National Assembly, ministers.

8. The country lacks a presidency entirely or there is a presidency, but the president is elected by the legislature.

Yes. The legislature elects the president.

Article 32
(8) The National Assembly shall have the power to elect, from among its members, by absolute majority vote of all its members, the President who shall serve for five years.

Article 41
(1) The President shall be elected from amongst the members of the National Assembly by a vote of the majority of its members. A candidate for the office of the President must be nominated by at least 20 percent vote of all the members of the National Assembly.

9. The legislature can vote no confidence in the government.

No. The legislature cannot vote no confidence in the government.

10. The legislature is immune from dissolution by the executive.

No. According to the 1997 constitution, the legislature is immune from dissolution. In practice, the president has refused to call the legislature into session when not doing so has served his interests.

11. Any executive initiative on legislation requires ratification or approval by the legislature before it takes effect; that is, the executive lacks decree power.

Yes. The president lacks decree power. While the president dominates policymaking in practice, all legislation formally passes through the legislature.

> Article 32
> (1) Pursuant to the provisions of this Constitution:
> a) The National Assembly shall have the power to enact laws and pass resolutions for the peace, stability, development and good governance of Eritrea;
> b) Unless, pursuant to the provisions of this Constitution or authorized by law enacted by the National Assembly, no person or organization shall have the power to make having the force of law.

12. Laws passed by the legislature are veto-proof or essentially veto-proof; that is, the executive lacks veto power, or has veto power but the veto can be overridden by a majority in the legislature.

Yes. The president lacks veto power.

> Article 33
> Any draft law approved by the National Assembly shall be transmitted to the President who, within thirty days, shall sign and have it published in the Gazette of Eritrean Laws.

13. The legislature's laws are supreme and not subject to judicial review.

No. The Supreme Court can review the constitutionality of laws.

> Article 49
> (2) The Supreme Court shall have the power of:
> a) sole jurisdiction of interpreting this Constitution and the constitutionality of any law enacted or any measure undertaken by government.

14. The legislature has the right to initiate bills in all policy jurisdictions; the executive lacks gatekeeping authority.

Yes. The legislature can initiate bills in all policy jurisdictions.

15. Expenditure of funds appropriated by the legislature is mandatory; the executive lacks the power to impound funds appropriated by the legislature.

No. The president can impound funds appropriated by the legislature.

16. The legislature controls the resources that finance its own internal operation and provide for the perquisites of its own members.

No. The legislature is dependent on the executive for the resources that finance its operations.

17. Members of the legislature are immune from arrest and/or criminal prosecution.

No. Formally, legislators are immune from arrest, but in practice, they have been arrested and held without charge for criticizing the president.

> Article 38
> (1) All members of the National Assembly shall maintain the high image of the National Assembly. They shall regard themselves as humble servants of the people and maintain close contact with them.
> (2) No member of the National Assembly or of its committees may be arrested or charged for any crimes he commits during the session of the National Assembly, unless he be apprehended in flagrante delicto. Nevertheless, where the National Assembly, by a majority vote of those present and voting, revokes his immunity, the member may be charged.
> (3) No member of the National Assembly may be arrested or charged for words uttered or written statements submitted by him at any meeting of the National Assembly or any meeting of its committees or any utterance or statement made outside the National Assembly in connection with his duty as member thereof.
> (4) The duties, responsibilities, immunities and compensation of the members of the National Assembly shall be determined by law; and all members shall be entitled to the protection of such immunities and shall perform the duties enumerated therein.

18. All members of the legislature are elected; the executive lacks the power to appoint any members of the legislature.

No. More than half of the members of the current transitional legislature were appointed by the ruling party. The others were elected at the regional level in nonparty elections on slates chosen by the ruling party and conducted under its supervision. This is despite the fact that the 1997 constitution states that all members of the legislature will be elected.

> Article 31
> (1) There shall be a National Assembly which shall be a supreme representative and legislative body.
> (2) The National Assembly shall be composed of representatives elected by the people.
> (3) Members of the National Assembly shall be elected by direct and secret ballot by all citizens who are qualified to vote.

19. The legislature alone, without the involvement of any other agencies, can change the Constitution.

No. In practice, it would be inconceivable for the legislature to change the constitution without the president's approval. According to the 1997 constitution, the legislature alone can change the constitution.

> Article 58
> (1) A proposal for the amendment of any provision of this Constitution may be initiated and tabled by

the President or 50 percent of all the members of the National Assembly.

(2) Any provision of this Constitution may be amended as follows:

a) where the National Assembly by a three-quarters majority vote of all its members proposes an amendment with reference to a specific Article of the Constitution tabled to be amended; and

b) where, one year after it has proposed such an amendment, the National Assembly, after deliberation, approves again the same amendment by four-fifths majority vote of all its members.

20. The legislature's approval is necessary for the declaration of war.

Yes. The legislature's approval is necessary for the declaration of war.

Article 32
(6) The National Assembly shall approve a state of peace, war or national emergency.

21. The legislature's approval is necessary to ratify treaties with foreign countries.

Yes. The legislature's approval is necessary to ratify international treaties.

Article 32
(4) The National Assembly shall ratify international agreements by law.

22. The legislature has the power to grant amnesty.

No. The president has the power to grant amnesty.

Article 42
The President shall have the following powers and duties:
12. pardon, grant amnesty or reprieve offenders.

23. The legislature has the power of pardon.

No. The president has the power of pardon.

Article 42
The President shall have the following powers and duties:
12. pardon, grant amnesty or reprieve offenders.

24. The legislature reviews and has the right to reject appointments to the judiciary; or the legislature itself appoints members of the judiciary.

No. Formally, the legislature's approval is required to confirm the president's appointments to the Supreme Court. In practice, the legislature does not challenge the president's decisions and plays no meaningful role in the appointments process.

Article 42
The President shall have the following powers and duties:
7. appoint with the approval of the National Assembly ... the Chief Justice of the Supreme Court and any

other person or persons who are required by any other provisions of this Constitution or other laws to be appointed by the President;
8. appoint justices of the Supreme Court upon proposal of the Judicial Service Commission and approval of the National Assembly.

25. The chairman of the central bank is appointed by the legislature.

No. The president appoints the governor of the National Bank of Eritrea.

Article 55
(2) The National Bank shall have a Governor appointed by the President with the approval of the National Assembly. There shall be a Board of Directors presided by the Governor and whose members shall be appointed by the President.

26. The legislature has a substantial voice in the operation of the state-owned media.

No. The legislature lacks a substantial voice in the operation of the public media.

27. The legislature is regularly in session.

No. The legislature meets in ordinary session for less than six months each year.

28. Each legislator has a personal secretary.

No.

29. Each legislator has at least one non-secretarial staff member with policy expertise.

No.

30. Legislators are eligible for re-election without any restriction.

Yes. There are no restrictions on re-election.

31. A seat in the legislature is an attractive enough position that legislators are generally interested in and seek re-election.

No. It is impossible to say with any certainty. Eritrea's "transitional assembly" has been in existence since the mid-1990s, and subsequent elections for a permanent body have not been held.

32. The re-election of incumbent legislators is common enough that at any given time the legislature contains a significant number of highly experienced members.

No. Members have served for well over a decade in the National Assembly, but the absence of elections since the founding of the transitional legislature means that there have been no opportunities for re-election, and service in the marginalized body has not translated into significant legislative experience.

PARLIAMENT OF ESTONIA (*RIIGIKOGU*)

Expert consultants: Jaak Allik, Piret Ehin, Mari-Ann Kelam, Tunne Kelam, Mikko Lagerspetz, Rein Taagepera

Score: .75

Influence over executive (8/9)		Institutional autonomy (7/9)		Specified powers (5/8)		Institutional capacity (4/6)	
1. replace	X	10. no dissolution		19. amendments	X	27. sessions	X
2. serve as ministers		11. no decree	X	20. war	X	28. secretary	
3. interpellate	X	12. no veto	X	21. treaties	X	29. staff	
4. investigate	X	13. no review		22. amnesty		30. no term limits	X
5. oversee police	X	14. no gatekeeping	X	23. pardon		31. seek re-election	X
6. appoint PM	X	15. no impoundment	X	24. judiciary	X	32. experience	X
7. appoint ministers	X	16. control resources	X	25. central bank			
8. lack president	X	17. immunity	X	26. media	X		
9. no confidence	X	18. all elected	X				

The Parliament (*Riigikogu*) of Estonia traces its roots to the country's 1920 constitution. Estonia's interwar independence was interrupted by occupation by Nazi Germany and the Soviet Union. In 1940 Estonia was formally absorbed into the Soviet Union. Following the collapse of the USSR, Estonia adopted a new constitution in 1992. The document establishes a unicameral legislature that elects the prime minister and the largely ceremonial president.

The legislature enjoys broad powers. It influences the executive with, among other powers, the right to interpellate and investigate executive branch officials and to remove the prime minister with a vote of no confidence. It also has a good deal of institutional autonomy. It is vested with a number of specified powers and prerogatives and enjoys some institutional capacity.

SURVEY

1. The legislature alone, without the involvement of any other agencies, can impeach the president or replace the prime minister.

Yes. The legislature can remove the prime minister with a vote of no confidence.

Article 92
(1) The Government of the Republic shall resign:

3) when the Parliament expresses no-confidence in the Government or the Prime Minister.

2. Ministers may serve simultaneously as members of the legislature.

No. Legislators who serve in government have a sleeping mandate, meaning that they may join the government but forfeit their voting rights in the legislature during their service in government. They may return to the legislature when their service in government ends.

Article 63
(1) A member of the Parliament may not hold any other public office.

Article 64
(1) The authority of a member of the Parliament shall be suspended on his or her appointment as a member of the Government of the Republic, and shall be restored on his or her being released from the duties as a member of government.

3. The legislature has powers of summons over executive branch officials and hearings with executive branch officials testifying before the legislature or its committees are regularly held.

Yes. The legislature regularly interpellates officials from the executive.

Article 74

(1) Members of the Parliament shall have the right to request explanations from the Government of the Republic and its members.

(2) Requests for explanations must be answered at a session of the Parliament within twenty session days.

4. The legislature can conduct independent investigation of the chief executive and the agencies of the executive.

Yes. The legislature can investigate the executive.

5. The legislature has effective powers of oversight over the agencies of coercion (the military, organs of law enforcement, intelligence services, and the secret police).

Yes. Legislative committees have effective powers of oversight over the agencies of coercion.

6. The legislature appoints the prime minister.

Yes. The president appoints a candidate for prime minister who must obtain majority support in the legislature. If the president presents two consecutive candidates who fail to obtain parliamentary approval, the parliament directly appoints the candidate for prime minister.

Article 65

The Parliament shall:

5) authorize the candidate for Prime Minister to form the Government of the Republic.

Article 78

The President of the Republic shall:

9) determine the candidate for Prime Minister in accordance with Article 89.

Article 89

(1) The President of the Republic, within fourteen days after the Government of the Republic has resigned, shall nominate a candidate for Prime Minister, who shall be tasked with forming a new government.

(2) The candidate for Prime Minister shall report to the Parliament, within fourteen days of being assigned the task of forming a government, the bases for the formation of the new government, after which the Parliament shall decide, without negotiation and by an open vote, on giving the candidate for Prime Minister the authority to form a Government.

(3) The candidate for Prime Minister who has received authority from the Parliament to form a government, shall present, within seven days, the composition of the Government to the President of the Republic, who shall appoint the Government within three days.

(4) If the candidate for Prime Minister, nominated by the President of the Republic, does not receive the majority of yes-votes in the Parliament, or is unable to form a Government, or abstains, the President of the Republic shall have the right to present another candidate for Prime Minister within seven days.

(5) If the President of the Republic does not present another candidate for Prime Minister within seven days, or abstains, or if this candidate is unable to obtain authority from the Parliament, in accordance with the conditions and time restraints in Paragraphs (2) and (3), or is unable to form a Government, or abstains, the right to present a candidate for Prime Minister shall be transferred to the Parliament.

(6) The Parliament shall present a candidate for Prime Minister, who shall present the composition of the Government to the President of the Republic. If, within fourteen days from the transfer of the right to present a candidate for Prime Minister to the Parliament, the composition of the Government has not been presented to the President of the Republic, the President of the Republic shall declare early elections for the Parliament.

7. The legislature's approval is required to confirm the appointment of ministers; or the legislature itself appoints ministers.

Yes. The legislature's approval is required to confirm ministerial appointments.

Article 78

The President of the Republic shall:

10) appoint and recall members of the Government, in accordance with Articles 89, 90, and 92.

Article 89

(1) The President of the Republic, within fourteen days after the Government of the Republic has resigned, shall nominate a candidate for Prime Minister, who shall be tasked with forming a new government.

(2) The candidate for Prime Minister shall report to the Parliament, within fourteen days of being assigned the task of forming a government, the bases for the formation of the new government, after which the Parliament shall decide, without negotiation and by an open vote, on giving the candidate for Prime Minister the authority to form a Government.

(3) The candidate for Prime Minister who has received authority from the Parliament to form a government, shall present, within seven days, the composition of the Government to the President of the Republic, who shall appoint the Government within three days.

(4) If the candidate for Prime Minister, nominated by the President of the Republic, does not receive the majority of yes-votes in the Parliament, or is unable to form a Government, or abstains, the President of the Republic shall have the right to present another candidate for Prime Minister within seven days.

(5) If the President of the Republic does not present another candidate for Prime Minister within seven days, or abstains, or if this candidate is unable to obtain authority from the Parliament, in accordance with the conditions and time restraints in Paragraphs (2) and (3), or is unable to form a Government, or abstains, the right to present a candidate for Prime Minister shall be transferred to the Parliament.

(6) The Parliament shall present a candidate for Prime Minister, who shall present the composition of the Government to the President of the Republic. If, within fourteen days from the transfer of the right to present a candidate for Prime Minister to the Parliament, the composition of the Government has not been presented to the President of the Republic, the President of the Republic shall declare early elections for the Parliament.

8. The country lacks a presidency entirely or there is a presidency, but the president is elected by the legislature.

Yes. The legislature elects the president. If no candidate for president obtains the requisite majority vote, a special electoral college containing members of the legislature and representatives of local governments elects the president.

Article 65
The Parliament shall:
3) elect the President of the Republic.

Article 79
1) The President of the Republic shall be elected by the Parliament, or, in the case described in Paragraph (4), by the Electoral Body.
4) The President of the Republic shall be elected by secret ballot. Each member of the Parliament shall have one vote. A candidate who is supported by a two-thirds majority of the complement of the Parliament shall be considered to be elected. Should no candidate receive the required majority, then a new vote shall be organized on the next day. Before the second round of voting, there shall be a new presentation of candidates. Should no candidate receive the required majority in the second round, then a third round of voting shall be organized on the same day between the two candidates who received the most votes in the second round. Should the President of the Republic still not be elected in the third round of voting, the Speaker of the Parliament shall convene, within one month, an Electoral Body to elect the President of the Republic.
5) The Electoral Body shall be comprised of the members of the Parliament and representatives of the local government council. Each local government council shall elect at least one representative, who must be an Estonian citizen, to the Electoral Body.
6) The Parliament shall present to the Electoral Body as candidates for President the two candidates who received the greatest number of votes in the Parliament. The right to present a presidential candidate shall also rest with at least twenty-one members of the Electoral Body.
7) The Electoral Body shall elect the President of the Republic with a majority of those members of the Electoral Body who are present. Should no candidate be elected in the first round, a second round of voting

shall be organized on the same day between the two candidates who received the highest number of votes.

9. The legislature can vote no confidence in the government.

Yes. The legislature can vote no confidence in the government.

Article 65
The Parliament shall:
13) decide on votes of no-confidence in the Government of the Republic, the Prime Minister or individual ministers.

Article 92
(1) The Government of the Republic shall resign:
  3) when the Parliament expresses no-confidence in the Government or the Prime Minister.

Article 97
(1) The Parliament may express no-confidence in either the Government of the Republic, the Prime Minister or a Minister
by a resolution adopted by the majority of the complement of the Parliament.
(2) The issue of no-confidence may be initiated by at least one-fifth of the complement of the Parliament by submitting a written motion at a session of the Parliament.
(3) The issue of expressing no-confidence may come up for resolution no earlier than two days after its being submitted, unless the Government demands speedier resolution.
(4) In the case of no-confidence being expressed in the Government or the Prime Minister, the President of the Republic may, on proposal by the Government and within three days, declare early elections.
(5) In the case of no-confidence being expressed in a Minister, the Speaker of the Parliament shall notify the President of the Republic, who shall recall the Minister from office.
(6) The expression of no-confidence on the same grounds may be re-initiated no earlier than three months after the previous no-confidence vote.

10. The legislature is immune from dissolution by the executive.

No. The president can dissolve the legislature.

Article 78
The President of the Republic shall:
3) declare regular Parliament elections, and early elections for the Parliament, in accordance with Articles 89, 97, 105, and 119.

Article 89
(1) The President of the Republic, within fourteen days after the Government of the Republic has resigned, shall nominate a candidate for Prime Minister, who shall be tasked with forming a new government.

(2) The candidate for Prime Minister shall report to the Parliament, within fourteen days of being assigned the task of forming a government, the bases for the formation of the new government, after which the Parliament shall decide, without negotiation and by an open vote, on giving the candidate for Prime Minister the authority to form a Government.

(3) The candidate for Prime Minister who has received authority from the Parliament to form a government, shall present, within seven days, the composition of the Government to the President of the Republic, who shall appoint the Government within three days.

(4) If the candidate for Prime Minister, nominated by the President of the Republic, does not receive the majority of yes-votes in the Parliament, or is unable to form a Government, or abstains, the President of the Republic shall have the right to present another candidate for Prime Minister within seven days.

(5) If the President of the Republic does not present another candidate for Prime Minister within seven days, or abstains, or if this candidate is unable to obtain authority from the Parliament, in accordance with the conditions and time restraints in Paragraphs (2) and (3), or is unable to form a Government, or abstains, the right to present a candidate for Prime Minister shall be transferred to the Parliament.

(6) The Parliament shall present a candidate for Prime Minister, who shall present the composition of the Government to the President of the Republic. If, within fourteen days from the transfer of the right to present a candidate for Prime Minister to the Parliament, the composition of the Government has not been presented to the President of the Republic, the President of the Republic shall declare early elections for the Parliament.

Article 97
(4) In the case of no-confidence being expressed in the Government or the Prime Minister, the President of the Republic may, on proposal by the Government and within three days, declare early elections.

Article 105
(1) The Parliament shall have the right to put draft legislation or other national issues to a referendum.
(2) The decision of the people shall be determined by the majority of those participating in the referendum.
(3) A law which has been adopted by referendum shall be immediately proclaimed by the President of the Republic. The referendum decision shall be binding on all state bodies.
(4) Should the draft law which has been put to referendum not receive a majority of yes-votes, the President of the Republic shall declare early elections for the Parliament.

Article 119
If the Parliament has not adopted the budget within two months of the beginning of the budget year, the President of the Republic shall declare early elections for the Parliament.

11. Any executive initiative on legislation requires ratification or approval by the legislature before it takes effect; that is, the executive lacks decree power.

Yes. The president lacks decree power. The president can, however, issue decrees in an emergency when the legislature is incapable of meeting. In such an event, the speaker of parliament and the prime minister must cosign the decrees. The decrees lapse if they are not subsequently approved by the legislature.

Article 109
(1) If the Parliament is prevented from convening, the President of the Republic shall have the right, in matters of national interest which cannot be postponed, to issue edicts which have the force of law, and which shall bear the co-signatures of the Speaker of the Parliament and the Prime Minister.
(2) When the Parliament convenes, the President of the Republic shall present such edicts to the Parliament, which shall immediately adopt a law either confirming or repealing the edicts.

Article 110
Neither the Constitution, the laws listed in Article 104, nor laws determining state taxes or the national budget can be enacted, amended or repealed by edicts issued by the President of the Republic.

12. Laws passed by the legislature are veto-proof or essentially veto-proof; that is, the executive lacks veto power, or has veto power but the veto can be overridden by a majority in the legislature.

Yes. The legislature can override a presidential veto by a majority vote of its present members. It merits note, however, that the president also has the ability to refer legislation to the National Court before signing it. This provision gives the president additional clout, as the legislature often prefers to accommodate the president's wishes before submitting the law for his or her signature rather than risk seeing the bill languish in court for an indefinite period of time.

Article 107
(1) Laws shall be proclaimed by the President of the Republic.
(2) The President of the Republic shall have the right not to proclaim a law adopted by the Parliament, and to return the law to the Parliament, within fourteen days of receiving it, together with the reasons for its rejection. If the Parliament [again] adopts a law which has been returned by the President of the Republic, without amendments, the President of the Republic shall proclaim the law, or propose to the National Court that

it declare the law to be in conflict with the Constitution. If the National Court declares the law to be in accordance with the Constitution, the President of the Republic shall proclaim the law.

13. The legislature's laws are supreme and not subject to judicial review.

No. The National Court can review the constitutionality of laws.

Article 107
(2) The President of the Republic shall have the right not to proclaim a law adopted by the Parliament, and to return the law to the Parliament, within fourteen days of receiving it, together with the reasons for its rejection. If the Parliament [again] adopts a law which has been returned by the President of the Republic, without amendments, the President of the Republic shall proclaim the law, or propose to the National Court that it declare the law to be in conflict with the Constitution. If the National Court declares the law to be in accordance with the Constitution, the President of the Republic shall proclaim the law.

Article 152
(2) If any law or other legal act is in conflict with the provisions and spirit of the Constitution, it shall be declared null and void by the National Court.

14. The legislature has the right to initiate bills in all policy jurisdictions; the executive lacks gatekeeping authority.

Yes. The legislature can initiate bills in all policy jurisdictions.

15. Expenditure of funds appropriated by the legislature is mandatory; the executive lacks the power to impound funds appropriated by the legislature.

Yes. The executive lacks the power to impound funds appropriated by the legislature.

16. The legislature controls the resources that finance its own internal operation and provide for the perquisites of its own members.

Yes. The legislature enjoys financial autonomy, including control over members' remuneration.

Article 75
The remuneration of members of the Parliament and restrictions on other income shall be determined by law, which may be amended for the next complement of the Parliament.

17. Members of the legislature are immune from arrest and/or criminal prosecution.

Yes. Legislators are immune.

Article 76
A member of the Parliament enjoys immunity. Criminal charges can only be brought against him or her

on proposal by the Legal Chancellor and with the consent of the majority of the complement of the Parliament.

18. All members of the legislature are elected; the executive lacks the power to appoint any members of the legislature.

Yes. All members of the legislature are elected.

Article 60
(1) Members of the Parliament shall be elected in free elections on the principle of proportionality.

19. The legislature alone, without the involvement of any other agencies, can change the Constitution.

Yes. The legislature alone can change the constitution through a complicated procedure. The sitting legislature can propose the amendment, and then, following an election, the subsequent legislature can approve the amendment with a three-fifths majority vote. The constitution can be amended as a "matter of urgency" by the same procedure with a four-fifths majority in one parliament and a two-thirds majority in the next.

Article 161
(1) The right to initiate amendments to the Constitution shall rest with at least one-fifth of the complement of the Parliament and with the President of the Republic.

Article 162
Chapter I 'General Provisions' and Chapter XV 'Amendments to the Constitution' may be amended only by referendum.

Article 163
(1) The Constitution may be amended by a law which is adopted by:
   1) referendum;
   2) two successive complements of the Parliament;
   3) the Parliament, in matters of urgency.
(2) A draft law to amend the Constitution shall be considered during three readings in the Parliament, whereby the interval between the first and second readings shall be at least three months, and the interval between the second and third readings shall be at least one month. The manner in which the Constitution is amended shall be decided at the third reading.

Article 165
(1) In order to amend the Constitution by two successive complements of the Parliament, the draft law to amend the Constitution must receive the support of the majority of the complement of the Parliament.
(2) If the next complement of the Parliament adopts the draft which received the support of the majority of the previous complement, without amendment, on its first reading and with a three-fifths majority of its

complement, the law to amend the Constitution shall be adopted.

Article 166

A proposal to consider a proposed amendment to the Constitution as a matter of urgency shall be adopted by the Parliament by a four-fifths majority. In such a case the law to amend the Constitution shall be adopted by a two-thirds majority of the complement of the Parliament.

20. The legislature's approval is necessary for the declaration of war.

Yes. The legislature alone can declare war on the proposal of the president with the common exception for foreign invasion. In cases of armed attack on the country, the president can declare war without prior legislative authorization.

Article 65

The Parliament shall:

15) on proposal by the President of the Republic declare a state of war, order mobilization and demobilization.

Article 78

The President of the Republic shall:

17) present proposals to the Parliament on declarations of a state of war, on orders for mobilization and demobilization and, in accordance with Article 129, on proclamations of a state of emergency.

Article 128

(1) The Parliament shall declare, on proposal by the President of the Republic, a state of war, order mobilization and de-mobilization, and shall decide on the utilization of the Defense Forces to fulfill the international obligations of the Estonian nation.

(2) In the case of aggression directed against the Republic of Estonia, the President of the Republic shall declare a state of war and mobilization, and shall appoint the Commander-in-Chief of the Defense Forces, without waiting for a resolution to be adopted by the Parliament.

21. The legislature's approval is necessary to ratify treaties with foreign countries.

Yes. The legislature's approval is necessary to ratify international treaties on most major issues.

Article 65

The Parliament shall:

4) ratify and denounce foreign treaties in accordance with Article 121.

Article 121

The Parliament shall ratify and denounce treaties of the Republic of Estonia:

1) which amend state borders;

2) the implementation of which requires the adoption, amendment or annulment of Estonian laws;

3) by which the Republic of Estonia joins international organizations or leagues;

4) by which the Republic of Estonia assumes military or assets obligations;

5) where ratification is prescribed.

22. The legislature has the power to grant amnesty.

No. Amnesty and pardon are not treated separately, and the legislature lacks the power to grant amnesty. See item 23.

23. The legislature has the power of pardon.

No. The president has the power of pardon (mercy).

Article 78

The President of the Republic shall:

19) grant mercy, on the request of prisoners, by freeing those sentenced or reducing the sentence.

24. The legislature reviews and has the right to reject appointments to the judiciary; or the legislature itself appoints members of the judiciary.

Yes. The legislature appoints the chairman and the judges of the National Court.

Article 65

The Parliament shall:

8) appoint, on proposal by the Chairman of the National Court, judges for the National Court.

Article 78

The President of the Republic shall:

11) present proposals to the Parliament for appointments to the offices of the Chairman of the National Court, the Chairman of the Council of the Bank of Estonia, the Legal Chancellor.

13) appoint judges on proposal by the National Court.

Article 150

(1) The Chairman of the National Court shall be appointed by the Parliament, on proposal by the President of the Republic.

(2) Members of the National Court shall be appointed by the Parliament, on proposal by the Chairman of the National Court.

(3) Other judges shall be appointed by the President of the Republic, on proposal by the National Court.

25. The chairman of the central bank is appointed by the legislature.

No. The president appoints the president of the Bank of Estonia.

Article 78

The President of the Republic shall:

12) appoint, on proposal by the Council of the Bank of Estonia, the President of the Bank of Estonia.

26. The legislature has a substantial voice in the operation of the state-owned media.

Yes. The media oversight council, which oversees the public media, includes legislators among its members.

27. The legislature is regularly in session.

Yes. The legislature meets in ordinary session for about seven months each year.

> Article 67
> Regular sessions of the Parliament shall take place from the second Monday of January to the third Thursday of June, and from the second Monday of September to the third Thursday of December.

28. Each legislator has a personal secretary.

No.

29. Each legislator has at least one non-secretarial staff member with policy expertise.

No.

30. Legislators are eligible for re-election without any restriction.

Yes. There are no restrictions on re-election.

31. A seat in the legislature is an attractive enough position that legislators are generally interested in and seek re-election.

Yes.

32. The re-election of incumbent legislators is common enough that at any given time the legislature contains a significant number of highly experienced members.

Yes. Re-election rates are sufficiently high to produce a significant number of highly experienced members.

PARLIAMENT OF ETHIOPIA (*MEKIR BET*)

Expert consultants: Jon Abbink, Wondem Asres Degu, Sisay Gebre-Egziabher, Samuel Haile, Hartmut Hess, Solomon Kebede, Kidane Mengisteab, David H. Shinn

Score: .50

Influence over executive (5/9)		Institutional autonomy (6/9)		Specified powers (2/8)		Institutional capacity (3/6)	
1. replace		10. no dissolution		19. amendments		27. sessions	X
2. serve as ministers	X	11. no decree		20. war	X	28. secretary	
3. interpellate	X	12. no veto	X	21. treaties	X	29. staff	
4. investigate		13. no review	X	22. amnesty		30. no term limits	X
5. oversee police		14. no gatekeeping	X	23. pardon		31. seek re-election	X
6. appoint PM	X	15. no impoundment		24. judiciary		32. experience	
7. appoint ministers	X	16. control resources	X	25. central bank			
8. lack president	X	17. immunity	X	26. media			
9. no confidence		18. all elected	X				

The Parliament (*Mekir Bet*) of Ethiopia was established in the 1994 constitution. The document calls for a bicameral legislature consisting of a lower house, the House of People's Representatives (*Yehizbtewekayoch Mekir Bet*), and an upper house, the House of Federation (*Yefedereshn Mekir Bet*). Before 1994 Ethiopia was ruled for twenty years by a military junta and prior to that by a traditional monarchy. Since its inception in 1994, the legislature has been in the firm control of a single party, the Ethiopian People's Revolutionary Democratic Front (EPRDF), and a single prime minister, Meles Zenawi. In Ethiopia the prime minister is the chief executive and the commander-in-chief of the armed forces; the president is the head of state but holds executive powers far inferior to those of the prime minister.

Parliament influences the executive through the rights, among others, to elect the president and the prime minister. It also enjoys some institutional autonomy. For example, legislation is not subject to an executive veto, and the legislature itself, rather than any high court, has the final word on the constitutionality of laws. On the other hand, parliament's autonomy is circumscribed by executive powers to dissolve the legislature and issue decrees that have the force of law. The legislature enjoys some specified powers and prerogatives, including the authority to declare war and ratify international treaties. It has some institutional capacity, although it lacks staff support and a significant number of experienced legislators.

SURVEY

1. The legislature alone, without the involvement of any other agencies, can impeach the president or replace the prime minister.

No. Formally, the legislature can remove the prime minister from office with a vote of no confidence. In practice, however, a vote of no confidence would be unthinkable. The prime minister has a tight grip on power, which he secures using personal control over the agencies of coercion and the hegemonic Ethiopian People's Revolutionary Democratic Front (EPRDF).

Article 60
(1) With the consent of the House, the Prime Minister may cause the dissolution of the House before the expiry of its term in order to hold new elections.
(2) The President may invite political parties to form a coalition government within one week, if the Council of Ministers of a previous coalition is dissolved because of the loss of its majority in the House. The House shall be dissolved and new elections shall be held if the political parties cannot agree to the continuation of the previous coalition or to form a new majority coalition.
(3) If the House is dissolved pursuant to sub-article 1 or 2 of this article, new elections shall be held within six months of its dissolution.
(4) The new House shall convene within thirty days of the conclusion of the elections.
(5) Following the dissolution of the House, the previous governing party of coalition of parties shall continue as a caretaker government. Beyond conducting the day to day affairs of government and organizing new elections, it may not enact new proclamations, regulations or decrees, nor may it repeal or amend any existing law.

2. Ministers may serve simultaneously as members of the legislature.

Yes. Legislators may serve simultaneously in ministerial positions.

Article 73
(1) The Prime Minister shall be elected from among members of the House of People's Representatives.

(2) Power of Government shall be assumed by the political party or a coalition of political parties that constitutes a majority in the House of People's Representatives.

Article 74
(2) The Prime Minister shall submit for approval to the House of People's Representatives nominees for ministerial posts from among members of the two Houses or from among persons who are not members of either House and possess the required qualifications.

3. The legislature has powers of summons over executive branch officials and hearings with executive branch officials testifying before the legislature or its committees are regularly held.

Yes. The House of People's Representatives regularly interpellates officials from the executive.

Article 55
(17) The House of People's Representatives has the power to call and to question the Prime Minister and other Federal officials and to investigate the Executive's conduct and discharge of its responsibilities.

4. The legislature can conduct independent investigation of the chief executive and the agencies of the executive.

No. The legislature cannot investigate the executive.

5. The legislature has effective powers of oversight over the agencies of coercion (the military, organs of law enforcement, intelligence services, and the secret police).

No. Despite constitutional provisions to the contrary, the legislature lacks effective powers of oversight over the agencies of coercion.

Article 55
(7) The House of People's Representatives shall determine the organization of national defence, public security, and a national police force. If the conduct of these forces infringes upon human rights and the nation's security, it shall carry out investigations and take necessary measures.

6. The legislature appoints the prime minister.

Yes. The prime minister is elected by the party, or coalition of parties, with the greatest number of seats in the lower house of parliament.

Article 56
A political party, or a coalition of political parties that has the greatest number of seats in the House of People's Representatives shall form the Executive and lead it.

Article 73
(1) The Prime Minister shall be elected from among members of the House of People's Representatives.

(2) Power of Government shall be assumed by the political party or a coalition of political parties that constitutes a majority in the House of People's Representatives.

7. The legislature's approval is required to confirm the appointment of ministers; or the legislature itself appoints ministers.

Yes. The approval of the House of People's Representatives is necessary to confirm the prime minister's ministerial appointments.

> Article 56
> A political party, or a coalition of political parties that has the greatest number of seats in the House of People's Representatives shall form the Executive and lead it.

> Article 74
> (2) The Prime Minister shall submit for approval to the House of People's Representatives nominees for ministerial posts from among members of the two Houses or from among persons who are not members of either House and possess the required qualifications.

8. The country lacks a presidency entirely or there is a presidency, but the president is elected by the legislature.

Yes. The House of People's Representatives elects the president.

> Article 70
> (1) The House of People's Representatives shall nominate the candidate for President.
> (2) The nominee shall be elected President if a joint session of the House of People's Representatives and the House of the Federation approves his candidacy by a two-thirds majority vote.

9. The legislature can vote no confidence in the government.

No. Formally, the legislature can vote no confidence in the government, but in practice, a vote of no confidence would be unthinkable. See item 1.

> Article 60
> (1) With the consent of the House, the Prime Minister may cause the dissolution of the House before the expiry of its term in order to hold new elections.
> (2) The President may invite political parties to form a coalition government within one week, if the Council of Ministers of a previous coalition is dissolved because of the loss of its majority in the House. The House shall be dissolved and new elections shall be held if the political parties cannot agree to the continuation of the previous coalition or to form a new majority coalition.
> (3) If the House is dissolved pursuant to sub-article 1 or 2 of this article, new elections shall be held within six months of its dissolution.
> (4) The new House shall convene within thirty days of the conclusion of the elections.

(5) Following the dissolution of the House, the previous governing party or coalition of parties shall continue as a caretaker government. Beyond conducting the day to day affairs of government and organizing new elections, it may not enact new proclamations, regulations or decrees, nor may it repeal or amend any existing law.

10. The legislature is immune from dissolution by the executive.

No. The prime minister can dissolve the lower house of parliament.

> Article 60
> (1) With the consent of the House, the Prime Minister may cause the dissolution of the House before the expiry of its term in order to hold new elections.

11. Any executive initiative on legislation requires ratification or approval by the legislature before it takes effect; that is, the executive lacks decree power.

No. The prime minister issues decrees that have the force of law.

12. Laws passed by the legislature are veto-proof or essentially veto-proof; that is, the executive lacks veto power, or has veto power but the veto can be overridden by a majority in the legislature.

Yes. The president lacks veto power.

> Article 57
> Laws deliberated upon and passed by the House shall be submitted to the Nation's President for signature. The President shall sign a law submitted to him within fifteen days. If the President does not sign the law within fifteen days it shall take effect without his signature.

13. The legislature's laws are supreme and not subject to judicial review.

Yes. The legislature has the final word on the constitutionality of laws.

> Article 83
> (1) All constitutional disputes shall be decided by the House of the Federation.
> (2) The House of the Federation shall, within thirty days of receipt, decide a constitutional dispute submitted to it by the Council of Constitutional Inquiry.

> Article 84
> (1) The Council of Constitutional Inquiry shall have powers to investigate constitutional disputes. Should the Council, upon consideration of the matter, find it necessary to interpret the Constitution, it shall submit its recommendations thereon to the House of the Federation.

14. The legislature has the right to initiate bills in all policy jurisdictions; the executive lacks gatekeeping authority.

Yes. The legislature can initiate bills in all policy jurisdictions.

15. Expenditure of funds appropriated by the legislature is mandatory; the executive lacks the power to impound funds appropriated by the legislature.

No. The executive can impound funds appropriated by the legislature.

16. The legislature controls the resources that finance its own internal operation and provide for the perquisites of its own members.

Yes. The legislature enjoys financial autonomy.

17. Members of the legislature are immune from arrest and/or criminal prosecution.

Yes. Legislators are immune with the common exception for cases of *flagrante delicto*. At the government's request, however, parliament has sometimes voted to remove the immunity of opposition members.

Article 54
(5) No member of the House may be prosecuted on account of any vote he casts or opinion he expresses in the House, nor shall any administrative action be taken against any member on such grounds.
(6) No member of the House may be arrested or prosecuted without the permission of the House except in the case of flagrante delicto.

Article 63
(1) No member of the House of the Federation may be prosecuted on account of any vote he casts or opinion he expresses in the House, nor shall any administrative action be taken against any member on such grounds.
(2) No member of the House of the Federation may be arrested or prosecuted without the permission of the House except in the case of flagrante delicto.

18. All members of the legislature are elected; the executive lacks the power to appoint any members of the legislature.

Yes. All members of the legislature are elected.

Article 54
(1) Members of the House of People's Representatives shall be elected by the People for a term of five years on the basis of universal suffrage and by direct, free and fair elections held by secret ballot.

Article 61
(1) The House of the Federation is composed of representatives of Nations, Nationalities and Peoples.
(2) Each Nation, Nationality and People shall be represented in the House of the Federation by at least one member. Each Nation or Nationality shall be represented by one additional representative for each one million of its population.

(3) Members of the House of the Federation shall be elected by the State Councils. The State Councils may themselves elect representatives to the House of the Federation, or they may hold elections to have the representatives elected by the people directly.

19. The legislature alone, without the involvement of any other agencies, can change the Constitution.

No. Constitutional amendments require approval in at least two-thirds of the state (provincial) assemblies.

Article 105
(1) All rights and freedoms specified in Chapter Three of this Constitution, this very article, and Article 104 can be amended only in the following manner:
    (a) When all State Councils, by a majority vote, approve the proposed amendment;
    (b) When the House of People's Representatives, by a two-thirds majority vote, approves the proposed amendment; and
    (c) When the House of the Federation, by a two-thirds majority vote, approves the proposed amendment.
(2) All provisions of this Constitution other than those specified in sub-article 1 of this article can be amended only in the following manner:
    (a) When the House of People's Representatives and the House of the Federation, in a joint session, approve a proposed amendment by a two-thirds majority vote; and
    (b) When two-thirds of the Councils of the member States of the Federation approve the proposed amendment by majority votes.

20. The legislature's approval is necessary for the declaration of war.

Yes. The approval of the House of People's Representatives is necessary for the declaration of war.

Article 55
(9) On the basis of a draft law submitted to it by the Council of Ministers [the House of People's Representatives] shall proclaim a state of war.

21. The legislature's approval is necessary to ratify treaties with foreign countries.

Yes. The legislature's approval is necessary to ratify international treaties.

Article 55
(12) [The House of People's Representatives] shall ratify international agreements concluded by the executive.

22. The legislature has the power to grant amnesty.

No. Amnesty and pardon are not treated separately, and the president has the power to grant amnesty.

Article 71
(7) He shall, in accordance with conditions and procedures established by law, grant pardon.

23. The legislature has the power of pardon.

No. The president has the power of pardon.

Article 71
(7) He shall, in accordance with conditions and procedures established by law, grant pardon.

24. The legislature reviews and has the right to reject appointments to the judiciary; or the legislature itself appoints members of the judiciary.

No. Although the legislature by law has the power to appoint the president and vice president of the Federal Supreme Court and other federal judges upon the nomination of the prime minister, the prime minister's control of the process, backed by his control of extraparliamentary levers of control that include the agencies of coercion and the hegemonic ruling party, render the parliament's authority a mere formality. In practice, the prime minister's office controls the judiciary; the parliament does not have a substantial say in judicial appointments.

Article 55
(13) It shall approve the appointment of Federal judges, members of the Council of Ministers, commissioners, the Auditor General, and of other officials whose appointment is required by law to be approved by it.

Article 81
(1) The President and Vice-President of the Federal Supreme Court shall, upon recommendation by the Prime Minister, be appointed by the House of People's Representatives.
(2) Regarding other Federal judges, the Prime Minister shall submit to the House of People's Representatives for appointment candidates selected by the Federal Judicial Administration Council.

Article 82
(2) The Council of Constitutional Inquiry shall have eleven members comprising:
   (a) The President of the Federal Supreme Court, who shall serve as its President;
   (b) The vice-president of the Federal Supreme Court, who shall serve as its Vice-President;
   (c) Six legal experts, appointed by the President of the Republic on recommendation by the House of People's Representatives, who shall have proven professional competence and high moral standing;
   (d) Three persons designated by the House of the Federation from among its members.

25. The chairman of the central bank is appointed by the legislature.

No. The Council of Ministers appoints the governor of the National Bank of Ethiopia.

Article 77
(4) The Council of Ministers shall ensure the proper execution of financial and monetary policies of the country; it shall administer the National Bank, decide on the printing of money and minting of coins, borrow money from domestic and external sources, and regulate foreign exchange matters.

26. The legislature has a substantial voice in the operation of the state-owned media.

No. The legislature lacks a substantial voice in the operation of the public media.

27. The legislature is regularly in session.

Yes. The legislature meets in ordinary session for about nine months each year, from the final week of *Meskerem* (which correlates with early to mid-October) to the 30th day of *Sene* (which falls in June).

Article 58
(1) The presence of more than half of the members of the House constitutes a quorum.
(2) The annual session of the House shall begin on Monday of the final week of the Ethiopian month of Meskerem and end on the 30th day of the Ethiopian month of Sene. The House may adjourn for one month of recess during its annual session.

28. Each legislator has a personal secretary.

No.

29. Each legislator has at least one non-secretarial staff member with policy expertise.

No.

30. Legislators are eligible for re-election without any restriction.

Yes. There are no restrictions on re-election.

31. A seat in the legislature is an attractive enough position that legislators are generally interested in and seek re-election.

Yes.

32. The re-election of incumbent legislators is common enough that at any given time the legislature contains a significant number of highly experienced members.

No. The rate of re-election is relatively low, and the legislature lacks a sizable cohort of highly experienced members.

PARLIAMENT OF FIJI

Expert consultants: Noel Cox, Jon Fraenkel, Kathryn Hawley, Brij V. Lal, Steven Ratuva

Score: .63

Influence over executive (7/9)		Institutional autonomy (5/9)		Specified powers (4/8)		Institutional capacity (4/6)	
1. replace	X	10. no dissolution		19. amendments	X	27. sessions	X
2. serve as ministers	X	11. no decree	X	20. war	X	28. secretary	
3. interpellate	X	12. no veto	X	21. treaties	X	29. staff	
4. investigate	X	13. no review		22. amnesty		30. no term limits	X
5. oversee police	X	14. no gatekeeping	X	23. pardon		31. seek re-election	X
6. appoint PM	X	15. no impoundment	X	24. judiciary		32. experience	X
7. appoint ministers		16. control resources	X	25. central bank			
8. lack president		17. immunity		26. media	X		
9. no confidence	X	18. all elected					

The Parliament of Fiji originated in the colonial Legislative Council, established in 1904 to advise the British governor. Fiji gained independence in 1970. A new constitution in 1990 and a series of constitutional amendments in 1997 formally enshrined, and then backed away from enshrining, the political dominance of the indigenous Fijians over the Indo-Fijians. Neither constitutional change substantially affected parliament's powers. Tensions between the major ethnic groups persist and have contributed to several attempts to overturn the constitutional order, most notably in military coups staged in 1987 and 2006.

The constitution calls for a bicameral parliament with an elected House of Representatives and an upper house, the Senate, that is appointed by the president. The legislature enjoys substantial powers. It does not elect the figurehead president, a power that is vested in the traditional Great Council of Chiefs, nor does it appoint or confirm individual ministers. In other respects, however, the legislature controls the executive. The legislature's own institutional autonomy is bolstered by provisions that deny the president and the government decree, veto, or gatekeeping powers. The legislature is granted a few specified powers and prerogatives and a fair amount of institutional capacity.

At the time of this writing, parliament is not playing its traditionally weighty role. Commodore Frank Bainimarama shut down the legislature after leading a military coup in late 2006. His junta has balked at reopening parliament. Under pressure from influential neighbors, Bainimarama has stated that he intends to hold new parliamentary elections in early 2009. The information presented below is based on conditions before the coup.

SURVEY

1. The legislature alone, without the involvement of any other agencies, can impeach the president or replace the prime minister.

Yes. The legislature can remove the prime minister with a vote of no confidence. Presidential impeachment requires the involvement of the Great Council of Chiefs (*Bose Levu Vakaturaga*) and the chief justice.

Section 93
(1) The President or Vice-President may be removed from office for inability to perform the functions of office (whether arising from infirmity of body or mind or any other cause) or for misbehaviour, and may not otherwise be removed.
(2) Removal of the President or Vice-President from office must be by the Bose Levu Vakaturaga pursuant to this section.

(3) If the Prime Minister considers that the question of removing the President or Vice-President from office ought to be investigated, then:
(a) the Prime Minister requests the Chief Justice to establish:
(i) in a case of alleged misbehaviour – a tribunal consisting of a chairperson and 2 other members each of whom is, or is eligible to be, a judge; and
(b) the Chief Justice, who must act on the request, establishes the tribunal.
(c) the tribunal . . . enquires into the matter and furnishes a written report to the Chief Justice;
(d) the Chief Justice refers the report to the Prime Minister together with, in the case of a report on alleged misbehaviour, written recommendations of the Chief Justice;
(e) the Prime Minister considers the report and any recommendations and:
(i) if he or she considers that the matter should be considered by the Bose Levu Vakaturaga – he or she refers the report and any recommendations to the Bose Levu Vakaturaga, with a request that it consider the matter, and notifies the President or Vice-President, as the case maybe, accordingly;
(f) upon receipt of a request from the Prime Minister under
subparagraph (e)(i), the Bose Levu Vakaturaga convenes to consider whether the President or Vice-President, as the case may be, should be removed from office.
(4) The President or Vice-President is taken to be unable to perform the functions of his or her office during the period starting on the day on which the President or Vice President received notification under paragraph (3)(a) and ending on:
(a) if the matter is not referred to the Bose Levu Vakaturaga – the day on which the President or Vice-President receives notification under subparagraph (3)(e)(iii); or
(b) if the matter is referred to the Bose Levu Vakaturaga – the day on which the matter is finally dealt with by the Bose Levu Vakaturaga.

Section 107
If:
(a) the Government is defeated at a general election; or
(b) the Government is defeated on the floor of the House of Representatives in a vote:
(i) after due notice, on whether the Government has the confidence of the House of Representatives;
(ii) that the Government treats as a vote of no confidence; or
(iii) the effect of which is to reject or fail to pass a Bill appropriating revenue or moneys for the ordinary services of the Government; and the Prime Minister considers that there is another person capable of forming a Government that has the confidence of the House of Representatives, the Prime Minister must immediately advise the President of the person whom the Prime Minister believes can

form a Government that has the confidence of the House and must thereupon resign.

2. Ministers may serve simultaneously as members of the legislature.

Yes. Ministers are selected from, and required to serve simultaneously in, the legislature.

Section 99
(1) The President appoints and dismisses other Ministers on the advice of the Prime Minister.
(2) To be eligible for appointment, a Minister must be a member of the House of Representatives or the Senate.

Section 105
(1) Subject to subsection (2), the appointment of a Minister terminates if;
(a) the Prime Minister resigns in the circumstances set out in section 107;
(b) the Prime Minister is dismissed;
(c) the Minister tenders his or her resignation to the President; or
(d) the Minister ceases to be a member of the Parliament.

3. The legislature has powers of summons over executive branch officials and hearings with executive branch officials testifying before the legislature or its committees are regularly held.

Yes. Parliamentary standing committees summon and hold hearings with executive branch officials.

Section 74
(3) The House of Representatives must, under its rules and orders, establish not less than 5 sector standing committees with the functions of scrutinizing Government administration and examining Bills and subordinate legislation and such other functions as are specified from time to time in the rules and orders of the House.

4. The legislature can conduct independent investigation of the chief executive and the agencies of the executive.

Yes. The legislature can make provisions for investigation of the executive.

Section 156
(1) This section applies to the President, Vice-President, Ministers, members of Parliament, holders of offices established by or continued in existence under this Constitution, members of commissions, Secretaries of departments, the Secretary to the Cabinet and persons who hold statutory appointments or governing or executive positions in statutory authorities.
(2) Persons to whom this section applies must so conduct themselves in relation to the performance of their public duties as not:
(a) to place themselves in positions in which they have, or could be seen as having, a conflict between their private interests and their public duties;

(b) to compromise the fair exercise of their public duties;

(c) to use their offices for private gain;

(d) to allow their integrity to be called into question; or

(e) to cause respect for, or confidence in, the integrity of the Government to be diminished.

(3) The Parliament must, as soon as practicable after the commencement of this Constitution, make a law:

(a) to implement more fully the conduct rules set out in subsection (2);

(b) to provide for the monitoring of standards of conduct in relation to the performance of public duties; and

(c) if the Parliament considers it appropriate, to make provision in relation to the investigation of alleged breaches of those standards and the enforcement of those standards.

Section 158

(1) Subject to this Part, the Ombudsman:

(a) must investigate action, being action that relates to a matter of administration.

(b) may, of his own motion or at the request of a member of the Parliament or of a committee of the Parliament, investigate any action, being action that relates to a matter of administration, taken either before or after the commencement of this Constitution by a department or by a prescribed authority.

(4) The authority of the Ombudsman to investigate complaints in relation to action relating to a matter of administration extends to action taken by a commission to the extent that:

(a) the action relates to a function conferred on it otherwise than by this Constitution; and

(b) the authority to investigate is conferred by a law made by the Parliament.

(5) The Ombudsman is not authorized to investigate:

(a) action taken by a Minister;

(b) action taken by a judge; or

(c) action taken by any body or person with respect to the appointment of a person to, or the removal of a person from, a public office, the taking of disciplinary action against the holder of a public office or the pension entitlement of a person who is or was the holder of a public office.

(6) The proceedings of the Ombudsman may not be called into question in any court of law.

5. The legislature has effective powers of oversight over the agencies of coercion (the military, organs of law enforcement, intelligence services, and the secret police).

Yes. Legislative committees (in particular the Standing Select Committee on Justice, Law and Order) have effective powers of oversight over the agencies of coercion.

Section 74

(3) The House of Representatives must, under its rules and orders, establish not less than 5 sector standing committees with the functions of scrutinizing Government administration and examining Bills and subordinate legislation and such other functions as are specified from time to time in the rules and orders of the House.

6. The legislature appoints the prime minister.

Yes. The president appoints the candidate for prime minister who enjoys the support of the House of Representatives.

Section 98

The President, acting in his or her own judgment, appoints as Prime Minister the member of the House of Representatives who, in the President's opinion, can form a government that has the confidence of the House of Representatives.

7. The legislature's approval is required to confirm the appointment of ministers; or the legislature itself appoints ministers.

No. The president appoints ministers on the recommendation of the prime minister, and the appointments do not require the legislature's approval. It bears note, however, that in Fiji's multiethnic polity, which is divided between ethnic Fijian and people of South Asian descent, the constitution recommends that the prime minister allocate ministerial portfolios in a manner that facilitates inclusion of the major parties represented in parliament.

Section 99

(1) The President appoints and dismisses other Ministers on the advice of the Prime Minister.

(3) The Prime Minister must establish a multi-party Cabinet in the way set out in this section comprising such number of Ministers as he or she determines.

(4) Subject to this section, the composition of the Cabinet should, as far as possible, fairly represent the parties represented in the House of Representatives.

(5) In establishing the Cabinet, the Prime Minister must invite all parties whose membership in the House of Representatives comprises at least 10% of the total membership of the House to be represented in the Cabinet in proportion to their numbers in the House.

(6) If the Prime Minister selects for appointment to the Cabinet a person from a party whose membership in the House of Representatives is less than 10% of the total membership of the House, that selection is deemed, for the purposes of this section, to be a selection of a person from the Prime Minister's own party.

(7) If a party declines an invitation from the Prime Minister to be represented in the Cabinet, the Prime Minister must allocate the Cabinet positions to which that

party would have been entitled amongst the other parties (including the Prime Minister's party) in proportion, as far as possible, to their respective entitlements under subsection (5).

(8) If all parties (apart from the Prime Minister's party and the party (if any) with which it is in coalition) decline an invitation from the Prime Minister to be represented in the Cabinet, the Prime Minister may look to his or her own party or coalition of parties to fill the places in the Cabinet.

(9) In selecting persons from parties other than his or her own party for appointment as Ministers, the Prime Minister must consult with the leaders of those parties.

8. The country lacks a presidency entirely or there is a presidency, but the president is elected by the legislature.

No. The president is appointed by the Great Council of Chiefs (*Bose Levu Vakaturaga*).

Section 90
The President and Vice-President are appointed by the Bose Levu Vakaturaga after consultation by the Bose Levu Vakaturaga with the Prime Minister.

9. The legislature can vote no confidence in the government.

Yes. The legislature can vote no confidence in the government.

Section 107
If:
(a) the Government is defeated at a general election; or
(b) the Government is defeated on the floor of the House of Representatives in a vote:
(i) after due notice, on whether the Government has the confidence of the House of Representatives;
(ii) that the Government treats as a vote of no confidence; or
(iii) the effect of which is to reject or fail to pass a Bill appropriating revenue or moneys for the ordinary services of the Government; and the Prime Minister considers that there is another person capable of forming a Government that has the confidence of the House of Representatives, the Prime Minister must immediately advise the President of the person whom the Prime Minister believes can form a Government that has the confidence of the House and must thereupon resign.

10. The legislature is immune from dissolution by the executive.

No. The president, on the advice of the prime minister, can dissolve the legislature.

Section 108
(1) If a Prime Minister who has lost the confidence of the House of Representatives (defeated Prime Minister) advises a dissolution of the House of Representatives, the President may, acting in his or her own judgment, ascertain whether or not there is another

person who can get the confidence of the House of Representatives (alternative Prime Minister) and:
(a) if the President ascertains that an alternative Prime Minister exists-ask the defeated Prime Minister to resign, dismiss him or her if he or she does not do so and appoint the alternative Prime Minister; or
(b) if the President cannot ascertain that an alternative Prime minister exists-grant the dissolution advised by the defeated Prime Minister.

(2) If the President appoints the alternative Prime Minister pursuant to paragraph (1)(a) but the alternative Prime Minister fails to get the confidence of the House of Representatives, the President must dismiss him or her, re-appoint his or her predecessor and grant that person the dissolution originally advised.

11. Any executive initiative on legislation requires ratification or approval by the legislature before it takes effect; that is, the executive lacks decree power.

Yes. The executive lacks decree power.

12. Laws passed by the legislature are veto-proof or essentially veto-proof; that is, the executive lacks veto power, or has veto power but the veto can be overridden by a majority in the legislature.

Yes. The executive lacks veto power.

Section 46
(1) Subject to this Constitution, the power of the Parliament to make laws is exercised through the enactment of Bills passed by both Houses of the Parliament and assented to by the President.
(2) The President must not refuse to assent to a Bill duly presented for his or her assent.
(3) A law made by the Parliament does not come into operation before the date on which it is published in the Gazette.

13. The legislature's laws are supreme and not subject to judicial review.

No. The High Court can review the constitutionality of laws.

Section 120
(1) The High Court has unlimited original jurisdiction to hear and determine any civil or criminal proceedings under any law and such other original jurisdiction as is conferred on it under this Constitution.
(2) The High Court also has original jurisdiction in any matter arising under this Constitution or involving its interpretation.

14. The legislature has the right to initiate bills in all policy jurisdictions; the executive lacks gatekeeping authority.

Yes. The legislature can initiate bills in all policy jurisdictions.

15. Expenditure of funds appropriated by the legislature is mandatory; the executive lacks the power to impound funds appropriated by the legislature.

Yes. The executive lacks the power to impound funds appropriated by the legislature.

16. The legislature controls the resources that finance its own internal operation and provide for the perquisites of its own members.

Yes. The legislature enjoys financial autonomy.

17. Members of the legislature are immune from arrest and/or criminal prosecution.

No. Legislative immunity extends to official parliamentary business only. Legislators are subject to arrest for common crimes.

18. All members of the legislature are elected; the executive lacks the power to appoint any members of the legislature.

No. All thirty-two members of the Senate are appointed by the president on the advice of various other institutions. All of the members of the House of Representatives are elected.

Section 50
The House of Representatives consists of 71 members elected in accordance with this Constitution to represent single-member constituencies.

Section 64
(1) The Senate consists of 32 members, of whom:
(a) 14 are appointed by the President on the advice of the Bose Levu Vakaturaga;
(b) 9 are appointed by the President on the advice of the Prime Minister;
(c) 8 are appointed by the President on the advice of the Leader of the Opposition; and
(d) 1 is appointed by the President on the advice of the Council of Rotuma.

19. The legislature alone, without the involvement of any other agencies, can change the Constitution.

Yes. The legislature can change the constitution in multiple readings by a two-thirds majority vote. If the bill to amend the constitution is declared urgent by the prime minister, the House can adopt a constitutional amendment with the support of at least fifty-three of its seventy-one members.

Section 191
(1) A Bill for the alteration of this Constitution must be expressed as a Bill for an Act to alter this Constitution.
(2) Subject to subsection (3) and section 192, the Bill, with or without amendments passed by either House of the Parliament, must be passed by both Houses in accordance with the following procedure:

(a) the Bill is read 3 times in each House and motions for the second and third readings are carried in each House;
(b) at the second and third readings it is supported by the votes of at least two-thirds of the members of each House;
(c) in the House of Representatives an interval of at least 60 days elapses between the second and third readings and each of those readings is preceded by full opportunity for debate;
(d) the third reading of the Bill in the House of Representatives does not take place until after the relevant standing committee has reported on the Bill to that House.
(3) Subject to section 192, if
(a) the Prime Minister certifies that a particular Bill for the alteration of the Constitution is an urgent measure that ought to be dealt with by the House of Representatives under this subsection; and
(b) the giving of that certificate is supported by a resolution passed by a majority of at least 53 members of the House; paragraphs (2)(b), (c) and (d) do not apply in relation to the consideration of the Bill by that House and the Bill is deemed to have been duly passed by that House if, on its third reading, it is passed by a majority of at least 53 members of that House.

20. The legislature's approval is necessary for the declaration of war.

Yes. There is no specific constitutional provision for the declaration of war. The legislature's approval is needed, however, for the president to declare a state of emergency.

Section 187
(1) The Parliament may make a law conferring power on the President, acting on the advice of the Cabinet, to proclaim a state of emergency in Fiji, or in a part of Fiji, in such circumstances as the law prescribes.

21. The legislature's approval is necessary to ratify treaties with foreign countries.

Yes. The legislature's approval is necessary to ratify international treaties.

22. The legislature has the power to grant amnesty.

No. The president has the power to grant amnesty. Amnesty and pardon are not treated separately. See item 23.

23. The legislature has the power of pardon.

No. The president has the power of pardon.

Section 115
(1) The President may:
(a) grant to a person convicted of an offence under the law of the State a pardon or a conditional pardon.

24. The legislature reviews and has the right to reject appointments to the judiciary; or the legislature itself appoints members of the judiciary.

No. The president appoints the members of the judiciary, and these appointments do not require the legislature's approval.

Section 132

(1) The Chief Justice is appointed by the President on the advice of the Prime Minister following consultation by him or her with the Leader of the Opposition.

(2) The judges of the Supreme Court, the Justices of Appeal (including the President of the Court of Appeal) and the puisne judges of the High Court are appointed by the President on the recommendation of the Judicial Service Commission following consultation by it with the Minister and the sector standing committee of the House of Representatives responsible for matters relating to the administration of justice.

(3) The President may, on the recommendation of the Judicial Service Commission following consultation by it with the Minister:

(a) appoint a judge or a person who is qualified for appointment as a judge to act as Chief Justice during any period, or during all periods, when the office of Chief Justice is vacant or when the Chief Justice is absent from duty or from Fiji or is, for any reason, unable to perform the functions of office; and

(b) appoint a person to act as a puisne judge of the High Court during any period, or during all periods, when an office of puisne judge of the High Court is vacant or when a puisne judge is absent from duty or from Fiji or is, for any reason, unable to perform the functions of office.

(4) A person is not eligible to be appointed under paragraph (3)(b) unless he or she is qualified for appointment as a judge.

25. The chairman of the central bank is appointed by the legislature.

No. The Constitutional Offices Commission, in consultation with the board of the Reserve Bank, appoints the governor of the Reserve Bank of Fiji.

Section 146

(1) The Constitutional Offices Commission has the function of making appointments, in accordance with this Constitution, to the following offices:

(g) Governor of the Reserve Bank of Fiji.

26. The legislature has a substantial voice in the operation of the state-owned media.

Yes. The Fiji Broadcasting Act makes provisions for the legislative scrutiny of the public media.

27. The legislature is regularly in session.

Yes. The legislature meets in ordinary session for at least six months each year.

28. Each legislator has a personal secretary.

No.

29. Each legislator has at least one non-secretarial staff member with policy expertise.

No.

30. Legislators are eligible for re-election without any restriction.

Yes. There are no restrictions on re-election.

31. A seat in the legislature is an attractive enough position that legislators are generally interested in and seek re-election.

Yes.

32. The re-election of incumbent legislators is common enough that at any given time the legislature contains a significant number of highly experienced members.

Yes. Re-election rates are sufficiently high to produce a significant number of highly experienced members. It should be noted, however, that several senior legislators were defeated in the 2001 parliamentary elections.

PARLIAMENT OF FINLAND (*EDUSKUNTA*)

Expert consultants: Ari Hyytinen, Mikko Mattila, Sari Pajula, Tapio Raunio, Eelis Roikonen

Score: .72

Influence over executive (6/9)		Institutional autonomy (6/9)		Specified powers (6/8)		Institutional capacity (5/6)	
1. replace		10. no dissolution		19. amendments	X	27. sessions	X
2. serve as ministers	X	11. no decree		20. war	X	28. secretary	
3. interpellate	X	12. no veto	X	21. treaties	X	29. staff	X
4. investigate	X	13. no review	X	22. amnesty	X	30. no term limits	X
5. oversee police		14. no gatekeeping	X	23. pardon		31. seek re-election	X
6. appoint PM	X	15. no impoundment	X	24. judiciary		32. experience	X
7. appoint ministers	X	16. control resources	X	25. central bank	X		
8. lack president		17. immunity		26. media	X		
9. no confidence	X	18. all elected	X				

The Parliament (*Eduskunta*) of Finland was established in the Parliament Act of 1906 while Finland was still under Russian rule. Finland achieved independence in 1919. Its fundamental law was embodied in four important measures: the Form of Government Act of 1919, the Ministerial Responsibility Act of 1922, the Court of the Realm Act of 1922, and the Parliament Act of 1928. Reforms in the 1980s and 1990s did not markedly alter parliament's powers. In 2000 Finland adopted a unified constitution that integrated the four abovementioned documents.

Parliament enjoys broad authority. It controls the executive with the powers to elect, interpellate, investigate, and vote no confidence in the government, and its members can serve in government. It enjoys substantial institutional autonomy. Most notably, the legislature's laws are not subject to judicial review. The legislature can pass "exceptive laws" that are enacted even if the courts judge them to be contrary to the constitution. Yet the legislature's autonomy is limited by the president's dissolution powers, the absence of immunity for legislators, and, most notably, the presence of executive decree authority. The legislature has numerous specified powers and enjoys a high level of institutional capacity.

SURVEY

1. The legislature alone, without the involvement of any other agencies, can impeach the president or replace the prime minister.

No. Presidential impeachment requires the involvement of the chancellor of justice, the ombudsman, or the government and prosecution by the prosecutor-general before the High Court of Impeachment. The legislature can vote no confidence in the government.

Section 43
(1) A group of at least twenty Representatives may address an interpellation to the Government or to an individual Minister on a matter within the competence of the Government or the Minister. The interpellation shall be replied to in a plenary session of the Parliament within fifteen days of the date when the interpellation was brought to the attention of the Government.
(2) At the conclusion of the consideration of the interpellation, a vote of confidence shall be taken by the Parliament, provided that a motion of no confidence in the Government or the Minister has been put forward during the debate.

Section 44
(1) The Government may present a statement or report to the Parliament on a matter relating to the governance of the country or its international relations.

(2) At the conclusion of the consideration of a state-ment, a vote of confidence in the Government or a Minister shall be taken, provided that a motion of no confidence in the Government or the Minister has been put forward during the debate. No decision on confi-dence in the Government or its Member shall be made in the consideration of a report.

Section 113

If the Chancellor of Justice, the Ombudsman or the Government deem that the President of the Republic is guilty of treason or high treason, or a crime against humanity, the matter shall be communicated to the Parliament. In this event, if the Parliament, by three fourths of the votes cast, decides that charges are to be brought, the Prosecutor-General shall prosecute the President in the High Court of Impeachment and the President shall abstain from office for the duration of the proceedings. In other cases, no charges shall be brought for the official acts of the President.

2. Ministers may serve simultaneously as members of the legislature.

Yes. Legislators may serve simultaneously in min-isterial positions.

3. The legislature has powers of summons over exec-utive branch officials and hearings with executive branch officials testifying before the legislature or its committees are regularly held.

Yes. The legislature regularly interpellates officials from the executive.

Section 4

(1) A group of at least twenty Representatives may address an interpellation to the Government or to an individual Minister on a matter within the competence of the Government or the Minister. The interpellation shall be replied to in a plenary session of the Parliament within fifteen days of the date when the interpellation was brought to the attention of the Government.

4. The legislature can conduct independent investi-gation of the chief executive and the agencies of the executive.

Yes. The legislature can investigate the executive.

Section 47

(1) The Parliament has the right to receive from the Government the information it needs in the consideration of matters. The appropriate Minister shall ensure that Committees and other parliamentary organs receive without delay the necessary documents and other information in the possession of the author-ities.

(2) A Committee has the right to receive information from the Government or the appropriate Ministry on a matter within its competence. The Committee may issue a statement to the Government or the Ministry on the basis of the information.

(3) A Representative has the right to information which is in the possession of authorities and which is necessary for the performance of the duties of the Representative, in so far as the information is not secret or it does not pertain to a State budget proposal under preparation.

(4) In addition, the right of the Parliament to informa-tion on international affairs is governed by the provi-sions included elsewhere in this Constitution.

5. The legislature has effective powers of oversight over the agencies of coercion (the military, organs of law enforcement, intelligence services, and the secret police).

No. The agencies of coercion report to the pres-ident and are not subject to effective legislative oversight.

Section 128

(1) The President of the Republic is the commander-in-chief of the defence forces. On the proposal of the Government, the President may relinquish this task to another Finnish citizen.

(2) The President appoints the officers of the defence forces.

6. The legislature appoints the prime minister.

Yes. The legislature elects the prime minister.

Section 61

(1) The Parliament elects the Prime Minister, who is thereafter appointed to the office by the President of the Republic. The President appoints the other Ministers in accordance with a proposal made by the Prime Minister.

(2) Before the Prime Minister is elected, the groups rep-resented in the Parliament negotiate on the political programme and composition of the Government. On the basis of the outcome of these negotiations, and after having heard the Speaker of the Parliament and the parliamentary groups, the President informs the Parlia-ment of the nominee for Prime Minister. The nominee is elected Prime Minister if his or her election has been supported by more than half of the votes cast in an open vote in the Parliament.

7. The legislature's approval is required to confirm the appointment of ministers; or the legislature itself appoints ministers.

Yes. Formally, the president appoints ministers, but in practice, ministerial positions are allotted according to the outcome of negotiations among the parliamentary groups.

Section 61

(1) The Parliament elects the Prime Minister, who is thereafter appointed to the office by the President of the Republic. The President appoints the other Ministers in accordance with a proposal made by the Prime Minister.

(2) Before the Prime Minister is elected, the groups rep-resented in the Parliament negotiate on the political programme and composition of the Government. On the basis of the outcome of these negotiations, and after

having heard the Speaker of the Parliament and the parliamentary groups, the President informs the Parliament of the nominee for Prime Minister. The nominee is elected Prime Minister if his or her election has been supported by more than half of the votes cast in an open vote in the Parliament.

8. The country lacks a presidency entirely or there is a presidency, but the president is elected by the legislature.

No. The president is directly elected.

Section 54
(1) The President of the Republic is elected by a direct vote for a term of six years.

9. The legislature can vote no confidence in the government.

Yes. The legislature can vote no confidence in the government.

Section 43
(1) A group of at least twenty Representatives may address an interpellation to the Government or to an individual Minister on a matter within the competence of the Government or the Minister. The interpellation shall be replied to in a plenary session of the Parliament within fifteen days of the date when the interpellation was brought to the attention of the Government.
(2) At the conclusion of the consideration of the interpellation, a vote of confidence shall be taken by the Parliament, provided that a motion of no confidence in the Government or the Minister has been put forward during the debate.

Section 44
(1) The Government may present a statement or report to the Parliament on a matter relating to the governance of the country or its international relations.
(2) At the conclusion of the consideration of a statement, a vote of confidence in the Government or a Minister shall be taken, provided that a motion of no confidence in the Government or the Minister has been put forward during the debate. No decision on confidence in the Government or its Member shall be made in the consideration of a report.

10. The legislature is immune from dissolution by the executive.

No. The president, on the recommendation of the prime minister, can dissolve the legislature.

Section 26
(1) The President of the Republic, in response to a reasoned proposal by the Prime Minister, and after having heard the parliamentary groups, and while the Parliament is in session, may order that extraordinary parliamentary elections shall be held. Thereafter, the Parliament shall decide the time when it concludes its work before the elections.

11. Any executive initiative on legislation requires ratification or approval by the legislature before it takes effect; that is, the executive lacks decree power.

No. The president and the government can issue decrees that have the force of law.

Section 80
(1) The President of the Republic, the Government and a Ministry may issue Decrees on the basis of authorisation given to them in this Constitution or in another Act. However, the principles governing the rights and obligations of private individuals and the other matters that under this Constitution are of a legislative nature shall be governed by Acts. If there is no specific provision on who shall issue a Decree, it is issued by the Government.

12. Laws passed by the legislature are veto-proof or essentially veto-proof; that is, the executive lacks veto power, or has veto power but the veto can be overridden by a majority in the legislature.

Yes. The legislature can override a presidential veto by a majority vote of its present members.

Section 77
(1) An Act adopted by the Parliament shall be submitted to the President of the Republic for confirmation. The President shall decide on the confirmation within three months of the submission of the Act. The President may obtain a statement on the Act from the Supreme Court or the Supreme Administrative Court.
(2) If the President does not confirm the Act, it is returned for the consideration of the Parliament. If the Parliament readopts the Act without material alterations, it enters into force without confirmation. If the Parliament does not readopt the Act, it shall be deemed to have lapsed.

13. The legislature's laws are supreme and not subject to judicial review.

Yes. The Constitutional Law Committee can issue statements on the constitutionality of laws but cannot void laws based on unconstitutionality. The president can refuse to sign a bill for constitutional concerns based on a report issued by the Constitutional Law Committee. The legislature can, nevertheless, pass what are sometimes called "exceptive laws" that go into force despite contravening the constitution.

Section 74
The Constitutional Law Committee shall issue statements on the constitutionality of legislative proposals and other matters brought for its consideration, as well as on their relation to international human rights treaties.

Section 77
(1) An Act adopted by the Parliament shall be submitted to the President of the Republic for confirmation.

The President shall decide on the confirmation within three months of the submission of the Act. The President may obtain a statement on the Act from the Supreme Court or the Supreme Administrative Court.

(2) If the President does not confirm the Act, it is returned for the consideration of the Parliament. If the Parliament readopts the Act without material alterations, it enters into force without confirmation. If the Parliament does not readopt the Act, it shall be deemed to have lapsed.

14. The legislature has the right to initiate bills in all policy jurisdictions; the executive lacks gatekeeping authority.

Yes. The legislature can initiate bills in all policy jurisdictions.

15. Expenditure of funds appropriated by the legislature is mandatory; the executive lacks the power to impound funds appropriated by the legislature.

Yes. The executive lacks the power to impound funds appropriated by the legislature.

16. The legislature controls the resources that finance its own internal operation and provide for the perquisites of its own members.

Yes. The legislature enjoys financial autonomy.

17. Members of the legislature are immune from arrest and/or criminal prosecution.

No. Legislators can be arrested and prosecuted for any crime for which the minimum punishment is at least six months.

Section 30
(1) A Representative shall not be prevented from carrying out his or her duties as a Representative.
(2) A Representative shall not be charged in a court of law nor be deprived of liberty owing to opinions expressed by the Representative in the Parliament or owing to conduct in the consideration of a matter, unless the Parliament has consented to the same by a decision supported by at least five sixths of the votes cast.
(3) If a Representative has been arrested or detained, the Speaker of the Parliament shall be immediately notified of this. A Representative shall not be arrested or detained before the commencement of a trial without the consent of the Parliament, unless he or she is for substantial reasons suspected of having committed a crime for which the minimum punishment is imprisonment for at least six months.

18. All members of the legislature are elected; the executive lacks the power to appoint any members of the legislature.

Yes. All members of the legislature are elected.

Section 25
(1) The Representatives shall be elected by a direct, proportional and secret vote.

19. The legislature alone, without the involvement of any other agencies, can change the Constitution.

Yes. The legislature can change the constitution through a complicated procedure. The sitting legislature can propose a constitutional amendment, and then, following an election, the subsequent legislature can pass the amendment with a two-thirds majority vote. The legislature can also pass an "urgent" constitutional amendment without waiting for new elections with a five-sixths majority vote.

Section 73
(1) A proposal on the enactment, amendment or repeal of the Constitution or on the enactment of a limited derogation of the Constitution shall in the second reading be left in abeyance, by a majority of the votes cast, until the first parliamentary session following parliamentary elections. The proposal shall then, once the Committee has issued its report, be adopted without material alterations in one reading in a plenary session by a decision supported by at least two thirds of the votes cast.
(2) However, the proposal may be declared urgent by a decision that has been supported by at least five sixths of the votes cast. In this event, the proposal is not left in abeyance and it can be adopted by a decision supported by at least two thirds of the votes cast.

20. The legislature's approval is necessary for the declaration of war.

Yes. The legislature's approval is necessary for presidential war declarations.

Section 93
(1) The foreign policy of Finland is directed by the President of the Republic in co-operation with the Government. However, the Parliament accepts Finland's international obligations and their denouncement and decides on the bringing into force of Finland's international obligations in so far as provided in this Constitution. The President decides on matters of war and peace, with the consent of the Parliament.

21. The legislature's approval is necessary to ratify treaties with foreign countries.

Yes. The legislature's approval is necessary to ratify international treaties.

Section 93
(1) The foreign policy of Finland is directed by the President of the Republic in co-operation with the Government. However, the Parliament accepts Finland's international obligations and their denouncement and decides on the bringing into force of Finland's international obligations in so far as provided in this Constitution. The President decides on matters of war and peace, with the consent of the Parliament.

Section 94
(1) The acceptance of the Parliament is required for such treaties and other international obligations that

contain provisions of a legislative nature, are otherwise significant, or otherwise require approval by the Parliament under this Constitution. The acceptance of the Parliament is required also for the denouncement of such obligations.

(2) A decision concerning the acceptance of an international obligation or the denouncement of it is made by a majority of the votes cast. However, if the proposal concerns the Constitution or an alteration of the national borders, the decision shall be made by at least two thirds of the votes cast.

(3) An international obligation shall not endanger the democratic foundations of the Constitution.

22. The legislature has the power to grant amnesty.

Yes. The legislature has the power to grant amnesty through law.

Section 105
(2) A general amnesty may be provided only by an Act.

23. The legislature has the power of pardon.

No. The president has the power of pardon.

Section 105
(1) In individual cases, the President of the Republic may, after obtaining a statement from the Supreme Court, grant full or partial pardon from a penalty or other criminal sanction imposed by a court of law.

24. The legislature reviews and has the right to reject appointments to the judiciary; or the legislature itself appoints members of the judiciary.

No. The president makes judicial appointments, and the appointments do not require the legislature's approval.

Section 102
Tenured judges are appointed by the President of the Republic in accordance with the procedure laid down by an Act.

25. The chairman of the central bank is appointed by the legislature.

Yes. The governor of the Bank of Finland is formally appointed by the president, but the president acts on the recommendation of the

Parliamentary Supervisory Council, a nine-member body appointed by parliament, and approval by the government. The legislature controls the appointments process.

Section 91
(1) The Bank of Finland operates under the guarantee and supervision of the Parliament, as provided by an Act. For the purpose of supervising the operations of the Bank of Finland, the Parliament elects its governors.

26. The legislature has a substantial voice in the operation of the state-owned media.

Yes. The Finnish Broadcasting Corporation is under parliament's control, although politicians do not generally interfere in its operational affairs.

27. The legislature is regularly in session.

Yes. The legislature is in session year round, except for breaks during the summer and the winter holidays.

28. Each legislator has a personal secretary.

No.

29. Each legislator has at least one non-secretarial staff member with policy expertise.

Yes.

30. Legislators are eligible for re-election without any restriction.

Yes. There are no restrictions on re-election.

31. A seat in the legislature is an attractive enough position that legislators are generally interested in and seek re-election.

Yes.

32. The re-election of incumbent legislators is common enough that at any given time the legislature contains a significant number of highly experienced members.

Yes. Re-election rates are sufficiently high to produce a significant number of highly experienced members.

PARLIAMENT OF FRANCE (*PARLEMENT*)

Expert consultants: Richard Balme, David S. Bell, Sylvain Brouard, Guy Carcassonne, Robert Elgie, Nicholas Jabko, Vivien Ann Schmidt, Yves Surel

Score: .56

Influence over executive (3/9)		Institutional autonomy (6/9)		Specified powers (3/8)		Institutional capacity (6/6)	
1. replace		10. no dissolution		19. amendments		27. sessions	X
2. serve as ministers		11. no decree	X	20. war	X	28. secretary	X
3. interpellate	X	12. no veto	X	21. treaties	X	29. staff	X
4. investigate	X	13. no review		22. amnesty	X	30. no term limits	X
5. oversee police		14. no gatekeeping	X	23. pardon		31. seek re-election	X
6. appoint PM		15. no impoundment		24. judiciary		32. experience	X
7. appoint ministers		16. control resources	X	25. central bank			
8. lack president		17. immunity	X	26. media			
9. no confidence	X	18. all elected	X				

The Parliament (*Parlement*) of France was established following the 1789 revolution that overthrew the *ancien régime*. Over the next two centuries, France was governed by fifteen different constitutions. The constitution of the Fifth Republic, adopted in 1958, stepped away from previous parliamentary systems by establishing a directly elected president and a semipresidential system. The bicameral parliament consists of a lower house, the National Assembly (*Assemblée nationale*), and an upper house, the Senate (*Sénat*).

Parliament is an important but not dominant actor in French politics and government. Its control over executive power is limited to the powers to interpellate and investigate the executive and to vote no confidence in the government. It lacks all other means for influencing the executive captured in this survey.

Parliament enjoys a fair degree of institutional autonomy. For example, it can override a presidential veto with a majority vote. It is endowed with a modest number of specified powers. Of the eight specified powers enumerated in this survey, the parliament of France is vested with only three: control over the declaration of war, control over ratification of treaties with foreign countries, and the power to grant amnesty. The legislature's muscle is most evident in the realm of

institutional capacity, for which parliament receives an affirmative answer for all six of the survey items.

SURVEY

1. The legislature alone, without the involvement of any other agencies, can impeach the president or replace the prime minister.

No. Presidential impeachment requires the involvement of the High Court of Justice. The legislature can remove the prime minister with a motion of censure.

Article 49
(1) The Prime Minister, after deliberation by the Council of Ministers, may commit the Government's responsibility before the National Assembly with regard to its program or, should the occasion arise, to a statement of general policy.
(2) The National Assembly may challenge the responsibility of the Government by passing a motion of censure. Such a motion shall be admissible only if signed by at least one tenth of the members of the National Assembly. The vote may not take place until forty-eight hours after the motion has been tabled; the only votes counted shall be those in favor of the motion of censure, which may be adopted only by a majority of the membership of the Assembly.

(3) The Prime Minister may, after deliberation by the Council of Ministers, commit the Government's responsibility to the National Assembly on the passing of a bill. In this case, the text shall be regarded as carried unless a motion of censure, tabled within the succeeding twenty-four hours, is passed under the conditions laid down in the previous paragraph.

(4) The Prime Minister may ask the Senate to approve a general policy statement.

Article 50

If the National Assembly adopts a motion of censure, or rejects the Government's program or a general policy statement by the latter, the Prime Minister must tender the Government's resignation to the President of the Republic.

Article 68

(1) The President of the Republic shall not be held accountable for actions performed in the exercise of his office except in the case of high treason. He may be indicted only by the two Assemblies ruling by identical vote in open balloting and by an absolute majority of their members. He shall be tried by the High Court of Justice.

2. Ministers may serve simultaneously as members of the legislature.

No. Legislators are prohibited from serving simultaneously in ministerial positions.

Article 23

(1) Membership of the Government shall be incompatible with the exercise of any Parliamentary mandate, with the holding of any representational office at national level in a trade organization, and with any public employment or professional activity.

3. The legislature has powers of summons over executive branch officials and hearings with executive branch officials testifying before the legislature or its committees are regularly held.

Yes. Legislators question the government during question time, held for one hour each Tuesday and Wednesday afternoon.

Article 48

(1) The discussion of bills tabled by the Government and of private members' bills agreed to by it shall have priority on the agendas of the Assemblies in the order decided by the Government.

(2) One meeting per week shall be reserved in priority for members' questions and the Government's replies.

4. The legislature can conduct independent investigation of the chief executive and the agencies of the executive.

Yes. The legislature can investigate the executive.

5. The legislature has effective powers of oversight over the agencies of coercion (the military, organs of

law enforcement, intelligence services, and the secret police).

No. The agencies of coercion report to the president and are not subject to legislative oversight.

6. The legislature appoints the prime minister.

No. The president appoints the prime minister, although in some cases in which opponents of his or her party control the legislature, the president appoints a partisan opponent to the post, producing a situation known as "cohabitation."

Article 8

(1) The President of the Republic shall appoint the Prime Minister. He shall terminate that appointment when the latter tenders the resignation of the Government.

(2) On the proposal of the Prime Minister, he shall appoint the other members of the Government and terminate their appointments.

7. The legislature's approval is required to confirm the appointment of ministers; or the legislature itself appoints ministers.

No. The president appoints ministers, and the appointments do not require the legislature's approval.

Article 8

(1) The President of the Republic shall appoint the Prime Minister. He shall terminate that appointment when the latter tenders the resignation of the Government.

(2) On the proposal of the Prime Minister, he shall appoint the other members of the Government and terminate their appointments.

8. The country lacks a presidency entirely or there is a presidency, but the president is elected by the legislature.

No. The president is directly elected.

Article 6

The President of the Republic shall be elected for five years by direct universal suffrage. The procedures implementing this Article shall be laid down in an organic act.

9. The legislature can vote no confidence in the government.

Yes. The legislature can pass a motion of censure in the government.

Article 49

(1) The Prime Minister, after deliberation by the Council of Ministers, may commit the Government's responsibility before the National Assembly with regard to its program or, should the occasion arise, to a statement of general policy.

(2) The National Assembly may challenge the responsibility of the Government by passing a motion of censure. Such a motion shall be admissible only if signed by at least one tenth of the members of the National Assembly. The vote may not take place until forty-eight hours after the motion has been tabled; the only votes counted shall be those in favor of the motion of censure, which may be adopted only by a majority of the membership of the Assembly. Should the motion of censure be rejected, its signatories may not introduce another such motion in the course of the same session, except in the case provided for in the following paragraph.

(3) The Prime Minister may, after deliberation by the Council of Ministers, commit the Government's responsibility to the National Assembly on the passing of a bill. In this case, the text shall be regarded as carried unless a motion of censure, tabled within the succeeding twenty-four hours, is passed under the conditions laid down in the previous paragraph.

(4) The Prime Minister may ask the Senate to approve a general policy statement.

Article 50

If the National Assembly adopts a motion of censure, or rejects the Government's program or a general policy statement by the latter, the Prime Minister must tender the Government's resignation to the President of the Republic.

10. The legislature is immune from dissolution by the executive.

No. The president can dissolve the legislature.

Article 12

(1) The President of the Republic may, after consultation with the Prime Minister and the Presidents of the Assemblies, pronounce the dissolution of the National Assembly. A General election shall take place not less than twenty days and not more than forty days after the dissolution.

11. Any executive initiative on legislation requires ratification or approval by the legislature before it takes effect; that is, the executive lacks decree power.

Yes. The executive lacks decree power. The government can, however, issue regulations to implement parliament's laws, and parliament can grant the government the power to issue temporary "ordinance measures."

Article 37

(1) Matters other than those that fall within the sphere of legislation shall be determined by regulation.

(2) Legislation concerning these matters may be amended by orders issued after consultation with the Conseil d'Etat. Any such legislative texts introduced after this Constitution has entered into force shall be amended by order only if the Constitutional Council has pronounced that the matters they deal with fall within the field subject to regulation as defined in the preceding paragraph.

Article 38

(1) The Government may, in order to carry out its program, ask Parliament to authorize it, for a limited period, to take by ordinance measures normally within the legislative sphere.

(2) Ordinances shall be enacted in meetings of the Council of Ministers after consultation with the Conseil d'Etat. They shall come into force upon their publication, but shall become null and void if the bill for their ratification is not submitted to Parliament before the date set by the enabling act.

(3) Upon expiry of the period referred to in the first paragraph of this article, the ordinances may be amended only by act of Parliament in respect of those matters which are within the legislative domain.

12. Laws passed by the legislature are veto-proof or essentially veto-proof; that is, the executive lacks veto power, or has veto power but the veto can be overridden by a majority in the legislature.

Yes. The legislature can override a presidential veto by a majority vote of its present members.

Article 10

(1) The President of the Republic shall promulgate laws within fifteen days following the transmission to the Government of the said laws as finally adopted.

(2) He may, before expiry of this time limit, ask Parliament to reconsider a law or certain of its articles.

13. The legislature's laws are supreme and not subject to judicial review.

No. The Constitutional Council can review the constitutionality of laws.

Article 46

(5) Organic acts may be promulgated only after the Constitutional Council has declared them constitutional.

Article 61

(1) Organic acts, before their promulgation, and standing orders of the parliamentary Assemblies, before their implementation, must be submitted to the Constitutional Council which shall rule on their constitutionality.

(2) To the same end, acts of Parliament may, before their promulgation, be submitted to the Constitutional Council by the President of the Republic, the Prime Minister, the President of the National Assembly, the President of the Senate, sixty deputies or sixty senators.

14. The legislature has the right to initiate bills in all policy jurisdictions; the executive lacks gatekeeping authority.

Yes. The legislature can initiate bills in all policy jurisdictions.

15. Expenditure of funds appropriated by the legislature is mandatory; the executive lacks the power to impound funds appropriated by the legislature.

No. The executive can impound funds appropriated by the legislature.

16. The legislature controls the resources that finance its own internal operation and provide for the perquisites of its own members.

Yes. The legislature enjoys financial autonomy, including control over members' salaries.

Article 25
(1) An organic act shall determine the term for which each Assembly is elected, the number of its members, their emoluments, the conditions of eligibility and ineligibility and the offices incompatible with membership of the Assemblies.

17. Members of the legislature are immune from arrest and/or criminal prosecution.

Yes. Legislators are immune with the common exception for cases of *flagrante delicto.*

Article 26
(1) No member of Parliament may be prosecuted or subjected to inquiry, arrest, detention, or trial on account of opinions expressed or votes cast in the course of his or her duties.
(2) No member of Parliament may, during parliamentary sessions, be prosecuted or arrested for a felony or misdemeanor without the authority of the Assembly of which he or she is a member, except in cases of flagrante delicto.
(3) When Parliament is not in session, no member of Parliament may be arrested without the authority of the bureau of the Assembly of which he or she is a member, except in the case of flagrante delicto, authorized prosecution, or final sentence.
(4) The detention or prosecution of a member of Parliament shall be suspended if the Assembly of which he or she is a member so demands.

18. All members of the legislature are elected; the executive lacks the power to appoint any members of the legislature.

Yes. All members of the legislature are elected.

Article 24
(1) Parliament shall consist of the National Assembly and the Senate.
(2) Deputies of the National Assembly shall be elected by direct suffrage.
(3) The Senate shall be elected by indirect suffrage. It shall ensure the representation of the territorial entities of the Republic. French nationals living outside France shall be represented in the Senate.

19. The legislature alone, without the involvement of any other agencies, can change the Constitution.

No. The constitution can be changed through two procedures, both of which require the involvement of actors other than the legislature. In one procedure, a legislative bill for constitutional amendment must be approved in a popular referendum. In the other, the president must initiate the amendment, which can then be approved by a three-fifths majority vote in the legislature.

Article 89
(1) The initiative for amending the Constitution shall belong both to the President of the Republic on the proposal of the Prime Minister and to the members of Parliament.
(2) A Government or private member's bill for amendment must be passed by the two Assemblies in identical terms. The amendment shall become definitive after approval by referendum.
(3) Nevertheless, the proposed amendment shall not be submitted to a referendum when the President of the Republic decides to submit it to Parliament convened in Congress; in this case, the proposed amendment shall be approved only if it is accepted by a three-fifths majority of the votes cast. The Bureau of the Congress shall be that of the National Assembly.
(4) No amendment procedure may be undertaken or followed when the integrity of the territory is in jeopardy.
(5) The republican form of government shall not be subject to amendment.

20. The legislature's approval is necessary for the declaration of war.

Yes. The legislature's approval is necessary for the declaration of war.

Article 35
A declaration of war must be authorized by Parliament.

21. The legislature's approval is necessary to ratify treaties with foreign countries.

Yes. The legislature's approval is necessary to ratify international treaties.

Article 53
(1) Peace treaties, commercial treaties and treaties, or agreements relating to international organization, or implying a financial commitment on the part of the State, or modifying provisions of a legislative nature, or relating to the status of persons, or entailing a cession, exchange or ad junction of territory, may be ratified or approved only by act of Parliament.
(2) They shall take effect only after having been ratified or approved.

22. The legislature has the power to grant amnesty.

Yes. The legislature has the power to grant amnesty.

Article 34
(2) Legislation shall establish the rules concerning: amnesty.

23. The legislature has the power of pardon.

No. The president has the power of pardon.

Article 17
The President of the Republic shall have the right of
pardon.

24. The legislature reviews and has the right to reject
appointments to the judiciary; or the legislature itself
appoints members of the judiciary.

No. The president appoints the members of the
Council of Magistrates (*Conseil Superieur de la
Magistrature*). The president, the president of the
Senate, and the president of the National Assembly
each appoint three members to the Constitutional
Council. The appointments do not require the legislature's approval. The legislature elects the members of the High Court of Justice, but this body,
which is called together to judge the president for
high treason, has never been convened in the Fifth
Republic.

Article 56
(1) The Constitutional Council shall consist of nine
members, whose term of office shall last nine years and
shall not be renewable. Three of its members shall be
appointed by the President of the Republic, three by
the President of the National Assembly, three by the
President of the Senate.

Article 65
(1) The Conseil Superieur de la Magistrature shall be
presided over by the President of the Republic.
(2) The Conseil Superieur shall, in addition, comprise
nine members appointed by the President of the Republic under the terms laid down by an organic act.

Article 67
(1) A High Court of Justice shall be instituted.
(2) It shall be composed of members elected in equal
number by the National Assembly and the Senate from
within their ranks after each general or partial election to these Assemblies. It shall elect its President from
among its members.

25. The chairman of the central bank is appointed by
the legislature.

No. The president appoints the governor of the
Bank of France.

26. The legislature has a substantial voice in the operation of the state-owned media.

No. The legislature lacks a substantial voice in the
operation of the public media.

27. The legislature is regularly in session.

Yes. According to the constitution adopted in 1958
and modified in 1963, the legislature met for two
ordinary sessions each year, totaling ninety days
in the spring and eighty in the fall. The brevity
of parliament's time in session, according to
critics, seriously limited the Assembly's capacity
and reduced its ability to influence the government. In 1995 the law was altered to allow for an

ordinary session that meets for 120 days stretch-
ing from October through June, as well as extraordinary sessions, which can be convoked at any
time by the prime minister and a majority of the
Assembly. While the constitution continues to create the impression that parliament is in session for
less than half of the year, in practice it meets for
roughly nine months each year.

Article 28
(1) Parliament shall convene ipso jure in two ordinary
sessions per year.
(2) The first session shall begin on 2 April and last for
thirty days.
(3) The second session shall open on 2 October and last
for not more than ninety days.
(4) If 2 October or 2 April is a public holiday, the session
shall open on the first working day thereafter.

Article 29
Parliament convenes in extraordinary session, at the
request of the Prime Minister or of the majority of the
members of the National Assembly, to consider a specific agenda.
When an extraordinary session is held at the request of
members of the National Assembly, the decree closing
it shall take effect once Parliament has dealt with the
agenda for which it was convened, or twelve days after
its first sitting, whichever shall be the earlier.
Only the Prime Minister can request a new session
before the end of the month following the decree closing an extraordinary session.

Article 30
Apart from the case when Parliament convenes as of
right, extraordinary sessions are opened and closed by
decree of the President of the Republic.

28. Each legislator has a personal secretary.

Yes.

29. Each legislator has at least one non-secretarial
staff member with policy expertise.

Yes.

30. Legislators are eligible for re-election without any
restriction.

Yes. There are no restrictions on re-election.

31. A seat in the legislature is an attractive enough
position that legislators are generally interested in and
seek re-election.

Yes.

32. The re-election of incumbent legislators is common enough that at any given time the legislature
contains a significant number of highly experienced
members.

Yes. Re-election rates are sufficiently high to produce a significant number of highly experienced
members.

PARLIAMENT OF GABON (*PARLEMENT*)

Expert consultants: Barrie Hofmann, François Ngolet, Guy Rossatanga-Rignault, Nicholas Shaxson, Douglas A. Yates

Score: .44

Influence over executive (2/9)		Institutional autonomy (4/9)		Specified powers (3/8)		Institutional capacity (5/6)	
1. replace		10. no dissolution		19. amendments	X	27. sessions	X
2. serve as ministers		11. no decree	X	20. war	X	28. secretary	X
3. interpellate	X	12. no veto		21. treaties	X	29. staff	
4. investigate		13. no review		22. amnesty		30. no term limits	X
5. oversee police		14. no gatekeeping	X	23. pardon		31. seek re-election	X
6. appoint PM		15. no impoundment		24. judiciary		32. experience	X
7. appoint ministers		16. control resources	X	25. central bank			
8. lack president		17. immunity		26. media			
9. no confidence	X	18. all elected	X				

The Parliament (*Parlement*) of Gabon was established in 1960 upon independence from France. For most of the next thirty years, the legislature was sidelined by the one-party state of President Omar Bongo. Economic instability threatened Bongo's control in the early 1990s, leading to the adoption of a new constitution in 1991 that reintroduced a multiparty system. A constitutional amendment in 1994 created an upper house of parliament, the Senate (*Sénat*). Prior to 1994 parliament was a unicameral body, consisting only of what is now the lower house, the National Assembly (*Assemblée nationale*). Amendments in 1997 and 2003 established the position of vice president and eliminated presidential term limits, respectively.

The Gabonese legislature has little sway over the executive branch. Its powers in this area are limited to the rights to question executive branch officials and to vote no confidence (in Gabon, to pass a motion of censure) in the government. The legislature's institutional autonomy is limited by the president's dissolution, veto, and impoundment powers. The legislature holds several specified powers and prerogatives, such as the power to approve presidential treaties and war declarations. It is endowed with some institutional capacity.

SURVEY

1. The legislature alone, without the involvement of any other agencies, can impeach the president or replace the prime minister.

No. Presidential impeachment requires the involvement of the High Court of Justice. The legislature can remove the prime minister with a motion of censure.

Article 15
He [the President] ends his [the Prime Minister's] functions... upon the presentation by the Prime Minister of the resignation of the Government, or following a vote of defiance or the adoption of a motion of censure by the National Assembly.

Article 63
The Prime Minister, after deliberation of the Council of Ministers, engages the responsibility of Government before the National Assembly, by posing the question of confidence, either on a declaration of general policy, or on the vote of a text of law. The debate on the question of confidence may only intervene three full days after it was raised. The confidence may only be refused by an absolute majority of the members composing the National Assembly.

Article 64
The National Assembly puts to issue the responsibility of the Government by the passing of a motion of censure. Such a motion can only be receivable if it is signed by at least one-quarter of the members of the National Assembly... The motion to censure can only be adopted by an absolute majority of the members of the National Assembly.

Article 65
When the National Assembly adopts a motion of censure or denies its confidence to the Prime Minister, he immediately submits his resignation to the President of the Republic.

Article 78
The High Court of Justice . . . judges the President of the Republic in the case of violation of the oath or high treason. The President of the Republic shall be impeached by Parliament deciding by a two-thirds majority of its members, by public ballot.

2. Ministers may serve simultaneously as members of the legislature.

No. Legislators are prohibited from serving simultaneously in ministerial positions.

Article 31
The Government is composed of the Prime Minister, and the other members of the Government.
The Prime Minister is the Head of the Government.
The members of the Government are chosen both from within the National Assembly and outside of it.

Article 32
The functions of a member of the Government are incompatible with the exercise of a parliamentary mandate.

3. The legislature has powers of summons over executive branch officials and hearings with executive branch officials testifying before the legislature or its committees are regularly held.

Yes. The legislature interpellates executive branch officials and questions them during a weekly question time.

Article 57
The Prime Minister and the other members of the Government . . . are heard at their demand or that of the parliamentary authorities.

Article 61
The means of control of the legislative upon the executive are the following: interpellations, written and oral questions, commissions of inquiry and control, the motion of censure exercised by the National Assembly under the conditions provided for in Article 63 of the present Constitution.
One meeting per week is reserved to the questions of the Parliamentarians and to the responses by members of the Government. The current questions may be the object of interpellations of the Government, even during the extraordinary sessions of Parliament.
The executive is held to furnish to Parliament all the elements of information which it has demanded on its conduct and its activities.

4. The legislature can conduct independent investigation of the chief executive and the agencies of the executive.

No. According to the constitution, the legislature can establish commissions of inquiry to investigate the executive. In practice, the legislature cannot investigate the executive.

Article 61
The means of control of the legislative upon the executive are the following: interpellations, written and oral questions, commissions of inquiry and control, the motion of censure exercised by the National Assembly under the conditions provided for in Article 63 of the present Constitution.
One meeting per week is reserved to the questions of the Parliamentarians and to the responses by members of the Government. The current questions may be the object of interpellations of the Government, even during the extraordinary sessions of Parliament. The executive is held to furnish to Parliament all the elements of information which it has demanded on its conduct and its activities.

5. The legislature has effective powers of oversight over the agencies of coercion (the military, organs of law enforcement, intelligence services, and the secret police).

No. The legislature lacks effective powers of oversight over the agencies of coercion.

6. The legislature appoints the prime minister.

No. The president appoints the prime minister.

Article 15
The President of the Republic names the Prime Minister.

7. The legislature's approval is required to confirm the appointment of ministers; or the legislature itself appoints ministers.

No. The president appoints ministers on the proposal of the prime minister, and the appointments do not require the legislature's approval.

Article 15
The President of the Republic names the Prime Minister . . . Upon the proposal of the Prime Minister, he names the other members of the Government and ends their functions.

8. The country lacks a presidency entirely or there is a presidency, but the president is elected by the legislature.

No. The president is directly elected.

Article 9
The President of the Republic is elected for seven years, by direct universal suffrage.

9. The legislature can vote no confidence in the government.

Yes. The legislature can adopt a motion of censure resulting in the resignation of the government.

Article 15
He [the President] ends his [the Prime Minister's] functions . . . upon the presentation by the Prime Minister of the resignation of the Government, or following a

vote of defiance or the adoption of a motion of censure by the National Assembly.

Article 64
The National Assembly puts to issue the responsibility of the Government by the passing of a motion of censure. Such a motion can only be receivable if it is signed by at least one-quarter of the members of the National Assembly. The vote of the motion to censure can only take place three days after its filing. The motion to censure can only be adopted by an absolute majority of the members of the National Assembly.

Article 65
When the National Assembly adopts a motion of censure or denies its confidence to the Prime Minister, he immediately submits his resignation to the President of the Republic.
The resignation of the Prime Minister encompasses the resignation of the entire Government.

10. The legislature is immune from dissolution by the executive.

No. The president can dissolve the legislature.

Article 19
The President of the Republic may, after consultation with the Prime Minister and the Presidents of the two Chambers of the Parliament pronounce the dissolution of the National Assembly.
However, the recourse to this prerogative, limited to two times over the course of the same Presidential mandate, may not intervene consecutively in the twelve months which follow the first dissolution.

11. Any executive initiative on legislation requires ratification or approval by the legislature before it takes effect; that is, the executive lacks decree power.

Yes. The executive lacks decree power. During emergency circumstances, however, the president can issue decree-laws. The legislature can also grant the government the authority to issue decrees under emergency circumstances. Both presidential and governmental decrees lapse if they are not subsequently approved by the legislature.

Article 26
When the institutions of the Republic, independence or the superior interests of the nation, territorial integrity or the execution of its international engagements are menaced in a grave and immediate manner and that the regular operation of constitutional public powers is interrupted, the President of the Republic takes by ordinance, during the intersessions, with the least delay, measures necessitated by the circumstances, and after consultation of the National Assembly as well as the Constitutional Court. He informs the nation of this by a message. During the sessions, these measures arise in the domain of the law.

Article 51
Matters other than those which are of the domain of the law have a regulatory character. They are made the objects of decrees of the President of the Republic. These matters may, for the application of these decrees, be the object of administrative decisions taken by the Prime Minister or, upon delegation of the Prime Minister, by the ministers responsible or by the other administrative authorities habituated to making them.

Article 52
The Government may, in case of emergency, for the execution of its program, demand of Parliament the authorization to be taken by ordinance during Parliamentary recess, measures which are normally of the domain of the law. The ordinances are taken in the Council of Ministers, after the advice of the Administrative Chamber and signed by the President of the Republic. They become effective upon their publication. They must be ratified by Parliament in the course of its next session. Parliament has the possibility to modify the ordinances by way of amendments. In the absence of a law of ratification, the ordinances are null and void.
Ordinances may be modified by another ordinance or by a law.

12. Laws passed by the legislature are veto-proof or essentially veto-proof; that is, the executive lacks veto power, or has veto power but the veto can be overridden by a majority in the legislature.

No. A two-thirds majority vote in the legislature is needed to override a presidential veto.

Article 17
The President of the Republic may, during the period of promulgation, demand of Parliament a new deliberation on the law or on certain articles. This new deliberation cannot be refused. The text thus submitted to a second deliberation is adopted by a two-thirds majority of its members, either in its original form, or after modification. The President of the Republic promulgates it within the time limits fixed above.

13. The legislature's laws are supreme and not subject to judicial review.

No. The Constitutional Court can review the constitutionality of laws.

Article 83
The Constitutional Court is the highest jurisdiction of the State in constitutional matters. It is the judge of the constitutionality of laws and it guarantees the fundamental rights of the human person and public liberties. It is the regulatory organ of the operation of the institutions and of the activities of the pubic powers.

14. The legislature has the right to initiate bills in all policy jurisdictions; the executive lacks gatekeeping authority.

Yes. The legislature can initiate bills in all policy jurisdictions.

15. Expenditure of funds appropriated by the legislature is mandatory; the executive lacks the power to impound funds appropriated by the legislature.

No. The president can impound funds appropriated by the legislature.

16. The legislature controls the resources that finance its own internal operation and provide for the perquisites of its own members.

Yes. The legislature enjoys financial autonomy.

Article 46
Each Chamber of Parliament enjoys administrative and financial autonomy.

17. Members of the legislature are immune from arrest and/or criminal prosecution.

No. By law, legislators are immune, but in practice, any legislator who dares to criticize the president cannot depend on the law for protection and may find himself or herself subject to persecution.

Article 38
No member of the Parliament may be prosecuted, investigated, arrested, detained or judged as a result of the opinions or votes he expressed in the exercise of his functions.
Any member of Parliament may, during sessions, only be prosecuted, investigated, arrested for a criminal, correctional or simple police matter, with the authorization of the Bureau of the concerned Chamber, except in the case of flagrant offense or definitive condemnation.
The detention or the prosecution of a member of Parliament will be suspended until the end of his mandate, except in the case of a waiver of parliamentary immunity.

18. All members of the legislature are elected; the executive lacks the power to appoint any members of the legislature.

Yes. All members of the legislature are elected.

Article 35
The legislative power is represented by a Parliament composed of two Chambers: the National Assembly and the Senate.
The members of the National Assembly carry the title of Deputy. They are elected for a duration of five years by direct universal suffrage.
The members of the Senate carry the title of Senator. They are elected for a duration of six years by indirect universal suffrage. They must be forty years of age, at least. The Senate assures the representation of the local collectivities.

19. The legislature alone, without the involvement of any other agencies, can change the Constitution.

Yes. The legislature alone can change the constitution with a two-thirds majority vote.

Article 116
The initiative of amendment belongs concurrently to the President of the Republic, the Council of Ministers thereupon focused, and the members of Parliament. Any proposal of amendment is filed with the Bureau of the National Assembly by at least one-third of the Deputies or with the Bureau of the Senate by at least one-third of the Senators. Any bill or proposal to revise the Constitution as well as any amendment concerning it, is submitted, for advice, to the Constitutional Court. The amendment is adopted either by way of referendum, or by the parliamentary [vote]. When the parliamentary [vote] is chosen, the bill or proposal to revise the Constitution must be voted upon respectively by the National Assembly and by the Senate in identical terms. The adoption of any bill or of any proposal of revision of the Constitution by the parliamentary [vote] requires the presence of at least two-thirds of the members of the Parliament convened in congress. The presidency of the congress is assured by the President of the National Assembly.
The Bureau of the congress is that of the National Assembly. A qualified majority of two-thirds of the expressed votes is required to adopt the bill or proposal to revise the Constitution.

20. The legislature's approval is necessary for the declaration of war.

Yes. The legislature's approval is necessary for presidential war declarations.

Article 49
A Declaration of War by the President of the Republic is authorized by the National Assembly by a two-thirds majority of its members.

21. The legislature's approval is necessary to ratify treaties with foreign countries.

Yes. The legislature's approval is necessary to ratify international treaties.

Article 113
The President of the Republic negotiates international treaties and accords and ratifies them after the vote of a law of authorization by the Parliament and the verification of their constitutionality by the Constitutional Court. The President of the Republic and the Presidents of the Chambers of the Parliament are informed of any negotiation leading to the conclusion of an international accord not submitted to ratification.

22. The legislature has the power to grant amnesty.

No. While "the rules concerning... [the] amnesty system" are formally established by law, the power to grant amnesty in practice rests with the president alone.

Article 47
Outside of the cases expressly provided for by the Constitution, the law establishes the rules concerning:

– the determination of crimes and misdemeanors as well as the penalties which are applicable to them, the penal procedure, the penitentiary and amnesty system.

23. The legislature has the power of pardon.

No. The president has the power of pardon.

Article 23
The President of the Republic has the right of pardon.

24. The legislature reviews and has the right to reject appointments to the judiciary; or the legislature itself appoints members of the judiciary.

No. Formally, the legislature has the right to elect a portion of the Superior Council of the Magistrature, but in practice, the legislature does not fulfill this role, and the president fully controls all appointments to the judiciary.

Article 71
The Superior Council of the Magistrature is presided over by the President of the Republic assisted by the Minister charged with Justice, [as] Vice President.
The legislative power is represented within the Superior Council of the Magistrature by three Deputies and two Senators chosen by the President of each Chamber of Parliament from the different parliamentary groups, and having consultative voice.
The Minister charged with Finance assists the Superior Council of the Magistrature with a consultative voice.

Article 80
The High Court of Justice is composed of thirteen members of which seven professional magistrates are designated by the Superior Council of the Magistrature and six members elected by Parliament from within, in proportion to the members *[effectifs]* of parliamentary groups.
The President and the Vice-President of the High Court of Justice are elected from among the resultant magistrates of the preceding paragraph by the group of members of this institution.

Article 89
The Constitutional Court consists of nine appointed members who carry the title of Counselors.
The duration of the mandate of the Counselors is seven years renewable once.
The nine members of the Constitutional Court are chosen as follows:
– three by the President of the Republic, one of which will be the President;
– three, by the President of the Senate;
– three, by the President of the National Assembly.

25. The chairman of the central bank is appointed by the legislature.

No. Gabon belongs to the Bank of Central African States, whose governor is selected by the member countries.

26. The legislature has a substantial voice in the operation of the state-owned media.

No. The legislature lacks a substantial voice in the operation of the public media.

27. The legislature is regularly in session.

Yes. The legislature meets in ordinary session for roughly eight months each year.

Article 41
The Parliament meets by right in the course of two sessions per year.
The first session opens on the first business day of March and end, at the latest on the last business day of June.
The second session opens on the first business day in September and end at the latest on the last business day of December.

28. Each legislator has a personal secretary.

Yes.

29. Each legislator has at least one non-secretarial staff member with policy expertise.

No.

30. Legislators are eligible for re-election without any restriction.

Yes. There are no restrictions on re-election.

31. A seat in the legislature is an attractive enough position that legislators are generally interested in and seek re-election.

Yes.

32. The re-election of incumbent legislators is common enough that at any given time the legislature contains a significant number of highly experienced members.

Yes. Re-election rates are sufficiently high to produce a significant number of highly experienced members. The party of President Omar Bongo, the Gabonese Democratic Party, has long held a lock on the legislature. The party's near-monopoly of seats was most recently confirmed in parliamentary elections held in 2001 and 2006. It should be noted that the president's de facto control of parliament means that long experience of membership does not necessarily spell substantial experience in legislative work.

NATIONAL ASSEMBLY OF THE GAMBIA

Expert consultants: Momodou N. Darboe, Ida-Denise Drameh, Eleanor Marchant, Hawa Sisay Sabally, Abdoulaye Saine

Score: .31

Influence over executive (2/9)		Institutional autonomy (3/9)		Specified powers (2/8)		Institutional capacity (3/6)	
1. replace		10. no dissolution	X	19. amendments		27. sessions	X
2. serve as ministers		11. no decree	X	20. war	X	28. secretary	
3. interpellate	X	12. no veto		21. treaties	X	29. staff	
4. investigate	X	13. no review		22. amnesty		30. no term limits	X
5. oversee police		14. no gatekeeping		23. pardon		31. seek re-election	X
6. appoint PM		15. no impoundment		24. judiciary		32. experience	
7. appoint ministers		16. control resources	X	25. central bank			
8. lack president		17. immunity		26. media			
9. no confidence		18. all elected					

The National Assembly of The Gambia was established in the country's 1970 constitution. For the half-decade before that, The Gambia was ruled by a legislative council under British colonial rule and with the assistance of traditional chiefs. The constitution was suspended following a military coup in 1994. It was replaced by a new constitution, adopted in 1996. Yahya Jammeh, a military leader, transformed himself and his military junta into a civilian administration in the 1996 presidential elections.

The unicameral National Assembly has little influence over the executive branch. Its own institutional autonomy is circumscribed by presidential gatekeeping powers and the president's power to appoint some members of the National Assembly. The legislature is granted only a couple of specified powers and has a fairly low level of institutional capacity.

SURVEY

1. The legislature alone, without the involvement of any other agencies, can impeach the president or replace the prime minister.

No. Presidential impeachment requires the establishment of a special tribunal appointed by the chief justice of the Supreme Court.

Article 67

(1) The President may be removed from office in accordance with this section on any of the following grounds –

(a) abuse of office, wilful violation of the oath of allegiance or the President's oath of office, or wilful violation of any provision of this Constitution, or

(b) misconduct in that –

(i) he or she has conducted himself in a manner which brings or is likely to bring the office of President into contempt or disrepute; or

(ii) he or she has dishonestly done any act which is prejudicial or inimical to the economy of The Gambia or dishonestly omitted to act with similar consequences.

(2) Where the Speaker receives a notice in writing signed by not less than one half of all the members of the National Assembly of a motion for the removal of the President on any of the grounds set out in subsection (1), specifying particulars of the allegations (with any necessary documentation), and requesting that a tribunal be appointed to investigate the allegations, the Speaker shall –

(a) inform the President of the notice;

(b) request the Chief Justice to appoint a tribunal consisting of a Justice of the Supreme Court, as Chairman, and not less than four other persons selected by the Chief Justice, at least two of whom shall be persons who hold or have held high judicial office.

(3) The tribunal shall investigate the matter and shall report to the National Assembly through the Speaker

whether or not it finds the allegations specified in the motion to have been substantiated. The President shall have the right to appear and be legally represented before the tribunal.

(4) If the tribunal reports to the National Assembly that it finds that the particulars of any allegation against the President contained in the motion have not been substantiated, no further proceedings shall be taken under this section in respect of that allegation.

(5) Where the tribunal reports to the National Assembly that it finds that the particulars of any such allegation have been substantiated, the National Assembly may, on a motion supported by the votes of not less than two thirds of all the members, resolve that the President has been guilty of such abuse of office, violation of oath, violation of the Constitution, or misconduct or misbehaviour as to render him or her unfit to continue to hold the office of President; and where the National Assembly so resolves, the President shall immediately cease to hold office.

2. Ministers may serve simultaneously as members of the legislature.

No. Legislators are prohibited from serving simultaneously in ministerial positions.

> Article 71
> (2) A person shall not be qualified to be appointed, or hold the office of a Secretary of State if, he or she is a member of the National Assembly.

3. The legislature has powers of summons over executive branch officials and hearings with executive branch officials testifying before the legislature or its committees are regularly held.

Yes. The legislature regularly interpellates officials from the executive.

> Article 77
> (2) The National Assembly may request the President to attend a sitting of the National Assembly for the discussion of a matter of national importance.
> (4) The Vice-President or a Secretary of State shall, when requested by the National Assembly, report to the National Assembly on any matter concerning a department or other business of Government committed to his or her charge.

4. The legislature can conduct independent investigation of the chief executive and the agencies of the executive.

Yes. The legislature can establish committees to investigate the executive.

> Article 109
> (2) Committees may be appointed –
> (a) to investigate or inquire into the activities or administration of ministries or departments of the Government, and such investigation or inquiry may extend to making proposals for legislation;
> (b) to investigate any matter of public importance.

5. The legislature has effective powers of oversight over the agencies of coercion (the military, organs of law enforcement, intelligence services, and the secret police).

No. Despite constitutional provisions to the contrary, the legislature lacks effective powers of oversight over the agencies of coercion.

> Article 109
> (1) The National Assembly shall appoint –
> (d) a Standing Committee on Defence and Security, and such other standing or other committees as it considers necessary for the exercise of its functions.

6. The legislature appoints the prime minister.

No. There is no prime minister.

7. The legislature's approval is required to confirm the appointment of ministers; or the legislature itself appoints ministers.

No. Ministers (secretaries of state) are appointed by the president, and the appointments do not require the legislature's approval.

> Article 71
> (3) Secretaries of State shall be appointed by the President and shall, before assuming the functions of their office, take and subscribe the prescribed oaths.

8. The country lacks a presidency entirely or there is a presidency, but the president is elected by the legislature.

No. The president is directly elected.

> Article 46
> There shall be an election for the office of President in the three months before the expiration of the term of the incumbent President.

9. The legislature can vote no confidence in the government.

No. The legislature can pass a vote of censure against individual ministers (secretaries of state), but not against the government as a whole.

> Article 75
> (1) The National Assembly may, by resolution supported by the votes of two-thirds of all the members, pass a vote of censure against a Secretary of State or Vice President on the grounds of –
> (a) his or her inability, arising from any cause, to perform the functions of his or her office;
> (b) abuse of office or violation of any provision of this Constitution;
> (c) his or her misconduct in office.
> (2) A vote of censure shall be initiated by a petition, signed by not less than one third of all the members of the National Assembly to the President through the

Speaker stating the grounds on which they are dissatisfied with the conduct or performance of the Secretary of State or Vice President.

(3) The President shall cause a copy of the petition to be given to the Secretary of State or Vice President immediately he or she receives it.

(4) The motion for the resolution of censure shall not be debated until after the expiry of fourteen days from the day the petition was sent to the President.

(5) The Secretary of State or Vice President concerned has the right to attend and be heard during the debate on the motion.

(6) In this section, "misconduct in office" means that the person concerned has –

(a) conducted himself or herself in a manner which brings or is likely to bring his or her office into contempt or disrepute;

(b) dishonestly done any act which is prejudicial or inimical to the economy of The Gambia or dishonestly omitted to act with similar consequences.

10. The legislature is immune from dissolution by the executive.

Yes. The legislature is immune from dissolution. Shortly before the 2006 presidential elections and during a period of political tension, however, the legislature voted to allow the president to dissolve it.

11. Any executive initiative on legislation requires ratification or approval by the legislature before it takes effect; that is, the executive lacks decree power.

Yes. The executive lacks decree power.

12. Laws passed by the legislature are veto-proof or essentially veto-proof; that is, the executive lacks veto power, or has veto power but the veto can be overridden by a majority in the legislature.

No. A two-thirds majority vote in the National Assembly is needed to override a presidential veto.

Article 100

(3) Where a Bill passed by the National Assembly is presented to the President for his or her assent, the President shall, within thirty days, assent to the Bill or return it to the National Assembly with the request that the National Assembly reconsider the Bill; and if he or she requests the National Assembly to reconsider the Bill, the President shall state the reasons for the request and any recommendations for amendment of the Bill.

(4) Where the National Assembly has reconsidered a Bill as so requested in accordance with subsection (3) and has resolved by a vote supported by not less than two thirds of all the members of the National Assembly that the Bill, with or without the amendments recommended by the President, be presented again to the

President for his or her assent, the President shall assent to the Bill within seven days of it being so presented.

13. The legislature's laws are supreme and not subject to judicial review.

No. The Supreme Court can review the constitutionality of laws.

Article 127

(1) The Supreme Court shall have an exclusive original jurisdiction –

(a) for the interpretation or enforcement of any provision of this Constitution other than any provision of sections 18 to 33 or section 36(5) (which relate to fundamental rights and freedoms);

(b) on any question whether any law was made in excess of the powers conferred by this Constitution or any other law upon the National Assembly or any other person or authority.

14. The legislature has the right to initiate bills in all policy jurisdictions; the executive lacks gatekeeping authority.

No. The legislature is prohibited from initiating legislation related to taxation, public expenditures, and government debt.

Article 101

(4) Without prejudice to the power of the National Assembly to make any amendment (whether by the increase or reduction of any tax or charges, or the amount of any payment or withdrawal, or otherwise), the National Assembly shall not give consideration to a Bill that in the opinion of the person presiding makes provision for any of the following purposes –

(i) for the imposition of taxation or the alteration of taxation;

(ii) for the imposition of any charges on the Consolidated Revenue Fund or any other public fund of The Gambia or the alteration of any such charge;

(iii) for the payment, issue or withdrawal from the Consolidated Revenue Fund or any other public fund of The Gambia of moneys not charged thereon or any increase in the amount of such payment, issue or withdrawal; or

(iv) for the composition or remission of any debt due to the Government, unless the Bill is introduced into the National Assembly by the President.

15. Expenditure of funds appropriated by the legislature is mandatory; the executive lacks the power to impound funds appropriated by the legislature.

No. The president can impound funds appropriated by the legislature.

16. The legislature controls the resources that finance its own internal operation and provide for the perquisites of its own members.

Yes. The legislature enjoys financial autonomy, including control over members' perquisites.

Article 95
The Speaker, the Deputy Speaker and the other members of the National Assembly shall receive such remuneration and benefits, including retirement benefits, as an Act of the National Assembly may prescribe.

17. Members of the legislature are immune from arrest and/or criminal prosecution.

No. Legislators can be arrested and prosecuted, although not for anything they say, nor for anything at all while they are on their way to, attending, or returning from a legislative session.

Article 113
There shall be freedom of speech and debate in the National Assembly and that freedom shall not be impeached or questioned in any court or place outside the National Assembly.

Article 114
Without prejudice to the generality of section 113, no civil or criminal proceedings shall be instituted against a member of the National Assembly in any court or other place outside the National Assembly by reason of anything said by him.

Article 115
No civil or criminal process issuing from any court or other place outside the National Assembly shall be served on or executed in relation to a member of the National Assembly while he or she is on his or her way to, attending or returning from any proceeding of the National Assembly.

18. All members of the legislature are elected; the executive lacks the power to appoint any members of the legislature.

No. The president appoints about 10 percent of the members of the National Assembly.

Article 88
(1) Members of the National Assembly shall comprise the following –
(a) thirty-nine members elected from the Chieftaincy Districts, each of which district shall constitute a constituency;
(b) three members elected from the constituencies in Banjul, namely, Banjul North, Banjul South and Banjul Central;
(c) three members elected from the constituencies in the Kanifing Municipality, namely, Serrekunda West, Serrekunda East and Bakau; and
(d) four members nominated by the President.

19. The legislature alone, without the involvement of any other agencies, can change the Constitution.

No. The legislature alone cannot change the constitution without the approval of the president. If the

president objects to a constitutional amendment that has been passed by a two-thirds majority vote in the Assembly, he or she can choose to put the amendment to a nationwide referendum.

Article 226
(1) Subject to the provisions of this section, an Act of the National Assembly may alter this Constitution.
(2) Subject to subsection (4), a bill for an Act of the National Assembly under this section shall not be passed by the National Assembly or presented to the President for assent unless –
(a) before the first reading of the Bill in the National Assembly, the Bill is published in at least two issues of the Gazette, the latest publication being not less than three months after the first, and the Bill is introduced into the National Assembly not earlier than ten days after the latest publication;
(b) the Bill is supported on the second and third readings by the votes of not less than three quarters of all the members of the National Assembly.
(3) If the President fails to assent within thirty days to a Bill passed by the National Assembly in accordance with subsection (2), the Bill shall be returned to the Speaker who shall refer it to the Independent Electoral Commission. The Independent Electoral Commission shall cause a referendum to be held on the Bill in accordance with subsection (4) and, if the Bill is supported on such a referendum by the majority provided for in that subsection, it shall again be presented to the President for his assent.

20. The legislature's approval is necessary for the declaration of war.

Yes. The legislature's approval is necessary for presidential war declarations.

Article 79
(1) The President shall be responsible for –
(d) subject to the prior approval of the National Assembly, the declaration of war and the making of peace.

21. The legislature's approval is necessary to ratify treaties with foreign countries.

Yes. The legislature's approval is necessary to ratify international treaties.

Article 79
(1) The President shall be responsible for –
(c) the negotiation and, subject to ratification by the National Assembly, the conclusion of treaties and other international agreements;
(2) The Gambia shall not –
(a) enter into any engagement with any other country which causes it to lose its sovereignty without the matter first being put to a referendum and passed by such majority as may be prescribed by an Act of the National Assembly;

(b) become a member of any international organization unless the National Assembly is satisfied that it is in the interest of The Gambia and that membership does not derogate from its sovereignty.

(3) The National Assembly may, by resolution, establish procedures for the ratification of treaties and other international agreements.

22. The legislature has the power to grant amnesty.

No. The president has the power to grant amnesty. Amnesty and pardon are not treated separately. See item 23.

23. The legislature has the power of pardon.

No. The president has the power of pardon.

Article 82
(1) The President may, after consulting the Committee established by subsection (2) –
(a) grant to any person convicted of any offence a pardon either free or subject to lawful conditions;
(b) grant to any person a respite, either indefinite or for a specified period, of the execution of any punishment imposed on that person for any offence;
(c) substitute a less severe form of punishment for any punishment imposed on any person for any offence;
(d) remit the whole or any part of any punishment imposed on any person for such an offence or any penalty otherwise due to the Republic on account of any offence.

24. The legislature reviews and has the right to reject appointments to the judiciary; or the legislature itself appoints members of the judiciary.

No. Formally, the legislature has a minimal role in selecting judges, but in practice, the president controls judicial appointments.

Article 134
(3) The members of the Special Criminal Court shall be appointed by the Judicial Service Commission subject to the approval of the National Assembly.

Article 138
(1) The Chief Justice shall be appointed by the President after consultation with the Judicial Service Commission.
(2) All other judges of the superior courts except the judges of the Special Criminal Court shall be appointed by the President on the recommendation of the Judicial Service Commission.

25. The chairman of the central bank is appointed by the legislature.

No. The president appoints the chairman of the Central Bank of Gambia.

Article 162
(1) The authority of the Central Bank shall vest in the Board of Directors of the Bank which shall comprise –
(a) a Chairman, who shall be the Governor and Chief Executive of the Bank; and
(b) four other Directors.
(2) The members of the Board of Directors shall be appointed from among persons of standing and experience in financial matters by the President, in consultation with the Public Service Commission.

26. The legislature has a substantial voice in the operation of the state-owned media.

No. The legislature lacks a substantial voice in the operation of the public media.

27. The legislature is regularly in session.

Yes. The legislature is required to meet in ordinary session for only five months each year, but in practice, it normally meets for six months or longer.

Article 98
(b) The National Assembly shall sit for a period of not less than one hundred and fifty days a year.

28. Each legislator has a personal secretary.

No.

29. Each legislator has at least one non-secretarial staff member with policy expertise.

No.

30. Legislators are eligible for re-election without any restriction.

Yes. There are no restrictions on re-election.

31. A seat in the legislature is an attractive enough position that legislators are generally interested in and seek re-election.

Yes.

32. The re-election of incumbent legislators is common enough that at any given time the legislature contains a significant number of highly experienced members.

No. The turnover rate is high, resulting in few highly experienced legislators.

SUPREME COUNCIL OF GEORGIA (*PARLAMENTI*)

Expert consultants: Ivlian Haindrava, Nina Khatiskatsi, Mark Mullen, Ghia Nodia, Colette Selman

Score: .59

Influence over executive (5/9)		Institutional autonomy (5/9)		Specified powers (5/8)		Institutional capacity (4/6)	
1. replace		10. no dissolution		19. amendments	X	27. sessions	X
2. serve as ministers		11. no decree		20. war	X	28. secretary	
3. interpellate	X	12. no veto		21. treaties	X	29. staff	
4. investigate	X	13. no review		22. amnesty		30. no term limits	X
5. oversee police	X	14. no gatekeeping	X	23. pardon		31. seek re-election	X
6. appoint PM		15. no impoundment	X	24. judiciary	X	32. experience	X
7. appoint ministers	X	16. control resources	X	25. central bank			
8. lack president		17. immunity	X	26. media	X		
9. no confidence	X	18. all elected	X				

The Supreme Council (*Parlamenti*) of Georgia first met in 1918 and was formally established in the country's 1921 constitution. Shortly after the constitution was drawn up, it was rendered inoperative by Georgia's incorporation into the Soviet Union. Georgia gained independence in 1991, and in 1995 parliament drafted and adopted the current constitution. The document calls for a unicameral legislature. Following the "Rose Revolution" of 2004, a sweeping constitutional amendment altered parliament's powers. The 2004 amendments introduced a government under a prime minister as a body of executive power separate from the presidency. Under the amendments, the legislature gained the power to vote no confidence in the government. Prior to 2004 parliament lacked the ability to vote no confidence. The amendment also gave the president the authority to dissolve the parliament under certain circumstances. Previously the parliament had been immune from dissolution.

The legislature enjoys some ability to influence the executive branch. In addition to holding the power of confirmation of the president's ministerial appointments, parliament can interpellate and investigate executive branch officials. Parliament has some institutional autonomy, although it is limited by presidential decree, veto, and the aforementioned dissolution powers. It is granted a few specified powers and prerogatives and has a fair amount of institutional capacity.

SURVEY

1. The legislature alone, without the involvement of any other agencies, can impeach the president or replace the prime minister.

No. Presidential impeachment for treason requires the involvement of the Supreme Court, and impeachment for violation of the constitution requires a decision by the Constitutional Court. The legislature can remove the prime minister with a vote of no confidence.

Article 63
1. Under the circumstances defined in the second paragraph of Article 75, not less than one third of the total number of the members of the Parliament shall be entitled to raise the question of the dismissal of the President of Georgia in accordance with impeachment procedure. The case shall be submitted to the Supreme Court or Constitutional Court for a conclusion.
2. If, by its conclusion, the Supreme Court confirmed corpus delicti in the act of the President or the Constitutional Court confirmed the violation of the Constitution, after having discussed the conclusion the Parliament shall adopt a decision by the majority of votes of the total number of the members of the Parliament on putting the issue of impeachment of the President to the vote.

3. The President shall be deemed to be dismissed from the office in accordance with impeachment procedure, if not less than two thirds of the total number of the members of the Parliament supported the decision.

Article 75
1. The President of Georgia shall enjoy personal immunity. While holding his/her position, his/her detention or proceeding shall be impermissible.
2. In case of the violation of the Constitution, commission of high treason and other criminal offence, the Parliament shall be authorized to dismiss the President in accordance with a procedures of Article 63 of the Constitution and in accordance with a procedures determined by the Organic Law if:
a. the violation of the Constitution is confirmed by a judgment of the Constitutional Court;
b. corpus delicti of high treason and other criminal offence is confirmed by a conclusion of the Supreme Court.

Article 81
1. The Parliament shall be entitled to declare non-confidence to the Government by the majority of the total number. Not less than one third of the total number of the members of the Parliament shall be entitled to raise a question of declaration of non-confidence. After the declaration of non-confidence to the Government the President of Georgia shall dismiss the Government or not approve the decision of the Parliament. In case the Parliament declares non-confidence to the Government again not earlier than 90 days and not later than 100 days, the President of Georgia shall dismiss the Government or dissolve the Parliament and schedule extraordinary elections. In case of circumstances provided for by subparagraphs "a"–"d" of Article 51 re-voting of non-confidence shall be held within 15 days from the end of these circumstances.
2. The Parliament shall be entitled to raise the question of declaration of unconditional non-confidence to the Government by a resolution. In case the Parliament declares non-confidence to the Government by the majority of three-fifth of the total number of the members of the Parliament not earlier than 15 days and not later than 20 days from the adoption of the resolution, the President shall dismiss the Government. In case the Parliament does not declare non-confidence to the Government, it shall be impermissible to put the question of non-confidence to the Government within next 6 months.

2. Ministers may serve simultaneously as members of the legislature.

No. Legislators are prohibited from serving simultaneously in ministerial positions.

Article 53
1. A member of the Parliament shall not be entitled to hold any position in public office or engage in an entrepreneurial activity. The conflict of interests shall be determined by law.

3. The legislature has powers of summons over executive branch officials and hearings with executive branch officials testifying before the legislature or its committees are regularly held.

Yes. The legislature regularly interpellates officials from the executive.

Article 59
1. A member of the Parliament shall be entitled to apply with a question to the bodies accountable to the Parliament, [including] a member of the Government . . . and to receive answers from them.
2. A group of at least ten members of the Parliament or a Parliamentary Faction shall be entitled to apply with a question to any body accountable to the Parliament, the Government, a particular member of the Government the latter being obliged to answer the raised questions at a sitting of the Parliament. The answer may become a matter of discussion of the Parliament.

4. The legislature can conduct independent investigation of the chief executive and the agencies of the executive.

Yes. The legislature can establish committees to investigate the executive.

Article 56
1. To prepare the legislative agenda, facilitate the implementation of decisions adopted by Parliament and to control the activities of the bodies accountable to Parliament and the Government, committees shall be set up for the duration of the term of Parliament.
2. In the cases defined in the Constitution and in the rules of procedure of Parliament, as well as upon the request of no fewer than one fourth of the members of Parliament, investigative or other temporary committees are established by Parliament. The representation of the parliamentary majority in such a committee shall not exceed half of the total number of its members.
3. At the request of the investigative committee, attendance at its meetings as well as the submission of documents required for the investigation of the matter under consideration are obligatory.

5. The legislature has effective powers of oversight over the agencies of coercion (the military, organs of law enforcement, intelligence services, and the secret police).

Yes. Legislative committees have effective oversight powers over the agencies of coercion. For example, in a recent episode, the opposition in the legislature came upon a secret Ministry of Security document that included proposals for spying on opposition parties. The Minister of Security was speedily summoned to a hearing in which he renounced the plan and sacked the employee who drafted the document.

Article 59

1. A member of the Parliament shall be entitled to apply with a question to the bodies accountable to the Parliament, [including] a member of the Government . . . and to receive answers from them.

2. A group of at least ten members of the Parliament or a Parliamentary Faction shall be entitled to apply with a question to any body accountable to the Parliament, the Government, a particular member of the Government the latter being obliged to answer the raised questions at a sitting of the Parliament. The answer may become a matter of discussion of the Parliament.

6. The legislature appoints the prime minister.

No. The president appoints the prime minister. Prior to 2004 there was no prime minister.

Article 73

1. The President of Georgia:
   b. appoints the Prime Minister and approves the appointments of the other members of Government, such as ministers, by the Prime Minister.

7. The legislature's approval is required to confirm the appointment of ministers; or the legislature itself appoints ministers.

Yes. The president appoints ministers on the recommendation of the prime minister, and the appointments require the legislature's approval. The legislature can disapprove of individual ministers by raising a "question of recusal." Prior to 2004 ministerial appointments did not require parliament's approval.

Article 73

1. The President of Georgia:
   b. appoints the Prime Minister and approves the appointments of the other members of Government, such as ministers, by the Prime Minister.

Article 79

5. The Prime Minister shall appoint other members of the Government by the consent of the President, be authorized to dismiss the members of the Government.

Article 80

3. Within a week from the submission of the composition of the Government by the President of Georgia the Parliament shall consider and vote the issue of declaration of confidence to the composition of the Government and the Governmental program. The confidence of the Parliament shall be gained by the majority of the total number of the members of the Parliament. The members of the Government shall be appointed within a term of three days from the declaration of confidence. The Parliament shall be entitled to declare non-confidence to the composition of the Government and raise a question of recusal of a particular member of the Government in the same decision. In case of approval of the decision of the Parliament on the recusal by the President the recused person shall not be

appointed in the same composition of the Government instead of a dismissed or resigned member.

8. The country lacks a presidency entirely or there is a presidency, but the president is elected by the legislature.

No. The president is directly elected.

Article 70

1. The President of Georgia shall be elected on the basis of universal, equal and direct suffrage by secret ballot for a term of five years.

9. The legislature can vote no confidence in the government.

Yes. The legislature can vote no confidence in the government.

Article 81

1. The Parliament shall be entitled to declare non-confidence to the Government by the majority of the total number. Not less than one third of the total number of the members of the Parliament shall be entitled to raise a question of declaration of non-confidence. After the declaration of non-confidence to the Government the President of Georgia shall dismiss the Government or not approve the decision of the Parliament. In case the Parliament declares non-confidence to the Government again not earlier than 90 days and not later than 100 days, the President of Georgia shall dismiss the Government or dissolve the Parliament and schedule extraordinary elections.

2. The Parliament shall be entitled to raise the question of declaration of unconditional non-confidence to the Government by a resolution. In case the Parliament declares non-confidence to the Government by the majority of three-fifth of the total number of the members of the Parliament not earlier than 15 days and not later than 20 days from the adoption of the resolution, the President shall dismiss the Government. In case the Parliament does not declare non-confidence to the Government, it shall be impermissible to put the question of non-confidence to the Government within next 6 months.

10. The legislature is immune from dissolution by the executive.

No. The president can dissolve the legislature. Prior to 2004 the legislature was immune from dissolution.

Article 51

The Parliament shall be dissolved by the President only in cases determined by the Constitution.

Article 73

1. The President of Georgia shall:
   c. be entitled to dissolve the Government, dismiss the Ministers of Internal Affairs, Defence and State Security of Georgia on his/her own initiative or in other cases envisaged by the Constitution;

o. dissolve the Parliament in accordance with a procedure and in cases established by the Constitution.

Article 80

5. In case a composition of the Government and the program of the Governmental thereof do not gain the confidence of the Parliament for three times, the President of Georgia shall nominate a new candidate of the Prime Minister within a term of 5 days or appoint the Prime Minister without consent of the Parliament, whereas the Prime Minister shall appoint the Ministers by the consent of the President of Georgia within a term of 5 days as well. In such a case the President of Georgia shall dissolve the Parliament and schedule extraordinary elections.

Article 81

1. The Parliament shall be entitled to declare non-confidence to the Government by the majority of the total number. Not less than one third of the total number of the members of the Parliament shall be entitled to raise a question of declaration of non-confidence. After the declaration of non-confidence to the Government the President of Georgia shall dismiss the Government or not approve the decision of the Parliament. In case the Parliament declares non-confidence to the Government again not earlier than 90 days and not later than 100 days, the President of Georgia shall dismiss the Government or dissolve the Parliament and schedule extraordinary elections.

Article 93

2. The Government shall submit the Draft Budget of next year to the Parliament not later than three months before the end of the budget year. Together with the Draft Budget, the Government shall submit a report on the progress of the fulfilment of the State Budget of the current year. The Government shall submit a report on the fulfilment of the State Budget to the Parliament for approval not later than three months from the end of the budget year. In case of non-fulfilment of the State Budget the Parliament does not approve a report on the fulfilment of the State Budget, the President of Georgia shall consider the issue of liability of the Government and inform the Parliament on his/her founded decision within a month.

6. If the Parliament fails to adopt the Budget submitted in accordance with a procedure established by paragraph 2 of this Article within three months, the President of Georgia shall be authorised to dismiss the Government or dissolve the Parliament and schedule extraordinary elections.

11. Any executive initiative on legislation requires ratification or approval by the legislature before it takes effect; that is, the executive lacks decree power.

No. The president can issue decrees that have the force of law on tax and budgetary issues between the dissolution of one parliament and the convocation of the next. The decrees lapse if they are not subsequently approved by parliament.

Article 73

1. The President of Georgia shall:

j. issue decrees and orders on the basis of the Constitution and law;

q. from the dissolution of the Parliament to the first convocation of the newly elected Parliament, in the exclusive cases, be entitled to issue a decree having the force of law on tax and budgetary issues, which shall be invalid in case it is not approved by the newly elected Parliament within a month from the first convocation.

12. Laws passed by the legislature are veto-proof or essentially veto-proof; that is, the executive lacks veto power, or has veto power but the veto can be overridden by a majority in the legislature.

No. A three-fifths majority vote in the legislature is needed to override a presidential veto.

Article 68

1. A draft law adopted by the Parliament shall be submitted to the President of Georgia within a term of seven days.

2. The President shall sign and promulgate the law within a term of ten days or return it to the Parliament with reasoned remarks.

3. If the President returns the draft law to the Parliament, the latter shall put to the vote the remarks of the President. For the adoption of the remarks the same number of votes shall suffice as determined for this kind of draft law by Article 66 of the Constitution. If the remarks are adopted, the final redaction of the draft law shall be submitted to the President who shall sign and promulgate it within a term of seven days.

4. If the Parliament rejects the remarks of the President, the initial redaction of the draft law shall be put to the vote. A law or an Organic Law shall be deemed to be adopted if it is supported by not less than three fifths of the number of the members of the Parliament on the current nominal list. The constitutional amendment shall be deemed to be passed if it is supported by not less than two thirds of the total number of the members of the Parliament.

5. If the President fails to promulgate the draft law within the defined term, the President of the Parliament shall sign and promulgate it.

13. The legislature's laws are supreme and not subject to judicial review.

No. The Constitutional Court can review the constitutionality of laws.

Article 89

1. The Constitutional Court of Georgia on the basis of a constitutional claim or a submission of the President of Georgia, the Government, not less than one fifth of the members of the Parliament, a court, the higher representative bodies the Autonomous Republic of Abkhazia and the Autonomous Republic of Ajara, the

Public Defender or a citizen in accordance with a procedure established by the Organic Law) shall:
  a. adjudicate upon the constitutionality of a Constitutional Agreement, law, [and] normative acts of the President and the Government.

14. The legislature has the right to initiate bills in all policy jurisdictions; the executive lacks gatekeeping authority.

Yes. The legislature can initiate bills in all policy jurisdictions.

15. Expenditure of funds appropriated by the legislature is mandatory; the executive lacks the power to impound funds appropriated by the legislature.

Yes. The executive lacks the power to impound funds appropriated by the legislature.

16. The legislature controls the resources that finance its own internal operation and provide for the perquisites of its own members.

Yes. The legislature enjoys financial autonomy, including control over members' remuneration.

Article 53
3. A member of the Parliament shall receive remuneration as determined by law.

17. Members of the legislature are immune from arrest and/or criminal prosecution.

Yes. Legislators are immune. Even in cases of *flagrante delicto*, legislators must be immediately released if the parliament does not consent to their prosecution.

Article 52
2. Arrest or detention of a member of the Parliament, the search of his/her apartment, car, workplace or his/her person shall be permissible only by the consent of the Parliament, except in the cases when he/she is caught flagrante delicto which shall immediately be notified to the Parliament. Unless the Parliament gives the consent, the arrested or detained member of the Parliament shall immediately be released.
3. A member of the Parliament shall have the right not to testify on the fact disclosed to him/her as to a member of the Parliament. Seizure of written materials connected with this matter shall be impermissible. The right shall also be reserved to a member of the Parliament after the termination of his/her office.
4. A member of the Parliament shall not be proceeded on the account of the ideas and opinions expressed by him/her in and outside the Parliament while performing his/her duties.

18. All members of the legislature are elected; the executive lacks the power to appoint any members of the legislature.

Yes. All members of the legislature are elected.

Article 49
1. The Parliament of Georgia shall consist of 150 members of the Parliament elected by a proportional system and 85 members elected by a majority system for a term of four years on the basis of universal, equal and direct suffrage by secret ballot.

19. The legislature alone, without the involvement of any other agencies, can change the Constitution.

Yes. The legislature can pass a bill to amend the constitution with a two-thirds majority vote. If the bill is vetoed by the president, the legislature can override the president's veto with a two-thirds majority vote.

Article 102
1. The following shall be entitled to submit a draft law on general or partial revision of the Constitution: the President; more than half of the total number of the members of the Parliament; not less than 200,000 electors.
2. A draft law on the revision of the Constitution shall be submitted to the Parliament, which shall promulgate the former for the public discussion. The Parliament shall begin the discussion of the draft law after a month from its promulgation.
3. The draft law on the revision of the Constitution shall be deemed to be adopted if it is supported by at least two thirds of the total number of the members of the Parliament of Georgia.
4. The law on the revision of the Constitution shall be signed and promulgated by the President of Georgia in accordance with a procedure provided for by Article 68 of the Constitution.

Article 68
1. A draft law adopted by the Parliament shall be submitted to the President of Georgia within a term of seven days.
2. The President shall sign and promulgate the law within a term of ten days or return it to the Parliament with reasoned remarks.
3. If the President returns the draft law to the Parliament, the latter shall put to the vote the remarks of the President. For the adoption of the remarks the same number of votes shall suffice as determined for this kind of draft law by Article 66 of the Constitution. If the remarks are adopted, the final redaction of the draft law shall be submitted to the President who shall sign and promulgate it within a term of seven days.
4. If the Parliament rejects the remarks of the President, the initial redaction of the draft law shall be put to the vote. A law or an Organic Law shall be deemed to be adopted if it is supported by not less than three fifths of the number of the members of the Parliament on the current nominal list. The constitutional amendment shall be deemed to be passed if it is supported by not less than two thirds of the total number of the members of the Parliament.

5. If the President fails to promulgate the draft law within the defined term, the President of the Parliament shall sign and promulgate it.

20. The legislature's approval is necessary for the declaration of war.

Yes. The legislature declares war. Since 2004 presidential decisions on the "use of the armed forces" require the legislature's approval. Prior to 2004 the president was not required to obtain parliamentary approval before dispatching troops abroad.

Article 62
Decision of the Parliament on the issues of war and peace, state of emergency or martial law and issues determined by Article 46 of the Constitution shall be adopted by the majority of the total number of the members of the Parliament.

Article 100
1. The President of Georgia shall adopt a decision on the use of the armed forces and submit it to the Parliament within 48 hours for approval. In addition the use of the armed forces for the honouring international obligations shall be impermissible without the consent of the Parliament of Georgia.
2. For the purpose of state defence in the exclusive cases and in cases envisaged by law, the decision about the entrance, use and movement of the armed forces of another state on the territory of Georgia shall be adopted by the President of Georgia. The decision shall immediately be submitted to the Parliament for approval and shall be enforced after the consent of the Parliament.

21. The legislature's approval is necessary to ratify treaties with foreign countries.

Yes. The legislature's approval is necessary to ratify international treaties on most major issues.

Article 65
1. The Parliament of Georgia by the majority of the total number of the members of the Parliament shall ratify, denounce and annul the international treaties and agreements.
2. Apart from the international treaties and agreements providing for ratification, it shall also be obligatory to ratify an international treaty and agreement which: provides for accession of Georgia to an international organisation or intergovernmental union; is of a military character; pertains to the territorial integrity of the state or change of the state frontiers; is related to borrowing or lending loans by the state; requires a change of domestic legislation, adoption of necessary laws and acts with force of law with the view of honouring the undertaken international obligations.
3. The Parliament shall be notified about the conclusion of other international treaties and agreements.

4. In case of lodging a constitutional claim or a submission with the Constitutional Court, ratification of the respective international treaty or agreement shall be impermissible before adjudication by the Constitutional Court.

22. The legislature has the power to grant amnesty.

No. The president has the power to grant amnesty. Amnesty and pardon are not treated separately. See item 23.

23. The legislature has the power of pardon.

No. The president has the power of pardon.

Article 73
1. The President of Georgia:
   n. grants pardon to convicted persons.

24. The legislature reviews and has the right to reject appointments to the judiciary; or the legislature itself appoints members of the judiciary.

Yes. The legislature elects three of the nine judges of the Constitutional Court and all of the judges on the Supreme Court.

Article 88
2. The Constitutional Court of Georgia shall consist of nine judges – the members of the Constitutional Court. Three members of the Constitutional Court shall be appointed by the President of Georgia, three members shall be elected by the Parliament by not less than three fifths of the number of the members of the Parliament on the current nominal list, three members shall be appointed by the Supreme Court.

Article 90
2. The President and the judges of the Supreme Court of Georgia shall be elected for a period of not less than ten years by the Parliament by the majority of the number of the members of Parliament on the current nominal list upon the submission of the President of Georgia.

25. The chairman of the central bank is appointed by the legislature.

No. The president appoints the president of the National Bank of Georgia.

Article 96
1. The Council of the National Bank shall be the higher body of the National Bank of Georgia. The members of the Council of the National Bank shall be elected for a term of seven years by the Parliament by the majority of the number of the members of the Parliament on the current nominal list upon the submission of the President of Georgia. The dismissal of the members of the Council of the National Bank shall be permissible only under a decision of the Parliament in accordance with Article 64.
2. The President of the National Bank shall be appointed and dismissed by the President of Georgia of the Bank

upon the submission of the Council of the National Bank among the members of the Council.

26. The legislature has a substantial voice in the operation of the state-owned media.

Yes. The Board of Trustees that oversees public broadcasting is elected by the legislature. The initial nine-member board was elected from a slate of eighteen candidates presented by the president. In order to fill openings on the board, the parliament selects one of three candidates proposed by the president.

27. The legislature is regularly in session.

Yes. The legislature meets in ordinary session for eight months each year.

> Article 61
> 1. The Parliament of Georgia shall assemble ex officio for a regular session twice a year. The autumn session shall open on the first Tuesday of September and close on the third Friday of December. The spring session shall open on the first Tuesday of February and close on the last Friday of June.

28. Each legislator has a personal secretary.

No. By law, legislators are entitled to personal staff, but in practice, legislative staffs have been limited by budgetary constraints.

29. Each legislator has at least one non-secretarial staff member with policy expertise.

No. See item 28.

30. Legislators are eligible for re-election without any restriction.

Yes. There are no restrictions on re-election.

31. A seat in the legislature is an attractive enough position that legislators are generally interested in and seek re-election.

Yes.

32. The re-election of incumbent legislators is common enough that at any given time the legislature contains a significant number of highly experienced members.

Yes. Re-election rates are sufficiently high to produce a significant number of highly experienced members.

PARLIAMENT OF THE FEDERAL REPUBLIC OF GERMANY (*BUNDESTAG*)

Expert consultants: Alison B. Alter, David Bach, Sebastian Karcher, Gerhard Loewenberg, Carsten Schneider, Tobias Schulze-Cleven, Christian Soe, J. Nicholas Ziegler

Score: .84

Influence over executive (8/9)		Institutional autonomy (7/9)		Specified powers (6/8)		Institutional capacity (6/6)	
1. replace	X	10. no dissolution		19. amendments	X	27. sessions	X
2. serve as ministers	X	11. no decree	X	20. war	X	28. secretary	X
3. interpellate	X	12. no veto	X	21. treaties	X	29. staff	X
4. investigate	X	13. no review		22. amnesty	X	30. no term limits	X
5. oversee police	X	14. no gatekeeping	X	23. pardon		31. seek re-election	X
6. appoint PM	X	15. no impoundment	X	24. judiciary	X	32. experience	X
7. appoint ministers		16. control resources	X	25. central bank			
8. lack president	X	17. immunity	X	26. media	X		
9. no confidence	X	18. all elected	X				

The Parliament (*Bundestag*) of the Federal Republic of Germany was founded in the Federal Republic's 1949 constitution. The bicameral legislature consists of the popularly elected House of Representatives (*Bundestag*) and the Senate (*Bundesrat*), whose members are appointed by the governments of the states. In 1990 East Germany acceded to the Federal Republic of Germany under the 1949 constitutional framework.

The legislature is the center of German politics and government. It exerts formidable influence over the executive. It appoints and removes the prime minister (chancellor), comprises half of the membership of the electoral college that elects the (largely ceremonial) president, and wields effective oversight and investigatory authority. Its members, moreover, serve in ministerial positions. Parliament also has great autonomy in the legislative process. It can introduce bills in all policy jurisdictions, and bills are not subject to veto, although most bills are introduced by the cabinet. In terms of specified powers and prerogatives, the legislature is also strong. Of the eight powers listed in this category, the German parliament has six. The legislature is also equipped with substantial institutional capacity, holding every measure of institutional capacity measured in this survey. It attracts and retains talented politicians, who are provided with adequate staff and resources.

A distinctive feature of the German system is the constructive vote of no confidence, according to which the parliament must designate a successor chancellor before passing a vote of no confidence in the sitting government or risk its own dissolution.

SURVEY

1. The legislature alone, without the involvement of any other agencies, can impeach the president or replace the prime minister.

Yes. The House of Representatives can replace the chancellor with a constructive vote of no confidence, meaning that the parliament must designate a successor chancellor before passing a vote of no confidence. Presidential impeachment requires the involvement of the Federal Constitutional Court.

Article 61
(1) The House of Representatives or the Senate may impeach the President before the Federal Constitutional Court for willful violation of this Constitution or any other federal statute. The motion of impeachment is filed by at least one quarter of the members of the House of Representatives or one quarter of the votes of the Senate. A decision to impeach requires a majority of two thirds of the members of the House of Representatives or of two thirds of the votes of the Senate. The impeachment is pleaded by a person commissioned by the impeaching body.

(2) Where the Federal Constitutional Court finds the President guilty of a willful violation of this Constitution or of another federal statute, it may declare him to have forfeited his office. After impeachment, it may issue an interim order preventing the President from exercising his functions.

Article 67
(1) The House of Representatives can express its lack of confidence in the Chancellor only by electing a successor with the majority of its members and by requesting the President to dismiss the Chancellor.

2. Ministers may serve simultaneously as members of the legislature.

Yes. Since 1949 the overwhelming majority of ministers have served simultaneously as members of the House of Representatives.

3. The legislature has powers of summons over executive branch officials and hearings with executive branch officials testifying before the legislature or its committees are regularly held.

Yes. The standing committees of the legislature often question the ministers.

4. The legislature can conduct independent investigation of the chief executive and the agencies of the executive.

Yes. The legislature can establish committees to investigate the executive.

Article 44
(1) The House of Representatives has the right, and upon the motion of one quarter of its members the duty, to set up a committee of investigation, which takes the requisite evidence at public hearings.

5. The legislature has effective powers of oversight over the agencies of coercion (the military, organs of law enforcement, intelligence services, and the secret police).

Yes. Legislative committees have effective powers of oversight over the agencies of coercion.

Article 45a
(1) The House of Representatives appoints a Committee on Foreign Affairs and Committee on Defence.
(2) The Committee on Defence also has the rights of a committee of investigation. Upon the motion of one quarter of its members it has the duty to make a specific matter the subject of investigation.

Article 45b
A Defence Commissioner of the House of Representatives is appointed to safeguard the basic rights and to assist the House of Representatives in exercising parliamentary control. Details are regulated by a federal statute.

6. The legislature appoints the prime minister.

Yes. The House of Representatives elects the chancellor.

> Article 63
> (1) The Chancellor is elected, without debate, by the House of Representatives upon the proposal of the President.
> (2) The person obtaining the votes of the majority of the members of the House of Representatives is elected. The person elected is appointed by the President.

7. The legislature's approval is required to confirm the appointment of ministers; or the legislature itself appoints ministers.

No. The president appoints ministers on the recommendation of the chancellor, and the appointments do not require the legislature's approval.

> Article 64
> (1) The Ministers are appointed and dismissed by the President upon the proposal of the Chancellor.

8. The country lacks a presidency entirely or there is a presidency, but the president is elected by the legislature.

Yes. The president is elected by a Federal Convention consisting of the members of the House of Representatives and members elected by the state parliaments.

> Article 54
> (1) The President is elected, without debate, by the Federal Convention. Every German who is entitled to vote in House of Representatives elections and has attained the age of forty years is eligible for election.
> (2) The term of office of the President is five years. Reelection for a consecutive term is permitted only once.
> (3) The Federal Convention consists of the members of the House of Representatives [*Bundestag*] and an equal number of members elected by the parliaments of the States according to the principles of proportional representation.

9. The legislature can vote no confidence in the government.

Yes. The House of Representatives has a constructive vote of no confidence, meaning that the parliament must designate a successor chancellor before passing a vote of no confidence.

> Article 67
> (1) The House of Representatives can express its lack of confidence in the Chancellor only by electing a successor with the majority of its members and by requesting the President to dismiss the Chancellor. The

President complies with the request and appoints the person elected.

> Article 68
> (1) Where a motion of the Chancellor for a vote of confidence is not carried by the majority of the members of the House of Representatives, the President may, upon the proposal of the Chancellor, dissolve the House of Representatives within twenty-one days. The right of dissolution lapses as soon as the House of Representatives elects another Chancellor with the majority of its members.

10. The legislature is immune from dissolution by the executive.

No. The president, on the proposal of the chancellor, can dissolve the House of Representatives.

> Article 68
> (1) Where a motion of the Chancellor for a vote of confidence is not carried by the majority of the members of the House of Representatives, the President may, upon the proposal of the Chancellor, dissolve the House of Representatives within twenty-one days. The right of dissolution lapses as soon as the House of Representatives elects another Chancellor with the majority of its members.

11. Any executive initiative on legislation requires ratification or approval by the legislature before it takes effect; that is, the executive lacks decree power.

Yes. The executive lacks decree power.

12. Laws passed by the legislature are veto-proof or essentially veto-proof; that is, the executive lacks veto power, or has veto power but the veto can be overridden by a majority in the legislature.

Yes. The president lacks veto power.

13. The legislature's laws are supreme and not subject to judicial review.

No. The Federal Constitutional Court can review the constitutionality of laws.

> Article 93
> (1) The Federal Constitutional Court decides:
> 2. in case of differences of opinion or doubts on the formal and material compatibility of federal law or State law with this Constitution . . . at the request of the Government, of a State government, or of one third of the House of Representatives members.

14. The legislature has the right to initiate bills in all policy jurisdictions; the executive lacks gatekeeping authority.

Yes. The legislature can initiate bills in all policy jurisdictions of federal (national) concern, meaning all areas except where power is reserved to the states.

15. Expenditure of funds appropriated by the legislature is mandatory; the executive lacks the power to impound funds appropriated by the legislature.

Yes. The executive lacks the power to impound funds appropriated by the legislature.

16. The legislature controls the resources that finance its own internal operation and provide for the perquisites of its own members.

Yes. The legislature enjoys financial autonomy. Members' salaries are protected by law.

Article 48
(3) Deputies are entitled to adequate remuneration ensuring their independence . . . Details are regulated by a federal statute.

17. Members of the legislature are immune from arrest and/or criminal prosecution.

Yes. Legislators are immune with the exceptions of "defamatory insults" and *flagrante delicto,* here expressed as "apprehended during commission of the offence or in the course of the following day." In practice, the exception for "defamatory insults" is not used to threaten or intimidate opponents.

Article 46
(1) A deputy may not at any time be subjected to court proceedings or disciplinary action or otherwise called to account outside the House of Representatives for a vote cast or a statement made by him in the House of Representatives or in any of its committees. This does not apply to defamatory insults.
(2) A deputy may not be called to account or arrested for a punishable offence except by permission of the House of Representatives, unless he is apprehended during commission of the offence or in the course of the following day.

18. All members of the legislature are elected; the executive lacks the power to appoint any members of the legislature.

Yes. The executive lacks the power to appoint members of the legislature. The members of the Senate are appointed at the state level.

Article 38
(1) The deputies to the German House of Representatives are elected in general, direct, free, equal, and secret elections.

Article 51
(1) The Senate consists of members of the State governments which appoint and recall them.

19. The legislature alone, without the involvement of any other agencies, can change the Constitution.

Yes. The legislature can change the constitution with a two-thirds majority vote.

Article 79
(1) This Constitution can be amended only by statutes which expressly amend or supplement the text thereof.
(2) Any such statute requires the consent of two thirds of the members of the House of Representatives and two thirds of the votes of the Senate.

20. The legislature's approval is necessary for the declaration of war.

Yes. The legislature's approval is required to declare a "state of defense." Recently, the House of Representatives played a major role in debating and approving the deployments of German troops outside the NATO area to the former Yugoslavia and Afghanistan.

Article 80a
(1) Where this Constitution or a federal statute on defence, including the protection of the civilian population, stipulates that legal provisions may only be applied in accordance with this Article, their application is, except in a state of defence, admissible only after the House of Representatives has determined that a state of tension exists or where it has specifically approved such application.

Article 115a
(1) The determination that federal territory is being attacked by armed force or that such an attack is directly imminent are made by the House of Representatives with the consent of the Senate. Such determination are made at the request of the Government and require a two-thirds majority of the votes cast, which include at least the majority of the members of the House of Representatives.
(2) Where the situation imperatively calls for immediate action and where insurmountable obstacles prevent the timely assembly of the House of Representatives, or where there is no quorum in the House of Representatives, the Joint Committee makes this determination with a two-thirds majority of the votes cast, which includes at least the majority of its members.
(4) Where the federal territory is being attacked by armed force and where the competent bodies of the Federation are not in a position at once to make the determination provided for in Paragraph (1) of this article, such determination is deemed to have been made and promulgated at the time the attack began. The President announces such time as soon as circumstances permit.
(5) Where the determination of the existence of a state of defence has been promulgated and where the federal territory is being attacked by armed force, the President may, with the consent of the House of Representatives, issue declarations under international law regarding the existence of such state of defence.

21. The legislature's approval is necessary to ratify treaties with foreign countries.

Yes. The legislature's approval is necessary to ratify international treaties.

Article 59
(2) Treaties which regulate the political relations of the Federation or relate to matters of federal legislation require the consent or participation, in the form of a federal statute, of the bodies competent in any specific case for such federal legislation.

22. The legislature has the power to grant amnesty.

Yes. The legislature has the power to pass an amnesty law.

23. The legislature has the power of pardon.

No. The president has the power of pardon.

Article 60
(2) [The president] exercises the right of pardon in individual cases on behalf of the Federation.

24. The legislature reviews and has the right to reject appointments to the judiciary; or the legislature itself appoints members of the judiciary.

Yes. The legislature elects the members of the Federal Constitutional Court.

Article 94
(1) The Federal Constitutional Court consists of federal judges and other members. Half of the members of the Federal Constitutional Court are elected by the House of Representatives and half by the Senate.

25. The chairman of the central bank is appointed by the legislature.

No. The president, on the recommendation of the government, appoints the president of the German Federal Bank.

26. The legislature has a substantial voice in the operation of the state-owned media.

Yes. The legislature appoints some members to the board that oversees public media.

27. The legislature is regularly in session.

Yes. The House of Representatives has the authority to determine its own sessions and chooses to meet regularly.

Article 39
(3) The House of Representatives determines the termination and resumption of its meetings. The President of the House of Representatives may convene it at an earlier date. He does so where one third of its members or the President or the Chancellor so demand.

28. Each legislator has a personal secretary.

Yes.

29. Each legislator has at least one non-secretarial staff member with policy expertise.

Yes.

30. Legislators are eligible for re-election without any restriction.

Yes. There are no restrictions on re-election.

31. A seat in the legislature is an attractive enough position that legislators are generally interested in and seek re-election.

Yes.

32. The re-election of incumbent legislators is common enough that at any given time the legislature contains a significant number of highly experienced members.

Yes. Re-election rates are sufficiently high to produce a significant number of highly experienced members.

PARLIAMENT OF GHANA

Expert consultants: Sophia A. B. Akuffo, Emmanuel Akwetey, Vitus A. Azeem, Staffan I. Lindberg, Minion K. C. Morrison

Score: .47

Influence over executive (4/9)		Institutional autonomy (4/9)		Specified powers (4/8)		Institutional capacity (3/6)	
1. replace		10. no dissolution	X	19. amendments	X	27. sessions	X
2. serve as ministers	X	11. no decree	X	20. war	X	28. secretary	
3. interpellate	X	12. no veto		21. treaties	X	29. staff	
4. investigate	X	13. no review		22. amnesty		30. no term limits	X
5. oversee police		14. no gatekeeping		23. pardon		31. seek re-election	X
6. appoint PM		15. no impoundment	X	24. judiciary	X	32. experience	
7. appoint ministers	X	16. control resources		25. central bank			
8. lack president		17. immunity		26. media			
9. no confidence		18. all elected	X				

The Parliament of Ghana originated during the years of British colonial rule, with the first legislative elections taking place under the Guggisberg Constitution of 1925. Under the new 1950 constitution, the legislature achieved some autonomy from the colonial power, and members were elected to this body in 1951, 1954, and 1956. Ghana attained independence and adopted a constitution in 1957. It thereafter operated a Westminster-type system until 1960, when it created a presidency, which was occupied by Kwame Nkrumah. In 1964 the constitution was amended to turn Ghana into a one-party state, dominated by Nkrumah's Convention People's Party (CPP), and Nkrumah was declared president-for-life. A military coup in 1966 deposed Nkrumah and led to the suspension of the constitution. Between then and the early 1990s, Ghana was mostly controlled by military governments, although there were brief intervals of more open politics in 1969–72 and 1979–81. In the early 1990s, the country began taking steps toward political opening. In 1992 it adopted the constitution of the Fourth Republic of Ghana and reconstituted a functioning parliament.

The legislature's powers are not insubstantial. Parliament can control the executive by rejecting the president's ministerial appointments and by interpellating and investigating executive branch officials. Moreover, most ministers are drawn from parliament. The legislature's own institutional autonomy is not expansive. It is circumscribed by presidential powers of veto and gatekeeping. Legislators also lack immunity from criminal prosecution. The legislature is granted a few specified powers, such as the authority to approve international treaties and declarations of war. The legislature also has some institutional capacity.

SURVEY

1. The legislature alone, without the involvement of any other agencies, can impeach the president or replace the prime minister.

No. Presidential impeachment requires the involvement of the Supreme Court.

Article 69

(1) The President shall be removed from office if he is found, in accordance with the provisions of this article –

    (a) to have acted in willful violation of the oath of allegiance and the presidential oath set out in the Second Schedule to, or in willful violation of any other provision of, this Constitution; or

    (b) to have conducted himself in a manner –

        (i) which brings or is likely to bring the high office of President into disrepute, ridicule or contempt; or

(ii) prejudicial or inimical to the economy or the security of the State; or

(c) to be incapable of performing the functions of his office by reason of infirmity of body or mind.

(2) For the purposes of the removal from office of the President, a notice

in writing –

(a) signed by not less than one-third of all the members of Parliament, and

(b) stating that the conduct or the physical or mental capacity of the President be investigated on any of the grounds specified in clause (1) of this article, shall be given to the Speaker who shall immediately inform the Chief Justice and deliver the notice to him copied to the President.

(3) The notice referred to in clause (2) of this article shall be accompanied by a statement in writing setting out in detail the facts, supported by the necessary documents, on which it is claimed that the conduct or the physical or mental capacity of the President be investigated for the purposes of his removal from office.

(4) Subject to clause (5) of this article, the Chief Justice shall, by constitutional instrument, immediately convene a tribunal consisting of the Chief Justice as Chairman and the four most senior Justices of the Supreme Court and the tribunal shall inquire, in camera, whether there is a prima facie case for the removal of the President.

(5) Where a notice under clause (2) of this article is delivered to the Chief Justice in respect of the removal from office of the President on the grounds of physical or mental incapacity, the Chief Justice shall, in consultation with the professional head of the Ghana Health Services, causes a medical board to be convened which shall consist of not less than four eminent medical specialists and the President shall be informed accordingly.

(6) The President shall be invited to submit himself for examination by the medical board within fourteen days after the appointment of the board.

(7) The President shall be entitled during the proceedings of the tribunal or of the medical board to be heard in his defence by himself or by a lawyer or other expert or person as the case may be, of his own choice.

(8) The Rules of Court Committee shall, by constitutional instrument, make rules for the practice and procedure of the tribunal or of the medical board for the removal of the President.

(9) Where the tribunal or medical board specified in clauses (4) and (5) of this article determines that there is a prima facie case for the removal of the President or that the President is by reason of physical or mental incapacity unable to perform the functions of his office, the findings shall immediately be submitted to the Speaker of Parliament through the Chief Justice and copied to the President.

(10) Parliament shall, within fourteen days after the date of the findings of the tribunal or medical board, move a resolution whether or not the President shall be removed from office.

(11) The resolution for the removal from office of the President shall be by a secret ballot and shall be taken to be approved by Parliament if supported by the votes of not less that two-thirds of all the members of Parliament after prior debate.

(12) The proceedings of Parliament for the removal of the President shall not be held in camera except where Parliament otherwise orders in the interest of national security.

(13) The President shall cease to hold office as President on the date Parliament decides that he be removed from office.

2. Ministers may serve simultaneously as members of the legislature.

Yes. A majority of the ministers are required to serve simultaneously in the legislature.

Article 78
(1) Ministers of State shall be appointed by the President with the prior approval of Parliament from among members of Parliament or persons qualified to be elected as members of Parliament, except that the majority of Ministers of State shall be appointed from among members of Parliament.

3. The legislature has powers of summons over executive branch officials and hearings with executive branch officials testifying before the legislature or its committees are regularly held.

Yes. The legislature regularly summons and holds hearings with executive branch officials.

Article 103
(1) Parliament shall appoint standing committees and other committees as may be necessary for the effective discharge of its functions.
(3) Committees of Parliament shall be charged with such functions, including the investigation and inquiry into the activities and administration of ministries and departments as Parliament may determine; and such investigation and inquiries may extend to proposals for legislation.
6) A committee appointed under this article shall have the powers, rights and privileges of the High Court or a Justice of the High Court at a trial for –
(a) enforcing the attendance of witnesses and examining them on oath, affirmation or otherwise;
(b) compelling the production of documents; and
(c) issuing a commission or request to examine witnesses abroad.

4. The legislature can conduct independent investigation of the chief executive and the agencies of the executive.

Yes. The legislature can establish committees to investigate the executive.

Article 103

(1) Parliament shall appoint standing committees and other committees as may be necessary for the effective discharge of its functions.

(3) Committees of Parliament shall be charged with such functions, including the investigation and inquiry into the activities and administration of ministries and departments as Parliament may determine; and such investigation and inquiries may extend to proposals for legislation.

6) A committee appointed under this article shall have the powers, rights and privileges of the High Court or a Justice of the High Court at a trial for –

(a) enforcing the attendance of witnesses and examining them on oath, affirmation or otherwise;

(b) compelling the production of documents; and

(c) issuing a commission or request to examine witnesses abroad.

5. The legislature has effective powers of oversight over the agencies of coercion (the military, organs of law enforcement, intelligence services, and the secret police).

No. The legislature lacks effective powers of oversight over the agencies of coercion.

6. The legislature appoints the prime minister.

No. There is no prime minister.

7. The legislature's approval is required to confirm the appointment of ministers; or the legislature itself appoints ministers.

Yes. The legislature's approval is necessary to confirm the president's ministerial appointments.

Article 78

(1) Ministers of State shall be appointed by the President with the prior approval of Parliament from among members of Parliament or persons qualified to be elected as members of Parliament, except that the majority of Ministers of State shall be appointed from among members of Parliament.

8. The country lacks a presidency entirely or there is a presidency, but the president is elected by the legislature.

No. The president is directly elected.

Article 63

(2) The election of the President shall be on the terms of universal adult suffrage and shall, subject to the provisions of this Constitution, be conducted in accordance with such regulations as may be prescribed by constitutional instrument by the Electoral Commission.

9. The legislature can vote no confidence in the government.

No. The legislature can pass a motion of censure in individual ministers, but not in the government as a whole.

Article 82

(1) Parliament may, by a resolution supported by the votes of not less than two-thirds of all the members of Parliament, pass a vote of censure on a Minister of State.

(3) The motion shall be debated in Parliament within fourteen days after the receipt by the Speaker of the notice for the motion.

(4) A Minister of State in respect of whom a vote of censure is debated under clause (3) of this article is entitled, during the debate, to be heard in his defence.

(5) Where a vote of censure is passed against a Minister under this article the President may, unless the Minister resigns his office, revoke his appointment as a Minister.

10. The legislature is immune from dissolution by the executive.

Yes. The legislature is immune from dissolution.

11. Any executive initiative on legislation requires ratification or approval by the legislature before it takes effect; that is, the executive lacks decree power.

Yes. The executive lacks decree power.

12. Laws passed by the legislature are veto-proof or essentially veto-proof; that is, the executive lacks veto power, or has veto power but the veto can be overridden by a majority in the legislature.

No. A two-thirds majority vote in the legislature is required to override a presidential veto.

Article 106

(8) Where the President refuses to assent to a bill, he shall, within fourteen days after the refusal –

(a) state in a memorandum to the Speaker any specific provisions of the bill which in his opinion should be reconsidered by Parliament, including his recommendations for amendments if any; or

(b) inform the Speaker that he has referred the bill to the Council of State for consideration and comment under article 90 of this Constitution.

(9) Parliament shall reconsider a bill taking into account the comments made by the President or the Council of State, as the case may be, under clause (8) of this article.

(10) Where a bill reconsidered under clause (9) of this article is passed by Parliament by a resolution supported by the votes of not less than two-thirds of all the members of Parliament, the President shall assent to it within thirty days after passing of the resolution.

13. The legislature's laws are supreme and not subject to judicial review.

No. The Supreme Court can review the constitutionality of laws.

Article 130

(1) Subject to the jurisdiction of the High Court in the enforcement of the Fundamental Human Rights and Freedoms as provided in article 33 of this Constitution,

the Supreme Court shall have exclusive original jurisdiction in –

(a) all matters relating to the enforcement or interpretation of this Constitution; and

(b) all matters arising as to whether an enactment
was made in excess of the powers conferred on Parliament or any other authority or person by law or
under this Constitution.

**14. The legislature has the right to initiate bills in all
policy jurisdictions; the executive lacks gatekeeping
authority.**

No. The legislature is prohibited from introducing
legislation related to taxation, public expenditures,
and government debt.

Article 108
Parliament shall not, unless the bill is introduced or
the motion is introduced by, or on behalf of, the President –

(a) proceed upon a bill including an amendment to a
bill, that, in the opinion of the person presiding, makes
provision for any of the following –

(i) the imposition of taxation or the alteration of taxation otherwise than by reduction; or

(ii) the imposition of a charge on the Consolidated
Fund or other public funds of Ghana or the alteration
of any such charge otherwise than by reduction; or

(iii) the payment, issue or withdrawal from the Consolidated Fund or other public funds of Ghana of any
moneys not charged on the Consolidated Fund or
any increase in the amount of that payment, issue or
withdrawal; or

(iv) the composition or remission of any debt due to
the Government of Ghana; or

(b) proceed upon a motion, including an amendment
to a motion, the effect of which, in the opinion of the
person presiding, would be to make provision for any
of the purpose specified in paragraph (a) of this article.

**15. Expenditure of funds appropriated by the legis-
lature is mandatory; the executive lacks the power to
impound funds appropriated by the legislature.**

Yes. The executive lacks the power to impound
funds appropriated by the legislature.

**16. The legislature controls the resources that finance
its own internal operation and provide for the
perquisites of its own members.**

No. The legislature is dependent on the executive
for the resources that finance its operations.

Article 71
(1) The salaries and allowances payable, and the facilities and privileges available, to –

(a) members of Parliament;

being expenditure charged on the Consolidated Fund,
shall be determined by the President on the recommendations of a committee of not more than five persons

appointed by the President, acting in accordance with
the advice of the Council of State.

Article 98
(1) A member of Parliament shall be paid such salary
and allowances and provided with such facilities as may
be determined in accordance with article 71 of this Constitution.

**17. Members of the legislature are immune from
arrest and/or criminal prosecution.**

No. Legislators are subject to arrest and prosecution. Legislators cannot be arrested or prosecuted,
however, for something that they say, or while
they are on their way to, attending, or returning
from a legislative session.

Article 115
There shall be freedom of speech, debate and proceedings in Parliament and that freedom shall not be
impeached or questioned in any court or place out of
Parliament.

Article 116
(1) Subject to the provisions of this article, but without
prejudice to the general effect of article 115 of this Constitution, civil or criminal proceedings shall not be instituted against a member of Parliament in any court or
place out of Parliament for any matter or thing brought
by him in or before Parliament by petition, bill, motion
or otherwise.

Article 117
Civil or criminal process coming from any court or place
out of Parliament shall not be served on, or executed
in relation to, the Speaker or a member or the clerk to
Parliament while he is on his way to, attending at or
returning from, any proceedings of Parliament.

**18. All members of the legislature are elected; the
executive lacks the power to appoint any members of
the legislature.**

Yes. All members of the legislature are elected.

Article 93
(1) There shall be a Parliament of Ghana which shall
consist of not less than one hundred and forty elected
members.

**19. The legislature alone, without the involvement of
any other agencies, can change the Constitution.**

Yes. The legislature can amend "non-entrenched
provisions" of the constitution in multiple readings of the bill with a two-thirds majority vote.
Changes to "entrenched provisions" of the constitution require approval in a popular referendum.

Article 289
(1) Subject to the provisions of this Constitution. Parliament may, by an Act of Parliament, amend any provision of this Constitution.

(2) This Constitution shall not be amended by an Act of Parliament or altered whether directly or indirectly unless –

(a) the sole purpose of the Act is to amend this Constitution; and

(b) the Act has been passed in accordance with this Chapter.

Article 290

(1) This article applies to the amendment of the following provisions of this Constitution, which are, in this Constitution referred to as "entrenched provisions" –

(a) The Constitution: articles 1, 2 and 3;

(b) The Territories of Ghana: articles 4 and 5;

(c) The Laws of Ghana: article 11;

(d) Fundamental Human Rights and Freedoms: Chapter 5;

(e) Representation of the People: articles 42, 43, 46, 49, 55 and 56;

(f) The Executive: Chapter 8;

(g) The Legislature: articles 93 and 106;

(h) The Judiciary: articles 125, 127, 129, 145 and 146;

(i) Freedom and Independence of the Media: article 162, clauses (1) to (5);

(j) Finance: articles 174 and 187;

(k) Police Service: article 200;

(l) The Armed Forces of Ghana: article 210;

(m) Commission on Human Rights and Administrative Justice: articles 216 and 225;

(n) National Commission for Civic Education: article 231;

(o) Decentralization and Local Government: articles 240 and 252;

(p) Chieftaincy: article 270;

(q) Code of Conduct for Public Officers: article 286;

(r) Amendment of the Constitution: Chapter 25; and

(s) Miscellaneous: articles 293 and 299.

(2) A bill for the amendment of an entrenched provision shall, before Parliament proceeds to consider it, be referred by the Speaker to the Council of State for its advice and the Council of State shall render advice on the bill within thirty days after receiving it.

(3) The bill shall be published in the *Gazette* but shall not be introduced into Parliament until the expiry of six months after the publication in the *Gazette* under this clause.

(4) After the bill has been read the first time in Parliament it shall not be proceeded with further unless it has been submitted to a referendum held throughout Ghana and at least forty percent of the persons entitled to vote, voted at the referendum and at least seventy-five percent of the persons who voted cast their votes in favour of the passing of the bill.

(5) Where the bill is approved at the referendum, Parliament shall pass it.

(6) Where a bill for the amendment of an entrenched provision has been passed by Parliament in accordance with this article, the President shall assent to it.

Article 291

(1) A bill to amend a provision of this Constitution which is not an entrenched provision shall not be introduced into Parliament unless –

(a) it has been published twice in the *Gazette* with the second publication being made at least three months after the first; and

(b) at least ten days have passed after the second publication.

(2) The Speaker shall, after the first reading of the bill in Parliament, refer it to the Council of State for consideration and advice and the Council of State shall render advice on the bill within thirty days after receiving it.

(3) Where Parliament approves the bill, it may only be presented to the President for his assent if it was approved at the second and third readings of it in Parliament by the votes of at least two thirds of all the members of Parliament.

(4) Where the bill has been passed in accordance with this article, the President shall assent to it.

20. The legislature's approval is necessary for the declaration of war.

Yes. There is no constitutional provision specifically addressing the declaration of war. In practice, the legislature's approval is necessary for presidential war declarations.

21. The legislature's approval is necessary to ratify treaties with foreign countries.

Yes. The legislature's approval is necessary to ratify international treaties.

Article 75

(1) The President may execute or cause to be executed treaties, agreements or conventions in the name of Ghana.

(2) A treaty, agreement or convention executed by or under the authority of the President shall be subject to ratification by –

(a) Act of Parliament; or

(b) a resolution of Parliament supported by the votes of more than one-half of all the members of Parliament.

22. The legislature has the power to grant amnesty.

No. The president has the power to grant amnesty. Amnesty and pardon are not treated separately. See item 23.

23. The legislature has the power of pardon.

No. The president has the power of pardon.

Article 72

(1) The President may, acting in consultation with the Council of State –

(a) grant to a person convicted of an offence a pardon either free or subject to lawful conditions; or

(b) grant to a person a respite, either indefinite or for a specified period, from the execution of punishment imposed on him for an offence; or

(c) substitute a less severe form of punishment for a punishment imposed on a person for an offence; or

(d) remit the whole or part of a punishment imposed on a person or of a penalty or forfeiture otherwise due to Government on account on any offence.

24. The legislature reviews and has the right to reject appointments to the judiciary; or the legislature itself appoints members of the judiciary.

Yes. The legislature's consent is required to approve the president's Supreme Court nominations.

Article 144
(1) The Chief Justice shall be appointed by the President acting in consultation with the Council of State and with the approval of Parliament.
(2) The other Supreme Court Justices shall be appointed by the President acting on the advice of the Judicial Council, in consultation with the Council of State and with the approval of Parliament.
(3) Justices of the Court of Appeal and of the High Court and Chairmen of Regional Tribunals shall be appointed by the President acting on the advice of the judicial Council.

25. The chairman of the central bank is appointed by the legislature.

No. The president appoints the governor of the Bank of Ghana.

Article 183
(4) The following shall apply to the Governor of the Bank of Ghana –
(a) he shall be appointed by the President acting in consultation with the Council of State for periods of four years.

26. The legislature has a substantial voice in the operation of the state-owned media.

No. The legislature lacks a substantial voice in the operation of the public media.

27. The legislature is regularly in session.

Yes. The legislature meets in three sessions, each lasting between eight and twelve weeks, every year.

Article 112
(1) A session of Parliament shall be held at such place within Ghana and shall commence at such time as the Speaker may, by constitutional instrument, appoint.
(2) A session of Parliament shall be held at least once a year, so that the period between the last sitting of Parliament in one session and the first sitting of Parliament in the next session does not amount to twelve months.

28. Each legislator has a personal secretary.

No.

29. Each legislator has at least one non-secretarial staff member with policy expertise.

No.

30. Legislators are eligible for re-election without any restriction.

Yes. There are no restrictions on re-election.

31. A seat in the legislature is an attractive enough position that legislators are generally interested in and seek re-election.

Yes.

32. The re-election of incumbent legislators is common enough that at any given time the legislature contains a significant number of highly experienced members.

No. Stability in membership has not been high through the four rounds of parliamentary elections held since the early 1990s. While the legislature is not entirely bereft of experienced members, the re-election rate has averaged well under 50 percent, and only a relative handful of legislators have retained their seats throughout the period of the Fourth Republic.

PARLIAMENT OF GREECE (*VOULI TON ELLINON*)

Expert consultants: P. Nikiforos Diamandouros, James Georgas, Georgia Gionna, Dimitris Keridis, Dimitris G. Papadimitriou

Score: .81

Influence over executive (8/9)		Institutional autonomy (7/9)		Specified powers (5/8)		Institutional capacity (6/6)	
1. replace	X	10. no dissolution		19. amendments	X	27. sessions	X
2. serve as ministers	X	11. no decree	X	20. war	X	28. secretary	X
3. interpellate	X	12. no veto	X	21. treaties	X	29. staff	X
4. investigate	X	13. no review		22. amnesty	X	30. no term limits	X
5. oversee police	X	14. no gatekeeping	X	23. pardon		31. seek re-election	X
6. appoint PM	X	15. no impoundment	X	24. judiciary		32. experience	X
7. appoint ministers		16. control resources	X	25. central bank	X		
8. lack president	X	17. immunity	X	26. media			
9. no confidence	X	18. all elected	X				

The Parliament of Greece (*Vouli ton Ellinon*) can trace its origins to the various national assemblies that gathered following independence from the Ottoman Empire in the 1830s. During 1864–1911 a national parliament operated as part of a "democratic monarchy." For much of the twentieth century, the legislature was sidelined as power alternated between authoritarian presidents and military juntas. In 1967 a group of military officers seized power in a coup d'état and ruled by decree until civilian rule was restored in 1975. A new constitution in that year called for a unicameral parliament paired with a powerful president who was vested with the authority to rule by decree and to appoint the government. In practice, the president rarely exercised the broad powers vested in the presidency, and in 1986 the president's more modest de facto powers were codified in a constitutional amendment. The amendment formally shifted executive powers to the prime minister, spelled out the government's responsibility to the legislature, and scaled back the president's decree power. A constitutional amendment in 2001 dealt with individual rights but did not directly affect legislative power.

The legislature is the main stage of national politics. Its control over executive power is formidable, and parliament enjoys substantial institutional autonomy. Parliament also holds numerous specified prerogatives, which include the power to change the constitution alone without the involvement of any other agencies. It has a high level of institutional capacity.

SURVEY

1. The legislature alone, without the involvement of any other agencies, can impeach the president or replace the prime minister.

Yes. The legislature can remove the prime minister with a vote of no confidence. Presidential impeachment requires the involvement of a special court.

Article 38
(1) The President of the Republic shall divest the Prime Minster of his duties when the latter has resigned and when the Government has been defeated in Parliament, in accordance with the provisions of Article 84.
(2) If the Prime Minister resigns or dies, the President of the Republic shall appoint at this post the person proposed by the deputies of its party, in a period no longer than three days.

Article 49
(1) The President of the Republic shall not be held in any way responsible for the acts carried out in the discharge of his duties, save in the case of high treason or wilful violation of the Constitution. Prosecution for acts unrelated to the discharge of his duties shall be postponed until the end of the presidential term.

(2) Impeachment motions against the President of the Republic shall be submitted to Parliament in writing signed by at least one third of the members thereof, and must be accepted by a decision taken by a two thirds majority of the total number of the members thereof.

(3) If such motion be accepted, the President of the Republic shall appear before the special court provided for by Article 86, and the provisions relating thereto shall apply also in this case.

(4) Following his impeachment, the President shall refrain from exercising his duties and shall be replaced in accordance with the provisions of Article 34. He shall resume again his duties, if his term of office has not expired after he has been acquitted by the court provided for by Article 86.

(5) A law to be passed by the plenum of Parliament shall regulate questions relating to the implementation of the provisions of this Article.

Article 84

(1) The Government must enjoy the confidence of Parliament. The Government must ask for a vote of confidence from Parliament within fifteen days from the swearing in of the Prime Minister and may do so at any other time. If Parliament should be in adjournment when the Government is formed, Parliament shall be convened within fifteen days in order to decide on the motion of confidence.

(2) Parliament may, by its decision, withdraw its confidence from the Government or from a member of the Government. A motion of no confidence in the Government may not be submitted before the lapse of six months from the rejection by Parliament of such a motion. The motion of no confidence must be signed by at least one sixth of the deputies and must contain in detail the topic to be discussed.

(3) By exception, a motion of no confidence may be submitted before the lapse of the said six month period if it be signed by the total number of deputies.

(4) The debate on the motion of confidence or no confidence shall commence two days after the submission of the said motion, unless the Government in the case of a motion of no confidence should ask for the debate to be held immediately, and may not be extended beyond three days from the commencement thereof.

(5) The vote on the motion of confidence or no confidence shall be taken immediately after the end of the debate; it may, however, be postponed for forty-eight hours if the Government should ask for such postponement.

(6) No motion of confidence shall be upheld unless it be approved by the absolute majority of the deputies present, which may not be less than two fifths of the total number thereof. A motion of no confidence shall only be upheld if approved by the absolute majority of the total number of deputies.

(7) The Ministers and Deputy Ministers who are also deputies shall be permitted to vote on such motions.

2. Ministers may serve simultaneously as members of the legislature.

Yes. Legislators may serve simultaneously in ministerial positions, although in recent years there have been debates about instituting an incompatibility law, the possibility of which is envisioned in the constitution.

Article 81

(4) A law may establish the incompatibility of the office of Minister or Deputy Minister with other functions as well.

3. The legislature has powers of summons over executive branch officials and hearings with executive branch officials testifying before the legislature or its committees are regularly held.

Yes. The legislature regularly interpellates officials from the executive.

Article 69

No one shall, without being summoned, appear before Parliament to report on any matter either orally or in writing. Petitions may be presented through a deputy or delivered to the Speaker. Parliament shall have the right to forward petitions addressed to it to the ministers and Deputy-Ministers who shall be obliged, whenever it be demanded, to provide explanations.

4. The legislature can conduct independent investigation of the chief executive and the agencies of the executive.

Yes. The legislature can establish committees of inquiry to investigate the executive.

Article 68

(1) At the beginning of each regular session, Parliament shall constitute Parliamentary committees the members whereof shall be deputies, with a view to processing and examining the bills and private members' bills which have been submitted and shall come before the Plenum and the Departments of Parliament.

(2) Parliament shall constitute committees of enquiry, the members whereof shall be deputies, by a majority of two fifths of the total number of deputies and following a proposal made by one fifth of the same number.

(3) The constitution of committees of enquiry on matters relating to foreign policy or national defence shall require a decision by Parliament taken by the absolute majority of the total number of deputies. Matters relating to the composition and functioning of the said committees shall be determined by the Regulations of Parliament.

(4) The Parliamentary committees, the committees of enquiry, and Departments of Parliament operating under Articles 70 and 71 shall be composed in proportion to the parliamentary strength of each party, group, or independent deputies, as laid down by the Regulations.

5. The legislature has effective powers of oversight over the agencies of coercion (the military, organs of law enforcement, intelligence services, and the secret police).

Yes. Legislative committees have effective powers of oversight over the agencies of coercion.

6. The legislature appoints the prime minister.

Yes. The president is required to appoint as prime minister the candidate who enjoys the support of parliament.

> Article 37
> (1) The President of the Republic shall appoint the Prime Minister and, at the recommendation of the latter, he shall also appoint the rest of the members of the Government and the Deputy Ministers.
> (2) The leader of the party which shall have the absolute majority in Parliament shall be appointed Prime Minister. If there is not such party, the President of the Republic shall give the leader of the party which commands the relative majority an exploratory mandate with a view to ascertain the possibility of forming a government which shall enjoy the confidence of Parliament.

7. The legislature's approval is required to confirm the appointment of ministers; or the legislature itself appoints ministers.

No. The president appoints ministers on the recommendation of the prime minister, and the appointments do not require the legislature's approval.

> Article 37
> (1) The President of the Republic shall appoint the Prime Minister and, at the recommendation of the latter, he shall also appoint the rest of the members of the Government and the Deputy Ministers.

8. The country lacks a presidency entirely or there is a presidency, but the president is elected by the legislature.

Yes. The legislature elects the president.

> Article 30
> (1) The President of the Republic shall regulate the functions of the powers of the State. He shall be elected by Parliament for a term of five years, according to the procedure specified in Articles 32 and 33.

9. The legislature can vote no confidence in the government.

Yes. The legislature can vote no confidence in the government.

> Article 84
> (1) The Government must enjoy the confidence of Parliament. The Government must ask for a vote of confidence from Parliament within fifteen days from the swearing in of the Prime Minister and may do so at any other time. If Parliament should be in adjournment

when the Government is formed, Parliament shall be convened within fifteen days in order to decide on the motion of confidence.
> (2) Parliament may, by its decision, withdraw its confidence from the Government or from a member of the Government. A motion of no confidence in the Government may not be submitted before the lapse of six months from the rejection by Parliament of such a motion. The motion of no confidence must be signed by at least one sixth of the deputies and must contain in detail the topic to be discussed.
> (3) By exception, a motion of no confidence may be submitted before the lapse of the said six month period if it be signed by the total number of deputies.
> (4) The debate on the motion of confidence or no confidence shall commence two days after the submission of the said motion, unless the Government in the case of a motion of no confidence should ask for the debate to be held immediately, and may not be extended beyond three days from the commencement thereof.
> (5) The vote on the motion of confidence or no confidence shall be taken immediately after the end of the debate; it may, however, be postponed for forty-eight hours if the Government should ask for such postponement.
> (6) No motion of confidence shall be upheld unless it be approved by the absolute majority of the deputies present, which may not be less than two fifths of the total number thereof. A motion of no confidence shall only be upheld if approved by the absolute majority of the total number of deputies.
> (7) The Ministers and Deputy Ministers who are also deputies shall be permitted to vote on such motions.

10. The legislature is immune from dissolution by the executive.

No. The president can dissolve the legislature.

> Article 32
> (4) If the said increased majority be not attained in the final vote, Parliament shall be dissolved within ten days from the said vote and elections for a new Parliament shall be proclaimed. The relevant decree shall be signed by the incumbent President of the Republic, and if this be not possible by the Speaker who shall replace him.

> Article 41
> (1) The President of the Republic may dissolve Parliament, if two Governments have resigned or defeated in the Parliament and its composition cannot achieve stability of government. The elections shall be organized by the Government enjoying the confidence of the dissolved Parliament. In every other case, the provisions of the last phrase of Article 37 (3) shall apply.
> (2) The President of the Republic shall dissolve the Parliament at the suggestion of a Government which has been given a vote of confidence, with a view to renewing its mandate in order to deal with a problem of extraordinary importance for the nation. The dissolution of the new Parliament for the same reason is prohibited.

11. Any executive initiative on legislation requires ratification or approval by the legislature before it takes effect; that is, the executive lacks decree power.

Yes. The executive lacks decree power. Under "extreme circumstances of the most urgent and unforeseen need," the president can, however, with the approval of the cabinet, issue decrees that have the force of law. The decrees lapse if they are not subsequently approved by the legislature.

Article 43

(1) The President of the Republic shall issue the decrees necessary for the execution of the laws, but he shall under no circumstances suspend the operation of the laws nor exempt anyone from the execution thereof.

Article 44

(1) In extraordinary circumstances of most urgent and unforeseen need, the President of the Republic may, at the suggestion of the Cabinet, issue acts of legislative content. These acts shall be brought before Parliament for approval, in accordance with the provisions of Article 72 (1), within forty days from the day of issuance or within forty days from the commencement of a Parliamentary session. If the said acts be not submitted to Parliament within the said time limits, or if they be not approved by Parliament within three months from each submission, they shall become invalid for the future.

Article 48

(1) In case of a state of war or mobilization due to external dangers or of manifest threat to the national security, or in case of armed revolt against the Democratic regime, the Parliament may, after proposition of the Cabinet, suspend throughout the country or in part thereof the operation of Articles 5 (4), 6, 8, 9, 11, 12 (1)–(4), 14, 19, 22, 23, 96 (4), and 97 or some of these Articles and put into effect the law on "state of siege" as this law may apply on each occasion, and establish extraordinary tribunals. The President of the Republic issues the resolution of the Parliament. This resolution defines also the duration of the imposed measures, that can not be longer than fifteen days.

(2) If the Parliament is in absence or it is not possible to convoke it in time, the measures of the aforegoing Paragraph shall be taken by presidential decree, after proposition of the Cabinet. This decree shall be brought to the Parliament when its convocations becomes possible, even if its term has ended or if it has been dissolved and, in any case, not later than fifteen days after its issuance.

(3) The duration of the measures of the aforegoing paragraphs can be extended beyond fifteen days only by decision of the Parliament, each time for a period of fifteen days. The Parliament is convoked therefore even if its term has ended or if it has been dissolve.

(4) The measures taken in accordance to the aforegoing paragraphs shall *ipso jure* be lifted after the termination of the war and, in any other case, after the expiration of the delays of the Paragraphs (1), (2) and (3) of the present Article.

(5) The President of the Republic may, after proposition of the Cabinet, issue Legislative Acts, with a view to coping with the situation and the speedy resumption of the operation of the constitutional institutions. These acts shall be brought before Parliament for approval within fifteen days from the day of issuance or from the day of the convocation of the Parliament. If the said acts be not submitted to Parliament within the said time limits, or if they be not approved by Parliament within fifteen days from their submission, they shall become invalid for the future. The law on the state of siege may not be amended while it is in force.

(6) The decisions of the Parliament in accordance to Paragraphs (2) and (3) are taken by the absolute majority of the total number of deputies, whereas the decision in accordance to the Paragraph (1) is taken by a majority of the three fifths of the total number thereof, in one only Session.

(7) During the application of measures of the state of siege the provisions of the Articles 61 and 62 shall remain *ipso jure* in force, even if the term of Parliament has ended or if it has been dissolved.

12. Laws passed by the legislature are veto-proof or essentially veto-proof; that is, the executive lacks veto power, or has veto power but the veto can be overridden by a majority in the legislature.

Yes. The legislature can override a presidential veto by a majority vote of its present members.

Article 42

(1) The President of the Republic shall issue and publish the laws passed by Parliament within one month from the passing thereof. The President of the Republic may, within the time limit specified in the aforegoing paragraph, send back to Parliament a bill passed thereby, stating the reasons for his veto.

(2) A bill or private member's bill vetoed by the President of the Republic shall be brought before the Plenary Session of Parliament, and should it be passed again by the absolute majority of the total number of deputies, according to the procedure laid down by Article 76 (2), the President of the Republic shall issue and publish such bill within ten days from the second passing thereof.

13. The legislature's laws are supreme and not subject to judicial review.

No. The Supreme Court can review the constitutionality of laws.

14. The legislature has the right to initiate bills in all policy jurisdictions; the executive lacks gatekeeping authority.

Yes. The legislature can initiate bills in all policy jurisdictions, with one minor exception. According to the constitution, legislation related to the granting of pensions can only be introduced by the minister of finance following a recommendation by the Council of Comptrollers.

Article 73

(1) The right of proposing laws shall belong to Parliament and the Government.

(2) Bills relating in any way to the granting of pensions and the prerequisites thereof shall be submitted only by the Minister of Finance following a recommendation by the Council of Comptrollers. In the case of pensions involving an increase in the budgetary expenditure of local authority bodies or other bodies corporate of public law, the bills in question shall be submitted by the competent Minister and the Minister of Finance. Such bills on pensions must be specific, the insertion of provisions regarding pensions in laws designed to settle other matters being prohibited and resulting in the annulment of the said bills.

15. Expenditure of funds appropriated by the legislature is mandatory; the executive lacks the power to impound funds appropriated by the legislature.

Yes. The executive lacks the power to impound funds appropriated by the legislature.

16. The legislature controls the resources that finance its own internal operation and provide for the perquisites of its own members.

Yes. The legislature enjoys financial autonomy, including control over members' salaries.

Article 63

(1) Deputies shall receive compensation and an expense allowance from the Public Treasury for the discharge of their duties. The amounts to cover both the aforegoing shall be fixed by a decision taken by the plenum of Parliament.

17. Members of the legislature are immune from arrest and/or criminal prosecution.

Yes. Legislators are immune with the common exception for cases of *flagrante delicto*.

Article 61

(1) Deputies shall not be persecuted or in any way questioned on account of an opinion or vote given by them in the discharge of their duties as deputies.

(2) Deputies may be prosecuted, with the leave of Parliament, for malicious slander, according to law. The competent court shall be the Appeal Court. Leave shall be deemed not granted if Parliament does not decide within forty five days from the day when the indictment was received by the Speaker. In the event that leave be not granted or the fixed period expire, the act shall be deemed unindicted. This paragraph shall be applicable as from the next parliamentary term.

(3) Deputies shall not be questioned in relation to information received or given by them in the discharge of their duties or in relation to persons who entrusted them with such information or to whom they provided the same.

Article 62

During the parliamentary term no deputy shall be prosecuted, arrested, imprisoned, or in any way restricted without the leave of Parliament. Likewise, no deputy of Parliament which has been dissolved shall be prosecuted for political crimes from the dissolution of the said Parliament and until the declaration of the deputies of the new Parliament. Leave shall be deemed not given if Parliament should not decide within three months from the day on which the application of the Public Prosecutor to press charges be submitted to the Speaker. The fixed period of three months shall be suspended during the recess of Parliament. Leave shall not be required for crimes committed *in flagrante delicto*.

18. All members of the legislature are elected; the executive lacks the power to appoint any members of the legislature.

Yes. All members of the legislature are elected.

Article 51

(3) The deputies shall be elected by direct, universal, and secret ballot and by citizens having the right to vote as the law provides.

19. The legislature alone, without the involvement of any other agencies, can change the Constitution.

Yes. The legislature can change the constitution through a complicated procedure. The sitting legislature can propose an amendment in multiple readings by a three-fifths majority vote, and then, following an election, the subsequent legislature can approve the amendment with a majority vote.

Article 110

(1) The provisions of the Constitution, save those which determine the basis and the form of government as a Parliamentary Republic with a President as Head of State and those of Articles 2 (1), 4 (1), (4) and (7), 5 (1) and (3), 13 (1) and 26 shall be subject to revision.

(2) The need to revise the Constitution shall be ascertained by a decision of Parliament taken following a motion by at least fifty deputies, approved by a majority of three fifths of the total number of deputies in two votes separated from each other by at least one month. The same decision shall determine in detail the provisions to be revised.

(3) Once the revision has been decided upon by Parliament, the following Parliament in its first session shall, with an absolute majority of all the members thereof, decide on the provisions to be revised.

(4) If the proposal for the revision of the Constitution be approved by the majority of the total number of deputies but not by the majority of three fifths specified in Paragraph (2), the following Parliament in its first session may decide on the provisions to be revised by a majority of three fifths of the total number thereof.

20. The legislature's approval is necessary for the declaration of war.

Yes. Formally, the president declares war. In practice, it would be unthinkable for the president to declare war without the legislature's approval.

Article 36
(1) The President of the Republic without any prejudice to the provisions of Article 35 (1) shall represent the State in its relations to other States, declare war, conclude treaties of peace, alliance, economic co-operation and participation in international organizations or unions, and announce the same to Parliament with the necessary clarifications, if the interests and security of the State so permit.

21. The legislature's approval is necessary to ratify treaties with foreign countries.

Yes. The legislature's approval is necessary to ratify international treaties.

Article 36
(1) The President of the Republic without any prejudice to the provisions of Article 35 (1) shall represent the State in its relations to other States, declare war, conclude treaties of peace, alliance, economic co-operation and participation in international organizations or unions, and announce the same to Parliament with the necessary clarifications, if the interests and security of the State so permit.
(2) Commercial treaties and those relating to taxation, economic co-operation, and participation in international organizations or unions, and such other treaties as contain concessions in regard to which, under the provisions of this Constitution, nothing can be determined without a law, or which entail a burden on Greeks as individuals, shall be invalid without the formal law which ratifies them.

22. The legislature has the power to grant amnesty.

Yes. The legislature can grant amnesty for political crimes by a three-fifths majority vote.

Article 47
(3) Amnesty may only be granted in cases of political crimes, by a law voted in Plenary Session of the Parliament by a majority of three fifths of the total number of deputies.
(4) Amnesty in the cases of common crimes may not be granted even by law.

23. The legislature has the power of pardon.

No. The president has the power of pardon. To grant pardon to a minister, however, the president must receive the consent of parliament.

Article 47
(1) The President of the Republic shall have the right, following a proposal by the Minister of Justice and having consulted the opinion of a council which contains a majority of judges, to pardon, commute, alter, or reduce sentences pronounced by the courts of law and to lift legal consequences of any kind emanating from sentences which have been pronounced and served.

(2) The President of the Republic shall have the right to grant a pardon to a minister sentenced according to Article 86 only with the consent of Parliament.

24. The legislature reviews and has the right to reject appointments to the judiciary; or the legislature itself appoints members of the judiciary.

No. The president appoints the judiciary, and the appointments do not require the legislature's approval.

Article 88
(1) All judicial functionaries shall be appointed by presidential decree, on the basis of a law determining their qualifications and the procedure of selection; judicial functionaries shall be appointed for life.

25. The chairman of the central bank is appointed by the legislature.

Yes. The legislature appoints the governor of the Bank of Greece.

26. The legislature has a substantial voice in the operation of the state-owned media.

No. The legislature lacks a substantial voice in the operation of the public media.

27. The legislature is regularly in session.

Yes. The legislature is required by law to meet in ordinary session for at least five months each year. In practice, the legislature is in session for well over six months each year.

Article 64
(1) Parliament shall meet *ipso jure* on the first Monday of October in regular session for the annual parliamentary work, unless the President of the Republic should convoke the same earlier under Article 40.
(2) The duration of the regular session shall be not less than five months which shall not include the period of suspension under Article 40.
(3) The regular session shall be obligatorily extended until the passing of the budget under Article 79 or the passing of the special law under the same article.

28. Each legislator has a personal secretary.

Yes.

29. Each legislator has at least one non-secretarial staff member with policy expertise.

Yes.

Article 65
(5) The Regulations may provide for the setting up of a Parliamentary experts committee which would assist in the legislative work of Parliament.

30. Legislators are eligible for re-election without any restriction.

Yes. There are no restrictions on re-election.

31. A seat in the legislature is an attractive enough position that legislators are generally interested in and seek re-election.

Yes.

32. The re-election of incumbent legislators is common enough that at any given time the legislature contains a significant number of highly experienced members.

Yes. Re-election rates are sufficiently high to produce a significant number of highly experienced members.

CONGRESS OF GUATEMALA (*CONGRESO*)

Expert consultants: Marco Fonseca, Natalia Ajenjo Fresno, Eduardo Díaz Reyna, Rachel Sieder, William Stanley, Anja Stuckert

Score: .50

Influence over executive (2/9)		Institutional autonomy (6/9)		Specified powers (5/8)		Institutional capacity (3/6)	
1. replace		10. no dissolution	X	19. amendments		27. sessions	X
2. serve as ministers		11. no decree	X	20. war	X	28. secretary	
3. interpellate	X	12. no veto		21. treaties	X	29. staff	
4. investigate	X	13. no review		22. amnesty	X	30. no term limits	X
5. oversee police		14. no gatekeeping	X	23. pardon	X	31. seek re-election	X
6. appoint PM		15. no impoundment	X	24. judiciary	X	32. experience	
7. appoint ministers		16. control resources	X	25. central bank			
8. lack president		17. immunity		26. media			
9. no confidence		18. all elected	X				

The Congress (*Congreso*) of Guatemala traces its origins to the first independence constitution of 1839. For much of Guatemala's history, however, the legislature's power failed to materialize, as generals and presidents staged coups and clashed with insurgents. From 1960 to 1996 the country was engulfed in a gruesome civil war. A political opening in the mid-1980s led to the adoption of the 1985 constitution and the establishment of a unicameral Congress. A constitutional amendment in 1994 gave the Supreme Court of Justice the power to lift legislators' parliamentary immunity. Prior to 1994 legislators enjoyed immunity.

The legislature has only slight leverage over the president. It does, however, enjoy significant institutional autonomy and holds numerous specific powers, including the sole authority to declare war and the powers of amnesty and pardon. The development of institutional capacity has been impeded by a dearth of experienced legislators and a lack of personal staff.

SURVEY

1. The legislature alone, without the involvement of any other agencies, can impeach the president or replace the prime minister.

No. The legislature cannot impeach the president.

2. Ministers may serve simultaneously as members of the legislature.

No. Legislators who serve in government have a sleeping mandate, meaning that they may join the government but forfeit their voting rights in the legislature during their government service. They may return to the legislature when their government service ends.

> Article 160
> A deputy can hold the position of minister or official of the State or any other decentralized or autonomous entity. In these cases permission must be granted to him for the period that his executive responsibilities last. During his temporary absence, one shall

proceed in conformity with the last paragraph of Article 157.

Article 157
In case of the definitive fault of a deputy the post shall be declared vacant. Vacancies shall be filled, according to the case, by calling the postulate that appears in the respective district list of candidates or national list immediately after the last post awarded.

3. The legislature has powers of summons over executive branch officials and hearings with executive branch officials testifying before the legislature or its committees are regularly held.

Yes. The legislature regularly interpellates officials from the executive.

Article 165
The Congress will have the power to do the following:
j. To interpellate ministers of State.

Article 166
The ministers of State have the obligation to appear in Congress in order to answer the interpellations formulated by one or more deputies. Those which refer to diplomatic or pending military operations are excepted. The basic questions must be addressed to the minister or ministers interpellated with forty-eight hours' notice. Neither the full Congress, nor any authority, will be able to limit the deputies to the Congress in their right to interpellate, qualify the questions, or restrict them. Any deputy can address additional questions that he deems pertinent and related to the matter or matters underlying the interpellation and it is from the latter that a vote of no confidence may originate, which must be petitioned by four deputies, at least, and carried out without delay, in the same session or in one of the two immediately subsequent ones.

Article 167
When an interpellation is made to a minister, the latter cannot absent himself from the country nor decline to answer in any form.

Article 168
Ministers of State are required to attend the sessions of Congress, Commissions and Legislative Blocks when they are invited for this purpose. Notwithstanding, they can attend in any case and participate with voice in all discussions concerning matters of their competence. They can have themselves represented by their Vice Ministers.
All the officials and public employees are obliged to appear and report to the Congress, when the latter, its commissions or legislative blocks consider it necessary.

Article 199
The Ministers have the obligation to appear before the Congress, with the purpose of answering the interpellations addressed to them.

4. The legislature can conduct independent investigation of the chief executive and the agencies of the executive.

Yes. The legislature can establish committees to investigate the executive.

Article 171
Other Powers of the Congress.
It is also among the powers of the Congress to do the following:
m. To appoint investigation committees in specific matters of the public administration, that may involve problems of national interest.

5. The legislature has effective powers of oversight over the agencies of coercion (the military, organs of law enforcement, intelligence services, and the secret police).

No. The legislature can interpellate national security officials, but the legislature lacks effective powers of oversight over the agencies of coercion.

6. The legislature appoints the prime minister.

No. There is no prime minister.

7. The legislature's approval is required to confirm the appointment of ministers; or the legislature itself appoints ministers.

No. The president appoints ministers, and the appointments do not require the legislature's approval.

Article 183
The following are functions of the President of the Republic:
s. To appoint and remove the Ministers of State, Vice Ministers, Secretaries and Undersecretaries of the Presidency, ambassadors and other officials which correspond to him in accordance with the law.

8. The country lacks a presidency entirely or there is a presidency, but the president is elected by the legislature.

No. The president is directly elected.

Article 184
The President and Vice President of the Republic will be elected by the people through universal and secret suffrage and for a single term of four years.

9. The legislature can vote no confidence in the government.

No. The legislature cannot vote no confidence in the government.

10. The legislature is immune from dissolution by the executive.

Yes. The legislature is immune from dissolution.

11. Any executive initiative on legislation requires ratification or approval by the legislature before it takes effect; that is, the executive lacks decree power.

Yes. The executive lacks decree power.

12. Laws passed by the legislature are veto-proof or essentially veto-proof; that is, the executive lacks veto power, or has veto power but the veto can be overridden by a majority in the legislature.

No. A two-thirds majority vote in Congress is needed to override a presidential veto.

Article 179
Once the decree is sent back to Congress, the Directive Board should bring it to the attention of the plenary in the next session, and Congress may reconsider it or reject it during a period not to exceed thirty days. If the observations made by the Executive are not accepted and the Congress rejects the veto by a vote of two-thirds of its members, the Executive will obligatorily have to approve and promulgate the decree within the eight subsequent days after receiving it. Should the Executive not do so, the Directive Board of the Congress shall order its publication in a period not to exceed three days so it may enter into effect as a law of the Republic.

13. The legislature's laws are supreme and not subject to judicial review.

No. The Court of Constitutionality can review the constitutionality of laws.

Article 266
In concrete cases, in every process of whatever competence or jurisdiction, in any instance, and in cassation and even before sentence is decreed, the parties will be able to press as an action, exception, or incident the total or partial unconstitutionality of a law. The court will have to make a determination in that respect.

Article 267
Actions against the laws, regulations or provisions of a general character which contain a partial or total absence of constitutionality will be heard directly by the Tribunal or Court of Constitutionality.

Article 268
The Court of Constitutionality is a permanent tribunal of exclusive jurisdiction, whose essential function is the defense of the constitutional order.

Article 272
The Court of Constitutionality has the following functions:
e. To issue an opinion on the constitutionality of treaties, agreements, and bills of law at the request of any of the organisms of the State.

14. The legislature has the right to initiate bills in all policy jurisdictions; the executive lacks gatekeeping authority.

Yes. The legislature can initiate bills in all policy jurisdictions.

15. Expenditure of funds appropriated by the legislature is mandatory; the executive lacks the power to impound funds appropriated by the legislature.

Yes. The executive lacks the power to impound funds appropriated by the legislature.

16. The legislature controls the resources that finance its own internal operation and provide for the perquisites of its own members.

Yes. The legislature enjoys financial autonomy, including control over members' compensation.

Article 170
The specific powers of the Congress are as follows:
b. To appoint and remove its administrative personnel. The relations of the Legislative Organism with its administrative, technical, and service personnel, will be regulated by a specific law, which will establish the regime of classification, pay, discipline, and dismissals. The labor benefits of the personnel of the Legislative Organism that may be obtained by law, internal accord, resolution, or custom, cannot be diminished or distorted.

17. Members of the legislature are immune from arrest and/or criminal prosecution.

No. Legislative immunity can be revoked by a decision of the Supreme Court of Justice. Prior to 1994 legislators were immune.

Article 161
Deputies are representatives of the people and dignitaries of the Nation; as a guarantee for the exercise of their functions they will enjoy, from the day they are declared elected, the following prerogatives:
a. Personal immunity from arrest or trial if the Supreme Court of Justice does not previously declare that there is probable cause, after examining the report of the investigating judge that will be named for this end. The case of flagrante delicto is excepted, for which that deputy shall be immediately placed at the disposition of the Directive Board or the Permanent Commission of the Congress for the purpose of the corresponding initial judgment.
b. They cannot be held responsible for their opinions, initiative, and the manner of handling public business in the performance of their work. All the dependencies of the State have the obligation to show deputies the consideration attaching to their high position. These prerogatives do not authorize arbitrariness, excess of personal initiative, or any type of action tending to undermine the principle of no reelection for the exercise of the Presidency of the Republic. Only the Congress will be competent to judge and determine if there has been arbitrariness or excess and to impose the appropriate disciplinary sanctions. Considering the declaration to which paragraph (a) in this article refers, those accused are subject to the jurisdiction of the competent judge. If he should decree provisional imprisonment for them, they shall be suspended from their functions as long as the incarceration decree is not revoked. In the case of firm condemnatory sentence, it shall remain vacant.

18. All members of the legislature are elected; the executive lacks the power to appoint any members of the legislature.

Yes. All members of the legislature are elected.

Article 157
Legislative power belongs to the Congress of the Republic made up of deputies elected directly by the people in universal and secret suffrage through the national list and electoral district system for a period of four years, allowing for reelection.

19. The legislature alone, without the involvement of any other agencies, can change the Constitution.

No. Amendments to Chapter I, Title II, of the constitution require the convocation of a National Constituent Assembly. Other constitutional amendments require approval in a popular referendum.

Article 277
The following have the initiative to propose amendments to the Constitution:
a. The President of the Republic in the Council of Ministers;
b. Ten or more deputies to the Congress of the Republic;
c. The Court of Constitutionality; and
d. The people through a petition addressed to the Congress of the Republic by no fewer than 5,000 citizens duly listed in the Register of Citizens.
In any of the cases above, the Congress of the Republic must address without delay whatsoever the issue raised.

Article 278
In order to amend this or any article contained in Chapter I of Title II of this Constitution, it is indispensable that the Congress of the Republic, with the affirmative vote of two-thirds of the members composing it, should call a National Constituent Assembly. In the decree of convocation, the article or articles to be amended shall be specified and shall be communicated to the Supreme Electoral Tribunal so that it may determine the date when the elections would be held within the maximum deadline of 120 days, proceeding in other respects in accordance with the Constitutional Electoral Law.

Article 279
The National Constituent Assembly and the Congress of the Republic will be able to function simultaneously. The characteristics required to be deputy to the National Constituent Assembly are the same as those that are required to be deputy to the Congress, and the constituent deputies shall enjoy equal immunities and privileges.
It will not be possible to be simultaneously deputy to the National Constituent Assembly and to the Congress of the Republic.
The elections of deputies to the National Constituent Assembly, the number of deputies to be elected, and the other questions relating to the electoral process will be regulated in an equal form as the elections to the Congress of the Republic.

Article 280
For any other constitutional amendment, it will be necessary that the Congress of the Republic approve it with an affirmative vote of two-thirds of the total number of deputies. Amendments will not enter into effect unless they are ratified through a referendum referred to in Article 173 of this Constitution.
If the result of the referendum were to ratify the amendment, the latter will enter into effect 60 days after the Supreme Electoral Court announced the result of the referendum.

Article 281
In no case can Articles 140, 141, 165 (paragraph g), 186, and 187 be amended, nor can any question relating to the republican form of government, to the principle of the non-reelectibility for the exercise of the Presidency of the Republic be raised in any form, neither may the effectiveness or application of the articles that provide for alternating the tenure of the Presidency of the Republic be suspended or their content changed or modified in any other way.

20. The legislature's approval is necessary for the declaration of war.

Yes. The legislature declares war.

Article 171
It is also among the powers of the Congress to do the following:
f. To declare war and approve or disapprove peace treaties.

21. The legislature's approval is necessary to ratify treaties with foreign countries.

Yes. The legislature's approval is necessary to ratify international treaties on most major issues.

Article 171
It is also among the powers of the Congress to do the following:
f. To declare war and approve or disapprove peace treaties.
l. To approve, before their ratification, the treaties, agreements, or any international settlement when:
1. They affect the existing laws where this Constitution may require the same majority of votes;
2. They affect the power of the Nation, establish the economic or political union of Central America, whether partial or total, or attribute or transfer competences to organs, institutions, or mechanisms created for an ordained juridical community to realize regional and common objectives in the Central American area;
3. They obligate the State financially in proportion that it exceeds one percent of the Budget of Ordinary Revenues or when the amount of the obligation is indeterminate;
4. They constitute a pledge [*compromiso*] to submit any matter to international judicial or arbitral decision;
5. They contain a general arbitration clause or one for submission to international jurisdiction; and

m. To appoint investigation committees in specific matters of the public administration, that may involve problems of national interest.

Article 172

To approve before their ratification, with a vote of two-thirds of the total number of deputies who make up the Congress, treaties, agreements, or any international settlement when:

a. They refer to the passage of foreign armed forces through the national territory or the temporary establishment of foreign military bases; and

b. They affect or can affect the security of the State or put an end to a state of war.

22. The legislature has the power to grant amnesty.

Yes. The legislature has the power to grant amnesty for political crimes.

Article 171

Other Powers of the Congress.

It is also among the powers of the Congress to do the following:

g. To decree amnesty for political and related common crimes when public convenience demands it.

23. The legislature has the power of pardon.

Yes. The legislature has the power of pardon, indicated here as "amnesty for . . . common crimes."

Article 171

Other Powers of the Congress.

It is also among the powers of the Congress to do the following:

g. To decree amnesty for political and related common crimes when public convenience demands it.

24. The legislature reviews and has the right to reject appointments to the judiciary; or the legislature itself appoints members of the judiciary.

Yes. The legislature elects all of the magistrates on the Supreme Court of Justice and the Court of Appeals and one of the five magistrates on the Court of Constitutionality.

Article 205

The following are established as guarantees of the Judicial Organism:

a. Functional independence;

b. Financial independence;

c. Irremovability of the magistrates and judges of the first instance, except in cases established by the law; and

d. The selection of personnel.

Article 209

Judges, secretaries, and auxiliary personnel will be appointed by the Supreme Court of Justice. The judicial career is established.

Article 215

Election of the Supreme Court of Justice.

The Magistrates of the Supreme Court of Justice shall be elected by the Congress of the Republic for a period of five years from a list of twenty-six candidates proposed by a postulation commission composed of a representative of the Rectors of the Universities of the country, who shall preside, the Deans of the Faculties of Law or Juridical and Social Sciences of each University of the country, an equivalent number of representatives elected by the General Assembly of the Association of Lawyers and Notaries of Guatemala and by an equal number of representatives elected by the titled judges of the Court of Appeals and other tribunals referred to in Article 217 of this Constitution.

Article 217

The titled magistrates [of the Court of Appeals] shall be elected by the Congress of the Republic from a panel of candidates with double the number to be elected, proposed by a postulation commission composed of one representative of the Rectors of the Universities of the country, who shall preside, the Deans of the Law or Juridical and Social Sciences Departments of each University of the country, an equivalent number of members elected by the General Assembly of the Association of Lawyers and Notaries of Guatemala and by an equal number of representatives elected by the judges of the Supreme Court of Justice.

Article 269

The Court of Constitutionality consists of five titled magistrates each of whom will have his respective alternate. When it is seized with matters of unconstitutionality against the Supreme Court of Justice, the Congress of the Republic, or the President or Vice President of the Republic, the number of its members will be raised to seven, the other two magistrates being selected by lot from among the alternates.

The magistrates serve in their functions five years and shall be appointed in the following manner:

a. One magistrate by the plenary of the Supreme Court of Justice;

b. One magistrate by the plenary of the Congress of the Republic;

c. One magistrate by the President of the Republic in the Council of Ministers;

d. One magistrate by the Higher University Council of the University of San Carlos de Guatemala; and

e. One magistrate by the Assembly of the Bar Association.

Simultaneously with the appointment of the magistrate, that of the respective alternate will occur before the Congress of the Republic.

The installation of the Court of Constitutionality will become effective 90 days after that of the Congress of the Republic.

25. The chairman of the central bank is appointed by the legislature.

No. The president appoints the president of the Bank of Guatemala.

26. The legislature has a substantial voice in the operation of the state-owned media.

No. The legislature lacks a substantial voice in the operation of the public media.

27. The legislature is regularly in session.

Yes. The legislature meets in ordinary session for at least seven months each year.

> Article 158
> The annual period of sessions of the Congress is initiated the fourteenth of January of each year without necessity of convocation. The Congress meets in ordinary sessions of the fourteenth of January to the fifteenth of May and of the first of August to the thirteenth of November of each year.

> Article 163
> Each year the Congress will elect its Directorate [*Junta Directiva*]. Before closing its period of ordinary sessions the Congress will elect its Permanent Committee, presided over by the President of the Congress, that will function while the Congress is not in session.

28. Each legislator has a personal secretary.

No.

29. Each legislator has at least one non-secretarial staff member with policy expertise.

No.

30. Legislators are eligible for re-election without any restriction.

Yes. There are no restrictions on re-election.

31. A seat in the legislature is an attractive enough position that legislators are generally interested in and seek re-election.

Yes.

32. The re-election of incumbent legislators is common enough that at any given time the legislature contains a significant number of highly experienced members.

No. The party system has been highly unstable, resulting in a great deal of turnover and a dearth of highly experienced legislators.

NATIONAL ASSEMBLY OF GUINEA (*ASSEMBLÉE NATIONALE*)

Expert consultants: Kaké Makanéra Al-Hassan, Mohamed Saliou Camara, Malick Diakite, Nanfadima Magassouba, Denis Marantz

Score: .31

Influence over executive (1/9)		Institutional autonomy (3/9)		Specified powers (3/8)		Institutional capacity (3/6)	
1. replace		10. no dissolution		19. amendments		27. sessions	
2. serve as ministers		11. no decree		20. war	X	28. secretary	
3. interpellate		12. no veto		21. treaties	X	29. staff	
4. investigate	X	13. no review		22. amnesty	X	30. no term limits	X
5. oversee police		14. no gatekeeping	X	23. pardon		31. seek re-election	X
6. appoint PM		15. no impoundment		24. judiciary		32. experience	X
7. appoint ministers		16. control resources	X	25. central bank			
8. lack president		17. immunity		26. media			
9. no confidence		18. all elected	X				

The National Assembly (*Assemblée nationale*) of Guinea has origins in the People's National Assembly (*Assemblée nationale populaire*) established in 1962 under the Marxist-Leninist government of President Sékou Touré. In practice, Touré sidelined the legislature and ruled by decree. Upon Touré's death in 1984, Lasana Conté seized power in a military coup and dissolved the legislature. A new constitution in 1990 called for the establishment of the unicameral National Assembly, and Guinea held its first multiparty elections in 1995. A constitutional amendment in 2001 gave the president the power to appoint Supreme Court justices. Prior to 2001 the National Assembly appointed them.

The legislature has almost no influence over the executive branch. It cannot remove the president, question executive branch officials, or reject the president's ministerial appointments. The legislature's own institutional autonomy is circumscribed by presidential veto and decree powers. The legislature has some specified powers, including the right to approve presidential declarations of war and to ratify international treaties. Its institutional capacity is modest.

SURVEY

1. The legislature alone, without the involvement of any other agencies, can impeach the president or replace the prime minister.

No. Presidential impeachment requires the involvement of the High Court of Justice.

> Article 86
> The President of the Republic shall be responsible for the acts accomplished in the exercise of his functions only in the case of high treason.
> He shall only be accused by the National Assembly deciding by a three-fifths majority in a secret vote. He shall be judged by the High Court of Justice. It may decide when the President of the Republic is accused, that the President of the National Assembly shall exercise his interim powers until the outcome is determined.

2. Ministers may serve simultaneously as members of the legislature.

No. Legislators are prohibited from serving simultaneously in ministerial positions.

3. The legislature has powers of summons over executive branch officials and hearings with executive branch officials testifying before the legislature or its committees are regularly held.

No. Formally, the legislature has the power to interpellate executive branch officials, but this right is not regularly exercised.

> Article 73
> The Deputies can ask the Ministers, who are obligated to respond, written and oral questions with or without debate. The responses given shall not be followed by a vote. They shall be published in the Official Journal. One meeting per week shall be reserved during the course of each extraordinary session, for oral questions without debate. The National Assembly can designate at its center commissions of inquiry. The regulations of the Assembly shall determine the powers of these commissions. They shall be created by law, which shall define their composition, functioning and objective, and which shall specify their powers.

4. The legislature can conduct independent investigation of the chief executive and the agencies of the executive.

Yes. The legislature can establish commissions of inquiry to investigate the executive.

> Article 73
> The Deputies can ask the Ministers, who are obligated to respond, written and oral questions with or without debate. The responses given shall not be followed by a vote. They shall be published in the Official Journal. One meeting per week shall be reserved during the course of each extraordinary session, for oral questions without debate. The National Assembly can designate at its center commissions of inquiry. The regulations of the Assembly shall determine the powers of these commissions. They shall be created by law, which shall define their composition, functioning and objective, and which shall specify their powers.

5. The legislature has effective powers of oversight over the agencies of coercion (the military, organs of law enforcement, intelligence services, and the secret police).

No. The legislature lacks effective powers of oversight over the agencies of coercion.

6. The legislature appoints the prime minister.

No. There is no prime minister.

7. The legislature's approval is required to confirm the appointment of ministers; or the legislature itself appoints ministers.

No. The president appoints the ministers, and the appointments do not require the legislature's approval.

> Article 39
> The President of the Republic shall appoint Ministers who shall assist him and shall be responsible only to him.

8. The country lacks a presidency entirely or there is a presidency, but the president is elected by the legislature.

No. The president is directly elected.

> Article 24
> The President of the Republic shall be elected by direct universal suffrage.

9. The legislature can vote no confidence in the government.

No. The legislature cannot vote no confidence in the government.

10. The legislature is immune from dissolution by the executive.

No. The president can dissolve the legislature.

Article 76
In the case of persistent disagreement between the President of the Republic and the National Assembly on fundamental questions, the President of the Republic can, after having consulted the President of the National Assembly, pronounce the dissolution of the Assembly.

11. Any executive initiative on legislation requires ratification or approval by the legislature before it takes effect; that is, the executive lacks decree power.

No. According to the constitution, the president may issue regulatory decrees and can issue decrees that have the force of law only when he or she is authorized to do so by the legislature. In practice, the president issues decrees that have the force of law without prior legislative authorization.

Article 38
The President of the Republic shall assure the execution of laws and prescribe regulatory power which he exercises by decree.

Article 66
The National Assembly can enable the President by a law to take measures normally relegated to the domain of the law, for a specified period of time and objectives that it specifies.
Within the time limits and domain fixed by the enabling act, the President of the Republic can make ordinances which shall be effective upon their publication, but become void if a bill of ratification is not presented before the National Assembly before the date fixed by the enabling act. After this last date, they may only be modified by law. They retain at all times their regulatory value until their ratification. They may be amended at the time of the vote of the law of ratification.

12. Laws passed by the legislature are veto-proof or essentially veto-proof; that is, the executive lacks veto power, or has veto power but the veto can be overridden by a majority in the legislature.

No. A two-thirds majority vote in the legislature is needed to override a presidential veto.

Article 63
In the ten days fixed for promulgation, the President of the Republic can, by message, demand a new deliberation of the National Assembly which cannot be refused. The delay period of promulgation is thereby suspended. The law shall only be voted upon a second time if two thirds of the members of the National Assembly are in favor. It shall take priority on the day's agenda if the majority of the members of the National Assembly demand it.

13. The legislature's laws are supreme and not subject to judicial review.

No. The Supreme Court can review the constitutionality of laws.

Article 64
In the full eight days which follow the adoption of a law, the President of the Republic or a tenth of the Deputies can convene the Supreme Court for close scrutiny to ensure the conformity of the law with the Fundamental Law. The delay period of promulgation is thus suspended. The Supreme Court shall decide within the thirty days that follow its convocation or, if the President of the republic makes the demand, in eight days. The decision of the Supreme Court shall be published in the Official Journal. A disposition of a law declared nonconforming to the Fundamental Law shall not be promulgated nor applied. The decision of the Supreme Court shall be binding on all.
The delay period of promulgation begins to run from the date of publication of the decision of the Supreme Court which declares the law in conformity with the Fundamental Law.

Article 83
The Supreme Court shall have the authority to declare the constitutionality of laws and international engagements, under the conditions established in Articles 64, 67 and 78.

14. The legislature has the right to initiate bills in all policy jurisdictions; the executive lacks gatekeeping authority.

Yes. The legislature can initiate bills in all policy jurisdictions.

15. Expenditure of funds appropriated by the legislature is mandatory; the executive lacks the power to impound funds appropriated by the legislature.

No. The executive can impound funds appropriated by the legislature. Legislative appropriations authorize, but do not require, the expenditure of funds.

16. The legislature controls the resources that finance its own internal operation and provide for the perquisites of its own members.

Yes. The legislature enjoys financial autonomy.

17. Members of the legislature are immune from arrest and/or criminal prosecution.

No. By law, legislators are immune, but in practice, opponents of the president are subject to arrest and prosecution. For example, in 1998 four members of the Assembly, including Alpha Condé, an opposition leader and a candidate for president that year, were arrested and imprisoned for "causing a breach of the peace." Although the law provides that members of the Assembly may be arrested only if their immunity is lifted by the Assembly, in these cases and others the executive and the agencies of coercion ignored the legal requirement for the authorization of the National Assembly.

Article 52
No member of the National Assembly shall be prosecuted, investigated, arrested, detained or tried because
of opinions or votes expressed by him while exercising
his functions as Deputy.
No deputy shall be prosecuted or arrested on penal
grounds while the National Assembly is in session
except with the Assembly's authorization, except in the
case of *flagrante delicto.*
No deputy can be arrested or detained while the Assembly is not in session without the authorization of the
office of the National Assembly except in the case of
flagrante delicto, prosecutions authorized by the Assembly or final condemnations. The preventive detention
or prosecution of a Deputy shall be suspended if the
Assembly requires it.

18. All members of the legislature are elected; the
executive lacks the power to appoint any members of
the legislature.

Yes. All members of the legislature are elected.

Article 47
The Deputies to the National Assembly shall be elected
by direct universal suffrage.
The duration of their term shall be five years, except in
the case of dissolution. They may be reelected.

19. The legislature alone, without the involvement of
any other agencies, can change the Constitution.

No. Constitutional amendments initiated by the
legislature require approval in a popular referendum.

Article 91
The initiative of the revision of the Fundamental Law
belongs to both the President of the Republic and to the
Deputies. The bill or proposition of revision adopted
by the National Assembly shall only become definitive after having been approved by referendum. At any
time, the bill of revision shall not be presented to referendum when the President of the Republic decides to
submit it only to the National Assembly. In this case
the bill of revision shall be approved by a two thirds
majority of the members of the National Assembly. It
shall consist of the same proposition of revision which
had received the approval of the President of the Republic.

20. The legislature's approval is necessary for the declaration of war.

Yes. The legislature's approval is necessary for presidential war declarations.

Article 75
The state of war shall be declared by the President of the
Republic after being authorized by the National Assem-
bly by a two thirds majority of its members.

21. The legislature's approval is necessary to ratify
treaties with foreign countries.

Yes. The legislature's approval is necessary to ratify
international treaties on most major issues.

Article 77
The President of the Republic negotiates international engagements. Peace treaties, commercial treaties,
treaties or accords relative to international organization, those which engage the finances of the State,
those which modify provisions of a legislative nature,
those which are relative to the state of persons, those
which encompass cession, exchange or adjunction
of territory, shall only be ratified or approved by a
law.

22. The legislature has the power to grant amnesty.

Yes. The National Assembly has the power to grant
amnesty.

Article 59
Subject to the provisions of Article 45, the National
Assembly alone shall pass laws.
The law shall only be prospective.
The law shall fix rules concerning:
  – amnesty.

23. The legislature has the power of pardon.

No. The president has the power of pardon.

Article 43
The President of the Republic exercises the power to
grant pardons.

24. The legislature reviews and has the right to reject
appointments to the judiciary; or the legislature itself
appoints members of the judiciary.

No. Formally, the legislature makes appointments
to the High Court of Justice, while the president
appoints the magistrates of the Supreme Court, but
in practice, the president fully controls all judicial
appointments, and the legislature lacks a meaningful role.

Article 81
Magistrates shall be named by the President of the
Republic, those of the bench after consultation of the
Superior Council of the Magistrate.

Article 85
The High Court of Justice shall be composed of members elected by the National Assembly, at its center, at
the beginning of each legislature.

25. The chairman of the central bank is appointed by
the legislature.

No. The president appoints the governor of the
Central Bank of Guinea.

26. The legislature has a substantial voice in the operation of the state-owned media.

No. The legislature lacks a substantial voice in the
operation of the public media.

27. The legislature is regularly in session.

No. The legislature meets in ordinary session for no more than three months each year.

> Article 55
> The National Assembly shall meet, as of right, in ordinary sessions twice a year.
> The first session shall open on April 5 and shall last no longer than thirty days.
> The second session shall open on October 5 and shall last no longer than sixty days.

28. Each legislator has a personal secretary.

No.

29. Each legislator has at least one non-secretarial staff member with policy expertise.

No.

30. Legislators are eligible for re-election without any restriction.

Yes. There are no restrictions on re-election.

> Article 47
> The Deputies to the National Assembly shall be elected by direct universal suffrage.

The duration of their term shall be five years, except in the case of dissolution. They may be reelected.

31. A seat in the legislature is an attractive enough position that legislators are generally interested in and seek re-election.

Yes.

32. The re-election of incumbent legislators is common enough that at any given time the legislature contains a significant number of highly experienced members.

Yes. Since the first multiparty elections in 1995, the re-election rate has been relatively high, producing a stable body of experienced members. President Lasana Conté's Party of Unity and Progress has long dominated parliament. Its hegemony was reconfirmed in the 2002 elections, in which it captured three-quarters of the seats in the legislature. The president's dominance of politics, including his de facto control of the National Assembly, means that even experienced members do not necessarily possess significant acumen as legislators.

NATIONAL PEOPLE'S ASSEMBLY OF GUINEA-BISSAU (*ASSEMBLEIA NACIONAL POPULAR*)

Expert consultants: Elisabete Azevedo, Joshua B. Forrest, Fodé Mané, Eleanor Marchant, P. M. Karibe Mendy, Lars Rudebeck

Score: .25

Influence over executive (0/9)	Institutional autonomy (3/9)		Specified powers (3/8)		Institutional capacity (2/6)	
1. replace	10. no dissolution		19. amendments	X	27. sessions	
2. serve as ministers	11. no decree		20. war	X	28. secretary	
3. interpellate	12. no veto		21. treaties	X	29. staff	
4. investigate	13. no review	X	22. amnesty		30. no term limits	X
5. oversee police	14. no gatekeeping	X	23. pardon		31. seek re-election	X
6. appoint PM	15. no impoundment		24. judiciary		32. experience	
7. appoint ministers	16. control resources		25. central bank			
8. lack president	17. immunity		26. media			
9. no confidence	18. all elected	X				

The National People's Assembly (*Assembleia Nacional Popular*) of Guinea-Bissau was established upon independence from Portugal in 1974. A new constitution was adopted in 1984 that called for a unicameral assembly. Constitutional amendments in 1991 and 1993 did not directly concern the legislature's power. In practice, the African Party for the Independence of Guinea-Bissau and Cape Verde

(PAIGC) dominated Guinea-Bissau after independence, and competitive multiparty elections were not held until 1994. A dispute over the 1999 presidential elections led to civil conflict and eventually the dissolution of the Assembly in November 2002. The Assembly drafted a new constitution in 2001, but the president never either promulgated or vetoed it, resulting in ambiguity about which constitution contains the country's legitimate fundamental law. The constitutional excerpts cited below are from the 1984 constitution. The Assembly reconvened following legislative elections in March 2004, which were again won by the PAIGC.

The Assembly has little clout. It cannot influence the executive. It also has little institutional autonomy; presidential powers that include veto and decree circumscribe the legislature's autonomy. The legislature holds three of the enumerated powers assessed here: It can change the constitution, declare war, and ratify treaties. The absence of staff, a paucity of legislators with substantial experience, and the absence of regular meeting sessions severely restrict the Assembly's institutional capacity.

SURVEY

1. The legislature alone, without the involvement of any other agencies, can impeach the president or replace the prime minister.

No. The legislature cannot impeach the president. The legislature can remove the prime minister with a vote of no confidence.

> Article 75
> The Government shall be politically responsible to the National Popular Assembly and to the Council of State.

2. Ministers may serve simultaneously as members of the legislature.

No. Legislators are prohibited from serving simultaneously in ministerial positions.

> Article 55
> 1. The National Popular Assembly shall elect its President and other members of his Cabinet at the first session of each legislature.
> 2. The Cabinet shall be composed of the President, one First Vice-President, one Second Vice-President, a First Secretary, and a Second Secretary, elected by the total legislature. The powers and jurisdiction of the Cabinet shall be regulated by the Rules and Procedures of the Assembly.
> 3. The office of the President of the National Popular Assembly shall be incompatible with that of Member of the Government.

> Article 59
> Members of the Political Bureau of the PAIGC and members of the Government who are not Deputies may sit and speak in plenary sessions of the Assembly.

3. The legislature has powers of summons over executive branch officials and hearings with executive branch officials testifying before the legislature or its committees are regularly held.

No. According to the constitution, the legislature can interpellate executive branch officials, but in practice, hearings are rare.

> Article 52
> A Deputy shall have the right to question members of the Council of State and of the Government, either orally or in written form; the respective answer must be provided to him during the same session or within two weeks, at the most, in written form, if an investigation is required.

4. The legislature can conduct independent investigation of the chief executive and the agencies of the executive.

No. Although the legislature formally has the right to create special commissions to investigate the executive, in practice, the legislature lacks the ability to investigate the executive.

> Article 52
> A Deputy shall have the right to question members of the Council of State and of the Government, either orally or in written form; the respective answer must be provided to him during the same session or within two weeks, at the most, in written form, if an investigation is required.

> Article 57
> The National Popular Assembly shall create permanent specialized Commissions according to various matters and create temporary committees to take up predetermined subjects.

5. The legislature has effective powers of oversight over the agencies of coercion (the military, organs of law enforcement, intelligence services, and the secret police).

No. The legislature lacks effective powers of oversight over the agencies of coercion.

6. The legislature appoints the prime minister.

No. The president appoints the prime minister.

> Article 67
> The attributions of the President of the Council of State shall be those which are conferred upon him by the National Popular Assembly or by this Constitution, namely:
> 4. to appoint and to recall the Prime Minister, Ministers, Secretaries of State, and the Governor of the Central Bank.

7. The legislature's approval is required to confirm the appointment of ministers; or the legislature itself appoints ministers.

No. The president appoints ministers, and the appointments do not require the legislature's approval.

Article 67
The attributions of the President of the Council of State shall be those which are conferred upon him by the National Popular Assembly or by this Constitution, namely:
4. to appoint and to recall the Prime Minister, Ministers, Secretaries of State, and the Governor of the Central Bank.

8. The country lacks a presidency entirely or there is a presidency, but the president is elected by the legislature.

No. According to the 1984 constitution cited here, the president is elected by the legislature, but the constitution does not provide a good guide to the means of election. In 1994, 1999, and 2005, the citizens of Guinea-Bissau elected the president directly.

Article 63
1. The Council of State shall comprise 15 members elected from among the Deputies by the National Popular Assembly in the first session of each legislature.
2. The National Popular Assembly shall elect the President of the Council of State from among members elected to the Council of State.

9. The legislature can vote no confidence in the government.

No. Although the government is formally "politically responsible" to the legislature, the legislature cannot vote no confidence in the government.

Article 75
The Government shall be politically responsible to the National Popular Assembly and to the Council of State.

10. The legislature is immune from dissolution by the executive.

No. Formally, the legislature is immune from dissolution. In practice, the president can dissolve the legislature, as he did in 2002.

11. Any executive initiative on legislation requires ratification or approval by the legislature before it takes effect; that is, the executive lacks decree power.

No. Formally, the president can issue decrees that have the force of law only with the prior authorization of the legislature. In practice, the president regularly issues decree-laws without such authorization.

Article 67
The attributions of the President of the Council of State shall be those which are conferred upon him by the National Popular Assembly or by this Constitution, namely:
11. to promulgate laws-by-decree, to sign and to order the publication of decisions of the Council of State and of decrees of the Cabinet Council in the *Official Bulletin.*

12. Laws passed by the legislature are veto-proof or essentially veto-proof; that is, the executive lacks veto power, or has veto power but the veto can be overridden by a majority in the legislature.

No. The legislature cannot override the president's veto. The constitution does not grant the president a veto of any type, but in practice, the president simply refuses to promulgate any legislation to which he objects.

13. The legislature's laws are supreme and not subject to judicial review.

Yes. According to the 1984 constitution, the legislature itself has the authority to review the constitutionality of laws. The new constitution, if adopted, will provide for a Supreme Court with the power to review the constitutionality of laws.

Article 56
The following shall be incumbent upon the National Popular Assembly:
5. to decide on the constitutionality of laws, laws-by-decree, and other legislation;
6. to approve, modify, or annul legislation and other measures adopted by organs of the State that are contrary to this Constitution and laws.

Article 98
1. Cases placed before the courts may not apply rules that infringe upon the provisions of the Constitution or principles herein consecrated.
2. The question of unconstitutionality may be raised officially by a court, by the Public Ministry, or by any of the parties.
3. Whenever a question of unconstitutionality is raised, the incident shall be separately submitted to the National Popular Assembly, which shall decide the matter.
4. All decisions made by the National Popular Assembly regarding unconstitutionality shall be generally mandatory and shall be published in the *Official Bulletin.*

14. The legislature has the right to initiate bills in all policy jurisdictions; the executive lacks gatekeeping authority.

Yes. The legislature can initiate bills in all policy jurisdictions.

15. Expenditure of funds appropriated by the legislature is mandatory; the executive lacks the power to impound funds appropriated by the legislature.

No. The president can impound funds appropriated by the legislature.

16. The legislature controls the resources that finance its own internal operation and provide for the perquisites of its own members.

No. The legislature is dependent on the executive for the resources that finance its operations.

17. Members of the legislature are immune from arrest and/or criminal prosecution.

No. Formally, legislators are immune, but in practice, this constitutional provision is overlooked, and legislators have been arrested and detained.

> Article 53
> 1. No deputy may be disturbed, prosecuted, arrested, imprisoned, judged, or condemned for his voting record or the opinions he expresses while performing his duties as Deputy.
> 2. Except if apprehended in the act of committing an offense *flagrante delicto* that bears a penalty equal to or greater than two years of forced labor, or with the previous consent of the National Popular Assembly or the Council of State, Deputies may not be prosecuted or imprisoned for a criminal or disciplinary question, whether judged or not.

18. All members of the legislature are elected; the executive lacks the power to appoint any members of the legislature.

Yes. All members of the legislature are elected.

> Article 47
> 1. Members of the Regional Councils shall be elected by free, universal, equal, direct, and secret suffrage. Voters shall be all citizens of the nation over 18 years old, except for those disqualified by law.
> 2. Members of the National Popular Assembly shall be elected by the Regional Councils from among their members, provided same are native citizens of the nation according to conditions and forms fixed by law.

19. The legislature alone, without the involvement of any other agencies, can change the Constitution.

Yes. The legislature can change the constitution with a two-thirds majority vote.

> Article 99
> 1. This Constitution may be amended at any time by the National Popular Assembly.
> 2. The initiative to revise the Constitution shall belong to Deputies, to the Council of State, and to the Government.

> Article 100
> 1. The proposal for revision shall indicate the articles that must be revised and the sense of the changes to be introduced.

> 2. A proposed law for revision must be submitted by at least one-third of the Deputies actively in office, by the Council of State, or by the Government.

> Article 101
> Proposals for revision must be approved by the majority of two-thirds of the Deputies comprising the Assembly.

> Article 102
> No proposal for revision may impose upon:
> a) the unitary structure or republican form of the State;
> b) the Laic Statute of the State;
> c) the integrity of national territory.

20. The legislature's approval is necessary for the declaration of war.

Yes. There is no constitutional provision that specifically addresses the declaration of war. The legislature alone can declare a state of martial law or a state of emergency.

> Article 56
> The following shall be incumbent upon the National Popular Assembly:
> 10. to declare a state of martial law or a state of emergency, according to terms of law.

21. The legislature's approval is necessary to ratify treaties with foreign countries.

Yes. The legislature's approval is necessary to ratify international treaties on most major issues.

> Article 56
> The following shall be incumbent upon the National Popular Assembly:
> 8. to approve treaties that concern the participation of Guinea-Bissau in international organizations, treaties for friendship, peace, defense, the changing of borders, and any others that the Government decides to submit for approval.

> Article 72
> The following shall be incumbent upon the Government in exercising its functions:
> h) to negotiate and to sign international pacts and conventions.

22. The legislature has the power to grant amnesty.

No. The legislature formally has the power to grant amnesty, but in practice, this power is reserved for the president.

> Article 56
> The following shall be incumbent upon the National Popular Assembly:
> 12. to grant amnesty.

23. The legislature has the power of pardon.

No. The cabinet (the Council of State) has the power of pardon.

> Article 64
> 1. The responsibilities of the Council of State are:
>   k) to pardon and to commute penalties.

24. The legislature reviews and has the right to reject appointments to the judiciary; or the legislature itself appoints members of the judiciary.

No. The president appoints judges, and the appointments do not require the legislature's approval.

> Article 67
> The attributions of the President of the Council of State shall be those which are conferred upon him by the National Popular Assembly or by this Constitution, namely:
> 5. to appoint and recall Judges of the Supreme Court of Justice and the Procurator-General of the Republic.

> Article 92
> The Supreme Court of Justice shall be the Republic's supreme judicial instance. Its judges shall be appointed by the President of the Council of State.

25. The chairman of the central bank is appointed by the legislature.

No. Guinea-Bissau is a member of the Central Bank of West African States, whose governor is selected by the member states.

26. The legislature has a substantial voice in the operation of the state-owned media.

No. The legislature lacks a substantial voice in the operation of the public media.

27. The legislature is regularly in session.

No. The legislature usually meets in only one annual ordinary session, which lasts two or three months.

> Article 58
> The National Popular Assembly shall meet in regular session once a year. It may also gather in special session when called by the Council of State at its own initiative, by the Council or Ministers, or when required by a majority of Deputies. All details of said operation shall be regulated by law.

28. Each legislator has a personal secretary.

No.

29. Each legislator has at least one non-secretarial staff member with policy expertise.

No.

30. Legislators are eligible for re-election without any restriction.

Yes. There are no restrictions on re-election.

31. A seat in the legislature is an attractive enough position that legislators are generally interested in and seek re-election.

Yes.

32. The re-election of incumbent legislators is common enough that at any given time the legislature contains a significant number of highly experienced members.

No. Political instability and irregular sittings of the legislature have prevented legislators from developing significant expertise.

NATIONAL ASSEMBLY OF GUYANA

Expert consultants: Deryck M. Bernard, Desiree Bernard, Percy C. Hintzen, Michael Murphy, Haslyn Parris

Score: .38

Influence over executive (2/9)		Institutional autonomy (4/9)		Specified powers (2/8)		Institutional capacity (4/6)	
1. replace		10. no dissolution		19. amendments	X	27. sessions	X
2. serve as ministers	X	11. no decree	X	20. war		28. secretary	
3. interpellate		12. no veto		21. treaties	X	29. staff	
4. investigate		13. no review		22. amnesty		30. no term limits	X
5. oversee police		14. no gatekeeping	X	23. pardon		31. seek re-election	X
6. appoint PM		15. no impoundment	X	24. judiciary		32. experience	X
7. appoint ministers		16. control resources		25. central bank			
8. lack president	X	17. immunity		26. media			
9. no confidence		18. all elected	X				

The National Assembly of Guyana was established in 1966 in the country's first post-independence constitution. The constitution called for a Westminster-style system with a prime minister and government appointed by, and responsible to, the legislature. A new constitution in 1980 instituted a semipresidential system. The president is the leader of the plurality party in the legislature, but the prime minister and other ministers are appointed by the president, and ministerial appointments do not require legislative approval. The legislature can no longer vote no confidence in the government or remove the chief executive from office.

The legislature has little control over the executive. The legislature's own institutional autonomy is circumscribed by presidential veto and dissolution powers. Many of the specified powers and prerogatives assessed in this survey are granted to the president. The legislature can, however, change the constitution without the involvement of any other actors. The legislature also has some institutional capacity, although legislators lack personal staff.

SURVEY

1. The legislature alone, without the involvement of any other agencies, can impeach the president or replace the prime minister.

No. Presidential impeachment requires the involvement of the judiciary.

Article 180
(1) If notice in writing is given to the Speaker of the National Assembly, signed by not less than one-half of all the elected members of the Assembly, of a motion alleging that the President has committed any violation of the Constitution or any gross misconduct and specifying the particulars of the allegations and proposing that a tribunal be established under this article to investigate those allegations, the Speaker shall –
    (a) if Parliament is then sitting or has been summoned to meet within five days, cause the motion to be considered by the Assembly within seven days of the notice; or
    (b) if Parliament is not then sitting (and notwithstanding that it may be prorogued) summon the Assembly to meet within twenty-one days of the notice and cause the motion to be considered at that meeting.
(2) Where a motion under this article is proposed for consideration by the National Assembly, the Assembly shall not debate the motion but the person presiding in the Assembly shall forthwith cause a vote to be taken on the motion and, if the motion is supported by the votes of not less than two-thirds of all the elected members of the Assembly, shall declare the motion to be passed.
(3) If the motion is declared to be passed under paragraph (2) –
    (a) the Chancellor shall appoint a tribunal which shall consist of a chairman and not less than two other members selected by the Chancellor from

among persons who hold or have held office as a Judge of a court having unlimited jurisdiction in civil and criminal matters in some part of the Commonwealth or a court having jurisdiction on appeal from any such court;

(b) the tribunal shall investigate the matter and shall report to the National Assembly whether it finds the particulars of the allegations specified in the motion to have been substantiated;

(c) the President shall have the right to appear and be represented before the tribunal during its investigation of the allegations against him.

(4) If the tribunal reports to the National Assembly that the tribunal finds that the particulars of any allegation against the President specified in the motion have not been substantiated no further proceedings shall be taken under this article in respect of that allegation.

(5) If the tribunal reports to the National Assembly that the tribunal finds that the particulars of any allegation specified in the motion have been substantiated, the Assembly may, on a motion supported by the votes of not less than three-quarters of all elected members of the Assembly, resolve that the President has been guilty of such violation of the Constitution or, as the case may be, such gross misconduct as is if the Assembly so resolves, the President shall cease to hold office upon the third day following the passage of the resolution unless he sooner dissolves Parliament.

2. Ministers may serve simultaneously as members of the legislature.

Yes. The prime minister and vice presidents must be selected from the members of the legislature. Other ministers may be appointed from inside or outside the legislature. Ministers who were not members of the legislature at the time of their appointment become nonvoting members of the legislature.

Article 103
(2) Subject to the provisions of article 101 (1), Vice Presidents and other Ministers shall be appointed by the President from among persons who are elected members of the National Assembly or are qualified to be elected as such members.

Article 105
A Minister who was not an elected member of the Assembly at the time of his appointment shall (unless he becomes such a member) be a member of the Assembly by virtue of holding the office of Minister but shall not vote in the Assembly.

3. The legislature has powers of summons over executive branch officials and hearings with executive branch officials testifying before the legislature or its committees are regularly held.

No. The legislature does not regularly question officials from the executive.

4. The legislature can conduct independent investigation of the chief executive and the agencies of the executive.

No. The legislature cannot investigate the executive.

5. The legislature has effective powers of oversight over the agencies of coercion (the military, organs of law enforcement, intelligence services, and the secret police).

No. The legislature lacks effective powers of oversight over the agencies of coercion.

6. The legislature appoints the prime minister.

No. The president appoints the prime minister.

Article 101
(1) The President shall appoint an elected member of the National Assembly to be Prime Minister of Guyana.

7. The legislature's approval is required to confirm the appointment of ministers; or the legislature itself appoints ministers.

No. The president appoints ministers, and the appointments do not require the legislature's approval.

Article 103
(2) Subject to the provisions of article 101 (1), Vice Presidents and other Ministers shall be appointed by the President from among persons who are elected members of the National Assembly or are qualified to be elected as such members.

8. The country lacks a presidency entirely or there is a presidency, but the president is elected by the legislature.

Yes. Although the constitution states that the president is "elected by the people," in practice, the president is the leader of the party that wins a plurality of seats in parliamentary elections.

Article 91
The President shall be elected by the people.

9. The legislature can vote no confidence in the government.

No. The legislature cannot vote no confidence in the government.

10. The legislature is immune from dissolution by the executive.

No. The president can dissolve the legislature.

Article 70
(2) The President may at any time by proclamation dissolve Parliament.

Article 85

(1) The President may at any time by proclamation summon, prorogue or dissolved on the occurrence of a dissolution of Parliament.

(2) The Supreme Congress of the People, unless sooner dissolved, shall stand dissolved on the occurrence of a dissolution of Parliament.

11. Any executive initiative on legislation requires ratification or approval by the legislature before it takes effect; that is, the executive lacks decree power.

Yes. The executive lacks decree power.

12. Laws passed by the legislature are veto-proof or essentially veto-proof; that is, the executive lacks veto power, or has veto power but the veto can be overridden by a majority in the legislature.

No. A two-thirds majority vote in the National Assembly is needed to override a presidential veto.

Article 170

(1) Subject to the provisions of article 164, the power of Parliament to make laws shall be exercised by Bills passed by the National Assembly and assented to by the President.

(2) When a Bill is presented to the President for assent, he shall signify that he assents or that he withholds assent.

(3) Where the President withholds his assent to a Bill, he shall return it to the Speaker within twenty-one days of the date when it was presented to him for assent with a message stating the reasons why he has withheld his assent.

(4) Where a Bill is so returned to the Speaker it shall not again be presented to the President for assent unless within six months of the Bill being so returned upon a motion supported by the votes of not less that two-thirds of all the elected members of the National Assembly the Assembly resolves that the Bill be again presented for assent.

13. The legislature's laws are supreme and not subject to judicial review.

No. The Supreme Court of Judicature can review the constitutionality of laws.

Article 123

(1) There shall be for Guyana a Supreme Court of Judicature consisting of a Court of Appeal and a High Court, with such jurisdiction and powers as are conferred on those Courts respectively by this Constitution or any other law.

(2) Each of those Courts shall be a superior court of record and, save as otherwise provided by Parliament, shall have all the powers of such a court.

(3) Parliament may confer on any court any part of the jurisdiction of and any powers conferred on the High Court by this Constitution or any other law.

14. The legislature has the right to initiate bills in all policy jurisdictions; the executive lacks gatekeeping authority.

Yes. The legislature can initiate bills in all policy jurisdictions.

15. Expenditure of funds appropriated by the legislature is mandatory; the executive lacks the power to impound funds appropriated by the legislature.

Yes. The executive lacks the power to impound funds appropriated by the legislature.

16. The legislature controls the resources that finance its own internal operation and provide for the perquisites of its own members.

No. The legislature is dependent on the executive for the resources that finance its operations.

17. Members of the legislature are immune from arrest and/or criminal prosecution.

No. Legislative immunity extends to official parliamentary business and civil debt only. Legislators are subject to arrest for common crimes.

Article 172

(1) Subject to the provisions of paragraphs (2), (3) and (4), Parliament may by law determine the privileges, immunities and powers of the National Assembly and the members thereof.

(2) No civil or criminal proceedings may be instituted against any member of the Assembly for words spoken before, or written in a report to, the Assembly or to a committee thereof or by reason of any matter or thing brought by him therein by petition, bill, resolution, motion or otherwise.

(3) For the duration of any session, members of the Assembly shall enjoy freedom from arrest for any civil debt.

(4) No process issued by any court in the exercise of its civil jurisdiction shall be served or executed within the precincts of the Assembly while the Assembly is sitting or through the Speaker, the Clerk or any officer of the Assembly.

Article 176

(1) Parliament may by law determine the privileges, immunities, and powers of the Supreme Congress of the People and the members thereof.

(2) No civil or criminal proceedings may be instituted against any member of the Congress for words spoken before or written in a report to, the Congress or to a committee thereof or by reason of any matter or thing brought by him therein by petition, resolution, motion or otherwise.

(3) For the duration of any session members of the Congress shall enjoy freedom from arrest for any civil debt.

(4) No process issued by any court in the exercise of its civil jurisdiction shall be served or executed within the precincts of the Congress while the Congress is sitting or through the Chairman, the Clerk or any officer of the Congress.

18. All members of the legislature are elected; the executive lacks the power to appoint any members of the legislature.

Yes. All members of the legislature are elected. The president can appoint ministers from outside the legislature, who become, by virtue of their ministerial position, nonvoting members of the legislature.

Article 52
(1) Subject to paragraph (2) and to articles 105, 185 and 186, the National Assembly shall consist of sixty-five members who shall be elected in accordance with the provisions of this Constitution and, subject thereto, in accordance with any law made by Parliament in that behalf.

19. The legislature alone, without the involvement of any other agencies, can change the Constitution.

Yes. The legislature can change the constitution with a majority vote.

Article 164
(1) Subject to the provisions of paragraphs (2) and (3), a Bill for an Act or Parliament to alter this Constitution shall not be passed by the National Assembly unless it is supported at the final voting in the Assembly by the votes of a majority of all the elected members of the Assembly.

20. The legislature's approval is necessary for the declaration of war.

No. The constitution does not specifically address the declaration of war. The president can issue a proclamation of emergency without the legislature's approval. If the legislature does not subsequently approve the proclamation, the state of emergency lapses after fourteen days.

Article 150
(1) This article applies to any period when –
(a) Guyana is at war; or
(b) there is in force a proclamation (in this article referred to as a "proclamation of emergency") made by the President declaring that a state of public emergency exists for the purposes of this article; or
(c) there is in force a resolution of the National Assembly, in favour of which there were cast the votes of not fewer that two-thirds of all the elected members, declaring that democratic institutions in Guyana are threatened by subversion.
(2) Nothing contained in or done under the authority of any laws shall be held to be inconsistent with or in contravention of article 139, 140 (2) or 143,

any provision of article 144 other than paragraph (4) thereof, or any provision of articles 145 to 149 (inclusive) to the extent that the law in question makes in relation to any period to which this article applies provision, or authorises the doing during any such period of anything, which is reasonably justifiable in the circumstances of any situation arising or existing during that period for the purpose of dealing with that situation.
(3a) Where any proclamation of emergency has been made, copies thereof shall as soon as practicable be laid before the National Assembly, and if, by reason of its adjournment or the prorogation of Parliament, the Assembly is not due to meet within five days the President shall, by proclamation, summon the Assembly to meet within five days, and the Assembly shall accordingly meet and sit upon the day appointed by the proclamation and shall continue to sit and act as if it had stood adjourned or Parliament had stood prorogued to that day.
(b) A proclamation of emergency shall, unless it is sooner revoked by the President, cease to be in force at the expiration of a period of fourteen days beginning on the date on which it was made or such longer period as may be provided under the next following subparagraph, but without prejudice to the making of another proclamation of emergency at or before the end of the period.
(c) If at any time while a proclamation of emergency is in force (including any time while it is in force by virtue of the provisions of this subparagraph) a resolution is passed by the Assembly approving its continuance in force for a further period, not exceeding six months, beginning on the date on which it would otherwise expire, the proclamation shall, if not sooner revoked, continue in force for that further period.
(4) A resolution such as is referred to in paragraph (1) (c) shall, unless it is sooner revoked by a resolution of the Assembly, ceased to be in force at the expiration of two years beginning on the date on which it was passed or such shorter period as may be specified therein, but without prejudice to the passing of another resolution by the Assembly in the manner prescribed by that paragraph at or before the end of that period.

21. The legislature's approval is necessary to ratify treaties with foreign countries.

Yes. The legislature's approval is necessary to ratify international treaties.

22. The legislature has the power to grant amnesty.

No. Amnesty and pardon are not treated separately, and the legislature lacks the power to grant amnesty. See item 23.

23. The legislature has the power of pardon.

No. The president has the power of pardon.

Article 121

The Prerogative of Mercy shall vest in the President and shall be exercised by him in accordance with the provisions of articles 191 to 196 (inclusive).

Article 188

(1) The President may –

(a) grant to any person concerned in or convicted of any offence under the law of Guyana, a pardon, either free or subject to lawful conditions;

(b) grant to any person a respite, either indefinite, or for a specified period, of the execution of any punishment imposed on that person for such an offence; or

(c) substitute a less severe form of punishment for any punishment imposed on any person for such an offence; or

(d) remit the whole or any part of any punishment imposed on any person for such an offence or of any penalty or forfeiture otherwise due to the State on account of such an offence.

24. The legislature reviews and has the right to reject appointments to the judiciary; or the legislature itself appoints members of the judiciary.

No. Members of the judiciary are appointed by the president, and the appointments do not require the legislature's approval.

Article 127

The Chancellor and the Chief Justice shall be appointed by the President acting after consultation with the Minority Leader.

Article 128

The Judges, other than the Chancellor and the Chief Justice, shall be appointed by the President, acting in accordance with the advice of the Judicial Service Commission.

25. The chairman of the central bank is appointed by the legislature.

No. The president appoints the governor of the Bank of Guyana.

26. The legislature has a substantial voice in the operation of the state-owned media.

No. The president appoints the members of the board that controls the public media.

27. The legislature is regularly in session.

Yes. The legislature meets in ordinary session for about ten months each year from October 10 until August 10.

Article 69

(1) Each session of Parliament shall be held at such place within Guyana and shall begin at such time (not being later than six months from the end of the preceding session if Parliament has been prorogued or sixteen months from the end of that session if Parliament has been dissolved) as the President shall appoint by proclamation.

(2) Subject to the provisions of the preceding paragraph, the sittings of the National Assembly shall be held at such time and place as the Assembly may, by its rules of procedure or otherwise, determine.

28. Each legislator has a personal secretary.

No.

29. Each legislator has at least one non-secretarial staff member with policy expertise.

No.

30. Legislators are eligible for re-election without any restriction.

Yes. There are no restrictions on re-election.

31. A seat in the legislature is an attractive enough position that legislators are generally interested in and seek re-election.

Yes.

32. The re-election of incumbent legislators is common enough that at any given time the legislature contains a significant number of highly experienced members.

Yes. Re-election rates are sufficiently high to produce a significant number of highly experienced members.

NATIONAL ASSEMBLY OF HAITI (*ASSEMBLÉE NATIONALE*)

Expert consultants: Joy Cadogan-Logie, Maria Del Pilar Gonzalez Morales, Jean-Germain Gros, Tim Pershing

Score: .44

Influence over executive (4/9)		Institutional autonomy (4/9)		Specified powers (3/8)		Institutional capacity (3/6)	
1. replace	X	10. no dissolution	X	19. amendments		27. sessions	X
2. serve as ministers		11. no decree	X	20. war	X	28. secretary	
3. interpellate	X	12. no veto	X	21. treaties	X	29. staff	
4. investigate		13. no review		22. amnesty		30. no term limits	X
5. oversee police		14. no gatekeeping		23. pardon		31. seek re-election	X
6. appoint PM		15. no impoundment		24. judiciary	X	32. experience	
7. appoint ministers	X	16. control resources		25. central bank			
8. lack president		17. immunity		26. media			
9. no confidence	X	18. all elected	X				

The National Assembly (*Assemblée nationale*) of Haiti traces its roots to Haiti's 1805 constitution, adopted following independence from France in 1804. For the next two centuries, political instability, foreign military occupation, and dictatorship prevented the development of a well-functioning legislature. In 1987 the country's current constitution was adopted. It calls for a bicameral legislature consisting of a lower house, the House of Deputies (*Chambre des députés*), and an upper house, the Senate (*Sénat*). In 1990 Jean-Bertrand Aristide became Haiti's first elected president, only to be ousted in a military coup the following year. The next decade and a half witnessed U.S. military intervention to restore civilian rule, the election of a civilian president who declared the expiration of parliament's term and proceeded to rule by decree, an attempted coup, civil strife leading to a president's exile, massive floods, and the deployment to of UN peacekeeping forces.

Despite grave political instability, the legislature, refreshed by legislative elections held in 2006, potentially has some authority. For example, the constitution grants the legislature the power to indict the president for treason with a two-thirds majority vote and to remove the government with a motion of censure. The formal absence of executive dissolution, decree, and veto powers provides the legislature with some institutional autonomy. The legislature holds several enumerated powers and has some institutional capacity.

SURVEY

1. The legislature alone, without the involvement of any other agencies, can impeach the president or replace the prime minister.

Yes. The House of Deputies can indict the president for treason by a two-thirds majority vote of its total membership. It can remove the prime minister with a vote of censure.

> Article 129-4
> When the interpellation request ends in a vote of censure on a question concerning a Government program or declaration of general policy, the Prime Minister must submit his Government's resignation to the President of the Republic.

> Article 186
> The House of Deputies, by a majority of two-thirds of its members, shall indict:
> a) The President of the Republic for the crime of high treason or any other crime or offense committed in the discharge of his duties.

2. Ministers may serve simultaneously as members of the legislature.

No. Legislators are prohibited from serving simultaneously in ministerial positions.

Article 129-1
Service as a member of the Legislature is incompatible with any other duty remunerated by the State, except that of teacher.

Article 132
Members of the Executive Branch and the Director Generals of Government departments may not be elected members of the Legislature unless they resign at least one (1) year before the date of the elections.

Article 164
The duties of the Prime Minister and of a member of the Government are incompatible with membership in the Parliament. If such a case occurs, the member of Parliament must choose one duty or the other.

3. The legislature has powers of summons over executive branch officials and hearings with executive branch officials testifying before the legislature or its committees are regularly held.

Yes. The legislature regularly interpellates officials from the executive.

Article 129-2
Every member of the two Houses has the right to question and interpellate a member of the Government or the entire Government on events and acts of the Administration.

Article 129-3
An interpellation request must be seconded by five members of the body concerned. It becomes a vote of confidence or of censure when passed by a majority of that body.

Article 129-4
When the interpellation request ends in a vote of censure on a question concerning a Government program or declaration of general policy, the Prime Minister must submit his Government's resignation to the President of the Republic.

Article 161
The Prime Minister and the Ministers may appear before the two Houses to support bills and the objections of the President of the Republic and to reply to interpellations.

4. The legislature can conduct independent investigation of the chief executive and the agencies of the executive.

No. The legislature cannot investigate the executive.

5. The legislature has effective powers of oversight over the agencies of coercion (the military, organs of law enforcement, intelligence services, and the secret police).

No. The legislature lacks effective powers of oversight over the agencies of coercion.

6. The legislature appoints the prime minister.

No. The president appoints the prime minister in consultation with the legislature.

Article 137
The President of the Republic shall choose a Prime Minister from among the members of the majority party of the Parliament. In the absence of such a majority, the President of the Republic shall choose his Prime Minister in consultation with the President of the Senate and the President of the House of Deputies. In either case, the President's choice must be ratified by the Parliament.

7. The legislature's approval is required to confirm the appointment of ministers; or the legislature itself appoints ministers.

Yes. The legislature's approval is required to confirm ministerial appointments.

Article 158
With the approval of the President, the Prime Minister shall choose the members of his Cabinet of Ministers and shall go before Parliament to obtain a vote of confidence on his declaration of general policy. The vote shall be taken in open ballot, and an absolute majority of both Houses is required.

8. The country lacks a presidency entirely or there is a presidency, but the president is elected by the legislature.

No. The president is directly elected.

Article 134
The President of the Republic is elected in direct universal suffrage by an absolute majority of votes. If that majority is not obtained in the first election, a second election is held.

9. The legislature can vote no confidence in the government.

Yes. The legislature can pass a vote of censure against the government.

Article 129-2
Every member of the two Houses has the right to question and interpellate a member of the Government or the entire Government on events and acts of the Administration.

Article 129-3
An interpellation request must be seconded by five members of the body concerned. It becomes a vote of confidence or of censure when passed by a majority of that body.

Article 129-4
When the interpellation request ends in a vote of censure on a question concerning a Government program or declaration of general policy, the Prime Minister must submit his Government's resignation to the President of the Republic.

10. The legislature is immune from dissolution by the executive.

Yes. The legislature is immune from dissolution.

> Article 111-8
> In no case may the House of Deputies or the Senate be dissolved or adjourned, nor shall the terms of their members be extended.

11. Any executive initiative on legislation requires ratification or approval by the legislature before it takes effect; that is, the executive lacks decree power.

Yes. The executive lacks decree power.

12. Laws passed by the legislature are veto-proof or essentially veto-proof; that is, the executive lacks veto power, or has veto power but the veto can be overridden by a majority in the legislature.

Yes. The legislature can override a presidential veto by a majority vote of its present members.

> Article 121
> Any bill passed by the Legislature shall be immediately forwarded to the President of the Republic, who, before promulgating it, has the right to make objections to it in all or in part.
>
> Article 121-1
> In such cases, the President of the Republic sends back the bill with his objections to the House where it was originally passed. If the bill is amended by that House, it is sent to the other House with the objections.
>
> Article 121-2
> If the bill thus amended is voted on by the second House, it will be sent back to the President of the Republic for promulgation.
>
> Article 121-3
> If the objections are rejected by the House that originally passed the bill, it shall be returned to the other House with the objections.
>
> Article 121-4
> If the second House also votes to reject it, the bill is sent back to the President of the Republic, who must then promulgate it.

13. The legislature's laws are supreme and not subject to judicial review.

No. The Supreme Court can review the constitutionality of laws.

> Article 128
> Only the Legislative Branch has the authority to interpret laws, which it does by passing a law.
>
> Article 183
> When litigation is referred to it, the Supreme Court, sitting as a full Court, shall rule on the unconstitutionality of the laws.

14. The legislature has the right to initiate bills in all policy jurisdictions; the executive lacks gatekeeping authority.

No. The legislature is prohibited from initiating bills related to taxation, government revenues, and government expenditures.

> Article 111-2
> However, only the Executive Branch may initiate budget laws, laws concerning the assessment, percentage and manner of collecting taxes and contributions, and laws designed to generate revenues or to increase revenues and expenditures of the Government. Bills introduced on these matters must be voted on first by the House of Deputies.

15. Expenditure of funds appropriated by the legislature is mandatory; the executive lacks the power to impound funds appropriated by the legislature.

No. The president can impound funds appropriated by the legislature.

16. The legislature controls the resources that finance its own internal operation and provide for the perquisites of its own members.

No. The legislature is dependent on the executive for the resources that finance its operations.

17. Members of the legislature are immune from arrest and/or criminal prosecution.

No. By law, legislators are immune, but in practice, many legislators have been subject to arrest and state-backed repression in the violence and waves of reprisals that frequently mar Haiti's electoral politics. The government has sometimes abused the *flagrante delicto* provision to deprive opposition members of parliament of their immunity.

> Article 114
> Members of the Legislature are inviolable from the day they take oath up to the expiration of their term, subject to the provisions of Article 115 below.
>
> Article 114-1
> They may at no time be prosecuted or attacked for the opinions and votes cast by them in the discharge of their duties.
>
> Article 114-2
> No member of the Legislature shall be subject to civil imprisonment during his term of office.
>
> Article 115
> No member of the Legislature may during his term be arrested under ordinary law for a crime, a minor offense or a petty violation, except by authorization of the House of which he is a member, unless he is apprehended in the act of committing an offense punishable by death, personal restraint or penal servitude or the loss of civil rights. In that case, the matter is referred to the House of Deputies or the Senate without delay if

the Legislature is in session, and if not, it shall be taken up at the next regular or special session.

18. All members of the legislature are elected; the executive lacks the power to appoint any members of the legislature.

Yes. All members of the legislature are elected.

Article 89
The House of Deputies is a body composed of members elected by direct suffrage by the citizens and is responsible for exercising, on their behalf and in concert with the Senate, the functions of the Legislative Branch.

Article 94
The Senate is a body composed of members elected by direct suffrage of the citizens and charged with exercising on their behalf, in concert with the House of Deputies, the duties of the Legislative Branch.

19. The legislature alone, without the involvement of any other agencies, can change the Constitution.

No. Formally, the legislature can change the constitution with a two-thirds majority vote in both houses, but in practice, such action would be unthinkable without presidential backing.

Article 98-3
The Assembly's powers are:
4) To amend the Constitution according to the procedure indicated herein.

Article 282
On the recommendation, with reasons given to support it, of one of the two Houses or of the Executive Branch, the Legislature may declare that the Constitution should be amended.

Article 282-1
This declaration must be supported by two-thirds of each of the two Houses. It may be made only in the course of the last Regular Session of the Legislative period and shall be published immediately throughout the territory.

20. The legislature's approval is necessary for the declaration of war.

Yes. The legislature's approval is necessary for presidential war declarations.

Article 98-3
The Assembly's powers are:
2) To ratify any decision to declare war when all efforts at conciliation have failed.

Article 140
[The president] declares war, and negotiates and signs peace treaties with the approval of the National Assembly.

21. The legislature's approval is necessary to ratify treaties with foreign countries.

Yes. The legislature's approval is necessary to ratify international treaties.

Article 98-3
The Assembly's powers are:
3) To approve or reject international treaties and conventions.

Article 139
[The president] shall negotiate and sign all international treaties, conventions and agreements and submit them to the National Assembly for ratification.

22. The legislature has the power to grant amnesty.

No. The president has the power to grant amnesty.

Article 147
[The president] may grant amnesty only for political matters as stipulated by law.

23. The legislature has the power of pardon.

No. The president has the power of pardon.

Article 146
The President of the Republic has the right to pardon and commute sentences in all *res judicata* cases, except for sentences handed down by the High Court of Justice as stipulated in this Constitution.

24. The legislature reviews and has the right to reject appointments to the judiciary; or the legislature itself appoints members of the judiciary.

Yes. The president appoints members of the Supreme Court from a list of candidates proposed by the Senate.

Article 97
In addition to the responsibilities incumbent upon it as a branch of the Legislature, the Senate shall have the following powers:
1) To propose to the Executive the list of Supreme Court justices according to the provisions of the Constitution;
2) Constitute itself as a High Court of Justice.

Article 175
Supreme Court justices are appointed by the President of the Republic from a list submitted by the Senate of three persons per court seat. Judges of the Courts of Appeal and Courts of First Instance are appointed from a list submitted by the Departmental Assembly concerned; Justices of the Peace are appointed from a list drawn up by the Communal Assemblies.

25. The chairman of the central bank is appointed by the legislature.

No. The president appoints the governor of the Central Bank of Haiti.

26. The legislature has a substantial voice in the operation of the state-owned media.

No. The legislature lacks a substantial voice in the operation of the public media.

27. The legislature is regularly in session.

Yes. The House of Deputies meets in ordinary session for seven months each year. The Senate is permanently in session.

> Article 92-2
> The first session [of the House of Deputies] runs from the second Monday of January to the second Monday of May; the second session, from the second Monday of June to the second Monday of September.

> Article 95-1
> The Senate is permanently in session.

> Article 95-2
> The Senate may however adjourn, but not during the Legislative Session. When it adjourns, it leaves a permanent committee charged with handling current business. The committee may not make any decisions, except to convene the Senate.

28. Each legislator has a personal secretary.

No.

29. Each legislator has at least one non-secretarial staff member with policy expertise.

No.

30. Legislators are eligible for re-election without any restriction.

Yes. There are no restrictions on re-election.

> Article 92
> Deputies are elected for four years and may be reelected an indefinite number of times.

> Article 95
> Senators are elected for six years and may be reelected an indefinite number of times.

31. A seat in the legislature is an attractive enough position that legislators are generally interested in and seek re-election.

Yes.

32. The re-election of incumbent legislators is common enough that at any given time the legislature contains a significant number of highly experienced members.

No. Political instability has prevented politicians from developing significant experience and legislative expertise.

NATIONAL CONGRESS OF HONDURAS (*CONGRESO NACIONAL*)

Expert consultants: Natalia Ajenjo Fresno, Peter Peetz, Michelle M. Taylor-Robinson, Ian Walker, Maureen Zamora

Score: .53

Influence over executive (3/9)		Institutional autonomy (6/9)		Specified powers (4/8)		Institutional capacity (4/6)	
1. replace		10. no dissolution	X	19. amendments	X	27. sessions	X
2. serve as ministers		11. no decree	X	20. war		28. secretary	
3. interpellate	X	12. no veto		21. treaties	X	29. staff	
4. investigate	X	13. no review		22. amnesty	X	30. no term limits	X
5. oversee police	X	14. no gatekeeping	X	23. pardon		31. seek re-election	X
6. appoint PM		15. no impoundment	X	24. judiciary	X	32. experience	X
7. appoint ministers		16. control resources	X	25. central bank			
8. lack president		17. immunity		26. media			
9. no confidence		18. all elected	X				

The National Congress (*Congreso Nacional*) of Honduras traces its roots to the country's independence in 1840. For most of its history, the legislature was not a key player because Honduras was ruled by a succession of high-handed presidents and military dictators. Civilian rule returned with a new constitution in 1982 – the sixteenth in Honduras's history – bringing with it a more assertive National Congress. A constitutional amendment in 2004 removed immunity for members of the National

Congress. Prior to 2004 legislators were immune from arrest and prosecution while in office.

The legislature enjoys some authority. It can influence the executive with its powers of interpellation, investigation, and oversight, although it does not elect the president and has no say in the formation of the government. It enjoys significant institutional autonomy, including a monopoly on lawmaking power and immunity from dissolution. It has a number of specified powers and a fair amount of institutional capacity.

SURVEY

1. The legislature alone, without the involvement of any other agencies, can impeach the president or replace the prime minister.

No. Presidential impeachment requires the involvement of the Supreme Court of Justice.

> Article 205
> The National Congress shall have the following powers:
> 15. To declare whether or not there are grounds for impeachment of the President.

> Article 319
> The Supreme Court of Justice shall have the following power:
> 2. To try official and common crimes of high functionaries of the Republic, when the National Congress has declared that there are grounds for impeachment.

2. Ministers may serve simultaneously as members of the legislature.

No. Legislators who serve in government have a sleeping mandate, meaning that they may join the government but forfeit their voting rights in the legislature during their government service. They may return to the legislature when their government service ends.

> Article 199
> The following may not be elected deputies:
> 3. Secretaries and Sub-secretaries of State.

> Article 203
> Deputies in office may not obtain remunerated public positions during the term for which they have been elected, except teaching and cultural positions and professional services related to social welfare. They may, however, be Secretaries or Sub-Secretaries of State, President or Manager of decentralized entities, Chief of Diplomatic or Consular missions, or serve in Ad Hoc Diplomatic Missions. In such cases they will be reinstated in the National Congress upon the termination of these functions. Alternates may hold public positions or employment without losing their status as alternates.

3. The legislature has powers of summons over executive branch officials and hearings with executive

branch officials testifying before the legislature or its committees are regularly held.

Yes. The legislature regularly interpellates officials from the executive.

> Article 205
> The National Congress shall have the following powers:
> 22. To interpellate Secretaries of State and other functionaries of the central government, decentralized organisms, state enterprises and any other entity in which the State has an interest, concerning matters related to the public administration.

> Article 251
> The National Congress may summon the Secretaries of State and these must answer any questions put to them concerning matters relating to public administration.

4. The legislature can conduct independent investigation of the chief executive and the agencies of the executive.

Yes. The legislature can establish special commissions to investigate the executive.

> Article 205
> The National Congress shall have the following powers:
> 21. To appoint special commissions for the investigation of matters of national interest. The summons of such commissions shall be compulsory under penalty of contempt similar to that observed in the judicial procedure.

5. The legislature has effective powers of oversight over the agencies of coercion (the military, organs of law enforcement, intelligence services, and the secret police).

Yes. Legislative committees have effective powers of oversight over the agencies of coercion.

6. The legislature appoints the prime minister.

No. There is no prime minister.

7. The legislature's approval is required to confirm the appointment of ministers; or the legislature itself appoints ministers.

No. The president appoints the ministers (secretaries), and the appointments do not require the legislature's approval.

> Article 245
> The President of the Republic shall be responsible for the general administration of the State; his powers:
> 5. To freely appoint and dismiss the Secretaries and Sub-secretaries of State and other functionaries and employees whose appointment is not attributed to other authorities.

8. The country lacks a presidency entirely or there is a presidency, but the president is elected by the legislature.

No. The president is directly elected.

Article 236
The President of the Republic and three Designates of the Presidency shall be elected jointly and directly by the people, by a simple majority of votes.

9. The legislature can vote no confidence in the government.

No. The legislature cannot vote no confidence in the government.

10. The legislature is immune from dissolution by the executive.

Yes. The legislature is immune from dissolution.

11. Any executive initiative on legislation requires ratification or approval by the legislature before it takes effect; that is, the executive lacks decree power.

Yes. The executive lacks decree power. The president can issue regulatory decrees.

Article 245
The President of the Republic shall be responsible for the general administration of the State; his powers:
11. To issue directives and decrees and to issue regulations and resolutions according to the Law.

Article 248
The decrees, regulations, directives, orders and executive acts of the President of the Republic must be authorized by the Secretaries of State in their respective areas or by the Sub-Secretaries, as the case may be. Without this requirement they shall not have legal force.
The Secretaries of State and the Sub-Secretaries shall be jointly responsible with the President of the Republic for the acts they authorize.
For decisions taken in the Council of Ministers, the Ministers present shall be responsible unless they have given grounds for their dissenting votes.

12. Laws passed by the legislature are veto-proof or essentially veto-proof; that is, the executive lacks veto power, or has veto power but the veto can be overridden by a majority in the legislature.

No. A two-thirds majority vote is needed to override a presidential veto.

Article 216
Should the Executive Power find impediments to the sanction of the Bill of Law, it shall return it to the National Congress within ten days with the formulation: "Return to Congress," and shall explain the grounds on which disapproval is based. If it does not object it within the period indicated, it shall be considered sanctioned and shall be promulgated as Law.
Whenever the Executive returns a Bill of Law, it shall again be debated in the National Congress, and if it is ratified by a two-thirds vote, it shall again be sent to the

Executive Power, with this formulation: "Constitutionally ratified" and the Executive Power shall publish it forthwith.
If the grounds for the veto are that the Bill of Law is unconstitutional, it may not be submitted to a new debate until the opinion of the Supreme Court of Justice has been obtained; it shall issue its opinion within such period as the National Congress shall specify.

13. The legislature's laws are supreme and not subject to judicial review.

No. The Supreme Court of Justice can review the constitutionality of laws.

Article 184
The Laws may be declared unconstitutional by reason of form or content.
The Supreme Court of Justice has original and exclusive competence over hearing and deciding such matters, and must render its decisions with the requirements of definitive sentences.

Article 319
The Supreme Court of Justice shall have the following powers:
12. To declare laws to be unconstitutional in the manner and cases provided in this Constitution.

14. The legislature has the right to initiate bills in all policy jurisdictions; the executive lacks gatekeeping authority.

Yes. The legislature can initiate bills in all policy jurisdictions.

15. Expenditure of funds appropriated by the legislature is mandatory; the executive lacks the power to impound funds appropriated by the legislature.

Yes. The executive lacks the power to impound funds that the legislature appropriates.

16. The legislature controls the resources that finance its own internal operation and provide for the perquisites of its own members.

Yes. The legislature enjoys financial autonomy. The executive is required to include the funds requested by the legislature for its operations in the state budget.

Article 211
The Executive Power shall include in the General Budget of Expenditures and Revenue of the Republic the funds budgeted by the Legislative Power for its functioning.

17. Members of the legislature are immune from arrest and/or criminal prosecution.

No. Legislators are subject to arrest and prosecution. A constitutional amendment in 2004 removed immunity. Prior to 2004 legislators were immune.

18. All members of the legislature are elected; the executive lacks the power to appoint any members of the legislature.

Yes. All members of the legislature are elected.

Article 189
The Legislative Power is exercised by a Congress of Deputies, who shall be elected by direct suffrage. It shall convene in the capital of the Republic in ordinary sessions on the twenty-fifth of January of each year without the necessity of convocation and shall adjourn on the thirty-first of October of the same year.

19. The legislature alone, without the involvement of any other agencies, can change the Constitution.

Yes. The legislature can change the constitution with a two-thirds majority vote.

Article 373
The amendment of this Constitution may be decreed by the National Congress, in ordinary sessions, with two-thirds of the votes of all its members. The Decree shall specify for that purpose the article or articles that are to be amended, which must be ratified by the subsequent ordinary legislature, by the same number of votes, in order to take effect.

20. The legislature's approval is necessary for the declaration of war.

No. The president can declare war while the legislature is in recess.

Article 205
The National Congress shall have the following powers:
26. To authorize or deny the transit of foreign troops through the territory of the country;
27. To authorize the Executive Power to order troops of the Armed Forces to serve in foreign territory, in accordance with international treaties and conventions;
28. To declare war and to make peace.

Article 245
The President of the Republic shall be responsible for the general administration of the State; his powers:
17. To declare war and make peace during a recess of the National Congress, which must be convened forthwith.

21. The legislature's approval is necessary to ratify treaties with foreign countries.

Yes. The legislature's approval is necessary to ratify international treaties on most major issues.

Article 16
All international treaties must be approved by the National Congress before their ratification by the Executive Power.

Article 205
The National Congress shall have the following powers:
30. To approve or disapprove international treaties signed by the Executive Power.

Article 245
The President of the Republic shall be responsible for the general administration of the State; his powers:
13. To conclude treaties and agreements and to ratify, following approval by the National Congress, International Treaties of a political and military character, those relating to the national territory, sovereignty and concessions, those entailing financial obligations for the Public Treasury, or those requiring amendment or repeal of any constitutional or legal provision, and those needing legislative measures for their execution.

22. The legislature has the power to grant amnesty.

Yes. The legislature has the power to grant amnesty.

Article 205
The National Congress shall have the following powers:
16. To grant amnesty for political offenses or related common offenses, except in such cases the National Congress may not make decisions on pardons.

23. The legislature has the power of pardon.

No. The president has the power of pardon.

Article 245
The President of the Republic shall be responsible for the general administration of the State; his powers:
24. To pardon and commute sentences according to the Law.

24. The legislature reviews and has the right to reject appointments to the judiciary; or the legislature itself appoints members of the judiciary.

Yes. The legislature appoints the nine magistrates, the seven alternates, and the president of the Supreme Court of Justice. Normally, the president submits a list of recommended candidates for the bench to the legislature, and the legislature chooses from names on the president's list, although it is not obligated to do so.

Article 205
The National Congress shall have the following powers:
9. To elect for the constitutional term, nine principal magistrates and seven alternates of the Supreme Court of Justice and to elect its President.

Article 303
The power to dispense justice emanates from the people and is administered free of charge on behalf of the State by independent magistrates and judges. The Judicial Power consists of a Supreme Court of Justice, the Courts of Appeals, and the Courts established by the Law.
The Supreme Court of Justice shall have its seat in the Capital of the Republic, shall be composed of nine principal magistrates and seven alternates, elected by the National Congress, and shall be divided into chambers, in accordance with the provisions of the Internal Regulations of that Court.

Article 304
The President of the Supreme Court of Justice shall be elected by the National Congress for a term of four years.

25. The chairman of the central bank is appointed by the legislature.

No. The president appoints the president of the Central Bank of Honduras.

26. The legislature has a substantial voice in the operation of the state-owned media.

No. The legislature lacks a substantial voice in the operation of the public media.

27. The legislature is regularly in session.

Yes. The legislature meets in ordinary session from late January until the end of October. The legislature's internal rules provide for a one-month recess during the summer, leaving Congress in session for a total of eight months.

Article 189
The Legislative Power is exercised by a Congress of Deputies, who shall be elected by direct suffrage. It shall convene in the capital of the Republic in ordinary sessions on the twenty-fifth of January of each year

without the necessity of convocation and shall adjourn on the thirty-first of October of the same year.

28. Each legislator has a personal secretary.

No. Political parties and legislative committees provide staff, but on average there is less than one staff person for each legislator.

29. Each legislator has at least one non-secretarial staff member with policy expertise.

No. See item 28.

30. Legislators are eligible for re-election without any restriction.

Yes. There are no restrictions on re-election.

31. A seat in the legislature is an attractive enough position that legislators are generally interested in and seek re-election.

Yes.

32. The re-election of incumbent legislators is common enough that at any given time the legislature contains a significant number of highly experienced members.

Yes. Re-election rates are sufficiently high to produce a significant number of highly experienced members.

NATIONAL ASSEMBLY OF HUNGARY (*ORSZÁGGYŰLÉS*)

Expert consultants: Kenneth Benoit, Mátyás Eörsi, Anna Grzymała-Busse, Renata Uitz, Jason Wittenberg

Score: .75

Influence over executive (8/9)		Institutional autonomy (7/9)		Specified powers (5/8)		Institutional capacity (4/6)	
1. replace	X	10. no dissolution		19. amendments	X	27. sessions	X
2. serve as ministers	X	11. no decree	X	20. war		28. secretary	
3. interpellate	X	12. no veto	X	21. treaties	X	29. staff	
4. investigate	X	13. no review		22. amnesty	X	30. no term limits	X
5. oversee police	X	14. no gatekeeping	X	23. pardon		31. seek re-election	X
6. appoint PM	X	15. no impoundment	X	24. judiciary	X	32. experience	X
7. appoint ministers		16. control resources	X	25. central bank			
8. lack president	X	17. immunity	X	26. media	X		
9. no confidence	X	18. all elected	X				

The National Assembly (*Országgyűlés*) of Hungary traces its origins to the country's first post-independence legislative body, the National

Council, established at the end of World War I. Hungary came under Soviet domination shortly after the end of World War II. The 1949 constitution institutionalized a National Assembly that formally enjoyed supreme authority, but in practice, the Communist Party dictated legislation. During the collapse of communist-party rule in 1989, the National Assembly passed a constitutional amendment that overhauled the fundamental law, providing for the open political system found in Hungary today. The renovated constitution granted the legislature oversight authority over the government, guaranteed a competitive multiparty system, established a Constitutional Court to review the constitutionality of laws, mandated that the legislature meet regularly, and established procedures for the election of the legislature. Subsequent amendments did not directly affect legislative power.

The National Assembly has considerable clout. Its approval is not needed for the appointment of ministers, but it holds every other means of controlling executive power assessed in this survey. It also enjoys considerable autonomy, including a monopoly on lawmaking powers, and is endowed with a number of specified powers. It has some institutional capacity, although legislators lack personal staff.

SURVEY

1. The legislature alone, without the involvement of any other agencies, can impeach the president or replace the prime minister.

Yes. The legislature can remove the prime minister with a vote of no confidence. Presidential impeachment requires the involvement of the Constitutional Court.

Article 33A
The Government's mandate shall end –
f) if the Parliament passes a motion of no-confidence in the Prime Minister and elects a new Prime Minister in accordance with the provisions of Par. (1), Article 39A.

Article 31A
(1) The person of the President of the Republic is inviolable; protection from criminal prosecution shall be granted by a separate law.
(2) Should the President of the Republic violate the Constitution or any other law while in office, a motion supported by one-fifth of the Members of Parliament may propose that impeachment proceedings be initiated against the President of the Republic.
(3) A majority of two-thirds of the votes of the Members of Parliament is required to initiate impeachment proceedings. Voting shall be held by secret ballot.
(4) From passage of this resolution by the Parliament until the conclusion of the impeachment proceedings, the President of the Republic may not attend to any of the duties of his office.

(5) The Constitutional Court shall have jurisdiction in such cases.
(6) Should the Constitutional Court determine that the law was violated, it shall have the authority to remove the President of the Republic from office.

Article 39A
(1) A motion of no-confidence in the Prime Minister may be initiated by a written petition, which includes the nomination for a candidate for the office of Prime Minister, by no less than one-fifth of the Members of Parliament. A motion of no-confidence in the Prime Minister is considered a motion of no-confidence in the Government as well. Should, on the basis of this motion, the majority of the Members of Parliament withdraw their confidence, then the candidate nominated for Prime Minister in the motion shall be considered to have been elected.
(2) The debate and vote on the motion of no-confidence shall be held no earlier than three days from the date of proposal and no later than eight days from the date of proposal.
(3) The Government, via the Prime Minister, may propose a vote of confidence in accordance with the period of time specified in Paragraph (2).
(4) The Government, via the Prime Minister, may propose that the vote on the motion it has made simultaneously be considered as a vote of confidence.
(5) Should the Parliament fail to give the Government a vote of confidence in accordance with the provisions of Paragraphs (3)–(4), the Government shall resign.

2. Ministers may serve simultaneously as members of the legislature.

Yes. Legislators may serve simultaneously in ministerial positions.

Article 20
(5) A Member of Parliament may not be the President of the Republic, a member of the Constitutional Court, the Ombudsman for Civil Rights, the President, Deputy President or auditor of the State Audit Office, a judge or prosecutor, an employee of a public administration body – with the exception of the Members of the Government and Parliamentary State Secretaries – nor a professional member of the armed forces, the police or other security organs. Other cases of conflict of interest may be established by law.

3. The legislature has powers of summons over executive branch officials and hearings with executive branch officials testifying before the legislature or its committees are regularly held.

Yes. The legislature regularly questions executive branch officials.

Article 27
Any Member of Parliament may direct a question ... to the Government or any of the Members of the Government ... on matters which fall within their respective sphere of authority.

Article 39

(1) The Government is responsible to the Parliament for its operation and is required to furnish the Parliament with regular reports on its work.

(2) Members of the Government are responsible to the Government and to the Parliament and shall provide the Government and the Parliament with reports on their activities. The legal status, compensation and method of accountability of Members of the Government and State Secretaries shall be regulated by law.

4. The legislature can conduct independent investigation of the chief executive and the agencies of the executive.

Yes. The legislature can establish committees to investigate the executive.

Article 21

(2) The Parliament shall establish standing committees from among its members and may delegate a committee for the investigation of any issue whatsoever.

(3) Everyone is obliged to provide Parliamentary Committees with the information requested and is obliged to testify before such committees.

5. The legislature has effective powers of oversight over the agencies of coercion (the military, organs of law enforcement, intelligence services, and the secret police).

Yes. Legislative committees have effective powers of oversight over the agencies of coercion.

6. The legislature appoints the prime minister.

Yes. The legislature elects the prime minister.

Article 19

(3) Within this sphere of authority, the Parliament shall –

k) elect ... the Prime Minister.

Article 33

(3) The Prime Minister shall be elected by a majority of the votes of the Members of Parliament, based on the recommendation made by the President of the Republic. The Parliament shall hold the vote on the election of the Prime Minister and on the passage of the Government's program at the same time.

7. The legislature's approval is required to confirm the appointment of ministers; or the legislature itself appoints ministers.

No. The president appoints the ministers on the recommendation of the prime minister, and the appointments do not require the legislature's approval.

Article 33

(4) The Ministers shall be appointed and dismissed by the President of the Republic, based on the recommendation made by the Prime Minister.

8. The country lacks a presidency entirely or there is a presidency, but the president is elected by the legislature.

Yes. The legislature elects the president.

Article 19

(3) Within this sphere of authority, the Parliament shall –

k) elect the President of the Republic.

Article 29A

(1) The Parliament shall elect the President of the Republic for a term of five years.

9. The legislature can vote no confidence in the government.

Yes. The legislature can vote no confidence in the government.

Article 33A

The Government's mandate shall end –

f) if the Parliament passes a motion of no-confidence in the Prime Minister and elects a new Prime Minister in accordance with the provisions of Par. (1), Article 39A.

Article 39A

(1) A motion of no-confidence in the Prime Minister may be initiated by a written petition, which includes the nomination for a candidate for the office of Prime Minister, by no less than one-fifth of the Members of Parliament. A motion of no-confidence in the Prime Minister is considered a motion of no-confidence in the Government as well. Should, on the basis of this motion, the majority of the Members of Parliament withdraw their confidence, then the candidate nominated for Prime Minister in the motion shall be considered to have been elected.

(2) The debate and vote on the motion of no-confidence shall be held no earlier than three days from the date of proposal and no later than eight days from the date of proposal.

(3) The Government, via the Prime Minister, may propose a vote of confidence in accordance with the period of time specified in Paragraph (2).

(4) The Government, via the Prime Minister, may propose that the vote on the motion it has made simultaneously be considered as a vote of confidence.

(5) Should the Parliament fail to give the Government a vote of confidence in accordance with the provisions of Paragraphs (3)–(4), the Government shall resign.

10. The legislature is immune from dissolution by the executive.

No. The president can dissolve the legislature.

Article 28

(1) The term of Parliament commences from its inaugural sitting.

(2) The Parliament has the right to declare its dissolution prior to the completion of its term.

(3) The President of the Republic has the right to dissolve the Parliament, simultaneously with the announcement of new elections, if –
  a) the Parliament passes a motion of no-confidence in the Government on no less than four occasions in a period of twelve months during the course of one term, or;
  b) in the event that the mandate of the Government ends, a candidate for Prime Minister proposed by the President of the Republic is not elected by the Parliament within a period of forty days from the day upon which the first candidate is nominated.

11. Any executive initiative on legislation requires ratification or approval by the legislature before it takes effect; that is, the executive lacks decree power.

Yes. The executive lacks decree power. During a state of martial law, however, the National Defense Council may pass decrees that have the force of law. If not subsequently passed by parliament, the decrees lapse at the end of the crisis.

Article 19B
(4) The National Defense Council may pass decrees, which may suspend the application of certain laws or which may deviate from the provisions of certain laws. Furthermore, it may take other extraordinary measures, but may not, however, suspend the application of the Constitution.
(5) Decrees passed by the National Defense Council shall lose validity upon cessation of the state of national crisis, unless the Parliament extends the validity of such decrees.

Article 19C
(4) Emergency measures introduced by decree shall remain in force for a period of thirty days, unless the Parliament or, should the Parliament be obstructed, the Parliamentary Defense Committee extends their validity.

12. Laws passed by the legislature are veto-proof or essentially veto-proof; that is, the executive lacks veto power, or has veto power but the veto can be overridden by a majority in the legislature.

Yes. The legislature can override a presidential veto by a majority vote of its present members.

Article 26
(1) The President of the Republic shall ensure promulgation of the law within a period of fifteen days following its receipt, or within a period of five days if the Speaker of Parliament requests that the issue be accorded urgency. The President of the Republic shall ratify the law sent for promulgation. The law shall be promulgated in the Official Gazette.
(2) Should the President of the Republic disagree with a law or with any provision of a law, prior to ratification, he shall refer such law, along with his comments, to the Parliament for reconsideration within the period of time specified in Par. (1).

(3) The Parliament shall debate the law again and hold another vote on its passage. The President of the Republic is required to ratify and promulgate the law sent to him by the Speaker of Parliament following this procedure, within a period of five days.

13. The legislature's laws are supreme and not subject to judicial review.

No. The Constitutional Court can review the constitutionality of laws.

Article 26
(4) Should the President of the Republic have reservations about the constitutionality of any provision of a law, he may refer such law to the Constitutional Court for review within the period of time specified in Par. (1) prior to ratification.
(5) Should the Constitutional Court – in special proceedings – determine the law to be unconstitutional, the President of the Republic shall refer such law to the Parliament; otherwise he shall ratify and promulgate the law within a period of five days.

Article 32A
(1) The Constitutional Court shall review the constitutionality of laws and attend to the duties assigned to its jurisdiction by law.
(2) The Constitutional Court shall annul any laws and other statutes that it finds to be unconstitutional.

14. The legislature has the right to initiate bills in all policy jurisdictions; the executive lacks gatekeeping authority.

Yes. The legislature can initiate bills in all policy jurisdictions.

15. Expenditure of funds appropriated by the legislature is mandatory; the executive lacks the power to impound funds appropriated by the legislature.

Yes. The executive lacks the power to impound funds appropriated by the legislature.

16. The legislature controls the resources that finance its own internal operation and provide for the perquisites of its own members.

Yes. The legislature enjoys financial autonomy, including control over members' perquisites.

Article 20
Members of Parliament are entitled to compensation adequate to ensure their independence, to specified allowances and to reimbursement of their expenses. A majority of two-thirds of the votes of the Members of Parliament present is required to pass the law on the amount of compensation, reimbursement of expenses and allowances.

17. Members of the legislature are immune from arrest and/or criminal prosecution.

Yes. Legislators are immune with the common exception for cases of *flagrante delicto*.

Article 20
Members of Parliament are granted parliamentary immunity, in accordance with the regulations of the law defining the legal status of Members of Parliament.

18. All members of the legislature are elected; the executive lacks the power to appoint any members of the legislature.

Yes. All members of the legislature are elected.

19. The legislature alone, without the involvement of any other agencies, can change the Constitution.

Yes. The legislature can change the constitution with a two-thirds majority vote.

Article 24
(3) A majority of two-thirds of the votes of the Members of Parliament is required to amend the Constitution and for certain decisions specified therein.

20. The legislature's approval is necessary for the declaration of war.

No. If the legislature is out of session and meeting is impossible, the president may declare war without the legislature's approval. The decision must be submitted to the legislature for subsequent approval.

Article 19
(3) Within this sphere of authority, the Parliament shall –
g) decide on the declaration of a state of war and on the conclusion of peace.

Article 19A
(1) Should the Parliament be obstructed in reaching such decisions, the President of the Republic shall have the right to declare a state of war, a state of national crisis and establish the National Defense Council, or to declare a state of emergency.
(2) The Parliament shall be considered to be obstructed in reaching such decisions, if it is not in session and convening it is impossible due to lack of time or due to the events responsible for the declaration of the state of war, state of national crisis or state of emergency.
(3) The Speaker of Parliament, the President of the Constitutional Court and the Prime Minister shall jointly determine whether the Parliament is obstructed, and whether a declaration of a state of war, a state of national crisis or a state of emergency is justified.
(4) At its first meeting following the end of the obstruction, the Parliament shall review the justification of the declaration of a state of war, state of national crisis or state of emergency, and shall rule on the legality of the measures taken. A majority of two-thirds of the votes of the Members of Parliament is required for this decision.

21. The legislature's approval is necessary to ratify treaties with foreign countries.

Yes. The legislature's approval is necessary to ratify international treaties.

Article 19
(3) Within this sphere of authority, the Parliament shall –
f) conclude international treaties of outstanding importance to the foreign relations of the Republic of Hungary.

Article 30A
(1) The President of the Republic shall –
b) conclude international treaties in the name of the Republic of Hungary; if the subject of the treaty falls within its legislative competence, prior ratification by the Parliament is necessary for conclusion of the treaty.

22. The legislature has the power to grant amnesty.

Yes. The legislature has the power to grant amnesty.

Article 19
(3) Within this sphere of authority, the Parliament shall –
m) exercise general amnesty.

23. The legislature has the power of pardon.

No. The president has the power of pardon.

Article 30A
(1) The President of the Republic shall –
k) exercise the right to grant individual pardons.

24. The legislature reviews and has the right to reject appointments to the judiciary; or the legislature itself appoints members of the judiciary.

Yes. The legislature appoints the members of the Constitutional Court and the president of the Supreme Court.

Article 19
(3) Within this sphere of authority, the Parliament shall –
k) elect ... the members of the Constitutional Court, ... [and] the President of the Supreme Court.

Article 32A
(4) The Constitutional Court shall consist of eleven members who are elected by the Parliament. Members of the Constitutional Court shall be nominated by the Nominating Committee which shall consist of one member of each political party represented in the Parliament. A majority of two-thirds of the votes of the Members of Parliament is required to elect a member of the Constitutional Court.

Article 48
(1) Based on the recommendation made by the President of the Republic, the Parliament shall elect the

President of the Supreme Court; based on the recommendation made by the President of the Supreme
Court, the President of the Republic shall appoint the
Deputy Presidents of the Supreme Court. A majority of
two-thirds of the votes of the Members of Parliament is
required to elect the President of the Supreme Court.

(2) The President of the Republic shall appoint professional judges in the manner specified by law.

(3) Judges may only be removed from office on the
grounds and in accordance with the procedures specified by law.

25. The chairman of the central bank is appointed by
the legislature.

No. The president appoints the president of the
National Bank of Hungary.

Article 30A

(1) The President of the Republic shall –
   i) appoint and dismiss the President and Vice-
   Presidents of the National Bank of Hungary.

Article 32D

(2) The President of the National Bank of Hungary is
appointed by the President of the Republic for a term
of six years.

26. The legislature has a substantial voice in the operation of the state-owned media.

Yes. The legislature has a substantial voice in the
operation of the public media. The parties represented in parliament elect the board of the state-
owned broadcasting companies.

27. The legislature is regularly in session.

Yes. The legislature is in session for roughly seven
months each year.

Article 22

(1) The Parliament shall hold two regular sessions
annually: every year from the 1st of February through
the 15th of June and from the 1st of September through
the 15th of December.

28. Each legislator has a personal secretary.

No. Political parties provide legislators with secretarial assistance, but on average there is less than
one staff person for each legislator.

29. Each legislator has at least one non-secretarial
staff member with policy expertise.

No. See item 28.

30. Legislators are eligible for re-election without any
restriction.

Yes. There are no restrictions on re-election.

31. A seat in the legislature is an attractive enough
position that legislators are generally interested in and
seek re-election.

Yes.

32. The re-election of incumbent legislators is common enough that at any given time the legislature
contains a significant number of highly experienced
members.

Yes. Re-election rates are sufficiently high to produce a significant number of highly experienced
members.

PARLIAMENT OF INDIA (*SANSAD*)

Expert consultants: Niraja Gopal Jayal, Kuldeep Mathur, Pratap Bhanu Mehta, Amit Prakash, Pai Ramachandra

Score: .63

Influence over executive (8/9)		Institutional autonomy (5/9)		Specified powers (2/8)		Institutional capacity (5/6)	
1. replace	X	10. no dissolution		19. amendments	X	27. sessions	X
2. serve as ministers	X	11. no decree		20. war		28. secretary	X
3. interpellate	X	12. no veto	X	21. treaties		29. staff	
4. investigate	X	13. no review		22. amnesty		30. no term limits	X
5. oversee police	X	14. no gatekeeping	X	23. pardon		31. seek re-election	X
6. appoint PM	X	15. no impoundment	X	24. judiciary		32. experience	X
7. appoint ministers		16. control resources	X	25. central bank			
8. lack president	X	17. immunity		26. media	X		
9. no confidence	X	18. all elected	X				

The Parliament (*Sansad*) of India traces its roots to the assemblies that met during British rule, which ended in 1947. Parliament was formally established in the 1950 constitution. The constitution called for a bicameral legislature with a lower chamber, the House of the People (*Lok Sabha*), and an upper chamber, the Council of States (*Rajya Sabha*). The constitution has been altered at a rate of about two amendments each year since independence, but none of these changes has appreciably affected parliament's power.

Parliament is a formidable center of authority. It has broad sway over executive power. Parliament's composition determines the identity of the prime minister, and parliament elects the president. Furthermore, parliament's members serve in government, and parliament can interpellate and investigate the executive branch, vote no confidence in the government, and remove the president from office. Parliament's institutional autonomy is circumscribed, however, by presidential decree and dissolution powers. Parliament has remarkably few specified powers and prerogatives, but it is endowed with a high level of institutional capacity.

SURVEY

1. The legislature alone, without the involvement of any other agencies, can impeach the president or replace the prime minister.

Yes. The legislature can remove the prime minister with a vote of no confidence. The legislature can remove the president from office by a two-thirds majority vote of its total membership in both houses.

Article 61
(1) When a President is to be impeached for violation of the Constitution, the charge shall be preferred by either House of Parliament.
(2) No such charge shall be preferred unless –
    (a) the proposal to prefer such charge is contained in a resolution which has been moved after at least fourteen days' notice in writing signed by not less than one-fourth of the total number of members of the House has been given of their intention to move the resolution, and
    (b) such resolution has been passed by a majority of not less than two-thirds of the total membership of the House.
(3) When a charge has been so preferred by either House of Parliament, the other House shall investigate the charge or cause the charge to be investigated and the President shall have the right to appear and to be represented at such investigation.
(4) If as a result of the investigation a resolution is passed by a majority of not less than two-thirds of the total membership of the House by which the charge was investigated or caused to be investigated, declaring that the charge preferred against the President has been sustained, such resolution shall have the effect of removing the President from his office as from the date on which the resolution is so passed.

Article 75
(3) The Council of Ministers shall be collectively responsible to the House of the People.

2. Ministers may serve simultaneously as members of the legislature.

Yes. Ministers are generally selected from, and required to serve simultaneously in, the legislature. Nonmembers can also be appointed for a period of six months, within which time they must be elected to the legislature or lose their position in government.

3. The legislature has powers of summons over executive branch officials and hearings with executive branch officials testifying before the legislature or its committees are regularly held.

Yes. The constitution grants parliament the authority to define its own powers but does not specifically address interpellation. In practice, the legislature regularly interpellates executive branch officials.

Article 105
(3) In other respects, the powers... of each House of Parliament... shall be such as may from time to time be defined by Parliament by law.

4. The legislature can conduct independent investigation of the chief executive and the agencies of the executive.

Yes. The constitution grants parliament the authority to define its own powers but does not specifically address investigations. In practice, the legislature can investigate the executive.

Article 105
(3) In other respects, the powers... of each House of Parliament... shall be such as may from time to time be defined by Parliament by law.

5. The legislature has effective powers of oversight over the agencies of coercion (the military, organs of law enforcement, intelligence services, and the secret police).

Yes. Legislative committees have effective powers of oversight over the agencies of coercion.

6. The legislature appoints the prime minister.

Yes. Formally, the president appoints the prime minister, but in practice, the president appoints as prime minister the candidate who enjoys the support of the legislature.

Article 75
(1) The Prime Minister shall be appointed by the President and the other Ministers shall be appointed by the President on the advice of the Prime Minister.

7. The legislature's approval is required to confirm the appointment of ministers; or the legislature itself appoints ministers.

No. The president appoints ministers on the advice of the prime minister, and the appointments do not require the legislature's approval.

Article 75
(1) The Prime Minister shall be appointed by the President and the other Ministers shall be appointed by the President on the advice of the Prime Minister.

8. The country lacks a presidency entirely or there is a presidency, but the president is elected by the legislature.

Yes. The legislature elects the president.

Article 54
The President shall be elected by the members of an electoral college consisting of –
(a) the elected members of both Houses of Parliament; and
(b) the elected members of the Legislative Assemblies of the States. Explanation: In this article and in article 55, "State" includes the National Capital Territory of Delhi and the Union territory of Pondicherry.

9. The legislature can vote no confidence in the government.

Yes. The House of the People can vote no confidence in the government (the Council of Ministers).

Article 75
(3) The Council of Ministers shall be collectively responsible to the House of the People.

10. The legislature is immune from dissolution by the executive.

No. The president can dissolve the legislature.

Article 83
(2) The House of the People, unless sooner dissolved, shall continue for five years from the date appointed for its first meeting and no longer and the expiration of the said period of five years shall operate as a dissolution of the House:
Provided that the said period may, while a Proclamation of Emergency is in operation, be extended by Parliament by law for a period not exceeding one year at a time and not extending in any case beyond a period of six months after the Proclamation has ceased to operate.

Article 85
(2) The President may from time to time –
(a) prorogue the Houses or either House;
(b) dissolve the House of the People.

11. Any executive initiative on legislation requires ratification or approval by the legislature before it takes effect; that is, the executive lacks decree power.

No. The president (or the government) can issue decrees (ordinances) that have the force of law when the legislature is not in session. The decrees lapse if they are not subsequently approved by the legislature.

Article 123

(1) If at any time, except when both Houses of Parliament are in session, the President is satisfied that circumstances exist which render it necessary for him to take immediate action, he may promulgate such Ordinances as the circumstances appear to him to require.

(2) An Ordinance promulgated under this article shall have the same force and effect as an Act of Parliament, but every such Ordinance –

(a) shall be laid before both Houses of Parliament and shall cease to operate at the expiration of six weeks from the reassembly of Parliament, or, if before the expiration of that period resolutions disapproving it are passed by both Houses, upon the passing of the second of those resolutions; and

(b) may be withdrawn at any time by the President.

Explanation: Where the Houses of Parliament are summoned to reassemble on different dates, the period of six weeks shall be reckoned from the later of those dates for the purposes of this clause.

(3) If and so far as an Ordinance under this article makes any provision which Parliament would not under this Constitution be competent to enact, it shall be void.

12. Laws passed by the legislature are veto-proof or essentially veto-proof; that is, the executive lacks veto power, or has veto power but the veto can be overridden by a majority in the legislature.

Yes. The legislature can override a presidential veto by a majority vote of its present members.

Article 111

When a Bill has been passed by the Houses of Parliament, it shall be presented to the President, and the President shall declare either that he assents to the Bill, or that he withholds assent therefrom. Provided that the President may, as soon as possible after the presentation to him of a Bill for assent, return the Bill if it is not a Money Bill to the Houses with a message requesting that they will reconsider the Bill or any specified provisions thereof and, in particular, will consider the desirability of introducing any such amendments as he may recommend in his message, and when a Bill is so returned, the Houses shall reconsider the Bill accordingly, and if the Bill is passed again by the Houses with or without amendment and presented to the President for assent, the President shall not withhold assent therefrom.

13. The legislature's laws are supreme and not subject to judicial review.

No. The Supreme Court can review the constitutionality of laws.

Article 132

(1) An appeal shall lie to the Supreme Court from any judgement, decree of final order of a High Court in the territory of India, whether in a civil, criminal or other proceeding, if the High Court certifies under article 134A that the case involves a substantial question of law as to the interpretation of this Constitution.

14. The legislature has the right to initiate bills in all policy jurisdictions; the executive lacks gatekeeping authority.

Yes. The legislature can initiate bills in all policy jurisdictions.

15. Expenditure of funds appropriated by the legislature is mandatory; the executive lacks the power to impound funds appropriated by the legislature.

Yes. The executive lacks the power to impound funds appropriated by the legislature.

16. The legislature controls the resources that finance its own internal operation and provide for the perquisites of its own members.

Yes. The legislature enjoys financial autonomy, including control over members' perquisites.

Article 106

Members of either House of Parliament shall be entitled to receive such salaries and allowances as may from time to time be determined by Parliament by law and, until provision in that respect is so made, allowances at such rates and upon such conditions as were immediately before the commencement of this Constitution applicable in the case of members of the Constituent Assembly of the Dominion of India.

17. Members of the legislature are immune from arrest and/or criminal prosecution.

No. Legislative immunity extends to official parliamentary business only. Legislators are subject to arrest for common crimes.

Article 105

(1) Subject to the provisions of this Constitution and to the rules and standing orders regulating the procedure of Parliament, there shall be freedom of speech in Parliament.

(2) No member of Parliament shall be liable to any proceedings in any court in respect of anything said or any vote given by him in Parliament or any committee thereof, and no person shall be so liable in respect of the publication by or under the authority of either House of Parliament of any report, paper, votes or proceedings.

(3) In other respects, the powers, privileges and immunities of each House of Parliament, and of the members and the committees of each House, shall be such as may from time to time be defined by Parliament by law, and, until so defined, shall be those of that House and of its members and committees immediately before

the coming into force of section 15 of the Constitution (Forty-fourth Amendment) Act. 1978.

(4) The provisions of clauses (1), (2) and (3) shall apply in relation to persons who by virtue of this Constitution have the right to speak in, and otherwise to take part in the proceedings of, a House of Parliament or any committee thereof as they apply in relation to members of Parliament.

18. All members of the legislature are elected; the executive lacks the power to appoint any members of the legislature.

Yes. All members of the legislature are elected, with two minor exceptions. The president appoints two of the 538 members of the House of the People to represent the Anglo-Indian community and twelve of the 238 members of the Council of States from the world of the arts, literature, science, and social service.

Article 80

(1) The Council of States shall consists of –

(a) twelve members to be nominated by the President in accordance with the provisions of clause (3); and

(b) not more than two hundred and thirty-eight representatives of the States and of the Union territories.

(2) The allocation of seats in the Council of States to be filled by representatives of the States and of the Union territories shall be in accordance with the provisions in that behalf contained in the Fourth Schedule.

(3) The members to be nominated by the President under sub-clause (a) and clause (1) shall consists of persons having special knowledge or practical experience in respect of such matters as the following, namely: Literature, science, art and social service.

(4) The representatives of each State in the Council of States shall be elected members of the Legislative Assembly of the State in accordance with the system of proportional representation by means of the single transferable vote.

(5) The representatives of the Union territories in the Council of States shall be chosen in such manner as Parliament may by law prescribe.

Article 81

(1) Subject to the provisions of article 331, the House of the People shall consists of –

(a) not more than five hundred and thirty members chosen by direct election from territorial constituencies in the States, and

(b) not more than twenty members to represent the Union territories, chosen in such manner as Parliament may by law provide.

19. The legislature alone, without the involvement of any other agencies, can change the Constitution.

Yes. The legislature can changes the constitution with a two-thirds majority vote in both houses. Amendments to select constitutional articles require approval by the state legislatures.

Article 368

(1) Notwithstanding anything in this Constitution, Parliament may in exercise of its constituent power amend by way of addition, variation or repeal any provision of this Constitution in accordance with the procedure laid down in this article.

(2) An amendment of this Constitution may be initiated only by the introduction of a Bill for the purpose in either House of Parliament, and when the Bill is passed in each House by a majority of the total membership of that House and by a majority of not less than two-thirds of the members of that House present and voting, it shall be presented to the President who shall give his assent to the Bill and thereupon the Constitution shall stand amended in accordance with the terms of the Bill: Provided that if such amendment seeks to make any change in –

(a) article 54, article 55, article 73, article 162 or article 241, or

(b) Chapter IV of Part V, Chapter V of Part VI, or Chapter I of Part XI, or

(c) any of the Lists in the Seventh Schedule, or

(d) the representation of States in Parliament, or

(e) the provisions of this article,

the amendment shall also require to be ratified by the Legislatures of not less than one-half of the States by resolutions to that effect passed by those Legislatures before the Bill making provision for such amendment is presented to the President for assent.

20. The legislature's approval is necessary for the declaration of war.

No. The president, with the cabinet's approval, can issue a proclamation of emergency without the legislature's prior approval. The proclamation lapses after one month if it is not subsequently approved by the legislature.

Article 352

(1) If the President is satisfied that a grave emergency exists whereby the security of India or of any part of the territory thereof is threatened, whether by war or external aggression or armed rebellion, he may, by proclamation, make a declaration to that effect in respect of the whole of India or of such part of the territory thereof as may be specified in the proclamation.

Explanation: A proclamation of Emergency declaring that the security of India or any part of the territory thereof is threatened by war or by external aggression or by armed rebellion may be made before the actual occurrence of war or of any such aggression or rebellion, if the President is satisfied that there is imminent danger thereof.

(3) The President shall not issue a Proclamation under clause (1) or a Proclamation varying such Proclamation unless the decision of the Union cabinet (that is to say, the Council consisting of the Prime Minister and other

Ministers of Cabinet rank appointed under article 75) that such a Proclamation may be issued has been communicated to him in writing.

(4) Every Proclamation issued under this article shall be laid before each House of Parliament and shall, except where it is a Proclamation revoking a previous Proclamation, cease to operate at the expiration of one month unless before the expiration of that period it has been approved by resolutions of both Houses of Parliament: Provided that if any such Proclamation (not being a Proclamation revoking a previous Proclamation) is issued at a time when the House of the People has been dissolved, or the dissolution of the House of the People takes place during the period of one month referred to in this clause, and if a resolution approving the Proclamation has been passed by the Council of States, but no resolution with respect to such Proclamation has been passed by the House of the People before the expiration of that period, the Proclamation shall cease to operate at the expiration of thirty days from the date on which the House of the People first sits after its reconstitution, unless before the expiration of the said period of thirty days a resolution approving the Proclamation has been also passed by the House of the People.

21. The legislature's approval is necessary to ratify treaties with foreign countries.

No. The president can conclude international treaties without the legislature's approval.

22. The legislature has the power to grant amnesty.

No. Amnesty and pardon are not treated separately, and the legislature lacks the power to grant amnesty. See item 23.

23. The legislature has the power of pardon.

No. The president has the power of pardon.

> Article 72
> (1) The President shall have the power to grant pardons, reprieves, respites or remissions of punishment or to suspend, remit or commute the sentence of any persons convicted of any offence.

24. The legislature reviews and has the right to reject appointments to the judiciary; or the legislature itself appoints members of the judiciary.

No. The president appoints the members of the Supreme Court, and the appointments do not require the legislature's approval.

> Article 124
> (1) There shall be a Supreme Court of India consisting of a Chief Justice of India and, until Parliament by law prescribes a larger number, of not more than seven other Judges.

(2) Every Judge of the Supreme Court shall be appointed by the President by warrant under his hand and seal after consultation with such of the Judges of the Supreme Court and of the High Courts in the States as the President may deem necessary for the purpose and shall hold office until he attains the age of sixty-five years.

25. The chairman of the central bank is appointed by the legislature.

No. The government appoints the governor of the Reserve Bank of India.

26. The legislature has a substantial voice in the operation of the state-owned media.

Yes. The legal framework and budgetary allocations of the public media are subjected to legislative scrutiny.

27. The legislature is regularly in session.

Yes. The legislature meets in ordinary session for about eight months each year. The "budget session" runs from February to May, the "monsoon session" occurs in July and August, and the "winter session" is held in November and December.

28. Each legislator has a personal secretary.

Yes. Legislators are paid a fixed sum toward secretarial assistance and office expenses.

> Article 98
> (1) Each House of Parliament shall have a separate secretarial staff.

29. Each legislator has at least one non-secretarial staff member with policy expertise.

No. Legislators are provided funds for staff, but not every legislator has a policy expert on staff.

30. Legislators are eligible for re-election without any restriction.

Yes. There are no restrictions on re-election.

31. A seat in the legislature is an attractive enough position that legislators are generally interested in and seek re-election.

Yes.

32. The re-election of incumbent legislators is common enough that at any given time the legislature contains a significant number of highly experienced members.

Yes. Re-election rates are sufficiently high to produce a significant number of highly experienced members.

HOUSE OF REPRESENTATIVES OF INDONESIA (*DEWAN PERWAKILAN RAKYAT*)

Expert consultants: Harry Bhaskara, Jonathan Chang, Harold Crouch, Hans J. Esderts, Muhamad Nadratuzzaman Hosen, Peter Lewis

Score: .56

Influence over executive (3/9)		Institutional autonomy (6/9)		Specified powers (4/8)		Institutional capacity (5/6)	
1. replace		10. no dissolution	X	19. amendments	X	27. sessions	X
2. serve as ministers		11. no decree		20. war	X	28. secretary	X
3. interpellate	X	12. no veto	X	21. treaties	X	29. staff	
4. investigate	X	13. no review		22. amnesty		30. no term limits	X
5. oversee police		14. no gatekeeping	X	23. pardon		31. seek re-election	X
6. appoint PM		15. no impoundment	X	24. judiciary	X	32. experience	X
7. appoint ministers		16. control resources	X	25. central bank			
8. lack president		17. immunity		26. media			
9. no confidence	X	18. all elected	X				

The House of Representatives (*Dewan Perwakilan Rakyat,* or DPR) of Indonesia was established in the 1945 constitution. The legislature of Indonesia as constituted today consists of three separate bodies. The House of Representatives is the primary lawmaking body. The House of Regional Representatives (*Dewan Perwakilan Daerah,* or DPD), created in a 2004 constitutional amendment, serves as an upper house of the legislature and is charged with providing the DPR with input on regional issues. The People's Consultative Assembly (*Majelis Permusyawaratan Rakyat,* or MPR) is a special body that consists of the members of the DPR and the DPD. It meets to amend the constitution and to inaugurate and impeach the president.

The legislature was largely sidelined under the rule of President Suharto, who held power from 1965 to 1997. Following Suharto's fall, the legislature was revitalized, and in 1999 Indonesia held its first free parliamentary election since 1955. A constitutional amendment in 1999 placed some constraints on the president's previously unlimited decree powers. In 2000 another constitutional amendment revoked the veto powers that the president had previously held. A 2001 amendment provided for direct presidential elections; prior to 2001 the MPR elected the president. The amendment also established a Constitutional Court with the power of judicial review; prior to 2001 the laws

of the legislature were supreme and not subject to judicial review. Another amendment in 2001 took away from the president the right to appoint members of the MPR; prior to 2001 the president appointed some of the MPR membership.

The legislature is a fairly weighty institution. It has some influence over the executive, including the ability to interpellate and investigate executive branch officials. It has a fair amount of institutional autonomy, although legislators lack immunity from arrest and criminal prosecution. It exercises a number of specified powers, and it has considerable institutional capacity.

SURVEY

1. The legislature alone, without the involvement of any other agencies, can impeach the president or replace the prime minister.

No. Presidential impeachment requires the involvement of the Constitutional Court.

Article 3
(3) The MPR may only dismiss the President and/or Vice-President during his/her term of office in accordance with the Constitution.

Article 7A
The President and/or the Vice-President may be dismissed from his/her position during his/her term of office by the MPR on the proposal of the House of

Representatives, both if it is proven that he/she has violated the law through an act of treason, corruption, bribery, or other act of a grave criminal nature, or through moral turpitude, and/or that the President and/or Vice-President no longer meets the qualifications to serve as President and/or Vice-President.

Article 7B

(1) Any proposal for the dismissal of the President and/or the Vice-President may be submitted by the DPR to the MPR only by first submitting a request to the Constitutional Court to investigate, bring to trial, and issue a decision on the opinion of the DPR either that the President and/or Vice-President has violated the law through an act of treason, corruption, bribery, or other act of a grave criminal nature, or through moral turpitude, and/or that the President and/or Vice-President no longer meets the qualifications to serve as President and/or Vice-President.

(2) The opinion of the DPR that the President and/or Vice-President has violated the law or no longer meets the qualifications to serve as President and/or Vice-President is undertaken in the course of implementation of the supervision function of the DPR.

(3) The submission of the request of the DPR to the Constitutional Court shall only be made with the support of at least 2/3 of the total members of the DPR who are present in a plenary session that is attended by at least 2/3 of the total membership of the DPR.

(4) The Constitutional Court has the obligation to investigate, bring to trial, and reach the most just decision on the opinion of the DPR at the latest ninety days after the request of the DPR was received by the Constitutional Court.

(5) If the Constitutional Court decides that the President and/or Vice-President is proved to have violated the law through an act of treason, corruption, bribery, or other act of a grave criminal nature, or through moral turpitude; and/or the President and/or Vice-President is proved no longer to meet the qualifications to serve as President and/or Vice-President, the DPR shall hold a plenary session to submit the proposal to impeach the President and/or Vice-President to the MPR.

(6) The MPR shall hold a session to decide on the proposal of the DPR at the latest thirty days after its receipt of the proposal.

(7) The decision of the MPR over the proposal to impeach the President and/or Vice-President shall be taken during a plenary session of the MPR which is attended by at least 3/4 of the total membership and shall require the approval of at least 2/3 of the total of members who are present, after the President and/or Vice-President have been given the opportunity to present his/her explanation to the plenary session of the MPR.

2. Ministers may serve simultaneously as members of the legislature.

No. Ministers may not serve simultaneously in the legislature.

3. The legislature has powers of summons over executive branch officials and hearings with executive branch officials testifying before the legislature or its committees are regularly held.

Yes. The legislature regularly interpellates officials from the executive.

Article 20A

(1) The DPR shall hold legislative, budgeting and oversight functions.

(2) In carrying out its functions, in addition to the rights regulated in other articles of this Constitution, the DPR shall hold the right of interpellation, the right of investigation, and the right to declare an opinion.

(3) Other than the rights regulated in other articles of this Constitution, every DPR member shall hold the right to submit questions, the right to propose suggestions and opinions, and the right of immunity.

(4) Further provisions on the rights of the DPR and the rights of DPR members shall be regulated by law.

4. The legislature can conduct independent investigation of the chief executive and the agencies of the executive.

Yes. The legislature can investigate the executive.

Article 20A

(1) The DPR shall hold legislative, budgeting and oversight functions.

(2) In carrying out its functions, in addition to the rights regulated in other articles of this Constitution, the DPR shall hold the right of interpellation, the right of investigation, and the right to declare an opinion.

(3) Other than the rights regulated in other articles of this Constitution, every DPR member shall hold the right to submit questions, the right to propose suggestions and opinions, and the right of immunity.

(4) Further provisions on the rights of the DPR and the rights of DPR members shall be regulated by law.

5. The legislature has effective powers of oversight over the agencies of coercion (the military, organs of law enforcement, intelligence services, and the secret police).

No. The legislature lacks effective powers of oversight over the agencies of coercion.

6. The legislature appoints the prime minister.

No. There is no prime minister.

7. The legislature's approval is required to confirm the appointment of ministers; or the legislature itself appoints ministers.

No. The president appoints ministers, and the appointments do not require the legislature's approval.

Article 17

(1) The President shall be assisted by Ministers of State.

(2) Ministers of State shall be appointed and dismissed by the President.

8. The country lacks a presidency entirely or there is a presidency, but the president is elected by the legislature.

No. The president is directly elected. Prior to 2001 the MPR elected the president.

> Article 6A
> (1) The President and Vice-President shall be elected as a single ticket directly by the people.

9. The legislature can vote no confidence in the government.

Yes. The legislature can vote to censure the government. The vote is merely symbolic, however. It does not result in the government's resignation.

10. The legislature is immune from dissolution by the executive.

Yes. The legislature is immune from dissolution.

> Article 7C
> The President may not freeze and/or dissolve the DPR.

11. Any executive initiative on legislation requires ratification or approval by the legislature before it takes effect; that is, the executive lacks decree power.

No. The president can issue decrees (here expressed as "regulations") that have the force of law "should exigencies compel." The decrees lapse if they are not subsequently approved by the legislature.

> Article 22
> (1) Should exigencies compel, the President shall have the right to establish government regulations in lieu of laws.
> (2) Such government regulations must obtain the approval of the DPR during its next session.
> (3) Should there be no such approval, these government regulations shall be revoked.

12. Laws passed by the legislature are veto-proof or essentially veto-proof; that is, the executive lacks veto power, or has veto power but the veto can be overridden by a majority in the legislature.

Yes. The executive lacks veto power. If the president refuses to sign a bill, it automatically becomes law within thirty days. Prior to a 2000 constitutional amendment, the president had veto powers.

> Article 20
> (1) The DPR shall hold the authority to establish laws.
> (2) Each bill shall be discussed by the DPR and the President to reach joint approval.
> (3) If a bill fails to reach joint approval, that bill shall not be reintroduced within the same DPR term of sessions.
> (4) The President signs a jointly approved bill to become a law.
> (5) If the President fails to sign a jointly approved bill within 30 days following such approval, that bill shall legally become a law and must be promulgated.

13. The legislature's laws are supreme and not subject to judicial review.

No. The Constitutional Court can review the constitutionality of laws.

> Article 24C
> (1) The Constitutional Court...shall have the final power of decision in reviewing laws against the Constitution.

14. The legislature has the right to initiate bills in all policy jurisdictions; the executive lacks gatekeeping authority.

Yes. The legislature can initiate bills in all policy jurisdictions.

15. Expenditure of funds appropriated by the legislature is mandatory; the executive lacks the power to impound funds appropriated by the legislature.

Yes. The executive lacks the power to impound funds appropriated by the legislature.

16. The legislature controls the resources that finance its own internal operation and provide for the perquisites of its own members.

Yes. The legislature enjoys financial autonomy.

17. Members of the legislature are immune from arrest and/or criminal prosecution.

No. The constitution specifies only that legislators have "the right of immunity." In practice, legislators can be arrested with the president's approval.

> Article 20A
> (3) Other than the rights regulated in other articles of this Constitution, every DPR member shall hold the right to submit questions, the right to propose suggestions and opinions, and the right of immunity.

18. All members of the legislature are elected; the executive lacks the power to appoint any members of the legislature.

Yes. All members of the three legislative bodies are elected. Prior to 2001 some of the members of the MPR were appointed.

> Article 2
> (1) The MPR shall consist of the members of the DPR and the members of the DPD who have been elected through general elections, and shall be regulated further by law.
>
> Article 19
> (1) Members of the DPR shall be elected through a general election.
>
> Article 22C
> (1) The members of the DPD shall be elected from every province through a general election.

19. The legislature alone, without the involvement of any other agencies, can change the Constitution.

Yes. The MPR can change the constitution with a two-thirds majority vote.

Article 3
(1) The MPR has the authority to amend and enact the Constitution.

Article 37
(1) A proposal to amend the Articles of this Constitution may be included in the agenda of an MPR session if it is submitted by at least 1/3 of the total MPR membership.
(2) Any proposal to amend the Articles of this Constitution shall be introduced in writing and must clearly state the articles to be amended and the reasons for the amendment.
(3) To amend the Articles of this Constitution, the session of the MPR requires at least 2/3 of the total membership of the MPR to be present.
(4) Any decision to amend the Articles of this Constitution shall be made with the agreement of at least fifty percent plus one member of the total membership of the MPR.
(5) Provisions relating to the form of the unitary state of the Republic of Indonesia may not be amended.

20. The legislature's approval is necessary for the declaration of war.

Yes. The House of Representatives' approval is necessary for presidential war declarations.

Article 11
(1) The President with the approval of the DPR may declare war, make peace and conclude treaties with other countries.

21. The legislature's approval is necessary to ratify treaties with foreign countries.

Yes. The legislature's approval is necessary to ratify international treaties.

Article 11
(1) The President with the approval of the DPR may declare war, make peace and conclude treaties with other countries.
(2) The President in making other international agreements that will produce an extensive and fundamental impact on the lives of the people which is linked to the state financial burden, and/or that will requires an amendment to or the enactment of a law, shall obtain the approval of the DPR.

22. The legislature has the power to grant amnesty.

No. The president has the power to grant amnesty.

Article 14
(1) The President may grant clemency and restoration of rights and shall in so doing have regard to the opinion of the Supreme Court.
(2) The President may grant amnesty and the dropping of charges and shall in so doing have regard to the opinion of the DPR.

23. The legislature has the power of pardon.

No. The president has the power of pardon.

Article 14
(1) The President may grant clemency and restoration of rights and shall in so doing have regard to the opinion of the Supreme Court.
(2) The President may grant amnesty and the dropping of charges and shall in so doing have regard to the opinion of the DPR.

24. The legislature reviews and has the right to reject appointments to the judiciary; or the legislature itself appoints members of the judiciary.

Yes. The legislature's consent is required to approve the president's appointments to the Supreme Court and the Judicial Commission.

Article 24A
(3) Candidate justices of the Supreme Court shall be proposed by the Judicial Commission to the DPR for approval and shall subsequently be formally appointed to office by the President.

Article 24B
(3) The members of the Judicial Commission shall be appointed and dismissed by the President with the approval of the DPR.

Article 24C
(3) The Constitutional Court shall be composed of nine persons who shall be constitutional justices and who shall be confirmed in office by the President, of whom three shall be nominated by the Supreme Court, three nominated by the DPR, and three nominated by the President.

25. The chairman of the central bank is appointed by the legislature.

No. The president appoints the governor of the Bank of Indonesia.

26. The legislature has a substantial voice in the operation of the state-owned media.

No. The legislature lacks substantial voice in the operation of the public media.

27. The legislature is regularly in session.

Yes. According to the constitution, the MPR must meet once every five years, and the DPR and the DPD must meet at least once a year. In practice, the MPR meets for about ten days each year, and the DPR meets regularly in ordinary session.

Article 2
(1) The MPR shall consist of the members of the DPR and the members of the DPD who have been elected through general elections, and shall be regulated further by law.

(2) The MPR shall convene in a session at least once in every five years in the capital of the State.

Article 19
(3) The DPR shall convene in a session at least once a year.

Article 22C
(3) The DPD shall hold a session at least once every year.

28. Each legislator has a personal secretary.

Yes.

29. Each legislator has at least one non-secretarial staff member with policy expertise.

No.

30. Legislators are eligible for re-election without any restriction.

Yes. There are no restrictions on re-election.

31. A seat in the legislature is an attractive enough position that legislators are generally interested in and seek re-election.

Yes.

32. The re-election of incumbent legislators is common enough that at any given time the legislature contains a significant number of highly experienced members.

Yes. Since the opening of the political system in the late 1990s, Indonesia has held two rounds of parliamentary elections, in 1999 and 2004. Re-election rates are sufficiently high to produce a significant number of highly experienced members.

ISLAMIC CONSULTATIVE ASSEMBLY OF THE ISLAMIC REPUBLIC OF IRAN (*MAJLES-E-SHURA-YE-ESLAMI*)

Expert consultants: Navabeh Espahbodi, Elahe Koolaee, Homeira Moshirzadeh, Babak Rahimi, Masoud Shafigh, Nargess Tavassolian, Güneş Murat Tezcür, Reza Yousefian

Score: .44

Influence over executive (4/9)		Institutional autonomy (5/9)		Specified powers (1/8)		Institutional capacity (4/6)	
1. replace		10. no dissolution	X	19. amendments		27. sessions	X
2. serve as ministers		11. no decree		20. war		28. secretary	X
3. interpellate	X	12. no veto		21. treaties	X	29. staff	
4. investigate	X	13. no review		22. amnesty		30. no term limits	X
5. oversee police		14. no gatekeeping	X	23. pardon		31. seek re-election	X
6. appoint PM		15. no impoundment	X	24. judiciary		32. experience	
7. appoint ministers	X	16. control resources	X	25. central bank			
8. lack president		17. immunity		26. media			
9. no confidence	X	18. all elected	X				

The Islamic Consultative Assembly (*Majles-e-Shura-ye-Eslami*) of Iran traces its roots to the legislature established in Iran's 1906 constitution. The legislature was subordinated to the shahs, however, except for a few years in the early twentieth century and between 1941 and 1953. The 1979 constitution, still in place today, created a system of dual authority with an elected legislature, prime minister, and president overseen by a religious Supreme Leader and Guardian Coun-

cil. A 1989 amendment eliminated the position of the prime minister. The 1989 amendment further cluttered the already crowded institutional landscape by creating the Council of Expediency of the State, which formally enjoys "supreme legislative authority" and is intended to mediate between the Guardian Council and the legislature.

The legislature nevertheless has some power. It can influence the executive with, among other powers, its ability to interpellate officials from the executive. The legislature also enjoys some institutional autonomy. Its lawmaking authority is severely circumscribed, however, by the Guardian Council, which reviews laws for "compatibility with Islam and the constitution" and thereby wields absolute veto power. The legislature wields only one of the specified powers assessed in this survey. Furthermore, its institutional capacity is limited by a lack of a significant number of highly experienced legislators. A low level of legislative expertise among members is partly the result of the Guardian Council's powers to disqualify electoral candidates and invalidate electoral results. In the 2004 parliamentary elections alone, the Guardian Council rejected over two thousand candidates, including scores of incumbent legislators.

SURVEY

1. The legislature alone, without the involvement of any other agencies, can impeach the president or replace the prime minister.

No. Removing the president from office requires the involvement of the Supreme Leader.

Article 89
(2) In the event at least one-third of the members of the Islamic Consultative Assembly interpellate the President concerning his executive responsibilities in relation with the Executive Power and the executive affairs of the country the President must be present in the Assembly within one month after the tabling of the interpellation in order to give adequate explanations in regard to the matters raised. In the event, after hearing the statements of the opposing and favoring members and the reply of the President, two-thirds of the members of the Assembly declare a vote of no confidence, the same will be communicated to the Leadership for information and implementation of Article 110 (10).

Article 110
(1) Following are the duties and powers of the Leadership:
   10. Dismissal of the President of the Republic, with due regard for the interests of the country, after the Supreme Court holds him guilty of the violation of his constitutional duties, or after a vote of the Islamic Consultative Assembly testifying to his incompetence on the basis of Article 89.

2. Ministers may serve simultaneously as members of the legislature.

No. Legislators are prohibited from serving simultaneously in ministerial positions.

Article 141
(1) The President, the deputies to the President, Ministers, and Government employees cannot hold more

than one Government position, and it is forbidden for them...to be a member of the Islamic Consultative Assembly.

3. The legislature has powers of summons over executive branch officials and hearings with executive branch officials testifying before the legislature or its committees are regularly held.

Yes. The legislature regularly interpellates officials from the executive.

Article 89
(1) Members of the Islamic Consultative Assembly can interpellate the Council of Ministers or an individual Minister in instances they deem necessary. Interpellations can be tabled if they bear the signatures of at least ten members. The Council of Ministers or interpellated Minister must be present in the Assembly within ten days after the tabling of the interpellation in order to answer it and seek a vote of confidence. If the Council of Ministers or the Minister concerned fails to attend the Assembly, the members who tabled the interpellation will explain their reasons, and the Assembly will declare a vote of no confidence if it deems it necessary. If the Assembly does not pronounce a vote of confidence, the Council of Ministers or the Minister subject to interpellation is dismissed. In both cases, the Ministers subject to interpellation cannot become members of the next Council of Ministers formed immediately afterwards.
(2) In the event at least one-third of the members of the Islamic Consultative Assembly interpellate the President concerning his executive responsibilities in relation with the Executive Power and the executive affairs of the country the President must be present in the Assembly within one month after the tabling of the interpellation in order to give adequate explanations in regard to the matters raised. In the event, after hearing the statements of the opposing and favoring members and the reply of the President, two-thirds of the members of the Assembly declare a vote of no confidence, the same will be communicated to the Leadership for information and implementation of Article 110 (10).

4. The legislature can conduct independent investigation of the chief executive and the agencies of the executive.

Yes. The legislature can investigate the executive.

Article 76
The Islamic Consultative Assembly has the right to investigate and examine all the affairs of the country.

Article 90
Whoever has a complaint concerning the work of the Assembly or the executive power or the judicial power can forward his complaint in writing to the Assembly. The Assembly must investigate his complaint and give a satisfactory reply. In cases where the complaint relates to the executive or the judiciary, the Assembly must

demand proper investigation in the matter and an adequate explanation from them, and announce the results within a reasonable time. In cases where the subject of the complaint is of public interest, the reply must be made public.

5. The legislature has effective powers of oversight over the agencies of coercion (the military, organs of law enforcement, intelligence services, and the secret police).

No. The legislature lacks effective powers of oversight over the agencies of coercion.

6. The legislature appoints the prime minister.

No. There has been no prime minister in Iran since 1989.

7. The legislature's approval is required to confirm the appointment of ministers; or the legislature itself appoints ministers.

Yes. The legislature's approval is required to confirm ministerial appointments.

> Article 133
> Ministers will be appointed by the President and will be presented to the Assembly for a vote of confidence. With the change of Assembly, a new vote of confidence will not be necessary.

8. The country lacks a presidency entirely or there is a presidency, but the president is elected by the legislature.

No. The president is directly elected.

> Article 114
> The President is elected for a four-year term by the direct vote of the people.

> Article 117
> The President is elected by an absolute majority of votes polled by the voters.

9. The legislature can vote no confidence in the government.

Yes. The legislature can vote no confidence in the government.

> Article 87
> The President must obtain, for the Council of Ministers, after being formed and before all other business, a vote of confidence from the Assembly. During his incumbency, he can also seek a vote of confidence for the Council of Ministers from the Assembly on important and controversial issues.

> Article 136
> The President can dismiss the Ministers and in such a case he must obtain a vote of confidence for the new Minister(s) from the Assembly. In case half of the members of the Council of Ministers are changed after the government has received its vote of confidence from

the Assembly, the government must seek a fresh vote of confidence from the Assembly.

10. The legislature is immune from dissolution by the executive.

Yes. The legislature is immune from dissolution.

11. Any executive initiative on legislation requires ratification or approval by the legislature before it takes effect; that is, the executive lacks decree power.

No. The president can issue decrees that have the force of law.

12. Laws passed by the legislature are veto-proof or essentially veto-proof; that is, the executive lacks veto power, or has veto power but the veto can be overridden by a majority in the legislature.

No. The president lacks veto power, but all laws are subject to an absolute veto by the Guardian Council.

> Article 123
> The President is obliged to sign legislation approved by the Assembly or the result of a referendum, after the legal procedures have been completed and it has been communicated to him. After signing, he must forward it to the responsible authorities for implementation.

13. The legislature's laws are supreme and not subject to judicial review.

No. The Guardian Council reviews laws to ensure their "compatibility with the criteria of Islam and the Constitution."

> Article 94
> All legislation passed by the Islamic Consultative Assembly must be sent to the Guardian Council. The Guardian Council must review it within a maximum of ten days from its receipt with a view to ensuring its compatibility with the criteria of Islam and the Constitution. If it finds the legislation incompatible, it will return it to the Assembly for review. Otherwise the legislation will be deemed enforceable.

14. The legislature has the right to initiate bills in all policy jurisdictions; the executive lacks gatekeeping authority.

Yes. The legislature can initiate bills in all policy jurisdictions.

15. Expenditure of funds appropriated by the legislature is mandatory; the executive lacks the power to impound funds appropriated by the legislature.

Yes. The executive lacks the power to impound funds appropriated by the legislature.

16. The legislature controls the resources that finance its own internal operation and provide for the perquisites of its own members.

Yes. The legislature enjoys financial autonomy.

17. Members of the legislature are immune from arrest and/or criminal prosecution.

No. Legislative immunity extends to official parliamentary business only. Legislators are subject to arrest for common crimes.

Article 86
Members of the Assembly are completely free in expressing their views and casting their votes in the course of performing their duties as representatives, and they cannot be prosecuted or arrested for opinions expressed in the Assembly or votes cast in the course of performing their duties as representatives.

18. All members of the legislature are elected; the executive lacks the power to appoint any members of the legislature.

Yes. All members of the legislature are elected. It bears note, however, that the Guardian Council, while unable directly to appoint members of the legislature, influences the composition of the body through its right to disqualify candidates.

Article 62
(1) The Islamic Consultative Assembly is constituted by the representatives of the people elected directly and by secret ballot.

19. The legislature alone, without the involvement of any other agencies, can change the Constitution.

No. The constitution can be amended only by a special Council for Revision of the Constitution, which includes representatives from all three branches of government, the Guardian Council, and other institutions.

Article 177
(1) The revision of the Constitution of the Islamic Republic of Iran, whenever needed by the circumstances, will be done in the following manner:
The Leader issues an edict to the President after consultation with the Nation's Exigency Council stipulating the amendments or additions to be made by the Council for Revision of the Constitution which consists of:
1. Members of the Guardian Council;
2. heads of the three branches of the government;
3. permanent members of the Nation's Exigency Council;
4. five members from among the Assembly of Experts;
5. ten representatives selected by the Leader;
6. three representatives from the Council of Ministers;
7. three representatives from the judiciary branch;
8. ten representatives from among the members of the Islamic Consultative Assembly; and
9. three representatives from among the university professors.

(2) The method of working, manner of selection and the terms and conditions of the Council shall be determined by law.
(3) The decisions of the Council, after the confirmation and signatures of the Leader, shall be valid if approved by an absolute majority vote in a national referendum.
(4) The provisions of Article 59 shall not apply to the referendum for the "Revision of the Constitution."
(5) The contents of the articles of the Constitution related to the Islamic character of the political system; the basis of all the rules and regulations according to Islamic criteria; the religious footing; the objectives of the Islamic Republic of Iran; the democratic character of the government; the holy principle; the Imamate of Ummah; and the administration of the affairs of the country based on national referenda, official religion of Iran and the religious school are unalterable.

20. The legislature's approval is necessary for the declaration of war.

No. The Supreme Leader can declare war without the legislature's approval.

Article 110
(1) Following are the duties and powers of the Leadership:
5. Declaration of war and peace and the mobilization of the Armed Forces.

21. The legislature's approval is necessary to ratify treaties with foreign countries.

Yes. The legislature's approval is necessary to ratify international treaties.

Article 77
International treaties, protocols, contracts, and agreements must be approved by the Islamic Consultative Assembly.

Article 125
The President or his legal representative has the authority to sign treaties, protocols, contracts, and agreements concluded by the Iranian government with other governments, as well as agreements pertaining to international organizations, after obtaining the approval of the Islamic Consultative Assembly.

22. The legislature has the power to grant amnesty.

No. Amnesty and pardon are not treated separately, and the legislature lacks the power to grant amnesty. See item 23.

23. The legislature has the power of pardon.

No. The Supreme Leader has the power of pardon.

Article 110
(1) Following are the duties and powers of the Leadership:
11. Pardoning or reducing the sentences of convicts, within the framework of Islamic criteria, on a recommendation from the Head of judicial power.

24. The legislature reviews and has the right to reject appointments to the judiciary; or the legislature itself appoints members of the judiciary.

No. The head of the judiciary is appointed by the Supreme Leader, and the Chief of the Supreme Court is nominated by the head of the judiciary. The appointments do not require the legislature's approval.

Article 91

With a view to safeguard the Islamic ordinances and the Constitution, in order to examine the compatibility of the legislation passed by the Islamic Consultative Assembly with Islam, a council to be known as the Guardian Council is to be constituted with the following composition:

1. six religious men, conscious of the present needs and the issues of the day, to be selected by the Leader, and
2. six jurists, specializing in different areas of law, to be elected by the Islamic Consultative Assembly from among the Muslim jurists nominated by the Head of the Judicial Power.

Article 157

In order to fulfil the responsibilities of the judiciary power in all the matters concerning judiciary, administrative and executive areas, the Leader shall appoint a just honorable man well versed in judiciary affairs and possessing prudence and administrative abilities as the head of the judiciary power for a period of five years who shall be the highest judicial authority.

Article 162

The Chief of the Supreme Court and the Prosecutor-General must both be just honorable men well versed in judicial matters. They will be nominated by the head of the judiciary branch for a period of five years, in consultation with the judges of the Supreme Court.

25. The chairman of the central bank is appointed by the legislature.

No. The governor of the Central Bank of the Islamic Republic of Iran is nominated by the president, confirmed by the general assembly of the Central Bank of the Islamic Republic of Iran, and then appointed by the president.

26. The legislature has a substantial voice in the operation of the state-owned media.

No. Despite the legislature's right to appoint two of the six members to the council that oversees the public media, the legislature lacks a substantial voice. The state-owned media is under the control of the Supreme Leader and the president.

Article 175

(1) The freedom of expression and dissemination of thoughts in the Radio and Television of the Islamic Republic of Iran must be guaranteed in keeping with the Islamic criteria and the best interests of the country.

(2) The appointment and dismissal of the head of the Radio and Television of the Islamic Republic of Iran rests with the Leader. A council consisting of two representatives each of the President, the head of the judiciary branch, and the Islamic Consultative Assembly shall supervise the functioning of this organization.

(3) The policies and the manner of managing the organization and its supervision will be determined by law.

27. The legislature is regularly in session.

Yes. The legislature regularly meets in ordinary session.

28. Each legislator has a personal secretary.

Yes.

29. Each legislator has at least one non-secretarial staff member with policy expertise.

No.

30. Legislators are eligible for re-election without any restriction.

Yes. There are no restrictions on re-election.

31. A seat in the legislature is an attractive enough position that legislators are generally interested in and seek re-election.

Yes.

32. The re-election of incumbent legislators is common enough that at any given time the legislature contains a significant number of highly experienced members.

No. The legislature lacks a significant number of highly experienced members. The Council of Guardians disqualified over two thousand candidates, including scores of incumbents, before the parliamentary elections of 2004.

COUNCIL OF REPRESENTATIVES OF IRAQ (*MEJLIS WATANI*)

Expert consultants: Adeed Dawisha, David Patel

Score: .63

Influence over executive (7/9)		Institutional autonomy (8/9)		Specified powers (3/8)		Institutional capacity (2/6)	
1. replace	X	10. no dissolution	X	19. amendments		27. sessions	X
2. serve as ministers		11. no decree	X	20. war	X	28. secretary	
3. interpellate	X	12. no veto	X	21. treaties	X	29. staff	
4. investigate	X	13. no review		22. amnesty		30. no term limits	X
5. oversee police		14. no gatekeeping	X	23. pardon		31. seek re-election	
6. appoint PM	X	15. no impoundment	X	24. judiciary	X	32. experience	
7. appoint ministers	X	16. control resources	X	25. central bank			
8. lack president	X	17. immunity	X	26. media			
9. no confidence	X	18. all elected	X				

The Council of Representatives (*Mejlis Watani*) of Iraq was established in the 2005 constitution adopted following the American-led invasion and occupation that overthrew the regime of Saddam Hussein. The document calls for a unicameral body that appoints the prime minister and elects a largely ceremonial head of state, the president.

The constitution grants the legislature significant authority. The Council enjoys broad influence over the executive branch, including powers to choose the prime minister, the ministers, and the president. The Council's laws are subject to judicial review, but otherwise the Council possesses every measure of institutional autonomy measured in this survey. It exercises a few specified powers and has some institutional capacity.

The legislature has continued to function even in the face of an active insurgency, but it is too early to say whether the body will be able effectively to exercise the substantial powers vested in it by the constitution. As of this writing, Iraq is under occupation and embroiled in civil war, and the future of the country, including its legislature, is entirely uncertain.

SURVEY

1. The legislature alone, without the involvement of any other agencies, can impeach the president or replace the prime minister.

Yes. The legislature can remove the prime minister with a vote of no confidence. Presidential impeachment requires the involvement of the Supreme Federal Court.

Article 58
The Council of Representatives shall have the following powers:
(6) A. To question the President of the Republic on the basis of a reasoned petition by an absolute majority of the members of the Council of Representatives.
B. To remove the President of the Republic from office by an absolute majority of the members of the Council of Representatives after he has been convicted by the Supreme Federal Court for one of the following offenses:
  1. Perjury of the constitutional oath.
  2. Violation the Constitution.
  3. High treason.
(8) A. The Council of Representatives may withdraw confidence from one of the Ministers by an absolute majority; in this case the Minister concerned is deemed to have resigned on the day on which the decision to withdraw the confidence has been taken. The issue of no-confidence in the Minister may be tabled only upon request by the Minister concerned or on a petition signed by fifty (50) members of the Council after an inquiry hearing directed at him. The Council of Representatives shall not issue its decision regarding the request or petition before seven (7) days have passed after its submission.
B. 1. The President of the Republic may submit a request to the Council of Representatives to withdraw confidence from the Prime Minister.

2. The Council of Representatives may withdraw confidence from the Prime Minister based on the request of one-fifth (1/5) of its members. This request may be submitted only after a question has been put to the Prime Minister and after at least seven (7) days from submitting the request.

3. The Council of Representatives shall decide to withdraw confidence from the Prime Minister by an absolute majority of its members.

C. In case of a withdrawal of confidence from the Prime Minister, the Government is deemed to have resigned.

D. In case of a vote of withdrawal of confidence in the Cabinet as a whole, the Prime Minister and the Ministers continue in their functions in order to administer the current affairs for a period not exceeding thirty (30) days until a new cabinet is formed in accordance with the provisions of Article 73 of this Constitution.

2. Ministers may serve simultaneously as members of the legislature.

No. Legislators are prohibited from serving simultaneously in the legislature.

> Article 47
> (6) No member of the Council of Representatives shall be allowed to hold any other official position or work.

3. The legislature has powers of summons over executive branch officials and hearings with executive branch officials testifying before the legislature or its committees are regularly held.

Yes. The legislature regularly questions executive branch officials.

> Article 58
> The Council of Representatives shall have the following powers:
> (6) A. To question the President of the Republic on the basis of a reasoned petition by an absolute majority of the members of the Council of Representatives.
> (7) A. Member(s) of the Council of Representatives may direct questions to the Prime Minister and the Ministers on any subject within their competence and they may answer the members' questions. The Member who has asked the question solely has the right to comment on the answer.

4. The legislature can conduct independent investigation of the chief executive and the agencies of the executive.

Yes. Legislative committees can investigate the executive.

5. The legislature has effective powers of oversight over the agencies of coercion (the military, organs of law enforcement, intelligence services, and the secret police).

No. While the new legal order intends the parliament to oversee the official agencies of coercion,

parliament has yet to demonstrate its powers of oversight over the army and the police.

6. The legislature appoints the prime minister.

Yes. The president is required to appoint as prime minister the candidate "from the ranks of the group with the highest numbers of members" in the legislature.

> Article 73
> (1) The President of the Republic shall charge a candidate designated from the ranks of the group with the highest numbers of members in the Council of Representatives with the formation of the Cabinet within fifteen (15) days from the date of the election of the President of the Republic.
> (2) The Prime Minister-designate shall name the members of his Cabinet within a period not exceeding thirty (30) days from the date of his designation.
> (3) In case the Prime Minister-designate fails to form the cabinet during the period specified in clause (2), the President of the Republic shall name a new candidate for the post of Prime Minister within fifteen (15) days.
> (4) The Prime Minister-designate shall present the names of his Cabinet members and the program of his government to the Council of Representatives. He is deemed to have gained its confidence upon the approval, by an absolute majority of the Council of Representatives, of the individual Ministers and of the program of government.

7. The legislature's approval is required to confirm the appointment of ministers; or the legislature itself appoints ministers.

Yes. The legislature's approval is required to confirm ministerial appointments.

> Article 73
> (1) The President of the Republic shall charge a candidate designated from the ranks of the group with the highest numbers of members in the Council of Representatives with the formation of the Cabinet within fifteen days from the date of the election of the President of the Republic.
> (2) The Prime Minister-designate shall name the members of his Cabinet within a period not exceeding thirty days from the date of his designation.
> (3) In case the Prime Minister-designate fails to form the cabinet during the period specified in clause (2), the President of the Republic shall name a new candidate for the post of Prime Minister within fifteen days.
> (4) The Prime Minister-designate shall present the names of his Cabinet members and the program of his government to the Council of Representatives. He is deemed to have gained its confidence upon the approval, by an absolute majority of the Council of Representatives, of the individual Ministers and of the program of government.

8. The country lacks a presidency entirely or there is a presidency, but the president is elected by the legislature.

Yes. The legislature elects the president.

> Article 58
> The Council of Representatives shall have the following powers:
> (3) To elect the President of the Republic.

> Article 67
> (1) The Council of Representatives shall elect, from amongst the nominees, the President of the Republic by a two-thirds majority of its members.

9. The legislature can vote no confidence in the government.

Yes. The legislature can vote no confidence in the government.

> Article 58
> The Council of Representatives shall have the following powers:
> (8) A. The Council of Representatives may withdraw confidence from one of the Ministers by an absolute majority; in this case the Minister concerned is deemed to have resigned on the day on which the decision to withdraw the confidence has been taken. The issue of no-confidence in the Minister may be tabled only upon request by the Minister concerned or on a petition signed by fifty members of the Council after an inquiry hearing directed at him. The Council of Representatives shall not issue its decision regarding the request or petition before seven days have passed after its submission.
> B. 1. The President of the Republic may submit a request to the Council of Representatives to withdraw confidence from the Prime Minister.
> 2. The Council of Representatives may withdraw confidence from the Prime Minister based on the request of one-fifth of its members. This request may be submitted only after a question has been put to the Prime Minister and after at least seven days from submitting the request.
> 3. The Council of Representatives shall decide to withdraw confidence from the Prime Minister by an absolute majority of its members.
> C. In case of a withdrawal of confidence from the Prime Minister, the Government is deemed to have resigned.
> D. In case of a vote of withdrawal of confidence in the Cabinet as a whole, the Prime Minister and the Ministers continue in their functions in order to administer the current affairs for a period not exceeding thirty days until a new cabinet is formed in accordance with the provisions of Article 73 of this Constitution.

10. The legislature is immune from dissolution by the executive.

Yes. The legislature is immune from dissolution.

11. Any executive initiative on legislation requires ratification or approval by the legislature before it takes effect; that is, the executive lacks decree power.

Yes. The executive lacks decree power. The president can issue administrative "decrees" to implement law.

> Article 70
> The President of the Republic shall have the following powers:
> G. To issue presidential decrees.

12. Laws passed by the legislature are veto-proof or essentially veto-proof; that is, the executive lacks veto power, or has veto power but the veto can be overridden by a majority in the legislature.

Yes. The executive lacks veto power.

> Article 70
> The President of the Republic shall have the following powers:
> C. To ratify and issue the laws enacted by the Council of Representatives. Such laws are considered ratified after fifteen days from the date of receipt.

13. The legislature's laws are supreme and not subject to judicial review.

No. The Federal Supreme Court can review the constitutionality of laws.

> Article 90
> The Federal Supreme Court shall have jurisdiction over the following matters:
> (1) Oversight of the constitutionality of laws and regulations in force.
> (2) Interpretation of the provisions of the Constitution.

14. The legislature has the right to initiate bills in all policy jurisdictions; the executive lacks gatekeeping authority.

Yes. The legislature has the right to initiate bills in all policy jurisdictions.

> Article 57
> (2) A. Bills shall be presented by the President of the Republic and the Prime Minister.

15. Expenditure of funds appropriated by the legislature is mandatory; the executive lacks the power to impound funds appropriated by the legislature.

Yes. The executive lacks the power to impound funds appropriated by the legislature.

16. The legislature controls the resources that finance its own internal operation and provide for the perquisites of its own members.

Yes. The legislature enjoys financial autonomy.

17. Members of the legislature are immune from arrest and/or criminal prosecution.

Yes. Legislators are immune with the common exception for cases of *flagrante delicto*.

Article 60
(2) A. Each member of the Council of Representatives shall enjoy immunity for statements made while the Council is in session, and the member may not be prosecuted before the courts for such.
B. A member of the Council of Representatives may not be placed under arrest during the legislative term of the Council of Representatives, unless the member is accused of a felony and the [other] members of the Council of Representatives consent by an absolute majority to lift his immunity or if caught in flagrante delicto in the commission of a felony.
C. A member of the Council of Representatives may not be arrested after the legislative term of the Council of Representatives, unless the member is accused of a felony and the President of the Council of Representatives agrees to lift his immunity or unless he is caught in flagrante delicto in the commission of a felony.

18. All members of the legislature are elected; the executive lacks the power to appoint any members of the legislature.

Yes. All members of the legislature are elected.

Article 47
(1) The Council of Representatives shall consist of a number of members at a ratio of one representative per one hundred thousand Iraqis, representing the entire Iraqi people. The members shall be elected by direct, secret and general ballot.

19. The legislature alone, without the involvement of any other agencies, can change the Constitution.

No. Constitutional amendments require approval by the public in a popular referendum and by the president.

Article 122
(1) The President of the Republic and the Council of the Ministers, jointly, or one-fifth of the members of the Council of Representatives may propose to amend the Constitution.
(2) The fundamental principles mentioned in Section One and the rights and liberties mentioned in Section Two of the Constitution may not be amended except after two successive electoral terms, with the approval of two-thirds of the Council members, the approval of the people in a general referendum and the ratification of the President of the Republic within seven days.
(3) Other Articles not stipulated in clause Second of this Article may not be amended, except with the approval of two-thirds of the members of the Council of Representatives, the approval of the people in a general referendum and the ratification of the President of the Republic within seven (7) days.
(4) Articles of the Constitution may not be amended if such amendment diminishes the powers of the regions

that are not part of the exclusive powers of the federal authorities, except with the consent of the legislative authority of the region concerned, and the approval of the majority of its citizens in a general referendum.
(5) A. The amendment is considered ratified by the President of the Republic after the expiration of the period stipulated in clauses Second and Third and of this Article in case he does not ratify it.
B. An amendment shall enter into force on the date of its publication in the *Official Gazette.*

20. The legislature's approval is necessary for the declaration of war.

Yes. The legislature's approval is required to approve war declarations, which are made on a joint request from the president and the prime minister.

Article 58
The Council of Representatives shall have the following powers:
(9) A. To consent to the declaration of war and the state of emergency by a two-thirds majority based on a joint request from the President of the Republic and the Prime Minister.

21. The legislature's approval is necessary to ratify treaties with foreign countries.

Yes. The legislature's approval is necessary to ratify international treaties.

Article 58
The Council of Representatives shall have the following powers:
(4) A law shall regulate the ratification of international treaties and agreements by a two-thirds majority of the members of the Council of Representatives.

Article 70
The President of the Republic shall have the following powers:
B. To ratify international treaties and agreements after approval by the Council of Representatives. Such international treaties and agreements are considered ratified after fifteen days from the date of receipt.

22. The legislature has the power to grant amnesty.

No. Amnesty and pardon are not treated separately, and the legislature lacks the power to grant amnesty. See item 23.

23. The legislature has the power of pardon.

No. The president has the power of pardon.

Article 70
The President of the Republic shall have the following powers:
A. To issue a special pardon on the recommendation of the Prime Minister, except for anything concerning private claims and those who have been convicted of

committing international crimes, terrorism, or financial and administrative corruption.

24. The legislature reviews and has the right to reject appointments to the judiciary; or the legislature itself appoints members of the judiciary.

Yes. The legislature appoints the president and members of the Federal Court of Cassation, the president of the Judicial Oversight Commission, and the members of the Federal Supreme Court.

Article 58
The Council of Representatives shall have the following powers:
(5) To approve the appointment of the following:
A. The President and members of the Federal Court of Cassation, the Chief Public Prosecutor and the President of Judicial Oversight Commission upon a proposal from the Higher Juridical Council, by an absolute majority.

Article 89
(2) The Federal Supreme Court shall be made up of a number of judges who are experts in Islamic jurisprudence and the law; their number, selection procedure and the work of the court shall be determined by a law enacted by a two-thirds majority of the members of the Council of Representatives.

25. The chairman of the central bank is appointed by the legislature.

No. The current governor of the Central Bank of Iraq was appointed by the Iraqi Governing Council, the transitional government.

26. The legislature has a substantial voice in the operation of the state-owned media.

No. The legislature lacks a substantial voice in the operation of the public media.

27. The legislature is regularly in session.

Yes. The legislature meets in ordinary session for eight months each year.

Article 55
The Council of Representatives shall have one annual term with two legislative sessions lasting eight months.

28. Each legislator has a personal secretary.

No.

29. Each legislator has at least one non-secretarial staff member with policy expertise.

No.

30. Legislators are eligible for re-election without any restriction.

Yes. There are no restrictions on re-election.

31. A seat in the legislature is an attractive enough position that legislators are generally interested in and seek re-election.

No. There has been only one election, so it is too early to tell how legislators will behave with regard to re-election. It bears note, however, that a large proportion of the legislators who served in the transitional legislature sought election to the permanent body.

32. The re-election of incumbent legislators is common enough that at any given time the legislature contains a significant number of highly experienced members.

No. The permanent legislature has gone through only one election, and members do not have substantial experience as legislators.

PARLIAMENT OF IRELAND (*OIREACHTAS*)

Expert consultants: Robert Elgie, Brian Girvin, Michael Marsh, Gary Murphy, Eoin O'Malley, Nicola Jo-Anne Smith

Score: .66

Influence over executive (8/9)		Institutional autonomy (5/9)		Specified powers (3/8)		Institutional capacity (5/6)	
1. replace	X	10. no dissolution		19. amendments		27. sessions	X
2. serve as ministers	X	11. no decree	X	20. war	X	28. secretary	X
3. interpellate	X	12. no veto	X	21. treaties	X	29. staff	
4. investigate	X	13. no review		22. amnesty	X	30. no term limits	X
5. oversee police	X	14. no gatekeeping	X	23. pardon		31. seek re-election	X
6. appoint PM	X	15. no impoundment		24. judiciary		32. experience	X
7. appoint ministers	X	16. control resources	X	25. central bank			
8. lack president		17. immunity		26. media			
9. no confidence	X	18. all elected	X				

The Parliament (*Oireachtas*) of Ireland originated in the representative bodies that began meeting in the thirteenth century. In 1800 the Act of Union abolished the Irish parliament and transferred legislative authority in Ireland to London. In 1920 the British parliament passed the Government of Ireland Act, reestablishing the Irish parliament. Ireland achieved independence the following year. The bicameral legislature consists of a lower house, the House of Representatives (*Dáil Éireann*), and an upper house, the Senate (*Seanad Éireann*). The Senate, much like the British House of Lords, serves as an advisory body. Its sole legislative power is to delay, not veto, the decisions of the lower house. The executive branch consists of a prime minister and government chosen by parliament, which operate alongside a directly elected president.

The legislature holds strong sway over the executive branch, including the power to remove both the prime minister and the president without the involvement of any other agencies. The legislature's autonomy is considerable but not unlimited. The executive branch, rather than the legislature, exercises many of the specified powers and prerogatives assessed here, including the power to appoint judges and the chairman of the central bank. The legislature has considerable institutional capacity.

SURVEY

1. The legislature alone, without the involvement of any other agencies, can impeach the president or replace the prime minister.

Yes. The House of Representatives can remove the prime minister with a vote of no confidence. The legislature, acting alone, can also impeach the president. Impeachment can be proposed by a two-thirds majority vote of the total membership in one house of parliament and, following a parliamentary investigation, approved by a two-thirds majority vote of the total membership in the other house of parliament.

Article 12
(10.1) The President may be impeached for stated misbehavior.
(10.2) The charge shall be preferred by either of the Houses of Parliament, subject to and in accordance with the provisions of this section.
(10.3) A proposal to either House of Parliament to prefer a charge against the President under this section shall not be entertained unless upon a notice of motion in writing signed by not less than thirty members of that House.
(10.4) No such proposal shall be adopted by either of the Houses of Parliament save upon a resolution of that House supported by not less than two-thirds of the total membership thereof.

(10.5) When a charge has been preferred by either House of Parliament, the other House shall investigate the charge, or cause the charge to be investigated.

(10.6) The President shall have the right to appear and to be represented at the investigation of the charge.

(10.7) If, as a result of the investigation, a resolution be passed supported by not less than two-thirds of the total membership of the House of Parliament by which the charge was investigated, or caused to be investigated, declaring that the charge preferred against the President has been sustained and that the misbehavior, the subject of the charge, was such as to render him unfit to continue in office, such resolution shall operate to remove the President from his office.

Article 28

(10) The Prime Minister shall resign from office upon his ceasing to retain the support of a majority in the House of Representatives unless on his advice the President dissolves the House of Representatives and on the reassembly of the House of Representatives after the dissolution the Prime Minister secures the support of a majority in the House of Representatives.

2. Ministers may serve simultaneously as members of the legislature.

Yes. Ministers are selected from, and required to serve simultaneously in, the House of Representatives.

Article 28

(7.1) The Prime Minister, the Vice Prime Minister and the member of the Government who is in charge of the Department of Finance must be members of the House of Representatives.

(7.2) The other members of the Government must be members of the House of Representatives or the Senate, but not more than two may be members of the Senate.

3. The legislature has powers of summons over executive branch officials and hearings with executive branch officials testifying before the legislature or its committees are regularly held.

Yes. The legislature regularly interpellates officials from the executive.

4. The legislature can conduct independent investigation of the chief executive and the agencies of the executive.

Yes. The legislature can investigate the executive.

5. The legislature has effective powers of oversight over the agencies of coercion (the military, organs of law enforcement, intelligence services, and the secret police).

Yes. The legislature has effective powers of oversight over the agencies of coercion.

6. The legislature appoints the prime minister.

Yes. The president is required to appoint as prime minister the candidate selected by the House of Representatives.

Article 13

(1.1) The President shall, on the nomination of the House of Representatives, appoint the Prime Minister.

(1.2) The President shall, on the nomination of the Prime Minister with the previous approval of the House of Representatives, appoint the other members of the Government.

7. The legislature's approval is required to confirm the appointment of ministers; or the legislature itself appoints ministers.

Yes. The president appoints ministers on the recommendation of the prime minister, and the legislature's approval is necessary to confirm the appointments.

Article 13

(1.1) The President shall, on the nomination of the House of Representatives, appoint the Prime Minister.

(1.2) The President shall, on the nomination of the Prime Minister with the previous approval of the House of Representatives, appoint the other members of the Government.

8. The country lacks a presidency entirely or there is a presidency, but the president is elected by the legislature.

No. The president is directly elected.

Article 12

(2.1) The President shall be elected by direct vote of the people.

9. The legislature can vote no confidence in the government.

Yes. The House of Representatives can vote no confidence in the government.

Article 28

(10) The Prime Minister shall resign from office upon his ceasing to retain the support of a majority in the House of Representatives unless on his advice the President dissolves the House of Representatives and on the reassembly of the House of Representatives after the dissolution the Prime Minister secures the support of a majority in the House of Representatives.

10. The legislature is immune from dissolution by the executive.

No. The president, on the advice of the prime minister, can dissolve the House of Representatives.

Article 13
(2.1) The House of Representatives shall be summoned and dissolved by the President on the advice of the Prime Minister.

Article 28
(10) The Prime Minister shall resign from office upon his ceasing to retain the support of a majority in the House of Representatives unless on his advice the President dissolves the House of Representatives and on the reassembly of the House of Representatives after the dissolution the Prime Minister secures the support of a majority in the House of Representatives.

11. Any executive initiative on legislation requires ratification or approval by the legislature before it takes effect; that is, the executive lacks decree power.

Yes. The executive lacks decree power.

12. Laws passed by the legislature are veto-proof or essentially veto-proof; that is, the executive lacks veto power, or has veto power but the veto can be overridden by a majority in the legislature.

Yes. The executive lacks veto power.

Article 25
(1) As soon as any Bill, other than a Bill expressed to be a Bill containing a proposal for the amendment of this Constitution, shall have been passed or deemed to have been passed by both Houses of Parliament, the Prime Minister shall present it to the President for his signature and for promulgation by him as a law in accordance with the provisions of this article.

13. The legislature's laws are supreme and not subject to judicial review.

No. The Supreme Court can review the constitutionality of laws.

Article 26
(1.1) The President may, after consultation with the Council of State, refer any Bill to which this article applies to the Supreme Court for a decision on the question as to whether such Bill or any specified provision or provisions of such Bill is or are repugnant to this Constitution or to any provision thereof.

14. The legislature has the right to initiate bills in all policy jurisdictions; the executive lacks gatekeeping authority.

Yes. The legislature can initiate bills in all policy jurisdictions.

15. Expenditure of funds appropriated by the legislature is mandatory; the executive lacks the power to impound funds appropriated by the legislature.

No. The executive can impound funds appropriated by the legislature. The House of Representatives' appropriations authorize, but do not require, the expenditure of funds.

16. The legislature controls the resources that finance its own internal operation and provide for the perquisites of its own members.

Yes. The legislature enjoys financial autonomy, including control over members' perquisites.

Article 15
(15) Parliament may make provision by law for the payment of allowances to the members of each House thereof in respect of their duties as public representatives and for the grant to them of free traveling and such other facilities (if any) in connection with those duties as Parliament may determine.

17. Members of the legislature are immune from arrest and/or criminal prosecution.

No. Legislative immunity extends to official parliamentary business only. Legislators are subject to arrest for common crimes.

Article 15
(13) The members of each House of Parliament shall, except in case of treason as defined in this Constitution, felony or breach of the peace, be privileged from arrest in going to and returning from, and while within the precincts of, either House, and shall not, in respect of any utterance in either House, be amenable to any court or any authority other than the House itself.

18. All members of the legislature are elected; the executive lacks the power to appoint any members of the legislature.

Yes. All members of the House of Representatives are elected. Eleven of the sixty-two members of the largely ceremonial Senate are appointed by the prime minister.

Article 16
(2.5) The members shall be elected on the system of proportional representation by means of the single transferable vote.

Article 18
(1) The Senate shall be composed of sixty members, of whom eleven shall be nominated members and forty-nine shall be elected members.
(2) A person to be eligible for membership of the Senate must be eligible to become a member of the House of Representatives.
(3) The nominated members of the Senate shall be nominated, with their prior consent, by the Prime Minister who is appointed next after the reassembly of the House of Representatives following the dissolution thereof which occasions the nomination of the said members.

19. The legislature alone, without the involvement of any other agencies, can change the Constitution.

No. Constitutional amendments require approval in a popular referendum.

Article 46

(1) Any provision of this Constitution may be amended, whether by way of variation, addition, or repeal, in the manner provided by this article.

(2) Every proposal for an amendment of this Constitution shall be initiated in the House of Representatives as a Bill, and shall upon having been passed or deemed to have been passed by both Houses of Parliament, be submitted by Referendum to the decision of the people in accordance with the law for the time being in force relating to the Referendum.

20. The legislature's approval is necessary for the declaration of war.

Yes. The legislature's approval is necessary for governmental war declarations, with the common exception for cases of foreign invasion. In cases of invasion, the government can declare war and seek retroactive authorization.

Article 28

(3.1) War shall not be declared and the State shall not participate in any war save with the assent of the House of Representatives.

(3.2) In the case of actual invasion, however, the Government may take whatever steps they may consider necessary for the protection of the State, and the House of Representatives if not sitting shall be summoned to meet at the earliest practicable date.

21. The legislature's approval is necessary to ratify treaties with foreign countries.

Yes. The House of Representatives' approval is necessary to ratify international treaties.

Article 29

(5.1) Every international agreement to which the State becomes a party shall be laid before the House of Representatives.

(5.2) The State shall not be bound by any international agreement involving a charge upon public funds unless the terms of the agreement shall have been approved by the House of Representatives.

22. The legislature has the power to grant amnesty.

Yes. The legislature can grant amnesty through law.

23. The legislature has the power of pardon.

No. The president has the power of pardon.

Article 13

(6) The right of pardon and the power to commute or remit punishment imposed by any court exercising criminal jurisdiction are hereby vested in the President, but such power of commutation or remission may, except in capital cases, also be conferred by law on other authorities.

24. The legislature reviews and has the right to reject appointments to the judiciary; or the legislature itself appoints members of the judiciary.

No. The president appoints the judges of the Supreme Court, the High Court, and all other courts, and the appointments do not require the legislature's approval.

Article 35

(1) The judges of the Supreme Court, the High Court and all other Courts established in pursuance of Article 34 hereof shall be appointed by the President.

25. The chairman of the central bank is appointed by the legislature.

No. The president, on the recommendation of the government, appoints the governor of the Central Bank and Financial Services Authority of Ireland.

26. The legislature has a substantial voice in the operation of the state-owned media.

No. The legislature lacks a substantial voice in the operation of the public media.

27. The legislature is regularly in session.

Yes. The legislature meets in ordinary session for about eight months each year, from January to July, and again from October to December.

Article 15

(7) Parliament shall hold at least one session every year.

28. Each legislator has a personal secretary.

Yes.

29. Each legislator has at least one non-secretarial staff member with policy expertise.

No.

30. Legislators are eligible for re-election without any restriction.

Yes. There are no restrictions on re-election.

31. A seat in the legislature is an attractive enough position that legislators are generally interested in and seek re-election.

Yes.

32. The re-election of incumbent legislators is common enough that at any given time the legislature contains a significant number of highly experienced members.

Yes. Re-election rates are sufficiently high to produce a significant number of highly experienced members.

PARLIAMENT OF ISRAEL (*KNESSET*)

Expert consultants: Gregory S. Mahler, Bettina Malka-Igelbusch, Emanuele Ottolenghi, Nadav Shelef, Alan S. Zuckerman

Score: .75

Influence over executive (9/9)		Institutional autonomy (7/9)		Specified powers (3/8)		Institutional capacity (5/6)	
1. replace	X	10. no dissolution		19. amendments	X	27. sessions	X
2. serve as ministers	X	11. no decree	X	20. war	X	28. secretary	X
3. interpellate	X	12. no veto	X	21. treaties	X	29. staff	
4. investigate	X	13. no review		22. amnesty		30. no term limits	X
5. oversee police	X	14. no gatekeeping	X	23. pardon		31. seek re-election	X
6. appoint PM	X	15. no impoundment	X	24. judiciary		32. experience	X
7. appoint ministers	X	16. control resources	X	25. central bank			
8. lack president	X	17. immunity	X	26. media			
9. no confidence	X	18. all elected	X				

The Parliament (*Knesset*) of Israel was established at the creation of the state of Israel in the late 1940s. At the time of the foundation of the new state in 1948, a Provisional State Council functioned as the country's legislature. In 1949 elections were held for the Constituent Assembly; legislators voted to change the name of the body to the Knesset soon after they convened. Israel lacks a formal constitution. Rather, a number of separate "basic laws" establish the fundamental law. The legislature adopted the Basic Law of the Knesset in 1950, which was subsequently amended nine times between 1958 and 2003. A 2003 change to the Basic Law provided for a constructive vote of no confidence. Between 1996 and 2003, Israel experimented with the direct election of the prime minister, but the provision for direct election was revoked in 2003.

The Knesset is the main stage of Israel politics. It holds every power over the executive included in this survey. It chooses the president and the prime minister and can remove them from office. It also has a monopoly on lawmaking authority; the executive lacks decree, veto, and gatekeeping powers. It holds several specified powers and prerogatives and has a high level of institutional capacity.

SURVEY

1. The legislature alone, without the involvement of any other agencies, can impeach the president or replace the prime minister.

Yes. The legislature can remove the prime minister from office by a majority vote of its total membership. It can remove the president from office by a three-fourths majority vote of its total membership.

Section 20
(a) The Knesset may, by resolution, remove the President of the State from office if it finds that he is unworthy of his office owing to conduct unbecoming his status as President of the State.
(b) The Knesset shall not remove the President of the State from office, save following a complaint brought before the House Committee by at least twenty members of the Knesset and upon the proposal of the House Committee passed by a three-quarters majority of the members of the Committee. A resolution by the Knesset to remove the President from office shall require a three-quarters majority of the Members of the Knesset.
(c) The House Committee shall not propose the removal of the President of the State from office before he has been given an opportunity to refute the complaint in accordance with procedure prescribed by the Committee with the approval of the Knesset, and the

Knesset shall not resolve to remove the President of the State from office before he has been given an opportunity to be heard in accordance with procedure prescribed by the House Committee with the approval of the Knesset.

(d) The President of the State may be represented before the House Committee and before the Knesset by an authorized representative. A Member of the Knesset shall not act as the representative of the President. The House Committee and the Knesset may summon the President of the State to be present at proceedings under this section.

(e) Proceedings of the Knesset under this section shall be taken at a meeting, or successive meetings, assigned solely for that purpose. The proceedings shall begin not later than twenty days after the resolution of the House Committee. The time of their beginning shall be notified by the Speaker of the Knesset to all the Members of the Knesset, in writing, at least ten days in advance. If the beginning of the proceedings does not fall in one of the session terms of the Knesset, the Speaker of the Knesset shall convene the Knesset for the proceedings.

Section 18

(a) Should the Prime Minister be convicted of an offense which the court defined as involving moral turpitude, the Knesset may remove him from office, pursuant to a decision of a majority of the Knesset members. Should the Knesset so decide, the Government shall be deemed to have resigned.

Section 28

(a) The Knesset may adopt an expression of no confidence in the Government.

(b) An expression of no confidence in the Government will be by a decision adopted by the majority of the Members of Knesset to request that the President assign the task of forming a Government to a certain Knesset member who gave his written consent thereto.

(c) If the Knesset has expressed no confidence in the Government, the Government shall be deemed to have resigned on the day of the expression of no confidence. The President will, within two days, charge the Knesset Member so named with the task of forming a Government.

(d) A Knesset Member to whom the task of forming a Government has been assigned under this section shall have a period of 28 days for its fulfillment. The President of the State may extend the period by additional periods not in the aggregate exceeding 14 days.

(e) Where the periods referred to in subsection (d) have passed and the Knesset Member has not notified the President of the State that he has formed a Government, or where he has notified him before then that he is unable to form a Government, the President will so notify the Speaker of the Knesset.

(f) If the President so informed the Speaker of the Knesset as per subsection (e) or where he presented a Government and the Knesset rejected his request for confidence under section 13(d), it will be deemed to be a Knesset decision to disperse prior to the completion of its period of service, and elections to the Knesset will be held on the last Tuesday before the end of 90 days of the President's announcement, or of the rejection of the request for confidence in the Government, as relevant.

2. Ministers may serve simultaneously as members of the legislature.

Yes. Legislators may serve simultaneously in ministerial positions.

Section 23

A cabinet member who is not a member of the Knesset shall, as to everything relating to the Knesset, have the same status as a cabinet member who is a member of the Knesset, except that he shall not have the right to vote.

(b) The Prime Minister shall be a member of the Knesset. A Minister need not be a member of the Knesset.

3. The legislature has powers of summons over executive branch officials and hearings with executive branch officials testifying before the legislature or its committees are regularly held.

Yes. The legislature regularly interpellates officials from the executive.

Section 42

(a) The Government will provide the Knesset and its committees with information upon request and will assist them in the discharging of their roles.

4. The legislature can conduct independent investigation of the chief executive and the agencies of the executive.

Yes. The legislature can establish commissions of inquiry to investigate the executive.

Section 22

The Knesset may appoint commissions of inquiry – either by empowering one of the permanent committees in that behalf or by electing a commission from among its members – to investigate matters designated by the Knesset; the powers and functions of a commission of inquiry shall be prescribed by the Knesset; every commission of inquiry shall include also representatives of party groups which do not participate in the Government, in accordance with the relative strength of the party groups in the Knesset.

5. The legislature has effective powers of oversight over the agencies of coercion (the military, organs of law enforcement, intelligence services, and the secret police).

Yes. The legislature has effective powers of oversight over the agencies of coercion.

6. The legislature appoints the prime minister.

Yes. The president appoints as prime minister the candidate who enjoys the support of the Knesset. From 1996 until 2003 the prime minister was directly elected.

Section 7

(a) When a new Government has to be constituted, the President of the State shall, after consultation with representatives of party groups in the Knesset, assign the task of forming a Government to a Knesset Member who has notified him that he is prepared to accept the task; the President shall do so within seven days of the publication of the election results, or should the need arise to form a new government; and in the case of the death of the Prime Minister, within 14 days of his death.

7. The legislature's approval is required to confirm the appointment of ministers; or the legislature itself appoints ministers.

Yes. The prime minister and the leading parliamentary groups allocate ministerial portfolios.

Section 7

(a) When a new Government has to be constituted, the President of the State shall, after consultation with representatives of party groups in the Knesset, assign the task of forming a Government to a Knesset Member who has notified him that he is prepared to accept the task; the President shall do so within seven days of the publication of the election results, or should the need arise to form a new government; and in the case of the death of the Prime Minister, within 14 days of his death.

(d) When a Government has been formed, it shall present itself to the Knesset, shall announce the basic lines of its policy, its composition and the distribution of functions among the Ministers, and shall ask for an expression of confidence. The Government is constituted when the Knesset has expressed confidence in it, and the Ministers shall thereupon assume office.

8. The country lacks a presidency entirely or there is a presidency, but the president is elected by the legislature.

Yes. The legislature elects the president.

Section 3

(a) The President of the State shall be elected by the Knesset for seven years.

9. The legislature can vote no confidence in the government.

Yes. Since 2003 the parliament has had the power to pass a constructive vote of no confidence, meaning that parliament must designate a successor prime minister before passing a vote of no confidence. Prior to 2003 the legislature could vote no confidence in the government without designating a successor prime minister.

Section 28

(a) The Knesset may adopt an expression of no confidence in the Government.

(b) An expression of no confidence in the Government will be by a decision adopted by the majority of the Members of Knesset to request that the President assign the task of forming a Government to a certain Knesset member who gave his written consent thereto.

(c) If the Knesset has expressed no confidence in the Government, the Government shall be deemed to have resigned on the day of the expression of no confidence. The President will, within two days, charge the Knesset Member so named with the task of forming a Government.

(d) A Knesset Member to whom the task of forming a Government has been assigned under this section shall have a period of 28 days for its fulfillment. The President of the State may extend the period by additional periods not in the aggregate exceeding 14 days.

(e) Where the periods referred to in subsection (d) have passed and the Knesset Member has not notified the President of the State that he has formed a Government, or where he has notified him before then that he is unable to form a Government, the President will so notify the Speaker of the Knesset.

(f) If the President so informed the Speaker of the Knesset as per subsection (e) or where he presented a Government and the Knesset rejected his request for confidence under section 13(d), it will be deemed to be a Knesset decision to disperse prior to the completion of its period of service, and elections to the Knesset will be held on the last Tuesday before the end of 90 days of the President's announcement, or of the rejection of the request for confidence in the Government, as relevant.

10. The legislature is immune from dissolution by the executive.

No. The prime minister, with the approval of the president, can dissolve the legislature.

Section 29

(a) Should the Prime Minister ascertain that a majority of the Knesset opposes the Government, and that the effective functioning of the Government is prevented as a result, he may, with the approval of the President of the State, disperse the Knesset by way of an order to be published in Reshumot. The order will enter into effect 21 days after its publication, unless a request is submitted under subsection (c), and the Government will be deemed to have resigned on the day of the order's publication.

Section 36

Once the Knesset decides to dissolve itself, the term of office of the next Knesset shall run until the next month of Cheshvan following the termination of four years from the day of its election.

(b) Should the President so inform the Knesset Speaker, or should a Knesset Member charged with forming a Government under section 10(a) present a Government and fail to win the confidence of the Knesset under section 13(d), then the Knesset shall be deemed to have decided to disperse prior to the completion of its period of service, and elections for the Knesset will be held on the last Tuesday before the end of 90 days of the President's announcement, or of the rejection of the request for confidence in the Government, as relevant.

11. Any executive initiative on legislation requires ratification or approval by the legislature before it takes effect; that is, the executive lacks decree power.

Yes. The executive lacks decree power.

12. Laws passed by the legislature are veto-proof or essentially veto-proof; that is, the executive lacks veto power, or has veto power but the veto can be overridden by a majority in the legislature.

Yes. The executive lacks veto power.

13. The legislature's laws are supreme and not subject to judicial review.

No. The Supreme Court has the power to review the constitutionality of laws, although, in practice, it has rarely struck down Knesset legislation.

14. The legislature has the right to initiate bills in all policy jurisdictions; the executive lacks gatekeeping authority.

Yes. The legislature can initiate bills in all policy jurisdictions.

15. Expenditure of funds appropriated by the legislature is mandatory; the executive lacks the power to impound funds appropriated by the legislature.

Yes. The executive lacks the power to impound funds appropriated by the legislature. In cases in which the legislature passes a law allocating funds that the government opposes, the government has organized a subsequent law to cancel the expenditure.

16. The legislature controls the resources that finance its own internal operation and provide for the perquisites of its own members.

Yes. The legislature enjoys financial autonomy, including control over members' salaries.

Section 36
The salaries of the Ministers and the Deputy Ministers and other payments paid to them during their period of service or thereafter, or to their next of kin after their deaths, will be specified by law, or by virtue of a decision of the Knesset, or a public committee appointed by the Knesset for that purpose.

17. Members of the legislature are immune from arrest and/or criminal prosecution.

Yes. Members of the legislature are immune.

Section 17
The members of the Knesset shall have immunity; particulars shall be prescribed by Law.

18. All members of the legislature are elected; the executive lacks the power to appoint any members of the legislature.

Yes. All members of the legislature are elected.

Section 4
The Knesset shall be elected by general, national, direct, equal, secret, and proportional elections, in accordance with the Knesset Elections Law; this section shall not be altered save by a majority of the members of the Knesset.

19. The legislature alone, without the involvement of any other agencies, can change the Constitution.

Yes. The legislature can change the fundamental law through the normal legislative process.

20. The legislature's approval is necessary for the declaration of war.

Yes. Formally, the government has the power to declare war. In practice, it would be unthinkable for the government to declare war without the legislature's approval.

Section 40
(a) The state may only begin a war pursuant to a Government decision.

21. The legislature's approval is necessary to ratify treaties with foreign countries.

Yes. The legislature's approval is necessary to ratify international treaties.

Section 11
(a) The President of the State
(5) shall sign such conventions with foreign states as have been ratified by the Knesset.

22. The legislature has the power to grant amnesty.

No. Amnesty and pardon are not treated separately, and the legislature lacks the power to grant amnesty. See item 23.

23. The legislature has the power of pardon.

No. The president has the power of pardon.

Section 11
(b) The President of the State shall have power to pardon offenders and to lighten penalties by the reduction or commutation thereof.

24. The legislature reviews and has the right to reject appointments to the judiciary; or the legislature itself appoints members of the judiciary.

No. The president appoints the members of the judiciary on the basis of recommendations made by a committee that consists of the minister of justice, several other members of the Knesset, and presiding judges. The appointments do not require the legislature's approval.

Section 4

(a) A judge shall be appointed by the President of the State upon election by a Judges' Election Committee.

25. The chairman of the central bank is appointed by the legislature.

No. The president, on the recommendation of the prime minister, appoints the governor of the Bank of Israel.

26. The legislature has a substantial voice in the operation of the state-owned media.

No. The legislature lacks a substantial voice in the operation of the public media.

27. The legislature is regularly in session.

Yes. The legislature meets for at least eight months each year.

Section 31

(a) The Knesset shall hold two sessions a year; one of them shall open within four weeks after the Feast of Tabernacles, the other within four weeks after Independence Day; the aggregate duration of the two sessions shall not be less than eight months.

28. Each legislator has a personal secretary.

Yes.

29. Each legislator has at least one non-secretarial staff member with policy expertise.

No.

30. Legislators are eligible for re-election without any restriction.

Yes. There are no restrictions on re-election.

31. A seat in the legislature is an attractive enough position that legislators are generally interested in and seek re-election.

Yes.

32. The re-election of incumbent legislators is common enough that at any given time the legislature contains a significant number of highly experienced members.

Yes. Re-election rates are sufficiently high to produce a significant number of highly experienced members.

PARLIAMENT OF ITALY (*PARLAMENTO*)

Expert consultants: Francesco Battegazzorre, Giliberto Capano, Giuseppe Di Palma, Marco Giuliani, Giuseppe Ieraci, Amie Kreppel, Roberta Maffio, Leonardo Morlino, Alan S. Zuckerman

Score: .84

Influence over executive (8/9)		Institutional autonomy (6/9)		Specified powers (7/8)		Institutional capacity (6/6)	
1. replace	X	10. no dissolution		19. amendments	X	27. sessions	X
2. serve as ministers	X	11. no decree	X	20. war	X	28. secretary	X
3. interpellate	X	12. no veto	X	21. treaties	X	29. staff	X
4. investigate	X	13. no review		22. amnesty	X	30. no term limits	X
5. oversee police	X	14. no gatekeeping	X	23. pardon	X	31. seek re-election	X
6. appoint PM	X	15. no impoundment	X	24. judiciary	X	32. experience	X
7. appoint ministers		16. control resources	X	25. central bank			
8. lack president	X	17. immunity		26. media	X		
9. no confidence	X	18. all elected	X				

The Parliament (*Parlamento*) of Italy was established in the 1861 constitution following the *Risorgimento* that unified Italy. The bicameral legislature consists of a lower house, the Chamber of Deputies (*Camera dei deputati*), and an upper house, the Senate (*Senato*). A new constitution was adopted in 1948, after the 1946 referendum that abolished the monarchy. The new constitution created a Constitutional Court to review the constitutionality of laws. Prior to 1948 parliament's laws were supreme and not subject to judicial review. A proposed constitutional amendment that would have given the prime minister the powers to dissolve parliament and to appoint ministers was defeated in a June 2006 referendum.

The legislature is the main stage of national politics. It holds all but one of the measures of influence over the executive assessed here. It has substantial institutional autonomy. It is vested with all but one of the specified powers measured in this survey, and it has formidable institutional capacity.

SURVEY

1. The legislature alone, without the involvement of any other agencies, can impeach the president or replace the prime minister.

Yes. The legislature can remove the prime minister with a vote of no confidence. A joint session of parliament can impeach the president by a majority vote of its total membership.

Article 90
(1) The president may not be held responsible for exercising his duties, except for high treason and attempts to overthrow the constitution.
(2) In these cases, he must be impeached by parliament in joint session by a majority of its members.

Article 94
(1) Government has to enjoy the confidence of both chambers.
(2) Confidence is granted or withdrawn by each chamber on a reasoned motion by vote using a roll-call.
(3) The government has to appear before each chamber no later than ten days after its appointment to get a vote of confidence.
(4) The rejection of a government proposal by a chamber does not force government resignation.
(5) The request for a vote of no-confidence requires the signatures of at least one-tenth of the members of either chamber and is not debated until three days after it has been filed.

2. Ministers may serve simultaneously as members of the legislature.

Yes. Ministers may serve simultaneously in the legislature.

3. The legislature has powers of summons over executive branch officials and hearings with executive branch officials testifying before the legislature or its committees are regularly held.

Yes. The legislature regularly interpellates officials from the executive.

4. The legislature can conduct independent investigation of the chief executive and the agencies of the executive.

Yes. The legislature can establish committees of inquiry to investigate the executive.

Article 82
(1) A chamber may start inquiries into matters of public interest.
(2) It therefore appoints a committee composed of its members in proportion to the size of the groups in parliament. The committee of enquiry investigates and examines the matters carrying the same powers and limitations as the judiciary.

5. The legislature has effective powers of oversight over the agencies of coercion (the military, organs of law enforcement, intelligence services, and the secret police).

Yes. The legislature has effective powers of oversight over the agencies of coercion.

6. The legislature appoints the prime minister.

Yes. Formally, the president appoints the prime minister. In practice, the president appoints as prime minister the candidate who enjoys the support of parliament.

Article 92
(2) The president appoints the prime minister and, on his advice, the ministers.

7. The legislature's approval is required to confirm the appointment of ministers; or the legislature itself appoints ministers.

No. The president appoints ministers on the recommendation of the prime minister, and the appointments do not require the legislature's approval.

Article 92
(2) The president appoints the prime minister and, on his advice, the ministers.

8. The country lacks a presidency entirely or there is a presidency, but the president is elected by the legislature.

Yes. Parliament elects the president.

Article 83
(1) The president is elected in joint session of parliament.
(2) Three delegates from every region, elected by the regional councils in a way guaranteeing minority representation, participate in the election. The Aosta Valley is represented by one delegate.
(3) Presidential elections, conducted by secret ballot, require a two-thirds majority of the assembly. After the third ballot a majority of the members is sufficient.

9. The legislature can vote no confidence in the government.

Yes. The legislature can vote no confidence in the government.

> Article 94
> (1) Government has to enjoy the confidence of both chambers.
> (2) Confidence is granted or withdrawn by each chamber on a reasoned motion by vote using a roll-call.
> (3) The government has to appear before each chamber no later than ten days after its appointment to get a vote of confidence.
> (4) The rejection of a government proposal by a chamber does not force government resignation.
> (5) The request for a vote of no-confidence requires the signatures of at least one-tenth of the members of either chamber and is not debated until three days after it has been filed.

10. The legislature is immune from dissolution by the executive.

No. The president can dissolve the legislature.

> Article 88
> (1) The president may dissolve one or both chambers after having consulted their speakers.
> (2) He may not exercise this power during the last six months of his term, provided this period does not coincide partly or entirely with the last six months of the term of chambers.

11. Any executive initiative on legislation requires ratification or approval by the legislature before it takes effect; that is, the executive lacks decree power.

Yes. The president and government lack decree power. Formally, the government can issue decrees that carry the force of law with prior authorization from the legislature or "as an exception by necessity and urgency." In practice, it would be unthinkable for the government to issue decrees without legislative approval.

> Article 77
> (1) The government may not issue decrees with the force of law unless empowered by a proper delegation of the chambers.
> (2) As an exception by necessity and urgency, government may issue provisional measures with the force of law and submits them on the same day to the chambers for confirmation; if the chambers are not in session, they have to be summoned for that purpose within five days.
> (3) Legal decrees lose effect at the date of issue if they are not confirmed within sixty days of their publication. However, chambers may sanction rights and obligations arising out of decrees are not confirmed.

12. Laws passed by the legislature are veto-proof or essentially veto-proof; that is, the executive lacks veto

power, or has veto power but the veto can be overridden by a majority in the legislature.

Yes. The legislature can override a presidential veto by a majority vote of its present members.

> Article 74
> (1) Before promulgation, the president may ask for further deliberation by message to the chambers giving the reasons for such request.
> (2) The law has to be promulgated if the chambers adopt the bill once more.

13. The legislature's laws are supreme and not subject to judicial review.

No. The Constitutional Court can review the constitutionality of laws.

> Article 134
> The constitutional court decides:
> – disputes concerning the constitutionality of laws and acts with the force of law adopted by state or regions.

14. The legislature has the right to initiate bills in all policy jurisdictions; the executive lacks gatekeeping authority.

Yes. The legislature can initiate bills in all policy jurisdictions.

15. Expenditure of funds appropriated by the legislature is mandatory; the executive lacks the power to impound funds appropriated by the legislature.

Yes. The executive lacks the power to impound funds appropriated by the legislature.

16. The legislature controls the resources that finance its own internal operation and provide for the perquisites of its own members.

Yes. The legislature enjoys financial autonomy, including control over members' perquisites.

> Article 69
> Members of parliament receive an allowance defined by law.

17. Members of the legislature are immune from arrest and/or criminal prosecution.

No. Prior to 1993 legislators were immune, but following the *mani pulite* (clean hands) corruption scandals and anticorruption campaign of the early 1990s, the constitution was altered to allow members to be prosecuted without parliament's permission. In 2003 parliament passed a law to grant immunity from prosecution to five top state officials, including the prime minister and the speaker of each house of parliament. The measure was designed by Forza Italia, the party of the then–prime minister, Silvio Berlusconi, to shield Berlusconi from charges he faced for allegedly bribing judges. In early 2004, just months after this peculiar law was enacted, the Constitutional Court voided it.

Article 68

(1) Members of parliament may not be called to answer for opinions expressed or votes cast in the exercise of their office.

(2) Members of parliament may not be subjected to searches of their person or home without prior authorization by their chamber, nor arrested or otherwise deprived of personal freedom, nor kept in a state of detention, except on an irrevocable conviction or caught in the act of a crime for which arrest is mandatory.

(3) The same authorization is required to subject members of parliament to any form of interception of their conversations or communications, and in order to seize their mail or correspondence.

18. All members of the legislature are elected; the executive lacks the power to appoint any members of the legislature.

Yes. All members of the legislature are elected, with two minor exceptions. The president may appoint five "senators for life" from the "social, scientific, artistic, and literary fields." Former presidents are also guaranteed a position as senator for life. As of May 2006, following the April 2006 elections, seven of the 315 members of the Senate were appointed senators for life (of which three were former presidents).

Article 56

(1) The Chamber of Deputies is elected by universal and direct suffrage.

Article 57

(1) The Senate is elected on a regional basis except for the seats assigned to the constituency of Italians abroad.

Article 59

(1) Anyone who was president of the republic is a senator for life unless waiving this privilege.

(2) The president may appoint as senators for life five citizens who have brought honor to the nation through their exceptional accomplishments in the social, scientific, artistic, and literary fields.

19. The legislature alone, without the involvement of any other agencies, can change the Constitution.

Yes. The legislature can amend the constitution in multiple readings with a two-thirds majority vote.

Article 138

(1) Law amending the constitution and other constitutional acts are adopted by each of the two chambers twice within no less than three months and need the approval of a majority of the members of each chamber in the second voting.

(2) Such laws are afterwards submitted to popular referendum when, within three months of their publication, a request is made by one fifth of the members of either chamber, by 500,000 electors, or by five regional councils. The law submitted to referendum is not promulgated if it does not receive the majority of valid votes.

(3) No referendum may be held if the law has been approved by each chamber in the second vote with a majority of two thirds of its members.

20. The legislature's approval is necessary for the declaration of war.

Yes. The legislature declares war.

Article 78

Chambers are competent to declare war and assign the necessary powers to government.

21. The legislature's approval is necessary to ratify treaties with foreign countries.

Yes. The legislature's approval is necessary to ratify international treaties on most major issues.

Article 80

Chambers ratify by law international treaties which are of political nature, provide for arbitration or judicial regulation, imply modifications of the territory, impose financial burdens, or result in modifications of the laws.

22. The legislature has the power to grant amnesty.

Yes. The legislature can grant amnesty by a two-thirds majority vote in both chambers.

Article 79

(1) Amnesties and pardons may be granted by a law which must be adopted both article by article and in its entirety by two thirds of the members of each chamber.

(2) A law granting amnesty or pardon has to establish time limits for its enforcement.

(3) In no instance may amnesty or pardon be extended to offences committed after the bill has been introduced.

23. The legislature has the power of pardon.

Yes. The legislature can grant pardons by a two-thirds majority vote in both chambers.

Article 79

(1) Amnesties and pardons may be granted by a law which must be adopted both article by article and in its entirety by two thirds of the members of each chamber.

(2) A law granting amnesty or pardon has to establish time limits for its enforcement.

(3) In no instance may amnesty or pardon be extended to offences committed after the bill has been introduced.

24. The legislature reviews and has the right to reject appointments to the judiciary; or the legislature itself appoints members of the judiciary.

Yes. The legislature elects one-third of the members of the Superior Council of the Judiciary and one-third of the members of the Constitutional Court.

Article 104
(2) The superior council of the judiciary is chaired by the president.
(3) The first president and the general public prosecutor of the court of cassation are members by law.
(4) Other members are elected with two-thirds majority by all ordinary judges belonging to the different categories, and one-third by parliament in joint session, from among full professors of law and lawyers with at least fifteen years of practice.
(5) The council elects a vice-chairman from among the members designated by parliament.
(6) The elected members have a term of for four years and may not be immediately re-elected.
(7) They are not allowed, while in office, to be registered as members of the legal profession, nor become members of parliament or of a regional council.

Article 106
(1) Appointment to the judiciary is based on competitive examinations.
(2) The law on the organization of the judiciary may provide for honorary magistrates, possibly by election, to perform the duties of single judges.
(3) By proposal of the superior council of the judiciary, full professors of law as well as lawyers with at least fifteen years practice and registered for practice in higher courts, may be appointed to the court of cassation for exceptional merits.

Article 135
(1) The constitutional court consists of fifteen justices; one third being appointed by the president, one third by parliament in joint session, and one third by ordinary and administrative supreme courts.

25. The chairman of the central bank is appointed by the legislature.

No. The government appoints the governor of the Bank of Italy with the approval of the president.

26. The legislature has a substantial voice in the operation of the state-owned media.

Yes. The legislature appoints the president of the state-owned radio and television networks and oversees their activity through a special committee. The presidents of the two chambers of the legislature also appoint the board that directs the state-owned media.

27. The legislature is regularly in session.

Yes. The legislature meets in ordinary session for about eight months each year.

Article 62
(1) Sessions commence on the first days of February and October that are not holidays.
(2) Each chamber may be summoned in extraordinary session on the initiative of its speaker, the president of the republic, or of one third of its members.
(3) If a chamber is summoned for an extraordinary session, the other chamber also convenes.

28. Each legislator has a personal secretary.

Yes.

29. Each legislator has at least one non-secretarial staff member with policy expertise.

Yes. Legislators receive a budget for staff expenditure, although not all legislators decide to hire a policy advisor.

30. Legislators are eligible for re-election without any restriction.

Yes. There are no restrictions on re-election.

31. A seat in the legislature is an attractive enough position that legislators are generally interested in and seek re-election.

Yes.

32. The re-election of incumbent legislators is common enough that at any given time the legislature contains a significant number of highly experienced members.

Yes. The "clean hands" (*mani pulite*) affair of the early 1990s shook the party system and the parliament's membership profile. Nevertheless, many former politicians have returned, and post-scandal re-election rates have been sufficiently high to ensure the presence of a significant number of highly experienced members.

PARLIAMENT OF JAMAICA

Expert consultants: Robert Buddan, Perry Mars, Derwin Munroe, Karen Turner

Score: .63

Influence over executive (8/9)		Institutional autonomy (4/9)		Specified powers (3/8)		Institutional capacity (5/6)	
1. replace	X	10. no dissolution		19. amendments	X	27. sessions	X
2. serve as ministers	X	11. no decree	X	20. war	X	28. secretary	X
3. interpellate	X	12. no veto	X	21. treaties	X	29. staff	
4. investigate	X	13. no review		22. amnesty		30. no term limits	X
5. oversee police	X	14. no gatekeeping		23. pardon		31. seek re-election	X
6. appoint PM	X	15. no impoundment	X	24. judiciary		32. experience	X
7. appoint ministers		16. control resources	X	25. central bank			
8. lack president	X	17. immunity		26. media			
9. no confidence	X	18. all elected					

The Parliament of Jamaica finds heritage in the early nineteenth century, in the assembly that represented the Jamaican colony in the British Empire. The legislature in its current form was established in the 1962 constitution upon independence from Great Britain. The bicameral parliament comprises an elected lower house, the House of Representatives, and an appointed upper house, the Senate. The Governor General is the symbolic head of state and formally is the representative of the Queen of England. A constitutional amendment in 1986 did not directly affect legislative power.

The legislature enjoys significant power. It has substantial control over the executive. It chooses the prime minister and can question and investigate the executive. Parliament has never voted no confidence in the government, however, perhaps because such a vote would likely result in its own dissolution. The legislature's institutional autonomy is circumscribed by the government's gatekeeping power and the Governor General's right to appoint the members of the Senate. The legislature is granted a few specified powers and possesses considerable institutional capacity.

SURVEY

1. The legislature alone, without the involvement of any other agencies, can impeach the president or replace the prime minister.

Yes. The legislature can remove the prime minister with a vote of no confidence.

Article 64

(5) In the exercise of his powers under this section the Governor-General shall act in accordance with the advice to the Prime Minister: Provided that if House of Representatives by a resolution which has received the affirmative vote of a majority of all the members thereof has resolved that it has no confidence in the Government, the Governor-General shall by Proclamation published in the *Gazette* dissolve Parliament.

2. Ministers may serve simultaneously as members of the legislature.

Yes. Ministers are selected from, and required to serve simultaneously in, the legislature. Between two and four of the ministers must be senators. The rest are drawn from the House of Representatives.

Article 70

(1) Whenever the Governor-General has occasion to appoint a Prime Minister he, acting in his discretion, shall appoint the member of the House of Representatives who, in his judgment, is best able to command the confidence of a majority of the members of that House and shall, acting in accordance with the advice of the Prime Minister, appoint from among the members of the two Houses such number of other Ministers as the Prime Minister may advise.

3. The legislature has powers of summons over executive branch officials and hearings with executive

branch officials testifying before the legislature or its committees are regularly held.

Yes. Legislators can question executive branch officials during weekly question time.

4. The legislature can conduct independent investigation of the chief executive and the agencies of the executive.

Yes. The legislature can investigate the executive.

5. The legislature has effective powers of oversight over the agencies of coercion (the military, organs of law enforcement, intelligence services, and the secret police).

Yes. The legislature has effective powers of oversight over the agencies of coercion.

6. The legislature appoints the prime minister.

Yes. The Governor General appoints as prime minister the candidate who enjoys the support of the legislature.

Article 70
(1) Whenever the Governor-General has occasion to appoint a Prime Minister he, acting in his discretion, shall appoint the member of the House of Representatives who, in his judgment, is best able to command the confidence of a majority of the members of that House and shall, acting in accordance with the advice of the Prime Minister, appoint from among the members of the two Houses such number of other Ministers as the Prime Minister may advise.

7. The legislature's approval is required to confirm the appointment of ministers; or the legislature itself appoints ministers.

No. The Governor General appoints ministers on the recommendation of the prime minister, and the appointments do not require legislative approval.

Article 70
(1) Whenever the Governor-General has occasion to appoint a Prime Minister he, acting in his discretion, shall appoint the member of the House of Representatives who, in his judgment, is best able to command the confidence of a majority of the members of that House and shall, acting in accordance with the advice of the Prime Minister, appoint from among the members of the two Houses such number of other Ministers as the Prime Minister may advise.

8. The country lacks a presidency entirely or there is a presidency, but the president is elected by the legislature.

Yes. The country lacks a presidency. The Governor General is the head of state.

Article 27
There shall be a Governor-General of Jamaica who shall be appointed by Her Majesty and shall hold office during Her Majesty's pleasure and who shall be Her Majesty's representative in Jamaica.

Article 68
(1) The executive authority of Jamaica is vested in Her Majesty.
(2) Subject to the provisions of this Constitution, the executive authority of Jamaica may be exercised on behalf of Her Majesty by the Governor-General either directly or through officers subordinate to him.

9. The legislature can vote no confidence in the government.

Yes. The legislature can vote no confidence in the government.

Article 64
(5) In the exercise of his powers under this section the Governor-General shall act in accordance with the advice to the Prime Minister: Provided that if House of Representatives by a resolution which has received the affirmative vote of a majority of all the members thereof has resolved that it has no confidence in the Government, the Governor-General shall by Proclamation published in the *Gazette* dissolve Parliament.

10. The legislature is immune from dissolution by the executive.

No. The Governor General, on the recommendation of the prime minister, can dissolve the legislature.

Article 64
(1) The Governor-General may at any time by Proclamation published in the *Gazette* prorogue or dissolve Parliament.
(5) In the exercise of his powers under this section the Governor-General shall act in accordance with the advice to the Prime Minister: Provided that if House of Representatives by a resolution which has received the affirmative vote of a majority of all the members thereof has resolved that it has no confidence in the Government, the Governor-General shall by Proclamation published in the *Gazette* dissolve Parliament.

11. Any executive initiative on legislation requires ratification or approval by the legislature before it takes effect; that is, the executive lacks decree power.

Yes. The executive lacks decree power.

12. Laws passed by the legislature are veto-proof or essentially veto-proof; that is, the executive lacks veto power, or has veto power but the veto can be overridden by a majority in the legislature.

Yes. The legislature's laws are veto-proof. Formally, the Governor General can refuse to assent to a law. This would amount to veto power. In practice, however, it would be unthinkable for the Governor General to withhold assent from a law.

Article 60

(1) A Bill shall not become law until the Governor-General has assented thereto in Her Majesty's name and on Her Majesty's behalf and has signed it in token of such assent.

(2) Subject to the provisions of sections 37, 49, 50, 56 and 57 of this Constitution, a Bill shall be presented to the Governor-General for assent if, and shall not be so presented unless, it has been approved by both Houses of Parliament either without amendment or with such amendments only as are agreed to by both Houses.

(3) When a Bill is presented to the Governor-General for assent he shall signify that he assents or that he withholds assent.

13. The legislature's laws are supreme and not subject to judicial review.

No. The legislature's laws are subject to judicial review.

14. The legislature has the right to initiate bills in all policy jurisdictions; the executive lacks gatekeeping authority.

No. The legislature is prohibited from introducing legislation related to increases in taxation, increases in government expenditures, or increases in government debt.

Article 55

(3) Except on the recommendation of the Governor-General signified by a Minister, the House of Representatives shall not proceed upon any Bill (including any amendment to a Bill) which Bill or amendment, as the case may be, in the opinion of the person presiding, makes provision for any of the following purposes, that is to say, for imposing or increasing any tax, for imposing or increasing any charge on the revenues or other funds of Jamaica or for altering any such charge otherwise than by reducing it, or for compounding or remitting any debt due to Jamaica; proceed upon any motion (including any amendment to a motion) the effect of which motion or amendment, as the case may be, in the opinion of the person presiding, is that provision should be made for any of the purposes aforesaid; or receive any petition which, in the opinion of the person presiding, requests that provision be made for any of the purposes aforesaid.

(4) The Senate shall not proceed upon any Bill, other than a Bill sent from the House of Representatives, or upon any amendment to a Bill, which Bill or amendment, as the case may be, in the opinion of person presiding, makes provision for any of the following purposes, that is to say, for imposing or altering any existing or proposed tax, for imposing or altering any existing or proposed charge on the revenues or other funds of Jamaica, or for compounding or remitting any

debt due to Jamaica; proceed upon any motion (including any amendment to a motion) the effect of which motion or amendment, as the case may be, in the opinion of the person presiding, is that provision should be made for any of the purposes aforesaid; or receive any petition which, in the opinion of the person presiding, requests that provision be made for any of the purposes aforesaid.

15. Expenditure of funds appropriated by the legislature is mandatory; the executive lacks the power to impound funds appropriated by the legislature.

Yes. The executive lacks the power to impound funds appropriated by the legislature.

16. The legislature controls the resources that finance its own internal operation and provide for the perquisites of its own members.

Yes. The legislature enjoys financial autonomy.

17. Members of the legislature are immune from arrest and/or criminal prosecution.

No. Legislators are immune for "civil debt" while the legislature is in session only. Legislators are subject to arrest for common crimes.

Article 48

(2) Without prejudice to the generality of subsection (1) and subject to the provisions of subsections (3), (4) and (5) of this section Parliament may by law determine the privileges, immunities and powers of the two Houses and the members thereof.

(3) No civil or criminal proceedings may be instituted against any member of either House for words spoken before, or written in a report to, the House of which he is a member or to a committee thereof or to any joint committee of both Houses or by reason of any matter or thing brought by him therein by petition, bill, resolution, motion or otherwise.

(4) For the duration of any session of both Houses shall enjoy freedom from arrest for any civil debt except a debt the contraction of which constitutes a criminal offence.

(5) No process issued by any court in the exercise of its civil jurisdiction shall be served or executed within the precincts of either House while such House is sitting or through the President or the Speaker, the Clerk or any officer of either House.

18. All members of the legislature are elected; the executive lacks the power to appoint any members of the legislature.

No. All twenty-one senators are appointed by the Governor General. Thirteen senators are appointed on the recommendation of the prime minister, and the remaining eight are appointed on the recommendation of the leader of the opposition. All members of the House of Representatives are elected.

Article 35

(1) The Senate shall consist of twenty-one persons who being qualified for appointment as Senators in accordance with this Constitution have been so appointed in accordance with the provisions of this section.

(2) Thirteen Senators shall be appointed by the Governor-General, acting in accordance with the advice of the Prime Minister, by instrument under the Broad Seal.

(3) The remaining eight Senators shall be appointed by the Governor-General, acting in accordance with the advice of the Leader of the Opposition, by instrument under the Broad Seal.

Article 36

The House of Representatives shall consist of persons who, being qualified for election as members in accordance with the provisions of this Constitution, have been so elected in the manner provided by or under any law for the time being in force in Jamaica and who shall be known as "Members of Parliament."

19. The legislature alone, without the involvement of any other agencies, can change the Constitution.

Yes. The legislature can change the constitution with a majority vote. A constitutional amendment to change the fundamental structure of government, however, requires approval in a national referendum.

Article 49

(1) Subject to the provisions of this section Parliament may by Act of Parliament passed by both Houses alter any of the provisions of this Constitution.

(2) In so far as it alters –

a. sections 13, 14, 15, 16, 17, 18, 19, 20, 21, 22, 23, 24, 25, 26, subsection (3) of section 48, sections 66, 67, 82, 83, 84, 85, 86, 87, 88, 89, 90, 91, 94, subsections (2), (3), (4), (5), (6) or (7) of section 96, sections 97, 98, 99, subsections (3), (4), (5), (6), (7), (8) or (9) of section 100, sections 101, 103, 104, 105, subsections (3), (4), (5), (6), (7), (8) or (9) of section 106, subsections (1), (2), (4), (5), (6), (7), (8), (9) or (10) of section 111, sections 112, 113, 114, 116, 117, 118, 119, 120, subsections (2), (3), (4), (5), (6) or (7) of section 121, sections 122, 124, 125, subsection (1) of section 126, sections 127, 129, 130, 131, 135 or 136 or the Second or Third Schedule to this Constitution; or a. section 1 of this Constitution in its application to any of the provisions specified in paragraph (a) of this subsection; a Bill for an Act of Parliament under this section shall not be submitted to the Governor-General for his assent unless a period of three months has elapsed between the introduction of the Bill into the House of Representatives and the commencement of the first debate on the whole text of that Bill in that House and a further period of three months has elapsed between the conclusion of that debate and the passing of that Bill by that House.

(3) In so far as it alters –

a. this section;

b. sections 2, 34, 35, 36, 39, subsection (2) of section 63, subsections (2), (3) or (5) of section 64, section 65, or subsection (1) of section 68 of this Constitution;

c. section 1 of this Constitution in its application to any of the provisions specified in paragraph (a) or (b) of this subsection; or

d. any of the provisions of the Jamaica Independence Act, 1962, a Bill for an Act of Parliament under this section shall not be submitted to the Governor-General for his assent unless –

i. a period of three months has elapsed between the introduction of the Bill into the House of Representatives and the commencement of the first debate on the whole text of that Bill in that House and a further period of three months has elapsed between the conclusion of that debate and the passing of that Bill by that House, and

ii. subject to the provisions of subsection (6) of this section, the Bill, not less than two nor more than six months after its passage through both Houses, has been submitted to the electors qualified to vote for the election of members of the House of Representatives and, on a vote taken in such manner as Parliament may prescribe, the majority of the electors voting have approved the Bill.

(4) A Bill for an Act of Parliament under this section shall not be deemed to be passed in either House unless at the final vote thereon it is supported –

e. in the case of a Bill which alters any of the provisions specified in subsection (2) or subsection (3) of this section by the votes of not less than two-thirds of all the members of that House, or

f. in any other case by the votes of a majority of all the members of that House.

(5) If a Bill for an Act of Parliament which alters any of the provisions specified in subsection (2) of this section is passed by the House of Representatives –

g. twice in the same session in the manner prescribed by subsection (2) and paragraph (a) of subsection (4) of this section and having been sent to the Senate on the first occasion at least seven months before the end of the session and on the second occasion at least one month before the end of the session, is rejected the Senate on each occasion, or

h. in two successive sessions (whether of the same Parliament or not) in the manner prescribed by subsection (2) and paragraph (a) of subsection (4) of this section, and having been sent to the Senate in each of those sessions at least one month before the end of the session, the second occasion being at least six months after the first occasion is rejected by the Senate in each of those sessions, that Bill may, not less than two nor more than six months after its rejection by the Senate for the second time, be submitted to the electors qualified to vote for the election of members of the House of Representatives and, if on a vote taken in such manner as Parliament may prescribe, three-fifths of the electors voting approve the Bill, the Bill may be presented to the Governor-General for assent.

(6) If a Bill for an Act of Parliament which alters any of the provisions specified in subsection (3) of this section is passed by the House of Representatives –

i. twice in the same session in the manner prescribed by subsection (3) and paragraph (a) of subsection (4) of this section and having been sent to the Senate on the first occasion at least seven months before the end of the session and on the second occasion at least one month before the end of the session, is rejected by the Senate on each occasion, or

j. in two successive sessions (whether of the same Parliament or not) in the manner prescribed by subsection (3) and paragraph (a) of subsection (4) of this section and, having been sent to the Senate in each of those sessions at least one month before the end of the session, the second occasion being at least six months after the first occasion, is rejected by the Senate in each of those sessions, that Bill may, not less than two nor more than six months after its rejection by the Senate for the second time, be submitted to the electors qualified to vote for the election of members of the House of Representatives and, if on a vote taken in such manner as Parliament may prescribe, two-thirds of the electors voting approve the Bill, the Bill may be presented to the Governor-General for assent.

(7) For the purposes of subsection (5) and subsection (6) of this section a Bill shall be deemed to be rejected by the Senate if –

k. it is not passed by the Senate in the manner prescribed by paragraph (a) of subsection (4) of this section within one month after it is sent to that House; or

l. it is passed by the Senate in the manner so prescribed with any amendment which is not agreed to by the House of Representatives.

(8) For the purposes of subsection (5) and subsection (6) of this section a Bill that is sent to the Senate from the House of Representatives in any session shall be deemed to be the same Bill as the former Bill sent to the Senate in the same or in the preceding session if, when it is sent to the Senate, it is identical with the former Bill or contains only such alterations as are specified by the Speaker to be necessary owing to the time that has elapsed since the date of the former Bill or to represent any amendments which have been made by the Senate in the former Bill.

(9) In this section –

m. reference to any of the provisions of this Constitution or the Jamaica Independence Act, 1962, includes references to any law that alters that provision; and

n. "alter" includes amend, modify, re-enact with or without amendment or modification, make different provision in lieu of, suspend, repeal or add to.

20. The legislature's approval is necessary for the declaration of war.

Yes. Formally, the Governor General declares war, but in practice, the legislature's approval is necessary for the Governor General to declare war.

21. The legislature's approval is necessary to ratify treaties with foreign countries.

Yes. The legislature's approval is necessary to ratify international treaties.

22. The legislature has the power to grant amnesty.

No. Amnesty and pardon are not treated separately, and the legislature lacks the power to grant amnesty. See item 23.

23. The legislature has the power of pardon.

No. The Governor General has the power of pardon.

Article 90
(1) The Governor-General may, in Her Majesty's name and on Her Majesty's behalf –
grant to any person convicted of any offence against the law of Jamaica a pardon, either free or subject to lawful conditions; grant to any person a respite, either indefinite or for a specified period, from the execution of any punishment imposed on that person for such an offence; substitute a less severe form of punishment for that imposed on any person for such an offence; or remit the whole or part of any punishment imposed on any person for such an offense or any penalty or forfeiture otherwise due to the Crown on account of such an offence.

24. The legislature reviews and has the right to reject appointments to the judiciary; or the legislature itself appoints members of the judiciary.

No. The Governor General and the Judicial Service Commission are responsible for judicial appointments, and the appointments do not require the legislature's approval. The approval of the prime minister and the leader of the opposition in the legislature is needed for the Governor General's appointment of the chief justice of the Supreme Court.

Article 98
(1) The Chief Justice shall be appointed by the Governor-General by instrument under the Broad Seal on the recommendation of the Prime Minister after consultation with the Leader of the Opposition.
(2) The Puisne Judges shall be appointed by the Governor-General by instrument under the Broad Seal acting on the advice of the Judicial Service Commission.
(3) The qualifications for appointment as a Judge of the Supreme Court shall be such as may be prescribed by any law for the time being in force:
Provided that a person who has been appointed as a Judge of the Supreme Court may continue in office

notwithstanding any subsequent variations in the qualifications so prescribed.

25. The chairman of the central bank is appointed by the legislature.

No. The minister of finance appoints the governor of the Bank of Jamaica.

26. The legislature has a substantial voice in the operation of the state-owned media.

No. The executive dominates the state-owned media and uses it to provide public service information on its own behalf.

27. The legislature is regularly in session.

Yes. The legislature meets regularly in ordinary session.

Article 63
(2) Sessions shall be held at such times so that a period of six months shall not intervene between the last sitting of Parliament in one session and the first sitting thereof in the next session.

28. Each legislator has a personal secretary.
Yes.

29. Each legislator has at least one non-secretarial staff member with policy expertise.
No.

30. Legislators are eligible for re-election without any restriction.

Yes. There are no restrictions on re-election.

31. A seat in the legislature is an attractive enough position that legislators are generally interested in and seek re-election.
Yes.

32. The re-election of incumbent legislators is common enough that at any given time the legislature contains a significant number of highly experienced members.

Yes. Re-election rates are sufficiently high to produce a significant number of highly experienced members.

NATIONAL DIET OF JAPAN (*KOKKAI*)

Expert consultants: Ellis S. Krauss, Mikitaka Masuyama, T. J. Pempel, Frances M. Rosenbluth, Richard J. Samuels, Steven K. Vogel

Score: .66

Influence over executive (8/9)		Institutional autonomy (5/9)		Specified powers (2/8)		Institutional capacity (6/6)	
1. replace	X	10. no dissolution		19. amendments		27. sessions	X
2. serve as ministers	X	11. no decree	X	20. war	X	28. secretary	X
3. interpellate	X	12. no veto	X	21. treaties	X	29. staff	X
4. investigate	X	13. no review		22. amnesty		30. no term limits	X
5. oversee police	X	14. no gatekeeping	X	23. pardon		31. seek re-election	X
6. appoint PM	X	15. no impoundment		24. judiciary		32. experience	X
7. appoint ministers		16. control resources	X	25. central bank			
8. lack president	X	17. immunity		26. media			
9. no confidence	X	18. all elected	X				

The National Diet (*Kokkai*) of Japan was established in the 1889 Meiji Constitution. The document, the first written constitution in Asia, called for a bicameral legislature consisting of a lower house, the House of Representatives (*Shūgi-in*), and an upper house, the House of Counselors (*Sangi-in*). In practice, the Meiji-era legislature exercised little influence; the emperor held supreme executive, legislative, and judicial power. In 1947 Japan adopted a new constitution that retained and invigorated the bicameral parliament. In the new political order, the emperor became head of state, and the position of prime minister was created to serve as head of government. The constitution granted the legislature the authority to appoint the prime minister and to vote no confidence in the government. The legislature also gained the power to question executive branch officials. The constitution further established the Supreme Court and judicial review, although in practice, judicial review in Japan has not become a robust, vigorous institution.

Today the National Diet enjoys broad authority, which includes numerous levers for influencing the executive, fairly extensive institutional autonomy, and robust institutional capacity, although the legislature enjoys few specified powers and prerogatives.

SURVEY

1. The legislature alone, without the involvement of any other agencies, can impeach the president or replace the prime minister.

Yes. The legislature can remove the prime minister with a vote of no confidence.

Article 69
If the House of Representatives passes a resolution of no confidence, or rejects a confidence resolution, the Cabinet shall resign altogether, unless the House of Representatives is dissolved within ten days.

2. Ministers may serve simultaneously as members of the legislature.

Yes. A majority of ministers must be selected from, and serve simultaneously in, the legislature.

Article 68
(1) The Prime Minister shall appoint the Ministers of State.
(2) However, a majority of their number must be chosen from among the members of the Diet.
(3) The Prime Minister may remove the Ministers of State as he chooses.

3. The legislature has powers of summons over executive branch officials and hearings with executive branch officials testifying before the legislature or its committees are regularly held.

Yes. The legislature regularly interpellates officials from the executive.

Article 63
(1) The Prime Minister and other Ministers of State may, at any time, appear in either House for the purpose of speaking on bills, regardless of whether they are members of the House or not.
(2) They must appear when their presence is required in order to give answers or explanations.

4. The legislature can conduct independent investigation of the chief executive and the agencies of the executive.

Yes. The legislature can investigate the executive.

Article 62
Each House may conduct investigations in relation to government, and may demand the presence and testimony of witnesses and the production of records.

5. The legislature has effective powers of oversight over the agencies of coercion (the military, organs of law enforcement, intelligence services, and the secret police).

Yes. The legislature has effective powers of oversight over the agencies of coercion.

6. The legislature appoints the prime minister.

Yes. The emperor appoints the Diet's choice for prime minister. It is noteworthy, however, that although the choice of prime minister ultimately rests with parliament, the influence of the bosses of the ruling party (the Liberal Democratic Party) on the selection of the prime minister is especially (and famously) weighty in Japanese politics.

Article 6
(1) The Emperor shall appoint the Prime Minister as designated by the Diet.

Article 67
(1) The Prime Minister shall be designated from among the members of the Diet by a resolution of the Diet.
(2) This designation shall precede all other business.
(3) If the House of Representatives and the House of Councilors disagree and if no agreement can be reached even through a joint committee of both Houses, provided for by law, or the House of Councilors fails to make designation within ten days, exclusive of the period of recess, after the House of Representatives has made designation, the decision of the House of Representatives shall be the decision of the Diet.

7. The legislature's approval is required to confirm the appointment of ministers; or the legislature itself appoints ministers.

No. The prime minister appoints ministers, and the appointments do not require the legislature's approval.

Article 68
(1) The Prime Minister shall appoint the Ministers of State.
(2) However, a majority of their number must be chosen from among the members of the Diet.

8. The country lacks a presidency entirely or there is a presidency, but the president is elected by the legislature.

Yes. The country lacks a presidency. The emperor is the head of state.

9. The legislature can vote no confidence in the government.

Yes. The House of Representatives can vote no confidence in the government.

> Article 69
> If the House of Representatives passes a resolution of no confidence, or rejects a confidence resolution, the Cabinet shall resign altogether, unless the House of Representatives is dissolved within ten days.

10. The legislature is immune from dissolution by the executive.

No. The emperor, on the advice of the government, can dissolve the House of Representatives.

> Article 7
> The Emperor, with the advice and approval of the Cabinet, shall perform the following acts in matters of state on behalf of the people:
> 3. Dissolution of the House of Representatives.

> Article 69
> If the House of Representatives passes a resolution of no confidence, or rejects a confidence resolution, the Cabinet shall resign altogether, unless the House of Representatives is dissolved within ten days.

11. Any executive initiative on legislation requires ratification or approval by the legislature before it takes effect; that is, the executive lacks decree power.

Yes. The executive lacks decree power.

12. Laws passed by the legislature are veto-proof or essentially veto-proof; that is, the executive lacks veto power, or has veto power but the veto can be overridden by a majority in the legislature.

Yes. The executive lacks veto power.

> Article 59
> (1) A bill becomes a law on passage by both Houses, except as otherwise provided by the Constitution.
> (2) A bill which is passed by the House of Representatives, and upon which the House of Councilors makes a decision different from that of the House of Representatives, becomes a law when passed a second time by the House of Representatives by the majority of two-thirds or more of the members present.
> (3) The provision of the preceding paragraph does not preclude the House of Representatives from calling for the meeting of a joint committee of both Houses, provided for by law.
> (4) Failure by the House of Councilors to take final action within sixty days after receipt of a bill passed by the House of Representatives, time in recess excepted, may be determined by the House of Representatives to constitute a rejection of the said bill by the House of Councilors.

13. The legislature's laws are supreme and not subject to judicial review.

No. The Supreme Court can review the constitutionality of laws.

> Article 81
> The Supreme Court is the court of last resort with power to determine the constitutionality of any law, order, regulation, or official act.

14. The legislature has the right to initiate bills in all policy jurisdictions; the executive lacks gatekeeping authority.

Yes. The legislature can initiate bills in all policy jurisdictions.

15. Expenditure of funds appropriated by the legislature is mandatory; the executive lacks the power to impound funds appropriated by the legislature.

No. The government can increase or decrease Diet-approved funds from the Fiscal Investment and Loan Program (FILP), Japan's distinctive "second budget" funded by postal savings, by up to 50 percent.

16. The legislature controls the resources that finance its own internal operation and provide for the perquisites of its own members.

Yes. The legislature enjoys financial autonomy, including control over members' salaries.

> Article 49
> Members of both Houses shall receive appropriate annual payment from the national treasury in accordance with law.

17. Members of the legislature are immune from arrest and/or criminal prosecution.

No. Legislators are immune while the legislature is in session only.

> Article 50
> Except in cases provided by law, members of both Houses shall be exempt from apprehension while the Diet is in session, and any members apprehended before the opening of the session shall be freed during the term of the session upon demand of the House.

> Article 51
> Members of both Houses shall not be held liable outside the House for speeches, debates, or votes cast inside the House.

18. All members of the legislature are elected; the executive lacks the power to appoint any members of the legislature.

Yes. All members of the legislature are elected.

> Article 43
> (1) Both Houses shall consist of elected members, representative of all the people.

(2) The number of the members of each House shall be fixed by law.

19. The legislature alone, without the involvement of any other agencies, can change the Constitution.

No. Constitutional amendments require approval in a popular referendum.

> Article 96
> (1) Amendments to this Constitution shall be initiated by the Diet, through a concurring vote of two-thirds or more of all the members of each House and shall thereupon be submitted to the people for ratification, which shall require the affirmative vote of a majority of all votes cast thereon, at a special referendum or at such election as the Diet shall specify.
> (2) Amendments when so ratified shall immediately be promulgated by the Emperor in the name of the people, as an integral part of this Constitution.

20. The legislature's approval is necessary for the declaration of war.

Yes. In the constitution Japan renounces war. In practice, the legislature's approval is necessary for the international deployment of Japanese troops and would be necessary for a war declaration.

> Article 9
> (1) Aspiring sincerely to an international peace based on justice and order, the Japanese people forever renounce war as a sovereign right of the nation and the threat or use of force as means of settling international disputes.
> (2) In order to accomplish the aim of the preceding paragraph, land, sea, and air forces, as well as other war potential, will never be maintained. The right of aggression of the state will not be recognized.

21. The legislature's approval is necessary to ratify treaties with foreign countries.

Yes. The legislature's approval is necessary to ratify international treaties.

> Article 60
> (1) The budget must first be submitted to the House of Representatives.
> (2) Upon consideration of the budget, when the House of Councilors makes a decision different from that of the House of Representatives, and when no agreement can be reached even through a joint committee of both Houses, provided for by law, or in the case of failure by the House of Councilors to take final action within thirty days, the period of recess excluded, after the receipt of the budget passed by the House of Representatives, the decision of the House of Representatives shall be the decision of the Diet.

> Article 61
> Article 60 (2) applies also to the Diet approval required for the conclusion of treaties.

> Article 73
> The Cabinet, in addition to other general administrative functions, shall perform the following functions:
> 3. Conclude treaties. However, it shall obtain prior or, depending on circumstances, subsequent approval of the Diet.

22. The legislature has the power to grant amnesty.

No. The emperor and the cabinet have the power to grant amnesty.

> Article 7
> The Emperor, with the advice and approval of the Cabinet, shall perform the following acts in matters of state on behalf of the people:
> 6. Attestation of general and special amnesty, commutation of punishment, reprieve, and restoration of rights.

> Article 73
> The Cabinet, in addition to other general administrative functions, shall perform the following functions:
> 7. Decide on general amnesty, special amnesty, commutation of punishment, reprieve, and restoration of rights.

23. The legislature has the power of pardon.

No. The emperor and the cabinet have the power of pardon, here expressed as "commutation of punishment, reprieve, and restoration of rights."

> Article 7
> The Emperor, with the advice and approval of the Cabinet, shall perform the following acts in matters of state on behalf of the people:
> 6. Attestation of general and special amnesty, commutation of punishment, reprieve, and restoration of rights.

> Article 73
> The Cabinet, in addition to other general administrative functions, shall perform the following functions:
> 7. Decide on general amnesty, special amnesty, commutation of punishment, reprieve, and restoration of rights.

24. The legislature reviews and has the right to reject appointments to the judiciary; or the legislature itself appoints members of the judiciary.

No. Supreme Court justices are appointed by the cabinet, and the appointments are reviewed by the people in a popular referendum every ten years. The appointments do not require the legislature's approval.

> Article 6
> (2) The Emperor shall appoint the Chief Judge of the Supreme Court as designated by the Cabinet.

> Article 76
> (1) The whole judicial power is vested in a Supreme Court and in such inferior courts as are established by law.

(2) No extraordinary tribunal shall be established, nor shall any organ or agency of the Executive be given final judicial power.

(3) All judges are independent in the exercise of their conscience and bound only by this Constitution and the laws.

Article 79

(1) The Supreme Court shall consist of a Chief Judge and such number of judges as may be determined by law; all such judges excepting the Chief Judge shall be appointed by the Cabinet.

(2) The appointment of the judges of the Supreme Court shall be reviewed by the people at the first general election of members of the House of Representatives following their appointment, and shall be reviewed again at the first general election of members of the House of Representatives after a lapse of ten years, and in the same manner thereafter.

(3) In cases mentioned in the preceding paragraph, when the majority of the voters favors the dismissal of a judge, he shall be dismissed.

(4) Matters pertaining to review shall be prescribed by law.

(5) The judges of the Supreme Court shall be retired upon the attainment of the ages as fixed by law.

(6) All such judges shall receive, at regular stated intervals, adequate compensation which shall not be decreased during their terms of office.

25. The chairman of the central bank is appointed by the legislature.

No. The cabinet appoints the governor of the Bank of Japan with the approval of the legislature.

26. The legislature has a substantial voice in the operation of the state-owned media.

No. The legislature lacks a substantial voice in the operation of the public media.

27. The legislature is regularly in session.

Yes. The legislature meets in ordinary session for roughly six months each year, and extra sessions are common.

Article 52
An ordinary session of the Diet shall be convoked once per year.

28. Each legislator has a personal secretary.

Yes.

29. Each legislator has at least one non-secretarial staff member with policy expertise.

Yes.

30. Legislators are eligible for re-election without any restriction.

Yes. There are no restrictions on re-election.

31. A seat in the legislature is an attractive enough position that legislators are generally interested in and seek re-election.

Yes.

32. The re-election of incumbent legislators is common enough that at any given time the legislature contains a significant number of highly experienced members.

Yes. Re-election rates are sufficiently high to produce a significant number of highly experienced members.

NATIONAL ASSEMBLY OF JORDAN (*MAJLIS AL-'UMMA*)

Expert consultants: Nizam Assaf, Canan Atilgan, Russell E. Lucas, Ellen Lust-Okar, Pete W. Moore, Jillian Schwedler, Jeff VanDenBerg

Score: .22

Influence over executive (4/9)		Institutional autonomy (0/9)	Specified powers (1/8)		Institutional capacity (2/6)	
1. replace		10. no dissolution	19. amendments		27. sessions	
2. serve as ministers	X	11. no decree	20. war		28. secretary	
3. interpellate	X	12. no veto	21. treaties	X	29. staff	
4. investigate		13. no review	22. amnesty		30. no term limits	X
5. oversee police		14. no gatekeeping	23. pardon		31. seek re-election	X
6. appoint PM		15. no impoundment	24. judiciary		32. experience	
7. appoint ministers		16. control resources	25. central bank			
8. lack president	X	17. immunity	26. media			
9. no confidence	X	18. all elected				

The National Assembly (*Majlis al-'Umma*) of Jordan was established in the 1952 constitution. It comprises a lower house, the Chamber of Deputies (*Majlis al-Nuwaab*), and an upper house, the Senate (*Majlis al-Ayan*). Since its inception the legislature has had little influence on national politics. It has been dissolved for long periods of time, and legislative elections were completely suspended from 1967 to 1989. During 2001–3 the legislature was dissolved, and King Abdullah ruled by decree.

Today the royal palace remains the hub of political power and the legislature a feeble body. The Assembly's leverage over the executive is modest. It is completely lacking in institutional autonomy. It has only one of the specified powers assessed here, the right to ratify international treaties, and very little institutional capacity.

SURVEY

1. The legislature alone, without the involvement of any other agencies, can impeach the president or replace the prime minister.

No. The legislature cannot impeach the king. The Chamber of Deputies can replace the prime minister with a vote of no confidence.

Article 30
The King is the Head of the State and is immune from any liability and responsibility.

Article 53
(i) A motion of no confidence in the Council of Ministers or in any Minister may be raised by the Chamber of Deputies.
(ii) If the Chamber of Deputies casts a vote of no confidence in the Council of Ministers by an absolute majority of all its members, the Council of Ministers shall resign.
(iii) If the vote of no confidence concerns an individual Minister, he shall resign his office.

2. Ministers may serve simultaneously as members of the legislature.

Yes. Legislators may serve simultaneously in ministerial positions.

Article 52
The Prime Minister, or the Minister who is a member of either the Chamber of Deputies or the Senate, shall be entitled to vote in the House to which he belongs and to speak in both Houses. However, Ministers who are not members of either House may speak in both Houses without the right to vote.

3. The legislature has powers of summons over executive branch officials and hearings with executive branch officials testifying before the legislature or its committees are regularly held.

Yes. The legislature regularly interpellates officials from the executive.

Article 96

Any Senator or Deputy may address questions or interpellations to the Ministers concerning any public matters, in accordance with the provisions of the Internal Regulations of the Senate or the House (as the case may be). No interpellation may be debated before the lapse of eight days from the date of its receipt by the Minister, unless the case is of an urgent nature and the Minister agrees to shorten this period.

4. The legislature can conduct independent investigation of the chief executive and the agencies of the executive.

No. The legislature can investigate the government, but not the royal palace.

5. The legislature has effective powers of oversight over the agencies of coercion (the military, organs of law enforcement, intelligence services, and the secret police).

No. The legislature lacks effective powers of oversight over the agencies of coercion.

6. The legislature appoints the prime minister.

No. The king appoints the prime minister.

Article 35

The King appoints the Prime Minister and may dismiss him or accept his resignation. He appoints the Ministers; he also dismisses them or accepts their resignation, upon the recommendation of the Prime Minister.

7. The legislature's approval is required to confirm the appointment of ministers; or the legislature itself appoints ministers.

No. The king appoints ministers, and the appointments do not require the legislature's approval.

Article 35

The King appoints the Prime Minister and may dismiss him or accept his resignation. He appoints the Ministers; he also dismisses them or accepts their resignation, upon the recommendation of the Prime Minister.

8. The country lacks a presidency entirely or there is a presidency, but the president is elected by the legislature.

Yes. The country lacks a presidency. The king is the head of state.

Article 26

The Executive Power shall be vested in the King, who shall exercise his powers through his Ministers in accordance with the provisions of the present Constitution.

9. The legislature can vote no confidence in the government.

Yes. The Chamber of Deputies can vote no confidence in the government. It is noteworthy, however, that the legislature has never passed a vote of

no confidence in a government because the king has dissolved, or threatened to dissolve, the legislature in advance.

Article 53

(i) A motion of no confidence in the Council of Ministers or in any Minister may be raised by the Chamber of Deputies.

(ii) If the Chamber of Deputies casts a vote of no confidence in the Council of Ministers by an absolute majority of all its members, the Council of Ministers shall resign.

(iii) If the vote of no confidence concerns an individual Minister, he shall resign his office.

Article 54

(i) A session to consider a vote of no confidence in the Council of Ministers or in any individual Minister shall be held either at the request of the Prime Minister or at a request signed by not less than ten Deputies.

(ii) A vote of no confidence in the Council of Ministers or in any individual Minister may be postponed only for one period, which shall not exceed ten days, either upon the request of the Minister concerned or of the Council of Ministers. The Chamber shall not be dissolved during this period.

(iii) Every newly formed Council of Ministers shall within one month of its formation, in cases where the Chamber of Deputies is in session, place before the Chamber of Deputies a statement of its policy and request a vote confidence on the basis of the said statement. If the Chamber of Deputies is not in session at the time, or stands dissolved, the Speech from the Throne shall be considered to be a statement of its policy for the purposes of this Article.

10. The legislature is immune from dissolution by the executive.

No. The king can dissolve both houses of the legislature.

Article 34

(iii) The King may dissolve the Chamber of Deputies.

(iv) The King may dissolve the Senate or relieve any Senator of his membership.

Article 74

If the Chamber of Deputies is dissolved for any reason, the new Chamber shall not be dissolved for the same reason. A Minister who intends to nominate himself for election shall resign fifteen days at least before the beginning of nomination.

11. Any executive initiative on legislation requires ratification or approval by the legislature before it takes effect; that is, the executive lacks decree power.

No. The king can issue decrees that have the force of law. The cabinet (Council of Ministers) can also issue decrees that have the force of law when the legislature is not in session or dissolved. The laws remain in force unless they are explicitly rejected by the National Assembly in its next sitting.

Article 40

The King shall exercise the powers vested in him by Royal Decree. Every such Decree shall be countersigned by the Prime Minister and the Minister or Ministers concerned. The King expresses his concurrence by placing his signature above the said signatures.

Article 94

(i) In cases where the National Assembly is not sitting or is dissolved, the Council of Ministers has, with the approval of the King, the power to issue provisional laws covering matters which require necessary measures which admit of no delay or which necessitate expenditures incapable of postponement. Such provisional laws, which shall not be contrary to the provisions of the Constitution, shall have the force of law, provided that they are placed before the Assembly at the beginning of its next session, and the Assembly may approve or amend such laws. In the event of the rejection of such provisional laws, the Council of Ministers shall, with the approval of the King, immediately declare their nullity, and from the date of such declaration these provisional laws shall cease to have force provided that such nullity shall not affect any contracts or acquired rights.

12. Laws passed by the legislature are veto-proof or essentially veto-proof; that is, the executive lacks veto power, or has veto power but the veto can be overridden by a majority in the legislature.

No. A two-thirds majority is needed to override the king's veto.

Article 93

(i) Every draft law passed by the Senate and the Chamber of Deputies shall be submitted to the King for ratification.

(ii) A law shall come into force after its promulgation by the King and the lapse of thirty days from the date of its publication in the Official Gazette unless it is specifically provided in that law that it shall come into force on any other date.

(iii) If the King does not see fit to ratify a law, He may, within six months from the date on which the law was submitted to him, refer it back to the House coupled with a statement showing the reasons for withholding his ratification.

(iv) If any draft law (other than the Constitution) is referred back within the period specified in the preceding paragraph and is passed for the second time by two-thirds of the members of each of the Senate and the Chamber of Deputies, it shall be promulgated. If the law is not returned with the Royal ratification within the period prescribed in paragraph (iii) above, it shall be considered as promulgated and effective. If any draft law fails to obtain the two-thirds majority of votes, it cannot be reconsidered during the same session, provided that the National Assembly may reconsider the draft during its next ordinary session.

13. The legislature's laws are supreme and not subject to judicial review.

No. The legislature's laws are subject to judicial review.

14. The legislature has the right to initiate bills in all policy jurisdictions; the executive lacks gatekeeping authority.

No. Formally, the legislature has the right to initiate bills in all policy jurisdictions. In practice, the king has complete gatekeeping authority. He can prevent the introduction of any bill as he sees fit.

15. Expenditure of funds appropriated by the legislature is mandatory; the executive lacks the power to impound funds appropriated by the legislature.

No. The king can impound funds appropriated by the legislature.

16. The legislature controls the resources that finance its own internal operation and provide for the perquisites of its own members.

No. The legislature is dependent on the king and the government for the resources that finance its operations.

17. Members of the legislature are immune from arrest and/or criminal prosecution.

No. Legislators are immune while the legislature is in session only.

Article 86

(i) No Senator or Deputy may be detained or tried during the currency of the sessions of the National Assembly unless the House to which he belongs decides by an absolute majority that there is sufficient reason for his detention or trial or unless he was arrested flagrant delicto. In the event of his arrest in this manner, the House to which he belongs shall be notified immediately.

(ii) If a member is detained for any reason while the National Assembly is not sitting, the Prime Minister shall notify the Senate or the Chamber of Deputies when it reassembles of the proceedings which were taken against him, coupled with the necessary explanation.

Article 87

Every Senator or Deputy shall have complete freedom of speech and expression of opinion within the limits of the Internal Regulations of the Senate or Chamber of Deputies, as the case may be, and shall not be answerable in respect of any vote which he had cast or opinion expressed or speech made by him during the meetings of the House.

18. All members of the legislature are elected; the executive lacks the power to appoint any members of the legislature.

No. Senators are appointed by the king. All members of the Chamber of Deputies are elected.

> Article 36
> The King appoints members of the Senate and appoints the Speaker from amongst them and accepts their resignation.
>
> Article 67
> The Chamber of Deputies shall consist of members, elected by secret ballot, in a general direct election.

19. The legislature alone, without the involvement of any other agencies, can change the Constitution.

No. Constitutional amendments require the king's approval.

> Article 126
> (i) The procedure prescribed in the present Constitution with regard to draft laws shall apply to any draft law for the amendment of this Constitution, provided that any such amendment is passed by a two-thirds majority of the members of each of the Senate and the Chamber of Deputies. In the event of a joint meeting of the Senate and the Chamber of Deputies in accordance with Article (92) of this Constitution, the amendment shall be passed by a two-thirds majority of the members of both Houses, provided that in both cases the amendment shall not come into force unless ratified by the King.
> (ii) No amendment of the Constitution affecting the rights of the King and the succession to the Throne may be passed during the period of Regency.

20. The legislature's approval is necessary for the declaration of war.

No. The king can declare war without the legislature's approval.

> Article 33
> (i) The King declares war, concludes peace and ratifies treaties and agreements.

21. The legislature's approval is necessary to ratify treaties with foreign countries.

Yes. The legislature's approval is necessary to ratify international treaties that involve financial commitments to the treasury or affect citizens' rights.

> Article 33
> (i) The King declares war, concludes peace and ratifies treaties and agreements.
> (ii) Treaties and agreements which involve financial commitments to the Treasury or affect the public or private rights of Jordanians shall not be valid unless approved by the National Assembly. In no circumstances shall any secret terms contained in any treaty or agreement be contrary to their overt terms.

22. The legislature has the power to grant amnesty.

No. According to the constitution, amnesty, here referred to as "general pardon," can be granted by legislation. In practice, the legislature could not grant amnesty without the king's approval.

> Article 38
> The King has the right to grant a special pardon or remit any sentence, but any general pardon shall be determined by special law.

23. The legislature has the power of pardon.

No. The king has the power of pardon, here referred to as "special pardon."

> Article 38
> The King has the right to grant a special pardon or remit any sentence, but any general pardon shall be determined by special law.

24. The legislature reviews and has the right to reject appointments to the judiciary; or the legislature itself appoints members of the judiciary.

No. The king appoints the members of the judiciary, and the appointments do not require the legislature's approval.

> Article 98
> Judges of the Civil and Sharia Courts shall be appointed and dismissed by a Royal Decree in accordance with the provisions of the law.

25. The chairman of the central bank is appointed by the legislature.

No. The king appoints the governor of the Central Bank of Jordan.

26. The legislature has a substantial voice in the operation of the state-owned media.

No. The legislature lacks a substantial voice in the operation of the public media.

27. The legislature is regularly in session.

No. The legislature meets in ordinary session for only four months each year.

> Article 78
> (iii) The ordinary session of the National Assembly shall begin on the date upon which it was summoned to meet in accordance with the two preceding paragraphs, and shall last for four months unless the House of Deputies is dissolved by the King before the expiration of that period. The session may be prolonged by the King for a further period not exceeding three months to allow for the despatch of pending matters. At the expiration of the four months or any such prolongation thereof, the King shall prorogue the Assembly.

28. Each legislator has a personal secretary.

No.

29. Each legislator has at least one non-secretarial staff member with policy expertise.

No.

30. Legislators are eligible for re-election without any restriction.

Yes. There are no restrictions on re-election.

31. A seat in the legislature is an attractive enough position that legislators are generally interested in and seek re-election.

Yes.

32. The re-election of incumbent legislators is common enough that at any given time the legislature contains a significant number of highly experienced members.

No. Long spells of suspension and inactivity have precluded the development of a sizable cohort of legislators with substantial experience. In the elections of 2003 for the Chamber of Deputies, members of the party called Allies of King Abdullah II obtained roughly three-fifths of all seats. Some of these loyalists served in parliament prior to its suspension during 2001–3, but given the lack of continuity in parliament's existence in recent decades, one cannot reasonably speak of re-election rates.

PARLIAMENT OF KAZAKHSTAN (*KENGES*)

Expert consultants: Irina Chernykh, Sally N. Cummings, Pauline Jones Luong, Alen Sabyrov, Dina Sharipova

Score: .38

Influence over executive (1/9)	Institutional autonomy (3/9)		Specified powers (3/8)		Institutional capacity (5/6)	
1. replace	10. no dissolution		19. amendments		27. sessions	X
2. serve as ministers	11. no decree		20. war	X	28. secretary	X
3. interpellate	12. no veto		21. treaties	X	29. staff	
4. investigate	13. no review		22. amnesty	X	30. no term limits	X
5. oversee police	14. no gatekeeping	X	23. pardon		31. seek re-election	X
6. appoint PM	15. no impoundment		24. judiciary		32. experience	X
7. appoint ministers	16. control resources	X	25. central bank			
8. lack president	17. immunity	X	26. media			
9. no confidence	X	18. all elected				

The Parliament (*Kenges*) of Kazakhstan was founded in the 1993 constitution following the collapse of the Soviet Union. The constitution called for a unicameral parliament. A new constitution in 1995 established a second chamber, creating a bicameral legislature with an upper house, the Senate (*Senat*), and a lower house, the Assembly (*Majilis*). A constitutional amendment in 1998 extended the president's term from five to seven years but did not directly affect legislative power.

The legislature has little authority. It has little meaningful ability to influence the executive branch. Its institutional autonomy is circumscribed by presidential powers to veto and decree legislation, appoint legislators, and dissolve the legislature. It has three of the eight specified powers assessed here, namely, the powers to declare war, ratify treaties, and grant amnesty. The legislature does posses some institutional capacity.

SURVEY

1. The legislature alone, without the involvement of any other agencies, can impeach the president or replace the prime minister.

No. Presidential impeachment requires the involvement of the Supreme Court and the Constitutional Council.

Article 47
2. The President of the Republic shall bear responsibility for the actions performed while exercising his duties and only in the case of high treason may be discharged from office by Parliament. The decision to bring an accusation and conduct its investigation may be adopted by the majority of the deputies of the Majilis at the initiative of no less than one-third of the total number of its deputies. Investigation of the accusation shall be organized by the Senate and by the majority of votes of the total number of the deputies of the Senate its results are transferred for consideration at a joint session of the Parliament's Chambers. The final decision of this issue shall be adopted at a joint session of the Parliament's Chambers by the majority of no less than three-fourths of the total number of the deputies of each Chamber, provided the Supreme Court concludes the validity of the accusation and conclusion by the Constitutional Council that the established constitutional procedures were observed. The failure to arrive at a final decision within two months from the moment of the accusation shall result in the recognition that the accusation against the President of the Republic is rejected. Rejection of the accusation of the President of the Republic in perpetration of high treason at any stage shall result in premature termination of the powers of the deputies of the Majilis who initiated the consideration of this issue.
3. The issue of discharge of the President of the Republic from office may not be initiated in the period when the President is considering premature termination of the powers of the Parliament of the Republic.

2. Ministers may serve simultaneously as members of the legislature.

No. Ministers are prohibited from serving simultaneously in the legislature.

> Article 68
> 2. Members of the Government shall not have right to be deputies of a representative body.

3. The legislature has powers of summons over executive branch officials and hearings with executive branch officials testifying before the legislature or its committees are regularly held.

No. According to the constitution, the legislature has the right to hear reports on the activities of the members of government, but in practice, the power is rarely exercised.

> Article 57
> Each Chamber of the Parliament independently, without participation of the other Chamber shall:
> 6) have the right to hear reports of the members of the Government of the Republic on the issues of their activities, at the initiative of no less than one-third from the total number of the deputies of the Chambers.

4. The legislature can conduct independent investigation of the chief executive and the agencies of the executive.

No. The legislature cannot investigate the executive.

5. The legislature has effective powers of oversight over the agencies of coercion (the military, organs of law enforcement, intelligence services, and the secret police).

No. The legislature lacks effective powers of oversight over the agencies of coercion.

6. The legislature appoints the prime minister.

No. The president appoints the prime minister.

> Article 44
> 1. The President of the Republic of Kazakhstan shall:
> 3) appoint a Prime Minister of the Republic with the Parliament's consent; release him from office; determine the structure of the Government of the Republic at the proposal of the Prime Minister, appoint to and release from office its members.

> Article 53
> Parliament at a joint session of the Chambers shall:
> 5) give consent to the appointment of the Prime Minister of the Republic.

7. The legislature's approval is required to confirm the appointment of ministers; or the legislature itself appoints ministers.

No. The president appoints ministers on the proposal of the prime minister, and the appointments do not require the legislature's approval.

> Article 44
> 1. The President of the Republic of Kazakhstan shall:
> 3) appoint a Prime Minister of the Republic with the Parliament's consent; release him from office; determine the structure of the Government of the Republic at the proposal of the Prime Minister, appoint to and release from office its members.

> Article 65
> 1. The Government shall be formed by the President of the Republic of Kazakhstan according to the procedure stipulated by this Constitution.
> 2. Suggestions about the structure and composition of the Government shall be submitted to the President of the Republic of Kazakhstan by the Prime Minister of the Republic within ten days after his appointment.

8. The country lacks a presidency entirely or there is a presidency, but the president is elected by the legislature.

No. The president is directly elected.

> Article 41
> 1. The President of the Republic shall be elected by universal, equal and direct suffrage under a secret ballot for

a seven-year term in accordance with the constitutional law by the citizens of the Republic who have come of age.

9. The legislature can vote no confidence in the government.

Yes. The legislature can vote no confidence in the government.

Article 53
Parliament at a joint session of the Chambers shall:
6) hear the report of the Prime Minister on the Government's program and approve or reject the program. A second rejection of the program brought about by the majority of two-thirds of votes from the total number of deputies of each Chamber denotes a vote of no confidence in the Government. The absence of such a majority implies the approval of the Government's program;
7) express a vote of no confidence in the Government by the majority of two-thirds of votes from the total number of deputies of each Chamber at the initiative of no less than one-fifth of the total number of the Parliament's deputies and in cases established by this Constitution.

Article 61
7. In the case when of a draft of law submitted by the Government is not adopted, the Prime-Minister shall have the right to raise an issue of nonconfidence in the Government at a joint session of the Chambers. Voting on this issue shall be held not earlier than within forty-eight hours from the moment of calling for a vote of confidence. If the call for a vote of no confidence does not receive the necessary number of votes established by this Constitution, a draft of law shall be deemed adopted without voting. However, the Government may not use this right more than twice a year.

10. The legislature is immune from dissolution by the executive.

No. The president can dissolve the legislature.

Article 63
1. The President of the Republic of Kazakhstan may dissolve Parliament in cases: expressing by Parliament of a vote of no confidence in the Government, twice refusal of Parliament to give consent to the appointment of the Prime Minister, political crisis resulting from of insurmountable differences between the Chambers of Parliament or Parliament and other branches of state power.
2. The Parliament may not be dissolved in the period of a state of emergency or martial law, during the last six months of the President's term, as well as within a year after a previous dissolution.

11. Any executive initiative on legislation requires ratification or approval by the legislature before it takes effect; that is, the executive lacks decree power.

No. The president issues decrees that have the force of law.

Article 45
1. The President of the Republic of Kazakhstan, on the basis of and with the exercise of the Constitution and the laws, shall issue decrees and resolutions which are binding on the entire territory of the Republic.
2. In the case envisioned by subparagraph 4 of Article 53 of the Constitution the President of the Republic shall issue laws, and in the case envisioned by subparagraph 2 of Article 61 of the Constitution, the President of the Republic shall issue decrees having the force of laws in the Republic.

Article 53
Parliament at a joint session of the Chambers shall:
4) have the right to delegate legislative Powers for a term not exceeding one year to the President by two-thirds of the votes from the total number of deputies of each Chamber at the initiative of the President.

12. Laws passed by the legislature are veto-proof or essentially veto-proof; that is, the executive lacks veto power, or has veto power but the veto can be overridden by a majority in the legislature.

No. A two-thirds majority vote in a plenary session of the legislature is needed to override a presidential veto.

Article 53
Parliament at a joint session of the Chambers shall:
3) conduct a second round of discussion and voting on the laws or articles of the law that caused objections of the President of the Republic within a month's term from the moment the objections were presented. Nonobservance of this term denotes the acceptance of the President's objections. If Parliament by the majority of two-thirds of votes from the total number of deputies from each Chamber confirms the decision adopted earlier, the President shall sign the law within seven days. If the President's objections are not overruled, the law shall be deemed not adopted or adopted in the version proposed by the President.

13. The legislature's laws are supreme and not subject to judicial review.

No. The Constitutional Council can review the constitutionality of laws.

Article 72
1. The Constitutional Council by appeal of the President of the Republic of Kazakhstan, the chairperson of the Senate, the Chairperson of Majilis, not less than one-fifth of the total number of deputies of Parliament, the Prime Minister shall:
   2) consider the laws adopted by Parliament with respect to their compliance with the Constitution of the Republic before they are signed by the President.

14. The legislature has the right to initiate bills in all policy jurisdictions; the executive lacks gatekeeping authority.

Yes. The legislature can initiate bills in all policy jurisdictions.

15. Expenditure of funds appropriated by the legislature is mandatory; the executive lacks the power to impound funds appropriated by the legislature.

No. The president can impound funds appropriated by the legislature.

16. The legislature controls the resources that finance its own internal operation and provide for the perquisites of its own members.

Yes. The legislature enjoys financial autonomy.

17. Members of the legislature are immune from arrest and/or criminal prosecution.

Yes. Legislators are immune with the common exception for cases of *flagrante delicto*, here expressed as "being apprehended on the scene of a crime or committing grave crimes."

> Article 52
> 4. A deputy of Parliament during the term of his office may not be arrested, subject to detention, measures of administrative punishment imposed by a court of law, arraigned on a criminal charge without the consent of a respective Chamber except for the cases of being apprehended on the scene of a crime or committing grave crimes.

18. All members of the legislature are elected; the executive lacks the power to appoint any members of the legislature.

No. The president appoints seven of the forty-seven senators. All members of the *Majilis* are elected.

> Article 50
> 1. Parliament shall consist of two Chambers acting on a permanent basis: the Senate and the Majilis.
> 2. The Senate shall be composed of deputies elected in twos from each oblast, major city and the capital of the Republic of Kazakhstan, at a joint session of the deputies of all representative bodies of the respective oblast, major city and the capital of the Republic. Seven deputies of the Senate shall be appointed by the President of the Republic for the term of the Senate.
> 3. The Majilis shall consist of seventy-seven deputies. Sixty-seven deputies shall be elected in constituencies having one mandate and formed according to the administrative-territorial division of the Republic with an approximately equal number of constituents. Ten deputies shall be elected on the basis of the Party Lists according to the system of proportional representation and in the territory of a unified national constituency.

19. The legislature alone, without the involvement of any other agencies, can change the Constitution.

No. Constitutional amendments must be approved either by the president or in a popular referendum.

> Article 53
> Parliament at a joint session of the Chambers shall:
> 1) introduce amendments and make additions to the Constitution; adopt constitutional laws, introduce amendments and make additions to the Constitution at the proposal of the President of the Republic of Kazakhstan.

> Article 62
> 3. Amendments and additions to the Constitution shall be introduced by the majority of no less than three-fourths of votes from the total number of the deputies of each chamber.
> 4. Constitutional laws shall be adopted on the issues stipulated by the Constitution by the majority of no less than two-thirds of votes from the total number of the deputies of each Chamber.

> Article 91
> 1. Amendments and additions to the Constitution of the Republic of Kazakhstan may be introduced only by an all-nation referendum held by the decision of the President of the Republic made on his own initiative, at the recommendation of Parliament or the Government. The draft of amendments and additions to the Constitution shall not be submitted to an all-nation referendum if the President decides to pass it to the consideration of Parliament. In this case, Parliament's decision shall be adopted according to the procedure established by this Constitution. In case the President of the Republic refuses the proposal of the Parliament on submission of amendments and additions to the Constitution for the consideration of the Republican referendum, the Parliament has the right by majority of not less than four-fifths of votes of the total number of deputies of each Chamber of the Parliament to adopt the law on making of these amendments and additions to the Constitution. In such case the President of the Republic shall sign this law or submit it for the consideration of the Republican referendum which shall be deemed valid if more than half of the Republican citizens, possessing the right to participate in the Republican referendum, take part in it. Amendments and additions to the Constitution, which are submitted for the consideration of the Republican referendum, shall be deemed adopted, if more than half of citizens, taking part in it, vote for it.
> 2. The unitary status and territorial integrity of the Republic, the forms of government may not be changed.

> Article 92
> 1. The constitutional laws must be adopted within a year from the day of enactment of the Constitution. If the laws called constitutional in the Constitution or the acts having the force thereof have been adopted by the moment of enactment of the Constitution, they are brought into accordance with the Constitution and deemed to be the constitutional laws of the Republic of Kazakhstan.
> 2. Other laws named in the Constitution must be adopted according to the procedure and within the

terms determined by the Parliament but no later than two years after the enactment of the Constitution.

20. The legislature's approval is necessary for the declaration of war.

Yes. The legislature declares war.

> Article 53
> Parliament at a joint session of the Chambers shall:
> 8) decide issues of war and peace.

21. The legislature's approval is necessary to ratify treaties with foreign countries.

Yes. The legislature's approval is necessary to ratify international treaties.

> Article 44
> 1. The President of the Republic of Kazakhstan shall:
> 11) conduct negotiations and sign international treaties of the Republic; sign ratification instruments; receive letters of credentials and recall from diplomatic and other representatives of foreign states accredited to him.

> Article 54
> Parliament at separate sessions of the Chambers through consecutive consideration of issues first in the Majilis and then in the Senate shall:
> 7) ratify and denounce international treaties of the Republic.

22. The legislature has the power to grant amnesty.

Yes. The legislature has the power to grant amnesty.

> Article 54
> Parliament at separate sessions of the Chambers through consecutive consideration of issues first in the Majilis and then in the Senate shall:
> 6) issue acts of amnesty to citizens.

23. The legislature has the power of pardon.

No. The president has the power of pardon.

> Article 44
> 1. The President of the Republic of Kazakhstan shall:
> 15) exercise pardon of citizens.

24. The legislature reviews and has the right to reject appointments to the judiciary; or the legislature itself appoints members of the judiciary.

No. The president appoints most judges. The Senate formally has some appointment authority, but its choices are made on the proposal of the president, and in practice, the Senate automatically accepts the president's nominations.

> Article 82
> 1. The Chairperson of the Supreme Court, the Chairpersons of the Collegiums and judges of the Supreme Court of the Republic of Kazakhstan shall be elected by

the Senate at the proposal of the President of the Republic based on a recommendation of the Highest Judicial Council of the Republic.
> 2. The Chairpersons of oblast and equivalent courts, the Chairpersons of the Collegiums and judges of the oblast and equivalent courts shall be appointed by the President of the Republic at the recommendation of the Highest Judicial Court of the Republic.
> 3. The Chairperson and judges of other courts of the Republic shall be appointed by the President of the Republic at the proposal of the Minister of Justice based on a recommendation of the Qualification Collegium of Justice.
> 4. The Highest Judicial Council shall be headed by the Chairperson who is appointed by the President of the Republic and consist of the Chairperson of the Constitutional Council, the Chairperson of the Supreme Court, the Procurator General, the Minister of Justice, deputies of the Senate, judges and other persons appointed by the President of the Republic.

25. The chairman of the central bank is appointed by the legislature.

No. The president appoints the chairman of the National Bank of Kazakhstan with the legislature's approval.

> Article 44
> 1. The President of the Republic of Kazakhstan shall:
> 4) appoint the Chairperson of the National Bank of the Republic of Kazakhstan with the Parliament's consent.

> Article 53
> Parliament at a joint session of the Chambers shall:
> 5) give consent to the appointment of the ... Chairperson of the National Bank of the Republic by the President of the Republic.

26. The legislature has a substantial voice in the operation of the state-owned media.

No. The legislature lacks a substantial voice in the operation of the public media.

27. The legislature is regularly in session.

Yes. The legislature meets in ordinary session for about ten months each year.

> Article 59
> 3. Regular sessions of the Parliament shall be held once a year from the first working day of September to the last working day of June.

28. Each legislator has a personal secretary.

Yes.

29. Each legislator has at least one non-secretarial staff member with policy expertise.

No.

30. Legislators are eligible for re-election without any restriction.

Yes. There are no restrictions on re-election.

31. A seat in the legislature is an attractive enough position that legislators are generally interested in and seek re-election.

Yes.

32. The re-election of incumbent legislators is common enough that at any given time the legislature contains a significant number of highly experienced members.

Yes. Re-election rates are sufficiently high to produce a significant number of highly experienced members. Maintaining a place, however, depends largely on loyalty to President Nursultan Nazarbaev and his Fatherland Party, which holds a monopoly on seats.

NATIONAL ASSEMBLY OF KENYA (*BUNGE*)

Expert consultants: June Gachui, Nairobi Legis, David K. Leonard, Gideon Ochanda, Bjarte Tørå

Score: .31

Influence over executive (3/9)		Institutional autonomy (1/9)		Specified powers (1/8)		Institutional capacity (5/6)	
1. replace		10. no dissolution		19. amendments	X	27. sessions	X
2. serve as ministers	X	11. no decree		20. war		28. secretary	X
3. interpellate	X	12. no veto		21. treaties		29. staff	
4. investigate		13. no review		22. amnesty		30. no term limits	X
5. oversee police		14. no gatekeeping		23. pardon		31. seek re-election	X
6. appoint PM		15. no impoundment		24. judiciary		32. experience	X
7. appoint ministers		16. control resources	X	25. central bank			
8. lack president		17. immunity		26. media			
9. no confidence	X	18. all elected					

The National Assembly (*Bunge*) of Kenya was established in the 1963 constitution upon independence from Great Britain. The document called for a bicameral legislature with an elected lower house, the National Assembly, and an upper house, the Senate. In 1966 the Senate was eliminated, leaving a unicameral National Assembly. From 1968 until 1992 presidential elections were not held, and the leader of the Kenyan African National Union (KANU) served as president. During this period KANU was the sole legal party and held all seats in the legislature. In the 1992 elections for both president and the National Assembly, the ban on alternative parties was lifted. A national referendum held in 2005 rejected a proposed constitutional amendment that would have created the post of prime minister.

The National Assembly is an ineffectual body. It has modest power over the executive. Presidential dissolution, decree, veto, and gatekeeping powers undermine the legislature's institutional autonomy. The Assembly is granted only one specified power, the power to amend the constitution, and has considerable institutional capacity.

SURVEY

1. The legislature alone, without the involvement of any other agencies, can impeach the president or replace the prime minister.

No. The legislature cannot impeach the president.

Article 14
1. No criminal proceedings whatsoever shall be instituted or continued against the President while he holds

office or against any person while he is exercising the functions of the office of President.

2. No civil proceedings in which relief is claimed in respect of anything done or omitted to be done shall be instituted or continued against the President while he holds office or against any person, while he is exercising the functions of the office of President.

3. Where provision is made by law limiting the time within which proceedings of any description may be brought against any person, a period of time during which a person holds or exercises the functions of the office of President shall not be taken into account in any period of time prescribed by that law which determines whether any such proceedings as are mentioned in subsection (1.) or (2.) may be brought against that person.

2. Ministers may serve simultaneously as members of the legislature.

Yes. Ministers are selected from, and required to serve simultaneously in, the legislature.

Article 16
(1) There shall be such offices of Minister of the Government of Kenya as may be established by Parliament or, subject to any provisions made by Parliament, by the President.
(2) The President shall, subject to the provisions of any written law, appoint the Ministers from among the members of the National Assembly. Provided that, if occasion arises for making an appointment to the office of any Minister while Parliament stands dissolved, a person who was a member of the National Assembly immediately before the dissolution may be appointed to that office.

3. The legislature has powers of summons over executive branch officials and hearings with executive branch officials testifying before the legislature or its committees are regularly held.

Yes. The legislature regularly interpellates officials from the executive.

4. The legislature can conduct independent investigation of the chief executive and the agencies of the executive.

No. Parliamentary select committees have some limited power to scrutinize the executive, but cannot conduct independent investigations.

5. The legislature has effective powers of oversight over the agencies of coercion (the military, organs of law enforcement, intelligence services, and the secret police).

No. The legislature lacks effective powers of oversight over the agencies of coercion.

6. The legislature appoints the prime minister.

No. There is no prime minister.

7. The legislature's approval is required to confirm the appointment of ministers; or the legislature itself appoints ministers.

No. The president appoints ministers, and the appointments do not require the legislature's approval.

Article 16
1. There shall be such offices of Minister of the Government of Kenya as may be established by Parliament or, subject to any provisions made by Parliament, by the President.
2. The President shall, subject to the provisions of any written law, appoint the Ministers from among the members of the National Assembly:
Provided that, if occasion arises for making an appointment to the office of any Minister while Parliament stands dissolved, a person who was a member of the National Assembly immediately before the dissolution may be appointed to that office.

Article 19
1. The President may appoint Assistant Ministers from among the members of the National Assembly to assist Ministers, The President, Vice-President and Ministers in the performance of their duties:
Provided that, if occasion arises for making an appointment while Parliament stands dissolved, a person who was a member of the National Assembly immediately before the dissolution may be appointed as an Assistant Minister.

8. The country lacks a presidency entirely or there is a presidency, but the president is elected by the legislature.

No. The president is directly elected.

Article 5
(1) The President shall be elected in accordance with this Chapter and, subject thereto, with any Act of Parliament regulating the election of a President.

9. The legislature can vote no confidence in the government.

Yes. The legislature can vote no confidence in the government.

Article 59
(3) If the National Assembly passes a resolution which is supported by the votes of a majority of all the members of the Assembly (excluding the *ex officio* members), and of which not less than seven days' notice has been given in accordance with the standing orders of the Assembly, declaring that it has no confidence in the Government of Kenya, and the President does not within three days of the passing of that resolution either resign from his office or dissolve Parliament, Parliament shall stand dissolved on the fourth day following the day on which that resolution was passed.

10. The legislature is immune from dissolution by the executive.

No. The president can dissolve the legislature.

> Article 59
> (2) The President may at any time dissolve Parliament.

11. Any executive initiative on legislation requires ratification or approval by the legislature before it takes effect; that is, the executive lacks decree power.

Yes. The executive lacks decree power.

12. Laws passed by the legislature are veto-proof or essentially veto-proof; that is, the executive lacks veto power, or has veto power but the veto can be overridden by a majority in the legislature.

No. A 65 percent majority is required to override a presidential veto.

> Article 46
> (1) Subject to this Constitution, the legislative power of Parliament shall be exercisable by Bills passed by the National Assembly.
> (2) When a Bill has been passed by the National Assembly, it shall be presented to the President for his assent.
> (3) The President shall, within twenty-one days after the Bill has been presented to him for assent under subsection (2), signify to the Speaker that he assents to the Bill or refuses to assent to the Bill.
> (4) Where the President refuses to assent to a Bill he shall, within fourteen days of the refusal, submit a memorandum to the Speaker indicating the specific provisions of the Bill which in his opinion should be reconsidered by the National Assembly including his recommendations for amendments.
> (5) The National Assembly shall reconsider a Bill referred to it by the President taking into account the comments of the President and shall either –
> (a) approve the recommendations proposed by the President with or without amendment and resubmit the Bill to the President for assent; or
> (b) refuse to accept the recommendations and approve the Bill in its original form by a resolution in that behalf supported by votes of not less than sixty-five per cent of all the Members of the National Assembly (excluding ex officio members) in which case the President shall assent to the Bill within fourteen days of the passing of the resolution.

13. The legislature's laws are supreme and not subject to judicial review.

No. The High Court can review the constitutionality of laws.

> Article 67
> (1) Where a question as to the interpretation of this Constitution arises in proceedings in a subordinate court and the court is of the opinion that the question involves a substantial question of law, the court may, and shall if a party to the proceedings so requests, refer the question to the High Court.

14. The legislature has the right to initiate bills in all policy jurisdictions; the executive lacks gatekeeping authority.

No. The legislature is prohibited from introducing legislation related to taxation, public expenditures, and government debt.

> Article 48
> Except upon the recommendation of the President signified by a Minister, the National Assembly shall not
> –
> (*a*) proceed upon a Bill (including an amendment to a Bill) that, in the opinion of the person presiding, makes provision for any of the following purposes –
>   (i) the imposition of taxation or the alteration of taxation otherwise than by reduction; or
>   (ii) the imposition of a charge on the Consolidated Fund or any other fund of the Government of Kenya or the alteration of any such charge otherwise than by reduction; or
>   (iii) the payment, issue or withdrawal from the Consolidated Fund or any other fund of the Government of Kenya of moneys not charged upon the fund or an increase in the amount of the payment, issue or withdrawal; or
>   (iv) the composition or remission of a debt due to the Government of Kenya; or
> (*b*) proceed upon a motion (including an amendment to a motion) the effect of which, in the opinion of the person presiding, would be to make provision for any of those purposes.

15. Expenditure of funds appropriated by the legislature is mandatory; the executive lacks the power to impound funds appropriated by the legislature.

No. The executive can impound funds appropriated by the legislature.

16. The legislature controls the resources that finance its own internal operation and provide for the perquisites of its own members.

Yes. The legislature enjoys financial autonomy.

17. Members of the legislature are immune from arrest and/or criminal prosecution.

No. According to the constitution, the legislature has the power to establish immunity. In practice, legislators are subject to arrest beyond the grounds of parliament for common crimes.

> Article 57
> Without prejudice to the powers conferred by section 56, Parliament may, for the purpose of the orderly and effective discharge of the business of the National Assembly, provide for the powers, privileges and immunities of the Assembly and its committees and members.

18. All members of the legislature are elected; the executive lacks the power to appoint any members of the legislature.

No. The president appoints twelve of the 224 members of the National Assembly to represent "special interests."

Article 31
Subject to this Constitution, the National Assembly shall consist of elected members elected in accordance with section 32, nominated members appointed in accordance with section 33 and the ex officio members.

Article 33
(1) Subject to this section, there shall be twelve nominated members of the National Assembly appointed by the President following a general election, to represent special interests.

19. The legislature alone, without the involvement of any other agencies, can change the Constitution.

Yes. The legislature can change the constitution in multiple readings by a 65 percent majority vote.

Article 47
(1) Subject to this section, Parliament may alter this Constitution.
(2) A Bill for an Act of Parliament to alter this Constitution shall not be passed by the National Assembly unless it has been supported on the second and third readings by the votes of not less than sixty-five per cent of all the members of the Assembly (excluding the ex officio members).
(3) If, on the taking of a vote for the purposes of subsection (2), the Bill is supported by a majority of the members of the Assembly voting but not by the number of votes required by that subsection, and the Bill is not opposed by thirty-five per cent of all the members of the Assembly or more, then, subject to such limitations and conditions as may be prescribed by the standing orders of the Assembly, a further vote may be taken.
(4) When a Bill for an Act of Parliament to alter this Constitution has been introduced into the National Assembly, no alterations shall be made in it before it is presented to the President for his assent, except alterations which are certified by the Speaker to be necessary because of the time that has elapsed since the Bill was first introduced into the Assembly.
(5) A certificate of the Speaker under subsection (4) shall be conclusive as regards proceedings in the Assembly, and shall not be questioned in any court.
(6) In this section –
(a) references to this Constitution are references to this Constitution as from time to time amended; and
(b) references to the alteration of this Constitution are references to the amendment, modification or reenactment, with or without amendment or modification, of any provision of this Constitution, the suspension or repeal of that provision and the making of a different provision in the place of that provision.

20. The legislature's approval is necessary for the declaration of war.

No. The president can declare war without the legislature's approval.

21. The legislature's approval is necessary to ratify treaties with foreign countries.

No. The legislature's approval is not necessary to ratify international treaties.

22. The legislature has the power to grant amnesty.

No. Pardon and amnesty are not treated separately, and the legislature lacks the power to grant amnesty. See item 23.

23. The legislature has the power of pardon.

No. The president has the power of pardon.

Article 27
The President may:
(a) grant to a person convicted of an offence a pardon, either free or subject to lawful conditions;
(b) grant to a person a respite, either indefinite or for a specified period, of the execution of a punishment imposed on that person for an offence;
(c) substitute a less severe form of punishment for a punishment imposed on a person for an offence;
(d) remit the whole or part of a punishment imposed on a person for an offence or of a penalty or forfeiture otherwise due to the Republic on account of an offence; and
(e) remove in whole or in part the non-qualification or the disqualification of a person, arising out of or in consequence of the report of an election court under the provisions of the National Assembly and Presidential Elections Act, from registration as an elector on a register of electors or from nomination for election as an elected member of the National Assembly.

24. The legislature reviews and has the right to reject appointments to the judiciary; or the legislature itself appoints members of the judiciary.

No. The president appoints the chief justice and other judges of the High Court, and the appointments do not require the legislature's approval.

Article 61
(1) The Chief Justice [of the High Court] shall be appointed by the President.
(2) The puisne judges [of the High Court] shall be appointed by the President acting in accordance with the advice of the Judicial Service Commission.

25. The chairman of the central bank is appointed by the legislature.

No. The president appoints the governor of the Central Bank of Kenya.

26. The legislature has a substantial voice in the operation of the state-owned media.

No. The legislature lacks a substantial voice in the operation of the public media.

27. The legislature is regularly in session.

Yes. The legislature meets regularly in ordinary session.

> Article 58
> (1) Subject to this section, each session of Parliament shall be held at such place within Kenya and shall commence at such time as the President may appoint.
> (2) There shall be a session of Parliament at least once in every year, so that a period of twelve months shall not intervene between the last sitting of the National Assembly in one session and the first sitting thereof in the next session.

28. Each legislator has a personal secretary.

Yes.

29. Each legislator has at least one non-secretarial staff member with policy expertise.

No.

30. Legislators are eligible for re-election without any restriction.

Yes. There are no restrictions on re-election.

31. A seat in the legislature is an attractive enough position that legislators are generally interested in and seek re-election.

Yes.

32. The re-election of incumbent legislators is common enough that at any given time the legislature contains a significant number of highly experienced members.

Yes. Although there was considerable electoral volatility across the 1992, 1997, and 2002 National Assembly elections, re-election rates have been sufficiently high to produce a significant number of highly experienced members.

SUPREME PEOPLE'S ASSEMBLY OF THE DEMOCRATIC PEOPLE'S REPUBLIC OF KOREA (NORTH KOREA) (*CH'OEGO INMIN HOEUI*)

Expert consultants: Peter Beck, Hong Yung Lee

Score: .13

Influence over executive (0/9)	Institutional autonomy (1/9)		Specified powers (0/8)	Institutional capacity (3/6)	
1. replace	10. no dissolution	X	19. amendments	27. sessions	
2. serve as ministers	11. no decree		20. war	28. secretary	
3. interpellate	12. no veto		21. treaties	29. staff	
4. investigate	13. no review		22. amnesty	30. no term limits	X
5. oversee police	14. no gatekeeping		23. pardon	31. seek re-election	X
6. appoint PM	15. no impoundment		24. judiciary	32. experience	X
7. appoint ministers	16. control resources		25. central bank		
8. lack president	17. immunity		26. media		
9. no confidence	18. all elected				

The Supreme People's Assembly (*Ch'oego Inmin Hoeui*) of the Democratic People's Republic of Korea was established in the 1948 constitution following the division of the Korean peninsula at the end of World War II. The document called for a unicameral legislature paired with a cabinet led by a premier. A subset of the Supreme People's Assembly (SPA), the SPA Presidium, meets when the larger SPA is not in session, which is all but a few days a year. Despite the formal state institutions, Kim Il Sung, the country's first premier and head of the dominant political party, the Korean Worker's Party (KWP), ruled as an absolute dictator. Following a constitutional amendment in 1972, Kim Il Sung assumed the newly created position of president. Upon his death in 1994, he was replaced as the head of state by his son, Kim Jong Il. The elder Kim was named "eternal president," and the younger Kim assumed the title of "Chairman of the National Defense Commission."

North Korea is a single-man dictatorship, and the legislature is essentially defunct. It lacks any ability to influence the executive. Its formal powers to appoint members of the executive branch are illusory. The legislature has negligible institutional autonomy. Its membership is completely selected by Kim Jong Il and the ruling KWP, and it merely rubber-stamps legislation decreed by the dictator. The legislature exercises none of the specified powers measured in this survey. It has a bit of institutional capacity.

SURVEY

1. The legislature alone, without the involvement of any other agencies, can impeach the president or replace the prime minister.

No. The legislature cannot remove the Chairman of the National Defense Commission, the highest executive position in the country; nor can it remove the premier (i.e., head) of the cabinet.

2. Ministers may serve simultaneously as members of the legislature.

No. Members of the Supreme People's Assembly cannot serve simultaneously in the cabinet and the National Defense Commission.

3. The legislature has powers of summons over executive branch officials and hearings with executive branch officials testifying before the legislature or its committees are regularly held.

No. The legislature cannot question officials from the executive.

4. The legislature can conduct independent investigation of the chief executive and the agencies of the executive.

No. The legislature cannot investigate the executive.

5. The legislature has effective powers of oversight over the agencies of coercion (the military, organs of law enforcement, intelligence services, and the secret police).

No. Formally, the NDC "is accountable to the SPA," but in practice, the legislature lacks effective powers of oversight over the agencies of coercion.

Article 15
The NDC is accountable to the SPA.

6. The legislature appoints the prime minister.

No. Formally, the legislature has the power to elect the prime minister (the premier of the cabinet), but in practice, the sole candidate for the post is selected by Kim Jong Il.

Article 91
The SPA has the authority to:
9. elect or transfer the Premier of the Cabinet.

7. The legislature's approval is required to confirm the appointment of ministers; or the legislature itself appoints ministers.

No. Formally, the legislature appoints the members of the cabinet on the recommendation of the premier. In practice, the legislature merely rubber-stamps the candidates selected by Kim Jong Il.

Article 91
The SPA has the authority to:
10. appoint the vice premiers of the Cabinet, chairmen of commissions, ministers and other members of the Cabinet according to the recommendation of the Premier of the Cabinet.

8. The country lacks a presidency entirely or there is a presidency, but the president is elected by the legislature.

No. Formally, the legislature elects the chairman of the National Defense Commission, the highest executive post, but in practice, Kim Jong Il, the current chairman of the National Defense Commission, inherited the position of head of state from his father, Kim Il Sung.

Article 91
The SPA has the authority to:
5. elect or transfer the Chairman of the DPRK National Defense Commission.

9. The legislature can vote no confidence in the government.

No. The legislature cannot vote no confidence in the government.

10. The legislature is immune from dissolution by the executive.

Yes. There is no institutionalized mechanism for dissolving the legislature.

11. Any executive initiative on legislation requires ratification or approval by the legislature before it takes effect; that is, the executive lacks decree power.

No. Formally, the executive lacks decree power, but in practice, Kim Jong Il issues decrees that have the force of law.

Article 114
The SPA Presidium issues decrees, decisions and directions.

Article 97
The SPA adopts laws and decisions.
Laws and decisions of the SPA are adopted when more than half of the deputies attending signify approval by a show of hands.

12. Laws passed by the legislature are veto-proof or essentially veto-proof; that is, the executive lacks veto power, or has veto power but the veto can be overridden by a majority in the legislature.

No. Formally, there is no provision for veto, but in practice, Kim Jong Il could veto legislation passed by the SPA and the SPA would have no recourse to override.

13. The legislature's laws are supreme and not subject to judicial review.

No. Formally, there is no judicial review and the legislature's laws are supreme, but in practice, the laws are in no respect the products of the Supreme People's Assembly. Rather, they are the products of the decisions of the National Defense Commission.

Article 110
The SPA Presidium has the duties and authority to
4. interpret the Constitution, departmental laws and regulations in force.
6. abolish State organs' decisions which violate the Constitution, SPA's laws and decisions, NDC's decisions and orders and the SPA Presidium's decrees, decisions and directions, and suspend the implementation of unwarranted decisions by a local people's assembly.

14. The legislature has the right to initiate bills in all policy jurisdictions; the executive lacks gatekeeping authority.

No. Formally, the legislature has the right to initiate bills in all policy jurisdictions, but in practice, Kim Jong Il possesses absolute gatekeeping authority.

15. Expenditure of funds appropriated by the legislature is mandatory; the executive lacks the power to impound funds appropriated by the legislature.

No. The executive can impound funds appropriated by the legislature.

16. The legislature controls the resources that finance its own internal operation and provide for the perquisites of its own members.

No. The legislature depends on the executive for the resources that finance its own operation.

17. Members of the legislature are immune from arrest and/or criminal prosecution.

No. Formally, legislators are immune from arrest with the common exception for cases of *flagrante*

delicto, here expressed as "flagrant offence." In practice, legislators can be arrested and worse if they fall out of favor with Kim Jong Il.

Article 99
Deputies to the SPA are guaranteed inviolability as such. No deputy to the SPA can be arrested or punished without the consent of the SPA or, when it is not in session, without the consent of the SPA Presidium, except for a flagrant offence.

18. All members of the legislature are elected; the executive lacks the power to appoint any members of the legislature.

No. Formally, all members of the legislature are elected, but in practice, the ruling party chooses a list of candidates who are elected without opposition.

Article 6
The organs of State power at all levels, from the county People's Assembly to the SPA, are elected on the principle of universal, equal and direct suffrage by secret ballot.

Article 89
The SPA is composed of deputies elected on the principle of universal, equal and direct suffrage by secret ballot.

19. The legislature alone, without the involvement of any other agencies, can change the Constitution.

No. Formally, the legislature can amend the constitution, but in practice, constitutional changes are decided upon by Kim Jong Il and the KWP.

Article 91
The SPA has the authority to:
1. amend and supplement the Constitution.

20. The legislature's approval is necessary for the declaration of war.

No. The NDC can declare war without need for the legislature's approval.

Article 13
The NDC has the duties and authority to:
5. proclaim a state of war and orders for mobilization.

21. The legislature's approval is necessary to ratify treaties with foreign countries.

No. Formally, the legislature must ratify international treaties, but in practice, Kim Jong Il can conclude treaties and the legislature's approval is not needed.

Article 91
The SPA has the authority to:
17. decide on the ratification or abrogation of treaties submitted to the SPA.

Article 110
The SPA Presidium has the duties and authority to
14. ratify or abrogate treaties concluded with other countries.

22. The legislature has the power to grant amnesty.

No. Formally, the legislature has the power to grant amnesty, but in practice, Kim Jong Il alone has the power to grant amnesty.

Article 110
The SPA Presidium has the duties and authority to
17. exercise the right to grant general amnesties or special pardon.

23. The legislature has the power of pardon.

No. Formally, the legislature has the power of pardon, but in practice, Kim Jong Il alone has the power of pardon.

Article 110
The SPA Presidium has the duties and authority to
17. exercise the right to grant general amnesties or special pardon.

24. The legislature reviews and has the right to reject appointments to the judiciary; or the legislature itself appoints members of the judiciary.

No. Formally, the legislature elects the chief justice and judges of the Central Court, but in practice, judges are selected by Kim Jong Il and the hegemonic party.

Article 91
The SPA has the authority to
12. elect or transfer the Chief Justice.

Article 110
The SPA Presidium has the duties and authority to
13. elect or transfer judges of the Central Court and people 's assessors.

Article 155
The Central Court appoints and removes the director and judges of the Special Court.

25. The chairman of the central bank is appointed by the legislature.

No. Kim Jong Il appoints the chairman of the Central Bank of the DPRK.

26. The legislature has a substantial voice in the operation of the state-owned media.

No. The legislature lacks a substantial voice in the operation of the public media.

27. The legislature is regularly in session.

No. Every year the legislature meets in two ordinary sessions, each lasting a few days.

Article 92
The SPA holds regular and extraordinary sessions. Regular sessions are convened once or twice a year by the SPA Presidium. Extraordinary sessions are convened when the SPA Presidium deems them necessary or at the request of a minimum of one-third of the total number of deputies.

28. Each legislator has a personal secretary.

No.

29. Each legislator has at least one non-secretarial staff member with policy expertise.

No.

30. Legislators are eligible for re-election without any restriction.

Yes. Legislators who remain in the good graces of Kim Jung Il face no formal restrictions on re-election.

31. A seat in the legislature is an attractive enough position that legislators are generally interested in and seek re-election.

Yes.

32. The re-election of incumbent legislators is common enough that at any given time the legislature contains a significant number of highly experienced members.

Yes. Loyal party cadres are regularly re-elected, thereby forming a body of highly experienced members.

NATIONAL ASSEMBLY OF THE REPUBLIC OF KOREA (SOUTH KOREA) (*KUKHOE*)

Expert consultants: Charles K. Armstrong, Peter Gey, David C. Kang, Samuel S. Kim, Kenji Kushida, Seong-ho Lim, Chan Wook Park

Score: .59

Influence over executive (4/9)		Institutional autonomy (6/9)		Specified powers (3/8)		Institutional capacity (6/6)	
1. replace		10. no dissolution	X	19. amendments		27. sessions	X
2. serve as ministers	X	11. no decree	X	20. war	X	28. secretary	X
3. interpellate	X	12. no veto		21. treaties	X	29. staff	X
4. investigate	X	13. no review		22. amnesty		30. no term limits	X
5. oversee police	X	14. no gatekeeping	X	23. pardon		31. seek re-election	X
6. appoint PM		15. no impoundment	X	24. judiciary	X	32. experience	X
7. appoint ministers		16. control resources	X	25. central bank			
8. lack president		17. immunity		26. media			
9. no confidence		18. all elected	X				

The National Assembly (*Kukhoe*) of the Republic of Korea was established in the 1948 constitution, which called for a unicameral body with a president elected by the assembly. For the next forty years, the legislature sat on the sidelines and the military ruled.

In 1987 a major set of changes in the constitution ushered in the current, more open political system, the Sixth Republic of South Korea. The amendments greatly expanded the power of the legislature. The legislature gained the right to remove the prime minister, or any other minister, from office with a majority vote, and the president lost the power to dissolve the legislature. The length of the ordinary sessions of the National Assembly was lengthened. The legislature gained powers of investigation into the operations of the executive branch and the power to review and reject the president's appointments to the Supreme Court.

The legislature is a major force in national politics. It has substantial influence over the executive branch and a fair amount of institutional autonomy. It enjoys some specified powers and prerogatives and scores perfectly in terms of institutional capacity.

SURVEY

1. The legislature alone, without the involvement of any other agencies, can impeach the president or replace the prime minister.

No. Presidential impeachment requires the involvement of the Constitutional Court. The legislature can remove the prime minister from office by a majority vote of its total membership.

Article 63
(1) The National Assembly may pass a recommendation for the removal of the Prime Minister or a State Council member from office.
(2) A recommendation for removal as referred to in Paragraph (1) may be introduced by one third or more of the total members of the National Assembly, and passed with the concurrent vote of a majority of the total members of the National Assembly.

Article 65
(1) In case the President [has] violated the Constitution or other laws in the performance of official duties, the National Assembly may pass motions for ... impeachment.
(2) A motion for impeachment prescribed in Paragraph (1) may be proposed by one-third or more of the total members of the National Assembly, and requires a concurrent vote of a majority of the total members of the

National Assembly for passage: Provided, that a motion for the impeachment of the President shall be proposed by a majority of the total members of the National Assembly and approved by two-thirds or more of the total members of the National Assembly.

(3) Any person against whom a motion for impeachment has been passed is suspended from exercising his power until the impeachment has been adjudicated.

(4) A decision on impeachment does not extend further than removal from public office. However, it does not exempt the person impeached from civil or criminal liability.

Article 111
(1) The Constitutional Court is competent to adjudicate the following matters:
    2) Impeachment.

2. Ministers may serve simultaneously as members of the legislature.

Yes. Legislators may serve simultaneously in ministerial positions.

3. The legislature has powers of summons over executive branch officials and hearings with executive branch officials testifying before the legislature or its committees are regularly held.

Yes. The legislature regularly interpellates officials from the executive.

Article 62
(1) The Prime Minister, members of the State Council, or government delegates may attend meetings of the National Assembly or its committees and report on the state administration or deliver opinions and answer questions.
(2) When requested by the National Assembly or its committees, the Prime Minister, members of the State Council, or government delegates have to attend any meeting of the National Assembly and answer questions. If the Prime Minister or State Council members are requested to attend, the Prime Minister or State Council members may have State Council members or government delegates attend any meeting of the National Assembly and answer questions.

4. The legislature can conduct independent investigation of the chief executive and the agencies of the executive.

Yes. The legislature can investigate the executive.

Article 61
(1) The National Assembly may inspect affairs of state or investigate specific matters of state affairs, and may demand the production of documents directly related thereto, the appearance of a witness in person, and the furnishing of testimony or statements of opinion.
(2) The procedures and other necessary matters concerning the inspection and investigation of state administration are determined by law.

5. The legislature has effective powers of oversight over the agencies of coercion (the military, organs of law enforcement, intelligence services, and the secret police).

Yes. The legislature has effective powers of oversight over the agencies of coercion.

6. The legislature appoints the prime minister.

No. The president appoints the prime minister with the consent of the National Assembly.

Article 86
(1) The Prime Minister is appointed by the President with the consent of the National Assembly.

7. The legislature's approval is required to confirm the appointment of ministers; or the legislature itself appoints ministers.

No. The president appoints ministers on the recommendation of the prime minister, and the appointments do not require the legislature's approval.

Article 87
(1) The members of the State Council are appointed by the President on the recommendation of the Prime Minister.

8. The country lacks a presidency entirely or there is a presidency, but the president is elected by the legislature.

No. The president is directly elected.

Article 67
(1) The President is elected by universal, equal, direct, and secret ballot by the people.

9. The legislature can vote no confidence in the government.

No. The legislature can vote to remove the prime minister and other individual ministers from office, but cannot vote no confidence in the government as a whole.

Article 63
(1) The National Assembly may pass a recommendation for the removal of the Prime Minister or a State Council member from office.
(2) A recommendation for removal as referred to in Paragraph (1) may be introduced by one third or more of the total members of the National Assembly, and passed with the concurrent vote of a majority of the total members of the National Assembly.

10. The legislature is immune from dissolution by the executive.

Yes. The legislature is immune from dissolution.

11. Any executive initiative on legislation requires ratification or approval by the legislature before it takes effect; that is, the executive lacks decree power.

Yes. The executive lacks decree power. The president can issue decrees only when explicitly authorized to do so by the legislature.

Article 75
The President may issue presidential decrees concerning matters delegated to him by law with the scope specifically defined and also matters necessary to enforce laws.

12. Laws passed by the legislature are veto-proof or essentially veto-proof; that is, the executive lacks veto power, or has veto power but the veto can be overridden by a majority in the legislature.

No. A two-thirds majority vote is required to override a presidential veto.

Article 53
(1) Each bill passed by the National Assembly shall be sent to the Executive, and the President shall promulgate it within fifteen days.
(2) In case of objection to the bill, the President may, within the period referred to in Paragraph (1), return it to the National Assembly with written explanation of his objection, and request it be reconsidered. The President may do the same during adjournment of the National Assembly.
(3) The President may not request the National Assembly to reconsider the bill in part, or with proposed amendments.
(4) In case there is a request for reconsideration of a bill, the National Assembly reconsiders it, and if the National Assembly repasses the bill in the original form with the attendance of more than one half of the total members, and with a concurrent vote of two-thirds or more of the members present, it becomes law.

13. The legislature's laws are supreme and not subject to judicial review.

No. The courts can review the constitutionality of laws.

Article 107
(1) When the constitutionality of a law is at issue in trial, the court requests a decision of the Constitutional Court, and judges according to the decision thereof.
(2) The Supreme Court has the power to make a final review of the constitutionality or legality of administrative decrees, regulations or actions, when their constitutionality or legality is at issue in a trial.
(3) Administrative appeals may be conducted as a procedure prior to a judicial trial. The procedure of administrative appeals are determined by law and are in conformity with the principles of judicial procedures.

14. The legislature has the right to initiate bills in all policy jurisdictions; the executive lacks gatekeeping authority.

Yes. The legislature can initiate bills in all policy jurisdictions.

15. Expenditure of funds appropriated by the legislature is mandatory; the executive lacks the power to impound funds appropriated by the legislature.

Yes. The executive lacks the power to impound funds appropriated by the legislature.

16. The legislature controls the resources that finance its own internal operation and provide for the perquisites of its own members.

Yes. The legislature enjoys financial autonomy.

17. Members of the legislature are immune from arrest and/or criminal prosecution.

No. Legislators are immune only while the legislature is in session.

Article 44
(1) During the sessions of the National Assembly, no member of the National Assembly may be arrested or detained without the consent of the National Assembly except in case of *flagrante delicto*.
(2) In case of apprehension or detention of a member of the National Assembly prior to the opening of a session, such member must be released during the session upon the request of the National Assembly, except in case of *flagrante delicto*.

18. All members of the legislature are elected; the executive lacks the power to appoint any members of the legislature.

Yes. All members of the legislature are elected.

Article 41
(1) The National Assembly is composed of members elected by universal, equal, direct, and secret ballot by the citizens.
(2) The number of members of the National Assembly is determined by law, but the number may not be less than 200.
(3) The constituencies of members of the National Assembly, proportional representation, and other matters pertaining to National Assembly elections are determined by law.

19. The legislature alone, without the involvement of any other agencies, can change the Constitution.

No. Constitutional amendments require approval in a popular referendum.

Article 128
(1) A proposal to amend the Constitution can be introduced either by a majority of the total members of the National Assembly or by the President.
(2) Amendments to the Constitution for the extension of the term of office of the President or for a change allowing for the re-election of the President are not

effective for the President in office at the time of the proposal for such amendments to the Constitution.

Article 130

(1) The National Assembly decides upon the proposed amendments within sixty days of the public announcement, and passage by the National Assembly requires the concurrent vote of two-thirds or more of the total members of the National Assembly.

(2) The proposed amendments to the Constitution are submitted to a national referendum not later than thirty days after passage by the National Assembly, and are confirmed by more than one half of all votes cast by more than one half of voters eligible to vote in elections for members of the National Assembly.

(3) When the proposed amendments to the Constitution receive the concurrence prescribed in Paragraph (2), the amendments to the Constitution is finalized, and the President promulgates it without delay.

20. The legislature's approval is necessary for the declaration of war.

Yes. The legislature's approval is necessary for presidential war declarations.

Article 60

(2) The National Assembly also has the right to consent to the declaration of war, the dispatch of armed forces to foreign states, and the stationing of alien forces in the territory of the Republic of Korea.

Article 73

The President concludes and ratifies treaties; accredits, receives, or dispatches diplomatic envoys; and declares war and concludes peace.

Article 89

The following matters are referred to the State Council for deliberation:

(1) Basic plans for state affairs, and general policies of the Executive;

(2) Declaration of war, conclusion of peace, and other important matters pertaining to foreign policy.

21. The legislature's approval is necessary to ratify treaties with foreign countries.

Yes. The legislature's approval is necessary to ratify international treaties on most major issues.

Article 60

(1) The National Assembly has the right to consent to the conclusion and ratification of

treaties pertaining to mutual assistance or mutual security; treaties concerning important international organizations; treaties of friendship, trade and navigation; treaties pertaining to any restriction in sovereignty; peace treaties; treaties which will burden the State or people with an important financial obligation; and treaties related to legislative matters.

Article 73

The President concludes and ratifies treaties; accredits, receives, or dispatches diplomatic envoys; and declares war and concludes peace.

22. The legislature has the power to grant amnesty.

No. The president grants amnesty with the consent of the National Assembly.

Article 79

(1) The President may grant amnesty, commutation and restoration of rights under the conditions as prescribed by law.

(2) The President needs the consent of the National Assembly in granting a general amnesty.

(3) Matters pertaining to amnesty, commutation and restoration of rights are determined by law.

Article 89

The following matters are referred to the State Council for deliberation:

9) Granting of amnesty, commutation, and restoration of rights.

23. The legislature has the power of pardon.

No. The president has the power of pardon, here expressed as "commutation and restoration of rights."

Article 79

(1) The President may grant amnesty, commutation and restoration of rights under the conditions as prescribed by law.

(2) The President needs the consent of the National Assembly in granting a general amnesty.

(3) Matters pertaining to amnesty, commutation and restoration of rights are determined by law.

Article 89

The following matters are referred to the State Council for deliberation:

9) Granting of amnesty, commutation, and restoration of rights.

24. The legislature reviews and has the right to reject appointments to the judiciary; or the legislature itself appoints members of the judiciary.

Yes. The legislature's consent is needed for the president's appointments to the Supreme Court.

Article 104

(1) The Chief Justice of the Supreme Court is appointed by the President with the consent of the National Assembly.

(2) The Supreme Court Justices are appointed by the President on the recommendation of the Chief Justice and with the consent of the National Assembly.

(3) Judges other than the Chief Justice and the Supreme Court Justices are appointed by the Chief Justice with the consent of the Conference of Supreme Court Justices.

25. The chairman of the central bank is appointed by the legislature.

No. The president appoints the governor of the Bank of Korea.

26. The legislature has a substantial voice in the operation of the state-owned media.

No. The legislature lacks a substantial voice in the operation of the public media.

27. The legislature is regularly in session.

Yes. Although the constitution stipulates that the legislature must meet for no more than 100 days each year in ordinary session, the legislature is normally in session for over six months each year.

> Article 47
> (1) A regular session of the National Assembly is convened once every year under the conditions prescribed by law, and extraordinary sessions of the National Assembly can be convened upon the request of the President or at least one-fourth of the members.
> (2) The period of regular sessions cannot exceed a hundred days, and that of extraordinary sessions, thirty days.
> (3) If the President requests the convening of an extraordinary session, the period of the session and the reasons for the request must be clearly specified.

28. Each legislator has a personal secretary.

Yes.

29. Each legislator has at least one non-secretarial staff member with policy expertise.

Yes.

30. Legislators are eligible for re-election without any restriction.

Yes. There are no restrictions on re-election.

31. A seat in the legislature is an attractive enough position that legislators are generally interested in and seek re-election.

Yes.

32. The re-election of incumbent legislators is common enough that at any given time the legislature contains a significant number of highly experienced members.

Yes. Re-election rates are sufficiently high to produce a significant number of highly experienced members.

NATIONAL ASSEMBLY OF KUWAIT (*MAJILIS AL-UMMA*)

Expert consultants: Essa Al-Ghazali, F. Gregory Gause, Michael Herb, Jacqueline S. Ismael, Pete W. Moore

Score: .38

Influence over executive (3/9)		Institutional autonomy (2/9)		Specified powers (2/8)		Institutional capacity (5/6)	
1. replace		10. no dissolution		19. amendments		27. sessions	X
2. serve as ministers	X	11. no decree		20. war		28. secretary	X
3. interpellate	X	12. no veto		21. treaties	X	29. staff	
4. investigate		13. no review		22. amnesty		30. no term limits	X
5. oversee police		14. no gatekeeping	X	23. pardon		31. seek re-election	X
6. appoint PM		15. no impoundment		24. judiciary		32. experience	X
7. appoint ministers		16. control resources	X	25. central bank			
8. lack president	X	17. immunity		26. media	X		
9. no confidence		18. all elected					

The National Assembly (*Majilis al-Umma*) of Kuwait partakes of the heritage of the *Majilis* movement of 1938, when the people of Kuwait elected a legislative assembly that met for over six months before the emir dispersed it. The post- independence constitution of 1962 inaugurated the National Assembly in its current form. The unicameral body consists of both elected and appointed members. The emir has the right to dissolve the legislature at will, and emirs have frequently invoked this power; the legislature was suspended during 1976–81 and 1986–92.

The legislature can influence the executive branch through powers of interpellation, and ministers are drawn in part from members of parliament. Its own institutional autonomy is limited, however, by the emir's powers to decree and veto legislation, to appoint legislators, and to dissolve the legislature. The emir, rather than the legislature, also exercises most of the specified powers and prerogatives – although, notably, the legislature's approval is necessary to ratify international treaties, and the legislature has a voice in the operation of the state-controlled media. The legislature has appreciable institutional capacity, receiving affirmative answers for five of the six measures of capacity scored in this survey.

SURVEY

1. The legislature alone, without the involvement of any other agencies, can impeach the president or replace the prime minister.

No. The legislature cannot impeach the emir. Only the emir can remove the prime minister.

Article 102

(1) The Prime Minister does not hold any portfolio; nor shall the question of confidence in him be raised before the National Assembly.

(2) Nevertheless, if the National Assembly decides, in the manner specified in the preceding Article, that it cannot co-operate with the Prime Minister, the matter is submitted to the Head of State. In such a case, the Emir may either relieve the Prime Minister of office and appoint a new Cabinet or dissolve the National Assembly.

2. Ministers may serve simultaneously as members of the legislature.

Yes. Ministers are required to serve simultaneously in the legislature. Ministers appointed from outside the legislature's ranks automatically become ex-officio members of the National Assembly.

Article 56

(2) Ministers are appointed from amongst the members of the National Assembly and from others.

3. The legislature has powers of summons over executive branch officials and hearings with executive branch officials testifying before the legislature or its committees are regularly held.

Yes. The legislature regularly interpellates officials from the executive.

Article 99

Every member of the National Assembly may put to the Prime Minister and to Ministers questions with a view to clarifying matters falling within their competence. The questioner alone has the right to comment once upon the answer.

Article 100

(1) Every member of the National Assembly may address to the Prime Minister and to Ministers interpellations with regard to matters falling within their competence.

(2) The debate on such an interpellation shall not take place until at least eight days have elapsed after its presentation, except in case of urgency and with the consent of the Minister concerned.

(3) Subject to the provisions of Articles 101 and 102, an interpellation may lead to the question of no-confidence being put to the Assembly.

4. The legislature can conduct independent investigation of the chief executive and the agencies of the executive.

No. The legislature is vested with the right to investigate ministers, but it cannot investigate the emir.

Article 114

The National Assembly at all times has the right to set up committees of inquiry or to delegate one or more of its members to investigate any matter within its competence. Ministers and all Government officials must produce testimonials, documents, and statements requested from them.

5. The legislature has effective powers of oversight over the agencies of coercion (the military, organs of law enforcement, intelligence services, and the secret police).

No. The legislature lacks effective powers of oversight over the agencies of coercion.

6. The legislature appoints the prime minister.

No. The emir appoints the prime minister.

Article 56

(1) The Emir, after the traditional consultations, appoints the Prime Minister and relieves him of office. The Emir also appoints Ministers and relieves them of office upon the recommendation of the Prime Minister.

7. The legislature's approval is required to confirm the appointment of ministers; or the legislature itself appoints ministers.

No. The emir appoints ministers on the recommendation of the prime minister, and the appointments do not require the legislature's approval.

Article 56

(1) The Emir, after the traditional consultations, appoints the Prime Minister and relieves him of office.

The Emir also appoints Ministers and relieves them of office upon the recommendation of the Prime Minister. (2) Ministers are appointed from amongst the members of the National Assembly and from others. (3) The number of Ministers in all shall not exceed one-third of the number of the members of the National Assembly.

8. The country lacks a presidency entirely or there is a presidency, but the president is elected by the legislature.

Yes. The country lacks a presidency. The emir is the head of state.

9. The legislature can vote no confidence in the government.

No. The legislature cannot vote no confidence in the government. It can notify the emir that it is unable to cooperate with the prime minister, and the emir can decide to remove the prime minister or dissolve the legislature. In May 2006 the legislature started the process to declare its inability to work with the prime minister. The emir called elections, which the opposition won. The emir reappointed the former prime minister to form a new government, but the new government conceded on the underlying policy dispute that had led to the elections.

Article 102
(1) The Prime Minister does not hold any portfolio; nor shall the question of confidence in him be raised before the National Assembly.
(2) Nevertheless, if the National Assembly decides, in the manner specified in the preceding Article, that it cannot co-operate with the Prime Minister, the matter is submitted to the Head of State. In such a case, the Emir may either relieve the Prime Minister of office and appoint a new Cabinet or dissolve the National Assembly.
(3) In the event of dissolution, if the new Assembly decides by the abovementioned majority vote that it cannot co-operate with the said Prime Minister, he shall be considered to have resigned as from the date of the decision of the Assembly in this respect, and a new Cabinet shall be formed.

10. The legislature is immune from dissolution by the executive.

No. The emir can dissolve the legislature.

Article 102
(1) The Prime Minister does not hold any portfolio; nor shall the question of confidence in him be raised before the National Assembly.
(2) Nevertheless, if the National Assembly decides, in the manner specified in the preceding Article, that it cannot co-operate with the Prime Minister, the matter is submitted to the Head of State. In such a case, the

Emir may either relieve the Prime Minister of office and appoint a new Cabinet or dissolve the National Assembly.
(3) In the event of dissolution, if the new Assembly decides by the abovementioned majority vote that it cannot co-operate with the said Prime Minister, he shall be considered to have resigned as from the date of the decision of the Assembly in this respect, and a new Cabinet shall be formed.

Article 107
(1) The Emir may dissolve the National Assembly by a decree in which the reasons for dissolution is indicated. However, dissolution of the Assembly may not be repeated for the same reasons.

11. Any executive initiative on legislation requires ratification or approval by the legislature before it takes effect; that is, the executive lacks decree power.

No. The emir can issue decrees that have the force of law while the legislature is out of session or dissolved. The decrees lapse if they are not subsequently approved by the legislature.

Article 71
(1) Should necessity arise for urgent measures to be taken while the National Assembly is not in session or is dissolved, the Emir may issue decrees in respect thereof which have the force of law, provided that they are not contrary to the Constitution or to the appropriations included in the budget law.
(2) Such decrees are referred to the National Assembly within the fifteen days following their issue if the Assembly is in session. If it is dissolved or its legislative term has expired, such decrees are referred to the next Assembly at its first sitting. If they are not thus referred, they retrospectively cease to have the force of law, without the necessity of any decision to that effect. If they are referred and the Assembly does not confirm them, they retrospectively cease to have the force of law, unless the Assembly approves their validity for the preceding period or settles in some other way the effects arising therefrom.

12. Laws passed by the legislature are veto-proof or essentially veto-proof; that is, the executive lacks veto power, or has veto power but the veto can be overridden by a majority in the legislature.

No. A two-thirds majority is needed to override the emir's veto.

Article 66
Reference of a bill for reconsideration is by a decree stating the grounds therefore. If the National Assembly confirms the bill by a two-thirds majority vote of its members, the Emir sanctions and promulgates the bill within thirty days from its submission to him. If the bill does not receive the said majority, it may not be reconsidered during the same session. If the National Assembly, in another session, considers the same bill by a majority vote of its members, the Emir sanctions

and promulgates the bill as law within thirty days from its submission to him.

13. The legislature's laws are supreme and not subject to judicial review.

No. The judiciary can review the constitutionality of laws.

> Article 173
> (1) The law specifies the judicial body competent to deciding disputes relating to the constitutionality of laws and regulations and determines its jurisdiction and procedure.
> (2) The law ensures the right of both the Government and the interested parties to challenge the constitutionality of laws and regulations before the said body.
> (3) If the said body decides that a law or a regulation is unconstitutional, it is considered null and void.

14. The legislature has the right to initiate bills in all policy jurisdictions; the executive lacks gatekeeping authority.

Yes. The legislature can initiate bills in all policy jurisdictions.

15. Expenditure of funds appropriated by the legislature is mandatory; the executive lacks the power to impound funds appropriated by the legislature.

No. The emir can impound funds appropriated by the legislature.

16. The legislature controls the resources that finance its own internal operation and provide for the perquisites of its own members.

Yes. The legislature enjoys financial autonomy, including control over members' salaries.

> Article 119
> The remuneration of the President of the National Assembly, the Deputy President, and the Members are fixed by law. In the event of a modification of the said remuneration, such modification may not take effect until the next legislative term.

17. Members of the legislature are immune from arrest and/or criminal prosecution.

No. Legislators are immune only while the legislature is in session.

> Article 111
> Except in cases of flagrante delicto, no measures of inquiry, search, arrest, detention, or any other penal measure may be taken against a member while the Assembly is in session, except with the authorization of the Assembly. The Assembly must be notified of any penal measure that may be taken during its session in accordance with the foregoing provision. The Assembly, at its first meeting, is always notified of any such measure taken against any of its members while it was not sitting. In all cases, if the Assembly does not give

a decision regarding a request for authorization within one month from the date of its receipt, permission is deemed to have been given.

18. All members of the legislature are elected; the executive lacks the power to appoint any members of the legislature.

No. The emir appoints many members of the legislature. There are fifty elected members and up to fifteen additional members appointed by the emir.

> Article 80
> (1) The National Assembly is composed of fifty members elected directly by universal suffrage and secret ballot in accordance with the provisions prescribed by the electoral law.
> (2) Ministers who are not elected members of the National Assembly are considered ex-officio members thereof.

19. The legislature alone, without the involvement of any other agencies, can change the Constitution.

No. Constitutional amendments require the emir's approval.

> Article 174
> (1) The Emir or one-third of the members of the National Assembly have the right to propose a revision of the Constitution by amending or deleting one or more of its provisions or by adding new provisions.
> (2) If the Emir and the majority of the members constituting the National Assembly approve the principle of revision and its subject matter, the Assembly debates the bill article by article. Approval by a two-thirds majority vote of the members constituting the Assembly is required for the bill to be passed. The revision comes into force only after being sanctioned and promulgated by the Emir regardless of the provisions of Articles 65 and 66.
> (3) If the principle of revision or its subject matter is rejected, it may not be presented again before the lapse of one year from the rejection.
> (4) No amendment to this Constitution may be proposed before the lapse of five years from its coming into force.

20. The legislature's approval is necessary for the declaration of war.

No. The emir declares war, and the legislature's approval is not required.

> Article 68
> The Emir declares defensive war by decree. Offensive war is prohibited.

21. The legislature's approval is necessary to ratify treaties with foreign countries.

Yes. The legislature's approval is necessary to ratify international treaties on most major issues.

Article 70

(1) The Emir concludes treaties by decree and transmits them immediately to the National Assembly with the appropriate statement. A treaty has the force of law after it is signed, ratified, and published in the Official Gazette.

(2) However, treaties of peace and alliance; treaties concerning the territory of the State, its natural resources or sovereign rights, or public or private rights of citizens; treaties of commerce, navigation, and residence; and treaties entailing additional expenditure not provided for in the budget, or involving amendment of the laws of Kuwait; shall come into force only when made by a law.

22. The legislature has the power to grant amnesty.

No. Amnesty is granted by law, but in practice, it would be unthinkable for the legislature to pass an amnesty law without the emir's approval.

Article 75

(1) The Emir may, by decree, grant a pardon or commute a sentence.

(2) However, general amnesty shall not be granted except by a law and then only in respect of offences committed prior to the proposal of the amnesty.

23. The legislature has the power of pardon.

No. The emir has the power of pardon.

Article 75

(1) The Emir may, by decree, grant a pardon or commute a sentence.

(2) However, general amnesty shall not be granted except by a law and then only in respect of offences committed prior to the proposal of the amnesty.

24. The legislature reviews and has the right to reject appointments to the judiciary; or the legislature itself appoints members of the judiciary.

No. The emir appoints the members of the judiciary, and the appointments do not require the legislature's approval.

25. The chairman of the central bank is appointed by the legislature.

No. The emir appoints the governor of the Central Bank of Kuwait.

26. The legislature has a substantial voice in the operation of the state-owned media.

Yes. The legislature has budgetary control over the media, and, along with the executive, the legislature also establishes the legal framework for the functioning of public media.

27. The legislature is regularly in session.

Yes. The legislature is in session for at least eight months each year.

Article 85

The National Assembly has an annual session of not less than eight months.

28. Each legislator has a personal secretary.

Yes.

29. Each legislator has at least one non-secretarial staff member with policy expertise.

No.

30. Legislators are eligible for re-election without any restriction.

Yes. There are no restrictions on re-election.

Article 83

(2) Members whose term of office expires may be re-elected.

31. A seat in the legislature is an attractive enough position that legislators are generally interested in and seek re-election.

Yes.

32. The re-election of incumbent legislators is common enough that at any given time the legislature contains a significant number of highly experienced members.

Yes. Re-election rates are sufficiently high to produce a significant number of highly experienced members.

LEGISLATIVE ASSEMBLY OF KYRGYZSTAN (*JOGORKU KENESH*)

Expert consultants: Saltanat Berdikeeva, Eugene Huskey, Pauline Jones Luong, Bhaswar Mukhopadhyay, Natalia Pisareva, Aigul Turgunbaeva

Score: .47

Influence over executive (3/9)		Institutional autonomy (1/9)		Specified powers (5/8)		Institutional capacity (6/6)	
1. replace		10. no dissolution		19. amendments	X	27. sessions	X
2. serve as ministers		11. no decree		20. war	X	28. secretary	X
3. interpellate		12. no veto		21. treaties	X	29. staff	X
4. investigate	X	13. no review		22. amnesty	X	30. no term limits	X
5. oversee police		14. no gatekeeping		23. pardon		31. seek re-election	X
6. appoint PM		15. no impoundment		24. judiciary	X	32. experience	X
7. appoint ministers	X	16. control resources		25. central bank			
8. lack president		17. immunity		26. media			
9. no confidence	X	18. all elected	X				

The Legislative Assembly (*Jogorku Kenesh*) of Kyrgyzstan was established in the 1993 constitution. The document called for an elected, unicameral legislature. A 1994 amendment brought a brief experiment with a bicameral body, but the unicameral legislature was restored in a 2003 constitutional amendment. Constitutional amendments in 1996 and 1998 did not directly affect the legislature's power. In November 2006 the country adopted a new constitution that strengthened the legislature's power, most notably, granting the legislature the right to appoint the prime minister. A constitutional amendment in December 2006, however, revoked the legislature's new powers and restored the power to appoint the prime minister to the president. The 2006 constitution is not yet available in English. The constitutional excerpts below are from the 1993 constitution.

Apart from the powers to investigate the government, approve ministerial appointments, and vote no confidence in the government, the legislature lacks control over the executive branch. The legislature has precious little autonomy; in this area, presidential decree, veto, gatekeeping, and dissolution powers weight heavily. The authority that the legislature does possess comes in the form of specified powers and prerogatives and a high level of institutional capacity.

As of this writing, Kyrgyzstan's constitutional order is in a state of upheaval. In October 2007, according to the official results of a disputed referendum, voters approved the adoption of a new constitution. The referendum was pushed by the president, Kurmanbek Bakiyev, who sought to enhance his office's powers at the expense of parliament. Shortly after the referendum, Bakiyev dissolved parliament and called new elections. Precisely how the changes will affect the legislature's power, and whether they will take hold and prove lasting, are uncertain at this time.

SURVEY

1. The legislature alone, without the involvement of any other agencies, can impeach the president or replace the prime minister.

No. Presidential impeachment requires the involvement of the Constitutional Court.

Article 51
1. The President of the Kyrgyz Republic can be removed from office only on the basis of a charge of state treason or committing another severe crime brought by the Jogorku Kenesh of the Kyrgyz Republic, confirmed by a conclusion of the Constitutional Court of the Kyrgyz Republic.

2. Ministers may serve simultaneously as members of the legislature.

No. Legislators are prohibited from serving simultaneously in ministerial positions.

> Article 56
> 5. A Deputy of the Jogorku Kenesh of the Kyrgyz Republic cannot simultaneously hold the office of a member of the Government of the Kyrgyz Republic and be a Deputy of a local Kenesh.

3. The legislature has powers of summons over executive branch officials and hearings with executive branch officials testifying before the legislature or its committees are regularly held.

No. Legislators do not regularly question executive branch officials.

4. The legislature can conduct independent investigation of the chief executive and the agencies of the executive.

Yes. The legislature can investigate the executive. For example, a parliamentary investigation recently uncovered a government scheme to embezzle the country's gold reserves.

> Article 57
> A Deputy of the Jogorku Kenesh of the Kyrgyz Republic has the right of inquiry with organs of executive power, local self-government, and their officials who are obligated to respond to the inquiry within one month's period.

5. The legislature has effective powers of oversight over the agencies of coercion (the military, organs of law enforcement, intelligence services, and the secret police).

No. The legislature lacks effective powers of oversight over the agencies of coercion.

6. The legislature appoints the prime minister.

No. The president appoints the prime minister with the assent of the legislature.

> Article 46
> 1. The President of the Kyrgyz Republic:
> 2) Appoints the Prime Minister of the Kyrgyz Republic with the consent of the Jogorku Kenesh of the Kyrgyz Republic.

7. The legislature's approval is required to confirm the appointment of ministers; or the legislature itself appoints ministers.

Yes. The president appoints ministers on the recommendation of the prime minister, and the legislature's approval is necessary to confirm the appointments.

> Article 46
> 1. The President of the Kyrgyz Republic:

> 3) Appoints members of the Government of the Kyrgyz Republic according to the proposal of the Prime Minister of the Kyrgyz Republic and with the consent of the Jogorku Kenesh of the Kyrgyz Republic.

8. The country lacks a presidency entirely or there is a presidency, but the president is elected by the legislature.

No. The president is directly elected.

> Article 43
> 1. The President of the Kyrgyz Republic shall be elected for a term of five years.

9. The legislature can vote no confidence in the government.

Yes. The legislature can vote no confidence in the government.

> Article 58
> 1. The following [powers] belong within the authority the Jogorku Kenesh of the Kyrgyz Republic:
> 10) Expression of no confidence in the Government of the Kyrgyz Republic by the majority of no less than two thirds of votes of the total number of Deputies in cases provided by the Constitution.

> Article 72
> 3. The Jogorku Kenesh of the Kyrgyz Republic may, as a result of considerations of the annual report of the Prime Minister of the Kyrgyz Republic, by the initiative of a majority of the total number of Deputies of the Jogorku Kenesh of the Kyrgyz Republic, consider the matter of expressing no confidence in the Government of the Kyrgyz Republic.
> 4. A resolution on expressing no confidence in the Government of the Kyrgyz Republic is adopted by a majority of no less than two thirds of votes of the total number of Deputies of the Jogorku Kenesh of the Kyrgyz Republic.
> 6. After the expression of no confidence in the Government of the Kyrgyz Republic the President of the Kyrgyz Republic has the right to decide to dissolve the Government of the Kyrgyz Republic or to disagree with the decision of the Jogorku Kenesh of the Kyrgyz Republic.
> 7. In the event that the Jogorku Kenesh of the Kyrgyz Republic within three months adopts a vote of no confidence in the Government of the Kyrgyz Republic once more, the President of the Kyrgyz Republic declares the dismissal of the Government of the Kyrgyz Republic or dissolves the Jogorku Kenesh of the Kyrgyz Republic.

10. The legislature is immune from dissolution by the executive.

No. The president can dissolve the legislature.

> Article 46
> 6. The President of the Kyrgyz Republic:
> 3) in cases provided by this Constitution dissolves the Jogorku Kenesh of the Kyrgyz Republic.

Article 72

3. The Jogorku Kenesh of the Kyrgyz Republic may, as a result of considerations of the annual report of the Prime Minister of the Kyrgyz Republic, by the initiative of a majority of the total number of Deputies of the Jogorku Kenesh of the Kyrgyz Republic, consider the matter of expressing no confidence in the Government of the Kyrgyz Republic.

4. A resolution on expressing no confidence in the Government of the Kyrgyz Republic is adopted by a majority of no less than two thirds of votes of the total number of Deputies of the Jogorku Kenesh of the Kyrgyz Republic.

6. After the expression of no confidence in the Government of the Kyrgyz Republic the President of the Kyrgyz Republic has the right to decide to dissolve the Government of the Kyrgyz Republic or to disagree with the decision of the Jogorku Kenesh of the Kyrgyz Republic.

7. In the event that the Jogorku Kenesh of the Kyrgyz Republic within three months adopts a vote of no confidence in the Government of the Kyrgyz Republic once more, the President of the Kyrgyz Republic declares the dismissal of the Government of the Kyrgyz Republic or dissolves the Jogorku Kenesh of the Kyrgyz Republic.

11. Any executive initiative on legislation requires ratification or approval by the legislature before it takes effect; that is, the executive lacks decree power.

No. The president issues decrees that have the force of law.

Article 47

1. The President of the Kyrgyz Republic issues decrees and orders.

2. Decrees and orders of the President of the Kyrgyz Republic must be executed on the entire territory of the Kyrgyz Republic.

3. Decrees issued by the President of the Kyrgyz Republic while exercising [his] legislative powers in correspondence with sub-point 6 of point 5 of Article 46 of the Constitution of the Kyrgyz Republic have the power of law.

12. Laws passed by the legislature are veto-proof or essentially veto-proof; that is, the executive lacks veto power, or has veto power but the veto can be overridden by a majority in the legislature.

No. A two-thirds majority vote is required to override a presidential veto. A four-fifths majority is needed to override a presidential veto on a constitutional amendment.

Article 66

1. A law adopted by the Jogorku Kenesh of the Kyrgyz Republic is submitted to the President of the Kyrgyz Republic for signature within one month.

2. The President of the Kyrgyz Republic signs the law or returns it with his objections to the Jogorku Kenesh of the Kyrgyz Republic for a another consideration within one month of receiving the law. A law may be reconsidered by the Jogorku Kenesh of the Kyrgyz Republic no earlier than six months after it was received with objections of the President of the Kyrgyz Republic. This rule does not apply if the Jogorku Kenesh of the Kyrgyz Republic agrees with the objections of the President of the Kyrgyz Republic. In case of agreement of the Jogorku Kenesh of the Kyrgyz Republic with the wording proposed by the President of the Kyrgyz Republic, the law is to be signed by the President of the Kyrgyz Republic within the time period provided by point 2 of this Article.

3. If during the re-consideration the law is approved in the formerly adopted wording by a majority of no less than two thirds of votes of the total number of Deputies, it is to be signed by the President of the Kyrgyz Republic within one month of the receipt.

4. A law returned by the President of the Kyrgyz Republic for a re-consideration indicated in point 6 of Article 65 [related to constitutional amendments] of this Constitution may be re-considered by the Jogorku Kenesh no earlier than after one year. This rule does not apply if the Jogorku Kenesh of the Kyrgyz Republic decides to agree with the objections of the President of the Kyrgyz Republic. In case of agreement of the Jogorku Kenesh of the Kyrgyz Republic with the wording proposed by the President of the Kyrgyz Republic, the law is to be signed by the President of the Kyrgyz Republic within the time period provided by point 2 of this article.

5. If during the re-consideration taking place no earlier than after one year, the law indicated in point 6 of Article 65 of this Constitution is adopted in the previous wording by a majority of no less than four fifths of the votes of the total number of the Deputies of the Jogorku Kenesh of the Kyrgyz Republic, it is to be signed by the President of the Kyrgyz Republic within one month.

13. The legislature's laws are supreme and not subject to judicial review.

No. The Constitutional Court can review the constitutionality of laws.

Article 81

3. The Constitutional Court of the Kyrgyz Republic:
   1) Deems laws and other normative legal acts unconstitutional in the event they contradict the Constitution of the Kyrgyz Republic.

14. The legislature has the right to initiate bills in all policy jurisdictions; the executive lacks gatekeeping authority.

No. The legislature is prohibited from initiating legislation related to taxation, government expenditures, government revenues, and government financial obligations.

Article 65

5. Changes to the law on the stated budget, draft laws on the introduction or cancellation of taxes, the exemption from their payment, on changes of the state

financial obligations, other draft laws providing for the increase in expenses covered from the state budget, as well as the decrease in income can be introduced to the Jogorku Kenesh of the Kyrgyz Republic and adopted only with the consent of the Government of the Kyrgyz Republic.

15. Expenditure of funds appropriated by the legislature is mandatory; the executive lacks the power to impound funds appropriated by the legislature.

No. The president can impound funds appropriated by the legislature.

16. The legislature controls the resources that finance its own internal operation and provide for the perquisites of its own members.

No. The legislature is dependent on the executive for the resources that finance its own operations.

17. Members of the legislature are immune from arrest and/or criminal prosecution.

No. Formally, legislators are immune, but in practice, this right is not consistently observed. For example, an opposition member of parliament, Emil Aliyev, was arrested in July 2003 on embezzlement charges.

Article 56
4. A Deputy of the Jogorku Kenesh of the Kyrgyz Republic enjoys the right to immunity. He cannot be subjected to persecution for opinions expressed in connection with the activity of a Deputy or for the results of voting in the Jogorku Kenesh of the Kyrgyz Republic. A Deputy may not be detained or arrested, subjected to search or body search, except for cases when caught at a crime scene. Bringing a Deputy to a criminal as well as administrative responsibility imposed according to a court procedure is only permitted with the consent of the Jogorku Kenesh of the Kyrgyz Republic.

18. All members of the legislature are elected; the executive lacks the power to appoint any members of the legislature.

Yes. All members of the legislature are elected.

Article 54
2. The Jogorku Kenesh of the Kyrgyz Republic consists of 75 Deputies who are elected for five years from single-mandate territorial electoral districts.

19. The legislature alone, without the involvement of any other agencies, can change the Constitution.

Yes. The legislature can amend the constitution with a two-thirds majority vote.

Article 96
1. Changes and amendments to this Constitution are adopted by a referendum called by the President of the Kyrgyz Republic.

2. Changes and amendments may be adopted by the Jogorku Kenesh of the Kyrgyz Republic upon proposal of the President of the Kyrgyz Republic, [by] a majority of the total number of Deputies of the Jogorku Kenesh of the Kyrgyz Republic, or on the initiative of no less than 300 thousand voters.
3. Proposals concerning introduction of changes and amendments to the Constitution of the Kyrgyz Republic are considered by the Jogorku Kenesh of the Kyrgyz Republic taking into account the conclusion of the Constitutional Court of the Kyrgyz Republic no earlier than three months and no later than six months from the day of presentation of the proposal to the Jogorku Kenesh of the Kyrgyz Republic.
4. The text of the draft law on the introduction of changes and amendments to the Constitution of the Kyrgyz Republic may not be changed in the course of its discussion by the Jogorku Kenesh of the Kyrgyz Republic.

Article 97
1. Changes and amendments to this Constitution are considered adopted by the Jogorku Kenesh of the Kyrgyz Republic if no less than two thirds of votes of the total number of Deputies of the Jogorku Kenesh of the Kyrgyz Republic voted for them.
2. A proposal which has not been adopted may be submitted to the Jogorku Kenesh of the Kyrgyz Republic for another consideration no earlier than after one year.

20. The legislature's approval is necessary for the declaration of war.

Yes. The legislature's approval is required for presidential war declarations with the common exception for cases of foreign invasion. In the "event of aggression" the president can declare war and then seek retroactive legislative approval.

Article 46
6. The President of the Kyrgyz Republic:
   8) The President of the Kyrgyz Republic declares universal or partial mobilization (of troops); shall announce the status of troops in the event of aggression or direct threat of aggression to the Kyrgyz Republic, and shall promptly submit this matter for the consideration of the Legislative Assembly; and declares the state of war, in the interests of the defense of the country and the safety of its citizens, and shall promptly submit this matter for the consideration of the Legislative Assembly.

Article 58
1. The following [powers] belong within the authority the Jogorku Kenesh of the Kyrgyz Republic:
   23) Decision on matters of war and peace; imposition of martial law, declaration of a state of war, confirmation or repeal of the decrees of the President of the Kyrgyz Republic concerning that matter.

21. The legislature's approval is necessary to ratify treaties with foreign countries.

Yes. The legislature's approval is necessary to ratify international treaties.

Article 46
3. The President of the Kyrgyz Republic:
 1) directs the foreign policy of the Kyrgyz Republic;
 2) conducts negotiations and signs the international treaties of the Kyrgyz Republic;
 3) signs instruments of ratification.

Article 58
1. Powers of the Jogorku Kenesh of the Kyrgyz Republic shall be as follows:
 21) to ratify and denounce international treaties except in the cases provided by Article 48 of this Constitution of the Kyrgyz Republic.

22. The legislature has the power to grant amnesty.

Yes. The legislature has the power to grant amnesty.

Article 58
1. The following [powers] belong within the authority the Jogorku Kenesh of the Kyrgyz Republic:
 27) Issuance of acts on amnesty.

23. The legislature has the power of pardon.

No. The president has the power of pardon.

Article 46
4. The President of the Kyrgyz Republic:
 4) Grants pardon.

24. The legislature reviews and has the right to reject appointments to the judiciary; or the legislature itself appoints members of the judiciary.

Yes. The legislature, on the proposal of the president, elects the chairman and judges of the Constitutional Court, the chairman and judges of the Supreme Court, and the judges of the Supreme Economic Court.

Article 46
2. The President of the Kyrgyz Republic:
 1) Presents to the Jogorku Kenesh of the Kyrgyz Republic the candidates for the election to the post of the Chairman of the Constitutional Court of the Kyrgyz Republic, his deputy and judges of the Constitutional Court of the Kyrgyz Republic;
 2) Presents to the Jogorku Kenesh of the Kyrgyz Republic the candidates for the election to the post of the Chairman of the Supreme Court of the Kyrgyz Republic, his deputies and judges of the Supreme Court of the Kyrgyz Republic.

Article 58
1. The following [powers] belong within the authority the Jogorku Kenesh of the Kyrgyz Republic:
 11) election, upon nomination by the President of the Kyrgyz Republic, of the Chairman of the Constitutional Court of the Kyrgyz Republic, his deputy, and the judges of the Constitutional Court of the Kyrgyz Republic;
 12) election, upon nomination by the President of the Kyrgyz Republic, of the Chairman of the Supreme Court of the Kyrgyz Republic, their deputies, and the judges of the Supreme Court and the Supreme Economic Court of the Kyrgyz Republic.

25. The chairman of the central bank is appointed by the legislature.

No. The president appoints the chairman of the National Bank of the Kyrgyz Republic.

Article 46
2. The President of the Kyrgyz Republic:
 4) Appoints with the consent of the Jogorku Kenesh of the Kyrgyz Republic the Chairman of the National Bank of the Kyrgyz Republic; according to the proposal of the Chairman of the National Bank of the Kyrgyz Republic appoints the deputies of the Chairman and members of the Board of the National Bank of the Kyrgyz Republic; releases them from office.

26. The legislature has a substantial voice in the operation of the state-owned media.

No. The legislature lacks a substantial voice in the operation of the public media.

27. The legislature is regularly in session.

Yes. The legislature meets in ordinary session ten months each year.

Article 62
1. Sessions of the Jogorku Kenesh of the Kyrgyz Republic are carried out in the form of a sitting and are conducted once a year, beginning the first working day of September and ending the last working day of June of the following year.

28. Each legislator has a personal secretary.

Yes.

29. Each legislator has at least one non-secretarial staff member with policy expertise.

Yes.

30. Legislators are eligible for re-election without any restriction.

Yes. There are no restrictions on re-election.

31. A seat in the legislature is an attractive enough position that legislators are generally interested in and seek re-election.

Yes.

32. The re-election of incumbent legislators is common enough that at any given time the legislature contains a significant number of highly experienced members.

Yes. Re-election rates are sufficiently high to produce a significant number of highly experienced members.

NATIONAL ASSEMBLY OF LAOS (*SAPHA HENG XAT*)

Expert consultant: Martin Stuart-Fox

Score: .28

Influence over executive (1/9)		Institutional autonomy (5/9)		Specified powers (0/8)	Institutional capacity (3/6)	
1. replace		10. no dissolution	X	19. amendments	27. sessions	
2. serve as ministers	X	11. no decree		20. war	28. secretary	
3. interpellate		12. no veto	X	21. treaties	29. staff	
4. investigate		13. no review		22. amnesty	30. no term limits	X
5. oversee police		14. no gatekeeping	X	23. pardon	31. seek re-election	X
6. appoint PM		15. no impoundment		24. judiciary	32. experience	X
7. appoint ministers		16. control resources		25. central bank		
8. lack president		17. immunity	X	26. media		
9. no confidence		18. all elected	X			

The National Assembly (*Sapha Heng Xat*) of Laos, as currently constituted, was provided for in the 1991 constitution. The document calls for a unicameral legislature that elects the president. In practice, Laos is ruled by the sole legal political party, the communist Lao People's Revolutionary Party (LPRP). As in most other Soviet-type systems, the party vets candidates for election to the legislature, it is the fount of all legislation, and its leader is the president of the country.

The legislature's role is negligible. Effective lawmaking authority rests with the LPRP. The National Assembly has virtually no influence over the executive. It has some institutional autonomy. In practice, it does not enjoy any of the specified powers examined in this survey. It has a bit of institutional capacity.

SURVEY

1. The legislature alone, without the involvement of any other agencies, can impeach the president or replace the prime minister.

No. The legislature cannot remove the president. Formally, it can remove the prime minister with a vote of no confidence. In practice, it would be unthinkable for the legislature to vote no confidence in the government without explicit direction from the LPRP.

Article 61
The National Assembly may pass a vote of no confidence in the government or any member of the government if the National Assembly Standing Committee or one-fourth of the total number of the National Assembly members raise the question.
Within twenty-four hours after the vote of no confidence in the government by the National Assembly, the President of state has the right to bring the no confidence question to the National Assembly for reconsideration. The second consideration must be held within the forty-eight hours interval from the first consideration. If the new vote of no confidence in the government is passed the government must resign.

2. Ministers may serve simultaneously as members of the legislature.

Yes. Ministers may serve simultaneously in the legislature.

3. The legislature has powers of summons over executive branch officials and hearings with executive branch officials testifying before the legislature or its committees are regularly held.

No. Formally, the legislature has the right to interpellate officials from the executive, but hearings are not regularly held.

Article 50
Members of the National Assembly have the right to interpellate the members of the government, the President of the People's Supreme Court and the Public Prosecutor-General.

Organisations or persons interpellated must give verbal or written answers at the National Assembly session.

4. The legislature can conduct independent investigation of the chief executive and the agencies of the executive.

No. The legislature cannot investigate the executive.

5. The legislature has effective powers of oversight over the agencies of coercion (the military, organs of law enforcement, intelligence services, and the secret police).

No. The legislature lacks effective powers of oversight over the agencies of coercion.

6. The legislature appoints the prime minister.

No. The president appoints the prime minister with the approval of the legislature.

Article 53
The President of state has the following rights and duties:
3. To appoint or remove the Prime Minister and the members of the government with the approval or resolution of no confidence of the National Assembly.

Article 59
The Prime Minister is appointed by the President of state with the approval of the National Assembly.

7. The legislature's approval is required to confirm the appointment of ministers; or the legislature itself appoints ministers.

No. Formally, the president makes ministerial appointments and the National Assembly must confirm them, but in practice, the legislature merely rubber-stamps the candidates selected by the LPRP.

Article 40
The National Assembly has the following rights and duties:
6. To consider and approve the appointment or removal of the members of the government on the recommendation of the President of State.

Article 53
The President of state has the following rights and duties:
3. To appoint or remove the Prime Minister and the members of the government with the approval or resolution of no confidence of the National Assembly.

8. The country lacks a presidency entirely or there is a presidency, but the president is elected by the legislature.

No. Formally, the National Assembly elects the president, but in practice, its decision is entirely predetermined by the LPRP leadership, and the National Assembly plays no meaningful role.

Article 40
The National Assembly has the following rights and duties:
5. To elect or remove the President of state and the Vice-President of state on the recommendation of the National Assembly Standing Committee.

Article 54
The President of state is elected by the National Assembly with two-thirds of the votes of all members of the National Assembly attending the session.

9. The legislature can vote no confidence in the government.

No. Formally, the legislature can vote no confidence in the government. In practice, it would be unthinkable for the legislature to vote no confidence in the government.

Article 61
The National Assembly may pass a vote of no confidence in the government or any member of the government if the National Assembly Standing Committee or one-fourth of the total number of the National Assembly members raise the question.
Within twenty-four hours after the vote of no confidence in the government by the National Assembly, the President of state has the right to bring the no confidence question to the National Assembly for reconsideration. The second consideration must be held within the forty-eight hours interval from the first consideration. If the new vote of no confidence in the government is passed the government must resign.

10. The legislature is immune from dissolution by the executive.

Yes. The legislature is immune from dissolution.

11. Any executive initiative on legislation requires ratification or approval by the legislature before it takes effect; that is, the executive lacks decree power.

No. The president and the government issue decrees that have the force of law.

Article 53
The President of state has the following rights and duties:
2. To issue state decrees and state acts on the recommendation of the National Assembly Standing Committee.

Article 57
The government has the following rights and duties:
4. To issue decrees and decisions on the management of socio-economic, scientific and technical fields; national defence and security; and foreign affairs.

12. Laws passed by the legislature are veto-proof or essentially veto-proof; that is, the executive lacks veto power, or has veto power but the veto can be overridden by a majority in the legislature.

Yes. The legislature can override a presidential veto with a majority vote. It merits note, however, that bills are drawn up and approved by the LPRP before being submitted to the legislature.

Article 46
Laws already adopted by the National Assembly must be promulgated by the President of state not later than thirty days after their endorsement. During this period, the President of state has the right to request the National Assembly to reconsider such laws. If the National Assembly affirms to adhere to its previous decision in reconsidering such laws, the President of state must promulgate them within fifteen days.

13. The legislature's laws are supreme and not subject to judicial review.

No. Formally, there is no judicial review and the legislature's laws are supreme, but in practice, the laws are in no respect the work of the National Assembly. Rather, they are the products of the LPRP's decisions.

Article 40
The National Assembly has the following rights and duties:
12. To supervise the observance of the Constitution and laws.

Article 48
The National Assembly Standing Committee has the following rights and duties:
2. To interpret and explain the provisions of the constitution and laws.

14. The legislature has the right to initiate bills in all policy jurisdictions; the executive lacks gatekeeping authority.

Yes. The legislature has the right to initiate bills in all policy jurisdictions.

15. Expenditure of funds appropriated by the legislature is mandatory; the executive lacks the power to impound funds appropriated by the legislature.

No. The executive can impound funds appropriated by the legislature.

16. The legislature controls the resources that finance its own internal operation and provide for the perquisites of its own members.

No. The legislature depends on the government and the LPRP for the resources that finance its own operation.

17. Members of the legislature are immune from arrest and/or criminal prosecution.

Yes. Legislators are immune.

Article 51
Members of the National Assembly shall not be prosecuted in court or detained without the approval of the National Assembly or the National Assembly Standing Committee during the two sessions of the National Assembly. In cases involving gross and urgent offenses, the organisations detaining members of the National Assembly must immediately report to the National Assembly or to the National Assembly Standing Committee during the two sessions of the National Assembly for consideration and decisions concerning them. Inquiries and interrogations shall not cause the absence of prosecuted members from the National Assembly session.

18. All members of the legislature are elected; the executive lacks the power to appoint any members of the legislature.

Yes. All members of the legislature are elected. It merits mention, however, that in legislative elections voters choose from among a narrow range of LPRP-approved candidates.

Article 41
Members of the National Assembly are elected by the Lao citizens in accordance with the provisions stipulated in the law.

19. The legislature alone, without the involvement of any other agencies, can change the Constitution.

No. Formally, the legislature can change the constitution with a two-thirds majority vote, but in practice, it would be unthinkable for the legislature to change the constitution without the LPRP's instructions.

Article 40
The National Assembly has the following rights and duties:
1. To establish, endorse or amend the Constitution.

Article 80
Only the National Assembly of the Lao People's Democratic Republic has the right to amend the Constitution. The amendment to the Constitution requires the votes of approval cast by at least two-thirds of the total number of the National Assembly members.

20. The legislature's approval is necessary for the declaration of war.

No. Formally, the legislature has responsibility for declaring war, but in practice, the power to declare war rests exclusively with the LPRP.

Article 40
The National Assembly has the following rights and duties:
11. To decide on matters of war or peace.

21. The legislature's approval is necessary to ratify treaties with foreign countries.

No. Formally, and in a peculiar constitutional formulation, both the legislature and the president are granted virtually identical responsibility for ratifying treaties; in practice, the power rests with the president and the LPRP.

> Article 40
> The National Assembly has the following rights and duties:
> 10. To decide on the ratification or abolition of treaties and agreements signed with foreign countries in accordance with international law and regulations.

> Article 53
> The President of state has the following rights and duties:
> 11. To declare on the ratification or abolition of all treaties and agreements signed with foreign countries.

22. The legislature has the power to grant amnesty.

No. Formally, the legislature has the power to grant amnesty, but in practice, the president and the LPRP, not the National Assembly, have the power to grant amnesty.

> Article 40
> The National Assembly has the following rights and duties:
> 9. To decide on granting general amnesties.

23. The legislature has the power of pardon.

No. The president has the power of pardon.

> Article 53
> The President of state has the following rights and duties:
> 9. To decide on granting pardons.

24. The legislature reviews and has the right to reject appointments to the judiciary; or the legislature itself appoints members of the judiciary.

No. Formally, the National Assembly Standing Committee appoints the president and vice president of the Supreme Court and the judges of the people's courts, but in practice, all personnel decisions are made by the LPRP.

> Article 40
> The National Assembly has the following rights and duties:
> 7. To elect or remove the President of the People's Supreme Court and the Public Prosecutor-General on the recommendation of the National Assembly Standing committee.

> Article 67
> The Vice-President of the People's Supreme Court and the judges of the people's courts at all levels are appointed or removed by the National Assembly Standing Committee.

25. The chairman of the central bank is appointed by the legislature.

No. The governor of the Bank of Laos is appointed by the president, on the recommendation of the prime minister, and with the approval of the National Assembly.

26. The legislature has a substantial voice in the operation of the state-owned media.

No. The LPRP tightly controls all media.

27. The legislature is regularly in session.

No. The National Assembly meets in two brief ordinary sessions each year. The National Assembly Standing Committee, however, is permanently in session.

> Article 43
> The National Assembly convenes its ordinary session twice a year at the summoning of the National Assembly Standing Committee. The National Assembly Standing Committee may convene an extraordinary session of the National Assembly if it deems necessary.

28. Each legislator has a personal secretary.

No.

29. Each legislator has at least one non-secretarial staff member with policy expertise.

No.

30. Legislators are eligible for re-election without any restriction.

Yes. There are no restrictions on re-election.

31. A seat in the legislature is an attractive enough position that legislators are generally interested in and seek re-election.

Yes.

32. The re-election of incumbent legislators is common enough that at any given time the legislature contains a significant number of highly experienced members.

Yes. Through the elections of 1992, 1997, 2002, and 2006, the legislature retained a small but significant core of highly experienced members. It merits note, however, that membership does not amount to genuine experience in legislative affairs. Most members' primary jobs are as district and provincial-level administrators, and their membership in the National Assembly is more of an honorary affiliation than a substantial occupation.

PARLIAMENT OF LATVIA (*SAEIMA*)

Expert consultants: Daunis Auers, Stephen Bloom, Jānis Ikstens, Ivars Indans, Katia Papagianni

Score: .78

Influence over executive (7/9)		Institutional autonomy (6/9)		Specified powers (7/8)		Institutional capacity (5/6)	
1. replace	X	10. no dissolution		19. amendments	X	27. sessions	X
2. serve as ministers	X	11. no decree		20. war	X	28. secretary	X
3. interpellate	X	12. no veto	X	21. treaties	X	29. staff	
4. investigate	X	13. no review		22. amnesty	X	30. no term limits	X
5. oversee police		14. no gatekeeping	X	23. pardon		31. seek re-election	X
6. appoint PM	X	15. no impoundment	X	24. judiciary	X	32. experience	X
7. appoint ministers		16. control resources	X	25. central bank	X		
8. lack president	X	17. immunity	X	26. media	X		
9. no confidence	X	18. all elected	X				

The Parliament (*Saeima*) of Latvia was established in the constitution of 1922. From 1940 to 1991 Latvia was incorporated into the Soviet Union and its parliament submerged. In 1990, near the end of the Soviet period, elections for the Supreme Soviet of the Latvian Soviet Socialist Republic brought many new, independence-minded politicians of various political stripes into the legislature and marked the end of communist-party control of the body. Shortly after the dissolution of the USSR, Latvia formally restored the 1922 constitution. In 1996 the Constitutional Court was created to review the constitutionality of laws. Prior to 1996 the legislature's laws were supreme and not subject to judicial review.

The legislature is powerful. It scores high in terms of influence over the executive well on the other indicators of power. The major exception to the legislature's preeminence is the government's power to issue decrees that have the force of law between legislative sessions.

SURVEY

1. The legislature alone, without the involvement of any other agencies, can impeach the president or replace the prime minister.

Yes. The legislature can remove the prime minister with a vote of no confidence. It can remove the president from office by a two-thirds majority vote of its total membership.

Article 51
Upon the proposal of not less than half of all of the members of the Parliament, the Parliament may decide, in closed session and with a majority vote of not less than two-thirds of all of its members, to remove the President from office.

Article 59
In order to fulfill their duties, the Prime Minister and other Ministers must have the confidence of the Parliament and they shall be accountable to the Parliament for their actions. If the Parliament expresses no confidence in the Prime Minister, the entire Government shall resign. If there is an expression of no confidence in an individual Minister, then the Minister shall resign and another person shall be invited to replace them by the Prime Minister.

2. Ministers may serve simultaneously as members of the legislature.

Yes. Legislators may serve simultaneously in ministerial positions.

Article 63
Ministers, even if they are not members of the Parliament, and responsible government officials authorised by a Minister, have the right to attend sittings of the Parliament and its committees and to submit additions and amendments to draft laws.

3. The legislature has powers of summons over executive branch officials and hearings with executive branch officials testifying before the legislature or its committees are regularly held.

Yes. The legislature regularly interpellates officials from the executive.

> **Article 27**
> The Parliament shall have the right to submit to the Prime Minister or to an individual Minister requests and questions which either they, or a responsible government official duly authorized by them, must answer. The Prime Minister or any Minister shall furnish the relevant documents and enactments requested by the Parliament or by any of its committees.

4. The legislature can conduct independent investigation of the chief executive and the agencies of the executive.

Yes. The legislature can appoint parliamentary committees to investigate the executive.

> **Article 26**
> The Parliament shall appoint parliamentary investigatory committees for specified matters if not less than one-third of its members request it.

5. The legislature has effective powers of oversight over the agencies of coercion (the military, organs of law enforcement, intelligence services, and the secret police).

No. The legislature lacks effective powers of oversight over the agencies of coercion.

6. The legislature appoints the prime minister.

Yes. The president appoints as prime minister the candidate who enjoys the support of the legislature.

> **Article 56**
> The Government shall be formed by the person who has been invited by the President to do so.

7. The legislature's approval is required to confirm the appointment of ministers; or the legislature itself appoints ministers.

No. The president appoints ministers on the recommendation of the prime minister, and the appointments do not require the legislature's approval.

> **Article 55**
> The Government shall be composed of the Prime Minister and the Ministers chosen by the Prime Minister.

8. The country lacks a presidency entirely or there is a presidency, but the president is elected by the legislature.

Yes. The legislature elects the president.

> **Article 35**
> The President shall be elected by the Parliament for a term of four years.

9. The legislature can vote no confidence in the government.

Yes. The legislature can vote no confidence in the government.

> **Article 59**
> In order to fulfill their duties, the Prime Minister and other Ministers must have the confidence of the Parliament and they shall be accountable to the Parliament for their actions. If the Parliament expresses no confidence in the Prime Minister, the entire Government shall resign. If there is an expression of no confidence in an individual Minister, then the Minister shall resign and another person shall be invited to replace them by the Prime Minister.

10. The legislature is immune from dissolution by the executive.

No. The president can dissolve the legislature after securing approval for the move in a popular referendum.

> **Article 48**
> The President shall be entitled to propose the dissolution of the Parliament. Following this proposal a national referendum shall be held. If in the referendum more than half of the votes are cast in favor of dissolution, the Parliament shall be considered dissolved, new elections called, and such elections held no later than two months after the date of the dissolution of the Parliament.

> **Article 50**
> If in the referendum more than half of the votes are cast against the dissolution of the Parliament, then the President shall be deemed to be removed from office, and the Parliament shall elect a new President to serve for the remaining term of office of the President so removed.

11. Any executive initiative on legislation requires ratification or approval by the legislature before it takes effect; that is, the executive lacks decree power.

No. The government can issue decrees that have the force of law between sessions of parliament. The decrees lapse if they are not subsequently approved by the legislature. The executive also issues regulations specifying the implementation of laws.

> **Article 81**
> During the time between sessions of the Parliament the Government has the right, if necessary and if not able to be postponed, to issue regulations which have the force of law. Such regulations may not amend the law regarding elections of the Parliament, laws governing the court system and court proceedings, the Budget and rights pertaining to the Budget, as well as laws adopted

during the term of the current Parliament, and they may not pertain to amnesty, state taxes, customs duties, and loans and they shall cease to be in force unless submitted to the Parliament not later than three days after the next session of the Parliament has been convened.

12. Laws passed by the legislature are veto-proof or essentially veto-proof; that is, the executive lacks veto power, or has veto power but the veto can be overridden by a majority in the legislature.

Yes. The legislature can override a presidential veto by a majority vote of its present members.

Article 71
Within seven days of the adoption of a law by the Parliament, the President, by means of a written and reasoned request to the Chairperson of the Parliament, may require that a law be reconsidered. If the Parliament does not amend the law, the President then may not raise objections a second time.

Article 72
The President has the right to suspend the proclamation of a law for a period of two months. The President shall suspend the proclamation of a law if so requested by not less than one-third of the members of the Parliament. This right may be exercised by the President, or by one-third of the members of the Parliament, within seven days of the adoption of the law by the Parliament. The law thus suspended shall be put to a national referendum if so requested by not less than one-tenth of the electorate. If no such request is received during the aforementioned two month period, the law shall then be proclaimed after the expiration of such period. A national referendum shall not take place, however, if the Parliament again votes on the law and not less than three-quarters of all members of the Parliament vote for the adoption of the law.

13. The legislature's laws are supreme and not subject to judicial review.

No. The Constitutional Court can review the constitutionality of laws.

Article 85
In Latvia, there shall be a Constitutional Court, which, within its jurisdiction as provided for by law, shall review cases concerning the compliance of laws with the Constitution, as well as other matters regarding which jurisdiction is conferred upon it by law. The Constitutional Court shall have the right to declare laws or other enactments or parts thereof invalid. The appointment of judges to the Constitutional Court shall be confirmed by the Parliament for the term provided for by law, by secret ballot with a majority of the votes of not less than fifty-one members of the Parliament.

14. The legislature has the right to initiate bills in all policy jurisdictions; the executive lacks gatekeeping authority.

Yes. The legislature can initiate bills in all policy jurisdictions.

15. Expenditure of funds appropriated by the legislature is mandatory; the executive lacks the power to impound funds appropriated by the legislature.

Yes. The executive lacks the power to impound funds appropriated by the legislature.

16. The legislature controls the resources that finance its own internal operation and provide for the perquisites of its own members.

Yes. The legislature enjoys financial autonomy.

17. Members of the legislature are immune from arrest and/or criminal prosecution.

Yes. Legislators are immune with the common exception for cases of *flagrante delicto,* here expressed as "apprehended in the act of committing a crime." There is another exception to immunity, this one utterly eccentric: Legislators can also be arrested for disseminating "defamatory statements which they know to be false, or defamatory statements about private or family life." This rule has no effect in practice.

Article 28
Members of the Parliament may not be called to account by any judicial, administrative or disciplinary process in connection with their voting or their views as expressed during the execution of their duties. Court proceedings may be brought against members of the Parliament if they, albeit in the course of performing parliamentary duties, disseminate:
1) defamatory statements which they know to be false, or
2) defamatory statements about private or family life.

Article 29
Members of the Parliament shall not be arrested, nor shall their premises be searched, nor shall their personal liberty be restricted in any way without the consent of the Parliament. Members of the Parliament may be arrested if apprehended in the act of committing a crime. The Presidium shall be notified within twenty-four hours of the arrest of any member of the Parliament; the Presidium shall raise the matter at the next sitting of the Parliament for decision as to whether the member shall continue to be held in detention or be released. When the Parliament is not in session, pending the opening of a session, the Presidium shall decide whether the member of the Parliament shall remain in detention.

Article 30
Without the consent of the Parliament, criminal prosecution may not be commenced and administrative fines may not be levied against its members.

18. All members of the legislature are elected; the executive lacks the power to appoint any members of the legislature.

Yes. All members of the legislature are elected.

Article 6
The Parliament shall be elected in general, equal, direct and secret elections, based on proportional representation.

19. The legislature alone, without the involvement of any other agencies, can change the Constitution.

Yes. The legislature can amend the constitution in multiple readings with a two-thirds majority vote.

Article 76
The Parliament may amend the Constitution in sittings at which at least two-thirds of the members of the Parliament participate. The amendments shall be passed in three readings by a majority of not less than two-thirds of the members present.

20. The legislature's approval is necessary for the declaration of war.

Yes. The legislature's approval is necessary for presidential war declarations with the common exception for cases of foreign invasion. In the case that Latvia is invaded, the president may declare war and seek retroactive legislative approval.

Article 43
The President shall declare war on the basis of a decision of the Parliament.

Article 44
The President has the right to take whatever steps are necessary for the military defence of the State should another state declare war on Latvia or an enemy invade its borders. Concurrently and without delay, the President shall convene the Parliament, which shall decide as to the declaration and commencement of war.

21. The legislature's approval is necessary to ratify treaties with foreign countries.

Yes. The legislature's approval is necessary to ratify international treaties.

Article 68
(1) All international agreements, which settle matters that may be decided by the legislative process, shall require ratification by the Parliament.
(3) Membership of Latvia in the European Union shall be decided by a national referendum, which is proposed by the Parliament.
(4) Substantial changes in the terms regarding the membership of Latvia in the European Union shall be decided by a national referendum if such referendum is requested by at least one-half of the members of the Parliament.

22. The legislature has the power to grant amnesty.

Yes. The legislature has the power to grant amnesty.

Article 45
The President has the right to grant clemency to criminals against whom judgment of the court has come

into legal effect. The extent of, and procedures for, the utilisation of this right shall be set out in a specific law. Amnesty is granted by the Parliament.

23. The legislature has the power of pardon.

No. The president has the power of pardon, here expressed as "clemency."

Article 45
The President has the right to grant clemency to criminals against whom judgment of the court has come into legal effect. The extent of, and procedures for, the utilisation of this right shall be set out in a specific law. Amnesty is granted by the Parliament.

24. The legislature reviews and has the right to reject appointments to the judiciary; or the legislature itself appoints members of the judiciary.

Yes. The legislature's consent is required to approve judicial appointments.

Article 84
Judicial appointments shall be confirmed by the Parliament and they shall be irrevocable.

25. The chairman of the central bank is appointed by the legislature.

Yes. The parliament appoints the governor of the Bank of Latvia.

26. The legislature has a substantial voice in the operation of the state-owned media.

Yes. The legislature has a substantial voice in the operation of the public media.

27. The legislature is regularly in session.

Yes. The legislature is regularly in session with the exception of brief recesses during winter holidays and the summer.

Article 19
The Presidium shall convene sessions of the Parliament and schedule regular and extraordinary sittings.

28. Each legislator has a personal secretary.

Yes. Each legislator is provided funds to hire personnel.

29. Each legislator has at least one non-secretarial staff member with policy expertise.

No. Some, but not all, legislators hire a staff member with policy expertise.

30. Legislators are eligible for re-election without any restriction.

Yes. There are no restrictions on re-election.

31. A seat in the legislature is an attractive enough position that legislators are generally interested in and seek re-election.

Yes.

32. The re-election of incumbent legislators is common enough that at any given time the legislature contains a significant number of highly experienced members.

Yes. Despite considerable instability in the party system and a fairly high rate of turnover in membership, the legislature retains a cohort of highly experienced members.

NATIONAL ASSEMBLY OF LEBANON (*MAJLIS AL-NUWAAB*)

Expert consultants: Mona Khalaf, Amer K. Mohsen, Marwan Sakr, Nadim Shehadi, Abdulkader Sinno

Score: .50

Influence over executive (3/8)		Institutional autonomy (5/9)		Specified powers (4/8)		Institutional capacity (4/6)	
1. replace		10. no dissolution		19. amendments	X	27. sessions	
2. serve as ministers	X	11. no decree		20. war		28. secretary	X
3. interpellate		12. no veto	X	21. treaties	X	29. staff	
4. investigate		13. no review		22. amnesty	X	30. no term limits	X
5. oversee police		14. no gatekeeping	X	23. pardon		31. seek re-election	X
6. appoint PM		15. no impoundment	X	24. judiciary	X	32. experience	X
7. appoint ministers		16. control resources	X	25. central bank			
8. lack president	X	17. immunity		26. media			
9. no confidence	X	18. all elected	X				

The National Assembly (*Majlis al-Nuwaab*) of Lebanon was established in the 1926 constitution, which called for a bicameral legislature consisting of an upper house, the Senate, and a lower house, the Chamber of Deputies. A constitutional amendment in 1927 merged the two houses to form a unicameral assembly. In 1943 Lebanon gained independence from France. From 1975 to 1989 the legislature was sidelined as Lebanon endured a civil war that was sparked by sectarian violence and that triggered intervention by foreign powers. Israel held the southern part of the country, while Syria established a presence in some other areas. Legislative elections were suspended during the conflict; the legislature elected in 1972 simply renewed its own term every two years. By 1990 stability had returned, imposed by a Syrian-backed government. Legislative elections, the first since 1972, resumed in 1992. In 2000 Israel withdrew from southern Lebanon. A controversial constitutional amendment in 2004 extended the president's term by three years but did not directly affect legislative power. In 2005 Syrian troops withdrew from Lebanon under mounting international pressure. In 2006 violence returned, as Israel once again invaded southern Lebanon.

The National Assembly, which is sometimes referred to as the Assembly of Deputies or the Chamber of Deputies (the last is used in the translation of the constitution excerpted below), has significant authority. Its influence over the executive is not expansive, although its members can serve in government, it elects the president, and it can vote no confidence in the government. The legislature must contend with executive decree and dissolution powers but nevertheless enjoys notable institutional autonomy. It can, for example, override a presidential veto with a majority vote. The legislature also possesses some specified powers and prerogatives and some institutional capacity.

SURVEY

1. The legislature alone, without the involvement of any other agencies, can impeach the president or replace the prime minister.

No. The impeachment of the president or the prime minister requires the involvement of the Supreme Council, a special body established to try impeachment cases. The legislature can remove the prime minister with a vote of no confidence.

Article 60

(1) While performing his functions, the President of the Republic may not be held responsible except when he violates the constitution or in the case of high treason.

(2) However, his responsibility in respect of ordinary crimes is subject to the ordinary laws. For such crimes, as well as for violation of the constitution and for high treason, he may not be impeached except by a majority of two thirds of the total membership of the Chamber of Deputies. He is to be tried by the Supreme Council provided for in Article 80. The functions of Public Prosecutor of the Supreme Council are performed by a judge appointed by the Supreme Council in plenary session.

Article 37

Every Deputy has the absolute right to raise the question of no-confidence in the government during ordinary or extraordinary sessions. Discussion of and voting on such a proposal may not take place until at least five days after submission to the secretariat of the Chamber and its communication to the ministers concerned.

Article 69

(1) The Government is considered resigned in the following circumstances:

f. when it loses the confidence of the Chamber of Deputies based on the Chamber's initiative or based on the Council's initiative to gain the Chamber's confidence.

(2) Ministers are to be dismissed by a Decree signed by the President and the Prime Minister in accordance with Article 65 of the constitution.

Article 70

(1) The Chamber of Deputies has the right to impeach the Prime Minister and Ministers for high treason or for serious neglect of their duties. The Decision to impeach may not be taken except by a majority of two thirds of the total membership of the Chamber.

(2) A special law is to be issued to determine the conditions of the civil responsibility of the Prime Minister and individual Ministers.

Article 71

The impeached Prime Minister or Minister are tried by the Supreme Council.

Article 72

A Prime Minister or Minister leaves office as soon as the Decision of impeachment concerning him is issued. If he resigns, his resignation does not prevent judicial proceedings from being instituted or continued against him.

2. Ministers may serve simultaneously as members of the legislature.

Yes. Legislators may serve simultaneously in ministerial positions.

Article 28

A Deputy may also occupy a ministerial position. Ministers, all or in part, may be selected from among the members of the Chamber or from persons outside the Chamber.

3. The legislature has powers of summons over executive branch officials and hearings with executive branch officials testifying before the legislature or its committees are regularly held.

No. Hearings with executive branch officials testifying before the legislature are rarely held.

4. The legislature can conduct independent investigation of the chief executive and the agencies of the executive.

No. The legislature cannot investigate the executive.

5. The legislature has effective powers of oversight over the agencies of coercion (the military, organs of law enforcement, intelligence services, and the secret police).

No. The legislature lacks effective powers of oversight over the agencies of coercion.

6. The legislature appoints the prime minister.

No. The president appoints the prime minister. It bears note, however, that the president's decision must take into account the wishes of the leading parties in parliament.

Article 53

2. The President designates the Prime Minister in consultation with the President of the Chamber of Deputies based on parliamentary consultations which are binding and the content of which the President formally discloses to the Prime Minister.

3. The President alone issues the Decree which designates the Prime Minister.

7. The legislature's approval is required to confirm the appointment of ministers; or the legislature itself appoints ministers.

No. The president appoints ministers on the recommendation of the prime minister, and the appointments do not require the legislature's approval.

Article 53

(4) The President issues, in agreement with the Prime Minister, the decree appointing the Cabinet and the decrees accepting the resignation of Ministers.

8. The country lacks a presidency entirely or there is a presidency, but the president is elected by the legislature.

Yes. The legislature elects the president. In the recent past, the Syrian government has also had a say in the presidential election.

Article 49
(2) The President of the Republic shall be elected by secret ballot and by a two thirds majority of the Chamber of Deputies. After a first ballot, an absolute majority shall be sufficient.

9. The legislature can vote no confidence in the government.

Yes. The legislature can vote no confidence in the government.

Article 37
Every Deputy has the absolute right to raise the question of no-confidence in the government during ordinary or extraordinary sessions.

Article 69
(1) The Government is considered resigned in the following circumstances:
  f. when it loses the confidence of the Chamber of Deputies based on the Chamber's initiative or based on the Council's initiative to gain the Chamber's confidence.
(2) Ministers are to be dismissed by a Decree signed by the President and the Prime Minister in accordance with Article 65 of the constitution.

10. The legislature is immune from dissolution by the executive.

No. The Council of Ministers, at the president's request, can dissolve the legislature.

Article 55
(1) The President of the Republic may, in accordance with the conditions stipulated in Articles 65 and 77 of this constitution, ask the Council of Ministers to dissolve the Chamber of Deputies before the expiration of its mandate. If the Council, based on this request, decides to dissolve the Chamber of Deputies, the President issues the Decree dissolving it, and in this case, the electoral bodies meet as provided for in Article 25, and the new Chamber is to be called to convene within fifteen days after the proclamation of the election.

Article 65
Executive authority is vested in the Council of Ministers. It is the authority to which the armed forces are subject. Among the powers that it exercises are the following:
(4) It dissolves the Chamber of Deputies upon the request of the President of the Republic if the Chamber of Deputies, for no compelling reasons, fails to meet during one of its regular periods and fails to meet throughout two successive extraordinary periods, each longer than one month, or if the Chamber returns an annual budget plan with the aim or paralyzing the Government. This right cannot be exercised a second time if it is for the same reasons which led to the dissolution of the Chamber the first time.

11. Any executive initiative on legislation requires ratification or approval by the legislature before it takes effect; that is, the executive lacks decree power.

No. The president issues decrees that have the force of law.

Article 56
(2) The President issues decrees and requests their promulgation; he has the right to ask the Council of Ministers to review any Decision that the Chamber has taken within fifteen days of the decision's transmission to the Presidency. If the Council of Ministers insists on the Decision or if the time limit passes without the Decree being issued or returned, the Decision or Decree is considered legally operative and must be promulgated.

12. Laws passed by the legislature are veto-proof or essentially veto-proof; that is, the executive lacks veto power, or has veto power but the veto can be overridden by a majority in the legislature.

Yes. The legislature can override a presidential veto by a majority vote of its total membership.

Article 57
The President of the Republic, after consultation with the Council of Ministers, has the right to request the reconsideration of a law once during the period prescribed for its promulgation. This request may not be refused. When the President exercises this right, he is not required to promulgate this law until it has been reconsidered and approved by an absolute majority of all the members legally composing the Chamber. If the time limits pass without the law being issued or returned, the law is considered legally operative and must be promulgated.

13. The legislature's laws are supreme and not subject to judicial review.

No. The Constitutional Council can review the constitutionality of laws.

Article 19
A Constitutional Council is established to supervise the constitutionality of laws and to arbitrate conflicts that arise from parliamentary and presidential elections. The President, the President of the Parliament, the Prime Minister, along with any ten Members of Parliament, have the right to consult this Council on matters that relate to the constitutionality of laws. The officially recognized heads of religious communities have the right to consult this Council only on laws relating to personal status, the freedom of belief and religious practice, and the freedom of religious education.

14. The legislature has the right to initiate bills in all policy jurisdictions; the executive lacks gatekeeping authority.

Yes. The legislature can initiate bills in all policy jurisdictions.

15. Expenditure of funds appropriated by the legislature is mandatory; the executive lacks the power to impound funds appropriated by the legislature.

Yes. The executive lacks the power to impound funds appropriated by the legislature.

16. The legislature controls the resources that finance its own internal operation and provide for the perquisites of its own members.

Yes. The legislature enjoys financial autonomy, including control over members' perquisites.

> Article 48
> The remuneration of members of the Chamber is determined by law.

17. Members of the legislature are immune from arrest and/or criminal prosecution.

No. Legislators are immune only while the legislature is in session.

> Article 39
> No member of the Chamber may be prosecuted because of ideas and opinions expressed during the period of his mandate.

> Article 40
> No member of the Chamber may, during the sessions, be prosecuted or arrested for a criminal offense without the permission of the Chamber, except when he is caught in the act.

18. All members of the legislature are elected; the executive lacks the power to appoint any members of the legislature.

Yes. All members of the legislature are elected.

> Article 22
> With the election of the first Parliament on a national, non-confessional basis, a Senate is established in which all the religious communities are represented.

> Article 24
> (1) The Chamber of Deputies is composed of elected members; their number and the method of their election is determined by the electoral laws in effect.

19. The legislature alone, without the involvement of any other agencies, can change the Constitution.

Yes. The legislature alone can change the constitution. The legislature can propose a constitutional amendment with a two-thirds majority vote. If the government returns the bill proposing the amendment for reconsideration, the legislature can override the government by a three-fourths majority vote. If the government still objects, it can dissolve the legislature. The amendment passes if the new legislature approves it.

Article 77

The constitution may also be revised upon the request of the Chamber of Deputies. In this case the following procedures are to be observed: During an ordinary session and at the request of at least ten of its members, the Chamber of Deputies may recommend, by a majority of two thirds of the total members lawfully composing the Chamber, the revision of the constitution. However, the articles and the questions referred to in the recommendation must be clearly defined and specified. The President of the Chamber then transmits the recommendation to the Government requesting it to prepare a draft law relating thereto. If the Government approves the recommendation of the Chamber by a majority of two thirds, it must prepare the draft amendment and submit it to the Chamber within four months; if it does not agree, it shall return the Decision to the Chamber for reconsideration. If the Chamber insists upon the necessity of the amendment by a majority of three fourths of the total members lawfully composing the Chamber, the President of the Republic has then either to accede to the Chamber's recommendation or to ask the Council of Ministers to dissolve the Chamber and to hold new elections within three months. If the new Chamber insists on the necessity of amending the constitution, the Government must yield and submit the draft amendment within four months.

20. The legislature's approval is necessary for the declaration of war.

No. The Council of Ministers' war declarations do not require legislative approval.

> Article 65
> Executive authority is vested in the Council of Ministers. It is the authority to which the armed forces are subject. Among the powers that it exercises are the following:
> 5. Basic national issues are considered the following: . . . war and peace.

21. The legislature's approval is necessary to ratify treaties with foreign countries.

Yes. The legislature's approval is necessary to ratify international treaties.

> Article 52
> The President of the Republic negotiates international treaties in coordination with the Prime Minister. These treaties are not considered ratified except after agreement of the Council of Ministers. They are to be made known to the Chamber whenever the national interest and security of the state permit. However, treaties involving the finances of the state, commercial treaties, and in general treaties that cannot be renounced every year are not considered ratified until they have been approved by the Chamber.

22. The legislature has the power to grant amnesty.

Yes. The legislature grants general amnesty through law.

Article 53
(9) [The president] grants particular pardons by Decree, but a general amnesty cannot be granted except by a law.

23. The legislature has the power of pardon.

No. The president has the power of pardon.

Article 53
(9) [The president] grants particular pardons by Decree, but a general amnesty cannot be granted except by a law.

24. The legislature reviews and has the right to reject appointments to the judiciary; or the legislature itself appoints members of the judiciary.

Yes. The legislature appoints five of ten members of the Constitutional Council and seven of the fifteen members of the Supreme Council.

Article 19
A Constitutional Council is established to supervise the constitutionality of laws and to arbitrate conflicts that arise from parliamentary and presidential elections. The President, the President of the Parliament, the Prime Minister, along with any ten Members of Parliament, have the right to consult this Council on matters that relate to the constitutionality of laws. The officially recognized heads of religious communities have the right to consult this Council only on laws relating to personal status, the freedom of belief and religious practice, and the freedom of religious education. The rules governing the organization, operation, composition, and modes of appeal of the Council are decided by a special law.

Article 80
The Supreme Council, whose function is to try Presidents and Ministers, consists of seven deputies elected by the Chamber of Deputies and of eight of the highest Lebanese judges, according to their rank in the judicial hierarchy, or, in case of equal ranks, in the order of seniority. They meet under the presidency of the judge of the highest rank. The Decisions of condemnation by the Supreme Council is rendered by a majority of ten votes. A special law is to be issued to determine the procedure to be followed by this Council.

25. The chairman of the central bank is appointed by the legislature.

No. The Council of Ministers, on the recommendation of the minister of finance, appoints the governor of the Central Bank of Lebanon.

26. The legislature has a substantial voice in the operation of the state-owned media.

No. The legislature lacks a substantial voice in the operation of the public media.

27. The legislature is regularly in session.

No. The legislature is in session for only five months each year.

Article 32
The Chamber meets each year in two ordinary sessions. The first session opens on the first Tuesday following 15 March and continues until the end of May. The second session begins on the first Tuesday following 15 Oct; its meetings is reserved for the discussion of and voting on the budget before any other work. This session lasts until the end of the year.

28. Each legislator has a personal secretary.

Yes.

29. Each legislator has at least one non-secretarial staff member with policy expertise.

No.

30. Legislators are eligible for re-election without any restriction.

Yes. There are no restrictions on re-election.

31. A seat in the legislature is an attractive enough position that legislators are generally interested in and seek re-election.

Yes.

32. The re-election of incumbent legislators is common enough that at any given time the legislature contains a significant number of highly experienced members.

Yes. Re-election rates are sufficiently high to produce a significant number of highly experienced members.

PARLIAMENT OF LESOTHO

Expert consultants: Jørgen Elklit, Leonard Letsepe, Chelete Monyane, Roger Southall, Richard F. Weisfelder

Score: .53

Influence over executive (8/9)		Institutional autonomy (4/9)		Specified powers (1/8)		Institutional capacity (4/6)	
1. replace	X	10. no dissolution		19. amendments	X	27. sessions	X
2. serve as ministers	X	11. no decree		20. war		28. secretary	
3. interpellate	X	12. no veto	X	21. treaties		29. staff	
4. investigate	X	13. no review		22. amnesty		30. no term limits	X
5. oversee police	X	14. no gatekeeping	X	23. pardon		31. seek re-election	X
6. appoint PM	X	15. no impoundment		24. judiciary		32. experience	X
7. appoint ministers		16. control resources	X	25. central bank			
8. lack president	X	17. immunity		26. media			
9. no confidence	X	18. all elected	X				

The Parliament of Lesotho was formally established in 1966 upon independence from Great Britain. It consists of an elected lower house, the National Assembly, and an appointed upper house, the Senate. When the opposition won the first legislative elections in 1970, the ruling Basotho National Party (BNP) refused to cede power, setting the stage for a protracted violent struggle. The legislature was impotent, and the BNP ruled by decree until 1986, when the military executed a coup and transferred executive and legislative powers to the monarch. In 1993 the current constitution was adopted, and the first legislative elections since 1970 were held. The 1990s also witnessed political instability, however, including military coups, suspension of the constitution, disputes over succession to the throne, and military intervention from neighboring South Africa and Botswana. Peaceful legislative elections, in which opposition parties won and were allowed to hold some seats, were held in 2002 and 2007.

Despite political instability, the legislature manages to exercise some authority. It has broad control over the executive, with powers to elect the prime minister and remove the government with a vote of no confidence. The legislature's weakness is demonstrated in the other measured categories. Its institutional autonomy is circumscribed by the prime minister's powers to decree legislation and dissolve the legislature. With the exception of its ability to change the constitution, the legislature is granted none of the specified powers and prerogatives assessed in this survey. It has some institutional capacity.

SURVEY

1. The legislature alone, without the involvement of any other agencies, can impeach the president or replace the prime minister.

Yes. The legislature can remove the prime minister with a vote of no confidence.

Article 87

(5) The King may, acting in accordance with the advice of the Council of State, remove the Prime Minister from office –

(a) if a resolution of no confidence in the Government of Lesotho is passed by the National Assembly and the Prime minister does not within three days thereafter, either resign from his office or advise a dissolution of Parliament; or

(b) if at any time between the holding of a general election to the National Assembly and the date on which the Assembly first meets thereafter, the King considers that, in consequence of changes in the membership of the Assembly resulting from that election, the Prime Minister will no longer be the leader of the political party or coalition of political parties that will command the support of a majority of the members of the Assembly.

2. Ministers may serve simultaneously as members of the legislature.

Yes. Ministers are selected from, and required to serve simultaneously in, the legislature.

Article 76
(1) A Minister or an Assistant Minister who is a member of the National Assembly shall be entitled to attend all meetings of the Senate and to take part in all proceedings thereof but he shall not be regarded as a member of, or be entitled to vote on any question before, the Senate; and a Minister or an Assistant Minister who is a Senator shall be entitled to attend all meetings of the National Assembly and to take part in all proceedings thereof but he shall not be regarded as a member of, or be entitled to vote on any question before, the National Assembly.

3. The legislature has powers of summons over executive branch officials and hearings with executive branch officials testifying before the legislature or its committees are regularly held.

Yes. Legislators question executive branch officials during weekly question time.

4. The legislature can conduct independent investigation of the chief executive and the agencies of the executive.

Yes. The legislature can form a commission of inquiry to investigate the executive.

5. The legislature has effective powers of oversight over the agencies of coercion (the military, organs of law enforcement, intelligence services, and the secret police).

Yes. The legislature has effective powers of oversight over the agencies of coercion.

6. The legislature appoints the prime minister.

Yes. The king is required to appoint as prime minister the candidate who enjoys majority support in the legislature.

Article 87
(1) There shall be a Prime Minister who shall be appointed by the King acting in accordance with the advice of the Council of State.
(2) The King shall appoint as Prime Minister the member of the National Assembly who appears to the Council of State to be the leader of the political party or coalition of political parties that will command the support of a majority of the members of the National Assembly: Provided that if occasion arises for making an appointment to the office of Prime Minister while Parliament stands dissolved, a person who was a member of the

National Assembly immediately before the dissolution may be appointed to the office of Prime Minister.

7. The legislature's approval is required to confirm the appointment of ministers; or the legislature itself appoints ministers.

No. The king appoints ministers on the advice of the prime minister, and the appointments do not require the legislature's approval.

Article 87
(3) There shall be, in addition to the office of Prime Minister, such other offices of Minister of the Government of Lesotho (not being less than seven in number and one of which shall be the office of Deputy Prime Minister) as may be established by Parliament or, subject to any provision made by Parliament, by the King, acting in accordance with the advice of the Prime Minister.
(4) The King shall, acting in accordance with the advice of the Prime Minister, appoint the other Ministers from among the members of the National Assembly or from among the Senators who are nominated as Senators by the King under section 55 of this Constitution:
Provided that if occasion arises for making an appointment to the office of Minister other than Prime Minister while Parliament stands dissolved a person who immediately before the dissolution was a member of the National Assembly or such a Senator may be appointed to the office of Minister.

8. The country lacks a presidency entirely or there is a presidency, but the president is elected by the legislature.

Yes. The country lacks a presidency. The king is the head of state.

Article 44
(1) There shall be a King of Lesotho who shall be a constitutional monarch and Head of State.
(2) The King shall do all things that belong to his office in accordance with the provisions of this Constitution and of all other laws for the time being in force and shall faithfully comply with the terms of the oath of the office of King set out in Schedule 1 to this Constitution.

Article 45
(1) The College of Chiefs may at any time designate, in accordance with the customary law of Lesotho, the person (or the persons, in order of prior right) who are entitled to succeed to the office of King upon the death of the holder of, or the occurrence of any vacancy in, that office and if on such death or vacancy, there is a person who has previously been designated in pursuance of this section and who is capable under the customary law of Lesotho of succeeding to that office, that person (or, if there is more than one such person, that one of them who has been designated as having the first right to succeed to the office) shall become King.

9. The legislature can vote no confidence in the government.

Yes. The legislature can pass a constructive vote no confidence, meaning that it must designate a successor prime minister before passing a vote of no confidence.

Article 83
(4) In the exercise of his powers to dissolve or prorogue Parliament, the King shall act in accordance with the advice of the Prime Minister:
Provided that –
(b) if the National Assembly passes a resolution of no confidence in the Government of Lesotho and the Prime Minister does not within three days thereafter either resign or advise a dissolution the King may, acting in accordance with the advice of the Council of State, dissolve Parliament; and
(5) A resolution of no confidence in the Government of Lesotho shall not be effective for the purposes of subsection (4)(b) unless it proposes the name of a member of the National Assembly for the King to appoint in the place of the Prime Minister.

10. The legislature is immune from dissolution by the executive.

No. The king, at the request of the prime minister, can dissolve the legislature.

Article 83
(1) The King may at any time prorogue or dissolve Parliament.
(2) Subject to the provisions of subsection (3), Parliament, unless sooner dissolved, shall continue for five years from the date when the two Houses of Parliament first meet after any dissolution and shall then stand dissolved.
(3) At any time when Lesotho is at war Parliament may from time to time extend the period of five years specified in subsection (2) for not more than twelve months at a time:
Provided that the life of Parliament shall not be extended under this subsection for more than five years.
(4) In the exercise of his powers to dissolve or prorogue Parliament, the King shall act in accordance with the advice of the Prime Minister:
Provided that –
(a) if the Prime Minister recommends a dissolution and the King considers that the Government of Lesotho can be carried on without a dissolution and that a dissolution would not be in the interests of Lesotho, he may, acting in accordance with the advice of the Council of State, refuse to dissolve Parliament;
(b) if the National Assembly passes a resolution of no confidence in the Government of Lesotho and the Prime Minister does not within three days thereafter either resign or advise a dissolution the King may, acting in accordance with the advice of the Council of State, dissolve Parliament; and

(c) if the office of Prime Minister is vacant and the King considers that there is no prospect of his being able within a reasonable time to find a person who is the leader of a political party or a coalition of political parties that will command the support of a majority of the members of the National Assembly, he may, acting in accordance with the advice of the Council of State, dissolve Parliament.

11. Any executive initiative on legislation requires ratification or approval by the legislature before it takes effect; that is, the executive lacks decree power.

No. The prime minister issues decrees that have the force of law.

12. Laws passed by the legislature are veto-proof or essentially veto-proof; that is, the executive lacks veto power, or has veto power but the veto can be overridden by a majority in the legislature.

Yes. Formally, the king can refuse to assent to a bill; in practice, it would be unthinkable for the king to withhold assent.

Article 78
(1) The power of Parliament to make laws shall be exercisable by bills passed by both Houses of Parliament (or, in the cases mentioned in section 80 of this Constitution, by the National Assembly) and assented to by the King.
(2) A bill may originate only in the National Assembly.
(3) When a bill has been passed by the National Assembly it shall be sent to the Senate and –
(a) when it has been passed by the Senate and agreement has been reached between the two Houses on any amendments made to it by the Senate; or
(b) when it is required to be presented under section 80 of this Constitution,
it shall be presented to the King for assent.
(4) When a bill has been presented to the King for assent in pursuance of subsection (3), he shall signify that he assents or that he withholds assent.
(5) When a bill that has been duly passed is assented to in accordance with the provisions of this Constitution it shall become law and the King shall thereupon cause it to be published in the Gazette as a law.

13. The legislature's laws are supreme and not subject to judicial review.

No. The High Court can review the constitutionality of laws.

Article 119
(1) There shall be a High Court which shall have unlimited original jurisdiction to hear and determine any civil or criminal proceedings and the power to review the decisions or proceedings of any subordinate or inferior court, court-martial, tribunal, board or officer exercising judicial, quasi-judicial or public administrative

functions under any law and such jurisdiction and powers as may be conferred on it by this Constitution or by or under any other law.

14. The legislature has the right to initiate bills in all policy jurisdictions; the executive lacks gatekeeping authority.

Yes. The legislature can initiate bills in all policy jurisdictions.

15. Expenditure of funds appropriated by the legislature is mandatory; the executive lacks the power to impound funds appropriated by the legislature.

No. Once funds are approved through the budgetary process, the executive is not required to spend them. In fact, the government usually fails to spend appropriated funds. The problem, however, is often a matter of capacity rather than deliberate executive challenge to the legislature's authority.

16. The legislature controls the resources that finance its own internal operation and provide for the perquisites of its own members.

Yes. The legislature enjoys financial autonomy.

17. Members of the legislature are immune from arrest and/or criminal prosecution.

No. Legislators are immune only while they are in the parliament buildings during a legislative session. They are subject to arrest at other times.

18. All members of the legislature are elected; the executive lacks the power to appoint any members of the legislature.

Yes. All members of the National Assembly are elected. The largely ceremonial Senate is composed of appointed members.

Article 55
The Senate shall consist of the twenty-two Principal Chiefs and eleven other Senators nominated in that behalf by the King acting in accordance with the advice of the Council of State.

Article 56
The National Assembly shall consist of eighty members elected in accordance with the provisions of this Constitution.

19. The legislature alone, without the involvement of any other agencies, can change the Constitution.

Yes. The legislature can change the constitution with a majority vote. Amendments to certain specified articles require approval in a popular referendum.

Article 85
(1) Subject to the provisions of this section, Parliament may alter this Constitution.

(2) A bill for an Act of Parliament under this section shall not be passed by Parliament unless it is supported at the final voting in the National Assembly by the votes of the majority of all the members of the Assembly and, having been sent to the Senate, has become a bill that, apart from this section, may be presented to the King for his assent under subsection 80(1) or (3) as the case may be, of this Constitution.
(3) A bill to alter any of the following provisions of this Constitution, that is to say –
(a) this section, sections 1(1) and 2, Chapter II except sections 18(4) and 24(3), sections 44 to 48 inclusive, 50(1) to (3), 52, 86, 91 (1) to (4), 92, 95, 103, 104, 107, 108, 118(1) and (2), 119(1) to (3), 120(1), (2), (4), and (5), 121, 123(1), (3), (4), 125, 128, 129, 132, 133 and sections 154 and 155 in their application to any of the provisions mentioned in this paragraph; and
(b) sections 37, 38, 54 to 60 inclusive; sections 66, 67, 68, 69(1) and (6), 70, 74, 75(1), 78(1), (2), (3) and (4), 80(1), (2), and (3), 82(1), 83 and 84; sections 134 to 142 inclusive, 150 and 151 and sections 154 and 155 in their application to any of the provisions mentioned in this paragraph, shall not be submitted to the King for his assent unless the bill, not less than two nor more than six months after its passage by Parliament, has, in such manner as may be prescribed by or under an Act of Parliament, been submitted to the vote of the electors qualified to vote in the election of the members of the National Assembly, and the majority of the electors voting have approved the bill:
Provided that if the bill does not alter any of the provisions mentioned in paragraph (a) and is supported at the final voting in each House of Parliament by the votes of no less than two-thirds of all the members of that House it shall not be necessary to submit the bill to the vote of the electors.

20. The legislature's approval is necessary for the declaration of war.

No. There is no provision for the declaration of war. In times of war, the prime minister can declare a state of emergency without the legislature's approval. The state of emergency lapses after fourteen days if it is not subsequently approved by the legislature.

Article 23
(1) In time of war or other public emergency which threatens the life of the nation, the Prime Minister may, acting in accordance with the advice of the Council of State, by proclamation which shall be published in the Gazette, declare that a state of emergency exists for the purposes of this Chapter.
(2) Every declaration of emergency shall lapse at the expiration of fourteen days, commencing with the day on which it was made, unless it has in the meantime been approved by a resolution of each House of Parliament.

(3) A declaration of emergency may at any time be revoked by the Prime Minister acting in accordance with the advice of the Council of State, by proclamation which shall be published in the Gazette.

(4) A declaration of emergency that has been approved by a resolution of each House of Parliament in pursuance of subsection (2) shall, subject to the provisions of subsection (3), remain in force so long as those resolutions remain in force and no longer.

21. The legislature's approval is necessary to ratify treaties with foreign countries.

No. The legislature's approval is not necessary to ratify international treaties.

22. The legislature has the power to grant amnesty.

No. Amnesty and pardon are not treated separately, and the legislature lacks the power to grant amnesty. See item 23.

23. The legislature has the power of pardon.

No. The king has the power of pardon.

Article 101
(1) The King may –
(a) grant to any person convicted of any offence under the law of Lesotho a pardon, either free or subject to lawful conditions.

24. The legislature reviews and has the right to reject appointments to the judiciary; or the legislature itself appoints members of the judiciary.

No. The king, the prime minister, and the Judicial Service Commission are responsible for judicial appointments, and the appointments do not require the legislature's approval.

Article 120
(1) The Chief Justice shall be appointed by the King acting in accordance with the advice of the Prime Minister.
(2) The puisne judges shall be appointed by the King, acting in accordance with the advice of the Judicial Service Commission.

Article 124
(1) The President shall be appointed by the King on the advice of the Prime Minister.
(2) The Justices of Appeal shall be appointed by the King, acting in accordance with the advice of the Judicial Service Commission after consultation with the President.

25. The chairman of the central bank is appointed by the legislature.

No. The king, on the advice of the prime minister, appoints the governor of the Central Bank of Lesotho.

26. The legislature has a substantial voice in the operation of the state-owned media.

No. The legislature lacks a voice in the operation of the public media.

27. The legislature is regularly in session.

Yes. The constitution does not specify the number and duration of the legislature's ordinary sessions. In practice, the legislature meets in ordinary session for between six and seven months each year.

Article 82
(1) Each session of Parliament shall be held at such place within Lesotho and shall begin at such time as the King shall appoint:
Provided that –
(a) the time appointed for the meeting of Parliament after Parliament has been prorogued shall be not later than twelve months from the end of the preceding session; and
(b) after Parliament has been dissolved, the time appointed for the meeting of the National Assembly shall not be later than fourteen days after the holding of a general election of members of the National Assembly and the time appointed for the meeting of the Senate shall be such time as may be convenient after the nomination of one or more Senators in accordance with section 55 of this Constitution.
(2) Subject to the provisions of subsection (1), the sittings of each House of Parliament shall be held at such time and place as that House may, by its rules of procedure or otherwise, determine.

28. Each legislator has a personal secretary.

No.

29. Each legislator has at least one non-secretarial staff member with policy expertise.

No.

30. Legislators are eligible for re-election without any restriction.

Yes. There are no restrictions on re-election.

31. A seat in the legislature is an attractive enough position that legislators are generally interested in and seek re-election.

Yes.

32. The re-election of incumbent legislators is common enough that at any given time the legislature contains a significant number of highly experienced members.

Yes. The dominant political parties and their leaders have managed to hold on to their seats in the legislature despite the country's political turmoil. The result is the presence of numerous seasoned legislators in the parliament.

NATIONAL ASSEMBLY OF LIBERIA

Expert consultants: Alfred Fofie, Barrie Hofmann, Jacques Paul Klein, Eleanor Marchant

Score: .44

Influence over executive (3/9)		Institutional autonomy (5/9)		Specified powers (3/8)		Institutional capacity (3/6)	
1. replace	X	10. no dissolution	X	19. amendments		27. sessions	X
2. serve as ministers		11. no decree	X	20. war	X	28. secretary	
3. interpellate		12. no veto		21. treaties	X	29. staff	
4. investigate		13. no review		22. amnesty		30. no term limits	X
5. oversee police		14. no gatekeeping	X	23. pardon		31. seek re-election	X
6. appoint PM		15. no impoundment		24. judiciary	X	32. experience	
7. appoint ministers	X	16. control resources	X	25. central bank			
8. lack president		17. immunity		26. media			
9. no confidence	X	18. all elected	X				

The National Assembly of Liberia was established in the 1847 constitution. The document called for a bicameral legislature with a lower house, the House of Representatives, and an upper house, the Senate. The country enjoyed relative stability for over a century. A coup d'état in 1980 sparked two decades of civil violence. In the midst of the conflict, a new constitution was adopted in 1986. Charles Taylor, a warlord-become-president, assumed office in 1997 and ruled without regard for the legislature. In 2003 Taylor stepped down under international pressure, paving the way for a transitional government. Liberia held legislative and presidential elections in 2005.

Given the recentness of Taylor's departure, it is too early to tell how exactly the legislature will function in practice, although on paper its powers are not insignificant. Its influence over the executive includes the powers to approve ministerial appointments and impeach the president. The legislature also has a degree of institutional autonomy. It is immune from dissolution and is not subject to presidential decree or gatekeeping powers. The legislature is also granted several specified powers and has some institutional capacity.

SURVEY

1. The legislature alone, without the involvement of any other agencies, can impeach the president or replace the prime minister.

Yes. The legislature can impeach the president. The impeachment is proposed by the House of Representatives and decided by a two-thirds majority vote of the total membership in the Senate.

Article 43
The power to prepare a bill of impeachment is vested solely in the House of Representatives, and the power to try all impeachments is vested solely in the Senate. When the President, Vice President or an Associate Justice is to be tried, the Chief Justice shall preside; when the Chief Justice or a judge of a subordinate court of record is to be tried, the President of the Senate shall preside. No person shall be impeached but by the concurrence of two-thirds of the total membership of the Senate. Judgments in such cases shall not extend beyond removal from office and disqualification to hold public office in the Republic; but the party may be tried at law for the same offense. The Legislature shall prescribe the procedure for impeachment proceedings which shall be in conformity with the requirements of due process of law.

Article 62
The President and the Vice-President may be removed

from office by impeachment for treason, bribery and other felonies, violation of the Constitution or gross misconduct.

2. Ministers may serve simultaneously as members of the legislature.

No. Legislators are prohibited from serving simultaneously in ministerial positions.

> **Article 3**
> Liberia is a unitary sovereign state divided into counties for administrative purposes. The form of government is Republican with three separate coordinate branches: the Legislative, the Executive and Judiciary. Consistent with the principles of separation of powers and checks and balances, no person holding office in one of these branches shall hold office in or exercise any of the powers assigned to either of the other two branches except as otherwise provided in this Constitution.

3. The legislature has powers of summons over executive branch officials and hearings with executive branch officials testifying before the legislature or its committees are regularly held.

No. The legislature lacks the power to interpellate executive branch officials.

4. The legislature can conduct independent investigation of the chief executive and the agencies of the executive.

No. The legislature cannot investigate the executive.

5. The legislature has effective powers of oversight over the agencies of coercion (the military, organs of law enforcement, intelligence services, and the secret police).

No. The legislature lacks effective powers of oversight over the agencies of coercion.

6. The legislature appoints the prime minister.

No. There is no prime minister.

7. The legislature's approval is required to confirm the appointment of ministers; or the legislature itself appoints ministers.

Yes. The Senate's approval is required to confirm the president's ministerial appointments.

> **Article 54**
> The President shall nominate and, with the consent of the Senate, appoint and commission –
> a. cabinet ministers, deputy and assistant cabinet ministers.

8. The country lacks a presidency entirely or there is a presidency, but the president is elected by the legislature.

No. The president is directly elected.

> **Article 50**
> The president shall be elected by universal adult suffrage of registered voters in the Republic and shall hold office for a term of six years commencing at noon on the third working Monday in January of the year immediately following the elections.

9. The legislature can vote no confidence in the government.

Yes. The legislature can vote no confidence in the government. It is too early, however, to know whether the legislature will ever use this power.

10. The legislature is immune from dissolution by the executive.

Yes. The legislature is immune from dissolution.

11. Any executive initiative on legislation requires ratification or approval by the legislature before it takes effect; that is, the executive lacks decree power.

Yes. The executive lacks decree power.

12. Laws passed by the legislature are veto-proof or essentially veto-proof; that is, the executive lacks veto power, or has veto power but the veto can be overridden by a majority in the legislature.

No. A two-thirds majority is needed to override a presidential veto.

> **Article 35**
> Each bill or resolution which shall have passed both Houses of the Legislature shall, before it becomes law, be laid before the President for his approval. If he grants approval, it shall become law. If the President does not approve such bill or resolution, he shall return it, with his objections, to the House in which it originated. In so doing, the President may disapprove of the entire bill or resolution or any item or items thereof. This veto may be overridden by the re-passage of such bill, resolution or item thereof by a veto of two-thirds of the members in each House, in which case it shall become law. If the President does not return the bill or resolution within twenty days after the same shall have been laid before him it shall become law in like manner as if he had signed it, unless the Legislature by adjournment prevents its return.
> No bill or resolution shall embrace more than one subject which shall be expressed in its title.

13. The legislature's laws are supreme and not subject to judicial review.

No. The Supreme Court can review the constitutionality of laws.

Article 2

This Constitution is the supreme and fundamental law of Liberia and its provisions shall have binding force and effect on all authorities and persons throughout the Republic.

Any laws, treaties, statutes, decrees, customs and regulations found to be inconsistent with it shall, to the extent of the inconsistency, be void and of no legal effect. The Supreme Court, pursuant to its power of judicial review, is empowered to declare any inconsistent laws unconstitutional.

Article 66

The Supreme Court shall be final arbiter of constitutional issues.

14. The legislature has the right to initiate bills in all policy jurisdictions; the executive lacks gatekeeping authority.

Yes. The legislature can initiate bills in all policy jurisdictions.

15. Expenditure of funds appropriated by the legislature is mandatory; the executive lacks the power to impound funds appropriated by the legislature.

No. The president can impound funds appropriated by the legislature.

16. The legislature controls the resources that finance its own internal operation and provide for the perquisites of its own members.

Yes. The legislature enjoys financial autonomy, including control over members' perquisites.

Article 36

The Senators and Representatives shall receive from the Republic remuneration for their services to be fixed by law, provided that any increase shall become effective at the beginning of the next fiscal year.

17. Members of the legislature are immune from arrest and/or criminal prosecution.

No. Legislators are subject to arrest and criminal prosecution. They are immune from arrest only while traveling to, attending, or returning from legislative sessions, and for votes cast and opinions expressed in the exercise of their duties.

Article 42

No member of the Senate or House of Representatives shall be arrested, detained, prosecuted or tried as a result of opinions expressed or votes cast in the exercise of the functions of his office. Members shall be privileged from arrest while attending, going to or returning from sessions of the Legislature, except for treason, felony or breach of the peace. All official acts done or performed and all statement made in the Chambers of the Legislature shall be privileged, and no Legislator shall be held accountable or punished therefor.

18. All members of the legislature are elected; the executive lacks the power to appoint any members of the legislature.

Yes. All members of the legislature are elected.

Article 48

The House of Representatives shall be composed of members elected for a term of six years by the registered voters in each of the legislative constituencies of the counties, but a member of the House of Representatives elected in a by-election to fill a vacancy created by death, resignation or otherwise, shall be elected to serve only the remainder of the unexpired term of the office. Members of the House of Representatives shall be eligible for re-election.

19. The legislature alone, without the involvement of any other agencies, can change the Constitution.

No. Constitutional amendments require approval in a popular referendum.

Article 91

This Constitution may be amended whenever a proposal by either (1) two-thirds of the membership of both Houses of the Legislature or (2) a petition submitted to the Legislature, by not fewer than 10,000 citizens which receives the concurrence of two-thirds of the membership of both Houses of the Legislature, is ratified by two-thirds of the registered voters, voting in a referendum conducted by the Elections Commission not sooner than one year after the action of the Legislature.

20. The legislature's approval is necessary for the declaration of war.

Yes. The legislature declares war.

Article 34

The Legislature shall have the power:
b. to provide for the security of the Republic;
c. to provide for the common defense, to declare war and authorize the Executive to conclude peace.

21. The legislature's approval is necessary to ratify treaties with foreign countries.

Yes. The legislature's approval is necessary to ratify international treaties.

Article 34

The Legislature shall have the power:
f. to approve treaties, conventions and such other international agreements negotiated or signed on behalf of the Republic.

Article 57

The President shall have the power to conduct the foreign affairs of the Republic and in that connection he is empowered to conclude treaties, conventions and similar international agreements with the concurrence of a majority of each House of the Legislature.

22. The legislature has the power to grant amnesty.

No. Amnesty and pardon are not treated separately, and the legislature lacks the power to grant amnesty. See item 23.

23. The legislature has the power of pardon.

No. The president has the power of pardon.

> Article 59
> The President may remit any public forfeitures and penalties, suspend fines and sentences, grant reprieves and pardons, and restore civil rights after conviction for all public offenses, except impeachment.

24. The legislature reviews and has the right to reject appointments to the judiciary; or the legislature itself appoints members of the judiciary.

Yes. The Senate's consent is necessary to approve the president's appointments to the Supreme Court.

> Article 67
> The Supreme Court shall comprise of one Chief Justice and four Associate Justices, a majority of whom shall be deemed competent to transact the business of the Court. If a quorum is not obtained to enable the Court to hear any case, a circuit judge in the order of seniority shall sit as an ad hoc justice of the Supreme Court.

> Article 68
> The Chief Justice and Associate Justices of the Supreme Court shall, with the consent of the Senate, be appointed and commissioned by the President.

> Article 69
> The judges of subordinate courts of record shall, with the consent of the Senate, be appointed and commissioned by the President.

25. The chairman of the central bank is appointed by the legislature.

No. The president appoints the governor of the Central Bank of Liberia.

26. The legislature has a substantial voice in the operation of the state-owned media.

No. The legislature lacks a substantial voice in the operation of the public media.

27. The legislature is regularly in session.

Yes. Since the 2005 elections, the legislature has regularly met in ordinary sessions.

> Article 32
> The Legislature shall assemble in regular session once a year on the second working Monday in January. The President shall, on his own initiative or upon receipt of a certificate signed by at least one-fourth of the total membership of each House, and by proclamation, extend a regular session of the Legislature beyond the date for adjournment or call a special extraordinary session of that body to discuss or act upon matters of national emergency and concern. When the extension or call is at the request of the Legislature, the proclamation shall be issued not later than forty-eight hours after receipt of the certificate by the President.

28. Each legislator has a personal secretary.

No.

29. Each legislator has at least one non-secretarial staff member with policy expertise.

No.

30. Legislators are eligible for re-election without any restriction.

Yes. There are no restrictions on re-election.

31. A seat in the legislature is an attractive enough position that legislators are generally interested in and seek re-election.

Yes.

32. The re-election of incumbent legislators is common enough that at any given time the legislature contains a significant number of highly experienced members.

No. Decades of civil violence and the absence of a meaningful legislature have prevented legislators from developing expertise.

GENERAL PEOPLE'S CONGRESS OF LIBYA (*MUTAMAR AL SHA'AB AL 'AAM*)

Expert consultants: Alessandro Bruno, Mujeeb R. Khan, Amer K. Mohsen, Ronald Bruce St. John, Diederik Vandewalle

Score: .13

Influence over executive (2/9)		Institutional autonomy (1/9)		Specified powers (0/8)	Institutional capacity (1/6)	
1. replace		10. no dissolution	X	19. amendments	27. sessions	
2. serve as ministers	X	11. no decree		20. war	28. secretary	
3. interpellate		12. no veto		21. treaties	29. staff	
4. investigate		13. no review		22. amnesty	30. no term limits	
5. oversee police		14. no gatekeeping		23. pardon	31. seek re-election	
6. appoint PM		15. no impoundment		24. judiciary	32. experience	X
7. appoint ministers		16. control resources		25. central bank		
8. lack president	X	17. immunity		26. media		
9. no confidence		18. all elected				

The General People's Congress (*Mutamar Al Sha'ab Al 'Aam*) of Libya was established by decree by Colonel Muammar al-Qadhafi in 1977. The General People's Congress sits at the apex of a nationwide system of local People's Congresses that include every adult citizen in the country. The General People's Congress contains over 1,000 members and meets for about two weeks every year. When Congress is not in session, its powers are delegated to the cabinet (the General People's Committee), headed by the Secretary General. The members of the General People's Committee are, at least formally, selected by the General People's Congress. In practice, Libya remains under the control of Colonel Qadhafi, who does not hold an official government position. Since Qadhafi assumed power in a 1969 military coup, the country has lacked a formal constitution. The excerpts cited below are from the 1969 *Constitutional Proclamation* and the 1979 *Declaration on the Establishment of the Authority of the People* (cited in italics). The *Constitutional Proclamation* refers to the cabinet as the "Revolutionary Command Council," whose name was changed to the "General People's Committee" in 1979. Therefore, excerpts from the *Constitution Proclamation* refer to the cabinet as the Revolutionary Command Council, whereas excerpts from the 1979 *Declaration* refer to the General People's Committee.

The legislature is a symbolic organization with no meaningful authority. It has little control over the executive and scant institutional autonomy. It passes legislation in the form of annual resolutions but otherwise is denied most normal legislative functions. The legislature exercises none of the specified powers measured in this survey. Finally, annual sessions that last a mere two weeks are among the handicaps that hamper the legislature's institutional capacity.

SURVEY

1. The legislature alone, without the involvement of any other agencies, can impeach the president or replace the prime minister.

No. The legislature can impeach neither the de facto head of state, Colonel Muammar al-Qadhafi, nor the formal head of state, the Secretary General.

2. Ministers may serve simultaneously as members of the legislature.

Yes. Ministers (secretaries) may serve simultaneously in the General People's Congress.

3. The legislature has powers of summons over executive branch officials and hearings with executive branch officials testifying before the legislature or its committees are regularly held.

No. The legislature does not regularly question executive branch officials.

4. The legislature can conduct independent investigation of the chief executive and the agencies of the executive.

No. The legislature cannot investigate the executive.

5. The legislature has effective powers of oversight over the agencies of coercion (the military, organs of law enforcement, intelligence services, and the secret police).

No. The legislature lacks effective powers of oversight over the agencies of coercion.

6. The legislature appoints the prime minister.

No. Formally, the General People's Congress chooses the prime minister (Secretary General). In practice, Qadhafi appoints the prime minister.

> *Article VI*
> *The General People's Congress chooses the Secretary General and the Secretaries, dismisses them and accepts their resignations from their posts.*

7. The legislature's approval is required to confirm the appointment of ministers; or the legislature itself appoints ministers.

No. Formally, the General People's Congress chooses the ministers (secretaries). In practice, Qadhafi appoints ministers at will.

> *Article VI*
> *The General People's Congress chooses the Secretary General and the Secretaries, dismisses them and accepts their resignations from their posts.*

8. The country lacks a presidency entirely or there is a presidency, but the president is elected by the legislature.

Yes. The country lacks a presidency. Qadhafi is the de facto head of state. The official head of state, the Secretary General of the General People's Committee, is formally selected by the General People's Congress. In practice, Qadhafi chooses the Secretary General.

9. The legislature can vote no confidence in the government.

No. The legislature cannot vote no confidence in the government.

10. The legislature is immune from dissolution by the executive.

Yes. There is no institutionalized mechanism for dissolving the legislature.

11. Any executive initiative on legislation requires ratification or approval by the legislature before it takes effect; that is, the executive lacks decree power.

No. The General People's Committee issues decrees that have the force of law.

> *Article 18*
> The Revolutionary Command Council constitutes the supreme authority in the Libyan Arab Republic. It will exercise the powers attached to national sovereignty, promulgate laws and decrees.

12. Laws passed by the legislature are veto-proof or essentially veto-proof; that is, the executive lacks veto power, or has veto power but the veto can be overridden by a majority in the legislature.

No. There is no provision for veto, but in practice, Qadhafi could simply ignore resolutions of the General People's Congress with which he does not agree, and the legislature would have no recourse to override.

13. The legislature's laws are supreme and not subject to judicial review.

No. There is no judicial review process, but laws and their interpretation are decided by the General People's Committee.

14. The legislature has the right to initiate bills in all policy jurisdictions; the executive lacks gatekeeping authority.

No. Qadhafi has complete gatekeeping authority. The agenda for the annual meeting of the General People's Congress is determined by the executive. The legislature cannot initiate any bills without formal executive approval.

15. Expenditure of funds appropriated by the legislature is mandatory; the executive lacks the power to impound funds appropriated by the legislature.

No. The General People's Committee can impound funds.

16. The legislature controls the resources that finance its own internal operation and provide for the perquisites of its own members.

No. The legislature relies on the General People's Committee for the resources that finance its own operation.

17. Members of the legislature are immune from arrest and/or criminal prosecution.

No. Legislators are subject to arrest and criminal prosecution.

18. All members of the legislature are elected; the executive lacks the power to appoint any members of the legislature.

No. The members of the General People's Congress are selected by local People's Congresses and other local organizations that are under control of the executive.

Article III
The General People's Congress is the national conference of the People's Congresses, People's Committees and Professional Unions.

19. The legislature alone, without the involvement of any other agencies, can change the Constitution.

No. Changes to the basic law without Qadhafi's approval would be unthinkable.

20. The legislature's approval is necessary for the declaration of war.

No. The General People's Committee can declare war without the legislature's approval.

Article 23
The Revolutionary Command Council shall declare war, conclude and ratify treaties and agreements, unless it authorizes the Council of Ministers to do so.

21. The legislature's approval is necessary to ratify treaties with foreign countries.

No. The General People's Committee can conclude international treaties without the legislature's approval.

Article 23
The Revolutionary Command Council shall declare war, conclude and ratify treaties and agreements, unless it authorizes the Council of Ministers to do so.

22. The legislature has the power to grant amnesty.

No. Formally, amnesty is granted by law. In practice, the General People's Committee grants amnesty.

Article 32
Annulment or reduction of sentences shall be proclaimed by decree of the Revolutionary Command Council, and general amnesty by law.

23. The legislature has the power of pardon.

No. The General People's Committee has the power of pardon.

Article 32
Annulment or reduction of sentences shall be proclaimed by decree of the Revolutionary Command Council, and general amnesty by law.

24. The legislature reviews and has the right to reject appointments to the judiciary; or the legislature itself appoints members of the judiciary.

No. Formally, the legislature has a role in the appointment of judicial branch officials. In practice, the General People's Committee appoints judges.

25. The chairman of the central bank is appointed by the legislature.

No. The General People's Committee appoints the governor of the Central Bank of Libya.

26. The legislature has a substantial voice in the operation of the state-owned media.

No. The legislature lacks a substantial voice in the operation of the public media.

27. The legislature is regularly in session.

No. The General People's Congress meets in ordinary session for about two weeks each year.

28. Each legislator has a personal secretary.

No.

29. Each legislator has at least one non-secretarial staff member with policy expertise.

No.

30. Legislators are eligible for re-election without any restriction.

No. There are no direct parliamentary elections. Legislators can, however, seek subsequent terms in the legislature without any formal restriction.

31. A seat in the legislature is an attractive enough position that legislators are generally interested in and seek re-election.

No. Membership carries some perks, but the legislature has so little power and so many members, and meets so infrequently, that membership is not highly sought after.

32. The re-election of incumbent legislators is common enough that at any given time the legislature contains a significant number of highly experienced members.

Yes. Many of the same politicians return to the General People's Congress year after year, producing a significant number of highly experienced members. Given the General People's Congress's lack of real lawmaking authority, however, the body's longstanding members cannot necessarily be regarded as holders of substantial legislative expertise.

PARLIAMENT OF LITHUANIA (*SEIMAS*)

Expert consultants: Terry D. Clark, Algis Krupavicius, Alvidas Lukosaitis, Andrius Pauga, Virgis Valentinavicius, Darius Zeruolis

Score: .78

Influence over executive (6/9)		Institutional autonomy (7/9)		Specified powers (7/8)		Institutional capacity (5/6)	
1. replace	X	10. no dissolution		19. amendments	X	27. sessions	X
2. serve as ministers	X	11. no decree	X	20. war	X	28. secretary	X
3. interpellate	X	12. no veto	X	21. treaties	X	29. staff	
4. investigate	X	13. no review		22. amnesty	X	30. no term limits	X
5. oversee police	X	14. no gatekeeping	X	23. pardon		31. seek re-election	X
6. appoint PM		15. no impoundment	X	24. judiciary	X	32. experience	X
7. appoint ministers		16. control resources	X	25. central bank	X		
8. lack president		17. immunity	X	26. media	X		
9. no confidence	X	18. all elected	X				

The Parliament (*Seimas*) of Lithuania was established in the 1922 constitution. Lithuania lost its independence during World War II and was subsequently incorporated into the USSR. In 1992, following the collapse of the Soviet Union, Lithuania adopted its current constitution, which provided for a directly elected president, a prime minister, and a unicameral legislature.

The legislature has formidable power. It has substantial influence over the executive. Parliamentarians can serve in the government, and parliament can interpellate and investigate the government and remove the prime minister and president from office. The legislature's institutional autonomy is exceptionally robust. The president can dissolve the legislature, but an unusual provision tempers dissolution power. When the president dissolves the legislature, the newly elected parliament can, in turn, call new presidential elections. The legislature possesses all but one of the specified powers and has substantial institutional capacity.

SURVEY

1. The legislature alone, without the involvement of any other agencies, can impeach the president or replace the prime minister.

Yes. The legislature can remove the prime minister with a vote of no confidence. It can impeach the president with a three-fifths majority vote of its total membership. In 2004 the legislature impeached the president on corruption charges, making Lithuania the first European country ever to impeach a president.

Article 61

(1) Parliament members shall have the right to submit inquiries to the Prime Minister, the individual Ministers, and the heads of other State institutions formed or elected by the Parliament. Said persons or bodies must respond orally or in writing at the Parliaments session in the manner established by the Parliament.

(2) At sessions of the Parliament, a group of no less than one-fifth of the Parliament members may interpellate the Prime Minister or a Minister.

(3) Upon considering the response of the Prime Minister or Minister to the interpellation, the Parliament may decide that the response is not satisfactory, and, by a majority vote of half of all the Parliament members, express non-confidence in the Prime Minister or a Minister.

(4) The voting procedure shall be established by law.

Article 74

For gross violation of the Constitution, breach of oath, or upon the disclosure of the commitment of felony, the Parliament may, by three-fifths majority vote of all the Parliament members, remove from office the

President of the Republic. Such actions shall be carried out in accordance with impeachment proceedings which shall be established by the Statute of the Parliament.

2. Ministers may serve simultaneously as members of the legislature.

Yes. Legislators may serve simultaneously in ministerial positions.

Article 60
(2) A Parliament member may be appointed only as Prime Minister or Minister.

3. The legislature has powers of summons over executive branch officials and hearings with executive branch officials testifying before the legislature or its committees are regularly held.

Yes. The legislature regularly interpellates officials from the executive.

Article 61
(1) Parliament members shall have the right to submit inquiries to the Prime Minister, the individual Ministers, and the heads of other State institutions formed or elected by the Parliament. Said persons or bodies must respond orally or in writing at the Parliaments session in the manner established by the Parliament.
(2) At sessions of the Parliament, a group of no less than one-fifth of the Parliament members may interpellate the Prime Minister or a Minister.

Article 101
(1) Upon the request of the Parliament, the Government or individual Ministers must give an account of their activities to the Parliament.

4. The legislature can conduct independent investigation of the chief executive and the agencies of the executive.

Yes. The legislature can investigate the executive.

5. The legislature has effective powers of oversight over the agencies of coercion (the military, organs of law enforcement, intelligence services, and the secret police).

Yes. The legislature has effective powers of oversight over the agencies of coercion.

6. The legislature appoints the prime minister.

No. The president appoints the prime minister, who must be confirmed by parliament.

Article 92
(1) The Prime Minister shall, with the approval of the Parliament, be appointed or dismissed by the President of the Republic. The Ministers shall be appointed by the President of the Republic on the nomination of the Prime Minister.

Article 67
The Parliament shall:
6) approve or reject the candidature of the Prime Minister proposed by the President of the Republic.

Article 84
The President of the Republic shall:
4) appoint, upon approval of the Parliament, the Prime Minister, charge him or her to form the Government, and approve its composition.

7. The legislature's approval is required to confirm the appointment of ministers; or the legislature itself appoints ministers.

No. The president appoints ministers on the recommendation of the prime minister, and ministerial appointments do not require the legislature's approval.

Article 92
(1) The Prime Minister shall, with the approval of the Parliament, be appointed or dismissed by the President of the Republic. The Ministers shall be appointed by the President of the Republic on the nomination of the Prime Minister.

Article 84
The President of the Republic shall:
9) appoint or dismiss individual Ministers upon the recommendation of the Prime Minister.

8. The country lacks a presidency entirely or there is a presidency, but the president is elected by the legislature.

No. The president is directly elected.

Article 78
(2) The President of the Republic shall be elected by the citizens of the Republic of Lithuania on the basis of universal, equal, and direct suffrage by secret ballot for a term of five years.

9. The legislature can vote no confidence in the government.

Yes. The legislature can vote no confidence in the government.

Article 58
(2) The President of the Republic of Lithuania may also announce pre-term elections to the Parliament:
1) if the Parliament fails to adopt a decision on the new program of the Government within 30 days of its presentation, or if the Parliament twice in succession disapproves of the Government program within 60 days of its initial presentation; or
2) on the proposal of the Government, if the Parliament expresses direct non-confidence in the Government.

10. The legislature is immune from dissolution by the executive.

No. The president can dissolve the legislature. It is worthy of note, however, that the president jeopardizes his or her own term by choosing to dissolve the legislature.

Article 58
(1) Pre-term elections to the Parliament may be held on the decision of the Parliament adopted by three-fifths majority vote of all the Parliament members.
(2) The President of the Republic of Lithuania may also announce pre-term elections to the Parliament:
    1) if the Parliament fails to adopt a decision on the new program of the Government within 30 days of its presentation, or if the Parliament twice in succession disapproves of the Government program within 60 days of its initial presentation; or
    2) on the proposal of the Government, if the Parliament expresses direct non-confidence in the Government.

Article 87
(1) When, in cases specified in Article 58 (2), the President of the Republic announces pre-term elections to the Parliament, the newly-elected Parliament may, by three-fifths majority vote of all the Parliament members and within 30 days of the first sitting, announce a pre-term election of the President of the Republic.
(2) If the President of the Republic wishes to compete in the election, he or she shall immediately be registered as a candidate.
(3) If the President of the Republic is re-elected in such an election, he or she shall be deemed elected for a second term, provided that more than three years of the first term had expired prior to the election. If the expired period of the first term is less than three years, the President of the Republic shall only be elected for the remainder of the first term, which shall not be considered a second term.
(4) If a pre-term election for the President of the Republic is announced during the President's second term, the current President of the Republic may only be elected for the remainder of the second term.

11. Any executive initiative on legislation requires ratification or approval by the legislature before it takes effect; that is, the executive lacks decree power.

Yes. The executive lacks decree power.

12. Laws passed by the legislature are veto-proof or essentially veto-proof; that is, the executive lacks veto power, or has veto power but the veto can be overridden by a majority in the legislature.

Yes. The legislature can override a presidential veto by a majority vote of its total membership. A three-fifths majority vote is needed to override a presidential veto of a constitutional amendment.

Article 72
(1) The Parliament may reconsider and enact laws which have been referred back by the President of the Republic.

(2) After reconsideration by the Parliament, a law shall be deemed enacted if the amendments and supplements submitted by the President of the Republic were adopted, or if more than half of all the Parliament members vote in the affirmative, and if it is a constitutional law – if at least three-fifths of all the Parliament members vote in the affirmative.
(3) The President of the Republic must, within three days, sign and forthwith officially promulgate laws re-enacted by the Parliament.

13. The legislature's laws are supreme and not subject to judicial review.

No. The Constitutional Court can review the constitutionality of laws.

Article 102
(1) The Constitutional Court shall decide whether the laws and other legal acts adopted by the Parliament are in conformity with the Constitution and legal acts adopted by the President and the Government, do not violate the Constitution or laws.

14. The legislature has the right to initiate bills in all policy jurisdictions; the executive lacks gatekeeping authority.

Yes. The legislature can initiate bills in all policy jurisdictions.

15. Expenditure of funds appropriated by the legislature is mandatory; the executive lacks the power to impound funds appropriated by the legislature.

Yes. The executive lacks the power to impound funds appropriated by the legislature.

16. The legislature controls the resources that finance its own internal operation and provide for the perquisites of its own members.

Yes. The legislature enjoys financial autonomy, including control over members' salaries.

Article 60
(3) The service of a Parliament member shall be remunerated, and all expenses incurred from parliamentary activities shall be reimbursed with funds from the State Budget. A Parliament member may not receive any other salary, with the exception of payment for creative activities.

17. Members of the legislature are immune from arrest and/or criminal prosecution.

Yes. Legislators are immune with exceptions for cases of "personal insult or slander." In practice, this exception is inoperative and does not affect politics.

Article 62
(1) The person of a Parliament member shall be inviolable.

(2) Parliament members may not be found criminally responsible, may not be arrested, and may not be subjected to any other restriction of personal freedom without the consent of the Parliament.

(3) Parliament members may not be persecuted for voting or speeches in the Parliament. However, legal actions may be instituted against Parliament members according to the general procedure if they are guilty of personal insult or slander.

18. All members of the legislature are elected; the executive lacks the power to appoint any members of the legislature.

Yes. All members of the legislature are elected.

Article 55
(1) The Parliament shall consist of 141 Parliament members –
 – representatives of the People, who shall be elected for a four-year term on the basis of universal, equal, and direct suffrage by secret ballot.

19. The legislature alone, without the involvement of any other agencies, can change the Constitution.

Yes. The legislature can amend the constitution with a three-fifths majority vote. Amendments to certain specified constitutional articles require approval in a popular referendum.

Article 69
(3) Constitutional laws of the Republic of Lithuania shall be deemed adopted if more than half of all the members of the Parliament vote in the affirmative. Constitutional laws shall be amended by at least a three-fifths majority vote of all the Parliament members. The Parliament shall establish a list of constitutional laws by a three-fifths majority vote of the Parliament members.
(4) Provisions of the laws of the Republic of Lithuania may also be adopted by referendum.

Article 72
(1) The Parliament may reconsider and enact laws which have been referred back by the President of the Republic.
(2) After reconsideration by the Parliament, a law shall be deemed enacted if the amendments and supplements submitted by the President of the Republic were adopted, or if more than half of all the Parliament members vote in the affirmative, and if it is a constitutional law – if at least three-fifths of all the Parliament members vote in the affirmative.
(3) The President of the Republic must, within three days, sign and forthwith officially promulgate laws re-enacted by the Parliament.

Article 147
(1) In order to amend or append the Constitution of the Republic of Lithuania, a proposal must be submitted to the Parliament by either no less than one-fourth of the members of the Parliament, or by at least 300,000 voters.

Article 148
(1) The provision of Article 1 that the State of Lithuania is an independent democratic republic may only be amended by a referendum in which at least three-fourths of the electorate of Lithuania vote in favor thereof.
(2) The provisions of Chapter 1 and Chapter 14 may be amended only by referendum.
(3) Amendments of other chapters of the Constitution must be considered and voted upon in the Parliament twice. There must be a lapse of at least three months between each vote. Bills for constitutional amendments shall be deemed adopted by the Parliament if, in each of the votes, at least two-thirds of all the members of the Parliament vote in favor of the enactment.
(4) An amendment to the Constitution which is rejected by the Parliament may not be submitted to the Parliament for reconsideration for the period of one year.

20. The legislature's approval is necessary for the declaration of war.

Yes. The legislature alone can declare war with the common exception for cases of foreign invasion. In the case of armed invasion, the president can declare war and submit the decision to parliament for retroactive approval.

Article 67
The Parliament shall:
20) impose direct administration and martial law, declare states of emergency, announce mobilization, and adopt decisions to use the Armed Forces.

Article 84
The President of the Republic shall:
16) adopt, in the event of an armed attack which threatens State sovereignty or territorial integrity, decisions concerning defence against such armed aggression, the imposition of martial law, and mobilization, and submit these decisions to the next sitting of the Parliament for approval.
17) declare states of emergency according to the procedures and situations established by law, and submit these decisions to the next sitting of the Parliament for approval.

Article 142
(1) The Parliament shall impose martial law, shall announce mobilization or demobilization, and shall adopt decisions to use the Armed Forces in defence of the homeland or for the fulfillment of the international obligations of Lithuania.
(2) In the event of an armed attack which threatens the sovereignty of the State or territorial integrity, the President of the Republic of Lithuania shall immediately pass a decision concerning defence against such armed aggression, shall impose martial law throughout the country or in separate parts thereof, shall declare mobilization, and shall submit these decisions to the

next sitting of the Parliament; in the period between sessions, the President shall immediately convene an unscheduled session of the Parliament. The Parliament shall approve or abolish the decision of the President of the Republic of Lithuania.

21. The legislature's approval is necessary to ratify treaties with foreign countries.

Yes. The legislature's approval is necessary to ratify international treaties.

Article 67
The Parliament shall:
16) ratify or denounce international treaties whereto the Republic of Lithuania is a party, and consider other issues of foreign policy.

22. The legislature has the power to grant amnesty.

Yes. The legislature has the power to grant amnesty.

Article 67
The Parliament shall:
19) issue acts of amnesty.

23. The legislature has the power of pardon.

No. The president has the power of pardon.

Article 84
The President of the Republic shall:
23) grant pardons to sentenced persons.

24. The legislature reviews and has the right to reject appointments to the judiciary; or the legislature itself appoints members of the judiciary.

Yes. The legislature, on the president's recommendation, appoints the judges and chairpersons of the Constitutional Court and the Supreme Court. The legislature's approval is needed for the president's appointments to the Court of Appeals.

Article 67
The Parliament shall:
10) appoint judges to, and Chairpersons of, the Constitutional Court and the Supreme Court.

Article 84
The President of the Republic shall:
11) propose Supreme Court judge candidates to the Parliament, and, upon the appointment of all the Supreme Court judges, recommend from among them a Supreme Court Chairperson to the Parliament; appoint, with the approval of the Parliament, Court of Appeal judges, and from among them – the Court of Appeal Chairperson; appoint judges and chairpersons of district and local district courts, and change their places of office.
12) propose to the Parliament the candidatures of three Constitutional Court judges, and, upon appointing all the judges of the Constitutional Court, propose, from

among them, a candidate for Constitutional Court Chairperson to the Parliament.

25. The chairman of the central bank is appointed by the legislature.

Yes. The legislature, on the recommendation of the president, appoints the chairman of the Bank of Lithuania.

Article 67
The Parliament shall:
11) appoint to, and dismiss from, office the State Controller as well as the Chairperson of the Board of the Bank of Lithuania.

Article 126
(2) The Board Chairperson of the Bank of Lithuania shall be appointed for a five-year term by the Parliament on the nomination of the President of the Republic of Lithuania.

26. The legislature has a substantial voice in the operation of the state-owned media.

Yes. The legislature appoints four of the twelve members of the council that oversees Lithuanian Radio and Television (LRT).

27. The legislature is regularly in session.

Yes. The legislature meets in ordinary session for over six months each year.

Article 64
(1) Every year, the Parliament shall convene for two regular sessions – one in spring and one in fall. The spring session shall commence on March 10th and shall end on June 30th. The fall session shall commence on September 10th and shall end on December 23rd. The Parliament may resolve to prolong a session.

28. Each legislator has a personal secretary.

Yes.

29. Each legislator has at least one non-secretarial staff member with policy expertise.

No. Some, but not all, legislators have staff with policy expertise.

30. Legislators are eligible for re-election without any restriction.

Yes. There are no restrictions on re-election.

31. A seat in the legislature is an attractive enough position that legislators are generally interested in and seek re-election.

Yes.

32. The re-election of incumbent legislators is common enough that at any given time the legislature contains a significant number of highly experienced members.

Yes. Despite a re-election rate that averaged only about 40 percent in the 1996, 2000, and 2004 elections, the legislature retains a core of highly experienced members.

ASSEMBLY OF THE REPUBLIC OF MACEDONIA (*SOBRANIE*)

Expert consultants: Robert Hislope, Lidija Hristova, Andreas Klein, Ana Petruseva, Goce Todoroski

Score: .81

Influence over executive (7/9)		Institutional autonomy (8/9)		Specified powers (7/8)		Institutional capacity (4/6)	
1. replace	X	10. no dissolution	X	19. amendments	X	27. sessions	X
2. serve as ministers		11. no decree	X	20. war	X	28. secretary	
3. interpellate	X	12. no veto	X	21. treaties	X	29. staff	
4. investigate	X	13. no review		22. amnesty	X	30. no term limits	X
5. oversee police	X	14. no gatekeeping	X	23. pardon		31. seek re-election	X
6. appoint PM	X	15. no impoundment	X	24. judiciary	X	32. experience	X
7. appoint ministers	X	16. control resources	X	25. central bank	X		
8. lack president		17. immunity	X	26. media	X		
9. no confidence	X	18. all elected	X				

The Assembly (*Sobranie*) of the Republic of Macedonia was established in the 1991 constitution upon independence from Yugoslavia. The constitution calls for a unicameral legislature that elects the prime minister and cabinet, as well as a popularly elected president. Constitutional amendments in 2001 and 2005 recognized Albanian as an official language, along with Macedonian, and made changes to the judiciary, but did not directly affect the powers of parliament.

The legislature is the main stage of national politics. It influences the executive in numerous ways, including with powers to appoint the government and remove it with a vote of no confidence. The legislature also has formidable institutional autonomy. In fact, with the exception of the Constitutional Court's power to review the constitutionality of laws, the legislature enjoys every measure of autonomy included in this survey. The legislature is also vested with all but one of the specified powers and prerogatives, and it has some institutional capacity.

SURVEY

1. The legislature alone, without the involvement of any other agencies, can impeach the president or replace the prime minister.

Yes. The legislature can remove the prime minister with a vote of no confidence. Presidential impeachment requires the involvement of the Constitutional Court.

Article 87
(1) The President is held accountable for any violations of the Constitution in exercising his/her rights and duties.
(2) The procedure for determining the President of the Republic's answerability is initiated by the Assembly with a two-thirds majority vote of all Representatives.
(3) It is the Constitutional Court that decides on the answerability of the President by a two-thirds majority vote of all judges.
(4) If the Constitutional Court considers the President answerable for a violation, his/her mandate is terminated by the force of the Constitution.

Article 89
(1) The Government is composed of a Prime Minister and Ministers.

Article 92
(1) The Government and each of its members are accountable to the Assembly.
(2) The Assembly may take a vote of no-confidence in the Government.
(3) A vote of no-confidence in the Government may be initiated by a minimum of 20 Representatives.
(4) The vote of no-confidence in the Government is taken after three days have elapsed since the last

vote, unless proposed by a majority of all Representatives.

(5) A vote of no-confidence in the Government is adopted by a majority vote of all the Representatives. If a vote of no-confidence in the Government is passed, the Government is obliged to submit its resignation.

2. Ministers may serve simultaneously as members of the legislature.

No. Legislators are prohibited from serving simultaneously in ministerial positions.

Article 89

(1) The Government is composed of a Prime Minister and Ministers.

(2) The Prime Minister and the Ministers cannot be Representatives in the Assembly.

3. The legislature has powers of summons over executive branch officials and hearings with executive branch officials testifying before the legislature or its committees are regularly held.

Yes. The legislature regularly interpellates officials from the executive.

Article 72

(1) An interpellation may be made concerning the work of any public office-holder, the Government and any of its members individually, as well as on issues concerning the performance of state bodies.

(2) Interpellations may be made by a minimum of five Representatives.

(3) All Representatives have the right to ask a Representative's question.

(4) The mode and procedure for submitting and debating on an interpellation and Representative's question are regulated by the Rules of Procedure.

4. The legislature can conduct independent investigation of the chief executive and the agencies of the executive.

Yes. The legislature can set up commissions to investigate the executive.

Article 76

(1) The Assembly sets up permanent and temporary working bodies.

(2) The Assembly may set up survey commissions for any domain or any matter of public interest.

(3) A proposal for setting up a survey of commission may be submitted by a minimum of 20 Representatives.

(4) The Assembly sets up a permanent survey commission for the protection of the freedoms and rights of citizens.

(5) The findings of the survey commissions form the basis for the initiation of proceedings to ascertain the answerability of public office-holders.

5. The legislature has effective powers of oversight over the agencies of coercion (the military, organs of law enforcement, intelligence services, and the secret police).

Yes. Legislative committees have effective powers of oversight over the agencies of coercion.

6. The legislature appoints the prime minister.

Yes. The president is required to appoint as prime minister the candidate who enjoys majority support in the legislature.

Article 90

(1) The President of the Republic of Macedonia is obliged, within 10 days of the constitution of the Assembly, to entrust the mandate for constituting the Government to a candidate from the party or parties which has/have a majority in the Assembly.

(2) Within 20 days from the day of being entrusted with the mandate, the mandator submits a program to the Assembly and proposes the composition of the Government.

(3) The Government is elected by the Assembly on the proposal of the mandator and on the basis of the program by a majority vote of the total number of Representatives.

7. The legislature's approval is required to confirm the appointment of ministers; or the legislature itself appoints ministers.

Yes. The legislature elects the government on the proposal of the prime minister.

Article 90

(1) The President of the Republic of Macedonia is obliged, within 10 days of the constitution of the Assembly, to entrust the mandate for constituting the Government to a candidate from the party or parties which has/have a majority in the Assembly.

(2) Within 20 days from the day of being entrusted with the mandate, the mandator submits a program to the Assembly and proposes the composition of the Government.

(3) The Government is elected by the Assembly on the proposal of the mandator and on the basis of the program by a majority vote of the total number of Representatives.

8. The country lacks a presidency entirely or there is a presidency, but the president is elected by the legislature.

No. The president is directly elected.

Article 80

(1) The President of the Republic of Macedonia is elected in general and direct elections, by secret ballot, for a term of five years.

9. The legislature can vote no confidence in the government.

Yes. The legislature can vote no confidence in the government.

Article 92

(1) The Government and each of its members are accountable to the Assembly.

(2) The Assembly may take a vote of no-confidence in the Government.

(3) A vote of no-confidence in the Government may be initiated by a minimum of 20 Representatives.

(4) The vote of no-confidence in the Government is taken after three days have elapsed since the last vote, unless proposed by a majority of all Representatives.

(5) A vote of no-confidence in the Government is adopted by a majority vote of all the Representatives. If a vote of no-confidence in the Government is passed, the Government is obliged to submit its resignation.

10. The legislature is immune from dissolution by the executive.

Yes. The legislature is immune from dissolution by the executive. The legislature can, however, vote to dissolve itself.

> Article 63
> (5) The Assembly is dissolved when more than half of the total number of Representatives vote for dissolution.

11. Any executive initiative on legislation requires ratification or approval by the legislature before it takes effect; that is, the executive lacks decree power.

Yes. The executive lacks decree power.

12. Laws passed by the legislature are veto-proof or essentially veto-proof; that is, the executive lacks veto power, or has veto power but the veto can be overridden by a majority in the legislature.

Yes. The legislature can override a presidential veto by a majority vote of its total membership, although the constitution is ambiguous, if not outright contradictory, on this question.

> Article 75
> (2) The promulgation declaring a law is signed by the President of the Republic and the President of the Assembly.
> (3) The President of the Republic may decide not to sign the promulgation declaring a law. The Assembly considers the President of the Republic is then obligated to sign the promulgation in so far as it is adopted by a majority vote of the total number of Representatives.
> (4) The President is obligated to sign a promulgation if the law has been adopted by a two-thirds majority vote of the total number of Representatives in accordance with the Constitution.

13. The legislature's laws are supreme and not subject to judicial review.

No. The Constitutional Court can review the constitutionality of laws.

> Article 110
> The Constitutional Court of Macedonia.

– decides on the conformity of laws with the Constitution.

14. The legislature has the right to initiate bills in all policy jurisdictions; the executive lacks gatekeeping authority.

Yes. The legislature can initiate bills in all policy jurisdictions.

15. Expenditure of funds appropriated by the legislature is mandatory; the executive lacks the power to impound funds appropriated by the legislature.

Yes. The executive lacks the power to impound funds appropriated by the legislature.

16. The legislature controls the resources that finance its own internal operation and provide for the perquisites of its own members.

Yes. The legislature enjoys financial autonomy, including control over members' salaries.

> Article 64
> (6) A Representative is entitled to remuneration determined by law.

17. Members of the legislature are immune from arrest and/or criminal prosecution.

Yes. Legislators are immune with the common exception for cases of *flagrante delicto* for major crimes, here expressed as "found committing a criminal offence for which a prison sentence of at least five years is prescribed."

> Article 64
> (1) Representatives enjoy immunity.
> (2) A Representative cannot be held to have committed a criminal offence or be detained owing to views he/she has expressed or to the way he/she has voted in the Assembly.
> (3) A Representative cannot be detained without the approval of the Assembly unless found committing a criminal offence for which a prison sentence of at least five years is prescribed.
> (4) The Assembly can decide to invoke immunity for a Representative without his/her request, should it be necessary for the performance of the Representative's office.

18. All members of the legislature are elected; the executive lacks the power to appoint any members of the legislature.

Yes. All members of the legislature are elected.

> Article 62
> (1) The Assembly of the Republic of Macedonia is composed of 120 to 140 Representatives.
> (2) The Representatives are elected at general, direct and free elections and by secret ballot.

19. The legislature alone, without the involvement of any other agencies, can change the Constitution.

Yes. The legislature can change the constitution with a two-thirds majority vote.

Article 68
(1) The Assembly of the Republic of Macedonia:
– adopts and changes the Constitution.

Article 131
(1) The decisions to initiate a change in the Constitution is made by the Assembly by a two-thirds majority vote of the total number of Representatives.
(2) The draft amendment of the Constitution is confirmed by the Assembly by a majority vote of the total number of Representatives and then submitted to public debate.
(3) The decision to change the Constitution is made by the Assembly by a two-thirds majority vote of the total number of Representatives.
(4) The change in the Constitution is declared by the Assembly.

20. The legislature's approval is necessary for the declaration of war.

Yes. The legislature declares war on the proposal of the president with the common exception for cases of foreign invasion. In the event of an attack or an impending attack during a time when the legislature is out of session and cannot meet, the president can declare war and then submit the decision to the legislature for retroactive authorization.

Article 68
(1) The Assembly of the Republic of Macedonia:
– decides on war and peace.

Article 124
(1) A state of war exists when direct danger of military attack on the Republic is impending, or when the Republic is attacked, or war is declared on it.
(2) A state of war is declared by the Assembly by a two-thirds majority vote of the total number of Representatives of the Assembly, on the proposal of the President of the Republic, the Government or at least 30 Representatives.
(3) If the Assembly cannot meet, the decision on the declaration of a state of war is made by the President of the Republic who submits it to the Assembly for confirmation as soon as it can meet.

21. The legislature's approval is necessary to ratify treaties with foreign countries.

Yes. The legislature's approval is necessary to ratify international treaties.

Article 68
(1) The Assembly of the Republic of Macedonia:
– ratifies international agreements.

Article 119
(1) International agreements are concluded in the name of the Republic of Macedonia by the President of the Republic of Macedonia.
(2) International agreements may also be concluded by the Government of the Republic of Macedonia, when it is so determined by law.

22. The legislature has the power to grant amnesty.

Yes. The legislature has the power to grant amnesty.

Article 68
(1) The Assembly of the Republic of Macedonia:
– proclaims amnesties.

23. The legislature has the power of pardon.

No. The president has the power of pardon.

Article 84
The President of the Republic of Macedonia
– grants pardons in accordance with the law.

24. The legislature reviews and has the right to reject appointments to the judiciary; or the legislature itself appoints members of the judiciary.

Yes. The legislature appoints the members of the Republican Judicial Council and the members of the Constitutional Court.

Article 104
(1) The Republican Judicial Council is composed of seven members.
(2) The Assembly elects the members of the Council.

Article 109
(1) The Constitutional Court of Macedonia is composed of nine judges.
(2) The Assembly elects the judges to the Constitutional Court by a majority vote of the total number of Representatives. The term of office of the judges is nine years without the right to reelection.

25. The chairman of the central bank is appointed by the legislature.

Yes. The legislature, on the recommendation of the president, appoints the governor of the National Bank of the Republic of Macedonia.

26. The legislature has a substantial voice in the operation of the state-owned media.

Yes. The legislature has a substantial voice in the operation of the public media.

27. The legislature is regularly in session.

Yes. The legislature is permanently in session.

Article 66
(1) The Assembly is in permanent session.

28. Each legislator has a personal secretary.

No. There is legislative staff, but on average there is less than one staff person for each legislator. For example, each parliamentary group has a single secretary, and policy expertise is provided by the Staff Service of the Assembly.

29. Each legislator has at least one non-secretarial staff member with policy expertise.

No. See item 28.

30. Legislators are eligible for re-election without any restriction.

Yes. There are no restrictions on re-election.

31. A seat in the legislature is an attractive enough position that legislators are generally interested in and seek re-election.

Yes.

32. The re-election of incumbent legislators is common enough that at any given time the legislature contains a significant number of highly experienced members.

Yes. Re-election rates are sufficiently high to produce a significant number of highly experienced members.

NATIONAL ASSEMBLY OF MADAGASCAR (*ANTENIMIERAM-PIRENENA/ ASSEMBLÉE NATIONALE*)

Expert consultants: Richard R. Marcus, Dominique Rakotomalala, Solofo Randrianja, Adrien M. Ratsimbaharison, Marc Spindler

Score: .41

Influence over executive (1/9)		Institutional autonomy (5/9)		Specified powers (4/8)		Institutional capacity (3/6)	
1. replace		10. no dissolution		19. amendments		27. sessions	
2. serve as ministers		11. no decree		20. war	X	28. secretary	
3. interpellate		12. no veto	X	21. treaties	X	29. staff	
4. investigate		13. no review		22. amnesty	X	30. no term limits	X
5. oversee police		14. no gatekeeping	X	23. pardon		31. seek re-election	X
6. appoint PM		15. no impoundment	X	24. judiciary	X	32. experience	X
7. appoint ministers		16. control resources	X	25. central bank			
8. lack president		17. immunity	X	26. media			
9. no confidence	X	18. all elected					

The National Assembly (*Antenimieram-Pirenena/ Assemblée nationale*) of Madagascar was established in 1960 upon independence from France. Between 1976 and 1991, President Didier Ratsiraka, who gained power in a military coup, instituted a socialist government with a hegemonic party that dominated the legislature. Political pressure led to reforms and the adoption of the current constitution in 1992. The constitution calls for a bicameral legislature consisting of a lower house, the National Assembly (*Antenimieram-Pirenena/Assemblée nationale*), and an upper house, the Senate (*Antenimieran-Doholona/Sénat*). The Senate was not established until 2001.

Constitutional amendments in 1995 and 1998 weakened the legislature, shifting power to appoint the prime minister from the Assembly to the president and granting the president the right to appoint members of the Senate. Once the Senate finally convened in 2001, one-third of its members were presidential appointees. The constitutional changes also expanded the president's power to dissolve the legislature and stripped the legislature of its prior right to change the constitution on its own. Since the changes of the 1990s, the legislature can alter the constitution only with the assent of the president or of the people as a whole in a popular referendum. In 2007 voters approved in a referendum constitutional changes that allowed the president the right to issue decrees in emergencies without first obtaining the legislature's approval. In fact, even prior to that time, the president issued decrees that had the force of law, even in nonemergency situations. The referendum merely formalized a power that was already being wielded in practice.

Despite these measures, the legislature retains some power. It possesses little meaningful control over the executive, but it has some institutional autonomy. The president lacks gatekeeping and veto powers, and legislators enjoy immunity from arrest. The legislature is granted several specified powers and has modest institutional capacity.

SURVEY

1. The legislature alone, without the involvement of any other agencies, can impeach the president or replace the prime minister.

No. Presidential impeachment requires the involvement of the High Court of Justice. The legislature can remove the prime minister with a vote of no confidence.

Article 91
The Prime Minister, after deliberation in the Council of Ministers, may commit the responsibility of his Government by raising the question of confidence.
The vote may only take place forty-eight hours after the filing of the question. If it is placed in minority by an absolute majority of the members composing the National Assembly, the Government remits its resignation to the President of the Republic.
The President of the Republic appoints a Prime Minister, according to Article 53.

Article 113
The President of the Republic is accountable for acts accomplished in the exercise or on the occasion of the exercise of his functions deciding only in case of high treason or severe and repeated violation of the Constitution.
He may be impeached only by the two parliamentary Assemblies deciding by a separate vote, by public ballot and a majority of two-thirds of the members composing each assembly.
He is justiciable by the High Court of Justice and may incur forfeiture.
If forfeiture is pronounced, the High Constitutional Court establishes the vacancy of the Presidency of the Republic; the election of a new President will be initiated within the conditions of Article 47 above. The President struck with forfeiture is no longer eligible to any elective public function.

2. Ministers may serve simultaneously as members of the legislature.

No. Ministers are prohibited from serving simultaneously in the legislature.

Article 62
The functions of member of the Government are incompatible with the exercise of any elected public mandate, of any function of professional representation, any public employment or any other remunerated professional activity.

Article 67
The mandate of Deputy is incompatible with the exercise of all other elected, public mandate and all public office except teaching.
A Deputy appointed as a member of the Government is relieved of the office of his mandate.

3. The legislature has powers of summons over executive branch officials and hearings with executive branch officials testifying before the legislature or its committees are regularly held.

No. Formally, the legislature can interpellate executive branch officials, but in practice, it rarely does so.

Article 93
(1) The National Assembly shall be informed of governmental action by means of oral questions, written questions, summonses, and commissions of inquiry.
(2) During ordinary sessions, one meeting a month shall be reserved for questions put to the Government by members of Parliament and for the Government's responses.

4. The legislature can conduct independent investigation of the chief executive and the agencies of the executive.

No. The legislature cannot investigate the executive.

5. The legislature has effective powers of oversight over the agencies of coercion (the military, organs of law enforcement, intelligence services, and the secret police).

No. The legislature lacks effective powers of oversight over the agencies of coercion.

6. The legislature appoints the prime minister.

No. The president appoints the prime minister.

Article 53
The President of the Republic appoints the Prime Minister.
He terminates his functions for any determinant reason.
Upon proposal of the Prime Minister, he appoints the other members of the Government and terminates their functions.

7. The legislature's approval is required to confirm the appointment of ministers; or the legislature itself appoints ministers.

No. The president appoints the ministers, and the appointments do not require the legislature's approval.

> Article 53
> The President of the Republic appoints the Prime Minister.
> He terminates his functions for any determinant reason.
> Upon proposal of the Prime Minister, he appoints the other members of the Government and terminates their functions.

8. The country lacks a presidency entirely or there is a presidency, but the president is elected by the legislature.

No. The president is directly elected.

> Article 45
> The President of the Republic shall be elected by universal direct suffrage for a five-year term. He may be re-elected for one additional term.

9. The legislature can vote no confidence in the government.

Yes. The legislature can vote no confidence in the government.

> Article 91
> The Prime Minister, after deliberation in the Council of Ministers, may commit the responsibility of his Government by raising the question of confidence.
> The vote may only take place forty-eight hours after the filing of the question. If it is placed in minority by an absolute majority of the members composing the National Assembly, the Government remits its resignation to the President of the Republic.
> The President of the Republic appoints a Prime Minister, according to Article 53.

10. The legislature is immune from dissolution by the executive.

No. The president can dissolve the legislature.

> Article 95
> The President of the Republic may dissolve the National Assembly for determinant causes.

11. Any executive initiative on legislation requires ratification or approval by the legislature before it takes effect; that is, the executive lacks decree power.

No. Prior to 2007 the president could rule by decree only when he or she has received prior authorization from the legislature to do so. In practice, the president issued decrees that had the force of law without prior legislative authorization. In a referendum held in 2007, voters endorsed giving the president the right to legislate by decree in emergencies. In practice, the president's use of decree powers, like before the new measure was passed in the referendum, is not limited to emergencies.

> Article 96
> The Parliament, by a vote of an absolute majority of the members composing each Assembly, may delegate its power to legislate to the President of the Republic, for a limited time and for a specific purpose.
> The delegation of power authorizes the President of the Republic to take, by ordinance in the Council of Ministers, general measures falling within the domain of the law. They enter into force on their publication but become lapsed if the bill of the law of ratification is not presented before the National Assembly prior to the date established by the enabling law.

12. Laws passed by the legislature are veto-proof or essentially veto-proof; that is, the executive lacks veto power, or has veto power but the veto can be overridden by a majority in the legislature.

Yes. The legislature can override a presidential veto by a majority vote of its present members.

> Article 57
> The President of the Republic promulgates the laws within three weeks of the transmission by the National Assembly of the law definitely adopted.
> Before the expiration of this time limit, the President of the Republic may demand the Parliament for a new deliberation of the law or of certain of its articles. This new deliberation may not be refused.

13. The legislature's laws are supreme and not subject to judicial review.

No. The High Constitutional Court can review the constitutionality of laws.

> Article 118
> In addition to the questions that are referred to it by other articles of the Constitution, the High Constitutional Court, within conditions determined by an organic law:
> – decides on the conformity to the Constitution of the treaties, the laws, the ordinances, the Interprovincial Conventions, and the autonomous regulations decreed the Central Power.

14. The legislature has the right to initiate bills in all policy jurisdictions; the executive lacks gatekeeping authority.

Yes. The legislature can initiate bills in all policy jurisdictions.

15. Expenditure of funds appropriated by the legislature is mandatory; the executive lacks the power to impound funds appropriated by the legislature.

Yes. The executive lacks the power to impound funds appropriated by the legislature.

16. The legislature controls the resources that finance its own internal operation and provide for the perquisites of its own members.

Yes. The legislature enjoys financial autonomy.

17. Members of the legislature are immune from arrest and/or criminal prosecution.

Yes. Legislators are immune with the common exception for cases of *flagrante delicto.*

Article 69
(1) No deputy may be prosecuted, investigated, arrested, detained, or judged for opinions and votes cast by him in the exercise of his duties.
(2) For the duration of legislative sessions, no deputy may be prosecuted or arrested in a criminal or correctional matter, without the authorization of the bureau of the Assembly, except in case of flagrante delicto.
(3) Outside of legislative sessions, no deputy may be arrested without the authorization of the bureau of the Assembly, except in case of flagrante delicto, authorized prosecution, or final conviction.
(4) Anyone may bring to the attention of the National Assembly the acts or omissions of a deputy. The permanent bureau must furnish a prompt response.

18. All members of the legislature are elected; the executive lacks the power to appoint any members of the legislature.

No. The president appoints one-third of the Senate's membership. All members of the National Assembly are elected.

Article 66
(1) The members of the National Assembly shall have the title of Deputies of Madagascar.
(2) They shall be elected by direct universal suffrage for four-year terms.

Article 77
(1) Two-thirds of the Senate shall consist of an equal number of members elected in each electoral district by elected representatives of the territorial entities, and one-third shall consist of members representing economic, social, cultural, and religious groups appointed by the President of the Republic upon nomination by legally constituted organizations and groups.

19. The legislature alone, without the involvement of any other agencies, can change the Constitution.

No. The legislature alone cannot change the constitution without the approval of the president. If the president objects to a constitutional amendment that has been passed by the legislature, he or she can choose to put the amendment to a nationwide referendum.

Article 140
The initiative of the revision of the Constitution belongs either to the President of the Republic who decides in the Council of Ministers, or to the parliamentary Assemblies deciding by a separate vote of the absolute majority of the members composing each assembly.
No project or proposal of revision may have the object of affecting the integrity of the national territory.

Article 141
The project or proposal of revision is adopted only by a majority of three-quarters of the members of the National Assembly and the Senate.

Article 142
The President of the Republic, in the Council of Ministers, may decide to submit the revision of the Constitution to a referendum.

20. The legislature's approval is necessary for the declaration of war.

Yes. The legislature declares war.

Article 58
(2) In addition to matters referred to the Parliament by other articles of the Constitution:
V) War may only be declared by Parliament.

21. The legislature's approval is necessary to ratify treaties with foreign countries.

Yes. The legislature's approval is necessary to ratify international treaties on most major issues.

Article 82
(2) In addition to matters referred to the Parliament by other articles of the Constitution:
VIII) The ratification or approval of treaties of alliance, treaties of commerce, treaties or agreements relating to international organization, of those which bind the finances of the State, of those which modify the provisions of legislative nature, of those which concern the state of persons, of treaties of peace, of those which entail modification of territory, must be authorized by the law. Prior to any ratification, the treaties are submitted by the President of the Republic to the control of constitutionality of the High Constitutional Court. In case of non-conformity to the Constitution, ratification may take place only after revision of it. The treaties or agreements regularly ratified or approved have, upon their publication, an authority superior to those of the laws, with reservation, for each agreement or treaty, of its application by the other party.

22. The legislature has the power to grant amnesty.

Yes. The legislature has the power to grant amnesty.

Article 82
(2) In addition to matters referred to the Parliament by other articles of the Constitution:
I) The law shall establish rules concerning ... amnesty.

23. The legislature has the power of pardon.

No. The president has the power of pardon.

Article 56
(6) [The president] shall have the right of pardon.

24. The legislature reviews and has the right to reject appointments to the judiciary; or the legislature itself appoints members of the judiciary.

Yes. The legislature appoints three of the nine members of the High Constitutional Court and four of the nine members of the High Court of Justice.

Article 98
The President of the Republic is the guarantor of the independence of Justice.
For this purpose, he is assisted by a Superior Council of the Magistrature of which he is the president. The Minister charged with Justice is the vice-president of it.

Article 98.1
The magistrate is appointed to the office corresponding to his rank or dismissed from his function by a decree of the President of the Republic taken according to the conditions determined by an organic law.

Article 106
The First President and the Procurator General of the Supreme Court are the heads of this high jurisdiction. They are respectively appointed in the Council of Ministers upon proposal of the Minister charged with Justice after consultation with the Superior Council of the Magistrature.

Article 106.1
The First President of the Supreme Court is seconded by three Vice-Presidents, entrusted respectively with the presidency of the Court of Cassation, of the Council of State and of the Court of Accounts. Each Vice-President is chosen among the magistrates in office in the Supreme Court, the most senior at the highest level of the judicial, administrative or financial order concerned.

Article 116
The High Court of Justice is composed of nine members:
– The First President of the Supreme Court, President, substituted by right, in case of incapacity, by the President of the Court of Cassation;
– two presidents of the Chamber of the Court of Cassation, and two substitutes, designated by the general assembly of the said Court;
– two first presidents of the Courts of Appeal, and two substitutes, designated by the First President of the Supreme Court;
– two titular Deputies and two substitute Deputies, elected by the National Assembly;
– two titular Senators and two substitute Senators, elected by the Senate.
The public Ministry is represented by the Procurator General of the Supreme Court assisted by one or several members of his general public prosecutor's department. In case of incapacity of the Procurator General, he is substituted by the chief clerk of the Court of Cassation.

Article 119
The High Constitutional Court is composed of nine members whose mandate lasts seven years.

Three of the members are appointed by the President of the Republic, two are designated by the National Assembly, two by the Senate, two are elected by the Superior Council of the Magistrature. The President of the High Constitutional Court is appointed by decree of the President of the Republic. The designation of the other members is established by decree of the President of the Republic.

25. The chairman of the central bank is appointed by the legislature.

No. The president appoints the governor of the Central Bank of Madagascar.

26. The legislature has a substantial voice in the operation of the state-owned media.

No. The legislature lacks a substantial voice in the operation of the public media.

27. The legislature is regularly in session.

No. Formally, the legislature meets in ordinary session for four to six months each year, and in practice, it is generally in session for less than half the year.

Article 71
The National Assembly shall meet officially in two ordinary sessions per year. The length of each session may not be less than sixty days nor more than ninety days. The first session shall begin on the first Tuesday in May, and the second, devoted principally to the adoption of the budget, on the last Tuesday in September.

28. Each legislator has a personal secretary.
No.

29. Each legislator has at least one non-secretarial staff member with policy expertise.
No.

30. Legislators are eligible for re-election without any restriction.
Yes. There are no restrictions on re-election.

31. A seat in the legislature is an attractive enough position that legislators are generally interested in and seek re-election.
Yes.

32. The re-election of incumbent legislators is common enough that at any given time the legislature contains a significant number of highly experienced members.

Yes. Re-election rates are sufficiently high to produce a significant number of highly experienced members.

NATIONAL ASSEMBLY OF MALAWI

Expert consultants: Blessings Chinsinga, Brionne Dawson, Lameck Gondwe, Rob Jamieson, Heiko Meinhardt, Eric Pelser, Kimberly Smiddy, Arne Tostensen

Score: .38

Influence over executive (3/9)		Institutional autonomy (4/9)		Specified powers (2/8)		Institutional capacity (3/6)	
1. replace		10. no dissolution	X	19. amendments	X	27. sessions	
2. serve as ministers	X	11. no decree	X	20. war		28. secretary	
3. interpellate	X	12. no veto	X	21. treaties	X	29. staff	
4. investigate	X	13. no review		22. amnesty		30. no term limits	X
5. oversee police		14. no gatekeeping		23. pardon		31. seek re-election	X
6. appoint PM		15. no impoundment		24. judiciary		32. experience	X
7. appoint ministers		16. control resources		25. central bank			
8. lack president		17. immunity		26. media			
9. no confidence		18. all elected	X				

The National Assembly of Malawi traces its beginnings to the Nyasaland African Congress that was established under British colonial rule. Malawi gained independence in 1964. The 1966 constitution, while calling for a legislative assembly, also created a single-party state. Shortly thereafter President Hastings Banda became president, and he dominated national politics for the next quarter-century. Banda exited power in 1993, paving the way for political change. The current constitution, established in 1994, calls for a bicameral legislature consisting of a lower house, the National Assembly, and an upper house, the Senate. To date the Senate has not yet convened, making the legislature de facto a unicameral body.

The legislature plays a part in national political life, although that role is not expansive. It has some ability to keep tabs on the government: Its members can serve in government, and it has the power to investigate and interpellate executive branch officials. The legislature's greatest strength is in the realm of institutional autonomy. It does not contend with presidential decree powers, it can overrule the president's veto with a majority vote, it cannot be dissolved by the president, and the president does not appoint any members of the legislature. The legislature possesses only two of the eight specified powers assessed in this survey, and its institutional capacity is slight.

SURVEY

1. The legislature alone, without the involvement of any other agencies, can impeach the president or replace the prime minister.

No. The legislature cannot impeach the president. This issue of impeachment is currently being discussed in parliament, however. The constitution states that the parliament should follow the procedures for impeachment in the standing orders, but the standing orders do not yet include these procedures.

Article 86

(1) The President and Vice-President shall be removed from office where the National Assembly has indicted and convicted the President or Vice-President by impeachment.

(2) The procedure for impeachment shall be as laid down by the Standing Orders of Parliament, provided that they are in full accord with the principles of natural justice and that –

(a) indictment and conviction by impeachment shall only be on the grounds of serious violation of the Constitution or serious breach of the written laws of the Republic that either occurred or came to light during the term of office of the President or the Vice-President;

(b) indictment on impeachment shall require the affirmative vote of two-thirds of the members of the National Assembly in a committee of the whole house;

(c) the Speaker shall preside over proceedings of indictment by impeachment and the Chief Justice shall preside over trial on impeachment;

(d) conviction on impeachment shall require the affirmative vote of two-thirds of the members of both Chambers;

(e) conviction in cases of impeachment shall cause the removal, and disqualification from future office, of the office holder; and

(f) conviction by way of impeachment shall not act as a bar to legal proceedings.

2. Ministers may serve simultaneously as members of the legislature.

Yes. At present, virtually all ministers are also legislators. The Supreme Court's interpretation of the constitution is that ministers may serve simultaneously in the legislature, although the matter is a subject of public debate.

> Article 88
> (3) The President and members of the Cabinet shall not hold any other public office and shall not perform remunerative work outside the duties of their office and shall fully disclose all of their assets, liabilities and business interests, those of their spouses, or held on their behalf upon election.

3. The legislature has powers of summons over executive branch officials and hearings with executive branch officials testifying before the legislature or its committees are regularly held.

Yes. The legislature regularly interpellates officials from the executive, although the responsible committees are dependent on external donor funding for their operations.

> Article 60
> (3) The National Assembly and the Senate shall each have the power to conduct investigations and exercise the power to subpoena the attendance of any person or office holder whosoever as required in connexion with the prudent exercise of the respective functions of each Chamber.
> (4) The President shall be called to Parliament to answer questions at such times as may be prescribed by the Standing Orders of Parliament or on a motion of the National Assembly or Senate.

4. The legislature can conduct independent investigation of the chief executive and the agencies of the executive.

Yes. The legislature can investigate the executive.

> Article 60
> (3) The National Assembly and the Senate shall each have the power to conduct investigations and exercise the power to subpoena the attendance of any person or office holder whosoever as required in connection with

the prudent exercise of the respective functions of each Chamber.

5. The legislature has effective powers of oversight over the agencies of coercion (the military, organs of law enforcement, intelligence services, and the secret police).

No. The legislature lacks effective powers of oversight over the agencies of coercion.

6. The legislature appoints the prime minister.

No. There is no prime minister.

7. The legislature's approval is required to confirm the appointment of ministers; or the legislature itself appoints ministers.

No. The president appoints ministers, and the appointments do not require the legislature's approval.

> Article 92
> (1) There shall be a Cabinet consisting of the President, the Vice-President and such Ministers and Deputy Ministers as may, from time to time, be appointed by the President.

> Article 93
> (1) There shall be Ministers and Deputy Ministers who shall be appointed by the President and who shall exercise such powers and functions, including the running of Government departments, as may be prescribed by the President subject to this Constitution.

8. The country lacks a presidency entirely or there is a presidency, but the president is elected by the legislature.

No. The president is directly elected.

> Article 80
> (2) The President shall be elected by a majority of the electorate through direct, universal and equal suffrage.

9. The legislature can vote no confidence in the government.

No. The legislature cannot vote no confidence in the government.

10. The legislature is immune from dissolution by the executive.

Yes. The legislature is immune from dissolution.

> Article 67
> (1) The National Assembly shall last for five years from the date of its swearing in and then shall stand dissolved.

> Article 72
> The Senate shall continue from the date of its first sitting, being no later than thirty days after a Local Government election after any dissolution, until it dissolves sixty days before the next Local Government elections:

Provided that the life of the Senate shall not, in any case, be longer than three years.

11. Any executive initiative on legislation requires ratification or approval by the legislature before it takes effect; that is, the executive lacks decree power.

Yes. The president lacks decree power.

12. Laws passed by the legislature are veto-proof or essentially veto-proof; that is, the executive lacks veto power, or has veto power but the veto can be overridden by a majority in the legislature.

Yes. The legislature can override a presidential veto by a majority vote of its present members.

> Article 73
> (1) Where a Bill is presented to the President for assent, the President shall either assent or withhold assent.
> (2) Where the President withholds assent to a Bill, the Bill shall be returned to the Speaker of the National Assembly by the President with a notification that the President's assent has been withheld, including reasons therefor, and the Bill shall not be again debated by the National Assembly until after the expiry of twenty-one days from the date of the notification of that withholding.
> (3) If the Bill is debated again and passed by a majority of the National Assembly at any time between the date of the expiry of the twenty-one days referred to in subsection (2) and six months from that date, the Bill shall again be presented for assent by the President.
> (4) Where a Bill is again presented to the President for assent in accordance with subsection (3), the President shall assent to the Bill within twenty-one days of its presentation.

13. The legislature's laws are supreme and not subject to judicial review.

No. The High Court of the Republic can review the constitutionality of laws.

> Article 108
> (2) The High Court shall have original jurisdiction to review any law, and any action or decision of the Government, for conformity with this Constitution, save as otherwise provided by this Constitution and shall have such other jurisdiction and powers as may be conferred on it by this Constitution or any other law.

14. The legislature has the right to initiate bills in all policy jurisdictions; the executive lacks gatekeeping authority.

No. The legislature is prohibited from introducing legislation related to taxation, public expenditures, and government debt.

> Article 57
> (1) Except upon the recommendation of the Minister responsible for Finance, signified in writing, the National Assembly shall not –

> (a) proceed upon any Bill or any amendment to a Bill that, in the opinion of the person presiding, makes provision for any of the following purposes –
> (i) for the imposition of tax or the alteration of tax;
> (ii) for the imposition of any charge upon the Consolidated Fund, or the alteration of any such charge;
> (iii) for the payment, issue or withdrawal from the Consolidated Fund of any moneys not charged thereon, or any increase in the amount of such payment, issue or withdrawal; or
> (iv) for the composition or remission of any debt due to the Government;
> (b) proceed upon any motion or any amendment to a motion the effect of which, in the opinion of the person presiding, would be to make provision for any of the purposes specified in subsection (a); or
> (c) receive any petition that, in the opinion of the person presiding, requests that provision be made for any of the purposes.

15. Expenditure of funds appropriated by the legislature is mandatory; the executive lacks the power to impound funds appropriated by the legislature.

No. The president can impound funds appropriated by the legislature. Malawi operates on a cash budget, which gives the president pretexts for impounding funds. Even so-called "protected" expenditure can be impounded.

16. The legislature controls the resources that finance its own internal operation and provide for the perquisites of its own members.

No. The legislature lacks financial autonomy. The budgetary allocations for parliamentary business are inadequate. The committees are largely dependent on external donor funding, and some cannot even meet because of a lack of funds. Entire parliamentary sessions have been canceled because the minister of finance refused to allocate the necessary funds.

17. Members of the legislature are immune from arrest and/or criminal prosecution.

No. Legislators are immune only for statements made in the legislature and while they are going to, returning from, or located on the grounds of the legislature. Otherwise they are subject to arrest.

> Article 60
> (1) The Speaker, every Deputy Speaker, every member of the National Assembly and every member of the Senate shall, except in cases of treason, be privileged from arrest while going to, returning from, or while in the precincts of the National Assembly or the Senate, and shall not, in respect of any utterance that forms part of the proceedings in the National Assembly or the Senate,

be amenable to any other action or proceedings in any court, tribunal or body other than Parliament.

18. All members of the legislature are elected; the executive lacks the power to appoint any members of the legislature.

Yes. The executive lacks the power to appoint any members of the legislature. All members of the National Assembly are directly elected. Election to the Senate is indirect but does not involve appointment by the executive. The Senate, although established in the 1994 constitution, has never convened.

Article 66
(1) The National Assembly shall be a directly elected Chamber.

Article 68
(1) The Senate shall consist of eighty members as follows –
(a) one Senator from each District, registered as a voter in that District and elected by the District Council of that District in secret ballot within thirty days of each local government election;
(b) one Senator from each District, being a Chief registered as a voter in that District and elected by a caucus of all the Chiefs of that District in secret ballot within thirty days of each local government election;
(c) thirty-two other Senators who shall be elected by a two-thirds majority of sitting members of the Senate on the basis of nominations by the Nominations Committee provided for in subsection
(2) from all of the following sectors –
(i) interest groups, who shall include representatives from women's organizations, the disabled and from health, education, farming and business sectors, and from trade unions;
(ii) society, who shall be such persons as are generally recognized for their outstanding service to the public or contribution to the social, cultural, or technological development of the nation; and
(iii) religion, who shall include representatives of the major religious faiths in Malawi.
Functions and powers of the Senate.

Article 70
The Senate shall be an indirectly elected chamber.

19. The legislature alone, without the involvement of any other agencies, can change the Constitution.

Yes. The legislature can change the constitution with a two-thirds majority vote. Amendments to the constitutional amendment process itself and to the chapters listed in the "schedule," which includes provisions on fundamental principles, human rights, and citizenship, require approval in a popular referendum.

Article 195
Parliament may amend this Constitution in accordance with this Chapter.

Article 196
(1) Subject to this section, Parliament may amend this Chapter and the sections of this Constitution listed in the Schedule only if –
(a) the provision to be amended and the proposed amended to it have been put to a referendum of the people of Malawi and the majority of those voting have voted for the amendment; and
(b) the Electoral Commission has so certified to the Speaker.
(2) The Parliament may pass a Bill proposing an amendment to which the conditions set out in subsection (1) have been satisfied by a simple majority.
(3) Notwithstanding subsection (1), Parliament may pass a Bill containing an amendment to the provisions referred to in that subsection without a referendum where –
(a) the amendment would not affect the substance of the effect of the Constitution;
(b) the Speaker has so certified; and
(c) the Bill is supported by a majority of at least two-thirds of the total number of members of the National Assembly entitled to vote.

Article 197
Subject to section 196, Parliament may amend those Chapters and sections of this Constitution not listed in the Schedule only if the Bill proposing the amendment is supported by at least two-thirds of the total number of members of the National Assembly entitled to vote.

20. The legislature's approval is necessary for the declaration of war.

No. In times of war or "threat of war," the president can declare a state of emergency without obtaining the legislature's approval. The state of emergency can be extended beyond twenty-one days only with the legislature's approval.

Article 45
(1) No derogation from rights contained in this Chapter shall be permissible save to the extent provided for by this section and no such derogation shall be made unless there has been a declaration of a state of emergency within the meaning of this section.
(2) The President may declare a state of emergency –
(a) only to the extent that it is provided for in this section;
(b) only with the approval of the Defence and Security Committee of the National Assembly;
(c) only in times of war, threat of war, civil war or widespread natural disaster;
(d) only with regard to the specific location where that emergency exists, and that any declaration of a state of emergency shall be publicly announced; and
(e) only after the state of emergency has been publicly announced.
(3) Derogation shall only be permissible during a state of emergency –
(a) with respect to freedom of expression, freedom of information, freedom of movement, freedom of

assembly and rights under section 19 (6) (a) and section 42 (2) (b);

(b) to the extent that such derogation is not inconsistent with the obligations of Malawi under International Law; and

(c) to the extent that –

(i) in the case of war or threat of war, it is strictly required to prevent the lives of defensive combatants and legitimate military objectives from being placed in direct jeopardy; or

(ii) in the case of a widespread natural disaster, it is strictly required for the protection and relief of those people in the disaster area.

(4) The declaration of a state of emergency and any action taken in consequence thereof shall be in force for a period of not more than twenty-one days, unless it is extended for a period of not longer than three months, or consecutive periods of not longer than three months at a time, by resolution of the National Assembly adopted by a majority of at least two-thirds of all its members.

21. The legislature's approval is necessary to ratify treaties with foreign countries.

Yes. Although the power to negotiate treaties is formally granted to the president, in practice, the legislature's approval is necessary to ratify international treaties.

Article 89

(1) The President shall have the following powers and duties –

(f) to negotiate, sign, enter into and accede to international agreements.

22. The legislature has the power to grant amnesty.

No. Amnesty and pardon are not treated separately, and the legislature lacks the power to grant amnesty. See item 23.

23. The legislature has the power of pardon.

No. The president has the power of pardon.

Article 89

(2) The President may pardon convicted offenders, grant stays of execution of sentence, reduce sentences, or remit sentences.

24. The legislature reviews and has the right to reject appointments to the judiciary; or the legislature itself appoints members of the judiciary.

No. The legislature's role is limited to confirming the president's appointment for chief justice of the High Court. The president appoints the other judges of the High Court, and these appointments do not require the legislature's approval.

Article 111

(1) The Chief Justice shall be appointed by the President and confirmed by the National Assembly by a majority of two-thirds of the members present and voting.

(2) All other judges shall be appointed by the President on the recommendation of the Judicial Service Commission.

(3) Magistrates and persons appointed to other judicial offices shall be appointed by the Chief Justice on the recommendation of the Judicial Service Commission and shall hold office until the age of seventy unless removed in accordance with section 119.

25. The chairman of the central bank is appointed by the legislature.

No. The president appoints the governor of the Reserve Bank of Malawi.

26. The legislature has a substantial voice in the operation of the state-owned media.

No. Formally, the media committee in parliament has oversight powers, but, in practice, the committee has never been funded by donors or by parliament.

27. The legislature is regularly in session.

No. The legislature typically meets between two and four times a year in two-to-six-week sessions.

Article 59

(1) Every session of the National Assembly and of the Senate shall be held at such place within Malawi and shall commence at such time as each Speaker, in consultation with the President, may appoint with respect to the Chamber in which that Speaker presides and the sittings of each Chamber after the commencement of that session shall be held at such times and on such days as that Chamber shall appoint:

Provided that –

(a) the President, in consultation with the Speaker of the relevant Chamber, may summon, on extraordinary occasions, a meeting of the National Assembly or the Senate; and

(b) the President may, in consultation with the Speaker of the relevant Chamber, prorogue the National Assembly or the Senate.

(2) There shall be at least two sittings of the National Assembly and of the Senate every year.

28. Each legislator has a personal secretary.

No.

29. Each legislator has at least one non-secretarial staff member with policy expertise.

No.

30. Legislators are eligible for re-election without any restriction.

Yes. There are no restrictions on re-election.

31. A seat in the legislature is an attractive enough position that legislators are generally interested in and seek re-election.

Yes.

32. The re-election of incumbent legislators is common enough that at any given time the legislature contains a significant number of highly experienced members.

Yes. Since 1994, re-election rates have been sufficiently high to produce a significant number of highly experienced members.

PARLIAMENT OF MALAYSIA (*PARLIMEN*)

Expert consultants: Muthiah Alagappa, William Case, Harold Crouch, Chris Fadzel, Francis Loh

Score: .34

Influence over executive (3/9)		Institutional autonomy (4/9)		Specified powers (1/8)		Institutional capacity (3/6)	
1. replace		10. no dissolution		19. amendments	X	27. sessions	X
2. serve as ministers	X	11. no decree	X	20. war		28. secretary	
3. interpellate		12. no veto	X	21. treaties		29. staff	
4. investigate		13. no review	X	22. amnesty		30. no term limits	
5. oversee police		14. no gatekeeping	X	23. pardon		31. seek re-election	X
6. appoint PM	X	15. no impoundment		24. judiciary		32. experience	X
7. appoint ministers		16. control resources		25. central bank			
8. lack president	X	17. immunity		26. media			
9. no confidence		18. all elected					

The Parliament (*Parlimen*) of Malaysia traces its origins to the legislative bodies that met under British colonial rule. It was formally encoded in Malaysia's 1957 constitution adopted upon independence from Great Britain. The constitution called for a bicameral legislature consisting of a lower house, the House of Representatives (*Dewan Rakyat*), and an upper house, the Senate (*Dewan Negara*). The monarch (*Yang di-Pertuan Agong*) is the head of state, and the prime minister is the head of government. A constitutional amendment in 1994 granted the judiciary the right to advise on the constitutionality of proposed legislation, but stopped short of granting the judiciary the power to declare laws unconstitutional.

The legislature appoints the prime minister and its members serve in government, but it has few other means to influence the executive. The legislature has some institutional autonomy. Most notably, the legislature's laws are not subject to judicial review. The ability to change the constitution is the legislature's only specified power. Its institutional capacity is slight.

SURVEY

1. The legislature alone, without the involvement of any other agencies, can impeach the president or replace the prime minister.

No. Formally, the legislature can remove the prime minister with a vote of no confidence. In practice, a vote of no confidence would be unthinkable.

Article 43
(4) If the Prime Minister ceases to command the confidence of the majority of the members of the House of Representatives, then, unless at his request the Yang di-Pertuan Agong dissolves Parliament, the Prime Minister shall tender the resignation of the Cabinet.

2. Ministers may serve simultaneously as members of the legislature.

Yes. Ministers are selected from, and required to serve simultaneously in, the legislature.

Article 43
(1) The Yang di-Pertuan Agong shall appoint a Jemaah Menteri (Cabinet of Ministers) to advise him in the exercise of his functions.

(2) The Cabinet shall be appointed as follows, that is to say –

(a) the Yang di-Pertuan Agong shall first appoint as Perdana Menteri (Prime Minister) to preside over the Cabinet a member of the House of Representative who in his judgment is likely to command the confidence of the majority of the members of that House; and

(b) he shall on the advice of the Prime Minister appoint other Menteri (Ministers) from among the members of either House of Parliament.

3. The legislature has powers of summons over executive branch officials and hearings with executive branch officials testifying before the legislature or its committees are regularly held.

No. The legislature does not regularly question executive branch officials, although a Westminster-style question time is occasionally held.

4. The legislature can conduct independent investigation of the chief executive and the agencies of the executive.

No. The legislature cannot investigate the executive.

5. The legislature has effective powers of oversight over the agencies of coercion (the military, organs of law enforcement, intelligence services, and the secret police).

No. The legislature lacks effective powers of oversight over the agencies of coercion.

6. The legislature appoints the prime minister.

Yes. Formally, the monarch appoints the prime minister, but in practice, the monarch appoints as prime minister the candidate who enjoys majority support in parliament.

Article 40a
(1) In the exercise of his functions under this Constitution or federal law the Yang di-Pertuan Agong (Monarch) shall act in accordance with the advice of the Cabinet or of a Minister acting under the general authority of the Cabinet, except as otherwise provided by this Constitution; but shall be entitled, at his request, to any information concerning the government of the Federation which is available to the Cabinet.
(2) The Yang di-Pertuan Agong may act in his discretion in the performance of the following functions, that is to say –
(a) the appointment of a Prime Minister.

Article 43
(1) The Yang di-Pertuan Agong shall appoint a Jemaah Menteri (Cabinet of Ministers) to advise him in the exercise of his functions.
(2) The Cabinet shall be appointed as follows, that is to say –
(a) the Yang di-Pertuan Agong shall first appoint as Perdana Menteri (Prime Minister) to preside over the

Cabinet a member of the House of Representative who in his judgment is likely to command the confidence of the majority of the members of that House; and
(b) he shall on the advice of the Prime Minister appoint other Menteri (Ministers) from among the members of either House of Parliament.

7. The legislature's approval is required to confirm the appointment of ministers; or the legislature itself appoints ministers.

No. The monarch appoints ministers on the recommendation of the prime minister, and ministerial appointments do not require the legislature's approval.

Article 43
(1) The Yang di-Pertuan Agong shall appoint a Jemaah Menteri (Cabinet of Ministers) to advise him in the exercise of his functions.
(2) The Cabinet shall be appointed as follows, that is to say –
(a) the Yang di-Pertuan Agong shall first appoint as Perdana Menteri (Prime Minister) to preside over the Cabinet a member of the House of Representative who in his judgment is likely to command the confidence of the majority of the members of that House; and
(b) he shall on the advice of the Prime Minister appoint other Menteri (Ministers) from among the members of either House of Parliament.

8. The country lacks a presidency entirely or there is a presidency, but the president is elected by the legislature.

Yes. The country lacks a presidency. The head of state is the monarch.

Article 32
(1) There shall be a Supreme Head of the Federation, to be called the Yang di-Pertuan Agong (Monarch), who shall take precedence over all persons in the Federation and shall not be liable to any proceedings whatsoever in any court.
(2) The Consort of the Yang di-Pertuan Agong (to be called the Raja Permaisuri Agong) shall take precedence next after the Yang di-Pertuan Agong over all other persons in the Federation.
(3) The Yang di-Pertuan Agong shall be elected by the Conference of Rulers for a term of five years, but may at any time resign his office by writing under his hand addressed to the Conference of Rulers or be removed from office by the Conference of Rulers, and shall cease to hold office on ceasing to be a Ruler.

Article 39
The executive authority of the Federation shall be vested in the Yang di-Pertuan Agong and exercisable, subject to the provisions of any federal law and of the Second Schedule, by him or by the Cabinet or any Minister authorised by the Cabinet, but Parliament may by law confer executive function on other persons.

9. The legislature can vote no confidence in the government.

No. Formally, the legislature can vote no confidence in the government, but in practice, a vote of no confidence would be unthinkable. See item 1.

Article 43
(4) If the Prime Minister ceases to command the confidence of the majority of the members of the House of Representatives, then, unless at his request the Yang di-Pertuan Agong dissolves Parliament, the Prime Minister shall tender the resignation of the Cabinet.

10. The legislature is immune from dissolution by the executive.

No. The monarch, at the request of the prime minister, can dissolve the legislature.

Article 43
(4) If the Prime Minister ceases to command the confidence of the majority of the members of the House of Representatives, then, unless at his request the Yang di-Pertuan Agong dissolves Parliament, the Prime Minister shall tender the resignation of the Cabinet.

11. Any executive initiative on legislation requires ratification or approval by the legislature before it takes effect; that is, the executive lacks decree power.

Yes. The executive lacks decree power.

12. Laws passed by the legislature are veto-proof or essentially veto-proof; that is, the executive lacks veto power, or has veto power but the veto can be overridden by a majority in the legislature.

Yes. The legislature can override the monarch's veto by a majority vote of its present members. A two-thirds majority is required to override a veto of a constitutional amendment.

Article 66
(1) The power of Parliament to make laws shall be exercised by Bills passed by both Houses (or, in the cases mentioned in Article 68, the House of Representatives) and, except as otherwise provided in this Article, assented to by the Yang di-Pertuan Agong.
(2) Subject to Article 67, a Bill may originate in either House.
(3) When a Bill has been passed by the House in which it originated it shall be sent to the other House; and it shall be presented to the Yang di-Pertuan Agong for his assent when it has been passed by the other House and agreement has been reached between the two Houses and any amendments made in it or when it is required to be so presented under Article 68.
(4) The Yang di-Pertuan Agong shall within thirty days after a Bill is presented to him –
　(a) assent to the Bill by causing the Public Seal to be affixed thereto; or
　(b) if it is not a money Bill, return the Bill to the House in which it originated with a statement of the reasons for his objection to the Bill, or to any provision thereof.

(4A) If the Yang di-Pertuan Agong returns a Bill to the House in which it originated in accordance with Clause (4) (b), the House shall as soon as possible proceed to reconsider the Bill. If after such reconsideration the Bill is passed by the votes of not less than two-thirds of the total number of members of that House in the case of a Bill for making any amendment to the Constitution other than any amendment excepted pursuant to Article 159, and by a simple majority in the case of any other Bill, with or without amendment, it shall be sent together with the objections to the other House, by which it shall likewise be reconsidered, and if similarly approved by members of that House, the Bill shall again be presented to the Yang di-Pertuan Agong for assent and the Yang di-Pertuan Agong shall give his assent thereto within thirty days after the Bill is presented to him.

13. The legislature's laws are supreme and not subject to judicial review.

Yes. The legislature's laws are supreme and not subject to judicial review.

14. The legislature has the right to initiate bills in all policy jurisdictions; the executive lacks gatekeeping authority.

Yes. The legislature can initiate bills in all policy jurisdictions.

15. Expenditure of funds appropriated by the legislature is mandatory; the executive lacks the power to impound funds appropriated by the legislature.

No. The prime minister and government can impound funds appropriated by the legislature.

16. The legislature controls the resources that finance its own internal operation and provide for the perquisites of its own members.

No. Formally, the legislature has the power to provide for its own financial operations. In practice, the legislature is dependent on the government for the resources that finance its own operations.

Article 43
(9) Parliament shall by law make provision for the remuneration of members of the Cabinet.

Article 62
(1) Subject to the provisions of this Constitution and of federal law, each House of Parliament shall regulate its own procedure.

Article 64
Parliament shall by law provide for the remuneration of members of each House.

17. Members of the legislature are immune from arrest and/or criminal prosecution.

No. Legislators are subject to arrest and criminal prosecution.

18. All members of the legislature are elected; the executive lacks the power to appoint any members of the legislature.

No. The monarch appoints forty of the seventy members of the Senate. All members of the House of Representatives are elected.

Article 45
(1) Subject to Clause (4), the Senate shall consist of elected and appointed members as follows:
    (a) two members for each State shall be elected in accordance with the Seventh Schedule; and
        (aa) two members for the Federal Territory of Kuala Lumpur and one member for the Federal Territory of Labuan shall be appointed by the Yang di-Pertuan Agong; and
    (b) forty members shall be appointed by the Yang di-Pertuan Agong.
(2) The members to be appointed by the Yang di-Pertuan Agong shall be persons who in his opinion have rendered distinguished public service or have achieved distinction in the professions, commerce, industry, agriculture, cultural activities or social service or are representative of racial minorities or are capable of representing the interests of aborigines.

Article 46
(1) The House of Representatives shall consist of one hundred and ninety two elected members.

19. The legislature alone, without the involvement of any other agencies, can change the Constitution.

Yes. The legislature can amend the constitution with a two-thirds majority vote.

Article 159
(1) Subject to the following provisions of this Article and to Article 161E the provisions of this Constitution may be amended by federal law.
(3) A Bill for making any amendment to the Constitution (other than an amendment except from the provisions of this Clause) and a Bill for making any amendment to a law passed under Clause (4) of Article 10 shall not be passed in either House of Parliament unless it has been supported on Second and Third Readings by the votes of not less than two-thirds of the total number of members of that House.

20. The legislature's approval is necessary for the declaration of war.

No. There is no constitutional provision for the declaration of war. The monarch, on the advice of the prime minister, can issue a proclamation of emergency in times of war and then seek retroactive legislative approval.

Article 150
(1) If the Yang di-Pertuan Agong is satisfied that a grave emergency exists whereby the security or economic life of the Federation or of any part thereof is threatened, whether by war or external aggression or internal disturbance, he may issue a Proclamation of Emergency.

(2) If a Proclamation of Emergency is issued when Parliament is not sitting, the Yang di-Pertuan Agong shall summon Parliament as soon as may be practicable, and may, until both Houses of Parliament are sitting, promulgate ordinances having the force of law, if satisfied that immediate action is required.

21. The legislature's approval is necessary to ratify treaties with foreign countries.

No. The government can conclude international treaties without the legislature's approval.

22. The legislature has the power to grant amnesty.

No. Amnesty and pardon are not treated separately, and the legislature lacks the power to grant amnesty. See item 23.

23. The legislature has the power of pardon.

No. The monarch has the power of pardon.

Article 42
(1) The Yang di-Pertuan Agong has power to grant pardons, reprieves and respites in respect of all offences which have been tried by court-martial and all offences committed in the Federal Territories of Kuala Lumpur and Labuan; and the Ruler or Yang di-Pertua Negeri of a State has power to grant pardons, reprieves and respites in respect of all other offences committed in his State.

24. The legislature reviews and has the right to reject appointments to the judiciary; or the legislature itself appoints members of the judiciary.

No. The monarch appoints judges on the advice of the prime minister, and the appointments do not require the legislature's approval.

Article 122
(1) The Supreme Court shall consist of a president of the Court (to be styled "the Lord President of the Supreme Court"), of the Chief Justices of the High Courts and, until the Yang di- Pertuan Agong by order otherwise provides, of four other judges and such additional judges as may be appointed pursuant to Clause (1A).
    (1A) Notwithstanding anything in this Constitution contained, the Yang di- Pertuan Agong acting on the advice of the Lord President of the Supreme Court may appoint for such purposes or for such period as he may specified any person who has held high judicial office in Malaysia to be an additional judge of the Supreme Court.

Article 122b
(1) The Lord President of the Supreme Court, and chief justices of the High Courts and (subject to Article 122C) the other judges of the Supreme Court and of the High Court shall be appointed by the Yang di- Pertuan Agong, acting on the advice of the Prime Minister, after consulting the Conference of Rulers.

25. The chairman of the central bank is appointed by the legislature.

No. The monarch, on the recommendation of the prime minister, appoints the governor of the Central Bank of Malaysia.

26. The legislature has a substantial voice in the operation of the state-owned media.

No. The legislature lacks a substantial voice in the operation of the public media.

27. The legislature is regularly in session.

Yes. The legislature regularly meets in ordinary session.

> Article 55
> (1) The Yang di-Pertuan Agong shall from time to time summon Parliament and shall not allow six months to elapse between the last sitting in one session and the date appointed for its first meeting in the next session.

28. Each legislator has a personal secretary.

No. Some, but not all, legislators have personal secretaries provided by the legislature.

29. Each legislator has at least one non-secretarial staff member with policy expertise.

No. Some leading legislators have personal advisers, but these arrangements are informal and are not funded by the legislature.

30. Legislators are eligible for re-election without any restriction.

No. Members of the House of Representatives are eligible for re-election without restriction. Senators, however, are limited to two terms.

> Article 45
> (3A) A member of the Senate shall not hold office for more than two terms either continuously or otherwise: Provided that where a person who has already completed two or more terms of office as a member of the Senate is immediately before the coming into force of this Clause a member of the Senate, he may continue to serve as such member for the remainder of his term.

31. A seat in the legislature is an attractive enough position that legislators are generally interested in and seek re-election.

Yes.

32. The re-election of incumbent legislators is common enough that at any given time the legislature contains a significant number of highly experienced members.

Yes. Re-election rates are sufficiently high to produce a significant number of highly experienced members.

NATIONAL ASSEMBLY OF MALI (*ASSEMBLÉE NATIONALE*)

Expert consultants: Rokia Ba, Earl Conteh-Morgan, Olly Owen, Susanna Wing, Mossa Yattara

Score: .34

Influence over executive (1/9)		Institutional autonomy (5/9)		Specified powers (2/8)		Institutional capacity (3/6)	
1. replace		10. no dissolution		19. amendments		27. sessions	
2. serve as ministers		11. no decree		20. war	X	28. secretary	
3. interpellate		12. no veto		21. treaties	X	29. staff	
4. investigate		13. no review		22. amnesty		30. no term limits	X
5. oversee police		14. no gatekeeping	X	23. pardon		31. seek re-election	X
6. appoint PM		15. no impoundment	X	24. judiciary		32. experience	X
7. appoint ministers		16. control resources	X	25. central bank			
8. lack president		17. immunity	X	26. media			
9. no confidence	X	18. all elected	X				

The National Assembly (*Assemblée nationale*) of Mali was established in the 1960 constitution upon independence from France. For the next three decades a military dictatorship ruled Mali, and the legislature functioned only sporadically. A movement toward greater political openness in

1992 brought a new constitution and the reestablishment of a functioning unicameral legislature.

Although the legislature is more powerful than in the past, it still takes a back seat to the president in national politics. With the exception of the power to vote no confidence in the government, the National Assembly has no meaningful ability to influence the executive. The president's decree, veto, and dissolution powers circumscribe the legislature's institutional autonomy. The legislature possesses two of the eight specified powers and prerogatives assessed here. It has little institutional capacity.

SURVEY

1. The legislature alone, without the involvement of any other agencies, can impeach the president or replace the prime minister.

No. The legislature cannot impeach the president. The legislature can remove the prime minister with a vote of no confidence.

Article 79
When the National Assembly adopts a motion of censure or when it disapproves the program or the declaration of general policy of the Government, the Prime Minister must submit to the President of the Republic the resignation of the Government.

2. Ministers may serve simultaneously as members of the legislature.

No. Legislators are prohibited from serving simultaneously in ministerial positions.

Article 58
The functions of a member of the Government are incompatible with the exercise of any parliamentary mandate, any function of professional representation at the national or local level, of any public employment or of any professional and lucrative activity... The replacement of members of Parliament who are appointed to the Government takes place in accordance with the provisions of Article 63.

3. The legislature has powers of summons over executive branch officials and hearings with executive branch officials testifying before the legislature or its committees are regularly held.

No. The legislature cannot interpellate executive branch officials.

4. The legislature can conduct independent investigation of the chief executive and the agencies of the executive.

No. The legislature cannot investigate the executive.

5. The legislature has effective powers of oversight over the agencies of coercion (the military, organs of law enforcement, intelligence services, and the secret police).

No. The legislature lacks effective powers of oversight over the agencies of coercion.

6. The legislature appoints the prime minister.

No. The president appoints the prime minister.

Article 38
The President of the Republic appoints the Prime Minister. He ends his functions upon his presentation of the resignation of the Government. Upon the proposition of the Prime Minister, he appoints the other members of the Government and sets limits upon their functions.

7. The legislature's approval is required to confirm the appointment of ministers; or the legislature itself appoints ministers.

No. The president appoints ministers on the recommendation of the prime minister, and the appointments do not require the legislature's approval.

Article 38
The President of the Republic appoints the Prime Minister. He ends his functions upon his presentation of the resignation of the Government. Upon the proposition of the Prime Minister, he appoints the other members of the Government and sets limits upon their functions.

8. The country lacks a presidency entirely or there is a presidency, but the president is elected by the legislature.

No. The president is directly elected.

Article 30
The President of the Republic is elected for five years by direct universal suffrage and by an absolute majority in two stages.

9. The legislature can vote no confidence in the government.

Yes. The legislature can pass a motion of censure in the government.

Article 78
The Prime Minister, after the deliberation of the Council of Ministers, assumes before the Assembly the responsibility of the Government with regard to its program or eventually with respect to a declaration of general policy. The National Assembly questions the responsibility of the Government by the vote of a motion of censure. Such a motion is only receivable if it is signed by at least one-tenth of the members of the National Assembly. The vote may only take place forty-eight hours after its introduction. The only votes counted are those favorable to the motion of censure which may only be adopted by a two-thirds majority of the members composing the Assembly. If the motion

of censure is rejected, the signatories may not propose a new one during the course of the same session. The Prime Minister can, after deliberation of the Council of Ministers, assume the responsibility of the Government before the National Assembly on the vote of a text. In this case, the text is considered adopted, unless a motion of censure, introduced in the following twenty-four hours, is passed.

Article 79
When the National Assembly adopts a motion of censure or when it disapproves the program or the declaration of general policy of the Government, the Prime Minister must submit to the President of the Republic the resignation of the Government.

10. The legislature is immune from dissolution by the executive.

No. The president can dissolve the legislature.

Article 42
The President of the Republic can, after consultation with the Prime Minister and the President of the National Assembly, pronounce the dissolution of the National Assembly. General elections take place twenty-one days at the least and forty days at the most, after the dissolution. The National Assembly cannot be dissolved in the year following these elections.

11. Any executive initiative on legislation requires ratification or approval by the legislature before it takes effect; that is, the executive lacks decree power.

No. Formally, the government can issue decrees that have the force of law only with the prior authorization of the legislature. In practice, the president issues decrees that have the force of law without prior authorization.

Article 74
The Government can, for the execution of its program or in areas determined by law, demand the authorization of Parliament to take by Ordinances, during a specified period of time or between the two sessions, measures that are normally within the domain of the law. The Ordinances are taken in the Council of Ministers after consultation with the Supreme Court. They enter into force from the time of their adoption, but become lapsed if the bill for their ratification is not deposited at the National Assembly before the date set by the enabling law. Upon the expiration of the date mentioned in the first paragraph of the present Article, Ordinances cannot be further modified except by the law in matters which are in the legislative domain.

12. Laws passed by the legislature are veto-proof or essentially veto-proof; that is, the executive lacks veto power, or has veto power but the veto can be overridden by a majority in the legislature.

No. The president has the power to return a bill to the legislature, but the constitution does not specify the legislative procedure for overriding a presidential veto. This constitutional oversight reflects the fact that, in practice, the president's veto power is absolute.

Article 40
The President of the Republic promulgates the laws within the 15 days that follow the transmission to the Government of the text definitively adopted. He can before the expiration of this time demand of the National Assembly a new deliberation of the law or of certain of its articles. This new deliberation cannot be refused and suspends the time period of the promulgation. In the case of urgency, the time of promulgation can be shortened to eight days.

13. The legislature's laws are supreme and not subject to judicial review.

No. The Constitutional Court can review the constitutionality of laws.

Article 85
The Constitutional Court is the judge of the constitutionality of the laws and guarantees the fundamental rights of the human person and the public liberties.

Article 86
The Constitutional Court rules obligatorily on:
– the constitutionality of organic laws and the laws before their promulgation.

Article 88
Organic laws are submitted by the Prime Minister to the Constitutional Court before their promulgation. The other categories of law, before their promulgation, can be deferred to the Constitutional Court be it by the President of the Republic, by the Prime Minister, the President of the National Assembly or one-tenth of the Deputies, the President of the High Council of the Collectivities or one-tenth of the National Councilors or the President of the Supreme Court.

14. The legislature has the right to initiate bills in all policy jurisdictions; the executive lacks gatekeeping authority.

Yes. The legislature can initiate bills in all policy jurisdictions.

15. Expenditure of funds appropriated by the legislature is mandatory; the executive lacks the power to impound funds appropriated by the legislature.

Yes. The executive lacks the power to impound funds appropriated by the legislature.

16. The legislature controls the resources that finance its own internal operation and provide for the perquisites of its own members.

Yes. The legislature enjoys financial autonomy.

17. Members of the legislature are immune from arrest and/or criminal prosecution.

Yes. Legislators are immune with the common exception for cases of *flagrante delicto,* here expressed as "flagrant offense."

Article 62
The Deputies benefit from parliamentary immunity. No member of the National Assembly may be prosecuted, sought, arrested, detained, or judged because of his opinions or votes expressed by him in the exercise of his functions. No member of the National Assembly can, during its sessions, be prosecuted or arrested for criminal or correctional offenses without the authorization of the National Assembly, except in the case of a flagrant offense. No member of the National Assembly may, out of session, be arrested without the authorization of the Bureau of the National Assembly, except in the case of flagrant offense, of authorized prosecutions or of definitive condemnation. The detention or the prosecution of a member of the National Assembly is suspended if the National Assembly so requests.

18. All members of the legislature are elected; the executive lacks the power to appoint any members of the legislature.

Yes. All members of the legislature are elected.

Article 61
The Deputies are elected for five years by universal direct suffrage. A law determines the modalities of this election.

19. The legislature alone, without the involvement of any other agencies, can change the Constitution.

No. Constitutional amendments require approval in a popular referendum.

Article 118
The initiative for the revision of the Constitution belongs concurrently to the President of the Republic and the Deputies. The project or proposition of revision must be adopted by the National Assembly by a two-thirds majority of its members. The revision is only definitive after having been approved by referendum. No procedure of revision can be engaged in or pursued if it infringes on the integrity of the State. The republican form and the secularity of the State as well as multipartyism cannot be the object of revision.

20. The legislature's approval is necessary for the declaration of war.

Yes. The legislature's approval is necessary for presidential war declarations.

Article 49
The President of the Republic decrees after deliberation in the Council of Ministers, the state of siege and the state of urgency.

Article 71
The declaration of war is authorized by the National Assembly specially convened for this purpose. The President of the Republic informs the Nation by a message.

21. The legislature's approval is necessary to ratify treaties with foreign countries.

Yes. The legislature's approval is necessary to ratify international treaties.

Article 114
The President of the Republic negotiates and ratifies treaties. He shall be informed of any negotiations likely to lead to an international agreement not submitted to ratification.

Article 115
Peace treaties, [treaties] of commerce, treaties or accords relating to international organizations, those involving State finances, those concerning the status of persons, those relating to cession, exchange or annexation of territory, cannot be approved except by virtue of the law. They only take effect after approval or ratification. No cession, no exchange, no annexation of territory is valid without the consent of the people.

22. The legislature has the power to grant amnesty.

No. The legislature can pass an amnesty law only on the president's recommendation.

Article 45
The President of the Republic is the President of the High Council of the Judiciary. He exercises the power of pardon. He proposes laws of amnesty.

23. The legislature has the power of pardon.

No. The president has the power of pardon.

Article 45
The President of the Republic is the President of the High Council of the Judiciary. He exercises the power of pardon. He proposes laws of amnesty.

24. The legislature reviews and has the right to reject appointments to the judiciary; or the legislature itself appoints members of the judiciary.

No. The legislature itself does not appoint members of the judiciary; nor is the legislature's approval required to appoint members of the judiciary.

Article 47
The Members of the Supreme Court are appointed by decree taken in the Council of Ministers.

Article 91
The Constitutional Court consists of nine members who carry the title of Councilor with a mandate of seven years renewable one time.
The nine members of the Constitutional Court are designated as follows:
– three are designated by the President of the Republic of which at least two [are] jurists;
– three are designated by the President of the National Assembly of which at least two [are] jurists;
– three Magistrates are designated by the High Council of the Judiciary.

25. The chairman of the central bank is appointed by the legislature.

No. Mali is a member of the Central Bank of West African States, whose governor is selected by the member states.

26. The legislature has a substantial voice in the operation of the state-owned media.

No. The legislature lacks a substantial voice in the operation of the public media.

27. The legislature is regularly in session.

No. The legislature meets in ordinary session for a maximum of five and a half months each year.

> Article 65
> The National Assembly convenes by right in two ordinary sessions per year.
> The first session begins the first Monday in October. It may not exceed 75 days. The second session begins the first Monday in April and may not exceed a duration of ninety days.

28. Each legislator has a personal secretary.

No.

29. Each legislator has at least one non-secretarial staff member with policy expertise.

No.

30. Legislators are eligible for re-election without any restriction.

Yes. There are no restrictions on re-election.

31. A seat in the legislature is an attractive enough position that legislators are generally interested in and seek re-election.

Yes.

32. The re-election of incumbent legislators is common enough that at any given time the legislature contains a significant number of highly experienced members.

Yes. Since the 1992 parliamentary elections, re-election rates have been sufficiently high to produce a significant number of highly experienced members.

PARLIAMENT OF MAURITANIA (*BARLAMANE*)

Expert consultants: Mohamed Abdellahi, Mohamed Elhacen, Cédric Jourde, Moktar Lam, Amer K. Mohsen, Boubacar N'Diaye, Regina Wegemund

Score: .31

Influence over executive (1/9)		Institutional autonomy (5/9)		Specified powers (2/8)		Institutional capacity (2/6)	
1. replace		10. no dissolution		19. amendments		27. sessions	
2. serve as ministers		11. no decree	X	20. war	X	28. secretary	
3. interpellate		12. no veto	X	21. treaties	X	29. staff	
4. investigate		13. no review		22. amnesty		30. no term limits	X
5. oversee police		14. no gatekeeping	X	23. pardon		31. seek re-election	X
6. appoint PM		15. no impoundment		24. judiciary		32. experience	
7. appoint ministers		16. control resources		25. central bank			
8. lack president		17. immunity	X	26. media			
9. no confidence	X	18. all elected	X				

The Parliament (*Barlamane*) of Mauritania was established in the 1961 constitution when Mauritania achieved independence from France. The document called for a bicameral legislature consisting of a lower house, the National Assembly (*Majlis al-Watani*), and an upper house, the Senate (*Majlis al-Shuyukh*). A new constitution enacted in 1991 granted the president the power to dissolve parliament. Prior to 1991 the legislature was immune from dissolution. A constitutional amendment in 2006 limited the president's term in office but did not directly affect the legislature's power.

From the time of independence until 1978, Mauritania was ruled by an autocratic president, Moktar Ould Daddah, who presided over a single-party regime. After Daddah's ouster in a military coup, Mauritania was ruled by a military council until 1992. In 1984 Maaouya Ould Sid'Ahmed Taya took control of the military government and became president. In 1992 Mauritania returned to civilian rule, and presidential and legislative elections were held. Taya held onto the presidency, and his party, the Democratic and Social Republican Party, won the vast majority of seats in the National Assembly. The party retained its hegemonic control in subsequent parliamentary elections in 1996 and 2001, and Taya was re-elected by overwhelming majorities in 1997 and 2003. In 2005 Taya's two decades of rule were ended by a military coup led by Colonel Ely Ould Mohamed Vall. In the aftermath of the coup, parliament was suspended for over a year. New elections for the National Assembly, which was expanded from eighty-one to ninety-five seats, were held in November and December of 2006.

It is too early to say whether the new, post-coup situation will bring substantial changes in the power of the legislature, but to date the legislature's role in politics and government has been negligible. The legislature has hardly any influence on the executive branch, although it does have some institutional autonomy. It has few specified powers and little institutional capacity.

SURVEY

1. The legislature alone, without the involvement of any other agencies, can impeach the president or replace the prime minister.

No. Presidential impeachment requires the involvement of the High Court of Justice. The legislature can remove the prime minister with a vote of no confidence.

Article 93
(1) The President of the Republic is held liable for the acts committed in the exercise of his duties only in the case of high treason.
(2) He may be impeached only by the two assemblies voting together in a public vote by an absolute majority of the members; he is tried before the High Court of Justice.

Article 74
(1) The Prime Minister, together with his ministers, is responsible to the National Assembly. A lack of

confidence or a motion of censure shall result in bringing into question his political responsibility.
(2) The Prime Minister, after deliberation with the Council of Ministers, shall take the responsibility of the Government before the National Assembly for his program and ultimately for a declaration of general policy.
(3) The National Assembly may challenge the responsibility of the Government by voting a motion of censure.
(4) A motion of censure brought by a deputy must expressly bear this title and the signature of its author. Such a motion is acceptable only if it is signed by at least one third of the members of the National Assembly. The vote may take place only forty-eight hours after raising the question of the lack of confidence or the motion of censure.

Article 75
(1) The vote of no confidence or the adoption of a motion of censure causes the immediate resignation of the Government. Such a vote or motion can only be reached by a majority of the deputies making up the National Assembly; only the votes of no confidence or the votes favorable in the motion of censure shall be counted.
(2) The resigned government continues to manage current business the nomination by the President of the Republic of a new Prime Minister and a new Government.
(3) If a motion of censure is rejected, its signatories may not propose a new one during the course of the same session except in the case set forth in the following paragraph.
(4) The Prime Minister, after deliberation with the Council of Ministers takes the responsibility of the Government before the National Assembly for the voting of a bill. In this case, this bill shall be considered adopted unless a motion of censure brought during the following twenty-four hours shall be voted under the conditions set forth in the first paragraph.
(5) The Prime Minister may ask the Senate for the approval of a declaration of general policy.

2. Ministers may serve simultaneously as members of the legislature.

No. Legislators are prohibited from serving simultaneously in ministerial positions.

Article 44
The functions of a member of the government are incompatible with the exercise of any parliamentary mandate, with any function of professional representation of a national character, with any professional activity, and in general with any public or private employment. An organic law shall determine the conditions under which the holders of such mandates, functions, or employment are replaced. The replacement of members of Parliament shall take place according to the dispositions of Article 48.

3. The legislature has powers of summons over executive branch officials and hearings with executive

branch officials testifying before the legislature or its committees are regularly held.

No. Formally, the legislature can question executive branch officials, but in practice, such hearings are rarely held.

> Article 69
> (3) One session per week shall be reserved by priority for questions by members of Parliament and for the answers from the Government.

4. The legislature can conduct independent investigation of the chief executive and the agencies of the executive.

No. Formally, the government is required to provide the legislature with "all explanations requested concerning its management and acts." In practice, the legislature cannot investigate the executive.

> Article 72
> The Government is required to provide to the Parliament, in the form established by law, all explanations requested concerning its management and its acts.

5. The legislature has effective powers of oversight over the agencies of coercion (the military, organs of law enforcement, intelligence services, and the secret police).

No. The legislature lacks effective powers of oversight over the agencies of coercion.

6. The legislature appoints the prime minister.

No. The president appoints the prime minister.

> Article 30
> (2) [The President of the Republic] shall appoint the Prime Minister and discharge him from his functions.

7. The legislature's approval is required to confirm the appointment of ministers; or the legislature itself appoints ministers.

No. The president appoints ministers on the recommendation of the prime minister, and ministerial appointments do not require legislative approval.

> Article 30
> (3) Upon the recommendation of the Prime Minister, the President shall appoint the Ministers to whom he may delegate by decree certain of his powers.

8. The country lacks a presidency entirely or there is a presidency, but the president is elected by the legislature.

No. The president is directly elected.

> Article 26
> (1) The President of the Republic is elected for six years by direct, universal suffrage.

9. The legislature can vote no confidence in the government.

Yes. The legislature can vote no confidence in the government.

> Article 74
> (1) The Prime Minister, together with his ministers, is responsible to the National Assembly. A lack of confidence or a motion of censure shall result in bringing into question his political responsibility.
> (2) The Prime Minister, after deliberation with the Council of Ministers, shall take the responsibility of the Government before the National Assembly for his program and ultimately for a declaration of general policy.
> (3) The National Assembly may challenge the responsibility of the Government by voting a motion of censure.
> (4) A motion of censure brought by a deputy must expressly bear this title and the signature of its author. Such a motion is acceptable only if it is signed by at least one third of the members of the National Assembly. The vote may take place only forty-eight hours after raising the question of the lack of confidence or the motion of censure.

> Article 75
> (1) The vote of no confidence or the adoption of a motion of censure causes the immediate resignation of the Government. Such a vote or motion can only be reached by a majority of the deputies making up the National Assembly; only the votes of no confidence or the votes favorable in the motion of censure shall be counted.
> (2) The resigned government continues to manage current business until the nomination by the President of the Republic of a new Prime Minister and a new Government.
> (3) If a motion of censure is rejected, its signatories may not propose a new one during the course of the same session except in the case set forth in the following paragraph.
> (4) The Prime Minister, after deliberation with the Council of Ministers takes the responsibility of the Government before the National Assembly for the voting of a bill. In this case, this bill shall be considered adopted unless a motion of censure brought during the following twenty-four hours shall be voted under the conditions set forth in the first paragraph.
> (5) The Prime Minister may ask the Senate for the approval of a declaration of general policy.

10. The legislature is immune from dissolution by the executive.

No. The president can dissolve the legislature.

> Article 31
> (1) The President of the Republic, after consultation with the Prime Minister and the Presidents of the Assemblies, may pronounce the dissolution of the National Assembly. General elections shall take place at least thirty days and at most sixty days after the dissolution.

(2) The National Assembly shall meet in regular session fifteen days after the elections. If this session takes place during a period outside of the periods set aside for ordinary sessions, a session shall be legally opened for a period of fifteen days.

(3) There cannot be a new dissolution of the Assembly during the twelve months which follow these elections.

11. Any executive initiative on legislation requires ratification or approval by the legislature before it takes effect; that is, the executive lacks decree power.

Yes. The president and the government lack decree power.

12. Laws passed by the legislature are veto-proof or essentially veto-proof; that is, the executive lacks veto power, or has veto power but the veto can be overridden by a majority in the legislature.

Yes. The legislature can override a presidential veto by a majority vote of its total membership.

Article 70

(1) The President of the Republic shall promulgate the laws within a time period of eight days at the earliest and thirty days at the latest, following the transmission to him of the laws by the Parliament.

(2) During this period, the President may send back the draft law or bill for a second reading. If the National Assembly decides on the adoption of the law by a majority of its members, the law shall be promulgated and published during the time period indicated in the preceding paragraph.

13. The legislature's laws are supreme and not subject to judicial review.

No. The Constitutional Council can review the constitutionality of laws.

Article 67

(5) Organic laws may he promulgated only after certification by the Constitutional Council of their conformity with the Constitution.

14. The legislature has the right to initiate bills in all policy jurisdictions; the executive lacks gatekeeping authority.

Yes. The legislature can initiate bills in all policy jurisdictions. The legislature can initiate bills that reduce government revenues or increase government expenditures only, however, if it also provides a bill that offsets the change in revenue.

Article 62

(2) The bills or amendments proposed by the members of Parliament shall not be accepted when their adoption would entail either a reduction in public revenues or the creation or enlargement of public expenses unless they are accompanied by a bill for increasing revenues or equivalent savings.

(3) They may be declared unacceptable when they bear upon a matter which comes under the regulatory power by virtue of Article 59 or are contrary to a delegation granted by virtue of Article 60.

(4) If the Parliament disregards the objections raised by the Government by virtue of one of the two preceding paragraphs, the President of the Republic has recourse to the Constitutional Council which rules within a period of one week.

15. Expenditure of funds appropriated by the legislature is mandatory; the executive lacks the power to impound funds appropriated by the legislature.

No. The president can impound funds appropriated by the legislature.

16. The legislature controls the resources that finance its own internal operation and provide for the perquisites of its own members.

No. The legislature is dependent on the executive for the resources that finance its own operations.

17. Members of the legislature are immune from arrest and/or criminal prosecution.

Yes. Legislators are immune with the common exception for cases of *flagrante delicto*.

Article 50

(1) No member of Parliament may be prosecuted, pursued, arrested, detained, or tried because of the opinions or votes voiced by him during the exercise of his functions.

(2) No member of Parliament, while Parliament is in session, may be prosecuted or arrested for a criminal or penal matter, except with the authorization of the assembly to which he belongs unless it is a case of *flagrante delicto* or authorized prosecution or a judicial sentence.

(3) No member of Parliament, while Parliament is out of session, may be arrested, except with the authorization of the office of the assembly to which he belongs unless it is a case of *flagrante delicto* or authorized prosecution or a judicial sentence.

(4) The detention or prosecution of a member of Parliament is suspended if the assembly to which he belongs demands it.

18. All members of the legislature are elected; the executive lacks the power to appoint any members of the legislature.

Yes. All members of the legislature are elected.

Article 47

(1) The Deputies to the National Assembly are elected for five years by direct suffrage.

(2) The Senators are elected for six years by indirect suffrage.

19. The legislature alone, without the involvement of any other agencies, can change the Constitution.

No. Constitutional amendments require approval in a popular referendum.

Article 99
(1) The initiative for a revision of the Constitution belongs jointly to the President of the Republic and to the members of Parliament. No proposed revision presented by the members of Parliament may be debated if it has not been signed by at least one third of the members of one of the assemblies.
(2) Any proposed revision must be passed by a two-thirds majority of the deputies in the National Assembly and a two-thirds majority of the senators in the Senate in order for it to be submitted for a referendum.
(3) No procedure for revision may be initiated if it challenges the existence of the State or undermines the integrity of the territory, the republican form of government, or the pluralist character of Mauritanian democracy.

20. The legislature's approval is necessary for the declaration of war.

Yes. The legislature's approval is necessary for the declaration of war.

Article 58
The declaration of war shall be authorized by the Parliament.

21. The legislature's approval is necessary to ratify treaties with foreign countries.

Yes. The legislature's approval is necessary to ratify international treaties.

Article 36
The President of the Republic signs and ratifies treaties.

Article 78
(1) Peace treaties, union treaties, commerce treaties, treaties or accords concerning an international organization, treaties which require the finances of the State, treaties which modify provisions of a legislative nature, treaties concerning the status of persons, and treaties concerning the borders of the State may only he ratified by a law.
(2) They may take effect only after being ratified or approved. No cession, no exchange, and no annexation of territory is valid without the consent of the people who shall decide through referendum.
(3) In the case set forth in the last paragraph of Article 2, the required majority is four-fifths of the votes cast.

22. The legislature has the power to grant amnesty.

No. According to the constitution, amnesty can be passed only by law. In practice, the president holds the power to grant amnesty.

Article 57
(1) The following subjects are the domain of the law:
– amnesty.

23. The legislature has the power of pardon.

No. The president has the power of pardon.

Article 37
The President of the Republic has the right to grant clemency and the right to remit or commute sentences.

24. The legislature reviews and has the right to reject appointments to the judiciary; or the legislature itself appoints members of the judiciary.

No. Formally, the legislature has the power to elect the members of the High Court of Justice. In practice, the legislature has no role in judicial branch appointments.

Article 92
(1) There is instituted a High Court of Justice.
(2) It is composed of members elected from its midst and in equal number by the National Assembly and the Senate after each complete or partial renewal of these assemblies. It elects its president from among its members.

Article 81
(1) The Constitutional Council is composed of six members whose mandate lasts nine years and is not renewable. One third of the Constitutional Council shall be chosen every three years. Three of the members shall be appointed by the President of the Republic, two by the President of the National Assembly, and one by the President of the Senate.

25. The chairman of the central bank is appointed by the legislature.

No. The president appoints the chairman of the central bank.

26. The legislature has a substantial voice in the operation of the state-owned media.

No. The legislature lacks a substantial voice in the operation of the public media.

27. The legislature is regularly in session.

No. The legislature meets in ordinary session for less than four months each year.

Article 52
The Parliament meets in regular session for two ordinary sessions each year. The first ordinary session will convene during the first fortnight in November. The second will convene during the first fortnight in May. The length of each ordinary session may not exceed two months.

28. Each legislator has a personal secretary.

No.

29. Each legislator has at least one non-secretarial staff member with policy expertise.

No.

30. Legislators are eligible for re-election without any restriction.

Yes. There are no restrictions on re-election.

31. A seat in the legislature is an attractive enough position that legislators are generally interested in and seek re-election.

Yes.

32. The re-election of incumbent legislators is common enough that at any given time the legislature contains a significant number of highly experienced members.

No. From the mid-1980s until 2005, during the dictatorship of Maaouya Ould Sid'Ahmed Taya, the National Assembly was either effectively inoperative or wholly dominated by Taya's Democratic and Social Republican Party. Re-election rates were high owing to an absence of genuine competition, although members did not acquire a great deal of genuine experience in legislative matters. The parliament was suspended for over a year following the military coup of August 2005. Elections for the National Assembly held at the end of 2006 produced a legislature that contains myriad new parties and is highly fragmented in terms of party affiliation. Some legislators survive from the Taya era, but the discontinuity induced by the coup and the extended suspension of parliament, along with the dissolution of the previously hegemonic party system, have created a body that lacks a significant body of highly experienced legislators.

NATIONAL ASSEMBLY OF MAURITIUS

Expert consultants: John Bridge, V. Coopoomootoo, Staffan I. Lindberg, Edward McMahon, Brendan McSherry

Score: .66

Influence over executive (8/9)		Institutional autonomy (5/9)		Specified powers (4/8)		Institutional capacity (4/6)	
1. replace	X	10. no dissolution		19. amendments	X	27. sessions	X
2. serve as ministers	X	11. no decree	X	20. war	X	28. secretary	
3. interpellate	X	12. no veto	X	21. treaties	X	29. staff	
4. investigate	X	13. no review		22. amnesty		30. no term limits	X
5. oversee police	X	14. no gatekeeping		23. pardon		31. seek re-election	X
6. appoint PM	X	15. no impoundment	X	24. judiciary		32. experience	X
7. appoint ministers		16. control resources	X	25. central bank			
8. lack president	X	17. immunity		26. media	X		
9. no confidence	X	18. all elected	X				

The National Assembly of Mauritius has origins in the legislative bodies that represented the country in the British Empire in the late nineteenth century. The constitution adopted upon independence in 1968 instituted a unicameral legislature with a prime minister as head of government and a Governor General as head of state. A constitutional amendment in 1992 replaced the Governor General with a president elected by the legislature. The 1992 amendment also granted the judiciary the power to review the constitutionality of laws. Prior to 1992 the National Assembly's legislation was supreme and not subject to judicial review. Further constitutional amendments in 2003 granted the president the powers to dissolve the legislature and to issue pardons. Before 2003 the legislature had the power of pardon and was immune from dissolution.

Even after the adoption of these amendments that reduced parliament's powers, parliament remains a muscular institution. It influences the executive with, among other powers, the right to appoint the president, appoint and remove the prime minister, and oversee the agencies of coercion. Its own institutional autonomy is limited by executive dissolution and gatekeeping powers and a lack of immunity for legislators. The legislature possesses some specified powers and prerogatives and a fair amount of institutional autonomy.

SURVEY

1. The legislature alone, without the involvement of any other agencies, can impeach the president or replace the prime minister.

Yes. The legislature can remove the prime minister with a vote of no confidence. Presidential impeachment requires the involvement of the prime minister and an independent tribunal appointed by the judicial branch.

Article 30
(1) The President or the Vice-President may be removed from office in accordance with this section for –
(a) violation of the Constitution or any other serious act of misconduct;
(b) inability to perform his functions whether arising from infirmity of mind or body or from any other cause.
(2) Where the President fails to comply with section 46(2), he may be removed from office on a motion made by the Prime Minister in the Assembly and supported by the votes of a majority of all the members of the Assembly.
(3) The President or the Vice-President shall not be removed from office for any other cause unless –
(a) a motion that the circumstances requiring the removal of the President or the Vice-President be investigated by a tribunal is made in the Assembly by the Prime Minister;
(b) the motion states with full particulars the ground on which the removal of the President or the Vice-President is sought;
(c) the motion is supported by the votes of not less than two-thirds of all the members of the Assembly;
(d) the tribunal, after its investigation, forwards a written report on the investigation addressed to the Assembly and delivered to the Speaker and recommends the removal of the President or the Vice-President; and
(e) subject to paragraph (f), a motion made by the Prime Minister and supported by the votes of a majority of all the members of the Assembly requires the removal of the President or the Vice-President on a recommendation to that effect by the tribunal;
(f) a motion under paragraph (e) is made –
(i) where the Assembly is sitting, within 20 days of the receipt of the report of the tribunal by the Speaker;
(ii) where the Assembly is not sitting, within 20 days of the day on which the Assembly resumes its sitting.

(4) The President or the Vice-President shall have the right to appear and to be represented before the tribunal during its investigation.
(5) Where the Assembly supports a motion under subsection (3)(c), it may suspend the President or the Vice-President from performing the functions of his office.
(6) A suspension under subsection (5) shall cease to have effect where –
(a) a report under subsection (3)(d) does not recommend that the President or the Vice-President ought to be removed from office; or
(b) the Assembly does not support a motion under subsection (3)(e) requiring the removal of the President or the Vice-President.
(7) Where the Assembly supports a motion under subsection (3)(e) requiring the removal of the President or the Vice-President, the office of the President or the Vice-President, as the case may be, shall become vacant.
(8) In this section, "tribunal" means a tribunal consisting of a chairman and 2 or 4 other members appointed by the Chief Justice from amongst persons who hold or have held office as a Judge of a court having unlimited jurisdiction in civil or criminal matters in some part of the Commonwealth or a court having jurisdiction in appeals from such a court.

Article 57
(1) The President, acting in accordance with the advice of the Prime Minister, may at any time prorogue or dissolve Parliament:
Provided that –
(a) where the Assembly passes a resolution that it has no confidence in the Government and the Prime Minister does not within 3 days either resign from his office or advise the President to dissolve Parliament within 7 days or at such later time as the President, acting in his own deliberate judgment, may consider reasonable, the President, acting in his own deliberate judgment, may dissolve Parliament.
(4) The office of a Minister (other than the Prime Minister) shall become vacant –
(a) where the President, acting in accordance with the advice of the Prime Minister, so directs;
(b) where the Prime Minister resigns from office within 3 days after the passage by the Assembly of a resolution of no confidence in the Government or is removed from office under subsection (1) or (2); or
(c) upon the appointment of any person to the office of Prime Minister.

Article 60
(1) Where a resolution of no confidence in the Government is passed by the Assembly and the Prime Minister does not within 3 days resign from his office, the President shall remove the Prime Minister from office unless, in pursuance of section 57(1), Parliament has been or is to be dissolved in consequence of such resolution.
(2) Where at any time between the holding of a general election and the first sitting of the Assembly thereafter the President, acting in his own deliberate judgment, considers that, in consequence of changes in the

membership of the Assembly resulting from that general election, the Prime Minister will not be able to command the support of a majority of the members of the Assembly, the President may remove the Prime Minister from office:

Provided that the President shall not remove the Prime Minister from office within the period of 10 days immediately following the date prescribed for polling at that general election unless he is satisfied that a party or party alliance in opposition to the Government and registered for the purposes of that general election under paragraph 2 of the First Schedule has at that general election gained a majority of all seats in the Assembly.
(4) The office of a Minister (other than the Prime Minister) shall become vacant –

   (b) where the Prime Minister resigns from office within 3 days after the passage by the Assembly of a resolution of no confidence in the Government or is removed from office under subsection (1) or (2).

2. Ministers may serve simultaneously as members of the legislature.

Yes. Legislators may serve simultaneously in ministerial positions.

3. The legislature has powers of summons over executive branch officials and hearings with executive branch officials testifying before the legislature or its committees are regularly held.

Yes. The legislature regularly interpellates officials from the executive.

4. The legislature can conduct independent investigation of the chief executive and the agencies of the executive.

Yes. The legislature can investigate the executive.

5. The legislature has effective powers of oversight over the agencies of coercion (the military, organs of law enforcement, intelligence services, and the secret police).

Yes. The legislature has effective powers of oversight over the agencies of coercion.

6. The legislature appoints the prime minister.

Yes. The president appoints as prime minister the candidate who enjoys the support of the legislature.

Article 59
(1) There shall be a Prime Minister and a Deputy Prime Minister who shall be appointed by the President.
(2) There shall be, in addition to the offices of Prime Minister, Deputy Prime Minister and Attorney-General, such other offices of Minister of the Government as may be prescribed by Parliament or, subject to any law, established by the President, acting in accordance with the advice of the Prime Minister:

Provided that the number of offices of Minister, other than the Prime Minister, shall not be more than 24.
(3) The President, acting in his own deliberate judgment, shall appoint as Prime Minister the member of the Assembly who appears to him best able to command the support of the majority of the members of the Assembly, and shall, acting in accordance with the advice of the Prime Minister, appoint the Deputy Prime Minister, the Attorney-General and the other Ministers from among the members of the Assembly:
Provided that –

   (a) where occasion arises for making an appointment while Parliament is dissolved, a person who was a member of the Assembly immediately before the dissolution may be appointed; and
   (b) a person may be appointed Attorney-General, notwithstanding that he is not (or, as the case may be, was not) a member of the Assembly.

7. The legislature's approval is required to confirm the appointment of ministers; or the legislature itself appoints ministers.

No. The president appoints ministers on the recommendation of the prime minister, and the appointments do not require the legislature's approval.

Article 59
(1) There shall be a Prime Minister and a Deputy Prime Minister who shall be appointed by the President.
(2) There shall be, in addition to the offices of Prime Minister, Deputy Prime Minister and Attorney-General, such other offices of Minister of the Government as may be prescribed by Parliament or, subject to any law, established by the President, acting in accordance with the advice of the Prime Minister:
Provided that the number of offices of Minister, other than the Prime Minister, shall not be more than 24.
(3) The President, acting in his own deliberate judgment, shall appoint as Prime Minister the member of the Assembly who appears to him best able to command the support of the majority of the members of the Assembly, and shall, acting in accordance with the advice of the Prime Minister, appoint the Deputy Prime Minister, the Attorney-General and the other Ministers from among the members of the Assembly:
Provided that –

   (a) where occasion arises for making an appointment while Parliament is dissolved, a person who was a member of the Assembly immediately before the dissolution may be appointed; and
   (b) a person may be appointed Attorney-General, notwithstanding that he is not (or, as the case may be, was not) a member of the Assembly.

8. The country lacks a presidency entirely or there is a presidency, but the president is elected by the legislature.

Yes. Parliament elects the president.

Article 28
(2) (a) The President shall –
(i) be elected by the Assembly on a motion made by the Prime Minister and supported by the votes of a majority of all the members of the Assembly.

9. The legislature can vote no confidence in the government.

Yes. The legislature can vote no confidence in the government.

Article 57
(1) The President, acting in accordance with the advice of the Prime Minister, may at any time prorogue or dissolve Parliament:
Provided that –
(a) where the Assembly passes a resolution that it has no confidence in the Government and the Prime Minister does not within 3 days either resign from his office or advise the President to dissolve Parliament within 7 days or at such later time as the President, acting in his own deliberate judgment, may consider reasonable, the President, acting in his own deliberate judgment, may dissolve Parliament.

Article 60
(1) Where a resolution of no confidence in the Government is passed by the Assembly and the Prime Minister does not within 3 days resign from his office, the President shall remove the Prime Minister from office unless, in pursuance of section 57(1), Parliament has been or is to be dissolved in consequence of such resolution.
(2) Where at any time between the holding of a general election and the first sitting of the Assembly thereafter the President, acting in his own deliberate judgment, considers that, in consequence of changes in the membership of the Assembly resulting from that general election, the Prime Minister will not be able to command the support of a majority of the members of the Assembly, the President may remove the Prime Minister from office:
Provided that the President shall not remove the Prime Minister from office within the period of 10 days immediately following the date prescribed for polling at that general election unless he is satisfied that a party or party alliance in opposition to the Government and registered for the purposes of that general election under paragraph 2 of the First Schedule has at that general election gained a majority of all seats in the Assembly.
(4) The office of a Minister (other than the Prime Minister) shall become vacant –
(b) where the Prime Minister resigns from office within 3 days after the passage by the Assembly of a resolution of no confidence in the Government or is removed from office under subsection (1) or (2).

10. The legislature is immune from dissolution by the executive.

No. The president can dissolve the legislature.

Article 57
(1) The President, acting in accordance with the advice of the Prime Minister, may at any time prorogue or dissolve Parliament:
Provided that –
(a) where the Assembly passes a resolution that it has no confidence in the Government and the Prime Minister does not within 3 days either resign from his office or advise the President to dissolve Parliament within 7 days or at such later time as the President, acting in his own deliberate judgment, may consider reasonable, the President, acting in his own deliberate judgment, may dissolve Parliament;
(b) where the office of Prime Minister is vacant and the President considers that there is no prospect of his being able within a reasonable time to appoint to that office a person who can command the support of a majority of the members of the Assembly, the President, acting in his own deliberate judgment, may dissolve Parliament.

11. Any executive initiative on legislation requires ratification or approval by the legislature before it takes effect; that is, the executive lacks decree power.

Yes. The executive lacks decree power.

12. Laws passed by the legislature are veto-proof or essentially veto-proof; that is, the executive lacks veto power, or has veto power but the veto can be overridden by a majority in the legislature.

Yes. The legislature can override a presidential veto by a majority vote of its present members.

Article 46
(1) The power of Parliament to make laws shall be exercisable by Bills passed by the Assembly and assented to by the President.
(2) (a) Subject to paragraphs (b) and (c), where a Bill is submitted to the President for assent in accordance with this Constitution, he shall signify that he assents or that he withholds assent.
(b) The President shall not withhold assent under paragraph (a) –
(i) in the case of a Bill which makes provision for any of the purposes specified in section 54;
(ii) in the case of a Bill which amends any provision of the Constitution and which is certified by the Speaker as having complied with the requirements of section 47;
(iii) in the case of any other Bill, unless he is of opinion, acting in his own deliberate judgment, that the Bill including any proposed amendment thereto, should be reconsidered by the Assembly.
(c) Where the President withholds assent under paragraph (b)(iii), he shall, within 21 days of the submission of the Bill for assent, return the Bill to the Assembly with a request that it should reconsider the Bill, including any proposed amendment thereto.
(d) Where a Bill is returned to the Assembly under paragraph (c), the Assembly shall reconsider the Bill

accordingly, and where it is passed again by the Assembly with or without amendment and submitted anew to the President for assent, the President shall signify his assent.

(3) Where the President assents to a Bill that has been submitted to him in accordance with this Constitution, the Bill shall become law and the President shall thereupon cause it to be published in the Gazette as a law.

13. The legislature's laws are supreme and not subject to judicial review.

No. The Supreme Court can review the constitutionality of laws.

Article 83
(1) Subject to sections 41(5), 64(5) and 101(1), where any person alleges that any provision of this Constitution (other than Chapter II) has been contravened and that his interests are being or are likely to be affected by such contravention, then, without prejudice to any other action with respect to the same matter which is lawfully available, that person may apply to the Supreme Court for a declaration and for relief under this section.
(2) The Supreme Court shall have jurisdiction, in any application made by any person in pursuance of subsection (1) or in any other proceedings lawfully brought before the court, to determine whether any provision of this Constitution (other than Chapter II) has been contravened and to make a declaration accordingly.

Article 84
(1) Where any question as to the interpretation of this Constitution arises in any court of law established for Mauritius (other than the Court of Appeal, the Supreme Court or a court martial) and the court is of opinion that the question involves a substantial question of law, the court shall refer the question to the Supreme Court.
(2) Where any question is referred to the Supreme Court in pursuance of this section, the Supreme Court shall give its decision upon the question and the court in which the question arose shall dispose of the case in accordance with that decision or, where the decision is the subject of an appeal to the Court of Appeal or the Judicial Committee, in accordance with the decision of the Court of Appeal or, as the case may be, of the Judicial Committee.

14. The legislature has the right to initiate bills in all policy jurisdictions; the executive lacks gatekeeping authority.

No. The legislature is prohibited from introducing legislation related to taxation, public expenditures, or government debt.

Article 54
Except upon the recommendation of a Minister, the Assembly shall not –
(a) proceed upon any Bill (including any amendment to a Bill) that, in the opinion of the person presiding, makes provision for any of the following purposes –

(i) for the imposition of taxation or the alteration of taxation otherwise than by reduction;
(ii) for the imposition of any charge upon the Consolidated Fund or other public funds of Mauritius or the alteration of any such charge otherwise than by reduction;
(iii) for the payment, issue or withdrawal from the Consolidated Fund or other public funds of Mauritius of any money not charged on it or any increase in the amount of such payment, issue or withdrawal; or
(iv) for the composition or remission of any debt to the Government;
(b) proceed upon any motion (including any amendment to a motion) the effect of which, in the opinion of the person presiding, would be to make provision for any of those purposes; or
(c) receive any petition that, in the opinion of the person presiding, requests that provision be made for any of those purposes.

15. Expenditure of funds appropriated by the legislature is mandatory; the executive lacks the power to impound funds appropriated by the legislature.

Yes. The executive lacks the power to impound funds appropriated by the legislature.

16. The legislature controls the resources that finance its own internal operation and provide for the perquisites of its own members.

Yes. The legislature enjoys financial autonomy.

17. Members of the legislature are immune from arrest and/or criminal prosecution.

No. Legislators are subject to arrest and criminal prosecution.

Article 38
(1) Subject to this section, where a member of the Assembly is sentenced by a court in any part of the Commonwealth to death or to imprisonment (by whatever name called) for a term exceeding 12 months, he shall forthwith cease to perform his functions as a member of the Assembly and his seat in the Assembly shall become vacant at the expiration of a period of 30 days thereafter.

18. All members of the legislature are elected; the executive lacks the power to appoint any members of the legislature.

Yes. All members of the legislature are elected.

Article 31
(1) There shall be a Parliament for Mauritius, which shall consist of the President and a National Assembly.
(2) The Assembly shall consist of persons elected in accordance with the First Schedule, which makes provision for the election of 70 members.

19. The legislature alone, without the involvement of any other agencies, can change the Constitution.

Yes. The legislature can change the constitution with a two-thirds majority vote.

Article 47
(1) Subject to this section, Parliament may alter this Constitution.
(2) A Bill for an Act of Parliament to alter any of the following provisions of this Constitution –
(3) A Bill for an Act of Parliament to alter the provisions of section 1 or 57(2) shall not be passed by the Assembly unless –
(a) the proposed Bill has before its introduction in the Assembly been submitted, by referendum, to the electorate of Mauritius and has been approved by the votes of not less than three quarters of the electorate;
(b) it is supported at the final voting in the Assembly by the votes of all the members of the Assembly.
(4) A Bill for an Act of Parliament to alter any provision of this Constitution (but which does not alter any of the provisions of this Constitution as specified in subsection (2)) shall not be passed by the Assembly unless it is supported at the final voting in the Assembly by the votes of not less than two-thirds of all the members of the Assembly.
(5) In this section, references to altering this Constitution or any part of this Constitution include references –
(a) to revoking it, with or without re-enactment or the making of different provision;
(b) to modifying it, whether by omitting or amending any of its provisions or inserting additional provisions in it or otherwise; and
(c) to suspending its operation for any period, or terminating any such suspension.

20. The legislature's approval is necessary for the declaration of war.

Yes. The legislature's approval is necessary for the declaration of war.

21. The legislature's approval is necessary to ratify treaties with foreign countries.

Yes. Although not stated explicitly in the constitution, the legislature's approval is necessary to ratify international treaties.

22. The legislature has the power to grant amnesty.

No. The legislature lacks the power to grant amnesty.

23. The legislature has the power of pardon.

No. The president has the power of pardon.

Article 75
(1) The President may –
(a) grant to any person convicted of any offence a pardon, either free or subject to lawful conditions.

24. The legislature reviews and has the right to reject appointments to the judiciary; or the legislature itself appoints members of the judiciary.

No. The president and the Judicial and Legal Service Commission are responsible for judicial appointments, and these appointments do not require the legislature's approval.

Article 77
(1) The Chief Justice shall be appointed by the President acting after consultation with the Prime Minister.
(2) The Senior Puisne Judge shall be appointed by the President, acting in accordance with the advice of the Chief Justice.
(3) The Puisne Judges shall be appointed by the President, acting in accordance with the advice of the Judicial and Legal Service Commission.

25. The chairman of the central bank is appointed by the legislature.

No. The president appoints the governor of the Bank of Mauritius.

26. The legislature has a substantial voice in the operation of the state-owned media.

Yes. The legislature has a substantial voice in the operation of the public media.

27. The legislature is regularly in session.

Yes. The legislature regularly meets in ordinary session.

Article 56
(1) The sessions of the Assembly shall be held in such place and begin at such time as the President by Proclamation may appoint:
Provided that the place at which any session of the Assembly is to be held may be altered from time to time during the course of the session by further Proclamation made by the President.
(2) A session of the Assembly shall be held from time to time so that a period of 12 months shall not intervene between the last sitting of the Assembly in one session and its first sitting in the next session.

28. Each legislator has a personal secretary.

No.

29. Each legislator has at least one non-secretarial staff member with policy expertise.

No.

30. Legislators are eligible for re-election without any restriction.

Yes. There are no restrictions on re-election.

31. A seat in the legislature is an attractive enough position that legislators are generally interested in and seek re-election.

Yes.

32. The re-election of incumbent legislators is common enough that at any given time the legislature contains a significant number of highly experienced members.

Yes. Re-election rates are sufficiently high to produce a significant number of highly experienced members.

MEXICAN CONGRESS (*CONGRESO*)

Expert consultants: Kathleen Bruhn, Roderic A. Camp, Ernesto Castaneda, Victor Hermosillo, José Manuel Minjares Jimenez, Benito Nacif, Jeffrey A. Weldon

Score: .44

Influence over executive (3/9)		Institutional autonomy (5/9)		Specified powers (4/8)		Institutional capacity (2/6)	
1. replace	X	10. no dissolution	X	19. amendments		27. sessions	
2. serve as ministers		11. no decree	X	20. war	X	28. secretary	X
3. interpellate	X	12. no veto		21. treaties	X	29. staff	X
4. investigate	X	13. no review		22. amnesty	X	30. no term limits	
5. oversee police		14. no gatekeeping	X	23. pardon		31. seek re-election	
6. appoint PM		15. no impoundment		24. judiciary	X	32. experience	
7. appoint ministers		16. control resources	X	25. central bank			
8. lack president		17. immunity		26. media			
9. no confidence		18. all elected	X				

The Mexican Congress (*Congreso*) was established in Mexico's 1824 constitution. This and other nineteenth-century constitutions were largely ignored by presidents, who tended to rule without close regard for the law. At the conclusion of the Mexican Revolution (1910–17), the constitution currently in force was drawn up. Framers sought to curtail the powers of the presidency, although the president remained a central actor in the post-revolutionary Mexican political system. As the leaders of the hegemonic Institutional Revolutionary Party (PRI), successive Mexican presidents exerted sway over the other branches of government. In 2000, for the first time, a candidate who did not come from the PRI, Vicente Fox, was elected president.

Congress has some meaningful authority, although its powers are not expansive. Its leverage over the executive is quite circumscribed, but it does enjoy some institutional autonomy. The legislature cannot be dissolved, and the president cannot issue decrees without prior authorization by Congress. The legislature holds four of the eight specified powers assessed here: It has the authority to grant amnesty, and its approval is needed to declare war, ratify treaties, and confirm some high-level judicial appointments. It has some institutional capacity, in part by virtue of the presence of staff. Yet overall institutional capacity is relatively low, for two reasons. First, legislators may not run for re-election in successive terms. This provision prevents legislators from developing experience and expertise in the legislature. Furthermore, the legislature is in session for only about five months each year, which further limits its institutional capacity.

SURVEY

1. The legislature alone, without the involvement of any other agencies, can impeach the president or replace the prime minister.

Yes. The legislature can impeach the president. The Chamber of Deputies can declare grounds for impeachment by a majority vote of its total membership. The Senate investigates the accusations and can remove the president from office by a two-thirds majority vote of its total membership.

Article 108
The President of the Republic, during his term of office, may be impeached only for treason to the country and serious common crimes.

Article 109
If the offense is of a common order, the Chamber of Deputies acting as a grand jury shall determine, by an absolute majority of votes of its total membership, whether or not there are grounds for proceeding against the accused.

Article 111
The Senate, constituted as a grand jury, shall take cognizance of all official offenses; but it may not open the pertinent investigation without a previous bill of impeachment by the Chamber of Deputies. If after conducting such proceedings as it deems advisable and hearing the accused, the Chamber of Senators shall decide by a two-thirds majority of all its members that he is guilty, the latter shall be removed from office by virtue of such decision and disqualified from holding any other office for a period determined by law.

2. Ministers may serve simultaneously as members of the legislature.

No. Legislators are prohibited from serving simultaneously in ministerial positions.

Article 62
Proprietary deputies and senators, during their terms of office, may not hold any other commission or employment of the Federation or of the States for which they receive a salary, without prior permission from the respective chamber; but their representative functions shall thereupon cease, while they are holding the new position.

3. The legislature has powers of summons over executive branch officials and hearings with executive branch officials testifying before the legislature or its committees are regularly held.

Yes. The legislature regularly interpellates officials from the executive. Additionally, the legislature questions the executive following the president's annual *Informe de Govierno*, which is similar to the State of the Union Address in the United States of America.

4. The legislature can conduct independent investigation of the chief executive and the agencies of the executive.

Yes. The legislature can investigate the executive.

5. The legislature has effective powers of oversight over the agencies of coercion (the military, organs of law enforcement, intelligence services, and the secret police).

No. The legislature lacks effective powers of oversight over the agencies of coercion.

6. The legislature appoints the prime minister.

No. There is no prime minister.

7. The legislature's approval is required to confirm the appointment of ministers; or the legislature itself appoints ministers.

No. The Senate must confirm only the attorney general. All other ministers are appointed by the president, and the appointments do not require the legislature's approval.

Article 89
The powers and duties of the President are the following:
1. To appoint and remove freely the secretaries of the Government... and to appoint and remove freely all other employees of the Union whose appointment or removal is not otherwise provided for in the Constitution or by law.

8. The country lacks a presidency entirely or there is a presidency, but the president is elected by the legislature.

No. The president is directly elected.

Article 81
The election of the President shall be direct and under the terms prescribed by the Electoral Law.

9. The legislature can vote no confidence in the government.

No. The legislature cannot vote no confidence in the government.

10. The legislature is immune from dissolution by the executive.

Yes. The legislature is immune from dissolution.

11. Any executive initiative on legislation requires ratification or approval by the legislature before it takes effect; that is, the executive lacks decree power.

Yes. The executive lacks decree power. The legislature can authorize the executive temporary decree power in specified issue areas.

12. Laws passed by the legislature are veto-proof or essentially veto-proof; that is, the executive lacks veto power, or has veto power but the veto can be overridden by a majority in the legislature.

No. A two-thirds vote of the total membership of both chambers of the legislature is required to override an executive veto.

Article 72
c. A bill or proposed decree rejected in whole or in part by the Executive shall be returned, with his objections, to the chamber of origin. It must be discussed anew by the latter, and if it is confirmed by a vote of two thirds of the total membership it shall again be sent to the

revisory chamber. If it is sanctioned by the latter by the same majority, the bill shall become a law or decree and shall be returned to the Executive for promulgation.

13. The legislature's laws are supreme and not subject to judicial review.

No. The Supreme Court of Justice has judicial review power. This power, however, is limited. The Court may hear only challenges brought by at least one-third of Congress itself, or the attorney general, within thirty days of the publication of the law.

14. The legislature has the right to initiate bills in all policy jurisdictions; the executive lacks gatekeeping authority.

Yes. The legislature can initiate bills in all other jurisdictions.

15. Expenditure of funds appropriated by the legislature is mandatory; the executive lacks the power to impound funds appropriated by the legislature.

No. The executive can introduce cuts to projected expenditures if actual revenues are lower than expected.

16. The legislature controls the resources that finance its own internal operation and provide for the perquisites of its own members.

Yes. The legislature enjoys financial autonomy.

Article 77
Each of the chambers, without the intervention of the other, may:
1. Dictate economic resolutions relating to its internal organization.

Article 127
The deputies and senators . . . shall receive a compensation for their services that shall be specified by law.

17. Members of the legislature are immune from arrest and/or criminal prosecution.

No. Members of the legislature enjoy immunity only for statements made in their work as legislators. They are subject to arrest for common crimes.

Article 61
Deputies and senators are inviolable for opinions expressed by them in the discharge of their offices and shall never be called to account for them.

Article 108
Senators and deputies of the Congress of the Union . . . are liable for common crimes that they may commit during their term of office, and also for crimes, offenses, or omissions that they incur in the exercise of their office.

18. All members of the legislature are elected; the executive lacks the power to appoint any members of the legislature.

Yes. All members of Congress are elected.

Article 51
The Chamber of Deputies is composed of representatives of the Nation, all elected every three years by the Mexican citizens.

Article 56
The Chamber of Senators shall be composed of two members for each State and two for the Federal District, all directly elected every six years.

19. The legislature alone, without the involvement of any other agencies, can change the Constitution.

No. Constitutional amendments require the approval of the majority of the provincial (state) legislatures.

Article 135
The present Constitution may be added to or amended. In order that the additions or amendments shall become a part thereof, it shall be required that the Congress of the Union, by a vote of two thirds of the individuals present, agree to the amendments or additions and that they be approved by a majority of the legislatures of the States.

20. The legislature's approval is necessary for the declaration of war.

Yes. The legislature's approval is necessary for presidential war declarations.

Article 73
The Congress has the power:
XII. To declare war, in the light of information submitted by the Executive.

Article 89
The powers and duties of the President are the following:
XX. To declare war in the name of the United Mexican States, pursuant to a previous law of the Congress of the Union.

21. The legislature's approval is necessary to ratify treaties with foreign countries.

Yes. The legislature's approval is necessary to ratify international treaties.

Article 76
The exclusive powers of the Senate are:
I. To approve the treaties and diplomatic conventions made by the President of the Republic with foreign powers.

22. The legislature has the power to grant amnesty.

Yes. The legislature has the power to grant amnesty.

Article 73
The Congress has the power:
XXII. To grant amnesties for crimes within the jurisdiction of the federal courts.

23. The legislature has the power of pardon.

No. The president has the power of pardon.

Article 89
The powers and duties of the President are the following:
XIV. To grant, according to law, pardons to criminals convicted of crimes within the jurisdiction of the federal courts, and to those convicted of common crimes in the Federal District and Territories.

24. The legislature reviews and has the right to reject appointments to the judiciary; or the legislature itself appoints members of the judiciary.

Yes. Congressional approval is necessary for some high-level judicial appointments.

Article 73
VI. 4. Appointments of the magistrates of the superior court of justice of the Federal District and of the Territories shall be made by the President of the Republic and submitted for the approval of the Chamber of Deputies, which shall grant or refuse such approval within a period of ten days, without extension.

Article 74
The exclusive powers of the Chamber of Deputies are:
vi. To grant or refuse its approval of appointments of magistrates of the superior court of justice of the Federal District and of the Territories, submitted to it by the President of the Republic.

Article 76
The exclusive powers of the Senate are:
vi. To grant or deny its approval of the appointments of ministers of the Supreme Court of Justice of the Nation . . . which the President of the Republic may submit to it.

Article 96
Appointments of the ministers of the Supreme Court shall be made by the President of the Republic and submitted to the approval of the Chamber of Senators, which shall grant or deny approval within the unalterable period of ten days.

25. The chairman of the central bank is appointed by the legislature.

No. The president appoints the governor of the Bank of Mexico.

26. The legislature has a substantial voice in the operation of the state-owned media.

No. The public media are largely controlled by executive branch bureaucracies with little input from the legislature.

27. The legislature is regularly in session.

No. The legislature is in session for only five months each year. Ordinary sessions are scheduled to last from September 1 to December 15 (except in a presidential election year when it may extend to December 31) and from March 15 to April 30. During interim periods, a smaller legislative commission meets and has legislative power. Congress may also vote to extend its own session.

28. Each legislator has a personal secretary.

Yes. The parliamentary groups provide personnel.

29. Each legislator has at least one non-secretarial staff member with policy expertise.

Yes. See item 28.

30. Legislators are eligible for re-election without any restriction.

No. Consecutive re-election is forbidden. Legislators can run for re-election only after sitting out at least one term.

Article 59
Senators and deputies to the Congress of the Union cannot be reelected for the immediately following term.

31. A seat in the legislature is an attractive enough position that legislators are generally interested in and seek re-election.

No. The ban on immediate re-election creates conditions under which most legislators treat their offices as stepping stones to other positions. Legislators generally are not interested in seeking re-election after sitting out for one or more terms, although some do seek to return to the legislature at some later point in their careers.

32. The re-election of incumbent legislators is common enough that at any given time the legislature contains a significant number of highly experienced members.

No. Since legislators are prohibited from serving consecutive terms, the legislature contains relatively few highly experienced members.

PARLIAMENT OF MOLDOVA (*PARLAMENTUL*)

Expert consultants: Igor Botan, Radu Gorincioi, Natalia Postica, Vladimir Solonari, Lucan A. Way

Score: .75

Influence over executive (8/9)		Institutional autonomy (6/9)		Specified powers (6/8)		Institutional capacity (4/6)	
1. replace	X	10. no dissolution		19. amendments		27. sessions	X
2. serve as ministers		11. no decree	X	20. war	X	28. secretary	
3. interpellate	X	12. no veto	X	21. treaties	X	29. staff	
4. investigate	X	13. no review		22. amnesty	X	30. no term limits	X
5. oversee police	X	14. no gatekeeping		23. pardon		31. seek re-election	X
6. appoint PM	X	15. no impoundment	X	24. judiciary	X	32. experience	X
7. appoint ministers	X	16. control resources	X	25. central bank	X		
8. lack president	X	17. immunity	X	26. media	X		
9. no confidence	X	18. all elected	X				

The Parliament (*Parlamentul*) of Moldova was born along with the new state following the dissolution of the USSR in 1992. A new constitution in 1994 established the institutional framework of the current legislature. The 1994 constitution called for a unicameral parliament with a popularly elected president. In 2000 a constitutional amendment granted parliament the power to elect the president.

The legislature influences the executive branch with robust oversight powers and with powers to elect the prime minister and the president and shape the government. It also has substantial institutional autonomy. It exercises many specified powers and prerogatives, including the powers to declare war, approve international treaties, and grant amnesty. It has some institutional capacity, although legislators lack personal staff.

SURVEY

1. The legislature alone, without the involvement of any other agencies, can impeach the president or replace the prime minister.

Yes. The legislature can dismiss the prime minister with a vote of no confidence. Presidential impeachment requires the involvement of the Supreme Court of Justice.

Article 81

(2) The President of the Republic of Moldova enjoys immunity. He may not be brought to juridical responsibility for opinions expressed in the exercise of his mandate.

(3) The Parliament may decide to impeach the President of the Republic of Moldova by the vote of two-thirds of the elected deputies if he commits a crime. The competence of judgment belongs to the Supreme Court of Justice in accordance with the law. The President is removed from office by right on the day on which the conviction is final (definitive).

Article 89

(1) In case of actions committed that violate the provisions of the Constitution, the President of the Republic of Moldova may be removed from office by the Parliament by the vote of two-thirds of the elected deputies.

(2) The proposal for the removal from office may be initiated by at least one-third of the deputies and must be brought to the attention of the President of the Republic Moldova without delay. The President may provide the Parliament and the Constitutional Court with explanations of the accusation brought against him.

Article 106

(1) The Parliament may, on the proposal of at least one quarter of the deputies, express no confidence in the Government by the majority vote of the deputies.

(2) The initiative to express no confidence is examined three days after the date when it was presented to the Parliament.

Article 106.1

(2) The Government resigns if the motion of censure brought within a three-month period from the moment of introducing a program, declaration of a general political character or a bill is adopted in accordance with Article 106.

(3) If the Government does not resign in accordance with paragraph (2), the presented bill is considered adopted, and the program or declaration of a general political character [becomes] obligatory for the Government.

2. Ministers may serve simultaneously as members of the legislature.

No. Legislators are prohibited from serving simultaneously in ministerial positions.

Article 70

(1) The position of a deputy is incompatible with the performance of any other remunerated function with the exception of teaching and scientific activity.

(2) Other incompatibilities are established by an organic law.

Article 99

(1) The function of a member of the Government is incompatible with the performance of any other remunerated function.

3. The legislature has powers of summons over executive branch officials and hearings with executive branch officials testifying before the legislature or its committees are regularly held.

Yes. The legislature regularly interpellates officials from the executive.

Article 105

(1) The Government and each of its members are obligated to respond to questions and interpellations formulated by deputies.

(2) Parliament may adopt a motion that expresses its position on the subject of the interpellation.

4. The legislature can conduct independent investigation of the chief executive and the agencies of the executive.

Yes. The legislature can investigate the executive.

5. The legislature has effective powers of oversight over the agencies of coercion (the military, organs of law enforcement, intelligence services, and the secret police).

Yes. The legislature has effective powers of oversight over the agencies of coercion.

6. The legislature appoints the prime minister.

Yes. The president appoints as prime minister the candidate who enjoys the support of the legislature.

Article 98

(1) After consultations with Parliamentary factions, the President of the Republic of Moldova nominates a candidate for the office of the Prime Minister.

(2) The candidate for the office of the Prime Minister shall request, within 15 days of his nomination, a vote of confidence from the Parliament regarding his action program and the entire composition of the Government.

7. The legislature's approval is required to confirm the appointment of ministers; or the legislature itself appoints ministers.

Yes. The legislature's approval is required to confirm ministerial appointments.

Article 98

(1) After consultations with Parliamentary factions, the President of the Republic of Moldova nominates a candidate for the office of the Prime Minister.

(2) The candidate for the office of the Prime Minister shall request, within 15 days of his nomination, a vote of confidence from the Parliament regarding his action program and the entire composition of the Government.

(3) The action program and the composition of the Government are debated in a session of the Parliament. [The Parliament] expresses confidence in the Government by the majority vote of the elected deputies.

(4) Based on the vote of confidence expressed by the Parliament, the President of the Republic of Moldova appoints the Government.

(5) The Government exercises its powers from the day its members take the oath before the President Republic of Moldova.

(6) In case of governmental changes or vacancies in the Government functions, the President of the Republic of Moldova, upon the proposal of the Prime Minister, dismisses from office and appoints individual members of the Government.

8. The country lacks a presidency entirely or there is a presidency, but the president is elected by the legislature.

Yes. The legislature elects the president. Prior to a constitutional amendment in 2000, the president was directly elected.

Article 78

(1) The President of the Republic of Moldova is elected by secret ballot.

9. The legislature can vote no confidence in the government.

Yes. The legislature can vote no confidence in the government.

Article 106

(1) The Parliament may, on the proposal of at least one quarter of the deputies, express no confidence in the Government by the majority vote of the deputies.

(2) The initiative to express no confidence is examined three days after the date when it was presented to the Parliament.

Article 106.1

(2) The Government resigns if the motion of censure brought within a three-month period from the moment of introducing a program, declaration of a general political character or a bill is adopted in accordance with Article 106.

(3) If the Government does not resign in accordance with paragraph (2), the presented bill is considered adopted, and the program or declaration of a general political character [becomes] obligatory for the Government.

10. The legislature is immune from dissolution by the executive.

No. The president can dissolve the legislature.

Article 85

(1) In cases [when it is] impossible to form the Government or [when] the procedure for adoption of new legislation has been blocked for a period of three months, the President of the Republic of Moldova, after consultation with parliamentary factions, may dissolve the Parliament.

(2) The Parliament may be dissolved if it did not express confidence in the formed Government within 45 days of the first request and also after rejecting, at least twice, the vote of confidence.

(3) In the course of a year, the Parliament may be dissolved only once.

(4) The Parliament may not be dissolved during the last six months of the term of the President of the Republic Moldova, with the exception of the case provided by Article 78, paragraph (5) as well as during the time of the state of urgency, siege or war.

11. Any executive initiative on legislation requires ratification or approval by the legislature before it takes effect; that is, the executive lacks decree power.

Yes. The president and the government both lack the power to issue decrees that have the force of law. The president can issue regulatory decrees but not decrees that have the force of law. The legislature can also delegate temporary decree powers to the government.

Article 94

(1) In the exercise of his powers, the President of the Republic of Moldova issues decrees obligatory for execution on the entire territory of the State. The decrees are published in the "Monitorul Oficial" of the Republic of Moldova.

(2) Decrees issued by the President in the exercise of his powers provided in Article 86, paragraph (2) and Article 87, paragraphs (2), (3) and (4) are countersigned by the Prime Minister.

Article 106.2

(1) For implementing Government program of activities, at its proposal Parliament may adopt a special law entitling Government to issue ordinances in the domains other than subjects of organic laws.

(2) Entitling law has to stipulated the domain and the term for issuing ordinances.

(3) Ordinances shall enter into force upon their publication, without being promulgated.

(4) Provided entitling law specifically stipulates so, ordinances shall be approved by Parliament. The draft law on approving the ordinances shall be submitted within the term set in the entitling law. Failure to observe the term results in annulment of the ordinance. Unless Parliament rejects the draft law on approving the ordinance, the later shall remain in force.

(5) After expiration of the term set for issuing ordinances, the latter may be abrogated, suspended or modified only by law.

12. Laws passed by the legislature are veto-proof or essentially veto-proof; that is, the executive lacks veto power, or has veto power but the veto can be overridden by a majority in the legislature.

Yes. The legislature can override a presidential veto by a majority vote of its present members.

Article 93

(1) The President of the Republic of Moldova promulgates laws.

(2) The President of the Republic of Moldova has the right, in case he objects to a law, to send it within the period of two weeks to the Parliament for reexamination. In the event that the Parliament maintains the previously adopted decision, the President promulgates the law.

13. The legislature's laws are supreme and not subject to judicial review.

No. The Constitutional Court can review the constitutionality of laws.

Article 135

(1) The Constitutional Court:
    a) Exercises, upon notification, control over the constitutionality of laws, decisions of the Parliament, decrees of the President of the Republic of Moldova, decisions and ordinances of the Government as well as international treaties to which the Republic of Moldova is a party;
    b) Interprets the Constitution.

14. The legislature has the right to initiate bills in all policy jurisdictions; the executive lacks gatekeeping authority.

No. The legislature is prohibited from passing legislation that affects budgetary incomes or expenses.

Article 131

(4) Any legislation or amendment increasing or reducing budget incomes or loans, as well as increasing or

reducing budgetary expenses, may be adopted only after Government approval.

15. Expenditure of funds appropriated by the legislature is mandatory; the executive lacks the power to impound funds appropriated by the legislature.

Yes. The executive lacks the power to impound funds appropriated by the legislature.

16. The legislature controls the resources that finance its own internal operation and provide for the perquisites of its own members.

Yes. The legislature enjoys financial autonomy.

17. Members of the legislature are immune from arrest and/or criminal prosecution.

Yes. Legislators are immune with the common exception for cases of *flagrante delicto,* here expressed as "cases of flagrant offense."

> Article 70
> (3) A deputy may not be detained, arrested, searched or prosecuted, with the exception of cases of flagrant offense, without the Parliament's consent [and] after a hearing.

18. All members of the legislature are elected; the executive lacks the power to appoint any members of the legislature.

Yes. All members of the legislature are elected.

> Article 61
> (1) The Parliament is elected on the basis of universal, equal, direct, secret and freely expressed suffrage.

19. The legislature alone, without the involvement of any other agencies, can change the Constitution.

No. Constitutional amendments can be presented to parliament only on the advice of the Constitutional Court.

> Article 141
> (1) Revision of the Constitution may be initiated by:
> a) At least 200,000 citizens of the Republic of Moldova who have the right to vote. The citizens who initiate the revision of the Constitution must represent at least a half of the administrative-territorial units of second level, and at least 20,000 signers in support of the initiative must be registered in each of them;
> b) At least one-third of the deputies of the Parliament;
> c) The Government.
> (2) Draft constitutional laws are presented to the Parliament only with the approval of the Constitutional Court adopted by at least four judges.

> Article 142
> (1) The provisions regarding the sovereignty, independence and unity of the State, as well as those related to the permanent neutrality of the State, may be revised

only with the approval of a referendum by the majority vote of citizens registered to vote.
(2) No revision may be done if it results in the suppression of the fundamental rights and freedoms of citizens or of the guarantees thereof.
(3) The Constitution may not be revised during the state of urgency, siege or war.

> Article 143
> (1) The Parliament has the right to adopt a law on the amendment to the Constitution after at least six months from the date when the corresponding initiative was presented. The law is adopted by the vote of two-thirds of the deputies.
> (2) If, within one year after the presentation of the initiative to amend the Constitution, the Parliament has not adopted the corresponding constitutional law, the proposal is considered null and void.

20. The legislature's approval is necessary for the declaration of war.

Yes. The legislature alone declares war with the common exception for cases of foreign invasion. In the event of foreign invasion, the president can declare war and seek retroactive legislative approval.

> Article 66
> The Parliament has the following basic powers:
> m) To declare the states of urgency, siege and war.

> Article 87
> (1) The President of the Republic of Moldova is the Commander-in-Chief of the armed forces.
> (2) The President of the Republic of Moldova may declare, upon prior approval of the Parliament, partial or general mobilization.
> (3) In the event of armed aggression against the country, the President of the Republic of Moldova takes measures to repel aggression, declares a state of war and informs the Parliament without delay. If the Parliament is not in session, it is convened by right within 24 hours of the start of the aggression.
> (4) The President of the Republic of Moldova may take other measures in order to ensure national security and public order within the limits and in accordance with the law.

21. The legislature's approval is necessary to ratify treaties with foreign countries.

Yes. The legislature's approval is necessary to ratify international treaties.

> Article 66
> The Parliament has the following basic powers:
> g) To ratify, denounce, suspend and annul international treaties concluded by the Republic of Moldova.

> Article 86
> (1) The President of the Republic of Moldova conducts talks and participates in negotiations, concludes international treaties in the name of the Republic of

Moldova and presents them, in the manner and time period established by the law, to the Parliament for ratification.

22. The legislature has the power to grant amnesty.

Yes. The legislature has the power to grant amnesty.

Article 66
The Parliament has the following basic powers:
p) To adopt acts of amnesty.

Article 72
(1) The Parliament adopts constitutional, organic and ordinary laws.
(2) Constitutional laws are those for the revision of the Constitution.
(3) Organic laws regulate [the following]:
  o) granting of amnesty and pardon.

23. The legislature has the power of pardon.

No. Formally, the parliament and the president both have the power of pardon, but in practice, the power of pardon is reserved for the president alone.

Article 72
(1) The Parliament adopts constitutional, organic and ordinary laws.
(2) Constitutional laws are those for the revision of the Constitution.
(3) Organic laws regulate [the following]:
  o) granting of amnesty and pardon.

Article 88
The President of the Republic of Moldova also exercises the following powers:
  e) Grants individual pardons.

24. The legislature reviews and has the right to reject appointments to the judiciary; or the legislature itself appoints members of the judiciary.

Yes. The legislature appoints two of the six judges on the Constitutional Court.

Article 136
(1) The Constitutional Court is composed of six judges appointed for a six-year term.
(2) Two judges are appointed by the Parliament, two by the Government and two by the Superior Council of the Magistrature.
(3) The judges of the Constitutional Court elect its president by secret ballot.

Article 116
(1) Judges of judicial instances are independent, impartial and irremovable according to the law.
(2) Judges of judicial instances are appointed by the President of the Republic of Moldova upon the proposal of the Superior Council of the Magistrature (Consiliului Superior al Magistraturii) according to the law. Judges

who have passed through the selection process (concursul) are initially appointed for a term of five years. After the expiration of the five-year term, judges are appointed [for a term lasting] until they reach the age limit established in accordance with the law.

25. The chairman of the central bank is appointed by the legislature.

Yes. The legislature appoints the governor of the National Bank of Moldova.

26. The legislature has a substantial voice in the operation of the state-owned media.

Yes. The legislature has a substantial voice in the operation of the public media.

27. The legislature is regularly in session.

Yes. The legislature meets in ordinary session for approximately eight months each year.

Article 67
(1) The Parliament meets in two ordinary sessions per year. The first session begins in February and may not last beyond the end of July. The second session begins in September and may not last beyond the end of December.
(2) The Parliament also meets in extraordinary or special sessions at the request of the President of the Republic of Moldova, the President of Parliament or one-third of the deputies.

28. Each legislator has a personal secretary.

No. There is legislative staff, but on average there is less than one staff person for each legislator. Legislative committees have between three and five staff members for every eight to ten members.

29. Each legislator has at least one non-secretarial staff member with policy expertise.

No. See item 28.

30. Legislators are eligible for re-election without any restriction.

Yes. There are no restrictions on re-election.

31. A seat in the legislature is an attractive enough position that legislators are generally interested in and seek re-election.

Yes.

32. The re-election of incumbent legislators is common enough that at any given time the legislature contains a significant number of highly experienced members.

Yes. Re-election rates are sufficiently high to produce a significant number of highly experienced members.

GREAT STATE ASSEMBLY OF MONGOLIA (*ULSIYN IKH-HURAL*)

Expert consultants: L. Burma, D. Byambajav, N. Enhbold, B. Enkhbat, L. Sumati

Score: .84

Influence over executive (8/9)		Institutional autonomy (7/9)		Specified powers (7/8)		Institutional capacity (5/6)	
1. replace	X	10. no dissolution	X	19. amendments	X	27. sessions	X
2. serve as ministers	X	11. no decree	X	20. war	X	28. secretary	X
3. interpellate	X	12. no veto		21. treaties	X	29. staff	
4. investigate	X	13. no review		22. amnesty	X	30. no term limits	X
5. oversee police	X	14. no gatekeeping	X	23. pardon		31. seek re-election	X
6. appoint PM	X	15. no impoundment	X	24. judiciary	X	32. experience	X
7. appoint ministers	X	16. control resources	X	25. central bank	X		
8. lack president		17. immunity	X	26. media	X		
9. no confidence	X	18. all elected	X				

The Great State Assembly (also translated as National Parliament; *Ulsiyn ikh-Hural*) of Mongolia was established in the 1924 constitution, which codified communist-party dominance that endured for nearly seven decades. As in all Soviet-type systems, the legislature hypothetically held supreme power but was fully subordinate to the hegemonic party in practice. The collapse of the Soviet Union paved the way for a more open political system and a new constitution in 1992. Post-communist Mongolia has a unicameral legislature, a prime minister as the head of government, and a directly elected president as the head of state. A constitutional amendment in 1999 granted legislators the right to serve simultaneously in government. Prior to 1999 legislators lacked the formal right to serve in government.

The legislature is a formidable force. It possesses every means of influencing the executive scored in this survey with the exception of the power to elect the president. Apart from presidential veto powers and the Constitutional Court's power to review the constitutionality of laws, moreover, the legislature has full institutional autonomy. Parliament also scores nearly perfectly in terms of specified powers and institutional capacity.

SURVEY

1. The legislature alone, without the involvement of any other agencies, can impeach the president or replace the prime minister.

Yes. The legislature can impeach the president. It can also remove the prime minister with a vote of no confidence.

Article 25
The National Parliament may consider, at its initiative, any issue pertaining to domestic and foreign policies of the country, and retains within its exclusive competence the following questions and decisions thereon:
5) to pass a law . . . to relieve or remove the President.

Article 43
(1) The Prime Minister may tender his resignation to the National Parliament before the expiry of his terms of office if he considers that the Government is unable to exercise its powers.
(2) The Government steps down in its entirety upon the resignation of the Prime Minister or if half of the members of the Government resign at the same time.
(3) The National Parliament considers the matter and makes a final decision within 15 days after taking initiative to dissolve the Government or receiving the President's proposal or the Prime Minister's statement on resignation.
(4) The National Parliament considers and takes decision on the dissolution of the Government if not less than one fourth of the members of the National Parliament formally propose the dissolution of the Government.

Article 44
If the Government submits a draft resolution requesting a vote of confidence, the National Parliament proceeds with the matter in accordance with Article 43 (3).

2. Ministers may serve simultaneously as members of the legislature.

Yes. Legislators may serve simultaneously in ministerial positions.

> Article 29
> (1) Members of the National Parliament receive remuneration from the State budget during their tenure and may not hold concurrently any posts and employment other than those assigned by law.

3. The legislature has powers of summons over executive branch officials and hearings with executive branch officials testifying before the legislature or its committees are regularly held.

Yes. The legislature regularly interpellates officials from the executive.

4. The legislature can conduct independent investigation of the chief executive and the agencies of the executive.

Yes. The legislature can investigate the executive.

5. The legislature has effective powers of oversight over the agencies of coercion (the military, organs of law enforcement, intelligence services, and the secret police).

Yes. The legislature has effective powers of oversight over the agencies of coercion.

6. The legislature appoints the prime minister.

Yes. The legislature appoints the prime minister.

> Article 25
> The National Parliament may consider, at its initiative, any issue pertaining to domestic and foreign policies of the country, and retains within its exclusive competence the following questions and decisions thereon:
> 6) Appointing, replacing or removing the Prime Minister, members of the Government and other bodies responsible and accountable to the National Parliament as provided for by law.

> Article 33
> The President enjoys the following prerogative rights:
> 2) to propose to the National Parliament the candidature for the appointment to the post of Prime Minister in consultation with the majority party or parties in the National Parliament if none of them has majority of seats.

7. The legislature's approval is required to confirm the appointment of ministers; or the legislature itself appoints ministers.

Yes. The legislature appoints ministers.

> Article 25
> The National Parliament may consider, at its initiative, any issue pertaining to domestic and foreign policies

of the country, and retains within its exclusive competence the following questions and decisions thereon:
> 6) Appointing, replacing or removing the Prime Minister, members of the Government and other bodies responsible and accountable to the National Parliament as provided for by law.

8. The country lacks a presidency entirely or there is a presidency, but the president is elected by the legislature.

No. The president is directly elected.

> Article 31
> (1) Presidential elections are conducted in two stages.
> (2) Political parties which have obtained seats in the National Parliament nominate individually or collectively presidential candidates, one candidate for each party or coalition of parties.
> (3) At the primary stage of the elections, citizens eligible to vote participate in electing the President on the basis of universal, free, and direct suffrage by secret ballot.
> (4) The National Parliament considers the candidate who has obtained a majority of all votes cast in the first voting as elected President and passes a law recognizing his or her mandate.
> (5) If none of the candidates obtains a majority vote in the first round, second voting takes place involving the two candidates who have obtained the largest number of votes in the first round. The candidate who wins a majority of all votes cast in the second ballot is considered elected President and a law recognizing his or her mandate is passed by the National Parliament.
> (6) If neither of the candidates wins in the second ballot, Presidential elections are held anew.

9. The legislature can vote no confidence in the government.

Yes. The legislature can vote no confidence in the government.

> Article 43
> (1) The Prime Minister may tender his resignation to the National Parliament before the expiry of his terms of office if he considers that the Government is unable to exercise its powers.
> (2) The Government steps down in its entirety upon the resignation of the Prime Minister or if half of the members of the Government resign at the same time.
> (3) The National Parliament considers the matter and makes a final decision within 15 days after taking initiative to dissolve the Government or receiving the President's proposal or the Prime Minister's statement on resignation.
> (4) The National Parliament considers and takes decision on the dissolution of the Government if not less than one fourth of the members of the National Parliament formally propose the dissolution of the Government.

Article 44
If the Government submits a draft resolution requesting a vote of confidence, the National Parliament proceeds with the matter in accordance with Article 43 (3).

10. The legislature is immune from dissolution by the executive.

Yes. The legislature is immune from dissolution by the executive, although it can vote to dissolve itself.

Article 22
(1) If regular elections of the National Parliament cannot be held due to extraordinary circumstances such as sudden calamities occurred in the whole or in part of the country, the National Parliament retains its power till the extraordinary circumstances cease to exist and the newly elected members of the National Parliament are sworn in.
(2) The National Parliament may decide on its dissolution if not less than two thirds of its members consider that the National Parliament is unable to carry out its mandate, or if the President, in consultation with the Chairman of the National Parliament, proposes to do so for the same reason. In case of such a decision, the National Parliament exercises its powers until the newly elected members of the National Parliament are sworn in.

11. Any executive initiative on legislation requires ratification or approval by the legislature before it takes effect; that is, the executive lacks decree power.

Yes. The executive cannot issue decrees that have the force of law. The president and government can issue regulatory "decrees" to implement law.

Article 33
The President enjoys the following prerogative rights:
3) to instruct the Government on issues within his competence. If the President issues a relevant decree it becomes effective upon signature by the Prime Minister.

Article 34
(1) The President, within his powers, issues decrees in conformity with the law.
(2) If a Presidential decree is incompatible with law, the President himself or the National Parliament invalidates it.

Article 45
(1) The Government shall, in conformity with legislation, issue decrees and ordinances which shall be signed by the Prime Minister and the Minister responsible for their application.
(2) If these decrees and ordinances are incompatible with laws and regulations, the Government itself or the National Parliament shall invalidate them.

12. Laws passed by the legislature are veto-proof or essentially veto-proof; that is, the executive lacks veto power, or has veto power but the veto can be overridden by a majority in the legislature.

No. A two-thirds majority vote is required to override a presidential veto.

Article 33
(1) The President enjoys the following prerogative rights:
1) to veto, partially or wholly, laws and other decisions adopted by the National Parliament. The laws or decisions remain in force if two-thirds of the members of the National Parliament present do not accept the President's veto.

13. The legislature's laws are supreme and not subject to judicial review.

No. The Constitutional Court can review the constitutionality of laws.

Article 64
(1) The Constitutional Court is an organ exercising supreme supervision over the implementation of the constitution, making judgment on the violation of its provisions, and resolving constitutional disputes. It is the guarantee for the strict observance of the Constitution.

14. The legislature has the right to initiate bills in all policy jurisdictions; the executive lacks gatekeeping authority.

Yes. The legislature can initiate bills in all policy jurisdictions.

15. Expenditure of funds appropriated by the legislature is mandatory; the executive lacks the power to impound funds appropriated by the legislature.

Yes. The executive lacks the power to impound funds appropriated by the legislature.

16. The legislature controls the resources that finance its own internal operation and provide for the perquisites of its own members.

Yes. The legislature enjoys financial autonomy.

17. Members of the legislature are immune from arrest and/or criminal prosecution.

Yes. Legislators are immune.

Article 29
(2) Immunity of members of the National Parliament is protected by law.
(3) If a question arises that a member of the National Parliament is involved in a crime, it is considered by the session of the National Parliament to decide on the suspension of his or her mandate. If the court proves the member in question to be guilty of crime, the National Parliament shall terminate his or her membership in the legislature.

18. All members of the legislature are elected; the executive lacks the power to appoint any members of the legislature.

Yes. All members of the legislature are elected.

Article 21
(2) The members of the National Parliament are elected by citizens qualified to vote, on the basis of universal, free, and direct suffrage by secret ballot for a term of four years.

19. The legislature alone, without the involvement of any other agencies, can change the Constitution.

Yes. The legislature can pass constitutional amendments with a three-fourths majority vote.

Article 68
(1) Amendments to the Constitution may be initiated by organizations and officials enjoying the right to legislative initiative and may be proposed by the Constitutional Court to the National Parliament.
(2) A national referendum on constitutional amendment may be held on the concurrence of not less than two-thirds of the members of the National Parliament. The referendum is held in accordance with the provisions of Article 25 (1) No. 16.

Article 69
(1) An amendment to the Constitution is adopted by not less that three-fourths of votes of all members of the National Parliament.
(2) A draft amendment to the Constitution which has twice failed to win three-fourths of votes of all members of the National Parliament is not subject to consideration until the National Parliament sits in a new composition following general elections.
(3) The National Parliament may not undertake amendment of the Constitution within six months pending the next general elections.
(4) Amendments which have been adopted are of the same force as the Constitution.

20. The legislature's approval is necessary for the declaration of war.

Yes. The legislature declares war with the common exception for cases of foreign invasion. In the event that the country is threatened by external invasion and the legislature is in recess, the president can declare war without first obtaining the legislature's approval. The war declaration must be retroactively approved by the legislature within seven days or the declaration becomes null and void.

Article 25
The National Parliament may consider, at its initiative, any issue pertaining to domestic and foreign policies of the country, and retains within its exclusive competence the following questions and decisions thereon:
17) to declare a state of war in case the sovereignty and independence of the state are threatened by armed actions on the part of a foreign power, and to abate it.

Article 33
The President enjoys the following prerogative rights:
12) to declare a state of emergency or a state of war on the whole or a part of the national territory and to order

the deployment of armed forces when extraordinary circumstances described in Article 25 (2) and (3) arise and the National Parliament concurrently in recess, cannot be summoned at short notice. The National Parliament considers within 7 days the Presidential decree declaring a state of emergency or a state of war and approves or disapproves it. If the National Parliament does not take decision on the matter, the Presidential decree becomes null and void.

21. The legislature's approval is necessary to ratify treaties with foreign countries.

Yes. The legislature's approval is necessary to ratify international treaties.

Article 25
The National Parliament may consider, at its initiative, any issue pertaining to domestic and foreign policies of the country, and retains within its exclusive competence the following questions and decisions thereon:
15) to ratify and denounce international agreements to which Mongolia is a Party and to establish and sever diplomatic relations with foreign States at the suggestion of the Government.

22. The legislature has the power to grant amnesty.

Yes. The legislature has the power to grant amnesty.

Article 25
The National Parliament may consider, at its initiative, any issue pertaining to domestic and foreign policies of the country, and retains within its exclusive competence the following questions and decisions thereon:
14) to issue acts of amnesty.

23. The legislature has the power of pardon.

No. The president has the power of pardon.

Article 33
The President enjoys the following prerogative rights:
8) to grant pardon.

24. The legislature reviews and has the right to reject appointments to the judiciary; or the legislature itself appoints members of the judiciary.

Yes. The legislature appoints the members of the Constitutional Court.

Article 51
(1) The Supreme Court comprises the Chief Justice and judges.
(2) The President appoints the judges of the Supreme Court upon their presentation to the National Parliament by the General Council of Courts and appoints judges of other courts on the proposal of the General Council of Courts.

Article 65
(1) The Constitutional Court consists of 9 members. Members of the Constitutional Court are appointed by the National Parliament for a term of six years upon

the nomination of three of them by the National Parliament, three by the President, and the remaining three by the Supreme Court.

(3) The Chairman of the Constitutional Court is elected from among 9 members for a term of three years by a majority vote of the members of Constitutional Court. He may be re-elected once.

25. The chairman of the central bank is appointed by the legislature.

Yes. The legislature appoints the governor of the Bank of Mongolia.

26. The legislature has a substantial voice in the operation of the state-owned media.

Yes. The legislature has a substantial voice in the operation of the public media.

27. The legislature is regularly in session.

Yes. The constitution requires that the legislature meets for at least two fifty-day sessions each year. In practice, the legislature is in regular session for well over half of the year.

Article 27
(2) The National Parliament holds a regular session, which lasts not less then 50 workdays per six-month.

28. Each legislator has a personal secretary.

Yes.

29. Each legislator has at least one non-secretarial staff member with policy expertise.

No.

30. Legislators are eligible for re-election without any restriction.

Yes. There are no restrictions on re-election.

31. A seat in the legislature is an attractive enough position that legislators are generally interested in and seek re-election.

Yes.

32. The re-election of incumbent legislators is common enough that at any given time the legislature contains a significant number of highly experienced members.

Yes. Postcommunist Mongolia has experienced several major alternations in power between rival parties following parliamentary elections, and the turnover rate of legislators has been substantial, but parliament nevertheless includes a cohort of experienced members.

PARLIAMENT OF MOROCCO (*BARLAMAN*)

Expert consultants: Sanket Dhruva, Silam El Yaghmouri, Abdou Filali-Ansary, Abdeslam M. Maghraoui, Saloua Zerhouni

Score: .31

Influence over executive (3/9)		Institutional autonomy (2/9)		Specified powers (1/8)		Institutional capacity (4/6)	
1. replace		10. no dissolution		19. amendments		27. sessions	X
2. serve as ministers		11. no decree		20. war		28. secretary	
3. interpellate	X	12. no veto		21. treaties		29. staff	
4. investigate		13. no review		22. amnesty		30. no term limits	X
5. oversee police		14. no gatekeeping		23. pardon		31. seek re-election	X
6. appoint PM		15. no impoundment		24. judiciary	X	32. experience	X
7. appoint ministers		16. control resources	X	25. central bank			
8. lack president	X	17. immunity		26. media			
9. no confidence	X	18. all elected	X				

The Parliament (*Barlaman*) of Morocco was established in the 1962 constitution. Since that time the king has dominated national politics, leaving the legislature with only modest power. In 1965 the king temporarily suspended parliament in the face of social unrest. A constitutional amendment in 1996 added a second house to create a bicameral legislature consisting of a lower house, the House of Representatives (*Majlis an-Nuwab*), and an upper house, the House of Counselors (*Majlis al-Mustasharin*).

The legislature's influence over the executive is severely limited, and its institutional autonomy is circumscribed by the king's veto, dissolution, decree, and gatekeeping powers. Of the specified powers covered in this survey, parliament possesses only one, the right to be involved in judicial appointments. The legislature does enjoy some institutional capacity.

SURVEY

1. The legislature alone, without the involvement of any other agencies, can impeach the president or replace the prime minister.

No. The legislature cannot impeach the king. The legislature can remove the prime minister from office with a vote of no confidence.

> Article 75
> The Prime Minister may engage the responsibility of the Government before the House of Representatives through a vote of confidence regarding a statement on a general policy or a proposal requesting the approval thereof. Confidence shall be withdrawn and a bill rejected only by an absolute majority vote of the Members of the House of' Representatives. The vote shall be held three clear days after the matter of the vote of confidence has been raised. Withdrawal of confidence shall entail the resignation of the Government in a body.

2. Ministers may serve simultaneously as members of the legislature.

No. Legislators are prohibited from serving simultaneously in ministerial positions.

3. The legislature has powers of summons over executive branch officials and hearings with executive branch officials testifying before the legislature or its committees are regularly held.

Yes. The legislature regularly interpellates officials from the executive.

4. The legislature can conduct independent investigation of the chief executive and the agencies of the executive.

No. Formally, the legislature can establish "parliamentary fact-finding committees" to investigate the executive. In practice, the legislature lacks the power to investigate the royal palace.

> Article 42
> Apart from the standing committees referred to in the preceding paragraph, parliamentary fact-finding

committees may be established on the King's initiative or upon the request of the majority of the members of one of the two Houses and within each House, with the mission of inquiring about specific facts and submitting findings thereon to that House. There shall be no fact-finding committees in cases involving prosecutions, and as long as these are being conducted. The mission of any fact-finding committee which may be established shall end with the opening of the judicial investigation pertaining to the instances bringing about the establishment thereof. Fact-finding committees shall by nature be temporary. Their mission shall end with the submission of their reports. The functioning of these committees shall be governed by an organic law.

5. The legislature has effective powers of oversight over the agencies of coercion (the military, organs of law enforcement, intelligence services, and the secret police).

No. The legislature lacks effective powers of oversight over the agencies of coercion.

6. The legislature appoints the prime minister.

No. The king appoints the prime minister.

> Article 24
> The King shall appoint the Prime Minister. Upon the Prime Minister's recommendation, the King shall appoint the other Cabinet members as he may terminate their services. The King shall terminate the services of the Government either on his own initiative or because of their resignation.

7. The legislature's approval is required to confirm the appointment of ministers; or the legislature itself appoints ministers.

No. The king appoints ministers on the prime minister's recommendation, and the appointments do not require the legislature's approval.

> Article 24
> The King shall appoint the Prime Minister. Upon the Prime Minister's recommendation, the King shall appoint the other Cabinet members as he may terminate their services. The King shall terminate the services of the Government either on his own initiative or because of their resignation.

8. The country lacks a presidency entirely or there is a presidency, but the president is elected by the legislature.

Yes. The country lacks a presidency. The monarch is the head of state.

> Article 20
> The Moroccan Crown and the constitutional rights thereof shall be hereditary and handed down, from father to son, to descendants in direct male line and by order of primogeniture among the offspring of His

Majesty King Hassan II, unless the King should, during his lifetime, designate a successor among his sons apart from the eldest one. In case of failing descendants in direct male line, the right of succession to the Throne shall, under the same conditions, be invested in the closest male in the collateral consanguinity.

9. The legislature can vote no confidence in the government.

Yes. The legislature can vote no confidence in the government.

Article 75
The Prime Minister may engage the responsibility of the Government before the House of Representatives through a vote of confidence regarding a statement on a general policy or a proposal requesting the approval thereof. Confidence shall be withdrawn and a bill rejected only by an absolute majority vote of the Members of the House of Representatives. The vote shall be held three clear days after the matter of the vote of confidence has been raised. Withdrawal of confidence shall entail the resignation of the Government in a body.

10. The legislature is immune from dissolution by the executive.

No. The king can dissolve the legislature.

Article 27
The King may dissolve the two Houses of Parliament or one thereof by Royal Decree, in accordance with the conditions prescribed in Articles 71 and 73.

Article 71
After consulting with the Presidents of the two Houses and the Chairman of the Constitutional Council and addressing the Nation, the King may decree the dissolution of the two Houses or of one of them only.

11. Any executive initiative on legislation requires ratification or approval by the legislature before it takes effect; that is, the executive lacks decree power.

No. The king issues decrees that have the force of law.

Article 29
The King shall, by Royal Decrees, exercise the statutory powers explicitly conferred upon him by the Constitution. Royal Decrees shall be countersigned by the Prime Minister, with the exception of those provided for in Articles 21 (Paragraph 2), 24 (paragraphs 1, 3 and 4), 35, 69, 71, 79, 84, 91, 99 and 105.

12. Laws passed by the legislature are veto-proof or essentially veto-proof; that is, the executive lacks veto power, or has veto power but the veto can be overridden by a majority in the legislature.

No. A two-thirds majority vote in both houses is required to override the monarch's veto.

Article 67
The King may request a second reading by the two Houses of any draft bill or proposed law.

Article 68
A second reading shall be requested in a message. Such a new reading shall not be refused.

Article 69
After a second reading, the King may, by Royal Decree, submit any draft bill or proposed law to referendum, except in the case of those submitted for a new reading which shall have been adopted or rejected by a two-third majority of the members of each one of the two Houses.

13. The legislature's laws are supreme and not subject to judicial review.

No. The Constitutional Council can review the constitutionality of laws.

Article 81
The Constitutional Council shall perform the functions assigned by the articles of the Constitution or the provisions of the organic laws... Organic laws – before promulgation – and the Rules of Procedure of each House before implementation – shall be submitted to the Constitutional Council to look into their consistence with the Constitution. Before promulgation, laws may, for the same reason, be referred to the Constitutional Council by the King, the Prime Minister, the President of the House of Representatives, the President of the House of Counselors or one-fourth of the members making up one House or the other. The Constitutional Council shall have one month to decide upon the special instances stated in the preceding two paragraphs. However, in case of emergency, the deadline may be reduced to eight days if so requested by the Government. Regarding the above mentioned instances, referring law to the Constitutional Council shall entail the suspension of the deadline of the promulgation thereof. No unconstitutional provision shall be promulgated or implemented. Decisions of the Constitutional Council shall, in no way, be put into question. They shall, furthermore, be binding upon all public authorities, administrative and judicial sectors.

14. The legislature has the right to initiate bills in all policy jurisdictions; the executive lacks gatekeeping authority.

No. The legislature is prohibited from initiating bills beyond a restricted domain of issues and generally may not initiate bills in areas that the government deems "outside the purview of the legislative power."

Article 46
Within the domain of the law are, in addition to the matters which are expressly assigned to it by other articles of the Constitution:
– individual and collective rights enumerated in Title One of the present Constitution;

– the determination of misdemeanors and the penalties which are applicable, penal procedure, civil procedure and the establishment and the creation of new categories of jurisdiction;
– the Statute of Magistrates;
– the General Statute of the Civil Service;
– the fundamental guarantees accorded to civil and military functionaries;
– the electoral regime of the assemblies and the Councils of local collectivities;
– the regime of civil and commercial liabilities;
– the creation of public establishments;
– the nationalization of enterprises and the transfer of enterprises from the public sector to the private sector. The Parliament is entitled to vote framework laws concerning fundamental objectives of the economic, social and cultural action of the State.

Article 47
All other matters which are not within the legislative domain belong to the regulatory domain.

Article 53
The Government may declare the unsuitability of any proposal or amendment considered outside the purview of the legislative power. In case of disagreement, the Constitutional Council shall take action within a period of eight days upon request of one of the two Houses or the Government.

15. Expenditure of funds appropriated by the legislature is mandatory; the executive lacks the power to impound funds appropriated by the legislature.

No. The king can impound funds appropriated by the legislature.

16. The legislature controls the resources that finance its own internal operation and provide for the perquisites of its own members.

Yes. The legislature enjoys financial autonomy.

17. Members of the legislature are immune from arrest and/or criminal prosecution.

No. Legislators can be prosecuted for the expression of any opinion that "may be injurious to the monarchical system and the religion of Islam or derogatory to the respect owed the king."

Article 39
No member of Parliament shall be prosecuted, arrested, put into custody or brought to trial as a result of expressing opinions or casting a vote while exercising office functions, except when the opinions expressed may be injurious to the monarchical system and the religion of Islam or derogatory to the respect owed the king. During parliamentary sessions, no member of Parliament shall be subject to prosecution or arrest for criminal charges or felonies, besides those mentioned in the preceding paragraph, without permission from the House except flagrante delicto.

Outside parliamentary sessions, no member of Parliament shall be subject to arrest without permission from the Board of the House, except flagrante delicto, or in the case of authorized prosecution or final judgment. The imprisonment or prosecution of a member of Parliament shall be suspended if so required by the House, except flagrante delicto or in the case of authorized prosecution or final judgment.

18. All members of the legislature are elected; the executive lacks the power to appoint any members of the legislature.

Yes. All members of the legislature are elected.

Article 37
Members of the House of Representatives shall be elected for a six- year term by direct universal suffrage. The legal legislative period shall end at the opening of the October session in the fifth year following the election of the House.

Article 38
For 3/5 of its membership, the House of Counsellors shall consist of members elected in each region by electoral colleges made up of elected members of trade chambers as well as members elected at the national level by an electoral college consisting of wage-earners' representatives.
Members of the House of Counsellors shall be elected for a nine-year term. One third of the House shall be renewed every three years. In the first and second renewal operations, seats shall be drawn by lot. The number of counsellors as well as the voting system, the number of members to be elected by each electoral college, the distribution of seats according to regions, eligibility requirements, incompatibility cases, balloting procedures mentioned above and legal contentions concerning elections shall be set out in an organic law.

19. The legislature alone, without the involvement of any other agencies, can change the Constitution.

No. All constitutional amendments have been initiated by the king, and any violation of this norm would be unimaginable. Formally, the legislature can amend the constitution with a two-thirds majority vote in both houses.

Article 103
The King, the House of Representatives and the House of Counsellors shall have the right to initiate a revision of the Constitution. The King shall have the right to submit, directly for referendum, the revision project he may initiate.

Article 104
A proposal for revision submitted by one or more members of one of the two Houses shall be adopted only if voted on by a two-thirds majority of the members of the House concerned. The proposal shall be submitted to the other House which may adopt it by a two-thirds majority of its members.

20. The legislature's approval is necessary for the declaration of war.

No. The king can declare war without obtaining the legislature's approval.

> Article 66
> The Cabinet shall be notified of the following, before any relevant decision is taken:
> (c) declaration of war.

> Article 74
> The declaration of war shall be announced after notifying the House of' Representatives and the House of Counsellors.

21. The legislature's approval is necessary to ratify treaties with foreign countries.

No. The king can conclude international treaties without the legislature's approval. Treaties requiring approval under law can be concluded with a royal decree (see item 11).

> Article 31
> The King shall sign and ratify treaties. However, treaties committing State finances shall not be ratified without having been approved under the law.

22. The legislature has the power to grant amnesty.

No. The king has the power to grant amnesty.

23. The legislature has the power of pardon.

No. The king has the power of pardon.

> Article 34
> The King shall exercise the right of granting pardon.

24. The legislature reviews and has the right to reject appointments to the judiciary; or the legislature itself appoints members of the judiciary.

Yes. The legislature elects some of the members of the High Court of Justice.

> Article 79
> The Constitutional Council shall be made up of six members appointed by the King for a nine-year period. Upon consultation with parliamentary groups, six other members shall be appointed for the same period, half of them by the President of the House of Representatives and the other half by the President of the House of Counsellors. A third of each category of members shall be renewed every three years. The chairman of the Constitutional Council shall be selected by the king among the members appointed by him.

> Article 84
> Upon recommendations made by the Supreme Council of Magistracy, Magistrates shall be appointed by Royal Decrees.

> Article 91
> The High Court of Justice shall consist of equal numbers of members elected from the House of Representatives and the House of Counsellors. Its President shall be appointed by Royal Decree.

25. The chairman of the central bank is appointed by the legislature.

No. The king appoints the governor of the Bank of Morocco.

26. The legislature has a substantial voice in the operation of the state-owned media.

No. The legislature lacks a substantial voice in the operation of the public media.

27. The legislature is regularly in session.

Yes. The legislature meets in two three-month sessions each year.

> Article 40
> The Parliament shall hold its meetings during two sessions a year. The King shall preside over the opening of the first session which shall begin on the second Friday in October. The second session shall begin on the second Friday in April. When the Parliament convenes for at least three months during one session, the session may be adjourned by decree.

28. Each legislator has a personal secretary.

No.

29. Each legislator has at least one non-secretarial staff member with policy expertise.

No.

30. Legislators are eligible for re-election without any restriction.

Yes. There are no restrictions on re-election.

31. A seat in the legislature is an attractive enough position that legislators are generally interested in and seek re-election.

Yes.

32. The re-election of incumbent legislators is common enough that at any given time the legislature contains a significant number of highly experienced members.

Yes. Re-election rates are sufficiently high to produce a significant number of highly experienced members.

ASSEMBLY OF MOZAMBIQUE (*ASSEMBLEIA*)

Expert consultants: João Carlos Colaço, Carrie L. Manning, Eduardo Sitoe, Zaida Maria Sultanegy, Jan Nico van Overbeeke, Elysa Vieira

Score: .44

Influence over executive (3/9)		Institutional autonomy (3/9)		Specified powers (5/8)		Institutional capacity (3/6)	
1. replace		10. no dissolution		19. amendments	X	27. sessions	
2. serve as ministers		11. no decree		20. war		28. secretary	
3. interpellate	X	12. no veto		21. treaties	X	29. staff	
4. investigate	X	13. no review		22. amnesty	X	30. no term limits	X
5. oversee police		14. no gatekeeping	X	23. pardon	X	31. seek re-election	X
6. appoint PM		15. no impoundment		24. judiciary	X	32. experience	X
7. appoint ministers		16. control resources		25. central bank			
8. lack president		17. immunity	X	26. media			
9. no confidence	X	18. all elected	X				

The Assembly (*Assembleia*) of Mozambique was established in 1975 upon independence from Portugal. For the next fifteen years, Mozambique was ruled as a single-party Marxist-Leninist regime and was engulfed in civil war. A new constitution in 1990 paved the way for multiparty elections in 1994 and an enhanced role for the legislature.

The legislature's ability to influence the executive branch is limited to powers to interpellate, investigate, and vote no confidence in the government. The executive lacks gatekeeping authority and the power to appoint members of the legislature, and legislators are immune from arrest, but otherwise the legislature lacks institutional autonomy. The one area where the legislature's authority is expansive is that of specified powers; it enjoys five of the eight such powers assessed in this survey. The legislature has weak institutional capacity.

SURVEY

1. The legislature alone, without the involvement of any other agencies, can impeach the president or replace the prime minister.

No. The legislature cannot impeach the president.

Article 132
1. The President of the Republic shall enjoy immunity from civil and criminal proceedings with respect to actions taken in the discharge of his duties.
2. During the term of his office the President of the Republic may not be sued in court for actions taken outside the discharge of his duties.

2. Ministers may serve simultaneously as members of the legislature.

No. As "established by law," ministers are prohibited from serving simultaneously in the legislature.

Article 192
1. No person may hold at the same time more than one of the following positions:
President of the Republic, President of the Assembly of the Republic, Prime Minister, President of the Supreme Court, Deputy President of the Supreme Court, President of the Constitutional Council, President of the Administrative Court, Attorney-General of the Republic, Deputy Attorney-General of the Republic, Provincial Governor, Secretary of State.
2. The position of member of Government (Cabinet) shall also be incompatible with the posts named above, except those of President of the Republic and Prime Minister, since these are themselves members of Government.
3. Other cases of incompatibility may be established by law.

3. The legislature has powers of summons over executive branch officials and hearings with executive

branch officials testifying before the legislature or its committees are regularly held.

Yes. The legislature regularly interpellates officials from the executive.

4. The legislature can conduct independent investigation of the chief executive and the agencies of the executive.

Yes. The legislature can investigate the executive.

5. The legislature has effective powers of oversight over the agencies of coercion (the military, organs of law enforcement, intelligence services, and the secret police).

No. The legislature lacks effective powers of oversight over the agencies of coercion.

6. The legislature appoints the prime minister.

No. The president appoints the prime minister.

> Article 121
> In the function of directing government activity, the President of the Republic shall have power to:
> b) appoint, exonerate, and dismiss the Prime Minister.

7. The legislature's approval is required to confirm the appointment of ministers; or the legislature itself appoints ministers.

No. The president appoints the ministers, and the appointments do not require the legislature's approval.

> Article 121
> In the function of directing government activity, the President of the Republic shall have power to:
> d) appoint, exonerate and dismiss:
> – Ministers and Deputy Ministers.

8. The country lacks a presidency entirely or there is a presidency, but the president is elected by the legislature.

No. The president is directly elected.

> Article 118
> 1. The President of the Republic shall be elected by direct universal suffrage and by personal and secret ballot.

9. The legislature can vote no confidence in the government.

Yes. The legislature can vote no confidence in the government (reject the government's program).

> Article 136
> 1. At the beginning of each legislative session, the Assembly of the Republic shall evaluate the programme of the Government.
> 2. The Government may present a revised programme that takes the conclusions of the debate into account.

> 3. Should the Assembly of the Republic, after debate, reject the Government's programme, the President of the Republic may dissolve the Assembly and call new general elections.

10. The legislature is immune from dissolution by the executive.

No. The president can dissolve the legislature.

> Article 120
> In his role as head of State, the President of the Republic shall have power to:
> e) dissolve on a onetime basis the Assembly of the Republic if the Assembly does not approve the program of the government.

> Article 136
> 1. At the beginning of each legislative session, the Assembly of the Republic shall evaluate the programme of the Government.
> 2. The Government may present a revised programme that takes the conclusions of the debate into account.
> 3. Should the Assembly of the Republic, after debate, reject the Government's programme, the President of the Republic may dissolve the Assembly and call new general elections.

11. Any executive initiative on legislation requires ratification or approval by the legislature before it takes effect; that is, the executive lacks decree power.

No. Formally, the president and the government can issue regulatory decrees and presidential orders only. In practice, the president and the government issue decrees that have the force of law.

> Article 131
> Regulatory acts of the President of the Republic shall take the form of presidential decrees. Other decisions arising from the President's constitutional powers shall take the form of presidential orders. Both are to be published in the Boletim da República.

> Article 157
> 1. Regulatory acts of the Council of Ministers shall take the form of decrees. Other decisions of the Council of Ministers shall take the form of resolutions.
> 2. Decrees and resolutions shall be signed by the Prime Minister and published in the Boletim da República.

12. Laws passed by the legislature are veto-proof or essentially veto-proof; that is, the executive lacks veto power, or has veto power but the veto can be overridden by a majority in the legislature.

No. A two-thirds majority vote is required to override a presidential veto.

> Article 124
> 3. The President of the Republic may return a bill to the Assembly of the Republic for reexamination, giving reasons in a message to the Assembly.

4. Should the bill, under reexamination, be approved by a two-thirds majority, the President of the Republic shall promulgate it as law and order its publication.

13. The legislature's laws are supreme and not subject to judicial review.

No. The Constitutional Council can review the constitutionality of laws.

> Article 181
> 1. The Constitutional Council shall have power to:
> a) adjudicate the constitutionality and legality of legislative and regulatory acts of State organs.

14. The legislature has the right to initiate bills in all policy jurisdictions; the executive lacks gatekeeping authority.

Yes. The legislature can initiate bills in all policy jurisdictions.

15. Expenditure of funds appropriated by the legislature is mandatory; the executive lacks the power to impound funds appropriated by the legislature.

No. The president can impound funds appropriated by the legislature.

16. The legislature controls the resources that finance its own internal operation and provide for the perquisites of its own members.

No. The legislature is dependent on the executive for the resources that finance its own operations.

17. Members of the legislature are immune from arrest and/or criminal prosecution.

Yes. Legislators are immune with the common exception for cases of *flagrante delicto,* here expressed as "in the very act of committing a criminal offense."

> Article 144
> 1. No deputy to the People's Assembly may be arrested, unless apprehended in the very act of committing a criminal offense. No deputy may be brought to trial without the consent of the Assembly or its Standing Commission.
> 2. Deputies to the People's Assembly shall be tried by the Supreme Court.

> Article 145
> 1. Deputies to the People's Assembly may not be sued, detained, or put on trial for opinions voiced or votes cast in exercising their functions as deputies.
> 2. The above does not apply to civil or criminal responsibility for defamation or slander.

18. All members of the legislature are elected; the executive lacks the power to appoint any members of the legislature.

Yes. All members of the legislature are elected.

> Article 134
> 1. The Assembly of the Republic shall be elected by direct universal suffrage and personal secret ballot.

19. The legislature alone, without the involvement of any other agencies, can change the Constitution.

Yes. The legislature can amend the constitution with a two-thirds majority vote.

> Article 120
> In his role as head of State, the President of the Republic shall have power to:
> c) decide on the holding of referenda on amendments to the Constitution or on matters of fundamental interest for the nation.

> Article 198
> 1. Amendments to the Constitution may be proposed by the President of the Republic or by at least one-third of the deputies to the Assembly of the Republic.
> 2. Draft amendments must be submitted to the Assembly of the Republic 90 days before the opening of debate.

> Article 199
> 1. If a proposed amendment implies fundamental changes in the rights of citizens or in the organization of public powers, the proposal, after adoption by the Assembly of the Republic, shall be submitted to public debate and to a referendum.
> 2. The results of the referendum and the approved constitutional text shall be adopted by the Assembly of the Republic in the form of a constitutional law, and shall be published by order of the President of the Republic.
> 3. In other cases, amendments to the Constitution shall be adopted by a two-thirds majority of the deputies of the Assembly of the Republic.

20. The legislature's approval is necessary for the declaration of war.

No. The president can declare war without the legislature's approval.

> Article 122
> In matters of national defense and public order, the President of the Republic shall have power to:
> a) declare a state of war and its termination, a state of siege or a state of emergency.

> Article 159
> In particular, the National Defense and Security Council shall have power to:
> a) pronounce upon a state of war before such is declared.

21. The legislature's approval is necessary to ratify treaties with foreign countries.

Yes. The legislature's approval is necessary to ratify international treaties.

> Article 122
> In matters of national defense and public order, the President of the Republic shall have power to:
> b) make treaties.

Article 135

1. The Assembly of the Republic shall have power to legislate on basic questions of the country's domestic and foreign policy.

2. In particular, the Assembly of the Republic shall have power to:

k) ratify and terminate international treaties.

22. The legislature has the power to grant amnesty.

Yes. The legislature has the power to grant amnesty.

Article 135

1. The Assembly of the Republic shall have power to legislate on basic questions of the country's domestic and foreign policy.

2. In particular, the Assembly of the Republic shall have power to:

l) grant amnesties and pardons.

23. The legislature has the power of pardon.

Yes. The legislature and the president both have the power of pardon.

Article 120

In his role as head of State, the President of the Republic shall have power to:

i) grant pardons and commute sentences.

Article 135

1. The Assembly of the Republic shall have power to legislate on basic questions of the country's domestic and foreign policy.

2. In particular, the Assembly of the Republic shall have power to:

l) grant amnesties and pardons.

24. The legislature reviews and has the right to reject appointments to the judiciary; or the legislature itself appoints members of the judiciary.

Yes. The legislature appoints some members of the Supreme Court.

Article 120

In his role as head of State, the President of the Republic shall have power to:

g) appoint the President and Deputy President of the Supreme Court, the President of the Constitutional Council, and the President of the Administrative Court.

Article 170

1. The Supreme Court shall be composed of professional judges and of elected judges, the number to be established by law.

2. The professional judges shall be appointed by the President of the Republic, after consultation with the Supreme Council of the Judiciary.

4. The Assembly of the Republic shall elect the other judges to the Supreme Court.

25. The chairman of the central bank is appointed by the legislature.

No. The president appoints the governor of the Bank of Mozambique.

Article 121

In the function of directing government activity, the President of the Republic shall have power to:

d) appoint, exonerate and dismiss:

– the Governor and Deputy Governor of the Bank of Mozambique.

26. The legislature has a substantial voice in the operation of the state-owned media.

No. The legislature lacks a substantial voice in the operation of the public media.

27. The legislature is regularly in session.

No. The legislature does not regularly meet in ordinary session.

Article 139

The Assembly of the Republic shall meet in ordinary session twice a year, and in extraordinary session whenever requested by the President of the Republic, by the Standing Commission of the Assembly of the Republic, or by at least one-third of the deputies of the Assembly of the Republic.

28. Each legislator has a personal secretary.

No.

29. Each legislator has at least one non-secretarial staff member with policy expertise.

No.

30. Legislators are eligible for re-election without any restriction.

Yes. There are no restrictions on re-election.

31. A seat in the legislature is an attractive enough position that legislators are generally interested in and seek re-election.

Yes.

32. The re-election of incumbent legislators is common enough that at any given time the legislature contains a significant number of highly experienced members.

Yes. Across the 1994, 1999, and 2004 Assembly elections, re-election rates were sufficiently high to produce a significant number of highly experienced members.

PEOPLE'S ASSEMBLY OF MYANMAR (BURMA) (*PYITHU HLUTTAW*)

Score: .00

Influence over executive (0/9)	Institutional autonomy (0/9)	Specified powers (0/8)	Institutional capacity (0/6)
1. replace	10. no dissolution	19. amendments	27. sessions
2. serve as ministers	11. no decree	20. war	28. secretary
3. interpellate	12. no veto	21. treaties	29. staff
4. investigate	13. no review	22. amnesty	30. no term limits
5. oversee police	14. no gatekeeping	23. pardon	31. seek re-election
6. appoint PM	15. no impoundment	24. judiciary	32. experience
7. appoint ministers	16. control resources	25. central bank	
8. lack president	17. immunity	26. media	
9. no confidence	18. all elected		

The People's Assembly (*Pyithu Hluttaw*) of Myanmar (Burma) has been suspended since 1988. The Assembly traces its origins to the 1948 Constitution of the Union of Burma, which called for the creation of a bicameral Union Parliament. In 1962 a military coup brought to power a socialist government. In 1974 the government established a new constitution and a unicameral People's Assembly. In 1988 a military junta named the State Law and Order Restoration Council (SLORC) suspended the constitution. Legislative elections were held in 1990, but the junta's displeasure with the results, which produced a landslide for the opposition National League for Democracy, prompted it to deny the legislature's right to assemble.

In 2008 a new draft constitution passed in a national referendum whose result was widely regarded as rigged. Although the new constitution may pave the way for parliamentary elections in 2010, the junta's track record in power leaves ample grounds for skepticism regarding the promise of future elections.

NATIONAL ASSEMBLY OF NAMIBIA

Expert consultants: Achieng Akumu, Joshua B. Forrest, Jakes Jacobs, G. J. C. Strydom, Diana Swain

Score: .50

Influence over executive (5/9)		Institutional autonomy (5/9)		Specified powers (2/8)		Institutional capacity (4/6)	
1. replace	X	10. no dissolution		19. amendments	X	27. sessions	X
2. serve as ministers	X	11. no decree	X	20. war		28. secretary	
3. interpellate	X	12. no veto		21. treaties	X	29. staff	
4. investigate	X	13. no review		22. amnesty		30. no term limits	X
5. oversee police	X	14. no gatekeeping	X	23. pardon		31. seek re-election	X
6. appoint PM		15. no impoundment	X	24. judiciary		32. experience	X
7. appoint ministers		16. control resources	X	25. central bank			
8. lack president		17. immunity		26. media			
9. no confidence		18. all elected	X				

The National Assembly of Namibia was established in the 1990 constitution upon independence from South Africa. The document called for a bicameral legislature consisting of a lower house, the National Assembly (from which the entire legislature takes its name), and an upper house, the National Council, whose members are elected by regional councils.

The legislature enjoys substantial influence over the executive. It can remove the president and appoint its members to the government, and it has effective powers of oversight over the executive branch. The legislature has some institutional autonomy but must live with presidential veto and dissolution powers and de facto lack of immunity for legislators. The legislature is granted few specified powers. It has a moderate amount of institutional capacity.

SURVEY

1. The legislature alone, without the involvement of any other agencies, can impeach the president or replace the prime minister.

Yes. The legislature can remove the president from office by a two-thirds majority vote of the total membership in both houses.

Article 29
(1)(a) The President's term of office shall be five years unless he or she dies or resigns before the expiry of the said term or is removed from office.

(b) In the event of the dissolution of the National Assembly in the circumstances provided for under Article 57 (1), the President's term of office shall also expire.
(2) A President shall be removed from office if a two-thirds majority of all the members of the National Assembly, confirmed by a two-thirds majority of all the members of the National Council, adopts a resolution impeaching the President on the ground that he or she has been guilty of a violation of the Constitution or guilty of a serious violation of the laws of the land or otherwise guilty of such gross misconduct or ineptitude as to render him or her unfit to hold with dignity and honour the office of President.

2. Ministers may serve simultaneously as members of the legislature.

Yes. Legislators may serve simultaneously in ministerial positions.

3. The legislature has powers of summons over executive branch officials and hearings with executive branch officials testifying before the legislature or its committees are regularly held.

Yes. The legislature regularly interpellates officials from the executive.

Article 59
(3) For the purpose of exercising its powers and performing its functions any committee of the National Assembly established in terms of Paragraph (1) shall have the power to subpoena persons to appear before it to give evidence on oath and to produce any documents required by it.

Article 63

(2) The National Assembly shall further have the power and function, subject to this Constitution:

(f) to receive reports on the activities of the Executive, including para-statal enterprises, and from time to time to require any senior official to appear before any of the committees of the National Assembly to account for and explain his or her acts and programmes.

4. The legislature can conduct independent investigation of the chief executive and the agencies of the executive.

Yes. The legislature can investigate the executive.

5. The legislature has effective powers of oversight over the agencies of coercion (the military, organs of law enforcement, intelligence services, and the secret police).

Yes. The legislature has effective powers of oversight over the agencies of coercion.

6. The legislature appoints the prime minister.

No. The president appoints the prime minister.

Article 32

(3) The President...shall have the power, subject to this Constitution to; i) appoint the following persons:

(aa) the Prime Minister.

7. The legislature's approval is required to confirm the appointment of ministers; or the legislature itself appoints ministers.

No. The president appoints ministers, and the appointments do not require the legislature's approval.

Article 32

(3) The President...shall have the power, subject to this Constitution to (i) appoint the following persons:

(bb) Ministers and Deputy-Ministers.

8. The country lacks a presidency entirely or there is a presidency, but the president is elected by the legislature.

No. The president is directly elected.

Article 28

(1) The President shall be elected in accordance with the provisions of this Constitution and subject thereto.

(2) Election of the President shall be:

(a) by direct, universal and equal suffrage.

9. The legislature can vote no confidence in the government.

No. The legislature can remove the president with a two-thirds majority vote and can vote no confidence in individual ministers with a majority vote, but it cannot vote no confidence in the government as a whole.

Article 29

(1)(a) The President's term of office shall be five years unless he or she dies or resigns before the expiry of the said term or is removed from office.

(b) In the event of the dissolution of the National Assembly in the circumstances provided for under Article 57 (1), the President's term of office shall also expire.

(2) A President shall be removed from office if a two-thirds majority of all the members of the National Assembly, confirmed by a two-thirds majority of all the members of the National Council, adopts a resolution impeaching the President on the ground that he or she has been guilty of a violation of the Constitution or guilty of a serious violation of the laws of the land or otherwise guilty of such gross misconduct or ineptitude as to render him or her unfit to hold with dignity and honour the office of President.

Article 39

The President shall be obliged to terminate the appointment of any member of the Cabinet, if the National Assembly by a majority of all its members resolves that it has no confidence in that member.

10. The legislature is immune from dissolution by the executive.

No. The president can dissolve the legislature.

Article 57

(1) The National Assembly may be dissolved by the President on the advice of the Cabinet if the Government is unable to govern effectively.

(2) Should the National Assembly be dissolved a national election for a new National Assembly and a new President shall take place within a period of ninety (90) days from the date of such dissolution.

11. Any executive initiative on legislation requires ratification or approval by the legislature before it takes effect; that is, the executive lacks decree power.

Yes. The executive lacks decree power.

12. Laws passed by the legislature are veto-proof or essentially veto-proof; that is, the executive lacks veto power, or has veto power but the veto can be overridden by a majority in the legislature.

No. A two-thirds majority is required to override a presidential veto.

Article 56

(1) Every bill passed by Parliament in terms of this Constitution in order to acquire the status of an Act of Parliament shall require the assent of the President to be signified by the signing of the bill and the publication of the Act in the Gazette.

(2) Where a bill is passed by a majority of two-thirds of all the members of the National Assembly

and has been confirmed by the National Council the President shall be obliged to give his or her assent thereto.

(3) Where a bill is passed by a majority of the members of the National Assembly but such majority consists of less than two-thirds of all the members of the National Assembly and has been confirmed by the National Council, but the President declines to assent to such bill, the President shall communicate such dissent to the Speaker.

(4) If the President has declined to assent to a bill under Paragraph (3), the National Assembly may reconsider the bill and, if it so decides, pass the bill in the form in which it was referred back to it, or in an amended form or it may decline to pass the bill. Should the bill then be passed by a majority of the National Assembly it will not require further confirmation by the National Council but, if the majority consists of less than two-thirds of all the members of the National Assembly, the President shall retain his or her power to withhold assent to the bill. If the President elects not to assent to the bill, it shall then lapse.

Article 64

(1) Subject to the provisions of this Constitution, the President shall be entitled to withhold his or her assent to a bill approved by the National Assembly if in the President's opinion such bill would upon adoption conflict with the provisions of this Constitution.

(2) Should the President withhold assent on the grounds of such opinion, he or she shall so inform the Speaker who shall inform the National Assembly thereof, and the Attorney-General, who may then take appropriate steps to have the matter decided by a competent Court.

(3) Should such Court thereafter conclude that such bill is not in conflict with the provisions of this Constitution, the President shall assent to the said bill if it was passed by the National Assembly by a two-thirds majority of all its members. If the bill was not passed with such majority, the President may withhold his or her assent to the bill, in which event the provisions of Article 56 (3) and (4) shall apply.

(4) Should such Court conclude that the disputed bill would be in conflict with any provisions of this Constitution, the said bill shall be deemed to have lapsed and the President shall not be entitled to assent thereto.

13. The legislature's laws are supreme and not subject to judicial review.

No. The High Court can review the constitutionality of laws.

Article 64

(1) Subject to the provisions of this Constitution, the President shall be entitled to withhold his or her assent to a bill approved by the National Assembly if in the President's opinion such bill would upon adoption conflict with the provisions of this Constitution.

(2) Should the President withhold assent on the grounds of such opinion, he or she shall so inform

the Speaker who shall inform the National Assembly thereof, and the Attorney-General, who may then take appropriate steps to have the matter decided by a competent Court.

(3) Should such Court thereafter conclude that such bill is not in conflict with the provisions of this Constitution, the President shall assent to the said bill if it was passed by the National Assembly by a two-thirds majority of all its members. If the bill was not passed with such majority, the President may withhold his or her assent to the bill, in which event the provisions of Article 56 (3) and (4) shall apply.

(4) Should such Court conclude that the disputed bill would be in conflict with any provisions of this Constitution, the said bill shall be deemed to have lapsed and the President shall not be entitled to assent thereto.

Article 80

(1) The High Court shall consist of a Judge-President and such additional Judges as the President, acting on the recommendation of the Judicial Service Commission, may determine.

(2) The High Court shall have original jurisdiction to hear and adjudicate upon all civil disputes and criminal prosecutions, including cases which involve the interpretation, implementation and upholding of this Constitution and the fundamental rights and freedoms guaranteed thereunder. The High Court shall also have jurisdiction to hear and adjudicate upon appeals from Lower Courts.

(3) The jurisdiction of the High Court with regard to appeals shall be determined by Act of Parliament.

14. The legislature has the right to initiate bills in all policy jurisdictions; the executive lacks gatekeeping authority.

Yes. The legislature can initiate bills in all policy jurisdictions.

15. Expenditure of funds appropriated by the legislature is mandatory; the executive lacks the power to impound funds appropriated by the legislature.

Yes. The executive lacks the power to impound funds appropriated by the legislature.

16. The legislature controls the resources that finance its own internal operation and provide for the perquisites of its own members.

Yes. The legislature enjoys financial autonomy.

17. Members of the legislature are immune from arrest and/or criminal prosecution.

No. According to the constitution, the legislature has the power to pass legislation on its members' immunity. In practice, legislators are subject to arrest and criminal prosecution.

Article 60

(3) Rules providing for the privileges and immunities of members of the National Assembly shall be made by

Act of Parliament and all members shall be entitled to the protection of such privileges and immunities.

18. All members of the legislature are elected; the executive lacks the power to appoint any members of the legislature.

Yes. All of the seventy-two members of the National Assembly are elected. The president can appoint up to six additional members, but these appointees do not have voting rights.

Article 46
(1) The composition of the National Assembly shall be as follows: a) seventy-two members to be elected by the registered voters by general, direct and secret ballot. Every Namibian citizen who has the qualifications described in Article 17 shall be entitled to vote in the elections for members of the National Assembly and, subject to Article 47, shall be eligible for candidature as a member of the National Assembly; b) not more than six persons appointed by the President under Article 32 (5)(c), by virtue of their special expertise, status, skill or experience: provided that such members shall have no vote in the National Assembly, and shall not be taken into account for the purpose of determining any specific majorities that are required under this Constitution or any other law.

Article 69
(1) The National Council shall consist of two members from each region referred to in Article 102, to be elected from amongst their members by the Regional Council for such region.
(2) The elections of members of the National Council shall be conducted according to procedures to be prescribed by Act of Parliament.

19. The legislature alone, without the involvement of any other agencies, can change the Constitution.

Yes. The legislature can change the constitution with a two-thirds majority vote in both houses.

Article 132
(1) Any bill seeking to repeal or amend any provision of this Constitution shall indicate the proposed repeals and/or amendments with reference to the specific articles sought to be repealed and/or amended and shall not deal with any matter other than the proposed repeals or amendments.
(2) The majorities required in Parliament for the repeal and/or amendment of any of the provisions of this Constitution shall be:
    (a) two-thirds of all the members of the National Assembly; and
    (b) two-thirds of all the members of the National Council.
(3)(a) Notwithstanding the provisions of Paragraph (2), if a bill proposing a repeal and/or amendment of any of the provisions of this Constitution secures a majority of two-thirds of all the members of the National Assembly, but fails to secure a majority of two-thirds of all the

members of the National Council, the President may by Proclamation make the bill containing the proposed repeals and/or amendments the subject of a national referendum.
    (b) The national referendum referred to in Paragraph (a) shall be conducted in accordance with procedures prescribed for the holding of referenda by Act of Parliament.
    (c) If upon the holding of such a referendum the bill containing the proposed repeals and/or amendments is approved by a two-thirds majority of all the votes cast in the referendum, the bill shall be deemed to have been passed in accordance with the provisions of this Constitution, and the President shall deal it in terms of Article 56.
(4) No repeal or amendment of this paragraph or Paragraphs (2) or (3) in so far as it seeks to diminish or detract from the majorities required in Parliament or in a referendum shall be permissible under this Constitution, and no such purported repeal or amendment shall be valid or have any force or effect.
(5) Nothing contained in this article: (a) shall detract in any way from the entrenchment provided for in Article 131 of the fundamental rights and freedoms contained and defined in Chapter 3;
    (b) shall prevent Parliament from changing its own composition or structures by amending or repealing any of the provisions of this Constitution: provided always that such repeals or amendments are effected in accordance with the provisions of this Constitution.

20. The legislature's approval is necessary for the declaration of war.

No. The constitution contains no explicit provision on the declaration of war, although in times of war the president may declare a state of "martial law" without obtaining the legislature's approval.

Article 26
(7) The President shall have the power to proclaim or terminate martial law. Martial law may be proclaimed only when a state of national defence involving another country exists or when civil war prevails in Namibia: provided that any proclamation of martial law shall cease to be valid if it is not approved within a reasonable time by a resolution passed by a two-third majority of all the members of the National Assembly.

21. The legislature's approval is necessary to ratify treaties with foreign countries.

Yes. The legislature's approval is necessary to ratify international treaties.

Article 32
(3) Without derogating from the generality of the functions and powers contemplated by Paragraph (1), the President shall . . . have the power, subject to this Constitution to:
    e) negotiate and sign international agreements, and to delegate such power.

Article 40

The members of the Cabinet shall have the following functions:

(i) to assist the President in determining what international agreements are to be concluded, acceded to or succeeded to and to report to the National Assembly thereon.

Article 63

(2) The National Assembly shall further have the power and function, subject to this Constitution:

(d) to consider and decide whether or not to succeed to such international agreements as may have been entered into prior to Independence by administrations within Namibia in which the majority of the Namibian people have historically not enjoyed democratic representation and participation; (e) to agree to the ratification of or accession to international agreements which have been negotiated and signed in terms of Article 32 (3)(e).

22. The legislature has the power to grant amnesty.

No. Amnesty and pardon are not treated separately, and the legislature lacks the power to grant amnesty. See item 23.

23. The legislature has the power of pardon.

No. The president has the power of pardon.

Article 32

(3) Without derogating from the generality of the functions and powers contemplated by Paragraph (1), the President shall have the power, subject to this Constitution to:

(d) pardon or reprieve offenders, either unconditionally or subject to such conditions as the President may deem fit.

24. The legislature reviews and has the right to reject appointments to the judiciary; or the legislature itself appoints members of the judiciary.

No. The president appoints the judiciary, and the appointments do not require the legislature's approval.

Article 82

(1) All appointments of Judges to the Supreme Court and the High Court shall be made by the President on the recommendation of the Judicial Service Commission and upon appointment Judges shall make an oath or affirmation of office in the terms set out in Schedule 1.

(2) At the request of the Chief Justice the President may appoint Acting Judges of the Supreme Court to fill casual vacancies in the Court from time to time, or as ad hoc appointments to sit in cases involving constitutional issues or the guarantee of fundamental rights and freedoms, if in the opinion of the Chief Justice it is desirable that such persons should be appointed to hear such cases by reason of their special knowledge of or expertise in such matters.

(3) At the request of the Judge-President, the President may appoint Acting Judges of the High Court from time to time to fill casual vacancies in the Court, or to enable the Court to deal expeditiously with its work.

25. The chairman of the central bank is appointed by the legislature.

No. The president appoints the governor of the Central Bank of Namibia.

Article 128

(2) The Governing Board of the Central Bank shall consist of a Governor, a Deputy-Governor and such other members of the Board as shall be prescribed by Act of Parliament, and all members of the Board shall be appointed by the President in accordance with procedures prescribed by such Act of Parliament.

26. The legislature has a substantial voice in the operation of the state-owned media.

No. The legislature lacks a substantial voice in the operation of the public media.

27. The legislature is regularly in session.

Yes. The legislature regularly meets in ordinary session.

Article 62

(1) The National Assembly shall sit:

(a) at its usual place of sitting determined by the National Assembly, unless the Speaker directs otherwise on the grounds of public interest, security or convenience;

(b) for at least two (2) sessions during each year, to commence and terminate on such dates as the National Assembly from time to time determines;

(c) for such special sessions as directed by Proclamation by the President from time to time.

(2) During such sessions the National Assembly shall sit on such days and during such times of the day or night as the National Assembly by its rules and standing orders may provide.

(3) The day of commencement of any session of the National Assembly may be altered by Proclamation by the President, if the President is requested to do so by the Speaker on grounds of public interest or convenience.

28. Each legislator has a personal secretary.

No.

29. Each legislator has at least one non-secretarial staff member with policy expertise.

No.

30. Legislators are eligible for re-election without any restriction.

Yes. There are no restrictions on re-election.

31. A seat in the legislature is an attractive enough position that legislators are generally interested in and seek re-election.

Yes.

32. The re-election of incumbent legislators is common enough that at any given time the legislature contains a significant number of highly experienced members.

Yes. Re-election rates are sufficiently high to pro-

duce a significant number of highly experienced members. The dominance of a single party, the South West Africa People's Organization (SWAPO), has contributed to high rates of re-election and membership stability. SWAPO has won between fifty-three and fifty-five of the seventy-two seats in the National Assembly in each of the three post-independence elections, held in 1994, 1999, and 2004.

PARLIAMENT OF NEPAL (*SANSAD*)

Expert consultants: Lok Raj Baral, Ram Guragain, Deepak Gyawali, Nick Langton, Prakash Raj Sapkota, Anil Kumar Sinha, Deepak Thapa

Score: .44

Influence over executive (6/9)		Institutional autonomy (3/9)		Specified powers (2/8)		Institutional capacity (3/6)	
1. replace	X	10. no dissolution		19. amendments	X	27. sessions	
2. serve as ministers	X	11. no decree		20. war		28. secretary	X
3. interpellate	X	12. no veto	X	21. treaties	X	29. staff	
4. investigate		13. no review		22. amnesty		30. no term limits	X
5. oversee police		14. no gatekeeping	X	23. pardon		31. seek re-election	X
6. appoint PM	X	15. no impoundment		24. judiciary		32. experience	
7. appoint ministers		16. control resources	X	25. central bank			
8. lack president	X	17. immunity		26. media			
9. no confidence	X	18. all elected					

The Parliament of Nepal (*Sansad*) traces its origins to the Assembly of Lords (*Bharadari Sabha*) that acted as a consultative court to Nepalese monarchs from 1851 to 1947. A 1948 constitution introduced a bicameral parliament, although the legislature did not exercise significant powers. Royal authority was buttressed by a new constitution adopted in 1959. The monarch ruled until 1990, when Nepal adopted a new constitution that limited the king's powers and established a bicameral legislature with a directly elected lower house, the House of Representatives (*Pratinidhi Sabha*), and a partly appointed upper house, the National Assembly (*Rashtriya Sabha*). In 2002 the king suspended parliament, and in 2005 he also dismissed the government and assumed absolute power, claiming that his action was needed to combat antigovernment rebels who controlled much of the coun-

tryside. In April 2006, under the pressure of massive public demonstrations, the king recalled parliament. In May of that year parliament voted to curtail the monarch's political power. New elections were held in January 2007. At the time of this writing, discussions are underway on replacing the parliament with a Constituent Assembly, elections for which have been repeatedly postponed and which are now scheduled to be held sometime in 2008. The character and role of the legislature remain contested and unsettled and are at the center of public debate in Nepal. The constitutional excerpts cited below are from the 1990 constitution.

The legislature has some ability to influence the executive. Notably, it can appoint and remove the prime minister. The legislature's institutional autonomy is limited by the monarch's powers to dissolve the legislature, decree legislation, and appoint members of the legislature. Apart from rights to change the constitution and approve treaties, the legislature lacks the specified powers assessed here. It has some institutional capacity.

SURVEY

1. The legislature alone, without the involvement of any other agencies, can impeach the president or replace the prime minister.

Yes. The legislature can remove the prime minister with a vote of no confidence. The king cannot be impeached.

Article 31
No question shall be raised in any court about any act performed by His Majesty:
Provided that nothing in this Article shall be deemed to restrict any right under law to initiate proceedings against His Majesty's Government or any employee of His Majesty.

Article 59
(1) The Prime Minister, while he holds office, may, whenever he is of the opinion that it is necessary or appropriate to obtain a vote of confidence from the members of the House of Representatives, present a resolution to that effect in the House of Representatives.
(2) One-fourth of the total number of members of the House of Representatives may present in writing a no-confidence motion against the Prime Minister: Provided that a no-confidence motion shall not be presented more than once in the same session.
(3) A decision on a resolution presented pursuant to clauses (1) and (2) shall be made by a majority of the total number of members of the House of Representatives.

2. Ministers may serve simultaneously as members of the legislature.

Yes. Ministers are required to serve simultaneously in the legislature.

Article 38
Notwithstanding anything contained in Articles 36 and 37, any person who is not a member of either House of Parliament may be appointed Deputy-Prime Minister, Minister, State Minister or Assistant-Minister:
Provided that such Deputy-Prime Minister, Minister, State Minister or Assistant-Minister shall be required to become a member of Parliament within six months from the date of his appointment.

3. The legislature has powers of summons over executive branch officials and hearings with executive branch officials testifying before the legislature or its committees are regularly held.

Yes. The legislature regularly interpellates officials from the executive.

4. The legislature can conduct independent investigation of the chief executive and the agencies of the executive.

No. The legislature cannot investigate the royal palace.

Article 31
No question shall be raised in any court about any act performed by His Majesty:
Provided that nothing in this Article shall be deemed to restrict any right under law to initiate proceedings against His Majesty's Government or any employee of His Majesty.

Article 56
(1) No discussion shall be held in either House of Parliament on the conduct of His Majesty, Her Majesty the Queen and the heir apparent to His Majesty: Provided that nothing in this Article shall be deemed to bar criticism of His Majesty's Government.

5. The legislature has effective powers of oversight over the agencies of coercion (the military, organs of law enforcement, intelligence services, and the secret police).

No. The legislature lacks effective oversight powers over the agencies of coercion.

6. The legislature appoints the prime minister.

Yes. The monarch appoints as prime minister the candidate who enjoys majority support in the House of Representatives.

Article 36
(1) His Majesty shall appoint the leader of the party which commands a majority in the House of Representatives as the Prime Minister, and shall constitute the Council of Ministers under his chairmanship.

7. The legislature's approval is required to confirm the appointment of ministers; or the legislature itself appoints ministers.

No. The monarch appoints ministers on the recommendation of the prime minister, and the appointments do not require the legislature's approval.

Article 37
(1) His Majesty shall, on the recommendation of the Prime Minister, appoint State Ministers from amongst the members of Parliament.
(2) His Majesty shall, upon the recommendation of the Prime Minister, appoint Assistant Ministers from amongst the members of Parliament to assist any Minister in carrying out his responsibilities.
(3) The provisions of clause (6) of Article 36 relating to Ministers shall also be applicable to State Ministers and Assistant Ministers.

8. The country lacks a presidency entirely or there is a presidency, but the president is elected by the legislature.

Yes. The country lacks a presidency. The monarch is the head of state.

Article 35

(1) The executive power of the Kingdom of Nepal shall, pursuant to this Constitution and other laws, be vested in His Majesty and the Council of Ministers.

9. The legislature can vote no confidence in the government.

Yes. The legislature can vote no confidence in the government.

Article 59

(1) The Prime Minister, while he holds office, may, whenever he is of the opinion that it is necessary or appropriate to obtain a vote of confidence from the members of the House of Representatives, present a resolution to that effect in the House of Representatives.

(2) One-fourth of the total number of members of the House of Representatives may present in writing a no-confidence motion against the Prime Minister: Provided that a no-confidence motion shall not be presented more than once in the same session.

(3) A decision on a resolution presented pursuant to clauses (1) and (2) shall be made by a majority of the total number of members of the House of Representatives.

10. The legislature is immune from dissolution by the executive.

No. The monarch, on the recommendation of the prime minister, can dissolve the House of Representatives.

Article 53

(4) His Majesty may dissolve the House of Representatives on the recommendation of the Prime Minister. His Majesty shall, when so dissolving the House of Representatives, specify a date, to be within six months, for new elections to the House of Representatives.

11. Any executive initiative on legislation requires ratification or approval by the legislature before it takes effect; that is, the executive lacks decree power.

No. The monarch can issue decrees ("ordinances") that have the force of law when parliament is not in session. The decrees lapse if they are not subsequently approved by the legislature.

Article 72

(1) If at any time, except when both Houses of Parliament are in session, His Majesty is satisfied that circumstances exist which render it necessary for him to take immediate action, He may, without prejudicing the provisions set forth in this Constitution, promulgate any Ordinance as He may deem necessary.

(2) An Ordinance promulgated under clause (1) shall have the same force and effect as an Act: Provided that every such Ordinance:

(a) shall be presented at the next session of both Houses of Parliament, and if not passed by both Houses, it shall ipso facto cease to be effective;

(b) may be repealed at any time by His Majesty; and

(c) shall, unless rendered ineffective or repealed under sub-clause (a) or (b), ipso-facto cease to have effect at the expiration of six months from its promulgation or sixty days from the commencement of a session of both the Houses. Explanation: If the two Houses of Parliament meet on different dates, the latter date on which a House commences its session shall be deemed to be the date of commencement of session for the purpose of computation of time under this clause.

12. Laws passed by the legislature are veto-proof or essentially veto-proof; that is, the executive lacks veto power, or has veto power but the veto can be overridden by a majority in the legislature.

Yes. The legislature can override a presidential veto by a majority vote of its present members.

Article 71

(1) A Bill which is to be presented to His Majesty for assent pursuant to Article 69 shall be so presented by the Speaker or the Chairman of the House in which the Bill originated after it has been duly certified by him under his hand:

Provided that in the case of a Finance Bill, the Speaker shall so certify.

(2) Upon His Majesty's assent to any Bill that has been presented to Him pursuant to this Article, both Houses shall be informed as soon as possible.

(3) Except for a Finance Bill, if His Majesty is of the opinion that any Bill needs further deliberations, he may send back the Bill with His message to the House of origin of the Bill within one month from the date of presentation of the Bill to Him.

(4) If any Bill is sent back with a message from His Majesty, it shall be reconsidered by a joint sitting of the two Houses and if the Bill so reconsidered is again passed as it was or with amendments, and it is again presented to him, His Majesty shall give assent to that Bill within thirty days of such presentation.

(5) A Bill shall become an Act after His Majesty grants his assent to it in accordance with this Article, and such assent shall be deemed to have been granted after the Royal Seal has been affixed thereon.

13. The legislature's laws are supreme and not subject to judicial review.

No. The Supreme Court can review the constitutionality of laws.

Article 88

(1) Any Nepali citizen may file a petition in the Supreme Court to have any law or any part thereof declared void on the ground of inconsistency with this Constitution because it imposes an unreasonable restriction on the enjoyment of the fundamental rights

conferred by this Constitution or on any other ground, and extraordinary power shall rest with the Supreme Court to declare that law as void either ab initio or from the date of its decision if it appears that the law in question is inconsistent with the Constitution.

(5) If His Majesty wishes to have an opinion of the Supreme Court on any complicated legal question of interpretation of this Constitution or of any other law, the Court shall, upon consideration on the question, report to His Majesty its opinion thereon.

14. The legislature has the right to initiate bills in all policy jurisdictions; the executive lacks gatekeeping authority.

Yes. The legislature can initiate bills in all policy jurisdictions.

15. Expenditure of funds appropriated by the legislature is mandatory; the executive lacks the power to impound funds appropriated by the legislature.

No. The monarch can impound funds appropriated by the legislature.

16. The legislature controls the resources that finance its own internal operation and provide for the perquisites of its own members.

Yes. The legislature enjoys financial autonomy, including control over members' perquisites.

> Article 67
> The remuneration and privileges of the . . . members of Parliament shall be determined by law.

17. Members of the legislature are immune from arrest and/or criminal prosecution.

No. Legislators are immune while the legislature is in session and for anything done as part of official parliamentary business, but they are subject to arrest for common crimes when the legislature is not in session.

> Article 62
> (1) Subject to the provisions of this Constitution, there shall be full freedom of speech in both Houses of Parliament and no member shall be arrested, detained or prosecuted in any court for anything said or any vote cast in the House.
> (2) Subject to the provisions of this Constitution, each House of Parliament shall have full power to regulate its internal business, and it shall be the exclusive right of the House concerned to decide whether or not any proceeding of the House is regular. No question shall be raised in any court in this regard.
> (3) Subject to the provisions of this Constitution, no comment shall be made about the good faith concerning any proceeding of either House of Parliament and no publication of any kind shall be made about anything said by any member which intentionally distorts or misinterprets the meaning of the speech.

(4) Subject to the provisions of this Constitution, the provisions of clauses (1) and (3) shall also apply to any person, other than a member, who is entitled to take part in a meeting of the House.

(5) No proceedings shall be initiated in any court against any person for publication of any document, report, vote or proceeding which is made under authority given, subject to the provisions of this Constitution, by a House of Parliament. Explanation: For the purposes of this clause and clauses (1), (2), (3) and (4), the word "House" shall mean and include the committees of a House and shall also mean a joint sitting of Parliament or a meeting of the Joint Committee.

(6) No member of Parliament shall be arrested between the date of issuance of the summons for a session and the date on which that session closes: Provided that nothing in this clause shall be deemed to prevent the arrest under any law of any member on a criminal charge. If any member is so arrested, the official making such arrest shall forthwith inform the person chairing the concerned House.

18. All members of the legislature are elected; the executive lacks the power to appoint any members of the legislature.

No. The monarch appoints ten of the sixty members of the National Assembly. All members of the House of Representatives are elected.

> Article 45
> (1) The House of Representatives shall consist of two hundred and five members.
> (2) For the purpose of election of members to the House of Representatives, administrative districts shall be treated as election districts, and the ratio of the number of seats allocated to any district shall be, so far as practicable, equal to the ratio of the population of that district to the national population as determined by the last census preceding the concerned election; and the number of election constituencies shall be equal to the number of seats so allocated; and one member shall be elected from each election constituency. Provided that the number of members to be elected from the districts shall be so determined and election constituency so delimitated that there be elected at least one member from each district irrespective of its population.

> Article 46
> (1) The National Assembly shall consist of sixty members as follows: –
> (a) ten members to be nominated by His Majesty from amongst persons of high reputation who have rendered prominent service in various fields of national life,
> (b) thirty-five members, including at least three women members, to be elected by the House of Representatives in accordance with the provisions of law, on the basis of the system of proportional representation by means of the single transferable vote, and
> (c) fifteen members, three from each of the Development Regions, to be elected in accordance with

law on the basis of the system of single transferable vote by an electoral college consisting of the Chief and the Deputy-Chief of the Village and Town level Local Authorities and the Chief, Deputy-Chief, and the members of the District level Local Authorities: Provided that until elections are held for the Local Authorities, such electoral college shall, for the first time, consist of the members of the House of Representatives elected from the concerned Development Region.

19. The legislature alone, without the involvement of any other agencies, can change the Constitution.

Yes. The legislature can change the constitution with a two-thirds majority vote in both houses.

Article 116
(1) A bill to amend or repeal any Article of this Constitution, without prejudicing the spirit of the Preamble of this Constitution, may be introduced in either House of Parliament: Provided that this Article shall not be subject to amendment.
(2) If each House, with a two-thirds majority of its total membership attending, passes a Bill introduced pursuant to clause (1) by a majority of at least two-thirds of the members present, the Bill shall be submitted to His Majesty for assent; and His Majesty may, within thirty days from the date of submission, either grant assent to such Bill or send the Bill back for reconsideration with His message to the House where the Bill originated.
(3) A Bill sent back by His Majesty pursuant to clause (2) above shall be reconsidered by both Houses of Parliament; and if both the Houses, upon following the procedures referred to in clause (2), resubmit the Bill in its original an amended form to His Majesty for assent, His Majesty shall grant assent to such Bill within thirty days of such submission.

20. The legislature's approval is necessary for the declaration of war.

No. In times of war, the king can declare a state of emergency without the legislature's approval. The state of emergency ceases if it is not approved by the legislature within three months.

Article 115
(1) If a grave crisis arises in regard to the sovereignty or integrity of the Kingdom of Nepal or the security of any part thereof, whether by war, external aggression, armed rebellion or extreme economic disarray, His Majesty may, by Proclamation, declare or order a State of Emergency in respect of the whole of the Kingdom of Nepal or of any specified part thereof.
(2) Every Proclamation or Order issued under clause (1) above shall be laid before a meeting of the House of Representatives for approval within three months from the date of issuance.
(3) If a Proclamation or Order laid for approval pursuant to clause (2) is approved by a two-thirds majority

of the House of Representatives present at that meeting, such Proclamation or Order shall continue in force for a period of six months from the date of issuance.
(4) If a Proclamation or Order laid for approval pursuant to clause (2) is not approved pursuant to clause (3), such Proclamation or Order shall be deemed ipso facto to cease to operate.
(5) Before the expiration of the period referred to in clause (3), if a meeting of the House of Representatives, by a majority of two-thirds of the members present, passes a resolution to the effect that circumstances referred to in clause (1) above continue to exist, it may extend the period of the Proclamation or Order of the State of Emergency for one other period, not exceeding six months as specified in such resolution, and the Speaker shall inform His Majesty of such extension.

21. The legislature's approval is necessary to ratify treaties with foreign countries.

Yes. The legislature's approval is necessary to ratify international treaties on most major issues.

Article 126
(1) The ratification of, accession to, acceptance of or approval of treaties or agreements to which the Kingdom of Nepal or His Majesty's Government is to become a party shall be as determined by law.
(2) The laws to be made pursuant to clause (1) shall, inter alia, require that the ratification of, accession to, acceptance of or approval of treaties or agreements on the following subjects be done by a majority of two-thirds of the members present at a joint sitting of both Houses of Parliament:
(a) peace and friendship;
(b) defence and strategic alliance;
(c) boundaries of the Kingdom of Nepal; and
(d) natural resources, and the distribution of their uses.
Provided that out of the treaties and agreements referred to in sub-clauses (a) and (d), if any treaty or agreement is of an ordinary nature, which does not affect the nation extensively, seriously, or in the long term, the ratification of, accession to, acceptance of or approval of such treaty or agreement may be done at a meeting of the House of Representatives by a simple majority of the members present.
(3) After the commencement of this Constitution, unless a treaty or agreement is ratified, acceded to, accepted or approved in accordance with this Article, it shall not be binding on His Majesty's Government or the Kingdom of Nepal.
(4) Notwithstanding anything contained in clauses (1) and (2), no treaty or agreement shall be concluded that is detrimental to the territorial integrity of the Kingdom of Nepal.

22. The legislature has the power to grant amnesty.

No. Amnesty and pardon are not treated separately, and the legislature lacks the power to grant amnesty. See item 23.

23. The legislature has the power of pardon.

No. The king has the power of pardon.

> Article 122 Pardons
> His Majesty shall have the power to grant pardons and to suspend, commute or remit any sentence passed by any court, special court, military court or by any other judicial, quasi-judicial or administrative authority or institution.

24. The legislature reviews and has the right to reject appointments to the judiciary; or the legislature itself appoints members of the judiciary.

No. The monarch controls judicial appointments.

> Article 87
> (1) His Majesty shall appoint the Chief Justice of Nepal on the recommendation of the Constitutional Council, and other Judges of the Supreme Court on the recommendation of the Judicial Council. The tenure of office of the Chief Justice shall be seven years from the date of appointment.

> Article 91
> (1) His Majesty shall, on the recommendation of the Judicial Council, appoint any Chief Judge and Judges of the Appellate Courts and any Judges of the District Courts: Provided that His Majesty may delegate His authority to the Chief Justice for the appointment of the District Judges to be made on the recommendation of the Judicial Council.

25. The chairman of the central bank is appointed by the legislature.

No. The government appoints the governor of the Central Bank of Nepal.

26. The legislature has a substantial voice in the operation of the state-owned media.

No. The legislature lacks a substantial voice in the operation of the public media.

27. The legislature is regularly in session.

No. The legislature has been subject to frequent suspensions by the monarch, including between 2002 and 2006.

> Article 53
> (1) His Majesty shall summon a session of parliament within one month after the elections to the House of Representatives are held. Thereafter, His Majesty shall summon other sessions from time to time in accordance with this Constitution. Provided that the interval between two consecutive sessions shall not be more than six months.

28. Each legislator has a personal secretary.

Yes.

29. Each legislator has at least one non-secretarial staff member with policy expertise.

No.

30. Legislators are eligible for re-election without any restriction.

Yes. There are no restrictions on re-election.

31. A seat in the legislature is an attractive enough position that legislators are generally interested in and seek re-election.

Yes.

32. The re-election of incumbent legislators is common enough that at any given time the legislature contains a significant number of highly experienced members.

No. The lengthy suspension of parliament by the monarch between 2002 and 2006 severely interrupted the rhythm of normal parliamentary elections and activity and the potential for the emergence of a cohort of highly experienced legislators.

STATES-GENERAL OF THE NETHERLANDS (*STATEN GENERAAL*)

Expert consultants: Kees Aarts, Rudy B. Andeweg, Richard Gerding, Jane Rebecca Gingrich, Michael Thurman

Score: .78

Influence over executive (7/9)		Institutional autonomy (7/9)		Specified powers (6/8)		Institutional capacity (5/6)	
1. replace	X	10. no dissolution		19. amendments	X	27. sessions	X
2. serve as ministers		11. no decree	X	20. war	X	28. secretary	X
3. interpellate	X	12. no veto	X	21. treaties	X	29. staff	
4. investigate	X	13. no review	X	22. amnesty	X	30. no term limits	X
5. oversee police	X	14. no gatekeeping	X	23. pardon	X	31. seek re-election	X
6. appoint PM	X	15. no impoundment	X	24. judiciary	X	32. experience	X
7. appoint ministers		16. control resources	X	25. central bank			
8. lack president	X	17. immunity		26. media			
9. no confidence	X	18. all elected	X				

The States-General (*Staten Generaal*) of the Netherlands traces its origins to the mid-fifteenth century, when it gathered as a body of representatives from the various Dutch provinces. In 1581 it proclaimed independence from the Spanish monarchy. The States-General was included in the first constitution of the Kingdom of the Netherlands, passed in 1814, and became a bicameral body in 1815. The legislature consists of the First Chamber (*Eerste Kamer*) and the Second Chamber (*Tweede Kamer*). Between 1815 and 1848 members of the Second Chamber were indirectly elected through the Provincial Estates, and members of the First Chamber were appointed by the crown. Since 1848 members of the Second Chamber have been elected by all enfranchised citizens, while members of the First Chamber have been indirectly elected by the Provincial Estates.

The parliament is a formidable force. It has substantial influence over the executive. It is subject to dissolution and its members lack immunity, but otherwise the legislature enjoys complete institutional autonomy. It holds all but two of the specified prerogatives measured in this survey. Its rating on institutional capacity is blemished only by the lack of at least one personal staff member with policy expertise for every legislator.

SURVEY

1. The legislature alone, without the involvement of any other agencies, can impeach the president or replace the prime minister.

Yes. The legislature can remove the prime minister with a vote of no confidence.

2. Ministers may serve simultaneously as members of the legislature.

No. Legislators are prohibited from serving simultaneously in ministerial positions.

Article 57
(2) A member of the Parliament may not be a Minister.

3. The legislature has powers of summons over executive branch officials and hearings with executive branch officials testifying before the legislature or its committees are regularly held.

Yes. The legislature regularly interpellates officials from the executive.

Article 68
Ministers and State Secretaries shall provide orally or in writing the Chambers either separately or in joint session, with any information requested by one or more members, provided that the provision of such information does not conflict with the interests of the State.

4. The legislature can conduct independent investigation of the chief executive and the agencies of the executive.

Yes. The legislature can establish bodies to investigate the executive.

> Article 108
> (1) The establishment, powers and procedures of any general independent bodies for investigating complaints relating to actions of the authorities shall be regulated by Act of Parliament.
> (2) Appointment to such bodies shall be made by the Second Chamber of the Parliament if their jurisdiction covers the actions of the central authorities. Members may be dismissed in cases prescribed by Act of Parliament.

5. The legislature has effective powers of oversight over the agencies of coercion (the military, organs of law enforcement, intelligence services, and the secret police).

Yes. The legislature has effective powers of oversight over the agencies of coercion.

6. The legislature appoints the prime minister.

Yes. While the king formally appoints the prime minister, he selects the candidate who enjoys the support of the legislature.

> Article 43
> The Prime Minister and the other Ministers shall be appointed and dismissed by Royal Decree.

7. The legislature's approval is required to confirm the appointment of ministers; or the legislature itself appoints ministers.

No. Formally, ministers are appointed by the crown. In practice, the king appoints ministers on the recommendation of the prime minister, and the appointments do not require the legislature's approval.

> Article 43
> The Prime Minister and the other Ministers shall be appointed and dismissed by Royal Decree.

8. The country lacks a presidency entirely or there is a presidency, but the president is elected by the legislature.

Yes. The country lacks a presidency. The monarch is the head of state.

> Article 24
> The title to the Throne shall be hereditary and shall vest in the legitimate descendants of King William I, Prince of Orange-Nassau.

> Article 30
> (1) A successor to the Throne may be appointed by Act of Parliament if it appears that there will otherwise be no successor. The Bill shall be presented by or on

behalf of the King, upon which the Chambers shall be dissolved. The newly convened Chambers shall discuss and decide upon the matter in joint session. Such a Bill shall be passed only if at least two-thirds of the votes cast are in favor.
> (2) The Chambers shall be dissolved if there is no successor on the death or abdication of the King. The newly convened Chambers shall meet in joint session within four months of the decease or abdication in order to decide on the appointment of a King. They may appoint a successor only if at least two-thirds of the votes cast are in favor.

9. The legislature can vote no confidence in the government.

Yes. The legislature can vote no confidence in the government.

10. The legislature is immune from dissolution by the executive.

No. The crown, on the advice of the prime minister, can dissolve the legislature.

> Article 64
> (1) Each of the Chambers may be dissolved by Royal Decree.

11. Any executive initiative on legislation requires ratification or approval by the legislature before it takes effect; that is, the executive lacks decree power.

Yes. Formally, the monarch has decree power. In practice, the crown and the government lack the power to issue decrees that have the force of law.

> Article 47
> All Acts of Parliament and Royal Decrees shall be signed by the King and by one or more Ministers or State Secretaries.

12. Laws passed by the legislature are veto-proof or essentially veto-proof; that is, the executive lacks veto power, or has veto power but the veto can be overridden by a majority in the legislature.

Yes. The executive lacks veto power.

13. The legislature's laws are supreme and not subject to judicial review.

Yes. The legislature's laws are supreme and not subject to judicial review.

> Article 120
> The constitutionality of Acts of Parliament and treaties shall not be reviewed by the courts.

14. The legislature has the right to initiate bills in all policy jurisdictions; the executive lacks gatekeeping authority.

Yes. The legislature can initiate bills in all policy jurisdictions.

15. Expenditure of funds appropriated by the legislature is mandatory; the executive lacks the power to impound funds appropriated by the legislature.

Yes. The executive lacks the power to impound funds appropriated by the legislature.

16. The legislature controls the resources that finance its own internal operation and provide for the perquisites of its own members.

Yes. The legislature enjoys financial autonomy.

17. Members of the legislature are immune from arrest and/or criminal prosecution.

No. Legislative immunity extends to official parliamentary business only. Legislators are subject to arrest for common crimes.

Article 71
Members of the Parliament, Ministers, State Secretaries, and other persons taking part in deliberations may not be prosecuted or otherwise held liable in law for anything they say during the sittings of the Parliament or of its committees or for anything they submit to them in writing.

18. All members of the legislature are elected; the executive lacks the power to appoint any members of the legislature.

Yes. All members of the legislature are elected.

Article 53
(1) The members of both Chambers shall be elected by proportional representation within the limits to be laid down by Act of Parliament.

19. The legislature alone, without the involvement of any other agencies, can change the Constitution.

Yes. The legislature can change the constitution through a complicated procedure. The sitting legislature can propose a constitutional amendment, and then, following an election, the subsequent legislature can approve the amendment with a two-thirds majority vote.

Article 137
(1) An Act of Parliament shall be passed stating that an amendment to the Constitution in the form proposed shall be considered.
(2) The Second Chamber may divide a Bill presented for this purpose into a number of separate Bills, either upon a proposal presented by or on behalf of the King or otherwise.
(3) The two Chambers of the Parliament shall be dissolved after the Act referred to in the first paragraph has been published.
(4) The newly elected Chambers shall consider the Bill and it shall be passed only if at least two thirds of the votes cast are in favor.

(5) The Second Chamber may divide a Bill for the amendment of the Constitution into a number of separate Bills, either upon a proposal presented by or on behalf of the King or otherwise, if at least two-thirds of the votes cast are in favor.

20. The legislature's approval is necessary for the declaration of war.

Yes. The legislature's approval is necessary for the declaration of war.

Article 96
(1) A declaration that the Kingdom is in a state of war shall not be made without the prior approval of the Parliament.
(2) Such approval shall not be required in cases where consultation with Parliament proves to be impossible as a consequence of the actual existence of a state of war.

21. The legislature's approval is necessary to ratify treaties with foreign countries.

Yes. The legislature's approval is necessary to ratify international treaties.

Article 91
(1) The Kingdom shall not be bound by treaties, nor shall such treaties be denounced without the prior approval of the Parliament. The cases in which approval is not required shall be specified by Act of Parliament.
(3) Any provisions of a treaty that conflict with the Constitution or which lead to conflicts with it may be approved by the Chambers of the Parliament only if at least two-thirds of the votes cast are in favor.

22. The legislature has the power to grant amnesty.

Yes. The legislature can grant amnesty through law.

23. The legislature has the power of pardon.

Yes. The legislature has the power of pardon.

Article 122
(2) Pardons shall be granted by or pursuant to Act of Parliament.

24. The legislature reviews and has the right to reject appointments to the judiciary; or the legislature itself appoints members of the judiciary.

Yes. The members of the Supreme Court are appointed by the crown on the nomination of the legislature.

Article 117
(1) Members of the judiciary responsible for the administration of justice and the Procurator General at the Supreme Court shall be appointed for life by Royal Decree.

Article 118
(1) The members of the Supreme Court of the Netherlands shall be appointed from a list of three persons drawn up by the Second Chamber of the Parliament.

25. The chairman of the central bank is appointed by the legislature.

No. The monarch appoints the governor of the Netherlands Bank.

26. The legislature has a substantial voice in the operation of the state-owned media.

No. The legislature lacks a substantial voice in the operation of the public media.

27. The legislature is regularly in session.

Yes. The legislature regularly meets in ordinary session.

28. Each legislator has a personal secretary.

Yes.

29. Each legislator has at least one non-secretarial staff member with policy expertise.

No.

30. Legislators are eligible for re-election without any restriction.

Yes. There are no restrictions on re-election.

31. A seat in the legislature is an attractive enough position that legislators are generally interested in and seek re-election.

Yes.

32. The re-election of incumbent legislators is common enough that at any given time the legislature contains a significant number of highly experienced members.

Yes. Re-election rates are sufficiently high to produce a significant number of highly experienced members.

PARLIAMENT OF NEW ZEALAND

Expert consultants: Jonathan Boston, Malcolm Mackerras, Elizabeth McLeay, Alan McRobie, Susan M. Smith

Score: .69

Influence over executive (8/9)		Institutional autonomy (7/9)		Specified powers (1/8)		Institutional capacity (6/6)	
1. replace	X	10. no dissolution		19. amendments	X	27. sessions	X
2. serve as ministers	X	11. no decree	X	20. war		28. secretary	X
3. interpellate	X	12. no veto	X	21. treaties		29. staff	X
4. investigate	X	13. no review	X	22. amnesty		30. no term limits	X
5. oversee police	X	14. no gatekeeping	X	23. pardon		31. seek re-election	X
6. appoint PM	X	15. no impoundment	X	24. judiciary		32. experience	X
7. appoint ministers		16. control resources	X	25. central bank			
8. lack president	X	17. immunity		26. media			
9. no confidence	X	18. all elected	X				

The Parliament of New Zealand was established in 1852 to represent the country in the British Empire. The directly elected legislature is paired with an executive branch that consists of a prime minister as the head of government and a Governor General (formerly the British monarch's representative) as the head of state. New Zealand achieved full independence from Britain in 1947. It lacks a formal constitution. Rather, its fundamental law consists of a series of legal documents and acts including the Constitution Act of 1986 (from which excerpts cited below are taken).

The legislature is the main stage of national politics. It possesses nearly every means of influencing the executive recorded in this survey. It is subject to dissolution and legislators lack criminal immunity, but otherwise the legislature has complete institutional autonomy. In sharp contrast to its powers in other areas, the legislature exercises but a single specified power (the right to change the constitution). The legislature has robust institutional capacity.

SURVEY

1. The legislature alone, without the involvement of any other agencies, can impeach the president or replace the prime minister.

Yes. The legislature can remove the prime minister with a vote of no confidence.

2. Ministers may serve simultaneously as members of the legislature.

Yes. Ministers are selected from, and required to serve simultaneously in, the legislature.

> Section 6
> A person may be appointed and may hold office as a member of the Executive Council or as a Minister of the Crown only if that person is a member of Parliament.

3. The legislature has powers of summons over executive branch officials and hearings with executive branch officials testifying before the legislature or its committees are regularly held.

Yes. Legislative committees regularly interpellate officials from the executive.

4. The legislature can conduct independent investigation of the chief executive and the agencies of the executive.

Yes. The legislature can investigate the executive.

5. The legislature has effective powers of oversight over the agencies of coercion (the military, organs of law enforcement, intelligence services, and the secret police).

Yes. The legislature has effective powers of oversight over the agencies of coercion.

6. The legislature appoints the prime minister.

Yes. The Governor General appoints as prime minister the candidate who enjoys the support of the legislature.

7. The legislature's approval is required to confirm the appointment of ministers; or the legislature itself appoints ministers.

No. The Governor General appoints ministers on the recommendation of the prime minister, and the appointments do not require the legislature's approval.

8. The country lacks a presidency entirely or there is a presidency, but the president is elected by the legislature.

Yes. The country lacks a presidency. The Governor General is the head of state.

> Article 2
> (1) The Sovereign in right of New Zealand is the head of State of New Zealand, and shall be known by the royal style and titles proclaimed from time to time.
> (2) The Governor-General appointed by the Sovereign is the Sovereign's representative in New Zealand.

9. The legislature can vote no confidence in the government.

Yes. The legislature can vote no confidence in the government.

10. The legislature is immune from dissolution by the executive.

No. The Governor General can, upon the advice of the prime minister, dissolve the legislature.

> Section 18
> (2) The Governor-General may by Proclamation prorogue or dissolve Parliament.

11. Any executive initiative on legislation requires ratification or approval by the legislature before it takes effect; that is, the executive lacks decree power.

Yes. The executive lacks decree power.

12. Laws passed by the legislature are veto-proof or essentially veto-proof; that is, the executive lacks veto power, or has veto power but the veto can be overridden by a majority in the legislature.

Yes. The executive lacks veto power. Formally, the Governor General could withhold assent from a bill. In practice, it would be unthinkable for the Governor General to withhold assent from a bill.

> Article 16
> A Bill passed by the House of Representatives shall become law when the Sovereign or the Governor-General assents to it and signs it in token of such assent.

13. The legislature's laws are supreme and not subject to judicial review.

Yes. The legislature's laws are supreme and not subject to judicial review.

14. The legislature has the right to initiate bills in all policy jurisdictions; the executive lacks gatekeeping authority.

Yes. The legislature can initiate bills in all policy jurisdictions.

15. Expenditure of funds appropriated by the legislature is mandatory; the executive lacks the power to impound funds appropriated by the legislature.

Yes. The executive lacks the power to impound funds appropriated by the legislature.

16. The legislature controls the resources that finance its own internal operation and provide for the perquisites of its own members.

Yes. The legislature enjoys financial autonomy. The running costs of the legislature and the salaries of legislators are a permanent charge on the government's budget and are not subject to annual appropriation. The payment of salary and allowances to the legislature is mandatory under an Act of Parliament and cannot be withheld.

17. Members of the legislature are immune from arrest and/or criminal prosecution.

No. Legislative immunity extends only to civil charges; it begins forty days before the start of a parliamentary session begins and extends to forty days after the session concludes. Legislators are subject to arrest at other times.

18. All members of the legislature are elected; the executive lacks the power to appoint any members of the legislature.

Yes. All members of the legislature are elected.

> Article 10
> (4) The House of Representatives shall have as its members those persons who are elected from time to time in accordance with the provisions of the Electoral Act 1956, and who shall be known as "members of Parliament."

19. The legislature alone, without the involvement of any other agencies, can change the Constitution.

Yes. The legislature can change the fundamental law through the normal legislative process.

20. The legislature's approval is necessary for the declaration of war.

No. The government can declare war without the legislature's approval.

21. The legislature's approval is necessary to ratify treaties with foreign countries.

No. The government can conclude international treaties without the legislature's approval.

22. The legislature has the power to grant amnesty.

No. The government has the power to grant amnesty.

23. The legislature has the power of pardon.

No. The Governor General has the power of pardon.

24. The legislature reviews and has the right to reject appointments to the judiciary; or the legislature itself appoints members of the judiciary.

No. The attorney general makes judicial appointments, and the appointments do not require the legislature's approval.

25. The chairman of the central bank is appointed by the legislature.

No. The government, on the recommendation of the State Services Commission, appoints the governor of the Reserve Bank of New Zealand.

26. The legislature has a substantial voice in the operation of the state-owned media.

No. Public television and public radio are governed by independent boards whose members are appointed by the government.

27. The legislature is regularly in session.

Yes. The legislature meets in ordinary session for about ten months each year.

> Section 17
> (1) The term of Parliament shall, unless Parliament is sooner dissolved, be 3 years from the day fixed for the return of the writs issued for the last preceding general election of members of the House of Representatives, and no longer.
> (2) Section 189 of the Electoral Act 1956 shall apply in respect of subsection (1) of this section.

28. Each legislator has a personal secretary.

Yes. As part of the running cost of parliament, each legislator is provided with a secretary in his or her parliamentary office and another secretary and office in his or her electoral district.

29. Each legislator has at least one non-secretarial staff member with policy expertise.

Yes. Each party has its own research unit within the parliament buildings paid for by the state. On average, there is at least one staff member with policy expertise for each legislator.

30. Legislators are eligible for re-election without any restriction.

Yes. There are no restrictions on re-election.

31. A seat in the legislature is an attractive enough position that legislators are generally interested in and seek re-election.

Yes.

32. The re-election of incumbent legislators is common enough that at any given time the legislature contains a significant number of highly experienced members.

Yes. Re-election rates are sufficiently high to produce a significant number of highly experienced members.

NATIONAL ASSEMBLY OF NICARAGUA (*ASAMBLEA NACIONAL*)

Expert consultants: Leslie E. Anderson, Nestor Davilo, Luís Humberto Guzmán, Nehemías López Carrión, José Luis Rivas Calero, Reinaldo Saily

Score: .69

Influence over executive (3/9)		Institutional autonomy (8/9)		Specified powers (6/8)		Institutional capacity (5/6)	
1. replace	X	10. no dissolution	X	19. amendments	X	27. sessions	X
2. serve as ministers		11. no decree	X	20. war	X	28. secretary	X
3. interpellate	X	12. no veto	X	21. treaties	X	29. staff	
4. investigate	X	13. no review		22. amnesty	X	30. no term limits	X
5. oversee police		14. no gatekeeping	X	23. pardon	X	31. seek re-election	X
6. appoint PM		15. no impoundment	X	24. judiciary	X	32. experience	X
7. appoint ministers		16. control resources	X	25. central bank			
8. lack president		17. immunity	X	26. media			
9. no confidence		18. all elected	X				

The National Assembly (*Asamblea Nacional*) of Nicaragua traces its origins to the 1809 colonial constitution established by Spain. Nicaragua became fully independent in 1838 but was ruled by the powerful Somoza family for the next century and a half. In 1979 the Somoza regime was overthrown amid a civil war. A new constitution in 1987 called for a unicameral National Assembly.

The legislature has significant power. Its ability to influence the executive is relatively modest. In other areas, however, the legislature's powers are considerable. The Assembly has significant institutional autonomy: Apart from the Supreme Court's power to review the constitutionality of laws, the National Assembly possesses every measure of institutional autonomy measured in this survey. It also enjoys the bulk of the specified powers and prerogatives scored here, and it has a high level of institutional capacity.

SURVEY

1. The legislature alone, without the involvement of any other agencies, can impeach the president or replace the prime minister.

Yes. The legislature can impeach the president, here expressed as "deprive the President of the Republic of this immunity" with a two-thirds majority vote of its total membership.

Article 130
The National Assembly, by resolution approved by two-thirds of the votes of its members, may deprive the President of the Republic of this immunity. Public officers enjoying immunity in accordance with the Constitution may not be detained or prosecuted if the aforementioned procedure has not been followed, except for matters relating to family and labor. Immunity may be waived. This matter will be regulated by law.

2. Ministers may serve simultaneously as members of the legislature.

No. Ministers are prohibited from serving simultaneously in the legislature.

Article 134
2. The following persons may not run for Deputies, Proprietors or Substitutes:
a. Government ministers or vice ministers . . . unless they resign the office at least 12 months in advance of the election date.

3. The legislature has powers of summons over executive branch officials and hearings with executive branch officials testifying before the legislature or its committees are regularly held.

Yes. The legislature regularly interpellates officials from the executive.

Article 138
The National Assembly has the following powers:
4. To request reports from Ministers and Vice Ministers of the State, presidents or directors of autonomous and governmental entities. The National Assembly may also request their personal appearance and interpellation. Their appearance will be obligatory under the same constraints that are observed in judicial proceedings. If, as a consequence of the interpellation, the National Assembly, by an absolute majority of its members should consider that there are grounds for it, the interpellated functionary shall lose his immunity from that moment.

4. The legislature can conduct independent investigation of the chief executive and the agencies of the executive.

Yes. The legislature can investigate the executive.

Article 138
The National Assembly has the following powers:
18. Create permanent, special, and investigative committees.

5. The legislature has effective powers of oversight over the agencies of coercion (the military, organs of law enforcement, intelligence services, and the secret police).

No. The legislature lacks effective powers of oversight over the agencies of coercion.

6. The legislature appoints the prime minister.

No. The country lacks a prime minister.

7. The legislature's approval is required to confirm the appointment of ministers; or the legislature itself appoints ministers.

No. The president appoints ministers, and the appointments do not require the legislature's approval.

Article 150
The functions of the President of the Republic are the following:
6. To appoint and remove Ministers and Vice Ministers of State.

8. The country lacks a presidency entirely or there is a presidency, but the president is elected by the legislature.

No. The president is directly elected.

Article 146
The election of the President and Vice President of the Republic is made by universal, equal, direct, free and secret vote.

9. The legislature can vote no confidence in the government.

No. The legislature cannot vote no confidence in the government.

10. The legislature is immune from dissolution by the executive.

Yes. The legislature is immune from dissolution.

11. Any executive initiative on legislation requires ratification or approval by the legislature before it takes effect; that is, the executive lacks decree power.

Yes. The president lacks decree powers. The president can issue "decrees" to implement laws, but aside from emergency powers, the president cannot issue decrees that have the force of law.

Article 138
The National Assembly has the following powers:
28. Approve, reject, or amend the Executive Decree which declares the suspension of constitutional rights and guarantees or the State of Emergency, as well as their extensions.

Article 150
The functions of the President of the Republic are the following:
4. To issue executive decrees in administrative matters.
9. To decree and put into effect the suspension of rights and guarantees in the cases provided by this Political Constitution and to send the appropriate decree to the National Assembly within a period no longer than seventy-two hours for its approval, modification, or rejection.

12. Laws passed by the legislature are veto-proof or essentially veto-proof; that is, the executive lacks veto power, or has veto power but the veto can be overridden by a majority in the legislature.

Yes. The legislature can override a presidential veto by a majority vote of its total membership.

Article 142
The President of the Republic may veto totally or in part a bill of law within the fifteen days following its receipt. If the President of the Republic does not exercise this power nor sanction, promulgate, or publish the bill, the President of the National Assembly shall order the law to be published in any national written diffusion media.

Article 143
A bill of law partially or totally vetoed by the President of the Republic must be returned to the National Assembly with expression of the reasons for the veto; it can reject it with a vote of half the total plus one of its Deputies, in which case the President of the National Assembly shall order the law to be published.

Article 150
The functions of the President of the Republic are the following:
3. To exercise the power of initiative of law and the right of veto, in conformity with that established by this Constitution.

13. The legislature's laws are supreme and not subject to judicial review.

No. The Supreme Court can review the constitutionality of laws.

> Article 164
> The functions of the Supreme Court of Justice are:
> 4. To take cognizance of and resolve the recourses of the unconstitutionality of laws.

14. The legislature has the right to initiate bills in all policy jurisdictions; the executive lacks gatekeeping authority.

Yes. The legislature can initiate bills in all policy jurisdictions.

15. Expenditure of funds appropriated by the legislature is mandatory; the executive lacks the power to impound funds appropriated by the legislature.

Yes. The executive lacks the power to impound funds appropriated by the legislature.

16. The legislature controls the resources that finance its own internal operation and provide for the perquisites of its own members.

Yes. The legislature enjoys financial autonomy.

17. Members of the legislature are immune from arrest and/or criminal prosecution.

Yes. Legislators are immune.

> Article 139
> Deputies shall be exempt from responsibility for their opinions and votes cast in the National Assembly and enjoy immunity in conformity with the law.

18. All members of the legislature are elected; the executive lacks the power to appoint any members of the legislature.

Yes. All members of the legislature are elected.

> Article 132
> The National Assembly is composed of ninety Deputies with their respective substitutes elected by universal, equal, direct, free, and secret suffrage through the system of proportional representation.

19. The legislature alone, without the involvement of any other agencies, can change the Constitution.

Yes. The legislature alone can change the constitution through a complicated procedure. For a "partial reform" amendment, the sitting legislature can propose the amendment, and then, following an election, the subsequent legislature can approve the amendment. A total constitutional revision requires a two-thirds majority vote from a specially elected Constituent National Assembly.

Article 191
The National Assembly has the authority to partially reform this Political Constitution and to take cognizance of and resolve concerning the initiative of its total revision. The initiative for partial reform corresponds to the President of the Republic or to one-third of the Deputies of the National Assembly. The initiative for total reform corresponds to half plus one of the Deputies of the National Assembly.

Article 192
The initiative of partial reform must specify the article or articles to be reformed with a statement of reasons. It must be sent to a special commission which shall dictate an opinion within a period of no more than sixty days. The bill of reform shall then follow the same process as for the creation of a law. The initiative of partial reform must be discussed in two legislatures.

Article 193
A total revision initiative shall follow the same process established in the previous article, in terms of its presentation and finding. Upon the approval of a total revision initiative, the National Assembly shall establish a time period for holding elections for a Constituent National Assembly. The National Assembly shall retain its mandate until the installation of the new Constituent National Assembly. While the new Constitution is not yet approved by the Constituent National Assembly, this Constitution shall remain in effect.

Article 194
Approval of a partial reform shall require a favorable vote by sixty percent of the Deputies. Two-thirds of the total number of Deputies are required in the case of approval of the total revision initiative. The President of the Republic shall promulgate the partial reform and in this case may not exercise the right to veto.

Article 195
The reform of constitutional laws shall be made in accordance with the procedure established for partial reform of the Constitution, with the exception of the requirement of the two legislatures.

20. The legislature's approval is necessary for the declaration of war.

Yes. The National Assembly's approval is necessary to authorize any external deployment of the armed forces.

> Article 138
> The National Assembly has the following powers:
> 26. Authorize or forbid armed forces from leaving the national territory.

21. The legislature's approval is necessary to ratify treaties with foreign countries.

Yes. The legislature's approval is necessary to ratify international treaties on most major issues.

> Article 138
> The National Assembly has the following powers:

12. Approving or rejecting international treaties, covenants, pacts, agreements, and contracts of an economic character, international commerce, regional integration, defense and security; those which increase external debt or risk the Nation's credit; and those which involve the juridical organization of the State. Said instruments will have to be presented to the National Assembly within a deadline of fifteen days beginning with their introduction; they may only be discussed and debated at that time in a general sense and will have to be approved or rejected at most within no more than sixty days counting from their presentation in the National Assembly. Once that deadline is past, for all legal purposes the instruments will be considered as having been approved.

Article 150
The functions of the President of the Republic are the following:
8. To direct the international relations of the Republic. To negotiate, hold and sign treaties, covenants, or agreements and other instruments provided for in paragraph 12 of Article 138 of the Political Constitution, for their approval by the National Assembly.

22. The legislature has the power to grant amnesty.

Yes. The legislature has the power to grant amnesty.

Article 138
The National Assembly has the following powers:
3. To grant amnesty and pardon on their own initiative or on the initiative of the President of the Republic.

23. The legislature has the power of pardon.

Yes. The legislature has the power of pardon.

Article 138
The National Assembly has the following powers:
3. To grant amnesty and pardon on their own initiative or on the initiative of the President of the Republic.

24. The legislature reviews and has the right to reject appointments to the judiciary; or the legislature itself appoints members of the judiciary.

Yes. The legislature elects the judges of the Supreme Court and of the Supreme Electoral Council.

Article 138
The National Assembly has the following powers:
7. To elect the Judges of the Supreme Court of Justice from separate lists proposed for every position by the President of the Republic and by the Deputies of the National Assembly, in consultation with the appropriate civilian associations. The deadline for presenting the lists will be fifteen days counting from the summoning of the National Assembly for their election. In the absence of lists presented by the President of the Republic, the proposals by Deputies of the National Assembly will be enough. Each Judge will be elected with the favorable vote of at least sixty percent of the Deputies of the National Assembly.

8. To elect Judges, proprietary and substitute, of the Supreme Electoral Council from separate lists proposed for each position by the President of the Republic and the Deputies of the National Assembly, in consultation with the appropriate civilian associations. The deadline for presenting the lists will be fifteen days counting from the summoning of the National Assembly for their election. In the absence of lists presented by the President of the Republic, the proposals by the Deputies of the National Assembly shall be enough. Each Judge shall be elected with the favorable vote of at least sixty percent of the Deputies of the National Assembly.

Article 163
The Supreme Court of Justice will consist of sixteen magistrates elected by the National Assembly for a period of five years... The National Assembly shall appoint a Co-judge for each magistrate. In the event of an absence, excuse, impediment or recusation of any of the magistrates, the Co-judges shall be called to serve in Full Court or in any of the Courts. The magistrates of the Supreme Court take office before the National Assembly, having previously taken the promise of law. They elect their President and Vice President, among themselves, by majority of votes and for a one-year term. They may be reelected.

25. The chairman of the central bank is appointed by the legislature.

No. The president appoints the president of the Central Bank of Nicaragua.

26. The legislature has a substantial voice in the operation of the state-owned media.

No. The legislature lacks a substantial voice in the operation of the public media.

27. The legislature is regularly in session.

Yes. The legislature regularly meets in ordinary session.

Article 138
The National Assembly has the following powers:
31. Hold ordinary and extraordinary sessions.

28. Each legislator has a personal secretary.

Yes.

29. Each legislator has at least one non-secretarial staff member with policy expertise.

No.

30. Legislators are eligible for re-election without any restriction.

Yes. There are no restrictions on re-election.

31. A seat in the legislature is an attractive enough position that legislators are generally interested in and seek re-election.

Yes.

32. The re-election of incumbent legislators is common enough that at any given time the legislature contains a significant number of highly experienced members.

Yes. Nicaragua held five rounds of parliamentary elections between 1984 and 2006, and re-election rates have been sufficiently high to produce a significant number of highly experienced members.

NATIONAL ASSEMBLY OF NIGER (*ASSEMBLÉE NATIONALE*)

Expert consultants: Monique Alexis, H. Badjé, Sheryl Cowan, Foukori Fati, Barrie Hofmann, Ahmed Mohamed

Score: .50

Influence over executive (3/9)		Institutional autonomy (7/9)		Specified powers (3/8)		Institutional capacity (3/6)	
1. replace		10. no dissolution		19. amendments		27. sessions	
2. serve as ministers		11. no decree	X	20. war	X	28. secretary	
3. interpellate	X	12. no veto	X	21. treaties	X	29. staff	
4. investigate	X	13. no review	X	22. amnesty	X	30. no term limits	X
5. oversee police		14. no gatekeeping	X	23. pardon		31. seek re-election	X
6. appoint PM		15. no impoundment		24. judiciary		32. experience	X
7. appoint ministers		16. control resources	X	25. central bank			
8. lack president		17. immunity	X	26. media			
9. no confidence	X	18. all elected	X				

The National Assembly (*Assemblée nationale*) of Niger was created in 1960 upon independence from France. Formally Niger had a Westminster-style system, but in practice, single-party, military-backed regimes ruled for the next thirty years. Civilian rule was reintroduced in 1989, but single-party dominance persisted. Reforms in 1992 paved the way for multiparty elections. The current constitution, adopted in 1999, is inspired by the French model and calls for a unicameral parliament, a directly elected president, and a prime minister and cabinet selected by the president.

The legislature has some meaningful power. It has little sway over the executive but enjoys considerable institutional autonomy. For example, the Assembly is unencumbered by presidential decree and veto powers, and its laws are de facto supreme and not subject to judicial review. The legislature exercises only two of the eight specified powers assessed here. Its institutional capacity is modest, curbed by the brevity of legislative sessions and the absence of staff support for legislators.

SURVEY

1. The legislature alone, without the involvement of any other agencies, can impeach the president or replace the prime minister.

No. Presidential impeachment requires the involvement of the High Court of Justice. The legislature can remove the prime minister with a vote of no confidence.

> Article 42
>
> In case of an impeachment of the President of the Republic before the High Court of Justice, his interim shall be performed by the President of the Constitutional Court who exercises all the duties of the President of the Republic, with the exception of the duties mentioned in paragraph 8 of this article. He may not stand as candidate in the presidential elections.

> Article 88
>
> The Prime Minister, after deliberation by the Council of Ministers, may make the Government's program or possibly a statement of its general policy an issue of its responsibility before the National Assembly. The National Assembly may raise an issue of the Government's responsibility by passing a motion censure. Such a motion is not admissible unless it is signed by at

least one-tenth of the members of the National Assembly. Voting may not take place within forty-eight hours after the motion has been introduced. Only the votes in favor of the motion censure are counted; the motion of censure is not adopted unless it is voted for by the majority of the members of the Assembly. The Prime Minister may, after deliberation by the Council of Ministers, make the passing of a bill an issue of the Government's responsibility before the National Assembly. In that event, the bill shall be considered adopted unless a motion of censure, introduced within the subsequent twenty-four hours, is carried as provided for in the preceding paragraph.

Article 89
When the National Assembly adopts a motion of censure or when it fails to endorse the program or a statement of general policy of the Government, the Prime Minister must tender the resignation of the Government to the President of the Republic.

2. Ministers may serve simultaneously as members of the legislature.

No. Ministers are prohibited from serving simultaneously in the legislature.

Article 64
The functions of a member of the Government shall be incompatible with the exercise of any parliamentary mandate, of any function of professional representation at the national or local level, of any public work and of any professional activity.

3. The legislature has powers of summons over executive branch officials and hearings with executive branch officials testifying before the legislature or its committees are regularly held.

Yes. The legislature regularly interpellates officials from the executive.

Article 80
The members of the National Assembly, either individually, or collectively may question the Prime Minister or any member of the Government by means of a petition.
The members of the National Assembly may as well obtain, by means of written or oral questions, all information on the activities or the administrative acts of the Government.

4. The legislature can conduct independent investigation of the chief executive and the agencies of the executive.

Yes. The legislature can investigate the executive.

5. The legislature has effective powers of oversight over the agencies of coercion (the military, organs of law enforcement, intelligence services, and the secret police).

No. The legislature lacks effective powers of oversight over the agencies of coercion.

6. The legislature appoints the prime minister.

No. The president appoints the prime minister from a list proposed by the legislature.

Article 45
The President of the Republic shall appoint the Prime Minister from a list of three (3) people proposed by the majority. The majority shall be composed of a party or of a coalition of parties detaining the majority in the National Assembly. On the proposal of the Prime Minister, the President shall appoint other members of the Government and terminate their appointments.
The President of the Republic shall put an end to the functions of the Prime Minister upon presentation by the Prime Minister of the Government's resignation.

7. The legislature's approval is required to confirm the appointment of ministers; or the legislature itself appoints ministers.

No. The president appoints ministers on the proposal of the prime minister, and the appointments do not require the legislature's approval.

Article 45
The President of the Republic shall appoint the Prime Minister from a list of three (3) people proposed by the majority. The majority shall be composed of a party or of a coalition of parties detaining the majority in the National Assembly. On the proposal of the Prime Minister, the President shall appoint other members of the Government and terminate their appointments.
The President of the Republic shall put an end to the functions of the Prime Minister upon presentation by the Prime Minister of the Government's resignation.

8. The country lacks a presidency entirely or there is a presidency, but the president is elected by the legislature.

No. The president is directly elected.

Article 36
The President of the Republic is elected for five years by universal, free, direct, equal and secret suffrage. The President shall be re-eligible only once.

9. The legislature can vote no confidence in the government.

Yes. The legislature can vote no confidence in the government.

Article 88
The Prime Minister, after deliberation by the Council of Ministers, may make the Government's program or possibly a statement of its general policy an issue of its responsibility before the National Assembly.
The National Assembly may raise an issue of the Government's responsibility by passing a motion censure. Such a motion is not admissible unless it is signed by at least one-tenth of the members of the National Assembly. Voting may not take place within forty-eight hours after the motion has been introduced. Only the votes

in favor of the motion censure are counted; the motion of censure is not adopted unless it is voted for by the majority of the members of the Assembly.

The Prime Minister may, after deliberation by the Council of Ministers, make the passing of a bill an issue of the Government's responsibility before the National Assembly. In that event, the bill shall be considered adopted unless a motion of censure, introduced within the subsequent twenty-four hours, is carried as provided for in the preceding paragraph.

Article 89

When the National Assembly adopts a motion of censure or when it fails to endorse the program or a statement of general policy of the Government, the Prime Minister must tender the resignation of the Government to the President of the Republic.

10. The legislature is immune from dissolution by the executive.

No. The president can dissolve the legislature.

Article 48

The President of the Republic may, after consultation of the Prime Minister and of the President of the National Assembly, pronounce the dissolution of the National Assembly.

11. Any executive initiative on legislation requires ratification or approval by the legislature before it takes effect; that is, the executive lacks decree power.

Yes. The president lacks decree power.

12. Laws passed by the legislature are veto-proof or essentially veto-proof; that is, the executive lacks veto power, or has veto power but the veto can be overridden by a majority in the legislature.

Yes. The legislature can override a presidential veto by a majority vote of its total membership.

Article 47

The President of the Republic shall promulgate the laws within fifteen days, following the transmission that is done to him by the President of the National Assembly.

This time limit shall be reduced to five days in case of urgency declared by the National Assembly. The President of the Republic may, before the expiry of these time limits, address a request to the National Assembly for a second deliberation of the law of some of its articles. This deliberation may not be rejected. If after a second reading, the National Assembly votes the text at the absolute majority of its members, the law shall be promulgated of full right and published in accordance to the procedure of urgency.

13. The legislature's laws are supreme and not subject to judicial review.

Yes. In practice, the legislature's laws are supreme because the Constitutional Court is unable to

exercise its formal authority to review the constitutionality of laws.

Article 84

Matters other than those that fall within the domain of the law are of a regulatory character.

Texts of legislative form passed concerning these matters prior to the entry into force of this Constitution may be amended by decree issued after consultation with the Constitutional Court.

Article 92

Bills, projects and amendments which are not matters for law or which violate morality shall not be admissible. The inadmissibility shall be pronounced by the President of the National Assembly.

In case of disagreement, the Constitutional Court, at the request of the Prime Minister or of the President of the National Assembly, shall rule within eight days.

Article 103

The Constitutional Court is the competent jurisdiction in constitutional and electoral matters. It is in charge of ascertaining the constitutionality of the laws, of ordinances as well as the conformity of international treaties and agreements to the Constitution. It interprets the provisions of the Constitution. It controls the conformity, the transparency and the sincerity of the referendum, the presidential, legislative and local elections. It has competence over electoral litigation and proclaims the definitive results of elections.

Article 115

The decisions of the Constitutional Court are not susceptible to any appeal. They are binding on public authorities and on all other administrative, civil, military and judicial authorities.

14. The legislature has the right to initiate bills in all policy jurisdictions; the executive lacks gatekeeping authority.

Yes. The legislature can initiate bills in all policy jurisdictions.

15. Expenditure of funds appropriated by the legislature is mandatory; the executive lacks the power to impound funds appropriated by the legislature.

No. The president can impound funds appropriated by the legislature.

16. The legislature controls the resources that finance its own internal operation and provide for the perquisites of its own members.

Yes. The legislature enjoys financial autonomy.

17. Members of the legislature are immune from arrest and/or criminal prosecution.

Yes. Legislators are immune with the common exception for cases of *flagrante delicto,* here expressed as a "flagrant offence."

Article 70

The members of the National Assembly enjoy parliamentary immunity. No deputy may be prosecuted, searched, arrested, detained or judged on the basis of the opinions or the votes expressed by him in the exercise of his functions. Except in case of flagrant offence, no deputy can be prosecuted or arrested, during the period of the sessions, in matters of misdemeanors or serious crimes except with the authorization of the National Assembly. A deputy may be arrested out of session only with the authorization of the Bureau of the National Assembly, except in case of flagrant offence, of authorized prosecutions or of final condemnations.

18. All members of the legislature are elected; the executive lacks the power to appoint any members of the legislature.

Yes. All members of the legislature are elected.

Article 67

The Deputies shall be elected by universal, free, direct, equal and secret suffrage.

19. The legislature alone, without the involvement of any other agencies, can change the Constitution.

No. Constitutional amendments require approval in a popular referendum.

Article 134

The initiative for the revision of the Constitution belongs concurrently to the President of the Republic and the members of the National Assembly.

Article 135

In order to be taken into consideration, the project or bill to amend the Constitution must be voted by a majority of three-fourths of the members composing the National Assembly. If the project to amend the Constitution has been approved by a majority of four-fifths of the members composing the National Assembly, the amendment is approved. In default, the project or bill to amend the Constitution is submitted to Referendum.

20. The legislature's approval is necessary for the declaration of war.

Yes. The legislature's approval is necessary for the declaration of war.

Article 54

The President of the Republic, after deliberation of the Council of Ministers, shall announce the State of urgency in the conditions determined by the law.

Article 85

A declaration of war and the sending of military troupes abroad shall be authorized by the National Assembly.

21. The legislature's approval is necessary to ratify treaties with foreign countries.

Yes. The legislature's approval is necessary to ratify international treaties.

Article 129

The President of the Republic negotiates and ratifies treaties and international agreements.

Article 130

Defense and peace treaties and agreements relating to international organizations, those which modify the internal laws of the State and those which commit the finances of the State may only be ratified by virtue of a law.

22. The legislature has the power to grant amnesty.

Yes. The legislature has the power to grant amnesty.

Article 81

The law establishes the regulations concerning… amnesty.

23. The legislature has the power of pardon.

No. The president has the power of pardon.

Article 55

The President of the Republic shall have the right of pardon.

24. The legislature reviews and has the right to reject appointments to the judiciary; or the legislature itself appoints members of the judiciary.

No. The president makes judicial appointments, and the appointments do not require the approval of the legislature. The legislature does, however, propose one of the seven members of the Constitutional Court.

Article 101

Judges shall be appointed by the President of the Republic on proposition of the Minister of Justice, Keeper of the Seals, after consultation with the High Council of the Judiciary.

Article 104

The Constitutional Court consists of seven members of at least of forty years of age.

The Court consists of: two persons having extended professional experiences with one being proposed by the Bureau of the National Assembly and one proposed by the President of the Republic; two magistrates elected by their peers; one lawyer elected by his peers; one professor from the Faculty of Law holding at least a doctorate in public law elected by his peers; a representative of the Associations of Defense of Human Rights recognized for his expertise in public law. The members of the Constitutional Court are appointed for six years by decree of the President of the Republic. Their mandate is not renewable. One-third of the membership of the Constitutional Court is renewed every two years.

25. The chairman of the central bank is appointed by the legislature.

No. Niger is a member of the Central Bank of West African States, whose governor is selected by the member states.

26. The legislature has a substantial voice in the operation of the state-owned media.

No. The legislature lacks a substantial voice in the operation of the public media.

27. The legislature is regularly in session.

No. The legislature meets in ordinary session for less than five months each year.

> Article 73
> Each year, the National Assembly meets as of right in two ordinary sessions on convocation of its President. The first session opens the first week of the month of March and must not exceed ninety days. The second session, called the budgetary session, shall open the first week of the month of October and must not exceed sixty days.

28. Each legislator has a personal secretary.

No.

29. Each legislator has at least one non-secretarial staff member with policy expertise.

No.

30. Legislators are eligible for re-election without any restriction.

Yes. There are no restrictions on re-election.

31. A seat in the legislature is an attractive enough position that legislators are generally interested in and seek re-election.

Yes.

32. The re-election of incumbent legislators is common enough that at any given time the legislature contains a significant number of highly experienced members.

Yes. Niger held five rounds of National Assembly elections between 1993 and 2004. Re-election rates are sufficiently high to produce a significant number of highly experienced members.

NATIONAL ASSEMBLY OF NIGERIA

Expert consultants: Etannibi Alemika, Peter Lewis, Oyeleye Oyediran, Rebecca Sako-John, Richard L. Sklar

Score: .47

Influence over executive (3/9)		Institutional autonomy (5/9)		Specified powers (2/8)		Institutional capacity (5/6)	
1. replace		10. no dissolution	X	19. amendments		27. sessions	X
2. serve as ministers		11. no decree	X	20. war	X	28. secretary	X
3. interpellate	X	12. no veto		21. treaties	X	29. staff	
4. investigate	X	13. no review		22. amnesty		30. no term limits	X
5. oversee police		14. no gatekeeping	X	23. pardon		31. seek re-election	X
6. appoint PM		15. no impoundment		24. judiciary		32. experience	X
7. appoint ministers	X	16. control resources	X	25. central bank			
8. lack president		17. immunity		26. media			
9. no confidence		18. all elected	X				

The National Assembly of Nigeria was formally established in the 1963 constitution, following the achievement of independence from Great Britain in 1960. The document called for a Westminster-style parliamentary system. In 1979 Nigeria adopted a new constitution that established a presidential system with a bicameral National Assembly consisting of a lower house, the House of Representatives, and an upper house, the Senate. The legislature was sidelined for much of the post-independence period as the country was ruled intermittently by military dictators. Military rule ended in 1999, leading to presidential and legislative elections.

The legislature has middling powers. Its influence over the executive is not expansive. It has some institutional autonomy; most notably, the president lacks the powers to rule by decree or to dissolve the legislature. The legislature holds two of the eight specified prerogatives assessed here. It also enjoys a good deal of institutional capacity.

SURVEY

1. The legislature alone, without the involvement of any other agencies, can impeach the president or replace the prime minister.

No. Presidential impeachment requires the involvement of a special panel appointed by the chief justice of Nigeria.

Article 143

(1) The President or Vice-President may be removed from office in accordance with the provisions of this section.

(2) Whenever a notice of any allegation in writing signed by not less than one-third of the members of the National Assembly –

(a) is presented to the President of the Senate;

(b) stating that the holder of the office of President or Vice-President is guilty of gross misconduct in the performance of the functions of his office, detailed particulars of which shall be specified, the President of the Senate shall within seven days of the receipt of the notice cause a copy thereof to be served on the holder of the office and on each member of the National Assembly, and shall also cause any statement made in reply to the allegation by the holder of the office to be served on each member of the National Assembly.

(3) Within fourteen days of the presentation of the notice to the President of the Senate (whether or not any statement was made by the holder of the office in reply to the allegation contained in the notice) each House of the National Assembly shall resolve by motion without any debate whether or not the allegation shall be investigated.

(4) A motion of the National Assembly that the allegation be investigated shall not be declared as having been passed, unless it is supported by the votes of not less than two-thirds majority of all the members of each House of the National Assembly.

(5) Within seven days of the passing of a motion under the foregoing provisions, the Chief Justice of Nigeria shall at the request of the President of the Senate appoint a Panel of seven persons who in his opinion are of unquestionable integrity, not being members of any public service, legislative house or political party, to investigate the allegation as provided in this section.

(6) The holder of an office whose conduct is being investigated under this section shall have the right to defend himself in person and be represented before the Panel by legal practitioners of his own choice.

(7) A Panel appointed under this section shall –

(a) have such powers and exercise its functions in accordance with such procedure as may be prescribed by the National Assembly; and

(b) within three months of its appointment report its findings to each House of the National Assembly.

(8) Where the Panel reports to each House of the National Assembly that the allegation has not been proved, no further proceedings shall be taken in respect of the matter.

(9) Where the report of the Panel is that the allegation against the holder of the office has been proved, then within fourteen days of the receipt of the report, each House of the National Assembly shall consider the report, and if by a resolution of each House of the National Assembly supported by not less than two-thirds majority of all its members, the report of the Panel is adopted, then the holder of the office shall stand removed from office as from the date of the adoption of the report.

(10) No proceedings or determination of the Panel or of the National Assembly or any matter relating thereto shall be entertained or questioned in any court.

(11) In this section –

"gross misconduct" means a grave violation or breach of the provisions of this Constitution or a misconduct of such nature as amounts in the opinion of the National Assembly to gross misconduct.

2. Ministers may serve simultaneously as members of the legislature.

No. Ministers are prohibited from serving simultaneously in the legislature.

Article 147

(4) Where a member of the National Assembly or of a House of Assembly is appointed as Minister of the Government of the Federation, he shall be deemed to have resigned his membership of the National Assembly or of the House of Assembly on his taking the oath of office as Minister.

3. The legislature has powers of summons over executive branch officials and hearings with executive branch officials testifying before the legislature or its committees are regularly held.

Yes. The legislature regularly interpellates officials from the executive.

Article 88

(1) Subject to the provisions of this Constitution, each House of the National Assembly shall have power by resolution published in its journal or in the Official Gazette of the Government of the Federation to direct or cause to be directed an investigation into –

(a) any matter or thing with respect to which it has power to make laws; and

(b) the conduct of affairs of any person, authority, Ministry or government department charged, or intended to be charged, with the duty of or responsibility for –

(i) executing or administering laws enacted by the National Assembly, and

(ii) disbursing or administering moneys appropriated or to be appropriated by the National Assembly.

(2) The powers conferred on the National Assembly under the provisions of this section are exercisable only for the purpose of enabling it to –

(a) make laws with respect to any matter within its legislative competence and correct any defects in existing laws; and

(b) expose corruption, inefficiency or waste in the execution or administration of laws within its legislative competence and in the disbursement or administration of funds appropriated by it.

Article 89

(1) For the purposes of any investigation under section 88 of this Constitution and subject to the provisions thereof, the Senate or the House of Representatives or a committee appointed in accordance with section 62 of this Constitution shall have power to –

(a) procure all such evidence, written or oral, direct or circumstantial, as it may think necessary or desirable, and examine all persons as witnesses whose evidence may be material or relevant to the subject matter;

(b) require such evidence to be given on oath;

(c) summon any person in Nigeria to give evidence at any place or produce any document or other thing in his possession or under his control, and examine him as a witness and require him to produce any document or other thing in his possession or under his control, subject to all just exceptions; and

(d) issue a warrant to compel the attendance of any person who, after having been summoned to attend, fails, refuses or neglects to do so and does not excuse such failure, refusal or neglect to the satisfaction of the House or the committee in question, and order him to pay all costs which may have been occasioned in compelling his attendance or by reason of his failure, refusal or neglect to obey the summons, and also to impose such fine as may be prescribed for any such failure, refusal or neglect; and any fine so imposed shall be recoverable in the same manner as a fine imposed by a court of law.

(2) A summons or warrant issued under this section may be served or executed by any member of the Nigeria Police Force or by any person authorised in that behalf by the President of the Senate or the Speaker of the House of Representatives, as the case may require.

4. The legislature can conduct independent investigation of the chief executive and the agencies of the executive.

Yes. The legislature can investigate the executive.

Article 88

(1) Subject to the provisions of this Constitution, each House of the National Assembly shall have power by resolution published in its journal or in the Official Gazette of the Government of the Federation to direct or cause to be directed an investigation into –

(a) any matter or thing with respect to which it has power to make laws; and

(b) the conduct of affairs of any person, authority, Ministry or government department charged, or intended to be charged, with the duty of or responsibility for –

(i) executing or administering laws enacted by the National Assembly, and

(ii) disbursing or administering moneys appropriated or to be appropriated by the National Assembly.

(2) The powers conferred on the National Assembly under the provisions of this section are exercisable only for the purpose of enabling it to –

(a) make laws with respect to any matter within its legislative competence and correct any defects in existing laws; and

(b) expose corruption, inefficiency or waste in the execution or administration of laws within its legislative competence and in the disbursement or administration of funds appropriated by it.

Article 89

(1) For the purposes of any investigation under section 88 of this Constitution and subject to the provisions thereof, the Senate or the House of Representatives or a committee appointed in accordance with section 62 of this Constitution shall have power to –

(a) procure all such evidence, written or oral, direct or circumstantial, as it may think necessary or desirable, and examine all persons as witnesses whose evidence may be material or relevant to the subject matter;

(b) require such evidence to be given on oath;

(c) summon any person in Nigeria to give evidence at any place or produce any document or other thing in his possession or under his control, and examine him as a witness and require him to produce any document or other thing in his possession or under his control, subject to all just exceptions; and

(d) issue a warrant to compel the attendance of any person who, after having been summoned to attend, fails, refuses or neglects to do so and does not excuse such failure, refusal or neglect to the satisfaction of the House or the committee in question, and order him to pay all costs which may have been occasioned in compelling his attendance or by reason of his failure, refusal or neglect to obey the summons, and also to impose such fine as may be prescribed for any such failure, refusal or neglect; and any fine so imposed shall be recoverable in the same manner as a fine imposed by a court of law.

(2) A summons or warrant issued under this section may be served or executed by any member of the Nigeria Police Force or by any person authorised in that behalf by the President of the Senate or the

Speaker of the House of Representatives, as the case may require.

5. The legislature has effective powers of oversight over the agencies of coercion (the military, organs of law enforcement, intelligence services, and the secret police).

No. The legislature lacks effective powers of oversight over the agencies of coercion.

6. The legislature appoints the prime minister.

No. There is no prime minister.

7. The legislature's approval is required to confirm the appointment of ministers; or the legislature itself appoints ministers.

Yes. The Senate's approval is necessary to confirm the president's ministerial appointments.

> Article 147
> (1) There shall be such offices of Ministers of the Government of the Federation as may be established by the President.
> (2) Any appointment to the office of Minister of the Government of the Federation shall, if the nomination of any person to such office is confirmed by the Senate, be made by the President.
> (3) Any appointment under subsection (2) of this section by the President shall be in conformity with the provisions of section 14(3) of this Constitution:
> Provided that in giving effect to the provisions aforesaid the President shall appoint at least one Minister from each State, who shall be an indigene of such State.

8. The country lacks a presidency entirely or there is a presidency, but the president is elected by the legislature.

No. The president is directly elected.

> Article 132
> (1) An election to the office of President shall be held on a date to be appointed by the Independent National Electoral Commission.

9. The legislature can vote no confidence in the government.

No. The legislature cannot vote no confidence in the government.

10. The legislature is immune from dissolution by the executive.

Yes. The legislature is immune from dissolution.

> Article 64
> (1) The Senate and the House of Representatives shall each stand dissolved at the expiration of a period of four years commencing from the date of the first sitting of the House.

11. Any executive initiative on legislation requires ratification or approval by the legislature before it takes effect; that is, the executive lacks decree power.

Yes. The president lacks decree power.

12. Laws passed by the legislature are veto-proof or essentially veto-proof; that is, the executive lacks veto power, or has veto power but the veto can be overridden by a majority in the legislature.

No. A two-thirds majority vote is required to override a presidential veto.

> Article 58
> (1) The power of the National Assembly to make laws shall be exercised by bills passed by both the Senate and the House of Representatives and, except as otherwise provided by subsection (5) of this section, assented to by the President.
> (2) A bill may originate in either the Senate or the House of Representatives and shall not become law unless it has been passed and, except as otherwise provided by this section and section 59 of this Constitution, assented to in accordance with the provisions of this section.
> (3) Where a bill has been passed by the House in which it originated, it shall be sent to the other House, and it shall be presented to the President for assent when it has been passed by that other House and agreement has been reached between the two Houses on any amendment made on it.
> (4) Where a bill is presented to the President for assent, he shall within thirty days thereof signify that he assents or that he withholds assent.
> (5) Where the President withholds his assent and the bill is again passed by each House by two-thirds majority, the bill shall become law and the assent of the President shall not be required.

13. The legislature's laws are supreme and not subject to judicial review.

No. The courts can review the constitutionality of laws.

> Article 295
> (1) Where any question as to the interpretation or application of this Constitution arises in any proceedings in any court of law in any part of Nigeria (other than in the Supreme Court, the Court of Appeal, the Federal High Court or a High Court) and the court is of the opinion that the question involves a substantial question of law, the court may, and shall if any of the parties to the proceedings so requests, refer the question to the Federal High Court or a High Court having jurisdiction in that part of Nigeria and the Federal High Court or the High Court shall
> (a) if it is of opinion that the question involves a substantial question of law, refer the question to the Court of Appeal; or

(b) if it is of opinion that the question does not involve a substantial question of law, remit the question to the court that made the reference to be disposed of in accordance with such directions as the Federal High Court or the High Court may think fit to give.

(2) Where any question as to the interpretation or application of this Constitution arises in any proceedings in the Federal High Court or a High Court, and the court is of opinion that the question involves a substantial question of law, the court may, and shall if any party to the proceedings so requests, refer the question to the Court of Appeal; and where any question is referred in pursuance of this subsection, the court shall give its decision upon the question and the court in which the question arose shall dispose of the case in accordance with that decision.

(3) Where any question as to the interpretation or application of this Constitution arises in any proceedings in the Court of Appeal and the court is of opinion that the question involves a substantial question of law, the court may, and shall if any party to the proceedings so requests, refer the question to the Supreme Court which shall give its decision upon the question and give such directions to the Court of Appeal as it deems appropriate.

14. The legislature has the right to initiate bills in all policy jurisdictions; the executive lacks gatekeeping authority.

Yes. The legislature can initiate bills in all policy jurisdictions.

15. Expenditure of funds appropriated by the legislature is mandatory; the executive lacks the power to impound funds appropriated by the legislature.

No. The president can impound funds appropriated by the legislature.

16. The legislature controls the resources that finance its own internal operation and provide for the perquisites of its own members.

Yes. The legislature enjoys financial autonomy. Members' remuneration is protected by law.

Article 70
A member of the Senate or of the House of Representatives shall receive such salary and other allowances as the Revenue Mobilisation Allocation and Fiscal Commission may determine.

17. Members of the legislature are immune from arrest and/or criminal prosecution.

No. Legislators are subject to arrest and criminal prosecution.

18. All members of the legislature are elected; the executive lacks the power to appoint any members of the legislature.

Yes. All members of the legislature are elected.

Article 65
(1) Subject to the provisions of section 66 of this Constitution, a person shall be qualified for election as a member of –
(a) the Senate, if he is a citizen of Nigeria and has attained the age of thirty-five years; and
(b) the House of Representatives, if he is a citizen of Nigeria and has attained the age of thirty years.

19. The legislature alone, without the involvement of any other agencies, can change the Constitution.

No. A constitutional amendment requires approval by a two-thirds majority of the provincial (state) legislatures.

Article 9
(1) The National Assembly may, subject to the provisions of this section, alter any of the provisions of this Constitution.
(2) An Act of the National Assembly for the alteration of this Constitution, not being an Act to which section 8 of this Constitution applies, shall not be passed in either House of the National Assembly unless the proposal is supported by the votes of not less than two-thirds majority of all the members of that House and approved by resolution of the Houses of Assembly of not less than two-thirds of all the States.
(3) An Act of the National Assembly for the purpose of altering the provisions of this section, section 8 or Chapter IV of this Constitution shall not be passed by either House of the National Assembly unless the proposal is approved by the votes of not less than four-fifths majority of all the members of each House, and also approved by resolution of the Houses of Assembly of not less than two-thirds of all the States.
(4) For the purposes of section 8 of this Constitution and of subsections (2) and (3) of this section, the number of members of each House of the National Assembly shall, notwithstanding any vacancy, be deemed to be the number of members specified in sections 48 and 49 of this Constitution.

20. The legislature's approval is necessary for the declaration of war.

Yes. The legislature's approval is required for the president to declare war.

Article 5
(a) the President shall not declare a state of war between the Federation and another country except with the sanction of a resolution of both Houses of the National Assembly sitting in a joint session.

21. The legislature's approval is necessary to ratify treaties with foreign countries.

Yes. The legislature's approval is necessary to ratify international treaties.

Article 12
(1) No treaty between the Federation and any other country shall have the force of law except to the extent to which any such treaty has been enacted into law by the National Assembly.

22. The legislature has the power to grant amnesty.

No. Amnesty and pardon are not treated separately, and the legislature lacks the power to grant amnesty. See item 23.

23. The legislature has the power of pardon.

No. The president has the power of pardon.

Article 175
(1) The President may –
(a) grant any person concerned with or convicted of any offence created by an Act of the National Assembly a pardon, either free or subject to lawful conditions;
(b) grant to any person a respite, either for an indefinite or for a specified period, of the execution of any punishment imposed on that person for such an offence;
(c) substitute a less severe form of punishment for any punishment imposed on that person for such an offence; or
(d) remit the whole or any part of any punishment imposed on that person for such an offence or of any penalty or forfeiture otherwise due to the State on account of such an offence.

24. The legislature reviews and has the right to reject appointments to the judiciary; or the legislature itself appoints members of the judiciary.

No. The president makes judicial appointments, and the appointments do not require the legislature's approval.

Article 231
(1) The appointment of a person to the office of Chief Justice of Nigeria shall be made by the President on the recommendation of the National Judicial Council subject to confirmation of such appointment by the Senate.
(2) The appointment of a person to the office of a Justice of the Supreme Court shall be made by the President on the recommendation of the National Judicial Council subject to confirmation of such appointment by the Senate.

25. The chairman of the central bank is appointed by the legislature.

No. The president appoints the governor of the Central Bank of Nigeria.

26. The legislature has a substantial voice in the operation of the state-owned media.

No. The legislature lacks a substantial voice in the operation of the public media.

27. The legislature is regularly in session.

Yes. The legislature meets in ordinary session for at least six months each year.

Article 63
The Senate and the House of Representatives shall each sit for a period of not less than one hundred and eighty-one days in a year.

28. Each legislator has a personal secretary.

Yes.

Article 51
There shall be a Clerk to the National Assembly and such other staff as may be prescribed by an Act of the National Assembly, and the method of appointment of the Clerk and other staff of the National Assembly shall be as prescribed by that Act.

29. Each legislator has at least one non-secretarial staff member with policy expertise.

No.

30. Legislators are eligible for re-election without any restriction.

Yes. There are no restrictions on re-election.

31. A seat in the legislature is an attractive enough position that legislators are generally interested in and seek re-election.

Yes.

32. The re-election of incumbent legislators is common enough that at any given time the legislature contains a significant number of highly experienced members.

Yes. Military interventions caused considerable turbulence and interruption in parliamentary life during the 1980s and the first half of the 1990s, but the National Assembly elections of 1999, 2003, and 2007 restored some stability and continuity, and re-election rates have been sufficiently high to produce a significant number of highly experienced members.

PARLIAMENT OF NORWAY (*STORTING*)

Expert consultants: Christine Ingebritsen, Tor Arne Morskogen, Bjørn Erik Rasch, Hilmar Rommetvedt, Eva Stabell, Lars Svåsand

Score: .72

Influence over executive (7/9)		Institutional autonomy (7/9)		Specified powers (4/8)		Institutional capacity (5/6)	
1. replace	X	10. no dissolution	X	19. amendments	X	27. sessions	X
2. serve as ministers		11. no decree	X	20. war	X	28. secretary	X
3. interpellate	X	12. no veto	X	21. treaties	X	29. staff	
4. investigate	X	13. no review		22. amnesty		30. no term limits	X
5. oversee police	X	14. no gatekeeping	X	23. pardon		31. seek re-election	X
6. appoint PM	X	15. no impoundment	X	24. judiciary		32. experience	X
7. appoint ministers		16. control resources	X	25. central bank			
8. lack president	X	17. immunity		26. media	X		
9. no confidence	X	18. all elected	X				

The Parliament (*Storting*) of Norway was established in the 1814 Eisvold Convention, the oldest constitution in Europe that is currently in force. After a period of Swedish rule, Norway regained independence in 1905. The Eisvold Convention provided for a constitutional monarchy and a unicameral parliament consisting of two separate departments, the Permanent Chamber (*Lagting*) and the General Chamber (*Odelsting*). A constitutional amendment passed in 2007 called for a unicameral legislature to be established following the 2009 general election. Since 1880 the monarch's executive powers have been exercised by the government. Judicial review was instituted in 1890 and then eliminated in 1930. From 1930 to 1975 the legislature's laws were supreme and not subject to judicial review. Judicial review was reinstated in 1976. In the 1990s a number of reforms were instituted to update procedures by which the parliament oversees the executive, including the creation of a new Standing Committee on Scrutiny and Constitutional Affairs.

The parliament is a weighty political actor. It has considerable influence over the executive and a great deal of institutional autonomy. It exercises some specified powers and has a high level of institutional capacity.

SURVEY

1. The legislature alone, without the involvement of any other agencies, can impeach the president or replace the prime minister.

Yes. Formally, the king has the power to remove the prime minister from office. In practice, the legislature can remove the prime minister with a vote of no confidence. The legislature cannot depose the king.

Article 5
The King's person is sacred; he cannot be censured or accused. The responsibility rests with his Council.

Article 22
(1) The Prime Minister and the other Members of the Council of State, together with the State Secretaries, may be dismissed by the King without any prior court judgment, after he has heard the opinion of the Council of State on the subject.

2. Ministers may serve simultaneously as members of the legislature.

No. Legislators are prohibited from serving simultaneously in ministerial positions.

Article 62
(1) Officials who are employed in government departments, except however the State Secretaries, or officials

and pensioners of the Court, may not be elected as representatives to the Parliament. The same applies to officials employed in the diplomatic or consular services.
(2) Members of the Council of State may not attend meetings of the Parliament as representatives while holding a seat in the Council of State. Nor may the State Secretaries attend as representatives while holding their appointments.

3. The legislature has powers of summons over executive branch officials and hearings with executive branch officials testifying before the legislature or its committees are regularly held.

Yes. The legislature regularly interpellates officials from the executive.

> Article 75
> It devolves upon the Parliament:
> h) to have the right to require anyone, the King and the Royal Family excepted, to appear before it on matters of State; the exception does not, however, apply to the Royal Princes if they hold any public office.

4. The legislature can conduct independent investigation of the chief executive and the agencies of the executive.

Yes. The legislature can investigate the executive.

5. The legislature has effective powers of oversight over the agencies of coercion (the military, organs of law enforcement, intelligence services, and the secret police).

Yes. The legislature has effective powers of oversight over the agencies of coercion.

6. The legislature appoints the prime minister.

Yes. The king appoints as prime minister the candidate who enjoys the support of the legislature.

> Article 12
> (1) The King himself chooses a Council from among Norwegian citizens who are entitled to vote. This Council shall consist of a Prime Minister and at least seven other Members.

7. The legislature's approval is required to confirm the appointment of ministers; or the legislature itself appoints ministers.

No. Formally, ministers are appointed by the crown. In practice, the king appoints ministers on the recommendation of the prime minister, and the appointments do not require the legislature's approval.

> Article 12
> (1) The King himself chooses a Council from among Norwegian citizens who are entitled to vote. This Council shall consist of a Prime Minister and at least seven other Members.

8. The country lacks a presidency entirely or there is a presidency, but the president is elected by the legislature.

Yes. The country lacks a presidency. The king is the head of state.

> Article 3
> The Executive Power is vested in the King, or in the Queen if she has succeeded to the Crown pursuant to the provisions of Article 6 or Article 7 or Article 48 of this Constitution. When the Executive Power is thus vested in the Queen, she has all the rights and obligations which pursuant to this Constitution and the Law of the Land are possessed by the King.

9. The legislature can vote no confidence in the government.

Yes. The legislature can vote no confidence in the government.

> Article 22
> (1) The Prime Minister and the other Members of the Council of State, together with the State Secretaries, may be dismissed by the King without any prior court judgment, after he has heard the opinion of the Council of State on the subject.

10. The legislature is immune from dissolution by the executive.

Yes. The legislature is immune from dissolution.

11. Any executive initiative on legislation requires ratification or approval by the legislature before it takes effect; that is, the executive lacks decree power.

Yes. The executive lacks decree power.

12. Laws passed by the legislature are veto-proof or essentially veto-proof; that is, the executive lacks veto power, or has veto power but the veto can be overridden by a majority in the legislature.

Yes. Formally, the king can refuse to assent to a bill, which would amount to a veto power. In practice, it would be unthinkable for the monarch to veto legislation. There is one noteworthy exception, however. In 1940 the king vetoed a bill that would have conceded Norway's military defeat by Nazi Germany.

> Article 78
> (1) If the King assents to the Bill, he appends his signature, whereby it becomes law.
> (2) If he does not assent to it, he returns it to the General Chamber with a statement that he does not for the time being find it expedient to sanction it. In that case the Bill must not again be submitted to the King by the Parliament then assembled.

Article 79

If a Bill has been passed unaltered by two sessions of the Parliament, constituted after two separate successive elections and separated from each other by at least two intervening sessions of the Parliament, without a divergent Bill having been passed by any Parliament in the period between the first and last adoption, and it is then submitted to the King with a petition that His Majesty shall not refuse his assent to a Bill which, after the most mature deliberation, the Parliament considers to be beneficial, it shall become law even if the Royal Assent is not accorded before the Parliament goes into recess.

13. The legislature's laws are supreme and not subject to judicial review.

No. The courts can review the constitutionality of laws.

14. The legislature has the right to initiate bills in all policy jurisdictions; the executive lacks gatekeeping authority.

Yes. The legislature can initiate bills in all policy jurisdictions.

15. Expenditure of funds appropriated by the legislature is mandatory; the executive lacks the power to impound funds appropriated by the legislature.

Yes. The executive lacks the power to impound funds appropriated by the legislature.

16. The legislature controls the resources that finance its own internal operation and provide for the perquisites of its own members.

Yes. The legislature enjoys financial autonomy, including control over members' perquisites.

Article 65

(1) Every representative and proxy called to the Parliament shall be entitled to receive from the Treasury such reimbursement as is prescribed by law for travelling expenses to and from the Parliament, and from the Parliament to his home and back again during vacations lasting at least fourteen days.

(2) He shall further be entitled to remuneration, likewise prescribed by law, for attending the Parliament.

17. Members of the legislature are immune from arrest and/or criminal prosecution.

No. Legislators are immune only for opinions expressed in the legislature or while they are in parliament or traveling to and from parliament.

Article 66

Representatives on their way to and from the Parliament, as well as during their attendance there, shall be exempt from personal arrest, unless they are apprehended in public crimes, nor may they be called to account outside the meetings of the Parliament for opinions expressed there.

18. All members of the legislature are elected; the executive lacks the power to appoint any members of the legislature.

Yes. All members of the legislature are elected.

Article 49

The people exercises the Legislative Power through the Parliament, which consists of two departments, the Permanent Chamber and the General Chamber.

Article 58

(1) Each county constitutes a constituency.

(2) One hundred and fifty-seven of the Representatives of the Parliament are elected as representatives of constituencies and the remaining 8 representatives are elected so as to achieve a greater degree of proportionality.

19. The legislature alone, without the involvement of any other agencies, can change the Constitution.

Yes. The legislature can change the constitution with a two-thirds majority vote.

Article 112

(1) If experience shows that any part of this Constitution of the Kingdom of Norway ought to be amended, the proposal to this effect shall be submitted to the first, second or third Parliament after a new General Election and be publicly announced in print. But it shall be left to the first, second or third Parliament after the following General Election to decide whether or not the proposed amendment shall be adopted. Such amendment must never, however, contradict the principles embodied in this Constitution, but solely relate to modifications of particular provisions which do not alter the spirit of the Constitution, and such amendment requires that two thirds of the Parliament agree thereto.

(2) An amendment to the Constitution adopted in the manner aforesaid shall be signed by the President and the Secretary of the Parliament, and shall be sent to the King for public announcement in print, as an applicable provision of the Constitution of the Kingdom of Norway.

20. The legislature's approval is necessary for the declaration of war.

Yes. The legislature's approval is required to deploy the armed forces abroad.

Article 25

(1) The King is Commander-in-Chief of the land and naval forces of the Realm. These forces may not be increased or reduced without the consent of the Parliament. They may not be transferred to the service of foreign powers, nor may the military forces of any foreign power, except auxiliary forces assisting against hostile attack, be brought into the Realm without the consent of the Parliament.

(2) The territorial army and the other troops which cannot be classed as troops of the line must never, without

the consent of the Parliament, be employed outside the borders of the Realm.

21. The legislature's approval is necessary to ratify treaties with foreign countries.

Yes. The legislature's approval is necessary to ratify international treaties.

> Article 26
> (2) Treaties on matters of special importance, and, in all cases, treaties whose implementation, according to the Constitution, necessitates a new law or a decision by the Parliament, are not binding until the Parliament has given its consent thereto.

22. The legislature has the power to grant amnesty.

No. Amnesty and pardon are not treated separately, and the legislature lacks the power to grant amnesty. See item 23.

23. The legislature has the power of pardon.

No. The king has the power of pardon.

> Article 20
> (1) The King shall have the right in the Council of State to pardon criminals after sentence has been passed. The criminal shall have the choice of accepting the King's pardon or submitting to the penalty imposed.

24. The legislature reviews and has the right to reject appointments to the judiciary; or the legislature itself appoints members of the judiciary.

No. The constitution does not specify how justices are to be appointed. In practice, the government appoints the judiciary, and the appointments do not require the legislature's approval.

> Article 88
> (2) The Supreme Court shall consist of a President and at least four other Members.

25. The chairman of the central bank is appointed by the legislature.

No. The king, on the recommendation of the government, appoints the governor of the Central Bank of Norway.

26. The legislature has a substantial voice in the operation of the state-owned media.

Yes. The legislature appoints the members of the board that oversees the operation of the public media.

27. The legislature is regularly in session.

Yes. The legislature regularly meets in ordinary session.

> Article 80
> (1) The Parliament shall remain in session as long as it deems it necessary and shall terminate its proceedings when it has concluded its business.
> (2) In accordance with the rules of procedure adopted by the Parliament, the proceedings may be resumed, but they shall terminate not later than the last Sunday in the month of September.

28. Each legislator has a personal secretary.

Yes.

29. Each legislator has at least one non-secretarial staff member with policy expertise.

No.

30. Legislators are eligible for re-election without any restriction.

Yes. There are no restrictions on re-election.

31. A seat in the legislature is an attractive enough position that legislators are generally interested in and seek re-election.

Yes.

32. The re-election of incumbent legislators is common enough that at any given time the legislature contains a significant number of highly experienced members.

Yes. Re-election rates are sufficiently high to produce a significant number of highly experienced members.

COUNCIL OF OMAN (*MAJLIS*)

Expert consultant: Michael Herb

Score: .16

Influence over executive (2/9)	Institutional autonomy (1/9)	Specified powers (0/8)	Institutional capacity (2/6)	
1. replace	10. no dissolution	19. amendments	27. sessions	X
2. serve as ministers	11. no decree	20. war	28. secretary	
3. interpellate X	12. no veto	21. treaties	29. staff	
4. investigate	13. no review	22. amnesty	30. no term X	
			limits	
5. oversee police	14. no gatekeeping	23. pardon	31. seek re-election	
6. appoint PM	15. no impoundment	24. judiciary	32. experience	
7. appoint ministers	16. control resources	25. central bank		
8. lack X president	17. immunity X	26. media		
9. no confidence	18. all elected			

The Council (*Majlis*) of Oman was established by royal decree of the sultan in 1981. It was formalized and expanded in the country's first written constitution, which was decreed by the sultan in 1996. The constitution devotes but a single article to the Council and its powers; its other responsibilities were defined in subsequent legislation. The bicameral Council consists of an elected lower house, the Consultative Council (*Majlis ash Shura*), and an appointed upper house, the Council of State (*Majlis al-Dawla*). Oman held its first legislative elections in 2003.

The Council is not a legislature in the traditional sense. It does not introduce or pass legislation, but serves in an advisory role to the sultan. The Council questions government officials but otherwise lacks influence over the executive. It is virtually bereft of institutional autonomy and entirely lacking in the specified powers assessed in this survey. Notably, however, the Council does have some institutional capacity.

SURVEY

1. The legislature alone, without the involvement of any other agencies, can impeach the president or replace the prime minister.

No. The legislature cannot remove the sultan from office.

Article 41
The Sultan is the Head of State and the Supreme Commander of the Armed Forces. His person is inviolable and must be respected and his orders must be obeyed.

2. Ministers may serve simultaneously as members of the legislature.

No. Legislators are prohibited from serving simultaneously in ministerial positions.

3. The legislature has powers of summons over executive branch officials and hearings with executive branch officials testifying before the legislature or its committees are regularly held.

Yes. The legislature regularly interpellates officials from the executive.

4. The legislature can conduct independent investigation of the chief executive and the agencies of the executive.

No. The legislature cannot investigate the executive.

5. The legislature has effective powers of oversight over the agencies of coercion (the military, organs of law enforcement, intelligence services, and the secret police).

No. The legislature lacks effective powers of oversight over the agencies of coercion.

6. The legislature appoints the prime minister.

No. The sultan, if he so chooses, can appoint a prime minister.

> Article 48
> If the Sultan appoints a Prime Minister, his competencies and powers shall be specified in the Decree appointing him.

7. The legislature's approval is required to confirm the appointment of ministers; or the legislature itself appoints ministers.

No. The sultan appoints ministers, and the appointments do not require the legislature's approval.

> Article 42
> The Sultan discharges the following functions:
> – appointing and dismissing Deputy Prime Ministers, Ministers and those of their rank.

8. The country lacks a presidency entirely or there is a presidency, but the president is elected by the legislature.

Yes. The country lacks a presidency. The sultan is the head of state.

> Article 41
> The Sultan is the Head of State and the Supreme Commander of the Armed Forces. His person is inviolable and must be respected and his orders must be obeyed.

9. The legislature can vote no confidence in the government.

No. The legislature cannot vote no confidence in the government.

10. The legislature is immune from dissolution by the executive.

No. The sultan can dissolve the legislature.

11. Any executive initiative on legislation requires ratification or approval by the legislature before it takes effect; that is, the executive lacks decree power.

No. The sultan issues decrees that have the force of law.

> Article 42
> The Sultan discharges the following functions:
> – issuing and ratifying laws.

12. Laws passed by the legislature are veto-proof or essentially veto-proof; that is, the executive lacks veto power, or has veto power but the veto can be overridden by a majority in the legislature.

No. The sultan has absolute control over legislation. The legislature does not pass legislation; it merely provides advice to the sultan.

13. The legislature's laws are supreme and not subject to judicial review.

No. The Council does not make laws. Furthermore, a judicial department can settle disputes related to the constitutionality of laws.

> Article 70
> The Law shall stipulate the judicial department concerned with settling disputes arising from the incompatibility of laws and regulations with the Basic Law of the State and ensuring that the latter's provisions are not contravened, and shall define that department's powers and procedures.

14. The legislature has the right to initiate bills in all policy jurisdictions; the executive lacks gatekeeping authority.

No. The sultan has absolute gatekeeping authority. The legislature is prohibited from initiating legislation.

> Article 42
> The Sultan discharges the following functions:
> – issuing and ratifying laws.

15. Expenditure of funds appropriated by the legislature is mandatory; the executive lacks the power to impound funds appropriated by the legislature.

No. The Council does not appropriate funds.

16. The legislature controls the resources that finance its own internal operation and provide for the perquisites of its own members.

No. The Council is dependent on the Sultan for the resources that finance its own operations.

17. Members of the legislature are immune from arrest and/or criminal prosecution.

Yes. Members of the Council are immune.

18. All members of the legislature are elected; the executive lacks the power to appoint any members of the legislature.

No. The sultan appoints all of the members of the Council of State. All members of the Consultative Council are elected.

19. The legislature alone, without the involvement of any other agencies, can change the Constitution.

No. Constitutional changes are made "in the same manner in which [the constitution] was promulgated," meaning by the sultan's decree.

> Article 81
> This Basic Law can only be amended in the same manner in which it was promulgated.

20. The legislature's approval is necessary for the declaration of war.

No. The sultan can declare war without the Council's approval.

> Article 42
> The Sultan discharges the following functions:
> – declaring...war, and making peace in accordance with the provisions of the Law.

21. The legislature's approval is necessary to ratify treaties with foreign countries.

No. The sultan can conclude international treaties without the Council's approval.

> Article 42
> The Sultan discharges the following functions:
> – signing international treaties and agreements in accordance with the provisions of the Law (or authorising a signatory to sign them) and issuing decrees ratifying them.

22. The legislature has the power to grant amnesty.

No. The sultan has the power to grant amnesty.

> Article 42
> The Sultan discharges the following functions:
> – waiving or commuting punishments.

23. The legislature has the power of pardon.

No. The sultan has the power of pardon.

> Article 42
> The Sultan discharges the following functions:
> – waiving or commuting punishments.

24. The legislature reviews and has the right to reject appointments to the judiciary; or the legislature itself appoints members of the judiciary.

No. The sultan appoints judges, and the appointments do not require the legislature's approval.

> Article 42
> The Sultan discharges the following functions:
> – appointing and dismissing senior judges.

25. The chairman of the central bank is appointed by the legislature.

No. The sultan appoints the chairman of the Central Bank of Oman.

26. The legislature has a substantial voice in the operation of the state-owned media.

No. The legislature lacks a substantial voice in the operation of the public media.

27. The legislature is regularly in session.

Yes. The Council regularly meets in ordinary session.

28. Each legislator has a personal secretary.

No.

29. Each legislator has at least one non-secretarial staff member with policy expertise.

No.

30. Legislators are eligible for re-election without any restriction.

Yes. There are no restrictions on re-election.

31. A seat in the legislature is an attractive enough position that legislators are generally interested in and seek re-election.

No. There has been only one legislative election in Oman, so legislators have not yet had the opportunity to seek re-election.

32. The re-election of incumbent legislators is common enough that at any given time the legislature contains a significant number of highly experienced members.

No. The first legislative elections were held in 2003. Since its creation in 1981, royal reappointment rates have been high, so the Council has seen some consistency in membership over the past several decades. Still, it is too early to speak of re-election rates and continuity of elected membership.

PARLIAMENT OF PAKISTAN (*MAJLIS-E-SHOORA*)

Expert consultants: Sanaullah Baloch, Mary Cummins, Charles H. Kennedy, Aqil Shah, Nusrat Sheikh

Score: .44

Influence over executive (5/9)		Institutional autonomy (5/9)		Specified powers (1/8)		Institutional capacity (3/6)	
1. replace	X	10. no dissolution		19. amendments	X	27. sessions	
2. serve as ministers	X	11. no decree		20. war		28. secretary	
3. interpellate	X	12. no veto	X	21. treaties		29. staff	
4. investigate		13. no review		22. amnesty		30. no term limits	X
5. oversee police		14. no gatekeeping	X	23. pardon		31. seek re-election	X
6. appoint PM	X	15. no impoundment	X	24. judiciary		32. experience	X
7. appoint ministers		16. control resources	X	25. central bank			
8. lack president		17. immunity		26. media			
9. no confidence	X	18. all elected	X				

The Parliament (*Majlis-e-Shoora*) of Pakistan formally came into being upon independence from Great Britain and the partition of British India in 1947. Pakistan's constitution of 1956 called for a bicameral legislature with a lower house, the National Assembly, and an upper house, the Senate. The year 1971 brought separation of what had been East Pakistan (now Bangladesh) from West Pakistan (now Pakistan) in the Bangladesh Liberation War. The constitution currently in effect was promulgated in 1973. The military has frequently intervened in politics. The 1973 constitution was suspended by military rulers in 1977 and then restored with amendments in 1985. Prior to 1997 the legislature was subject to dissolution, but in that year Prime Minister Nawaz Sharif repealed the president's power to dismiss the legislature. In 1999 General Pervez Musharraf took over the country in a bloodless coup, declared himself president, and suspended parliament and the constitution. In 2002 the legislature again convened, but Musharraf reinstated the president's power to dissolve the legislature. The constitution was restored in stages. In late 2007 Musharraf declared a state of emergency and suspended the parliament. In early 2008 the country returned to civilian rule when Musharraf, under international pressure, resigned as army chief of staff. Musharraf retained his position as civilian president and held fresh elections that reinstated the parliament and brought to power a new, coalition government.

The legislature, while often hamstrung by military governments, is not devoid of power. It has some influence over the executive. Its powers in this area include the right to impeach the president and remove the prime minister with a vote of no confidence and to interpellate officials from the executive. Its institutional autonomy is not inconsiderable but is circumscribed by presidential decree and dissolution powers. The legislature exercises only one specified power, the right to change the constitution, and has modest institutional capacity.

SURVEY

1. The legislature alone, without the involvement of any other agencies, can impeach the president or replace the prime minister.

[A]Yes. The legislature can impeach the president by a two-thirds majority vote of its total membership. It can remove the prime minister with a vote of no confidence.

Article 47

(1) Notwithstanding anything contained in the Constitution, the President may, in accordance with the provisions of this Article, be removed from office on the ground of physical or mental incapacity or impeached on a charge of violating the Constitution or gross misconduct.

(2) Not less than one-half of the total membership of either House may give to the Speaker of the National

Assembly or, as the case may be, the Chairman written notice of its intention to move a resolution for the removal of, or, as the case may be, to impeach, the President; and such notice shall set out the particulars of his incapacity or of the charge against him.

(3) If a notice under clause (2) is received by the Chairman, he shall transmit it forthwith to the Speaker.

(4) The Speaker shall, within three days of the receipt of a notice under clause (2) or clause (3), cause a copy of the notice to be transmitted to the President.

(5) The Speaker shall summon the two Houses to meet in a joint sitting not earlier than seven days and not later than fourteen days after the receipt of the notice by him.

(6) The joint sitting may investigate or cause to be investigated the ground or the charge upon which the notice is founded.

(7) The President shall have the right to appear and be represented during the investigation, if any, and before the joint sitting.

(8) If, after consideration of the result of the investigation, if any, a resolution is passed at the joint sitting by the votes of not less than two-thirds of the total membership of declaring that the President is unfit to hold the office due to incapacity or is guilty of violating the Constitution or of gross misconduct, the President shall cease to hold office immediately on the passing of the resolution.

Article 95

(1) A resolution for a vote of no-confidence moved by not less than twenty per centum of the total membership of the National Assembly may be passed against the Prime Minister by the National Assembly.

(2) A resolution referred to in clause (1) shall not be voted upon before the expiration of three days, or later than seven days, from the day on which such resolution is moved in the National Assembly.

(3) A resolution referred to in clause (1) shall not be moved in the National Assembly while the National Assembly is considering demands for grants submitted to it in the Annual Budget Statement.

(4) If the resolution referred to in clause (1) is passed by a majority of the total membership of the National Assembly, the Prime Minister shall cease to hold office.

2. Ministers may serve simultaneously as members of the legislature.

[A]Yes. Ministers are chosen from, and required to serve simultaneously in, the legislature.

Article 91

(7) A Minister who for any period of six consecutive months is not a member of the National Assembly shall, at the expiration of that period, cease to be a Minister and shall not before the dissolution of that Assembly be again appointed a Minister unless he is elected a member of that Assembly; provided that nothing contained in this clause shall apply to a Minister who is a member of the Senate.

3. The legislature has powers of summons over executive branch officials and hearings with executive branch officials testifying before the legislature or its committees are regularly held.

Yes. The legislature regularly interpellates officials from the executive.

4. The legislature can conduct independent investigation of the chief executive and the agencies of the executive.

No. The legislature cannot investigate the executive.

5. The legislature has effective powers of oversight over the agencies of coercion (the military, organs of law enforcement, intelligence services, and the secret police).

No. The legislature lacks effective powers of oversight over the agencies of coercion.

6. The legislature appoints the prime minister.

Yes. The president appoints as prime minister the candidate who enjoys the support of the legislature.

Article 91

(1) There shall be a Cabinet of Ministers, with the Prime Minister at its head, to aid and advise the President in the exercise of his functions.

(2) The President shall in his discretion appoint from amongst the members of the National Assembly a Prime Minister who, in his opinion, is most likely to command the confidence of the majority of the members of the National Assembly.

[(2A) Notwithstanding anything contained in clause (2), after the twentieth day of March, one thousand nine hundred and ninety, the President shall invite the member of the National Assembly to be the Prime Minister who commands the confidence of the majority of the members of the National Assembly, as ascertained in a session of the Assembly summoned for the purpose in accordance with the provisions of the Constitution.]

7. The legislature's approval is required to confirm the appointment of ministers; or the legislature itself appoints ministers.

No. The legislature's approval is not required to confirm the appointment of individual ministers.

Article 91

(1) There shall be a Cabinet of Ministers, with the Prime Minister at its head, to aid and advise the President in the exercise of his functions.

(2) The President shall in his discretion appoint from amongst the members of the National Assembly a Prime Minister who, in his opinion, is most likely to command the confidence of the majority of the members of the National Assembly.

[(2A) Notwithstanding anything contained in clause (2), after the twentieth day of March, one thousand nine hundred and ninety, the President shall invite the member of the National Assembly to be the Prime Minister who commands the confidence of the majority of the members of the National Assembly, as ascertained in a session of the Assembly summoned for the purpose in accordance with the provisions of the Constitution.]

(3) The person appointed under clause (2), [or, as the case may be, invited under clause (2A)] shall, before entering upon the office, make before the president oath in the form set out in the Third Schedule and shall within a period of sixty days thereof obtain a vote of confidence from the National Assembly.

(4) The Cabinet, together with the Ministers of State, shall be collectively responsible to the National Assembly.

8. The country lacks a presidency entirely or there is a presidency, but the president is elected by the legislature.

No. According to the constitution, the legislature and provincial assemblies together form an electoral college that selects the president. In practice, since the 1999 coup General Musharraf has appointed himself president.

Article 41

(1) There shall be a President of Pakistan who shall be the Head of State and shall represent the unity of the Republic.

(3) The President to be elected after the expiration of the term specified in clause (7) shall be elected in accordance with the provisions of the Second Schedule by the members of an electoral college consisting of –

(a) the members of both Houses; and

(b) the members of the Provincial Assemblies.

(4) Election to the office of President shall be held not earlier than sixty days and not later than thirty days before the expiration of the term of the President in office:

Provided that, if the election cannot be held within the period aforesaid because the National Assembly is dissolved, it shall be held within thirty days of the general election to the Assembly.

9. The legislature can vote no confidence in the government.

Yes. The legislature can vote no confidence in the government.

Article 95

(1) A resolution for a vote of no-confidence moved by not less than twenty per centum of the total membership of the National Assembly may be passed against the Prime Minister by the National Assembly.

(2) A resolution referred to in clause (1) shall not be voted upon before the expiration of three days, or later than seven days, from the day on which such resolution is moved in the National Assembly.

(3) A resolution referred to in clause (1) shall not be moved in the National Assembly while the National Assembly is considering demands for grants submitted to it in the Annual Budget Statement.

(4) If the resolution referred to in clause (1) is passed by a majority of the total membership of the National Assembly, the Prime Minister shall cease to hold office.

10. The legislature is immune from dissolution by the executive.

No. The president, on the advice of the prime minister, can dissolve the legislature.

Article 58

(1) The President shall dissolve the National Assembly if so advised by the Prime Minister; and the National Assembly shall, unless sooner dissolved, stand dissolved at the expiration of forty-eight hours after the Prime Minister has so advised.

Explanation. – Reference in this Article to "Prime Minister" shall not be construed to include reference to a Prime Minister against whom a [notice of a resolution for a vote of no-confidence has been given] in the National Assembly but has not been voted upon or against whom such a resolution has been passed or who is continuing in office after his resignation or after the dissolution of the National Assembly

(2) Notwithstanding anything contained in clause (2) of Article 48, the President may also dissolve the National Assembly in his discretion where, in his opinion, –

(a) a vote of no-confidence having been passed against the Prime Minister, no other member of the National Assembly is likely to command the confidence of the majority of the members of the National Assembly in accordance with the provisions of the Constitution, as ascertained in a session of the National Assembly summoned for the purpose; or

(b) A situation has been arisen in which the government of the Federation cannot be carried on in accordance with the provisions of the constitution and an appeal to the electorate is necessary.

11. Any executive initiative on legislation requires ratification or approval by the legislature before it takes effect; that is, the executive lacks decree power.

No. The president can issue decrees that have the force of law, here called "ordinances," while the legislature is out of session. The decrees lapse if they are subsequently rejected by the legislature.

Article 89

(1) The President may, except when the National Assembly is in session, if satisfied that circumstances exist which render it necessary to take immediate action, make and promulgate an Ordinance as the circumstances may require.

(2) An Ordinance promulgated under this Article shall have the same force and effect as an Act of Parliament and shall be subject to like restrictions as the power of Parliament to make law, but every such ordinance –

(a) shall be laid –

(i) before the National Assembly if it [contains provisions dealing with all or any of the matters specified in clause (2) of Article 73], and shall stand repealed at the expiration of four months from its promulgation or, if before the expiration of that period a resolution disapproving it is passed by the Assembly, upon the passing of that resolution;

(ii) before both Houses if it [does not contain provisions dealing with any of the matters referred to in sub-paragraph (i)], and shall stand repealed at the expiration of four months from its promulgation or, if before the expiration of that period a resolution disapproving it is passed by either House, upon the passing of that resolution; and

(b) may be withdrawn at any time by the President.

(3) Without prejudice to the provisions of clause (2), and Ordinance laid before the National Assembly shall be deemed to be a Bill introduced in the National Assembly.

12. Laws passed by the legislature are veto-proof or essentially veto-proof; that is, the executive lacks veto power, or has veto power but the veto can be overridden by a majority in the legislature.

Yes. The legislature can override a presidential veto by a majority vote of its present members.

Article 75
(1) When a Bill is presented to the President for assent, the President shall, within [thirty] days, –

(a) assent to the Bill; or

(b) in the case of a Bill other than a Money Bill, return the Bill to the Majlis-e-Shoora with a message requesting that the Bill, or any specified provision thereof, be reconsidered and that any amendment specified in the message be considered.

(2) When the President has returned a Bill to the Majlis-e-Shoora, it shall be reconsidered by the Majlis-e-Shoora and, if it is again passed, with or without amendment, by the Majlis-e-Shoora, [in accordance with Article 70,] it shall be deemed for the purposes of the Constitution to have been passed by both Houses and shall be presented to the President and the President shall not withhold assent therefrom.

(3) When the President has assented to a Bill, it shall become law and be called an Act of Majlis-e-Shoora.

(4) No Act of Majlis-e-Shoora, and no provision in any such Act, shall be invalid by reason only that some recommendation, previous sanction or consent required by the Constitution was not given if that Act was assented to in accordance with the Constitution.

13. The legislature's laws are supreme and not subject to judicial review.

No. The Supreme Court can review the constitutionality of laws.

Article 185
(2) An appeal shall lie to the Supreme Court from any judgment, decree, final order or sentence of a High Court –

(f) if the High Court certifies that the case involves a substantial question of law as to the interpretation of the Constitution.

14. The legislature has the right to initiate bills in all policy jurisdictions; the executive lacks gatekeeping authority.

Yes. The legislature can initiate bills in all policy jurisdictions.

15. Expenditure of funds appropriated by the legislature is mandatory; the executive lacks the power to impound funds appropriated by the legislature.

Yes. The executive lacks the power to impound funds appropriated by the legislature.

16. The legislature controls the resources that finance its own internal operation and provide for the perquisites of its own members.

Yes. The legislature enjoys financial autonomy, including control over members' perquisites.

Article 250
(1) Within two years from the commencing day, provision shall be made by law for determining the salaries, allowances and privileges of . . . a member of the National Assembly . . . and a member of the Senate.

(2) Until other provision is made by law, –

(a) the salaries, allowances and privileges of . . . a member of the National Assembly shall be the same as the salaries, allowances and privileges to which the President, the Speaker or Deputy Speaker or a member of the National Assembly of Pakistan or a Provincial Assembly, a Federal Minister, a Minister of State, a Chief Minister, a Provincial Minister or, as the case may be, the Chief Election Commissioner was entitled immediately before the commencing day; and

(b) the salaries, allowances and privileges of the Chairman, the Deputy Chairman, the Prime Minister and a member of the Senate shall be such as the President may by Order determine.

17. Members of the legislature are immune from arrest and/or criminal prosecution.

No. Legislative immunity extends to official parliamentary business only. Legislators are subject to arrest for common crimes.

Article 66
(1) Subject to the Constitution and to the rules of procedure of Majlis-e-Shoora, there shall be freedom of speech in Majlis-e-Shoora and no member shall be liable to any proceedings in any court in respect of anything

said or any vote given by him in [Majlis-e-Shoora], and no person shall be so liable in respect of the publication by or under the authority of Majlis-e-Shoora of any report, paper, votes or proceedings.

(2) In other respects, the powers, immunities and privileges of Majlis-e-Shoora, and the immunities and privileges of the members of Majlis-e-Shoora, shall be such as may from time to time be defined by law and, until so defined, shall be such as were, immediately before the commencing day, enjoyed by the National Assembly of Pakistan and the committees thereof and its members.

18. All members of the legislature are elected; the executive lacks the power to appoint any members of the legislature.

Yes. All members of the legislature are elected.

Article 51
(1) There shall be three hundred and forty-two seats of the members in the National Assembly, including seats reserved for women and non-Muslims.
(4) For the purpose of election to the National Assembly, –
  (a) The constituencies for the general seats shall be single member territorial constituencies and the members to fill such seats shall be elected by direct and free vote in accordance with Law;
  (b) Each Province shall be a single constituency for all seats reserved for women which are allocated to the respective Provinces under clause (1A);
  (c) The constituency for all seats reserved for non-Muslims shall be the whole country;
  (d) members to the seats reserved for women which are allocated to a Province under clause (1A) shall be elected in accordance with law through proportional representation system of political parties' lists of candidates on the basis of total number of general seats secured by each political party from the Province concerned in the National Assembly[:]
  [Provided that for the purpose of this sub-clause the total number of general seats won by a political party shall include the independent returned candidate or candidates who may duly join such political party within three days of the publication in the official Gazette of the names of the returned candidates;]
  (e) members to the seats reserved for non-Muslims shall be elected in accordance with law through proportional representation system of political parties lists of candidates on the basis of total number of general seats won by each political party in the National Assembly:
  Provided that for the purpose of this sub-clause the total number of general seats won by a political party shall include the independent returned candidate or candidates who may duly join such political party within three days of the publication in the official Gazette of the names of the returned candidates.

Article 59
(1) The Senate shall consist of one hundred members, of whom –

  (a) fourteen shall be elected by the members of each Provincial Assembly;
  (b) eight shall be elected from the Federally Administered Tribal Areas in such manner as the President may, by order prescribe;
  (c) two on general seats, and one technocrat including Aalim shall be elected from the Federal Capital in such manner as the President may, by Order, prescribe;
  (d) four women shall be elected by the members of each Provincial Assembly;
  (e) four technocrats including Ulema shall be elected by the members of each provincial Assembly;
(2) Election to fill seats in the Senate allocated to each Province shall be held in accordance with the system of proportional representation by means of the single transferable vote.

19. The legislature alone, without the involvement of any other agencies, can change the Constitution.

Yes. The legislature can change the constitution with a two-thirds majority vote in both houses.

Article 238
Subject to this Part, the Constitution may be amended by Act of [Majlis-e-Shoora].

Article 239
(1) A Bill to amend the Constitution may originate in either House and, when the Bill has been passed by the votes of not less than two-thirds of the total membership of the House, it shall be transmitted to the other House.
(2) If the Bill is passed without amendment by the votes of not less than two-thirds of the total membership of the House to which it is transmitted under clause (1), it shall, subject to the provisions of clause (4), be presented to the President for assent.
(3) If the Bill is passed with amendment by the votes of not less than two-thirds of the total membership of the House to which it is transmitted under clause (1), it shall be reconsidered by the House in which it had originated, and if the Bill as amended by the former House is passed by the latter by the votes of not less than two-thirds of its total membership it shall, subject to the provisions of clause (4), be presented to the president for assent.
(4) A Bill to amend the Constitution which would have the effect of altering the limits of a Province shall not be presented to the President for assent unless it has been passed by the Provincial Assembly of that Province by the votes of not less than two-thirds of its total membership.
(5) No amendment of the Constitution shall be called in question in any court on any ground whatsoever.
(6) For the removal of doubt, it is hereby declared that there is no limitation whatever on the power of the Majlis-e-Shoora to amend any of the provisions of the Constitution.

20. The legislature's approval is necessary for the declaration of war.

No. In times of war the president can issue a proclamation of emergency without the legislature's approval. The proclamation lapses after two months if it is not subsequently approved by both houses of the legislature.

> Article 232
> (1) If the president is satisfied that a grave emergency exists in which the security of Pakistan, or any part thereof, is threatened by war or external aggression, or by internal disturbance beyond the power of a Provincial Government to control, he may issue a Proclamation of Emergency.
> (7) A Proclamation of Emergency shall be laid before a joint sitting which shall be summoned by the President to meet within thirty days of the Proclamation being issued and –
> > (a) shall cease to be in force at the expiration of two months unless before the expiration of that period it has been approved by a resolution of the joint sitting; and
> > (b) shall, subject to the provisions of paragraph (a), cease to be in force upon a resolution disapproving the Proclamation being passed by the votes of the majority of the total membership of the two Houses in joint sitting.
> (8) Notwithstanding anything contained in clause (7), if the National Assembly stands dissolved at the time when a Proclamation of Emergency is issued, the Proclamation shall continue in force for a period of four months but, if a general election to the Assembly is not held before the expiration of that period, it shall cease to be in force at the expiration of that period unless it has earlier been approved by a resolution of the Senate.

21. The legislature's approval is necessary to ratify treaties with foreign countries.

No. The legislature's approval is not necessary to ratify international treaties, although the power to implement treaties is listed as a legislative power in the constitution.

> Article 70(4) (Taken from the Fourth Schedule, which lists the legislature's powers):
> 3. External affairs; the implementing of treaties and agreements, including educational and cultural pacts and agreements, with other countries; extradition, including the surrender of criminals and accused persons to Governments outside Pakistan.

22. The legislature has the power to grant amnesty.

No. Amnesty and pardon are not treated separately, and the legislature lacks the power to grant amnesty. See item 23.

23. The legislature has the power of pardon.

No. The president has the power of pardon.

> Article 45
> The president shall have power to grant pardon, reprieve and respite, and to remit, suspend or commute any sentence passed by any court, tribunal or other authority.

24. The legislature reviews and has the right to reject appointments to the judiciary; or the legislature itself appoints members of the judiciary.

No. The president appoints members of the judiciary, and the appointments do not require parliament's approval.

> Article 176
> The Supreme Court shall consist of a Chief Justice to be known as the Chief Justice of Pakistan and so many other Judges as may be determined by Act of [Majlis-e-Shoora] or, until so determined, as may be fixed by the President.

> Article 177
> (1) The Chief Justice of Pakistan shall be appointed by President, and each of the other Judges shall be appointed by the President after consultation with the Chief Justice.

> Article 193
> (1) A Judge of a High Court shall be appointed by the President after consultation –
> > (a) with the Chief Justice of Pakistan;
> > (b) with the Governor concerned; and
> > (c) except where the appointment is that of Chief Justice, with the Chief Justice of the High Court.

25. The chairman of the central bank is appointed by the legislature.

No. The president appoints the governor of State Bank of Pakistan.

26. The legislature has a substantial voice in the operation of the state-owned media.

No. The legislature lacks a substantial voice in the operation of the public media.

27. The legislature is regularly in session.

No. The legislature does not regularly meet in ordinary session.

> Article 54
> (1) The President may, from time to time, summon either House or both Houses or [Majlis-e-Shoora] in joint sitting to meet at such time and place as he thinks fit and may also prorogue the same.
> (2) There shall be at least [three] sessions of the National Assembly every year, and not more than one hundred and twenty days shall intervene between the last sitting of the Assembly in one session and the date appointed for its first sitting in the next session:
> Provided that the National Assembly shall meet for not less than one hundred and [thirty] working days in each year.

28. Each legislator has a personal secretary.

No. The constitution provides for secretarial staff, although in practice there is less than one staff person for each legislator.

> Article 87
> (1) Each House shall have a separate Secretariat: Provided that nothing in this clause shall be construed as preventing the creation of posts common to both Houses.
> (2) Majlis-e-Shoora may by law regulate the recruitment and the conditions of service of persons appointed to the secretarial staff of either House.
> (3) Until provision is made by Majlis-e-Shoora under clause (2), the Speaker or, as the case may be, the Chairman may, with the approval of the President, make rules regulating the recruitment, and the conditions of service, of persons appointed to the secretarial staff of the National Assembly or the Senate.

29. Each legislator has at least one non-secretarial staff member with policy expertise.

No. See item 28.

30. Legislators are eligible for re-election without any restriction.

Yes. There are no restrictions on re-election.

31. A seat in the legislature is an attractive enough position that legislators are generally interested in and seek re-election.

Yes.

32. The re-election of incumbent legislators is common enough that at any given time the legislature contains a significant number of highly experienced members.

Yes. Despite frequent military interventions in politics, five rounds of parliamentary elections were held between 1988 and 2002, and re-election rates are sufficiently high to produce a significant number of highly experienced members.

NATIONAL ASSEMBLY OF PANAMA (*ASAMBLEA NACIONAL*)

Expert consultants: Natalia Ajenjo Fresno, Maria Del Pilar Gonzales Morales, Robert Harding, Carlos Guevara Mann, Orlando J. Pérez

Score: .50

Influence over executive (3/9)		Institutional autonomy (4/9)		Specified powers (5/8)		Institutional capacity (4/6)	
1. replace	X	10. no dissolution	X	19. amendments	X	27. sessions	X
2. serve as ministers	X	11. no decree		20. war	X	28. secretary	X
3. interpellate	X	12. no veto		21. treaties	X	29. staff	
4. investigate		13. no review		22. amnesty	X	30. no term limits	X
5. oversee police		14. no gatekeeping		23. pardon		31. seek re-election	X
6. appoint PM		15. no impoundment	X	24. judiciary	X	32. experience	
7. appoint ministers		16. control resources	X	25. central bank			
8. lack president		17. immunity		26. media			
9. no confidence		18. all elected	X				

The National Assembly (*Asamblea Nacional*) of Panama was established in the 1904 constitution, following Panama's declaration of independence from Colombia. The legislature has been denied authority for much of its history. From 1968 to 1981 a military leader, General Omar Torrijos Herrera, ruled Panama. Shortly thereafter, Manuel Noriega, another military ruler, came to power. His ouster by U.S. forces in 1989 paved the way for civilian rule. Panama's current constitution was adopted in 1972. In 1983 constitutional amendments set the formal parameters of a unicameral legislature as it exists today. Constitutional amendments in 1994 and 2004 did not noticeably affect the legislature's power.

The legislature has moderate authority. It can influence the executive with powers to remove the president and interpellate executive branch officials. Furthermore, its members can serve in government. The legislature's institutional autonomy is bolstered by the president's lack of dissolution powers. The legislature exercises many specified powers and has some institutional capacity.

SURVEY

1. The legislature alone, without the involvement of any other agencies, can impeach the president or replace the prime minister.

Yes. The legislature can remove the president from office.

> Article 154
> Judicial functions of the Legislative Assembly are:
> 1. To take cognizance of the accusations or charges lodged against the President of the Republic and the Justices of the Supreme Court, and to judge them, should the occasion arise, for acts performed in the exercise of the free functioning of the public power, or in violation of the Constitution or laws.

> Article 186
> The President and the Vice-Presidents of the Republic are responsible only in the following cases:
> 1. For exceeding their constitutional powers;
> 2. For acts of violence or coercion during the electoral process; for impeding the meeting of the Legislative Assembly, for blocking its exercise of functions, and the exercise of functions of the rest of the public organizations or authorities that are established by this Constitution;
> 3. For offenses against the international personality of the State, or against public authority. In the first and second cases, the penalty shall be removal from office, and disqualification to hold public office for a period of time fixed by law. In the third case ordinary law shall apply.

2. Ministers may serve simultaneously as members of the legislature.

Yes. Legislators may serve simultaneously in ministerial positions.

3. The legislature has powers of summons over executive branch officials and hearings with executive branch officials testifying before the legislature or its committees are regularly held.

Yes. The legislature regularly interpellates officials from the executive.

> Article 155
> 9. To call, or request, from officials that the Legislative Branch of Government appoints or confirms, from the Ministers of State, the General Directors or Managers of all Autonomous and Semi-autonomous Entities, decentralized organizations, industrial or commercial state enterprises, as well as mixed enterprises referred to in Number 11 of Article 153, the submission of written or oral reports on subjects under their authority, that

the Legislative Assembly requires, to better discharge its duties, or to have knowledge of administration actions, except for that which is stated in Number 7 of Article 157. When the reports are to be oral, the call should be delivered at least forty-eight hours ahead of time, and in the form of specific written questions. The officials who are asked to give such reports must attend and be heard during the session for which they were called, regardless of the debate to continue in later sessions for a decision by the Legislative Assembly. Such a debate shall not extend to subjects unrelated to the specific question.

4. The legislature can conduct independent investigation of the chief executive and the agencies of the executive.

No. Formally, the legislature can establish committees to investigate the executive, but in practice, the legislature lacks the ability to investigate the president.

> Article 155
> Administrative functions of the Legislative Assembly are the following:
> 6. To appoint the permanent Committees of the Legislative Assembly, and Committees of Investigation over any matters of public interest, in accordance with this Constitution and the rules for its internal proceedings, for the information of a full session of the Assembly so that measures considered appropriate will be issued.

5. The legislature has effective powers of oversight over the agencies of coercion (the military, organs of law enforcement, intelligence services, and the secret police).

No. The legislature lacks effective powers of oversight over the agencies of coercion.

6. The legislature appoints the prime minister.

No. There is no prime minister.

7. The legislature's approval is required to confirm the appointment of ministers; or the legislature itself appoints ministers.

No. The president appoints ministers, and the appointments do not require the legislature's approval.

> Article 178
> Functions which may be exercised by the President of the Republic by himself are:
> 1. To appoint and remove freely the Ministers of State.

8. The country lacks a presidency entirely or there is a presidency, but the president is elected by the legislature.

No. The president is directly elected.

Article 172
The President of the Republic shall be elected by a majority of votes in popular, direct suffrage for a period of five years.

9. The legislature can vote no confidence in the government.

No. Legislators can censure individual ministers but cannot vote no confidence in the government as a whole.

Article 155
Administrative functions of the Legislative Assembly are the following:
7. To give votes of censure against the Ministers of State when they, in the opinion of the Legislative Assembly, are responsible for threatening or illegal acts, or for grave errors that are considered detrimental to the interests of the State. In order that the vote of censure may be in order, it must be proposed in writing six days before its debate, by no less than half of the Legislators, and approved by the vote of two thirds of the Assembly.

10. The legislature is immune from dissolution by the executive.

Yes. The legislature is immune from dissolution.

11. Any executive initiative on legislation requires ratification or approval by the legislature before it takes effect; that is, the executive lacks decree power.

No. Formally, the president can issue decrees only when granted explicit authority to do so by the legislature, but in practice, this provision is abused, and the president regularly issues decrees that have the force of law.

Article 153
Legislative functions of the Nation are vested in the Legislative Assembly and consist in issuing laws necessary for the fulfillment of the purposes of the performance functions, of the State declared in this Constitution, and especially for the following:
16. To grant the Executive Branch of Government, when it so requests, and when the need exists, precise extraordinary powers that shall be exercised during the Legislative Assembly recess by means of Decree Laws. The law which confers such powers shall express specifically the matters and purposes that shall be the object of the Decree Laws and shall not include the matters mentioned in Numbers 3, 4, and 10 of this Article, nor the development of fundamental guarantees, suffrage, political party regulations and specification of crimes and punishments. The extraordinary powers law shall expire when the next ordinary session of the Legislative Assembly begins. Every Decree Law that the Executive Authority issues in the exercise of powers that are conferred upon it, must be submitted to the Legislative Branch of Government, so that the latter may legislate upon the matter, in ordinary session, immediately following promulgation of the respective Decree-Law. The

Legislative Branch shall have the power at all times, and on its own initiative, to repeal, amend, or add to without limitation as to matters, the Decree-Laws that have been issued.

12. Laws passed by the legislature are veto-proof or essentially veto-proof; that is, the executive lacks veto power, or has veto power but the veto can be overridden by a majority in the legislature.

No. A two-thirds majority is required to override a presidential veto.

Article 163
The Executive Authority shall be allowed a period of no more than thirty working days to return a bill with objections. If the Executive Authority does not return the bill with his objections within the terms prescribed therefor, he must approve it and order it to be promulgated.

Article 164
A bill vetoed as a whole by the Executive Authority, will be returned to the Legislative Assembly for a third reading. If it has been objected to only in part, it will be returned for a second reading for the sole purpose of the objections being considered. If the objections having been considered by the Legislative Assembly the bill is approved by the two-thirds of the Legislators composing the Assembly, the Executive Authority will approve it and have it promulgated without power to present new objections. If it does not obtain the approval of that number of Legislators, the bill shall be rejected.

13. The legislature's laws are supreme and not subject to judicial review.

No. The Supreme Court can review the constitutionality of laws.

Article 203
In the course of exercising from its Constitutional and legal powers, the Supreme Court of Justice shall:
1. Guard the integrity of the Constitution. For this purpose, and after hearing the opinion of the Attorney General of the Nation or the Solicitor General of the Administration, the Court in plenary session shall try and rule on cases concerning the unconstitutionality of laws, decrees, decisions, resolutions and other acts that for reasons of substance or form are challenged before it, by any person.

14. The legislature has the right to initiate bills in all policy jurisdictions; the executive lacks gatekeeping authority.

No. The legislature is prohibited from initiating legislation related to public sector salaries and other major financial issues.

15. Expenditure of funds appropriated by the legislature is mandatory; the executive lacks the power to impound funds appropriated by the legislature.

Yes. The executive lacks the power to impound funds appropriated by the legislature.

16. The legislature controls the resources that finance its own internal operation and provide for the perquisites of its own members.

Yes. The legislature enjoys financial autonomy, including control over members' salaries.

> Article 151
> Legislators shall receive emoluments as provided by law which shall be paid by the National Treasury, but an increase in such emoluments shall not become effective until after the Legislative Assembly term in which it was approved has expired.

17. Members of the legislature are immune from arrest and/or criminal prosecution.

No. Legislators' immunity is limited to the time period surrounding the legislative session only. Legislators are subject to arrest at other times.

> Article 149
> Five days before the period of each Legislature, during it, and up to five days after, members of the Legislative Assembly shall be granted immunity. In such a period they may not be prosecuted or arrested for penal or police reasons without prior authorization by the Legislative Assembly. This immunity shall have no effect when the Legislator renounces his immunity, or if he's caught in the act of committing a crime. The Legislator shall be subject to civil jurisdiction, but not subject to garnishment, attachment or other prejudgment remedies, against his property, from the day of his election to the end of his term.

18. All members of the legislature are elected; the executive lacks the power to appoint any members of the legislature.

Yes. All members of the legislature are elected.

> Article 140
> The Legislative Branch of Government shall be composed of a body named the Legislative Assembly, whose members shall be elected by means of party nominations, and direct popular vote, in accordance with that which is established in this Constitution.

19. The legislature alone, without the involvement of any other agencies, can change the Constitution.

Yes. The legislature can change the constitution through a complicated procedure. The sitting legislature can propose the amendment in three separate readings, and then, following an election, the subsequent legislature can approve the amendment.

> Article 308
> The initiative to propose Constitutional amendments belongs to the Legislative Assembly, the Cabinet Council, or the Supreme Court of Justice. Such amendments must be approved by one of the following procedures:
> 1. Through a Legislative Act, approved in three readings by an absolute majority of Legislative Assembly members, which must be published in the Official Gazette and sent from the Executive Branch of Government to the same Assembly within the first five days of ordinary sessions following elections for the new Legislative Branch of Government, for the purpose of, in this final Legislature, begin newly read and approved, without modification, in a single reading and by an absolute majority of all members of the Assembly.
> 2. Through a Legislative Act approved in three readings by an absolute majority of Legislative Assembly members, in one Legislature period, and approved equally, in three readings by an absolute majority of the members of the already mentioned Assembly, in the Legislature period immediately following. At this time the text approved during the previous Legislature period may be modified. The Legislative Act approved in this manner must be published in the Official Gazette and submitted to the people for direct, popular consideration through a referendum that shall be held on the date designated by the Legislative Assembly, within a time period no less than three months, nor more than six months from the date of the Act's approval by the second Legislature. The Legislative Act approved according to either of the two procedures mentioned will enter into force upon its publication in the Official Gazette, which shall be accomplished by the Executive Branch of Government within ten (10) working days following its ratification by the Legislative Assembly, or within thirty (30) working days following its approval through referendum, whichever the case may be, without a later publication being the cause of the Act's being unconstitutional.

20. The legislature's approval is necessary for the declaration of war.

Yes. The legislature declares war.

> Article 153
> Legislative functions of the Nation are vested in the Legislative Assembly and consist in issuing laws necessary for the fulfillment of the purposes of the performance functions, of the State declared in this Constitution, and especially for the following:
> 5. To declare war and to empower the Executive Branch of Government to negotiate peace.

21. The legislature's approval is necessary to ratify treaties with foreign countries.

Yes. The legislature's approval is necessary to ratify international treaties.

> Article 179
> The following functions shall be exercised by the President of the Republic with the participation of the respective Minister:

9. To direct foreign relations, to negotiate Treaties and international Agreements, which shall be submitted to the consideration of the Legislative Branch and authorize and to assign and receive diplomatic and consular agents.

22. The legislature has the power to grant amnesty.

Yes. The legislature has the power to grant amnesty.

> Article 153
> Legislative functions of the Nation are vested in the Legislative Assembly and consist in issuing laws necessary for the fulfillment of the purposes of the performance functions, of the State declared in this Constitution, and especially for the following:
> 6. To declare amnesty for political offenses.

23. The legislature has the power of pardon.

No. The president has the power of pardon.

> Article 179
> The following functions shall be exercised by the President of the Republic with the participation of the respective Minister:
> 12. To decree pardons for political offenses, reduce penalties and grant conditional freedom to common crimes convicts.

24. The legislature reviews and has the right to reject appointments to the judiciary; or the legislature itself appoints members of the judiciary.

Yes. The legislature's consent is required to approve the president's appointments to the Supreme Court.

> Article 155
> Administrative functions of the Legislative Assembly are the following:
> 4. To approve or disapprove appointments of Justices to the Supreme Court...that are made by the Executive Power and under this Constitution, or by law, requiring ratification by the Legislative Assembly.

> Article 200
> The Supreme Court of Justice shall be composed of the number of Justices determined by law, appointed with the agreement of the Cabinet Council, subject to the approval of the Legislative Branch of Government, for a ten year term.

25. The chairman of the central bank is appointed by the legislature.

No. The president appoints the president of the National Bank of Panama.

26. The legislature has a substantial voice in the operation of the state-owned media.

No. The legislature lacks a substantial voice in the operation of the public media.

27. The legislature is regularly in session.

Yes. The legislature meets in ordinary session for eight months each year.

> Article 143
> The Legislative Assembly shall convene, in its own right, without need for previous convocation, in the capital city for sessions that last eight months in a one year period, divided into two ordinary legislative sessions of four month's duration. Such sessions shall extend from September 1 through December 31, and March 1 through June 30. The Legislative Assembly shall meet in extraordinary session when convoked by the Executive Branch of Government and during the time it designates, to hear exclusively, matters that the Branch submits for the Legislators' consideration.

28. Each legislator has a personal secretary.

Yes.

29. Each legislator has at least one non-secretarial staff member with policy expertise.

No.

30. Legislators are eligible for re-election without any restriction.

Yes. There are no restrictions on re-election.

31. A seat in the legislature is an attractive enough position that legislators are generally interested in and seek re-election.

Yes.

32. The re-election of incumbent legislators is common enough that at any given time the legislature contains a significant number of highly experienced members.

No. Turnover rates are high, preventing the maintenance of a substantial cohort of highly experienced legislators.

NATIONAL PARLIAMENT OF PAPUA NEW GUINEA

Expert consultants: Donald Denoon, Graham Hassall, Joseph Ketan, Peter Larmour, Michael Morgan

Score: .66

Influence over executive (8/9)		Institutional autonomy (6/9)		Specified powers (3/8)		Institutional capacity (4/6)	
1. replace	X	10. no dissolution		19. amendments	X	27. sessions	
2. serve as ministers	X	11. no decree	X	20. war	X	28. secretary	X
3. interpellate	X	12. no veto	X	21. treaties	X	29. staff	X
4. investigate	X	13. no review		22. amnesty		30. no term limits	X
5. oversee police	X	14. no gatekeeping	X	23. pardon		31. seek re-election	X
6. appoint PM	X	15. no impoundment	X	24. judiciary		32. experience	
7. appoint ministers		16. control resources	X	25. central bank			
8. lack president	X	17. immunity		26. media			
9. no confidence	X	18. all elected	X				

The National Parliament of Papua New Guinea was established in the 1975 constitution upon independence from Australia. The constitution, which is not a paradigm of concision and lucidity, calls for a unicameral parliament. The executive comprises a prime minister as the head of government and a Governor General (formally representing the Queen of England) as the head of state.

The legislature has broad powers. With the exception of the power to appoint ministers, it possesses every means of influencing the executive captured in this survey. It also enjoys significant institutional autonomy, evidenced by a lack of executive decree, veto, and gatekeeping powers. The legislature exercises few specified powers, however. It enjoys some institutional capacity, but its capacity is limited by infrequent legislative sessions and a dearth of highly experienced legislators.

SURVEY

1. The legislature alone, without the involvement of any other agencies, can impeach the president or replace the prime minister.

Yes. The legislature can remove the prime minister from office with a vote of no confidence.

Article 142

(5) The Prime Minister –
(a) shall be dismissed from office by the Head of State if the Parliament passes, in accordance with Section

145 (motions of no confidence), a motion of no confidence in him or the Ministry.

2. Ministers may serve simultaneously as members of the legislature.

Yes. Ministers are chosen from, and required to serve simultaneously in, the legislature.

Article 141
The Ministry is a Parliamentary Executive, and therefore –
(a) no person who is not a member of the Parliament is eligible to be appointed to be a Minister, and, except as is expressly provided in this Constitution to the contrary, a Minister who ceases to be a member of the Parliament ceases to hold office as a Minister.

3. The legislature has powers of summons over executive branch officials and hearings with executive branch officials testifying before the legislature or its committees are regularly held.

Yes. The legislature regularly interpellates officials from the executive.

4. The legislature can conduct independent investigation of the chief executive and the agencies of the executive.

Yes. The legislature can order a special investigative body, the Ombudsman Commission, to investigate the executive.

Article 219
(1) Subject to this section and to any Organic Law made for the purposes of Subsection (7), the functions of the Ombudsman Commission are –

(a) to investigate, on its own initiative or on complaint by a person affected, any conduct on the part of –

(i) any State Service or provincial service, or a member of any such service; or

(ii) any other governmental body, or an officer or employee of a governmental body; or

(iii) any local government body or an officer or employee of any such body; or

(iv) any other body set up by statute –

(A) that is wholly or mainly supported out of public moneys of Papua New Guinea; or

(B) all of, or the majority of, the members of the controlling authority of which are appointed by the National Executive, or an officer of employee of any such body; and

(v) any member of the personal staff of the Governor-General, a Minister or the Leader or Deputy Leader of the Opposition; or

(vi) any other body or person prescribed for the purpose by an Act of the Parliament, specified by or under an Organic Law in the exercise of a power or function vested in it or him by law in cases where the conduct is or may be wrong, taking into account, amongst other things, the National Goals and Directive Principles, the Basic Rights and the Basic Social Obligations; and

(b) to investigate any defects in any law or administrative practice appearing from any such investigation; and

(c) to investigate, either on its own initiative or on complaint by a person affected, any case of an alleged or suspected discriminatory practice within the meaning of a law prohibiting such practices; and

(d) any functions conferred on it under Division III.2 (leadership code); and

(e) any other functions conferred upon it by or under an Organic Law.

(Subsection (1) amended by Constitutional Amendment No. 3).

(See: Organic Law on the Ombudsman Commission).

(2) Subject to Subsections (3), (4) and (5), and without otherwise limiting the generality of the expression, for the purposes of Subsection (1)(a) conduct is wrong if it is –

(a) contrary to law; or

(b) unreasonable, unjust, oppressive or improperly discriminatory, whether or not it is in accordance with law or practice; or

(c) based wholly or partly on improper motives, irrelevant grounds or irrelevant considerations; or

(d) based wholly or partly on a mistake of law or of fact; or

(e) conduct for which reasons should be given but were not, whether or not the act was supposed to be done in the exercise of deliberate judgement within the meaning of Section 62.

5. The legislature has effective powers of oversight over the agencies of coercion (the military, organs of law enforcement, intelligence services, and the secret police).

Yes. The legislature has effective powers of oversight over the agencies of coercion.

6. The legislature appoints the prime minister.

Yes. The Governor General appoints as prime minister the candidate who enjoys the support of the legislature.

Article 142

(1) An office of Prime Minister is hereby established.

(2) The Prime Minister shall be appointed, at the first meeting of the Parliament after a general election and otherwise from time to time as the occasion for the appointment of a Prime Minister arises, by the Head of State, acting in accordance with a decision of the Parliament.

7. The legislature's approval is required to confirm the appointment of ministers; or the legislature itself appoints ministers.

No. The Governor General appoints ministers on the advice of the prime minister, and the appointments do not require the legislature's approval.

Article 144

(1) There shall be such number of Ministers (other than the Prime Minister), not being less than six or more than one quarter of the number of members of the Parliament from time to time, as is determined by or under an Organic Law.

(2) The Ministers, other than the Prime Minister, shall be appointed by the Head of State, acting with, and in accordance with, the advice of the Prime Minister.

8. The country lacks a presidency entirely or there is a presidency, but the president is elected by the legislature.

Yes. The country lacks a presidency. The Governor General is the head of state.

Article 82

(1) Her Majesty the Queen –

(a) having been requested by the people of Papua New Guinea, through their Constituent Assembly, to become the Queen and Head of State of Papua New Guinea; and

(b) having graciously consented so to become, is the Queen and Head of State of Papua New Guinea.

(2) Subject to and in accordance with this Constitution, the privileges, powers, functions, duties and responsibilities of the Head of State may be had, exercised and performed through a Governor-General appointed in accordance with Division 3 (appointment, etc., of Governor-General) and, except where the contrary intention appears, reference in any law to the Head of State shall be read accordingly.

9. The legislature can vote no confidence in the government.

Yes. The legislature can vote no confidence in the government.

Article 145

(1) For the purposes of Sections 142 (the Prime Minister) and 144 (other Ministers), a motion of no confidence is a motion –
  (a) that is expressed to be a motion of no confidence in the Prime Minister, the Ministry or a Minister, as the case may be; and
  (b) of which not less than one week's notice, signed by a number of members of the Parliament being not less than one-tenth of the total number of seats in the Parliament, has been given in accordance with the Standing Orders of the Parliament.
(2) A motion of no confidence in the Prime Minister or the Ministry –
  (a) moved during the first four years of the life of Parliament shall not be allowed unless it nominates the next Prime Minister; and
  (b) moved within 12 months before the fifth anniversary of the date fixed for the return of the writs at the previous general election shall not be allowed if it nominates the next Prime Minister.
(3) A motion of no confidence in the Prime Minister or the Ministry moved in accordance with Subsection (2)(a) may not be amended in respect of the name of the person nominated as the next Prime Minister except by substituting the name of some other person.
(4) A motion of no confidence in the Prime Minister or in the Ministry may not be moved during the period of eighteen months commencing on the date of the appointment of the Prime Minister.

10. The legislature is immune from dissolution by the executive.

No. The Governor General, on the advice of the prime minister, can dissolve the legislature.

Article 105

(1) A general election to the Parliament shall be held –
  (a) within the period of three months before the fifth anniversary of the day fixed for the return of the writs for the previous general election; or
  (b) if, during the last 12 months before the fifth anniversary of the day fixed for the return of the writs for the previous general election –
    (i) a vote of no confidence in the Prime Minister or the Ministry is passed in accordance with Section 145 (motions of no confidence); or
    (ii) the Government is defeated on the vote on a question that the Prime Minister has declared to the Parliament to be a question of confidence; or
  (c) if the Parliament, by an absolute majority vote, so decides.
(2) The Head of State, acting with, and in accordance with, the advice of the Electoral Commission, shall fix the first and last days of the period during which polling

shall take place and the date by which the writs for a general election shall be returned.
(3) In advising the Head of State under Subsection (2), and in conducting the election, the Electoral Commission shall do its best to ensure that –
  (a) in a case to which Subsection (1)(a) applies – the date for the return of the writs is fixed as nearly as may reasonably be to the fifth anniversary of the date fixed for the return of the writs for the previous general election; and
  (b) in a case to which Subsection (1)(b) or (c) applies – the date for the return of the writs is fixed as soon as may reasonably be after the date of the relevant decision of the Parliament.

11. Any executive initiative on legislation requires ratification or approval by the legislature before it takes effect; that is, the executive lacks decree power.

Yes. The executive lacks decree power.

12. Laws passed by the legislature are veto-proof or essentially veto-proof; that is, the executive lacks veto power, or has veto power but the veto can be overridden by a majority in the legislature.

Yes. The executive lacks veto power. Formally, the Governor General could refuse to assent to legislation, but in practice, it would be unthinkable for the Governor General to withhold assent to a bill.

13. The legislature's laws are supreme and not subject to judicial review.

No. The Supreme Court can review the constitutionality of laws.

14. The legislature has the right to initiate bills in all policy jurisdictions; the executive lacks gatekeeping authority.

Yes. The legislature can initiate bills in all policy jurisdictions.

15. Expenditure of funds appropriated by the legislature is mandatory; the executive lacks the power to impound funds appropriated by the legislature.

Yes. The executive lacks the power to impound funds appropriated by the legislature.

16. The legislature controls the resources that finance its own internal operation and provide for the perquisites of its own members.

Yes. The legislature enjoys financial autonomy.

17. Members of the legislature are immune from arrest and/or criminal prosecution.

No. Immunity extends only to official parliamentary business and to criminal proceedings while the legislature is in session only. Legislators are subject to arrest for common crimes when the legislature is not in session.

Article 115

(1) The powers (other than legislative powers), privileges and immunities of the Parliament and of its members and committees are as prescribed by or under this section and by any other provision of this Constitution.
(2) There shall be freedom of speech, debate and proceeding in the Parliament, and the exercise of those freedoms shall not be questioned in any court or in any proceedings whatever (otherwise than in proceedings in the Parliament or before a committee of the Parliament).
(3) No member of the Parliament is subject to the jurisdiction of any court in respect of the exercise of his powers or the performance of his functions, duties or responsibilities as such, but this subsection does not affect the operation of Division III.2 (leadership code).
(4) No member of the Parliament is liable to civil or criminal proceedings, arrest, imprisonment, fine, damages or compensation by reason of any matter or thing that he has brought by petition, question, bill, resolution, motion or otherwise, or has said before or submitted to the Parliament or a committee of the Parliament.
(5) No member of the Parliament or other person is liable to civil or criminal proceedings, arrest, imprisonment, fine, damages or compensation by reason of –
  (a) an act done under the authority of the Parliament or under an order of the Parliament or a committee of the Parliament; or
  (b) words spoken or used, or a document or writing made or produced, under an order or summons made or issued under the authority of the Parliament or a committee of the Parliament.
(6) Members of the Parliament are free from arrest for civil debt during meetings of the Parliament and during the period commencing three days before, and ending three days after, a meeting when they are traveling from their respective electorates to attend the meeting or are returning to their electorates from the meeting.

18. All members of the legislature are elected; the executive lacks the power to appoint any members of the legislature.

Yes. All members of the legislature are elected, with one exception. The legislature itself may, by a two-thirds majority vote, appoint a single member of parliament.

Article 101

(1) Subject to this section, the Parliament is a single-chamber legislature, consisting of –
  (a) a number of members elected from single-member open electorates; and
  (b) a number of members elected from single-member provincial electorates; and
  (c) not more than three nominated members, appointed and holding office in accordance with Section 102.

Article 102

The Parliament may, from time to time, by a two-thirds absolute majority vote, appoint a person (other than a member) to be a nominated member of the Parliament.

19. The legislature alone, without the involvement of any other agencies, can change the Constitution.

Yes. The legislature can change the constitution in multiple readings with a two-thirds majority vote.

Article 13

This Constitution may be altered only by law made by the Parliament that –
(a) is expressed to be a law to alter this Constitution; and
(b) is made and certified in accordance with Section 14 (making of alterations to the Constitution and Organic Laws).

Article 14

(1) Subject to Sections 12(3) (Organic Laws) and 15 (urgent alterations), a proposed law to alter this Constitution, or a proposed Organic Law, must be supported on a division in accordance with the Standing Orders of the Parliament by the prescribed majority of votes determined in accordance with Section 17 ("prescribed majority of votes") expressed on at least two occasions after opportunity for debate on the merits.

Article 17

(1) Subject to this section, in relation to a proposed law to alter any provision of this Constitution the prescribed majority of votes for the purposes of Section 14 (making of alterations to the Constitution and Organic Laws) is the majority of votes prescribed by this Constitution in relation to that provision, or if no majority is prescribed a two-thirds absolute majority vote.

20. The legislature's approval is necessary for the declaration of war.

Yes. Formally, the Governor General, on the advice of the government (National Executive Council), can declare war. In practice, a declaration of war would be unthinkable without the legislature's approval.

Article 227

The Head of State, acting with, and in accordance with, the advice of the National Executive Council, may publicly declare that Papua New Guinea is at war with another country.

21. The legislature's approval is necessary to ratify treaties with foreign countries.

Yes. The legislature's approval is necessary to ratify international treaties.

Article 117

(3) Subject to Subsection (5), the consent of Papua New Guinea to be bound as a party to a treaty shall not be given –

(a) unless a treaty document relating to the treaty has been presented to the Parliament for at least ten sitting days; or

(b) if within ten sitting days of the Parliament after the day on which the treaty document was presented to the Parliament the Parliament, by an absolute majority vote, disapproves the giving of the consent.

(4) The fact that the Parliament has disapproved the giving of the consent of Papua New Guinea to be bound as a party to a treaty does not prevent the re-presentation to the Parliament of a treaty document relating to the treaty, and in that event Subsection (3) once again applies.

22. The legislature has the power to grant amnesty.

No. Amnesty and pardon are not treated separately, and the legislature lacks the power to grant amnesty. See item 23.

23. The legislature has the power of pardon.

No. The Governor General has the power of pardon.

Article 151

(1) Subject to this Subdivision, the Head of State, acting with, and in accordance with, the advice of the National Executive Council, may grant to a person convicted of an offence or held in penal detention under a law of Papua New Guinea –

(a) a pardon, either free or conditional; or

(b) a remission or commutation of sentence; or

(c) a respite of the execution of sentence; or

(d) a less severe form of punishment for that imposed by any sentence, and may remit or refund, in whole or in part, any fine, penalty or forfeiture paid or payable to a governmental body.

(2) Where an offence has been committed, the Head of State, acting with, and in accordance with, the advice of the National Executive Council, may grant a pardon, either free or conditional, to an accomplice who gives evidence that leads to the conviction of a principal offender.

24. The legislature reviews and has the right to reject appointments to the judiciary; or the legislature itself appoints members of the judiciary.

No. The Governor General, on the advice of the government, appoints the Chief Justice. Other justices are selected by a judicial services commission. The appointments do not require the legislature's approval.

Article 169

(1) An office of Chief Justice of Papua New Guinea is hereby established.

The Chief Justice shall be appointed by the Head of State, acting with, and in accordance with, the advice of the National Executive Council given after consultation with the Minister responsible for the National Justice Administration.

Article 170

(1) An office of Deputy Chief Justice of Papua New Guinea is hereby established.

(2) The Deputy Chief Justice and the other Judges of the National Court (other than the Chief Justice) and acting Judges shall be appointed by the Judicial and Legal Services Commission.

25. The chairman of the central bank is appointed by the legislature.

No. The government appoints the governor of the Bank of Papua New Guinea with the legislature's approval.

26. The legislature has a substantial voice in the operation of the state-owned media.

No. The legislature lacks a substantial voice in the operation of the public media.

27. The legislature is regularly in session.

No. Formally, the legislature is required to meet at least three times each year, in sessions that are to last for at least nine weeks. In practice, the legislature does not regularly meet because governments fearing a vote of no confidence often limit legislative sessions.

Article 124

(1) The Parliament shall be called to meet not more than seven days after the day fixed for the return of the writs for a general election, and shall meet not less frequently than three times in each period of 12 months, and, in principle, for not less than nine weeks in each such period.

28. Each legislator has a personal secretary.

Yes.

29. Each legislator has at least one non-secretarial staff member with policy expertise.

Yes.

30. Legislators are eligible for re-election without any restriction.

Yes. There are no restrictions on re-election.

31. A seat in the legislature is an attractive enough position that legislators are generally interested in and seek re-election.

Yes.

32. The re-election of incumbent legislators is common enough that at any given time the legislature contains a significant number of highly experienced members.

No. The legislature lacks a significant number of highly experienced members. In 2002, for example, eighty-three of 109 legislators were voted out of office.

CONGRESS OF PARAGUAY (*CONGRESO*)

Expert consultants: Esteban Areco, Rafael Filizzola, Phil Kelly, Desirèe Masi, Sebastian M. Saiegh, Brian Turner

Score: .56

Influence over executive (3/9)		Institutional autonomy (7/9)		Specified powers (4/8)		Institutional capacity (4/6)	
1. replace	X	10. no dissolution	X	19. amendments		27. sessions	X
2. serve as ministers		11. no decree	X	20. war	X	28. secretary	X
3. interpellate	X	12. no veto	X	21. treaties	X	29. staff	
4. investigate	X	13. no review		22. amnesty	X	30. no term limits	X
5. oversee police		14. no gatekeeping	X	23. pardon		31. seek re-election	X
6. appoint PM		15. no impoundment		24. judiciary	X	32. experience	
7. appoint ministers		16. control resources	X	25. central bank			
8. lack president		17. immunity	X	26. media			
9. no confidence		18. all elected	X				

The Congress (*Congreso*) of Paraguay was established in 1813 upon independence from Spain. Within a decade the 1,000-member assembly was disbanded, and President José Gaspar Rodríguez de Francia ruled until his death in 1840. In 1844 a new constitution recreated a substantial role for Congress, a part it retained for the next century. In 1954 General Alfredo Stroessner seized power and subsequently ruled for over three decades. He was deposed in 1989, leading to parliamentary and presidential elections and the adoption of a new constitution in 1992. The constitution called for a bicameral parliament consisting of a lower house, the House of Deputies (*Cámara de Diputados*), and an upper house, the Senate (*Cámara de Senadores*).

Congress has substantial powers overall, but its authority is unevenly distributed. Its opportunity to influence the executive is relatively modest. It cannot appoint the president or ministers, its members cannot serve in government, and it cannot vote no confidence in the government. It also lacks meaningful powers of oversight over the agencies of coercion. Its institutional autonomy, on the other hand, is formidable. With the exception of freedom from judicial review, the legislature possesses every measure of institutional autonomy captured in this survey. The legislature exercises some specified powers and has a fair amount of institutional capacity.

SURVEY

1. The legislature alone, without the involvement of any other agencies, can impeach the president or replace the prime minister.

Yes. The legislature can impeach the president. The Chamber of Deputies presses charges by a two-thirds majority vote, and the Senate conducts a public trial and removes the president from office by a majority vote.

Article 225
(1) The president of the Republic . . . may be forced to undergo impeachment proceedings for malfeasance in office, for crimes committed in office, or for common crimes.
(2) The Chamber of Deputies, by a two-thirds majority, will press the respective charges. The Senate, by a two-thirds absolute majority, will conduct a public trial of those charged by the Chamber of Deputies and, if appropriate, will declare them guilty for the sole purpose of removing them from office. In cases in which it appears that common crimes have been committed, the files on the respective impeachment proceedings will be referred to a competent court.

2. Ministers may serve simultaneously as members of the legislature.

No. Legislators are prohibited from serving simultaneously in ministerial positions.

Article 196

(1) Advisors of public offices or officials and employees who are on the payroll of the State or of municipalities, irrespective of their position and the nature of their remuneration, may be elected to a legislative office but cannot exercise legislative functions as long as their appointment to such positions is in force.

3. The legislature has powers of summons over executive branch officials and hearings with executive branch officials testifying before the legislature or its committees are regularly held.

Yes. The legislature regularly interpellates officials from the executive.

Article 193

(1) Each chamber, by an absolute majority, may individually summon and interpellate ministers and other senior administration officials and directors and directors and administrators of autonomous, self-supported, or decentralized companies, as well as directors and administrators of organizations charged with administering state funds and those in which the State is a majority shareholder, when the chamber is discussing a law or is studying a matter pertaining to their respective activities. The respective questions must be conveyed to the summoned official at least five days in advance. Except for those cases in which the summoned individual may claim a legal cause for being excused, it will be mandatory for him to appear before the respective chamber, to answer the questions, and to provide all the information he has been asked to give.

(2) The law will determine the participation of majority and minority blocs in the formulation of the questions.

(3) Neither the president of the Republic, the vice president, nor the members of the judicial branch may be summoned or interpellated on matters pertaining to their jurisdictional activity.

4. The legislature can conduct independent investigation of the chief executive and the agencies of the executive.

Yes. The legislature can investigate the executive.

Article 192

(1) Each chamber may ask other branches of government, as well as autonomous, self-supported, decentralized companies, or public officials, to submit reports on matters of public interest that it deems necessary, with the exception of matters pertaining to jurisdictional activities.

(2) The affected parties will have to submit the respective report within an established deadline, which will not be under 15 days.

Article 195

(1) Both chambers of Congress may create joint investigating committees on any matter of public interest, as well as on the conduct of their members.

(2) Directors and administrators of autonomous, self-supported, or decentralized companies, those of companies in which the State is a majority shareholder, and those charged with administering state funds, as well as public officials and private citizens, must appear before the two chambers to supply the information and documents they are asked to give. The law will establish sanctions for those failing to comply with this obligation.

(5) The judges will order, in accordance with the law, those actions and discovery proceedings that are required for the purpose of the investigation.

5. The legislature has effective powers of oversight over the agencies of coercion (the military, organs of law enforcement, intelligence services, and the secret police).

No. The legislature lacks effective powers of oversight over the agencies of coercion.

6. The legislature appoints the prime minister.

No. There is no prime minister.

7. The legislature's approval is required to confirm the appointment of ministers; or the legislature itself appoints ministers.

No. The president appoints ministers, and the appointments do not require the legislature's approval.

Article 238

The president of the Republic has the following duties and powers:

6. To appoint or remove cabinet ministers.

8. The country lacks a presidency entirely or there is a presidency, but the president is elected by the legislature.

No. The president is directly elected.

Article 230

The president and vice president of the Republic will be elected jointly and directly by the people, by a simple majority of voters, in general elections held between 90 and 120 days prior to the expiration of the ongoing constitutional term.

9. The legislature can vote no confidence in the government.

No. The legislature can censure individual ministers but cannot vote no confidence in the government as a whole.

Article 194

(1) If a summoned official fails to appear before the respective chamber, or if this chamber considers his briefing to be unsatisfactory, the two chambers, by a two-thirds absolute majority, will issue a vote of censure against him and will recommend that the president

of the Republic or the official's immediate supervisor remove him from office.

(2) If a motion of censure is not approved, no other motion may be proposed during that same period of sessions on the same subject with regard to the same minister or official.

10. The legislature is immune from dissolution by the executive.

Yes. The legislature is immune from dissolution.

11. Any executive initiative on legislation requires ratification or approval by the legislature before it takes effect; that is, the executive lacks decree power.

Yes. The executive lacks decree power.

12. Laws passed by the legislature are veto-proof or essentially veto-proof; that is, the executive lacks veto power, or has veto power but the veto can be overridden by a majority in the legislature.

Yes. The legislature can override a presidential veto by a majority vote of its total membership.

Article 238
The president of the Republic has the following duties and powers:
4. To veto, either totally or partially, laws approved by Congress through observations or objections he may deem appropriate.

Article 208
(1) A draft law that has been partially vetoed by the executive branch will be returned to the originating chamber, which will study and pass judgment on the objections. If this chamber, by an absolute majority, overrides the executive veto, the draft law will be passed on to the reviewing chamber, which will also pass judgment on the objections. If the reviewing chamber, by the same majority vote, also overrides the executive veto, the original version of the law will have been approved, and the executive branch will have to promulgate it by ordering its publication within five days. If both chambers fail to agree to override the objections, the respective draft law cannot be reconsidered during that period of sessions.

(2) The executive branch objections may be totally or partially accepted or rejected by the two chambers. If they were totally or partially accepted, the two chambers may decide, by an absolute majority, to approve the unquestioned portion of the draft law, which will then have to be promulgated by the executive branch.

(3) The originating chamber will have to consider these objections within 60 days. The reviewing chamber will also have 60 days.

Article 209
If a draft law is totally rejected by the executive branch, it will be returned to the originating chamber, which will discuss it again. If the originating chamber, by an absolute majority, reaffirms its earlier approval, the draft law will be passed on to the reviewing chamber. If

this chamber approves it too, by the same majority, the executive branch will have to promulgate it within five working days and will order its publication. If the two chambers fail to agree to override the total rejection, that draft law cannot be considered again during that period of sessions.

13. The legislature's laws are supreme and not subject to judicial review.

No. The Supreme Court can review the constitutionality of laws.

Article 132
The Supreme Court of Justice has the power to declare any legal provision or decision by the courts unconstitutional, in the manner and within the scope established in this Constitution and the law.

14. The legislature has the right to initiate bills in all policy jurisdictions; the executive lacks gatekeeping authority.

Yes. The legislature can initiate bills in all policy jurisdictions.

15. Expenditure of funds appropriated by the legislature is mandatory; the executive lacks the power to impound funds appropriated by the legislature.

No. The executive often fails to spend funds allocated by the legislature, particularly in the areas of public works and social service provision.

16. The legislature controls the resources that finance its own internal operation and provide for the perquisites of its own members.

Yes. The legislature enjoys financial autonomy.

17. Members of the legislature are immune from arrest and/or criminal prosecution.

Yes. Legislators are immune with the common exception for cases of *flagrante delicto*.

Article 191
(1) No charge may be pressed in court against a member of Congress for the opinions he may have expressed in discharging his duties. No senator or deputy may be arrested from the day of his election until the end of his term, unless he is caught in flagrante delicto in relation to a crime meriting a prison sentence. In this case, the official intervening will place the legislator under house arrest and report the arrest to the respective chamber and to a competent judge immediately, to whom he will submit the case files as soon as possible.

(2) If a court of law orders a pretrial inquest against a senator or a deputy, the presiding judge will send a copy of the case files to the respective chamber, which will examine the merits of the inquest and, by a two-thirds majority vote, will decide whether the senator or deputy involved should be stripped of his immunity in order to stand trial. If the chamber votes against the

legislator, it will suspend his immunity so that he may be brought to trial.

18. All members of the legislature are elected; the executive lacks the power to appoint any members of the legislature.

Yes. All members of the legislature are elected.

Article 182
(1) The legislative branch will be exercised by Congress, which consists of the Senate and of the Chamber of Deputies.
(2) Members and alternate members of both chambers will be directly elected by the people in accordance with the law.

19. The legislature alone, without the involvement of any other agencies, can change the Constitution.

No. Constitutional amendments require approval in a popular referendum. A total revision of the constitution requires a constituent assembly convened for the purpose.

Article 289
(1) This Constitution may be removed only 10 years after its promulgation.
(2) Its reform may be requested by 25 percent of the members of any of the two chambers of Congress, by the president of the Republic, or by 30,000 voters through a signed petition.
(3) By a two-thirds absolute majority vote of its members, the two chambers of Congress may declare the need for constitutional reform.
(4) Once the need for the reform has been declared, the Supreme Electoral Court will call general elections that must not coincide with any other scheduled election within a period of 180 days.
(5) The number of members of the National Constituent Assembly will not exceed the total number of the members of Congress. The causes for their ineligibility or incompatibility will be established by law.
(6) Members of a constituent assembly will enjoy the same immunities established for the members of Congress.
(7) As soon as the new Constitution is approved by the National Constituent Assembly, it will be considered to have been automatically promulgated.

Article 290
(1) This Constitution may be amended three years after it has been promulgated, at the initiative of one-fourth of the members of any of the two chambers of Congress, of the president of the Republic, or of 30,000 voters through a signed petition;
(2) The full text of the amendment will, have to be approved by an absolute majority by the originating chamber. A similar procedure will be followed at the reviewing chamber. If the majority required for its approval is not met in either of the two chambers, it will be considered that the proposed amendment has

been rejected, and it may not be proposed again within a period of one year.
(3) If the amendment has been approved by the two chambers of Congress, the full text of it will be submitted to the Superior Electoral Court, which, within a period of 180 days will call a referendum. If the outcome of the referendum is in favor of the amendment, it will be considered that it has been approved and promulgated and considered part of the Constitution.
(4) If the amendment repeals any provision of the Constitution, no amendment may again be proposed on the same subject for three years.
(5) The procedures established for the reform of the Constitution, rather than those established for its amendment, will be followed with regard to those provisions affecting the election, composition, term in office, or powers of any of the three branches of government or the provisions of Chapters I, II, III and IV of Title II of Part I.

20. The legislature's approval is necessary for the declaration of war.

Yes. The legislature's approval is required for the president to declare a "state of national defense" in the event of foreign aggression.

Article 238
The president of the Republic has the following duties and powers:
7. In case of foreign aggression he will declare – having first been authorized by Congress – a State of National Defense or make efforts to seek peace.

21. The legislature's approval is necessary to ratify treaties with foreign countries.

Yes. The legislature's approval is necessary to ratify international treaties.

Article 141
International treaties that were properly concluded and approved by a law of Congress and the instruments of ratification which have been exchanged or deposited are part of the domestic legal system in keeping with the order of preeminence established under Article 136.

Article 202
Congress has the following duties and powers:
9. To approve or to reject treaties or other international agreements signed by the executive branch.

22. The legislature has the power to grant amnesty.

Yes. The legislature has the power to grant amnesty.

Article 202
Congress has the following duties and powers:
18. To grant amnesties.

23. The legislature has the power of pardon.

No. The president has the power of pardon.

Article 238

The president of the Republic has the following duties and powers:

10. Based on reports by the Supreme Court of Justice, he may pardon or commute sentences imposed by the judges or courts of the Republic.

24. The legislature reviews and has the right to reject appointments to the judiciary; or the legislature itself appoints members of the judiciary.

Yes. The Senate appoints the members of the Supreme Court of Justice and the Superior Electoral Court on the proposal of the Council for Magistrates and with the approval of the executive.

Article 251

Members of appellate or lower courts of the Republic will be appointed by the Supreme Court of Justice from a list of three candidates proposed by the Council for Magistrates.

Article 264

The Council for Magistrates has the following duties and powers:

1. To propose a list of three candidates – selected on the basis of their abilities, qualifications, and merits – for each seat of the Supreme Court of Justice, and to submit such lists to the Senate, which will appoint said justices with the concurrence of the executive branch;

2. To propose a list of three candidates, following the above selection criteria and guidelines, for each member of appellate and lower courts, as well as for members of the Attorney General's Office.

Article 275

(1) The Superior Electoral Court will consist of three members who may be elected or removed following procedures established for the justices of the Supreme Court of Justice.

25. The chairman of the central bank is appointed by the legislature.

No. The president appoints the president of the Central Bank of Paraguay with the Senate's approval.

Article 224

The Senate has the following exclusive Powers:

6. To agree to the appointment of the president and the members of the board of directors of the Paraguayan Central Bank.

26. The legislature has a substantial voice in the operation of the state-owned media.

No. The legislature lacks a substantial voice in the operation of the public media.

27. The legislature is regularly in session.

Yes. The legislature meets in ordinary session for about ten months each year.

Article 184

(1) Both chambers of Congress will convene yearly in ordinance sessions that will last from 1 July to 30 June of the following year, with a period of recession from 31 December to 1 March, date on which the President of the Republic will give his report. Both chambers will call special sessions or will extend their ordinary sessions through a decision approved by one-fourth of the members of either house, by two-thirds of the Standing Congressional Committee, or by an executive branch decree. The president of Congress, or of the Standing Committee, must call the session within the peremptory term of 48 hours.

28. Each legislator has a personal secretary.

Yes.

29. Each legislator has at least one non-secretarial staff member with policy expertise.

No.

30. Legislators are eligible for re-election without any restriction.

Yes. There are no restrictions on re-election.

Article 187

(2) The term in office of legislators, which will be five years, will begin on 1 July. They may be reelected.

31. A seat in the legislature is an attractive enough position that legislators are generally interested in and seek re-election.

Yes.

32. The re-election of incumbent legislators is common enough that at any given time the legislature contains a significant number of highly experienced members.

No. The re-election rate is relatively low, resulting in a relatively small number of highly experienced legislators. For example, in 1998 only 60 percent of deputies ran for re-election, and only about 18 percent of the total membership won in the primaries and general elections to serve a second term in the lower house.

CONGRESS OF PERU (*CONGRESO*)

Expert consultants: Julio Javier Aguayo, Guillermo Garcia, Rüdiger Graichen, Cynthia McClintock, Percy Medina

Score: .66

Influence over executive (5/9)		Institutional autonomy (6/9)		Specified powers (4/8)		Institutional capacity (6/6)	
1. replace	X	10. no dissolution		19. amendments	X	27. sessions	X
2. serve as ministers	X	11. no decree		20. war	X	28. secretary	X
3. interpellate	X	12. no veto	X	21. treaties	X	29. staff	X
4. investigate	X	13. no review		22. amnesty	X	30. no term limits	X
5. oversee police		14. no gatekeeping	X	23. pardon		31. seek re-election	X
6. appoint PM		15. no impoundment	X	24. judiciary		32. experience	X
7. appoint ministers		16. control resources	X	25. central bank			
8. lack president		17. immunity	X	26. media			
9. no confidence	X	18. all elected	X				

The Congress (*Congreso*) of Peru was established in 1824 upon independence from Spain. The legislature enjoyed moderate influence in the civilian governments that alternated with military dictatorships throughout the twentieth century. In the 1980s and 1990s, a Maoist guerilla insurgency beleaguered Peru. In 1992 President Alberto Fujimori, with the army's backing, suspended the constitution and dissolved Congress. Fujimori's move paved the way for a new constitution in 1993, which currently remains in force. The document calls for a unicameral legislature and a directly elected president. The president appoints a president of the Council of Ministers. The latter in practice serves as an aide to the president. Yet, like a prime minister, the president of the Council of Ministers is subject to votes of confidence by the legislature.

The legislature has substantial authority. It influences the executive with, among other powers, the right to impeach the president, interpellate and investigate officials from the executive branch, and vote no confidence in the government. It also enjoys significant institutional autonomy. It exercises many of the specified powers measured in this survey, and it has a high level of institutional capacity.

SURVEY

1. The legislature alone, without the involvement of any other agencies, can impeach the president or replace the prime minister.

Yes. The legislature can impeach the president. It can remove the president of the Council of Ministers with a vote of no confidence.

Article 99
It is the responsibility of the Standing Committee to impeach... the President of the Republic... for violations of the Constitution and for any offense that (he or she) may commit in the exercise of (his or her) functions and up to five years after (he or she has) relinquished them.

Article 113
The [the office of the] President of the Republic may become vacant for the following reasons:
2. His permanent intellectual or physical incapacity is declared by Congress.
4. He leaves Peru's territory without permission from Congress or does not return within the set deadline. And,
5. He is removed from office after being sentenced for any of the violations mentioned in Article 117 of the Constitution.

Article 117
The President of the Republic may be impeached only during his term of office for treason to the country;

for blocking presidential, parliamentary, regional, or municipal elections; for dissolving Congress except in those cases provided for in Article 134 of the Constitution; and for impeding its meeting or the functioning of the National Board of Elections and other organs of the electoral system.

Article 130

Within 30 days of assuming his functions, the President of the Council of Ministers attends Congress accompanied by the other ministers to expound and discuss the government's general policy and the principal measures necessary for their implementation. For that purpose, a vote of confidence is taken.

Article 132

Congress implements the political responsibility of the Council of Ministers, or of the ministers individually, by means of a vote of censure or by defeating a vote of confidence. The latter may only be proposed upon a ministerial initiative. Any motion of censure of the Council of Ministers or of any of the ministers must be introduced by no fewer than 25 percent of the legal number of members of Congress. It is debated between the fourth and tenth calendar day following its introduction. Its approval requires the vote of over half the legal number of the members of Congress. The Council of Ministers or the censured minister must then resign. The President of the Republic accepts his resignation within the subsequent 72 hours.

The defeat of a ministerial initiative does not obligate the minister to resign, unless its approval was made a question of confidence.

Article 133

The President of the Council of Ministers may introduce before Congress a question of confidence on behalf of the Council of Ministers. If confidence is denied, or if the President is censured, or if he resigns or is removed by the President of the Republic, a total crisis of the Cabinet is produced.

2. Ministers may serve simultaneously as members of the legislature.

Yes. Ministers may not run for Congress, but legislators may be appointed to, and serve simultaneously in, ministerial positions.

Article 91

The following persons may not be elected members of Congress if they have not resigned from office six months before the election:

1. Ministers and deputy ministers of State, the Comptroller General, and regional authorities.

Article 92

The function of a member of Congress is full-time. The member is forbidden to hold any other post or exercise any profession or office during the hours when Congress is in session.

3. The legislature has powers of summons over executive branch officials and hearings with executive branch officials testifying before the legislature or its committees are regularly held.

Yes. The legislature regularly interpellates officials from the executive.

Article 96

Any representative in Congress may request from the Ministers of State, the National Board of Elections, the Comptroller General, the Central Reserve Bank, the Superintendency of Banking, Insurance and Privately Administered Funds, the Regional and Local Governments and the institutions determined by law the information which he deems necessary.

The request must be done in writing and in accordance with Congressional rules of procedure. Failure to respond may be sanctioned as provided by law.

Article 131

When summoned by Congress for an interpellation, attendance by the Council of Ministers or any of the ministers is mandatory. Interpellation is done in writing. It must be submitted by no fewer than 15 percent of the legal number of members of Congress. For their acceptance, the vote of one-third of the number of competent representatives is necessary. A vote must be taken without fail at the subsequent session. Congress determines the day and hour for the ministers to respond to the interpellation. The latter may not occur or be voted upon before the third day of its receipt or after the 10th day.

4. The legislature can conduct independent investigation of the chief executive and the agencies of the executive.

Yes. The legislature can investigate the executive.

Article 97

Congress may initiate an inquiry into any matter of public interest. It is mandatory to appear, upon their request, before the committees charged with such inquiries, subject to the same sanctions as in judicial proceedings. For the implementation of their purposes, said committees may have access to any information, which may involve the lifting of banking secrecy and tax confidentiality, with the exception of information that may bear on intimate personal matters. Their conclusions are not binding upon the judicial organs.

5. The legislature has effective powers of oversight over the agencies of coercion (the military, organs of law enforcement, intelligence services, and the secret police).

No. The legislature lacks effective powers of oversight over the agencies of coercion.

6. The legislature appoints the prime minister.

No. There is no prime minister. The president of the Council of Ministers, who fulfills some of the same roles as a prime minister, is appointed by the president without the need for legislative approval.

Article 122
The President of the Republic appoints and removes the President of the Council of Ministers. He also appoints and removes the other ministers on the recommendation and agreement, respectively, of the President of the Council of Ministers.

7. The legislature's approval is required to confirm the appointment of ministers; or the legislature itself appoints ministers.

No. The president appoints ministers on the recommendation of the president of the Council of Ministers, and the appointments do not require the legislature's approval.

Article 122
The President of the Republic appoints and removes the President of the Council of Ministers. He also appoints and removes the other ministers on the recommendation and agreement, respectively, of the President of the Council of Ministers.

8. The country lacks a presidency entirely or there is a presidency, but the president is elected by the legislature.

No. The president is directly elected.

Article 110
The President of the Republic is the Head of State and personifies the Nation.
In order to be elected President of the Republic one must be Peruvian by birth, be over 35 years of age at the time of his candidacy, and enjoy the right of suffrage.

9. The legislature can vote no confidence in the government.

Yes. The legislature can vote no confidence in the government.

Article 130
Within 30 days of assuming his functions, the President of the Council of Ministers attends Congress accompanied by the other ministers to expound and discuss the government's general policy and the principal measures necessary for their implementation. For that purpose, a vote of confidence is taken.

Article 132
Congress implements the political responsibility of the Council of Ministers, or of the ministers individually, by means of a vote of censure or by defeating a vote of confidence. The latter may only be proposed upon a ministerial initiative. Any motion of censure of the Council of Ministers or of any of the ministers must be introduced by no fewer than 25 percent of the legal number of members of Congress. It is debated between the fourth and tenth calendar day following its introduction. Its approval requires the vote of over half the legal number of the members of Congress. The Council of Ministers or the censured minister must then resign.

The President of the Republic accepts his resignation within the subsequent 72 hours.
The defeat of a ministerial initiative does not obligate the minister to resign, unless its approval was made a question of confidence.

Article 133
The President of the Council of Ministers may introduce before Congress a question of confidence on behalf of the Council of Ministers. If confidence is denied, or if the President is censured, or if he resigns or is removed by the President of the Republic, a total crisis of the Cabinet is produced.

10. The legislature is immune from dissolution by the executive.

No. The president can dissolve the legislature.

Article 134
The President of the Republic has the power to dissolve Congress if the latter has censured or denied its confidence to two Councils of Ministers. The dissolution decree contains a call for the election of a new Congress. Said election must take place within four months of the dissolution of Congress without any alteration to the existing electoral system. Congress may not be dissolved in the final year of its mandate. Once Congress is dissolved, its Standing Committee, which cannot be dissolved, maintains its functions. The parliamentary mandate may not be revoked in any other form. Under a state of siege, Congress may not be dissolved.

11. Any executive initiative on legislation requires ratification or approval by the legislature before it takes effect; that is, the executive lacks decree power.

No. The president can issue decrees that have the force of law in economic and financial matters "when required by the national interest." The decrees lapse if they are subsequently nullified by the legislature. The president can also issue decrees that have the force of law when authorized to do so by the legislature.

Article 104
Congress may delegate to the Executive Branch the responsibility of legislating by means of legislative decrees relating to a specific subject and for a stated period established by the authorizing law. Matters may not be delegated by Congress which cannot be delegated to its Standing Committee. Legislative decrees are treated under the same rules that apply to laws as regards their promulgation, publication, scope, and effects. The President of the Republic is accountable to Congress or its Standing Committee for each legislative decree.

Article 118
It is the responsibility of the President of the Republic:
19. To decree extraordinary measures by means of urgency decrees with the force of law in economic and

financial matters when required by the national interest, while being accountable to Congress. Congress can modify or nullify the said emergency decrees.

12. Laws passed by the legislature are veto-proof or essentially veto-proof; that is, the executive lacks veto power, or has veto power but the veto can be overridden by a majority in the legislature.

Yes. The legislature can override a presidential veto by a majority vote of its present members.

Article 108
A law approved according to a provision in the Constitution is sent to the President of the Republic for his promulgation within a period of 15 days. In case the President of the Republic does not promulgate a law, the President of Congress or its Standing Committee does so, as appropriate. If the President of the Republic has comments to make on the entire law or part of the law approved by Congress, he transmits these to the latter within the stated deadline of 15 days.
Once Congress reconsiders the law, its President promulgates it as long as more than half of the legal number of members approve it.

13. The legislature's laws are supreme and not subject to judicial review.

No. The Constitutional Court can review the constitutionality of laws.

Article 201
The Constitutional Court is the organ that oversees adherence to the Constitution.

Article 202
The Constitutional Court has the following responsibilities:
1. To adjudicate, as the unique instance, actions of unconstitutionality.

14. The legislature has the right to initiate bills in all policy jurisdictions; the executive lacks gatekeeping authority.

Yes. The legislature can initiate bills in all policy jurisdictions.

15. Expenditure of funds appropriated by the legislature is mandatory; the executive lacks the power to impound funds appropriated by the legislature.

Yes. The executive lacks the power to impound funds appropriated by the legislature.

16. The legislature controls the resources that finance its own internal operation and provide for the perquisites of its own members.

Yes. The legislature enjoys financial autonomy.

17. Members of the legislature are immune from arrest and/or criminal prosecution.

Yes. Legislators are immune with the common exception for cases of *flagrante delicto*.

Article 93
Members of Congress represent the Nation. They are not subject to an imperative mandate or to interpellation. They are not responsible before any authority or court for opinions held and votes cast in the exercise of their functions. They may not be prosecuted or arrested without prior authorization of Congress or its Standing Committee. Members of Congress have tenure from the time of their election to a month after the termination of their functions, except for an offense in flagrante delicto, in which case they are placed at the disposal of Congress or its Standing Committee within 24 hours to determine whether their imprisonment and trial may be authorized or not.

18. All members of the legislature are elected; the executive lacks the power to appoint any members of the legislature.

Yes. All members of the legislature are elected.

Article 90
The Legislative Power is vested in Congress, which is unicameral. The number of members of Congress is 120. Congress is elected for a period of five years by means of elections organized according to law.

19. The legislature alone, without the involvement of any other agencies, can change the Constitution.

Yes. The legislature alone can change the constitution through a complicated procedure. The sitting legislature can propose the amendment with a two-thirds majority vote, and then, following an election, the subsequent legislature can approve the amendment with a two-thirds majority vote.

Article 206
Every constitutional amendment must be approved by Congress with an absolute majority of the legal number of its members and ratified by referendum. The referendum may be omitted when the amendment is approved by Congress in two successive ordinary sessions by a favorable vote which exceeds, in each case, two-thirds of the legal number of members of Congress.
The constitutional amendment law is not subject to comments by the President of the Republic.
The right to initiate constitutional reform belongs to the President of the Republic, with the approval of the Council of Ministers; to the members of Congress, and to a number of citizens equivalent to three-tenths of one percent (0.3%) of the voters, with signatures verified by the elections authority.

20. The legislature's approval is necessary for the declaration of war.

Yes. The legislature's approval is required for presidential war declarations.

Article 118
It is the responsibility of the President of the Republic:
16. To declare war and make peace, with the approval of Congress.

21. The legislature's approval is necessary to ratify treaties with foreign countries.

Yes. The legislature's approval is necessary to ratify international treaties on most major issues.

Article 56
Treaties must be approved by Congress before their ratification by the President of the Republic if they involve the following matters:
1. Human rights.
2. Sovereignty, dominion, or integrity of the State.
3. National defense.
4. Financial obligations of the State.
Congress must also approve the treaties that create, amend, or eliminate taxes; those that require the modification or repeal of any law; and those that require legislative measures for their execution.

Article 57
The President of the Republic may accept or ratify treaties without need for the prior approval of Congress in matters not covered in the previous article. In all these cases, he must account to Congress. When the treaty affects constitutional provisions, it must be approved by the same procedure that applies to amending the Constitution before being ratified by the President of the Republic. The denunciation of treaties falls under the authority of the President of the Republic who is obliged to account to Congress. In the case of treaties subject to the approval of Congress, their denunciation requires its prior approval.

Article 102
The duties of Congress are as follows:
3. To approve treaties, in accordance with the Constitution.

Article 118
It is the responsibility of the President of the Republic:
11. To direct foreign policy and international relations and to sign and ratify treaties.

22. The legislature has the power to grant amnesty.

Yes. The legislature has the power to grant amnesty.

Article 102
The duties of Congress are as follows:
6. To exercise the right of amnesty.

23. The legislature has the power of pardon.

No. The president has the power of pardon.

Article 118
It is the responsibility of the President of the Republic:
21. To grant pardons and commute sentences. To exercise the power of pardon in processes where the

period of investigation has exceeded twice its maximum deadline.

24. The legislature reviews and has the right to reject appointments to the judiciary; or the legislature itself appoints members of the judiciary.

No. Formally, the legislature elects the members of the Constitutional Court, while other members of the judiciary are self-selected, but in practice, the president and the judiciary control judicial appointments without the legislature's participation.

Article 150
The National Council of the Magistracy is charged with the selection and appointment of judges and prosecutors, except when these are popularly elected.

Article 152
Justices of the Peace are popularly elected.

Article 154
The following are the duties of the National Council of the Magistracy:
1. To appoint, following a prior public competitive examination and personal evaluation, judges and prosecutors at all levels. Said appointments require a vote of two-thirds of the legal number of its members.

Article 155
The members of the National Council of the Magistracy, in accordance with the law on the subject, are as follows:
1. One elected by the Supreme Court by secret ballot in plenary session.
2. One elected by secret ballot by the Board of Senior Prosecutors.
3. One elected by secret ballot by members of the Bar Association.
4. Two elected by secret ballot by the members of the other national professional colleges, in accordance with the law.
5. One elected by secret ballot by the rectors of national universities.
6. One elected by secret ballot by the rectors of private universities.

Article 201
The members of the Constitutional Court are elected by the National Congress with the affirmative votes of two-thirds of the legal number of its members. Judges of the Constitutional Court, judges or prosecutors who have not relinquished their position for a year prior, cannot be voted into membership.

25. The chairman of the central bank is appointed by the legislature.

No. The executive branch appoints the directorate of the Central Reserve Bank of Peru with the approval of Congress.

Article 86

The Bank is managed by a seven-member Directorate. The Executive Branch appoints four, among them the President [of the Directorate]. Congress ratifies the latter and elects the other three members, with approval by an absolute majority of the legal number of its members. All the directors of the Bank are appointed for the constitutional period concurrent with the term of the President of the Republic. The board members do not represent any particular interests. Congress may remove them for grave error. In case of removal, the new directors complete the applicable constitutional term.

26. The legislature has a substantial voice in the operation of the state-owned media.

No. The legislature lacks a substantial voice in the operation of the public media.

27. The legislature is regularly in session.

Yes. The legislature regularly meets in ordinary session.

28. Each legislator has a personal secretary.

Yes.

29. Each legislator has at least one non-secretarial staff member with policy expertise.

Yes.

30. Legislators are eligible for re-election without any restriction.

Yes. There are no restrictions on re-election.

31. A seat in the legislature is an attractive enough position that legislators are generally interested in and seek re-election.

Yes.

32. The re-election of incumbent legislators is common enough that at any given time the legislature contains a significant number of highly experienced members.

Yes. Re-election rates are sufficiently high to produce a significant number of highly experienced members.

CONGRESS OF THE PHILIPPINES (*KONGRESO*)

Expert consultants: Yvonne T. Chua, Maria Socorro I. Diokno, David C. Kang, Carl H. Landé, James Putzel, Geronimo Velasco

Score: .56

Influence over executive (5/9)		Institutional autonomy (6/9)		Specified powers (2/8)		Institutional capacity (5/6)	
1. replace	X	10. no dissolution	X	19. amendments		27. sessions	X
2. serve as ministers		11. no decree	X	20. war	X	28. secretary	X
3. interpellate	X	12. no veto		21. treaties	X	29. staff	X
4. investigate	X	13. no review		22. amnesty		30. no term limits	
5. oversee police	X	14. no gatekeeping	X	23. pardon		31. seek re-election	X
6. appoint PM		15. no impoundment	X	24. judiciary		32. experience	X
7. appoint ministers	X	16. control resources	X	25. central bank			
8. lack president		17. immunity		26. media			
9. no confidence		18. all elected	X				

The Congress (*Kongreso*) of the Philippines was established in 1946 upon independence from the United States. In 1972 President Ferdinand Marcos suspended parliament and declared martial law. A new constitution in the following year formalized Marcos's absolute authority. Marcos relinquished power in 1986 amid demonstrations sparked by massive fraud in a presidential election. He subse-

quently fled the country, and in 1987 the Philippines adopted its current constitution. The document calls for a bicameral legislature with an upper house, the Senate (*Senado*), and a lower house, the House of Representatives (*Kapulungan Ng Mga Kinatawan*). In 2006 President Gloria Macapagal Arroyo, who is obligated by the constitution to vacate the presidency after the end of her term in 2010, proposed to rewrite the constitution to disband the Senate and establish a powerful unicameral legislature, thereby enabling her to remain in power, as prime minister rather than president, after 2010. Arroyo's attempt to transform the country from a presidential to a parliamentary political system in order to enable herself to retain the helm indefinitely met with vigorous and widespread opposition, and Arroyo and her supporters backed down following a brief political crisis.

Congress has significant, albeit not vast, authority. Its ability to influence the executive branch includes powers to impeach the president, interpellate and investigate the government, and review the president's ministerial appointments. It has some degree of institutional autonomy, as evidenced by the president's lack of decree, dissolution, and gatekeeping authority. With the exception of the powers to declare war and approve international treaties, however, the legislature exercises none of the specified powers measured in this survey. It has substantial institutional capacity.

SURVEY

1. The legislature alone, without the involvement of any other agencies, can impeach the president or replace the prime minister.

Yes. The legislature can impeach the president. One-third of the House's total membership can propose the impeachment. The Senate then conducts the trial and can impeach the president by a two-thirds majority vote of its total membership.

Article 11
Section 2. The President, the Vice-President, the Members of the Supreme Court, the Members of the Constitutional Commissions, and the Ombudsman may be removed from office, on impeachment for, and conviction of, culpable violation of the Constitution, treason, bribery, graft and corruption, other high crimes, or betrayal of public trust. All other public officers and employees may be removed from office as provided by law, but not by impeachment.
Section 3. (1) The House of Representatives shall have the exclusive power to initiate all cases of impeachment.
(2) A verified compliant for impeachment may be filed by any Member of the House of Representatives or by any citizen upon a resolution of endorsement by any Member thereof, which shall be included in the Order of Business within ten session days, and referred to the proper Committee within three session days thereafter. The Committee, after hearing, and by a majority vote of all its Members, shall submit its report to the House within sixty session days from such referral, together with the corresponding

resolution. The resolution shall be calendared for consideration by the House within ten session days from receipt thereof.
(3) A vote of at least one-third of all the Members of the House shall be necessary either to affirm a favorable resolution with the Articles of Impeachment of the Committee, or override its contrary resolution. The vote of each Member shall be recorded.
(4) In case the verified compliant or resolution of impeachment is filed by at least one-third of all the Members of the House, the same shall constitute the Articles of Impeachment, and trial by the Senate shall forthwith proceed.
(5) No impeachment proceedings shall be initiated against the same official more than once within a period of one year.
(6) The Senate shall have the sole power to try and decide all cases of impeachment. When sitting for that purpose, the Senators shall be on oath or affirmation. When the President of the Philippines is on trial, the Chief Justice of the Supreme Court shall preside, but shall not vote. No person shall be convicted without the concurrence of two-thirds of all the Members of the Senate.
(7) Judgment in cases of impeachment shall not extend further than removal from office and disqualification to hold any office under the Republic of the Philippines, but the party convicted shall nevertheless be liable and subject to prosecution, trial, and punishment according to law.
(8) The Congress shall promulgate its rules on impeachment to effectively carry out the purpose of this section.

2. Ministers may serve simultaneously as members of the legislature.

No. Legislators are prohibited from serving simultaneously in ministerial positions.

Article 6
Section 13. No Senator or Member of the House of Representatives may hold any other office or employment in the Government.

3. The legislature has powers of summons over executive branch officials and hearings with executive branch officials testifying before the legislature or its committees are regularly held.

Yes. The legislature regularly interpellates officials from the executive.

Section 22. The heads of departments may upon their own initiative, with the consent of the President, or upon the request of either House, as the rules of each House shall provide, appear before and be heard by such House on any matter pertaining to their departments. Written questions shall be submitted to the President of the Senate or the Speaker of the House of Representatives at least three days before their scheduled appearance. Interpellations shall not be limited to written questions, but may cover matters related thereto.

When the security of the State or the public interest so requires and the President so states in writing, the appearance shall be conducted in executive session.

4. The legislature can conduct independent investigation of the chief executive and the agencies of the executive.

Yes. The legislature can investigate the executive.

> Section 21. The Senate or the House of Representatives or any of its respective committees may conduct inquiries in aid of legislation in accordance with its duly published rules of procedure. The rights of persons appearing in or affected by such inquiries shall be respected.

5. The legislature has effective powers of oversight over the agencies of coercion (the military, organs of law enforcement, intelligence services, and the secret police).

Yes. The House Committee on Oversight oversees all executive branch agencies, both civilian and military.

6. The legislature appoints the prime minister.

No. There is no prime minister.

7. The legislature's approval is required to confirm the appointment of ministers; or the legislature itself appoints ministers.

Yes. The president's ministerial appointments require the approval of the Commission on Appointments, a body composed of the leaders of the legislative branch.

> Article 16
> Section 18. There shall be a Commission on Appointments consisting of the President of the Senate, as ex officio Chairman, twelve Senators, and twelve Members of the House of Representatives, elected by each House on the basis of proportional representation from the political parties and parties or organizations registered under the party-list system represented therein. The Chairman of the Commission shall not vote, except in case of a tie. The Commission shall act on all appointments submitted to it within thirty session days of the Congress from their submission. The Commission shall rule by a majority vote of all the Members.

> Article 7
> Section 16. The President shall nominate and, with the consent of the Commission on Appointments, appoint the heads of the executive departments, ambassadors, other public ministers and consuls, or officers of the armed forces from the rank of colonel or naval captain, and other officers whose appointments are vested in him in this Constitution. He shall also appoint all other officers of the Government whose appointments are not otherwise provided for by law, and those whom he may be authorized by law to appoint.

8. The country lacks a presidency entirely or there is a presidency, but the president is elected by the legislature.

No. The president is directly elected.

> Article 7
> Section 4. The President and the Vice-President shall be elected by direct vote of the people for a term of six years which shall begin at noon on the thirtieth day of June next following the day of the election and shall end at noon of the same date six years thereafter. The President shall not be eligible for any reelection. No person who has succeeded as President and has served as such for more than four years shall be qualified for election to the same office at any time.

9. The legislature can vote no confidence in the government.

No. The legislature cannot vote no confidence in the government.

10. The legislature is immune from dissolution by the executive.

Yes. The legislature is immune from dissolution.

11. Any executive initiative on legislation requires ratification or approval by the legislature before it takes effect; that is, the executive lacks decree power.

Yes. The executive lacks decree power.

12. Laws passed by the legislature are veto-proof or essentially veto-proof; that is, the executive lacks veto power, or has veto power but the veto can be overridden by a majority in the legislature.

No. A two-thirds majority vote is required to override a presidential veto.

> Article 6
> Section 27. (1) Every bill passed by the Congress shall, before it becomes a law, be presented to the President. If he approves the same he shall sign it; otherwise, he shall veto it and return the same with his objections to the House where it originated, which shall enter the objections at large in its Journal and proceed to reconsider it. If, after such reconsideration, two-thirds of all the Members of such House shall agree to pass the bill, it shall be sent, together with the objections, to the other House by which it shall likewise be reconsidered, and if approved by two-thirds of all the Members of that House, it shall become a law. In all such cases, the votes of each House shall be determined by yeas or nays, and the names of the Members voting for or against shall be entered in its Journal. The President shall communicate his veto of any bill to the House where it originated within thirty days after the date of receipt thereof, otherwise, it shall become a law as if he had signed it.
>
> (2) The President shall have the power to veto any particular item or items in an appropriation, revenue, or tariff bill, but the veto shall not affect the item or items to which he does not object.

13. The legislature's laws are supreme and not subject to judicial review.

No. The Supreme Court can review the constitutionality of laws.

Article 8
Section 4. (2) All cases involving the constitutionality of a treaty, international or executive agreement, or law, which shall be heard by the Supreme Court en banc, and all other cases which under the Rules of Court are required to be heard en banc, including those involving the constitutionality, application, or operation of presidential decrees, proclamations, orders, instructions, ordinances, and other regulations, shall be decided with the concurrence of a majority of the Members who actually took part in the deliberations on the issues in the case and voted thereon.
Section 5. The Supreme Court shall have the following powers:
(2) Review, revise, reverse, modify, or affirm on appeal or certiorari, as the law or the Rules of Court may provide, final judgments and orders of lower courts in:
(a) All cases in which the constitutionality or validity of any treaty, international or executive agreement, law, presidential decree, proclamation, order, instruction, ordinance, or regulation is in question.

14. The legislature has the right to initiate bills in all policy jurisdictions; the executive lacks gatekeeping authority.

Yes. The legislature can initiate bills in all policy jurisdictions.

15. Expenditure of funds appropriated by the legislature is mandatory; the executive lacks the power to impound funds appropriated by the legislature.

Yes. The executive lacks the power to impound funds appropriated by the legislature.

16. The legislature controls the resources that finance its own internal operation and provide for the perquisites of its own members.

Yes. The legislature enjoys financial autonomy, including control over members' salaries.

Article 6
Section 10. The salaries of Senators and Members of the House of Representatives shall be determined by law. No increase in said compensation shall take effect until after the expiration of the full term of all the Members of the Senate and the House of Representatives approving such increase.

17. Members of the legislature are immune from arrest and/or criminal prosecution.

No. Legislators are immune only while the legislature is in session. They are subject to arrest at other times.

Article 6
Section 11. A Senator or Member of the House of Representatives shall, in all offenses punishable by not more than six years imprisonment, be privileged from arrest while the Congress is in session. No Member shall be questioned nor be held liable in any other place for any speech or debate in the Congress or in any committee thereof.

18. All members of the legislature are elected; the executive lacks the power to appoint any members of the legislature.

Yes. All members of the legislature are elected.

Article 6
Section 2. The Senate shall be composed of twenty-four Senators who shall be elected at large by the qualified voters of the Philippines, as may be provided by law.
Section 5. (1) The House of Representatives shall be composed of not more than two hundred and fifty members, unless otherwise fixed by law, who shall be elected from legislative districts apportioned among the provinces, cities, and the Metropolitan Manila area in accordance with the number of their respective inhabitants, and on the basis of a uniform and progressive ratio, and those who, as provided by law, shall be elected through a party-list system of registered national, regional, and sectoral parties or organizations.

19. The legislature alone, without the involvement of any other agencies, can change the Constitution.

No. Constitutional amendments require approval in a popular referendum.

Article 17
Section 1. Any amendment to, or revision of, this Constitution may be proposed by:
(1) The Congress, upon a vote of three-fourths of all its Members; or
(2) A constitutional convention.
Section 2. Amendments to this Constitution may likewise be directly proposed by the people through initiative upon a petition of at least twelve per centum of the total number of registered voters, of which every legislative district must be represented by at least three per centum of the registered voters therein. No amendment under this section shall be authorized within five years following the ratification of this Constitution nor oftener than once every five years thereafter.
The Congress shall provide for the implementation of the exercise of this right.
Section 3. The Congress may, by a vote of two-thirds of all its Members, call a constitutional convention, or by a majority vote of all its Members, submit to the electorate the question of calling such a convention.
Section 4. Any amendment to, or revision of, this Constitution under Section 1 hereof shall be valid when ratified by a majority of the votes cast in a plebiscite which shall be held not earlier than sixty days nor later than ninety days after the approval of such amendment or revision.

Any amendment under Section 2 hereof shall be valid when ratified by a majority of the votes cast in a plebiscite which shall be held not earlier than sixty days nor later than ninety days after the certification by the Commission on Elections of the sufficiency of the petition.

20. The legislature's approval is necessary for the declaration of war.

Yes. The legislature declares war.

> Article 6
> Section 23. (1) The Congress, by a vote of two-thirds of both Houses in joint session assembled, voting separately, shall have the sole power to declare the existence of a state of war.

21. The legislature's approval is necessary to ratify treaties with foreign countries.

Yes. The Senate's approval is necessary to ratify international treaties.

> Article 7
> Section 21. No treaty or international agreement shall be valid and effective unless concurred in by at least two-thirds of all the Members of the Senate.

22. The legislature has the power to grant amnesty.

No. The president grants amnesty with the legislature's approval.

> Article 7
> Section 19. Except in cases of impeachment, or as otherwise provided in this Constitution, the President may grant reprieves, commutations, and pardons, and remit fines and forfeitures, after conviction by final judgment. He shall also have the power to grant amnesty with the concurrence of a majority of all the Members of Congress.

23. The legislature has the power of pardon.

No. The president has the power of pardon.

> Article 7
> Section 19. Except in cases of impeachment, or as otherwise provided in this Constitution, the President may grant reprieves, commutations, and pardons, and remit fines and forfeitures, after conviction by final judgment.

24. The legislature reviews and has the right to reject appointments to the judiciary; or the legislature itself appoints members of the judiciary.

No. The president appoints magistrates on the proposal of the Judicial and Bar Council, and the appointments do not require the legislature's approval.

> Article 8
> Section 9. The Members of the Supreme Court and judges of lower courts shall be appointed by the Presi-

dent from a list of at least three nominees prepared by the Judicial and Bar Council for every vacancy. Such appointments need no confirmation.

25. The chairman of the central bank is appointed by the legislature.

No. The president appoints the governor of the Central Bank of the Philippines.

26. The legislature has a substantial voice in the operation of the state-owned media.

No. The legislature lacks a substantial voice in the operation of the public media.

27. The legislature is regularly in session.

Yes. The legislature regularly meets in ordinary session.

> Article 6
> Section 15. The Congress shall convene once every year on the fourth Monday of July for its regular session, unless a different date is fixed by law, and shall continue to be in session for such number of days as it may determine until thirty days before the opening of its next regular session, exclusive of Saturdays, Sundays, and legal holidays.

28. Each legislator has a personal secretary.

Yes.

29. Each legislator has at least one non-secretarial staff member with policy expertise.

Yes.

30. Legislators are eligible for re-election without any restriction.

No. Senators are limited to two consecutive terms. Deputies are limited to three consecutive terms.

> Article 6
> Section 4. The term of office of the Senators shall be six years and shall commence, unless otherwise provided by law, at noon on the thirteenth day of June next following their election.
> No Senator shall serve for more than two consecutive terms.
> Section 7. The Members of the House of Representatives shall be elected for a term of three years which shall begin, unless otherwise provided by law, at noon on the thirtieth day of June next following their election.
> No Member of the House of Representatives shall serve for more than three consecutive terms.

31. A seat in the legislature is an attractive enough position that legislators are generally interested in and seek re-election.

Yes.

32. The re-election of incumbent legislators is common enough that at any given time the legislature contains a significant number of highly experienced members.

Yes. Re-election rates are sufficiently high to produce a significant number of highly experienced members.

PARLIAMENT OF POLAND (*PARLAMENT*)

Expert consultants: Michael Bernhard, Anna Grzymała-Busse, Krzysztof Jasiewicz, Conor O'Dwyer, Wei-fang Wang, Jakub Zielinski

Score: .75

Influence over executive (7/9)		Institutional autonomy (6/9)		Specified powers (5/8)		Institutional capacity (6/6)	
1. replace		10. no dissolution		19. amendments	X	27. sessions	X
2. serve as ministers	X	11. no decree	X	20. war	X	28. secretary	X
3. interpellate	X	12. no veto		21. treaties	X	29. staff	X
4. investigate	X	13. no review		22. amnesty		30. no term limits	X
5. oversee police	X	14. no gatekeeping	X	23. pardon		31. seek re-election	X
6. appoint PM	X	15. no impoundment	X	24. judiciary		32. experience	X
7. appoint ministers	X	16. control resources	X	25. central bank	X		
8. lack president		17. immunity	X	26. media	X		
9. no confidence	X	18. all elected	X				

The Parliament (*Parlament*) of Poland was founded, along with an independent Polish state, at the end of World War I. In 1926 the legislature's role was diminished by a military coup and the establishment of an authoritarian government. Following World War II, Poland was incorporated into the communist bloc and, in 1952, enacted a Soviet-style constitution. In 1989 Poland adopted sweeping constitutional amendments that removed the provisions that enshrined communist-party dominance. In 1992 these changes and others were formalized in the "little constitution" – so called because it set out a structure of government but did not contain sections on individual rights and liberties – that called for a bicameral legislature consisting of a lower house, the Diet (*Sejm*), and an upper house, the Senate (*Senat*). In 1997 the country adopted a new permanent constitution.

The legislature has a good deal of power. It holds considerable influence over the executive and enjoys a high degree of institutional autonomy, although it is subject to presidential veto and dissolution powers. It exercises numerous specified powers and prerogatives, including the power to declare war. It also enjoys every aspect of institutional capacity scored in this survey.

SURVEY

1. The legislature alone, without the involvement of any other agencies, can impeach the president or replace the prime minister.

No. Presidential impeachment requires the involvement of a judicial body, the Tribunal of State. The legislature can remove the prime minister with a vote of no confidence.

Article 145

(1) The President of the Republic may be held accountable before the Tribunal of State for an infringement of the Constitution or statute, or for commission of an offence.

(2) Bringing an indictment against the President of the Republic shall be done by resolution of the National Assembly passed by a majority of at least two-thirds of the statutory number of members of the National Assembly, on the motion of at least 140 members of the Assembly.

(3) On the day on which an indictment, to be heard before the Tribunal of State, is brought against the President of the Republic, he shall be suspended from

discharging all functions of his office. The provisions of Article 131 shall apply as appropriate.

Article 158

(1) The Diet shall pass a vote of no confidence by a majority of votes of the statutory number of Deputies, on a motion moved by at least 46 Deputies and which shall specify the name of a candidate for Prime Minister. If such a resolution has been passed by the Diet, the President of the Republic shall accept the resignation of the Council of Ministers and appoint a new Prime Minister as chosen by the Diet, and, on his application, the other members of the Council of Ministers and accept their oath of office.

2. Ministers may serve simultaneously as members of the legislature.

Yes. Legislators may serve simultaneously in ministerial positions.

Article 103

(1) The mandate of a Deputy shall not be held jointly with the office of the President of the National Bank of Poland, the President of the Supreme Chamber of Control, the Commissioner for Citizens' Rights, the Commissioner for Children's Rights or their deputies, a member of the Council for Monetary Policy, a member of the National Council of Radio Broadcasting and Television, ambassador, or with employment in the Chancellory of the Diet, Chancellery of the Senate, Chancellery of the President of the Republic, or with employment in government administration. This prohibition shall not apply to members of the Council of Ministers and secretaries of state in government administration.

3. The legislature has powers of summons over executive branch officials and hearings with executive branch officials testifying before the legislature or its committees are regularly held.

Yes. The legislature regularly interpellates officials from the executive.

Article 115

(1) The Prime Minister and other members of the Council of Ministers shall furnish answers to interpellations and Deputies' questions within 21 days. (2) The Prime Minister and other members of the Council of Ministers shall furnish answers to matters raised in the course of each sitting of the Diet.

4. The legislature can conduct independent investigation of the chief executive and the agencies of the executive.

Yes. The legislature can establish a committee to investigate the executive.

Article 111

(1) The Diet may appoint an investigative committee to examine a particular matter.
(2) The procedures for work by an investigative committee shall be specified by statute.

5. The legislature has effective powers of oversight over the agencies of coercion (the military, organs of law enforcement, intelligence services, and the secret police).

Yes. The legislature has effective powers of oversight over the agencies of coercion.

6. The legislature appoints the prime minister.

Yes. The president appoints as prime minister the candidate who enjoys the support of the legislature.

Article 144

(1) The President of the Republic, exercising his constitutional and statutory authority, shall issue Official Acts.
(2) Official Acts of the President shall require, for their validity, the signature of the Prime Minister who, by such signature, accepts responsibility therefor to the House of Representatives.
(3) The provisions of (2) above shall not relate to:
    11) nominating and appointing the Prime Minister.

Article 154

(1) The President of the Republic shall nominate a Prime Minister who shall propose the composition of a Council of Ministers. The President of the Republic shall, within 14 days of the first sitting of the Diet or acceptance of the resignation of the previous Council of Ministers, appoint a Prime Minister together with other members of a Council of Ministers and accept the oaths of office of members of such newly appointed Council of Ministers.
(2) The Prime Minister shall, within 14 days following the day of his appointment by the President of the Republic, submit a programme of activity of the Council of Ministers to the Diet, together with a motion requiring a vote of confidence. The Diet shall pass such vote of confidence by an absolute majority of votes in the presence of at least half of the statutory number of Deputies.
(3) In the event that a Council of Ministers has not been appointed pursuant to Paragraph (1) above or has failed to obtain a vote of confidence in accordance with Paragraph (2) above, the Diet, within 14 days of the end of the time periods specified in Paragraphs (1) and (2), shall choose a Prime Minister as well as members of the Council of Ministers as proposed by him, by an absolute majority of votes in the presence of at least half of the statutory number of Deputies. The President of the Republic shall appoint the Council of Ministers so chosen and accept the oaths of office of its members.

7. The legislature's approval is required to confirm the appointment of ministers; or the legislature itself appoints ministers.

Yes. The legislature's approval is required to confirm ministerial appointments.

Article 154

(1) The President of the Republic shall nominate a Prime Minister who shall propose the composition of a Council of Ministers. The President of the Republic shall, within 14 days of the first sitting of the Diet or acceptance of the resignation of the previous Council of Ministers, appoint a Prime Minister together with other members of a Council of Ministers and accept the oaths of office of members of such newly appointed Council of Ministers.

(2) The Prime Minister shall, within 14 days following the day of his appointment by the President of the Republic, submit a programme of activity of the Council of Ministers to the Diet, together with a motion requiring a vote of confidence. The Diet shall pass such vote of confidence by an absolute majority of votes in the presence of at least half of the statutory number of Deputies.

(3) In the event that a Council of Ministers has not been appointed pursuant to Paragraph (1) above or has failed to obtain a vote of confidence in accordance with Paragraph (2) above, the Diet, within 14 days of the end of the time periods specified in Paragraphs (1) and (2), shall choose a Prime Minister as well as members of the Council of Ministers as proposed by him, by an absolute majority of votes in the presence of at least half of the statutory number of Deputies. The President of the Republic shall appoint the Council of Ministers so chosen and accept the oaths of office of its members.

8. The country lacks a presidency entirely or there is a presidency, but the president is elected by the legislature.

No. The president is directly elected.

Article 127

(1) The President of the Republic shall be elected by the Nation, in universal, equal and direct elections, conducted by secret ballot.

9. The legislature can vote no confidence in the government.

Yes. The legislature has a constructive vote of no confidence, meaning that the parliament must designate a successor prime minister before passing a vote of no confidence.

Article 155

(1) In the event that a Council of Ministers has not been appointed pursuant to the provisions of Article 154 (3), the President of the Republic shall, within a period of 14 days, appoint a Prime Minister and, on his application, other members of the Council of Ministers. The Diet, within 14 days following the appointment of the Council of Ministers by the President of the Republic, shall hold, in the presence of at least half of the statutory number of Deputies, a vote of confidence thereto.

(2) In the event that a vote of confidence has not been granted to the Council of Ministers pursuant to Paragraph (1), the President of the Republic shall shorten the term of office of the Diet and order elections to be held.

Article 158

(1) The Diet shall pass a vote of no confidence by a majority of votes of the statutory number of Deputies, on a motion moved by at least 46 Deputies and which shall specify the name of a candidate for Prime Minister. If such a resolution has been passed by the Diet, the President of the Republic shall accept the resignation of the Council of Ministers and appoint a new Prime Minister as chosen by the Diet, and, on his application, the other members of the Council of Ministers and accept their oath of office.

(2) A motion to pass a resolution referred to in Paragraph (1) above, may be put to a vote no sooner than 7 days after it has been submitted. A subsequent motion of a like kind may be submitted no sooner than after the end of 3 months from the day the previous motion was submitted. A subsequent motion may be submitted before the end of 3 months if such motion is submitted by at least 115 Deputies.

Article 160

The Prime Minister may submit to the Diet (Sejm) a motion requiring a vote of confidence in the Council of Ministers. A vote of confidence in the Council of Ministers shall be granted by a majority of votes in the presence of at least half of the statutory number of Deputies.

10. The legislature is immune from dissolution by the executive.

No. The president can dissolve the legislature.

Article 155

(1) In the event that a Council of Ministers has not been appointed pursuant to the provisions of Article 154 (3), the President of the Republic shall, within a period of 14 days, appoint a Prime Minister and, on his application, other members of the Council of Ministers. The Diet, within 14 days following the appointment of the Council of Ministers by the President of the Republic, shall hold, in the presence of at least half of the statutory number of Deputies, a vote of confidence thereto.

(2) In the event that a vote of confidence has not been granted to the Council of Ministers pursuant to Paragraph (1), the President of the Republic shall shorten the term of office of the Diet and order elections to be held.

11. Any executive initiative on legislation requires ratification or approval by the legislature before it takes effect; that is, the executive lacks decree power.

Yes. The executive lacks decree power.

12. Laws passed by the legislature are veto-proof or essentially veto-proof; that is, the executive lacks veto power, or has veto power but the veto can be overridden by a majority in the legislature.

No. A three-fifths majority vote in the Diet is required to override a presidential veto.

> Article 122
> (1) After the completion of the procedure specified in Article 121, the Marshal of the Diet shall submit an adopted bill to the President of the Republic for signature.
> (2) The President of the Republic shall sign a bill within 21 days of its submission and shall order its promulgation in the Journal of Laws of the Republic of Poland.
> (3) The President of the Republic may, before signing a bill, refer it to the Constitutional Tribunal for an adjudication upon its conformity to the Constitution. The President of the Republic shall not refuse to sign a bill which has been judged by the Constitutional Tribunal as conforming to the Constitution.
> (4) The President of the Republic shall refuse to sign a bill which the Constitutional Tribunal has judged not to be in conformity to the Constitution. If, however, the non-conformity to the Constitution relates to particular provisions of the bill, and the Tribunal has not judged that they are inseparably connected with the whole bill, then, the President of the Republic, after seeking the opinion of the Marshal of the Diet, shall sign the bill with the omission of those provisions considered as being in non-conformity to the Constitution or shall return the bill to the Diet for the purpose of removing the non-conformity.
> (5) If the President of the Republic has not made reference to the Constitutional Tribunal in accordance with Paragraph (3), he may refer the bill, with reasons given, to the Diet for its reconsideration. If the said bill is repassed by the Diet by a three-fifths majority vote in the presence of at least half of the statutory number of Deputies, then, the President of the Republic shall sign it within 7 days and shall order its promulgation in the Journal of Laws of the Republic of Poland. If the said bill has been repassed by the Diet, the President of the Republic shall have no right to refer it to the Constitutional Tribunal in accordance with the procedure prescribed in Paragraph (3).
> (6) Any such reference by the President of the Republic to the Constitutional Tribunal for an adjudication upon the conformity of a statute to the Constitution, or any application for reconsideration of a bill, shall suspend the period of time allowed for its signature, specified in Paragraph (2) above.

13. The legislature's laws are supreme and not subject to judicial review.

No. The Constitutional Tribunal can review the constitutionality of laws.

> Article 188
> The Constitutional Tribunal shall adjudicate regarding the following matters:
> 1) the conformity of statutes and international agreements to the Constitution.

14. The legislature has the right to initiate bills in all policy jurisdictions; the executive lacks gatekeeping authority.

Yes. The legislature can initiate bills in all policy jurisdictions.

15. Expenditure of funds appropriated by the legislature is mandatory; the executive lacks the power to impound funds appropriated by the legislature.

Yes. The executive lacks the power to impound funds appropriated by the legislature.

16. The legislature controls the resources that finance its own internal operation and provide for the perquisites of its own members.

Yes. The legislature enjoys financial autonomy.

17. Members of the legislature are immune from arrest and/or criminal prosecution.

Yes. Legislators are immune with the common exception for cases of *flagrante delicto*.

> Article 105
> (1) A Deputy shall not be held accountable for his activity performed within the scope of a Deputy's mandate during the term thereof nor after its completion. Regarding such activities, a Deputy can only be held accountable before the Diet and, in a case where he has infringed the rights of third parties, he may only be proceeded against before a court with the consent of the Diet.
> (2) From the day of announcement of the results of the elections until the day of the expiry of his mandate, a Deputy shall not be subjected to criminal accountability without the consent of the Diet.
> (3) Criminal proceedings instituted against a person before the day of his election as Deputy, shall be suspended at the request of the Diet until the time of expiry of the mandate. In such instance, the statute of limitation with respect to criminal proceedings shall be extended for the equivalent time.
> (4) A Deputy may consent to be brought to criminal accountability. In such instance, the provisions of Paragraphs (2) and (3) shall not apply.
> (5) A Deputy shall be neither detained nor arrested without the consent of the Diet, except for cases in flagrante delicto and in which his detention is necessary for securing the proper course of proceedings. Any such detention shall be immediately communicated to the Marshal of the Diet, who may order an immediate release of the Deputy.

18. All members of the legislature are elected; the executive lacks the power to appoint any members of the legislature.

Yes. All members of the legislature are elected.

Article 96

(1) The Diet shall be composed of 460 Deputies.

(2) Elections to the Diet shall be universal, equal, direct and proportional and shall be conducted by secret ballot.

Article 97

(1) The Senate shall be composed of 100 Senators.

(2) Elections to the Senate shall be universal, direct and shall be conducted by secret ballot.

19. The legislature alone, without the involvement of any other agencies, can change the Constitution.

Yes. The legislature can change the constitution with a two-thirds majority vote in the Diet and with a majority vote in the Senate. Amendments to select chapters require approval in a popular referendum.

Article 235

(1) A bill to amend the Constitution may be submitted by the following: at least one-fifth of the statutory number of Deputies; the Senate; or the President of the Republic.

(2) Amendments to the Constitution shall be made by means of a statute adopted by the Diet and, thereafter, adopted in the same wording by the Senate within a period of 60 days.

(3) The first reading of a bill to amend the Constitution may take place no sooner than 30 days after the submission of the bill to the Diet.

(4) A bill to amend the Constitution shall be adopted by the Diet by a majority of at least two-thirds of votes in the presence of at least half of the statutory number of Deputies, and by the Senate by an absolute majority of votes in the presence of at least half of the statutory number of Senators.

(5) The adoption by the Diet of a bill amending the provisions of Chapters I, II or XII of the Constitution shall take place no sooner than 60 days after the first reading of the bill.

(6) If a bill to amend the Constitution relates to the provisions Chapters I, II or XII, the subjects specified in Paragraph (1) above may require, within 45 days of the adoption of the bill by the Senate, the holding of a confirmatory referendum. Such subjects shall make application in the matter to the Marshal of the Diet, who shall order the holding of a referendum within 60 days of the day of receipt of the application. The amendment to the Constitution shall be deemed accepted if the majority of those voting express support for such amendment.

(7) After conclusion of the procedures specified in Paragraphs (4) and (6) above, the Marshal of the Diet shall submit the adopted statute to the President of the Republic for signature. The President of the Republic shall sign the statute within 21 days of its submission and order its promulgation in the Journal of Laws of the Republic of Poland.

20. The legislature's approval is necessary for the declaration of war.

Yes. The legislature declares war.

Article 116

(1) The Diet shall declare, in the name of the Republic of Poland, a state of war and the conclusion of peace.

(2) The Diet may adopt a resolution on a state of war only in the event of armed aggression against the territory of the Republic of Poland or when an obligation of common defence against aggression arises by virtue of international agreements. If the Diet cannot assemble for a sitting, the President of the Republic may declare a state of war.

21. The legislature's approval is necessary to ratify treaties with foreign countries.

Yes. The legislature's approval is necessary to ratify international treaties on most major issues.

Article 89

(1) Ratification of an international agreement by the Republic of Poland, as well as denunciation thereof, shall require prior consent granted by statute – if such agreement concerns:

    1) peace, alliances, political or military treaties;

    2) freedoms, rights or obligations of citizens, as specified in the Constitution;

    3) the Republic of Poland's membership in an international organization;

    4) considerable financial responsibilities imposed on the State;

    5) matters regulated by statute or those in respect of which the Constitution requires the form of a statute.

(2) The President of the Council of Ministers (the Prime Minister) shall inform the Diet of any intention to submit, for ratification by the President of the Republic, any international agreements whose ratification does not require consent granted by statute.

(3) The principles of and procedures for the conclusion and renunciation of international agreements shall be specified by statute.

Article 133

(1) The President of the Republic, as representative of the State in foreign affairs, shall: 1) ratify and renounce international agreements, and shall notify the Diet and the Senate thereof;

(2) The President of the Republic, before ratifying an international agreement may refer it to the Constitutional Tribunal with a request to adjudicate upon its conformity to the Constitution.

22. The legislature has the power to grant amnesty.

No. Amnesty and pardon are not treated separately, and the legislature lacks the power to grant amnesty. See item 23.

23. The legislature has the power of pardon.

No. The president has the power of pardon.

Article 139
The President of the Republic shall have the power of pardon. The power of pardon may not be extended to individuals convicted by the Tribunal of State.

24. The legislature reviews and has the right to reject appointments to the judiciary; or the legislature itself appoints members of the judiciary.

No. The president makes judicial appointments, and the appointments do not require the legislature's approval.

Article 179
Judges shall be appointed for an indefinite period by the President of the Republic on the motion of the National Council of the Judiciary.

Article 183
(3) The First President of the Supreme Court shall be appointed by the President of the Republic for a 6-year term of office from amongst candidates proposed by the General Assembly of the Judges of the Supreme Court.

25. The chairman of the central bank is appointed by the legislature.

Yes. The Diet, on the recommendation of the president, appoints the president of the National Bank of Poland.

Article 227
(3) The Diet, on request of the President of the Republic, shall appoint the President of the National Bank of Poland for a period of 6 years.

26. The legislature has a substantial voice in the operation of the state-owned media.

Yes. The legislature appoints members to the National Council of Radio Broadcasting and Television, the body that oversees the public media.

Article 214
(1) The members of the National Council of Radio Broadcasting and Television shall be appointed by the Diet, the Senate and the President of the Republic.

27. The legislature is regularly in session.

Yes. The legislature regularly meets in ordinary session.

28. Each legislator has a personal secretary.

Yes.

29. Each legislator has at least one non-secretarial staff member with policy expertise.

Yes.

30. Legislators are eligible for re-election without any restriction.

Yes. There are no restrictions on re-election.

31. A seat in the legislature is an attractive enough position that legislators are generally interested in and seek re-election.

Yes.

32. The re-election of incumbent legislators is common enough that at any given time the legislature contains a significant number of highly experienced members.

Yes. Re-election rates are sufficiently high to produce a significant number of highly experienced members.

ASSEMBLY OF PORTUGAL (*ASSEMBLEIA*)

Expert consultants: Ana Freitas, Lawrence S. Graham, Pedro Magalhães, José M. Magone, Paul Christopher Manuel

Score: .63

Influence over executive (6/9)		Institutional autonomy (3/9)		Specified powers (7/8)		Institutional capacity (4/6)	
1. replace	X	10. no dissolution		19. amendments	X	27. sessions	X
2. serve as ministers		11. no decree		20. war	X	28. secretary	
3. interpellate	X	12. no veto	X	21. treaties	X	29. staff	
4. investigate	X	13. no review		22. amnesty	X	30. no term limits	X
5. oversee police	X	14. no gatekeeping		23. pardon	X	31. seek re-election	X
6. appoint PM	X	15. no impoundment		24. judiciary	X	32. experience	X
7. appoint ministers		16. control resources	X	25. central bank			
8. lack president		17. immunity		26. media	X		
9. no confidence	X	18. all elected	X				

The Assembly (*Assembleia*) of Portugal traces it origins to the early nineteenth century. For most of its history, the legislature wielded little power. Portugal was ruled by a constitutional monarch until the early twentieth century and by the dictatorship of António de Oliveira Salazar from the early 1930s until the late 1960s. Reforms carried out from the mid-1970s to the early 1980s established a semipresidential system with a strong prime minister and government and provided a basis for open political competition. A new constitution in 1976 created a unicameral parliament. A 1982 amendment established a civilian government and created a Constitutional Court to review the constitutionality of laws.

The Assembly has significant powers. It has considerable influence over the executive but a relatively modest measure of institutional autonomy. Its autonomy is circumscribed by executive decree, dissolution, impoundment, and gatekeeping powers. The Assembly exercises many specified powers. Its institutional capacity is limited by a lack of personal legislative staff.

SURVEY

1. The legislature alone, without the involvement of any other agencies, can impeach the president or replace the prime minister.

Yes. The legislature can remove the prime minister with a vote of no confidence. Removing the president from office requires the involvement of the Supreme Court of Justice.

Article 133
(1) The President of the Republic is answerable before the Supreme Court of Justice for offences committed in the performance of his duties.
(2) It shall be the duty of the Assembly of the Republic to initiate proceedings at the proposal of one fifth and by a decision of two thirds of its members entitled to vote.
(3) Conviction results in dismissal from office and excludes re-election.
(4) The President of the Republic is answerable to the common courts after the end of his term of office for offences not committed in the performance of his duties.

Article 186
Taking and leaving office
1. The Prime Minister shall take office upon his installation and shall leave office when he is discharged by the President of the Republic.
4. In the event that the Government resigns or is removed, the Prime Minister of the outgoing Government shall be discharged on the date of the appointment and installation of the new Prime Minister.

Article 195
1. The Government shall resign upon:
  a) The beginning of a new legislature;
  b) Acceptance by the President of the Republic of the Prime Minister's resignation;
  c) The Prime Minister's death or lasting physical incapacitation;

d) Rejection of the Government's Programme;

e) The failure of any confidence motion;

f) Passage of a no confidence motion by an absolute majority of all the Members in full exercise of their office.

2. The President of the Republic may only remove the Government when it becomes necessary to do so in order to ensure the normal functioning of the democratic institutions and after first consulting the Council of State.

2. Ministers may serve simultaneously as members of the legislature.

No. Legislators are prohibited from serving simultaneously in ministerial positions.

Article 154

1. Members who are appointed to the Government shall not exercise the office of Member until they leave the Government, and shall be temporarily substituted in accordance with the previous Article.

3. The legislature has powers of summons over executive branch officials and hearings with executive branch officials testifying before the legislature or its committees are regularly held.

Yes. The legislature regularly interpellates officials from the executive.

Article 156

Members shall have the following powers:

d) To question the Government about any of its acts or those of the Public Administration, and to obtain answers within a reasonable period of time, save the provisions of the law concerning state secrets;

e) To request and obtain from the Government or the governing bodies of any public entity, such information and documents and official publications as the Member or Members in question may deem useful to the exercise of their mandate.

4. The legislature can conduct independent investigation of the chief executive and the agencies of the executive.

Yes. The legislature can establish committees of inquiry to investigate the executive.

Article 156

Members shall have the following powers:

f) To request the formation of parliamentary committees of inquiry.

5. The legislature has effective powers of oversight over the agencies of coercion (the military, organs of law enforcement, intelligence services, and the secret police).

Yes. The legislature has effective powers of oversight over the agencies of coercion.

6. The legislature appoints the prime minister.

Yes. The president appoints as prime minister the candidate who enjoys the support of the legislature.

Article 133

In relation to other bodies the President of the Republic shall be responsible for:

f) Appointing the Prime Minister pursuant to Article 187(1);

h) Upon a proposal from the Prime Minister, appointing members of the Government and discharging them from office.

Article 187

1. The President of the Republic shall appoint the Prime Minister after consulting the parties with seats in Assembly of the Republic and in the light of the electoral results.

2. The President of the Republic shall appoint the remaining members of the Government upon a proposal from the Prime Minister.

7. The legislature's approval is required to confirm the appointment of ministers; or the legislature itself appoints ministers.

No. The president appoints ministers on the recommendation of the prime minister, and the appointments do not require the legislature's approval.

Article 133

In relation to other bodies the President of the Republic shall be responsible for:

f) Appointing the Prime Minister pursuant to Article 187(1);

h) Upon a proposal from the Prime Minister, appointing members of the Government and discharging them from office.

Article 187

1. The President of the Republic shall appoint the Prime Minister after consulting the parties with seats in Assembly of the Republic and in the light of the electoral results.

2. The President of the Republic shall appoint the remaining members of the Government upon a proposal from the Prime Minister.

8. The country lacks a presidency entirely or there is a presidency, but the president is elected by the legislature.

No. The president is directly elected.

Article 121

1. The President of the Republic shall be elected by the universal, direct, secret suffrage of all Portuguese citizens who are registered to vote in Portuguese territory and, in accordance with the following paragraph, of all Portuguese citizens who reside abroad.

9. The legislature can vote no confidence in the government.

Yes. The legislature can vote no confidence in the government.

> Article 166
> With respect to other organs, the Assembly of the Republic has the following powers:
> e) To pass motions of confidence in and censure of the Government.

> Article 195
> 1. The Government shall resign upon:
> e) The failure of any confidence motion;
> f) Passage of a no confidence motion by an absolute majority of all the Members in full exercise of their office.
> 2. The President of the Republic may only remove the Government when it becomes necessary to do so in order to ensure the normal functioning of the democratic institutions and after first consulting the Council of State.

10. The legislature is immune from dissolution by the executive.

No. The president can dissolve the legislature.

> Article 133
> In relation to other bodies the President of the Republic shall be responsible for:
> b) In accordance with electoral law, setting the date for elections for President of the Republic, Members of the Assembly of the Republic, Members of the European Parliament and members of the Legislative Assemblies of the autonomous regions;
> e) Subject to the provisions of Article 172 and after first consulting both the parties with seats in the Assembly and the Council of State, dissolving the Assembly of the Republic.

> Article 195
> 1. The Government shall resign upon:
> e) The failure of any confidence motion;
> f) Passage of a no confidence motion by an absolute majority of all the Members in full exercise of their office.
> 2. The President of the Republic may only remove the Government when it becomes necessary to do so in order to ensure the normal functioning of the democratic institutions and after first consulting the Council of State.

11. Any executive initiative on legislation requires ratification or approval by the legislature before it takes effect; that is, the executive lacks decree power.

No. The government issues decrees that have the force of law.

> Article 201
> 1. The Government has the following powers:
> a) To issue decree-laws on matters not reserved to the Assembly of the Republic;

> b) To issue decree-laws on matters relatively reserved to the Assembly of the Republic subject to its authorization;
> c) To issue decree-laws in application of laws laying down legal principles or bases.
> 2. The Government has exclusive competence in matters concerning its own organization and working.
> 3. The decree-laws provided for in Paragraph (1)(b) and (c) expressly mention the law granting legislative authorization or the law laying down bases under cover of which they are approved.

12. Laws passed by the legislature are veto-proof or essentially veto-proof; that is, the executive lacks veto power, or has veto power but the veto can be overridden by a majority in the legislature.

Yes. The legislature can override a presidential veto by a majority vote of its total membership. A two-thirds majority is required to override a presidential veto on laws in a handful of extraordinary areas, including those relating to national defense and states of emergency.

> Article 136
> 1. Within twenty days of the receipt of any decree of the Assembly of the Republic for enactment as a law, or of the publication of a Constitutional Court ruling that does not declare any of the decree's provisions unconstitutional, the President of the Republic shall either enact the decree or exercise the right of veto. In the latter case he shall send a message setting out the grounds therefore and requesting that the statute be reconsidered.
> 2. If the Assembly of the Republic confirms its original vote by an absolute majority of all the Members in full exercise of their office, the President of the Republic shall enact the decree within eight days of receiving it.
> 3. However, a majority that is at least equal to two thirds of all Members present and greater than an absolute majority of all the Members in full exercise of their office shall be required to confirm decrees that take the form of organic laws, as well as to confirm those concerning the following matters:
> a) External relations;
> b) Boundaries between the public, private and cooperative sectors in relation to the ownership of the means of production;
> c) Such regulations governing the electoral acts provided for by this Constitution as do not take the form of an organic law.
> 4. Within forty days of the receipt of any Government decree for enactment, or of the publication of a Constitutional Court ruling that does not declare any of the decree's provisions unconstitutional, the President of the Republic shall either enact the decree or exercise his right of veto. In the latter case he shall inform the Government in writing of the reasons for doing so.
> 5. The President of the Republic shall also exercise the right of veto pursuant to Articles 278 and 279.

13. The legislature's laws are supreme and not subject to judicial review.

No. The Constitutional Court can review the constitutionality of laws.

Article 223
1. The Constitutional Court shall assess cases of unconstitutionality and illegality in accordance with Articles 277 et sequitur.

Article 277
(1) Provisions of law that infringe a provision of the Constitution or the principles laid down therein are unconstitutional.
(2) The organic or formal unconstitutionality of international treaties that have been regularly ratified do not prevent the application of their provisions in Portuguese law as long as the provisions are applied in the law of the other party, except if the said unconstitutionality results from the violation of a fundamental principle.

Article 278
(1) The President of the Republic may request the Constitutional Court to judge preventively the constitutionality of any provision of any international treaty that has been submitted to him for ratification, an act sent to him for promulgation as a law or decree-law or an international agreement the act of approval of which has been sent to him for signature.

14. The legislature has the right to initiate bills in all policy jurisdictions; the executive lacks gatekeeping authority.

No. The legislature is prohibited from introducing bills that increase government expenditures or reduce government revenue in the financial year.

Article 170
(2) The Members, the parliamentary groups, and the regional legislative assemblies may not table bills or move amendments involving in the financial year running any increase in State expenditure, or any reduction in State revenue, allowed in the Budget.
(3) The Members and the parliamentary groups may not propose referenda involving in the financial year running any increase in State expenditure, or any reduction in State revenue, allowed in the Budget.

15. Expenditure of funds appropriated by the legislature is mandatory; the executive lacks the power to impound funds appropriated by the legislature.

No. The government can impound funds appropriated by the legislature.

16. The legislature controls the resources that finance its own internal operation and provide for the perquisites of its own members.

Yes. The legislature enjoys financial autonomy.

17. Members of the legislature are immune from arrest and/or criminal prosecution.

No. Legislators are subject to arrest "in the event of strong evidence of the commission of a serious crime punishable by imprisonment for a maximum term of more than three years." In these cases the legislature "shall obligatorily authorize a Member's appearance as defendant."

Article 117
1. Political officeholders shall be politically, civilly and criminally liable for their actions and omissions in the exercise of their functions.
2. The law shall lay down both the duties, responsibilities, liabilities and incompatibilities of political office and the consequences of any breach thereof, and the rights, privileges and immunities that apply thereto.
3. The law shall specify the special crimes for which political officeholders may be held liable, together with the applicable penalties and the effects thereof, which may include removal from office or loss of seat.

Article 157
1. Members shall not be civilly or criminally liable for or subject to disciplinary proceedings in relation to their votes or the opinions they express in the performance of their functions.
2. Members shall not appear as makers of declarations or defendants without the Assembly's authorisation. In the event of strong evidence of the commission of a serious crime punishable by imprisonment for a maximum term of more than three years, the Assembly shall obligatorily authorise a Member's appearance as defendant.
3. No Member may be detained, arrested or imprisoned without the Assembly's authorisation, save for a serious crime punishable by the type of prison term referred to in the previous paragraph and in flagrante delicto.
4. In the event that criminal proceedings are brought against any Member and he is definitively charged, the Assembly shall decide whether or not he is to be suspended so that the proceedings can take their course. In the event of a crime of the type referred to in the previous paragraphs, the Assembly shall obligatorily suspend the Member.

18. All members of the legislature are elected; the executive lacks the power to appoint any members of the legislature.

Yes. All members of the legislature are elected.

Article 149
1. Members shall be elected for constituencies that shall be geographically defined by law. The law may create plurinominal and uninominal constituencies and lay down the nature and complementarity thereof, all in such a way as to ensure that votes are converted into seats in accordance with the proportional representation system and using d'Hondt's highest-average rule.

19. The legislature alone, without the involvement of any other agencies, can change the Constitution.

Yes. The legislature can change the constitution with a two-thirds majority vote.

Article 156
Members shall have the following powers:
a) To submit draft amendments to the Constitution.

Article 286
(1) Amendments to the Constitution are approved by a two-thirds majority of the members of the Assembly entitled to vote.
(2) Changes in the Constitution which are approved are incorporated in a single revision law.
(3) The President of the Republic may not refuse to promulgate the revision law.

20. The legislature's approval is necessary for the declaration of war.

Yes. The legislature's approval is required for presidential war declarations.

Article 138
Declaration of a state of siege or a state of emergency shall require prior consultation of the Government and authorisation by the Assembly of the Republic, or, if the Assembly is not sitting and it is not possible to arrange for it to sit immediately, by its Standing Committee.
2. In the event that a declaration of a state of siege or a state of emergency is authorised by the Assembly of the Republic's Standing Committee, such declaration shall require confirmation by the Plenary as soon as it is possible to arrange for it to sit.

Article 161
The Assembly of the Republic shall be responsible for:
m) Authorising the President of the Republic to declare war or to make peace.

21. The legislature's approval is necessary to ratify treaties with foreign countries.

Yes. The legislature's approval is necessary to ratify international treaties on most major issues.

Article 138
The President of the Republic is competent in international relations to:
a) Appoint ambassadors and envoys extraordinary at the proposal of the Government, and accept the credentials of foreign diplomatic representatives;
b) Ratify international treaties once they have been duly approved.

Article 161
The Assembly of the Republic shall be responsible for:
i) Passing treaties, particularly those that entail Portugal's participation in international organisations, friendship, peace, defence, the rectification of borders or military affairs, as well as international agreements that address matters which are the exclusive responsibility of the Assembly, or which the Government deems fit to submit to the Assembly for consideration.

22. The legislature has the power to grant amnesty.

Yes. The legislature has the power to grant amnesty.

Article 161
Political and legislative responsibilities –
f) Granting generic amnesties and pardons.

23. The legislature has the power of pardon.

Yes. The legislature has the power of pardon.

Article 161
Political and legislative responsibilities –
f) Granting generic amnesties and pardons.

24. The legislature reviews and has the right to reject appointments to the judiciary; or the legislature itself appoints members of the judiciary.

Yes. The legislature appoints seven of the sixteen members of the Higher Council of the Bench and ten of the thirteen members of the Constitutional Court.

Article 133
In relation to other bodies the President of the Republic shall be responsible for:
m) Upon a proposal from the Government, appointing the President of the Audit Court.
n) Appointing . . . two members of the Supreme Judicial Council.

Article 217
1. The appointment, assignment, transfer and promotion of judges of the courts of law and the exercise of discipline over them shall be the responsibility of the Supreme Judicial Council, as laid down by law.
2. The appointment, assignment, transfer and promotion of judges of the administrative and tax courts and the exercise of discipline over them shall be the responsibility of the respective Supreme Council, as laid down by law.
3. Subject to the guarantees provided for by this Constitution, the law shall define the rules governing the assignment, transfer and promotion of judges of the remaining courts and the exercise of discipline over them, and shall determine the responsibility to do so.

Article 219
(1) The Higher Council of the Bench has the powers to appoint, assign, transfer, and promote the judges of the courts of law; it also has the powers to exercise disciplinary action against the latter. Such powers must be used in conformity with the law.

Article 220
(1) The Higher Council of the Bench are presided over by the President of the Supreme Court of Justice; its membership is as follows:
a) Two members appointed by the President of the Republic, one of which is to be a judge;
b) Seven members elected by the Assembly of the Republic;
c) Seven judges elected by their peers in accordance with the principle of proportional representation.

Article 224
(1) The Constitutional Court is made up of thirteen judges, of which ten are appointed by the Assembly of the Republic and the remaining three are co-opted.

25. The chairman of the central bank is appointed by the legislature.

No. The prime minister appoints the governor of the Bank of Portugal.

26. The legislature has a substantial voice in the operation of the state-owned media.

Yes. The legislature has a substantial voice in the operation of the public media.

27. The legislature is regularly in session.

Yes. The legislature meets in ordinary session for nine months each year.

> Article 174
> 1. Legislative sessions shall last for one year commencing on 15 September.
> 2. Without prejudice to suspensions decided by a two-thirds majority of all Members present, the Assembly of the Republic's normal parliamentary term shall be from 15 September to 15 June.
> 3. Following a Plenary decision to extend the normal parliamentary term, or on the initiative of the Standing Committee, or, in the event that the said Committee is unable to function and there is a dire emergency, on the initiative of more than half of all the Members, the Assembly may conduct proceedings outside the term set out in the previous paragraph.
> 4. The President of the Republic may also call the Assembly on an extraordinary basis in order to address specific matters.

> 5. When the Assembly so decides under the same terms as those set out in (2) above, committees may conduct proceedings regardless of whether the Assembly's Plenary is in full session.

28. Each legislator has a personal secretary.

No. There is legislative staff, but on average there is less than one staff person for each legislator.

29. Each legislator has at least one non-secretarial staff member with policy expertise.

No. See item 28.

30. Legislators are eligible for re-election without any restriction.

Yes. There are no restrictions on re-election.

31. A seat in the legislature is an attractive enough position that legislators are generally interested in and seek re-election.

Yes.

32. The re-election of incumbent legislators is common enough that at any given time the legislature contains a significant number of highly experienced members.

Yes. Re-election rates are sufficiently high to produce a significant number of highly experienced members.

CONSULTATIVE COUNCIL OF QATAR (*MAJLIS AL-SHURA*)

Expert consultant: Michael Herb

Score: .22

Influence over executive (3/9)		Institutional autonomy (2/9)		Specified powers (1/8)		Institutional capacity (1/6)	
1. replace		10. no dissolution		19. amendments		27. sessions	
2. serve as ministers	X	11. no decree		20. war		28. secretary	
3. interpellate	X	12. no veto		21. treaties	X	29. staff	
4. investigate		13. no review		22. amnesty		30. no term limits	X
5. oversee police		14. no gatekeeping	X	23. pardon		31. seek re-election	
6. appoint PM		15. no impoundment		24. judiciary		32. experience	
7. appoint ministers		16. control resources		25. central bank			
8. lack president	X	17. immunity	X	26. media			
9. no confidence		18. all elected					

The Consultative Council (*Majlis al-Shura*) of Qatar was established in the 1972 provisional constitution following national independence in 1971. The original body was partly elected and partly appointed, although legislative elections have not been repeated since the early 1970s, and the original legislators have simply been reappointed by the emir every four years. For the past three decades, the legislature has functioned as an advisory body to the emir.

Qatari voters endorsed a new constitution in 2003 that, at least formally, gives the Council some powers. Under the new system, which came into effect in 2005, the Council may initiate legislation. Formerly it merely commented on government legislation. The new constitution also affords powers to question executive branch officials and approve international treaties. Legislative elections, the first in over three decades, are scheduled for 2008.

SURVEY

1. The legislature alone, without the involvement of any other agencies, can impeach the president or replace the prime minister.

No. The legislature cannot remove the chief executive, the emir. Only the emir can replace the prime minister.

> Article 72
> The Emir shall appoint the Prime Minister, accept his resignation and remove him from office by an Emiri Order; and the resignation of the Prime Minister or his removal from office shall entail all Ministers. In the event of acceptance or resignation or removal from the office, the same Council shall continue to run urgent matters until such time the new Council is appointed.

2. Ministers may serve simultaneously as members of the legislature.

Yes. Ministers may serve simultaneously in the Council.

> Article 77
> Al-Shoura Council shall consist of forty-five Members thirty of whom shall be elected by direct, general secret ballot; and the Emir shall appoint the remaining fifteen Members from amongst the Ministers or any other persons. The term of service of the appointed Members in Al-Shoura Council shall expire when these Members resign their seats or are relieved from their posts.

3. The legislature has powers of summons over executive branch officials and hearings with executive branch officials testifying before the legislature or its committees are regularly held.

Yes. The Council regularly interpellates officials of the executive.

> Article 110
> Every Member of Al-Shoura Council may address an interpellation to Ministers on matters within their jurisdiction. An interpellation may not be made unless it is agreed on by one third of the Members of the Council.

4. The legislature can conduct independent investigation of the chief executive and the agencies of the executive.

No. The Council cannot investigate the emir.

5. The legislature has effective powers of oversight over the agencies of coercion (the military, organs of law enforcement, intelligence services, and the secret police).

No. The Council lacks effective powers of oversight over the agencies of coercion.

6. The legislature appoints the prime minister.

No. The emir appoints the prime minister.

> Article 72
> The Emir shall appoint the Prime Minister, accept his resignation and remove him from office by an Emiri Order; and the resignation of the Prime Minister or his removal from office shall entail all Ministers. In the event of acceptance or resignation or removal from the office, the same Council shall continue to run urgent matters until such time the new Council is appointed.

7. The legislature's approval is required to confirm the appointment of ministers; or the legislature itself appoints ministers.

No. The emir appoints ministers, and the appointments do not require the legislature's approval.

> Article 73
> The Emir shall appoint Ministers by an Emiri Order upon nomination by the Prime Minister; and he shall accept resignations of Ministers and relieve them from office in a like manner. Where a resignation of a minister has been accepted, the Minister may be entrusted with running urgent matters until his successor is appointed.

8. The country lacks a presidency entirely or there is a presidency, but the president is elected by the legislature.

Yes. The country lacks a presidency. The emir is the head of state.

> Article 64
> The Emir is the head of State.

9. The legislature can vote no confidence in the government.

No. The Council cannot vote no confidence in the government.

10. The legislature is immune from dissolution by the executive.

No. The emir can dissolve the Council.

> Article 104
> The Emir may dissolve the Council by a decree in which the reasons for the dissolution shall be stated; however,

the Council shall not be dissolved twice for the same reasons. Where the Council is dissolved, the elections of the new Council shall take place within a period not exceeding six months as of the date of dissolution. Until a new Council is elected, the Emir with the assistance of the Council of Ministers shall assume the power of legislation.

11. Any executive initiative on legislation requires ratification or approval by the legislature before it takes effect; that is, the executive lacks decree power.

No. The emir may rule by decree in "exceptional cases" when the Council is not in session. Decrees remain in force unless they are explicitly rejected by the Council.

Article 69
The Emir may, by a decree, declare Martial Laws in the country in the event of exceptional cases specified by the law; and in such cases, he may take all urgent necessary measures to counter any threat that undermine the safety of the State, the integrity of its territories or the security of its people and interests or obstruct the organs of the State from performing their duties. However, the decree must specify the nature of such exceptional cases for which the martial laws have been declared and clarify the measures taken to address this situation. Al-Shoura Council shall be notified of this decree within the fifteen days following its issue; and in the event that the Council is not in session for any reason whatsoever, the Council shall be notified of the decree at its first convening. Martial laws shall be declared for a limited period and the same shall not be extended unless approved by Al-Shoura Council.

Article 70
The Emir may, in the event of exceptional cases that require measures of utmost urgency which necessitate the issue of special laws and in case that Al-Shoura Council is not in session, issue pertinent decrees that have the power of law. Such decree-laws shall be submitted to Al-Shoura Council at its first meeting; and the Council may within a maximum period of forty days from the date of submission and with a two-thirds majority of its Members reject any of these decree-laws or request amendment thereof to be effected within a specified period of time; such decree-laws shall cease to have the power of law from the date of their rejection by the Council or where the period for effecting the amendments have expired.

Article 104
The Emir may dissolve the Council by a decree in which the reasons for the dissolution shall be stated; however, the Council shall not be dissolved twice for the same reasons. Where the Council is dissolved, the elections of the new Council shall take place within a period not exceeding six months as of the date of dissolution. Until a new Council is elected, the Emir with the assistance of the Council of Ministers shall assume the power of legislation.

12. Laws passed by the legislature are veto-proof or essentially veto-proof; that is, the executive lacks veto power, or has veto power but the veto can be overridden by a majority in the legislature.

No. A two-thirds majority is needed to override the emir's veto.

Article 106
1. Any draft law passed by the Council shall be referred to the Emir for ratification.
2. If the Emir declines to approve the draft law, he shall return it a long with the reasons for such declination to the Council within a period of three months from the date of referral.
3. In the event that a draft law is returned to the Council within the period specified in the preceding paragraph and the Council passes the same once more with a two-thirds majority of all its Members, the Emir shall ratify and promulgate it. The Emir may in compelling circumstances order the suspension of this law for the period that he deems necessary to serve the higher interests of the country.

13. The legislature's laws are supreme and not subject to judicial review.

No. The constitution calls for the establishment of a judicial body to review the constitutionality of laws.

Article 140
The law shall specify the competent judicial body for settling of disputes pertaining to the constitutionality of laws and regulations, define its powers and method of challenging and procedures to be followed before the said body. It shall also specify the consequences of judgment regarding unconstitutionality.

14. The legislature has the right to initiate bills in all policy jurisdictions; the executive lacks gatekeeping authority.

Yes. The new constitution does not explicitly grant the executive gatekeeping authority.

15. Expenditure of funds appropriated by the legislature is mandatory; the executive lacks the power to impound funds appropriated by the legislature.

No. The emir can impound funds appropriated by the Council.

16. The legislature controls the resources that finance its own internal operation and provide for the perquisites of its own members.

No. The Council is dependent on the emir for the resources that finance its own operations.

17. Members of the legislature are immune from arrest and/or criminal prosecution.

Yes. According to the 2003 constitution, legislators are immune with the common exception for cases of *flagrante delicto*.

Article 112
The Minister of the Council shall in no circumstances be accountable for opinions or statements he makes in respect of matters within the jurisdiction of the Council.

Article 113
1. Save when a Member of Al-Shoura Council is found flagrante delicto, he shall not be arrested, detained, searched or subject to investigation without prior permission from the Council. Where the Council has not issued a resolution on the request for permission within a period of one month from the date of receipt of the said request, this shall be virtually considered a permission. The permission shall be issued by the Speaker of the Council when the latter is not in session.
2. In case of flagrante delicto, the Council must be notified of the measures taken against the offending Member; and where the Council is not in session, such notification should be made at the first subsequent session.

18. All members of the legislature are elected; the executive lacks the power to appoint any members of the legislature.

No. According to the 2003 constitution, the emir appoints fifteen of the forty-five members of the Al-Shoura Council. Legislative elections have not been held since the early 1970s but are scheduled for 2008.

Article 77
Al-Shoura Council shall consist of forty-five Members thirty of whom shall be elected by direct, general secret ballot; and the Emir shall appoint the remaining fifteen Members from amongst the Ministers or any other persons. The term of service of the appointed Members in Al-Shoura Council shall expire when these Members resign their seats or are relieved from their posts.

19. The legislature alone, without the involvement of any other agencies, can change the Constitution.

No. Constitutional amendments require the emir's approval.

Article 144
The Emir or one third of the Members of Al-Shoura Council each shall have the prerogative to apply for the amendment of one or more of the articles of this Constitution. If the majority of Members of the Council accept the amendment in principle, the Council may discuss it article by article. The amendment shall be passed by a two-thirds majority of the Members of the Council. The said amendment shall not be into force before the approval of the Emir and its publication in the official Gazette. If, on the other hand, the proposal for amendment is rejected in principle or in subject, it

may not be re-introduced before the lapse of one year from the date of its rejection.

20. The legislature's approval is necessary for the declaration of war.

No. The emir can declare war without the legislature's approval.

Article 71
Defensive war shall be declared by an Emiri decree and aggressive war is prohibited.

21. The legislature's approval is necessary to ratify treaties with foreign countries.

Yes. The Council's approval is necessary to ratify international treaties.

Article 68
The Emir shall conclude treaties and agreements by a decree and refer them to Al-Shoura Council accompanied with appropriate explanatory notes. The treaty or agreement shall have the power of law after ratification and publication in the official Gazette; however, reconciliation treaties and treaties pertaining to the territory of the State or those relating to the right of sovereignty or public or private rights of the citizens, or those that involve an amendment of the laws of the State shall come into force when the same are issued as a law. Under no case may a treaty include secret conditions contradicting its publicized conditions.

22. The legislature has the power to grant amnesty.

No. Amnesty and pardon are not treated separately, and the Council lacks the power to grant amnesty. See item 23.

23. The legislature has the power of pardon.

No. The emir has the power of pardon.

Article 67
The Emir shall discharge the following functions:
6. Granting pardon or commuting penalty in accordance with the law.

24. The legislature reviews and has the right to reject appointments to the judiciary; or the legislature itself appoints members of the judiciary.

No. The Council has no role in judicial branch appointments.

Article 137
The judiciary shall have a Supreme Council to supervise the proper functioning of courts of law and their auxiliary organs. The law shall determine the composition, powers and functions of the said Council.

25. The chairman of the central bank is appointed by the legislature.

No. The monarch appoints the governor of the Qatar Central Bank.

26. The legislature has a substantial voice in the operation of the state-owned media.

No. The Council lacks a substantial voice in the operation of the public media.

27. The legislature is regularly in session.

No. According to the 2003 constitution, the Council meets in ordinary session for at least eight months each year. In practice, it does not regularly meet in ordinary session.

> Article 84
> The annual term of session of the Council shall at least be eight months and the Council may not be allowed to adjourn the session until the budget of the State is approved.

28. Each legislator has a personal secretary.

No.

29. Each legislator has at least one non-secretarial staff member with policy expertise.

No.

30. Legislators are eligible for re-election without any restriction.

Yes. According to the 2003 constitution, there are no restrictions on re-election.

> Article 81
> The term of Al-Shoura Council shall be four calendar years commencing from the date of the first meeting; and the elections of the new Council shall be conducted during the last ninety days of the aforementioned term. The Member whose term of service expires may be re-elected; and where the elections are not held at the expiry of the term of the Council or delayed for any reason whatsoever, the term of the Council shall remain intact until a new Council is elected.

31. A seat in the legislature is an attractive enough position that legislators are generally interested in and seek re-election.

No. There have been no elections since the early 1970s, so Council members have not had the opportunity to seek re-election. It bears note, however, that Council members generally welcome re-appointment.

32. The re-election of incumbent legislators is common enough that at any given time the legislature contains a significant number of highly experienced members.

No. The re-election of incumbent legislators is not possible because elections have never been held.

PARLIAMENT OF ROMANIA (*PARLAMENTUL*)

Expert consultants: Florin Fesnic, Venelin I. Ganev, Claudiu Lucaci, Alina Mungiu-Pippidi, Grigore Pop-Eleches, Marina Popescu, Michael Shafir

Score: .72

Influence over executive (6/9)		Institutional autonomy (7/9)		Specified powers (6/8)		Institutional capacity (4/6)	
1. replace		10. no dissolution		19. amendments		27. sessions	X
2. serve as ministers	X	11. no decree	X	20. war	X	28. secretary	
3. interpellate	X	12. no veto	X	21. treaties	X	29. staff	
4. investigate	X	13. no review		22. amnesty	X	30. no term limits	X
5. oversee police	X	14. no gatekeeping	X	23. pardon		31. seek re-election	X
6. appoint PM	X	15. no impoundment	X	24. judiciary	X	32. experience	X
7. appoint ministers		16. control resources	X	25. central bank	X		
8. lack president		17. immunity	X	26. media	X		
9. no confidence	X	18. all elected	X				

The Parliament (*Parlamentul*) of Romania traces its origins to the country's various representative assemblies that met as part of the constitutional monarchy in the nineteenth century. The monar-chical system gave way to a Soviet-backed communist regime at the end of World War II. Romania adopted a new constitution in 1991, following the dissolution of the Soviet bloc. The document calls for a bicameral parliament consisting of a lower house, the Chamber of Deputies (*Camera Deputatilor*), and an upper house, the Senate (*Senat*). The legislature is paired with a directly elected president. Prior to 2003 the legislature's laws were supreme, but a constitutional amendment in that year revoked parliament's power to overrule Supreme Court decisions.

The legislature is a formidable body. It enjoys extensive control over the executive, although it does not elect the president and cannot, acting along, remove the president from office. The executive's lack of decree, veto, and gatekeeping powers enhance the institutional autonomy of parliament. The legislature exercises many specified powers, including the powers to declare war and appoint the governor of the central bank. The legislature enjoys some institutional capacity, although its rating on this dimension is limited by the paucity of parliamentary staffers.

SURVEY

1. The legislature alone, without the involvement of any other agencies, can impeach the president or replace the prime minister.

No. Presidential impeachment requires the involvement of the Constitutional Court and approval in a national referendum. The legislature can remove the prime minister with a vote of no confidence.

Article 95

(1) In case of having committed grave acts infringing upon Constitutional provisions, the President of Romania may be suspended from office by the Chamber of Deputies and the Senate, in joint session, by a majority vote of Deputies and Senators, and after consultation with the Constitutional Court. The President may explain before Parliament with regard to imputations brought against him.

(2) The proposal of suspension from office may be initiated by at least one third of the number of Deputies and Senators, and the President shall be immediately notified thereof.

(3) If the proposal of suspension from office has been approved, a referendum shall be held within 30 days, in order to remove the President from office.

Article 112

(1) The Chamber of Deputies and the Senate may, in joint session, withdraw confidence granted to the Government, by carrying a motion of censure by a majority vote of the Deputies and Senators.

(2) The motion of censure may be initiated by at least one fourth of the total number of Deputies and Senators, and shall be notified to the Government upon the date of its tabling.

(3) The motion of censure shall be debated upon three days after its presentation in the joint session of the Chambers.

(4) If the motion of censure fails to be passed, the Deputies and the Senators who signed it may not submit another one during the same session, except for the case that the Government assumes responsibility in conformity with Article 113.

Article 113

(1) The Government may assume responsibility before the Chamber of Deputies and the Senate, in joint session, upon a program, a general policy statement, or a bill.

(2) The Government shall be dismissed if a motion of censure, tabled within three days from the date of presenting the program, the general policy statement, or the bill, has been passed in accordance with provisions under Article 112.

(3) If the Government has not been dismissed in accordance with Paragraph (2), the bill presented shall be considered as passed, and the program or the general policy statement become binding on the Government.

(4) In case the President of Romania demands reconsideration of the law passed according to Paragraph (3), the debate thereon shall be carried in the joint session of both Chambers.

2. Ministers may serve simultaneously as members of the legislature.

Yes. Legislators may serve simultaneously in ministerial positions.

Article 68

(1) No one may be a Deputy and a Senator at one and the same time.

(2) The capacity as a Deputy or Senator is incompatible with the exercise of any public office in authority, with the exception of Government membership.

(3) Other incompatibilities shall be established by an organic law.

3. The legislature has powers of summons over executive branch officials and hearings with executive branch officials testifying before the legislature or its committees are regularly held.

Yes. The legislature regularly interpellates officials from the executive.

Article 110

(1) The Government and other agencies of Public Administration shall, within the Parliamentary control over their activity, be bound to present any information and documents requested by the Chamber of Deputies, the Senate, or Parliamentary Committees, through their respective Presidents. In case a legislative initiative involves amendment of provisions of the State Budget or the State social security budget, the request for information shall be compulsory.

(2) Members of the Government are entitled to attend the proceedings of Parliament. If they are requested to be present, participation shall be compulsory.

4. The legislature can conduct independent investigation of the chief executive and the agencies of the executive.

Yes. The legislature can investigate the executive.

Article 108
(1) The Government is politically responsible for its entire activity only before Parliament. Each member of the Government is politically and jointly answerable with the others for the activity and acts of the Government.
(2) It is only the Chamber of Deputies, the Senate, and the President of Romania that shall have the right to demand criminal prosecutions be taken against members of the Government for acts committed in the exercise of their office. If such criminal prosecution has been requested, the President of Romania may decree that they be suspended from office. Institution of proceedings against a member of the Government entails suspension from office. The case shall be within the competence of the Supreme Court of Justice.
(3) Cases of liability, and penalties applicable to members of the Government shall be regulated by a law on Ministerial responsibility.

Article 110
(1) The Government and other agencies of Public Administration shall, within the Parliamentary control over their activity, be bound to present any information and documents requested by the Chamber of Deputies, the Senate, or Parliamentary Committees, through their respective Presidents. In case a legislative initiative involves amendment of provisions of the State Budget or the State social security budget, the request for information shall be compulsory.
(2) Members of the Government are entitled to attend the proceedings of Parliament. If they are requested to be present, participation shall be compulsory.

5. The legislature has effective powers of oversight over the agencies of coercion (the military, organs of law enforcement, intelligence services, and the secret police).

Yes. The legislature has effective powers of oversight over the agencies of coercion.

6. The legislature appoints the prime minister.

Yes. The president appoints the candidate as prime minister who enjoys the support of the legislature.

Article 85
(1) The President of Romania shall designate a candidate to the office of Prime Minister and appoint the Government on the vote of confidence of Parliament.

Article 102
(1) The President of Romania shall designate a candidate to the office of Prime Minister, as a result of his

consultation with the party which has obtained absolute majority in Parliament, or – if no such majority exists – with the parties represented in Parliament.

7. The legislature's approval is required to confirm the appointment of ministers; or the legislature itself appoints ministers.

No. The president appoints ministers on the recommendation of the prime minister. The legislature's approval is necessary to confirm the government as a whole, but it cannot vote to approve or reject individual ministers.

Article 85
(1) The President of Romania shall designate a candidate to the office of Prime Minister and appoint the Government on the vote of confidence of Parliament.

Article 102
(1) The President of Romania shall designate a candidate to the office of Prime Minister, as a result of his consultation with the party which has obtained absolute majority in Parliament, or – unless such majority exists – with the parties represented in Parliament.
(2) The candidate to the office of Prime Minister shall, within ten days after his designation, seek the vote of confidence of Parliament upon the program and complete list of the Government.
(3) The program and list of the Government shall be debated upon by the Chamber of Deputies and Senate in joint session. Parliament shall grant confidence to the Government by a majority vote of Deputies and Senators.

8. The country lacks a presidency entirely or there is a presidency, but the president is elected by the legislature.

No. The president is directly elected.

Article 81
(1) The President of Romania shall be elected by universal, equal, direct, secret, and free suffrage.

9. The legislature can vote no confidence in the government.

Yes. The legislature can vote no confidence in the government.

Article 112
(1) The Chamber of Deputies and the Senate may, in joint session, withdraw confidence granted to the Government, by carrying a motion of censure by a majority vote of the Deputies and Senators.
(2) The motion of censure may be initiated by at least one fourth of the total number of Deputies and Senators, and shall be notified to the Government upon the date of its tabling.
(3) The motion of censure shall be debated upon three days after its presentation in the joint session of the Chambers.

(4) If the motion of censure fails to be passed, the Deputies and the Senators who signed it may not submit another one during the same session, except for the case that the Government assumes responsibility in conformity with Article 113.

Article 113

(1) The Government may assume responsibility before the Chamber of Deputies and the Senate, in joint session, upon a program, a general policy statement, or a bill.

(2) The Government shall be dismissed if a motion of censure, tabled within three days from the date of presenting the program, the general policy statement, or the bill, has been passed in accordance with provisions under Article 112.

(3) If the Government has not been dismissed in accordance with Paragraph (2), the bill presented shall be considered as passed, and the program or the general policy statement become binding on the Government.

(4) In case the President of Romania demands reconsideration of the law passed according to Paragraph (3), the debate thereon shall be carried in the joint session of both Chambers.

10. The legislature is immune from dissolution by the executive.

No. The president can dissolve the legislature.

Article 89

(1) After consultation with the Presidents of both Chambers and the leaders of the Parliamentary groups, the President of Romania may dissolve the Parliament, if no vote of confidence has been obtained to form a government within 60 days after the first request was made, and only after rejection of at least two requests for investiture.

(2) During the same year, Parliament can be dissolved only once.

(3) Parliament cannot be dissolved during the last six months of the term of office of the President of Romania, nor can it be dissolved during a state of siege or emergency.

11. Any executive initiative on legislation requires ratification or approval by the legislature before it takes effect; that is, the executive lacks decree power.

Yes. The executive lacks decree power. The constitution apparently provides for decree powers, but these are actually usable only in emergency, or take the form of "enabling laws" under which the legislature grants the government temporary powers to issue decrees in specified issue areas.

Article 99

(1) In the exercise of his powers, the President of Romania shall issue decrees which shall be published in the Official Gazette of Romania. Absence of publicity entails the non-existence of a decree.

(2) The decrees issued by the President of Romania in the exercise of his powers, as provided for under Article 91 (1) and (2), 92 (2) and (3), 93 (1), and 94 (a), (b) and (d) shall be countersigned by the Prime Minister.

Article 114

(1) Parliament may pass a special law enabling the Government to issue orders in fields outside the scope of organic laws.

(2) The enabling law shall compulsorily establish the field and the date up to which orders can be issued.

(3) If the enabling law so requests, orders shall be submitted to Parliament for approval, according to the legislative procedure, until expiration of the enabling term. Non-compliance with the term entails discontinuation of effectiveness of the order.

(4) In exceptional cases, the Government may adopt emergency orders, which shall come into force only after their submission to Parliament for approval. If Parliament does not sit in a session, it shall obligatorily be convened.

(5) Orders shall be approved or rejected by a law which must also contain the orders that ceased to be effective in accordance with Paragraph (3).

12. Laws passed by the legislature are veto-proof or essentially veto-proof; that is, the executive lacks veto power, or has veto power but the veto can be overridden by a majority in the legislature.

Yes. The legislature can override a presidential veto by a majority vote of its present members.

Article 77

(1) A law shall be submitted for promulgation to the President of Romania. Promulgation shall be given within twenty days after receipt of the law.

(2) Before promulgation, the President of Romania may return the law to Parliament for reconsideration, and he may do so only once.

(3) In case the President has requested that the law be reconsidered or a review has been asked about its conformity with the Constitution, promulgation shall be made within ten days from receiving the law passed after its reconsideration, or the decision of the Constitutional Court confirming its Constitutionality.

13. The legislature's laws are supreme and not subject to judicial review.

No. The Constitutional Court can review the constitutionality of laws.

Article 144

The Constitutional Court shall have the following powers: a) to adjudicate on the constitutionality of laws, before promulgation, upon notification by the President of Romania, by the President of either Chamber of Parliament, by the Government, the Supreme Court of Justice, by a number of at least 50 Deputies or at least 25 Senators, as well as, ex officio, on initiatives to revise the Constitution; b) to adjudicate on the constitutionality of the Standing Orders of Parliament, upon notification by the President of either Chamber, by a parliamentary group or a number of at least 50 Deputies or at least

25 Senators; c) to decide on exceptions brought to the Courts of law as to the unconstitutionality of laws and orders.

14. The legislature has the right to initiate bills in all policy jurisdictions; the executive lacks gatekeeping authority.

Yes. The legislature can initiate bills in all policy jurisdictions.

15. Expenditure of funds appropriated by the legislature is mandatory; the executive lacks the power to impound funds appropriated by the legislature.

Yes. The executive lacks the power to impound funds appropriated by the legislature.

16. The legislature controls the resources that finance its own internal operation and provide for the perquisites of its own members.

Yes. The legislature enjoys financial autonomy.

Article 61
(1) The organization and functioning of each Chamber shall be regulated by its own Standing Orders. Financial resources of the Chambers shall be provided for in the budgets approved by them.

17. Members of the legislature are immune from arrest and/or criminal prosecution.

Yes. Legislators are immune with the common exception for cases of *flagrante delicto*.

Article 69
(1) No Deputy or Senator shall be detained, arrested, searched, or prosecuted for a criminal or minor offence without authorization of the Chamber he is a member of, after being given a hearing. The case shall be in the competence of the Supreme Court of Justice.
(2) In the case of flagrante delicto, he may be detained and searched. The Minister of Justice shall promptly inform the President of the respective Chamber about the detention and search. In case the Chamber thus notified finds no grounds for his detention, it shall immediately order that this detainment be repealed.

18. All members of the legislature are elected; the executive lacks the power to appoint any members of the legislature.

Yes. All members of the legislature are elected.

Article 59
(1) The Chamber of Deputies and the Senate are elected by universal, equal, direct, secret, and free suffrage, in accordance with the electoral law.

19. The legislature alone, without the involvement of any other agencies, can change the Constitution.

No. Constitutional amendments require approval in a popular referendum.

Article 146
(1) Revision of the Constitution may be initiated by the President of Romania on proposal of the Government, by at least one quarter of the number of Deputies or Senators, as well as by at least 500,000 citizens with the right to vote.
(2) The citizens who initiate the revision of the Constitution must belong to at least half the number of the counties in the country, and in each of the respective counties or in the City of Bucharest, at least 20,000 signatures must be recorded in support of this initiative.

Article 147
(1) The draft or proposed revision must be adopted by the Chamber of Deputies and the Senate by a majority of at least two thirds of the members of each Chamber.
(2) If no agreement can be reached by a mediation procedure, the Chamber of Deputies and the Senate shall decide thereupon, in joint session, by the vote of at least three quarters of the number of Deputies and Senators.
(3) The revision shall be final after approval by a referendum held within 30 days from the date of passing the draft or proposed revision.

20. The legislature's approval is necessary for the declaration of war.

Yes. The legislature declares war.

Article 62
(2) The Chambers shall meet in joint sessions in order:
  d) to declare a state of war.

21. The legislature's approval is necessary to ratify treaties with foreign countries.

Yes. The legislature's approval is necessary to ratify international treaties.

Article 11
(1) The Romanian State pledges to fulfill as such and in good faith its obligations as deriving from the treaties it is a party to.
(2) Treaties ratified by Parliament, according to the law, are part of national law.

Article 91
(1) The President shall, in the name of Romania, conclude international treaties negotiated by the Government, and then submit them to Parliament for ratification within 60 days.

22. The legislature has the power to grant amnesty.

Yes. The legislature has the power to grant amnesty.

Article 72
(1) Parliament passes constitutional, organic, and ordinary laws.
(2) Constitutional laws shall be pertaining to the revision of the Constitution.
(3) Organic laws shall regulate:
  g) granting of amnesty or collective pardon.

23. The legislature has the power of pardon.

No. The president has the power of pardon.

> Article 94
> The President of Romania shall also have the following powers:
> d) to grant individual pardon.

24. The legislature reviews and has the right to reject appointments to the judiciary; or the legislature itself appoints members of the judiciary.

Yes. The legislature elects the members of the Superior Council of the Magistracy and six of the nine judges of the Constitutional Court.

> Article 124
> (1) Judges appointed by the President of Romania shall be irremovable, according to the law. The President and other judges of the Supreme Court of Justice shall be appointed for a term of six years, and may be reinvested in office. Promotion, transfer, and sanctions against Judges may be decided upon only by the Superior Council of the Magistracy, in accordance with the law.
> (2) The office of a Judge shall be incompatible with any other public or private office, except that of an academic professorial activity.

> Article 132
> The Superior Council of the Magistracy shall consist of magistrates elected for a term of four years by the Chamber of Deputies and the Senate, in a joint session.

> Article 140
> (1) The Constitutional Court consists of nine Judges, appointed for a term of office of nine years, that cannot be prolonged or renewed.
> (2) Three Judges shall be appointed by the Chamber of Deputies, three by the Senate, and three by the President of Romania.

25. The chairman of the central bank is appointed by the legislature.

Yes. The legislature elects the governor of the National Bank of Romania.

26. The legislature has a substantial voice in the operation of the state-owned media.

Yes. The legislature has a substantial voice in the operation of the public media.

> Article 31
> (5) Public radio and television services shall be autonomous. They must guarantee for any important social and political group the exercise of the right to be on the air. The organization of these services and the Parliamentary control over their activity shall be regulated by an organic law.

27. The legislature is regularly in session.

Yes. The legislature meets in ordinary session for about eight months each year.

> Article 63
> (1) The Chamber of Deputies and the Senate shall meet in two ordinary sessions every year. The first session begins in February and is due to last by the end of June at the latest. The second session begins in September and is due to last by the end of December at the latest.
> (2) The Chamber of Deputies and the Senate may also meet in extraordinary sessions, upon request of the President of Romania, the Standing Bureau of each Chamber, or of at least one third of the number of Deputies or Senators.
> (3) Each Chamber shall be convened by its President.

28. Each legislator has a personal secretary.

No.

29. Each legislator has at least one non-secretarial staff member with policy expertise.

No.

30. Legislators are eligible for re-election without any restriction.

Yes. There are no restrictions on re-election.

31. A seat in the legislature is an attractive enough position that legislators are generally interested in and seek re-election.

Yes.

32. The re-election of incumbent legislators is common enough that at any given time the legislature contains a significant number of highly experienced members.

Yes. Re-election rates are sufficiently high to produce a significant number of highly experienced members.

FEDERAL ASSEMBLY OF THE RUSSIAN FEDERATION (*FEDERALNOE SOBRANIE*)

Expert consultants: Gerald M. Easter, Grigorii Golosov, Andrei Kunov, Joel M. Ostrow, Thomas F. Remington, Andrei Riabov, Robert Sharlet

Score: .44

Influence over executive (1/9)	Institutional autonomy (3/9)		Specified powers (4/8)		Institutional capacity (6/6)	
1. replace	10. no dissolution		19. amendments		27. sessions	X
2. serve as ministers	11. no decree		20. war	X	28. secretary	X
3. interpellate	12. no veto		21. treaties	X	29. staff	X
4. investigate	13. no review		22. amnesty	X	30. no term limits	X
5. oversee police	14. no gatekeeping	X	23. pardon		31. seek re-election	X
6. appoint PM	15. no impoundment		24. judiciary	X	32. experience	X
7. appoint ministers	16. control resources		25. central bank			
8. lack president	17. immunity	X	26. media			
9. no confidence X	18. all elected	X				

The Federal Assembly (*Federalnoe Sobranie*) of Russia traces its origins to the State Duma that was established following the 1905 revolution. During the half-decade following the demise of the Russian Empire and the seizure of power by the Bolsheviks in 1918, the Soviet Union came into existence and its legislature, the Supreme Soviet, was subordinated to the Communist Party. In 1989 and 1990, during the twilight of the Soviet era, both the Supreme Soviet of the USSR and the republican-level Supreme Soviet of the Russian Soviet Federated Socialist Republic (RSFSR) were reorganized, and popular elections were held for each. In 1991 a constitutional referendum created a presidency to function alongside the Russian Supreme Soviet. The demise of the USSR at the end of 1991 left the newly created Russian Federation operating under a Soviet-era constitution that had been heavily amended to reflect the reforms of the late Soviet period. A new constitution adopted by referendum in 1993 replaced the Supreme Soviet with the Federal Assembly, a bicameral legislature consisting of a lower house, the State Duma (*Gosudarstvennaia duma*), and an upper house, the Federation Council (*Sovet federatsii*).

The legislature's powers are markedly unbalanced and, on the whole, tightly circumscribed. The legislature has almost no ability to influence the executive branch, and its own institutional autonomy is severely hampered by the president's expansive powers. Such potency as the legislature

does possess comes in part in the form of scattered specified prerogatives, which include rights over the declaration of war, ratification of treaties, and granting of amnesty. The other area in which the legislature has some muscle is in its institutional capacity: The legislature is regularly in session, has staff, and contains a significant corpus of experienced members.

SURVEY

1. The legislature alone, without the involvement of any other agencies, can impeach the president or replace the prime minister.

No. Presidential impeachment requires the involvement of the Supreme Court and the Constitutional Court.

Article 93
(1) The President of the Russian Federation may be impeached by the Federation Council only on the basis of charges put forward against him of high treason or some other grave crime, confirmed by a ruling of the Supreme Court of the Russian Federation on the presence of indicia of crime in the President's actions and by a ruling of the Constitutional Court of the Russian Federation confirming that the procedure of bringing charges has been observed.
(2) The ruling of the State Duma on putting forward charges and the decision of the Federation Council on impeachment of the President is passed by the votes of two-thirds of the total number in each of the chambers

at the initiative of at least one-third of the deputies of the State Duma and in the presence of the opinion of a special commission formed by the State Duma.

(3) The decision of the Federation Council on impeaching the President of the Russian Federation is passed within three months of the charges being brought against the President by the State Duma. The charges against the President are considered to be rejected if the decision of the Federation Council is not passed.

2. Ministers may serve simultaneously as members of the legislature.

No. Legislators are prohibited from serving simultaneously in ministerial positions.

3. The legislature has powers of summons over executive branch officials and hearings with executive branch officials testifying before the legislature or its committees are regularly held.

No. The legislature can request executive branch officials to testify, but hearings are not a part of normal practice.

4. The legislature can conduct independent investigation of the chief executive and the agencies of the executive.

No. Formally, the legislature can establish commissions to investigate the government. In practice, however, investigations are rare and subject to executive influence.

5. The legislature has effective powers of oversight over the agencies of coercion (the military, organs of law enforcement, intelligence services, and the secret police).

No. The legislature lacks effective powers of oversight over the agencies of coercion.

6. The legislature appoints the prime minister.

No. The president appoints the prime minister (here called chairman of the government) with the consent of the State Duma.

Article 83
The President of the Russian Federation shall:
a) appoint Chairman of the Government of the Russian Federation subject to consent of the State Duma.

Article 111
(1) The Chairman of the Government of the Russian Federation is appointed by the President of the Russian Federation with consent of the State Duma.
(2) The proposal on the candidacy of the Chairman of the Government of the Russian Federation is made no later than two weeks after the inauguration of the newly-elected President of the Russian Federation or after the resignation of the Government of the Russian Federation or within one week after the rejection of the candidate by the State Duma.

(3) The State Duma considers the candidacy of the Chairman of the Government of the Russian Federation submitted by the President of the Russian Federation within one week after the nomination.
(4) After the State Duma thrice rejects candidates for Chairman of the Government of the Russian Federation nominated by the President of the Russian Federation, the President of the Russian Federation appoints the Chairman of the Government of the Russian Federation, dissolves the State Duma and calls a new election.

7. The legislature's approval is required to confirm the appointment of ministers; or the legislature itself appoints ministers.

No. The president appoints ministers on the recommendation of the prime minister, and the appointments do not require legislative approval.

Article 112
(1) The Chairman of the Government of the Russian Federation shall, not later than one week after appointment, submit to the President of the Russian Federation proposals on the structures of the federal bodies of executive power.
(2) The Chairman of the Government of the Russian Federation proposes to the President of the Russian Federation candidates for the office of Deputy Chairmen of the Government of the Russian Federation and federal ministers.

8. The country lacks a presidency entirely or there is a presidency, but the president is elected by the legislature.

No. The president is directly elected.

Article 81
(1) The President of the Russian Federation is elected for a term of four years by the citizens of the Russian Federation on the basis of general, equal and direct vote by secret ballot.

9. The legislature can vote no confidence in the government.

Yes. The legislature can vote no confidence in the government.

Article 117
(3) The State Duma may express non-confidence in the Government of the Russian Federation. The non-confidence resolution is approved by a simple majority of deputies in the State Duma. In the event the State Duma again expresses non-confidence in the Government of the Russian Federation within three months, the President of the Russian Federation announces the resignation of the Government or dissolves the State Duma.
(4) The Chairman of the Government of the Russian Federation may put the question of confidence in the Government of the Russian Federation before the State Duma. In the case of a non-confidence vote by the State Duma, the President decides within seven days about

the resignation of the Government of the Russian Federation or about the dissolution of the State Duma and calls a new election.

(5) If the Government of the Russian Federation resigns or lays down its powers, it shall, following instructions by the President of the Russian Federation, continue working until the formation of a new government of the Russian Federation.

10. The legislature is immune from dissolution by the executive.

No. The president can dissolve the State Duma.

Article 84
The President of the Russian Federation shall:
b) dissolve the State Duma in cases and under procedures envisaged by the Constitution.

Article 109
(1) The State Duma may be dissolved by the President of the Russian Federation in cases stipulated in Articles 111 and 117 of the Constitution.
(2) In the event of the dissolution of the State Duma, the President of the Russian Federation determines the date of elections so that the newly-elected State Duma convenes not later than four months since the time of dissolution.
(3) The State Duma may not be dissolved on grounds provided for by Article 117 of the Constitution within one year after its election.
(4) The State Duma may not be dissolved since the time it has brought accusations against the President of the Russian Federation and until a corresponding decision has been taken by the Federation Council.
(5) The State Duma may not be dissolved during the period of the state of emergency or martial law throughout the territory of the Russian Federation, as well as within six months of the expiry of the term of office of the President of the Russian Federation.

11. Any executive initiative on legislation requires ratification or approval by the legislature before it takes effect; that is, the executive lacks decree power.

No. The president issues decrees that have the force of law.

Article 90
(1) The President of the Russian Federation issues decrees and executive orders.
(2) The decrees and orders of the President of the Russian Federation are binding throughout the territory of the Russian Federation.
(3) The decrees and orders of the President of the Russian Federation may not contravene the Constitution or federal laws.

12. Laws passed by the legislature are veto-proof or essentially veto-proof; that is, the executive lacks veto power, or has veto power but the veto can be overridden by a majority in the legislature.

No. A two-thirds majority is required to override a presidential veto.

Article 107
(1) An adopted federal law is sent to the President of the Russian Federation for signing and publication within five days.
(2) The President of the Russian Federation shall, within fourteen days, sign a federal law and publish it.
(3) If the President rejects a federal law within fourteen days since it was sent to him, the State Duma and the Federation Council again consider the law in accordance with the procedure established by the Constitution. If, during the second hearings, the federal law is approved in its earlier draft by a majority of not less than two thirds of the total number of deputies of the Federation Council and the State Duma, it is signed by the President of the Russian Federation within seven days and published.

13. The legislature's laws are supreme and not subject to judicial review.

No. The Constitutional Court can review the constitutionality of laws.

Article 125
(2) The Constitutional Court of the Russian Federation on request by the President of the Russian Federation, the State Duma, one-fifth of the members of the Federation Council or deputies of the State Duma, the Government of the Russian Federation, the Supreme Court of the Russian Federation and Supreme Arbitration Court of the Russian Federation, bodies of legislative and executive power of subjects of the Russian Federation resolves cases about compliance with the Constitution of:
   a) federal laws, normative acts of the President of the Russian Federation, the Federation Council, State Duma and the Government of the Russian Federation;
   b) republican constitutions, charters, as well as laws and other normative acts of subjects of the Russian Federation published on issues pertaining to the jurisdiction of bodies of state power of the Russian Federation and joint jurisdiction of bodies of state power of the Russian Federation and bodies of state power of subjects of the Russian Federation;
   c) agreements between bodies of state power of the Russian Federation and bodies of state power of subjects of the Russian Federation, agreements between bodies of state power of subjects of the Russian Federation;
   d) international agreements of the Russian Federation that have not entered into force.
(4) The Constitutional Court of the Russian Federation, proceeding from complaints about violation of constitutional rights and freedoms of citizens and requests from courts reviews the constitutionality of the law applied or due to be applied in a specific case in accordance with procedures established by federal law.

(5) The Constitutional Court of the Russian Federation on request by the President of the Russian Federation, the Federation Council, State Duma, the Government of the Russian Federation, legislative bodies of subjects of the Russian Federation interprets the Constitution.

(6) Acts and their provisions deemed unconstitutional loose force thereof; international agreements of the Russian Federation may not be enforced and applied if they violate the Constitution.

14. The legislature has the right to initiate bills in all policy jurisdictions; the executive lacks gatekeeping authority.

Yes. The legislature can initiate bills in all policy jurisdictions.

15. Expenditure of funds appropriated by the legislature is mandatory; the executive lacks the power to impound funds appropriated by the legislature.

No. The president can impound funds appropriated by the legislature.

16. The legislature controls the resources that finance its own internal operation and provide for the perquisites of its own members.

No. The legislature is dependent on the president for the resources that finance its own operations. An office in the presidential apparatus controls legislators' perks and is regularly deployed by the president to sway legislators' behavior.

17. Members of the legislature are immune from arrest and/or criminal prosecution.

Yes. Legislators are immune with the common exception for cases of *flagrante delicto,* here expressed as "in the act of perpetrating a crime."

Article 98

(1) Deputies to the Federation Council and deputies to the State Duma possess immunity throughout their term in office. A deputy may not be detained, arrested, searched except when detained in the act of perpetrating a crime, and may not be subject to personal search except when such search is authorized by law to ensure the safety of other people.

(2) The question of stripping a deputy of immunity is decided on the recommendation of the Prosecutor-General of the Russian Federation by the corresponding chamber of the Federal Assembly.

18. All members of the legislature are elected; the executive lacks the power to appoint any members of the legislature.

Yes. All members of the legislature are elected.

Article 96

(1) The State Duma is elected for a term of four years.

19. The legislature alone, without the involvement of any other agencies, can change the Constitution.

No. Much of the constitution can be amended only with the involvement of actors besides the legislature. Amendments to chapters 3 (federation) and 8 (local self-government) require approval by two-thirds of the provincial governments. Amendments to chapters 1 (fundamental principles), 2 (rights and liberties), and 9 (constitutional amendments) require the convocation of a constitutional assembly.

Article 108

(1) Federal constitutional laws are passed on issues specified in the Constitution.

(2) A federal constitutional law is considered adopted, if it has been approved by a majority of at least three quarters of the total number of deputies of the Federation Council and at least two thirds of the total number of deputies of the House of Representatives [State Duma]. The adopted federal constitutional law is signed by the President of the Russian Federation within fourteen days and published.

Article 134

Proposals on amendments and revision of constitutional provisions may be made by the President of the Russian Federation, the Federation Council, the State Duma, the Government of the Russian Federation, legislative (representative) bodies of the subjects of the Russian Federation as well as groups of deputies numbering not less than one-fifth of the total number of deputies of the Federation Council or the State Duma.

Article 135

(1) The provisions of Chapters 1, 2 and 9 of the Constitution may not be revised by the Federal Assembly.

(2) In the event a proposal to revise any provisions in Chapters 1, and 9 of the Constitution is supported by three-fifths of the total number of deputies of the Federation Council and the State Duma, a Constitutional Assembly is convened in accordance with the federal constitutional law.

(3) The Constitutional Assembly may either confirm the inviolability of the Constitution or develop a new draft of the Constitution which is adopted by two-thirds of the total number of deputies to the Constitutional Assembly or submitted to popular voting. The Constitution is considered adopted during such poll if more than half of its participants have voted for it, provided more than half of the electorate have taken part in the poll.

Article 136

Amendments to Chapters 3 to 8 of the Constitution are adopted in accordance with the procedures envisaged for the adoption of a federal constitutional law and come into force following the approval thereof by no less than two-thirds of the subjects of the Russian Federation.

Article 137

(1) Changes to Article 65 of the Constitution which determines the composition of the Russian Federation,

are made on the basis of the federal constitutional law on admission to the Russian Federation and the formation within the Russian Federation of a new subject and on a change of the constitutional-legal status of the subject of the Russian Federation.

(2) In the event of a change in the name of the republic, territory, region, federal cities, autonomous region and autonomous area, the new name of the subject of the Russian Federation is included in Article 65 of the Constitution.

20. The legislature's approval is necessary for the declaration of war.

Yes. The legislature declares war.

Article 106
The federal laws adopted by the State Duma are considered by the Federation Council on a mandatory basis if such laws deal with the issues of:
f) war and peace.

21. The legislature's approval is necessary to ratify treaties with foreign countries.

Yes. The legislature's approval is necessary to ratify international treaties.

Article 86
The President of the Russian Federation shall:
b) conduct negotiations and sign international treaties of the Russian Federation;
c) sign instruments of ratification.

Article 106
The federal laws adopted by the State Duma are considered by the Federation Council on a mandatory basis if such laws deal with the issues of:
d) ratification and denunciation of international treaties of the Russian Federation.

22. The legislature has the power to grant amnesty.

Yes. The legislature has the power to grant amnesty.

Article 103
(1) The jurisdiction of the State Duma includes:
f) granting amnesty.

23. The legislature has the power of pardon.

No. The president has the power of pardon.

Article 89
The President of the Russian Federation shall:
c) grant pardon.

24. The legislature reviews and has the right to reject appointments to the judiciary; or the legislature itself appoints members of the judiciary.

Yes. The Federation Council appoints the judges to the Constitutional Court, the Supreme Court, and the Supreme Arbitration Court on the recommendation of the president.

Article 102
The jurisdiction of the Federation Council includes:
g) the appointment of judges of the Constitutional Court of the Russian Federation, the Supreme Court of the Russian Federation, and the Supreme Court of Arbitration of the Russian Federation.

Article 83
The President of the Russian Federation shall:
f) submit to the Federation Council candidates for appointment to the office of judges of the Constitutional Court of the Russian Federation, the Supreme Court of the Russian Federation and the Supreme Arbitration Court of the Russian Federation as well as the candidate for Prosecutor-General of the Russian Federation; submit to the Federation Council the proposal on relieving the Prosecutor-General of the Russian Federation of his duties; appoint the judges of other federal courts.

Article 128
(1) Judges of the Constitutional Court of the Russian Federation, of the Supreme Court of the Russian Federation, of the Supreme Arbitration Court of the Russian Federation are appointed by the Federation Council following nomination by the President of the Russian Federation.
(2) Judges of other federal courts are appointed by the President of the Russian Federation in accordance with procedures established by federal law.
(3) The powers, and procedure of the formation and activities of the Constitutional Court of the Russian Federation, the Supreme Court of the Russian Federation and the Supreme Arbitration Court of the Russian Federation and other federal courts are established by federal constitutional law.

25. The chairman of the central bank is appointed by the legislature.

No. Formally, the legislature, on the recommendation of the president, appoints the chairman of the Central Bank of the Russian Federation, but in practice, appointment authority rests exclusively with the president.

Article 83
The President of the Russian Federation shall:
d) introduce to the State Duma a candidature for appointment to the office of the Chairman of the Central Bank of the Russian Federation.

Article 103
(1) The jurisdiction of the House of Representatives [State Duma] includes:
   a) granting consent to the President of the Russian Federation for the appointment of the Chairman of the Government of the Russian Federation;
   b) decisions on confidence in the government of the Russian Federation;
   c) the appointment and dismissal of the Chairman of the Central Bank of the Russian Federation.

26. The legislature has a substantial voice in the operation of the state-owned media.

No. The legislature lacks a substantial voice in the operation of the public media.

27. The legislature is regularly in session.

Yes. The legislature regularly meets in ordinary session.

> Article 99
> (2) The State Duma holds its first session on the 30th day after its election. The President of the Russian Federation may convene a session of the State Duma before this term.
> (3) The first session of the State Duma is opened by the oldest deputy.

28. Each legislator has a personal secretary.

Yes.

29. Each legislator has at least one non-secretarial staff member with policy expertise.

Yes.

30. Legislators are eligible for re-election without any restriction.

Yes. There are no restrictions on re-election.

31. A seat in the legislature is an attractive enough position that legislators are generally interested in and seek re-election.

Yes.

32. The re-election of incumbent legislators is common enough that at any given time the legislature contains a significant number of highly experienced members.

Yes. Electoral volatility has been quite high across the parliamentary elections held since 1993, and turnover rates have been high, but a body of members has maintained membership from session to session, creating a substantial cohort of highly experienced members.

PARLIAMENT OF RWANDA (*INTEKO ISHINGA AMATEGEKO*)

Expert consultants: Timothy Longman, Aloys Muberanziza, Charles Ntampaka, Tito Rutaremara, Colin Waugh

Score: .47

Influence over executive (3/9)		Institutional autonomy (5/9)		Specified powers (3/8)		Institutional capacity (4/6)	
1. replace		10. no dissolution		19. amendments	X	27. sessions	X
2. serve as ministers		11. no decree		20. war		28. secretary	X
3. interpellate	X	12. no veto		21. treaties	X	29. staff	
4. investigate	X	13. no review	X	22. amnesty		30. no term limits	X
5. oversee police		14. no gatekeeping	X	23. pardon		31. seek re-election	X
6. appoint PM		15. no impoundment	X	24. judiciary	X	32. experience	
7. appoint ministers		16. control resources	X	25. central bank			
8. lack president		17. immunity	X	26. media			
9. no confidence	X	18. all elected					

The Parliament of Rwanda (*Inteko Ishinga Amategeko*) was established upon independence from Belgium in 1962. The bicameral legislature consists of a lower house, the Chamber of Deputies (*Umutwe w'Abadepite*), and an upper house, the Senate (*Umutwe wa Sena*). In 1991 a new constitution was adopted that allowed for greater multiparty competition. Ethnic violence and genocide shredded the country and undermined the legislature's influence in the mid-1990s. In 2003 a new constitution banned the incitement of ethnic hatred, and parliamentary elections, the first since 1994, were held.

The legislature has only modest sway over the executive, although it does enjoy substantial institutional autonomy. Most notably, the legislature's laws are supreme and not subject to judicial review. The legislature exercises few specified powers, but it does enjoy some institutional capacity.

SURVEY

1. The legislature alone, without the involvement of any other agencies, can impeach the president or replace the prime minister.

No. The legislature cannot impeach the president. It can remove the prime minister with a motion of censure or a vote of no confidence.

> Article 130
> The Chamber of Deputies may put the performance of Government or of one or several members into question through a vote of censure. A motion of censure is not receivable except after interpellation and only on condition that the motion is signed by at least a fifth of the members of the Chamber of Deputies in the case against one member of the Government, or by at least a third of the members of the Chamber of Deputies if it concerns the entire Government. A motion of censure cannot be voted upon prior to the expiry of at least forty-eight hours after its introduction and it shall be adopted through a secret ballot by a majority of at least two-thirds of the members of the Chamber of Deputies. The conclusion of ordinary or extraordinary sessions is by right postponed to ensure the application of the provisions of this article.

> Article 131
> A member of the Government against whom a vote of censure is passed must tender his resignation to the President of the Republic through the Prime Minister. When the vote of censure is passed against the Government, the Prime Minister tenders the resignation of the Government to the President of the Republic.
> If a motion of censure is rejected, signatories to the motion cannot introduce another motion for a vote of censure during the same session.

> Article 132
> The Prime Minister may, upon the proposal of the Government, request the Chamber of Deputies to pass a motion on a vote of confidence either in respect of the Government program or the adoption of the text of a bill. The debate on the request for a vote of confidence may not take place prior to the expiry of at least three full days from the time the request was submitted. A vote on the motion of confidence may only be rejected through a secret ballot by a majority of two-thirds of the members to the Chamber of Deputies. If the confidence is refused, the Prime Minister submits the resignation of the Government to the President of the Republic, within twenty-four hours.

2. Ministers may serve simultaneously as members of the legislature.

No. Legislators are prohibited from serving simultaneously in ministerial positions.

> Article 68
> No one shall at the same time be a member of the Chamber of Deputies and the Senate.
> The office of a Parliamentarian shall not be compatible with being a member of the Government.
> An organic law determines other offices which are incompatible with the office of a Parliamentarian.

3. The legislature has powers of summons over executive branch officials and hearings with executive branch officials testifying before the legislature or its committees are regularly held.

Yes. The legislature regularly questions executive branch officials.

> Article 129
> In the context of obtaining information and exercising oversight of government action, members of the Senate may address oral or written questions to the Prime Minister to which he shall either respond in person if the questions relate to the government as a whole or to several Ministries collectively or through the Ministers who are responsible for the matters in question.
> The Senate may, in addition, set up commissions of inquiry for oversight of government action.
> However, it may not conduct interpellation or initiate a motion of censure.

4. The legislature can conduct independent investigation of the chief executive and the agencies of the executive.

Yes. The Senate can set up commissions of inquiry to investigate the executive.

> Article 129
> In the context of obtaining information and exercising oversight of government action, members of the Senate may address oral or written questions to the Prime Minister to which he shall either respond in person if the questions relate to the government as a whole or to several Ministries collectively or through the Ministers who are responsible for the matters in question.
> The Senate may, in addition, set up commissions of inquiry for oversight of government action.
> However, it may not conduct interpellation or initiate a motion of censure.

5. The legislature has effective powers of oversight over the agencies of coercion (the military, organs of law enforcement, intelligence services, and the secret police).

No. The legislature lacks effective powers of oversight over the agencies of coercion.

6. The legislature appoints the prime minister.

No. The president appoints the prime minister.

> Article 116
> The Government is composed of the Prime Minister, Ministers, Ministers of State and other members who

may be determined, if necessary, by the President of the Republic.

The Prime Minister is chosen, appointed and removed from office by the President of the Republic. Other members of Government are appointed and removed from office by the President of the Republic upon proposal of the Prime Minister.

7. The legislature's approval is required to confirm the appointment of ministers; or the legislature itself appoints ministers.

No. The president appoints ministers, and the appointments do not require the legislature's approval.

Article 116

The Government is composed of the Prime Minister, Ministers, Ministers of State and other members who may be determined, if necessary, by the President of the Republic.

The Prime Minister is chosen, appointed and removed from office by the President of the Republic. Other members of Government are appointed and removed from office by the President of the Republic upon proposal of the Prime Minister.

8. The country lacks a presidency entirely or there is a presidency, but the president is elected by the legislature.

No. The president is directly elected.

Article 100

The election of the President of the Republic shall be by universal suffrage through a direct and secret ballot with a simple majority of the votes cast.

9. The legislature can vote no confidence in the government.

Yes. The legislature can vote no confidence in the government.

Article 130

The Chamber of Deputies may put the performance of Government or of one or several members into question through a vote of censure. A motion of censure is not receivable except after interpellation and only on condition that the motion is signed by at least a fifth of the members of the Chamber of Deputies in the case against one member of the Government, or by at least a third of the members of the Chamber of Deputies if it concerns the entire Government. A motion of censure cannot be voted upon prior to the expiry of at least forty-eight hours after its introduction and it shall be adopted through a secret ballot by a majority of at least two-thirds of the members of the Chamber of Deputies. The conclusion of ordinary or extraordinary sessions is by right postponed to ensure the application of the provisions of this article.

Article 131

A member of the Government against whom a vote of censure is passed must tender his resignation to the President of the Republic through the Prime Minister. When the vote of censure is passed against the Government, the Prime Minister tenders the resignation of the Government to the President of the Republic.

If a motion of censure is rejected, signatories to the motion cannot introduce another motion for a vote of censure during the same session.

Article 132

The Prime Minister may, upon the proposal of the Government, request the Chamber of Deputies to pass a motion on a vote of confidence either in respect of the Government program or the adoption of the text of a bill. The debate on the request for a vote of confidence may not take place prior to the expiry of at least three full days from the time the request was submitted. A vote on the motion of confidence may only be rejected through a secret ballot by a majority of two-thirds of the members to the Chamber of Deputies. If the confidence is refused, the Prime Minister submits the resignation of the Government to the President of the Republic, within twenty-four hours.

10. The legislature is immune from dissolution by the executive.

No. The president can dissolve the Chamber of Deputies, although the Senate is immune from dissolution.

Article 133

The President of the Republic, after consultation with the Prime Minister, the Presidents of the two Chambers of Parliament and the President of the Supreme Court, may dissolve the Chamber of Deputies. Elections of Deputies take place within ninety days after the dissolution.

The President of the Republic cannot dissolve the Chamber of Deputies more than once in the same presidential term of office. The Senate cannot be dissolved.

11. Any executive initiative on legislation requires ratification or approval by the legislature before it takes effect; that is, the executive lacks decree power.

No. The president can issue decrees that have the force of law when the legislature is not in session. The decrees lapse if they are not subsequently approved by the legislature.

Article 63

In the event of an absolute impossibility of Parliament holding a session, the President of the Republic during such a period promulgates decree-laws adopted by the Government and those decree-laws have the same effect as ordinary laws. These decree-laws lose their obligatory force, if they are not adopted by Parliament at its next session.

12. Laws passed by the legislature are veto-proof or essentially veto-proof; that is, the executive lacks veto power, or has veto power but the veto can be overridden by a majority in the legislature.

No. A two-thirds majority vote is required to override a presidential veto of ordinary laws, and a three-fourths majority vote is required to override a presidential veto of organic laws.

> Article 108
> The President of the Republic promulgates laws within fifteen days from the day on which the adopted definitive text is delivered to the Government.
> However, the President of the Republic may before promulgation of laws request Parliament to proceed to a second reading (lecture).
> In such a case, if Parliament adopts the same laws, a majority of two-thirds in the case of ordinary laws, and in the case of the organic laws, a majority of three-quarters, the President of the Republic must promulgate the laws within the period referred to in paragraph 1 of this article.

13. The legislature's laws are supreme and not subject to judicial review.

Yes. The legislature's laws are not subject to judicial review. The legislature is responsible for the "authentic interpretation" of laws.

> Article 96
> The authentic interpretation of laws belongs to both Chambers of Parliament acting jointly after the Supreme Court has given an opinion on the matter; each Chamber shall decide on the basis of the majority referred to in Article 93 of this Constitution. The authentic interpretation of the laws may be requested by the Government, a member of one of the Chambers of Parliament or by the Bar Association (l'Ordre des Avocats). Any interested person may request the authentic interpretation of laws through the members of Parliament or the Bar Association.

14. The legislature has the right to initiate bills in all policy jurisdictions; the executive lacks gatekeeping authority.

Yes. The legislature can initiate bills in all policy jurisdictions.

15. Expenditure of funds appropriated by the legislature is mandatory; the executive lacks the power to impound funds appropriated by the legislature.

Yes. The executive lacks the power to impound funds appropriated by the legislature.

16. The legislature controls the resources that finance its own internal operation and provide for the perquisites of its own members.

Yes. The legislature enjoys financial autonomy.

> Article 74
> Each Chamber of Parliament disposes over its own budget and shall enjoy financial and administrative autonomy.

17. Members of the legislature are immune from arrest and/or criminal prosecution.

Yes. Legislators are immune with the common exception for cases of *flagrante delicto*.

> Article 69
> The members of Parliament enjoy parliamentary immunity in the following manner:
> 1. no Member of Parliament may be prosecuted, pursued, arrested, detained or judged for any opinions expressed or votes made by him in the exercise of his functions;
> 2. during the session period, no Member of Parliament may be arrested for a crime or felony without the authorization of the Chamber to which he belongs;
> 3. when Parliament is not in session, no Member of Parliament may be arrested without the authorization of the Bureau of the Chamber to which he belongs, unless he or she is caught flagrante delicto committing a felony or the Bureau of the Chamber to which he belongs has previously authorized his prosecution or a court of law has passed a final verdict and sentence against him. Any Member of Parliament convicted of a felony by a court of law of last instance is automatically stripped of his parliamentary seat by the Chamber to which he belongs, after confirmation by the Supreme Court. Likewise, each Chamber of Parliament may, in its internal regulations, make provisions for serious misconduct as a consequence of which a member of that Chamber may be removed from office. In such a case, the decision to remove the member from office shall be taken by a majority of three-fifths of the members of the Chamber concerned.

18. All members of the legislature are elected; the executive lacks the power to appoint any members of the legislature.

No. The president appoints eight of the twenty-six members of the Senate to ensure the representation of "historically marginalized communities." All members of the Chamber of Deputies are elected.

> Article 76
> The Chamber of Deputies is composed of eighty members as follows:
> 1. fifty-three are elected in accordance with the provisions of Article 77 of this Constitution;
> 2. twenty-four women; that is: two from each Province and the City of Kigali. These shall be elected by a joint assembly composed of members of the respective District, Municipality, Town or Kigali City Councils and members of the Executive Committees of women's organizations at the Province, Kigali City, District, Municipalities, Towns and Sector levels;

3. two members elected by the National Youth Council;
4. one member elected by the Federation of the Associations of the Disabled.

Article 82

The Senate is composed of twenty-six members serving for a term of eight (8) years and at least thirty per cent of whom are women. In addition, the former Heads of State become members of the Senate upon their request as provided for in paragraph 4 of this article.

These twenty-six members are elected or appointed as follows:

1. twelve members representing each Province and the City of Kigali are elected through secret ballot by members of the Executive Committees of Sectors and District, Municipality, Town or City Councils of each Province and the City of Kigali;
2. eight members appointed by the President of the Republic who shall ensure the representation of historically marginalized communities;
3. four members designated by the Forum of Political Organizations;
4. one university lecturer of at least the academic rank of Associate Professor elected by the academic and research staff of public universities and institutions of higher learning;
5. one university lecturer of at least the rank of Associate Professor elected by the academic and research staff of private universities and institutions of higher learning.

The organs responsible for the nomination of Senators shall take into account national unity and equal representation of both sexes. Former Heads of State who honorably completed their terms or voluntarily resigned from office become members of the Senate by submitting a request to the Supreme Court. Dispute relating to the application of Article 82 and 83 of this Constitution which may arise, shall be adjudicated by the Supreme Court.

19. The legislature alone, without the involvement of any other agencies, can change the Constitution.

Yes. The legislature can change the constitution with a three-fourths majority vote. Amendments to select articles, including those concerning the president's term in office, require approval in a popular referendum.

Article 193

The power to initiate amendment of the Constitution is vested concurrently in the President of the Republic, upon the proposal of the Government, and each Chamber of Parliament, upon a resolution passed by a two-thirds majority vote of its members. The passage of a constitutional amendment requires a three-quarters majority vote of the members of each chamber of Parliament.

However, if the constitutional amendment concerns the term of the President of the Republic or the system of democratic government based on political pluralism, or the constitutional regime established by this Constitution, especially the republican form of the government or national sovereignty, the amendment must be passed by referendum after adoption by each Chamber of Parliament. No amendment to this article is permitted.

20. The legislature's approval is necessary for the declaration of war.

No. The president can declare war and then seek retroactive legislative approval.

Article 110

The President of the Republic is the Commander-in-Chief of the Rwanda Defense Forces.

He declares war in accordance with the provisions of Article 136 of this Constitution.

He signs armistice and peace agreements. He declares a state of siege and a state of emergency in accordance with the provisions of the Constitution and the law.

Article 136

The President of the Republic has the right to declare war and inform the Parliament within seven days. Parliament votes on the declaration of war by a simple majority of the members of each Chamber.

21. The legislature's approval is necessary to ratify treaties with foreign countries.

Yes. The legislature's approval is necessary to ratify treaties on most major issues.

Article 189

The President of the Republic negotiates international treaties and agreements and ratifies them. The Parliament is notified of such treaties and agreements following their conclusion.

However, peace treaties and treaties or agreements relating to commerce and international organizations and those which commit state finances, modify provisions of laws already adopted by Parliament or relate to the status of persons can only be ratified after authorization by Parliament.

22. The legislature has the power to grant amnesty.

No. Amnesty and pardon are not treated separately, and the legislature lacks the power to grant amnesty. See item 23.

23. The legislature has the power of pardon.

No. The president has the power of pardon.

Article 111

The President of the Republic has authority to exercise the prerogative of mercy in accordance with the procedure determined by law and after consulting the Supreme Court.

24. The legislature reviews and has the right to reject appointments to the judiciary; or the legislature itself appoints members of the judiciary.

Yes. The Senate appoints Supreme Court judges on the recommendation of the president.

Article 148

The President of the Republic, after consultation with the Council of Ministers and the Supreme Council of the Magistrature, shall submit to the Senate a list of candidates for appointment as judges of the Supreme Court. The list must have two candidates per post in respect of which there is an election. The candidates shall be elected by an absolute majority vote of the members of the Senate.

25. The chairman of the central bank is appointed by the legislature.

No. The president appoints the governor of the National Bank of Rwanda.

Article 113

The President of the Republic signs Presidential orders deliberated in the Council of Ministers concerning:
5. the promotion and appointment of:
  e) the Governor of the Central Bank.

26. The legislature has a substantial voice in the operation of the state-owned media.

No. The legislature lacks a substantial voice in the operation of the public media.

27. The legislature is regularly in session.

Yes. The legislature meets in three two-month ordinary sessions each year.

Article 71

The Chambers of Parliament shall hold three ordinary sessions of two months each.

1. the first session shall commence on February 5th;
2. the second session shall commence on June 5th;
3. the third session shall commence on October 5th.
Where the commencement date of a session falls on a non-working day, the opening of the session shall be postponed to the following day; or, if the following day is a holiday, to the next working day.

28. Each legislator has a personal secretary.

Yes.

29. Each legislator has at least one non-secretarial staff member with policy expertise.

No.

30. Legislators are eligible for re-election without any restriction.

Yes. There are no restrictions on re-election.

31. A seat in the legislature is an attractive enough position that legislators are generally interested in and seek re-election.

Yes.

32. The re-election of incumbent legislators is common enough that at any given time the legislature contains a significant number of highly experienced members.

No. It is too early to tell. In 2003 the first parliamentary elections were held since 1994.

CONSULTATIVE COUNCIL OF SAUDI ARABIA (*MAJLIS ASH-SHURA*)

Expert consultants: Şener Aktürk, Awadh Al-Badi, Hind Al-Sheikh, Michael Herb

Score: .09

Influence over executive (2/9)		Institutional autonomy (0/9)	Specified powers (0/8)	Institutional capacity (1/6)	
1. replace		10. no dissolution	19. amendments	27. sessions	X
2. serve as ministers		11. no decree	20. war	28. secretary	
3. interpellate	X	12. no veto	21. treaties	29. staff	
4. investigate		13. no review	22. amnesty	30. no term limits	
5. oversee police		14. no gatekeeping	23. pardon	31. seek re-election	
6. appoint PM		15. no impoundment	24. judiciary	32. experience	
7. appoint ministers		16. control resources	25. central bank		
8. lack president	X	17. immunity	26. media		
9. no confidence		18. all elected			

The Consultative Council (*Majlis Ash-Shura*) of Saudi Arabia was established in 1993. The Consultative Council is not a legislature in the traditional sense. It has very little legislative or oversight power. Its membership is entirely appointed, and it serves as an advisory body to the monarch, who retains ultimate political authority.

The fundamental law of Saudi Arabia is contained in a number of royal decrees. Those most relevant to the Consultative Council include The Basic Form of Government, The Consultative Council Establishment Act, and The Consultative Council Sanctions Statute, each promulgated in 1993. Unless otherwise noted, constitutional citations excerpted below are drawn from The Basic Form of Government.

The Council lacks the powers of a normal legislature. It has minimal influence over the executive and no institutional autonomy. In fact, the monarch can choose, at any time, completely to disband the Council by decree. The legislature does not exercise any specified powers and enjoys scant institutional capacity.

SURVEY

1. The legislature alone, without the involvement of any other agencies, can impeach the president or replace the prime minister.

No. The legislature cannot remove the chief executive, the king, from office. The prime minister can be replaced only by the king.

2. Ministers may serve simultaneously as members of the legislature.

No. Legislators are prohibited from serving simultaneously in ministerial positions.

> Article 9 (Consultative Council Establishment Act)
> It is not permitted to combine membership of the Shura Council and any other government post or to manage any other company unless the King sees fit that there is a need for this.

3. The legislature has powers of summons over executive branch officials and hearings with executive branch officials testifying before the legislature or its committees are regularly held.

Yes. The legislature summons government officials to testify, and hearings are regularly held.

> Article 22 (Consultative Council Establishment Act)
> The chairman of the Shura Council has to submit to the Chairman of the Council of Ministers requests to summon any government official to the meetings of the Shura Council when it discusses matters relating to that official's jurisdiction. The official will have the right to debate but not the right to vote.

4. The legislature can conduct independent investigation of the chief executive and the agencies of the executive.

No. The Council can request documents from the cabinet but cannot investigate the king or the government.

> Article 24 (Consultative Council Establishment Act)
> The chairman of the Shura Council should submit a request to the prime minister to provide the Council with statements and documents in the possession of the government apparatus which the council believes are necessary for facilitating its work.

5. The legislature has effective powers of oversight over the agencies of coercion (the military, organs of law enforcement, intelligence services, and the secret police).

No. The Council lacks effective powers of oversight over the agencies of coercion.

6. The legislature appoints the prime minister.

No. The king appoints the prime minister.

7. The legislature's approval is required to confirm the appointment of ministers; or the legislature itself appoints ministers.

No. The king appoints ministers, and the appointments do not require the legislature's approval.

> Article 57
> (a) The King appoints and relieves deputies of the prime minister and ministers and members of the Council of Ministers by Royal decree.

> Article 58
> The King appoints those who enjoy the rank of ministers, deputy ministers and those of higher rank, and relieves them of their posts by Royal decree in accordance with the explanations included in the law. Ministers and heads of independent departments are responsible before the prime minister for the ministries and departments which they supervise.

8. The country lacks a presidency entirely or there is a presidency, but the president is elected by the legislature.

Yes. The country lacks a presidency. The king is the head of state.

9. The legislature can vote no confidence in the government.

No. The legislature cannot vote no confidence in the government.

10. The legislature is immune from dissolution by the executive.

No. The king can dissolve the legislature.

11. Any executive initiative on legislation requires ratification or approval by the legislature before it takes effect; that is, the executive lacks decree power.

No. All legislation is issued by royal decree. The Council makes suggestions to the king but does not legislate.

12. Laws passed by the legislature are veto-proof or essentially veto-proof; that is, the executive lacks veto power, or has veto power but the veto can be over-ridden by a majority in the legislature.

No. The king has absolute veto power. The king can take the legislature's suggestions but "has the right to decide what he deems fit."

> Article 17
> The decisions of the Shura Council will be submitted to the chairman of the Council of Ministers for delibera-tion. If the views of both Councils are concordant, they will be issued following the King's consent; if the views are different, the King has the right to decide what he deems fit.

13. The legislature's laws are supreme and not sub-ject to judicial review.

No. The Council is an advisory body and does not make laws.

14. The legislature has the right to initiate bills in all policy jurisdictions; the executive lacks gatekeeping authority.

No. The Shura Council is prohibited from pursuing lawmaking at all. It is not, however, restricted in its ability to propose bills to the king.

> Article 23 (Consultative Council Establishment Act)
> Every ten members of the Shura Council have the right to propose a new draft law or amendment of an execu-tive law and submit them to the chairman of the Shura Council; the chairman should submit the proposal to the King.

15. Expenditure of funds appropriated by the legis-lature is mandatory; the executive lacks the power to impound funds appropriated by the legislature.

No. The legislature does not appropriate funds.

16. The legislature controls the resources that finance its own internal operation and provide for the perquisites of its own members.

No. The legislature is dependent on the king for the resources that finance its own operations.

> Article 27 (Consultative Council Establishment Act)
> The Shura Council is to be allocated a special budget by the King; it will be spent in accordance with rules to be issued by a Royal decree.

> Article 28 (Consultative Council Establishment Act)
> The Shura Council's financial matters, financial control and final statement of accounts are to be organized in accordance with special rules to be issued by a Royal decree.

17. Members of the legislature are immune from arrest and/or criminal prosecution.

No. Legislators are subject to arrest and criminal prosecution.

18. All members of the legislature are elected; the executive lacks the power to appoint any members of the legislature.

No. The king appoints all of the members of the Shura Council.

> Article 3 (Consultative Council Establishment Act)
> The Shura Council is composed of a chairman and sixty members chosen by the King from amongst scholars and men of knowledge and expertise, and the rights and duties of members and all their affairs are defined by a Royal decree.

19. The legislature alone, without the involvement of any other agencies, can change the Constitution.

No. Constitutional amendments are made in the "same way as [the constitution] was promulgated," meaning by royal decree.

> Article 83
> This law may only be amended in the same way as it was promulgated.

20. The legislature's approval is necessary for the dec-laration of war.

No. The king can declare war without the Council's approval.

> Article 61
> The King declares a state of emergency, general mobi-lization and war, and the law defines the rules for this.

21. The legislature's approval is necessary to ratify treaties with foreign countries.

No. The king can conclude international treaties without the Council's approval. The Council does, however, have the right to examine treaties and offer advice on them to the king.

> Article 70
> International treaties, agreements, regulations and con-cessions are approved and amended by Royal decree.

> Article 18 (Consultative Council Establishment Act)
> International treaties, agreements, orders and conces-sions are issued and amended by Royal decrees after being studied by the Shura Council.

22. The legislature has the power to grant amnesty.

No. The king has the power to grant amnesty.

23. The legislature has the power of pardon.

No. The king has the power of pardon.

24. The legislature reviews and has the right to reject appointments to the judiciary; or the legislature itself appoints members of the judiciary.

No. The king appoints the members of the judiciary, and the appointments do not require the Council's approval.

> Article 52
> The appointment of judges and the termination of their duties is carried out by Royal decree by a proposal from the Higher Council of Justice in accordance with the provisions of the law.

25. The chairman of the central bank is appointed by the legislature.

No. The king appoints the governor of the Saudi Arabian Monetary Agency.

26. The legislature has a substantial voice in the operation of the state-owned media.

No. The legislature lacks a substantial voice in the operation of the public media.

27. The legislature is regularly in session.

Yes. The legislature regularly meets in ordinary session.

> Article 12 (Consultative Council Sanctions Statute)
> The Consultative Council shall hold an ordinary session at least once every two weeks. The date and time of the session shall be decided by the chairman of the Council who has the right to bring it forward or to postpone it should the need arise.

28. Each legislator has a personal secretary.

No. There is legislative staff, but on average there is less than one staff person for each legislator. One secretary is provided for every three members of the Council.

29. Each legislator has at least one non-secretarial staff member with policy expertise.

No. See item 28.

30. Legislators are eligible for re-election without any restriction.

No. The law requires that more than half of the sitting legislators must be turned out every four years at the end of each term.

> Article 13 (Consultative Council Establishment Act)
> The period of the Shura Council will be four Hijrah years starting from the date specified in the Royal decree issued regarding its establishment. A new Council will be formed at least two months before the end of its predecessor's term. In the event of the term ending before the formation of a new Council, the outgoing Council will continue to function until a new Council is formed. When a new Council is formed, it has to be observed that new members must be selected, whose number must not be less than half of the total number of council members.

31. A seat in the legislature is an attractive enough position that legislators are generally interested in and seek re-election.

No. There are no elections, so Council members cannot seek re-election. It bears note, however, that Council members generally welcome re-appointment.

32. The re-election of incumbent legislators is common enough that at any given time the legislature contains a significant number of highly experienced members.

No. There have not been elections for the Council, nor does the Council legislate, so one cannot speak of re-election rates or members' experience as legislators. Furthermore, the law requires that more than half of the sitting Council members must be turned out every four years.

> Article 13 (Consultative Council Establishment Act)
> The period of the Shura Council will be four Hijrah years starting from the date specified in the Royal decree issued regarding its establishment. A new Council will be formed at least two months before the end of its predecessor's term. In the event of the term ending before the formation of a new Council, the outgoing Council will continue to function until a new Council is formed. When a new Council is formed, it has to be observed that new members must be selected, whose number must not be less than half of the total number of council members.

NATIONAL ASSEMBLY OF SENEGAL (*ASSEMBLÉE NATIONALE*)

Expert consultants: Mamadou Diouf, Martha Gning, Gerti Hesseling, Mayke Kaag, Boubacar Niane, Nicholas van de Walle

Score: .44

Influence over executive (3/9)		Institutional autonomy (5/9)		Specified powers (2/8)		Institutional capacity (4/6)	
1. replace		10. no dissolution		19. amendments		27. sessions	X
2. serve as ministers		11. no decree	X	20. war	X	28. secretary	
3. interpellate	X	12. no veto		21. treaties	X	29. staff	
4. investigate	X	13. no review		22. amnesty		30. no term limits	X
5. oversee police		14. no gatekeeping	X	23. pardon		31. seek re-election	X
6. appoint PM		15. no impoundment	X	24. judiciary		32. experience	X
7. appoint ministers		16. control resources	X	25. central bank			
8. lack president		17. immunity		26. media			
9. no confidence	X	18. all elected	X				

The National Assembly (*Assemblée nationale*) of Senegal was established upon independence from France in 1960. Like many other former French colonies, Senegal borrowed key aspects of its political system from the French model. The National Assembly is rare among African legislatures in that it has enjoyed decades of influence under uninterrupted civilian rule. In 2001 the Senegal adopted a new constitution that called for a unicameral legislature, thereby abolishing the Senate that had existed in what had been a bicameral legislature. The new document also granted the president the power to dissolve the legislature. Prior to 2001 the legislature was immune from dissolution.

The legislature is a significant, although not commanding, political actor. Its ability to influence the executive is limited to the powers to interpellate and investigate executive branch officials and to vote no confidence in the government. It has considerable institutional autonomy. Its specified powers are limited to responsibilities for confirming declarations of war and for ratifying international treaties. It has some institutional capacity.

SURVEY

1. The legislature alone, without the involvement of any other agencies, can impeach the president or replace the prime minister.

No. Presidential impeachment requires the involvement of the High Court of Justice. The legislature can remove the prime minister with a vote of no confidence.

Article 86
The Prime Minister may, after deliberation of the Council of Ministers, decide to pose a question of confidence in a program or a declaration of general policy. The vote on the question of confidence may not take place until two full days after it has been presented. Confidence is refused by a public vote by the absolute majority of the members of the National Assembly. The refusal entails a collective resignation of the Government. The National Assembly may provoke the resignation of the Government by the vote of a motion of censure. The motion of censure must, on pain of irreceivability, be accompanied by the signatures of one-tenth of the members composing the National Assembly. The vote of censure can only take place two full days after its filing with the bureau of the National Assembly. The motion of censure is voted by public ballot, by an absolute majority of the members composing the National Assembly; only the votes in favor of the motion of censure are counted. If the motion of censure is adopted, the Prime Minister immediately presents the Government to the President of the Republic. A new motion of censure cannot be presented in the course of the same session.

Article 101
The President of the Republic is only responsible for acts accomplished in the exercise of his functions in the case of high treason. He can be impeached only by the National Assembly, declared by secret ballot, by a

majority of three-fifths of the members composing it; he is judged by the High Court of Justice.

2. Ministers may serve simultaneously as members of the legislature.

No. Ministers are prohibited from serving simultaneously in the legislature.

Article 54
The office of a member of the Government is incompatible with a parliamentary mandate or any paid public or private professional activity.

3. The legislature has powers of summons over executive branch officials and hearings with executive branch officials testifying before the legislature or its committees are regularly held.

Yes. The legislature regularly questions executive branch officials.

Article 85
The Deputies may pose to the Prime Minister and to the other members of the Government who are held to respond to it, written questions and oral questions with or without debate. The questions or the responses which are made to them are not put to a vote.
The National Assembly can designate, from its midst, commissions of inquiry.
The law determines the conditions of the organization and of the functioning as well as the powers of the commissions of inquiry.

4. The legislature can conduct independent investigation of the chief executive and the agencies of the executive.

Yes. The legislature can establish commissions of inquiry to investigate the executive.

Article 85
The Deputies may pose to the Prime Minister and to the other members of the Government who are held to respond to it, written questions and oral questions with or without debate. The questions or the responses which are made to them are not put to a vote.
The National Assembly can designate, from its midst, commissions of inquiry.
The law determines the conditions of the organization and of the functioning as well as the powers of the commissions of inquiry.

5. The legislature has effective powers of oversight over the agencies of coercion (the military, organs of law enforcement, intelligence services, and the secret police).

No. The legislature lacks effective powers of oversight over the agencies of coercion.

6. The legislature appoints the prime minister.

No. The president appoints the prime minister.

Article 49
The President of the Republic appoints the Prime Minister and ends his functions. On the proposal of the Prime Minister, the President of the Republic appoints the Ministers, establishes their attributions and ends their functions.

7. The legislature's approval is required to confirm the appointment of ministers; or the legislature itself appoints ministers.

No. The president appoints ministers on the proposal of the prime minister, and the appointments do not require the legislature's approval.

Article 49
The President of the Republic appoints the Prime Minister and ends his functions. On the proposal of the Prime Minister, the President of the Republic appoints the Ministers, establishes their attributions and ends their functions.

8. The country lacks a presidency entirely or there is a presidency, but the president is elected by the legislature.

No. The president is directly elected.

Article 26
The President of the Republic is elected by direct universal suffrage and by majority vote in two rounds.

9. The legislature can vote no confidence in the government.

Yes. The legislature can vote no confidence in the government.

Article 86
The Prime Minister may, after deliberation of the Council of Ministers, decide to pose a question of confidence in a program or a declaration of general policy. The vote on the question of confidence may not take place until two full days after it has been presented. Confidence is refused by a public vote by the absolute majority of the members of the National Assembly. The refusal entails a collective resignation of the Government. The National Assembly may provoke the resignation of the Government by the vote of a motion of censure. The motion of censure must, on pain of irreceivability, be accompanied by the signatures of one-tenth of the members composing the National Assembly. The vote of censure can only take place two full days after its filing with the bureau of the National Assembly. The motion of censure is voted by public ballot, by an absolute majority of the members composing the National Assembly; only the votes in favor of the motion of censure are counted. If the motion of censure is adopted, the Prime Minister immediately presents the Government to the President of the Republic. A new motion of censure cannot be presented in the course of the same session.

10. The legislature is immune from dissolution by the executive.

No. The president can dissolve the legislature.

Article 87

The President of the Republic may pronounce, by decree, the dissolution of the National Assembly, after consulting its President, when it has adopted a motion of censure in opposition to the Government under the conditions established by Article 75.

11. Any executive initiative on legislation requires ratification or approval by the legislature before it takes effect; that is, the executive lacks decree power.

Yes. The executive lacks decree power. The legislature can, however, delegate temporary decree powers to the president on limited issue areas.

Article 77

The National Assembly can by a law empower the President of the Republic to take the measures which are normally of the domain the law. Within the limits of time and competences established by the enabling law, the President of the Republic takes the ordinances which enter in force on their publication but become lapsed if the bill of law of ratification is not presented to the Bureau of the National Assembly before the date established by the enabling law. The Parliament can amend them at the time of the vote (on) the law of ratification.

12. Laws passed by the legislature are veto-proof or essentially veto-proof; that is, the executive lacks veto power, or has veto power but the veto can be overridden by a majority in the legislature.

No. A three-fifths majority vote is required to override a presidential veto.

Article 72

The President of the Republic promulgates the definitely adopted law within eight days which follow the expiration of the time period of recourse specified in Article 74.

The time period of promulgation is reduced by half in case of urgency declared by the National Assembly.

Article 73

Within the time period specified for promulgation, the President of the Republic may, by a motivated message, demand of the National Assembly a new deliberation which cannot be refused. The law cannot be voted in second reading unless three-fifths of the members composing the National Assembly pronounce themselves in favor.

13. The legislature's laws are supreme and not subject to judicial review.

No. The Constitutional Court can review the constitutionality of laws.

Article 74

The Constitutional Court may be seated for the purpose of having a law declared unconstitutional:

a) by the President of the Republic, within six full days of the transmission to him of the definitely adopted law;

b) by a number of deputies equal to at least one-tenth of the members of the National Assembly, within six full days which follow its definitive adoption.

Article 92

The Constitutional Council takes cognizance of the constitutionality of the laws and of the international obligations, of conflicts of competence between the executive and the legislative, of conflicts of competence between the Council of State and the Court of Cassation, as well as of exceptions of unconstitutionality raised before the Council of State or the Court of Cassation.

14. The legislature has the right to initiate bills in all policy jurisdictions; the executive lacks gatekeeping authority.

Yes. The legislature can initiate bills in all policy jurisdictions.

15. Expenditure of funds appropriated by the legislature is mandatory; the executive lacks the power to impound funds appropriated by the legislature.

Yes. The executive lacks the power to impound funds appropriated by the legislature.

16. The legislature controls the resources that finance its own internal operation and provide for the perquisites of its own members.

Yes. The legislature enjoys financial autonomy.

17. Members of the legislature are immune from arrest and/or criminal prosecution.

No. Legislators are immune only while the legislature is in session. They are subject to arrest at other times.

Article 61

No deputy may be prosecuted, sought, arrested, detained or judged as the result of opinions expressed by him in the exercise of his functions. No deputy may, during the sessions, be prosecuted or arrested in a criminal or correctional mater without the authorization of the National Assembly. The deputy apprehended in flagrant offense or in flight after the perpetration of a punishable act can be arrested, prosecuted and imprisoned without the authorization of the bureau of the National Assembly.

18. All members of the legislature are elected; the executive lacks the power to appoint any members of the legislature.

Yes. All members of the legislature are elected.

Article 60

The deputies to the National Assembly are elected by universal direct suffrage.

19. The legislature alone, without the involvement of any other agencies, can change the Constitution.

No. The legislature alone cannot change the constitution. Constitutional amendments must be approved in a popular referendum or be introduced by the president and approved by the legislature.

Article 103
The initiative for the revision of the Constitution belongs concurrently to the President of the Republic and to the deputies. The Prime Minister can propose to the President of the Republic a revision of the Constitution. The bill or the proposal of revision must be adopted by the National Assembly. The revision is definite after it has been approved by referendum.
However, the bill or the proposal is not presented to referendum when the President of the Republic presents them to the National Assembly only. In this case the bill or the proposal is approved if it receives a majority of three-fifths of the members composing the National Assembly.

20. The legislature's approval is necessary for the declaration of war.

Yes. The legislature's approval is necessary for the declaration of war.

Article 70
The declaration of war is authorized by the National Assembly.

21. The legislature's approval is necessary to ratify treaties with foreign countries.

Yes. The legislature's approval is necessary to ratify international treaties.

Article 95
The President of the Republic negotiates international obligations. He ratifies them or approves them.

Article 96
The peace treaties, the commercial treaties, the treaties or agreements relating to international organizations, those which engage the finances of the State, those which modify the provisions of a legislative nature, those which concern the status of persons, (and) those which entail a cession, exchange or acquisition of territory can only be ratified or approved by virtue of a law.
They take effect only after they have been ratified or approved. No cession, no annexation of territory is valid without the consent of the population concerned. The Republic of Senegal can conclude with any African State treaties of association or of community including the partial or complete relinquishment of sovereignty with the purpose of realizing the African unity.

22. The legislature has the power to grant amnesty.

No. Formally, the legislature has the power to grant amnesty. In practice, the president has this power.

Article 67
The National Assembly holds the legislative power. It alone votes the law. The law establishes the rules concerning . . . amnesty.

23. The legislature has the power of pardon.

No. The president has the power of pardon.

Article 47
The President of the Republic has the right of pardon.

24. The legislature reviews and has the right to reject appointments to the judiciary; or the legislature itself appoints members of the judiciary.

No. The president makes judicial appointments, and the appointments do not require the legislature's approval.

Article 89
The members of the Constitutional Council are appointed by the President of the Republic.

Article 90
The magistrates other than the members of the Constitutional Council and the Court of Accounts are appointed by the President of the Republic after the advice of the Superior Council of the Magistrature. The magistrates of the Court of Accounts are appointed by the President of the Republic after the advice of the Superior Council of the Court of Accounts.

25. The chairman of the central bank is appointed by the legislature.

No. Senegal is a member of the Central Bank of West African States, whose governor is selected by the member states.

26. The legislature has a substantial voice in the operation of the state-owned media.

No. The legislature lacks a substantial voice in the operation of the public media.

27. The legislature is regularly in session.

Yes. Each year the legislature meets in two ordinary sessions, each of which may not exceed four months.

Article 63
With the exception of the date of the opening of the first session of the newly elected Assembly, which is determined by the President of the Republic, the National Assembly establishes the date of the opening and the duration of the ordinary session. These are, however, governed by the following rules:
a) the first is opened during the second trimester of the year;
b) the second is opened obligatorily during the first fifteen days of the month of October.
The duration of each ordinary session may not exceed four months.

28. Each legislator has a personal secretary.

No.

29. Each legislator has at least one non-secretarial staff member with policy expertise.

No.

30. Legislators are eligible for re-election without any restriction.

Yes. There are no restrictions on re-election.

31. A seat in the legislature is an attractive enough position that legislators are generally interested in and seek re-election.

Yes.

32. The re-election of incumbent legislators is common enough that at any given time the legislature contains a significant number of highly experienced members.

Yes. Re-election rates are sufficiently high to produce a significant number of highly experienced members.

NATIONAL ASSEMBLY OF SERBIA (*NARODNA SKUPSHTINA*)

Expert consultants: Ruzica Dabić, Jadranka Jelinčić, Nemanja Nenadić, Danijel Pantić, Vladimir Petrović, Jelena Simjanović

Score: .69

Influence over executive (5/9)		Institutional autonomy (7/9)		Specified powers (6/8)		Institutional capacity (4/6)	
1. replace		10. no dissolution		19. amendments	X	27. sessions	X
2. serve as ministers		11. no decree	X	20. war		28. secretary	
3. interpellate	X	12. no veto	X	21. treaties	X	29. staff	
4. investigate	X	13. no review		22. amnesty	X	30. no term limits	X
5. oversee police		14. no gatekeeping	X	23. pardon		31. seek re-election	X
6. appoint PM	X	15. no impoundment	X	24. judiciary	X	32. experience	X
7. appoint ministers	X	16. control resources	X	25. central bank	X		
8. lack president		17. immunity	X	26. media	X		
9. no confidence	X	18. all elected	X				

The National Assembly (*Narodna skupshtina*) of Serbia, as currently structured, was established in the country's 2006 constitution as the Union of Serbia and Montenegro disintegrated. The constitution established a unicameral legislature. From 1992 until 2006 Serbia had been joined with Montenegro to form first the Federal Republic of Yugoslavia (1992–2003) and then the short-lived Union of Serbia and Montenegro (2003–6). In May 2006 Montenegro voted for independence in a popular referendum. Serbia responded by declaring itself independent and drafting a new constitution.

The National Assembly has considerable powers. It influences the executive with, among other powers, the right to appoint, oversee, and remove the government. The legislature can be dissolved, and its laws are subject to judicial review, but oth-

erwise it enjoys complete institutional autonomy. It holds numerous specific powers and has some institutional capacity.

SURVEY

1. The legislature alone, without the involvement of any other agencies, can impeach the president or replace the prime minister.

No. The dismissal of the president requires the involvement of the Constitutional Court. The legislature can remove the prime minister with a vote of no confidence.

Article 118
The President of the Republic shall be dismissed for the violation of the Constitution, upon the decision of the National Assembly, by the votes of at least two thirds of deputies. Procedure for the dismissal may be

initiated by the National Assembly, upon the proposal of at least two thirds of deputies. The Constitutional Court shall have the obligation to decide on the violation of the Constitution, upon the initiated procedure for dismissal, not later than within 45 days.

Article 130

A vote of no confidence in the Government or the particular member of the Government may be requested by at least 60 deputies. The proposal for the vote of no confidence in the Government or the particular member of the Government shall be discussed by the National Assembly at the next first session, not later than five days after the submission of the proposal. After the discussion is concluded, they shall vote on the proposal. The proposal for the vote of no confidence in the Government or the member of the Government shall be accepted by the National Assembly, if more than a half of the total number of deputies votes for it. If the National Assembly passes a vote of no confidence in the Government, the President of the Republic shall be obliged to initiate proceedings for election of the new Government. If the National Assembly fails to elect the new Government within 30 days from the passing of a vote of no confidence, the President of the Republic shall be obliged to dissolve the National Assembly and schedule elections. If the National Assembly passes a vote of no confidence in the member of the Government, the President of the Republic shall be obliged to initiate proceedings for election of a new member of the Government, in accordance with the Law. If the National Assembly fails to pass a vote of no confidence in the Government or the member of the Government, signatories of the proposal may not submit a new proposal for a vote of no confidence before the expiry of the 180-day deadline.

Article 131

The Government may require a vote of its confidence. Upon the request of the Government, proposal for a vote of confidence in the Government may be discussed at the current session of the National Assembly, and if the Government has failed to submit such a proposal, the proposal shall be discussed on the next first session, not later than five days from its submission. After the discussion is concluded, they shall vote on the proposal. The proposal for the vote of confidence in the Government or the member of the Government shall be accepted by the National Assembly, if more than a half of the total number of deputies votes for it. If the National Assembly fails to pass a vote of confidence in the Government, the term of office of the Government ends and the President of the Republic shall be obliged to initiate proceedings for election of the new Government. If the National Assembly fails to elect the new Government within 30 days from the day of passing of vote of no confidence, the President of the Republic shall be obliged to dissolve the National Assembly and schedule elections.

2. Ministers may serve simultaneously as members of the legislature.

No. Legislators are prohibited from serving simultaneously in ministerial positions.

Article 102

Deputy may not be a deputy in the Assembly of the autonomous province, nor an official in bodies of executive government and judiciary, nor may he or she perform other functions, affairs and duties, which represent a conflict of interest, according to the Law.

Article 126

Member of the Government may not be a deputy in the National Assembly.

3. The legislature has powers of summons over executive branch officials and hearings with executive branch officials testifying before the legislature or its committees are regularly held.

Yes. The legislature regularly interpellates officials from the executive.

Article 105

The National Assembly shall adopt decisions by majority vote of deputies at the session at which majority of deputies are present.
By means of majority vote of all deputies the National Assembly shall:
10. decide on response to interpellation.

Article 129

At least 50 deputies may propose interpellation in relation to the work of the Government or particular member of the Government.
The Government shall have the obligation to respond to interpellation within 30 days.

4. The legislature can conduct independent investigation of the chief executive and the agencies of the executive.

Yes. The legislature can investigate the executive.

5. The legislature has effective powers of oversight over the agencies of coercion (the military, organs of law enforcement, intelligence services, and the secret police).

No. The legislature lacks effective powers of oversight over the agencies of coercion.

6. The legislature appoints the prime minister.

Yes. The legislature elects the prime minister on the recommendation of the president.

Article 112

The President of the Republic shall:
3. propose to the National Assembly a candidate for the Prime Minister, after considering views of representatives of elected lists of candidates.

Article 127

A candidate for the Prime Minister shall be proposed to the National Assembly by the President of the

Republic, after he or she considers the opinions of representatives of elected election lists. The candidate for the Prime Minister shall present to the National Assembly the Government's Programme and propose its constitution. The National Assembly shall simultaneously vote on the Government's Programme and election of the Prime Minister and members of the Government. The Government shall be elected if the majority of the total number of deputies votes for its election.

7. The legislature's approval is required to confirm the appointment of ministers; or the legislature itself appoints ministers.

Yes. The legislature elects ministers.

Article 99
Within its election rights, the National Assembly shall:
1. elect the Government, supervise its work and decide on expiry of the term of office of the Government and ministers.

Article 105
The National Assembly shall adopt decisions by majority vote of deputies at the session at which majority of deputies are present.
By means of majority vote of all deputies the National Assembly shall:
9. elect members of the Government and decide on the end of the term of office of the Government and ministers.

8. The country lacks a presidency entirely or there is a presidency, but the president is elected by the legislature.

No. The president is directly elected.

Article 114
The President of the Republic shall be elected on direct elections, by secret ballot, in accordance with the Law.

9. The legislature can vote no confidence in the government.

Yes. The legislature can vote no confidence in the government.

Article 130
A vote of no confidence in the Government or the particular member of the Government may be requested by at least 60 deputies. The proposal for the vote of no confidence in the Government or the particular member of the Government shall be discussed by the National Assembly at the next first session, not later than five days after the submission of the proposal. After the discussion is concluded, they shall vote on the proposal. The proposal for the vote of no confidence in the Government or the member of the Government shall be accepted by the National Assembly, if more than a half of the total number of deputies votes for it. If the National Assembly passes a vote of no confidence in the Government, the President of the Republic shall be obliged to initiate proceedings for election of the new Government. If the National Assembly fails to elect the

new Government within 30 days from the passing of a vote of no confidence, the President of the Republic shall be obliged to dissolve the National Assembly and schedule elections. If the National Assembly passes a vote of no confidence in the member of the Government, the President of the Republic shall be obliged to initiate proceedings for election of a new member of the Government, in accordance with the Law. If the National Assembly fails to pass a vote of no confidence in the Government or the member of the Government, signatories of the proposal may not submit a new proposal for a vote of no confidence before the expiry of the 180-day deadline.

Article 131
The Government may require a vote of its confidence. Upon the request of the Government, proposal for a vote of confidence in the Government may be discussed at the current session of the National Assembly, and if the Government has failed to submit such a proposal, the proposal shall be discussed on the next first session, not later than five days from its submission. After the discussion is concluded, they shall vote on the proposal. The proposal for the vote of confidence in the Government or the member of the Government shall be accepted by the National Assembly, if more than a half of the total number of deputies votes for it. If the National Assembly fails to pass a vote of confidence in the Government, the term of office of the Government ends and the President of the Republic shall be obliged to initiate proceedings for election of the new Government. If the National Assembly fails to elect the new Government within 30 days from the day of passing of vote of no confidence, the President of the Republic shall be obliged to dissolve the National Assembly and schedule elections.

10. The legislature is immune from dissolution by the executive.

No. The president can dissolve the legislature.

Article 109
The President of the Republic may dissolve the National Assembly, upon the elaborated proposal of the Government. The Government may not propose dissolution of the National Assembly, if a proposal has been submitted for the vote of no confidence in the Government or if the issue of its confidence has been raised. The National Assembly shall be dissolved if it fails to elect the government within 90 days from the day of its constitution. The National Assembly may not be dissolved during the state of war and emergency. The President of the Republic shall be obliged to dissolve the National Assembly upon his/her decree, in cases stipulated by the Constitution.
Simultaneously with the dissolution of the National Assembly, the President of the Republic shall schedule elections for deputies, so that elections finish not later than 60 days from the day of their announcement. The National Assembly, which has been dissolved, shall only perform current or urgent tasks, stipulated by the

Law. In case of declaration of the state of war or emergency, its full competence shall be reestablished and last until the end of the state of war, that is, emergency.

11. Any executive initiative on legislation requires ratification or approval by the legislature before it takes effect; that is, the executive lacks decree power.

Yes. The executive lacks decree power.

12. Laws passed by the legislature are veto-proof or essentially veto-proof; that is, the executive lacks veto power, or has veto power but the veto can be overridden by a majority in the legislature.

Yes. The legislature can override a presidential veto by a majority vote of its total membership.

Article 113
The President of the Republic shall be obliged to issue a decree on promulgation of laws or to return the law for reconsideration with a written explanation to the National Assembly, within maximum 15 days from the day of adoption of the law, that is, not later than within seven days, if the law has been adopted by emergency procedure. If the National Assembly decides to vote again on the law, which has been returned for reconsideration by the President of the Republic, the law shall be adopted by the majority vote from the total number of deputies. The President of the Republic shall be obliged to promulgate the newly adopted Law. If the President of the Republic fails to issue a decree on promulgation of the law within the deadline stipulated by the constitution, the decree shall be issued by the Chairman of the National Assembly.

13. The legislature's laws are supreme and not subject to judicial review.

No. The Constitutional Court reviews the constitutionality of laws.

Article 167
The Constitutional Court shall decide on:
1. compliance of laws and other general acts with the Constitution, generally accepted rules of the international law and ratified international treaties,
2. compliance of ratified international treaties with the Constitution.

14. The legislature has the right to initiate bills in all policy jurisdictions; the executive lacks gatekeeping authority.

Yes. The legislature can initiate bills in all policy jurisdictions.

15. Expenditure of funds appropriated by the legislature is mandatory; the executive lacks the power to impound funds appropriated by the legislature.

Yes. The executive lacks the power to impound funds appropriated by the legislature.

16. The legislature controls the resources that finance its own internal operation and provide for the perquisites of its own members.

Yes. The legislature enjoys financial autonomy.

17. Members of the legislature are immune from arrest and/or criminal prosecution.

Yes. Legislators are immune with the common exception for cases of *flagrante delicto,* here expressed as "found in the act of committing any criminal offence."

Article 103
Deputies shall enjoy immunity. Deputies may not accept criminal or other liability for the expressed opinion or cast vote in performing the deputy's function. Deputy who uses his/her immunity may not be detained, nor may he or she be involved in criminal or other proceedings in which prison sentence may be pronounced, without previous approval by the National Assembly.
Deputy found in the act of committing any criminal offence for which the prison sentence longer than five years is not envisaged, may be detained without previous approval by the National Assembly. There shall be no deadlines stipulated for the criminal or other proceedings in which the immunity is established. Failure to use the immunity shall not exclude the right of the National Assembly to establish the immunity.

18. All members of the legislature are elected; the executive lacks the power to appoint any members of the legislature.

Yes. All members of the legislature are elected.

Article 100
The National Assembly shall consist of 250 deputies, who are elected in direct elections by secret ballot, in accordance with the Law.

19. The legislature alone, without the involvement of any other agencies, can change the Constitution.

Yes. The legislature can change the constitution by a two-thirds majority vote of its total membership. Amendments to select articles of the constitution also require approval in a popular referendum.

Article 99
The National Assembly shall:
1. adopt and amend the Constitution.

Article 203
A proposal to amend the Constitution may be submitted by at least one third of the total number of deputies, the President of the Republic, the Government and at least 150,000 voters. The National Assembly shall decide on amending the Constitution. A proposal to amend the Constitution shall be adopted by a two-third majority of the total number of deputies . . . The National Assembly shall adopt an act on amending the

582   National Assembly of Serbia (*Narodna skupshtina*)

Constitution by a two-third majority of the total number of deputies and may decide to have it endorsed in the republic referendum by the citizens. The National Assembly shall be obliged to put forward the act on amending the Constitution in the republic referendum to have it endorsed, in cases when the amendment of the Constitution pertains to the preamble of the Constitution, principles of the Constitution, human and minority rights and freedoms, the system of authority, proclamation the state of war and emergency, derogation from human and minority rights in the state of emergency or war or the proceedings of amending the Constitution.

20. The legislature's approval is necessary for the declaration of war.

No. If the legislature is unable to meet, the president, together with the president of the National Assembly and the prime minister, can declare war.

Article 99
The National Assembly shall:
5. decide on war and peace and declare state of war and emergency.

Article 140
The Army of Serbia may be used outside the borders of the Republic of Serbia only upon the decision of the National Assembly of the Republic of Serbia.

Article 201
The National Assembly shall proclaim the state of war. When the National Assembly is not in a position to convene, the decision on proclamation of the state of war shall be passed by the President of the Republic together with the President of the National Assembly and the Prime Minister.

21. The legislature's approval is necessary to ratify treaties with foreign countries.

Yes. The legislature's approval is necessary to ratify international treaties.

Article 99
The National Assembly shall:
4. ratify international contracts when the obligation of their ratification is stipulated by the Law.

Article 105
By means of majority vote of all deputies, the National Assembly shall:
6. conclude and ratify international contracts.

22. The legislature has the power to grant amnesty.

Yes. Both the legislature and the president have the power to grant amnesty.

Article 99
The National Assembly shall:
12. grant amnesty for criminal offences.

Article 105
The National Assembly shall adopt decisions by majority vote of deputies at the session at which majority of deputies are present.
By means of majority vote of all deputies the National Assembly shall:
1. grant amnesty for criminal offences.

Article 112
The President of the Republic shall:
7. grant amnesties and award honours.

23. The legislature has the power of pardon.

No. The president has the power of pardon.

24. The legislature reviews and has the right to reject appointments to the judiciary; or the legislature itself appoints members of the judiciary.

Yes. The legislature elects some of the judges of the Constitutional Court, the president of the Supreme Court of Cessation, and other judges.

Article 99
The National Assembly shall:
2. appoint and dismiss judges of the Constitutional Court.
3. appoint the President of the Supreme Court of Cassation, presidents of courts, Republic Public Prosecutor, public prosecutors, judges and deputy public prosecutors, in accordance with the Constitution.

Article 105
The National Assembly shall adopt decisions by majority vote of deputies at the session at which majority of deputies are present.
By means of majority vote of all deputies the National Assembly shall:
11. elect judges of the Constitutional Court and decide on their dismissal and end of their term of office.
12. elect the President of the Supreme Court of Cessation, presidents of courts, Republic Public Prosecutor and public prosecutors and decide on the end of their term of office.
13. elect judges and deputy public prosecutors, in accordance with the Constitution.

Article 144
President of the Supreme Court of Cassation shall be elected by the National Assembly, upon the proposal of the High Judicial Council and received opinion of the meeting of the Supreme Court of Cassation and competent committee of the National Assembly.

Article 147
On proposal of the High Judicial Council, the National Assembly shall elect as a judge the person who is elected to the post of judge for the first time.

Article 172
The Constitutional Court shall have 15 justices who shall be elected and appointed for the period of nine years. Five justices of the Constitutional Court shall

be appointed by the National Assembly, another five by the President of the Republic, and another five at the general session of the Supreme Court of Cassation. The National Assembly shall appoint five justices of the Constitutional Court form among ten candidates proposed by the President of the Republic, the President of the Republic shall appoint five justices of the Constitutional Court from among ten candidates proposed by the National Assembly, and the general session of the Supreme Court of Cassation shall appoint five justices from among ten candidates proposed at a general session by the High Judicial Court and the State Prosecutor Council.

25. The chairman of the central bank is appointed by the legislature.

Yes. The legislature elects the governor of the National Bank of Serbia.

Article 95
The National Bank of Serbia shall be managed by the Governor elected by the National Assembly.

Article 99
The National Assembly shall:
4. appoint and dismiss the Governor of the National Bank of Serbia and supervise his/her work.

Article 105
The National Assembly shall adopt decisions by majority vote of deputies at the session at which majority of deputies are present.
By means of majority vote of all deputies the National Assembly shall:
14. elect and dismiss the Governor of the National Bank of Serbia, Governors' Council and Civic Defender.

26. The legislature has a substantial voice in the operation of the state-owned media.

Yes. The legislature has a substantial voice in the operation of the public media.

27. The legislature is regularly in session.

Yes. The legislature meets in ordinary session for a maximum of 180 days each year. In practice, including special sessions, the legislature meets for more than six months each year.

Article 106
The National Assembly shall be convoked for two regular sessions per year. The first regular session shall start on the first weekday of March, while the second regular session shall start on the first weekday of October. Regular sessions may not last longer than 90 days. The National Assembly shall be convoked for extraordinary session upon the request of at least one third of deputies or upon the request of the Government, with previously determined agenda.

28. Each legislator has a personal secretary.

No.

29. Each legislator has at least one non-secretarial staff member with policy expertise.

No.

30. Legislators are eligible for re-election without any restriction.

Yes. There are no restrictions on re-election.

31. A seat in the legislature is an attractive enough position that legislators are generally interested in and seek re-election.

Yes.

32. The re-election of incumbent legislators is common enough that at any given time the legislature contains a significant number of highly experienced members.

Yes. Re-election rates are sufficiently high to produce a significant number of highly experienced members.

PARLIAMENT OF SIERRA LEONE

Expert consultants: Daniel Gbondo, Lawrence Harding, Sheku Mesali, George Ola-Davies, R. H. O. Robbin-Coker

Score: .41

Influence over executive (1/9)		Institutional autonomy (5/9)		Specified powers (4/8)		Institutional capacity (3/6)	
1. replace		10. no dissolution	X	19. amendments	X	27. sessions	
2. serve as ministers		11. no decree	X	20. war	X	28. secretary	
3. interpellate		12. no veto		21. treaties	X	29. staff	
4. investigate		13. no review		22. amnesty		30. no term limits	X
5. oversee police		14. no gatekeeping	X	23. pardon		31. seek re-election	X
6. appoint PM	X	15. no impoundment	X	24. judiciary	X	32. experience	X
7. appoint ministers		16. control resources		25. central bank			
8. lack president		17. immunity		26. media			
9. no confidence		18. all elected	X				

The Parliament of Sierra Leone was established in 1961 upon independence from Great Britain. For most of its history, the legislature was suspended or sidelined due to single-party regimes, military coups, and civil wars. The country's current constitution, adopted in 1991, calls for a unicameral legislature. In 2002, with the help of UN peacekeeping forces, the most recent round of civil violence ceased, and parliamentary elections were held.

Despite a shaky history, the legislature has regained some power. Its ability to influence the executive is negligible, although its confirmation is needed for ministerial appointments. A degree of institutional autonomy is conferred by the president's inability to dissolve the legislature, decree legislation, or appoint legislators. The legislature exercises several specified powers and has modest institutional capacity.

SURVEY

1. The legislature alone, without the involvement of any other agencies, can impeach the president or replace the prime minister.

No. Presidential impeachment requires the involvement of a special tribunal established by the chief justice of the Supreme Court.

Article 51

(1) If notice in writing is given to the Speaker signed by not less than one-half of all the Members of Parliament of a motion alleging that the President has committed any violation of the Constitution or any gross misconduct in the performance of the functions of his office and specifying the particulars of the allegations and proposing that a tribunal be appointed under this section to investigate those allegations, the Speaker shall: if Parliament is then sitting or has been summoned to meet within five days, cause the motion to be considered by Parliament within seven days of the receipt of the notice; or if Parliament is not then sitting (and notwithstanding that it may be prorogued), summon Parliament to meet within twenty-one days of the receipt of the notice, and cause the motion to be considered by Parliament.

(2) Where a motion under this section is proposed for consideration by Parliament, it shall meet in secret session and shall not debate the motion, but the Speaker or the person presiding in Parliament shall forthwith cause a vote to be taken on the motion and, if the motion is supported by the votes of not less than two thirds of all Members of Parliament, shall declare the motion to be passed.

(3). If a motion is declared to be passed under subsection (2), the Speaker shall immediately notify the Chief Justice who shall appoint a tribunal which shall consist of a Chairman who shall be a Justice of the Supreme Court and not less than four others selected by the Chief Justice, at least two of whom shall hold or shall have held high judicial office; the Tribunal shall investigate the matter and shall within the period of three months from the date on which the motion was passed report to Parliament through the Speaker whether or not it finds the particulars of the allegation specified in the motion to have been sustained; the President shall have the right to appear and be represented before the Tribunal during its investigation of the allegations against him.

(4) If the Tribunal reports to Parliament that if finds that the particulars of any allegations against the President specified in the motion have not been substantiated, no further proceedings shall be taken under this Section in respect of that allegation.

(5) Where the Tribunal reports to Parliament that it finds that the particulars of any allegation specified in the motion have been substantiated, Parliament may, in secret session, on a motion supported by not less than two-thirds of all the Members of Parliament, resolve that the President has been guilty of such violation of the Constitution or, as the case may, such gross misconduct as is incompatible with his continuance in office as President; and where Parliament so resolves, the President shall thereupon cease to hold office and a vacancy shall then be deemed to have occurred in the office of President and subsection (4) of Section 49 of this Constitution shall apply accordingly.

2. Ministers may serve simultaneously as members of the legislature.

No. Legislators are prohibited from serving simultaneously in ministerial positions.

Article 56
(1) There shall be, in addition to the office of Vice-President, such other offices of Ministers and Deputy Ministers as may be established by the President: Provided that no Member of Parliament shall be appointed a Minister or Deputy Minister.
(3) A Minister or a Deputy Minister shall not, while he continues in office, hold any other office of profit or emolument whether by way of allowances or otherwise, whether private or public, and either directly or indirectly.

3. The legislature has powers of summons over executive branch officials and hearings with executive branch officials testifying before the legislature or its committees are regularly held.

No. Formally, legislative committees can "enforc[e] the attendance of witnesses," but in practice, the legislature lacks such power and testimony is rare.

Article 93
(1) At the beginning of each session of Parliament, but in any case not later than twenty-one days thereafter, there shall be appointed from among its members the following Standing Committees, that is to say –
(a) the Legislative Committee;
(b) the Finance Committee;

(c) the Committee on Appointments and Public Service;
(d) the Foreign Affairs and International Co-operation Committee;
(e) the Public Accounts Committee;
(f) the Committee of Privileges;
(g) the Standing Orders Committee;
(h) such other Committees of Parliament as the rules of procedure of Parliament shall provide.

(2) In addition to the Committees referred to in subsection (1), Parliament shall appoint other Committees which shall perform the functions specified in subsection (3).

(3) It shall be the duty of any such Committee as is referred to in subsection (2) to investigate or inquire into the activities or administration of such Ministries or Departments as may be assigned to it, and such investigation or inquiry may extend to proposals for legislation.

(4) Notwithstanding anything contained in subsections (1) and (2), Parliament may at any time appoint any other Committee to investigate any matter of public importance.

(5) The composition of each of the Committees appointed under subsections (1), (2) and (4) shall, as much as possible, reflect the strength of the political parties and Independent Members in Parliament.

(6) For the purposes of effectively performing its functions, each of the Committees shall have all such powers, rights and privileges as are vested in the High Court at a trial in respect of –
(a) enforcing the attendance of witnesses and examining them on oath, affirmation or otherwise;
(b) compelling the production of documents; and
(c) the issue of a commission or request to examine witnesses abroad.

Article 107
(1) A Minister may introduce a Bill in Parliament and take part, but without a vote, in the deliberations of Parliament on that Bill.
(2) A Minister may be summoned before Parliament or a Committee thereof –
(a) to give an account of any matter falling within his portfolio; or (b) to explain any aspect of Government policy.

4. The legislature can conduct independent investigation of the chief executive and the agencies of the executive.

No. Although the constitution provides legislative committees with the right to investigate the executive, they lack the ability to do so in practice.

Article 93
(1) At the beginning of each session of Parliament, but in any case not later than twenty-one days thereafter, there shall be appointed from among its members the following Standing Committees, that is to say –
(a) the Legislative Committee;

(b) the Finance Committee;

(c) the Committee on Appointments and Public Service;

(d) the Foreign Affairs and International Co-operation Committee;

(e) the Public Accounts Committee;

(f) the Committee of Privileges;

(g) the Standing Orders Committee;

(h) such other Committees of Parliament as the rules of procedure of Parliament shall provide.

(2) In addition to the Committees referred to in subsection (1), Parliament shall appoint other Committees which shall perform the functions specified in subsection (3).

(3) It shall be the duty of any such Committee as is referred to in subsection (2) to investigate or inquire into the activities or administration of such Ministries or Departments as may be assigned to it, and such investigation or inquiry may extend to proposals for legislation.

(4) Notwithstanding anything contained in subsections (1) and (2), Parliament may at any time appoint any other Committee to investigate any matter of public importance.

(5) The composition of each of the Committees appointed under subsections (1), (2) and (4) shall, as much as possible, reflect the strength of the political parties and Independent Members in Parliament.

(6) For the purposes of effectively performing its functions, each of the Committees shall have all such powers, rights and privileges as are vested in the High Court at a trial in respect of –

(a) enforcing the attendance of witnesses and examining them on oath, affirmation or otherwise;

(b) compelling the production of documents; and

(c) the issue of a commission or request to examine witnesses abroad.

5. The legislature has effective powers of oversight over the agencies of coercion (the military, organs of law enforcement, intelligence services, and the secret police).

No. The legislature lacks effective powers of oversight over the agencies of coercion.

6. The legislature appoints the prime minister.

No. There is no prime minister.

7. The legislature's approval is required to confirm the appointment of ministers; or the legislature itself appoints ministers.

Yes. The legislature's approval is required to confirm the president's ministerial appointments.

Article 56

(1) There shall be, in addition to the office of Vice-President, such other offices of Ministers and Deputy Ministers as may be established by the President:

Provided that no Member of Parliament shall be appointed a Minister or Deputy Minister.

(2) A person shall not be appointed a Minister or Deputy Minister unless – he is qualified to be elected as a Member of Parliament; and he has not contested and lost as a candidate in the general election immediately preceding his nomination for appointment; and his nomination is approved by Parliament.

(3) A Minister or a Deputy Minister shall not, while he continues in office, hold any other office of profit or emolument whether by way of allowances or otherwise, whether private or public, and either directly or indirectly.

Article 59

(1) There shall be a Cabinet whose functions shall be to advise the President in the government of Sierra Leone and which shall consist of the President, the Vice-President and such Ministers as the President may from time to time appoint.

8. The country lacks a presidency entirely or there is a presidency, but the president is elected by the legislature.

No. The president is directly elected.

Article 40

There shall be a President of the Republic of Sierra Leone who shall be Head of State, the supreme executive authority of the Republic and the Commander-in-Chief of the Armed Forces.

Article 42

(2) The following provisions shall apply to an election to the office of President –

(a) all persons registered in Sierra Leone as voters for the purposes of election to Parliament shall be entitled to vote in the election;

(b) the poll shall be taken by a secret ballot on such day or days, at such time, and in such manner as may be prescribed by or under an Act of Parliament;

(c) a candidate for an election to the office of President shall be deemed to have been duly elected to such office where he is the only candidate nominated for the election after the close of nomination;

(d) where in an election to the office of President a candidate nominated for the election dies, is incapacitated or disqualified, the party which nominated him shall within seven days of such death, incapacitation or disqualification, nominate another candidate;

(e) no person shall be elected as President of Sierra Leone unless at the Presidential election he has polled not less than fifty-five per cent of the valid votes in his favour; and

(f) in default of a candidate being duly elected under paragraph (e), the two candidates with the highest number or numbers of votes shall go forward to a second election which shall be held within fourteen days of the announcement of the result of the previous election, and the candidate polling the higher number of votes cast in his favour shall be declared President.

(3) A person elected to the office of President under this section shall assume that office on the day upon which

he is declared elected by the Returning Officer, or upon the date that his predecessor's term of office expires, whichever is the latter.

9. The legislature can vote no confidence in the government.

No. The legislature cannot vote no confidence in the government.

10. The legislature is immune from dissolution by the executive.

Yes. The legislature is immune from dissolution.

11. Any executive initiative on legislation requires ratification or approval by the legislature before it takes effect; that is, the executive lacks decree power.

Yes. The executive lacks decree power.

12. Laws passed by the legislature are veto-proof or essentially veto-proof; that is, the executive lacks veto power, or has veto power but the veto can be overridden by a majority in the legislature.

No. A two-thirds majority is required to override a presidential veto.

> Article 106
> (7) Where a Bill has been passed by Parliament but the President refuses to sign it, the President shall within fourteen days of the presentation of the Bill for his signature cause the unsigned Bill to be returned to Parliament giving reasons for his refusal.
> (8) Where a Bill is returned to Parliament pursuant to subsection (7) and that Bill is thereafter passed by the votes of not less than two-thirds of the Members of Parliament, it shall immediately become law and the Speaker shall thereupon cause it to be published in the *Gazette.*

13. The legislature's laws are supreme and not subject to judicial review.

No. The Supreme Court can review the constitutionality of laws.

> Article 124
> (1) The Supreme Court shall, save as otherwise provided in section 122 of this Constitution, have original jurisdiction, to the exclusion of all other Courts – in all matters relating to the enforcement or interpretation of any provision of this Constitution; and where any question arises whether an enactment was made in excess of the power conferred upon Parliament or any other authority or person by law or under this Constitution.
> (2) Where any question relating to any matter or question as is referred to in subsection (1) arises in any proceedings in any Court, other than the Supreme Court, that Court shall stay the proceedings and refer the question of law involved to the Supreme Court for determination; and the Court in which the question arose shall

dispose of the case in accordance with the decision of the Supreme Court.

14. The legislature has the right to initiate bills in all policy jurisdictions; the executive lacks gatekeeping authority.

Yes. The legislature can initiate bills in all policy jurisdictions.

15. Expenditure of funds appropriated by the legislature is mandatory; the executive lacks the power to impound funds appropriated by the legislature.

Yes. The executive lacks the power to impound funds appropriated by the legislature.

16. The legislature controls the resources that finance its own internal operation and provide for the perquisites of its own members.

No. The legislature is dependent on the executive for the resources that finance its own operations.

17. Members of the legislature are immune from arrest and/or criminal prosecution.

No. Legislative immunity extends only to anything said in parliament and while legislators are in, or traveling to and from, the parliament buildings only. They can be arrested for common crimes at other times.

> Article 98
> There shall be freedom of speech, debate and proceedings in Parliament and that freedom shall not be impeached or questioned in any court or place out of Parliament.

> Article 99
> (1) Subject to the provisions of this section, but without prejudice to the generality of section 97, no civil or criminal proceedings shall be instituted against a Member of Parliament in any court or place out of Parliament by reason of anything said by him in Parliament.

> Article 100
> No civil or criminal process issuing from any court or place out of Parliament shall be served on or executed in relation to the Speaker or a Member or the Clerk of Parliament while he is on his way to attending or returning from any proceedings of Parliament.

18. All members of the legislature are elected; the executive lacks the power to appoint any members of the legislature.

Yes. All members of the legislature are elected.

> Article 74
> (1) Members of Parliament shall comprise the following –
> (a) one Member of Parliament for each District who shall, subject to the provisions of this Constitution, be elected in such manner as may be prescribed by or under any law from among the persons who, under

any law, are for the time being Paramount Chiefs; and (b) such number of Members as Parliament may prescribe who, subject to the provisions of this Constitution, shall be elected in such manner as may be prescribed by or under any law.

(2) The number of Members of Parliament to be elected pursuant to paragraphs (a) and (b) of subsection (1) shall not together be less than sixty.

(3) In any election of Members of Parliament the votes of the electors shall be given by ballot in such manner as not to disclose how any particular elector votes.

19. The legislature alone, without the involvement of any other agencies, can change the Constitution.

Yes. The legislature can change the constitution on multiple readings with a two-thirds majority vote. Amendments to selected sections of the constitution require approval in a popular referendum.

Article 108

(1) Subject to the provisions of this section, Parliament may alter this Constitution.

(2) A Bill for an Act of Parliament under this section shall not be passed by Parliament unless –

(a) before the first reading of the Bill in Parliament the text of the Bill is published in at least two issues of the *Gazette:* Provided that not less than nine days shall elapse between the first publication of the Bill in the *Gazette* and the second publication; and

(b) the Bill is supported on the second and third readings by the votes of not less than two-thirds of the Members of Parliament.

(3) A Bill for an Act of Parliament enacting a new Constitution or altering any of the following provisions of this Constitution, that is to say –

(a) this section,

(b) Chapter III,

(c) sections 46, 56, 72, 73, 74(2), 74(3), 84(2), 85, 87, 105, 110–119, 120, 121, 122, 123, 124, 128, 129, 131, 132, 133, 135, 136, 137, 140, 151, 156, 167, shall not be submitted to the President for his assent and shall not become law unless the Bill, after it has been passed by Parliament and in the form in which it was so passed, has, in accordance with the provisions of any law in that behalf, been submitted to and been approved at a referendum.

(4) Every person who is entitled to vote in the elections of Members of Parliament shall be entitled to vote at a referendum held for the purposes of subsection (3) and no other person may so vote; and the Bill shall not be regarded as having been approved at the referendum unless it was so approved by the votes of not less than one-half of all such persons and by not less than two-thirds of all the votes validly cast at the referendum: Provided that in calculating the total number of persons entitled to vote at such referendum, the names of deceased persons, of persons disqualified as electors, and of persons duplicated in the register of electors and so certified by the Electoral Commission, shall not be taken into account.

(5) The conduct of any referendum for the purposes of subsection (3) of this section shall be under the general supervision of the Electoral Commission and the provisions of subsections (4), (5) and (6) of section 38 of this Constitution shall apply in relation to the exercise by the Electoral Commission of its functions with respect to a referendum as they apply in relation to the exercise of its functions with respect to elections of Members of Parliament.

(6) A Bill for an Act of Parliament under this section shall not be submitted to the President for his signature unless it is accompanied by a certificate under the hand of the Speaker of Parliament (or, if the Speaker is for any reason unable to exercise the functions of his office, the Deputy Speaker) that the provisions of subsections (3) and (4) of this section have been complied with, and every such certificate shall be conclusive for all purposes and shall not be inquired in any court.

(7) No Act of Parliament shall be deemed to amend, add to or repeal or in any way alter any of the provisions of this Constitution unless it does so in express terms.

(8) Any suspension, alteration, or repeal of this Constitution other than on the authority of Parliament shall be deemed to be an act of Treason.

(9) In this section –

(a) references to this Constitution include references to any law that amends or replaces any of the provisions of this Constitution; and

(b) references to the alteration of this Constitution or of any Chapter or section of this Constitution include references to the amendment, modification or re-enactment, with or without amendment or modification, of any provision for the time being contained in this Constitution or Chapter or section thereof, the suspension or repeal of any such provision, the making of different provision in lieu of such provision and the addition of new provisions to this Constitution or Chapter or section thereof, and references to the alteration of any particular provision of this Constitution shall be construed likewise.

20. The legislature's approval is necessary for the declaration of war.

Yes. The legislature's approval is necessary for the declaration of war.

Article 40

(4) Notwithstanding any provisions of this Constitution or any other law to the contrary, the President shall, without prejudice to any such law as may for the time being be adopted by Parliament, be responsible, in addition to the functions conferred upon him in the Constitution, for –

(g) the declaration of war.

Provided that any Treaty, Agreement or Convention executed by or under the authority of the President which relates to any matter within the legislative competence of Parliament, or which in any way alters the law of Sierra Leone or imposes any charge on, or authorises any expenditure out of, the Consolidated Fund or any other fund of Sierra Leone, and any declaration of war made by the President shall be subject to ratification by Parliament.

21. The legislature's approval is necessary to ratify treaties with foreign countries.

Yes. The legislature's approval is necessary to ratify international treaties.

> Article 40
> (4) Notwithstanding any provisions of this Constitution or any other law to the contrary, the President shall, without prejudice to any such law as may for the time being be adopted by Parliament, be responsible, in addition to the functions conferred upon him in the Constitution, for –
> (d) the execution of treaties, agreements or conventions in the name of Sierra Leone;
> Provided that any Treaty, Agreement or Convention executed by or under the authority of the President which relates to any matter within the legislative competence of Parliament, or which in any way alters the law of Sierra Leone or imposes any charge on, or authorises any expenditure out of, the Consolidated Fund or any other fund of Sierra Leone, and any declaration of war made by the President shall be subject to ratification by Parliament.

22. The legislature has the power to grant amnesty.

No. Amnesty and pardon are not treated separately, and the legislature lacks the power to grant amnesty. See item 23.

23. The legislature has the power of pardon.

No. The president has the power of pardon (mercy).

> Article 40
> (4) Notwithstanding any provisions of this Constitution or any other law to the contrary, the President shall, without prejudice to any such law as may for the time being be adopted by Parliament, be responsible, in addition to the functions conferred upon him in the Constitution, for –
> (e) the exercise of the Prerogative of Mercy.

24. The legislature reviews and has the right to reject appointments to the judiciary; or the legislature itself appoints members of the judiciary.

Yes. The legislature's approval is necessary to confirm the president's appointments to the Supreme Court.

> Article 135
> (1) The President shall, acting on the advice of the Judicial and Legal Service Commission and subject to the approval of Parliament, appoint the Chief Justice by warrant under his hand from among persons qualified to hold office as Justice of the Supreme Court.
> (2) The other Judges of the Superior Court of Judicature shall be appointed by the President by warrant under his hand acting on the advice of the Judicial and Legal

Service Commission and subject to the approval of Parliament.

25. The chairman of the central bank is appointed by the legislature.

No. The president appoints the governor of the Bank of Sierra Leone.

> Article 71
> Notwithstanding the provisions of section 152 of this Constitution and save as otherwise provided in this Constitution, the President shall, in accordance with the provisions of this Constitution or any other law, appoint –
> (c) the Governor and the other members of the governing body of any State Bank, Banking or Financial Institutions.

26. The legislature has a substantial voice in the operation of the state-owned media.

No. The legislature lacks a substantial voice in the operation of the public media.

27. The legislature is regularly in session.

No. In practice, the legislature does not regularly meet in ordinary session.

> Article 84
> (1) Each session in Parliament shall be held at such place within Sierra Leone and shall commence at such time as the President may be Proclamation appoint.
> (2) There shall be a session of Parliament at least once in every year, so that a period of twelve months shall not intervene between the last sitting of Parliament in one session and the first sitting thereof in the next session: Provided that there shall be a session of Parliament not later than twenty-eight days from the holding of a general election of Members of Parliament.
> (3) The President shall at the beginning of each session of Parliament present to Parliament an address on the state of the nation.

28. Each legislator has a personal secretary.

No.

29. Each legislator has at least one non-secretarial staff member with policy expertise.

No.

30. Legislators are eligible for re-election without any restriction.

Yes. There are no restrictions on re-election.

31. A seat in the legislature is an attractive enough position that legislators are generally interested in and seek re-election.

Yes.

32. The re-election of incumbent legislators is common enough that at any given time the legislature

contains a significant number of highly experienced members.

Yes. Despite instability, military interventions, and electoral volatility, the elections of 1996, 2002, and 2007 created parliaments in which there was some continuity in membership, and the legislature contains a significant number of highly experienced members.

PARLIAMENT OF SINGAPORE

Expert consultants: Jens Kayser, Diane K. Mauzy, Ern Ser Tan, Kevin Tan, Li-ann Thio

Score: .38

Influence over executive (2/9)		Institutional autonomy (5/9)		Specified powers (1/8)		Institutional capacity (4/6)	
1. replace		10. no dissolution		19. amendments	X	27. sessions	X
2. serve as ministers	X	11. no decree	X	20. war		28. secretary	
3. interpellate		12. no veto	X	21. treaties		29. staff	
4. investigate		13. no review		22. amnesty		30. no term limits	X
5. oversee police		14. no gatekeeping		23. pardon		31. seek re-election	X
6. appoint PM	X	15. no impoundment	X	24. judiciary		32. experience	X
7. appoint ministers		16. control resources	X	25. central bank			
8. lack president		17. immunity		26. media			
9. no confidence		18. all elected	X				

The Parliament of Singapore was established in the country's 1959 constitution that declared Singapore an autonomous state. The document called for a unicameral legislature led by a powerful prime minister. Singapore separated from Malaysia in 1965, achieving full independence. Constitutional amendments in 1984 and 1990 introduced non-constituency members of parliament and nominated members of parliament, respectively. The stated purpose of these "nonelected" legislators was to increase the opportunities of participation for opposition parties and underrepresented minorities. Prior to 1993 the president was elected by the legislature, but in that year Singapore introduced direct election of the president.

The legislature's powers are few and scattered. Apart from its members serving in government and its choosing the prime minister, parliament has no meaningful ability to influence the executive branch. Its institutional autonomy is limited by substantial executive powers. Most notably, executive gatekeeping authority prevents parliament from introducing legislation related to taxation, government debt, and other financial issues. The legislature lacks all but one of the specified powers and prerogatives included in this survey. It does, however, have some institutional capacity.

SURVEY

1. The legislature alone, without the involvement of any other agencies, can impeach the president or replace the prime minister.

No. The legislature cannot remove the prime minister from office. Presidential impeachment requires the involvement of a special tribunal established by the chief justice of the Supreme Court.

Article 221

(3) The Prime Minister or not less than one-quarter of the total number of the elected Members of Parliament referred to in Article 39 (1)(a) may give notice of a motion alleging that the President is permanently incapable of discharging the functions of his office by reason of mental or physical infirmity or that the President has been guilty of

(a) intentional violation of the Constitution;

(b) treason;

(c) misconduct or corruption involving the abuse of the powers of his office; or

(d) any offence involving fraud, dishonesty or moral turpitude, and setting out full particulars of the allegations made and seeking an inquiry and report thereon.

(4) Where the motion referred to in clause (3) has been adopted by not less than half of the total number of the elected Members of Parliament referred to in Article 39 (1)(a), the Chief Justice shall appoint a tribunal to inquire into the allegations made against the President.

(5) A tribunal appointed by the Chief Justice shall consist of not less than 5 Judges of the Supreme Court of whom the Chief Justice shall be one, unless he otherwise decides and such tribunal may regulate its own procedure and make rules for that purpose.

(6) A tribunal shall, after due inquiry at which the President shall have the right to appear and to be heard in person or by counsel, make a report of its determination to the Speaker together with the reasons therefor.

(7) Where the tribunal reports to the Speaker that in its opinion the President is permanently incapable of discharging the functions of his office by reason of mental or physical infirmity or that the President has been guilty of any of the other allegations contained in such resolution, Parliament may by a resolution passed by not less than three-quarters of the total number of the elected Members of Parliament referred to in Article 39 (1)(a) remove the President from office.

2. Ministers may serve simultaneously as members of the legislature.

Yes. Ministers are chosen from, and required to serve simultaneously in, the legislature.

Article 25
(1) The President shall appoint as Prime Minister a Member of Parliament who in his judgment is likely to command the confidence of the majority of the Members of Parliament, and shall, acting in accordance with the advice of the Prime Minister, appoint other Ministers from among the Members of Parliament: Provided that, if an appointment is made while Parliament is dissolved, a person who was a Member of the last Parliament may be appointed but shall not continue to hold office after the first sitting of the next Parliament unless he is a Member thereof.

3. The legislature has powers of summons over executive branch officials and hearings with executive branch officials testifying before the legislature or its committees are regularly held.

No. The legislature cannot interpellate executive branch officials.

4. The legislature can conduct independent investigation of the chief executive and the agencies of the executive.

No. The legislature cannot investigate the executive.

5. The legislature has effective powers of oversight over the agencies of coercion (the military, organs of law enforcement, intelligence services, and the secret police).

No. The legislature lacks effective powers of oversight over the agencies of coercion.

6. The legislature appoints the prime minister.

Yes. The president appoints as prime minister the candidate who enjoys the support of the legislature.

Article 25
(1) The President shall appoint as Prime Minister a Member of Parliament who in his judgment is likely to command the confidence of the majority of the Members of Parliament, and shall, acting in accordance with the advice of the Prime Minister, appoint other Ministers from among the Members of Parliament: Provided that, if an appointment is made while Parliament is dissolved, a person who was a Member of the last Parliament may be appointed but shall not continue to hold office after the first sitting of the next Parliament unless he is a Member thereof.

7. The legislature's approval is required to confirm the appointment of ministers; or the legislature itself appoints ministers.

No. The president appoints ministers on the advice of the prime minister, and ministerial appointments do not require the legislature's approval.

Article 25
(1) The President shall appoint as Prime Minister a Member of Parliament who in his judgment is likely to command the confidence of the majority of the Members of Parliament, and shall, acting in accordance with the advice of the Prime Minister, appoint other Ministers from among the Members of Parliament: Provided that, if an appointment is made while Parliament is dissolved, a person who was a Member of the last Parliament may be appointed but shall not continue to hold office after the first sitting of the next Parliament unless he is a Member thereof.

8. The country lacks a presidency entirely or there is a presidency, but the president is elected by the legislature.

No. Since 1993 the president has been directly elected. Prior to 1993 the legislature elected the president.

Article 17
(1) There shall be a President of Singapore who shall be the Head of State and shall exercise and perform such powers and functions as are conferred on the President by this Constitution and any other written law.
(2) The President shall be elected by the citizens of Singapore in accordance with any law made by the Legislature.

9. The legislature can vote no confidence in the government.

No. The legislature cannot vote no confidence in the government. The president can, however, choose to remove the prime minister from office if he or she believes that the prime minister has ceased to command the confidence of a majority of the legislature.

> Article 26
> (1) The President shall, by writing under the public seal, declare the office of Prime Minister vacant
>> (b) if the President, acting in his discretion, is satisfied that the Prime Minister has ceased to command the confidence of a majority of the Members of Parliament: Provided that, before declaring the office of Prime Minister vacant under this paragraph, the President shall inform the Prime Minister that he is satisfied as aforesaid, and, if the Prime Minister so requests, the President may dissolve Parliament instead of making such a declaration.

10. The legislature is immune from dissolution by the executive.

No. The president can dissolve the legislature.

> Article 65
> (1) The President may, at any time, by Proclamation in the Gazette, prorogue Parliament.
> (2) If, at any time, the office of Prime Minister is vacant, the President shall, by Proclamation in the Gazette, dissolve Parliament as soon as he is satisfied, acting in his discretion, that a reasonable period has elapsed since that office was last vacated and that there is no Member of Parliament likely to command the confidence of a majority of the Members thereof.
> (3) The President may, at any time, by Proclamation in the Gazette, dissolve Parliament if he is advised by the Prime Minister to do so, but he shall not be obliged to act in this respect in accordance with the advice of the Prime Minister unless he is satisfied that, in tendering that advice the Prime Minister commands the confidence of a majority of the Members of Parliament.
> (3a) The President shall not dissolve Parliament after a notice of motion proposing an inquiry into the conduct of the President has been given under Article 221 (3) unless
>> (a) a resolution is not passed pursuant to the notice of such motion under Article 221 (4);
>> (b) where a resolution has been passed pursuant to the notice of such motion under Article 221 (4), the tribunal appointed under Article 221 (5) determines and reports that the President has not become permanently incapable of discharging the functions of his office or that the President has not been guilty of any of the other allegations contained in such motion;
>> (c) the consequent resolution for the removal of the President is not passed under Article 221 (7); or
>> (d) Parliament by resolution requests the President to dissolve Parliament.

11. Any executive initiative on legislation requires ratification or approval by the legislature before it takes effect; that is, the executive lacks decree power.

Yes. The executive lacks decree power.

12. Laws passed by the legislature are veto-proof or essentially veto-proof; that is, the executive lacks veto power, or has veto power but the veto can be overridden by a majority in the legislature.

Yes. The executive lacks veto power.

> Article 58
> (1) Subject to the provisions of Part VII, the power of the Legislature to make laws shall be exercised by Bills passed by Parliament and assented to by the President.
> (2) A Bill shall become law on being assented to by the President and such law shall come into operation on the date of its publication in the Gazette or, if it is enacted either in such law or in any other law for the time being in force in Singapore that it shall come into operation on some other date, on that date.

13. The legislature's laws are supreme and not subject to judicial review.

No. The judiciary can review the constitutionality of laws.

> Article 4
> This Constitution is the supreme law of the Republic of Singapore and any law enacted by the Legislature after the commencement of this Constitution which is inconsistent with this Constitution shall to the extent of the inconsistency, be void.

14. The legislature has the right to initiate bills in all policy jurisdictions; the executive lacks gatekeeping authority.

No. The legislature is prohibited from introducing legislation related to taxation, government expenditures, government debt, and other financial issues.

> Article 59
> (1) Subject to the provisions of this Constitution and of Standing Orders of Parliament, any Member may introduce any Bill or propose any motion for debate in, or may present any petition to, Parliament, and the same shall be debated and disposed of according to the Standing Orders of Parliament.
> (2) A Bill or amendment making provision (whether directly or indirectly) for
>> (a) imposing or increasing any tax or abolishing, reducing or remitting any existing tax;
>> (b) the borrowing of money, or the giving of any guarantee, by the Government, or the amendment of the law relating to the financial obligations of the Government;
>> (c) the custody of the Consolidated Fund, the charging of any money on the Consolidated Fund or the abolition or alteration of any such charge;

(d) the payment of moneys into the Consolidated Fund or the payment, issue or withdrawal from the Consolidated Fund of any moneys not charged thereon, or any increase in the amount of such a payment, issue or withdrawal; or

(e) the receipt of any moneys on account of the Consolidated Fund or the custody or issue of such moneys, being provision as respects which the Minister charged with responsibility for finance signifies that it goes beyond what is incidental only and not of a substantial nature having regard to the purposes of the Bill or amendment, shall not be introduced or moved except on the recommendation of the President signified by a Minister.

(3) A Bill or amendment shall not be deemed to make provision for any of the said matters by reason only that it provides for the imposition or alteration of any fine or other pecuniary penalty or for the payment or demand of a license fee or a fee or charge for any service rendered.

15. Expenditure of funds appropriated by the legislature is mandatory; the executive lacks the power to impound funds appropriated by the legislature.

Yes. The executive lacks the power to impound funds appropriated by the legislature.

16. The legislature controls the resources that finance its own internal operation and provide for the perquisites of its own members.

Yes. The legislature enjoys financial autonomy.

17. Members of the legislature are immune from arrest and/or criminal prosecution.

No. Formally, the legislature has the power to pass laws on immunity, but in practice, legislators are subject to arrest and criminal prosecution.

> Article 63
> It shall be lawful for the Legislature by law to determine and regulate the privileges, immunities or powers of Parliament.

18. All members of the legislature are elected; the executive lacks the power to appoint any members of the legislature.

Yes. The executive lacks the power to appoint any members of the legislature. Not all members of the legislature are elected in the strict sense, however. "Non-constituency members" of parliament are the top three members of the opposition who failed to get elected but received at least 35 percent of the vote. "Nominated members" of parliament are chosen by a parliamentary select committee. These nonelected members have limited voting privileges in parliament.

> Article 39
> (1) Parliament shall consist of

(a) such number of elected Members as is required to be returned at a general election by the constituencies prescribed by or under any law made by the Legislature;

(b) such other Members, not exceeding 6 in number, who shall be known as non-constituency Members, as the Legislature may provide in any law relating to Parliamentary elections to ensure the representation in Parliament of a minimum number of Members from a political party or parties not forming the Government; and

(c) such other Members not exceeding 6 in number, who shall be known as nominated Members, as may be appointed by the President in accordance with the provisions of the Fourth Schedule.

(2) A non-constituency Member or a nominated Member shall not vote in Parliament on any motion pertaining to

(a) a Bill to amend the Constitution;

(b) a Supply Bill, Supplementary Supply Bill, or Final Supply Bill;

(c) a Money Bill as defined in Article 68;

(d) a vote of no confidence in the Government; and

(e) removing the President from office under Article 22l.

(3) In this article and in Articles 39a and 47, a constituency shall be construed as an electoral division for the purposes of Parliamentary elections.

(4) If any person who is not a Member of Parliament is elected as Speaker or Deputy Speaker, he shall, by virtue of holding the office of Speaker or Deputy Speaker, be a Member of Parliament in addition to the Members aforesaid, except for the purposes of Chapter 2 of Part V and of Article 46.

19. The legislature alone, without the involvement of any other agencies, can change the Constitution.

Yes. The legislature can change the constitution with a two-thirds majority vote. Amendments to select articles of the constitution require approval in a popular referendum.

> Article 5
> (1) Subject to this article and Article 8, the provisions of this Constitution may be amended by a law enacted by the Legislature.
>
> (2) A Bill seeking to amend any provision in this Constitution shall not be passed by Parliament unless it has been supported on Second and Third Readings by the votes of not less than two-thirds of the total number of the elected Members of Parliament referred to in Article 39 (1)(a).
>
> (2a) Unless the President, acting in his discretion, otherwise directs the Speaker in writing, a Bill seeking to amend this clause, Articles 17 to 22, 22a to 22o, 35, 65, 66, 69, 70, 93a, 94, 95, 105, 107, 110a, 110b, 151 or any provision in Part IV or XI shall not be passed by Parliament unless it has been supported at a national referendum by not less than two-thirds of the total

number of votes cast by the electors registered under the Parliamentary Elections Act.

(3) In this article, "amendment" includes addition and repeal.

Article 8

(1) A Bill for making an amendment to this Part shall not be passed by Parliament unless it has been supported, at a national referendum, by not less than two-thirds of the total number of votes cast by the electors registered under the Parliamentary Elections Act.

(2) In this article, "amendment" includes addition and repeal.

20. The legislature's approval is necessary for the declaration of war.

No. There is no constitutional provision for the declaration of war. The president can, however, declare a state of emergency in response to security threats without the legislature's approval. The state of emergency expires if it is not subsequently approved by the legislature.

Article 150

(1) If the President is satisfied that a grave emergency exists whereby the security or economic life of Singapore is threatened, he may issue a Proclamation of Emergency.

(2) If a Proclamation of Emergency is issued when Parliament is not sitting, the President shall summon Parliament as soon as practicable, and may, until Parliament is sitting, promulgate ordinances having the force of law, if satisfied that immediate action is required.

(3) A Proclamation of Emergency and any ordinance promulgated under clause (2) shall be presented to Parliament and, if not sooner revoked, shall cease to have effect if a resolution is passed by Parliament annulling such Proclamation or ordinance, but without prejudice to anything previously done by virtue thereof or to the power of the President to issue a new Proclamation under clause (1) or promulgate any ordinance under clause (2).

(4) Subject to clause (5) (b), while a Proclamation of Emergency is in force, Parliament may, notwithstanding anything in this Constitution, make laws with respect to any matter, if it appears to Parliament that the law is required by reason of the emergency; and any provision of this Constitution (except Articles 22e, 22h, 144 (2) and 148a) or of any written law which requires any consent or concurrence to the passing of a law or any consultation with respect thereto, or which restricts the coming into force of a law after it is passed or the presentation of a Bill to the President for his assent, shall not apply to a Bill for such a law or an amendment to such a Bill.

(5)(a) Subject to Paragraph (b), no provision of any ordinance promulgated under this article, and no provision of any Act which is passed while a Proclamation of Emergency is in force and which declares that the law appears to Parliament to be required

by reason of the emergency, shall be invalid on the ground of inconsistency with any provision of this Constitution.

(b) Paragraph (a) shall not validate any provision inconsistent with

(i) Article 5 (2a);

(ii) the provisions of this Constitution specified in Article 5 (2a) conferring discretionary powers on the President; and

(iii) the provisions of this Constitution relating to religion, citizenship or language.

(6) At the expiration of a period of 6 months beginning with the date on which a Proclamation of Emergency ceases to be in force, any ordinance promulgated in pursuance of the Proclamation and, to the extent that it could not have been validly made but for this article, any law made while the Proclamation was in force, shall cease to have effect, except as to things done or omitted to be done before the expiration of that period.

21. The legislature's approval is necessary to ratify treaties with foreign countries.

No. The legislature's approval is not necessary to ratify international treaties.

22. The legislature has the power to grant amnesty.

No. The government has the power to grant amnesty.

23. The legislature has the power of pardon.

No. The president, on the advice of the government, has the power of pardon.

24. The legislature reviews and has the right to reject appointments to the judiciary; or the legislature itself appoints members of the judiciary.

No. Judges are appointed by the president on the advice of the prime minister, and the appointments do not require the legislature's approval.

Article 95

(1) The Chief Justice, the Judges of Appeal, and the Judges of the High Court shall be appointed by the President if he, acting in his discretion, concurs with the advice of the Prime Minister.

25. The chairman of the central bank is appointed by the legislature.

No. The government appoints the chairman of the Monetary Authority of Singapore.

26. The legislature has a substantial voice in the operation of the state-owned media.

No. The legislature lacks a substantial voice in the operation of the public media.

27. The legislature is regularly in session.

Yes. The legislature regularly meets in ordinary session.

Article 64

(1) There shall be a session of Parliament once at least in every year and a period of 6 months shall not intervene between the last sitting of Parliament in any one session and the first sitting thereof in the next session.

(2) The sessions of Parliament shall be held in such places and shall commence at such times as the President may, from time to time, by Proclamation in the Gazette, appoint.

28. Each legislator has a personal secretary.

No.

29. Each legislator has at least one non-secretarial staff member with policy expertise.

No.

30. Legislators are eligible for re-election without any restriction.

Yes. There are no restrictions on re-election.

31. A seat in the legislature is an attractive enough position that legislators are generally interested in and seek re-election.

Yes.

32. The re-election of incumbent legislators is common enough that at any given time the legislature contains a significant number of highly experienced members.

Yes. Re-election rates are sufficiently high to produce a significant number of highly experienced members.

NATIONAL COUNCIL OF THE SLOVAK REPUBLIC (*NÁRODNÁ RADA*)

Expert consultants: Jan Fidrmuc, Darina Malovà, Peter Matijek, Grigorij Mesežnikov, Conor O'Dwyer, Geoffrey Pridham

Score: .72

Influence over executive (6/9)		Institutional autonomy (7/9)		Specified powers (5/8)		Institutional capacity (5/6)	
1. replace	X	10. no dissolution		19. amendments	X	27. sessions	X
2. serve as ministers		11. no decree	X	20. war	X	28. secretary	X
3. interpellate	X	12. no veto	X	21. treaties	X	29. staff	
4. investigate	X	13. no review		22. amnesty		30. no term limits	X
5. oversee police	X	14. no gatekeeping	X	23. pardon		31. seek re-election	X
6. appoint PM	X	15. no impoundment	X	24. judiciary	X	32. experience	X
7. appoint ministers		16. control resources	X	25. central bank			
8. lack president		17. immunity	X	26. media	X		
9. no confidence	X	18. all elected	X				

The National Council (*Národná Rada*) of the Slovak Republic was established in the 1993 constitution upon the breakup of Czechoslovakia. The Council is a unicameral body. Prior to 1999 the legislature elected the president, but in that year a constitutional crisis led to a constitutional amendment that established the direct election of the president.

The legislature has considerable muscle. It can influence the executive with the powers to interpellate and investigate the government, and remove the government with a vote of no confidence. Furthermore, although the president formally has the right to appoint the prime minister, the outcome of parliamentary elections predetermines the president's choice, meaning that the legislature effectively chooses the prime minister. The legislature's institutional autonomy is ensured by an absence of executive decree, veto, and gatekeeping authorities. The legislature is, however, subject to dissolution. It exercises a number of specified powers and prerogatives and has much institutional capacity.

SURVEY

1. The legislature alone, without the involvement of any other agencies, can impeach the president or replace the prime minister.

Yes. The legislature can remove the prime minister with a vote of no confidence. Presidential impeachment requires the involvement of the Constitutional Court.

Article 107
The President can be prosecuted only for the intentional violation of the Constitution or for treason. The issuance of an accusation against the President of the Republic is decided by the National Council of the Slovak Republic by a three-fifths majority of the votes of all Deputies. The accusation is presented by the National Council of the Slovak Republic to the Constitutional Court of the Slovak Republic, which decides on it in its plenary session. The sentencing decision of the Constitutional Court of the Slovak Republic results in the loss of the function of the President and the capacity to seek this function again.

Article 115
(1) The president of the Slovak Republic will recall the Government if the National Council of the Slovak Republic passes a vote of no confidence in it or if it turns down the Government's request to pass a vote of confidence in it.
(2) If the president of the Slovak Republic accepts the Government's resignation, he will entrust it with the execution of its duties until a new Government is appointed.

2. Ministers may serve simultaneously as members of the legislature.

No. Legislators who serve in government have a sleeping mandate, meaning that they may join the government but forfeit their voting rights in the legislature during their government service. They may return to the legislature when their government service ends.

Article 77
(2) If a deputy is appointed member of the Government of the Slovak Republic, his mandate as a deputy does not cease while he executes the government post, but is just not being exercised.

3. The legislature has powers of summons over executive branch officials and hearings with executive branch officials testifying before the legislature or its committees are regularly held.

Yes. The legislature regularly interpellates officials from the executive.

Article 80
(1) A deputy may address an interpellation to the Government of the Slovak Republic, a member of the Government of the Slovak Republic, or the head of another central body of state administration concerning matters within their jurisdiction. The deputy must receive a reply within 30 days.
(2) The reply to an interpellation shall become the subject of a debate in the National Council of the Slovak Republic that may be linked with a vote of confidence.

4. The legislature can conduct independent investigation of the chief executive and the agencies of the executive.

Yes. The legislature can investigate the executive.

5. The legislature has effective powers of oversight over the agencies of coercion (the military, organs of law enforcement, intelligence services, and the secret police).

Yes. The legislature has effective powers of oversight over the agencies of coercion.

6. The legislature appoints the prime minister.

Yes. Formally, the president appoints the prime minister, but in practice, the president appoints the candidate who enjoys the support of the legislature.

Article 102
The president
f) appoints and recalls the prime minister and other members of the Government of the Slovak Republic.

Article 110
(1) The prime minister is appointed and recalled by the president of the Slovak Republic.
(2) Any citizen of the Slovak Republic who can be elected to the National Council of the Slovak Republic can be appointed prime minister.

7. The legislature's approval is required to confirm the appointment of ministers; or the legislature itself appoints ministers.

No. The president appoints ministers on the recommendation of the prime minister, and the appointments do not require the legislature's approval.

Article 102
The president
f) appoints and recalls the prime minister and other members of the Government of the Slovak Republic.

Article 111
At the recommendation of the prime minister, the president of the Slovak Republic appoints and recalls other members of the Government and entrusts them with the management of ministries. The president can appoint as deputy prime minister and minister any citizen who can be elected to the National Council of the Slovak Republic.

8. The country lacks a presidency entirely or there is a presidency, but the president is elected by the legislature.

No. Since 1999 the president has been directly elected. Prior to 1999 the president was elected by the legislature.

Article 101
(1) The Head of the Slovak Republic is the President. The President represents the Slovak Republic externally and internally and by his decisions safeguards the orderly conduct of the Constitutional organs. The President conducts his office according to his conscience and convictions and is not bound by any orders.
(2) The President is elected by the citizens of the Slovak Republic in direct elections by secret voting for five years. (All) citizens who have the right to vote for the National Council have the right to vote for the President.

9. The legislature can vote no confidence in the government.

Yes. The legislature can vote no confidence in the government without jeopardizing its own term.

Article 88
(1) The motion to pass a vote of no-confidence in the Government of the Slovak Republic or a member of it will be discussed by the National Council of the Slovak Republic if requested by at least one-fifth of its deputies.
(2) The consent of more than 50 percent of all deputies is required to pass a vote of no-confidence in the Government of the Slovak Republic or a member of it.

Article 115
(1) The president of the Slovak Republic will recall the Government if the National Council of the Slovak Republic passes a vote of no confidence in it or if it turns down the Government's request to pass a vote of confidence in it.
(2) If the president of the Slovak Republic accepts the Government's resignation, he will entrust it with the execution of its duties until a new Government is appointed.

10. The legislature is immune from dissolution by the executive.

No. The president can dissolve the legislature.

Article 102
(1) The President:
  e) may dissolve the National Council of the Slovak Republic within six months of the appointment of the Government of the Slovak Republic, if it did not approve its announced program, if the National Council of the Slovak Republic did not agree within three months on a proposed Government law which the Government connected with a vote of confidence, if the National Council of the Slovak Republic was not able within no more than three months to

agree either that its session was interrupted or that it was, during this period, repeatedly called into session, or that the session of the National Council of the Slovak Republic was interrupted for a longer period than the Constitution permits. (The President) cannot make use of this right during the last six months of his electoral term, in times of war, martial law or a state of exception. (The President) dissolves the National Council of the Slovak Republic in case of a popular voting on the recall of the President, the President was not recalled.

11. Any executive initiative on legislation requires ratification or approval by the legislature before it takes effect; that is, the executive lacks decree power.

Yes. The executive lacks decree power.

12. Laws passed by the legislature are veto-proof or essentially veto-proof; that is, the executive lacks veto power, or has veto power but the veto can be overridden by a majority in the legislature.

Yes. The legislature can override a presidential veto by a majority vote of its total membership.

Article 87
(1) Bills may be introduced by the Committees of the National Council of the Slovak Republic, members of the National Council and the Government of the Slovak Republic.
(2) If the President of the Slovak Republic returns a bill with comments, the National Council shall reconsider it and in case of its approval such a law must be promulgated.
(3) The law is signed by the President of the Slovak Republic, the Chairman of the National Council and the Prime Minister of the Slovak Republic. If the National Council of the Slovak Republic after reconsideration in spite of the comments of the President of the Slovak Republic, and the President of the Slovak Republic does not sign the law, the law is published without the signature of the President of the Slovak Republic.

13. The legislature's laws are supreme and not subject to judicial review.

No. The Constitutional Court can review the constitutionality of laws.

Article 125
(1) The Constitutional Court rules on the consonance –
  a) of laws with the Constitution, constitutional laws with international treaties, with which the National Council of the Slovak Republic has expressed its treaty and which were ratified and promulgated in the manner established by law.

Article 128
The Constitutional Court provides an interpretation of the Constitution or the constitutional law if the matter is in dispute.

14. The legislature has the right to initiate bills in all policy jurisdictions; the executive lacks gatekeeping authority.

Yes. The legislature can initiate bills in all policy jurisdictions.

15. Expenditure of funds appropriated by the legislature is mandatory; the executive lacks the power to impound funds appropriated by the legislature.

Yes. The executive lacks the power to impound funds appropriated by the legislature.

16. The legislature controls the resources that finance its own internal operation and provide for the perquisites of its own members.

Yes. The legislature enjoys financial autonomy.

17. Members of the legislature are immune from arrest and/or criminal prosecution.

Yes. Legislators are immune.

> Article 78
> (1) No deputy shall be prosecuted for his vote in the national council or its committees, and this even after the expiration of his mandate.
> (2) For statements made in the National Council of the Slovak Republic in the exercise of the function of deputy, no deputy can be criminally prosecuted and this even after the expiration of his mandate. The deputy is subject to the disciplinary powers of the National Council of the Slovak Republic. The responsibility of the deputy under civil law is not affected thereby.
> (3) A deputy cannot be criminally or disciplinarily prosecuted, not taken into custody without the approval of the National Council of the Slovak Republic. If the National Council rejects a criminal prosecution or an arrest is excluded for the duration of the mandate of the deputy, in such a case the suspension of his mandate does not count.
> (4) If a deputy was apprehended and detained while committing a criminal offence, the competent organ is obligated to inform immediately the Chairman of the National Council of the Slovak Republic. If the mandate and community committee does not give the required approval for the arrest, the deputy must be immediately released.
> (5) If the deputy is in custody his mandate does not end, but it is not taken into account.

18. All members of the legislature are elected; the executive lacks the power to appoint any members of the legislature.

Yes. All members of the legislature are elected.

> Article 74
> (1) Deputies are elected by secret ballot in general, equal, and direct elections.

19. The legislature alone, without the involvement of any other agencies, can change the Constitution.

Yes. The legislature can change the constitution with a three-fifths majority vote.

> Article 84
> (4) For ... amending the Constitution ... the consent of at least a three-fifths majority of all deputies is required.

20. The legislature's approval is necessary for the declaration of war.

Yes. The legislature's approval is required for presidential war declarations.

> Article 86
> The powers of the National Council of the Slovak Republic shall be mainly to:
> j) to resolve to declare war, if the Slovak Republic is attacked or if a declaration ensues from obligations of international treaties of common defense against attack and after the end of war and conclusion of peace.

> Article 102
> (1) The President:
> l) declares war on the basis of a resolution by the National Council of the Slovak Republic when the Slovak Republic is attacked or when this ensues from obligations of international treaties concerning joint defense against assault, and concludes peace.

21. The legislature's approval is necessary to ratify treaties with foreign countries.

Yes. The legislature's approval is necessary to ratify international treaties on most major issues.

> Article 86
> The powers of the National Council of the Slovak Republic shall be mainly to:
> d) prior to their ratification, give consent to international treaties concerning human rights and fundamental freedoms, international political treaties, international treaties of a military nature, from which arise for the Slovak Republic membership in international organizations, international economic treaties of a general nature, international treaties for whose implementation a law is required, as well as from international treaties, which directly establish rights and obligations of physical persons or juridical persons, and also to decide whether it concerns international treaties according to Art. 7 paragraph (5).

> Article 102
> (1) The President:
> a) represents the Slovak Republic externally, negotiates and ratifies international treaties. He can delegate negotiation of international treaties to the Government of the Slovak Republic or, with the consent of the Government, to individual members thereof.

22. The legislature has the power to grant amnesty.

No. The president has the power to grant amnesty.

Article 102

(1) The President:

    j) pardons and commutes sentences imposed by courts in criminal proceedings and mitigates sentences in the form of individual grace or amnesty.

23. The legislature has the power of pardon.

No. The president has the power of pardon.

Article 102

The president

i) grants amnesty and pardon, lowers punishments meted out by criminal courts, issues orders not to initiate or not to continue criminal proceedings, and nullifies punishments.

24. The legislature reviews and has the right to reject appointments to the judiciary; or the legislature itself appoints members of the judiciary.

Yes. The president appoints the twelve judges of the Constitutional Court from a group of twenty-four candidates nominated by the legislature.

Article 134

(1) The Constitutional Court is composed of thirteen judges.

(2) The judges of the Constitutional Court are appointed for twelve years by the President of the Slovak Republic. The National Council of the Slovak Republic nominates a twofold number of candidates for judgeships, which the President shall appoint.

Article 145

(1) The judges are appointed and recalled by the President of the Slovak Republic on the proposal of the Judicial Council of the Slovak Republic; he appoints them without time limits.

(3) The President of the Supreme Court of the Slovak Republic and the Vice President of the Supreme Court of the Slovak Republic are appointed from the judges of the Supreme Court of the Slovak Republic by the President of the Republic for five years.

25. The chairman of the central bank is appointed by the legislature.

No. The president appoints the governor of the National Bank of Slovakia.

26. The legislature has a substantial voice in the operation of the state-owned media.

Yes. The legislature has a substantial voice in the operation of the public media.

27. The legislature is regularly in session.

Yes. The legislature regularly meets in ordinary session.

Article 82

(1) The National Council of the Slovak Republic holds permanent sessions.

(2) The constituent meeting of the National Council of the Slovak Republic is called by the president of the Slovak Republic within 30 days after the announcement of election results. If he fails to do so, the National Council of the Slovak Republic convenes on the 30th day after the announcement of the election results.

(3) The National Council of the Slovak Republic may interrupt its session by means of a resolution. The length of interruption must not exceed four months in a year. The chairman, deputy chairmen, and bodies of the National Council of the Slovak Republic perform their duties while the National Council of the Slovak Republic is in recess.

(4) While the session is interrupted, the chairman of the National Council of the Slovak Republic may call a meeting of the National Council of the Slovak Republic even prior to the set date. He will call a meeting whenever requested to do so by the Government of the Slovak Republic or at least one-fifth of the deputies.

(5) The session of the National Council of the Slovak Republic ends with the expiration of the electoral term or with its dissolution.

28. Each legislator has a personal secretary.

Yes.

29. Each legislator has at least one non-secretarial staff member with policy expertise.

No.

30. Legislators are eligible for re-election without any restriction.

Yes. There are no restrictions on re-election.

31. A seat in the legislature is an attractive enough position that legislators are generally interested in and seek re-election.

Yes.

32. The re-election of incumbent legislators is common enough that at any given time the legislature contains a significant number of highly experienced members.

Yes. Re-election rates are sufficiently high to produce a significant number of highly experienced members.

PARLIAMENT OF SLOVENIA (*PARLAMENT*)

Expert consultants: Milica Antić-Gaber, Erika Harris, Damjan Lajh, Nicole Lindstrom, Jurij Toplak

Score: .75

Influence over executive (7/9)		Institutional autonomy (7/9)		Specified powers (6/8)		Institutional capacity (4/6)	
1. replace	X	10. no dissolution		19. amendments	X	27. sessions	X
2. serve as ministers		11. no decree	X	20. war	X	28. secretary	
3. interpellate	X	12. no veto	X	21. treaties	X	29. staff	
4. investigate	X	13. no review		22. amnesty		30. no term limits	X
5. oversee police	X	14. no gatekeeping	X	23. pardon		31. seek re-election	X
6. appoint PM	X	15. no impoundment	X	24. judiciary	X	32. experience	X
7. appoint ministers	X	16. control resources	X	25. central bank	X		
8. lack president		17. immunity	X	26. media	X		
9. no confidence	X	18. all elected	X				

The Parliament (*Parlament*) of Slovenia traces its origins to the Slovene parliament in the Yugoslav federation. In 1989 the Slovene parliament seceded from the Yugoslav federation. Slovenia subsequently declared independence. Its 1991 constitution called for a bicameral parliament consisting of a lower house, the National Assembly (*Državni zbor*), and an upper house, the National Council (*Državni svet*).

Parliament occupies a commanding position in national politics. It controls the executive with powers to remove the prime minister (referred to as the "president of the government") and to appoint, effectively oversee, and remove the government. The legislature can be dissolved by the president and its laws are subject to judicial review, but otherwise the legislature enjoys complete institutional autonomy. It exercises six of the eight specified powers measured in this survey and has moderate institutional capacity.

SURVEY

1. The legislature alone, without the involvement of any other agencies, can impeach the president or replace the prime minister.

Yes. The legislature can remove the prime minister (president of the government) with a vote of no confidence. Presidential impeachment requires the involvement of the Constitutional Court.

Article 109
If in the performance of his office the President of the Republic violates the Constitution or seriously violates the law, he may be impeached by the National Assembly before the Constitutional Court. The Constitutional Court shall decide either that the impeachment charges are justified or it shall dismiss the charges, and it may further decide on relieving the President of office by a two-thirds majority vote of all judges. Upon receiving a resolution on impeachment from the National Assembly, the Constitutional Court may decide that pending a decision on impeachment the President of the Republic may not perform his office.

Article 116
(1) The National Assembly may pass a vote of no confidence in the Government only by electing a new President of the Government on the proposal of at least ten deputies and by a majority vote of all deputies. The incumbent President of the Government is thereby dismissed, but together with his ministers he must continue to perform his regular duties until the swearing in of a new Government.
(2) No less than forty-eight hours must elapse between the lodging of a proposal to elect a new President of the Government and the vote itself, unless the National Assembly decides otherwise by a two-thirds majority vote of all deputies, or if the country is at war or in a state of emergency.
(3) Where a President of the Government has been elected on the basis of the fourth paragraph of Article 111 a vote on no confidence is expressed in him if on the proposal of at least ten deputies, the National

Assembly elects a new President of the Government by a majority of votes cast.

Article 119
The National Assembly may impeach the President of the Government or ministers before the Constitutional Court on charges of violating the Constitution and laws during the performance of their office. The Constitutional Court considers the charges in such a manner as determined in Article 109.

2. Ministers may serve simultaneously as members of the legislature.

No. Legislators are prohibited from serving simultaneously in ministerial positions.

3. The legislature has powers of summons over executive branch officials and hearings with executive branch officials testifying before the legislature or its committees are regularly held.

Yes. The legislature regularly interpellates officials from the executive.

Article 118
(1) An interpellation with respect to the work of the Government or an individual minister may be initiated in the National Assembly by at least ten deputies.
(2) If, after the debate following such interpellation, a majority of all deputies carries a vote of no confidence in the Government or in an individual minister, the National Assembly dismisses the Government or said minister.

4. The legislature can conduct independent investigation of the chief executive and the agencies of the executive.

Yes. The legislature can investigate the executive.

Article 93
The National Assembly may order inquiries on matters of public importance, and it must do so when required by a third of the deputies of the National Assembly or when required by the National Council. For this purpose it shall appoint a commission which in matters of investigation and examination has powers comparable to those of judicial authorities.

5. The legislature has effective powers of oversight over the agencies of coercion (the military, organs of law enforcement, intelligence services, and the secret police).

Yes. The legislature has effective powers of oversight over the agencies of coercion.

6. The legislature appoints the prime minister.

Yes. The legislature appoints the prime minister (president of the government).

Article 111
(1) After consultation with the leaders of parliamentary groups the President of the Republic proposes to the National Assembly a candidate for President of the Government.
(2) The President of the Government is elected by the National Assembly by a majority vote of all deputies unless otherwise provided by this Constitution. Voting is by secret ballot.
(3) If such candidate does not receive the necessary majority of votes, the President of the Republic may after renewed consultation propose within fourteen days a new candidate, or the same candidate again, and candidates may also be proposed by parliamentary groups or a minimum of ten deputies. If within this period several candidates have been proposed, each one is voted on separately beginning with the candidate proposed by the President of the Republic, and if this candidate is not elected, a vote is taken on the other candidates in the order in which they were proposed.
(4) If no candidate is elected, the President of the Republic dissolves the National Assembly and calls new elections, unless within eighty-four hours the National Assembly decides by a majority of votes cast by those deputies present to hold new elections for President of the Government, whereby a majority of votes cast by those deputies present is sufficient for the election of the candidate. In such new elections a vote is taken on candidates individually in order of the number of votes received in the earlier voting and then on the new candidates proposed prior to the new vote, wherein any candidate proposed by the President of the Republic takes precedence.
(5) If in such elections no candidate receives the necessary number of votes, the President of the Republic dissolves the National Assembly and calls new elections.

7. The legislature's approval is required to confirm the appointment of ministers; or the legislature itself appoints ministers.

Yes. The legislature appoints ministers on the recommendation of the prime minister (president of the government).

Article 112
(1) Ministers are appointed and dismissed by the National Assembly on the proposal of the President of the Government.

8. The country lacks a presidency entirely or there is a presidency, but the president is elected by the legislature.

No. The president is directly elected.

Article 103
(1) The President of the Republic is elected in direct, general elections by secret ballot.

9. The legislature can vote no confidence in the government.

Yes. The legislature can pass a constructive vote of no confidence in the government, meaning that the legislature must designate a successor prime minister (president of the government) before passing a vote of no confidence.

Article 116

(1) The National Assembly may pass a vote of no confidence in the Government only by electing a new President of the Government on the proposal of at least ten deputies and by a majority vote of all deputies. The incumbent President of the Government is thereby dismissed, but together with his ministers he must continue to perform his regular duties until the swearing in of a new Government.

(2) No less than forty-eight hours must elapse between the lodging of a proposal to elect a new President of the Government and the vote itself, unless the National Assembly decides otherwise by a two-thirds majority vote of all deputies, or if the country is at war or in a state of emergency.

(3) Where a President of the Government has been elected on the basis of the fourth paragraph of Article 111 a vote on no confidence is expressed in him if on the proposal of at least ten deputies, the National Assembly elects a new President of the Government by a majority of votes cast.

10. The legislature is immune from dissolution by the executive.

No. The president can dissolve the legislature.

Article 117

(1) The President of the Government may require a vote of confidence in the Government. If the Government does not receive the support of a majority vote of all deputies, the National Assembly must elect within thirty days a new President of the Government or in a new vote express its confidence in the incumbent President of the Government, or failing this, the President of the Republic dissolves the National Assembly and calls new elections. The President of the Government may tie the issue of confidence to the adoption of a law or to some other decision in the National Assembly. If such decision is not adopted, it is deemed that a vote of no confidence in the Government has been passed.

(2) No less than forty-eight hours must elapse between the requirement of a vote of confidence and the vote itself.

11. Any executive initiative on legislation requires ratification or approval by the legislature before it takes effect; that is, the executive lacks decree power.

Yes. In normal political circumstances, the executive lacks decree power. The president can issue decrees that have the force of law only when the legislature is unable to meet because of war or a state of emergency.

Article 108

(1) In the event that the National Assembly is unable to convene due to a state of emergency or war, the President of the Republic may, on the proposal of the Government, issue decrees with the force of law.

(2) Such decrees may, in exception, restrict individual rights and fundamental freedoms as provided by Article 16 of this Constitution.

(3) The President of the Republic must submit decrees with the force of law to the National Assembly for confirmation immediately upon it next convening.

12. Laws passed by the legislature are veto-proof or essentially veto-proof; that is, the executive lacks veto power, or has veto power but the veto can be overridden by a majority in the legislature.

Yes. The executive lacks veto power.

Article 91

(1) Laws are promulgated by the President of the Republic no later than eight days after they have been passed.

(2) The National Council may within seven days of the passing of a law and prior to its promulgation require the National Assembly to decide again on such law. In deciding again, a majority of all deputies must vote for such law to be passed unless the Constitution envisages a higher majority for the passing of the law under consideration. Such new decision by the National Assembly is final.

13. The legislature's laws are supreme and not subject to judicial review.

No. The Constitutional Court can review the constitutionality of laws.

Article 153

(1) Laws, regulations and other general legal acts must be in conformity with the Constitution.

(2) Laws must be in conformity with generally accepted principles of international law and with valid treaties ratified by the National Assembly, whereas regulations and other general legal acts must also be in conformity with other ratified treaties.

(3) Regulations and other general legal acts must be in conformity with the Constitution and laws.

(4) Individual acts and actions of state authorities, local community authorities and bearers of public authority must be based on a law or regulation adopted pursuant to law.

Article 160

(1) The Constitutional Court decides:
 – on the conformity of laws with the Constitution.

14. The legislature has the right to initiate bills in all policy jurisdictions; the executive lacks gatekeeping authority.

Yes. The legislature can initiate bills in all policy jurisdictions.

15. Expenditure of funds appropriated by the legislature is mandatory; the executive lacks the power to impound funds appropriated by the legislature.

Yes. The executive lacks the power to impound funds appropriated by the legislature.

16. The legislature controls the resources that finance its own internal operation and provide for the perquisites of its own members.

Yes. The legislature enjoys financial autonomy.

17. Members of the legislature are immune from arrest and/or criminal prosecution.

Yes. Legislators are immune with the common exception for cases of *flagrante delicto*, here expressed as "apprehended committing a criminal offence for which a prison sentence of over five years is prescribed."

> Article 83
> (1) No deputy of the National Assembly shall be criminally liable for any opinion expressed or vote cast at sessions of the National Assembly or its working bodies.
> (2) No deputy may be detained nor, where such deputy claims immunity, may criminal proceedings be initiated against him without the permission of the National Assembly, except where such deputy has been apprehended committing a criminal offence for which a prison sentence of over five years is prescribed.
> (3) The National Assembly may also grant immunity to a deputy who has not claimed such immunity or who has been apprehended committing such criminal offence as referred to in the preceding paragraph.

18. All members of the legislature are elected; the executive lacks the power to appoint any members of the legislature.

Yes. All members of the legislature are elected.

> Article 80
> (1) The National Assembly is composed of deputies of the citizens of Slovenia and comprises ninety deputies.
> (2) Deputies are elected by universal, equal, direct and secret voting.

19. The legislature alone, without the involvement of any other agencies, can change the Constitution.

Yes. The legislature can change the constitution with a two-thirds majority vote.

> Article 168
> (1) A proposal to initiate the procedure for amending the Constitution may be made by twenty deputies of the National Assembly, the Government or at least thirty thousand voters.
> (2) Such proposal is decided upon by the National Assembly by a two-thirds majority vote of deputies present.
>
> Article 169
> The National Assembly adopts acts amending the Constitution by a two-thirds majority vote of all deputies.
>
> Article 170
> (1) The National Assembly must submit a proposed constitutional amendment to voters for adoption in a referendum, if so required by at least thirty deputies.
> (2) A constitutional amendment is adopted in a referendum if a majority of those voting voted in favour of the same, provided that a majority of all voters participated in the referendum.

20. The legislature's approval is necessary for the declaration of war.

Yes. The legislature declares war with the common exception for foreign invasion. If "a great and general danger threatens the existence of the state" at a time when the legislature is unable to meet, the president can declare war and seek retroactive approval.

> Article 92
> (1) A state of emergency shall be declared whenever a great and general danger threatens the existence of the state. The declaration of war or state of emergency, urgent measures and their repeal shall be decided upon by the National Assembly on the proposal of the Government.
> (2) The National Assembly decides on the use of the defence forces.
> (3) In the event that the National Assembly is unable to convene, the President of the Republic shall decide on matters from the first and second paragraphs of this article. Such decisions must be submitted for confirmation to the National Assembly immediately upon it next convening.

21. The legislature's approval is necessary to ratify treaties with foreign countries.

Yes. The legislature's approval is necessary to ratify international treaties.

> Article 86
> The National Assembly adopts laws and other decisions and ratifies treaties by a majority of votes cast by those deputies present, save where a different type of majority is provided by the Constitution or by law.

22. The legislature has the power to grant amnesty.

No. Amnesty and pardon are not treated separately, and the legislature lacks the power to grant amnesty. See item 23.

23. The legislature has the power of pardon.

No. The president has the power of pardon.

> Article 107
> (1) The President of the Republic:
> – decides on the granting of clemency.

24. The legislature reviews and has the right to reject appointments to the judiciary; or the legislature itself appoints members of the judiciary.

Yes. The legislature elects judges on the proposal of the Judicial Council.

Article 130
Judges are elected by the National Assembly on the pro-posal of the Judicial Council.

25. The chairman of the central bank is appointed by the legislature.

Yes. The legislature appoints the governor of the Bank of Slovenia.

Article 152
(2) The governor of the central bank is appointed by the National Assembly.

26. The legislature has a substantial voice in the operation of the state-owned media.

Yes. The legislature appoints members to the board that oversees the operations of the public media.

27. The legislature is regularly in session.

Yes. The legislature regularly meets in ordinary session.

Article 85
(1) The National Assembly meets in regular and extraordinary sessions.
(2) Regular and extraordinary sessions are called by the President of the National Assembly; an extraordinary session must be called if so required by at least a quarter

of the deputies of the National Assembly or by the President of the Republic.

28. Each legislator has a personal secretary.

No.

29. Each legislator has at least one non-secretarial staff member with policy expertise.

No.

30. Legislators are eligible for re-election without any restriction.

Yes. There are no restrictions on re-election.

31. A seat in the legislature is an attractive enough position that legislators are generally interested in and seek re-election.

Yes.

32. The re-election of incumbent legislators is common enough that at any given time the legislature contains a significant number of highly experienced members.

Yes. Re-election rates are sufficiently high to produce a significant number of highly experienced members.

TRANSITIONAL FEDERAL ASSEMBLY OF SOMALIA

Score: .00

Influence over executive (0/9)	Institutional autonomy (0/9)	Specified powers (0/8)	Institutional capacity (0/8)
1. replace	10. no dissolution	19. amendments	27. sessions
2. serve as ministers	11. no decree	20. war	28. secretary
3. interpellate	12. no veto	21. treaties	29. staff
4. investigate	13. no review	22. amnesty	30. no term limits
5. oversee police	14. no gatekeeping	23. pardon	31. seek re-election
6. appoint PM	15. no impoundment	24. judiciary	32. experience
7. appoint ministers	16. control resources	25. central bank	
8. lack president	17. immunity	26. media	
9. no confidence	18. all elected		

The Transitional Federal Assembly (TFA) of Somalia traces its origins to the legislature that was established upon independence in 1960. Somalia was ruled by Siad Barre from 1969 until his ouster in 1991, after which the country descended into the anarchy that prevails to this day.

The TFA was established in August 2004 as part of a new transitional government. The conference establishing the legislature was held in neighboring Kenya. The members of the new legislature elected a transitional president, who then appointed a prime minister and a transitional federal government. In June 2005 some members of the legislature moved back to Somalia. An insurgency, the Union of Islamic Courts, subsequently forced the government from the capital, Mogadishu. Ethiopian troops then intervened and pushed the Union of Islamic Courts out of Mogadishu.

The legislature exerts no meaningful power in an anarchic Somalia. In early 2007 a legislative session convened and voted to declare martial law, giving the government the power to rule by decree. The session was not held in the capital, but in the town of Baidoa. Only about one-third of the members of the legislature attended; the rest were in Mogadishu, Kenya, or scattered throughout other locations. The legislature does not have a parliament building in the capital.

PARLIAMENT OF SOUTH AFRICA

Expert consultants: Thomas A. Koelble, Nancy Msibi, Robert M. Price, Robert I. Rotberg, Ros Sagnelli, Robert Schrire

Score: .63

Influence over executive (7/9)		Institutional autonomy (6/9)		Specified powers (3/8)		Institutional capacity (4/6)	
1. replace	X	10. no dissolution		19. amendments	X	27. sessions	X
2. serve as ministers	X	11. no decree	X	20. war		28. secretary	
3. interpellate	X	12. no veto	X	21. treaties	X	29. staff	
4. investigate	X	13. no review		22. amnesty		30. no term limits	X
5. oversee police	X	14. no gatekeeping	X	23. pardon		31. seek re-election	X
6. appoint PM		15. no impoundment	X	24. judiciary		32. experience	X
7. appoint ministers		16. control resources	X	25. central bank			
8. lack president	X	17. immunity		26. media	X		
9. no confidence	X	18. all elected	X				

The Parliament of South Africa traces its origins to the 1910 constitution that established a self-governing Union of South Africa within the British Empire. In 1961 a new constitution declared an independent state. Under the subsequent post-independence apartheid rule, only white South Africans were able to occupy legislative seats; separate representative bodies were established for other racial groups. The apartheid system came to an end in 1994, and South Africa adopted a new constitution in 1996. The document called for a bicameral parliament consisting of a lower house, the National Assembly, and an upper house, the National Council of Provinces, which comprises representatives drawn from each of the nine provincial legislatures.

The legislature has considerable powers, including extensive control over the executive. Among other powers, the legislature elects the president, can interpellate and investigate officials from the executive, and can remove the president from office. It merits note that the South African president, despite the name of the office, plays the role typically associated with that of a prime minister. The South African president is elected by and presides over the legislature and heads the government in the manner of a prime minister. The legislature also enjoys broad institutional autonomy that is limited only by the threat of dissolution, judicial review, and a lack of immunity for legislators. The legislature exercises relatively few of the specified powers and prerogatives measured in this survey. Its institutional capacity is limited by lack of staff.

SURVEY

1. The legislature alone, without the involvement of any other agencies, can impeach the president or replace the prime minister.

Yes. The legislature can remove the president with a vote of no confidence, or by a two-thirds majority vote of its total membership, it can remove the president from office for violations of the constitution, misconduct, or inability to perform the functions of office.

Section 89
(1) The National Assembly, by a resolution adopted with a supporting vote of at least two thirds of its members, may remove the President from office only on the grounds of –
(a) a serious violation of the Constitution or the law;
(b) serious misconduct; or
(c) inability to perform the functions of office.
(2) Anyone who has been removed from the office of President in terms of subsection (1) (a) or (b) may not receive any benefits of that office, and may not serve in any public office.

Section 102
(1) If the National Assembly, by a vote supported by a majority of its members, passes a motion of no confidence in the Cabinet excluding the President, the President must reconstitute the Cabinet.
(2) If the National Assembly, by a vote supported by a majority of its members, passes a motion of no confidence in the President, the President and the other members of the Cabinet and any Deputy Ministers must resign.

2. Ministers may serve simultaneously as members of the legislature.

Yes. Ministers are generally selected from, and may serve simultaneously in, the legislature.

Section 91
(2) The President appoints the Deputy President and Ministers, assigns their powers and functions, and may dismiss them.
(3) The President –
(a) must select the Deputy President from among the members of the National Assembly;
(b) may select any number of Ministers from among the members of the Assembly; and
(c) may select no more than two Ministers from outside the Assembly.

3. The legislature has powers of summons over executive branch officials and hearings with executive branch officials testifying before the legislature or its committees are regularly held.

Yes. The legislature regularly summons executive branch officials.

Section 56
The National Assembly or any of its committees may –
(a) summon any person to appear before it to give evidence on oath or affirmation, or to produce documents;
(b) require any person or institution to report to it;
(c) compel, in terms of national legislation or the rules and orders, any person or institution to comply with a summons or requirement in terms of paragraph (a) or (b); and
(d) receive petitions, representations or submissions from any interested persons or institutions.

4. The legislature can conduct independent investigation of the chief executive and the agencies of the executive.

Yes. The legislature can investigate the executive.

5. The legislature has effective powers of oversight over the agencies of coercion (the military, organs of law enforcement, intelligence services, and the secret police).

Yes. The legislature has effective powers of oversight over the agencies of coercion.

6. The legislature appoints the prime minister.

No. There is no prime minister.

7. The legislature's approval is required to confirm the appointment of ministers; or the legislature itself appoints ministers.

No. The president appoints ministers, and the appointments do not require the legislature's approval.

Section 91
(2) The President appoints the Deputy President and Ministers, assigns their powers and functions, and may dismiss them.

8. The country lacks a presidency entirely or there is a presidency, but the president is elected by the legislature.

Yes. The National Assembly elects the president, who is chosen from among members of the Assembly.

Section 86
(1) At its first sitting after its election, and whenever necessary to fill a vacancy, the National Assembly must elect a woman or a man from among its members to be the President.

9. The legislature can vote no confidence in the government.

Yes. The legislature can vote no confidence in the government.

Section 102

(1) If the National Assembly, by a vote supported by a majority of its members, passes a motion of no confidence in the Cabinet excluding the President, the President must reconstitute the Cabinet.

(2) If the National Assembly, by a vote supported by a majority of its members, passes a motion of no confidence in the President, the President and the other members of the Cabinet and any Deputy Ministers must resign.

10. The legislature is immune from dissolution by the executive.

No. The president can dissolve the legislature.

Section 50

(1) The President must dissolve the National Assembly if –

(a) the Assembly has adopted a resolution to dissolve with a supporting vote of a majority of its members; and

(b) three years have passed since the Assembly was elected.

(2) The Acting President must dissolve the National Assembly if –

(a) there is a vacancy in the office of President; and

(b) the Assembly fails to elect a new President within 30 days after the vacancy occurred.

11. Any executive initiative on legislation requires ratification or approval by the legislature before it takes effect; that is, the executive lacks decree power.

Yes. The executive lacks decree power.

12. Laws passed by the legislature are veto-proof or essentially veto-proof; that is, the executive lacks veto power, or has veto power but the veto can be overridden by a majority in the legislature.

Yes. The legislature can override a presidential veto by a majority vote of its present members.

Section 79

(1) The President must either assent to and sign a Bill passed in terms of this Chapter or, if the President has reservations about the constitutionality of the Bill, refer it back to the National Assembly for reconsideration.

(2) The joint rules and orders must provide for the procedure for the reconsideration of a Bill by the National Assembly and the participation of the National Council of Provinces in the process.

(3) The National Council of Provinces must participate in the reconsideration of a Bill that the President has referred back to the National Assembly if –

(a) the President's reservations about the constitutionality of the Bill relate to a procedural matter that involves the Council; or

(b) section 74(1), (2) or (3)(b) or 76 was applicable in the passing of the Bill.

(4) If, after reconsideration, a Bill fully accommodates the President's reservations, the President must assent to and sign the Bill; if not, the President must either –

(a) assent to and sign the Bill; or

(b) refer it to the Constitutional Court for a decision on its constitutionality.

(5) If the Constitutional Court decides that the Bill is constitutional, the President must assent to and sign it.

13. The legislature's laws are supreme and not subject to judicial review.

No. The Constitutional Court can review the constitutionality of laws.

Section 80

(1) Members of the National Assembly may apply to the Constitutional Court for an order declaring that all or part of an Act of Parliament is unconstitutional.

(2) An application –

(a) must be supported by at least one third of the members of the Assembly; and

(b) must be made within 30 days of the date on which the President assented to and signed the Act.

(3) The Constitutional Court may order that all or part of an Act that is the subject of an application in terms of subsection (1) has no force until the Court has decided the application if –

(a) the interests of justice require this; and

(b) the application has a reasonable prospect of success.

(4) If an application is unsuccessful, and did not have a reasonable prospect of success, the Constitutional Court may order the applicants to pay costs.

Section 84

(1) The President has the powers entrusted by the Constitution and legislation, including those necessary to perform the functions of Head of State and head of the national executive.

(2) The President is responsible for –

(b) referring a Bill back to the National Assembly for reconsideration of the Bill's constitutionality;

(c) referring a Bill to the Constitutional Court for a decision on the Bill's constitutionality.

Section 172

(1) When deciding a constitutional matter within its power, a court –

(a) must declare that any law or conduct that is inconsistent with the Constitution is invalid to the extent of its inconsistency; and

(b) may make any order that is just and equitable, including –

(i) an order limiting the retrospective effect of the declaration of invalidity; and

(ii) an order suspending the declaration of invalidity for any period and on any conditions, to allow the competent authority to correct the defect.

(2) (a) The Supreme Court of Appeal, a High Court or a court of similar status may make an order concerning the constitutional validity of an Act of Parliament, a provincial Act or any conduct of the President, but an

order of constitutional invalidity has no force unless it is confirmed by the Constitutional Court.

14. The legislature has the right to initiate bills in all policy jurisdictions; the executive lacks gatekeeping authority.

Yes. The legislature can initiate bills in all policy jurisdictions.

15. Expenditure of funds appropriated by the legislature is mandatory; the executive lacks the power to impound funds appropriated by the legislature.

Yes. The executive lacks the power to impound funds appropriated by the legislature.

16. The legislature controls the resources that finance its own internal operation and provide for the perquisites of its own members.

Yes. The legislature enjoys financial autonomy, including control over members' perquisites.

> Section 58
> (3) Salaries, allowances and benefits payable to members of the National Assembly are a direct charge against the National Revenue Fund.

17. Members of the legislature are immune from arrest and/or criminal prosecution.

No. Legislative immunity extends to official parliamentary business only. Legislators are subject to arrest for common crimes.

> Section 58
> (1) Cabinet members and members of the National Assembly –
> (a) have freedom of speech in the Assembly and in its committees, subject to its rules and orders; and
> (b) are not liable to civil or criminal proceedings, arrest, imprisonment or damages for –
> (i) anything that they have said in, produced before or submitted to the Assembly or any of its committees; or
> (ii) anything revealed as a result of anything that they have said in, produced before or submitted to the Assembly or any of its committees.
> (2) Other privileges and immunities of the National Assembly, Cabinet members and members of the Assembly may be prescribed by national legislation.

18. All members of the legislature are elected; the executive lacks the power to appoint any members of the legislature.

Yes. All members of the National Assembly are elected. Sixty percent of the National Council of Provinces is elected, with the remainder appointed by provincial legislatures. The National Council of Provinces is, for the most part, a ceremonial body.

Section 46
(1) The National Assembly consists of no fewer than 350 and no more than 400 women and men elected as members in terms of an electoral system that –
(a) is prescribed by national legislation;
(b) is based on the national common voters roll;
(c) provides for a minimum voting age of 18 years; and
(d) results, in general, in proportional representation.
(2) An Act of Parliament must provide a formula for determining the number of members of the National Assembly.

19. The legislature alone, without the involvement of any other agencies, can change the Constitution.

Yes. The legislature can change the constitution with a three-fourths majority vote in the National Assembly and with the approval of at least six of the provinces represented in the National Council.

> Section 74
> (1) Section 1 and this subsection may be amended by a Bill passed
> by –
> (a) the National Assembly, with a supporting vote of at least 75 per cent of its members; and
> (b) the National Council of Provinces, with a supporting vote of at least six provinces.
> (2) Chapter 2 may be amended by a Bill passed by –
> (a) the National Assembly, with a supporting vote of at least two thirds of its members; and
> (b) the National Council of Provinces, with a supporting vote of at least six provinces.
> (3) Any other provision of the Constitution may be amended by a Bill passed –
> (a) by the National Assembly, with a supporting vote of at least two thirds of its members; and
> (b) also by the National Council of Provinces, with a supporting vote of at least six provinces, if the amendment –
> (i) relates to a matter that affects the Council;
> (ii) alters provincial boundaries, powers, functions or institutions; or
> (iii) amends a provision that deals specifically with a provincial matter.
> (9) A Bill amending the Constitution that has been passed by the National Assembly and, where applicable, by the National Council of Provinces, must be referred to the President for assent.

20. The legislature's approval is necessary for the declaration of war.

No. The president can declare war without the legislature's approval. The declaration of war lapses if it is not subsequently approved by the legislature within seven days.

Section 203

(1) The President as head of the national executive may declare a state of national defence, and must inform Parliament promptly and in appropriate detail of –

(a) the reasons for the declaration;

(b) any place where the defence force is being employed; and

(c) the number of people involved.

(2) If Parliament is not sitting when a state of national defence is declared, the President must summon Parliament to an extraordinary sitting within seven days of the declaration.

(3) A declaration of a state of national defence lapses unless it is approved by Parliament within seven days of the declaration.

21. The legislature's approval is necessary to ratify treaties with foreign countries.

Yes. The legislature's approval is necessary to ratify international treaties on most major issues.

Section 231

(1) The negotiating and signing of all international agreements is the responsibility of the national executive.

(2) An international agreement binds the Republic only after it has been approved by resolution in both the National Assembly and the National Council of Provinces, unless it is an agreement referred to in subsection (3).

(3) An international agreement of a technical, administrative or executive nature, or an agreement which does not require either ratification or accession, entered into by the national executive, binds the Republic without approval by the National Assembly and the National Council of Provinces, but must be tabled in the Assembly and the Council within a reasonable time.

(4) Any international agreement becomes law in the Republic when it is enacted into law by national legislation; but a self-executing provision of an agreement that has been approved by Parliament is law in the Republic unless it is inconsistent with the Constitution or an Act of Parliament.

(5) The Republic is bound by international agreements which were binding on the Republic when this Constitution took effect.

22. The legislature has the power to grant amnesty.

No. Amnesty and pardon are not treated separately, and the legislature lacks the power to grant amnesty. See item 23.

23. The legislature has the power of pardon.

No. The president has the power of pardon.

Section 84

(2) The President is responsible for –

(j) pardoning or reprieving offenders and remitting any fines, penalties or forfeitures.

24. The legislature reviews and has the right to reject appointments to the judiciary; or the legislature itself appoints members of the judiciary.

No. The president's judicial nominations do not require the legislature's approval, although for some appointments to high positions on the bench the president is obliged to consult with "the leaders of parties represented in the National Assembly."

Section 174

(3) The President as head of the national executive, after consulting the Judicial Service Commission and the leaders of parties represented in the National Assembly, appoints the President and Deputy President of the Constitutional Court and, after consulting the Judicial Service Commission, appoints the Chief Justice and Deputy Chief Justice.

(4) The other judges of the Constitutional Court are appointed by the President as head of the national executive, after consulting the President of the Constitutional Court and the leaders of parties represented in the National Assembly, in accordance with the following procedure:

(a) The Judicial Service Commission must prepare a list of nominees with three names more than the number of appointments to be made, and submit the list to the President.

(b) The President may make appointments from the list, and must advise the Judicial Service Commission, with reasons, if any of the nominees are unacceptable and any appointment remains to be made.

(c) The Judicial Service Commission must supplement the list with further nominees and the President must make the remaining appointments from the supplemented list.

(5) At all times, at least four members of the Constitutional Court must be persons who were judges at the time they were appointed to the Constitutional Court.

(6) The President must appoint the judges of all other courts on the advice of the Judicial Service Commission.

(7) Other judicial officers must be appointed in terms of an Act of Parliament which must ensure that the appointment, promotion, transfer or dismissal of, or disciplinary steps against, these judicial officers take place without favour or prejudice.

(8) Before judicial officers begin to perform their functions, they must take an oath or affirm, in accordance with Schedule 2, that they will uphold and protect the Constitution.

25. The chairman of the central bank is appointed by the legislature.

No. The president appoints the governor of the South African Reserve Bank.

26. The legislature has a substantial voice in the operation of the state-owned media.

Yes. The legislature has influence over the board that regulates public broadcasting.

Section 192
National legislation must establish an independent authority to regulate broadcasting in the public interest, and to ensure fairness and a diversity of views broadly representing South African society.

27. The legislature is regularly in session.

Yes. The legislature regularly meets in ordinary session.

Section 51
(1) After an election, the first sitting of the National Assembly must take place at a time and on a date determined by the President of the Constitutional Court, but not more than 14 days after the election result has been declared. The National Assembly may determine the time and duration of its other sittings and its recess periods.

28. Each legislator has a personal secretary.

No.

29. Each legislator has at least one non-secretarial staff member with policy expertise.

No.

30. Legislators are eligible for re-election without any restriction.

Yes. There are no restrictions on re-election.

31. A seat in the legislature is an attractive enough position that legislators are generally interested in and seek re-election.

Yes.

32. The re-election of incumbent legislators is common enough that at any given time the legislature contains a significant number of highly experienced members.

Yes. Re-election rates are sufficiently high to produce a significant number of highly experienced members. The dominance of a single party, the African National Congress (ANC), has contributed to high rates of re-election and stability of membership. In the 1994 election for the National Assembly, the ANC captured 252 of 400 seats. The ANC subsequently won 266 seats in 1999 and 279 seats in 2004.

THE GENERAL COURTS OF SPAIN (*LAS CORTES GENERALES*)

Expert consultants: Carles Campuzano, Blanca Martin Delgado, Oscar Luengo, Jaime Rodríguez-Arana, Sebastián Royo

Score: .72

Influence over executive (8/9)		Institutional autonomy (6/9)		Specified powers (5/8)		Institutional capacity (4/6)	
1. replace	X	10. no dissolution		19. amendments	X	27. sessions	X
2. serve as ministers	X	11. no decree	X	20. war	X	28. secretary	
3. interpellate	X	12. no veto	X	21. treaties	X	29. staff	
4. investigate	X	13. no review		22. amnesty		30. no term limits	X
5. oversee police	X	14. no gatekeeping	X	23. pardon		31. seek re-election	X
6. appoint PM	X	15. no impoundment		24. judiciary	X	32. experience	X
7. appoint ministers		16. control resources	X	25. central bank			
8. lack president	X	17. immunity	X	26. media	X		
9. no confidence	X	18. all elected	X				

The General Courts (*Las Cortes Generales*) of Spain came into being during first decade of the nineteenth century. For much of its history, however, the General Courts, or parliament, was sidelined by dominant executives: a constitutional monarch in the nineteenth century and Francisco Franco's military-backed dictatorship in the twentieth century. After Franco's death in 1975, Spain drew up a new constitution, which came into effect in 1978. The document established a bicameral legislature consisting of a directly elected lower house, the Congress of Deputies (*Congreso de los Diputados*), and an upper house, the Senate (*Senado*). The constitutional excerpts cited below translate *Congreso de los Diputados* as House of Representatives.

The king retains considerable moral authority in Spain's constitutional monarchy, but the legislature is the center of national politics and government. It enjoys many controls over the executive. Its institutional autonomy is protected by the absence of executive decree, veto, and gatekeeping powers. The legislature has a number of specified powers, including the authority to change the constitution. It has some institutional capacity.

SURVEY

1. The legislature alone, without the involvement of any other agencies, can impeach the president or replace the prime minister.

Yes. The legislature can remove the prime minister (referred to as the "president of the government") with a vote of no confidence.

Article 101
(1) The Government shall resign after the holding of general elections in the cases of the loss of confidence by parliament as stipulated in the Constitution, or because of the resignation or death of its President.
(2) But the outgoing Government shall continue in its functions until the new Government takes office.

Article 113
(1) The House of Representatives may require political responsibility from the Government by means of the adoption by an absolute majority of a motion of censure.
(2) The motion of censure must be proposed by at least one-tenth of the Deputies and must include a candidate to the office of the Presidency of the Government.
(3) The motion of censure cannot be voted on until five days after its presentation. During the first two days of this period, alternative motions may be presented.
(4) If the motion of censure is not approved by the House of Representatives, its signers cannot present another during the same period of sessions.

Article 114
(1) If the House of Representatives denies its confidence to the Government, it must present its resignation to the King, the President of the Government then to be designated pursuant to the provisions of Article 99.
(2) If the House of Representatives adopts a motion of censure, the Government shall present its resignation to the King and the candidate included in it shall be understood to have the confidence of the Chamber for the purposes specified in Article 92. The King shall appoint him President of the Government.

2. Ministers may serve simultaneously as members of the legislature.

Yes. Ministers may serve simultaneously in the legislature.

Article 98
(3) The members of the Government may not exercise representative functions other than those of the parliamentary mandate itself, nor any other public function which does not derive from their office, nor any professional or mercantile activity whatsoever.
(4) A law shall regulate the Statute and the incompatibilities of the members of the Government.

3. The legislature has powers of summons over executive branch officials and hearings with executive branch officials testifying before the legislature or its committees are regularly held.

Yes. The legislature regularly interpellates officials from the executive.

Article 111
(1) The Government and each of its members are subject to interpellations or questions put to them in the Chambers. The rules shall establish a weekly minimum time for this type of debate.
(2) Any interpellation may lead to a motion in which the Chamber can express its position.

4. The legislature can conduct independent investigation of the chief executive and the agencies of the executive.

Yes. The legislature can establish commissions to investigate the executive.

Article 76
(1) The House of Representatives and the Senate, and if necessary both Chambers jointly, may appoint investigating Commissions on any subject of public interest. Their conclusions shall not be binding on the courts nor will they affect judicial decisions, but they may be transmitted to the Public Prosecutor for the exercise of the necessary actions when required.
(2) Appearance before the Chambers on request shall be obligatory. The law shall regulate the sanctions which may be imposed for noncompliance with this obligation.

5. The legislature has effective powers of oversight over the agencies of coercion (the military, organs of law enforcement, intelligence services, and the secret police).

Yes. The legislature has effective powers of oversight over the agencies of coercion.

6. The legislature appoints the prime minister.

Yes. The king appoints as prime minister (president of the government) the candidate who enjoys majority support in the legislature.

Article 99

(1) After each renewal of the House of Representatives and in the other cases provided for by the Constitution, the King shall, after consultation with the representatives designated by the political groups represented in parliament, and through the President of the House of Representatives, propose a candidate for the Presidency of the Government.

(2) The proposed candidate, in conformity with the provisions of the foregoing paragraph, shall submit to the House of Representatives the political program of the Government he intends to form and shall seek the confidence of the Chamber.

(3) If the House of Representatives, by an absolute majority of its members, grants its confidence to said candidate, the King will appoint him President. If said majority is not obtained, the same proposal shall be submitted to a new vote 98 hours after the former, and confidence shall be understood to have been granted if a simple majority is obtained.

(4) If after the aforementioned votes are cast, confidence is not granted for investiture, successive proposals will be made in the manner foreseen in the foregoing paragraphs.

(5) If within two months from the first voting for investiture no candidate has obtained the confidence of the House of Representatives, the King shall dissolve both Chambers and call for new elections with the concurrence of the President of the House of Representatives.

7. The legislature's approval is required to confirm the appointment of ministers; or the legislature itself appoints ministers.

No. The king appoints ministers on the recommendation of the prime minister (president of the government), and the appointments do not require the legislature's approval.

Article 100

The other members of the Government shall be appointed and dismissed by the King at the proposal of its President.

8. The country lacks a presidency entirely or there is a presidency, but the president is elected by the legislature.

Yes. The country lacks a presidency. The king is the head of state.

Article 56

(1) The King is the Head of State, the symbol of its unity and permanence. He arbitrates and moderates the regular functioning of the institutions, assumes the highest representation of the Spanish State in international relations, especially with the nations of its historical community, and exercises the functions expressly attributed to him by the Constitution and the laws.

9. The legislature can vote no confidence in the government.

Yes. The legislature can pass a constructive vote of no confidence in the government, meaning that the legislature must designate a successor prime minister (president of the government) before passing a vote of no confidence.

Article 101

(1) The Government shall resign after the holding of general elections in the cases of the loss of confidence by parliament as stipulated in the Constitution, or because of the resignation or death of its President.

(2) But the outgoing Government shall continue in its functions until the new Government takes office.

Article 113

(1) The House of Representatives may require political responsibility from the Government by means of the adoption by an absolute majority of a motion of censure.

(2) The motion of censure must be proposed by at least one-tenth of the Deputies and must include a candidate to the office of the Presidency of the Government.

(3) The motion of censure cannot be voted on until five days after its presentation. During the first two days of this period, alternative motions may be presented.

(4) If the motion of censure is not approved by the House of Representatives, its signers cannot present another during the same period of sessions.

Article 114

(1) If the House of Representatives denies its confidence to the Government, it must present its resignation to the King, the President of the Government then to be designated pursuant to the provisions of Article 99.

(2) If the House of Representatives adopts a motion of censure, the Government shall present its resignation to the King and the candidate included in it shall be understood to have the confidence of the Chamber for the purposes specified in Article 92. The King shall appoint him President of the Government.

10. The legislature is immune from dissolution by the executive.

No. The king can dissolve the legislature on the proposal of the prime minister (president of the government).

Article 99

(5) If within two months from the first voting for investiture no candidate has obtained the confidence of the House of Representatives, the King shall dissolve both Chambers and call for new elections with the concurrence of the President of the House of Representatives.

Article 115

(1) The President of the Government, after deliberation of the Council of Ministers, and on his exclusive responsibility, may propose the dissolution of the House of Representatives, the Senate, and the Parliament, which shall be decreed by the King. The dissolution decree shall establish the date of the elections.

(2) The proposal for dissolution may not be presented when a motion of censure is in process.

(3) No new dissolution may take place before a year has passed since the previous one, except as provided for in Article 99 (5).

11. Any executive initiative on legislation requires ratification or approval by the legislature before it takes effect; that is, the executive lacks decree power.

Yes. The executive lacks decree power in normal political circumstances. In cases of "extraordinary and urgent necessity," however, the government can issue decrees that have the force of law. The laws subsequently lapse if they are not explicitly approved by the legislature.

Article 86
(1) In the case of extraordinary and urgent necessity, the Government may issue provisional legislative decisions which shall take the form of decree-laws and which may not affect the regulation of the basic institution of the State, the rights, duties, and liberties of the citizens which are regulated in Title I, the systems of Autonomous Communities, or the general electoral Law.
(2) The Decree-laws must be immediately submitted for debate and voting by the entire House of Representatives of Deputies convoked for that purpose, if it is not already in session, within a period of thirty days after their promulgation. The House of Representatives must expressly declare within that period its approval or repeal, for which purpose the Regulation shall establish a special and summary procedure.
(3) During the period established in the foregoing paragraph, the Parliament may treat them as draft laws by emergency procedure.

12. Laws passed by the legislature are veto-proof or essentially veto-proof; that is, the executive lacks veto power, or has veto power but the veto can be overridden by a majority in the legislature.

Yes. The executive lacks veto power.

13. The legislature's laws are supreme and not subject to judicial review.

No. The Constitutional Court can review the constitutionality of laws.

Article 161
(1) The Constitutional Court has jurisdiction over the whole of Spanish territory and is competent to hear:
  a) appeals on the grounds of unconstitutionality against laws and regulations having the force of law; a declaration of unconstitutionality of a legal rule with the status of law, interpreted by jurisprudence, shall also affect the latter, although an overturned sentence or sentences shall not lose the validity of a judgment.

Article 163
If a judicial organ considers, in some action, that a regulation with the status of law which is applicable thereto and upon the validity of which the judgment depends, may be contrary to the Constitution, it may bring the matter before the Constitutional Court in the cases, manner, and with the consequences which the law establishes, which in no case shall be suspensive.

14. The legislature has the right to initiate bills in all policy jurisdictions; the executive lacks gatekeeping authority.

Yes. The legislature can initiate bills in all policy jurisdictions.

15. Expenditure of funds appropriated by the legislature is mandatory; the executive lacks the power to impound funds appropriated by the legislature.

No. The executive can impound funds. The legislature's budgetary allocations authorize, but do not require, the expenditure of funds.

16. The legislature controls the resources that finance its own internal operation and provide for the perquisites of its own members.

Yes. The legislature enjoys financial autonomy.

Article 71
(4) The Deputies and Senators shall receive a remuneration which shall be fixed by the respective Chamber.

Article 72
(1) The Chambers establish their own regulations, autonomously approve their own budgets, and by common accord regulate the Personnel Statute of the Parliament. The Regulations and their reform shall be submitted to a final voting in their entirety which shall require an absolute majority.

17. Members of the legislature are immune from arrest and/or criminal prosecution.

Yes. Legislators enjoy immunity with the common exception for cases of *flagrante delicto*.

Article 71
(1) The Deputies and Senators enjoy indemnity for the opinions expressed during the exercise of their functions.
(2) During the period of their mandate, the Deputies and Senators enjoy immunity and may only be arrested in case of flagrante delicto. They may not be indicted or tried without prior authorization of the respective Chamber.
(3) In actions against Deputies and Senators, the Criminal Section of the Supreme Court shall be competent.

18. All members of the legislature are elected; the executive lacks the power to appoint any members of the legislature.

Yes. All members of the legislature are elected.

Article 68

(1) The House of Representatives is composed of a minimum of 300 and a maximum of 400 Deputies elected by universal, free, equal, direct, and secret suffrage under the terms established by law.

Article 69

(1) The Senate is the chamber of territorial representation.

(2) In each province, four senators will be elected by universal, free, equal, direct, and secret suffrage by the voters of each of them under the terms established by an organic law.

(3) In the island provinces, each island or grouping of them with a representation or insular council shall be a voting district for the purposes of the election of senators, three of them going to each of the major islands – Grand Canary, Mallorca, and Tenerife – and one each to the following islands or groupings: Ibiza-Formentera, Menorca, Fuerteventura, Gomera, Hierro, Lanzarote, and La Palma.

(4) The cities of Ceuta and Melilla shall elect two senators each.

(5) The Autonomous Communities shall also designate one senator and one additional senator for each million inhabitants in their respective territories. The designation shall be made by the legislative assembly, or in its absence, by the higher collective body of the Autonomous Community pursuant to the provisions of the Statutes, which in any case, shall insure adequate proportional representation.

19. The legislature alone, without the involvement of any other agencies, can change the Constitution.

Yes. The legislature can change the constitution with a three-fifths majority vote in each chamber or by an absolute majority vote in the Senate and a two-thirds majority vote in the Congress of Deputies.

Article 167

(1) Bills on Constitutional amendment must be approved by a majority of three-fifths of the members of each Chamber. If there is no agreement between the Chambers, an effort to reach it shall be made by setting up a Joint Commission of Deputies and Senators which shall submit a text to be voted on by the House of Representatives and the Senate.

(2) If adoption is not obtained by means of the procedure outlined in the foregoing paragraph, and provided that the text has obtained a favorable vote by an absolute majority of the Senate, the House of Representatives may approve the amendment by a two-thirds vote.

(3) Once the amendment has been passed by the Parliament, it shall be submitted to a referendum for its ratification, if so requested by one tenth of the members of either Chamber within fifteen days after its passage.

20. The legislature's approval is necessary for the declaration of war.

Yes. The legislature's approval is required for the king to declare war.

Article 63

(3) It is incumbent on the King, after authorization by the Parliament, to declare war and make peace.

21. The legislature's approval is necessary to ratify treaties with foreign countries.

Yes. The legislature's approval is necessary to ratify international treaties on most major issues.

Article 63

(2) It is incumbent on the King to express the consent of the State to obligate itself internationally through treaties in conformity with the Constitution and the laws.

Article 93

By means of an organic law, authorization may be established for the conclusion of treaties which attribute to an international organization or institution the exercise of competences derived from the Constitution. It is the responsibility of the Parliament or the Government, depending on the cases, to guarantee compliance with these treaties and the resolutions emanating from the international or supranational organizations who have been entitled by this cession.

Article 94

(1) The giving of the consent of the State to obligate itself to something by means of treaties or agreements shall require prior authorization of the Parliament in the following cases:

a) Treaties of a political nature;

b) Treaties or agreements of a military nature;

c) Treaties or agreements which affect the territorial integrity of the State or the fundamental rights and duties established in Title I;

d) Treaties or agreements which imply important obligations for the public treasury;

e) Treaties or agreements which involve modification or repeal of some law or require legislative measures for their execution.

(2) The House of Representatives and the Senate shall be immediately informed of the conclusion of the treaties or agreements.

Article 95

(1) The conclusion of an international treaty which contains stipulations contrary to the Constitution shall require a prior constitutional revision.

(2) The Government or either of the Chambers may request the Constitutional Court to declare whether or not such a contradiction exists.

22. The legislature has the power to grant amnesty.

No. Amnesty and pardon are not treated separately, and the legislature lacks the power to grant amnesty. See item 23.

23. The legislature has the power of pardon.

No. The king has the power of pardon.

Article 62
It is incumbent upon the King:
i) to exercise the right of clemency pursuant to a law, which cannot authorize general pardons.

24. The legislature reviews and has the right to reject appointments to the judiciary; or the legislature itself appoints members of the judiciary.

Yes. The legislature nominates eight of the twelve members of the Constitutional Court. The king's subsequent appointment of these nominations is a mere formality.

Article 123
(2) The President of the Supreme Court shall be appointed by the King at the proposal of the General Council of the judicial branch in the manner determined by law.

Article 159
(1) The Constitutional Court is composed of twelve members appointed by the King. Of these, four shall be nominated by the House of Representatives by a majority of three-fifths of its members, four shall be nominated by the Senate with the same majority; two shall be nominated by the Government, and two by the General Council of the Judiciary.

25. The chairman of the central bank is appointed by the legislature.

No. The king, on the recommendation of the prime minister, appoints the governor of the Bank of Spain.

26. The legislature has a substantial voice in the operation of the state-owned media.

Yes. The legislature appoints the members of the board that oversees public media.

27. The legislature is regularly in session.

Yes. The legislature meets in ordinary session for about seven months each year.

Article 73
(1) The Chambers shall meet annually in two ordinary periods of sessions, the first from September to December and the second from February to June.
(2) The Chambers may meet in extraordinary periods of sessions at the request of the Government, the Permanent Deputation, or by the absolute majority of the members of either of the two Chambers. The extraordinary periods of sessions must be convoked with a specific agenda and shall be closed once it has been dealt with.

28. Each legislator has a personal secretary.

No.

29. Each legislator has at least one non-secretarial staff member with policy expertise.

No.

30. Legislators are eligible for re-election without any restriction.

Yes. There are no restrictions on re-election.

31. A seat in the legislature is an attractive enough position that legislators are generally interested in and seek re-election.

Yes.

32. The re-election of incumbent legislators is common enough that at any given time the legislature contains a significant number of highly experienced members.

Yes. Re-election rates are sufficiently high to produce a significant number of highly experienced members.

PARLIAMENT OF SRI LANKA

Expert consultants: Sunanda Deshapriya, Basil Ilangakoon, Jehan Perera, Jayadeva Uyangoda, Hasitha Wickremasinghe

Score: .50

Influence over executive (4/9)		Institutional autonomy (5/9)		Specified powers (2/8)		Institutional capacity (5/6)	
1. replace		10. no dissolution		19. amendments	X	27. sessions	X
2. serve as ministers	X	11. no decree		20. war		28. secretary	X
3. interpellate	X	12. no veto	X	21. treaties	X	29. staff	
4. investigate	X	13. no review	X	22. amnesty		30. no term limits	X
5. oversee police		14. no gatekeeping		23. pardon		31. seek re-election	X
6. appoint PM		15. no impoundment	X	24. judiciary		32. experience	X
7. appoint ministers		16. control resources	X	25. central bank			
8. lack president		17. immunity		26. media			
9. no confidence	X	18. all elected	X				

The Parliament of Sri Lanka was established in the 1948 constitution upon independence from Great Britain. The constitution called for a bicameral legislature and a Westminster-style government headed by the prime minister. A new constitution in 1972 changed the country's name from Ceylon to Sri Lanka, established a unicameral legislature, and replaced the Governor General, the British monarch's local representative, with a ceremonial president as head of state. In political practice the president gathered substantial power, and this tendency was formalized in 1978 in a new constitution, which established a directly elected president.

The legislature has a moderate amount of power. It has some sway over the executive, but its institutional autonomy is limited by executive prerogatives. For example, executive gatekeeping authority prohibits the legislature from initiating legislation related to taxation or public expenditures. Yet the legislature's laws provide the final word; although the Supreme Court can review legislation that is under consideration in parliament, once a bill is enacted it is not subject to judicial review. The legislature's specified powers do not extend beyond the authority to change the constitution and to ratify international treaties. The legislature does enjoy a considerable amount of institutional capacity.

SURVEY

1. The legislature alone, without the involvement of any other agencies, can impeach the president or replace the prime minister.

No. Presidential impeachment requires the involvement of the Supreme Court. The legislature can remove the prime minister with a vote of no confidence.

Article 38
(2) (a) Any Member of Parliament may, by a writing addressed to the Speaker, give notice of a resolution alleging that the President is permanently incapable of discharging the functions of his office by reason of mental or physical infirmity or that the President has been guilty of –
  (i) intentional violation of the Constitution,
  (ii) treason,
  (iii) bribery,
  (iv) misconduct or corruption involving the abuse of the powers of his office, or
  (v) any offense under any law, involving moral turpitude, and setting out full particulars of the allegation or allegations made and seeking an inquiry and report thereon by the Supreme Court.
(b) No notice of such resolution shall be entertained by the Speaker or placed on the Order Paper of Parliament unless it complies with the provisions of sub-paragraph (a) and –

(i) such notice of resolution is signed by not less than two-thirds of the whole number of Members of Parliament, or

(ii) such notice of resolution is signed by not less than one-half of the whole number of Members of Parliament, and the Speaker is satisfied that such allegation or allegations merit inquiry and report by the Supreme Court.

(c) Where such resolution is passed by not less than two-thirds of the whole number of Members (including those not present) voting in its favor, the allegation or allegations contained in such resolution shall be referred by the Speaker to the Supreme Court for inquiry and report.

(d) The Supreme Court shall, after due inquiry at which the President shall have the right to appear and to be heard, in person or by an attorney-at-law, make a report of its determination to Parliament together with the reasons therefor.

(e) Where the Supreme Court reports to Parliament that in its opinion the President is permanently incapable of discharging the functions of his office by reason of mental or physical infirmity or that the President has been guilty of any of the other allegations contained in such resolution, as the case may be, Parliament may by a resolution passed by not less than two-thirds of the whole number of Members (including those not present) voting in its favor remove the President from office.

Article 49
(2) If Parliament rejects the Statement of Government Policy or the Appropriation Bill or passes a vote of no-confidence in the Government, the Cabinet of Ministers shall stand dissolved, and the President shall, unless he has in the exercise of his powers under Article 70, dissolved Parliament, appoint a Prime Minister, Ministers of the Cabinet of Ministers, other Ministers and Deputy Ministers in terms of Articles 43, 44, 45 and 46.

2. Ministers may serve simultaneously as members of the legislature.

Yes. Ministers are selected from, and required to serve simultaneously in, the legislature.

Article 44
(1) The President shall, from time to time, in consultation with the Prime Minister, where he considers such consultation to be necessary –
  (a) determine the number of Ministers of the Cabinet of Ministers and the Ministries and the assignment of subjects and functions to such Ministers; and
  (b) appoint from among the Members of Parliament, Ministers to be in charge of the Ministries so determined.

3. The legislature has powers of summons over executive branch officials and hearings with executive branch officials testifying before the legislature or its committees are regularly held.

Yes. Parliamentary select committees regularly summon executive branch officials.

4. The legislature can conduct independent investigation of the chief executive and the agencies of the executive.

Yes. Parliamentary select committees can investigate the executive.

5. The legislature has effective powers of oversight over the agencies of coercion (the military, organs of law enforcement, intelligence services, and the secret police).

No. The legislature lacks effective powers of oversight over the agencies of coercion.

6. The legislature appoints the prime minister.

No. Formally, the president appoints as prime minister the candidate who enjoys majority support in the legislature. In practice, the president has wide leeway in choosing the prime minister.

Article 43
(3) The President shall appoint as Prime Minister the Member of Parliament who in his opinion is most likely to command the confidence of Parliament.

7. The legislature's approval is required to confirm the appointment of ministers; or the legislature itself appoints ministers.

No. The president appoints ministers in consultation with the prime minister, and the appointments do not require the legislature's approval.

Article 44
(1) The President shall, from time to time, in consultation with the Prime Minister, where he considers such consultation to be necessary –
  (a) determine the number of Ministers of the Cabinet of Ministers and the Ministries and the assignment of subjects and functions to such Ministers; and
  (b) appoint from among the Members of Parliament, Ministers to be in charge of the Ministries so determined.

8. The country lacks a presidency entirely or there is a presidency, but the president is elected by the legislature.

No. The president is directly elected.

Article 30
(2) The President of the Republic shall be elected by the People, and shall hold office for a term of six years.

9. The legislature can vote no confidence in the government.

Yes. The legislature can vote no confidence in the government.

Article 49
(2) If Parliament rejects the Statement of Government Policy or the Appropriation Bill or passes a vote of no-confidence in the Government, the Cabinet of Ministers shall stand dissolved, and the President shall, unless he has in the exercise of his powers under Article 70, dissolved Parliament, appoint a Prime Minister, Ministers of the Cabinet of Ministers, other Ministers and Deputy Ministers in terms of Articles 43, 44, 45 and 46.

10. The legislature is immune from dissolution by the executive.

No. The president can dissolve the legislature.

Article 70
(1) The President may, from time to time, by Proclamation summon, prorogue and dissolve Parliament:
Provided that –
(a) subject to the provisions of sub-paragraph (d), when a General Election has been held consequent upon a dissolution of Parliament by the President, the President shall not thereafter dissolve Parliament until the expiration of a period of one year from the date of such General Election, unless Parliament by resolution requests the President to dissolve Parliament;
(b) the President shall not dissolve Parliament on the rejection of the Statement of Government Policy at the commencement of the first session of Parliament after a General Election;
(c) subject to the provisions of sub-paragraph (d), the President shall not dissolve Parliament after the Speaker has entertained a resolution complying with the requirements of sub-paragraphs (a) and (b) of paragraph (2) of Article 38, unless –
(i) such resolution is not passed as required by sub-paragraph (c) of paragraph (2) of Article 38;
(ii) the Supreme Court determines and reports that the President has not become permanently incapable of discharging the functions of his office or that the President has not been guilty of any of the other allegations contained in such resolution;
(iii) the consequent resolution for the removal of the President is not passed as required by sub-paragraph (e) of paragraph (2) of Article 38; or
(iv) Parliament by resolution requests the President to dissolve Parliament;
(d) where the President has not dissolved Parliament consequent upon the rejection by Parliament of the Appropriation Bill, the President shall dissolve Parliament if Parliament rejects the next Appropriation Bill.

11. Any executive initiative on legislation requires ratification or approval by the legislature before it takes effect; that is, the executive lacks decree power.

No. Formally, the president can issue decrees that have the force of law only in emergency situations. In practice, the issuance of decrees by the president is part of ordinary political practice.

Article 155
(2) The power to make emergency regulations under the *Public Security Ordinance* or the law for the time being in force relating to public security shall include the power to make regulations having the legal effect of over-riding, amending or suspending the operation of the provisions of any law, except the provisions of the Constitution.
(3) The provisions of any law relating to public security, empowering the President to make emergency regulations which have the legal effect of over-riding, amending or suspending the operation of the provisions of any law, shall not come into operation, except upon the making of a Proclamation under such law, bringing such provisions into operation.

12. Laws passed by the legislature are veto-proof or essentially veto-proof; that is, the executive lacks veto power, or has veto power but the veto can be overridden by a majority in the legislature.

Yes. The executive lacks veto power.

Article 80
(1) Subject to the provisions of paragraph (2) of this Article, a Bill passed by Parliament shall become law when the certificate of the Speaker is endorsed thereon.

13. The legislature's laws are supreme and not subject to judicial review.

Yes. The Supreme Court can review and reject bills under consideration by the legislature, but laws, once enacted, are not subject to judicial review.

Article 80
(3) Where a Bill becomes law upon the certificate of the President or the Speaker, as the case may be, being endorsed thereon, no court or tribunal shall inquire into, pronounce upon or in any manner call in question, the validity of such Act on any ground whatsoever.

Article 120
The Supreme Court shall have sole and exclusive jurisdiction to determine any question as to whether any Bill or any provision thereof is inconsistent with the Constitution.

14. The legislature has the right to initiate bills in all policy jurisdictions; the executive lacks gatekeeping authority.

No. The legislature is prohibited from introducing legislation related to taxation or public expenditures.

Article 152
No Bill or motion, authorizing the disposal of, or the imposition of charges upon, the Consolidated Fund or other funds of the Republic, or the imposition of any tax or the repeal, augmentation or reduction of any tax for the time being in force shall be introduced in Parliament except by a Minister, and unless such Bill or motion has been approved either by the Cabinet of

Ministers or in such manner as the Cabinet of Ministers may authorize.

15. Expenditure of funds appropriated by the legislature is mandatory; the executive lacks the power to impound funds appropriated by the legislature.

Yes. The executive lacks the power to impound funds appropriated by the legislature.

16. The legislature controls the resources that finance its own internal operation and provide for the perquisites of its own members.

Yes. The legislature enjoys financial autonomy.

17. Members of the legislature are immune from arrest and/or criminal prosecution.

No. According to the constitution, the legislature can regulate issues of legislators' immunity. In practice, legislators are subject to arrest and prosecution.

Article 67
The privileges, immunities, and powers of Parliament and of its Members may be determined and regulated by Parliament by law, and until so determined and regulated, the provisions of the Parliament (Powers and Privileges) Act, shall, mutatis mutandis, apply.

18. All members of the legislature are elected; the executive lacks the power to appoint any members of the legislature.

Yes. All members of the legislature are elected.

Article 62
(1) There shall be a Parliament which shall consist of two hundred and twenty-five Members elected in accordance with the provisions of the Constitution.

19. The legislature alone, without the involvement of any other agencies, can change the Constitution.

Yes. The legislature can change the constitution with a two-thirds majority vote. Amendments to select articles of the constitution require approval in a popular referendum.

Article 82
(1) No Bill for the amendment of any provision of the Constitution shall be placed on the Order Paper of Parliament, unless the provision to be repealed, altered or added, and consequential amendments, if any, are expressly specified in the Bill and is described in the long title thereof as being an Act for the amendment of the Constitution.
(2) No Bill for the repeal of the Constitution shall be placed on the Order Paper of Parliament unless the Bill contains provisions replacing the Constitution and is described in the long title thereof as being an Act for the repeal and replacement of the Constitution.

(3) If in the opinion of the Speaker, a Bill does not comply with the requirements of paragraph (1) or paragraph (2) of this Article, he shall direct that such Bill be not proceeded with unless it is amended so as to comply with those requirements.
(4) Notwithstanding anything in the preceding provisions of this Article, it shall be lawful for a Bill which complies with the requirements of paragraph (1) or paragraph (2) of this Article to be amended by Parliament provided that the Bill as so amended shall comply with those requirements.
(5) A Bill for the amendment of any provision of the Constitution or for the repeal and replacement of the Constitution, shall become law if the number of votes cast in favor thereof amounts to not less than two-thirds of the whole number of Members (including those not present) and upon a certificate by the President or the Speaker, as the case may be, being endorsed thereon in accordance with the provisions of Article 80 or 79.
(6) No provision in any law shall, or shall be deemed to, amend, repeal or replace the Constitution or any provision thereof, or be so interpreted or construed, unless enacted in accordance with the requirements of the preceding provisions of this Article.
(7) In this Chapter, "amendment" includes repeal, alteration and addition.

Article 83
Notwithstanding anything to the contrary in the provisions of Article 82 –
(a) a Bill for the amendment or for the repeal and replacement of or which is inconsistent with any of the provisions of Articles 1, 2, 3, 6, 7, 8, 9, 10 and 11, or of this Article, and
(b) a Bill for the amendment or for the repeal and replacement of or which is inconsistent with the provisions of paragraph (2) of Article 30 or of paragraph (2) of Article 62 which would extend the term of office of the President or the duration of Parliament, as the case may be, to over six years, shall become law if the number of votes cast in favor thereof amounts to not less than two-thirds of the whole number of Members (including those not present), is approved by the People at a Referendum and a certificate is endorsed thereon by the President in accordance with Article 80.

20. The legislature's approval is necessary for the declaration of war.

No. The president can declare war without the legislature's approval.

Article 33
In addition to the powers and functions expressly conferred on or assigned to him by the Constitution or by any written law whether enacted before or after the commencement of the Constitution, the President shall have the power –
(e) to declare war and peace.

21. The legislature's approval is necessary to ratify treaties with foreign countries.

Yes. The legislature's approval is necessary to ratify international treaties.

Article 157
Where Parliament by resolution passed by not less than two-thirds of the whole number of Members of Parliament (including those not present) voting in its favor, approves as being essential for the development of the national economy, any Treaty or Agreement between the Government of Sri Lanka and the Government of any foreign State for the promotion and protection of the investments in Sri Lanka of such foreign State, its nationals, or of corporations, companies and other associations incorporated or constituted under its laws, such Treaty or Agreement shall have the force of law in Sri Lanka, and otherwise than in the interests of national security no written law shall be enacted or made, and no executive or administrative action shall be taken, in contravention of the provisions of such Treaty or Agreement.

22. The legislature has the power to grant amnesty.

No. Amnesty and pardon are not treated separately, and the legislature lacks the power to grant amnesty. See item 23.

23. The legislature has the power of pardon.

No. The president has the power of pardon.

Article 34
(1) The President may in the case of any offender convicted of any offense in any court within the Republic of Sri Lanka –
(a) grant a pardon, either free or subject to lawful conditions;
Provided that where any offender shall have been condemned to suffer death by the sentence of any court, the President shall cause a report to be made to him by the Judge who tried the case and shall forward such report to the Attorney-General with instructions that after the Attorney-General has advised thereon, the report shall be sent together with the Attorney-General's advice to the Minister in charge of the subject of Justice, who shall forward the report with his recommendation to the President.

24. The legislature reviews and has the right to reject appointments to the judiciary; or the legislature itself appoints members of the judiciary.

No. The president makes judicial appointments, and the appointments do not require the legislature's approval.

Article 107
(1) The Chief Justice, the President of the Court of Appeal and every other Judge of the Supreme Court and Court of Appeal shall . . . be appointed by the President by warrant under his hand.

25. The chairman of the central bank is appointed by the legislature.

No. The president appoints the governor of the Central Bank of Sri Lanka.

26. The legislature has a substantial voice in the operation of the state-owned media.

No. The legislature lacks a substantial voice in the operation of the public media.

27. The legislature is regularly in session.

Yes. The legislature regularly meets in ordinary session.

Article 70
(2) Parliament shall be summoned to meet once at least in every year.

28. Each legislator has a personal secretary.

Yes.

29. Each legislator has at least one non-secretarial staff member with policy expertise.

No.

30. Legislators are eligible for re-election without any restriction.

Yes. There are no restrictions on re-election.

31. A seat in the legislature is an attractive enough position that legislators are generally interested in and seek re-election.

Yes.

32. The re-election of incumbent legislators is common enough that at any given time the legislature contains a significant number of highly experienced members.

Yes. Re-election rates are sufficiently high to produce a significant number of highly experienced members.

NATIONAL LEGISLATURE OF SUDAN

Expert consultants: Richard Lobban, Jok Madut, Philip G. Roessler

Score: .22

Influence over executive (1/9)	Institutional autonomy (1/9)	Specified powers (2/8)	Institutional capacity (3/6)
1. replace	10. no dissolution	19. amendments	27. sessions X
2. serve as ministers	11. no decree	20. war X	28. secretary
3. interpellate X	12. no veto	21. treaties X	29. staff
4. investigate	13. no review	22. amnesty	30. no term X limits
5. oversee police	14. no gatekeeping X	23. pardon	31. seek X re-election
6. appoint PM	15. no impoundment	24. judiciary	32. experience
7. appoint ministers	16. control resources	25. central bank	
8. lack president	17. immunity	26. media	
9. no confidence	18. all elected		

The National Legislature of Sudan traces its origins to the waning years of the country's domination by outside powers. In 1953 Britain and Egypt agreed to give Sudan independence within three years and to establish a Senate and a House of Representatives. In late 1953 elections were held for the new parliament, and in 1956 Sudan achieved full independence. General Ibrahim Abboud staged a military coup in 1958, and for the next half-century the legislature was often marginalized, as the armed forces frequently controlled the government and waged civil wars in the south and the northwest, although there were intervals of parliamentary activity. In 1964 Abboud was overthrown, and during the subsequent few years parliamentary activity revived. The legislature was marginalized again after 1969, when Gaafar Mohamed el-Nimeiri seized power in a military coup. Nimeiri's ouster in 1985 was followed by a revival of parliament in the second half of the 1980s.

Since 1989 politics have been marked by military coups and mass violence. In 1998 the ruling National Islamic Front promulgated a new constitution that called for a unicameral National Assembly. In the following year, however, President Umar Hassan Ahmad al-Bashir partially suspended the constitution, dissolved the National Assembly, and declared a state of emergency. In 2000 there were new parliamentary elections in which Bashir's National Congress/National Islamic Front Party obtained a virtual monopoly on seats. In 2002 the government and southern rebel groups reached a cease fire. Although fighting continued during the negotiations, talks helped produce a peace agreement and the 2005 Interim National Constitution, which is the document from which excerpts are drawn here. In 2004, just as the war in the south appeared to be ebbing, conflict in the northwestern Darfur region flared, and continues to rage as of this writing.

In addition to granting southern Sudan considerable autonomy, the new constitution calls for a bicameral National Legislature consisting of the directly elected National Assembly (*Majlis Watani*) and the Council of States (*Majlis Welayat*), which is comprised of members elected by state legislatures. Members of the National Assembly as it is currently constituted were appointed by the president in 2005 on the recommendation of political parties to represent the country's diverse and often warring groups. The first parliamentary elections are scheduled for 2009.

At least in its current form, the legislature's power is negligible. It interpellates ministers but otherwise lacks meaningful influence over the executive branch. Any potential institutional autonomy is squeezed out by presidential decree, dissolution, and veto powers. The legislature exercises few specified powers. It has a bit of institutional capacity.

SURVEY

1. The legislature alone, without the involvement of any other agencies, can impeach the president or replace the prime minister.

No. Presidential impeachment requires the involvement of the Constitutional Court.

Article 59

The Office of the President of the Republic shall fall vacant in any of the following cases: –

(d) impeachment in accordance with the provisions of this Constitution.

Article 60

(1) The President of the Republic and the First Vice President shall be immune from any legal proceedings and shall not be charged or sued in any court of law during their tenure of office.

(2) Notwithstanding sub-Article (1) above, and in case of high treason, gross violation of this Constitution or gross misconduct in relation to State affairs, the President or the First Vice President may be charged before the Constitutional Court upon a resolution passed by three quarters of all members of the National Legislature.

(3) In the event of conviction of the President of the Republic or the First Vice President, in accordance with sub-Article (2) above, he shall be deemed to have forfeited his office.

Article 91

(2) Without prejudice to the generality of sub-Article (1) above, the National Legislature shall convene for the following purposes to: –

(h) impeach the President of the Republic.

2. Ministers may serve simultaneously as members of the legislature.

No. Ministers are prohibited from serving simultaneously in the legislature.

3. The legislature has powers of summons over executive branch officials and hearings with executive branch officials testifying before the legislature or its committees are regularly held.

Yes. The legislature regularly questions executive branch officials. For example, in December 2006 the minister of defense was summoned to the National Assembly to testify on violence in Malakal, southern Sudan, between the Sudan Armed Forces (SAF) and the Sudan People's Liberation Army (SPLA).

Article 91

(3) The National Assembly shall be competent to:–

(g) summon national ministers to present reports on the executive performance of the government in general or of specified ministries or particular activities,

(h) interrogate, at will, national ministers about their performance or the performance of their ministries

and may recommend to the President of the Republic, in a subsequent sitting, the removal of a national minister, if he is deemed to have lost the confidence of the National Assembly.

Article 105

(1) The National Assembly or any of its committees may summon any public official or any person, other than the President of the Republic and the two Vice Presidents to testify before it, give opinion to the Assembly or any of its committees.

(2) Inquiry on any matter that falls within the direct responsibility of the National Executive may only be made after notifying the President of the Republic.

4. The legislature can conduct independent investigation of the chief executive and the agencies of the executive.

No. The legislature cannot investigate the executive.

5. The legislature has effective powers of oversight over the agencies of coercion (the military, organs of law enforcement, intelligence services, and the secret police).

No. The legislature lacks effective powers of oversight over the agencies of coercion. The military and intelligence organs serve the executive and operate beyond the reach of the legislature. They secretly execute many security activities throughout the country, including the provision of military support to irregular armed groups.

6. The legislature appoints the prime minister.

No. There is no prime minister.

7. The legislature's approval is required to confirm the appointment of ministers; or the legislature itself appoints ministers.

No. The president appoints ministers, and the appointments do not require the legislature's approval.

Article 70

(1) The President of the Republic shall, after consultation within the Presidency, appoint the National Council of Ministers.

8. The country lacks a presidency entirely or there is a presidency, but the president is elected by the legislature.

No. The president is directly elected.

Article 52

There shall be a President for the Republic of the Sudan to be directly elected by the people in national elections according to the law and the regulations set by the National Elections Commission.

9. The legislature can vote no confidence in the government.

No. The legislature can vote no confidence in individual ministers, but not in the government as a whole.

Article 91
(1) The National Legislature represents the will of the people and shall foster national unity, exercise national legislative functions, oversee the National Executive, and promote the decentralized system of government.
(2) Without prejudice to the generality of sub-Article (1) above, the National Legislature shall convene for the following purposes to: –
(h) interrogate, at will, national ministers about their performance or the performance of their ministries and may recommend to the President of the Republic, in a subsequent sitting, the removal of a national minister, if he is deemed to have lost the confidence of the National Assembly.

10. The legislature is immune from dissolution by the executive.

No. The president can dissolve the legislature.

Article 58
(1) The President of the Republic is the Head of the State and Government and represents the will of the people and the authority of the State; he shall exercise the powers vested in him by this Constitution and the Comprehensive Peace Agreement and shall, without prejudice to the generality of the foregoing, perform the following functions: –
(e) summon, adjourn or prorogue the National Legislature.

Article 211
The President of the Republic, with the consent of the First Vice President, may during the state of emergency take, by virtue of law or exceptional order, any measures that shall not derogate from the provisions of this Constitution and the Comprehensive Peace Agreement except as may be provided herein: –
(b) to dissolve or suspend any of the state organs or suspend such powers, as may be conferred upon the states under this Constitution. The President of the Republic with the consent of the First Vice President shall assume the functions of such organs and exercise the powers or prescribe the manner in which the affairs of the state concerned may be managed.

11. Any executive initiative on legislation requires ratification or approval by the legislature before it takes effect; that is, the executive lacks decree power.

No. The president can issue decrees that have the force of law "whenever he deems it appropriate for public interests." The decrees lapse if they are subsequently rejected by the legislature. The legislature can also choose to delegate "subsidiary" decree power to the president.

Article 113
(1) Notwithstanding the provisions of Article 109(2) above, the President of the Republic may wherever he deems it appropriate for public interests, make a presidential order having the force of law, providing that the imposition of any tax, or fee or the amendment thereof shall come into force, pending submission of a bill requiring the same to the National Assembly. When that financial bill is adopted or rejected, the force of the presidential order shall cease without the rejection or amendment of the bill having retrospective effect.

Article 115
The National Legislature or any of its Chambers may, by law, delegate to the President of the Republic, the National Council of Ministers or any public body, the power to make any subsidiary regulations, rules, orders or any other subsidiary instrument having the force of law; provided that such subsidiary legislation shall be tabled before the concerned Chamber and be subject to adoption or amendment by a resolution of that Chamber in accordance with the provisions of its regulations.

12. Laws passed by the legislature are veto-proof or essentially veto-proof; that is, the executive lacks veto power, or has veto power but the veto can be overridden by a majority in the legislature.

No. A two-thirds majority vote is required to override a presidential veto.

Article 91
(2) Without prejudice to the generality of sub-Article (1) above, the National Legislature shall convene for the following purposes to: –
(d) reconsider a bill which has been rejected by the President of the Republic under Article 108.

Article 108
(1) Any bill approved by the National Legislature shall not become law unless the President of the Republic assents to it and signs it into law. If the President withholds assent for thirty days without giving reasons, the bill shall be deemed to have been so signed.
(2) Should the President of the Republic withhold assent to the bill and give reasons within the aforementioned thirty days, the bill shall be re-introduced to the National Legislature to consider the observations of the President of the Republic.
(3) The bill shall become law if the National Legislature again passes it by a two-thirds majority of all the members and representatives of the two Chambers; the assent of the President of the Republic shall not be required for that bill to come into force.

13. The legislature's laws are supreme and not subject to judicial review.

No. The Constitutional Court can review the constitutionality of laws.

Article 122

(1) The Constitutional Court shall be the custodian of this Constitution, the constitutions of southern Sudan and the states; its decisions shall be final and binding, it shall: –

(e) adjudicate on the constitutionality of laws or provisions in accordance with this Constitution, the Interim Constitution of Southern Sudan or the relevant state constitutions.

14. The legislature has the right to initiate bills in all policy jurisdictions; the executive lacks gatekeeping authority.

Yes. The legislature can initiate bills in all policy jurisdictions.

15. Expenditure of funds appropriated by the legislature is mandatory; the executive lacks the power to impound funds appropriated by the legislature.

No. The president can impound funds appropriated by the legislature.

16. The legislature controls the resources that finance its own internal operation and provide for the perquisites of its own members.

No. The legislature is dependent on the executive for the resources that finance its own operations.

17. Members of the legislature are immune from arrest and/or criminal prosecution.

No. By law, legislators are immune, but in practice, opponents of the executive may be subject to persecution. For example, in 2004 Ali Dosa, a member of parliament, was arrested and imprisoned on charges of collaborating with rebels from the Darfur region. By law, members may be arrested only if the legislature lifts their immunity. Dosa was arrested and imprisoned even in the absence of any action by the legislature to lift his immunity.

Article 92

(1) Except where he is caught in the act of crime, no criminal proceedings shall be initiated against a member of the National Legislature; neither shall any measure be taken against his person or belongings without permission from the Speaker of the appropriate Chamber.

(2) In case the member or representative is charged with a serious crime the appropriate Chamber may waive the immunity of the accused member or representative.

18. All members of the legislature are elected; the executive lacks the power to appoint any members of the legislature.

No. Following the 2005 peace agreement between the government and the SPLM, all 450 members of the National Assembly were appointed by the president following the recommendations of political parties. The first parliamentary election under the new constitution is scheduled for 2009.

Article 84

(1) The National Assembly shall be composed of members elected in free and fair elections.

(2) The National Elections Law shall determine the number of members and composition of the National Assembly.

Article 85

(1) The Council of States shall be composed of two representatives from each state, elected by the state legislature in accordance with the National Elections Law and regulations set forth by the National Elections Commission.

19. The legislature alone, without the involvement of any other agencies, can change the Constitution.

No. Constitutional amendments can be initiated only by the president.

Article 58

(1) The President of the Republic is the Head of the State and Government and represents the will of the people and the authority of the State; he shall exercise the powers vested in him by this Constitution and the Comprehensive Peace Agreement and shall, without prejudice to the generality of the foregoing, perform the following functions: –

(h) initiate constitutional amendments and legislations and assent to laws.

Article 91

(2) Without prejudice to the generality of sub-Article (1) above, the National Legislature shall convene for the following purposes to: –

(a) amend this Constitution and approve amendments affecting the Comprehensive Peace Agreement that are presented by its signatories in accordance with Article 224 of this Constitution.

Article 224

(1) This Constitution shall not be amended unless the amendments are approved by three-quarters of all the members of each Chamber of the National Legislature sitting separately and only after introduction of the draft amendment at least two months prior to deliberations.

(2) Any amendment affecting the provisions of the Comprehensive Peace Agreement shall be introduced only with the approval of both Parties signatory to the Comprehensive Peace Agreement.

20. The legislature's approval is necessary for the declaration of war.

Yes. The legislature's approval is required for presidential war declarations.

Article 58

(1) The President of the Republic is the Head of the State and Government and represents the will of the people and the authority of the State; he shall exercise the powers vested in him by this Constitution and the Comprehensive Peace Agreement and shall, without prejudice to the generality of the foregoing, perform the following functions: –

(f) declare war in accordance with this Constitution and the law.

Article 91

(2) Without prejudice to the generality of sub-Article (1) above, the National Legislature shall convene for the following purposes to: –

(f) approve declaration of war.

Article 213

The President of the Republic, with the consent of the First Vice President, shall declare war whenever they decide that the country is under external aggression. Such declaration shall be legally enforceable upon approval by the National Legislature.

21. The legislature's approval is necessary to ratify treaties with foreign countries.

Yes. The legislature's approval is necessary to ratify international treaties.

Article 58

(1) The President of the Republic is the Head of the State and Government and represents the will of the people and the authority of the State; he shall exercise the powers vested in him by this Constitution and the Comprehensive Peace Agreement and shall, without prejudice to the generality of the foregoing, perform the following functions: –

(k) direct and supervise the foreign policy of the State and ratify treaties and international agreements with the approval of the National Legislature.

Article 91

(3) The National Assembly shall be competent to: –

(d) ratify international treaties, conventions and agreements.

22. The legislature has the power to grant amnesty.

No. Amnesty and pardon are not treated separately, and the legislature lacks the power to grant amnesty. See item 23.

23. The legislature has the power of pardon.

No. The president has the power of pardon.

Article 58

(1) The President of the Republic is the Head of the State and Government and represents the will of the people and the authority of the State; he shall exercise the powers vested in him by this Constitution and the Comprehensive Peace Agreement and shall, without prejudice to the generality of the foregoing, perform the following functions: –

(i) approve death sentences, grant pardon, lift convictions and remit penalties according to this Constitution and the national law.

24. The legislature reviews and has the right to reject appointments to the judiciary; or the legislature itself appoints members of the judiciary.

No. According to the constitution, the Council of States must approve the president's appointments to the Constitutional Court, while other judges are named by the president without need for the legislature's consent, but in practice, the executive has full control over all judicial appointments. The legislature has no genuine review authority on appointments to the Constitutional Court or any other judicial organ.

Article 121

(1) All Justices of the Constitutional Court shall be appointed by the President of the Republic in accordance with Article 58 (2) (c) herein and upon the recommendation of the National Judicial Service Commission and subject to approval by a two-thirds majority of all the representatives at the Council of States.

Article 130

(1) Having regard to competence, integrity and credibility, the Chief Justice of the Republic of the Sudan, his deputies, Justices and Judges shall be appointed by the President of the Republic in accordance with Article 58(2)(c) herein, where applicable, and upon the recommendation of the National Judicial Service Commission.

Article 132

The President of Government of Southern Sudan shall, within one week after the adoption of the Interim Constitution of Southern Sudan, appoint, without prejudice to Article 130(1) herein, the President and Justices of Southern Sudan Supreme Court, Judges of Courts of Appeal and other courts having regard to competence, integrity, credibility and impartiality as shall be determined by that Constitution and the law.

25. The chairman of the central bank is appointed by the legislature.

No. The president appoints the governor of the Central Bank of Sudan.

Article 202

(6) The Governor of the Central Bank of Sudan and his two Deputies shall be appointed by the President of the Republic in accordance with Article 58(2)(c) herein.

26. The legislature has a substantial voice in the operation of the state-owned media.

No. The legislature lacks a substantial voice in the operation of the public media.

27. The legislature is regularly in session.

Yes. The legislature regularly meets in ordinary session.

Article 93

(1) Each Chamber of the National Legislature shall hold its first sitting upon convocation by the President of the Republic within thirty days following the official declaration of the results of the elections. The first sitting shall be chaired by the eldest of the members/representatives present.

(2) Without prejudice to Article 58(2)(d), each Chamber shall determine the commencement and closure dates of its sessions.

(3) Either Chamber may convene an emergency or extraordinary session on the request of half of its members or representatives or upon call from the President of the Republic.

28. Each legislator has a personal secretary.

No. Some prominent members of the legislature have personal secretaries, but most legislators do not.

29. Each legislator has at least one non-secretarial staff member with policy expertise.

No. See item 28.

30. Legislators are eligible for re-election without any restriction.

Yes. There are no restrictions on re-election.

31. A seat in the legislature is an attractive enough position that legislators are generally interested in and seek re-election.

Yes.

32. The re-election of incumbent legislators is common enough that at any given time the legislature contains a significant number of highly experienced members.

No. The legislature is made up of members appointed by the president in 2005. This group includes some experienced politicians, but the absence of elections and the infancy of the current body leave the legislature without a cohort of experienced legislators.

PARLIAMENT OF SWAZILAND (*LIBANDLA*)

Expert consultants: Matthias Basedau, Khabele Matlosa, H. M. Mushala, Mark Y. Rosenberg, one anonymous expert

Score: .25

Influence over executive (2/9)		Institutional autonomy (1/9)		Specified powers (1/8)		Institutional capacity (4/6)	
1. replace		10. no dissolution		19. amendments		27. sessions	X
2. serve as ministers	X	11. no decree	X	20. war		28. secretary	
3. interpellate		12. no veto		21. treaties	X	29. staff	
4. investigate		13. no review		22. amnesty		30. no term limits	X
5. oversee police		14. no gatekeeping		23. pardon		31. seek re-election	X
6. appoint PM		15. no impoundment		24. judiciary		32. experience	X
7. appoint ministers		16. control resources		25. central bank			
8. lack president	X	17. immunity		26. media			
9. no confidence		18. all elected					

The Parliament (*Libandla*) of Swaziland was formally established in the country's 1968 constitution upon independence from Great Britain. The constitution provided for a bicameral parliament with a lower house, the House of Assembly, and an upper house, the Senate. In 1973 the king suspended parliament and banned political parties. The legislature was reestablished in 1978 along with the *tinkhundla* electoral system, in which legislative candidates are vetted by local tribal leaders.

A new constitution in 2005 maintained the ban on political parties but removed the king's decree powers.

Even after the elimination of the king's decree authority, the legislature remains feckless. It cannot appoint, oversee, or remove executive branch officials and generally has little sway over the king. Expansive royal powers that include the right to appoint a large proportion of the members of both the House of Assembly and the Senate ensure that the legislature is virtually bereft of institutional autonomy. The legislature exercises only one of the specified powers measured in this survey, although it does enjoy some institutional capacity.

SURVEY

1. The legislature alone, without the involvement of any other agencies, can impeach the president or replace the prime minister.

No. The legislature cannot remove the king from office. Formally, it can remove the prime minister with a vote no confidence, but in practice, this would be unthinkable without the king's assent.

> Article 11
> The King and *iNgwenyama* shall be immune from –
> (a) suit or legal process in any cause in respect of all things done or omitted to be done by him.

> Article 68
> (1) The office of the Prime Minister shall become vacant where –
> (d) after a resolution of no confidence in the Prime Minister is passed by at least two thirds majority of all members of the House, the King removes the Prime Minister.

2. Ministers may serve simultaneously as members of the legislature.

Yes. Ministers are selected from, and required to serve simultaneously in, the legislature.

> Article 67
> (1) The King shall appoint the Prime Minister from among members of the House acting on recommendation of the King's Advisory Council.
> (2) The King shall appoint Ministers from both chambers of Parliament on the recommendation of the Prime Minister.

3. The legislature has powers of summons over executive branch officials and hearings with executive branch officials testifying before the legislature or its committees are regularly held.

No. The legislature does not have the power to summon and question officials from the executive.

4. The legislature can conduct independent investigation of the chief executive and the agencies of the executive.

No. Formally, the legislature can establish committees of investigation. In practice, the legislature cannot investigate the king and his inner circle.

> Article 129
> (1) Each chamber of Parliament shall appoint sessional committees and other committees as may be necessary for the effective discharge of the functions of that chamber.
> (2) The standing committees shall be charged with such functions, including the investigation and inquiry into the activities and administration of ministries and departments as Parliament may determine and the investigations and enquiries may extend to proposals for legislation.

5. The legislature has effective powers of oversight over the agencies of coercion (the military, organs of law enforcement, intelligence services, and the secret police).

No. The legislature lacks effective powers of oversight over the agencies of coercion.

6. The legislature appoints the prime minister.

No. The king appoints the prime minister.

> Article 67
> (1) The King shall appoint the Prime Minister from among members of the House acting on recommendation of the King's Advisory Council.

7. The legislature's approval is required to confirm the appointment of ministers; or the legislature itself appoints ministers.

No. The king appoints ministers, and the appointments do not require the legislature's approval.

> Article 67
> (1) The King shall appoint the Prime Minister from among members of the House acting on recommendation of the King's Advisory Council.
> (2) The King shall appoint Ministers from both chambers of Parliament on the recommendation of the Prime Minister.

8. The country lacks a presidency entirely or there is a presidency, but the president is elected by the legislature.

Yes. The country lacks a presidency. The king is the head of state.

> Article 64
> (1) The executive authority of Swaziland vests in the King as Head of State and shall be exercised in accordance with the provisions of this Constitution.

9. The legislature can vote no confidence in the government.

No. Formally, the legislature can vote no confidence in the government, but in practice, this would be unthinkable without the king's assent.

Article 68
(1) The office of the Prime Minister shall become vacant where –
(d) after a resolution of no confidence in the Prime Minister is passed by at least two thirds majority of all members of the House, the King removes the Prime Minister.
(5) Where a resolution of no confidence is passed on the Cabinet by a three-fifths majority of all members of the House the King shall dissolve the Cabinet.

10. The legislature is immune from dissolution by the executive.

No. The king can dissolve the legislature.

Article 64
(4) The King in his capacity as Head of State has authority, in accordance with this Constitution or any other law, among other things to –
(b) summon and dissolve Parliament.

Article 134
(1) The King may at any time –
(b) dissolve Parliament.

11. Any executive initiative on legislation requires ratification or approval by the legislature before it takes effect; that is, the executive lacks decree power.

Yes. The king lacks decree power. Prior to 2005 the king issued decrees with the force of law, but the 2005 constitution removed the king's power of decree.

12. Laws passed by the legislature are veto-proof or essentially veto-proof; that is, the executive lacks veto power, or has veto power but the veto can be overridden by a majority in the legislature.

No. The king has absolute veto power. All bills require the king's assent in order to become law.

Article 108
(1) A bill shall not become law unless the King has assented to it and signed it in token of that assent.

13. The legislature's laws are supreme and not subject to judicial review.

No. Although there is no judicial review, the legislature's laws are not supreme, as the king wields ultimate executive and legislative authority.

14. The legislature has the right to initiate bills in all policy jurisdictions; the executive lacks gatekeeping authority.

No. The legislature is prohibited from introducing legislation related to taxation, public expenditures, or government debt.

Article 111
Except with the consent of the Cabinet signified by the Prime Minister or the Minister responsible for finance, neither chamber of Parliament shall –
(a) proceed upon any bill including an amendment to a bill that in the opinion of the person presiding makes provision for any of the following –
(i) the imposition of taxation or the alteration of taxation otherwise than by reduction;
(ii) the imposition of any charge upon the Consolidated Fund or other public funds of Swaziland or the alteration of any such charge otherwise than by reduction;
(iii) the payment, issue or withdrawal, from the Consolidated Fund or other public funds of Swaziland of any moneys not charged on the Consolidated Fund or any increase in the amount of that payment, issue or withdrawal, or the composition or remission of any debt due to the Government; or
(b) proceed upon any motion including an amendment to a motion the effect of which, in the opinion of the person presiding, would be to make provision for any of the purposes specified in paragraph (a) of this section.

15. Expenditure of funds appropriated by the legislature is mandatory; the executive lacks the power to impound funds appropriated by the legislature.

No. The king can impound funds.

16. The legislature controls the resources that finance its own internal operation and provide for the perquisites of its own members.

No. The legislature is dependent on the king for the resources that finance its own operations.

17. Members of the legislature are immune from arrest and/or criminal prosecution.

No. Formally, the legislature can prescribe laws for the immunity of its members, but in practice, legislators are subject to arrest and prosecution.

Article 130
(1) The President, Speaker, members of Parliament and any other person participating or assisting in or acting in connection with or reporting the proceedings of Parliament or any of its committees shall be entitled to such immunities and privileges as Parliament may by law prescribe.

18. All members of the legislature are elected; the executive lacks the power to appoint any members of the legislature.

No. The king appoints ten of the seventy-six members of the House of Assembly and twenty of the thirty-one members of the Senate.

Article 94

(1) The Senate shall consist of not more than thirty-one members (in this Constitution referred to as "Senators") who shall be elected or appointed in accordance with this section.

(2) Ten Senators, at least half of whom shall be female, shall be elected by the members of the House in such manner as may be prescribed by or under any law at their first meeting so as to represent a cross-section of the Swazi society.

(3) Twenty Senators, at least eight of whom shall be female, shall be appointed by the King acting in his discretion after consultation with such bodies as the King may deem appropriate.

Article 95

(1) Subject to the provisions of this Constitution, the House of Assembly shall consist of not more than seventy-six members composed as follows–

(a) not more than sixty members elected from *tinkhundla* areas serving as constituencies;

(b) not more than ten members nominated by the King acting in his discretion after consultation with such bodies as the King may deem appropriate;

(c) four female members specially elected from the four Regions subject to subsection (3);

(d) the Attorney-General who shall be an *ex officio* member.

19. The legislature alone, without the involvement of any other agencies, can change the Constitution.

No. Constitutional amendments require the king's assent.

Article 245

(1) Subject to the provisions of this chapter, Parliament may amend any provision of this Constitution by the introduction of a bill expressly providing that the Constitution shall be amended as proposed in that bill.

(2) A bill to amend this Constitution shall only be introduced at a joint sitting of the Senate and the House summoned for the purpose in accordance with the provisions of the First Schedule.

(5) If, after the prescribed period the bill is passed at the joint sitting and or at a referendum with the requisite majority, the bill shall be submitted to the King for assent.

Article 246

(1) Where a bill in terms of this Chapter contains provision for amending any of the specially entrenched provisions of this Constitution as set out in sub-section (2), the bill shall not be passed at the joint sitting unless it is supported on its final reading by the votes of not less than three-quarters of all the members of the two chambers.

(2) The specially entrenched provisions are as follows –

(a) The Kingdom and its Constitution: section 2;

(b) Monarchy: section 4, 5, 7(2), 7(3), 8(2), 9, 10, 11;

(c) Protection and Promotion of Fundamental Rights and Freedoms Chapter III

(d) The Executive: section 64, 65, 66(1), 69(1), 69(2);

(e) The Legislature: section 79, 84, 93, 106, 108, 115, 119(1), 134;

(f) The Judicature: section 138, 139, 140, 141, 146, 151, 153(1) 155, 158, 159 except 159(5);

(g) Director of Public Prosecutions and the Commission on Human Rights: section 162(1), 162(4), 162(6);

(h) Public Finance: section 207(1);

(i) Land, Minerals, etc: section 210(1), 211(1), 213;

(j) Traditional Institutions: section 227, 228, 229; 230; 231;

(k) Amendment of the Constitution: Chapter XVII;

(l) Miscellaneous: Chapter XVIII in its application to any of the provisions referred to in this section except section 251;

(m) The First Schedule in its application to any of the provisions referred to in this section.

(3) Where a bill in terms of this section has been duly passed at a joint sitting that bill shall not be presented to the King for assent unless it is approved by a simple majority of all votes validly cast at a referendum in such manner as may be prescribed, at which every person who at the time of the referendum is registered as a voter for purposes of the elected members of the House shall be entitled to vote.

20. The legislature's approval is necessary for the declaration of war.

No. The king can declare a state of emergency in times of war without first obtaining legislative approval. The state of emergency lapses if it is not subsequently approved by the legislature.

Article 36

(1) The king may, on the advice of the Prime Minister, by proclamation which shall be published in the *Gazette*, declare that a state of emergency exists in Swaziland or any part of Swaziland for the purposes of this Chapter.

(2) The provisions of subsection (1) shall not apply and a proclamation shall not be issued under that subsection and where issued that proclamation shall not be effective in law unless –

(a) Swaziland is at war or circumstances have arisen making imminent a state of war between Swaziland and a foreign State;

(b) there is in Swaziland a natural disaster or imminent threat of a natural disaster; or

(c) there is action taken or immediately threatened by a person or body of persons of such a nature or on so extensive a scale as to be likely to endanger the public safety or to deprive the community or a significant part of that community of supplies or services essential to the life of the community.

(4) A declaration under subsection (1) if not sooner revoked, shall cease to have effect –

(a) in the case of a declaration made when Parliament is sitting or has been summoned to meet within three days, at the expiration of a period of seven days beginning with the date of publication of the declaration;

(b) in any other case, at the expiration of a period of twenty-one days beginning with the date of publication of the declaration, unless, before the expiration of that period, the declaration is approved by a resolution passed by a two-thirds majority at a joint sitting of all the members of the Senate and the House.

21. The legislature's approval is necessary to ratify treaties with foreign countries.

Yes. The legislature's approval is necessary to ratify international treaties.

Article 238
(1) The Government may execute or cause to be executed an international agreement in the name of the Crown.
(2) An international agreement executed by or under the authority of the Government shall be subject to ratification and become binding on the government by –
(a) an Act of Parliament; or
(b) a resolution of at least two-thirds of the members at a joint sitting of the two Chambers of Parliament.
(3) The provisions of sub-section (2) do not apply where the agreement is of a technical, administrative or executive nature or is an agreement which does not require ratification or accession.
(4) Unless it is self-executing, an international agreement becomes law in Swaziland only when enacted into law by Parliament.
(5) Accession to an international agreement shall be done in the same manner as ratification under sub-section (2).

22. The legislature has the power to grant amnesty.

No. Amnesty and pardon are not treated separately, and the legislature lacks the power to grant amnesty. See item 23.

23. The legislature has the power of pardon.

No. The king has the power of pardon.

Article 64
(4) The King in his capacity as Head of State has authority, in accordance with this Constitution or any other law, among other things to –
(a) issue pardons, reprieves or commute sentences.

Article 78
(1) The King may, in respect of a person sentenced to death or life imprisonment –
(a) grant a pardon, either free or subject to lawful conditions;
(b) grant to any person a respite, either indefinite or for a specified period;
(c) substitute a less severe form of punishment for any punishment imposed on any person for such an offence; or
(d) remit the whole or part of that sentence, penalty or forfeiture otherwise due to the Government on account of that offence.

24. The legislature reviews and has the right to reject appointments to the judiciary; or the legislature itself appoints members of the judiciary.

No. The king makes judicial appointments on the recommendation of a special commission, and the appointments do not require the legislature's approval.

Article 153
(1) The Chief Justice and the other Justices of the superior courts shall be appointed by the King on the advice of the Judicial Service Commission.

25. The chairman of the central bank is appointed by the legislature.

No. The king appoints the minister of finance, who heads the Central Bank of Swaziland.

Article 206
(1) There shall be the Central Bank of Swaziland consisting of the Governor and such other staff and having such powers and functions as Parliament shall determine.
(4) The Governor shall be appointed by the King on the advice of the Prime Minister based on the recommendation of the Board.

26. The legislature has a substantial voice in the operation of the state-owned media.

No. The monarch controls the state-owned media.

27. The legislature is regularly in session.

Yes. The legislature regularly meets in ordinary session.

Article 133
(1) There shall be a session of Parliament at least once in every year so that a period of six months shall not intervene between the last sitting of Parliament in one session and the first sitting of Parliament in the next session.

28. Each legislator has a personal secretary.

No.

29. Each legislator has at least one non-secretarial staff member with policy expertise.

No.

30. Legislators are eligible for re-election without any restriction.

Yes. There are no restrictions on re-election.

31. A seat in the legislature is an attractive enough position that legislators are generally interested in and seek re-election.

Yes.

32. The re-election of incumbent legislators is common enough that at any given time the legislature contains a significant number of highly experienced members.

Yes. Re-election rates are sufficiently high to produce a significant number of highly experienced members.

PARLIAMENT OF SWEDEN (*RIKSDAG*)

Expert consultants: Nicholas Aylott, Magnus Hagevi, Jonas Hinnfors, Johannes Lindvall, Jon Pierre

Score: .72

Influence over executive (7/9)		Institutional autonomy (7/9)		Specified powers (5/8)		Institutional capacity (4/6)	
1. replace	X	10. no dissolution		19. amendments	X	27. sessions	X
2. serve as ministers		11. no decree	X	20. war	X	28. secretary	
3. interpellate	X	12. no veto	X	21. treaties	X	29. staff	
4. investigate	X	13. no review	X	22. amnesty		30. no term limits	X
5. oversee police	X	14. no gatekeeping	X	23. pardon		31. seek re-election	X
6. appoint PM	X	15. no impoundment	X	24. judiciary		32. experience	X
7. appoint ministers		16. control resources	X	25. central bank	X		
8. lack president	X	17. immunity		26. media	X		
9. no confidence	X	18. all elected	X				

The Parliament (*Riksdag*) of Sweden first met in 1435. Its existence was formalized in 1719, when Sweden adopted its first constitution. The constitution granted executive power to the king and divided legislative power between the king and parliament. Over the centuries the legislature's powers gradually expanded. In 1975 a sweeping constitutional amendment formalized the monarch's ceremonial role.

The legislature dominates national politics and government. The executive is dependent on and responsible to the legislature. For example, the legislature chooses the prime minister and can remove the government from office with a vote of no confidence. The legislature also has broad institutional autonomy. Most notably, its laws are supreme and not subject to judicial review. It holds numerous specified powers and has some institutional capacity.

SURVEY

1. The legislature alone, without the involvement of any other agencies, can impeach the president or replace the prime minister.

Yes. The legislature can remove the prime minister with a vote of no confidence.

Chapter 6, Article 5
If the Parliament declares that the Prime Minister or any other Minister no longer enjoys its confidence, the Speaker shall discharge the Minister concerned. When the Government is in a position to order an extra election, however, no decision shall be made to discharge the Minister if the Government issues an order for an extra election within one week from the declaration of no confidence.

2. Ministers may serve simultaneously as members of the legislature.

No. Legislators who serve in government have a sleeping mandate, meaning that they may join the government but forfeit their voting rights in the legislature during their government service. They may return to the legislature when their government service ends.

Chapter 4, Article 9
(1) While a member of the Parliament is acting as Speaker of the Parliament or is a member of the Government, his mandate as a member of the Parliament shall be exercised by an alternate member. The Parliament may prescribe in the Parliament Act that an alternate

member shall replace a member of the Parliament while the latter is on leave of absence.

3. The legislature has powers of summons over executive branch officials and hearings with executive branch officials testifying before the legislature or its committees are regularly held.

Yes. The legislature regularly interpellates officials from the executive.

> Chapter 12, Article 5
> Under provisions laid down in the Parliament Act, any member of the Parliament may submit an interpellation or put down a question for a Minister in any matter concerning the Minister's performance of his duties.

4. The legislature can conduct independent investigation of the chief executive and the agencies of the executive.

Yes. The legislature can investigate the executive.

> Chapter 12, Article 1
> The Committee on the Constitution shall examine Ministers' performance of their duties and the handling of Government business. The Committee is entitled for this purpose to have access to the records of the decisions made in Cabinet matters and to all documents pertaining to such matters. Any other Parliament Committee and any member of the Parliament shall be entitled to raise in writing with the Committee on the Constitution any issue concerning a Minister's performance of his duties or concerning the handling of Cabinet business.

> Chapter 12, Article 6
> (1) The Parliament shall elect one or more Ombudsmen to supervise under instructions laid down by the Parliament the application in public service of laws and other statutes. An Ombudsman may initiate legal proceedings in the cases indicated in these instructions.
> (2) An Ombudsman may be present at the deliberations of a court or an administrative authority and shall have access to the minutes and other documents of any such court or authority. Any court or administrative authority and any State or local government official shall provide an Ombudsman with such information and reports as he may request. A similar obligation shall also be incumbent on any other person coming under the supervision of the Ombudsman. A public prosecutor shall assist an Ombudsman on request.
> (3) Further provisions concerning the Ombudsmen are set forth in the Parliament Act.

> Chapter 12, Article 7
> (1) The Parliament shall elect auditors from among its members to examine the activities of the State. The Parliament may decide that the auditors' scrutiny shall extend also to other activities. The Parliament draws up standing orders for the auditors.
> (2) Under provisions set forth in law, the auditors may demand such documents, data, and reports as are necessary for their scrutiny.

> (3) Further provisions concerning the auditors are set out in the Parliament Act.

5. The legislature has effective powers of oversight over the agencies of coercion (the military, organs of law enforcement, intelligence services, and the secret police).

Yes. The legislature has effective powers of oversight over the agencies of coercion.

6. The legislature appoints the prime minister.

Yes. The legislature appoints the prime minister.

> Chapter 6, Article 1
> The Government comprises the Prime Minister and other members of the Cabinet. The Prime Minister is appointed in the manner prescribed in Articles 2 to 4. The Prime Minister appoints the other members of the Cabinet.

> Chapter 6, Article 2
> (1) When a Prime Minister is to be appointed, the Speaker shall summon for consultation one or more representatives from each party group in the Parliament. The Speaker shall confer with the Deputy Speakers and shall then submit a proposal to the Parliament.
> (2) The Parliament shall proceed to vote on the proposal, no later than the fourth day thereafter, without preparation in committee. If more than half the members of the Parliament vote against the proposal, it is rejected. In all other circumstances it is approved.

7. The legislature's approval is required to confirm the appointment of ministers; or the legislature itself appoints ministers.

No. The prime minister appoints ministers, and the appointments do not require the legislature's approval.

> Chapter 6, Article 1
> The Government comprises the Prime Minister and other members of the Cabinet. The Prime Minister is appointed in the manner prescribed in Articles 2 to 4. The Prime Minister appoints the other members of the Cabinet.

8. The country lacks a presidency entirely or there is a presidency, but the president is elected by the legislature.

Yes. The country lacks a presidency. The monarch is the head of state.

> Chapter 1, Article 5
> (1) The King or Queen who occupies the throne of Sweden in accordance with the Act of Succession shall be the Head of State.

9. The legislature can vote no confidence in the government.

Yes. The legislature can vote no confidence in the government.

Chapter 6, Article 2

(1) When a Prime Minister is to be appointed, the Speaker shall summon for consultation one or more representatives from each party group in the Parliament. The Speaker shall confer with the Deputy Speakers and shall then submit a proposal to the Parliament.

(2) The Parliament shall proceed to vote on the proposal, no later than the fourth day thereafter, without preparation in committee. If more than half the members of the Parliament vote against the proposal, it is rejected. In all other circumstances it is approved.

Chapter 6, Article 3

If the Parliament rejects the Speaker's proposal the procedure laid down in Article 2 shall be resumed. If the Parliament rejects the Speaker's proposal four times in succession, the procedure for appointing a Prime Minister is discontinued and resumed only after an election for the Parliament has been held. Unless ordinary elections must in any case be held within three months, an extra election shall be held within that same period.

Chapter 6, Article 5

If the Parliament declares that the Prime Minister or any other Minister no longer enjoys its confidence, the Speaker shall discharge the Minister concerned. When the Government is in a position to order an extra election, however, no decision shall be made to discharge the Minister if the Government issues an order for an extra election within one week from the declaration of no confidence.

Chapter 12, Article 4

(1) The Parliament may declare that a particular Minister does not enjoy the confidence of Parliament. Such a declaration of no confidence requires the concurrence therein of more than half the members of the Parliament.

(2) A motion for a declaration of no confidence shall be taken up for consideration only if it is introduced by no fewer than one tenth of the members of the Parliament. It shall not be taken up for consideration during the period between the date on which an ordinary election has been held or an extra election has been declared and the Parliament elected in such an election has convened. A motion which concerns a Minister holding office under the terms of Chapter 6, Article 8 after having been discharged may not be taken up for consideration in any circumstances.

(3) A motion calling for a declaration of no confidence shall not be prepared in committee.

10. The legislature is immune from dissolution by the executive.

No. The government can dissolve the legislature. Dissolution is here expressed as "order an extra election."

Chapter 3, Article 4

(1) The Government may order an extra election to be held between ordinary elections. Extra elections shall

be held within three months of the issue of such an order.

(2) After an election for the Parliament has been held, the Government is debarred from issuing an order for an extra election until three months have elapsed from the first meeting of the newly-elected Parliament. Nor may the Government issue an order for an extra election while ministers retain their posts, after having all been formally discharged, pending the assumption of office by a new Government.

(3) Provisions concerning an extra election in a particular case are set forth in Chapter 6, Article 3.

Chapter 6, Article 2

(1) When a Prime Minister is to be appointed, the Speaker shall summon for consultation one or more representatives from each party group in the Parliament. The Speaker shall confer with the Deputy Speakers and shall then submit a proposal to the Parliament.

(2) The Parliament shall proceed to vote on the proposal, no later than the fourth day thereafter, without preparation in committee. If more than half the members of the Parliament vote against the proposal, it is rejected. In all other circumstances it is approved.

Chapter 6, Article 3

If the Parliament rejects the Speaker's proposal the procedure laid down in Article 2 shall be resumed. If the Parliament rejects the Speaker's proposal four times in succession, the procedure for appointing a Prime Minister is discontinued and resumed only after an election for the Parliament has been held. Unless ordinary elections must in any case be held within three months, an extra election shall be held within that same period.

11. Any executive initiative on legislation requires ratification or approval by the legislature before it takes effect; that is, the executive lacks decree power.

Yes. The executive lacks decree power.

12. Laws passed by the legislature are veto-proof or essentially veto-proof; that is, the executive lacks veto power, or has veto power but the veto can be overridden by a majority in the legislature.

Yes. The executive lacks veto power.

13. The legislature's laws are supreme and not subject to judicial review.

Yes. In practice, the legislature's laws are supreme and not subject to judicial review. Formally, courts can refuse a law only if its contravention of the constitution is totally indisputable or "manifest," and there has been but a single case of such a decision, involving a minor matter. The case arose in the 1990s, when a court voided an archaic law from the 1930s concerning political uniforms.

Chapter 11, Article 14

If a court or any other public body considers that a provision conflicts with a provision of a fundamental law or with a provision of any other superior statute, or that the procedure prescribed was set aside in any important respect when the provision was introduced, the provision may not be applied. However, if the provision has been approved by the Parliament or by the Government, it may be set aside only if the fault is manifest.

14. The legislature has the right to initiate bills in all policy jurisdictions; the executive lacks gatekeeping authority.

Yes. The legislature can initiate bills in all policy jurisdictions.

15. Expenditure of funds appropriated by the legislature is mandatory; the executive lacks the power to impound funds appropriated by the legislature.

Yes. The executive lacks the power to impound funds appropriated by the legislature.

Chapter 9, Article 2
(1) State funds may not be used in any way other than that determined by the Parliament.
(2) The Parliament approves the use of such funds for different purposes by adopting a budget in accordance with Articles 3 to 5. The Parliament may, however, decide that funds are to be employed in another manner.

16. The legislature controls the resources that finance its own internal operation and provide for the perquisites of its own members.

Yes. The legislature enjoys financial autonomy.

17. Members of the legislature are immune from arrest and/or criminal prosecution.

No. Legislators are subject to arrest for crimes that carry a minimum penalty of not less than two years' imprisonment.

Chapter 4, Article 8
(1) No one may bring an action against any person who holds a mandate, or has held a mandate, as a member of the Parliament, deprive him of his liberty, or prevent him from traveling within the country, on account of his actions or statements in the fulfillment of his mandate, unless the Parliament has given its consent by means of a decision in which no fewer than five sixths of those present and voting have concurred.
(2) If, in any other case, a member of the Parliament is suspected of having committed a criminal act, the relevant provisions of law relating to arrest, detention or remand are applicable only if he admits guilt or was caught in the act, or if the minimum penalty for the crime is not less than two years' imprisonment.

18. All members of the legislature are elected; the executive lacks the power to appoint any members of the legislature.

Yes. All members of the legislature are elected.

Chapter 3, Article 1
(1) The Parliament is appointed by free, secret and direct elections.

19. The legislature alone, without the involvement of any other agencies, can change the Constitution.

Yes. The legislature can change the constitution with a three-fourths majority vote. It can also change the constitution through a more complicated procedure. The sitting legislature can propose the constitutional amendment in multiple readings with a majority vote, and, following an election, the subsequent legislature can approve the amendment.

Chapter 8, Article 15
(1) A fundamental law shall be adopted by means of two decisions of identical wording. The second decision may not be taken until elections for the Parliament have been held throughout the country following the first decision, and the newly-elected Parliament has been convened. Not less than nine months shall furthermore elapse between the time when the matter was first submitted to the Chamber of the Parliament and the time of the election, unless the Constitutional Committee of the Parliament grants an exemption from this provision by means of a decision taken not later than the Committee stage, and in which no fewer than five sixths of the members concur.

Chapter 8, Article 16
The Parliament Act shall be adopted as prescribed in Article 15 (1), first and second sentences, and (2). It may also be adopted by means of a single decision, provided that it is approved by no fewer than three fourths of those present and voting and by more than half the members of the Parliament. Supplementary provisions of the Parliament Act shall however be adopted in the same way as ordinary laws.

20. The legislature's approval is necessary for the declaration of war.

Yes. The legislature's approval is necessary for the declaration of war, with the common exception for cases of foreign invasion. In order to "repel an armed attack," the government can unilaterally deploy the country's armed forces.

Chapter 10, Article 9
(1) The Government may commit the country's defence forces, or any part of them, to battle in order to repel an armed attack upon the Realm. Swedish armed forces may otherwise be committed to battle or sent to another country only if
    1) the Parliament has assented thereto;
    2) it is permitted under a law which sets out the prerequisites for such action;
    3) an obligation to take such action follows from an international agreement or obligation which has been approved by the Parliament.

(2) No declaration of war may be made without the consent of the Parliament, except in the event of an armed attack against Sweden.

(3) The Government may authorize the defence forces to use force in accordance with international law and custom to prevent a violation of Swedish soil in time of peace or during a war between foreign states.

21. The legislature's approval is necessary to ratify treaties with foreign countries.

Yes. The legislature's approval is necessary to ratify international treaties.

Chapter 10, Article 1
Agreements with other states or with international organizations shall be concluded by the Government.

Chapter 10, Article 2
(1) The Government may not conclude any international agreement binding upon the Realm without Parliament approval, if the agreement presupposes the amendment or abrogation of a law or the enactment of a new law, or if it otherwise concerns a matter which is for the Parliament to decide.

(2) If in a case under Paragraph (1) a special procedure has been prescribed for the decision of the Parliament, the same procedure shall be followed in connection with the approval of the agreement.

(3) Nor may the Government in cases other than cases under Paragraph (1) without the approval of the Parliament conclude any international agreement which is binding upon the Realm, if the agreement is of major importance. The Government may, however, act without obtaining the Parliament's approval of the agreement if the interest of the Realm so requires. In such a case the Government shall confer instead with the Foreign Affairs Advisory Council before concluding the agreement.

22. The legislature has the power to grant amnesty.

No. Amnesty and pardon are not treated separately, and the legislature lacks the power to grant amnesty. See item 23.

23. The legislature has the power of pardon.

No. The government has the power of pardon.

Chapter 1, Article 13
(1) The Government may by exercising mercy remit or reduce a penal sanction or other legal effect of a criminal act, and may remit or reduce any other similar intervention affecting the person or property of a private subject made by a public authority.

(2) Where exceptional reasons so warrant, the Government may order that no further action be taken to investigate or prosecute a criminal act.

24. The legislature reviews and has the right to reject appointments to the judiciary; or the legislature itself appoints members of the judiciary.

No. The government makes judicial appointments,

and the appointments do not require the legislature's approval.

Chapter 11, Article 9
(1) Appointments to a post in a court or in an administrative authority under the Government shall be made by the Government or by an authority designated by the Government.

(2) When making appointments to posts within the State administration attention shall be directed only to objective factors such as merit and competence.

(3) Only a Swedish citizen may hold or exercise the functions of a judicial office, an office directly subordinate to the Government, a post or commission as head of an authority directly subordinate to the Parliament or to the Government, or as a member of such an authority or its board, a post in the Government Chancery immediately subordinate to a Minister or a post as a Swedish envoy. Also in other cases no one who is not a Swedish citizen may hold an office or carry out a commission, if the holder of such an office or commission is elected by the Parliament. Swedish nationality may otherwise be made a prerequisite of the right to hold or exercise an office or commission under the State or a local authority only if laid down in law or under conditions prescribed by law.

25. The chairman of the central bank is appointed by the legislature.

Yes. Parliament appoints the governor of the Bank of Sweden, although it does so indirectly, by electing the body that names the governor.

Chapter 9, Article 12
(2) The Bank of Sweden is an authority under the Parliament.

(3) The Bank of Sweden is administered by eight Trustees. Seven of the Trustees are elected by the Parliament. These Trustees elect a Trustee to act also as Governor of the Bank for a five-year period. The Trustees elected by the Parliament elect a chairman from among their number. This chairman may not exercise any other commission or hold any office within the executive direction of the Bank. Rules concerning the Parliament's election of Trustees, concerning the direction of the Bank of Sweden in other respects, and concerning its operations are laid down in the Parliament Act and elsewhere in law.

(4) A Trustee for whom the Parliament does not grant discharge of responsibility is thereby severed from his appointment. The Trustees elected by the Parliament may remove the chairman from office and the person who is a Trustee and the Governor of the Bank from his appointment.

26. The legislature has a substantial voice in the operation of the state-owned media.

Yes. The legislature has authority over the funding and organization of the public media, although it is forbidden from interfering with programs' content.

27. The legislature is regularly in session.

Yes. The legislature regularly meets in ordinary session.

> Chapter 4, Article 1
> The Parliament shall convene in session every year. Sessions shall be held in Stockholm, unless otherwise decided by the Parliament, or by the Speaker, having regard to the safety or liberty of Parliament.
>
> Chapter 1, Article 4
> (1) An ordinary session which has begun during August, September or October shall be prorogued no later than 31 May the following year. If special grounds exist the Parliament can prolong the session up to and including 15 June, but no longer. Other sessions continue for as long as the Parliament finds necessary. If a motion has been raised calling for the holding of a referendum on a matter concerning a fundamental law, the session shall continue until the motion has been considered, notwithstanding what has been stated above in this article. A session shall be prorogued not later than the day on which the next ordinary session shall begin.
> (2) If the Government has ordered an extra election, it may decide to suspend a session for the remainder of the electoral period. The Parliament shall be dissolved immediately after the decision has been announced at a meeting of the Chamber.

28. Each legislator has a personal secretary.

No. Party groups provide secretarial assistance, but on average there is less than one staff person for each legislator.

29. Each legislator has at least one non-secretarial staff member with policy expertise.

No. See item 28.

30. Legislators are eligible for re-election without any restriction.

Yes. There are no restrictions on re-election.

31. A seat in the legislature is an attractive enough position that legislators are generally interested in and seek re-election.

Yes.

32. The re-election of incumbent legislators is common enough that at any given time the legislature contains a significant number of highly experienced members.

Yes. Re-election rates are sufficiently high to produce a significant number of highly experienced members.

FEDERAL ASSEMBLY OF SWITZERLAND (*BUNDESVERSAMMLUNG/ASSEMBLÉE FÉDÉRALE/ASSEMBLEA FEDERALE*)

Expert consultants: Clive H. Church, Paolo Dardanelli, Hans Hirter, Wolf Linder, Gerald Schneider, Susanne Alice Wengle

Score: .72

Influence over executive (6/9)		Institutional autonomy (9/9)		Specified powers (5/8)		Institutional capacity (3/6)	
1. replace		10. no dissolution	X	19. amendments		27. sessions	
2. serve as ministers		11. no decree	X	20. war	X	28. secretary	
3. interpellate	X	12. no veto	X	21. treaties	X	29. staff	
4. investigate	X	13. no review	X	22. amnesty	X	30. no term limits	X
5. oversee police	X	14. no gatekeeping	X	23. pardon	X	31. seek re-election	X
6. appoint PM	X	15. no impoundment	X	24. judiciary	X	32. experience	X
7. appoint ministers	X	16. control resources	X	25. central bank			
8. lack president	X	17. immunity	X	26. media			
9. no confidence		18. all elected	X				

The Federal Assembly (*Bundesversammlung/ Assemblée fédérale/Assemblea federale*) of Switzerland traces its origins to the meetings of representative diets in the late thirteenth century. The diets were formalized in the country's 1815 constitution. The 1848 constitution established the present bicameral legislature, consisting of a lower house, the National Council (*Nationalrat/Conseil national/Consiglio nazionale*), and an upper house, the Council of States (*Ständerat/Conseil des états/ Consiglio degli stati*). The constitution also established the Federal Council, a seven-person executive elected by the legislature. The ceremonial presidency rotates every year among the members of the Federal Council.

The legislature is the center of national politics. It selects and effectively oversees the members of government. The legislature enjoys complete institutional autonomy. It is noteworthy, however, that although the executive lacks decree power, the legislature's laws can be rejected in a popular referendum. The legislature exercises many specified powers and has some institutional capacity.

SURVEY

1. The legislature alone, without the involvement of any other agencies, can impeach the president or replace the prime minister.

No. The legislature cannot vote no confidence in, or impeach, the president.

2. Ministers may serve simultaneously as members of the legislature.

No. Legislators are prohibited from serving simultaneously in ministerial positions.

> Article 144
> (1) Members of the National Council, of the Council of States, of the Federal Government, and Judges of the Federal Court may not at the same time be members of another of these bodies.

3. The legislature has powers of summons over executive branch officials and hearings with executive branch officials testifying before the legislature or its committees are regularly held.

Yes. The legislature regularly interpellates officials from the executive.

> Article 169
> (1) The Federal Parliament shall exercise the high supervision over the Federal Government, the Federal Administration, the Federal Courts and the other organs entrusted with tasks of the Federation.
> (2) Official secrecy shall not be opposable to those special delegations of supervisory commissions that are appointed as provided by Statute.

4. The legislature can conduct independent investigation of the chief executive and the agencies of the executive.

Yes. The legislature can investigate the executive.

> Article 169
> (1) The Federal Parliament shall exercise the high supervision over the Federal Government, the Federal Administration, the Federal Courts and the other organs entrusted with tasks of the Federation.
> (2) Official secrecy shall not be opposable to those special delegations of supervisory commissions that are appointed as provided by Statute.

5. The legislature has effective powers of oversight over the agencies of coercion (the military, organs of law enforcement, intelligence services, and the secret police).

Yes. The legislature has effective powers of oversight over the agencies of coercion.

6. The legislature appoints the prime minister.

Yes. The legislature appoints the members of the Federal Council, among whom the federal president rotates annually.

> Article 168
> (1) The Federal Parliament shall elect the members of the Federal Government, the Federal Chancellor, the judges of the Federal Court and the General.

> Article 175
> (1) The Federal Government shall consist of seven members.
> (2) The members of the Federal Government shall be elected by the Federal Parliament after each full renewal of the National Council.

> Article 176
> (1) The President of the Federation shall chair the Federal Government.
> (2) The Federal Parliament shall elect, for a term of one year, one of the members of the Federal Government as President of the Federation, and another as Vice-President of the Federal Government.
> (3) These mandates may not be renewed for the following year. The President of the Federation shall not be eligible to be Vice-President for the following year.

7. The legislature's approval is required to confirm the appointment of ministers; or the legislature itself appoints ministers.

Yes. The legislature elects the members of the federal government.

> Article 168
> (1) The Federal Parliament shall elect the members of the Federal Government, the Federal Chancellor, the judges of the Federal Court and the General.

> Article 175
> (1) The Federal Government shall consist of seven members.
> (2) The members of the Federal Government shall be elected by the Federal Parliament after each full renewal of the National Council.

8. The country lacks a presidency entirely or there is a presidency, but the president is elected by the legislature.

Yes. The country lacks a presidency in the usual sense of the term. The legislature does, however, elect the president of the federation from among the members of the federal government.

> Article 176
> (1) The President of the Federation shall chair the Federal Government.
> (2) The Federal Parliament shall elect, for a term of one year, one of the members of the Federal Government as President of the Federation, and another as Vice-President of the Federal Government.
> (3) These mandates may not be renewed for the following year. The President of the Federation shall not be eligible to be Vice-President for the following year.

9. The legislature can vote no confidence in the government.

No. The legislature cannot vote no confidence in the government.

10. The legislature is immune from dissolution by the executive.

Yes. The legislature is immune from dissolution.

11. Any executive initiative on legislation requires ratification or approval by the legislature before it takes effect; that is, the executive lacks decree power.

Yes. The executive lacks decree power. The government can issue "ordinances" to ensure the implementation of laws.

> Article 182
> (1) The Federal Government shall legislate in the form of ordinances, insofar as the Constitution or the statute empower it to do so.
> (2) It shall ensure the implementation of statutes, of decrees of the Federal Parliament, and of judgments of the federal judiciary.

12. Laws passed by the legislature are veto-proof or essentially veto-proof; that is, the executive lacks veto power, or has veto power but the veto can be overridden by a majority in the legislature.

Yes. The executive lacks veto power. Laws can be vetoed, however, in a popular referendum.

13. The legislature's laws are supreme and not subject to judicial review.

Yes. The legislature's laws are supreme and not subject to judicial review.

14. The legislature has the right to initiate bills in all policy jurisdictions; the executive lacks gatekeeping authority.

Yes. The legislature can initiate bills in all policy jurisdictions.

15. Expenditure of funds appropriated by the legislature is mandatory; the executive lacks the power to impound funds appropriated by the legislature.

Yes. The executive lacks the power to impound funds appropriated by the legislature.

16. The legislature controls the resources that finance its own internal operation and provide for the perquisites of its own members.

Yes. The legislature enjoys financial autonomy.

17. Members of the legislature are immune from arrest and/or criminal prosecution.

Yes. Legislators are immune.

> Article 162
> (1) The members of the Federal Parliament and the Federal Government, and the Federal Chancellor may not be held responsible for their statements in the Chambers and before parliamentary organs.
> (2) The statute may provide for further forms of immunity, and extend them to other persons.

18. All members of the legislature are elected; the executive lacks the power to appoint any members of the legislature.

Yes. All members of the legislature are elected.

> Article 149
> (1) The National Council shall be composed of 200 representatives of the People.
> (2) The representatives shall be elected directly by the People according to the system of proportional representation. The National Council shall be renewed in full every four years.

> Article 150
> (1) The Council of States shall consist of 46 delegates of the Cantons.
> (2) The Cantons of Obwald, Nidwald, Basle-City, Basle-Land, Appenzell Outer-Rhodes and Appenzell Inner-Rhodes shall elect one Senator each, the other Cantons shall elect two Senators.

19. The legislature alone, without the involvement of any other agencies, can change the Constitution.

No. Constitutional amendments require approval in a popular referendum.

> Article 138
> (1) 100,000 citizens entitled to vote may propose a total revision of the Federal Constitution.
> (2) This proposal has to be submitted to the people by referendum.

> Article 140
> (1) The following shall be submitted to the vote of the People and the Cantons:

a. Revisions of the Federal Constitution.

Article 193

(1) A total revision of the Federal Constitution may be proposed by the People or by one of the Chambers, or may be decreed by the Federal Parliament.

(2) If the initiative emanates from the People or if the Chambers disagree, the People shall decide whether a total revision shall be undertaken.

(3) Should the People accept a total revision, both Chambers shall be newly elected.

(4) The mandatory provisions of international law may not be violated.

Article 194

(1) A partial revision of the Federal Constitution may be requested by the People, or be decreed by the Federal Parliament.

(2) A partial revision must respect the principle of the unity of subject matter; it may not violate the mandatory provisions of international law.

(3) A popular initiative for partial revision must, moreover, respect the principle of the unity of form.

20. The legislature's approval is necessary for the declaration of war.

Yes. Switzerland maintains permanent neutrality, and the constitution does not provide for a declaration of war. The legislature's approval is required for a sustained mobilization of a substantial number of troops.

Article 185

(1) The Federal Government shall take measures to secure the external security, the independence, and the neutrality of Switzerland.

(2) It shall take measures to safeguard the inner security.

(3) It may base itself directly on the present article to issue ordinances and orders to obviate existing or imminent great disturbances of the public order, the external or the inner security. Such ordinances shall be limited in time.

(4) In urgent cases, it may mobilize troops. If it mobilizes more than 4000 members of the armed forces for active duty, or if the mobilization for active duty is expected to last more than three weeks, the Federal Parliament must be convened without delay.

21. The legislature's approval is necessary to ratify treaties with foreign countries.

Yes. The legislature's approval is necessary to ratify international treaties with the exception for treaties that "are within the powers of the federal government."

Article 141a

(1) If the approval of an international treaty is subject to a mandatory public referendum, the Federal Parliament may include into the approval act those amendments to the Constitution necessary for the implementation of the treaty.

(2) If the approval of an international treaty is subject to a facultative public referendum, the Federal Parliament may include into the approval act those changes of the law necessary for the implementation of the treaty.

Article 166

(1) The Federal Parliament shall participate in shaping foreign policy, and shall supervise foreign relations.

(2) It shall approve international treaties, with the exception of those which by statute or international treaty are within the powers of the Federal Government.

Article 184

(1) The Federal Government shall conduct foreign relations safeguarding the Federal Parliament's participation rights; it shall represent Switzerland abroad.

(2) It shall sign treaties and ratify them. It shall submit them to the Federal Parliament for approval.

(3) When the safeguard of the interests of the country so require, the Federal Government may issue ordinances and orders. Ordinances must be limited in time.

22. The legislature has the power to grant amnesty.

Yes. The legislature has the power to grant amnesty.

Article 173

(1) The Federal Parliament shall further have the following tasks and powers:

   k. It shall decide on petitions for pardon and declare amnesties.

23. The legislature has the power of pardon.

Yes. The legislature has the power of pardon.

Article 157

(1) The National Council and the Council of States shall deliberate in common as the Federal Parliament in Joint Session under the chairmanship of the President of the National Council in order to:

   c. to rule on petitions for pardon.

Article 173

(1) The Federal Parliament shall further have the following tasks and powers:

   k. It shall decide on petitions for pardon and declare amnesties.

24. The legislature reviews and has the right to reject appointments to the judiciary; or the legislature itself appoints members of the judiciary.

Yes. The legislature elects the members of the judiciary.

Article 168

(1) The Federal Parliament shall elect the judges of the Federal Court.

25. The chairman of the central bank is appointed by the legislature.

No. The Federal Council appoints the chairman of the Swiss National Bank.

26. The legislature has a substantial voice in the operation of the state-owned media.

No. The legislature lacks a substantial voice in the operation of the public media.

27. The legislature is regularly in session.

No. Parliament is in session for only four three-week meetings each year.

> Article 151
> (1) The Chambers shall meet regularly for sessions. The Statute shall regulate the calling of sessions.

28. Each legislator has a personal secretary.

No. Legislators receive a modest fixed sum for personal staff, although not all legislators have a secretary.

29. Each legislator has at least one non-secretarial staff member with policy expertise.

No. See item 28.

30. Legislators are eligible for re-election without any restriction.

Yes. There are no restrictions on re-election.

31. A seat in the legislature is an attractive enough position that legislators are generally interested in and seek re-election.

Yes.

32. The re-election of incumbent legislators is common enough that at any given time the legislature contains a significant number of highly experienced members.

Yes. Re-election rates are sufficiently high to produce a significant number of highly experienced members.

PEOPLE'S ASSEMBLY OF SYRIA (*MAJLIS AL-SHAAB*)

Expert consultants: Taima Aljayoush, Souhaïl Belhadj, Ellen Lust-Okar, Daniel Neep, Eyal Zisser

Score: .31

Influence over executive (2/9)		Institutional autonomy (2/9)		Specified powers (2/8)		Institutional capacity (4/6)	
1. replace		10. no dissolution		19. amendments		27. sessions	X
2. serve as ministers	X	11. no decree		20. war	X	28. secretary	
3. interpellate		12. no veto		21. treaties	X	29. staff	
4. investigate		13. no review		22. amnesty		30. no term limits	X
5. oversee police		14. no gatekeeping	X	23. pardon		31. seek re-election	X
6. appoint PM		15. no impoundment		24. judiciary		32. experience	X
7. appoint ministers		16. control resources		25. central bank			
8. lack president		17. immunity		26. media			
9. no confidence	X	18. all elected	X				

The People's Assembly (*Majlis al-Shaab*) of Syria traces its origins to the Syrian National Congress established by the French in 1919. Over the course of its history, the Syrian legislature has had few opportunities to assert itself. After achieving independence from France in 1946, Syria briefly (1958–61) united with Egypt to create the United Arab Republic. Following its separation from Egypt, Syria was ruled by emergency law in the Arab Socialist Baath Party's one-party state. A new constitution in 1973 established the unicameral People's Assembly. Under this constitution the president is nominated by the Baath Party and approved in a popular referendum.

The Assembly has little meaningful power. It has meager influence over the executive. The Assembly's own autonomy is circumscribed by the president's dissolution, decree, and veto powers. It exercises strikingly few specified powers but does enjoy some institutional capacity.

SURVEY

1. The legislature alone, without the involvement of any other agencies, can impeach the president or replace the prime minister.

No. The legislature alone cannot impeach the president. According to law, the president can be removed from office in a procedure involving both the legislature and the Supreme Constitutional Court. In practice, the president cannot be removed from office at all by constitutional means. The legislature can remove the prime minister with a vote of no confidence.

> Article 72
> Confidence may not be withheld without the interrogation of the cabinet or a minister. A request for withholding confidence has to be made in accordance with a proposal submitted by at least one-fifth of the members of the Assembly. Confidence in the cabinet or a minister may be withheld by a majority of the members of the Assembly. In the event of no confidence in the cabinet, the Prime Minister must submit the cabinet's resignation to the President of the Republic. A minister from whom confidence has been withheld must also resign.

> Article 91
> The President cannot be held responsible for actions pertaining directly to his duties, except in the case of high treason. A request for his indictment requires a proposal of at least one-third of the members of the People's Assembly and an Assembly decision adopted by a two-thirds majority in an open vote at a special secret session. His trial takes place only before the Supreme Constitutional Court.

2. Ministers may serve simultaneously as members of the legislature.

Yes. Legislators may serve simultaneously in ministerial positions.

> Article 125
> Cabinet and People's Assembly membership may be combined.

3. The legislature has powers of summons over executive branch officials and hearings with executive branch officials testifying before the legislature or its committees are regularly held.

No. Formally, the legislature can question executive branch officials, but in practice, it lacks this power.

> Article 70
> The members of the Assembly have the right to... address questions and inquiries to the cabinet or any minister in accordance with the Assembly's internal organization.

4. The legislature can conduct independent investigation of the chief executive and the agencies of the executive.

No. The legislature cannot investigate the executive.

5. The legislature has effective powers of oversight over the agencies of coercion (the military, organs of law enforcement, intelligence services, and the secret police).

No. The legislature lacks effective powers of oversight over the agencies of coercion.

6. The legislature appoints the prime minister.

No. The president appoints the prime minister.

> Article 95
> The President of the Republic appoints one or more Vice Presidents and delegates some of his duties to them. The President also appoints the Prime Minister and his deputies and the ministers and their deputies, accepts their resignations, and dismisses them from their posts.

7. The legislature's approval is required to confirm the appointment of ministers; or the legislature itself appoints ministers.

No. The president appoints ministers, and the appointments do not require the legislature's approval.

> Article 95
> The President of the Republic appoints one or more Vice Presidents and delegates some of his duties to them. The President also appoints the Prime Minister and his deputies and the ministers and their deputies, accepts their resignations, and dismisses them from their posts.

8. The country lacks a presidency entirely or there is a presidency, but the president is elected by the legislature.

No. The president is elected in a popular referendum on the proposal of the Arab Socialist Baath Party.

> Article 84
> Upon the proposal of the Arab Socialist Baath Party regional command, the Assembly issues the order for election of the President:
> 1) the candidacy is proposed to the citizens for referendum;
> 2) the referendum takes place upon the request of the President of the Assembly;
> 3) the new president is elected before termination of the term of the present President, within a period of not less than 30 days and not more than 60 days;
> 4) the candidate becomes President of the Republic if he obtains an absolute majority of the total votes. If he fails to obtain this majority, the Assembly names another candidate. The same procedures are followed concerning the election, provided this takes place within 1 month from the time the results of the first plebiscite were announced.

9. The legislature can vote no confidence in the government.

Yes. The legislature can vote no confidence in the government.

> Article 72
> Confidence may not be withheld without the interrogation of the cabinet or a minister. A request for withholding confidence has to be made in accordance with a proposal submitted by at least one-fifth of the members of the Assembly. Confidence in the cabinet or a minister may be withheld by a majority of the members of the Assembly. In the event of no confidence in the cabinet, the Prime Minister must submit the cabinet's resignation to the President of the Republic. A minister from whom confidence has been withheld must also resign.

10. The legislature is immune from dissolution by the executive.

No. The president can dissolve the legislature.

> Article 107
> (1) The President of the Republic can dissolve the People's Assembly through a decision giving the reasons. Elections are held within 90 days from the date of the dissolution.
> (2) He may not dissolve the People's Assembly more than once for the same reason.

11. Any executive initiative on legislation requires ratification or approval by the legislature before it takes effect; that is, the executive lacks decree power.

No. The president issues decrees that have the force of law.

> Article 99
> The President of the Republic issues decrees, decisions, and orders in accordance with the legislation in effect.

12. Laws passed by the legislature are veto-proof or essentially veto-proof; that is, the executive lacks veto power, or has veto power but the veto can be overridden by a majority in the legislature.

No. A two-thirds majority vote is required to override the president's veto.

> Article 98
> The President of the Republic promulgates the laws approved by the People's Assembly, he may veto these laws through a decision, giving the reasons for this objection, within a month after their receipt by the President. If the Assembly again approves them by a two-thirds majority, the President of the Republic has to issue them.

13. The legislature's laws are supreme and not subject to judicial review.

No. The Supreme Constitutional Court can review the constitutionality of laws made by the legislature. In an unusual twist on the practice of judicial review, the Supreme Constitutional Court may review laws enacted by the legislature, but not those made by the president and approved by public referendum.

> Article 145
> The Supreme Constitutional Court looks into and decides on the constitutionality of laws in accordance with the following:
> 1) Should the President of the Republic or a quarter of the People's Assembly members challenge the constitutionality of a law before its promulgation, the promulgation of such law is suspended until the court makes a decision on it within 15 days from the date the appeal was filed with it. Should the law be of an urgent nature, the Supreme Constitutional Court must make a decision within 7 days.
> 2) Should a quarter of the People's Assembly members object to the constitutionality of a legislative decree within 15 days of the date of the People's Assembly session, the Supreme Constitutional Court must decide on it within 15 days from the date the objection was filed with it.
> 3) Should the Supreme Constitutional Court decide that a law or a decree is contrary to the Constitution, whatever is contrary to the text of the Constitution is considered null and void with retroactive effect and has no consequence.

> Article 146
> The Supreme Constitutional Court has no right to look into laws which the President of the Republic submits to public referendum and are approved by the people.

> Article 147
> The Supreme Constitutional Court, at the request of the President of the Republic, gives its opinion on the constitutionality of bills and legislative decrees and the legality of draft decrees.

14. The legislature has the right to initiate bills in all policy jurisdictions; the executive lacks gatekeeping authority.

Yes. The legislature can initiate bills in all policy jurisdictions.

15. Expenditure of funds appropriated by the legislature is mandatory; the executive lacks the power to impound funds appropriated by the legislature.

No. The president can impound funds appropriated by the legislature.

16. The legislature controls the resources that finance its own internal operation and provide for the perquisites of its own members.

No. The legislature is dependent on the executive for the resources that finance its own operations.

17. Members of the legislature are immune from arrest and/or criminal prosecution.

No. Formally, legislators are immune for official parliamentary business, but in practice, legislators lack immunity. For example, in 2002 two legislators urging political reform were stripped of their parliamentary immunity and charged with "attempting to illegally change the constitution."

Article 66
Members of the Assembly are not accountable before criminal or civil courts for any occurrences or views they express, in voting in public or secret sessions, or in the activities of the various committees.

18. All members of the legislature are elected; the executive lacks the power to appoint any members of the legislature.

Yes. All members of the legislature are elected.

Article 50
(2) The members of the People's Assembly are elected by general, secret, direct, and equal ballot in accordance with the provisions of the election law.

19. The legislature alone, without the involvement of any other agencies, can change the Constitution.

No. Constitutional amendments require the president's approval.

Article 149
(1) The President of the Republic as well as a two-thirds majority of the People's Assembly members have a right to propose amending the Constitution.
(2) The amendment proposal includes the provisions to be amended and the reasons for it.
(3) Upon receipt of the proposal, the People's Assembly sets up a special committee to investigate it.
(4) The Assembly discusses the amendment proposal, and if approved by a two-thirds majority of its members, the amendment is considered final, provided it is approved by the President of the Republic. It will then be included in the body of the Constitution.

20. The legislature's approval is necessary for the declaration of war.

Yes. The legislature's approval is required for presidential war declarations.

Article 100
The President of the Republic can declare war and general mobilization and conclude peace following the approval by the People's Assembly.

21. The legislature's approval is necessary to ratify treaties with foreign countries.

Yes. The legislature's approval is necessary to ratify international treaties on most major issues.

Article 71
The People's Assembly assumes the following powers:
5) Approval of international treaties and agreements connected with state security; namely, peace and alliance treaties, all treaties connected with the rights of

sovereignty or agreements which grant concessions to foreign companies or establishments, as well as treaties and agreements which entail expenditures of the state treasury not included in the treasury's budget, and treaties and agreements which run counter to the provisions of the laws in force or treaties and agreements which require promulgation of new legislation to be implemented.

22. The legislature has the power to grant amnesty.

No. The legislature's approval is necessary to confirm the president's decisions to grant amnesty, but the legislature cannot grant amnesty itself.

Article 71
The People's Assembly assumes the following powers:
6) Approval of general amnesty.

Article 105
The President of the Republic can issue amnesty and reinstatement decisions.

23. The legislature has the power of pardon.

No. The president has the power of pardon.

24. The legislature reviews and has the right to reject appointments to the judiciary; or the legislature itself appoints members of the judiciary.

No. The president appoints the members of the Supreme Constitutional Court and other courts, and the appointments do not require the legislature's approval.

Article 139
The Supreme Constitutional Court is composed of five members, of whom one will be the President, and all of whom are appointed by the President of the Republic by decree.

25. The chairman of the central bank is appointed by the legislature.

No. The president appoints the governor of the Central Bank of Syria.

26. The legislature has a substantial voice in the operation of the state-owned media.

No. The legislature lacks a voice in the operation of the public media.

27. The legislature is regularly in session.

Yes. The legislature regularly meets in ordinary session.

Article 61
The People's Assembly is convened in three ordinary sessions yearly. It may also be convened in extraordinary sessions. The Assembly's table of organization sets the dates and periods of the sessions. The Assembly is invited to meet at extraordinary sessions by a decision of the President of the Assembly, at the written request

of the President of the Republic, or at the request of one-third of the members of the Assembly.

28. Each legislator has a personal secretary.

No.

29. Each legislator has at least one non-secretarial staff member with policy expertise.

No.

30. Legislators are eligible for re-election without any restriction.

Yes. There are no restrictions on re-election.

31. A seat in the legislature is an attractive enough position that legislators are generally interested in and seek re-election.

Yes.

32. The re-election of incumbent legislators is common enough that at any given time the legislature contains a significant number of highly experienced members.

Yes. Re-election rates are sufficiently high to produce a significant number of highly experienced members. It merits note, however, that remaining in the good graces of the president and his hegemonic Baath Party, rather than maintaining popular support in elections, is the key to members' retention of seats and to the presence of continuity of membership in the legislature.

LEGISLATIVE YUAN OF TAIWAN, REPUBLIC OF CHINA (*LÌFĂ YÙAN*)

Expert consultants: Jean-Pierre Cabestan, Tun-jen Cheng, Yun Fan, Thomas B. Gold, Pei-Shan Lee, I-Chou Liu, Alexander C. Tan, Yu-Shan Wu

Score: .59

Influence over executive (3/9)		Institutional autonomy (6/9)		Specified powers (4/8)		Institutional capacity (6/6)	
1. replace		10. no dissolution		19. amendments		27. sessions	X
2. serve as ministers		11. no decree	X	20. war	X	28. secretary	X
3. interpellate	X	12. no veto		21. treaties	X	29. staff	X
4. investigate	X	13. no review		22. amnesty	X	30. no term limits	X
5. oversee police	X	14. no gatekeeping	X	23. pardon		31. seek re-election	X
6. appoint PM		15. no impoundment	X	24. judiciary	X	32. experience	X
7. appoint ministers		16. control resources	X	25. central bank			
8. lack president		17. immunity	X	26. media			
9. no confidence		18. all elected	X				

The Legislative Yuan (*Lìfǎ Yùan*) of Taiwan traces its origins to the Republic of China's 1931 provisional constitution. The constitution set up a system of government with five branches: the Legislative Yuan, the Executive Yuan, the Judicial Yuan, as well as the Control Yuan (responsible for ensuring that public officials obey the law) and the Examination Yuan (responsible for recruitment, training, and promotion of civil servants). The constitution also called for an elected National Assembly responsible for electing a new president and changing the constitution.

Following the Kuomintang's evacuation from mainland China to Taiwan in 1948, the island came under martial law and single-party rule, which lasted until 1991. During this period, legislative elections were irregularly held and constitutional limits on presidential re-election were ignored. Public officials chosen in the last elections before leaving the mainland remained in office, partly to maintain the legitimacy of the claim that the government of Taiwan represented all of China. In the late 1980s, Taiwan began a period of liberalization, which led to the formal abolition of emergency measures in 1991 and to legislative elections in 1992.

A constitutional amendment in 1992 provided for the direct election of the president, and a presidential election was held in 1996. Prior to 1996 the president was elected by the National Assembly. According to a constitutional amendment of 2000, which went into effect in 2003, the president, vice president, and grand justices of the Judicial Yuan are appointed by the president with the consent of the Legislative Yuan. Prior to 2003 the president appointed the members of the judiciary, and the appointments were confirmed by the Control Yuan. In 2005 the National Assembly passed a constitutional amendment to abolish itself. In the future, constitutional amendments will be proposed by the Legislative Yuan and approved in a national referendum. In 2004 the Legislative Yuan voted to cut the number of seats from 225 to 113. The change took effect at the time of the legislative elections in January 2008.

There are currently discussions underway to further amend the constitution to clarify the separation of powers in Taiwan's semipresidential system. Those who favor change disagree about whether the reforms should move the system closer to parliamentarism or presidentialism.

The Legislative Yuan enjoys substantial powers. It can control the executive branch through powers of interpellation and investigation, as well as oversight over the agencies of coercion. The legislature has considerable institutional autonomy. The members of the legislature are immune from arrest, and the executive lacks gatekeeping and decree powers. The legislature also enjoys a number of specified prerogatives and has a high level of institutional capacity.

SURVEY

1. The legislature alone, without the involvement of any other agencies, can impeach the president or replace the prime minister.

No. Presidential impeachment can be initiated only by the Control Yuan, an institution whose purpose is to exercise the powers of censure and impeachment. According to a 2005 amendment, the impeachment proceedings are then carried out by the Judicial Yuan. Prior to 2005 presidential impeachment was initiated by the Control Yuan, and the proceedings were held in the National Assembly.

Article 100
Impeachment proceedings initiated by the Control Yuan against the President or the Vice President shall be instituted upon the proposal of one fourth or more than

one fourth of all Members of the Control Yuan and the resolution, after careful consideration, by a majority of all Members of the Control Yuan.

2. Ministers may serve simultaneously as members of the legislature.

No. Legislators are prohibited from serving simultaneously in ministerial positions.

Article 75
No Member of the Legislative Yuan shall concurrently hold a government post.

3. The legislature has powers of summons over executive branch officials and hearings with executive branch officials testifying before the legislature or its committees are regularly held.

Yes. The legislature regularly interpellates officials from the executive.

Article 57
The Executive Yuan shall be responsible to the Legislative Yuan in accordance with the following provisions:
1. When the Legislative Yuan is in session, its Members have the right to interpellate the President of the Executive Yuan and Ministers and Chairmen of Commissions of the said Yuan.

4. The legislature can conduct independent investigation of the chief executive and the agencies of the executive.

Yes. The legislature can set up committees to investigate the executive.

Article 67
(1) The Legislative Yuan may set up various committees.
(2) The various committees of the Legislative Yuan may invite government officials and concerned individuals in society at large to be present at the committee meetings to present their views.

5. The legislature has effective powers of oversight over the agencies of coercion (the military, organs of law enforcement, intelligence services, and the secret police).

Yes. Legislative committees have effective powers of oversight over the agencies of coercion.

6. The legislature appoints the prime minister.

No. The president appoints the prime minister, called the president of the Executive Yuan.

Article 55
(1) The President of the Executive Yuan shall be nominated and . . . appointed by the President of the Republic.

7. The legislature's approval is required to confirm the appointment of ministers; or the legislature itself appoints ministers.

No. The president appoints ministers on the rec-ommendation of the president of the Executive Yuan, and the appointments do not require the legislature's approval.

Article 56
The Vice President of the Executive Yuan, Ministers and Chairmen of Commissions, and Ministers without Port-folio shall be appointed by the President of the Republic upon the recommendation of the President of the Exec-utive Yuan.

8. The country lacks a presidency entirely or there is a presidency, but the president is elected by the legislature.

No. A 1992 amendment calls for the direct election of the president, and the first nationwide presiden-tial elections were held in 1996. Prior to 1996 the president was elected by the National Assembly.

9. The legislature can vote no confidence in the gov-ernment.

No. The legislature cannot vote no confidence in the government.

10. The legislature is immune from dissolution by the executive.

No. The president can dissolve the Legislative Yuan.

11. Any executive initiative on legislation requires rat-ification or approval by the legislature before it takes effect; that is, the executive lacks decree power.

Yes. The executive lacks decree power.

12. Laws passed by the legislature are veto-proof or essentially veto-proof; that is, the executive lacks veto power, or has veto power but the veto can be over-ridden by a majority in the legislature.

No. The president does not have a direct veto but can request his own government, the Executive Yuan, to ask the Legislative Yuan to reconsider legislation. A two-thirds majority from the Leg-islative Yuan is needed to override an executive veto.

Article 57
The Executive Yuan shall be responsible to the Legisla-tive Yuan in accordance with the following provisions:
3. In case the Executive Yuan deems an enactment, a budget, or a treaty passed by the Legislative Yuan difficult to enforce, it may, with the approval of the President of the Republic and within ten days after the transmission of the Legislative Yuan's message, request the latter for reconsideration. If, during reconsidera-tion, two thirds of the members of the Legislative Yuan present at the meeting uphold the original resolution, the President of the Executive Yuan shall either abide

by the Legislative Yuan's resolution or tender his resig-nation.

Article 72
Law bills passed by the Legislative Yuan shall be trans-mitted to the President of the Republic and the Exec-utive Yuan. The President shall, within ten days after receipt of the bills, promulgate them, but he may also deal with them in accordance with the provisions of Article 57 of this Constitution.

13. The legislature's laws are supreme and not sub-ject to judicial review.

No. The Judicial Yuan can review the constitution-ality of laws.

Article 78
The Judicial Yuan shall interpret the Constitution and shall have the power to unify the interpretation of laws and ordinances.

Article 171
(1) Laws that contravene the Constitution shall be null and void.
(2) In case of doubt as to whether a given law contra-venes the Constitution, the matter shall be settled by interpretation by the Judicial Yuan.

14. The legislature has the right to initiate bills in all policy jurisdictions; the executive lacks gatekeeping authority.

Yes. The legislature can initiate bills in all policy jurisdictions.

15. Expenditure of funds appropriated by the legis-lature is mandatory; the executive lacks the power to impound funds appropriated by the legislature.

Yes. The executive cannot impound funds appro-priated by the legislature.

16. The legislature controls the resources that finance its own internal operation and provide for the perquisites of its own members.

Yes. The legislature has financial autonomy.

17. Members of the legislature are immune from arrest and/or criminal prosecution.

Yes. Legislators are immune with the common exception for cases of *flagrante delicto*.

Article 73
No Member of the Legislative Yuan shall be held respon-sible outside the Yuan for opinions expressed or votes cast in the Yuan.

Article 74
No Member of the Legislative Yuan shall, except in case of flagrante delicto, be arrested or detained without the permission of the Legislative Yuan.

18. All members of the legislature are elected; the executive lacks the power to appoint any members of the legislature.

Yes. Since 1992, all members of the legislature are elected. From 1948 to 1992, in an attempt to claim that the Republic of China was the official government of mainland China, the legislature retained the legislators who had been elected in the final elections held on the mainland before fleeing to Taiwan. During this time periodic elections were held to replace deceased members and to expand the size of the legislature.

> Article 62
> The Legislative Yuan...shall be composed of Members elected by the people and shall exercise legislative power on their behalf.

19. The legislature alone, without the involvement of any other agencies, can change the Constitution.

No. Constitutional amendments require approval in a popular referendum.

20. The legislature's approval is necessary for the declaration of war.

Yes. The legislature's approval is required for the declaration of war.

> Article 63
> The Legislative Yuan shall have the power to pass bills on laws, budgets, martial law, and amnesty, declaration of war, conclusion of peace, treaties, and other important matters of State.

21. The legislature's approval is necessary to ratify treaties with foreign countries.

Yes. The legislature's approval is necessary to ratify international treaties on most major issues.

> Article 38
> The President shall, in accordance with the provisions of this Constitution, exercise the powers of concluding treaties, declaring war, and making peace.

> Article 63
> The Legislative Yuan shall have the power to pass bills on laws, budgets, martial law, amnesty, declaration of war, conclusion of peace, treaties, and other important matters of State.

22. The legislature has the power to grant amnesty.

Yes. The legislature has the power to grant amnesty.

> Article 63
> The Legislative Yuan shall have the power to pass bills on laws, budgets, martial law, amnesty, declaration of war, conclusion of peace, treaties, and other important matters of State.

23. The legislature has the power of pardon.

No. The president has the power of pardon.

> Article 40
> The President shall, in accordance with law, exercise the powers of amnesty, pardon, remission of sentence, and restitution of civil rights.

24. The legislature reviews and has the right to reject appointments to the judiciary; or the legislature itself appoints members of the judiciary.

Yes. According to a constitution amendment of 2000, which entered into effect in 2003, the president, vice president, and grand justices of the Judicial Yuan are appointed by the president with the consent of the Legislative Yuan. Prior to 2003 the president appointed the members of the judiciary, and the appointments, which were confirmed by the Control Yuan, did not require the legislature's approval.

> Article 79
> (1) The Judicial Yuan shall have a President and a Vice President. The President and the Vice President of the Judicial Yuan shall be nominated and, upon confirmation by the Control Yuan, appointed by the President of the Republic.
> (2) The Judicial Yuan shall have a number of Grand Justices to be responsible for the matters specified in Article 78 of this Constitution. The Grand Justices shall be nominated and, upon confirmation by the Control Yuan, appointed by the President of the Republic.

25. The chairman of the central bank is appointed by the legislature.

No. The president appoints the chairman of the Bank of Taiwan.

26. The legislature has a substantial voice in the operation of the state-owned media.

No. The legislature lacks a voice in the operation of the public media.

27. The legislature is regularly in session.

Yes. The legislature meets in ordinary session for at least eight months each year.

> Article 68
> The Legislative Yuan shall hold two sessions each year and shall convene of its own accord. The first session shall be from February to the end of May, and the second from September to the end of December. Any session may be prolonged, if necessary.

28. Each legislator has a personal secretary.

Yes.

29. Each legislator has at least one non-secretarial staff member with policy expertise.

Yes.

30. Legislators are eligible for re-election without any restriction.

Yes. There are no restrictions on re-election.

Article 65
Members of the Legislative Yuan shall serve a term of three years and shall be re-eligible.

31. A seat in the legislature is an attractive enough position that legislators are generally interested in and seek re-election.

Yes.

32. The re-election of incumbent legislators is common enough that at any given time the legislature contains a significant number of highly experienced members.

Yes. Re-election rates are sufficiently high to produce a significant number of highly experienced members.

SUPREME ASSEMBLY OF TAJIKISTAN (*MAJLISI OLI*)

Expert consultants: Mehrdad Haghayeghi, Zuhra Halimova, Lidia Isamova, Sarmad Khawaja, Faizullokhodzha Nasrulloev

Score: .31

Influence over executive (1/9)		Institutional autonomy (2/9)		Specified powers (2/8)		Institutional capacity (5/6)	
1. replace		10. no dissolution	X	19. amendments		27. sessions	X
2. serve as ministers		11. no decree		20. war	X	28. secretary	X
3. interpellate		12. no veto		21. treaties	X	29. staff	
4. investigate		13. no review		22. amnesty		30. no term limits	X
5. oversee police		14. no gatekeeping		23. pardon		31. seek re-election	X
6. appoint PM	X	15. no impoundment		24. judiciary		32. experience	X
7. appoint ministers		16. control resources		25. central bank			
8. lack president		17. immunity	X	26. media			
9. no confidence		18. all elected					

The Supreme Assembly (*Majlisi Oli*) of Tajikistan traces its origins to the Regional Congress of the Soviets held in Tashkent in 1917. Beginning in 1921, the country that is now Tajikistan fell under seven decades of Soviet rule. Tajikistan achieved independence in 1991, paving the way for the adoption of the 1994 constitution. The document called for a bicameral legislature consisting of the lower house, the Assembly of Representatives (*Majlisi Namoyandagon*), and an upper house, the National Assembly (*Majlisi Milli*). A constitutional amendment in 2003 extended the length of the president's term but did not directly affect the legislature's powers.

During much of the 1990s, Tajikistan was torn by civil war, and the legislature did not function normally. During the first decade of the 2000s, the Assembly took on more of its formal functions, but its role in national politics is still diminu-

tive. Tajikistan is dominated by its president, Emomali Rakhmon, and the legislature has almost no influence on the executive branch. For example, it cannot choose the president or the prime minister, effectively oversee the government, or remove members of the executive from office. The legislature's own institutional autonomy is limited by a president whose powers include decree authority and the right to appoint one-quarter of the upper house of the legislature. The legislature exercises few specified powers. It does possess some institutional capacity, which is bolstered by the presence of personal legislative staff.

SURVEY

1. The legislature alone, without the involvement of any other agencies, can impeach the president or replace the prime minister.

No. Presidential impeachment requires the approval of the Constitutional Court. The president must initiate removal of the prime minister.

Article 55
Powers of the Majlisi Milli and the Majlisi Namoyandagon while conducting joint sessions:
Approval of presidential decrees on appointment and dismissal of the Prime Minster and other members of the Government.

Article 72
The President has the right to immunity.
The President is deprived of immunity in the event of committing a State treason based on the conclusion of the Constitutional Court by two thirds of votes of all the members of the Majlisi Milli and the deputies of the Majlisi Namoyandagon voting in each Majlisi separately.

2. Ministers may serve simultaneously as members of the legislature.

No. Ministers are prohibited from serving simultaneously in the legislature.

Article 50
Members of the Government . . . may not become members of the Majlisi Milli.

Article 73
The members of the Government do not have the right to hold another office, be deputies of representative organs, or engage in entrepreneurial activity with the exception of scientific, creative, and educational activity.

3. The legislature has powers of summons over executive branch officials and hearings with executive branch officials testifying before the legislature or its committees are regularly held.

No. The legislature does not regularly question executive branch officials.

4. The legislature can conduct independent investigation of the chief executive and the agencies of the executive.

No. The legislature cannot investigate the executive.

5. The legislature has effective powers of oversight over the agencies of coercion (the military, organs of law enforcement, intelligence services, and the secret police).

No. The legislature lacks effective powers of oversight over the agencies of coercion.

6. The legislature appoints the prime minister.

No. The president appoints the prime minister.

Article 69
Powers of the President:

Appoints and dismisses the Prime Minister and other members of the Government; presents decrees appointing and dismissing the Prime Minister and other members of the Government to the joint session of the Majlisi Milli and the Majlisi Namoyandagon for approval.

7. The legislature's approval is required to confirm the appointment of ministers; or the legislature itself appoints ministers.

Yes. The legislature's approval is necessary to confirm the president's ministerial appointments.

Article 69
Powers of the President:
Appoints and dismisses the Prime Minister and other members of the Government; presents decrees appointing and dismissing the Prime Minister and other members of the Government to the joint session of the Majlisi Milli and the Majlisi Namoyandagon for approval.

8. The country lacks a presidency entirely or there is a presidency, but the president is elected by the legislature.

No. The president is directly elected.

Article 65
The President is elected by the citizens of Tajikistan on the basis of universal, equal and direct suffrage by a secret ballot for a term of seven years.

9. The legislature can vote no confidence in the government.

No. The legislature cannot, acting alone, vote no confidence in the government. The legislature's approval, however, is necessary for the president to dismiss the prime minister.

Article 55
Powers of the Majlisi Milli and the Majlisi Namoyandagon while conducting joint sessions:
Approval of presidential decrees on appointment and dismissal of the Prime Minster and other members of the Government.

10. The legislature is immune from dissolution by the executive.

Yes. The legislature is immune from dissolution by the executive, although the legislature can vote to dissolve itself.

Article 63
The Majlisi Milli and the Majlisi Namoyandagon in a joint session may dissolve themselves prematurely with the support of no less than two thirds of the members of the Majlisi Milli and deputies of the Majlisi Namoyandagon.
The Majlisi Milli and the Majlisi Namoyandagon may not be dissolved during the state of emergency and martial law.

11. Any executive initiative on legislation requires ratification or approval by the legislature before it takes effect; that is, the executive lacks decree power.

No. The president issues decrees that have the force of law.

Article 70
The President within the limits of his powers issues decrees and orders, informs the joint session of the Majlisi Milli and the Majlisi Namoyandagon about the country's situation, [and] submits important and necessary issues for discussion to the joint session of the Majlisi Milli and the Majlisi Namoyandagon.

12. Laws passed by the legislature are veto-proof or essentially veto-proof; that is, the executive lacks veto power, or has veto power but the veto can be overridden by a majority in the legislature.

No. A two-thirds majority vote is required to override a presidential veto.

Article 62
Laws are presented to the President of the Republic of Tajikistan for signature and promulgation. If the President does not agree with a law or its part, he returns it within fifteen days to the Majlisi Namoyandagon with his objections. The Majlisi Milli and the Majlisi Namoyandagon reconsider the given law according to the procedure established by the Constitution. If during the reconsideration the law is approved in the earlier adopted wording by a majority of no less than two thirds of all the members of the Majlisi Milli and the deputies of the Majlisi Namoyandagon, the President shall sign the law and promulgate it within 10 days.
During reconsideration of a law returned by the President previously adopted by the Majlisi Namoyandagon by two thirds of the votes, the Majlisi Milli and the Majlisi Namoyandagon approve the law again by a majority of no less than two thirds of the votes.
If the President returns a constitutional law, the Majlisi Namoyandagon and the Majlisi Milli reconsider the given law according to the procedure established by the Constitution. If during the reconsideration the constitutional law is approved in the earlier adopted wording by a majority of no less than two thirds of all the members of the Majlisi Milli and deputies of the Majlisi Namoyandagon, the President shall sign the law and promulgate it within 10 days.

13. The legislature's laws are supreme and not subject to judicial review.

No. The Constitutional Court can review the constitutionality of laws.

Article 89
Powers of the Constitutional Court:
Determining of the conformity to the Constitution of laws.

14. The legislature has the right to initiate bills in all policy jurisdictions; the executive lacks gatekeeping authority.

No. The legislature is prohibited from initiating legislation related to taxation and amnesty.

Article 59
Amnesty bills are introduced to the Majlisi Namoyandagon by the President of the Republic of Tajistan. Budget bills and bills establishing and abolishing taxes are introduced to the Majlisi Namoyandagon by the Government of the Republic of Tajikistan.

15. Expenditure of funds appropriated by the legislature is mandatory; the executive lacks the power to impound funds appropriated by the legislature.

No. The president can impound funds appropriated by the legislature.

16. The legislature controls the resources that finance its own internal operation and provide for the perquisites of its own members.

No. The legislature is dependent on the president for the resources that finance its own operations.

17. Members of the legislature are immune from arrest and/or criminal prosecution.

Yes. Legislators are immune with the common exception for cases of *flagrante delicto*, here expressed as "detainment at a scene of a crime."

Article 51
A member of the Majlisi Milli and a deputy of the Majlisi Namoyandagon have the right to immunity; he may not be arrested, detained, taken into custody, [and] searched, except in cases of detainment at a scene of a crime. A member of the Majlisi Milli and a deputy of the Majlisi Namoyandagon may not be subjected to a personal search except in cases provided for by law in order to ensure safety of other people. Issues regarding the deprivation of a member of the Majlisi Milli and a deputy of the Majlisi Namoyandagon of their immunity are resolved by the corresponding Majlisi upon a presentation of the General Procurator.

18. All members of the legislature are elected; the executive lacks the power to appoint any members of the legislature.

No. The president appoints eight of the thirty-four members of the National Assembly. All members of the Assembly of Representatives are elected.

Article 48
The Majlisi Oli – the Parliament of the Republic of Tajikistan – is the highest representative and legislative organ of the Republic of Tajikistan.
The Majlisi Oli consists of two Majlisis (assemblies) – the Majlisi Milli and the Majlisi Namoyandagon.
The term of the Majlisi Milli and the Majlisi Namoyandagon is five years. The powers of the Majlisi Milli and the Majlisi Namoyandagon are terminated on

the day on which the activity of the Majlisi Milli and the Majlisi Namoyandagon of the new convocation begins. The organization and activity of the Majlisi Oli are determined by a constitutional law.

Article 49
The Majlisi Namoyandagon is elected on the basis of universal, equal, and direct suffrage by secret ballot... Three quarters of the members of the Majlisi Milli are elected indirectly by way of secret ballot at joint assemblies of people's deputies of the Gorno-Badakhshan Autonomous Oblast and its cities and rayons, oblasts and their cities and rayons, the city of Dushanbe and its rayons, cities and rayons of republican subordination (jointly). In the Majlisi Milli, the Gorno-Badakhshan Autonomous Oblast, oblasts, the city of Dushanbe, [and] cities and rayons of republican subordination have an equal number of representatives. One quarter of the members of the Majlisi Milli is appointed by the President of the Republic of Tajikistan.

19. The legislature alone, without the involvement of any other agencies, can change the Constitution.

No. Constitutional amendments require approval in a popular referendum.

Article 98
Amendments and supplements to the Constitution take place by means of a national referendum.
A referendum is called by the President or the Majlisi Namoyandagon with the support of no less than two thirds of the total number of deputies.

Article 99
Proposed amendments and supplements to the Constitution are introduced by the President or by no less than one third of all members of the Majlisi Milli and deputies of the Majlisi Namoyandagon. Proposed amendments and supplements to the Constitution are published in the press three months before the referendum.

20. The legislature's approval is necessary for the declaration of war.

Yes. There is no formal provision for the declaration of war. The legislature's approval is necessary, however, for presidential declarations of martial law and a state of emergency.

Article 55
Powers of the Majlisi Milli and the Majlisi Namoyandagon while conducting joint sessions:
Approval of the presidential decree on declaration of martial law and state of emergency

Article 69
Powers of the President:
Declares a state of emergency on the entire territory of the Republic or in individual locations with an immediate presentation of a corresponding decree for approval to the joint session of the Majlisi Milli and the Majlisi Namoyandagon and notification of the United Nations.

21. The legislature's approval is necessary to ratify treaties with foreign countries.

Yes. The approval of the Assembly of Representatives is necessary to ratify international treaties.

Article 57
Powers of the Majlisi Namoyandagon:
Ratification and denouncement international treaties

Article 69
Powers of the President:
Leads the conduct of foreign policy, signs international treaties and presents them for the approval of the Majlisi Namoyandagon.

22. The legislature has the power to grant amnesty.

No. Amnesty bills are introduced by the president and approved by the Assembly of Representatives.

Article 59
Amnesty bills are introduced to the Majlisi Namoyandagon by the President of the Republic of Tajikistan.

Article 60
The laws on the State budget and amnesty are adopted only by the Majlisi Namoyandagon.

23. The legislature has the power of pardon.

No. The president has the power of pardon.

Article 69
Powers of the President:
Grants pardons.

24. The legislature reviews and has the right to reject appointments to the judiciary; or the legislature itself appoints members of the judiciary.

No. The National Assembly elects the judges of the Constitutional Court, the Supreme Court, and the Highest Economic Court "upon the presentation of the president," but in practice, the president's "presentation" is the final word, and the legislature has no substantial voice in the appointments. Other judges are appointed by the president on the recommendation of the Council of Justice.

Article 56
Powers of the Majlisi Milli:
Election and recall of the Chairman, Deputy Chairmen, and judges of the Constitutional Court, the Supreme Court, and the Highest Economic Court upon the presentation of the President.

Article 86
Judges of the Military Court, judges of the court of the Gorno-Badakhshan Autonomous Oblast, oblasts, the city of Dushanbe, city and rayon courts, judges of the economic court of the Gorno-Badakhshan Autonomous Oblast, oblasts, and the city of Dushanbe are appointed and dismissed by the President upon the presentation of the Council of Justice.

25. The chairman of the central bank is appointed by the legislature.

No. The president appoints the chairman of the National Bank of Tajikistan with the approval of the legislature.

> Article 69
> Powers of the President:
> Appoints and dismisses the Chairman of the National Bank, his deputies, and presents relevant decrees for the approval of the Majlisi Namoyandagon.

26. The legislature has a substantial voice in the operation of the state-owned media.

No. The legislature lacks a voice in the operation of the public media.

27. The legislature is regularly in session.

Yes. The legislature meets in ordinary session for about eight months each year.

> Article 52
> The activity of the Majlisi Namoyandagon is conducted in the form of sessions. Regular session of the Majlisi Namoyandagon is held once a year from the first working day of October until the last working day of June.

28. Each legislator has a personal secretary.

Yes.

29. Each legislator has at least one non-secretarial staff member with policy expertise.

No.

30. Legislators are eligible for re-election without any restriction.

Yes. There are no restrictions on re-election.

31. A seat in the legislature is an attractive enough position that legislators are generally interested in and seek re-election.

Yes.

32. The re-election of incumbent legislators is common enough that at any given time the legislature contains a significant number of highly experienced members.

Yes. Legislative elections were held in 1995, 2000, and 2005, and the legislature is staffed with a significant number of experienced politicians. It bears note, however, that legislators' loyalty to the president, who dominates politics by controlling the agencies of coercion, the media, and the hegemonic People's Democratic Party, is the key to maintaining a seat in the Assembly.

NATIONAL ASSEMBLY OF TANZANIA (*BUNGE*)

Expert consultants: Paul J. Kaiser, Apollonia Kerenge, David K. Leonard, Rwekaza Mukandala, Vibeke Wang

Score: .31

Influence over executive (4/9)		Institutional autonomy (1/9)		Specified powers (1/8)		Institutional capacity (4/6)	
1. replace		10. no dissolution		19. amendments		27. sessions	X
2. serve as ministers	X	11. no decree		20. war		28. secretary	
3. interpellate	X	12. no veto		21. treaties	X	29. staff	
4. investigate	X	13. no review		22. amnesty		30. no term limits	X
5. oversee police		14. no gatekeeping		23. pardon		31. seek re-election	X
6. appoint PM		15. no impoundment		24. judiciary		32. experience	X
7. appoint ministers		16. control resources	X	25. central bank			
8. lack president		17. immunity		26. media			
9. no confidence	X	18. all elected					

The National Assembly (*Bunge*) of Tanzania traces its origins to the Executive Council established in 1920 to provide representation in Britain's colonial government. Tanzania achieved independence in 1962, but for the next few decades the legislature was marginalized under the single-party system erected by President Julius Nyerere. The country's current constitution was adopted in 1977 and calls for a unicameral legislature. Nyerere's retirement in 1985 paved the way for multiparty politics and the adoption of a constitutional amendment in 1992, which provides the legislature with a vote of no confidence.

The Assembly's modest powers are distributed unevenly. The Assembly enjoys some influence over the executive branch. It members serve in government. Furthermore, it can interpellate and investigate the government and remove the government with a vote of no confidence. The legislature's own institutional autonomy, however, is negligible. Furthermore, the legislature exercises only one of the specified powers assessed in this survey, but it does have some institutional capacity.

SURVEY

1. The legislature alone, without the involvement of any other agencies, can impeach the president or replace the prime minister.

No. Presidential impeachment requires the involvement of a Special Committee of Inquiry, whose membership includes extraparliamentary judicial authorities. The legislature can remove the prime minister with a vote of no confidence.

Article 46
(1) Notwithstanding the provisions of Article 46 of this Constitution the National Assembly may pass a resolution to remove the President from office if a motion to impeach the President is moved and passed in accordance with the provisions of this Article.
(2) Subject to the other provisions of this Article, no motion to impeach the President shall be moved save only if it is alleged that the President –
    (a) has committed acts which generally violate the Constitution or the law concerning the ethics of public leaders;
    (b) has committed acts which contravene the conditions concerning the registration of political parties specified in Article 20(2) of this Constitution; or
    (c) has conducted himself in a manner which lowers the esteem of the office of President of the United Republic, and no such motion shall be moved within twenty months from the time when a similar motion was previously moved and rejected by the National Assembly.
(3) The National Assembly shall not pass a motion to impeach the President save only if –
    (a) a written notice signed and supported by not less the twenty per cent of all the member of Parliament is submitted to the Speaker thirty days prior to the sitting at which such motion is intended to be moved in the National Assembly, specifying the

wrong committed by the President and proposing that a Special Committee of Inquiry be constituted to inquire into the charges brought against the President.
    (b) at any time after the Speaker receives the notice duly signed by the Member of Parliament and satisfies himself that the provisions of the Constitution for the moving of the motion have been complied with, to vote on the motion to constitute a Special Committee of Inquiry, and if it is supported by not less than two thirds of all the Member of Parliament, the Speaker shall announce the names of the member of the Special Committee of Inquiry.
(4) The Special Committee of Inquiry for the purpose of this Article shall consist of the following members, that is to say –
    (a) the Chief Justice of the United Republic who shall be the Chairman of the Committee;
    (b) the Chief Justice of Tanzania Zanzibar; and
    (c) seven members appointed by the Speaker in accordance with the Standing Orders of the National Assembly and taking into account the proportional representation amongst the political parties represented in the National Assembly.
(5) In the event that the National Assembly passes the motion to constitute a Special Committee of Inquiry, the President shall be deemed to be out of office, and the duties and functions of the office of President shall be discharged in accordance with the provisions of Article 37(3) of this Constitution until the Speaker shall inform the President about the resolution of the National Assembly in connection with the charges brought against him.
(6) Within seven days after the Special Committee of Inquiry is constituted, it shall sit, inquire into and analyse the charges preferred against the President, including affording the President the opportunity to be heard in his defence in accordance with the procedure prescribed by the Standing Orders of the National Assembly.
(7) As soon as possible and in any event within a period of not more than ninety days, the Special Committee of Inquiry shall submit its report to the Speaker.
(8) After the Speaker receives the report of the Special Committee of Inquiry, the report shall be tabled before the National Assembly in accordance with the procedure prescribed by the Standing Orders of the National Assembly.
(9) After the report of the Special Committee of Inquiry is submitted pursuant to subarticle (8) the National Assembly shall discuss the report and shall afford the President the opportunity to be heard, and then by the votes of not less than two thirds majority of all the Members of Parliament, the National Assembly shall pass a resolution either that the charges against the President have been proved and that he is unworthy of continuing to hold the office of President, or that the charges have not been proved.
(10) In the event the National Assembly passes a resolution that the charges against the President have been

proved and that he is unworthy of continuing to hold the office of President, the Speaker shall inform the President and the Chairman of the Electoral Commission about such resolution of the National Assembly, whereupon the President shall be obliged to resign before the expiry of three days from the day the National Assembly passed the resolution.

(11) In the event the President ceases to hold the office of President by reason of the charges against him being proved he shall not be entitled to receive any payment by way of pension or to receive any benefits or other privileges which he has under the Constitution or any other law enacted by Parliament.

Article 51
(1) There shall be a Prime Minister of the United Republic who shall be appointed by the President in accordance with the provisions of this Article and who, before assuming his office, shall take and subscribe before the President such oath of office of Prime Minister as may be prescribed by Parliament.
(2) As soon as possible, and in any event within fourteen days after assuming his office, the President shall appoint a Member of Parliament elected from a constituency from a political party having a majority of Members of Parliament in the National Assembly or, if no political party has a majority, who appears to have the support of the majority of the Members of Parliament, to be Prime Minister of the United Republic, and he shall not assume office until his appointment is first confirmed by a resolution of the National Assembly supported by a majority vote of Members of Parliament.

2. Ministers may serve simultaneously as members of the legislature.

Yes. Ministers are required to serve simultaneously in the legislature.

Article 55
(4) All Ministers and Deputy Ministers shall be appointed from among Members of Parliament.

3. The legislature has powers of summons over executive branch officials and hearings with executive branch officials testifying before the legislature or its committees are regularly held.

Yes. The legislature regularly interpellates officials from the executive.

Article 63
(3) For the purposes of discharging its functions the National Assembly may –
   (a) put any question to any Minister concerning public affairs in the United Republic which are within his responsibility.

4. The legislature can conduct independent investigation of the chief executive and the agencies of the executive.

Yes. The legislature can establish special committees to investigate the executive.

5. The legislature has effective powers of oversight over the agencies of coercion (the military, organs of law enforcement, intelligence services, and the secret police).

No. The legislature lacks effective powers of oversight over the agencies of coercion.

6. The legislature appoints the prime minister.

No. The president appoints the prime minister with the consent of the National Assembly.

Article 51
(1) There shall be a Prime Minister of the United Republic who shall be appointed by the President in accordance with the provisions of this Article and who, before assuming his office, shall take and subscribe before the President such oath of office of Prime Minister as may be prescribed by Parliament.
(2) As soon as possible, and in any event within fourteen days after assuming his office, the President shall appoint a Member of Parliament elected from a constituency from a political party having a majority of Members of Parliament in the National Assembly or, if no political party has a majority, who appears to have the support of the majority of the Members of Parliament, to be Prime Minister of the United Republic, and he shall not assume office until his appointment is first confirmed by a resolution of the National Assembly supported by a majority vote of Members of Parliament.

7. The legislature's approval is required to confirm the appointment of ministers; or the legislature itself appoints ministers.

No. The president appoints ministers on the advice of the prime minister, and the appointments do not require the legislature's approval.

Article 55
(1) All Ministers who are members of the Cabinet by virtue of Article 54 shall be appointed by the President after consultation with the Prime Minister, and they shall be responsible for such offices as the President may, from time to time, by writing under his hand and the Public Seal, establish.
(2) In addition to the Ministers referred to in subarticle (1) the President may, after consultation with the Prime Minister, appoint Deputy Ministers. All Deputy Ministers shall not be members of the Cabinet.
(3) The President may appoint any number of Deputy Ministers who shall assist Ministers in the discharge of their duties and functions.
(4) All Ministers and Deputy Ministers shall be appointed from among Members of Parliament.
(5) Notwithstanding the provisions of subarticle (4), in the event that the President is obliged to appoint a Minister or a Deputy Minister after dissolution of Parliament then he may appoint any person who was a Member of Parliament before Parliament was dissolved.

8. The country lacks a presidency entirely or there is a presidency, but the president is elected by the legislature.

No. The president is directly elected.

Article 33

(1) There shall be a President of the United Republic.

Article 38

(1) The President shall be elected by the people in accordance with the provisions of this Constitution and in accordance with the law enacted by Parliament pursuant to the provisions of this Constitution, making provisions concerning the election of the President.

9. The legislature can vote no confidence in the government.

Yes. The legislature can vote no confidence in the government.

Article 53A

(1) Notwithstanding the provisions of Article 51 of this Constitution, the National Assembly may pass a vote of no confidence in the Prime Minister if a motion proposing in that behalf is moved and passed in accordance with the provisions of this Article.

(2) Subject to the other provisions of this Article, any motion for a vote of no confidence in the Prime Minister shall not be moved in the National Assembly if –

(a) either it has no relation with the discharge of the responsibilities of the Prime Minister in accordance with Article 52 of the Constitution) or there are no allegations that the Prime Minister has contravened the law concerning the ethics of public leaders;

(b) six months have not lapsed since he was appointed;

(c) nine months have not lapsed since a similar motion was moved in and rejected by the National Assembly.

(3) A motion for a vote of no confidence in the Prime Minister shall not be passed by the National Assembly save only if:

(a) a written notice, signed and supported by not less than twenty percentum of all the Members of Parliament is submitted to the Speaker, at least fourteen days prior to the day on which the motion is intended to be moved before the National Assembly;

(b) The Speaker satisfies himself that the provisions of the Constitution governing the moving of the motion have been complied with.

(4) A motion which satisfies the provisions of this Article shall be moved before the National Assembly as soon as possible in accordance with the Standing Orders of the National Assembly.

(5) A motion for a vote of no confidence in the Prime Minister shall be passed only if it is supported by a majority of the Members of Parliament.

(6) In the event the motion for a vote of no confidence in the Prime Minister is supported by a majority of the Members of Parliament, the Speaker shall submit the resolution to the President, and as soon as possible and in any event within two days from the day the National Assembly passed the vote of no confidence in the Prime Minister, the Prime Minister shall be required to resign, and the President shall appoint another Member of Parliament to be Prime Minister.

10. The legislature is immune from dissolution by the executive.

No. The president can dissolve the legislature.

Article 90

(2) The President shall not have power to dissolve Parliament at any time save only –

(a) if the life of Parliament has expired in terms of Article 65 of the Constitution or at any time within the last twelve months of the life of Parliament, save only if the Speaker receives a formal notice under Article 46A of this Constitution proposing the formation of a Special Committee of Inquiry with a view to impeaching the President;

(b) if the National Assembly refuses to approve a budget proposed by the Government;

(c) if Parliament fails to pass a Bill in terms of the provisions of Article 97(4);

(d) if the National Assembly declines to pass a motion which is of fundamental importance to Government policies and the President considers that the way out is not to appoint another Prime Minister but to call for a general election; or

(e) if, having regard to the proportional representation of political parties in the National Assembly the President considers that it is no longer legitimate for the Government in power to continue in office, and it is not feasible to form a new Government.

(3) Upon the expiration of the life of Parliament, Parliament shall stand dissolved: Save that if the life of Parliament expires at any time when the United Republic is at war, the National Assembly may, from time to time, extend the period mentioned in Article 65 of this Constitution for a period not exceeding twelve months each time; provided that the life of Parliament shall not be extended under the provisions of this subarticle for a period of more than five years.

(4) If an emergency arises or exists which, in the opinion of the President, necessitates the summoning of a Parliament at a time when Parliament stands dissolved, and the majority of results in the general election following the dissolution have not been declared, the President may, by Proclamation, summon Parliament and direct that the Speaker and all the persons who were the Members of Parliament immediately before the dissolution of Parliament attend such meeting of Parliament and such persons together with the Speaker shall be deemed to be the Members of the National Assembly for the purposes of that meeting and shall be so deemed until midnight of the day the majority of the results of the general election are declared.

11. Any executive initiative on legislation requires ratification or approval by the legislature before it takes effect; that is, the executive lacks decree power.

No. Formally, the executive lacks decree power. In practice, the president issues decrees that have the force of law.

12. Laws passed by the legislature are veto-proof or essentially veto-proof; that is, the executive lacks veto power, or has veto power but the veto can be overridden by a majority in the legislature.

No. A two-thirds majority vote is required to override a presidential veto. Moreover, an override does not necessarily result in the passage of a bill. Even after the legislature votes to override the president's veto, the president can still choose to dissolve the legislature rather than assent to the bill.

Article 97

(1) Subject to the provisions contained in this Constitution, the National Assembly shall exercise its legislative power through the process of debating and passing Bills which eventually shall have to be assented to by the President, and a Bill shall not become law unless it is so passed by the National Assembly and assented to by the President in accordance with the provisions of this Article.

(2) After a Bill is presented to the President for his assent, the President may either assent to the Bill or withhold his assent, and in the event the President withholds his assent to a Bill, he shall return it to the National Assembly together with a statement of his reasons for withholding his assent to the Bill.

(3) After a Bill is returned to the National Assembly pursuant to the provisions of this Article, it shall not be presented again to the President for his assent before the expiration of six months since it was so returned, except if at the last stage in the National Assembly before it is again presented to the President it is supported by the votes of not less than two-thirds of all the Members of Parliament.

(4) If a Bill is returned to the National Assembly by the President, and it is then supported in the National Assembly by not less than two-thirds of all Members of Parliament as provided in subarticle (3) and it is presented a second time to the President for assent within six months of its being so returned, then the President shall be obliged to assent to the Bill within twenty-one days of its being presented to him, otherwise he shall have to dissolve Parliament.

(5) The provisions contained in this Article or in Article 64 of this Constitution shall not prevent Parliament from enacting laws making provisions conferring on any person or department of Government the power to make regulations having the force of law or conferring the force of law on any regulations made by any person, or any department of Government.

13. The legislature's laws are supreme and not subject to judicial review.

No. The High Court can review the constitutionality of laws.

Article 30

(5) Where in any proceedings it is alleged that any law enacted or any action taken by the Government or any other authority abrogates or abridges any of the basic rights, freedoms and duties set out in Articles 12 to 29 of this Constitution, and the High Court is satisfied that the law or action concerned, to the extent that it conflicts with this Constitution, is void, or is inconsistent with this Constitution, then the High Court, if it deems fit, or if the circumstances or public interest so requires, instead of declaring that such law or action is void, shall have power to decide to afford the Government or other authority concerned an opportunity to rectify the defect found in the law or action concerned within such a period and in such manner as the High Court shall determine, and such law or action shall be deemed to be valid until such time the defect is rectified or the period determined by the High Court lapses, whichever is the earlier.

14. The legislature has the right to initiate bills in all policy jurisdictions; the executive lacks gatekeeping authority.

No. The legislature is prohibited from introducing legislation related to taxation, public expenditures, or government debt.

Article 99

(1) The National Assembly shall not deal with any of the matters to which this Article relates except if the President has proposed that the matter be dealt with by the National Assembly and the proposal has been submitted to the National Assembly by a Minister.

(2) The matters to which this Article relate are the following:

(a) a Bill to enact a law providing for any of the following –

(i) to levy a tax or to alter taxation otherwise than by reduction;

(ii) the imposition of any charge upon the Consolidated Fund or any other public fund or the alteration of any such charge otherwise than by reduction;

(iii) the payment, issue or withdrawal from the Consolidated Fund or any other public fund of any moneys not charged thereon, or any increase in the amount of such payment, issue or withdrawal;

(iv) the composition or remission of any debt due or payable to the United Republic;

(b) a motion or any amendment of a motion for the purposes of any of the matters referred to in paragraph (a) of this subarticle.

(3) The provisions of this Article shall not apply to a Bill or any amendment to a Bill introduced by or a motion or an amendment to a motion moved by a Minister or a Deputy Minister.

15. Expenditure of funds appropriated by the legislature is mandatory; the executive lacks the power to impound funds appropriated by the legislature.

No. The president can impound funds appropriated by the legislature.

16. The legislature controls the resources that finance its own internal operation and provide for the perquisites of its own members.

Yes. The legislature enjoys financial autonomy.

17. Members of the legislature are immune from arrest and/or criminal prosecution.

No. Legislative immunity extends to official parliamentary business only. Legislators are subject to arrest for common crimes.

Article 100
(1) There shall be freedom of opinion, debate and in the National Assembly, and that freedom shall not be breached or questioned by any organ in the United Republic or in any court or elsewhere outside the National Assembly.
(2) Subject to this Constitution or to the provisions of any other relevant law, a Member of Parliament shall not be prosecuted and no civil proceedings may be instituted against him in a court in relation to any thing which he has said or done in the National Assembly or has submitted to the National Assembly by way of a petition, bill, motion or otherwise.

18. All members of the legislature are elected; the executive lacks the power to appoint any members of the legislature.

No. The executive can appoint members of the legislature. The executive branch, relying on constitutional provisions that allow the Electoral Commission a say in ensuring adequate female membership, enjoys some effective appointment powers. The attorney general, who is appointed by the president, also serves as a legislator.

Article 66
(1) Subject to the other provisions of this Article, there shall be the following categories of Members of Parliament, that is to say: –
  (a) members elected to represent, constituencies;
  (b) women members being not less than fifteen percent of the members mentioned in paragraphs (a), (c) and (d) elected by the political parties represented in the National Assembly in terms of Article 78 and on the basis of proportional representation amongst those parties;
  (c) five members elected by the House of Representatives from among its members;
  (d) the Attorney General.
(2) The President and the Vice-President shall each not be a Member of Parliament.

(3) Where a Regional Commissioner is elected a Member of Parliament representing a constituency or where a Member of Parliament representing a constituency is appointed a Regional Commissioner, the National Assembly shall be deemed to consist of the requisite number of members and its proceedings shall be valid notwithstanding that the ordinary total number of members in terms of this Article shall have been reduced by reason of such election of the Regional Commissioner or such appointment of a constituency member.

Article 78
(1) For the purposes of the election of women Members of Parliament mentioned in Article 66(1) (b), political parties which took part in the election shall in accordance with the procedure laid down propose to the Electoral Commission the names of women on the basis of the proportional representation among the parties which won elections in constituencies and secured seats in the National Assembly. If the Commission is satisfied that any person so proposed has the qualifications to be Member of Parliament it shall declare that that person has been elected Member of Parliament and the provisions of Article 83 of this Constitution shall apply in connection with the election of that person to be Member of Parliament.
(2) No person may be proposed by any political party for the purposes of election in accordance with this Article save only if that person has the requisite qualifications for election in terms of Article 67 of this Constitution.
(3) The names of the persons proposed to the Electoral Commission in accordance with subarticle (1) shall be declared to be the results of the election after the Commission is satisfied that the relevant provisions of the Constitution and of other legislation have been complied with.

19. The legislature alone, without the involvement of any other agencies, can change the Constitution.

No. Constitutional amendments require the president's approval.

Article 97
(1) Subject to the provisions contained in this Constitution, the National Assembly shall exercise its legislative power through the process of debating and passing Bills which eventually shall have to be assented to by the President, and a Bill shall not become law unless it is so passed by the National Assembly and assented to by the President in accordance with the provisions of this Article.

Article 98
(1) Parliament may enact legislation for altering any provision of this Constitution in accordance with the following principles:
  (a) A Bill for an Act to alter any provisions of this Constitution (other than those relating to paragraph (b) of this subarticle) or any provisions of any law

specified in List One of the Second Schedule to this Constitution shall be supported by the votes of not less than two-thirds of all the Members of Parliament;
(b) A Bill for an Act to alter any provisions of this Constitution or any provisions of any law relating to any of the matters specified in List Two of the Second Schedule to this Constitution shall be passed only if it is supported by the votes of not less than two-thirds of all Members of Parliament from Mainland Tanzania and not less than two-thirds of all Members of Parliament from Tanzania Zanzibar.
(2) For the purposes of construing the provisions of subarticle (1), alteration of provisions of this Constitution or the provisions of a law shall be understood to include modification, or correction of those provisions or repeal and replacement of those provisions or the re-enactment or modification of the application of the provisions.

20. The legislature's approval is necessary for the declaration of war.

No. The president can declare war without the legislature's approval. The president is required to seek the legislature's "support" for the war declaration within fourteen days.

Article 44
(1) Subject to this Constitution or to any Act of Parliament providing in that behalf, the President may declare the existence of a state of war between the United Republic and any other country.
(2) After making the declaration, the President shall transmit a copy of such declaration to the Speaker of the National Assembly who, after consultation with the Leader of Government Business in the National Assembly, shall within fourteen days from the date of the declaration, convene a meeting of the National Assembly to deliberate on the prevailing situation and to consider whether or not to pass a resolution in support of the declaration of war made by the President.

21. The legislature's approval is necessary to ratify treaties with foreign countries.

Yes. The legislature's approval is necessary to ratify international treaties.

Article 63
(3) For the purposes of discharging its functions the National Assembly may –
(e) deliberate upon and ratify all treaties and agreements to which the United Republic is party and the provisions of which require ratification.

22. The legislature has the power to grant amnesty.

No. Amnesty and pardon are not treated separately, and the legislature lacks the power to grant amnesty. See item 23.

23. The legislature has the power of pardon.

No. The president has the power of pardon.

Article 45
(1) Subject to the other provisions contained in this Article, the President may do any of the following:
(a) grant a pardon to any person convicted by a court of law of any offence, and he may grant such pardon unconditionally or on conditions, subject to law;
(b) grant any person a respite, either indefinitely or for a specified period, of the execution of any punishment imposed on that person for any offence;
(c) substitute a less severe form of punishment for any punishment imposed on any person for any offence; and
(d) remit the whole or part of any punishment imposed on any person for any offence, or remit the whole or part of any penalty of fine or forfeiture of property belonging to a convicted person which would otherwise be due to the Government of the United Republic on account of any offence.

24. The legislature reviews and has the right to reject appointments to the judiciary; or the legislature itself appoints members of the judiciary.

No. The president makes judicial appointments, and the appointments do not require the legislature's approval.

Article 109
(1) There shall be a Principal Judge of the High Court (who in the following provisions of this Constitution shall be referred to as the "Principal Judge") and other Judges of the High Court who shall be not less than fifteen.
(2) The Principal Judge and other Judges of the High Court shall be appointed by the President after consultation with the Judicial Service Commission.

Article 113
(1) Subject to the provisions of any law enacted by Parliament concerning the appointment of magistrates and other Judicial officers, the division of power for that purpose shall be as follows:
(a) the power to appoint persons to hold offices prescribed in subarticle (2) of this Article (including the power to confirm such persons in office and to promote them) is hereby vested in the President;
(2) The offices to which this Article applies are the offices of the Registrar of the Court of Appeal of Tanzania and his Deputy of any grade, the offices of the Registrar of the High Court and his Deputy of any grade, the office of Resident Magistrate and of a magistrate of any other category, and any other office connected with any court (other than a court-martial) as may be specified by a law enacted by Parliament in accordance with the provisions of this Constitution.

Article 118
(1) There shall be a Chief Justice of the Court of Appeal (who in the subsequent Articles of this Constitution shall be referred to in short as "the Chief Justice") and not less than two other Justices of Appeal; save that a

full bench of the Court of Appeal shall consist of not less than five Justices of Appeal.

(2) The Chief Justice shall be appointed by the President, and shall be the Head of the Court of Appeal and of the Judiciary as defined in Article 116 of this Constitution.

(3) The other Justices of Appeal shall be appointed by the President after consultation with the Chief Justice, from among persons who qualify to be appointed Judges of the High Court of the United Republic as provided for in Article 109 of this Constitution, or from among persons who qualify to be appointed Judges of the High Court of Zanzibar in accordance with the laws applicable in Zanzibar.

25. The chairman of the central bank is appointed by the legislature.

No. The president appoints the governor of the Bank of Tanzania.

26. The legislature has a substantial voice in the operation of the state-owned media.

No. The legislature lacks a substantial voice in the operation of the public media.

27. The legislature is regularly in session.

Yes. The legislature regularly meets in ordinary session.

28. Each legislator has a personal secretary.

No.

29. Each legislator has at least one non-secretarial staff member with policy expertise.

No.

30. Legislators are eligible for re-election without any restriction.

Yes. There are no restrictions on re-election.

31. A seat in the legislature is an attractive enough position that legislators are generally interested in and seek re-election.

Yes.

32. The re-election of incumbent legislators is common enough that at any given time the legislature contains a significant number of highly experienced members.

Yes. Re-election rates are sufficiently high to produce a significant number of highly experienced members.

NATIONAL ASSEMBLY OF THAILAND (*RATHASAPHA*)

Expert consultants: Chris Baker, Paul Chambers, Allen Hicken, James R. Klein, Michael Nelson, Pasuk Phongpaichit, Aaron M. Stern

Score: .59

Influence over executive (7/9)		Institutional autonomy (3/9)		Specified powers (4/8)		Institutional capacity (5/6)	
1. replace	X	10. no dissolution		19. amendments	X	27. sessions	X
2. serve as ministers	X	11. no decree		20. war	X	28. secretary	X
3. interpellate	X	12. no veto		21. treaties	X	29. staff	X
4. investigate	X	13. no review		22. amnesty		30. no term limits	
5. oversee police		14. no gatekeeping		23. pardon		31. seek re-election	X
6. appoint PM	X	15. no impoundment	X	24. judiciary	X	32. experience	X
7. appoint ministers		16. control resources	X	25. central bank			
8. lack president	X	17. immunity	X	26. media			
9. no confidence	X	18. all elected					

The National Assembly (*Rathasapha*) of Thailand was established in the 1932 constitution, which set forth a constitutional monarchy with a prime minister as the head of government and the king as the head of state. A new constitution in 1947 instituted the current bicameral legislative structure with a lower house, the House of Representatives (*Sapha Phuthaen Ratsadon*), and an upper house, the Senate (*Wuthisapha*). A 1994 amendment mandated that the prime minister must be an elected member of the parliamentary majority. Prior to 1994 the monarch had wide discretion in choosing the prime minister.

For much of its history, the legislature was a sideshow in successive military dictatorships. The early 1990s brought military withdrawal to the barracks and the onset of more regular parliamentary politics. In 2006, however, the military again staged a coup, this one allegedly to rid the country of the overweening and corrupting influence of the then-prime minister, Thaksin Shinawatra. The new military regime appointed an interim National Assembly and drafted a new constitution, the country's current fundamental law, which was passed in a popular referendum in 2007. The new constitution allows ministers to serve simultaneously in the House of Representatives. Prior to 2007 the prime minister and other ministers were required by law to vacate their seats in the legislature in order to assume a government position. The new constitution also grants the king the power to appoint the members of the Senate on the recommendation of a special commission. Prior to 2007 all members of the legislature were elected.

The legislature has substantial, albeit not overwhelming, power. It can influence the government by choosing the prime minister, interpellating and investigating executive branch officials, and removing the prime minister with a vote of no confidence. The legislature's institutional autonomy is limited by the executive branch's gatekeeping, veto, dissolution, and decree powers. For example, the legislature is prohibited from initiating money bills, bills relating to taxes, public expenditure, loans, and currency without the endorsement of the prime minister. It has several specified powers and significant institutional capacity.

SURVEY

1. The legislature alone, without the involvement of any other agencies, can impeach the president or replace the prime minister.

Yes. The legislature can replace the prime minister with a vote of no confidence. It cannot remove the king from the throne.

Section 8
The King shall be enthroned in a position of revered worship and shall not be violated. No person shall expose the King to any sort of accusation or action.

Section 158
Members of the House of Representatives of not less than one-fifth of the total number of the existing members of the House have the right to submit a motion for a general debate for the purpose of passing a vote of no-confidence in the Prime Minister. Such motion must nominate the suitable next Prime Minister who is also a person under section 171 paragraph two and, when the motion has been submitted, the dissolution of the House of Representatives shall not be permitted, except that the motion is withdrawn or the resolution is passed without being supported by the vote in accordance with paragraph three. If the general debate is concluded with a resolution not to pass over the agenda of the general debate, the House of Representatives shall pass a vote of confidence or no-confidence. Voting in such case shall not take place on the date of the conclusion of the debate. The vote of no-confidence must be passed by more than one-half of the total number of the existing members of the House of Representatives.

2. Ministers may serve simultaneously as members of the legislature.

Yes. The prime minister is chosen from, and required to serve simultaneously in, the House of Representatives.

Section 116
A senator shall not be a Minister or a person holding any political position or a person holding position in the independent constitutional organ.

Section 171
The Prime Minister must be a member of the House of Representatives appointed under section 172.

3. The legislature has powers of summons over executive branch officials and hearings with executive branch officials testifying before the legislature or its committees are regularly held.

Yes. The legislature regularly interpellates officials from the executive.

Section 156
Every member of the House of Representatives or senator has the right to interpellate a Minister on any matter within the scope of his authority, but the Minister has the right to refuse to answer it if the Council of Ministers is of the opinion that the matter should not yet be disclosed on the ground of safety or vital interest of the State.

Section 157
In the administration of State affairs on any matter which involves an important problem of public concern, affects national or public interest, or requires urgency, a member of the House of Representatives may notify the President of the House of Representatives in writing prior to the commencement of the sitting of the day, that he will interpellate the Prime Minister or the Minister responsible for the administration of State affairs on that matter without specifying the question,

and the President of the House of Representatives shall place such matter on the agenda of the meeting of that day.

The interpellation and the answer to the interpellation under paragraph one may be made once a week, and a verbal interpellation by a member of the House of Representatives on a matter involving the administration of State affairs may be made not exceeding three times on each matter in accordance with the rules of procedure of the House of Representatives.

4. The legislature can conduct independent investigation of the chief executive and the agencies of the executive.

Yes. The legislature can establish committees to investigate the executive.

Section 135
The House of Representatives and the Senate have the power to select and appoint members of each house to constitute a standing committee and have the power to select and appoint persons, being or not being its members, to constitute an non-standing committee in order to perform any act, inquire into or study any matter within the powers and duties of the House and report its findings to the House. The resolution appointing such non-standing committee must specify its activities or the responsible matters clearly and without repetition or duplication. The committee under paragraph one has the power to demand documents from any person or summon any person to give statements of fact or opinions on the act or the matter under its inquiry or study and such demand or summoning is enforceable as provided by law but it is not applicable to a judge performing his powers and duties in trial of the case or to the personnel management of each Court and to the Ombudsman or members of the independent Constitutional organ in the performance of their powers and duties under the Constitution or the organic laws, as the case may be. In the case where the person under paragraph two is a government official, official or employee of government agency, State agency, State enterprise or local government organ, the Chairperson of the committee shall notify the Minister who supervises and controls the agency to which such person is attached in order to instruct him to act as prescribed in paragraph two, except that, in the case of the safety of or important benefit to the State, it shall be deemed as a ground for the exemption to the compliance with paragraph two.

5. The legislature has effective powers of oversight over the agencies of coercion (the military, organs of law enforcement, intelligence services, and the secret police).

No. The legislature lacks effective powers of oversight over the agencies of coercion.

6. The legislature appoints the prime minister.

Yes. The king is required to appoint as prime minister the candidate nominated by a majority vote in the House of Representatives.

Section 171
The King appoints the Prime Minister and not more than thirty-five other Ministers to constitute the Council of Ministers having the duty to carry out the administration of State affairs with collective accountability.

Section 172
The House of Representatives shall complete its consideration and approval of the person suitable to be appointed as Prime Minister within thirty days as from the day the National Assembly is convoked for the first sitting under section 127. The nomination of a person who is suitable to be appointed as Prime Minister under paragraph one shall be endorsed by members of the House of Representatives of not less than one-fifth of the total number of the existing members of the House. The resolution of the House of Representatives approving the appointment of a person as Prime Minister shall be passed by the votes of more than one-half of the total number of the existing members of the House of Representatives. The passing of the resolution in such case shall be by open votes.

Section 173
In the case where the period of thirty days as from the date the National Assembly is convoked for the first sitting of members of the House of Representatives has elapsed and no one has been approved for appointment as Prime Minister under section 172 paragraph three, the President of the House of Representatives shall, within fifteen days as from the lapse of such period, present to the King for the issuance of a Royal Command appointing the person who has received the highest votes as Prime Minister.

7. The legislature's approval is required to confirm the appointment of ministers; or the legislature itself appoints ministers.

No. The king appoints ministers on the recommendation of the prime minister, and ministerial appointments do not require legislative approval.

Section 171
The King appoints the Prime Minister and not more than thirty-five other Ministers to constitute the Council of Ministers having the duty to carry out the administration of State affairs with collective accountability.

8. The country lacks a presidency entirely or there is a presidency, but the president is elected by the legislature.

Yes. The country lacks a presidency. The king is the head of state.

Section 2
Thailand adopts a democratic regime of government with the King as Head of State.

9. The legislature can vote no confidence in the government.

Yes. The legislature can pass a constructive vote of no confidence in the government, which means that parliament must designate a successor prime minister before passing a vote of no confidence.

Section 158
Members of the House of Representatives of not less than one-fifth of the total number of the existing members of the House have the right to submit a motion for a general debate for the purpose of passing a vote of no-confidence in the Prime Minister. Such motion must nominate the suitable next Prime Minister who is also a person under section 171 paragraph two and, when the motion has been submitted, the dissolution of the House of Representatives shall not be permitted, except that the motion is withdrawn or the resolution is passed without being supported by the vote in accordance with paragraph three. If the general debate is concluded with a resolution not to pass over the agenda of the general debate, the House of Representatives shall pass a vote of confidence or no-confidence. Voting in such case shall not take place on the date of the conclusion of the debate. The vote of no-confidence must be passed by more than one-half of the total number of the existing members of the House of Representatives.

10. The legislature is immune from dissolution by the executive.

No. The king, on the advice of the prime minister, can dissolve the legislature.

Section 108
The King has the prerogative to dissolve the House of Representatives for a new election of members of the House. The dissolution of the House of Representatives shall be made in the form of a Royal Decree in which the day for a new general election must be fixed for not less than forty-five days but not more than sixty days as from the day the House of Representatives has been dissolved and such election day must be the same throughout the Kingdom. The dissolution of the House of Representatives may be made only once under the same circumstance.

11. Any executive initiative on legislation requires ratification or approval by the legislature before it takes effect; that is, the executive lacks decree power.

No. The king issues royal decrees that have the force of law. The king, on the advice of the government, can also decree laws in emergency situations. If the emergency decree is not subsequently approved by the legislature, it lapses. The government has made liberal use of its emergency decree powers; it held such powers continually for over a year prior to the military coup of 2006 in order to grapple with a separatist movement in the southern part of the country.

Section 184
For the purpose of maintaining national or public safety or national economic security, or averting public calamity, the King may issue an Emergency Decree which shall have the force as an Act.
The issuance of an Emergency Decree under paragraph one shall be made only when the Council of Ministers is of the opinion that it is the case of emergency and necessary urgency which is unavoidable. In the next succeeding sitting of the National Assembly, the Council of Ministers shall submit the Emergency Decree to the National Assembly for its consideration without delay. If it is out of session and it would be a delay to wait for the opening of an ordinary session, the Council of Ministers must proceed to convoke an extraordinary session of the National Assembly in order to consider whether to approve or disapprove the Emergency Decree without delay. If the House of Representatives disapproves it or approves it but the Senate disapproves it and the House of Representatives reaffirms its approval by the votes of not more than one-half of the total number of the existing members of the House, the Emergency Decree shall lapse; provided that it shall not affect any act done during the enforcement of such Emergency Decree.

Section 187
The King has the prerogative to issue a Royal Decree which is not contrary to the law.

12. Laws passed by the legislature are veto-proof or essentially veto-proof; that is, the executive lacks veto power, or has veto power but the veto can be overridden by a simple majority in the legislature.

No. A two-thirds majority vote is required to override the king's veto.

Section 151
If the King refuses His assent to a bill and either returns it to the National Assembly or does not return it within ninety days, the National Assembly must reconsider such bill. If the National Assembly resolves to reaffirm the bill with the votes of not less than two-thirds of the total number of existing members of both Houses, the Prime Minister shall present such bill to the King for signature once again. If the King does not sign and return the bill within thirty days, the Prime Minister shall cause the bill to be promulgated as an Act in the Government Gazette as if the King had signed it.

13. The legislature's laws are supreme and not subject to judicial review.

No. The Constitutional Court reviews the constitutionality of laws.

Section 141
Before presenting the organic law bill as approved by the National Assembly to the King for His signature, it shall be submitted to the Constitutional Court for considering of its constitutionality and, it such case, the Constitutional Court shall have a decision thereon

within thirty days as from the date of receiving thereof. If the Constitutional Court decides that the provisions of an organic law bill are contrary to or inconsistent with the Constitution, such provisions shall lapse and if the Constitutional Court decides that such provisions are the essential element thereof or the organic law bill is enacted inconsistent with the provisions of the Constitution, such organic law bill shall lapse.

14. The legislature has the right to initiate bills in all policy jurisdictions; the executive lacks gatekeeping authority.

No. The legislature is prohibited from introducing legislation related to taxation, public expenditure, government loans, or currency.

Section 142
Subject to section 139, a bill may be introduced only by the followings:
(1) the Council of Ministers;
(2) members of the House of Representatives of not less than twenty in number;
(3) the Court or the independent Constitutional organs only for the bills relating to their organization over the execution of which the President of such Court or organ has control;
(4) the persons having the right to vote of not less than ten thousand in number whom jointly introduce a bill under section 163.
If the bill under (2), (3) or (4) is a money bill, it shall be introduced only with the endorsement of the Prime Minister.

Section 143
A money bill means a bill with provisions dealing with any of the following matters:
(1) the imposition, repeal, reduction, alteration, modification, remission, or regulation of taxes or duties;
(2) the allocation, receipt, custody, payment of the State funds, or transfer of expenditure estimates of the State;
(3) the raising of loans, or guarantee or redemption of loans, or any binding of State's properties;
(4) currency.

15. Expenditure of funds appropriated by the legislature is mandatory; the executive lacks the power to impound funds appropriated by the legislature.

Yes. The executive lacks the power to impound funds appropriated by the legislature.

16. The legislature controls the resources that finance its own internal operation and provide for the perquisites of its own members.

Yes. The legislature enjoys financial autonomy.

17. Members of the legislature are immune from arrest and/or criminal prosecution.

Yes. Legislators are immune with the common exception for cases of *flagrante delicto*.

Section 131
No member of the House of Representatives or senator shall, during a session, be arrested, detained or summoned by a warrant for inquiry as the suspect in a criminal case unless permission of the House of which he is a member is obtained or he is arrested in flagrante delicto. In the case where a member of the House of Representatives or a senator has been arrested in flagrante delicto, it shall be forthwith reported to the President of the House of which he is a member and such President may order the release of the person so arrested. In the case where a criminal charge is brought against a member of the House of Representatives or a senator, whether the House is in session or not, the Court shall not try the case during a session, unless permission of the House of which he is a member is obtained or it is a case concerning the organic law on election of members of the House of Representatives and acquisition of senators, the organic law on Election Commission or the organic law on political parties; provided that the trial of the Court shall not hinder such member from attending the sitting of the House. The trial and adjudication of the Court conducted before it is invoked that the accused is a member of either House are valid.
If a member of the House of Representatives or a senator is detained during the inquiry or trial before the beginning of a session, when the session begins, the inquiry official or the Court, as the case may be, must order his release as soon as the President of the House of which he is a member has so requested. The order of release under paragraph one shall be effective as from the date of such order until the last day of the session.

18. All members of the legislature are elected; the executive lacks the power to appoint any members of the legislature.

No. Some members of the Senate are appointed by a special commission, and others are elected. All members of the House of Representatives are elected.

Section 93
The House of Representatives consists of four hundred and eighty members, four hundred of whom are from the election on a constituency basis and eighty of whom are from the election on a proportional basis. The election of member of the House of Representatives shall be by direct suffrage and secret ballot, and the ballot to be used in an election shall be varied upon the election basis.

Section 111
The Senate consists of one hundred and fifty members acquired upon the basis of election in each Changwat, one elected senator for each Changwat, and upon the selection basis in an amount equal to the total number of senators deducted by the number of senators from the election basis.

Section 112
In an election of senators, the area of Changwat shall be regarded as one constituency and the number of senator

for each Changwat is one. The person having the right to vote at an election of senators may cast ballot, at the election, for one candidate and the election shall be by direct suffrage and secret ballot. For the purpose of the election of senators, the campaign to be launched by the candidates in the election is limited to the matters related to the performance of duties of the Senate.

Section 113

There shall be the Senators Selection Committee consisting of the President of the Constitutional Court, the Chairperson of the Election Commission, the President of the Ombudsmen, the Chairperson of the National Counter Corruption Commission, the Chairperson of the State Audit Commission, a judge of the Supreme Court of Justice holding the position of not lower than judge of the Supreme Court of Justice as entrusted by the general meeting of the Supreme Court of Justice and a judge of the Supreme Administrative Court as entrusted by the general meeting of the Supreme Administrative Court, having a duty to select persons under section 114 within thirty days as from the date of receiving the list of candidates from the Election Commission and to notify the selection result to the Election Commission for publication of the persons selected as senators.

Section 114

The Senators Selection Committee shall carry out the selection process for persons who may be beneficial to the performance of powers and duties of the Senate from persons nominated by academic institutions, public sector, private sector, professional organizations and other organizations to be senators in an amount as prescribed in section 111 paragraph one. In selection of person under paragraph one, regard shall be had to knowledge, skills or experience of the nominated persons which will be beneficial to the performance of the Senate, and the composition of the selected persons shall be regarded to interdisciplinary knowledge and experience, genders opportunity and equality, closely apportion of the persons nominated by the organizations under paragraph one and opportunity of social vulnerable groups.

19. The legislature alone, without the involvement of any other agencies, can change the Constitution.

Yes. The legislature can change the constitution in multiple readings with a majority vote.

Section 291

An amendment of the Constitution may be made only under the rules and procedure as follows:

(1) a motion for amendment must be proposed either by the Council of Ministers or members of the House of Representatives of not less than one-fifth of the total number of the existing members of the House of Representatives or members of both Houses of not less than one-fifth of the total number of the existing members thereof or persons having the right to votes of not less than fifty thousand in number under the law on the public submission of a bill;

A motion for amendment which has the effect of changing the democratic regime of government with the King as Head of State or changing the form of State shall be prohibited;

(2) a motion for amendment must be proposed in the form of a draft Constitution Amendment and the National Assembly shall consider it in three readings;

(3) the voting in the first reading for acceptance in principle shall be by roll call and open voting, and the amendment must be approved by votes of not less than one-half of the total number of the existing members of both Houses;

(4) in the consideration section by section in the second reading, consultation with the people who submit a draft Constitution Amendment shall be held;

The voting in the second reading for consideration section by section shall be decided by a simple majority of votes;

(5) at the conclusion of the second reading, there shall be an interval of fifteen days after which the National Assembly shall proceed with its third reading;

(6) the voting in the third and final reading shall be by roll call and open voting, and its promulgation as the Constitution must be approved by votes of more than one-half of the total number of the existing members of both Houses;

(7) after the resolution has been passed in accordance with the above rules and procedure, the draft Constitution Amendment shall be presented to the King, and the provisions of section 150 and section 151 shall apply mutatis mutandis.

20. The legislature's approval is necessary for the declaration of war.

Yes. The legislature's approval is required for the king's war declarations.

Section 189

The King has the prerogative to declare war with the approval of the National Assembly. The approval resolution of the National Assembly must be passed by the votes of not less than two-thirds of the total number of the existing members of both Houses. During the expiration of the term or the dissolution of the House of Representatives, the Senate shall perform the function of the National Assembly in giving the approval under paragraph one, and the resolution shall be passed by the votes of not less than two-thirds of the total number of the existing senators.

21. The legislature's approval is necessary to ratify treaties with foreign countries.

Yes. The legislature's approval is necessary to ratify international treaties.

Section 190

The King has the prerogative to conclude a peace treaty, armistice and other treaties with other countries or international organizations. A treaty which provides for a change in the Thai territories or the Thai external territories that Thailand has sovereign right or jurisdiction over such territories under any treaty or an international law or requires the enactment of an Act for its implementation or affects immensely to economic or social security of the country or results in the binding of trade, investment budget of the country significantly must be approved by the National Assembly.

22. The legislature has the power to grant amnesty.

No. Amnesty and pardon are not treated separately, and the legislature lacks the power to grant amnesty. See item 23.

23. The legislature has the power of pardon.

No. The king has the power of pardon.

> Section 191
> The King has the prerogative to grant a pardon.

24. The legislature reviews and has the right to reject appointments to the judiciary; or the legislature itself appoints members of the judiciary.

Yes. The king appoints the members of the Constitutional Court on the recommendation of the Senate. The king appoints other judges on the recommendation of the appropriate judicial commission.

> Section 200
> The King appoints and removes judges except in the case of removal from office upon death.
> The appointment and removal from office of a judge of any Court other than the Constitutional Court, the Court of Justice, the Administrative Court and the Military Court as well as the adjudicative jurisdiction and procedure of such Courts shall be in accordance with the law on the establishment of such Courts.

> Section 204
> The Constitutional Court consists of the President and eight judges of the Constitutional Court to be appointed by the King upon advice of the Senate from the following persons:
> (1) three judges of the Supreme Court of Justice holding a position of not lower than judge of the Supreme Court of Justice and elected at a general meeting of the Supreme Court of Justice by secret ballot;
> (2) two judges of the Supreme Administrative Court elected at a general meeting of the Supreme Administrative Court by secret ballot;
> (3) two qualified persons in law who having orientated knowledge and experience in this field and having been selected under section 206;
> (4) two qualified persons in political science, public administration or other social sciences who having orientated knowledge and experience in the administration of State affairs and having been selected under section 206.

> Section 220
> The appointment and removal from office of a judge of a Court of Justice must be approved by the Judicial

Commission of the Courts of Justice before they are tendered to the King.

> Section 224
> The appointment and removal from office of an administrative judge must be approved by the Judicial Commission of the Administrative Courts as provided by law before they are tendered to the King.

25. The chairman of the central bank is appointed by the legislature.

No. The government appoints the governor of the Bank of Thailand.

26. The legislature has a substantial voice in the operation of the state-owned media.

No. The legislature lacks a substantial voice in the operation of the public media.

> Section 47
> Transmission frequencies for radio or television broadcasting and telecommunication are national communication resources for public interest. There shall be an independent regulatory body having the duty to distribute the frequencies under paragraph one and supervise radio or television broadcasting and telecommunication businesses as provided by the law.

27. The legislature is regularly in session.

Yes. The constitution requires only 120 days of meeting each year. In practice, the legislature normally is in session for at least half of the year.

> Section 127
> The National Assembly shall, within thirty days as from the date of the election of members of the House of Representatives, be summoned for the first sitting. Each year, there shall be a general ordinary session and a legislative ordinary session. An ordinary session of the National Assembly shall last one hundred and twenty days but the King may prolong it. An ordinary session may be prorogued before the end of one hundred and twenty days only with the approval of the National Assembly.

28. Each legislator has a personal secretary.

Yes.

29. Each legislator has at least one non-secretarial staff member with policy expertise.

Yes.

30. Legislators are eligible for re-election without any restriction.

No. Senators may serve only one term and may not seek reappointment.

> Section 117
> The term of membership of the senates is six years as from the election day or the day the Election Commission publishes the result of the selection, as the case

may be, and no senator shall hold office more than one term.

31. A seat in the legislature is an attractive enough position that legislators are generally interested in and seek re-election.

Yes.

32. The re-election of incumbent legislators is common enough that at any given time the legislature

contains a significant number of highly experienced members.

Yes. Prior to the 2006 coup, legislators regularly sought and achieved re-election, and the legislature contained a body of experienced members. It is unclear whether this pattern will hold in the post-coup environment.

NATIONAL PARLIAMENT OF TIMOR-LESTE

Expert consultants: Naazneen Barma, Nicole Seibel

Score: .47

Influence over executive (2/9)		Institutional autonomy (5/9)		Specified powers (5/8)		Institutional capacity (3/6)	
1. replace		10. no dissolution		19. amendments	X	27. sessions	X
2. serve as ministers		11. no decree	X	20. war	X	28. secretary	
3. interpellate		12. no veto	X	21. treaties	X	29. staff	
4. investigate		13. no review		22. amnesty	X	30. no term limits	X
5. oversee police		14. no gatekeeping		23. pardon		31. seek re-election	X
6. appoint PM	X	15. no impoundment	X	24. judiciary	X	32. experience	
7. appoint ministers		16. control resources	X	25. central bank			
8. lack president		17. immunity		26. media			
9. no confidence	X	18. all elected	X				

The National Parliament of Timor-Leste (also called East Timor) was established in the country's 2002 constitution upon independence from Indonesia. The document calls for a unicameral legislature, a prime minister as head of the government, and a directly elected president as the head of state. Timor-Leste held parliamentary elections in August 2001, before the country formally gained independence. The first legislative elections since independence were held in June 2007.

It is too early to say with any certainty how the legislature will function in the new polity. From the constitution and early indications, it appears that the legislature has a moderate amount of power, although it has very little ability to influence the executive. It chooses the prime minister but cannot effectively oversee the executive or remove executive branch officials. The legislature does have some institutional autonomy, and it holds five of the eight specified powers and pre-

rogatives assessed in this survey. The legislature has some institutional capacity.

SURVEY

1. The legislature alone, without the involvement of any other agencies, can impeach the president or replace the prime minister.

No. Presidential impeachment requires the involvement of the Supreme Court of Justice. The president's approval is needed to remove the prime minister following a vote of no confidence.

Article 79
1. The President of the Republic enjoys immunity in the exercise of his or her functions.
2. The President of the Republic is responsible before the Supreme Court of Justice for crimes committed in the exercise of his or her functions and for clear and serious violation of constitutional obligations.

3. It is the incumbent upon the National Parliament to initiate the criminal proceedings, following a proposal made by one-fifth, and deliberation approved by a two-third majority, of its Members.

4. The Plenary of the Supreme Court of Justice shall issue a judgment within a maximum of 30 days.

5. Conviction shall result in forfeiture of office and disqualification from re-election.

6. For crimes not committed in the exercise of his or her functions, the President of the Republic shall also be answerable before the Supreme Court of Justice, and forfeiture of office shall only occur in case of sentence to prison.

Article 111

1. The National Parliament may, following proposal by one-quarter of the Members in full exercise of their functions, pass a vote of no confidence on the Government with respect to the implementation of its program or any relevant matter of national interest.

2. When a vote of no confidence is not approved, its signatories shall not move another vote of no confidence during the same legislative session.

Article 112

1. The dismissal of the Government shall occur when:
   a. at the beginning of a new legislative;
   b. by the acceptance by the President of the Republic of the resignation of the Prime Minister;
   c. by the death of the Prime Minister or by suffering a permanent physical incapacity;
   d. by the rejection of its program for the second consecutive time;
   e. by the non-approval of a vote of confidence;
   f. by the approval of a vote of no confidence by a absolute majority of the Members in full exercise of their functions;

2. The President of the Republic can only dismiss the Prime Minister in accordance with the cases provided for in the previous number and when it is deemed necessary to ensure the regular functioning of the democratic institutions, after consultation with the Council of State.

2. Ministers may serve simultaneously as members of the legislature.

No. The constitution states that incompatibilities will be determined by law. In practice, legislators are prohibited from serving simultaneously in ministerial positions.

Article 68

2. The law shall define other incompatibilities.

3. The legislature has powers of summons over executive branch officials and hearings with executive branch officials testifying before the legislature or its committees are regularly held.

No. Formally, legislators can question government officials, but in practice, ministers do not regularly respond to the legislature's requests.

Article 101

1. The Members of the Government have the right to attend plenary sessions of the National Parliament and may take the floor as provided for in the rules of procedures.

2. Sittings shall be scheduled at which members of the Government shall be present to answer questions from Members of Parliament in accordance with the Rules of Procedure.

3. The National Parliament or its Committees may request members of the Governments to take part in their proceedings.

4. The legislature can conduct independent investigation of the chief executive and the agencies of the executive.

No. The legislature cannot investigate the executive.

5. The legislature has effective powers of oversight over the agencies of coercion (the military, organs of law enforcement, intelligence services, and the secret police).

No. The legislature lacks effective powers of oversight over the agencies of coercion.

6. The legislature appoints the prime minister.

Yes. The president is required to appoint as prime minister the candidate who enjoys majority support in the legislature.

Article 85

It is exclusively incumbent upon the President of the Republic:
   d. to appoint and swear in the Prime Minister designated by the party or alliance parties with parliamentary majority after consultation with the political parties sitting in the National Parliament.

Article 106

1. The Prime Minister shall be designated by the political party or alliance of political parties with parliamentary majority and shall be appointed by the President of the Republic, after consultation with the political parties sitting in the National Parliament.

7. The legislature's approval is required to confirm the appointment of ministers; or the legislature itself appoints ministers.

No. The president appoints ministers on the proposal of the prime minister, and ministerial appointments do not require the legislature's approval.

Article 86

It is incumbent upon the President of the Republic, with regard to other organs:

h. to appoint, swear in and remove Government Members from office, following a proposal by the Prime Minister, in accordance with number 2, Article 106.

Article 106

2. The remaining members of the Government shall be appointed by the President of the Republic on the proposal by the Prime Minister.

8. The country lacks a presidency entirely or there is a presidency, but the president is elected by the legislature.

No. The president is directly elected.

Article 76

1. The President of the Republic is elected by universal, free, direct, secret and personal suffrage.

9. The legislature can vote no confidence in the government.

Yes. The legislature can vote no confidence in the government.

Article 111

1. The National Parliament may, following proposal by one-quarter of the Members in full exercise of their functions, pass a vote of no confidence on the Government with respect to the implementation of its program or any relevant matter of national interest.

2. When a vote of no confidence is not approved, its signatories shall not move another vote of no confidence during the same legislative session.

Article 112

1. The dismissal of the Government shall occur when:

f. by the approval of a vote of no confidence by a absolute majority of the Members in full exercise of their functions;

2. The President of the Republic can only dismiss the Prime Minister in accordance with the cases provided for in the previous number and when it is deemed necessary to ensure the regular functioning of the democratic institutions, after consultation with the Council of State.

10. The legislature is immune from dissolution by the executive.

No. The president can dissolve the legislature.

Article 86

It is incumbent upon the President of the Republic, with regard to other organs:

f. to dissolve the National Parliament in case of a serious institutional crisis preventing the formation of a government or the approval of the State Budget and lasting more than sixty days, after consultation with political parties sitting in the Parliament and with the Council of State, on pain of rendering the act of dissolution null and void, taking into consideration provisions of Article 100.

Article 100

1. The National Parliament shall not be dissolved during the six months immediately following its election, during the last half-year of the term of office of the President of the Republic or during a state of siege or a state of emergency, on pain of rendering the act of dissolution null and void.

2. The dissolution of the National Parliament does not affect the continuance of the mandates of its Members until the first meeting of the National Parliament after the ensuing election.

11. Any executive initiative on legislation requires ratification or approval by the legislature before it takes effect; that is, the executive lacks decree power.

Yes. The executive lacks decree power. The legislature can, however, grant the government temporary decree powers on certain issue areas.

Article 96

1. The National Parliament may authorize the government to make laws concerning the following matters:

a. definition of crimes, sentences, security measures and respective prerequisites;

b. definition of civil and criminal procedure;

c. organization of the Judiciary and status of magistrates;

d. general rules and regulations for the public service, the status of the civil servants and the responsibility of the State;

e. general bases for the organization of public administration;

f. monetary system;

g. banking and financial system;

h. definition of the bases for a policy of protection of the environment and sustainable development;

i. general rules and regulations for radio and television broadcasting and other mass media communication;

j. military or civic service;

k. general rules and regulations for the requisition and expropriation for public utility;

l. means and ways of intervention, expropriation, nationalization and privatization of means of production and soils on grounds of public interest, as well as criteria for the establishment of compensation in such cases.

2. Laws on legislative authorization shall define the subject, sense, scope and duration of the authorization, which may be renewed.

3. Laws on legislative authorization cannot be used more than once and shall lapse with the dismissal of the Government, with the end of the legislative term or with the dissolution of the National Parliament.

12. Laws passed by the legislature are veto-proof or essentially veto-proof; that is, the executive lacks veto power, or has veto power but the veto can be overridden by a majority in the legislature.

Yes. The legislature can override a presidential veto by a majority vote of its total membership.

Article 88

1. Within thirty days after receiving any draft law from the National Parliament for the purpose of its promulgation as law, the President of the Republic shall either promulgate the law or exercise the right of veto, based on substantive grounds, send a message to the National Parliament requesting a new appraisal of the statute.

2. If, within ninety days, the National Parliament confirms its vote by an absolute majority of its Members in full exercise of their functions, the President of the Republic shall promulgate the law within eight days after receiving it.

3. However, a majority of two-thirds of the Members present shall be required to ratify laws on matters provided for in Article 95 when that majority exceeds an absolute majority of the Members in full exercise of their functions.

4. Within forty days after receiving any draft law from the Government for the purpose of its promulgation as law, the President of the Republic shall either promulgate it or exercise the right of veto by way of a written communication to the Government containing the reasons for the veto.

13. The legislature's laws are supreme and not subject to judicial review.

No. The Supreme Court of Justice can review the constitutionality of laws.

Article 120
The courts shall not apply rules that contravene the Constitution or the principles contained therein.

Article 126
1. It is incumbent upon the Supreme Court of Justice, in the domain of juridico-constitutional questions:
  a. to review and declare the unconstitutionality and illegality of normative and legislative bills by the organs of the State;
  b. to provide an anticipatory verification of the legality and constitutionality of the bills and referenda;
  c. to verify cases of unconstitutionality by commission;
  d. to verify cases of unconstitutionality by omission;
  e. to verify the legality of the establishment of political parties and their coalitions and order their registration or dissolution, in accordance with the Constitution and the law;
  f. to exercise all other competences provided for by the Constitution or the law.

Article 152
1. The Supreme Court of Justice has jurisdiction to hear appeals against any of the following court decisions:
  a. decisions refusing to apply a legal rule on the grounds of unconstitutionality;
  b. decisions applying a legal rule the constitutionality of which was challenged during the proceedings.
2. An appeal under paragraph (1) (b) above may be brought only by the party who raised the question of unconstitutionality.

14. The legislature has the right to initiate bills in all policy jurisdictions; the executive lacks gatekeeping authority.

No. The legislature is prohibited from introducing legislation that would increase state expenditures or reduce state revenues.

Article 97
2. There cannot be any presentation of bills, draft legislation or amendments involving, in any given fiscal year, any increase in State expenditure or any reduction in State revenues provided for in the Budget or Rectifying Budgets.

15. Expenditure of funds appropriated by the legislature is mandatory; the executive lacks the power to impound funds appropriated by the legislature.

Yes. The executive lacks the power to impound funds appropriated by the legislature.

16. The legislature controls the resources that finance its own internal operation and provide for the perquisites of its own members.

Yes. The legislature enjoys financial autonomy.

17. Members of the legislature are immune from arrest and/or criminal prosecution.

No. Legislators are subject to arrest for felonies that carry a maximum sentence of more than two years.

Article 114
No member of the Government may be detained or imprisoned without the permission of the National Parliament, except for a felonious crime punishable with a maximum sentence of imprisonment for more than two years and in *flagrante delicto.*

18. All members of the legislature are elected; the executive lacks the power to appoint any members of the legislature.

Yes. All members of the legislature are elected.

Article 93
1. The National Parliament is elected by universal, free, direct, equal, secret and personal suffrage.

19. The legislature alone, without the involvement of any other agencies, can change the Constitution.

Yes. The legislature can assume the power to revise the constitution with a four-fifths majority vote and can change the constitution with a two-thirds majority vote.

Article 154
1. The initiative for constitutional revision is incumbent upon the Members of Parliament and the Parliamentary Groups.
2. The National Parliament may revise the Constitution after six years have elapsed since the last date of

publication of the last law revising the Constitution was published.

3. The period of six years for the first constitutional review is counted from the day the present Constitution enters into force.

4. The National Parliament, regardless of any time frame, can take on powers to revise the Constitution by a majority of four-fifths of the Members of Parliament in full exercise of their functions.

5. Proposals for revision must be deposited with the National Parliament one hundred and twenty days prior to the date of the commencement of the debate.

6. After submission of a proposal for constitutional revision under the terms of number 5 above, any other proposal shall be submitted within thirty days.

Article 155

1. Amendments to the Constitution shall be approved by a majority of two-thirds of the Members of Parliament in full exercise of their functions.

2. The new text of the Constitution shall be published together with the revision law.

3. The President of the Republic shall not refuse to promulgate a revision law.

20. The legislature's approval is necessary for the declaration of war.

Yes. The legislature's approval is required for the president's war declarations.

Article 85

It is exclusively incumbent upon the President of the Republic:

h. to declare war and make peace following a Government proposal, after consultation with the Council of State and the Supreme Council of Defense and Security, under authorization of the National Parliament.

Article 87

It is incumbent upon the President of the Republic, in the field of international relations:

a. to declare war in case of actual or imminent aggression and to make peace, following proposal by the Government, after consultation with the Supreme Council for Defense and Security and following authorization of the National Parliament or of its Standing Committee.

21. The legislature's approval is necessary to ratify treaties with foreign countries.

Yes. The legislature's approval is necessary to ratify international treaties.

Article 85

It is exclusively incumbent upon the President of the Republic:

a. to promulgate statutes and order the publication of resolutions by the National Parliament approving agreements and ratifying international treaties and conventions.

Article 95

3. It is also incumbent upon (the National Parliament):

f. to approve and renounce agreements and to ratify treaties and international conventions.

Article 115

1. It is incumbent upon the Government:

f. to prepare and negotiate treaties and enter into, approve, accede and renounce international agreements which do not fall within the competence of the National parliament or of the President of the Republic.

22. The legislature has the power to grant amnesty.

Yes. The legislature has the power to grant amnesty.

Article 95

3. It is also incumbent upon (the National Parliament):

g. to grant amnesty.

23. The legislature has the power of pardon.

No. The president has the power of pardon.

Article 85

It is exclusively incumbent upon the President of the Republic:

i. to grant pardons and commute sentences after consultation with the Government.

24. The legislature reviews and has the right to reject appointments to the judiciary; or the legislature itself appoints members of the judiciary.

Yes. The legislature elects one of the members of the Supreme Court of Justice, and its approval is required to ratify the president's appointments to head the Supreme Court of Justice, the High Administrative Court, the Tax Court, and the Audit Court.

Article 86

It is incumbent upon the President of the Republic, with regard to other organs:

j. to appoint the President of the Supreme Court of Justice and swear in the President of the High Administrative Court, the Tax Court and the Court of Accounts.

Article 95

3. It is also incumbent upon (the National Parliament):

a. to ratify the appointment of the President of the Supreme Court of Justice and of the High Administrative, Tax and Audit Court.

Article 125

2. The Supreme Court of Justice is composed of career judges, magistrates of the Public Prosecution or jurists of recognized merit in number to be established by law, as follows:

a. one elected by the National Parliament;

b. and all the others designated by the Superior Council for the Judiciary.

25. The chairman of the central bank is appointed by the legislature.

No. According to the constitution, the governance of the central bank will be determined by law. In practice, the central bank has not yet been established.

> Article 143
> 1. The State shall establish a national central bank jointly responsible for the definition and implementation of the monetary and financial policy.
> 2. The law defines the functions and the relationship of the Central Bank with the National Parliament and the Government, safeguarding the management autonomy of the financial institution.
> 3. The Central Bank has exclusive competence for issuing the national currency.

26. The legislature has a substantial voice in the operation of the state-owned media.

No. The legislature lacks a substantial voice in the operation of the public media.

27. The legislature is regularly in session.

Yes. The legislature regularly meets in ordinary session.

> Article 99
> 1. The legislative term comprises five legislative sessions, and each legislative session shall have the duration of one year.
> 2. The regular period of functioning of the National Parliament is defined by the Rules of Procedure.

> 3. The National Parliament convenes on a regular basis following notice by its President.
> 4. The National Parliament convenes on an extraordinary basis whenever so decided by the Standing Committee, at the request of one-third of Members or following notice of the President of the Republic with a view to addressing specific issues.

28. Each legislator has a personal secretary.

No.

29. Each legislator has at least one non-secretarial staff member with policy expertise.

No.

30. Legislators are eligible for re-election without any restriction.

Yes. There are no restrictions on re-election.

31. A seat in the legislature is an attractive enough position that legislators are generally interested in and seek re-election.

Yes.

32. The re-election of incumbent legislators is common enough that at any given time the legislature contains a significant number of highly experienced members.

No. The legislature is relatively new, preventing legislators from yet having much experience.

NATIONAL ASSEMBLY OF TOGO (*ASSEMBLÉE NATIONALE*)

Expert consultants: Markoua Dadjo, Alain Faupin, El Hadj Kassim Mensah, Mathurin Houngnikpo, Comi M. Toulabor

Score: .38

Influence over executive (2/9)		Institutional autonomy (3/9)		Specified powers (3/8)		Institutional capacity (4/6)	
1. replace		10. no dissolution		19. amendments	X	27. sessions	X
2. serve as ministers		11. no decree		20. war	X	28. secretary	
3. interpellate	X	12. no veto	X	21. treaties	X	29. staff	
4. investigate		13. no review		22. amnesty		30. no term limits	X
5. oversee police		14. no gatekeeping	X	23. pardon		31. seek re-election	X
6. appoint PM		15. no impoundment		24. judiciary		32. experience	X
7. appoint ministers		16. control resources		25. central bank			
8. lack president		17. immunity		26. media			
9. no confidence	X	18. all elected	X				

The National Assembly (*Assemblée nationale*) of Togo was established in the 1961 constitution, following independence from France in 1960.

The assembly was dissolved in 1967 by President Gnassingbé Eyadéma, who also suspended the constitution and proceeded to monopolize executive and legislative power for the next several decades. A new constitution in 1992 called for a popularly elected unicameral legislature. A second house, the Senate, was called for in a 2002 constitutional amendment, although the Senate has not yet been established. Eyadéma's death in 2005 led to a brief spate of political violence and the establishment of a transitional government. Eyadéma's son, Faure Gnassingbé, subsequently assumed the presidency, thereby completing a dynastic succession.

The legislature is a diminutive political actor. It has scant influence over the executive. The legislature's autonomy is circumscribed by, among other things, presidential decree powers and a failure to observe the formal institutions of immunity for legislators. The legislature exercises several specified powers and has some institutional capacity.

SURVEY

1. The legislature alone, without the involvement of any other agencies, can impeach the president or replace the prime minister.

No. The legislature cannot impeach the president. The legislature can remove the prime minister with a vote of no confidence.

> Article 97
> The Prime Minister, after deliberation by the Council of Ministers, may commit the responsibility of the Government before the National Assembly with regard to its program or to a declaration of general policy. The National Assembly, after debate, shall cast a vote. The Government may only be denied a vote of confidence by a majority of two-thirds of the deputies of the National Assembly. In the event that the vote of confidence is refused, the Prime Minister must submit the resignation of the Government to the President of the Republic.

> Article 127
> The High Court of Justice is the only jurisdiction with competence to judge infringements committed by the President of the Republic. The President of the Republic shall not be held politically liable except in case of high treason.

2. Ministers may serve simultaneously as members of the legislature.

No. Ministers are prohibited from serving simultaneously in ministerial positions.

> Article 76
> The functions of a member of the Government are incompatible with the exercise of any parliamentary mandate, of any function of professional representation with national character and of any private or public, civil or military employment or of any other pro-

fessional activity. An organic law shall determine the status of former members of the Government concerning, in particular, their compensation and security.

3. The legislature has powers of summons over executive branch officials and hearings with executive branch officials testifying before the legislature or its committees are regularly held.

Yes. The legislature regularly interpellates officials from the executive.

> Article 96
> Members of the Government have access to the National Assembly, the Senate and their committees. They shall also be heard on interpellation, by the National Assembly, on written or oral questions which are addressed to them.

4. The legislature can conduct independent investigation of the chief executive and the agencies of the executive.

No. The legislature cannot investigate the executive.

5. The legislature has effective powers of oversight over the agencies of coercion (the military, organs of law enforcement, intelligence services, and the secret police).

No. The legislature lacks effective powers of oversight over the agencies of coercion.

6. The legislature appoints the prime minister.

No. The president appoints the prime minister.

> Article 66
> The President of the Republic shall appoint the Prime Minister. He shall terminate the functions of the Prime Minister. Upon the proposal of the Prime Minister, he shall appoint the other members of the Government and shall terminate their functions.

7. The legislature's approval is required to confirm the appointment of ministers; or the legislature itself appoints ministers.

No. The president appoints ministers, and the appointments do not require the legislature's approval.

> Article 66
> The President of the Republic shall appoint the Prime Minister. He shall terminate the functions of the Prime Minister. Upon the proposal of the Prime Minister, he shall appoint the other members of the Government and shall terminate their functions.

8. The country lacks a presidency entirely or there is a presidency, but the president is elected by the legislature.

No. The president is directly elected.

Article 59
The President of the Republic is elected by universal, direct and secret suffrage for a mandate of five years.

9. The legislature can vote no confidence in the government.

Yes. The legislature can vote no confidence in the government.

Article 97
The Prime Minister, after deliberation by the Council of Ministers, may commit the responsibility of the Government before the National Assembly with regard to its program or to a declaration of general policy. The National Assembly, after debate, shall cast a vote. The Government may only be denied a vote of confidence by a majority of two-thirds of the deputies of the National Assembly. In the event that the vote of confidence is refused, the Prime Minister must submit the resignation of the Government to the President of the Republic.

Article 98
The National Assembly may challenge the responsibility of the Government by passing a motion of censure. Such a motion, in order to be admissible, must be signed by at least one-third of the deputies of the National Assembly. The vote may only be called five days after the motion has been introduced. The National Assembly may only pass a vote to censure the Government by a majority of two-thirds of its members. If the motion of censure is adopted, the Prime Minister shall hand in his resignation of Government. The President of the Republic shall appoint a new Prime Minister. If the motion of censure is rejected, its signatories may not propose a new motion during the same session.

10. The legislature is immune from dissolution by the executive.

No. The president can dissolve the legislature.

Article 68
The President of the Republic, after consultation with the Prime Minister and the President of the National Assembly, may pronounce the dissolution of the National Assembly. This dissolution may not take place during the first year of the legislature. A new Assembly shall have to be elected within sixty days following the dissolution. The National Assembly shall meet as of right on the second Tuesday following its election; if this meeting takes place out of determined periods for the ordinary sessions, a session shall take place as of right for a duration of fifteen days. A new dissolution may not take place during the year following these elections.

11. Any executive initiative on legislation requires ratification or approval by the legislature before it takes effect; that is, the executive lacks decree power.

No. The president issues decrees that have the force of law.

Article 69
The President of the Republic shall sign the ordinances and decrees deliberated upon in the Council of Ministers.

12. Laws passed by the legislature are veto-proof or essentially veto-proof; that is, the executive lacks veto power, or has veto power but the veto can be overridden by a majority in the legislature.

Yes. The legislature can override a presidential veto by a majority vote of its present members.

Article 67
The President of the Republic shall promulgate the laws within fifteen days following the transmission to the Government of the law definitively adopted by the National Assembly; during this time period, he may request a new deliberation of the law or of certain articles, the request must be justified. The new deliberation may not be refused.

13. The legislature's laws are supreme and not subject to judicial review.

No. The Constitutional Court can review the constitutionality of laws.

Article 92
The projects or bills of organic laws shall be submitted to the deliberation and vote of the National Assembly at the end of a time period of fifteen days after their registration. Organic laws may not be promulgated before a declaration by the Constitutional Court of their conformity with the Constitution.

Article 99
The Constitutional Court is the highest jurisdiction of the State in constitutional matters. It shall judge the constitutionality of the law and it shall guarantee the fundamental rights of the human person and of public freedoms. It shall be the regulatory organ for the functioning of the institutions and of the activity of the public powers.

Article 104
The Constitutional Court is the jurisdiction charged with ensuring respect for the disciplines of the Constitution... It is the judge of the constitutionality of laws.

14. The legislature has the right to initiate bills in all policy jurisdictions; the executive lacks gatekeeping authority.

Yes. The legislature can initiate bills in all policy jurisdictions.

15. Expenditure of funds appropriated by the legislature is mandatory; the executive lacks the power to impound funds appropriated by the legislature.

No. The executive can impound funds allocated by the legislature.

16. The legislature controls the resources that finance its own internal operation and provide for the perquisites of its own members.

No. The legislature is dependent on the president for the resources that finance its own operations.

17. Members of the legislature are immune from arrest and/or criminal prosecution.

No. Formally, legislators enjoy immunity, but in practice, opposition legislators have been arrested and even killed.

Article 53
Deputies and senators shall enjoy parliamentary immunity. No deputy or senator may be prosecuted, searched, arrested, detained or judged on the basis of the opinions or the votes expressed by him in the exercise of his functions, even after the expiration of his mandate. Except in case of flagrant offense, deputies and senators can only be arrested or prosecuted for crimes or offenses after their parliamentary immunity has been removed by their respective Assembly. Any proceeding relating to a flagrant offense against a deputy or against a senator shall be brought without delay to the knowledge of the board of their Assembly. A deputy or a senator may not be arrested out of session without the authorization of the board of the Assembly to which he belongs. The detention or prosecution of a deputy or a senator shall be suspended if the Assembly to which he belongs requests it.

18. All members of the legislature are elected; the executive lacks the power to appoint any members of the legislature.

Yes. All members of the National Assembly are elected. According to the constitution, the president will appoint one-third of the members of the Senate. The Senate has not yet been established, however. Moreover, the Senate will not be a weighty legislative body. It cannot initiate legislation or take part in votes of confidence.

Article 52
The deputies are elected for five years by universal, direct and secret suffrage by uninominal majority vote with one ballot. They may be reelected. Each deputy shall be the representative of the entire Nation. Any imperative mandate is void... The Senate is composed of two-thirds by personalities elected by the representatives of the Territorial Collectivities and of one-third by personalities designated by the President of the Republic.

Article 83
The introduction of laws shall lie concurrently in the hands of the deputies and of the Government.

Article 98
The National Assembly may challenge the responsibility of the Government by passing a motion of censure.

Such a motion, in order to be admissible, must be signed by at least one-third of the deputies of the National Assembly. The vote may only be called five days after the motion has been introduced. The National Assembly may only pass a vote to censure the Government by a majority of two-thirds of its members. If the motion of censure is adopted, the Prime Minister shall hand in his resignation of Government. The President of the Republic shall appoint a new Prime Minister. If the motion of censure is rejected, its signatories may not propose a new motion during the same session.

19. The legislature alone, without the involvement of any other agencies, can change the Constitution.

Yes. The legislature can change the constitution with a four-fifths majority vote.

Article 144
The initiative for revision of the Constitution belongs concurrently to the President of the Republic and to at least one-fifth of the deputies composing the National Assembly. The project or bill for revision shall be considered adopted if it is voted upon by a majority of four-fifths of the deputies composing the National Assembly. When this majority is not reached, the project or bill for revision adopted by a majority of two-thirds of the deputies composing the National Assembly shall be submitted to referendum. The President of the Republic may submit any constitutional law bill to referendum. No procedure for revision can be engaged in or pursued during an interim period or a vacancy or when the integrity of the territory is being violated. The Republican form of the State and the State's secularity shall not be subject to revision.

20. The legislature's approval is necessary for the declaration of war.

Yes. The legislature's approval is necessary for the president's war declarations.

Article 93
The declaration of war is authorized by the National Assembly.

Article 72
The President of the Republic shall be the head of the Army. He shall preside over the Defense Councils. He shall declare war upon authorization of the National Assembly.

21. The legislature's approval is necessary to ratify treaties with foreign countries.

Yes. The legislature's approval is necessary to ratify international treaties on most major issues.

Article 137
The President of the Republic negotiates and ratifies international treaties and agreements.

Article 138
Peace treaties, commercial treaties, treaties relating to international organizations, those that involve use of

the State's finances, those that modify the provisions of a legislative nature, those relating to the state of people and to Human Rights, those that involve cession, exchange or addition of territory, shall only be ratified pursuant to a law. Such treaties shall only take effect after having been ratified and published. No cession, no exchange or addition of territory shall be valid without the consent of the population concerned.

22. The legislature has the power to grant amnesty.

No. Pardon and amnesty are not treated separately, and the legislature lacks the power to grant amnesty. See item 23.

23. The legislature has the power of pardon.

No. The president has the power of pardon (grace).

Article 73
The President of the Republic exercises the right of grace after consultation of the High Council of the Judiciary.

24. The legislature reviews and has the right to reject appointments to the judiciary; or the legislature itself appoints members of the judiciary.

No. Formally, the legislature has broad judicial appointment powers, but in practice, the president controls judicial appointments.

Article 100
The Constitutional Court is composed of nine members designated for seven renewable years. Three are designated by the President of the Republic including one because of his juridical competence(s). Three are elected by the National Assembly by a majority of two-thirds of its members. They must be chosen from the outside of the deputies. One among them must be designated because of his juridical competence(s). Three shall be elected by the Senate by a majority of two-thirds of its members. They shall be chosen from outside the pool of senators. One among them must be designated because of his juridical competence(s).

Article 108
The Court of Audit is composed of: the President, the Chamber Presidents, the Master-Counselors, the Audit Counselors, and the Auditors. The public ministry of the Court of Audit shall be directed by the Prosecutor General and General Attorneys. The President, the Prosecutor General, the General Attorneys, the Chamber Presidents and the Master-Counselors are appointed by decree of the President of the Republic taken in the Council of Ministers. The Audit Counselors and the Auditors are appointed by the President of the Republic on proposal of the Prime Minister after consultation with the Minister of Finance and favorable opinion by the National Assembly.

Article 121
The President of the Supreme Court is of necessity a professional magistrate. He is appointed by a decree of the President of the Republic taken in the Council of

Ministers on the proposal of the High Council of the Judiciary.

Article 126
The High Court of Justice is composed of the President and the Chamber Presidents of the Supreme Court and of four deputies elected by the National Assembly.

25. The chairman of the central bank is appointed by the legislature.

No. Togo is a member of the Central Bank of West African States, whose governor is selected by the member states.

26. The legislature has a substantial voice in the operation of the state-owned media.

No. The legislature lacks a substantial voice in the operation of the public media.

27. The legislature is regularly in session.

Yes. The legislature meets in ordinary session for six months each year.

Article 55
The National Assembly shall meet as of right in two ordinary sessions per year.
The first session shall open on the first Tuesday of April.
The second session shall open on the first Tuesday of October.
The Senate shall meet as of right in two ordinary sessions per year.
The first session shall open on the first Thursday of April.
The second session shall open on the first Thursday of October.
Each session shall last three months.

28. Each legislator has a personal secretary.

No.

29. Each legislator has at least one non-secretarial staff member with policy expertise.

No.

30. Legislators are eligible for re-election without any restriction.

Yes. There are no restrictions on re-election.

Article 52
The deputies are elected for five years by universal, direct and secret suffrage by uninominal majority vote with one ballot. They may be reelected.

31. A seat in the legislature is an attractive enough position that legislators are generally interested in and seek re-election.

Yes.

32. The re-election of incumbent legislators is common enough that at any given time the legislature

contains a significant number of highly experienced members.

Yes. Re-election rates are sufficiently high to produce a significant number of highly experienced members. Re-election, however, depends largely on maintaining fealty to the president and the hegemonic party, the Rally of the Togolese People.

PARLIAMENT OF TRINIDAD AND TOBAGO

Expert consultants: Kirk Meighoo, Dennis Pantin, Rita Pemberton, Ralph R. Premdas, Selwyn D. Ryan

Score: .53

Influence over executive (6/9)		Institutional autonomy (5/9)		Specified powers (2/8)		Institutional capacity (4/6)	
1. replace	X	10. no dissolution		19. amendments	X	27. sessions	X
2. serve as ministers	X	11. no decree	X	20. war		28. secretary	
3. interpellate	X	12. no veto	X	21. treaties	X	29. staff	
4. investigate		13. no review		22. amnesty		30. no term limits	X
5. oversee police		14. no gatekeeping	X	23. pardon		31. seek re-election	X
6. appoint PM	X	15. no impoundment	X	24. judiciary		32. experience	X
7. appoint ministers		16. control resources	X	25. central bank			
8. lack president	X	17. immunity		26. media			
9. no confidence	X	18. all elected					

The Parliament of Trinidad and Tobago traces its roots to the body that represented the country in the British Empire. Upon independence from Great Britain in 1962, Trinidad and Tobago retained a Westminster-style system with a prime minister as the head of government and a Governor General, acting as the British monarch's representative, as the head of state. A new constitution, adopted in 1976, abolished the Governor General and established a presidency. The bicameral legislature consists of a lower house, the House of Representatives, and an upper house, the Senate. Subsequent constitutional amendments have not directly affected legislative power.

The legislature possesses moderate powers. Its influence over the executive includes powers to select the president and the prime minister. The legislature's institutional autonomy is bolstered by the executive's lack of veto, decree, and gatekeeping powers. Yet parliament exercises relatively few specified powers and prerogatives. Its institutional capacity is limited by the absence of staff.

SURVEY

1. The legislature alone, without the involvement of any other agencies, can impeach the president or replace the prime minister.

Yes. The legislature can remove the prime minister with a vote of no confidence. Presidential impeachment requires the involvement of a special judicial tribunal.

Article 36

1. The President shall be removed from office where –

   (a) a motion that his removal from office should be investigated by a tribunal is proposed in the House of Representatives;

   (b) the motion states with full particulars the grounds on which his removal from office is proposed, and is signed by not less than one-third of the total membership of the House of Representatives;

   (c) the motion is adopted by the vote of not less than two-thirds of the total membership of the Senate and the House of Representatives assembled together;

   (d) a tribunal consisting of the Chief Justice and four other Judges appointed by him, being as far as practicable the most senior Judges, investigate the complaint and report on the facts to the House of Representatives;

   (e) the Senate and the House of Representatives assembled together on the summons of the Speaker consider the report and by resolution supported by the votes of not less than two-thirds of the total membership of the Senate and the House of Representatives assembles together declare that he shall be removed from office.

2. Where a motion is adopted as is provided for in subsection (1)(a), (b) and (c) the President shall cease to perform any of his functions as President and the President of the Senate shall act temporarily as President.

3. The procedure of the tribunal shall be such as is prescribed, but, subject to such procedure, the tribunal may regulate its own procedure.

4. Upon the adoption of the resolution in accordance with subsection (1)(c) the office shall become vacant.

Article 77

1. Where the House of Representatives passes a resolution, supported by the votes of a majority of all the members of the House, declaring that it has no confidence in the Prime Minister and the Prime Minister does not within seven days of the passing of such a resolution either resign or advise the President to dissolve Parliament, the President shall revoke the appointment of the Prime Minister.

2. Ministers may serve simultaneously as members of the legislature.

Yes. Ministers are chosen from, and serve simultaneously in, the legislature.

Article 76

3. The Ministers other than the Prime Minister shall be such persons as the President, acting in accordance with the advice of the Prime Minister, shall appoint from among the members of the House of Representatives and the Senators.

3. The legislature has powers of summons over executive branch officials and hearings with executive branch officials testifying before the legislature or its committees are regularly held.

Yes. The legislature regularly questions officials of the executive.

4. The legislature can conduct independent investigation of the chief executive and the agencies of the executive.

No. The legislature cannot investigate the executive. Investigations are conducted by the Ombudsman.

Article 93

1. Subject to this section and to sections 94 and 95 the principal function of the Ombudsman shall be to investigate any decision or recommendation made, including any advice given or recommendation made to a Minister, or any act done or omitted by any department of Government or any other authority to which this section applies, or by officers or members of such a department or authority, being action taken in exercise of the administrative functions of that department or authority.

2. The Ombudsman may investigate any such matter in any of the following circumstances –

(a) where a complaint is duly made to the Ombudsman by any person alleging that the complainant has sustained an injustice as a result of a fault in administration;

(b) where a member of the House of Representatives requests the Ombudsman to investigate the matter on the ground that a person or body of persons specified in the request has or may have sustained such injustice;

(c) in any other circumstances in which the Ombudsman considers that he ought to investigate the matter on the ground that some person or body of persons has or may have sustained such injustice.

3. The authorities other than departments of Government to which this section applies are –

(a) local authorities or other bodies established for purposes of the public service or of local Government;

(b) authorities or bodies the majority of whose members are appointed by the President or by a Minister or whose revenues consist wholly or mainly of moneys provided out of public funds;

(c) any authority empowered to determine the person with whom any contract shall be entered into by or on behalf of Government;

(d) such other authorities as may be prescribed.

5. The legislature has effective powers of oversight over the agencies of coercion (the military, organs of law enforcement, intelligence services, and the secret police).

No. The legislature lacks effective powers of oversight over the agencies of coercion.

6. The legislature appoints the prime minister.

Yes. The president appoints as prime minister the candidate who enjoys the support of the legislature.

Article 76

1. Where there is occasion for the appointment of a Prime Minister, the President shall appoint as Prime Minister –

(a) a member of the House of Representatives who is the Leader in that House of the party which commands the support of the majority of members of that House; or

(b) where it appears to him that party does not have an undisputed leader in that House or that no party commands the supports of such a majority, the member of the House of Representatives who, in his judgment, is most likely to command the support of the majority of members of that House; and who is willing to accept the office of Prime Minister.

7. The legislature's approval is required to confirm the appointment of ministers; or the legislature itself appoints ministers.

No. The president appoints ministers on the recommendation of the prime minister, and ministerial appointments do not require the legislature's approval.

Article 76
3. The Ministers other than the Prime Minister shall be such persons as the President, acting in accordance with the advice of the Prime Minister, shall appoint from among the members of the House of Representatives and the Senators.

8. The country lacks a presidency entirely or there is a presidency, but the president is elected by the legislature.

Yes. The legislature elects the president.

Article 22
There shall be a President of Trinidad and Tobago elected in accordance with the provisions of this Chapter who shall be the Head of State and Commander-in-Chief of the armed forces.

Article 28
1. There shall be an Electoral College for the purposes of this Chapter which shall be a unicameral body consisting of all the members of the Senate and all the members of the House of Representatives assembled together.
2. The Electoral College shall be convened by the Speaker.
3. The Speaker shall preside as Chairman over the proceedings of the Electoral College and shall have an original vote.
4. Subject to this Chapter, the Electoral College may regulate its own procedure and may make provision for the postponement or adjournment of its meetings and such other provisions as may be necessary to deal with difficulties that may arise in the carrying out of elections under this Chapter.
5. Ten Senators, the Speaker and twelve other members of the House of Representatives shall constitute a quorum of the Electoral College.

Article 29
The President shall be elected by the Electoral College voting by secret ballot.

9. The legislature can vote no confidence in the government.

Yes. The legislature can vote no confidence in the government.

Article 77
1. Where the House of Representatives passes a resolution, supported by the votes of a majority of all the members of the House, declaring that it has no confidence in the Prime Minister and the Prime Minister does not within seven days of the passing of such a resolution either resign or advise the President to dissolve Parliament, the President shall revoke the appointment of the Prime Minister.

10. The legislature is immune from dissolution by the executive.

No. The president, acting on the advice of the prime minister, can dissolve the legislature.

Article 68
1. The President, acting in accordance with the advice of the Prime Minister, may at any time prorogue or dissolve Parliament.

11. Any executive initiative on legislation requires ratification or approval by the legislature before it takes effect; that is, the executive lacks decree power.

Yes. The executive lacks decree power.

12. Laws passed by the legislature are veto-proof or essentially veto-proof; that is, the executive lacks veto power, or has veto power but the veto can be overridden by a majority in the legislature.

Yes. The executive lacks veto power. Formally, the president can withhold assent from a bill. In practice, it would be unthinkable for the president to do so.

Article 61
1. Subject to the provisions of this Constitution, the power of Parliament to make laws shall, except where otherwise authorized by statute, be exercised by Bills passed by the House of Representatives and the Senate and assented to by the President.
2. When a bill is presented to the President for assent, he shall signify that he assents or that he withholds assent.
3. A Bill shall not become law unless it has been duly passed and assented to in accordance with this Constitution.
4. A Bill may be assented to during the period occurring between the end of one session of Parliament and the beginning of the next or at any subsequent time during the life of that Parliament.

13. The legislature's laws are supreme and not subject to judicial review.

No. The judiciary can review the constitutionality of laws.

14. The legislature has the right to initiate bills in all policy jurisdictions; the executive lacks gatekeeping authority.

Yes. The legislature can initiate bills in all policy jurisdictions.

15. Expenditure of funds appropriated by the legislature is mandatory; the executive lacks the power to impound funds appropriated by the legislature.

Yes. The executive lacks the power to impound funds appropriated by the legislature.

16. The legislature controls the resources that finance its own internal operation and provide for the perquisites of its own members.

Yes. The legislature enjoys financial autonomy.

17. Members of the legislature are immune from arrest and/or criminal prosecution.

No. Legislative immunity extends to official parliamentary business only. Legislators are subject to arrest for common crimes.

Article 55
2. No civil or criminal proceedings may be instituted against any member of either House for words spoken before, or written in a report to, the House of which he is a member or in which he has a right of audience under section 62 or a committee thereof or any joint committee or meeting of the Senate and House of Representatives or by reason of any matter or thing brought by him therein by petition, bill, resolution, motion or otherwise; or for the publication by or under the authority of either House of any report, paper, votes or proceedings.

18. All members of the legislature are elected; the executive lacks the power to appoint any members of the legislature.

No. All members of the Senate are appointed. All members of the House of Representatives are elected.

Article 46
1. Subject to the provisions of this section, the House of Representatives shall consist of members who shall be elected in the manner provided by Parliament.
2. There shall be thirty-six members of the House of Representatives or such other number of members as corresponds with the number of constituencies as provided for by an Order made by the President under section 72.
3. Where any person who is not a member of the House of Representatives is elected to be Speaker of the House he shall, by virtue of holding the office of Speaker, be a member of the House in addition to the thirty-six or other number of members aforesaid.

Article 40
1. The Senate shall consist of thirty-one members who shall be appointed by the President in accordance with this section.
2. Of the thirty-one Senators –
    (*a*) sixteen shall be appointed by the President acting in accordance with the advice of the Prime Minister;
    (*b*) six shall be appointed by the President acting in accordance with the advice of the Leader of the Opposition; and
    (*c*) nine shall be appointed by the President in his discretion from outstanding persons from economic or social or community organizations and other major fields of endeavour.

19. The legislature alone, without the involvement of any other agencies, can change the Constitution.

Yes. The legislature can change the constitution through the normal legislative process.

Article 54
1. Subject to the provisions of this section, Parliament may alter any of the provisions of this Constitution or (in so far as it forms part of the law of Trinidad and Tobago) any of the provisions of the Trinidad and Tobago Independence Act, 1962.

20. The legislature's approval is necessary for the declaration of war.

No. There is no provision for the declaration of war, although the president can declare a state of emergency without the legislature's approval. The state of emergency lapses after fifteen days if it is not subsequently extended by the legislature.

Part III
8.
(1) Subject to this section, for the purposes of this Chapter, the President may from time to time make a Proclamation declaring that a state of public emergency exists.
(2) A Proclamation made by the President under subsection (1) shall not be effective unless it contains a declaration that the President is satisfied –
    (*a*) that a public emergency has arisen as a result of the imminence of a state of war between Trinidad and Tobago and a foreign State;
    (*b*) that a public emergency has arisen as a result of the occurrence of any earthquake, hurricane, flood, fire, outbreak of pestilence or of infectious disease, or other calamity whether similar to the foregoing or not; or
    (*c*) that action has been taken, or is immediately threatened, by any person, of such a nature and on so extensive a scale, as to be likely to endanger the public safety or to deprive the community or any substantial portion of the community of supplies or services essential to life.
9.
(1) Within three days of the making of the Proclamation, the President shall deliver to the Speaker for presentation to the House of Representatives a statement setting out the specific grounds on which the decision to declare the existence of a state of public emergency was based, and a date shall be fixed for a debate on this statement as soon as practicable but in any event not later that fifteen days from the date of the Proclamation.
(2) A Proclamation made by the President for the purposes of and in accordance with this section shall, unless previously revoked, remain in force for fifteen days.
10.
(1) Before its expiration the Proclamation may be extended from time to time by resolution supported by

a simple majority vote of the House of Representatives, so however, that no extension exceeds three months and the extensions do not in the aggregate exceed six months.

(2) The Proclamation may be further extended from time to time for not more than three months at any one time, by a resolution passed by both Houses of Parliament and supported by the votes of not less that three-fifths of all the members of each House.

(3) The Proclamation may be revoked at any time by a resolution supported by a simple majority vote of the House of Representatives.

21. The legislature's approval is necessary to ratify treaties with foreign countries.

Yes. The legislature's approval is necessary to ratify international treaties.

22. The legislature has the power to grant amnesty.

No. Amnesty and pardon are not treated separately, and the legislature lacks the power to grant amnesty. See item 23.

23. The legislature has the power of pardon.

No. The president has the power of pardon.

Article 87
1. The President may grant to any person a pardon, either free or subject to lawful conditions, respecting any offences that he may have committed. The power of the President under this subsection may be exercised by him either before or after the person is charged with any offence and before he is convicted thereof.
2. The President may –
(*a*) grant to any person convicted of any offence against the law of Trinidad and Tobago a pardon, either free or subject to lawful conditions;
(*b*) grant to any person a respite, either indefinite or for a specified period, from the execution of any punishment imposed on that person for such an offence;
(*c*) substitute a less severe form of punishment for that imposed by any sentence for such an offence; or
(*d*) remitted the whole or any part of any sentence passed for such an offence or any penalty or forfeiture otherwise due to the State on account of such an offence.
3. The power of the President under subsection (2) may be exercised by him in accordance with the advice of a Minister designated by him, acting in accordance with the advice of the Prime Minister.

24. The legislature reviews and has the right to reject appointments to the judiciary; or the legislature itself appoints members of the judiciary.

No. The president appoints the Chief Justice of the Supreme Court after consultation with the prime minister and the leader of the opposition. Other

judges are appointed by the president on the advice of the Judicial and Legal Service Commission. The legislature's approval is not required for judicial appointments.

Article 102
The Chief Justice shall be appointed by the President after consultation with the Prime Minister and the Leader of the Opposition.

Article 104
1. The Judges, other than the Chief Justice, shall be appointed by the President, acting in accordance with the advice of the Judicial and Legal Service Commission.

25. The chairman of the central bank is appointed by the legislature.

No. The legislature does not have a role in the appointment of the governor of the Central Bank of Trinidad and Tobago.

26. The legislature has a substantial voice in the operation of the state-owned media.

No. The legislature lacks a substantial voice in the operation of the public media.

27. The legislature is regularly in session.

Yes. The legislature regularly meets in ordinary session.

Article 67
1. Each session of Parliament shall be held at such place within Trinidad and Tobago and shall commence at such time as the President may by Proclamation appoint.
2. There shall be a session of each House once at least in every year, so that a period of six months shall not intervene between the last sitting of Parliament in one session and the first sitting thereof in the next session.

28. Each legislator has a personal secretary.

No.

29. Each legislator has at least one non-secretarial staff member with policy expertise.

No.

30. Legislators are eligible for re-election without any restriction.

Yes. There are no restrictions on re-election.

31. A seat in the legislature is an attractive enough position that legislators are generally interested in and seek re-election.

Yes.

32. The re-election of incumbent legislators is common enough that at any given time the legislature

contains a significant number of highly experienced members.

Yes. Re-election rates are sufficiently high to produce a significant number of highly experienced members.

NATIONAL PARLIAMENT OF TUNISIA (*MAJLIS AL-NUWAAB*)

Expert consultants: Michele Penner Angrist, Jean-Philippe Bras, Mujeeb R. Khan, Amer K. Mohsen, Kenneth Perkins, Peter J. Schraeder

Score: .28

Influence over executive (2/9)		Institutional autonomy (1/9)		Specified powers (1/8)		Institutional capacity (5/6)	
1. replace		10. no dissolution		19. amendments	X	27. sessions	X
2. serve as ministers	X	11. no decree		20. war		28. secretary	X
3. interpellate		12. no veto		21. treaties		29. staff	
4. investigate		13. no review		22. amnesty		30. no term limits	X
5. oversee police		14. no gatekeeping	X	23. pardon		31. seek re-election	X
6. appoint PM		15. no impoundment		24. judiciary		32. experience	X
7. appoint ministers		16. control resources		25. central bank			
8. lack president		17. immunity		26. media			
9. no confidence	X	18. all elected					

The National Parliament (*Majlis al-Nuwaab*) of Tunisia was established in the 1959 constitution upon independence from France. The document called for a unicameral legislature with a directly elected president. Since then the legislature has played a small role in national politics, as the country has been ruled by two successive autocratic presidents: Habib Bourguiba (1956–87) and Zine El Abidine Ben Ali (1987–present). A constitutional amendment in 2005 created an upper house, the Chamber of Advisers (*Majlis al-Mustasharin*).

The legislature exerts little influence in national politics. It cannot choose, effectively oversee, or remove the executive. Its own institutional autonomy is eviscerated by executive powers of decree, dissolution, veto, and review, as well as by the president's right to appoint one-third of the members of the Chamber of Advisers. The legislature exercises only a single specified power, the right to change the constitution. Perhaps surprisingly, the legislature does enjoy some institutional capacity.

SURVEY

1. The legislature alone, without the involvement of any other agencies, can impeach the president or replace the prime minister.

No. The legislature cannot remove the president. It can remove the prime minister with a motion of censure.

Article 62

(1) The National Parliament may, by a vote on a motion of censure, oppose the continuation of the responsibilities of the government, if it finds that the government is not following the general policy and the fundamental options provided for in Articles 49 and 58.

(2) The motion is not receivable unless it is motivated and signed by at least half of the membership of the National Parliament.

(3) The vote may not take place until 48 hours have elapsed after the motion of censure.

(4) When a motion of censure is adopted by a majority of two-thirds of the deputies, the President of the Republic accepts the resignation of the government presented by the Prime Minister.

2. Ministers may serve simultaneously as members of the legislature.

Yes. Legislators may serve simultaneously in ministerial positions.

3. The legislature has powers of summons over executive branch officials and hearings with executive branch officials testifying before the legislature or its committees are regularly held.

No. According to the constitution, the legislature can address questions to executive branch officials, but in practice, this power is not effectively exercised.

Article 61
(2) Any deputy may address written or oral questions to the Government.

4. The legislature can conduct independent investigation of the chief executive and the agencies of the executive.

No. The legislature cannot investigate the executive.

5. The legislature has effective powers of oversight over the agencies of coercion (the military, organs of law enforcement, intelligence services, and the secret police).

No. The legislature lacks effective powers of oversight over the agencies of coercion.

6. The legislature appoints the prime minister.

No. The president appoints the prime minister.

Article 50
(1) The President of the Republic nominates the Prime Minister, and on his suggestion, the other members of the Government.

7. The legislature's approval is required to confirm the appointment of ministers; or the legislature itself appoints ministers.

No. The president appoints ministers on the recommendation of the prime minister, and ministerial appointments do not require the legislature's approval.

Article 50
(1) The President of the Republic nominates the Prime Minister, and on his suggestion, the other members of the Government.

8. The country lacks a presidency entirely or there is a presidency, but the president is elected by the legislature.

No. The president is directly elected.

Article 37
The executive power is vested in the President of the Republic assisted by a Government directed by a Prime Minister.

Article 39
(1) The President of the Republic is elected for five years by universal, free, direct, and secret suffrage, within the last thirty days of the term of office and under the conditions specified by the electoral law.

9. The legislature can vote no confidence in the government.

Yes. The legislature can pass a motion of censure in the government. It bears note, however, that it has never done so.

Article 62
(1) The National Parliament may, by a vote on a motion of censure, oppose the continuation of the responsibilities of the government, if it finds that the government is not following the general policy and the fundamental options provided for in Articles 49 and 58.
(2) The motion is not receivable unless it is motivated and signed by at least half of the membership of the National Parliament.
(3) The vote may not take place until 48 hours have elapsed after the motion of censure.
(4) When a motion of censure is adopted by a majority of two-thirds of the deputies, the President of the Republic accepts the resignation of the government presented by the Prime Minister.

10. The legislature is immune from dissolution by the executive.

No. The president can dissolve the legislature.

Article 63
(1) If the National Parliament has adopted a second motion of censure with a two-thirds majority during the same legislative period, the President of the Republic may either accept the resignation of the government or dissolve the National Parliament.
(2) The decree dissolving the National Parliament must include the calling of new elections within a maximum period of thirty days.

11. Any executive initiative on legislation requires ratification or approval by the legislature before it takes effect; that is, the executive lacks decree power.

No. The president can issue decrees that have the force of law while the legislature is out of session. The decrees lapse if they are not subsequently approved by the legislature. The legislature can also delegate temporary decree powers to the president.

Article 28
(2) The National Parliament may authorize the President of the Republic to issue decree-laws within a fixed time limit and for a specific purpose which must be submitted for ratification to the National Parliament upon expiration of that time limit.

Article 31
During the vacation of the National Parliament, the President of the Republic may, with the consent of the interested permanent committee, issue decree-laws which must be submitted to the ratification by the National Parliament during the next ordinary session.

12. Laws passed by the legislature are veto-proof or essentially veto-proof; that is, the executive lacks veto power, or has veto power but the veto can be over-ridden by a majority in the legislature.

No. A two-thirds majority vote is required to override a presidential veto.

Article 52
(1) The President of the Republic promulgates constitutional, organic, or ordinary laws and ensures their publication in the Official Journal of the Tunisian Republic within a maximum period of fifteen days counting from the transmission by the President of the National Parliament.
(2) The President of the Republic may, during this period, return the bill to the National Parliament for a second reading. If the bill is adopted by the National Parliament with a majority of two-thirds of its members, the law is promulgated and published within a second period of fifteen days.

13. The legislature's laws are supreme and not subject to judicial review.

No. The legislature's laws are not subject to judicial review, but they are not supreme. They can be overruled on legal grounds by the executive branch.

14. The legislature has the right to initiate bills in all policy jurisdictions; the executive lacks gatekeeping authority.

Yes. The legislature can initiate bills in all policy jurisdictions.

15. Expenditure of funds appropriated by the legislature is mandatory; the executive lacks the power to impound funds appropriated by the legislature.

No. The president can impound funds appropriated by the legislature.

16. The legislature controls the resources that finance its own internal operation and provide for the perquisites of its own members.

No. The legislature is dependent on the executive for the resources that finance its own operations.

17. Members of the legislature are immune from arrest and/or criminal prosecution.

No. Formally, legislators are immune with the common exception for *flagrante delicto*, but in practice, members of the opposition have been arrested.

Article 26
A deputy cannot be prosecuted, arrested, or tried for opinions expressed, proposals made, or acts carried out in the exercise of his mandate in the National Parliament.

Article 27
No deputy can be arrested or prosecuted for the duration of his mandate for a crime or misdemeanor as long as the National Parliament has not lifted the immunity which covers him. However, in the event of flagrante delicto, arrest procedure is permitted, in such a case, the National Parliament is to be informed without delay. The detention of a deputy is suspended if the National Parliament so requests.

18. All members of the legislature are elected; the executive lacks the power to appoint any members of the legislature.

No. One-third of the members of the newly created Chamber of Advisers are to be appointed by the president. All members of the lower chamber are elected.

Article 19
The members of the National Parliament are elected by universal, free, direct, and secret suffrage, according to the modalities and conditions determined by the Electoral Law.

19. The legislature alone, without the involvement of any other agencies, can change the Constitution.

Yes. The legislature can change the constitution in multiple readings with a two-thirds majority vote.

Article 72
The initiative for the amendment of the Constitution belongs to the President of the Republic or to at least one-third of the members of the National Parliament, with the reservation that it does not affect the republican form of the State.

Article 73
(1) The National Parliament may not deliberate on the proposed amendment except following a resolution passed by an absolute majority and after a special ad hoc committee has determined and studied the objective.
(2) The Constitution cannot be amended except following the adoption by the National Parliament of the amendment proposal with a majority of two-thirds of its members after two readings, the second of which may not take place until at least three months after the first.

20. The legislature's approval is necessary for the declaration of war.

No. Formally, the legislature's approval is necessary for presidential war declarations. In practice, the president can declare war without the legislature's approval.

Article 48
(1) The President of the Republic ratifies the treaties.
(2) He declares war and concludes peace with the approval of the National Parliament.

21. The legislature's approval is necessary to ratify treaties with foreign countries.

No. Formally, treaties "are approved by law." In practice, the legislature's approval is not necessary to ratify international treaties.

> Article 32
> Treaties do not have the force of law until after their ratification. Treaties duly ratified have an authority superior to laws.

> Article 33
> The treaties are approved by law.

> Article 48
> (1) The President of the Republic ratifies the treaties.

22. The legislature has the power to grant amnesty.

No. Formally, amnesty is regulated by law. In practice, the legislature lacks this power.

> Article 34
> Matters relating to the following are regulated in the form of laws:
> – amnesty.

23. The legislature has the power of pardon.

No. The president has the power of pardon.

> Article 48
> (3) [The President of the Republic] exercises the right of pardon.

24. The legislature reviews and has the right to reject appointments to the judiciary; or the legislature itself appoints members of the judiciary.

No. The president appoints the judiciary, and the appointments do not require the legislature's approval.

> Article 66
> Magistrates are nominated by decree of the President of the Republic upon the recommendation of the Superior Council of the Magistrature.

25. The chairman of the central bank is appointed by the legislature.

No. The president appoints the governor of the Central Bank of Tunisia.

26. The legislature has a substantial voice in the operation of the state-owned media.

No. The president tightly controls the state-run Tunisian Radio and Television Establishment (ERTT).

27. The legislature is regularly in session.

Yes. The legislature meets in ordinary session for about nine months each year.

> Article 29
> (1) The National Parliament meets each year in ordinary session which begins during the month of October and ends during the month of July.
> (2) However, the first session of every legislature begins during the first fifteen days of November.

28. Each legislator has a personal secretary.

Yes.

29. Each legislator has at least one non-secretarial staff member with policy expertise.

No.

30. Legislators are eligible for re-election without any restriction.

Yes. There are no restrictions on re-election.

31. A seat in the legislature is an attractive enough position that legislators are generally interested in and seek re-election.

Yes.

32. The re-election of incumbent legislators is common enough that at any given time the legislature contains a significant number of highly experienced members.

Yes. Since 1987 members of President Ben Ali's hegemonic political party, the Democratic Constitutional Rally, have rarely been defeated at the polls, providing the legislature with a significant number of highly experienced members.

TURKISH GRAND NATIONAL ASSEMBLY (*BÜYÜK MILLET MECLISI*)

Expert consultants: Şener Aktürk, Doğu Ergil, Ömer Gençkaya, Kerim Can Kavakli, Ziya Öniş

Score: .78

Influence over executive (7/9)		Institutional autonomy (8/9)		Specified powers (4/8)		Institutional capacity (6/6)	
1. replace	X	10. no dissolution	X	19. amendments		27. sessions	X
2. serve as ministers	X	11. no decree	X	20. war	X	28. secretary	X
3. interpellate	X	12. no veto	X	21. treaties	X	29. staff	X
4. investigate	X	13. no review		22. amnesty	X	30. no term limits	X
5. oversee police		14. no gatekeeping	X	23. pardon	X	31. seek re-election	X
6. appoint PM		15. no impoundment	X	24. judiciary		32. experience	X
7. appoint ministers	X	16. control resources	X	25. central bank			
8. lack president	X	17. immunity	X	26. media			
9. no confidence	X	18. all elected	X				

The Turkish Grand National Assembly (*Büyük Millet Meclisi*) was established in the 1920s following the breakup of the Ottoman Empire. The 1962 constitution established a Constitutional Court to review the constitutionality of laws. Prior to 1962 the legislature's laws were supreme. Turkey's current constitution was adopted in 1982. It calls for a unicameral legislature, a prime minister as the head of government, and a president, elected by the legislature, as the head of state. The document gave the president the power to submit constitutional amendments proposed by the legislature to popular referendum. Prior to 1982 the legislature could, acting alone, change the constitution.

The Assembly wields broad powers. It influences the executive with, among other powers, the right to choose the president, oversee the executive branch, and remove the president and the prime minister from office. The Assembly's laws are subject to judicial review, but otherwise the Assembly possesses complete institutional autonomy. It exercises some specified powers and enjoys every measure of institutional capacity captured in this survey.

SURVEY

1. The legislature alone, without the involvement of any other agencies, can impeach the president or replace the prime minister.

Yes. The legislature can remove the prime minister with a vote of no confidence. It can impeach the president with a three-fourths majority vote of its total membership.

Article 105
(3) The President of the Republic may be impeached for high treason on the proposal of at least one-third of the total number of members of the Turkish Grand National Assembly, and by the decision of at least three-quarters of the total number of members.

Article 111
(1) If the Prime Minister deems it necessary, and after discussing the matter in the Council of Ministers, he/she may ask for a vote of confidence in the Turkish Grand National Assembly.
(2) The request for a vote of confidence shall not be debated before one full day has elapsed from the time it was submitted to the Turkish Grand National Assembly and shall not be put to the vote until one full day has passed after debate.
(3) A request for a vote of confidence shall be rejected only by an absolute majority of the total number of members.

2. Ministers may serve simultaneously as members of the legislature.

Yes. Legislators may serve simultaneously in ministerial positions.

Article 109

(1) The Council of Ministers shall consist of the Prime Minister and the ministers.

(2) The Prime Minister shall be appointed by the President of the Republic from among the members of the Turkish Grand National Assembly.

(3) The ministers shall be nominated by the Prime Minister and appointed by the Turkish Grand National Assembly, or from among those eligible for election as deputies; and they can be dismissed, by the President of the Republic, upon the proposal of the Prime Minister when deemed necessary.

3. The legislature has powers of summons over executive branch officials and hearings with executive branch officials testifying before the legislature or its committees are regularly held.

Yes. The legislature regularly interpellates officials from the executive.

Article 98

(1) The Turkish Grand National Assembly shall exercise its supervisory power by means of questions, parliamentary inquiries, general debates interpellation and parliamentary investigations.

(2) A question is a request for information addressed to the Prime Minister or ministers to be answered orally or in writing on behalf of the Council of Ministers.

(3) A parliamentary inquiry is an examination conducted to obtain information on a specific subject.

(4) A general debate is the consideration of a specific subject relating to the community and the activities of the State at the plenary sessions of the Turkish Grand National Assembly.

(5) The form of presentation, content, and scope of the motions concerning questions, parliamentary inquiries and general debates, and the procedures for answering, debating and investigating them, shall be regulated by the Rules of Procedure.

4. The legislature can conduct independent investigation of the chief executive and the agencies of the executive.

Yes. The legislature can investigate the executive.

Article 98

(1) The Turkish Grand National Assembly shall exercise its supervisory power by means of questions, parliamentary inquiries, general debates interpellation and parliamentary investigations.

(2) A question is a request for information addressed to the Prime Minister or ministers to be answered orally or in writing on behalf of the Council of Ministers.

(3) A parliamentary inquiry is an examination conducted to obtain information on a specific subject.

(4) A general debate is the consideration of a specific subject relating to the community and the activities of the State at the plenary sessions of the Turkish Grand National Assembly.

(5) The form of presentation, content, and scope of the motions concerning questions, parliamentary inquiries and general debates, and the procedures for answering, debating and investigating them, shall be regulated by the Rules of Procedure.

Article 100

(1) Parliamentary investigation concerning the Prime Minister or other ministers may be requested with a motion tabled by at least one-tenth of the total number of members of the Turkish Grand National Assembly. The Assembly shall consider and decide on this request within one month at the latest.

(2) In the event of a decision to initiate an investigation, this investigation shall be conducted by a commission of fifteen members chosen by lot on behalf of each party from among three times the number of members the party is entitled to have on the commission, representation being proportional to the parliamentary membership of the party. The commission shall submit its report on the result of the investigation to the Assembly within two months. If the investigation is not completed within the time allotted, the commission shall be granted a further and final period of two months.

(3) The Assembly shall debate the report with priority and, if found necessary, may decide to bring the person involved before the Supreme Court. The decision to bring a person before the Supreme Court shall be taken only by an absolute majority of the total number of members.

(4) Political party groups in the Assembly shall not hold discussions or take decisions regarding parliamentary investigations.

5. The legislature has effective powers of oversight over the agencies of coercion (the military, organs of law enforcement, intelligence services, and the secret police).

No. The legislature lacks effective powers of oversight over the agencies of coercion.

6. The legislature appoints the prime minister.

No. The president appoints the prime minister.

Article 104

(2) To this end, the duties [the President] shall perform, and the powers he/she shall exercise, in accordance with the conditions stipulated in the relevant articles of the Constitution are as follows:

  b) Those relating to the executive functions:

    – To appoint the Prime Minister and to accept his/her resignation.

Article 109

(2) The Prime Minister shall be appointed by the President of the Republic from among the members of the Turkish Grand National Assembly.

(3) The ministers shall be nominated by the Prime Minister and appointed by the Turkish Grand National Assembly, or from among those eligible for election as

deputies; and they can be dismissed, by the President of the Republic, upon the proposal of the Prime Minister when deemed necessary.

7. The legislature's approval is required to confirm the appointment of ministers; or the legislature itself appoints ministers.

Yes. The legislature's approval is required to confirm ministerial appointments.

> Article 104
> (2) To this end, the duties [the President] shall perform, and the powers he/she shall exercise, in accordance with the conditions stipulated in the relevant articles of the Constitution are as follows:
>   b) Those relating to the executive functions:
>   – To appoint and dismiss Ministers on the proposal of the Prime Minister.

> Article 109
> (1) The Council of Ministers shall consist of the Prime Minister and the ministers.
> (2) The Prime Minister shall be appointed by the President of the Republic from among the members of the Turkish Grand National Assembly.
> (3) The ministers shall be nominated by the Prime Minister and appointed by the Turkish Grand National Assembly or from among those eligible for election as deputies; and they can be dismissed, by the President of the Republic, upon the proposal of the Prime Minister when deemed necessary.

> Article 110
> (1) The complete list of members of the Council of Ministers shall be submitted to the Turkish Grand National Assembly. If the Turkish Grand National Assembly is in recess, it shall be summoned to meet.
> (2) The Government Programme of the Council of Ministers shall be read by the Prime Minister or by one of the ministers before the Turkish Grand National Assembly within a week of the formation of the Council of Ministers following which a vote of confidence shall be taken. Debate on the vote of confidence shall begin two full days after the reading of the programme and the vote shall be taken one full day after the end of debate.

8. The country lacks a presidency entirely or there is a presidency, but the president is elected by the legislature.

Yes. The legislature elects the president. In a referendum held in October 2007, however, voters endorsed holding direct popular elections for the president. Future elections may be held on such a basis, in which case parliament will lose its power of presidential election.

> Article 101
> (1) The President of the Republic shall be elected for a term of office of seven years by the Turkish Grand National Assembly from among its own members who

are over 40 years of age and who have completed their higher education or from among Turkish citizens who fulfill these requirements and are eligible to be deputies.

> Article 102
> (1) The President of the Republic shall be elected by a two-thirds majority of the total number of members of the Turkish Grand National Assembly and by secret ballot. If the Turkish Grand National Assembly is not in session, it shall be summoned immediately to meet.

9. The legislature can vote no confidence in the government.

Yes. The legislature can vote no confidence in the government.

> Article 111
> (1) If the Prime Minister deems it necessary, and after discussing the matter in the Council of Ministers, he/she may ask for a vote of confidence in the Turkish Grand National Assembly.
> (2) The request for a vote of confidence shall not be debated before one full day has elapsed from the time it was submitted to the Turkish Grand National Assembly and shall not be put to the vote until one full day has passed after debate.
> (3) A request for a vote of confidence shall be rejected only by an absolute majority of the total number of members.

10. The legislature is immune from dissolution by the executive.

Yes. The legislature is immune from dissolution.

11. Any executive initiative on legislation requires ratification or approval by the legislature before it takes effect; that is, the executive lacks decree power.

Yes. The executive lacks decree power. The legislature can, however, grant temporary decree powers to the president to deal with specific issue areas.

> Article 91
> (1) The Turkish Grand National Assembly may empower the Council of Ministers to issue decrees having force of law. However, the fundamental rights, individual rights and duties included in the First and Second Chapter of the Second Part of the Constitution and the political rights and duties listed in the Fourth Chapter, cannot be regulated by decrees having force of law except during periods of martial law and states of emergency.
> (2) The empowering law shall define the purpose, scope, principles, and operative period of the decree having force of law, and whether more than one decree will be issued within the same period.
> (4) When approving a decree having force of law before the end of the prescribed period, the Turkish Grand National Assembly shall also state whether the power has terminated or will continue until the expiry of the said period.

(5) Provisions relating to the decrees having force of law issued by the Council of Ministers meeting under the chairmanship of the President of the Republic in time of martial law or states of emergency, are reserved.
(6) Decrees having force of law shall come into force on the day of their publication in the Official Gazette. However, a later date may be indicated in the decree as the date of entry into force.
(7) Decrees are submitted to the Turkish Grand National Assembly on the day of their publication in the Official Gazette.
(8) Laws of empowering and decrees having force of law which are based on these, shall be discussed in the committees and in the plenary session of the Turkish Grand National Assembly with priority and urgency.
(9) Decrees not submitted to the Turkish Grand National Assembly on the day of their publication shall cease to have effect on that day and decrees rejected by the Turkish Grand National Assembly shall cease to have effect on the day of publication of the decision in the Official Gazette. The amended provisions of the decrees which are approved as amended shall go into force on the day of their publication in the Official Gazette.

12. Laws passed by the legislature are veto-proof or essentially veto-proof; that is, the executive lacks veto power, or has veto power but the veto can be overridden by a majority in the legislature.

Yes. The legislature can override a presidential veto by a majority vote of its present members.

Article 89
(1) The President of the Republic shall promulgate the laws adopted by the Turkish Grand National Assembly within fifteen days.
(2) He shall, within the same period, refer to the Turkish Grand National Assembly for further consideration, laws which he deems unsuitable for promulgation, together with a statement of his reasons. Budget laws shall not be subject to this provision.
(3) If the Turkish Grand National Assembly adopts in its unchanged form the law referred back, the President of the Republic shall promulgate it; if the Assembly amends the law which was referred back, the President of the Republic may again refer the amended law back to the Assembly.
(4) Provisions relating to Constitutional amendments are reserved.

13. The legislature's laws are supreme and not subject to judicial review.

No. The Constitutional Court can review the constitutionality of laws.

Article 104
(2) To this end, the duties [the president] shall perform, and the powers he/she shall exercise, in accordance with the conditions stipulated in the relevant articles of the Constitution are as follows:
 a) Those relating to legislation:

– To appeal to the Constitutional Court for the annulment in part or entirety of certain provisions of laws, decrees having force of law, and the Rules of Procedure of the Turkish Grand National Assembly on the grounds that they are unconstitutional in form or in content.

Article 148
(1) The Constitutional Court shall examine the constitutionality, in respect of both form and substance, of laws, decrees having force of law, and the Rules of Procedure of the Turkish Grand National Assembly. Constitutional amendments shall be examined and verified only with regard to their form. However, no action shall be brought before the Constitutional Court alleging unconstitutionality as to the form or substance of decrees having force of law issued during a state of emergency, martial law or in time of war.

14. The legislature has the right to initiate bills in all policy jurisdictions; the executive lacks gatekeeping authority.

Yes. The legislature can initiate bills in all policy jurisdictions.

15. Expenditure of funds appropriated by the legislature is mandatory; the executive lacks the power to impound funds appropriated by the legislature.

Yes. The executive lacks the power to impound funds appropriated by the legislature.

16. The legislature controls the resources that finance its own internal operation and provide for the perquisites of its own members.

Yes. The legislature enjoys financial autonomy, including control over members' salaries.

Article 86
(1) The salaries and allowances of the members of the Turkish Grand National Assembly shall be regulated by law. The monthly amount of the salary shall not exceed the salary of the most senior civil servant; the travel allowance shall not exceed half of that salary.
(2) The salaries and allowances paid to the members of the Turkish Grand National Assembly shall not necessitate the suspension of payments of pensions and similar benefits by social security agencies.
(3) A maximum of three months' salaries and allowances may be paid in advance.

17. Members of the legislature are immune from arrest and/or criminal prosecution.

Yes. Legislators are immune with the common exception for cases of *flagrante delicto*, here expressed as "caught in the act of committing a crime punishable by a heavy penalty."

Article 83
(1) Members of the Turkish Grand National Assembly shall not be liable for their votes and statements

concerning parliamentary functions, for the views they express before the Assembly, or unless the Assembly decides otherwise on the proposal of the Bureau for that sitting, for repeating or revealing these outside the Assembly.

(2) A deputy who is alleged to have committed an offence before or after election, shall not be arrested, interrogated, detained or tried unless the Assembly decides otherwise. This provision shall not apply in cases where a member is caught in the act of committing a crime punishable by a heavy penalty and in cases subject to Article 14 of the Constitution if an investigation has been initiated before the election. However, in such situations the competent authority shall notify the Turkish Grand National Assembly immediately and directly.

(3) The execution of a criminal sentence imposed on a member of the Turkish Grand National Assembly either before or after his election shall be suspended until he ceases to be a member; the statute of limitations does not apply during the term of membership.

(4) Investigation and prosecution of a re-elected deputy shall be subject to the renewed waiver of immunity by the Assembly.

(5) Political party groups in the Turkish Grand National Assembly shall not hold discussions or take decisions regarding parliamentary immunity.

18. All members of the legislature are elected; the executive lacks the power to appoint any members of the legislature.

Yes. All members of the legislature are elected.

Article 75
The Turkish Grand National Assembly shall be composed of five hundred fifty deputies elected by universal suffrage.

19. The legislature alone, without the involvement of any other agencies, can change the Constitution.

No. The legislature alone cannot change the constitution without the approval of the president. If the president objects to a constitutional amendment that has been passed by the legislature, he or she can choose to put the amendment to a nationwide referendum.

Article 175
(1) The constitutional amendment shall be proposed in writing by at least one-third of the total number of members of the Turkish Grand National Assembly. Proposals to amend the Constitution shall be debated twice in the Plenary Session. The adoption of a proposal for an amendment shall require a three-fifths majority of the total number of members of the Assembly by a secret ballot.

(2) The consideration and adopting of proposals for the amendment of the Constitution shall be subject to the provisions governing the consideration and adoption

of legislation, with the exception of the conditions set forth in this article.

(3) The President of the Republic may refer the laws related to the Constitutional amendments for further consideration. If the Assembly adopts the draft law referred by the President by a two-thirds majority, the President may submit the law to referendum.

(4) If a law is adopted by a three-fifths or less than two-thirds majority of the total number of votes of the Assembly and is not referred by the President for further consideration, it shall be published in the Official Gazette and shall be submitted to referendum.

(5) A law on the Constitutional amendment adopted by a two-thirds majority of the total number of members of the Turkish Grand National Assembly directly or if referred by the President for further consideration, or its articles as considered necessary may be submitted to a referendum by the President. Laws or related articles of the Constitutional amendment not submitted to referendum shall be published in the Official Gazette.

(6) Laws related to Constitutional amendment which are submitted to referendum, shall require the approval of more than half of the valid votes cast.

20. The legislature's approval is necessary for the declaration of war.

Yes. The legislature's approval is necessary for presidential war declarations with the common exception for cases of foreign invasion.

Article 92
(1) The Power to authorise the declaration of a state of war in cases deemed legitimate by international law and, except where required by international treaties to which Turkey is a party or by the rules of international courtesy to send Turkish Armed Forces to foreign countries and to allow foreign armed forces to be stationed in Turkey, is vested in the Turkish Grand National Assembly.

(2) If the country is subjected, while the Turkish Grand National Assembly is adjourned or in recess, to sudden armed aggression and it thus becomes imperative to decide immediately on the use of the armed forces, the President of the Republic can decide on the use of the Turkish Armed Forces.

21. The legislature's approval is necessary to ratify treaties with foreign countries.

Yes. The legislature's approval is necessary to ratify international treaties on most major issues.

Article 90
(1) The ratification of treaties concluded with foreign states and international organisations on behalf of the Republic of Turkey, shall be subject to adoption by the Turkish Grand National Assembly by a law approving the ratification.

(2) Agreements regulating economic, commercial and technical relations, and covering a period of no more than one year, may be put into effect through

promulgation, provided they do not entail any financial commitment by the State, and provided they do not infringe upon the status of individuals or upon the property rights of Turkish citizens abroad. In such cases, these agreements must be brought to the knowledge of the Turkish Grand National Assembly within two months of their promulgation.

(3) Agreements in connection with the implementation of an international treaty, and economic, commercial, technical, or administrative agreements which are concluded depending on an authorisation given by law shall not require approval by the Turkish Grand National Assembly. However, agreements concluded under the provision of this paragraph and affecting the economic, or commercial relations and private rights of individuals shall not be put into effect unless promulgated.

(4) Agreements resulting in amendments to Turkish laws shall be subject to the provisions of the first paragraph.

(5) International agreements duly put into effect carry the force of law. No appeal to the Constitutional Court can be made with regard to these agreements, on the ground that they are unconstitutional.

Article 104
(2) To this end, the duties [the president] shall perform, and the powers he/she shall exercise, in accordance with the conditions stipulated in the relevant articles of the Constitution are as follows:
  b) Those relating to the executive functions:
    – To ratify and promulgate international treaties.

22. The legislature has the power to grant amnesty.

Yes. The legislature has the power to grant amnesty.

Article 87
The functions and powers of the Turkish Grand National Assembly comprise . . . deciding on the proclamation of amnesties and pardons excluding those who have been convicted for activities set out in Article 14 of the Constitution.

23. The legislature has the power of pardon.

Yes. The legislature has the power of pardon.

Article 87
The functions and powers of the Turkish Grand National Assembly comprise . . . deciding on the proclamation of amnesties and pardons excluding those who have been convicted for activities set out in Article 14 of the Constitution.

24. The legislature reviews and has the right to reject appointments to the judiciary; or the legislature itself appoints members of the judiciary.

No. The president and members of the judiciary make judicial appointments, and the appointments do not require the legislature's approval.

Article 104
(2) To this end, the duties [the president] shall perform, and the powers he/she shall exercise, in accordance with the conditions stipulated in the relevant articles of the Constitution are as follows:
  c) Those relating to the judiciary:
To appoint the members of the Constitutional Court, one-fourth of the members of the Council of State, the Chief Public Prosecutor and the Deputy Chief Public Prosecutor of the High Court of Appeals, the members of the Military High Court of Appeals, the members of the Supreme Military Administrative Court and the members of the Supreme Council of Judges and Public Prosecutors.

Article 146
(1) The Constitutional Court shall be composed of eleven regular and four substitute members.
(2) The President of the Republic shall appoint two regular and two substitute members from the High Court of Appeals, two regular and one substitute member from the Council of State, and one member each from the Military High Court of Appeals, the High Military Administrative Court and the Audit Court, three candidates being nominated for each vacant office by the Plenary Assemblies of each court from among their respective presidents and members, by an absolute majority of the total number of members; the President of the Republic shall also appoint one member from a list of three candidates nominated by the Higher Education Council from among members of the teaching staff of institutions of higher education who are not members of the Council, and three members and one substitute member from among senior administrative officers and lawyers.

Article 154
(2) Members of the High Court of Appeals shall be appointed by the Supreme Council of Judges and Public Prosecutors from among first category judges and public prosecutors of the Republic, of the courts of justice, or those considered to be members of this profession, by secret ballot and by an absolute majority of the total number of members.

Article 156
(2) Members of the Military High Court of Appeals shall be appointed by the President of the Republic from among three candidates nominated for each vacant office by the Plenary Assembly of the Military High Court of Appeals from among military judges of the first category, by secret ballot and by an absolute majority of the total number of members.

Article 157
(2) Members of the High Military Administrative Court of Appeals who are military judges shall be appointed by the President of the Republic from a list of three candidates nominated for each vacant office by the president and members of the Court, who are also military judges, by secret ballot and by an absolute majority of the total number of such members, from among

military judges of the first category; members who are not military judges shall be appointed by the President of the Republic from a list of three candidates nominated for each vacant office by the Chief of the General Staff from among officers holding the rank and qualifications prescribed by law.

Article 159

(1) The Supreme Council of Judges and Public Prosecutors shall be established and shall exercise its functions in accordance with the principles of the independence of the courts and the security of tenure of judges.

(2) The President of the Council is the Minister of Justice. The Undersecretary to the Minister of Justice shall be an ex-officio member of the Council. Three regular and three substitute members of the Council shall be appointed by the President of the Republic for a term of four years from a list of three candidates nominated for each vacant office by the Plenary Assembly of the High Court of Appeals from among its own members and two regular and two substitute members shall be similarly appointed from a list of three candidates nominated for each vacant office by the Plenary Assembly of the Council of State. They may be re-elected at the end of their term of office. The Council shall elect a deputy president from among its elected regular members.

25. The chairman of the central bank is appointed by the legislature.

No. The government appoints the governor of the Central Bank of the Republic of Turkey.

26. The legislature has a substantial voice in the operation of the state-owned media.

No. The government appoints the head of the Turkish Radio-Television Corporation.

27. The legislature is regularly in session.

Yes. The legislature meets in ordinary session for nine months each year.

Article 93

(1) The Turkish Grand National Assembly shall convene of its own accord on the first day of October each year.

(2) The Assembly may be in recess for a maximum of three months in the course of a legislative year. During an adjournment and recess it may be summoned by the President of the Republic either on his own initiative or at the request of the Council of Ministers.

(3) The President of the Assembly may also summon the Assembly either on his own initiative or at the written request of one-fifth of the members.

(4) If the Turkish Grand National Assembly is convened during an adjournment or recess, it shall not adjourn or go into recess again before having given priority consideration to the matter requiring the summons.

28. Each legislator has a personal secretary.

Yes.

29. Each legislator has at least one non-secretarial staff member with policy expertise.

Yes.

30. Legislators are eligible for re-election without any restriction.

Yes. There are no restrictions on re-election.

31. A seat in the legislature is an attractive enough position that legislators are generally interested in and seek re-election.

Yes.

32. The re-election of incumbent legislators is common enough that at any given time the legislature contains a significant number of highly experienced members.

Yes. Re-election rates are sufficiently high to produce a significant number of highly experienced members.

PEOPLE'S COUNCIL OF TURKMENISTAN (*KHALK MASLAKHATY*)

Expert consultants: Şener Aktürk, Robia Charles, Michael J. Denison, Jody LaPorte, Regine Spector

Score: .06

Influence over executive (1/9)	Institutional autonomy (0/9)	Specified powers (0/8)	Institutional capacity (1/6)
1. replace	10. no dissolution	19. amendments	27. sessions
2. serve as **X**	11. no decree	20. war	28. secretary
ministers	12. no veto	21. treaties	29. staff
3. interpellate	13. no review	22. amnesty	30. no term
4. investigate			limits
5. oversee	14. no	23. pardon	31. seek
police	gatekeeping		re-election
6. appoint PM	15. no	24. judiciary	32. experience **X**
	impoundment		
7. appoint	16. control	25. central bank	
ministers	resources		
8. lack	17. immunity	26. media	
president			
9. no	18. all elected		
confidence			

The People's Council (*Khalk Maslakhaty*) of Turkmenistan was established in the country's 1992 constitution following independence from the Soviet Union. The constitution calls for two legislative bodies: the *Majlis* (parliament) and the more expansive People's Council. The latter includes all of the members of the *Majlis*, the president, the cabinet, judges, leaders of political parties, and local representatives. In 2003 a constitutional amendment clarified the powers of the two bodies and named the People's Council, led by the president, the nation's supreme legislative authority. The People's Council is the body whose powers are assessed here.

The People's Council is not a genuine legislature. The People's Council has been merely a decoration in a firmament of adornments that make up the cult of the president, Saparmurat Niyazov. Between the dissolution of the USSR at the end of 1991 and Niyazov's death in December 2006, Turkmenistan endured the erection of the modern world's most all-embracing and farcical personality cult. The legislature's functions, in practice, have been limited to bestowing awards upon and singing the praises of Niyazov, who was referred to universally in Turkmenistan's press as Turkmenbashi (Father of the Turkmen) the Great, and whom the legislature made president for life in 1999. The death of Niyazov in December 2006 presents the possibility of a more meaningful role for the legislature in Turkmenistan, but what part it might play in the future remains open.

The legislature lacks a voice in the formation of the executive branch and cannot effectively oversee or remove executive branch officials. The president decrees legislation, appoints members of the legislature, and can dissolve the legislature, leaving the legislature without institutional autonomy. The legislature does not exercise any of the specified powers measured in this survey and has minimal institutional capacity.

SURVEY

1. The legislature alone, without the involvement of any other agencies, can impeach the president or replace the prime minister.

No. Presidential impeachment requires approval in a national referendum.

Article 59

In case of violation of the Constitution and laws by the President of Turkmenistan, the Khalk Maslakhaty may express no confidence in the President of Turkmenistan and put the issue of his removal to a national vote. The issue of no confidence in the President of Turkmenistan may be considered upon the request of no less than one-third of the established number of members of the Khalk Maslakhaty. The decision of no confidence in the President of Turkmenistan is adopted by no less than two-thirds of the votes of the established number of members of the Khalk Maslakhaty.

2. Ministers may serve simultaneously as members of the legislature.

Yes. Ministers are prohibited from serving simultaneously in the *Majlis* but are automatically members of the *Khalk Maslakhaty*.

> Article 46
> The members of the Khalk Maslakhaty are:
> The President of Turkmenistan;
> Deputies of the Majlis, the Chairman of the Supreme Court, the General Procurator, members of the Cabinet of Ministers, khyakims of velayets [and] the khyakim of the city of Ashgabat;
> Khalk vekilleri;
> Leaders of political parties, the Youth Organization, professional unions, the Union of Women, who are members of the Nation-wide Movement "Galkynysh," leaders of public organizations in the State [and] the representatives of the elders of Turkmenistan;
> Khyakims of cities that are administrative centers of velayets and etraps [and] archyns of cities and villages that are administrative centers of etraps.
> The Khalk Maslakhaty consists of 2,507 members.
>
> Article 70
> The Majlis is a standing body of state, and a deputy may not simultaneously serve as a member of the Cabinet of Ministers, the hyakim of a velayat, city, or etrap, an archyn or kazy, or a prosecutor.

3. The legislature has powers of summons over executive branch officials and hearings with executive branch officials testifying before the legislature or its committees are regularly held.

No. Formally, legislators can question executive branch officials, but in practice, ministers rarely undergo questioning before the legislature.

> Article 68
> Deputies of the Majlis have the right of inquiry [in form of] oral or written questions to the Cabinet of Ministers, the ministers [and] the leaders of other State organs.

4. The legislature can conduct independent investigation of the chief executive and the agencies of the executive.

No. The legislature cannot investigate the executive.

5. The legislature has effective powers of oversight over the agencies of coercion (the military, organs of law enforcement, intelligence services, and the secret police).

No. The legislature lacks effective powers of oversight over the agencies of coercion.

6. The legislature appoints the prime minister.

No. There is no prime minister. The president is the head of the cabinet of ministers.

7. The legislature's approval is required to confirm the appointment of ministers; or the legislature itself appoints ministers.

No. The president appoints ministers, and the appointments do not require the legislature's approval.

> Article 74
> The Cabinet of Ministers includes Deputy Chairmen of the Cabinet of Ministers and minister. The President of Turkmenistan may appoint other officials who are the heads of central executive bodies of government to the Cabinet of Ministers. The Cabinet of Ministers is formed by the President within one month after taking office and is dissolved before a newly elected President takes office.

8. The country lacks a presidency entirely or there is a presidency, but the president is elected by the legislature.

No. The president is directly elected. President Niyazov served as an elected president from 1992 to 1999. From 1999 to 2006 President Niyazov ruled as president for life, a position granted to him by the People's Council. Presidential elections to replace Niyazov were held in February 2007.

> Article 54
> The President of Turkmenistan is elected directly by the people of Turkmenistan for a term of five years and enters office immediately after taking an oath at a session of the Khalk Maslakhaty.

9. The legislature can vote no confidence in the government.

No. The legislature cannot vote no confidence in the government.

10. The legislature is immune from dissolution by the executive.

No. The president can dissolve the *Majlis*.

> Article 63
> The Majlis may be dissolved early:
> 1. By the decision of a referendum;
> 2. By a resolution of the Khalk Maslakhaty;
> 3. By a resolution of the Majlis, adopted by a majority of no less than two-thirds of the established number of deputies (self-dissolution);
> 4. By the President of Turkmenistan, in cases of not forming within six months the leadership of the Majlis.

11. Any executive initiative on legislation requires ratification or approval by the legislature before it takes effect; that is, the executive lacks decree power.

No. The president issues decrees that have the force of law.

Article 56
The President of Turkmenistan issues decrees, ordinances and orders, which are binding throughout Turkmenistan.

12. Laws passed by the legislature are veto-proof or essentially veto-proof; that is, the executive lacks veto power, or has veto power but the veto can be overridden by a majority in the legislature.

No. A two-thirds majority is required to override a presidential veto.

Article 55
The President of Turkmenistan:
6. Signs laws [and] has the right, within a two-week period to the use of the delaying veto to return legislation with his objections to the Majlis for a repeated debate and vote. If the Majlis confirms its previously adopted decision by a majority of two-thirds of the votes of the deputies, the President of Turkmenistan shall sign the law. The President of Turkmenistan does not have the right of delaying veto in respect to laws on amendments and supplements to the Constitution adopted by the Khalk Maslakhaty.

13. The legislature's laws are supreme and not subject to judicial review.

No. The legislature's laws are not supreme. Formally, the legislature is granted the power to review the constitutionality of laws. In practice, the "legislature's laws" do not exist, as the president is the country's sole lawgiver.

Article 66
The competence of the Majlis includes:
7. Determining whether the normative acts of organs of State power and administration are in accordance with the Constitution.

Article 111
Laws [and] other legal acts of State organs and officials are issued on the basis of and in accordance with the Constitution.
In case of a discrepancy between the provisions indicated by the Constitution and laws, the provisions of the Constitution are in effect.

14. The legislature has the right to initiate bills in all policy jurisdictions; the executive lacks gatekeeping authority.

No. The legislature is prohibited from initiating bills beyond a restricted domain of issues.

Article 48
The competence of the Khalk Maslakhaty includes:
1. Adoption of the Constitution of Turkmenistan, constitutional laws [and] the introductions of amendments and supplements to them;
2. Creation of the Central Commission for Elections and Conduct of Referenda in Turkmenistan [and] making changes to its composition;

3. Decision on the issue of conducting nation-wide referenda;
4. Calling the election of the President of Turkmenistan, deputies of the Mejlis, khalk vekilleri and members of Gengeshes;
5. Consideration and approval of programs of basic directions of political, economic and social development of the country;
6. Change of the State border and administratively-territorial division of Turkmenistan;
9. Declaration of individual unlawful acts as treason against the Homeland, declaration as traitors of the Homeland of persons recognized as guilty and convicted of committing such acts and the decision on the issue of permitting the application of an exceptional measure of punishment in the form of life-long deprivation of liberty. The right to apply the exceptional measure of punishment in the form of life-long deprivation of liberty belongs to the Supreme Court of Turkmenistan with the subsequent consideration at a session of the Khalk Maslakhaty of the issue of approving such sentences pronounced by the court.

15. Expenditure of funds appropriated by the legislature is mandatory; the executive lacks the power to impound funds appropriated by the legislature.

No. The president can impound funds appropriated by the legislature.

16. The legislature controls the resources that finance its own internal operation and provide for the perquisites of its own members.

No. The legislature is dependent on the executive for the resources that finance its own operations.

17. Members of the legislature are immune from arrest and/or criminal prosecution.

No. Formally, members of the *Majlis* are immune, but in practice, legislators enjoy immunity only at the pleasure of the president.

Article 69
A deputy may be deprived of his deputy powers only by the Majlis. The decision on this issue is adopted by a majority of no less than two-thirds of the votes of the established number of deputies of the Majlis. A deputy may not be brought to criminal responsibility, arrested or in another manner deprived of liberty without the consent of the Majlis.

18. All members of the legislature are elected; the executive lacks the power to appoint any members of the legislature.

No. The members of the legislature include the president and officials appointed by him, including ministers and judges. Even the formally elected members are indirectly selected by the executive branch. For example, the government chooses the candidates eligible for election to the *Majlis*.

Article 46
The members of the Khalk Maslakhaty are:
The President of Turkmenistan;
Deputies of the Majlis, the Chairman of the Supreme Court, the General Procurator, members of the Cabinet of Ministers, khyakims of velayets [and] the khyakim of the city of Ashgabat;
Khalk vekilleri;
Leaders of political parties, the Youth Organization, professional unions, the Union of Women, who are members of the Nation-wide Movement "Galkynysh," leaders of public organizations in the State [and] the representatives of the elders of Turkmenistan;
Khyakims of cities that are administrative centers of velayets and etraps [and] archyns of cities and villages that are administrative centers of etraps.
The Khalk Maslakhaty consists of 2,507 members.

Article 62
The Majlis consists of 50 deputies elected by territorial districts, which contain an approximately equal number of electors, for a term of five years.

19. The legislature alone, without the involvement of any other agencies, can change the Constitution.

No. In practice, it would be unthinkable for the legislature to change the constitution without the president's approval. Formally, the *Khalk Maslakhaty* can change the constitution with a two-thirds majority vote.

Article 113
A law on the amendment to the Constitution is considered adopted if no less than two-thirds of the established number of members of the Khalk Maslakhaty voted in its favor.

20. The legislature's approval is necessary for the declaration of war.

No. The constitution does not contain a provision addressing the declaration of war. In practice, the president could declare war without the legislature's approval.

21. The legislature's approval is necessary to ratify treaties with foreign countries.

No. Formally, the *Khalk Maslakhaty* has the power to ratify international treaties. In practice, the president concludes international treaties without the legislature's approval.

Article 48
The competence of the Khalk Maslakhaty includes:
10. Ratification and denunciation of treaties on international unions and other formations.

22. The legislature has the power to grant amnesty.

No. The president has the power to grant amnesty.

Article 55
The President of Turkmenistan:

11. Grants pardons and amnesty.

23. The legislature has the power of pardon.

No. The president has the power of pardon.

Article 55
The President of Turkmenistan:
11. Grants pardons and amnesty.

24. The legislature reviews and has the right to reject appointments to the judiciary; or the legislature itself appoints members of the judiciary.

No. The president appoints the judiciary, and the appointments do not require the legislature's approval.

Article 100
Judges of all courts are appointed by the President of Turkmenistan for a term of five years.

25. The chairman of the central bank is appointed by the legislature.

No. The president appoints the chairman of State Central Bank of Turkmenistan.

26. The legislature has a substantial voice in the operation of the state-owned media.

No. The legislature lacks a substantial voice in the operation of the public media.

27. The legislature is regularly in session.

No. The legislature is called into session by the president and meets infrequently and for short sessions.

Article 50
The Khalk Maslakhaty is convened by the Chairman of the Khalk Maslakhaty or the President of Turkmenistan as necessary but not less frequently than once a year by the Chairman of the Khalk Maslakhaty, the President of Turkmenistan, the Majlis or one-third of the Khalk Maslakhaty members.

28. Each legislator has a personal secretary.

No.

29. Each legislator has at least one non-secretarial staff member with policy expertise.

No.

30. Legislators are eligible for re-election without any restriction.

No. There are no elections for the vast majority of seats in the legislature.

31. A seat in the legislature is an attractive enough position that legislators are generally interested in and seek re-election.

No. The vast majority of seats in the legislature are filled by appointment rather than election so one cannot speak of re-election. It is also impossible to know with certainty whether members seek re-appointment. The stipends that members receive may be sufficient to make membership attractive, and a seat may be regarded as prestigious. It is normally obtained through service to the president or by virtue of tribal or clan seniority.

32. The re-election of incumbent legislators is common enough that at any given time the legislature contains a significant number of highly experienced members.

Yes. Despite frequent shuffles and purges by the president, there remains a core of experienced presidential loyalists in the legislature. Most members of the legislature are experienced in managing affairs at local or district levels, but do not necessarily have competence or expertise in matters of legislation.

NATIONAL ASSEMBLY OF UGANDA

Expert consultants: Onek Adyanga, Giovanni Carbone, David K. Leonard, Anne Mugisha, Zahara Nampewo

Score: .44

Influence over executive (3/9)		Institutional autonomy (5/9)		Specified powers (2/8)		Institutional capacity (4/6)	
1. replace		10. no dissolution	X	19. amendments		27. sessions	X
2. serve as ministers	X	11. no decree	X	20. war		28. secretary	
3. interpellate	X	12. no veto		21. treaties	X	29. staff	
4. investigate		13. no review		22. amnesty		30. no term limits	X
5. oversee police		14. no gatekeeping		23. pardon		31. seek re-election	X
6. appoint PM		15. no impoundment	X	24. judiciary	X	32. experience	X
7. appoint ministers	X	16. control resources	X	25. central bank			
8. lack president		17. immunity		26. media			
9. no confidence		18. all elected	X				

The National Assembly of Uganda was established upon the country's independence from Great Britain in 1962. For most of its history, the National Assembly was sidelined as the country suffered military coups, international and civil wars, and dictatorial rulers. Beginning in 1986, with the coming to power of Yoweri Museveni, Uganda underwent gradual reforms that culminated in the 1995 constitution. The document calls for a unicameral legislature and a directly elected president.

The legislature has middling powers. Its influence over the executive is not extensive. It cannot choose the president, oversee the executive branch, or remove executive branch officials from office. The legislature does have some institutional autonomy, although that autonomy is limited by presidential veto and gatekeeping powers. It exercises few specified powers, yet it does have a role in approving judicial branch appointments. Its institutional capacity is limited by a lack of staff.

SURVEY

1. The legislature alone, without the involvement of any other agencies, can impeach the president or replace the prime minister.

No. Presidential impeachment requires the involvement of the Supreme Court.

Article 107
(1) The President may be removed from office in accordance with this article on any of the following grounds –
　(a) abuse of office or willful violation of the oath of allegiance and the presidential oath or any provision of this Constitution;

(b) misconduct or misbehavior –
(i) that he or she has conducted himself or herself in a manner which brings or is likely to bring the office of President into hatred, ridicule, contempt or disrepute; or
(ii) that he or she has dishonestly done any act or omission which is prejudicial or inimical to the economy or security of Uganda; or

(2) For the purpose of removal of the President under paragraph (a) or (b) of clause (1) of this article, a notice in writing signed by not less than one-third of all the members of Parliament shall be submitted to the Speaker –
(a) stating that they intend to move a motion for a resolution in Parliament for the removal of the President on the charge that the President has –
(i) wilfully abused his or her office or wilfully violated the oath of allegiance and the Presidential oath or any other provision of this Constitution in terms of paragraph (a) of clause (1) of this article;
(ii) misconducted himself or herself or misbehaved in terms of paragraph (b) of clause (1) of this article; and
(b) setting out the particulars of the charge supported by the necessary documents on which it is claimed that the conduct of the President be investigated for the purposes of his or her removal.

(3) The Speaker shall, within twenty-four hours after receipt of the notice referred to in clause (2) of this article, cause a copy to be transmitted to the President and the Chief Justice.

(4) The Chief Justice shall, within seven days after receipt of the notice transmitted under clause (3) of this article, constitute a tribunal comprising three Justices of the Supreme Court to investigate the allegation in the notice and to report its findings to Parliament stating whether or not there is a prima facie case for the removal of the President.

(6) If the tribunal determines that there is a prima facie case for the removal of the President under paragraph (a) or (b) of clause (1) of this article, then if Parliament passes the resolution supported by the votes of not less than two-thirds of all members of Parliament, the President shall cease to hold office.

2. Ministers may serve simultaneously as members of the legislature.

Yes. Legislators may serve simultaneously in ministerial positions.

Article 113
(1) Cabinet Ministers shall be appointed by the President with the approval of Parliament from among members of Parliament or persons qualified to be elected members of Parliament.

3. The legislature has powers of summons over executive branch officials and hearings with executive branch officials testifying before the legislature or its committees are regularly held.

Yes. The legislature regularly questions executive branch officials.

Article 89
(3) The functions of standing committees shall include the following –
(c) to assess and evaluate activities of Government and other bodies;
(4) In the exercise of their functions under this article, committees of Parliament –
(a) may call any Minister or any person holding public office and private individuals to submit memoranda or appear before them to give evidence;
(c) shall have the powers of the High Court for –
(i) enforcing the attendance of witnesses and examining them on oath, affirmation or otherwise;
(ii) compelling the production of documents.

4. The legislature can conduct independent investigation of the chief executive and the agencies of the executive.

No. The legislature cannot investigate the executive.

5. The legislature has effective powers of oversight over the agencies of coercion (the military, organs of law enforcement, intelligence services, and the secret police).

No. The legislature lacks effective powers of oversight over the agencies of coercion.

6. The legislature appoints the prime minister.

No. There is no prime minister.

7. The legislature's approval is required to confirm the appointment of ministers; or the legislature itself appoints ministers.

Yes. The legislature's approval is required to confirm the president's ministerial appointments.

Article 113
(1) Cabinet Ministers shall be appointed by the President with the approval of Parliament from among members of Parliament or persons qualified to be elected members of Parliament.

8. The country lacks a presidency entirely or there is a presidency, but the president is elected by the legislature.

No. The president is directly elected.

Article 103
(1) The election of the President shall be by universal adult suffrage through a secret ballot.

9. The legislature can vote no confidence in the government.

No. The legislature cannot vote no confidence in the government. It can pass a motion of censure against individual ministers, but it cannot pass a motion of censure in the government as a whole.

Article 118

(1) Parliament may, by resolution supported by more than half of all members of Parliament, pass a vote of censure against a Minister on any of the following grounds –

(a) abuse of office or wilful violation of the oath of allegiance or oath of office;

(b) misconduct or misbehaviour;

(c) physical or mental incapacity, namely, that he or she is incapable of performing the functions of his or her office by reason of physical or mental incapacity;

(d) mismanagement; or

(e) incompetence.

(2) Upon a vote of censure being passed against a Minister, the President shall, unless the Minister resigns his or her office, take appropriate action in the matter.

(3) Proceedings for censure of a Minister shall be initiated by a petition to the President through the Speaker signed by not less than one-third of all members of Parliament giving notice that they are dissatisfied with the conduct or performance of the Minister and intend to move a motion for a resolution of censure and setting out particulars of the grounds in support of the motion.

(4) The President shall, upon receipt of the petition, cause a copy of it to be given to the Minister in question.

(5) The motion for the resolution of censure shall not be debated until the expiry of thirty days after the petition was sent to the President.

(6) A Minister in respect of whom a vote of censure is debated under clause (5) of this article is entitled during the debate to be heard in his or her defence.

10. The legislature is immune from dissolution by the executive.

Yes. The legislature is immune from dissolution.

Article 96

Parliament shall stand dissolved upon the expiration of its term as prescribed by article 77 of this Constitution.

11. Any executive initiative on legislation requires ratification or approval by the legislature before it takes effect; that is, the executive lacks decree power.

Yes. The executive lacks decree power.

Article 79

(2) Except as provided in this Constitution, no person or body other than Parliament shall have power to make provisions having the force of law in Uganda except under authority conferred by an Act of Parliament.

12. Laws passed by the legislature are veto-proof or essentially veto-proof; that is, the executive lacks veto power, or has veto power but the veto can be overridden by a majority in the legislature.

No. A two-thirds majority vote is required to override a presidential veto.

Article 91

(1) Subject to the provisions of this Constitution, the power of Parliament to make laws shall be exercised through bills passed by Parliament and assented to by the President.

(2) A bill passed by Parliament shall, as soon as possible, be presented to the President for assent.

(3) The President shall, within thirty days after a bill is presented to him or her –

(a) assent to the bill; or

(b) return the bill to Parliament with a request that the bill or a particular provision of it be reconsidered by Parliament; or

(c) notify the Speaker in writing that he or she refuses to assent to the bill.

(4) Where a bill has been returned to Parliament under paragraph (b) of clause (3) of this article, Parliament shall reconsider it and if passed again, it shall be presented for a second time to the President for assent.

(5) Where the President returns the same bill twice under paragraph (b) of clause (3) of this article and the bill is passed for the third time, with the support of at least two-thirds of all members of Parliament, the Speaker shall cause a copy of the bill to be laid before Parliament and the bill shall become law without the assent of the President.

(6) Where the President –

(a) refuses to assent to a bill under paragraph (c) of clause (3) of this article, Parliament may reconsider the bill and if passed, the bill shall be presented to the President for assent;

(b) refuses to assent to a bill which has been reconsidered and passed under paragraph (a) of this clause or under clause (4) of this article, the Speaker shall, upon the refusal, if the bill was so passed with the support of at least two-thirds of all members of Parliament, cause a copy of the bill to be laid before Parliament and the bill shall become law without the assent of the President.

13. The legislature's laws are supreme and not subject to judicial review.

No. The Constitutional Court can review the constitutionality of laws.

Article 137

(1) Any question as to the interpretation of this Constitution shall be determined by the Court of Appeal sitting as the Constitutional Court.

(2) When sitting as a Constitutional Court, the Court of Appeal shall consist of a bench of five members of that Court.

(3) A person who alleges that –

(a) an Act of Parliament or any other law or anything in or done under the authority of any law; or

(b) any act or omission by any person or authority, is inconsistent with or in contravention of a provision of this Constitution, may petition the Constitutional Court for a declaration to that effect, and for redress where appropriate.

14. The legislature has the right to initiate bills in all policy jurisdictions; the executive lacks gatekeeping authority.

No. The legislature is prohibited from introducing legislation related to taxation, public expenditure, or government debt.

Article 93

Parliament shall not, unless the bill or the motion is introduced on behalf of the Government –

(a) proceed upon a bill, including an amendment bill, that makes provision for any of the following –

(i) the imposition of taxation or the alteration of taxation otherwise than by reduction; or

(ii) the imposition of a charge on the Consolidated Fund or other public fund of Uganda or the alteration of any such charge otherwise than by reduction; or

(iii) the payment, issue or withdrawal from the Consolidated Fund or other public fund of Uganda of any moneys not charged on that fund or any increase in the amount of that payment, issue or withdrawal; or

(iv) the composition or remission of any debt due to the Government of Uganda; or

(b) proceed upon a motion, including an amendment to a motion, the effect of which would be to make provision for any of the purposes specified in paragraph (a) of this article.

15. Expenditure of funds appropriated by the legislature is mandatory; the executive lacks the power to impound funds appropriated by the legislature.

Yes. The executive lacks the power to impound funds appropriated by the legislature.

16. The legislature controls the resources that finance its own internal operation and provide for the perquisites of its own members.

Yes. The legislature enjoys financial autonomy, including control over members' salaries.

Article 85

(1) A member of Parliament shall be paid such emoluments and such gratuity and shall be provided with such facilities as may be determined by Parliament.

(2) A member of Parliament shall not hold any office of profit or emolument likely to compromise his or her office.

17. Members of the legislature are immune from arrest and/or criminal prosecution.

No. The constitution states that parliament shall prescribe immunities by law, but in practice, legislators are subject to arrest.

Article 97

The Speaker, the Deputy Speaker, members of Parliament and any other person participating or assisting in or acting in connection with or reporting the proceedings of Parliament or any of its committees shall be entitled to such immunities and privileges as Parliament shall by law prescribe.

18. All members of the legislature are elected; the executive lacks the power to appoint any members of the legislature.

Yes. All members of the legislature are elected with the exception of the vice president and the ministers, who, if not already members of the legislature, become ex-officio members without voting rights.

Article 78

(1) Parliament shall consist of –

(a) members directly elected to represent constituencies;

(b) one woman representative for every district;

(c) such numbers of representatives of the army, youth, workers, persons with disabilities and other groups as Parliament may determine; and

(d) the Vice-President and Ministers, who, if not already elected members of Parliament, shall be ex-officio members of Parliament without the right to vote on any issue requiring a vote in Parliament.

Article 81

(1) A general election of members of Parliament shall be held within thirty days before the expiration of the term of Parliament.

19. The legislature alone, without the involvement of any other agencies, can change the Constitution.

No. In practice, any substantial constitutional change would be impossible without the president's blessing. Formally, the legislature can change most of the articles of the constitution in multiple readings with a two-thirds majority vote. Amendments to select articles of the constitution require approval in either a popular referendum or by regional representative bodies.

Article 258

(1) Subject to the provisions of this Constitution, Parliament may amend by way of addition, variation or repeal, any provision of this Constitution in accordance with the procedure laid down in this Chapter.

(2) This Constitution shall not be amended except by an Act of Parliament –

(a) the sole purpose of which is to amend this Constitution; and

(b) the Act has been passed in accordance with this Chapter.

Article 259

(1) A bill for an Act of Parliament seeking to amend any of the provisions specified in clause (2) of this article shall not be taken as passed unless –

(a) it is supported at the second and third readings in Parliament by not less than two-thirds of all members of Parliament; and

(b) it has been referred to a decision of the people and approved by them in a referendum.

(2) The provisions referred to in clause (1) of this article are –

(a) this article;

(b) Chapter One – articles 1 and 2;

(c) Chapter Four – article 44;

(d) Chapter Five – articles 69, 74 and 75;

(e) Chapter Six – article 79 clause (2);

(f) Chapter Seven – article 105 clause (1);

(g) Chapter Eight – article 128 clause (1); and

(h) Chapter Sixteen.

Article 260

(1) A bill for an Act of Parliament seeking to amend any of the provisions specified in clause (2) of this article shall not be taken as passed unless –

(a) it is supported at the second and third readings in Parliament by not less than two-thirds of all members of Parliament; and

(b) it has been ratified by at least two-thirds of the members of the district council in each of at least two-thirds of all the districts of Uganda.

(2) The provisions referred to in clause (1) of this article are –

(a) this article;

(b) Chapter Two – article 5, clause (2);

(c) Chapter Nine – article 152;

(d) Chapter Eleven – article 176, clause (1) and articles 178, 189 and 197.

Article 261

A bill for an Act of Parliament to amend any provision of the Constitution, other than those referred to in articles 259 and 260 of this Constitution, shall not be taken as passed unless it is supported at the second and third readings by the votes of not less than two-thirds of all members of Parliament.

Article 262

(1) The votes on the second and third readings referred to in articles 259 and 260 of this Constitution shall be separated by at least fourteen sitting days of Parliament.

(2) A bill for the amendment of this Constitution which has been passed in accordance with this Chapter shall be assented to by the President only if –

(a) it is accompanied by a certificate of the Speaker that the provisions of this Chapter have been complied with in relation to it; and

(b) in the case of a bill to amend a provision to which article 259 or 260 of this Constitution applies, it is accompanied by a certificate of the Electoral Commission that the amendment has been approved at a referendum or, as the case may be, ratified by the district councils in accordance with this Chapter.

(3) Where the provisions of clause (2) of this article are complied with in the case of a bill to which article 259 or 260 of this Constitution applies, the President shall not refuse to assent to the bill.

(4) Where in the case of a bill to which clause (3) of this article applies the President –

(a) refuses to assent to the bill; or

(b) fails to assent to the bill within thirty days after the bill is submitted, the President shall be taken to have assented to the bill and the Speaker shall cause a copy of the bill to be laid before Parliament and the bill shall become law without the assent of the President.

20. The legislature's approval is necessary for the declaration of war.

No. The president can declare war without the legislature's approval when consulting the legislature would be "impracticable." The president then must seek retroactive approval within seventy-two hours.

Article 124

(1) The President may, with the approval of Parliament, given by resolution supported by not less than two-thirds of all the members of Parliament, declare that a state of war exists between Uganda and any other country.

(2) Where it is impracticable to seek the approval of Parliament before declaration of a state of war, the President may declare a state of war without the approval but shall seek the approval immediately after the declaration and in any case not later than seventy-two hours after the declaration.

(3) Where the President makes the declaration of a state of war under clause (2) when Parliament is in recess, the Speaker shall, immediately summon Parliament to an emergency session to sit within seventy-two hours after the declaration of a state of war.

(4) The President may, with the approval of Parliament, given by resolution, revoke a declaration of a state of war made under clause (1) or (2) of this article.

21. The legislature's approval is necessary to ratify treaties with foreign countries.

Yes. The legislature's approval is necessary to ratify international treaties.

Article 123

(1) The President or a person authorised by the President may make treaties, conventions, agreements, or other arrangements between Uganda and any other country or between Uganda and any international organisation or body, in respect of any matter.

(2) Parliament shall make laws to govern ratification of treaties, conventions, agreements or other arrangements made under clause (1) of this article.

22. The legislature has the power to grant amnesty.

No. Amnesty and pardon are not treated separately, and the legislature lacks the power to grant amnesty. See item 22.

23. The legislature has the power of pardon.

No. The president, acting on the advice of the Advisory Committee on the Prerogative of Mercy, has the power of pardon (mercy).

Article 121

(1) There shall be an Advisory Committee on the Prerogative of Mercy which shall consist of –

(a) the Attorney-General who shall be Chairperson; and

(b) six prominent citizens of Uganda appointed by the President.

(2) A person shall not be qualified for appointment as a member of the Committee if he or she is a member of Parliament, the Uganda Law Society or a District Council.

(3) A member appointed under paragraph (b) of clause (1) of this article shall serve for a period of four years and shall cease to be a member of the Committee –

(a) if circumstances arise that would disqualify him or her from appointment; or

(b) if removed by the President for inability to perform the functions of his or her office arising from infirmity of body or mind or for misbehaviour, misconduct or incompetence.

(4) The President may, on the advice of the Committee –

(a) grant to any person convicted of an offence, a pardon either free or subject to lawful conditions;

(b) grant to a person a respite, either indefinite or for a specified period, from the execution of punishment imposed on him or her for an offence;

(c) substitute a less severe form of punishment for a punishment imposed on a person for an offence; or

(d) remit the whole or part of a punishment imposed on a person or of a penalty or forfeiture otherwise due to Government on account of any offence.

(5) Where a person is sentenced to death for an offence, a written report of the case from the trial judge or judges or person presiding over the court or tribunal, together with such other information derived from the record of the case or elsewhere as may be necessary, shall be submitted to the Advisory Committee on the Prerogative of Mercy.

(6) A reference in this article to conviction or imposition of a punishment, sentence, or forfeiture includes conviction or imposition of a punishment, penalty, sentence or forfeiture by a court martial or other military tribunal except a Field Court Martial.

24. The legislature reviews and has the right to reject appointments to the judiciary; or the legislature itself appoints members of the judiciary.

Yes. The legislature's approval is necessary for the president's judicial appointments.

Article 142

(1) The Chief Justice, the Deputy Chief Justice, the Principal Judge, a Justice of the Supreme Court, a Justice of Appeal and a Judge of the High Court shall be appointed by the President acting on the advice of the Judicial Service Commission and with the approval of Parliament.

Article 148

Subject to the provisions of this Constitution, the Judicial Service Commission may appoint persons to hold

or act in any judicial office other than the offices specified in clause (3) of article 147 of this Constitution and confirm appointments in and exercise disciplinary control over persons holding or acting in such offices and remove such persons from office.

25. The chairman of the central bank is appointed by the legislature.

No. The president appoints the governor of the Bank of Uganda with the approval of parliament.

Article 161

(1) The Bank of Uganda shall be the central bank of Uganda and it shall be the only authority to issue the currency of Uganda.

(2) The authority of the Bank of Uganda shall vest in a Board which shall consist of a Governor, a Deputy Governor and not more than five other members.

(3) The Governor, the Deputy Governor and all other members of the Board shall –

(a) be appointed by the President with the approval of Parliament.

26. The legislature has a substantial voice in the operation of the state-owned media.

No. The president and the Ministry of Information control the public media.

27. The legislature is regularly in session.

Yes. The legislature regularly meets in ordinary session.

Article 95

(1) Where a new Parliament is elected, the President shall, by proclamation, appoint the place and a date not beyond seven days after the expiry of the term of Parliament or of the extended period, as the case may be, for the first sitting of the new Parliament.

(2) A session of Parliament shall be held at such place within Uganda and shall commence at such time as the Speaker may, by proclamation, appoint.

(3) The Speaker may, after consultation with the President, prorogue Parliament by proclamation.

(4) A session of Parliament shall be held at least once a year but the period between one session and the next following session shall be less than twelve months.

(5) Notwithstanding any other provision of this article, at least one-third of all members of Parliament may, in writing signed by them, request a meeting of Parliament; and the Speaker shall summon Parliament to meet within twenty-one days after receipt of the request.

28. Each legislator has a personal secretary.

No.

29. Each legislator has at least one non-secretarial staff member with policy expertise.

No.

30. Legislators are eligible for re-election without any restriction.

Yes. There are no restrictions on re-election.

31. A seat in the legislature is an attractive enough position that legislators are generally interested in and seek re-election.

Yes.

32. The re-election of incumbent legislators is common enough that at any given time the legislature contains a significant number of highly experienced members.

Yes. Uganda held parliamentary elections in 1996, 2001, and 2006. There was considerable stability in membership across elections, contributing to the formation of a sizable cohort of highly experienced members. The ostensibly nonpartisan organization of President Yoweri Museveni, the National Resistance Movement, functions as the legislature's hegemonic party.

SUPREME COUNCIL OF UKRAINE (*VERKHOVNA RADA*)

Expert consultants: Nadia Diuk, Andrew Konitzer-Smirnov, Oleh Protsyk, A. Tobias Schedlbauer, Lucan A. Way

Score: .59

Influence over executive (4/9)		Institutional autonomy (4/9)		Specified powers (6/8)		Institutional capacity (5/6)	
1. replace		10. no dissolution		19. amendments		27. sessions	X
2. serve as ministers		11. no decree		20. war	X	28. secretary	X
3. interpellate	X	12. no veto		21. treaties	X	29. staff	
4. investigate		13. no review		22. amnesty	X	30. no term limits	X
5. oversee police		14. no gatekeeping	X	23. pardon		31. seek re-election	X
6. appoint PM	X	15. no impoundment		24. judiciary	X	32. experience	X
7. appoint ministers	X	16. control resources	X	25. central bank	X		
8. lack president		17. immunity	X	26. media	X		
9. no confidence	X	18. all elected	X				

The Supreme Council (*Verkhovna Rada*) of Ukraine traces its roots to the Central Council set up in Kiev following the collapse of the Russian Empire in 1917. Independence was short lived, as Ukraine was incorporated into the Soviet Union at the beginning of the 1920s. During the collapse of the Soviet Union in late 1991, Ukraine declared independence. In 1996 the country adopted its post-independence constitution, which called for a unicameral legislature. Some constitutional amendments that were passed during the "Orange Revolution" of 2004 strengthened the legislature. The legislature gained the power to choose the prime minister and the other ministers of the cabinet. Prior to that time, the president appointed the prime minister and the government. Not all constitutional changes bolstered the legislature's powers, however. The president obtained the power to dissolve the legislature, whereas prior to 2004 the legislature was immune from dissolution.

The legislature enjoys considerable clout. Influence over the executive is ensured by powers to choose the prime minister and government, question executive branch officials, and remove the government with a vote of no confidence. The legislature possesses a fair degree of institutional autonomy and five of the eight specified powers assessed in this survey. It has considerable institutional capacity, lacking only personal staff with policy expertise.

SURVEY

1. The legislature alone, without the involvement of any other agencies, can impeach the president or replace the prime minister.

No. Presidential impeachment requires the involvement of the Constitutional Court. The legislature can remove the prime minister with a vote of no confidence.

Article 87
The Verkhovna Rada of Ukraine, on the proposal of no fewer National Deputies of Ukraine than one-third of its constitutional composition, may consider the issue of responsibility of the Cabinet of Ministers of Ukraine and adopt a resolution of no confidence in the Cabinet of Ministers of Ukraine by the majority of the constitutional composition of the Verkhovna Rada of Ukraine. The issue of responsibility of the Cabinet of Ministers of Ukraine shall not be considered by the Verkhovna Rada of Ukraine more than once during one regular session, and also within one year after the approval of the Programme of Activity of the Cabinet of Ministers of Ukraine.

Article 111
The President of Ukraine may be removed from office by the Verkhovna Rada of Ukraine by the procedure of impeachment, in the event that he or she commits state treason or other crime.
The issue of the removal of the President of Ukraine from office by the procedure of impeachment is initiated by the majority of the constitutional composition of the Verkhovna Rada of Ukraine.
To conduct the investigation, the Verkhovna Rada of Ukraine establishes a special temporary investigatory commission whose composition includes a special procurator and special investigators. The conclusions and proposals of the temporary investigatory commission are considered at a meeting of the Verkhovna Rada of Ukraine. For cause, the Verkhovna Rada of Ukraine, by no less than two-thirds of its constitutional composition, adopts a decision on the accusation of the President of Ukraine. The decision on the removal of the President of Ukraine from office by the procedure of impeachment is adopted by the Verkhovna Rada of Ukraine by no less than three-quarters of its constitutional composition, after the review of the case by the Constitutional Court of Ukraine and the receipt of its opinion on the observance of the constitutional procedure of investigation and consideration of the case of impeachment, and the receipt of the opinion of the Supreme Court of Ukraine to the effect that the acts, of which the President of Ukraine is accused, contain elements of state treason or other crime.

Article 115
The adoption of a resolution of no confidence in the Cabinet of Ministers of Ukraine by the Verkhovna Rada of Ukraine results in the resignation of the Cabinet of Ministers of Ukraine.

2. Ministers may serve simultaneously as members of the legislature.

No. Ministers are prohibited from serving in the legislature.

Article 78
Requirements concerning the incompatibility of the mandate of the deputy with other types of activity are established by law.

Article 120
Members of the Cabinet of Ministers of Ukraine and chief officers of central and local bodies of executive power do not have the right to combine their official activity with other work, except teaching, scholarly and creative activity outside of working hours, or to be members of an administrative body or board of supervisors of an enterprise that is aimed at making profit.

3. The legislature has powers of summons over executive branch officials and hearings with executive branch officials testifying before the legislature or its committees are regularly held.

Yes. The legislature regularly interpellates officials from the executive.

Article 86
At a session of the Verkhovna Rada of Ukraine, a National Deputy of Ukraine has the right to present an inquiry to the bodies of the Verkhovna Rada of Ukraine, the Cabinet of Ministers of Ukraine, chief officers of other bodies of state power and bodies of local self-government, and also to the chief executives of enterprises, institutions and organisations located on the territory of Ukraine, irrespective of their subordination and forms of ownership. Chief officers of bodies of state power and bodies of local self-government, chief executives of enterprises, institutions and organisations are obliged to notify a National Deputy of Ukraine of the results of the consideration of his or her inquiry.

4. The legislature can conduct independent investigation of the chief executive and the agencies of the executive.

No. The legislature cannot investigate the executive.

5. The legislature has effective powers of oversight over the agencies of coercion (the military, organs of law enforcement, intelligence services, and the secret police).

No. The legislature lacks effective powers of oversight over the agencies of coercion.

6. The legislature appoints the prime minister.

Yes. Since 2006 the legislature selects the prime minister. Prior to 2006 the president appointed the prime minister with the consent of the legislature.

Article 85
Powers of the Verkhovna Rada of Ukraine shall include:
(12) appointing to office – upon the submission by the President of Ukraine – the Prime Minister of Ukraine, the Minister of Defense, the Minister of Foreign Affairs of Ukraine; appointing to office – upon the submission

by the Prime Minister of Ukraine – other members of the Cabinet of Ministers of Ukraine.

Article 106
The President of Ukraine:
(9) puts forward, following the relevant proposal by the parliamentary coalition formed in the Verkhovna Rada of Ukraine as provided for by Article 83 of the Constitution of Ukraine, the name of a candidate to be appointed to the office of the Prime Minister of Ukraine by the Verkhovna Rada of Ukraine, no later than fifteen days after the receipt of such a proposal.

Article 114
The Prime Minister of Ukraine is appointed by the Verkhovna Rada of Ukraine upon the submission by the President of Ukraine.
The name of a candidate for the office of the Prime Minister of Ukraine shall be put forward by the President of Ukraine following the relevant proposal by the parliamentary coalition formed in the Verkhovna Rada of Ukraine as provided for in Article 83 of the Constitution of Ukraine or by a parliamentary faction whose National Deputies of Ukraine make up a majority of the constitutional membership of the Verkhovna Rada of Ukraine.

Article 83
A coalition of parliamentary groups in the Verkhovna Rada of Ukraine submits to the President of Ukraine, in accordance with this Constitution, proposals concerning a person's candidature for the office of the Prime Minister of Ukraine and also, in accordance with this Constitution, proposes candidates for the membership of the Cabinet of Ministers of Ukraine.

7. The legislature's approval is required to confirm the appointment of ministers; or the legislature itself appoints ministers.

Yes. Since 2006 the legislature appoints ministers. Prior to 2006 the president appointed ministers, and the appointments did not require the legislature's approval.

Article 85
Powers of the Verkhovna Rada of Ukraine shall include:
(12) appointing to office – upon the submission by the President of Ukraine – the Prime Minister of Ukraine, the Minister of Defense, the Minister of Foreign Affairs of Ukraine; appointing to office – upon the submission by the Prime Minister of Ukraine – other members of the Cabinet of Ministers of Ukraine.

Article 106
The President of Ukraine:
(10) puts forward to the Verkhovna Rada of Ukraine the name of a candidate to be appointed to the office of the Minister of Defense of Ukraine and the Minister of Foreign Affairs of Ukraine.

Article 114
The Minister of Defense and the Minister of Foreign Affairs of Ukraine are appointed by the Verkhovna Rada of Ukraine upon proposal by the President of Ukraine; the other members of the Cabinet of Ministers of Ukraine are appointed upon proposal by the Prime Minister of Ukraine.

Article 83
A coalition of parliamentary groups in the Verkhovna Rada of Ukraine submits to the President of Ukraine, in accordance with this Constitution, proposals concerning a person's candidature for the office of the Prime Minister of Ukraine and also, in accordance with this Constitution, proposes candidates for the membership of the Cabinet of Ministers of Ukraine.

8. The country lacks a presidency entirely or there is a presidency, but the president is elected by the legislature.

No. The president is directly elected.

Article 103
The President of Ukraine is elected by the citizens of Ukraine for a five-year term, on the basis of universal, equal and direct suffrage, by secret ballot.

9. The legislature can vote no confidence in the government.

Yes. The legislature can vote no confidence in the government.

Article 87
The Verkhovna Rada of Ukraine, on the proposal of no fewer National Deputies of Ukraine than one-third of its constitutional composition, may consider the issue of responsibility of the Cabinet of Ministers of Ukraine and adopt a resolution of no confidence in the Cabinet of Ministers of Ukraine by the majority of the constitutional composition of the Verkhovna Rada of Ukraine. The issue of responsibility of the Cabinet of Ministers of Ukraine shall not be considered by the Verkhovna Rada of Ukraine more than once during one regular session, and also within one year after the approval of the Programme of Activity of the Cabinet of Ministers of Ukraine.

Article 115
The adoption of a resolution of no confidence in the Cabinet of Ministers of Ukraine by the Verkhovna Rada of Ukraine results in the resignation of the Cabinet of Ministers of Ukraine.

10. The legislature is immune from dissolution by the executive.

No. A constitutional amendment passed in 2004 granted the president the power to dissolve the legislature. Prior to that time the legislature was immune from dissolution.

Article 90
Powers of the Verkhovna Rada of Ukraine shall terminate on the date when the Verkhovna Rada of Ukraine of a new convocation opens its first meeting.

The President of Ukraine may order the early termination of powers of the Verkhovna Rada of Ukraine where:
(1) there is a failure to form within one month a coalition of parliamentary factions in the Verkhovna Rada of Ukraine as provided for in Article 83 of this Constitution;
(2) there is a failure, within sixty days following the resignation of the Cabinet of Ministers of Ukraine, to appoint members of the Cabinet of Ministers of Ukraine;
(3) the Verkhovna Rada of Ukraine fails, within thirty days of a single regular session, to commence its plenary meetings.
The early termination of powers of the Verkhovna Rada of Ukraine shall be decided by the President of Ukraine following relevant consultations with the Chairperson and Deputy Chairpersons of the Verkhovna Rada of Ukraine and with Chairpersons of Verkhovna Rada parliamentary factions.

11. Any executive initiative on legislation requires ratification or approval by the legislature before it takes effect; that is, the executive lacks decree power.

No. The president issues decrees that have the force of law.

Article 106
The President of Ukraine, on the basis and for the execution of the Constitution and the laws of Ukraine, issues decrees and directives that are mandatory for execution on the territory of Ukraine.
Acts issued by the President of Ukraine within the scope of his or her competence as provided for in subparagraphs 5, 18, 21, 22, and 23 of this Article shall be co-signed by the Prime Minister of Ukraine and the Minister responsible for the act and its implementation.

CHAPTER XV [from "Transitional Provisions" portion of the constitution]
4. The President of Ukraine, within three years after the Constitution of Ukraine enters into force, has the right to issue decrees approved by the Cabinet of Ministers of Ukraine and signed by the Prime Minister of Ukraine on economic issues not regulated by laws, with simultaneous submission of the respective draft law to the Verkhovna Rada of Ukraine, by the procedure established by Article 93 of this Constitution. Such a decree of the President of Ukraine takes effect, if within thirty calendar days from the day of submission of the draft law (except the days between sessions), the Verkhovna Rada of Ukraine does not adopt the law or does not reject the submitted draft law by the majority of its constitutional composition, and is effective until a law adopted by the Verkhovna Rada of Ukraine on these issues enters into force.

12. Laws passed by the legislature are veto-proof or essentially veto-proof; that is, the executive lacks veto power, or has veto power but the veto can be overridden by a majority in the legislature.

No. A two-thirds majority vote is required to override a presidential veto.

Article 94
The Chairman of the Verkhovna Rada of Ukraine signs a law and forwards it without delay to the President of Ukraine.
Within fifteen days of the receipt of a law, the President of Ukraine signs it, accepting it for execution, and officially promulgates it, or returns it to the Verkhovna Rada of Ukraine with substantiated and formulated proposals for repeat consideration.
In the event that the President of Ukraine has not returned a law for repeat consideration within the established term, the law is deemed to be approved by the President of Ukraine and shall be signed and officially promulgated.
If a law, during its repeat consideration, is again adopted by the Verkhovna Rada of Ukraine by no less than two-thirds of its constitutional composition, the President of Ukraine is obliged to sign and to officially promulgate it within ten days.
A law enters into force in ten days from the day of its official promulgation, unless otherwise envisaged by the law itself, but not prior to the day of its publication.

13. The legislature's laws are supreme and not subject to judicial review.

No. The Constitutional Court can review the constitutionality of laws.

Article 147
The Constitutional Court of Ukraine is the sole body of constitutional jurisdiction in Ukraine.
The Constitutional Court of Ukraine decides on issues of conformity of laws and other legal acts with the Constitution of Ukraine and provides the official interpretation of the Constitution of Ukraine and the laws of Ukraine.

14. The legislature has the right to initiate bills in all policy jurisdictions; the executive lacks gatekeeping authority.

Yes. The legislature can initiate bills in all policy jurisdictions.

15. Expenditure of funds appropriated by the legislature is mandatory; the executive lacks the power to impound funds appropriated by the legislature.

No. The executive can impound funds appropriated by the legislature.

16. The legislature controls the resources that finance its own internal operation and provide for the perquisites of its own members.

Yes. The legislature enjoys financial autonomy.

Article 85
The authority of the Verkhovna Rada of Ukraine comprises:

35) approving the budget of the Verkhovna Rada of Ukraine and the structure of its staff.

17. Members of the legislature are immune from arrest and/or criminal prosecution.

Yes. Legislators are immune. By law, members are not exempted from "liability for insult or defamation," but in practice, this exception is not used as a basis for arresting and prosecuting members.

Article 80
National Deputies of Ukraine are guaranteed parliamentary immunity.
National Deputies of Ukraine are not legally liable for the results of voting or for statements made in Parliament and in its bodies, with the exception of liability for insult or defamation.
National Deputies of Ukraine shall not be held criminally liable, detained or arrested without the consent of the Verkhovna Rada of Ukraine.

18. All members of the legislature are elected; the executive lacks the power to appoint any members of the legislature.

Yes. All members of the legislature are elected.

Article 76
The constitutional composition of the Verkhovna Rada of Ukraine consists of 450 National Deputies of Ukraine who are elected for a four-year term on the basis of universal, equal and direct suffrage, by secret ballot.

19. The legislature alone, without the involvement of any other agencies, can change the Constitution.

No. Constitutional amendments require approval from the Constitutional Court. Amendments to select articles of the constitution also require approval in a popular referendum.

Article 154
A draft law on introducing amendments to the Constitution of Ukraine may be submitted to the Verkhovna Rada of Ukraine by the President of Ukraine, or by no fewer National Deputies of Ukraine than one-third of the constitutional composition of the Verkhovna Rada of Ukraine.

Article 155
A draft law on introducing amendments to the Constitution of Ukraine, with the exception of Chapter I – "General Principles," Chapter III – "Elections. Referendum," and Chapter XIII – "Introducing Amendments to the Constitution of Ukraine," previously adopted by the majority of the constitutional composition of the Verkhovna Rada of Ukraine, is deemed to be adopted, if at the next regular session of the Verkhovna Rada of Ukraine, no less than two-thirds of the constitutional composition of the Verkhovyna Rada of Ukraine have voted in favour thereof.

Article 156
A draft law on introducing amendments to Chapter I – "General Principles," Chapter III – "Elections. Referendum," and Chapter XIII – "Introducing Amendments to the Constitution of Ukraine," is submitted to the Verkhovna Rada of Ukraine by the President of Ukraine, or by no less than two-thirds of the constitutional composition of the Verkhovna Rada of Ukraine, and on the condition that it is adopted by no less than two-thirds of the constitutional composition of the Verkhovna Rada of Ukraine, and is approved by an All-Ukrainian referendum designated by the President of Ukraine. The repeat submission of a draft law on introducing amendments to Chapters I, III and XIII of this Constitution on one and the same issue is possible only to the Verkhovna Rada of Ukraine of the next convocation.

Article 157
The Constitution of Ukraine shall not be amended, if the amendments foresee the abolition or restriction of human and citizens' rights and freedoms, or if they are oriented toward the liquidation of the independence or violation of the territorial indivisibility of Ukraine. The Constitution of Ukraine shall not be amended in conditions of martial law or a state of emergency.

Article 158
The draft law on introducing amendments to the Constitution of Ukraine, considered by the Verkhovna Rada of Ukraine and not adopted, may be submitted to the Verkhovna Rada of Ukraine no sooner than one year from the day of the adoption of the decision on this draft law. Within the term of its authority, the Verkhovna Rada of Ukraine shall not amend twice the same provisions of the Constitution.

Article 159
A draft law on introducing amendments to the Constitution of Ukraine is considered by the Verkhovna Rada of Ukraine upon the availability of an opinion of the Constitutional Court of Ukraine on the conformity of the draft law with the requirements of Articles 157 and 158 of this Constitution.

20. The legislature's approval is necessary for the declaration of war.

Yes. The legislature's approval is necessary for presidential war declarations.

Article 85
The authority of the Verkhovna Rada of Ukraine comprises:
9) declaring war upon the submission of the President of Ukraine and concluding peace, approving the decision of the President of Ukraine on the use of the Armed Forces of Ukraine and other military formations in the event of armed aggression against Ukraine.

Article 106
The President of Ukraine:
19) forwards the submission to the Verkhovna Rada of Ukraine on the declaration of a state of war, and adopts

the decision on the use of the Armed Forces in the event of armed aggression against Ukraine.

21. The legislature's approval is necessary to ratify treaties with foreign countries.

Yes. The legislature's approval is necessary to ratify international treaties.

Article 85
The authority of the Verkhovna Rada of Ukraine comprises:
32) granting consent to the binding character of international treaties of Ukraine within the term established by law, and denouncing international treaties of Ukraine.

Article 106
The President of Ukraine:
3) represents the state in international relations, administers the foreign political activity of the State, conducts negotiations and concludes international treaties of Ukraine.

22. The legislature has the power to grant amnesty.

Yes. The legislature has the power to grant amnesty.

Article 92
The following are determined exclusively by the laws of Ukraine:
Amnesty is declared by the law of Ukraine.

23. The legislature has the power of pardon.

No. The president has the power of pardon.

Article 106
The President of Ukraine:
27) grants pardons.

24. The legislature reviews and has the right to reject appointments to the judiciary; or the legislature itself appoints members of the judiciary.

Yes. The legislature appoints some members of the judiciary, including six of the eighteen members of the Constitutional Court.

Article 85
The authority of the Verkhovna Rada of Ukraine comprises:
26) appointing one-third of the composition of the Constitutional Court of Ukraine.

Article 128
The first appointment of a professional judge to office for a five-year term is made by the President of Ukraine. All other judges, except the judges of the Constitutional Court of Ukraine, are elected by the Verkhovna Rada of Ukraine for permanent terms by the procedure established by law. The Chairman of the Supreme Court of Ukraine is elected to office and dismissed from office by the Plenary Assembly of the Supreme Court of Ukraine by secret ballot, by the procedure established by law.

Article 148
The Constitutional Court of Ukraine is composed of eighteen judges of the Constitutional Court of Ukraine. The President of Ukraine, the Verkhovna Rada of Ukraine and the Congress of Judges of Ukraine each appoint six judges to the Constitutional Court of Ukraine.

25. The chairman of the central bank is appointed by the legislature.

Yes. The legislature, on the recommendation of the president, appoints the chairman of the National Bank of Ukraine.

Article 85
The authority of the Verkhovna Rada of Ukraine comprises:
18) appointing to office and dismissing from office the Chairman of the National Bank of Ukraine on the submission of the President of Ukraine.

26. The legislature has a substantial voice in the operation of the state-owned media.

Yes. The legislature influences the public media through its power to appoint half the members of the National Council of Ukraine on Television and Radio Broadcasting.

Article 85
The authority of the Verkhovna Rada of Ukraine comprises:
20) appointing one-half of the composition of the National Council of Ukraine on Television and Radio Broadcasting.

Article 106
The President of Ukraine:
13) appoints and dismisses one-half of the membership of the National Council of Ukraine on Television and Radio Broadcasting.

27. The legislature is regularly in session.

Yes. The legislature regularly meets in ordinary session.

Article 83
Regular sessions of the Verkhovna Rada of Ukraine commence on the first Tuesday of February and on the first Tuesday of September each year. Special sessions of the Verkhovna Rada of Ukraine, with the stipulation of their agenda, are convoked by the Chairman of the Verkhovna Rada of Ukraine, on the demand of no fewer National Deputies of Ukraine than one-third of the constitutional composition of the Verkhovna Rada of Ukraine, or on the demand of the President of Ukraine.

28. Each legislator has a personal secretary.

Yes. The legislature provides each legislator with four staff members.

29. Each legislator has at least one non-secretarial staff member with policy expertise.

No. Despite a state-funded legislative staff, not every legislator has at least one policy expert.

30. Legislators are eligible for re-election without any restriction.

Yes. There are no restrictions on re-election.

31. A seat in the legislature is an attractive enough position that legislators are generally interested in and seek re-election.

Yes.

32. The re-election of incumbent legislators is common enough that at any given time the legislature contains a significant number of highly experienced members.

Yes. Many legislators have maintained their seat for over a decade, resulting in a significant number of highly experienced members.

FEDERAL NATIONAL COUNCIL OF THE UNITED ARAB EMIRATES (*MAJLIS AL-ITTIHAD AL-WATANI*)

Expert consultants: Abdulkhaleq Abdulla, Abdulrazak Al-Faris, Ebtisam Al-Kitbi, Mariam Gamal, Michael Herb

Score: .06

Influence over executive (0/9)	Institutional autonomy (1/9)	Specified powers (0/8)	Institutional capacity (1/6)
1. replace	10. no dissolution	19. amendments	27. sessions
2. serve as ministers	11. no decree	20. war	28. secretary
3. interpellate	12. no veto	21. treaties	29. staff
4. investigate	13. no review	22. amnesty	30. no term limits X
5. oversee police	14. no gatekeeping	23. pardon	31. seek re-election
6. appoint PM	15. no impoundment	24. judiciary	32. experience
7. appoint ministers	16. control resources	25. central bank	
8. lack president	17. immunity X	26. media	
9. no confidence	18. all elected		

The Federal National Council (*Majlis Al-Ittihad Al-Watani*) of the United Arab Emirates was established in the 1971 constitution upon independence from Great Britain and the formation of the United Arab Emirates. The document calls for a unicameral body appointed by the leaders of the constituent states (emirates) and a large executive branch that includes a president, a government (the Council of Ministers), and a supreme executive body (the Supreme Council). The country's first-ever legislative elections were held in December 2006. Candidates vied for twenty seats that were chosen by 6,700 eligible voters handpicked by the government out of a national population of 800,000. The other twenty seats on the Federal National Council will still be appointed by their respective emirates.

The Federal National Council serves an advisory role and has no real legislative power. It lacks the powers to introduce and pass legislation; laws are normally made by executive decree. The Federal National Council has no ability to choose, oversee, or remove executive branch officials. It can debate legislation, but the Council of Ministers may halt debate if it decides that it is "contrary to the highest interests of the union." The legislature does not meet regularly; a year or more sometimes passes between the end of one session and the beginning of another. It has negligible institutional capacity.

SURVEY

1. The legislature alone, without the involvement of any other agencies, can impeach the president or replace the prime minister.

No. The legislature cannot remove the president or the prime minister (the chairman of the Council of Ministers) from office.

2. Ministers may serve simultaneously as members of the legislature.

No. Legislators are prohibited from serving simultaneously in ministerial positions.

> Article 71
> Membership of the Federal National Council may not be combined with the holding of any public office in the Union, including Ministerial positions.

3. The legislature has powers of summons over executive branch officials and hearings with executive branch officials testifying before the legislature or its committees are regularly held.

No. The legislature can submit questions, and the relevant minister formally is obliged to answer them, but in practice, this power is not effectively exercised.

> Article 93
> The Government of the Union shall be represented at sessions of the Federal National Council by the Chairman of the Council of Ministers or his deputy or one member of the Union Cabinet at least. The Prime Minister or his deputy or the competent Minister shall answer questions put to them by any member of the Council requesting explanation of any matters within its jurisdiction, in accordance with the procedures prescribed in the internal regulations of the Council.

4. The legislature can conduct independent investigation of the chief executive and the agencies of the executive.

No. The legislature cannot investigate the executive.

5. The legislature has effective powers of oversight over the agencies of coercion (the military, organs of law enforcement, intelligence services, and the secret police).

No. The legislature lacks effective powers of oversight over the agencies of coercion.

6. The legislature appoints the prime minister.

No. The chairman of the Council of Ministers is appointed by the president with the agreement of the Supreme Council.

> Article 47
> The Supreme Council of the Union shall be responsible for the following matters: –
> 5. Agreement to the appointment of the Chairman of the Council of Ministers of the Union, acceptance of his resignation and his dismissal from office, following a proposal from the President of the Union.

> Article 54
> The President of the Union shall have the following responsibilities:
> 5. He shall appoint the Chairman of the Council of Ministers, receive his resignation and dismiss him from office with the agreement of the Supreme Council. He shall also appoint the Deputy Chairman of the Council of Ministers and the Ministers.

7. The legislature's approval is required to confirm the appointment of ministers; or the legislature itself appoints ministers.

No. The president appoints ministers, and the appointments do not require the legislature's approval.

> Article 54
> The President of the Union shall have the following responsibilities:
> 5. He shall appoint the Chairman of the Council of Ministers, receive his resignation and dismiss him from office with the agreement of the Supreme Council. He shall also appoint the Deputy Chairman of the Council of Ministers and the Ministers.

8. The country lacks a presidency entirely or there is a presidency, but the president is elected by the legislature.

No. The Supreme Council elects the president.

> Article 51
> The Supreme Council of the Union shall elect from among its members a President of the Union and a Deputy to the President of the Union.

9. The legislature can vote no confidence in the government.

No. The legislature cannot vote no confidence in the government.

10. The legislature is immune from dissolution by the executive.

No. The president, with the agreement of the Supreme Council, can dissolve the legislature.

> Article 88
> The Federal National Council may also be dissolved by a decree promulgated by the President of the Union with the agreement of the Supreme Council of the Union, provided that the decree of dissolution includes a summons to the new Council to come into session within sixty days of the date of the decree of dissolution. The

Council may not be dissolved again for the same reasons.

11. Any executive initiative on legislation requires ratification or approval by the legislature before it takes effect; that is, the executive lacks decree power.

No. The executive issues decrees that have the force of law. When the legislature is not in session, the Council of Ministers can issue decrees through the Supreme Council and the president. When the Supreme Council is not in session, the president and the Council of Ministers can issue decree laws.

Article 110
4. Notwithstanding the foregoing, if the situation demands the promulgation of Union laws when the Federal National Council is not sitting, the Council of Ministers of the Union may issue them through the Supreme Council and the President of the Union, provided that the Federal National Council are advised of them at their next meeting.

Article 113
If, between meetings of the Supreme Council, the speedy promulgation of Union laws, which cannot be delayed, is required, the President of the Union and the Council of Ministers may together promulgate the necessary laws in the form of decrees which shall have the force of law, provided they are not inconsistent with the Constitution.
Such decree laws must be submitted to the Supreme Council within a week at the maximum for assent or rejection. In the case of assent the force of law shall be confirmed and the Federal National Council shall be informed accordingly at its next meeting.
In the event that the Supreme Council does not assent, such decree laws shall cease to have force of law, except that it may be decided to sanction their effectiveness during the earlier period, or to sanction adjustment of their effects.

Article 115
The Supreme Council may authorise the President of the Union and the Council of Ministers collectively to promulgate, when the Supreme Council is not in session, such decrees as necessity dictates and whose ratification is within the power of the Supreme Council. Provided that such authority shall not include authority to conclude international agreements and treaties, to impose or rescind martial law, to declare a state of defensive war or to appoint the President or Judges of the Supreme Union Court.

12. Laws passed by the legislature are veto-proof or essentially veto-proof; that is, the executive lacks veto power, or has veto power but the veto can be overridden by a majority in the legislature.

No. The president has absolute veto power. The Federal National Council does not legislate at all.

Article 110
2. A draft law shall become law after the adoption of the following procedure: –
   a. The Council of Ministers shall prepare a draft law and submit it to the Federal National Council.
   b. The Council of Ministers shall submit the draft law to the President of the Union for his agreement and presentation to the Supreme Council for their ratification.
   c. The President of the Union shall sign the law after ratification by the Supreme Council and shall promulgate it.
3. a. If the Federal National Council inserts any amendment in the draft law and this amendment is not acceptable to the President of the Union or the Supreme Council, or if the Federal National Council rejects the draft, the President of the Union or the Supreme Council shall refer it back to the Federal National Council. If the Federal National Council inserts any amendment on that occasion which is not acceptable to the President of the Union or the Supreme Council, or if the Federal National Council deems fit to reject the draft, the President of the Union may promulgate the law after ratification by the Supreme Council.

13. The legislature's laws are supreme and not subject to judicial review.

No. The Supreme Court can review the constitutionality of laws.

Article 99
The Supreme Court of the Union shall be competent to render judgment in the following matters: –
2. Examination of the constitutional legality of Union laws, if they are challenged by one or more of the Emirates on the grounds of violating the Constitution of the Union.
Examination of the constitutional legality of legislation promulgated by one of the Emirates, if it is challenged by one of the Union authorities on the grounds of violation of the Constitution of the Union or of Union laws.
3. Examination of the constitutional legality of laws, legislation and regulations generally, if such a request is remitted to it by any State Court during a case under consideration before it. The Court aforesaid shall be bound to accept the ruling of the Supreme Court of the Union in this case.

14. The legislature has the right to initiate bills in all policy jurisdictions; the executive lacks gatekeeping authority.

No. The legislature is prohibited from initiating legislation at all. It merely debates bills under consideration by the government and provides recommendations.

Article 89
Insofar as this does not conflict with the provisions of Article 110, draft Union laws, including draft financial

laws, shall be submitted to the Federal National Council before their submission to the President of the Union for presentation to the Supreme Council for ratification. The Federal National Council shall debate these drafts and may agree to them, amend them or reject them.

Article 92

The Federal National Council shall debate any general subject pertaining to the affairs of the Union unless the Council of Ministers informs the Federal National Council that debate of any subject is contrary to the highest interests of the Union. The Prime Minister or the competent Minister shall attend the debates. The Federal National Council may express its recommendations and may define the subjects for debate. If the Council of Ministers does not approve of these recommendations, it shall notify the Federal National Council of its reasons.

15. Expenditure of funds appropriated by the legislature is mandatory; the executive lacks the power to impound funds appropriated by the legislature.

No. The executive can impound funds appropriated by the legislature.

16. The legislature controls the resources that finance its own internal operation and provide for the perquisites of its own members.

No. The legislature is dependent on the other organs of government for the resources that finance its own operations.

Article 83

The Chairman of the Council and its other members shall be entitled, from the date of taking the oath before the Council, to a salary which shall be determined by law, and to traveling expenses from their place of residence to the place in which the Council is meeting.

17. Members of the legislature are immune from arrest and/or criminal prosecution.

Yes. Legislators are immune with the common exception for cases of *flagrante delicto*.

Article 81

Members of the Council shall not be censured for any opinions or views expressed in the course of carrying out their duties within the Council or its Committees.

Article 82

No penal proceedings may be instituted against any member while the Council is in session, except in cases of "flagrante delicto," without the permission of the Council. The Council must be informed if such proceedings are instituted while it is not in session.

18. All members of the legislature are elected; the executive lacks the power to appoint any members of the legislature.

No. Half of the legislators are appointed by the members of the constituent states (emirates).

In 2006 the country's first legislative elections selected the other half of the members of the legislature. Prior to 2006 all legislators were appointed by the members of the constituent states (emirates).

Article 69

Each Emirate shall be left to determine the method of selection of the citizens who shall represent it on the Federal National Council.

19. The legislature alone, without the involvement of any other agencies, can change the Constitution.

No. Constitutional amendments can be initiated only by the Supreme Council and require the approval of the president.

Article 144

2. a. If the Supreme Council considers that the supreme interests of the Union require the amendment of this Constitution it shall submit a draft constitutional amendment to the Federal National Council.

   b. The procedure for approving the constitutional amendment shall be the same as the procedure for approving the law.

   c. The approval of the Federal National Council for a draft constitutional amendment shall require the agreement of two-thirds of the votes of members present.

   d. The President of the Union shall sign the constitutional amendment in the name of the Supreme Council and as its representative and shall promulgate the amendment.

20. The legislature's approval is necessary for the declaration of war.

No. The president can declare war without the legislature's approval. Presidential war declarations require the approval of the Supreme Council but do not require the approval of the Federal National Council.

Article 140

The declaration of a state of defensive war shall be made by means of a Union decree issued by the President of the Union after its approval by the Supreme Council. Offensive war shall be prohibited in accordance with the provisions of international charters.

21. The legislature's approval is necessary to ratify treaties with foreign countries.

No. The legislature's approval is not necessary to ratify international treaties, although the government is responsible for informing the legislature of international agreements.

Article 47

The Supreme Council of the Union shall be responsible for the following matters:

4. The ratification of treaties and international agreements. Such ratification shall be accomplished by decree.

Article 91
The Government shall be responsible for informing the Federal National Council of international treaties and agreements concluded with other states and the various international organisations, together with appropriate explanations.

22. The legislature has the power to grant amnesty.

No. Amnesty laws are passed like other pieces of legislation. They require the approval of the Supreme Council, the president, and the Council of Ministers, but not the legislature.

Article 109
There shall be no general amnesty for crimes generally or for specified crimes except by law. The promulgation of an amnesty law shall result in such crimes being deemed never to have been committed, and in the remission of sentences imposed therefore in full or to the extent of that part remaining to be served.

Article 110
2. A draft law shall become law after the adoption of the following procedure: –
    a. The Council of Ministers shall prepare a draft law and submit it to the Federal National Council.
    b. The Council of Ministers shall submit the draft law to the President of the Union for his agreement and presentation to the Supreme Council for their ratification.
    c. The President of the Union shall sign the law after ratification by the Supreme Council and shall promulgate it.
3. a. If the Federal National Council inserts any amendment in the draft law and this amendment is not acceptable to the President of the Union or the Supreme Council, or if the Federal National Council rejects the draft, the President of the Union or the Supreme Council shall refer it back to the Federal National Council. If the Federal National Council inserts any amendment on that occasion which is not acceptable to the President of the Union or the Supreme Council, or if the Federal National Council deems fit to reject the draft, the President of the Union may promulgate the law after ratification by the Supreme Council.

23. The legislature has the power of pardon.

No. The president has the power of pardon.

Article 54
The President of the Union shall have the following responsibilities:
10. He shall exercise the right of pardon and commutation of sentences and confirm capital sentences according to the provisions of this Constitution and Union laws.

Article 107
The President of the Union may grant pardon from the execution of any sentence passed by the Union judicature before it is carried out or while it is being served or may reduce such sentence, on the basis of the recommendation of the Union Minister of Justice, after obtaining the approval of a committee formed under the chairmanship of the Minister and consisting of six members selected by the Union Council of Ministers for a term of three years which may be renewed.

24. The legislature reviews and has the right to reject appointments to the judiciary; or the legislature itself appoints members of the judiciary.

No. The president appoints members of the judiciary with the approval of the Supreme Council, and the appointments do not require the legislature's approval.

Article 47
The Supreme Council of the Union shall be responsible for the following matters: –
6. Agreement to the appointment of the President and Judges of the Supreme Union Court, acceptance of their resignations and their dismissal in the circumstances stipulated by this Constitution. These acts shall be accomplished by decrees.

Article 96
The Supreme Court of the Union shall consist of a President and a number of Judges, not exceeding five in all, who shall be appointed by decree, issued by the President of the Union after approval by the Supreme Council.

25. The chairman of the central bank is appointed by the legislature.

No. The legislature lacks a role in the appointment of the governor of the Central Bank of the United Arab Emirates.

26. The legislature has a substantial voice in the operation of the state-owned media.

No. The legislature lacks a substantial voice in the operation of the public media.

27. The legislature is regularly in session.

No. Legislative sessions are mandated by the constitution to last "not less than six months." Gaps of a year or more between the end of one session and the beginning of a new one, however, are common.

Article 78
The Council shall hold an annual ordinary session lasting not less than six months, commencing in the third week of November each year. It may be called into extraordinary session whenever the need arises.

28. Each legislator has a personal secretary.

No.

29. Each legislator has at least one non-secretarial staff member with policy expertise.

No.

30. Legislators are eligible for re-election without any restriction.

Yes. There are no restrictions on re-election.

31. A seat in the legislature is an attractive enough position that legislators are generally interested in and seek re-election.

No. There has only been one legislative election, held in December 2006, so it is impossible yet to speak of re-election. It bears note, however, that members of the Federal National Council generally have welcomed reappointment.

32. The re-election of incumbent legislators is common enough that at any given time the legislature contains a significant number of highly experienced members.

No. There has only been one legislative election, which was held in December 2006. Reappointment to the Federal National Council has been common, but it is too early to speak of re-election or of the accumulation of legislative experience on the part of members.

PARLIAMENT OF THE UNITED KINGDOM

Expert consultants: Philip Cowley, Frank Cranmer, Thomas Lundberg, Bryn Morgan, David J. Sanders

Score: .78

Influence over executive (8/9)		Institutional autonomy (7/9)		Specified powers (4/8)		Institutional capacity (6/6)	
1. replace	X	10. no dissolution		19. amendments	X	27. sessions	X
2. serve as ministers	X	11. no decree	X	20. war		28. secretary	X
3. interpellate	X	12. no veto	X	21. treaties	X	29. staff	X
4. investigate	X	13. no review	X	22. amnesty	X	30. no term limits	X
5. oversee police	X	14. no gatekeeping	X	23. pardon		31. seek re-election	X
6. appoint PM	X	15. no impoundment	X	24. judiciary		32. experience	X
7. appoint ministers		16. control resources	X	25. central bank			
8. lack president	X	17. immunity		26. media	X		
9. no confidence	X	18. all elected	X				

The Parliament of the United Kingdom has its origins in the thirteenth century, when English nobles met with the king to discuss matters of mutual interest. These informal parleys eventually became the first formal parliament in 1295.

Many of the features of modern legislatures developed organically in England over the course of centuries. Parliament's legislative role originated in the 1362 statute requiring parliamentary approval for all lay taxation. The origins of legislative oversight over the government can be traced to the "good parliament" of 1376 that accused the royal government of corruption and fraud and impeached some officials in a trial before the House of Lords. Parliamentary immunity was established in 1513, when parliament passed a bill to release one of its members, Richard Strode, who had been jailed for introducing a bill alleged to hurt the tin mining industry. Following the "Glorious Revolution," in 1689 the Bill of Rights and the Crown and Parliament Recognition Act encoded the distribution of power between parliament and the crown that had evolved over the previous centuries. In 1721 King George I turned over the task of running the government's day-to-day affairs to a member of parliament, Sir Robert Walpole. This move established the position of prime minister and began the gradual transfer of executive power from the monarch to the parliament.

To this day the United Kingdom lacks a formal constitution. Instead, the fundamental law is a compilation of evolving conventions, customs, and statutes. The "constitutional" citations below come from a compilation of material originally provided by the British government for purposes of publication. The bicameral parliament consists of a lower house, the House of Commons, and an upper house, the House of Lords.

Parliament is the supreme political power in the United Kingdom. It has broad sway over the executive, which is bolstered by its right to interpellate and investigate the government and to remove the government from office with a vote of no confidence. Parliament also enjoys a high degree of institutional autonomy. Among other sources of autonomy, parliament's laws are supreme and not subject to judicial review. Parliament has several of the specified powers assessed here and a high level of institutional capacity.

SURVEY

1. The legislature alone, without the involvement of any other agencies, can impeach the president or replace the prime minister.

Yes. The legislature can replace the prime minister if the governing party votes to replace its leader or with a vote of no confidence in the government.

2. Ministers may serve simultaneously as members of the legislature.

Yes. Ministers are selected from, and required to serve simultaneously serve in, the legislature.

> Section 42
> (1) The Prime Minister is appointed by the Queen, and all other ministers are appointed by the Queen on the recommendation of the Prime Minister. Most ministers are members of the Commons, although the Government is also fully represented by ministers in the Lords. The Lord Chancellor is always a member of the House of Lords.

3. The legislature has powers of summons over executive branch officials and hearings with executive branch officials testifying before the legislature or its committees are regularly held.

Yes. Parliament regularly questions the government during weekly question time.

> Section 37
> There are opportunities for criticism and examination of government policy in the House of Lords at daily question time and during debates on general motions. Other opportunities include 'unstarred' questions, which can be debated at the end of the day's business, and debates on proposed legislation.

4. The legislature can conduct independent investigation of the chief executive and the agencies of the executive.

Yes. The legislature can establish select committees to scrutinize the work of the government and its agencies. The committees conduct investigations, request written evidence, and summon witnesses.

> Section 36
> (2) Select committees are appointed, normally for the duration of a Parliament, to examine subjects by taking written and oral evidence.

5. The legislature has effective powers of oversight over the agencies of coercion (the military, organs of law enforcement, intelligence services, and the secret police).

Yes. Parliamentary committees have effective powers of oversight over the agencies of coercion.

6. The legislature appoints the prime minister.

Yes. Formally, the British monarch appoints the prime minister. In practice, the monarch appoints the candidate who enjoys the support of parliament.

> Section 42
> (1) The Prime Minister is appointed by the Queen, and all other ministers are appointed by the Queen on the recommendation of the Prime Minister.

7. The legislature's approval is required to confirm the appointment of ministers; or the legislature itself appoints ministers.

No. The British monarch appoints ministers on the recommendation of the prime minister, and the appointments do not require the legislature's approval.

> Section 42
> (1) The Prime Minister is appointed by the Queen, and all other ministers are appointed by the Queen on the recommendation of the Prime Minister.

8. The country lacks a presidency entirely or there is a presidency, but the president is elected by the legislature.

Yes. The country lacks a presidency. The British monarch is the head of state.

9. The legislature can vote no confidence in the government.

Yes. The legislature can vote no confidence in the government.

10. The legislature is immune from dissolution by the executive.

No. The British monarch, on the advice of the prime minister, can dissolve the legislature. The maximum length of a parliament is five years.

11. Any executive initiative on legislation requires ratification or approval by the legislature before it takes effect; that is, the executive lacks decree power.

Yes. The executive lacks decree power.

12. Laws passed by the legislature are veto-proof or essentially veto-proof; that is, the executive lacks veto power, or has veto power but the veto can be overridden by a majority in the legislature.

Yes. The executive lacks veto power. Bills must receive royal assent, but this requirement is purely a formality.

> Section 35
> (3) Bills must normally be passed by both Houses. They must then receive the Royal Assent before becoming Acts. In practice this is a formality.

13. The legislature's laws are supreme and not subject to judicial review.

Yes. Parliament's laws are supreme. The judiciary reviews the conformity of the decisions of public bodies with the law but does not review the law itself.

14. The legislature has the right to initiate bills in all policy jurisdictions; the executive lacks gatekeeping authority.

Yes. The legislature can initiate bills in all policy jurisdictions.

15. Expenditure of funds appropriated by the legislature is mandatory; the executive lacks the power to impound funds appropriated by the legislature.

Yes. The executive lacks the power to impound funds appropriated by the legislature.

16. The legislature controls the resources that finance its own internal operation and provide for the perquisites of its own members.

Yes. The legislature enjoys financial autonomy.

17. Members of the legislature are immune from arrest and/or criminal prosecution.

No. Legislators enjoy civil immunity but are subject to criminal prosecution.

> Section 40
> (2) The privileges of the members of the Commons include freedom of speech; freedom from arrest in civil actions; exemption from serving on juries, or being compelled to attend court as witnesses; and the right of access to the Crown, which is a collective privilege of the House.

18. All members of the legislature are elected; the executive lacks the power to appoint any members of the legislature.

Yes. All members of the House of Commons are elected. The House of Lords is a much less powerful body whose members are appointed.

> Section 32
> (3) Elections: For electoral purposes Britain is divided into 651 constituencies, each of which returns one member to the House of Commons...Candidates are elected if they have more votes than any of the other candidates, although not necessarily an absolute majority over all other candidates.

19. The legislature alone, without the involvement of any other agencies, can change the Constitution.

Yes. The legislature can change the fundamental law through the normal legislative process.

20. The legislature's approval is necessary for the declaration of war.

No. The British monarch, on the government's recommendation, can declare war without the legislature's approval.

21. The legislature's approval is necessary to ratify treaties with foreign countries.

Yes. Formally, the power to make treaties is vested in the prime minister on behalf of the crown. Treaties that require a change in the law or the expenditure of public funds must be approved through normal parliamentary legislation.

22. The legislature has the power to grant amnesty.

Yes. A general amnesty can be granted only through legislation.

23. The legislature has the power of pardon.

No. The British monarch has the power of pardon.

24. The legislature reviews and has the right to reject appointments to the judiciary; or the legislature itself appoints members of the judiciary.

No. The Constitutional Reform Act of 2005 created a special commission independent from parliament to make judicial appointments. Prior to 2005 the British monarch appointed members of the judiciary based on the recommendation of the prime minister.

25. The chairman of the central bank is appointed by the legislature.

No. The British monarch, on the recommendation of the prime minister, appoints the governor of the Bank of England.

26. The legislature has a substantial voice in the operation of the state-owned media.

Yes. The British Broadcasting Committee (BBC) has operational independence, but its work is scrutinized by select committees in the legislature.

27. The legislature is regularly in session.

Yes. The legislature regularly meets in ordinary session.

28. Each legislator has a personal secretary.

Yes.

29. Each legislator has at least one non-secretarial staff member with policy expertise.

Yes.

30. Legislators are eligible for re-election without any restriction.

Yes. There are no restrictions on re-election.

31. A seat in the legislature is an attractive enough position that legislators are generally interested in and seek re-election.

Yes.

32. The re-election of incumbent legislators is common enough that at any given time the legislature contains a significant number of highly experienced members.

Yes. Re-election rates are sufficiently high to produce a significant number of highly experienced members.

CONGRESS OF THE UNITED STATES OF AMERICA

Expert consultants: Richard F. Fenno, Richard G. Niemi, Eric Schickler, Charles R. Shipan, Raymond E. Wolfinger

Score: .63

Influence over executive (5/9)		Institutional autonomy (6/9)		Specified powers (3/8)		Institutional capacity (6/6)	
1. replace	X	10. no dissolution	X	19. amendments		27. sessions	X
2. serve as ministers		11. no decree	X	20. war	X	28. secretary	X
3. interpellate	X	12. no veto		21. treaties	X	29. staff	X
4. investigate	X	13. no review		22. amnesty		30. no term limits	X
5. oversee police	X	14. no gatekeeping	X	23. pardon		31. seek re-election	X
6. appoint PM		15. no impoundment	X	24. judiciary	X	32. experience	X
7. appoint ministers	X	16. control resources	X	25. central bank			
8. lack president		17. immunity		26. media			
9. no confidence		18. all elected	X				

The Congress of the United States of America traces its origins to the Continental Congress established at the onset of America's war of independence with Great Britain in the mid-1770s. In 1781 the legislature was formalized in the country's first post-independence constitution, the Articles of Confederation. The current constitution was adopted in 1787. It calls for a bicameral legislature consisting of a lower house, the House of Representatives, and an upper house, the Senate. In 1803 the *Marbury v. Madison* court decision established judicial review, providing the Supreme Court with the power to pass judgment on the constitutionality of laws.

Prior to 1803 judicial review had not yet been created, and the legislature's laws were supreme. The seventeenth amendment to the constitution, ratified in 1913, provided for direct election of the Senate. Prior to that time Senators were elected or appointed by state legislators. Other amendments to the constitution did not directly alter the legislature's power.

Congress has significant authority. Its influence over the executive branch includes powers to review ministerial appointments, question and investigate agencies of the executive, and impeach the president. The legislature's institutional autonomy is protected by a lack of presidential decree, dissolution, and gatekeeping powers. The president does enjoy veto powers, however, and legislators are not immune from arrest and prosecution. The legislature exercises three of the eight specified powers and prerogatives assessed in this survey. It has a very high level of institutional capacity.

SURVEY

1. The legislature alone, without the involvement of any other agencies, can impeach the president or replace the prime minister.

Yes. The House of Representatives can impeach the president. The Senate, presided over by the chief justice of the Supreme Court, can try and remove the president from office by a two-thirds majority vote of its present members.

> Article 1, Section 2
> (5) The House of Representatives shall chuse their Speaker and other Officers; and shall have the sole Power of Impeachment.
>
> Article 2, Section 4
> (4) The President, Vice President and all civil Officers of the United States, shall be removed from Office on Impeachment for, and Conviction of, Treason, Bribery, or other high Crimes and Misdemeanors.
>
> Article 1, Section 3
> (6) The Senate shall have the sole Power to try all Impeachments. When sitting for that Purpose, they shall be on Oath or Affirmation. When the President of the United States is tried, the Chief Justice shall preside: And no Person shall be convicted without the Concurrence of two thirds of the Members present.
> (7) Judgment in Cases of Impeachment shall not extend further than to removal from Office, and disqualification to hold and enjoy any Office of honor, Trust, or Profit under the United States: but the Party convicted shall nevertheless be liable and subject to Indictment, Trial, Judgment, and Punishment, according to Law.

2. Ministers may serve simultaneously as members of the legislature.

No. Legislators are prohibited from serving simultaneously in ministerial positions.

> Article 1, Section 6
> (2) No Senator or Representative shall, during the Time for which he was elected, be appointed to any civil Office under the Authority of the United States, which shall have been created, or the Emoluments whereof shall have been increased during such time; and no Person holding any Office under the United States, shall be a Member of either House during his Continuance in Office.

3. The legislature has powers of summons over executive branch officials and hearings with executive branch officials testifying before the legislature or its committees are regularly held.

Yes. The legislature regularly interpellates officials from the executive.

4. The legislature can conduct independent investigation of the chief executive and the agencies of the executive.

Yes. The legislature can investigate the executive.

5. The legislature has effective powers of oversight over the agencies of coercion (the military, organs of law enforcement, intelligence services, and the secret police).

Yes. The legislature has effective powers of oversight over the agencies of coercion.

6. The legislature appoints the prime minister.

No. There is no prime minister.

7. The legislature's approval is required to confirm the appointment of ministers; or the legislature itself appoints ministers.

Yes. The Senate's consent is required to confirm the president's ministerial appointments.

> Article 2, Section 2
> (2) [The president] shall nominate, and by and with the Advice and Consent of the Senate, shall appoint Ambassadors, other public Ministers and Consuls, Judges of the supreme Court, and all other Officers of the United States, whose Appointments are not herein otherwise provided for, and which shall be established by Law; but the Congress may by Law vest the Appointment of such inferior Officers, as they think proper, in the President alone, in the Courts of Law, or in the Heads of Departments.

8. The country lacks a presidency entirely or there is a presidency, but the president is elected by the legislature.

No. The president is elected by popular vote through an electoral college.

> Article 2, Section 1
> (1) The executive Power shall be vested in a President of the United States of America. He shall hold his Office during the Term of four Years, and, together with the Vice President, chosen for the same Term, be elected, as follows:
> 3) The Electors shall meet in their respective States, and vote by Ballot for two Persons, of whom one at least shall not be an Inhabitant of the same State with themselves. And they shall make a List of all the Persons voted for, and of the Number of Votes for each; which List they shall sign and certify, and transmit sealed to the Seat of the Government of the

United States, directed to the President of the Senate. The President of the Senate shall, in the Presence of the Senate and House of Representatives, open all the Certificates, and the Votes shall then be counted. The Person having the greatest Number of Votes shall be the President, if such Number be a Majority of the whole Number of Electors appointed; and if there be more than one who have such Majority, and have an equal Number of Votes, then the House of Representatives shall immediately chuse by Ballot one of them for President; and if no Person have a Majority, then from the five highest on the List the said House shall in like Manner chuse the President. But in chusing the President, the Votes shall be taken by States the Representation from each State having one Vote; A quorum for this Purpose shall consist of a Member or Members from two thirds of the States, and a Majority of all the States shall be necessary to a Choice. In every Case, after the Choice of the President, the Person having the greater Number of Votes of the Electors shall be the Vice President. But if there should remain two or more who have equal Votes, the Senate shall chuse from them by Ballot the Vice President.

9. The legislature can vote no confidence in the government.

No. The legislature cannot vote no confidence in the government.

10. The legislature is immune from dissolution by the executive.

Yes. The legislature is immune from dissolution.

11. Any executive initiative on legislation requires ratification or approval by the legislature before it takes effect; that is, the executive lacks decree power.

Yes. The executive lacks decree power.

12. Laws passed by the legislature are veto-proof or essentially veto-proof; that is, the executive lacks veto power, or has veto power but the veto can be overridden by a majority in the legislature.

No. A two-thirds majority vote in both houses is required to override a presidential veto.

Article 1, Section 7
(2) All Bills for raising Revenue shall originate in the House of Representatives; but the Senate may propose or concur with Amendments as on other Bills. Every Bill which shall have passed the House of Representatives and the Senate, shall, before it become a Law, be presented to the President of the United States; If he approve he shall sign it, but if not he shall return it, with his Objections to the House in which it shall have originated, who shall enter the Objections at large on their Journal, and proceed to reconsider it. If after such Reconsideration two thirds of that House shall agree to pass the Bill, it shall be sent together with the Objec-

tions, to the other House, by which it shall likewise be reconsidered, and if approved by two thirds of that House, it shall become a Law.
(3) Every Order, Resolution, or Vote, to Which the Concurrence of the Senate and House of Representatives may be necessary (except on a question of Adjournment) shall be presented to the President of the United States; and before the Same shall take Effect, shall be approved by him, or being disapproved by him, shall be repassed by two thirds of the Senate and House of Representatives, according to the Rules and Limitations prescribed in the Case of a Bill.

13. The legislature's laws are supreme and not subject to judicial review.

No. Since 1803 the Supreme Court has possessed the power to review the constitutionality of laws. Prior to 1803 the institution of judicial review had not yet been created.

Article 3, Section 2
(1) The judicial Power shall extend to all Cases, in Law and Equity, arising under this Constitution, the Laws of the United States, and Treaties made, or which shall be made, under their Authority; – to all Cases affecting Ambassadors, other public Ministers and Consuls; – to all Cases of admiralty and maritime Jurisdiction; – to Controversies to which the United States shall be a Party; – to Controversies between two or more States; – between a State and Citizens of another State; – between Citizens of different States, – between Citizens of the same State claiming Lands under the Grants of different States, and between a State, or the Citizens thereof, and foreign States, Citizens or Subjects.

14. The legislature has the right to initiate bills in all policy jurisdictions; the executive lacks gatekeeping authority.

Yes. The legislature can initiate bills in all policy jurisdictions.

15. Expenditure of funds appropriated by the legislature is mandatory; the executive lacks the power to impound funds appropriated by the legislature.

Yes. The executive lacks the power to impound funds appropriated by the legislature.

16. The legislature controls the resources that finance its own internal operation and provide for the perquisites of its own members.

Yes. The legislature enjoys financial autonomy, including control over members' salaries.

Article 1, Section 6
(1) The Senators and Representatives shall receive a Compensation for their Services, to be ascertained by Law, and paid out of the Treasury of the United States. They shall in all Cases, except Treason, Felony and Breach of the Peace, be privileged from Arrest during their Attendance at the Session of their respective

Houses, and in going to and returning from the same; and for any Speech or Debate in either House, they shall not be questioned in any other Place.

17. Members of the legislature are immune from arrest and/or criminal prosecution.

No. Legislators are subject to arrest and prosecution. Immunity is in force only while legislators are in, or traveling to and from, the legislative buildings, and for speeches and debates made in the legislature.

Article 1, Section 6
(1) The Senators and Representatives shall receive a Compensation for their Services, to be ascertained by Law, and paid out of the Treasury of the United States. They shall in all Cases, except Treason, Felony and Breach of the Peace, be privileged from Arrest during their Attendance at the Session of their respective Houses, and in going to and returning from the same; and for any Speech or Debate in either House, they shall not be questioned in any other Place.

18. All members of the legislature are elected; the executive lacks the power to appoint any members of the legislature.

Yes. All members of the legislature are elected.

Article 1, Section 2
(1) The House of Representatives shall be composed of Members chosen every second Year by the People of the several States, and the Electors in each State shall have the Qualifications requisite for Electors of the most numerous Branch of the State Legislature.

Article 1, Section 3
(1) The Senate of the United States shall be composed of two Senators from each State, chosen by the Legislature thereof, for six Years; and each Senator shall have one Vote.

Amendment XVII
(1) The Senate of the United States shall be composed of two Senators from each State, elected by the people thereof, for six years; and each Senator shall have one vote. The electors in each State shall have the qualifications requisite for electors of the most numerous branch of the State legislatures.
(2) When vacancies happen in the representation of any State in the Senate, the executive authority of such State shall issue writs of election to fill such vacancies: Provided, That the legislature of any State may empower the executive thereof to make temporary appointments until the people fill the vacancies by election as the legislature may direct.
(3) This amendment shall not be so construed as to affect the election or term of any Senator chosen before it becomes valid as part of the Constitution.

19. The legislature alone, without the involvement of any other agencies, can change the Constitution.

No. Constitutional amendments require the approval of three-fourths of the fifty states in the federation.

Article 5
The Congress, whenever two thirds of both Houses shall deem it necessary, shall propose Amendments to this Constitution, or, on the Application of the Legislatures of two thirds of the several States, shall call a Convention for proposing Amendments, which, in either Case, shall be valid to all Intents and Purposes, as part of this Constitution, when ratified by the Legislatures of three fourths of the several States, or by Conventions in three fourths thereof, as the one or the other Mode of Ratification may be proposed by the Congress; Provided that no Amendment which may be made prior to the Year One thousand eight hundred and eight shall in any Manner affect the first and fourth Clauses in the Ninth Section of the first Article; and that no State, without its Consent, shall be deprived of its equal Suffrage in the Senate.

20. The legislature's approval is necessary for the declaration of war.

Yes. The legislature declares war.

Article 1, Section 8
(11) The Congress shall have Power:
    To declare War.

21. The legislature's approval is necessary to ratify treaties with foreign countries.

Yes. The Senate's approval is necessary to ratify international treaties.

Article 2, Section 2
(2) [The president] shall have Power, by and with the Advice and Consent of the Senate to make Treaties, provided two thirds of the Senators present concur.

22. The legislature has the power to grant amnesty.

No. Amnesty and pardon are not treated separately, and the legislature lacks the power to grant amnesty. See item 23.

23. The legislature has the power of pardon.

No. The president has the power of pardon.

Article 2, Section 2
(1) The President shall be Commander in Chief of the Army and Navy of the United States, and of the militia of the several States, when called into the actual Service of the United States; he may require the Opinion, in writing, of the principal Officer in each of the Executive Departments, upon any Subject relating to the Duties of their respective Offices, and he shall have Power to grant Reprieves and Pardons for Offenses against the United States, except in Cases of Impeachment.

24. The legislature reviews and has the right to reject appointments to the judiciary; or the legislature itself appoints members of the judiciary.

Yes. The Senate's consent is necessary to confirm the president's appointments to the Supreme Court.

> Article 2, Section 2
> (2) [The president] shall nominate, and by and with the Advice and Consent of the Senate, shall appoint...Judges of the Supreme Court.

25. The chairman of the central bank is appointed by the legislature.

No. The president appoints the chairman of the Federal Reserve Bank with the approval of the Senate.

26. The legislature has a substantial voice in the operation of the state-owned media.

No. The legislature lacks a substantial voice in the operation of the public media.

27. The legislature is regularly in session.

Yes. The legislature meets in ordinary session for about ten months each year.

> Amendment 20
> (2) The Congress shall assemble at least once in every year, and such meeting shall begin at noon on the

3d day of January, unless they shall by law appoint a different day.

28. Each legislator has a personal secretary.

Yes.

29. Each legislator has at least one non-secretarial staff member with policy expertise.

Yes.

30. Legislators are eligible for re-election without any restriction.

Yes. There are no restrictions on re-election.

31. A seat in the legislature is an attractive enough position that legislators are generally interested in and seek re-election.

Yes.

32. The re-election of incumbent legislators is common enough that at any given time the legislature contains a significant number of highly experienced members.

Yes. The re-election of incumbent legislators is exceedingly common, resulting in a very large number of highly experienced legislators.

URUGUAYAN GENERAL ASSEMBLY (*ASAMBLEA GENERAL*)

Expert consultants: David Altman, Scott Morgenstern, Francisco Panizza, Juan Rial, Karen van Rompaey

Score: .66

Influence over executive (6/9)		Institutional autonomy (5/9)		Specified powers (5/8)		Institutional capacity (5/6)	
1. replace	X	10. no dissolution		19. amendments		27. sessions	X
2. serve as ministers		11. no decree	X	20. war	X	28. secretary	X
3. interpellate	X	12. no veto		21. treaties	X	29. staff	X
4. investigate	X	13. no review		22. amnesty	X	30. no term limits	X
5. oversee police	X	14. no gatekeeping		23. pardon	X	31. seek re-election	X
6. appoint PM		15. no impoundment	X	24. judiciary	X	32. experience	
7. appoint ministers	X	16. control resources	X	25. central bank			
8. lack president		17. immunity	X	26. media			
9. no confidence	X	18. all elected	X				

Uruguay's bicameral General Assembly (*Asamblea General*) was established under the 1830 constitution upon independence from Brazil and Argentina. Uruguay subsequently promulgated four more constitutions, in 1917, 1934, 1952, and 1967.

The 1967 constitution, in effect today, resembles its predecessors in calling for a presidential system with a bicameral legislature, composed of the Chamber of Representatives (*Cámara de Representantes*) and the Chamber of Senators (*Cámara de Senadores*). A military takeover in 1976 stripped the Assembly of power and granted legislative and executive authority to an oligarchic body named the Council of the Nation. Civilian rule and the constitution were restored in 1985. Amendments made in 1996 altered the legislative procedures for overriding a presidential veto and for influencing a presidentially declared state of emergency, although these amendments did not appreciably affect the legislature's power.

The Assembly enjoys substantial muscle. It has some influence over the executive, which it holds by virtue of its ability to impeach the president, interpellate ministers, investigate the government, oversee the agencies of coercion, and vote no confidence in the government. Its institutional autonomy is not expansive, however, and is limited by the president's veto, gatekeeping, and dissolution powers. The Assembly holds five of the eight specified powers assessed in this survey. Its institutional capacity is substantial and limited only by the relative dearth of highly experienced members.

SURVEY

1. The legislature alone, without the involvement of any other agencies, can impeach the president or replace the prime minister.

Yes. The Chamber of Representatives can impeach the president, and the Chamber of Senators can then remove the president from office by a two-thirds majority vote of its total membership.

> Article 93
> The Chamber of Representatives has the exclusive right of impeachment . . . of the President . . . of the Republic . . . for violation of the Constitution or for other serious offenses.

> Article 102
> The Chamber of Senators is competent to initiate the public trial of those impeached by the Chamber of Representatives . . . and to pronounce sentence, by a two-thirds vote of its full membership, and such sentence shall have the sole effect of removal from office.

2. Ministers may serve simultaneously as members of the legislature.

No. Legislators who serve in government have a sleeping mandate, meaning that they may join the government but forfeit their voting rights in the legislature during their government service. They may return to the legislature when their government service ends.

> Article 122
> Whenever Senators and Representatives are called to serve as Ministers or Under Secretaries of State, their legislative functions are suspended, and during such suspension their corresponding alternates shall replace them.

> Article 174
> The President of the Republic shall allot the Ministries to citizens who, by virtue of their parliamentary support, are assured of remaining in office.

3. The legislature has powers of summons over executive branch officials and hearings with executive branch officials testifying before the legislature or its committees are regularly held.

Yes. The legislature regularly interpellates officials from the executive.

> Article 119
> Each Chamber has the right, by a resolution of one-third of its full membership, to require the presence on its floor of the Ministers of state in order to question them and receive from them information which it considers appropriate, whether for legislative purposes or for purposes of inspection or investigation.

4. The legislature can conduct independent investigation of the chief executive and the agencies of the executive.

Yes. The legislature can establish committees to investigate the executive.

> Article 118
> Any Legislator may ask a Minister of state, the Supreme Court of Justice, the Electoral Court, the Contentious-Administrative Tribunal, and the Tribunal of Accounts, for such data and information as he may consider necessary for the discharge of his duties.

> Article 119
> Each Chamber has the right, by a resolution of one-third of its full membership, to require the presence on its floor of the Ministers of state in order to question them and receive from them information which it considers appropriate, whether for legislative purposes or for purposes of inspection or investigation.

> Article 120
> Each Chamber may appoint parliamentary committees for making investigations or for obtaining data for legislative purposes.

5. The legislature has effective powers of oversight over the agencies of coercion (the military, organs of law enforcement, intelligence services, and the secret police).

Yes. The legislature has effective powers of oversight over the agencies of coercion.

6. The legislature appoints the prime minister.

No. There is no prime minister.

7. The legislature's approval is required to confirm the appointment of ministers; or the legislature itself appoints ministers.

Yes. The legislature's approval is required to confirm ministerial appointments.

> Article 168
>
> 26) The President of the Republic may freely appoint a Secretary and an Assistant Secretary, who shall serve as such in the Council of Ministers.
>
> Both shall cease to serve along with the President and they may be removed or replaced by him at any time.

> Article 174
>
> The President of the Republic shall allot the Ministries to citizens who, by virtue of their parliamentary support, are assured of remaining in office. The President of the Republic may require an express vote of confidence from the General Assembly for the Council of Ministers. For this purpose, he shall appear before the General Assembly, which shall make a decision without debate, by a vote of the absolute majority of all of its members and within a period not longer than seventy-two hours from when the General Assembly receives the communication from the President of the Republic. If the [General Assembly] does not meet within the stipulated period or, having met, does not adopt a decision, it shall be understood that the vote of confidence is granted.

8. The country lacks a presidency entirely or there is a presidency, but the president is elected by the legislature.

No. The president is directly elected.

> Article 151
>
> The President . . . shall be elected jointly and directly by the people by an absolute majority of voters.

9. The legislature can vote no confidence in the government.

Yes. The legislature can pass a motion of censure against the government.

> Article 147
>
> Either of the Chambers may pass judgment on the conduct of Ministers of State by proposing that the General Assembly in joint session shall declare that their acts of administration or of government are censured.

> Article 148
>
> The disapproval may be individual, plural, or collective, but in all cases it must be adopted by an absolute majority of the votes of the full membership of the General Assembly, at a special and public session. Individual disapproval is one that affects one Minister; plural disapproval one that affects more than one Minister; and collective disapproval is one that affects a majority of the Council of Ministers. Disapproval adopted in accordance with the foregoing articles shall mean the resignation of the Minister, the Ministers, or the Council of Ministers, as the case may be. The President of the Republic may veto the vote of disapproval whenever it has been adopted by less than two-thirds of the full membership of the body . . . If the General Assembly maintains its vote by less than three-fifths of its full membership, the President of the Republic, within the next forty-eight hours, may, by express decision, retain the censured Minister, Ministers, or Council of Ministers, and dissolve the Chambers.

10. The legislature is immune from dissolution by the executive.

No. The president can dissolve the Assembly. It bears note, however, that the requirements for dissolution are quite stringent.

> Article 148
>
> The disapproval may be individual, plural, or collective, but in all cases it must be adopted by an absolute majority of the votes of the full membership of the General Assembly, at a special and public session. Individual disapproval is one that affects one Minister; plural disapproval one that affects more than one Minister; and collective disapproval is one that affects a majority of the Council of Ministers. Disapproval adopted in accordance with the foregoing articles shall mean the resignation of the Minister, the Ministers, or the Council of Ministers, as the case may be. The President of the Republic may veto the vote of disapproval whenever it has been adopted by less than two-thirds of the full membership of the body . . . If the General Assembly maintains its vote by less than three-fifths of its full membership, the President of the Republic, within the next forty-eight hours, may, by express decision, retain the censured Minister, Ministers, or Council of Ministers, and dissolve the Chambers.

11. Any executive initiative on legislation requires ratification or approval by the legislature before it takes effect; that is, the executive lacks decree power.

Yes. The executive lacks decree power, with one minor exception. If the legislature does not act quickly enough (within thirty days) to reconsider a bill vetoed by the president, the bill becomes law with the president's suggested changes included.

12. Laws passed by the legislature are veto-proof or essentially veto-proof; that is, the executive lacks veto power, or has veto power but the veto can be overridden by a majority in the legislature.

No. The General Assembly can override a presidential veto only with a three-fifths majority vote.

Article 138

Whenever a bill shall have been returned by the Executive Power with total or partial objections or observations, the General Assembly shall be convoked and the matter shall be decided by a three-fifths vote of the members present of each of the Chambers, who may incorporate the observations or reject them, maintaining the adopted bill.

13. The legislature's laws are supreme and not subject to judicial review.

No. The Supreme Court can review the constitutionality of laws.

Article 256

Laws may be declared unconstitutional by reason of form or content, in accordance with the provisions of the following articles.

Article 257

The Supreme Court of Justice has original and exclusive jurisdiction in the hearing and decision of such matters; and must render its decision in accordance with the requirement for final decisions.

14. The legislature has the right to initiate bills in all policy jurisdictions; the executive lacks gatekeeping authority.

No. The legislature is prohibited from introducing legislation related to tax exemptions or to price floors and ceilings, including the minimum wage.

Article 133

The initiative of the Executive Power shall be required for any bill specifying tax exemptions or fixing minimum wages or prices for the purchase of the products or goods of public or private enterprise. The Legislative Power may not increase the tax exemptions nor the minimums proposed by the Executive Power for wages and prices, nor may it lower the proposed maximum prices.

15. Expenditure of funds appropriated by the legislature is mandatory; the executive lacks the power to impound funds appropriated by the legislature.

Yes. The executive lacks the power to impound funds appropriated by the legislature.

16. The legislature controls the resources that finance its own internal operation and provide for the perquisites of its own members.

Yes. The legislature enjoys financial autonomy, including control over members' salaries.

Article 117

Senators and Representatives shall be compensated for their services by a monthly salary which they shall receive during their term of office...The salary shall be fixed by a two-thirds vote of the full membership of the General Assembly, meeting in joint session, during the last period of each legislative term, for the members

of the succeeding term. This compensation shall be paid with absolute independence from the Executive Power.

17. Members of the legislature are immune from arrest and/or criminal prosecution.

Yes. Legislators are immune with the common exception for cases of *flagrante delicto*.

Article 112

Senators and Representatives shall never be held liable for the votes they cast or opinions expressed during the discharge of their duties.

Article 113

No Senator or Representative, from the day of his election until that of his termination, may be arrested except in case of *flagrante delicto* and then notice shall immediately be given to the respective Chamber, with a summary report of the case.

Article 114

No Senator or Representative, from the day of his election until that of his termination, may be indicted on a criminal charge, or even for common offenses which are not specified in Article 93 [dealing with impeachment for "serious offenses"], except before his own Chamber, which, by two-thirds of the votes of its full membership, shall decide whether or not there are grounds for prosecution and if so, shall declare him suspended from office, and he shall be placed at the disposition of a competent Tribunal.

18. All members of the legislature are elected; the executive lacks the power to appoint any members of the legislature.

Yes. All members of the legislature are elected.

Article 88

The Chamber of Representatives shall consist of ninety-nine members elected directly by the people.

Article 94

The Chamber of Senators shall be composed of thirty members, elected directly by the people.

19. The legislature alone, without the involvement of any other agencies, can change the Constitution.

No. Constitutional amendments require approval in a popular referendum.

Article 331

The present Constitution may be amended, in whole or in part, in accordance with the following procedures:

a) Upon the initiative of ten percent of the citizens inscribed in the National Civil Register, by presenting a detailed proposal which shall be referred to the President of the General Assembly, to be submitted for popular decision at the next election.

b) By proposal of amendment approved by two-fifths of the full membership of the General Assembly, presented to the President thereof, and submitted to plebiscite at the next ensuing election.

c) The Senators, Representatives, and the Executive Power may present proposed amendments which must be approved by an absolute majority of the full membership of the General Assembly... Upon the approval of a proposal and its promulgation by the President of the General Assembly, the Executive Power, within ninety days thereafter, shall call for the election of a National Constituent Convention, which shall consider and decide upon approved proposals for amendment as well as upon any other proposals that may be presented to the Convention... The proposal or proposals drawn up by the Convention must be ratified by the body electorate.

d) The Constitution may be amended, also, by constitutional laws which shall require for their sanction two-thirds of the full membership of each Chamber in the same legislative period. Constitutional laws may not be vetoed by the Executive Power and shall take effect as soon as the electorate specially convoked on the date specified in such laws shall have expressed their approval by an absolute majority of the votes cast.

20. The legislature's approval is necessary for the declaration of war.

Yes. The legislature declares war.

Article 85
The General Assembly is competent:
7) To declare war and to approve or disapprove, by an absolute majority of the full membership of both Chambers, the treaties of peace, alliance, commerce, and conventions or contracts of any nature which the Executive Power may make with foreign powers.

21. The legislature's approval is necessary to ratify treaties with foreign countries.

Yes. The legislature's approval is necessary to ratify treaties.

Article 168
The President of the Republic, acting with the respective Minister or Ministers, or with the Council of Ministers, has the following duties:
20) To conclude and sign treaties, the approval of the Legislative Power being necessary for their ratification.

22. The legislature has the power to grant amnesty.

Yes. The legislature has the power to grant amnesty.

Article 85
The General Assembly is competent:
14) To grant pardons by a two-thirds vote of the full membership of the General Assembly in joint session, and to grant amnesties in extraordinary cases, by an absolute majority vote of the full membership of each Chamber.

23. The legislature has the power of pardon.

Yes. The legislature has the power of pardon.

Article 85
The General Assembly is competent:
14) To grant pardons by a two-thirds vote of the full membership of the General Assembly in joint session, and to grant amnesties in extraordinary cases, by an absolute majority vote of the full membership of each Chamber.

24. The legislature reviews and has the right to reject appointments to the judiciary; or the legislature itself appoints members of the judiciary.

Yes. Members of the Supreme Court of Justice are appointed by the General Assembly by a two-thirds vote of its members.

Article 85
The General Assembly is competent:
18) To elect, in joint session of both Chambers, the members of the Supreme Court of Justice [and] of the Electoral Court... subject to the provisions of the respective Sections.

Article 236
The members of the Supreme Court of Justice shall be appointed by the General Assembly by a two-thirds vote of its full membership.

25. The chairman of the central bank is appointed by the legislature.

No. The president appoints the governor of the Central Bank of Uruguay with the approval of the Senate.

26. The legislature has a substantial voice in the operation of the state-owned media.

No. The legislature lacks substantial voice in the operation of the public media.

27. The legislature is regularly in session.

Yes. The specified length of legislative sessions is from March to December. A permanent committee functions during summer breaks and other times when there is no regular session. There can also be extra sessions.

Article 104
The General Assembly shall begin its sessions on the first of March of each year, meeting until the fifteenth of December, or only until the fifteenth of September, in the event that there are elections, and the new Assembly must in that event begin its sessions on the fifteenth of the following February.

28. Each legislator has a personal secretary.

Yes. Each legislator has a budget to hire up to five advisors and secretaries.

29. Each legislator has at least one non-secretarial staff member with policy expertise.

Yes. See item 28.

30. Legislators are eligible for re-election without any restriction.

Yes. There are no restrictions on re-election.

31. A seat in the legislature is an attractive enough position that legislators are generally interested in and seek re-election.

Yes. A seat in the legislature is attractive even though salaries are quite low.

32. The re-election of incumbent legislators is common enough that at any given time the legislature contains a significant number of highly experienced members.

No. The rate of turnover is quite high, leading to a relatively small cohort of experienced members.

SUPREME ASSEMBLY OF UZBEKISTAN (*OLIY MAJLIS*)

Expert consultants: Rustam Burnashev, Bakhodirzhon Ergashev, Bakhtiyor Ergashev, Pauline Jones Luong, Vladimir Paramonov

Score: .28

Influence over executive (1/9)		Institutional autonomy (3/9)		Specified powers (2/8)		Institutional capacity (3/6)	
1. replace		10. no dissolution		19. amendments		27. sessions	
2. serve as ministers		11. no decree		20. war	X	28. secretary	
3. interpellate		12. no veto		21. treaties	X	29. staff	
4. investigate		13. no review		22. amnesty		30. no term limits	X
5. oversee police		14. no gatekeeping	X	23. pardon		31. seek re-election	X
6. appoint PM		15. no impoundment		24. judiciary		32. experience	X
7. appoint ministers	X	16. control resources		25. central bank			
8. lack president		17. immunity	X	26. media			
9. no confidence		18. all elected	X				

The Supreme Assembly (*Oliy Majlis*) of Uzbekistan traces its origins to the Uzbek Soviet Socialist Republic's Supreme Soviet that operated during the time of the Soviet Union. The Supreme Assembly was established in Uzbekistan's constitution in 1992 following the dissolution of the Soviet Union. The document calls for a unicameral legislature. Constitutional amendments in 1995 and 2002 extended the president's term in office and created a bicameral legislature.

The legislature has minimal powers. It has no ability to influence the executive branch save the power to confirm the president's ministerial appointments. Its institutional autonomy is diminutive and is circumscribed by presidential decree, dissolution, impoundment, and veto powers. The legislature exercises a few specified powers and has a bit of institutional capacity.

SURVEY

1. The legislature alone, without the involvement of any other agencies, can impeach the president or replace the prime minister.

No. The legislature cannot impeach the president.

Article 91
The President shall enjoy personal immunity and protection under law.

2. Ministers may serve simultaneously as members of the legislature.

No. Legislators are prohibited from serving simultaneously in ministerial positions.

Article 87
The expenses of the deputies connected with their work for the Oliy Majlis shall be reimbursed in prescribed manner. The deputies working for the Oliy Majlis on a permanent basis may not hold any other paid posts,

nor engage in commercial activity during their term of office.

3. The legislature has powers of summons over executive branch officials and hearings with executive branch officials testifying before the legislature or its committees are regularly held.

No. The legislature does not regularly question executive branch officials.

4. The legislature can conduct independent investigation of the chief executive and the agencies of the executive.

No. The legislature cannot investigate the executive.

5. The legislature has effective powers of oversight over the agencies of coercion (the military, organs of law enforcement, intelligence services, and the secret police).

No. The legislature lacks effective powers of oversight over the agencies of coercion.

6. The legislature appoints the prime minister.

No. The president appoints the prime minister.

> Article 78
> The exclusive powers of the Oliy Majlis of the Republic of Uzbekistan shall include:
> 16) ratification of the decrees of the President of the Republic of Uzbekistan on the appointment and removal of the Prime Minister, the First Deputy Prime Minister, the Deputy Prime Ministers and the members of the Cabinet of Ministers.

> Article 93
> The President of the Republic of Uzbekistan shall:
> 9) appoint and dismiss the Prime Minister, his First Deputy, the Deputy Prime Ministers, the members of the Cabinet of Ministers of the Republic of Uzbekistan, the Procurator-General of the Republic of Uzbekistan and his Deputies, with subsequent confirmation by the Oliy Majlis.

7. The legislature's approval is required to confirm the appointment of ministers; or the legislature itself appoints ministers.

Yes. The legislature's approval is necessary to confirm the president's ministerial appointments.

> Article 78
> The exclusive powers of the Oliy Majlis of the Republic of Uzbekistan shall include:
> 16) ratification of the decrees of the President of the Republic of Uzbekistan on the appointment and removal of the Prime Minister, the First Deputy Prime Minister, the Deputy Prime Ministers and the members of the Cabinet of Ministers.

> Article 93
> The President of the Republic of Uzbekistan shall:

> 9) appoint and dismiss the Prime Minister, his First Deputy, the Deputy Prime Ministers, the members of the Cabinet of Ministers of the Republic of Uzbekistan, the Procurator-General of the Republic of Uzbekistan and his Deputies, with subsequent confirmation by the Oliy Majlis.

> Article 98
> The Cabinet of Ministers shall be formed by the President of the Republic of Uzbekistan and approved by the Oliy Majlis.

8. The country lacks a presidency entirely or there is a presidency, but the president is elected by the legislature.

No. The president is directly elected.

> Article 90
> The President of the Republic of Uzbekistan shall be elected for a term of five years. He shall be elected by citizens of the Republic of Uzbekistan on the basis of the universal, equal and direct suffrage by secret ballot. The procedure for electing President shall be specified by the electoral law of the Republic of Uzbekistan.

9. The legislature can vote no confidence in the government.

No. The legislature cannot vote no confidence in the government.

10. The legislature is immune from dissolution by the executive.

No. The president can dissolve the legislature.

> Article 95
> Should any insurmountable differences arise between the deputies of the Oliy Majlis, jeopardizing its normal functioning, or should it repeatedly make decisions in opposition to the Constitution, the Oliy Majlis may be dissolved by a decision of the President, sanctioned by the Constitutional Court. In the event of the dissolution of the Oliy Majlis, elections shall be held within three months. The Oliy Majlis may not be dissolved during a state of emergency.

11. Any executive initiative on legislation requires ratification or approval by the legislature before it takes effect; that is, the executive lacks decree power.

No. The president issues decrees that have the force of law.

> Article 94
> The President of the Republic of Uzbekistan, shall issue decrees, enactments and ordinances binding on the entire territory of the Republic on the basis of and for enforcement of the Constitution and the laws of the Republic of Uzbekistan.

> Article 98
> The Cabinet of Ministers shall provide guidance for the economic, social and cultural development of the Republic of Uzbekistan. It should also be responsible for

the execution of the laws and other decisions of the Oliy Majlis, as well as of the decrees and other enactments issued by the President of the Republic of Uzbekistan.

12. Laws passed by the legislature are veto-proof or essentially veto-proof; that is, the executive lacks veto power, or has veto power but the veto can be overridden by a majority in the legislature.

No. A two-thirds majority vote is required to override a presidential veto.

> Article 93
> The President of the Republic of Uzbekistan shall:
> 14) sign the laws of the Republic of Uzbekistan. The President may refer any law, with his own amendments, to the Oliy Majlis for additional consideration and vote. Should the Oliy Majlis confirm its earlier decision by a majority of 2/3 of its total voting power, the President shall sign the law.

13. The legislature's laws are supreme and not subject to judicial review.

No. The Constitutional Court can review the constitutionality of laws.

> Article 108
> The Constitutional Court of the Republic of Uzbekistan shall hear cases relating to the Constitutionality of acts passed by the legislative and executive branches.

> Article 109
> The Constitutional Court of the Republic of Uzbekistan shall:
> 1) judge the constitutionality of the laws of the Republic of Uzbekistan and other acts passed by the Oliy Majlis of the Republic of Uzbekistan, the decrees issued by the President of the Republic of Uzbekistan, the enactments of the government and the ordinances of local authorities, as well as obligations of the Republic of Uzbekistan under inter-state treaties and other documents;
> 2) conform the constitutionality of the Constitution and laws of the Republic of Karakalpakstan to the Constitution and laws of the Republic of Uzbekistan;
> 3) interpret the Constitution and the laws of the Republic of Uzbekistan.

14. The legislature has the right to initiate bills in all policy jurisdictions; the executive lacks gatekeeping authority.

Yes. The legislature can initiate bills in all policy jurisdictions.

15. Expenditure of funds appropriated by the legislature is mandatory; the executive lacks the power to impound funds appropriated by the legislature.

No. The president can impound funds appropriated by the legislature.

16. The legislature controls the resources that finance its own internal operation and provide for the perquisites of its own members.

No. The legislature is dependent on the president for the resources that finance its own operations.

17. Members of the legislature are immune from arrest and/or criminal prosecution.

Yes. Legislators are immune.

> Article 88
> Deputies of the Oliy Majlis shall have the right of immunity. They may not be prosecuted, arrested or incur a court-imposed administrative penalty without the sanction of the Oliy Majlis.

18. All members of the legislature are elected; the executive lacks the power to appoint any members of the legislature.

Yes. All members of the legislature are elected.

> Article 77
> The Oliy Majlis of the Republic of Uzbekistan shall consist of 150 deputies, elected by territorial constituencies on a multi-party basis for a term of five years.

19. The legislature alone, without the involvement of any other agencies, can change the Constitution.

No. Formally, the legislature can change the constitution with a two-thirds majority vote, but in practice, it would be unthinkable for the legislature to change the constitution except on the president's instruction.

> Article 127
> The Constitution of the Republic of Uzbekistan shall be amended by laws, passed by at least 2/3 of the deputies of the Oliy Majlis of the Republic.

> Article 128
> The Oliy Majlis of the Republic of Uzbekistan may pass a law altering or amending the Constitution within six months of submission of the relevant proposal, with due regard for its nation-wide discussion. Should the Oliy Majlis of the Republic of Uzbekistan reject an amendment to the Constitution, a repeated proposal may not be submitted for one year.

20. The legislature's approval is necessary for the declaration of war.

Yes. The legislature's approval is necessary for presidential war declarations.

> Article 93
> The President of the Republic of Uzbekistan shall:
> 17) proclaim a state of war in the event of an armed attack on the Republic of Uzbekistan or when it is necessary to meet international obligations relating to mutual defence against aggression, and submit the decision to the Oliy Majlis of the Republic of Uzbekistan for confirmation.

21. The legislature's approval is necessary to ratify treaties with foreign countries.

Yes. The legislature's approval is necessary to ratify international treaties.

Article 78
The exclusive powers of the Oliy Majlis of the Republic of Uzbekistan shall include:
21) ratification and denouncement of international treaties and agreements.

Article 93
The President of the Republic of Uzbekistan shall:
4) conduct negotiations, sign treaties and agreements on behalf of the Republic of Uzbekistan, and ensure the observance of the treaties and agreements signed by the Republic and the fulfilment of its commitments.

22. The legislature has the power to grant amnesty.

No. The president has the power to grant amnesty.

Article 93
The President of the Republic of Uzbekistan shall:
20) issue acts of amnesty and grant pardon to citizens convicted by the courts of the Republic of Uzbekistan.

23. The legislature has the power of pardon.

No. The president has the power of pardon.

Article 93
The President of the Republic of Uzbekistan shall:
20) issue acts of amnesty and grant pardon to citizens convicted by the courts of the Republic of Uzbekistan.

24. The legislature reviews and has the right to reject appointments to the judiciary; or the legislature itself appoints members of the judiciary.

No. Formally, the president nominates members of the judiciary, who are then elected by the legislature. In practice, the president's nominations are the last word; the legislature does not scrutinize the president's choices.

Article 78
The exclusive powers of the Oliy Majlis of the Republic of Uzbekistan shall include:
12) election of the Constitutional Court of the Republic of Uzbekistan;
13) election of the Supreme Court of the Republic of Uzbekistan;
14) election of the Higher Arbitration Court of the Republic of Uzbekistan.

Article 93
The President of the Republic of Uzbekistan shall:
10) present to the Oliy Majlis of the Republic of Uzbekistan his nominees for the posts of Chairman and members of the Constitutional Court, the Supreme Court,

and the Higher Economic Court, as well as the Chairman of the Board of the Central Bank of the Republic of Uzbekistan, and the Chairman of the State Committee for the Protection of Nature of the Republic of Uzbekistan;
11) appoint and dismiss judges of regional, district, city and arbitration courts.

25. The chairman of the central bank is appointed by the legislature.

No. The president appoints the chairman of the Central Bank of Uzbekistan.

26. The legislature has a substantial voice in the operation of the state-owned media.

No. The legislature lacks a substantial voice in the operation of the public media.

27. The legislature is regularly in session.

No. The legislature meets irregularly and is in session for less than half the year.

28. Each legislator has a personal secretary.

No.

29. Each legislator has at least one non-secretarial staff member with policy expertise.

No.

30. Legislators are eligible for re-election without any restriction.

Yes.

31. A seat in the legislature is an attractive enough position that legislators are generally interested in and seek re-election.

Yes.

32. The re-election of incumbent legislators is common enough that at any given time the legislature contains a significant number of highly experienced members.

Yes. Re-election rates are sufficiently high to produce a significant number of highly experienced members. Maintaining a seat is the legislature, however, is strictly a matter of loyalty to the president, Islam Karimov. The president's party, the People's Democratic Party, and several minor satellite parties that also support the president are the sole presence in the legislature. Any party that pretends to genuine opposition status is banned from participation.

NATIONAL ASSEMBLY OF VENEZUELA (*ASAMBLEA NACIONAL*)

Expert consultants: Michael Coppedge, Daniel Hellinger, José Molina, David Myers, Jason Seawright

Score: .53

Influence over executive (3/9)		Institutional autonomy (6/9)		Specified powers (4/8)		Institutional capacity (4/6)	
1. replace		10. no dissolution		19. amendments		27. sessions	X
2. serve as ministers		11. no decree		20. war	X	28. secretary	
3. interpellate	X	12. no veto	X	21. treaties	X	29. staff	
4. investigate	X	13. no review		22. amnesty	X	30. no term limits	X
5. oversee police	X	14. no gatekeeping	X	23. pardon		31. seek re-election	X
6. appoint PM		15. no impoundment	X	24. judiciary	X	32. experience	X
7. appoint ministers		16. control resources	X	25. central bank			
8. lack president		17. immunity	X	26. media			
9. no confidence		18. all elected	X				

The National Assembly (*Asamblea Nacional*) of Venezuela was established in the country's 1830 constitution adopted upon independence from Gran Colombia. For the next century, Venezuela suffered political instability and military rule, and the legislature did not play a major role in national politics. In 1961 a new constitution reinstated civilian authority. For the next three decades, the bicameral legislature and national politics were controlled by two political parties, the Democratic Action Party and the Social Christian Party. In 1998 Hugo Chavez, a populist leftist, was elected president. Chavez broke the control of the previously dominant parties over politics. He pushed for a constitutional change to increase the powers of the president and obtained it in a popular referendum at the end of 1999. Prior to that year the legislature was immune from dissolution by the president, but the amendment approved in the referendum disbanded one house of the legislature to create a unicameral body and granted the president the power to dissolve it. The amendment also created the office of the executive vice president, who is appointed by the president, serves as a top aide to him or her, and presides over the cabinet.

The National Assembly has a moderate amount of power, although its influence over the executive is sharply limited. It cannot shape the formation of the government or remove the government from office, yet it does hold some powers of oversight.

The legislature enjoys a fair amount of institutional autonomy, but on this score its strength is limited by presidential decree and dissolution powers. It exercises some specified powers and has a moderate amount of institutional capacity.

SURVEY

1. The legislature alone, without the involvement of any other agencies, can impeach the president or replace the prime minister.

No. The legislature cannot impeach the president.

2. Ministers may serve simultaneously as members of the legislature.

No. Legislators are prohibited from serving simultaneously in ministerial positions.

Article 189
[The following] cannot be elected deputies:
1. Ministers.

Article 191
The deputies to the National Assembly cannot accept or perform public positions without losing their investiture, except in teaching, academic, incidental or assistance activities, as long as they do not involve exclusive dedication.

3. The legislature has powers of summons over executive branch officials and hearings with executive

branch officials testifying before the legislature or its committees are regularly held.

Yes. The legislature regularly interpellates officials from the executive.

Article 222
The National Assembly can perform its function of control by means of the following mechanisms: parliamentarian interpellations, authorizations and approvals provided in this Constitution and in the law and any other mechanism that the laws and its Regulations establish. In exercise of the parliamentary control they can declare the political responsibility of the public functionaries and request the Civic Power to try the actions for which there is cause to make such responsibility effective.

4. The legislature can conduct independent investigation of the chief executive and the agencies of the executive.

Yes. The legislature can investigate the executive.

Article 193
The National Assembly will name Permanent Commissions, ordinary and special commissions. The Permanent Commissions, in a number no greater than fifteen, will correspond to the sectors of national activity. Likewise, it can create Commissions with a temporary character for investigation and study, all of which in conformity with its Regulations. The National Assembly can create or suppress Permanent Commissions with the favorable vote of two-thirds of its members.

Article 223
The Assembly or its Commissions can make the investigations that they deem fitting in the matters of their competence, in conformity with the Regulations.
All public functionaries are obligated, under the sanctions that the laws establish, to appear before said Commissions and to provide them with the information and documents they require for the fulfillment of their functions.
This obligation also comprises the individuals; preserving the rights and guarantees that this Constitution consecrates.

Article 224
The exercise of the faculty of investigation does not affect the attributions of the other public powers. The judges will be obligated to furnish the evidence for which they receive [the] commission of the legislative bodies.

5. The legislature has effective powers of oversight over the agencies of coercion (the military, organs of law enforcement, intelligence services, and the secret police).

Yes. Legislative commissions have effective powers of oversight over the agencies of coercion.

6. The legislature appoints the prime minister.

No. There is no prime minister.

7. The legislature's approval is required to confirm the appointment of ministers; or the legislature itself appoints ministers.

No. The president appoints ministers, and the appointments do not require the legislature's approval.

Article 243
The President of the Republic can appoint Ministers of State, who, in addition to participating in the Council of Ministers will advise the President of the Republic and the Executive Vice President in the matters assigned to them.

8. The country lacks a presidency entirely or there is a presidency, but the president is elected by the legislature.

No. The president is directly elected.

Article 228
The election of the President of the Republic will be made by universal, direct and secret ballot, in conformity with the law. The candidate who has obtained the majority of the valid votes will be proclaimed elected.

9. The legislature can vote no confidence in the government.

No. The legislature can pass a vote of censure against the executive vice president and individual ministers but cannot vote no confidence in the government as a whole.

Article 187
It corresponds to the National Assembly:
10. To express a vote of censure [against] the Executive Vice President and [against] the Ministers. The motion of censure can only be discussed two days after being presented to the Assembly, which can decide, by three-fifths of the deputies, that the vote of censure leads to the dismissal of the Executive Vice President or the Minister.

Article 240
The approval of a motion of censure [against] the Executive Vice President, by a vote [of] no less than two-thirds of the members of the National Assembly, implies his removal. The removed functionary cannot opt for the position of Executive Vice President or Minister for the rest of the presidential term.
The removal of the Executive Vice President on three occasions within the same constitutional term, as a consequence of the approval of motions of censure, enables the President of the Republic to dissolve the National Assembly. The decree of dissolution gives rise to the convocation of elections for a new legislature within the sixty days following its dissolution. The Assembly cannot be dissolved in the last year of its constitutional term.

Article 246

The approval of a motion of censure [against] a Minister by a vote [of] no less than three-fifths of the members present of the National Assembly, implies his removal. The removed functionary cannot opt for the position of Minister or Executive Vice President for the rest of the presidential term.

10. The legislature is immune from dissolution by the executive.

No. The president can dissolve the legislature.

Article 236

Attributions and obligations of the President of the Republic are:

21. To dissolve the National Assembly in the case established in this Constitution.

Article 240

The approval of a motion of censure [against] the Executive Vice President, by a vote [of] no less than two-thirds of the members of the National Assembly, implies his removal. The removed functionary cannot opt for the position of Executive Vice President or Minister for the rest of the presidential term. The removal of the Executive Vice President on three occasions within the same constitutional term, as a consequence of the approval of motions of censure, enables the President of the Republic to dissolve the National Assembly. The decree of dissolution gives rise to the convocation of elections for a new legislature within the sixty days following its dissolution.

The Assembly cannot be dissolved in the last year of its constitutional term.

11. Any executive initiative on legislation requires ratification or approval by the legislature before it takes effect; that is, the executive lacks decree power.

No. Formally, the president can issue decrees that have the force of law only when authorized to do so by the legislature. In practice, the president regularly issues decree-laws.

Article 236

Attributions and obligations of the President of the Republic are:

8. To issue, with prior authorization by an enabling law, decrees with the force of law.

12. Laws passed by the legislature are veto-proof or essentially veto-proof; that is, the executive lacks veto power, or has veto power but the veto can be overridden by a majority in the legislature.

Yes. The legislature can override a presidential veto by a majority vote of its present members.

Article 214

The President of the Republic will promulgate the law within the ten days following that in which he has received it. Within this period he can, with the agreement of the Council of Ministers, request the National Assembly, by means of a reasoned exposition, to modify any of the provisions of the law or raise the sanction to the entire law or to part of it. The National Assembly will decide on the issues posed by the President of the Republic, by absolute majority of the deputies present and will submit the law to him for promulgation. The President of the Republic must proceed to promulgate the law within the five days following its receipt, without being able to formulate new observations.

13. The legislature's laws are supreme and not subject to judicial review.

No. The Constitutional Chamber of the Supreme Tribunal of Justice can review the constitutionality of laws.

Article 214

When the President of the Republic considers that the law or any of its articles is unconstitutional he will request the pronouncement of the Constitutional Chamber of the Supreme Tribunal of Justice, in the period of ten days that he has to promulgate the same. The Supreme Tribunal of Justice will decide in the period of fifteen days counting from the receipt of the communication from the President of the Republic. Should the Tribunal deny the unconstitutionality invoked or should it not decide in the aforementioned period, the President of the Republic will promulgate the law within the five days following the decision of the Tribunal or the expiration of said period.

Article 334

All the judges of the Republic, within the scope of their competences and in conformity with that provided in this Constitution and in the law, have the obligation to ensure the integrity of the Constitution.

In case of incompatibility between this Constitution and some law or other juridical norm, the constitutional provisions will be applied, corresponding to the tribunals in any cause, even of office, to decide what is fitting.

It corresponds exclusively to the Constitutional Chamber of the Supreme Tribunal of Justice as constitutional jurisdiction, to declare the nullity of the laws and other acts of the organs that exercise the Public Power dictated in direct and immediate execution of the Constitution or that have rank of law.

Article 336

Attributions of the Constitutional Chamber of the Supreme Tribunal of Justice are:

1. To declare the total or partial nullity of the national laws and other acts with rank of law from the national legislative bodies that conflict with this Constitution.

2. To declare the total or partial nullity of the Constitutions and state laws, municipal ordinances and other acts of the deliberative bodies of the States and Municipalities dictated in direct and immediate execution of the Constitution and that conflict with the latter.

3. To declare the total or partial nullity of the acts with rank of law dictated by the National Executive that conflict with this Constitution.

14. The legislature has the right to initiate bills in all policy jurisdictions; the executive lacks gatekeeping authority.

Yes. The legislature can initiate bills in all policy jurisdictions.

15. Expenditure of funds appropriated by the legislature is mandatory; the executive lacks the power to impound funds appropriated by the legislature.

Yes. The executive lacks the power to impound funds appropriated by the legislature.

16. The legislature controls the resources that finance its own internal operation and provide for the perquisites of its own members.

Yes. The legislature enjoys financial autonomy.

17. Members of the legislature are immune from arrest and/or criminal prosecution.

Yes. Legislators are immune with the common exception for cases of *flagrante delicto,* here expressed as "flagrant crime."

Article 199
The deputies to the National Assembly are not responsible for votes and opinions expressed in the performance of their functions. They will only be responsible before the electors and the legislative body in accordance with the Constitution and the Regulations.

Article 200
The deputies to the National Assembly will enjoy immunity in the performance of their functions from their proclamation until the conclusion of their mandate or the renunciation of the same. The Supreme Tribunal of Justice will hear the alleged crimes that the members of the National Assembly commit, [which is the] only authority that will be able to order, with prior authorization from the National Assembly, their detention and continue their judgment. In case of flagrant crime committed by a parliamentarian, the competent authority will put him in custody in his residence and will communicate the fact to the Supreme Tribunal of Justice. The public functionaries who violate the immunity of the members of the National Assembly will incur in penal responsibility and will be punished in conformity with the law.

18. All members of the legislature are elected; the executive lacks the power to appoint any members of the legislature.

Yes. All members of the legislature are elected.

Article 186
The National Assembly will be composed of deputies elected in each federal entity by universal, direct,

personalized and secret vote with proportional representation, according to a population base of one point one per cent of the total population of the country.

19. The legislature alone, without the involvement of any other agencies, can change the Constitution.

No. Constitutional amendments require approval in a popular referendum.

Article 341
The amendments to the Constitution will be transacted in the following form:
1. The initiative can come from fifteen per cent of the citizens registered in the Civil and Electoral Register; or by thirty per cent of the members of the National Assembly or [from] the President of the Republic in the Council of Ministers.
2. When the initiative comes from the National Assembly, the amendment will require the approval of the latter by the majority of its members and will be discussed, according to the procedure established in this Constitution for the formation of laws.
3. The Electoral Power will submit the amendments to referendum in thirty days following their formal reception.
4. The amendments will be considered approved in accordance with that established in this Constitution and the law regarding the approving referendum.
5. The amendments will be numbered consecutively and will be published after the Constitution without altering the text of the latter, but noting [in] a foot[note] to the amended article or articles the reference of the number and date of the amendment that modified it.

Article 342
The Constitutional Reform has for its object a partial revision of this Constitution and the substitution of one or several of its norms that do not modify the structure and fundamental principles of the Constitutional text. The initiative of the Reform of the Constitution is exercised by the National Assembly by means of an agreement approved by the vote of the majority of its members, by the President of the Republic in the Council of Ministers or by request of a number no less than the fifteen per cent of the electors registered in the Civil and Electoral Register.

Article 343
The initiative of Constitutional Reform will be transacted by the National Assembly in the following form:
1. The Bill of Constitutional Reform will have a first debate in the period of sessions corresponding to the presentation of the same.
2. A second debate by Title or Chapter, as the case may be.
3. A third and final debate article by article.
4. The National Assembly will adopt the Bill of Constitutional Reform in a period [of] no greater than two years, counted from the date on which it took cognizance of and approved the request for [the] reform.

5. The bill of reform will be considered adopted with the vote of two-thirds of the members of the National Constituent Assembly.

Article 344

The Bill of Constitutional Reform approved by the National Assembly will be submitted to referendum within the thirty days following its sanction. The referendum will pronounce on the entirety of the Reform, but it will be possible to vote separately [on] up to one-third of it, if a number no less than one-third of the National Assembly so approved or if in the initiative of the reform the President of the Republic or a number no less than five per cent of the electors registered in the Civil and Electoral Registry so requested.

Article 345

The Constitutional Reform will be declared approved if the number of affirmative votes is greater than the number of negative votes. The initiative of revised Constitutional Reform cannot be presented again in the same constitutional term of the National Assembly.

Article 346

The President of the Republic will be obligated to promulgate the Amendments and Reforms within the ten days following their approval. Should he not do it, that provided in this Constitution will be applied.

20. The legislature's approval is necessary for the declaration of war.

Yes. The constitution does not specifically address the declaration war. The legislature's approval is required to authorize the deployment of military forces abroad.

Article 187

It corresponds to the National Assembly:
11. To authorize the deployment of Venezuelan military missions abroad or foreign ones in the country.

21. The legislature's approval is necessary to ratify treaties with foreign countries.

Yes. The legislature's approval is necessary to ratify international treaties.

Article 154

The treaties concluded by the Republic must be approved by the National Assembly before their ratification by the President of the Republic, with the exception of those by means of which it is attempted to execute or perfect preexisting obligations of the Republic, apply principles expressly recognized in it, execute ordinary acts in the international relations to exercise powers that the law expressly attributes to the National Executive.

Article 187

It corresponds to the National Assembly:
18. To approve by law the international treaties or covenants that the National Executive makes, save the exceptions consecrated in this Constitution.

22. The legislature has the power to grant amnesty.

Yes. The legislature has the power to grant amnesty.

Article 187

It corresponds to the National Assembly:
5. To decree amnesties.

23. The legislature has the power of pardon.

No. The president has the power of pardon.

Article 236

Attributions and obligations of the President of the Republic are:
19. To grant pardons.

24. The legislature reviews and has the right to reject appointments to the judiciary; or the legislature itself appoints members of the judiciary.

Yes. The legislature appoints the members of the Supreme Tribunal of Justice on the recommendation of the Judicial Postulations Committee and the Civic Power.

Article 264

The magistrates of the Supreme Tribunal of Justice will be elected for a sole period of twelve years. The law will determine the procedure of election. In any case, candidates will be able to submit their candidature before the Committee of Judicial Postulations, by their own initiative or by organizations linked to the juridical activity. The Committee, after hearing the opinion of the community, will make a pre-selection for its presentation to the Civic Power, which will make a second pre-selection that will be presented to the National Assembly, which will make a third pre-selection for the definitive selection. Citizens can present objections on good grounds [concerning] any of the candidatures before the Committee of Judicial Postulations, or before the National Assembly.

25. The chairman of the central bank is appointed by the legislature.

No. The president appoints the governor of the Central Bank of Venezuela.

26. The legislature has a substantial voice in the operation of the state-owned media.

No. A new law passed in December 2004 effectively expanded the president's control over the public media.

27. The legislature is regularly in session.

Yes. The legislature meets in ordinary session for about nine months each year.

Article 219

The first period of the ordinary sessions of the National Assembly will begin, without prior convocation, [on] the fifth of January of every year or [on] the subsequent most immediately possible day and will last until the fifteenth of August.

The second period will begin [on] the fifteenth of September or [on] the subsequent most immediate possible day and will end [on] the fifteenth of December.

28. Each legislator has a personal secretary.

No.

29. Each legislator has at least one non-secretarial staff member with policy expertise.

No.

30. Legislators are eligible for re-election without any restriction.

Yes. There are no restrictions on re-election.

31. A seat in the legislature is an attractive enough position that legislators are generally interested in and seek re-election.

Yes.

32. The re-election of incumbent legislators is common enough that at any given time the legislature contains a significant number of highly experienced members.

Yes. Re-election rates are sufficiently high to produce a significant number of highly experienced members.

NATIONAL ASSEMBLY OF VIETNAM (*Qu^óc h^ọi*)

Expert consultants: Pach Ngoc Chien, David Payne, Pete Peterson, Tuong Vu

Score: .34

Influence over executive (3/9)		Institutional autonomy (5/9)		Specified powers (0/8)	Institutional capacity (3/6)	
1. replace		10. no dissolution	X	19. amendments	27. sessions	
2. serve as ministers	X	11. no decree		20. war	28. secretary	
3. interpellate	X	12. no veto	X	21. treaties	29. staff	
4. investigate		13. no review		22. amnesty	30. no term limits	X
5. oversee police		14. no gatekeeping	X	23. pardon	31. seek re-election	X
6. appoint PM		15. no impoundment		24. judiciary	32. experience	X
7. appoint ministers	X	16. control resources		25. central bank		
8. lack president		17. immunity	X	26. media		
9. no confidence		18. all elected	X			

The National Assembly (*Qu^óc h^ọi*) of Vietnam traces its origins to the bodies established by the Democratic Republic of Vietnam upon its declaration of independence from France in 1945. After decades of war, the Democratic Republic of Vietnam in the north and the Republic of South Vietnam were united to form the Socialist Republic of Vietnam in 1976. The unicameral legislature was established in its current form in the country's 1992 constitution.

Power is concentrated in the Communist Party of Vietnam (CPV), leaving the National Assembly without a major role. As is typical in Soviet-style systems, the party is the source of legislation as well as personnel decisions and administration. Notably, however, the legislature occasionally has been able to influence the CPV's ministerial appointments. Legislative oversight over the executive has also improved in recent years; some hearings with executive branch officials testifying before the legislature have been televised. The legislature basically lacks institutional autonomy, although it cannot be dissolved and its members enjoy immunity. The legislature's institutional capacity is restricted by exceedingly short sessions and the lack of staff.

SURVEY

1. The legislature alone, without the involvement of any other agencies, can impeach the president or replace the prime minister.

No. Formally, the legislature can remove the president and the prime minister from office, but in practice, the Communist Party of Vietnam makes all personnel decisions.

Article 84
The National Assembly has the following duties and powers:
7. To... remove from office the State President and Vice-President, ... the Prime Minister... [and] to cast a vote of confidence on persons holding positions elected or approved by the National Assembly.

2. Ministers may serve simultaneously as members of the legislature.

Yes. Ministers may, but with the exception of the prime minister are not required to, serve simultaneously in the National Assembly.

Article 110
(1) The Government shall be composed of the Prime Minister, the Deputy Prime Ministers, the Cabinet Ministers, and other members. With the exception of the Prime Minister, its members are not necessarily members of the National Assembly.

3. The legislature has powers of summons over executive branch officials and hearings with executive branch officials testifying before the legislature or its committees are regularly held.

Yes. Ministers often testify before the legislature. In recent years some hearings have even been televised.

Article 98
(1) The deputy to the National Assembly has the right to interpellate the State President, the Chairman of the National Assembly, the Prime Minister, Cabinet Ministers and other members of the Government, the President of the Supreme People's Court, and the Head of the Supreme People's Office of Supervision and Control.
(2) The interpellated officials must give an answer at the current session; in case an inquiry is needed the National Assembly may decide that the answer should be given to its Standing Committee or at one of its own subsequent sessions, or may allow the answer to be given in writing.
(3) The deputy to the National Assembly has the right to request State organs, social organizations, economic bodies, and units of the armed forces to answer questions on matters with which he is concerned. The people in charge of those organs, organizations, bodies and units have the responsibility to answer questions put by the deputy within the time limit set by the law.

4. The legislature can conduct independent investigation of the chief executive and the agencies of the executive.

No. Formally, the legislature can investigate the executive, but in practice, this power does not exist.

Article 96
(1) The Nationalities Council and the Committees of the National Assembly can require members of the Government, the President of the Supreme People's Court, the Head of the Supreme People's Office of Supervision and Control, and other State officials to report or supply documents on certain necessary matters. Those to whom such requests are made must satisfy them.
(2) It is the responsibility of State organs to examine and answer the proposals made by the Nationalities Council and the Committees of the National Assembly.

5. The legislature has effective powers of oversight over the agencies of coercion (the military, organs of law enforcement, intelligence services, and the secret police).

No. The military reports solely to the CPV. The legislature does have some oversight power over the other agencies.

6. The legislature appoints the prime minister.

No. Formally, the legislature elects the prime minister, but in fact, the CPV chooses the prime minister.

Article 84
The National Assembly has the following duties and powers:
7. To elect... the Prime Minister.

7. The legislature's approval is required to confirm the appointment of ministers; or the legislature itself appoints ministers.

Yes. The legislature's approval is necessary to confirm the ministers chosen by the CPV and appointed by the president. Generally, the legislature rubber-stamps the CPV's decisions, but in rare instances the legislature has prevailed upon the party to change its choice of candidates.

Article 103
The State President has the following duties and powers:
4. On the basis of resolutions of the National Assembly, to appoint, release from duty or dismiss Deputy Prime Ministers, Ministers and other members of the Government.

8. The country lacks a presidency entirely or there is a presidency, but the president is elected by the legislature.

No. Formally, the National Assembly elects the president, but in practice, its decision is entirely predetermined by the CPV leadership, and the legislature plays no meaningful role.

Article 84
The National Assembly has the following duties and powers:
7. To elect... the State President.

Article 102
(1) The State President shall be elected by the National Assembly from among its members.

9. The legislature can vote no confidence in the government.

No. The legislature can vote no confidence in individual ministers, but not in the government as a whole.

Article 84
The National Assembly has the following duties and powers:
7. to cast a vote of confidence on persons holding positions elected or approved by the National Assembly.

10. The legislature is immune from dissolution by the executive.

Yes. The legislature is immune from dissolution.

11. Any executive initiative on legislation requires ratification or approval by the legislature before it takes effect; that is, the executive lacks decree power.

No. The government and the president can issue decrees that have the force of law.

Article 91
The Standing Committee of the National Assembly has the following duties and powers:
3. To interpret the Constitution, the law, and decree-laws;
4. To enact decree-laws on matters entrusted to it by the National Assembly.

Article 103
The State President has the following duties and powers:
1. To promulgate the Constitution, laws and decree-laws.

Article 115
(1) On the basis of the Constitution, the law, and the resolutions of the National Assembly, the decree-laws and resolutions of the latter's Standing Committee, the orders and decisions of the State President, the Government shall issue resolutions and decrees, the Prime Minister shall issue decisions and directives and shall supervise the execution of those formal written orders.

12. Laws passed by the legislature are veto-proof or essentially veto-proof; that is, the executive lacks veto power, or has veto power but the veto can be overridden by a majority in the legislature.

Yes. The legislature can override a presidential veto by a majority vote of its present members. One should note, however, that bills are written and approved by the CPV before being submitted to the legislature.

Article 103
The State President has the following duties and powers:
7. To propose to the National Assembly Standing Committee to revise its ordinances within ten days from the date these ordinances were passed; if such ordinances are still voted for by the National Assembly Standing Committee against the State President's disapproval, the State President shall report it to the National Assembly for decision at its nearest session.

13. The legislature's laws are supreme and not subject to judicial review.

No. Judicial review is not practiced, but the laws are in no respect the handiwork of the National Assembly. Rather, they are the products of the CPV's decisions.

14. The legislature has the right to initiate bills in all policy jurisdictions; the executive lacks gatekeeping authority.

Yes. The legislature can initiate bills in all policy jurisdictions.

15. Expenditure of funds appropriated by the legislature is mandatory; the executive lacks the power to impound funds appropriated by the legislature.

No. The CPV can impound funds appropriated by the legislature.

16. The legislature controls the resources that finance its own internal operation and provide for the perquisites of its own members.

No. The legislature is dependent on the executive and the CPV for the resources that finance its own operations.

Article 100
(1) The deputy to the National Assembly must devote the necessary time to his work.
(2) It is the responsibility of the Standing Committee of the National Assembly, the Prime Minister, the Cabinet Ministers, the other members of the Government, and the other State organs to supply him with the material he requires and to create the necessary conditions for him to fulfill his duty.
(3) The State shall ensure that he has the money necessary to his activities.

17. Members of the legislature are immune from arrest and/or criminal prosecution.

Yes. Legislators are immune. Even in cases of *flagrante delicto,* here expressed as "flagrant offence," an arrest must be reported to the legislature for a decision on whether to lift the legislator's immunity.

Article 99

(1) A member of the National Assembly cannot be arrested or prosecuted without the consent of the National Assembly and, in the intervals between its sessions, without the consent of its Standing Committee.

(2) In case of a flagrant offence and the deputy is taken into temporary custody, the organ effecting his arrest must immediately report the facts to the National Assembly or its Standing Committee for it to examine them and take a decision.

18. All members of the legislature are elected; the executive lacks the power to appoint any members of the legislature.

Yes. All members of the legislature are elected. It is worthy of mention, however, that in legislative elections voters choose from among a narrow range of CPV-approved candidates.

Article 85

(1) The duration of each National Assembly is five years.

(2) Two months before the end of its tenure, a new National Assembly shall have been elected. The electoral procedure and the number of members of the National Assembly shall be established by law.

19. The legislature alone, without the involvement of any other agencies, can change the Constitution.

No. Formally, the legislature can change the constitution with a two-thirds majority vote. In practice, it would be unthinkable for the legislature to change the constitution without the CPV's approval.

Article 84

The National Assembly has the following duties and powers:

1. To make and amend the Constitution; to make and amend laws; to work out a programme for making laws and decree-laws.

Article 147

The National Assembly alone shall have the right to amend the Constitution. An amendment to the Constitution must be approved by at least two-thirds of its total membership.

20. The legislature's approval is necessary for the declaration of war.

No. Formally, the president declares war on the recommendation of the legislature. In practice, the president can declare war without the legislature's approval.

Article 84

The National Assembly has the following duties and powers:

12. To decide issues of war and peace.

Article 103

The State President has the following duties and powers:

5. On the basis of resolutions of the National Assembly or its Standing Committee to proclaim a state of war.

21. The legislature's approval is necessary to ratify treaties with foreign countries.

No. Formally, the legislature's approval is necessary to ratify international treaties. In practice, the president can conclude treaties without the legislature's approval.

Article 84

The National Assembly has the following duties and powers:

13. To decide on fundamental policies in external relations; to ratify or nullify international treaties signed directly by the State President; to ratify or nullify other international treaties signed or acceded to at the proposal of the State President.

Article 103

The State President has the following duties and powers:

10. To ... negotiate and conclude international agreements in the name of the State of the Socialist Republic of Vietnam with the heads of other States; to submit to the National Assembly for ratification international agreements directly signed by him/her; to decide on ratification of, or accession to international treaties, except where they must be submitted to the National Assembly for decision.

22. The legislature has the power to grant amnesty.

No. Formally, the president declares amnesty on the recommendation of the legislature. In practice, the president can declare amnesty without involvement of the legislature.

Article 84

The National Assembly has the following duties and powers:

10. To proclaim an amnesty.

Article 103

The State President has the following duties and powers:

5. On the basis of resolutions of the National Assembly or its Standing Committee ... to proclaim an amnesty.

23. The legislature has the power of pardon.

No. The president has the power of pardon.

Article 103

The State President has the following duties and powers:

12. To grant pardons.

24. The legislature reviews and has the right to reject appointments to the judiciary; or the legislature itself appoints members of the judiciary.

No. Formally, the legislature elects the president of the Supreme People's Court. In practice, all personnel decisions are made by the CPV.

> Article 103
> The State President has the following duties and powers:
> 3. To propose to the National Assembly to elect ... the President of the Supreme People's Court.
> 8. To appoint, release from duty, dismiss the Vice-Presidents and judges of the Supreme People's Court, the Deputy Head and members of the Supreme People's Office of Supervision and Control.
>
> Article 84
> The National Assembly has the following duties and powers:
> 7. To elect ... the President of the Supreme People's Court.

25. The chairman of the central bank is appointed by the legislature.

No. Formally, the prime minister appoints the governor of the State Bank of Vietnam. In practice, all personnel decisions are made by the CPV.

26. The legislature has a substantial voice in the operation of the state-owned media.

No. The CPV controls the public media.

27. The legislature is regularly in session.

No. The legislature meets in two ordinary sessions each year, lasting about one month each. The Standing Committee of the legislature, however, is regularly in session.

> Article 86
> (1) The National Assembly shall hold two sessions each year, to be convened by its Standing Committee.
> (2) When so required by the State President, the Prime Minister, or at least one-third of the total member-ship of the National Assembly, or in pursuance of its own decision, the Standing Committee may convene an extraordinary session of the National Assembly.
> (3) The first session of the newly-elected National Assembly shall be convened two months after its election at the latest; it shall be opened and presided over by the chairman of the outgoing Assembly until the election by the incoming Assembly of its chairman.

28. Each legislator has a personal secretary.

No. Only legislators in leadership positions have a personal staff.

29. Each legislator has at least one non-secretarial staff member with policy expertise.

No. See item 28.

30. Legislators are eligible for re-election without any restriction.

Yes. Provided that legislators can remain in the good graces of the CPV, there are no restrictions on re-election.

31. A seat in the legislature is an attractive enough position that legislators are generally interested in and seek re-election.

Yes.

32. The re-election of incumbent legislators is common enough that at any given time the legislature contains a significant number of highly experienced members.

Yes. The legislature contains many multiterm members. It merits mention, however that few members are full-time lawmakers. Almost all also work in the executive branch, the CPV, or other professions.

PARLIAMENT OF YEMEN (*MAJLIS AL-NUWAAB*)

Expert consultants: Sheila Carapico, Iris Glosemeyer, Jefferson Morton Gray, Paul Harris, Jillian Schwedler

Score: .44

Influence over executive (4/9)		Institutional autonomy (5/9)		Specified powers (1/8)		Institutional capacity (4/6)	
1. replace		10. no dissolution		19. amendments		27. sessions	X
2. serve as ministers	X	11. no decree		20. war		28. secretary	
3. interpellate	X	12. no veto	X	21. treaties	X	29. staff	
4. investigate		13. no review		22. amnesty		30. no term limits	X
5. oversee police		14. no gatekeeping	X	23. pardon		31. seek re-election	X
6. appoint PM		15. no impoundment		24. judiciary		32. experience	X
7. appoint ministers	X	16. control resources	X	25. central bank			
8. lack president		17. immunity	X	26. media			
9. no confidence	X	18. all elected	X				

The Parliament of Yemen was established in the country's 1991 constitution upon the unification of North and South Yemen. It took the form of an Assembly of Deputies (*Majlis Al-Nuwaab*, which is also translated, as it is in the constitutional excerpts cited below, as House of Representatives). A constitutional amendment in 2001 added an upper house, the Consultative Council (*Majlis Al-Shura*), which is appointed by the president and performs a purely advisory role. The parliament as a whole is still usually referred to as the *Majlis Al-Nuwaab*.

The legislature's powers are not expansive. Its influence over the executive is not great. The legislature has some institutional autonomy, but that autonomy is limited by presidential decree and dissolution powers. It is very short on specified powers; of the eight such powers assessed in this survey, Yemen's legislature has but one, the responsibility for ratifying international treaties. The legislature has some institutional capacity, although its members lack staff.

SURVEY

1. The legislature alone, without the involvement of any other agencies, can impeach the president or replace the prime minister.

No. Presidential impeachment requires the involvement of the judiciary. The legislature can remove the prime minister with a vote of no confidence.

Article 97
The House of Representatives may withdraw confidence from the government. The House may not withdraw confidence from the government before an interpolation directed at the Prime Minister or he who is acting on his behalf. The request for interpolation must by signed by a third of the members of the House. The House cannot vote on the issue of no-confidence in the government without seven days' notification of such a vote. A majority is necessary to pass a vote of no-confidence.

Article 126
The President of the Republic may be charged with grand treason, violation of the Constitution, or any other action that prejudices the independence and sovereignty of the country. Such a charge requires the petitioning of half of the House of Representatives. The indictment decision on this matter requires the support of two thirds of the House of Representatives and the law stipulates the procedures of the trial. If the charge is directed at the President and his deputy, then the Presidency Board of the House of Representatives temporarily assumes the duties of the President and until the giving of the court's verdict on the charges brought against the President. The House of Representatives shall pass the above mentioned law in the first regular round of its sessions once this Constitution takes effect. If the court's verdict finds either of the two guilty, then he is relieved of his post by the Constitution, and is then

subject to the normal penalties of the law. In all cases, Prescription shall not be applied to crimes stipulated in this article.

Article 140

If the Prime Minister becomes unable to carry out his responsibilities, or if the House of Representatives withdraws confidence from the Council of Ministers, or a general election for the House of Representatives is undertaken, the Prime Minister is obliged to tender the resignation of his government to the President of the Republic.

2. Ministers may serve simultaneously as members of the legislature.

Yes. Legislators may serve simultaneously in ministerial positions.

Article 79

Membership of the Council of Ministers may concur with membership of the House of Representatives.

3. The legislature has powers of summons over executive branch officials and hearings with executive branch officials testifying before the legislature or its committees are regularly held.

Yes. The legislature regularly questions executive branch officials.

Article 95

The responsibility of the Council of Ministers is both collective and individual. Every member of the House of Representatives may pose questions to the Prime Minister, any of his deputies, ministers or deputy ministers on any matter falling within their responsibilities and they are under obligation to provide answers accordingly. The questioning may not be converted into an interpolation during the same sitting.

Article 96

Every member of the House has the right to direct an interpolation to the Prime Minister, his deputies and ministers to hold them accountable for matters under their charge. Responses to and discussions of such interpolations shall take place after at least one week, except in cases which the House deems urgent, and to which the government agrees.

4. The legislature can conduct independent investigation of the chief executive and the agencies of the executive.

No. Formally, the legislature can investigate the executive, but in practice, this power does not exist.

Article 94

Upon a request signed by at least ten of its members, the House of Representatives may create a special committee or instruct one of its committees to investigate any issue which is contrary to public interest or to investigate the actions of any ministry, government

agency, board, public/mixed corporation, or local councils. To carry out such investigations, the committee may gather proof and hold hearings by seeking testimony from any party/person it deems necessary. All executive and special authorities shall comply by laying all information or documentation they possess at the disposal of the relevant committee.

5. The legislature has effective powers of oversight over the agencies of coercion (the military, organs of law enforcement, intelligence services, and the secret police).

No. The legislature lacks effective powers of oversight over the agencies of coercion.

6. The legislature appoints the prime minister.

No. The president appoints the prime minister.

7. The legislature's approval is required to confirm the appointment of ministers; or the legislature itself appoints ministers.

Yes. The legislature's approval is required to confirm ministerial appointments.

Article 130

In consultation with the President of the Republic, the Prime Minister chooses the members of his cabinet, and seeks the confidence of the House of Representatives on the basis of a program he submits to the House.

8. The country lacks a presidency entirely or there is a presidency, but the president is elected by the legislature.

No. The president is directly elected.

Article 105

The President of the Republic is the President of the state and shall be elected according to the Constitution.

9. The legislature can vote no confidence in the government.

Yes. The legislature can vote no confidence in the government.

Article 97

The House of Representatives may withdraw confidence from the government. The House may not withdraw confidence from the government before an interpolation directed at the Prime Minister or he who is acting on his behalf. The request for interpolation must by signed by a third of the members of the House. The House cannot vote on the issue of no-confidence in the government without seven days' notification of such a vote. A majority is necessary to pass a vote of no-confidence.

Article 140

If the Prime Minister becomes unable to carry out his responsibilities, or if the House of Representatives withdraws confidence from the Council of Ministers, or a general election for the House of Representatives is undertaken, the Prime Minister is obliged to tender the resignation of his government to the President of the Republic.

10. The legislature is immune from dissolution by the executive.

No. The president can dissolve the legislature with the support of a popular referendum.

Article 100
The President of the Republic may not dissolve the House of Representatives except in urgent circumstances and only after a nation-wide referendum on the reasons for the dissolution. The President of the Republic shall issue a decree that suspends the sessions of the House and calls for the referendum within thirty days. If an absolute majority of the voters are in favour of the dissolution, the President shall issue a decree of dissolution. The decree shall simultaneously call voters to elect a new House of Representatives within a date that does not exceed sixty days from the date of the announcement of the results of the referendum. If the dissolution decree does not include the above-mentioned call, or elections did not take-place, the dissolution is considered void and null and the House shall meet by under the power of the Constitution. The House shall also meet under the power of the Constitution if a referendum does not take place within thirty days or does not gain the required majority. If elections are held, the new House must hold its first session within ten days following the completion of elections. If the House is not called to meet, it must hold its first session by the end of the said ten days in accordance with the rules of the Constitution. Once the House of Representatives is dissolved, the new House of Representatives may not be dissolved again for the same reason. In all cases, the House of Representatives may not be dissolved in its first session.

11. Any executive initiative on legislation requires ratification or approval by the legislature before it takes effect; that is, the executive lacks decree power.

No. The president can issue decree-laws when the legislature is not in session. The decrees lapse if they are not subsequently approved by the legislature.

Article 119
If, while the House of Representatives is in recess or under dissolution, urgent decisions are required, then the President of the Republic can issue decrees which have the power of law, provided such decrees do not contradict the Constitution or the budgetary estimates. Such decrees have to be presented to the first meeting of the House of Representatives. If they are not presented, the House may discuss them and take appropriate decisions thereon. If the House of Representatives rejects those decrees, they become null and void from the date the House decides and the House of Representatives determines how the consequences are to be settled.

12. Laws passed by the legislature are veto-proof or essentially veto-proof; that is, the executive lacks veto power, or has veto power but the veto can be overridden by a majority in the legislature.

Yes. The legislature can override a presidential veto by a majority vote of its present members.

Article 101
The President of the Republic has the right to request a review of any bill which is approved by the House. Based on a reasoned decision, he must then return the bill to the House of Representatives within thirty days of its submission. If he does not return the bill to the House within this period, or if the requested review is not heeded the Bill is then approved once again by the majority of the House, it shall be considered a law, and the President shall issue it within two weeks. If the President does not issue the law, it comes into effect under the power of the Constitution, and is, at once, published in the Official Gazette and come into operation two weeks later.

13. The legislature's laws are supreme and not subject to judicial review.

No. The Supreme Court of the Republic can review the constitutionality of laws.

Article 151
The Supreme Court of the Republic is the highest judicial authority. The law shall specify how it can be formed, clarify its functions and the procedures to be followed before it. It shall undertake to do the following:
a. Judge cases and pleas that laws, regulations, bylaws and decisions are not constitutional.

14. The legislature has the right to initiate bills in all policy jurisdictions; the executive lacks gatekeeping authority.

Yes. The legislature can initiate bills in all policy jurisdictions. Bills related to taxation and public expenditure, however, must be proposed by either the government or at least 20 percent of the representatives.

Article 61
The House of Representatives is the legislative authority of the state. It shall enact laws, sanction general state policy and the socio-economic plan, and approve government budgets and final accounts. It shall also direct and monitor the activities of the Executive Authority as stipulated in this constitution.

Article 84
A member of the House of Representatives and the government has the right to propose bills for laws, and their amendments. In the case of financial laws that aim at increasing or abolishing an existing tax, or decrease or give exemption from part of it, or aim at allocating part of the state funds for a certain project, these may only be proposed by the government or by at least 20% of

the representatives. All the proposed laws presented by a member or additional members of the House shall not be referred to one of the committees of the House before being studied by a special committee which will determine whether the proposal meets the requirements for action by the House. If the House decides to discuss any of these it can be transferred to the committee responsible for examining and reporting thereon. Any proposed law submitted by others than the government may not be submitted again during the same session.

15. Expenditure of funds appropriated by the legislature is mandatory; the executive lacks the power to impound funds appropriated by the legislature.

No. The president can impound funds appropriated by the legislature.

16. The legislature controls the resources that finance its own internal operation and provide for the perquisites of its own members.

Yes. The legislature enjoys financial autonomy.

17. Members of the legislature are immune from arrest and/or criminal prosecution.

Yes. Legislators are immune with the common exception for cases of *flagrante delicto,* here expressed as "being caught in the act."

Article 81
A member of the House of Representatives may not be subject to procedures of investigation, inspection, arrest, imprisonment, or punishment except with the permission of the House of Representatives save in the case his being caught in the act, and in such a case, the House shall be notified forthwith. The House shall make sure of the rectitude of the procedures followed in such cases. If the House is in recess, permission shall be sought from the Presidency Board of the House, and the House of Representatives shall be notified at the first meeting following the procedures taken.

18. All members of the legislature are elected; the executive lacks the power to appoint any members of the legislature.

Yes. All members of the House of Representatives are elected. The president appoints the members of the Consultative Council, but this body lacks real legislative power and serves a mere advisory role.

Article 62
The House of Representatives consists of 301 members, who shall be elected in a secret, free and equal vote directly by the people.

Article 125
A decree by the President of the Republic shall form a Consultative Council from experienced and qualified specialists in order to expand the base of participation through consultation and to make use of national expertise and qualifications available in different areas

of Yemen. The law shall clarify the special rules that concern the Council.

19. The legislature alone, without the involvement of any other agencies, can change the Constitution.

No. Constitutional amendments require approval in a popular referendum.

Article 156
The President of the Republic and the House of Representatives have the right to request an amendment to one or more articles of the Constitution. The request must mention the articles that require amendment, the reasons and justification for this amendment. If the request was issued by the House of Representatives it must be signed by a third of its members, and in all cases, the House shall discuss the principle of amendment and take a decision only with a majority of its members. If the request is rejected, another request for the amendment of the same articles may not be submitted until the lapse of one year. If the House of Representatives agrees to the principle of the amendment, the House shall discuss the articles which require amendment after a break of two months. If three quarters of the House agree on the amendment, it shall be presented to the people in a general referendum. If the absolute majority of those who vote are in favour of the amendment, the amendment is considered valid as of the date of announcing the results of the referendum.

20. The legislature's approval is necessary for the declaration of war.

No. In "circumstances of war, internal discord, or natural disasters" the president can declare a state of emergency without the legislature's consent. The legislature's subsequent approval is required, but a time frame for approval is not specified.

Article 118
The responsibilities of the President of the Republic are as follows:
17) To proclaim states of emergency and general mobilization according to the Law.

Article 121
The President declares a state of emergency by a republican decree according to the law. The House of Representatives shall be called to session within one week and be presented with the declaration of emergency. If the House of Representatives is dissolved, then the old House of Representatives is called to session by the Constitution. If the House is not called to session, or the declaration of the state of emergency has not been presented to it, then the state of emergency shall cease to exist according to the Constitution. In all cases, a state of emergency is only declared in circumstances of war, internal discord, or natural disasters. Declaring the state of emergency shall only be for a limited time, and may not be extended, except with the approval of the House of Representatives.

21. The legislature's approval is necessary to ratify treaties with foreign countries.

Yes. The legislature's approval is necessary to ratify international treaties.

Article 91
The House of Representatives shall ratify international political and economic treaties and conventions of a general nature, of whatsoever form or level, and in particular those connected to defense, alliance, truce, peace or border alterations, and those, which involve financial commitments on the slate or for which their execution needs the enactment of a law.

Article 118
The responsibilities of the President of the Republic are as follows:
12) To issue decrees endorsing Treaties and Conventions approved by the House of Representatives.

Article 135
The Council of Ministers is responsible for the execution of overall state policies in the political, economic, social, cultural, and defense fields, according to the laws and regulations. In particular, it shall exercise the following:
d. To approve Treaties and Conventions before presenting them to the House of Representatives or the President of the Republic according to the responsibilities of each.

22. The legislature has the power to grant amnesty.

No. The president has the power to grant amnesty.

23. The legislature has the power of pardon.

No. The president has the power of pardon.

24. The legislature reviews and has the right to reject appointments to the judiciary; or the legislature itself appoints members of the judiciary.

No. The constitution states only that the appointment of judges will be determined by law. In practice, the executive controls the judiciary, and the legislature does not have a role in selecting or confirming judicial appointments.

Article 147
The Judiciary authority is an autonomous authority in its judicial, financial and administrative aspects and the General Prosecution is one of its sub-bodies. The courts shall judge all disputes and crimes. The judges are independent and not subject to any authority, except the law. No other body may interfere in any way in the affairs and procedures of justice. Such interference shall be considered a crime that must be punished by law. A charge regarding such interference cannot be nullified with the passing of time.

Article 148
The judiciary is an integrated system. The law organizes this system in terms of ranks, responsibilities, the terms and procedures of appointment, transfer and promotion of judges, and their other privileges and guarantees. Exceptional courts may not be established under any conditions.

25. The chairman of the central bank is appointed by the legislature.

No. The president appoints the governor of the Central Bank of Yemen.

26. The legislature has a substantial voice in the operation of the state-owned media.

No. The Ministry of Information controls the public media.

27. The legislature is regularly in session.

Yes. The legislature regularly meets in ordinary session.

Article 73
The House shall annually hold two ordinary sessions. It may be called to hold extraordinary sessions. The internal regulations of the House shall specify the dates of the ordinary sessions and their duration. In times of necessity, the House may call for extraordinary sessions by Presidential decree, a decision by the Presiding Board of the House, or a written request from one third of the members. The House session shall not be adjourned during the last quarter of the year before the endorsement of the General Budget of the state.

28. Each legislator has a personal secretary.

No.

29. Each legislator has at least one non-secretarial staff member with policy expertise.

No.

30. Legislators are eligible for re-election without any restriction.

Yes. There are no restrictions on re-election.

31. A seat in the legislature is an attractive enough position that legislators are generally interested in and seek re-election.

Yes.

32. The re-election of incumbent legislators is common enough that at any given time the legislature contains a significant number of highly experienced members.

Yes. Although there is a fair degree of turnover in the legislature, the leadership of the General People's Congress, the hegemonic party in the legislature, remains largely constant, producing a significant number of highly experienced legislators.

NATIONAL ASSEMBLY OF ZAMBIA

Expert consultants: Peter Burnell, Leonard Mulenga, Adrian Muunga, Naison Ngoma, Lise Rakner

Score: .28

Influence over executive (1/9)	Institutional autonomy (2/9)	Specified powers (2/8)	Institutional capacity (4/6)
1. replace	10. no dissolution	19. amendments X	27. sessions X
2. serve as X ministers	11. no decree	20. war	28. secretary
3. interpellate	12. no veto	21. treaties	29. staff
4. investigate	13. no review	22. amnesty	30. no term X limits
5. oversee police	14. no gatekeeping	23. pardon	31. seek X re-election
6. appoint PM	15. no X impoundment	24. judiciary X	32. experience X
7. appoint ministers	16. control X resources	25. central bank	
8. lack president	17. immunity	26. media	
9. no confidence	18. all elected		

The National Assembly of Zambia was founded upon independence from Great Britain in 1964. For the next few decades the legislature was shunted aside, and the country ruled as an official one-party state. New constitutions in 1991 and 1996 allowed for multiparty politics but did not redistribute power from the presidency to the legislature. The 1996 constitution, which is currently in force, calls for a unicameral legislature.

The National Assembly is virtually devoid of power. It has little control over the executive, and its institutional autonomy is restricted by presidential dissolution, decree, veto, and gatekeeping powers. Most of the specified powers measured in this survey are reserved for the president rather than the legislature. Apart from a lack of personal legislative staff, however, the legislature does have some institutional capacity.

SURVEY

1. The legislature alone, without the involvement of any other agencies, can impeach the president or replace the prime minister.

No. Presidential impeachment requires the involvement of a special tribunal appointed by the chief justice of the Supreme Court.

Article 37

(1) If notice in writing is given to the Speaker of the National Assembly signed by not less than one-third of all the members of the Assembly of a motion alleging that the President has committed any violation of the Constitution or any gross misconduct and specifying the particulars of the allegations and proposing that a tribunal be established under this Article to investigate those allegations, the Speaker shall –

(a) if Parliament is then sitting or has been summoned to meet within five days, cause the motion to be considered by the Assembly within seven days of the notice;

(b) if Parliament is not then sitting (and notwithstanding that it may be prorogued) summon the Assembly to meet within twenty-one days of the notice and cause the motion to be considered at that meeting.

(2) Where a motion under this Article is proposed for consideration by the National Assembly, the Assembly shall not debate the motion but the person presiding in the Assembly shall forthwith cause a vote to be taken on the motion and if the motion is supported by the votes of not less than two-thirds of all the members of the Assembly, shall declare the motion to be passed.

(3) If the motion is declared to be passed under clause (2) –

(a) the Chief Justice shall appoint a tribunal which shall consist of a Chairman and not less than two other members selected by the Chief Justice from among persons who hold or have held high judicial office;

(b) the tribunal shall investigate the matter and shall report to the National Assembly whether it finds the particulars of the allegations specified in the motion to have been substantiated;

(c) the President shall have the right to appear and be represented before the tribunal during its investigation of the allegations against him.

(4) If the tribunal reports to the National Assembly that the tribunal finds that the particulars of any allegation against the President specified in the motion have not been substantiated no further proceedings shall be taken under this Article in respect of that allegation.

(5) If the tribunal reports to the National Assembly that the tribunal finds that the particulars of any allegation specified in the motion have been substantiated, the Assembly may, on a motion supported by the votes of not less than three-quarters of all members of the Assembly, resolve that the President has been guilty of such violation of the Constitution or, as the case may be such gross misconduct as it is incompatible with his continuance in office as President and, if the Assembly so resolves, the President shall cease to hold office upon the third day following the passage of the resolution.

(6) No proceedings shall be taken or continued under this Article at any time when Parliament is dissolved.

2. Ministers may serve simultaneously as members of the legislature.

Yes. Ministers are chosen from, and required to serve simultaneously in, the legislature.

Article 46
(1) There shall be such Ministers as may be appointed by the President.
(2) Appointment to the office of Minister shall be made from among the members of the National Assembly.

3. The legislature has powers of summons over executive branch officials and hearings with executive branch officials testifying before the legislature or its committees are regularly held.

No. The legislature does not regularly question executive branch officials.

4. The legislature can conduct independent investigation of the chief executive and the agencies of the executive.

No. The legislature cannot investigate the executive.

5. The legislature has effective powers of oversight over the agencies of coercion (the military, organs of law enforcement, intelligence services, and the secret police).

No. The legislature lacks effective powers of oversight over the agencies of coercion.

6. The legislature appoints the prime minister.

No. There is no prime minister.

7. The legislature's approval is required to confirm the appointment of ministers; or the legislature itself appoints ministers.

No. The president appoints ministers, and the appointments do not require the legislature's approval.

Article 46
(1) There shall be such Ministers as may be appointed by the President.
(2) Appointment to the office of Minister shall be made from among the members of the National Assembly.

8. The country lacks a presidency entirely or there is a presidency, but the president is elected by the legislature.

No. The president is directly elected.

Article 33
(1) There shall be a President of the Republic of Zambia who shall be the Head of State and of the Government and the Commander-in-Chief of the Defence Forces.

Article 34
(1) The election of the President shall be direct by universal adult suffrage and by secret ballot and shall be conducted in accordance with this Article and as may be prescribed by or under an Act of Parliament.

9. The legislature can vote no confidence in the government.

No. The legislature cannot vote no confidence in the government.

10. The legislature is immune from dissolution by the executive.

No. The president can dissolve the legislature.

Article 44
(2) Without prejudice to the generality of clause (1), the President may preside over meetings of the Cabinet and shall have the power, subject to this Constitution, to –
    (a) dissolve the National Assembly as provided in Article 88.

Article 88
(6) Subject to clause (9) the National Assembly –
(c) may be dissolved by the President at any time.

11. Any executive initiative on legislation requires ratification or approval by the legislature before it takes effect; that is, the executive lacks decree power.

No. Formally, the president lacks decree power. In practice, the president issues decrees that have the force of law.

12. Laws passed by the legislature are veto-proof or essentially veto-proof; that is, the executive lacks veto power, or has veto power but the veto can be overridden by a majority in the legislature.

No. The legislature cannot override a presidential veto. After the legislature passes a bill for the second time, the president can choose to dissolve the legislature rather than assent to the legislation.

Article 78
(1) Subject to the provisions of this Constitution, the legislative power of Parliament shall be exercised by bills passed by the National Assembly and assented to by the President.
(2) No bill (other than such a bill as is mentioned in Article 27 (8)) shall be presented to the President until after the expiration of three days from the third reading of the bill by the National Assembly, and where a bill is referred to a tribunal in accordance with Article 27 that bill shall not be presented to the President for assent until the tribunal has reported on the bill or the time for making a report has expired, whichever is the earlier.
(3) Where a bill is presented to the President for assent he shall either assent or withhold his assent.
(4) Where the President withholds his assent to a bill, the bill shall be returned to the National Assembly: Provided that if the President withholds his assent to a bill in respect of which a tribunal has reported under Article 27 that it would, if enacted, be inconsistent with Part III, the bill shall be returned to the Assembly only if the President so directs.
(6) Where a bill is again presented to the President for assent in accordance with the provisions of clause (5) the President shall assent to the bill within twenty-one days of its presentation, unless he sooner dissolves Parliament.

13. The legislature's laws are supreme and not subject to judicial review.

No. An ad hoc Constitutional Council can review the constitutionality of laws.

14. The legislature has the right to initiate bills in all policy jurisdictions; the executive lacks gatekeeping authority.

No. The legislature is prohibited from initiating legislation related to taxation, public expenditures, or government debt.

Article 81
Except upon the recommendation of the President signified by the Vice President or a Minister, the National Assembly shall not –
(a) proceed upon any bill (including any amendment to a bill) that, in the opinion of the person presiding, makes provision for any of the following purposes:
(i) for the imposition of taxation or the alteration of taxation otherwise than by reduction;
(ii) for the imposition of any charge upon the general revenues of the Republic or the alteration of any such charge otherwise than by reduction;
(iii) for the payment, issue or withdrawal from the general revenues of the Republic of any moneys not charged thereon or any increase in the amount of such payment, issue or withdrawal; or
(iv) for the composition or remission of any debt due to the Government; or
(b) proceed upon any motion (including any amendment to a motion) the effect of which, in the opinion of the person presiding, would be to make provision for any of those purposes.

15. Expenditure of funds appropriated by the legislature is mandatory; the executive lacks the power to impound funds appropriated by the legislature.

Yes. The executive lacks the power to impound funds appropriated by the legislature.

16. The legislature controls the resources that finance its own internal operation and provide for the perquisites of its own members.

Yes. The legislature enjoys financial autonomy.

17. Members of the legislature are immune from arrest and/or criminal prosecution.

No. According to the constitution, legislative immunity will be "prescribed by an Act of Parliament" following "law and custom of the Parliament of England." In practice, legislators are subject to arrest and criminal prosecution.

Article 87
Privileges and Immunities of National Assembly
(1) The National Assembly and its members shall have such privileges, powers and immunities as may be prescribed by an Act of Parliament.
(2) Notwithstanding subclause (1) the law and custom of the Parliament of England shall apply to the National Assembly with such modifications as may be prescribed by or under an Act of Parliament.

18. All members of the legislature are elected; the executive lacks the power to appoint any members of the legislature.

No. The president appoints eight of the 158 members of the National Assembly.

Article 63
(2) Subject to the provisions of this Constitution, the election of members of the National Assembly shall be direct, by universal adult suffrage and by secret ballot and shall be conducted in accordance with the provisions of this Constitution and as may be prescribed by or under an Act of Parliament.

Article 68
(1) The President may, at any time after a general election to the National Assembly and before the National Assembly is next dissolved, appoint such number of persons as he thinks fit to be nominated members of

the National Assembly, so, however, that there are not more than eight such members as any one time.

19. The legislature alone, without the involvement of any other agencies, can change the Constitution.

Yes. The legislature can change the constitution in multiple readings with a two-thirds majority vote. Amendments to the part of the constitution that deals with fundamental rights also require approval in a popular referendum.

Article 79
(1) Subject to the provisions of this Article, Parliament may alter this Constitution or the Constitution of Zambia Act, 1991.
(2) Subject to cause (3) a bill for the alteration of this Constitution or the Constitution of Zambia Act, 1991 shall not be passed unless –
  (a) not less than thirty days before the first reading of the bill in the National Assembly the text of the bill is published in the Gazette; and
  (b) the bill is supported on second and third readings by the votes of not less than two thirds of all the members of the Assembly.
(3) A bill for the alteration of Part III of this Constitution or of this Article shall not be passed unless before the first reading of the bill in the National Assembly it has been put to a National referendum with or without amendment by not less than fifty per cent of persons entitled to be registered as voters for the purposes of Presidential and parliamentary elections.
(4) Any referendum conducted for the purposes of clause (3) shall be so conducted and supervised in such manner as may be prescribed by or under an Act of Parliament.
(5) In this Article –
  (a) references to this Constitution or the Constitution of Zambia Act, 1991 include reference to any law that amends or replaces any of the provisions of this Constitution or that Act; and
  (b) references to the alteration of this Constitution or the Constitution of Zambia Act, 1991 or of any Part of Article include references to the amendment, modification or re-enactment with or without amendment or modification, of any provision for the time being contained in this Constitution, that Act, Part or Article, the suspension or repeal or any such provision and the making of different provision in lieu of such provision, and the addition of new provisions, to this Constitution, that Act, Part or Article.
(6) Nothing in this Article shall be so construed as to require the publication of any amendment to any such bill as is referred to in clause (2) proposed to be moved in the National Assembly.

20. The legislature's approval is necessary for the declaration of war.

No. The president can declare war without the legislature's approval.

Article 29
(1) The President may, in consultation with Cabinet, at any time, by Proclamation published in the Gazette declare war.
(2) A declaration made under clause (1) shall continue in force until the cessation of hostilities.
(3) An Act of Parliament shall provide for the conditions and circumstances under which a declaration may be made under clause (1).

21. The legislature's approval is necessary to ratify treaties with foreign countries.

No. The president can conclude international treaties without legislative approval.

Article 44
(2) Without prejudice to the generality of clause (1), the President may preside over meetings of the Cabinet and shall have the power, subject to this Constitution, to –
(d) negotiate and sign international agreements and to delegate the power to do so.

22. The legislature has the power to grant amnesty.

No. Pardon and amnesty are not treated separately, and the legislature lacks the power to grant amnesty. See item 23.

23. The legislature has the power of pardon.

No. The president has the power of pardon.

Article 44
(2) Without prejudice to the generality of clause (1), the President may preside over meetings of the Cabinet and shall have the power, subject to this Constitution, to –
(c) pardon or reprieve offenders, either unconditionally or subject to such conditions as he may consider fit.

Article 59
The President may –
  (a) grant to any person convicted of any offence a pardon, either free or subject to lawful conditions.

24. The legislature reviews and has the right to reject appointments to the judiciary; or the legislature itself appoints members of the judiciary.

Yes. The legislature's consent is needed for the president's nominations to the Supreme Court. Other judges are appointed by the president on the recommendation of the Judicial Service Commission.

Article 93
(1) The Chief Justice shall be appointed by the President subject to ratification by the National Assembly.
(2) The judges of the Supreme Court shall, subject to ratification by the National Assembly, be appointed by the President.

Article 95

(1) The puisne judges shall, subject to ratification by the National Assembly, be appointed by the President on the advice of the Judicial Service Commission.

25. The chairman of the central bank is appointed by the legislature.

No. The president appoints the governor of the Bank of Zambia.

26. The legislature has a substantial voice in the operation of the state-owned media.

No. The government controls the Zambia National Broadcasting Corporation and has influence over two widely circulated newspapers.

27. The legislature is regularly in session.

Yes. The legislature regularly meets in ordinary session.

Article 88

(1) Subject to the provisions of clauses (2) and (8), each session of Parliament shall be held at such place within Zambia and shall commence at such time as the President may appoint.

(2) There shall be a session of Parliament at least once every year so that a period of twelve months shall not intervene between the last sitting of the National Assembly in one session and the commencement of the next session.

28. Each legislator has a personal secretary.

No.

29. Each legislator has at least one non-secretarial staff member with policy expertise.

No.

30. Legislators are eligible for re-election without any restriction.

Yes. There are no restrictions on re-election.

31. A seat in the legislature is an attractive enough position that legislators are generally interested in and seek re-election.

Yes.

32. The re-election of incumbent legislators is common enough that at any given time the legislature contains a significant number of highly experienced members.

Yes. Re-election rates are sufficiently high to produce a significant number of highly experienced members.

PARLIAMENT OF ZIMBABWE

Expert consultants: Annie Dzenga, Liisa Laakso, Adrienne LeBas, Valerie Tsanga, Joel Zowa

Score: .31

Influence over executive (4/9)		Institutional autonomy (1/9)		Specified powers (1/8)		Institutional capacity (4/6)	
1. replace	X	10. no dissolution		19. amendments	X	27. sessions	X
2. serve as ministers	X	11. no decree		20. war		28. secretary	
3. interpellate	X	12. no veto		21. treaties		29. staff	
4. investigate		13. no review		22. amnesty		30. no term limits	X
5. oversee police		14. no gatekeeping		23. pardon		31. seek re-election	X
6. appoint PM		15. no impoundment		24. judiciary		32. experience	X
7. appoint ministers		16. control resources	X	25. central bank			
8. lack president		17. immunity		26. media			
9. no confidence	X	18. all elected					

The Parliament of Zimbabwe traces its origins to the Legislative Council of Southern Rhodesia established by Great Britain in the late nineteenth century to represent the colony in the British Empire. Zimbabwe did not receive formal independence from Great Britain until 1980. The country's first constitution called for a Westminster-style system with a bicameral legislature consisting of a lower house, the House of Assembly, and an upper house, the Senate. Over time, the powers of the figurehead president gradually increased, until a 1987 constitutional amendment abolished the Senate and the office of prime minister and made the president the head of government. The change enabled Robert Mugabe, theretofore the prime minister, to assume the office of president and augment his own powers in the process. During the subsequent two decades, Mugabe's rule became increasingly arbitrary and authoritarian. Mugabe has used his party, the Zimbabwe African National Union/Patriotic Front (ZANU-PF), as his organizational weapon. Engineering large majorities for the party in parliamentary elections by means of fraud and coercion, Mugabe has maintained effective control of the legislature. ZANU-PF's large majority in the House of Assembly enabled it, at Mugabe's urging, to amend the constitution to reestablish the Senate in August 2005, and elections were held for it in November of that year. Both houses of parliament contain popularly elected members as well as members appointed by the president.

The legislature is nearly impotent. It cannot effectively oversee the executive, protect its own institutional autonomy, or exercise specified powers and prerogatives. The minimal power it does have includes the formal right to remove the president from office and some institutional capacity.

SURVEY

1. The legislature alone, without the involvement of any other agencies, can impeach the president or replace the prime minister.

Yes. Both houses of the legislature, sitting in plenary session, can remove the president with a two-thirds majority vote of their total membership.

Article 29
(3) The President shall cease to hold office if a report prepared by a joint committee of the Senate and the House of Assembly, appointed by the Speaker in consultation with the President of Senate upon the request of not fewer than one-third of the members of House of Assembly, has recommended the removal of the President on the ground –
(a) that he has acted in willful violation of this Constitution; or
(c) of gross misconduct; and the Senators and members of the House of Assembly sitting together have resolved by the affirmative votes of not less than two-thirds of their total number that the President should be removed from office.

2. Ministers may serve simultaneously as members of the legislature.

Yes. Ministers are required to serve simultaneously in the legislature.

Article 31E
(1) The office of a Vice-President, Minister or Deputy Minister shall become vacant –
(2) No person shall hold office as Vice-President, Minister or Deputy Minister for longer than three months unless he is a member of Parliament:
Provided that, if during that period Parliament is dissolved, he may continue to hold such office without being a member of Parliament until Parliament first meets after the dissolution.
(3) A person who has held office as Vice-President, Minister or Deputy Minister without also being a member of Parliament shall not be eligible for reappointment to that office before Parliament is next dissolved unless in the meantime he has become a member of Parliament.

3. The legislature has powers of summons over executive branch officials and hearings with executive branch officials testifying before the legislature or its committees are regularly held.

Yes. The legislature questions executive branch officials during regular question time.

4. The legislature can conduct independent investigation of the chief executive and the agencies of the executive.

No. The legislature cannot investigate the executive.

5. The legislature has effective powers of oversight over the agencies of coercion (the military, organs of law enforcement, intelligence services, and the secret police).

No. The legislature lacks effective powers of oversight over the agencies of coercion.

6. The legislature appoints the prime minister.

No. There is no prime minister.

7. The legislature's approval is required to confirm the appointment of ministers; or the legislature itself appoints ministers.

No. The president appoints ministers, and the appointments do not require the legislature's approval.

Article 31
(1) The President –
(a) shall appoint Ministers and may assign functions to such Ministers, including the administration of any Act of Parliament or of any Ministry or department; and

(b) may appoint Deputy Ministers of any Ministry or department or of such other description as the President may determine, and may authorize any Deputy Minister to exercise or perform on behalf of a Minister any of the functions entrusted to such Minister.

8. The country lacks a presidency entirely or there is a presidency, but the president is elected by the legislature.

No. The president is directly elected.

> Article 28
> (2) The President shall be elected by voters.

9. The legislature can vote no confidence in the government.

Yes. The legislature can vote no confidence in the government.

> Article 31F
> (1) Parliament may, by resolution supported by the votes of not less than two-thirds of all the members of each House, pass a vote of no confidence in the Government.
> (2) A motion for the resolution referred to in subsection (1) shall not be moved in the House of Assembly unless –
>
> (a) not less than seven days' notice of the motion has been given to the Speaker; and
> (b) the notice of the motion has been signed by not less than one-third of all the members of the House of Assembly; and shall be debated in the House of Assembly within twenty-one days after the receipt by the Speaker of the notice of the motion.
> (3) Where a vote of no confidence in the Government is passed by Parliament in terms of this section, the President shall within fourteen days do one of the following –
>
> (a) dissolve Parliament; or
> (b) remove every Vice-President, Minister and Deputy Minister from his office unless he has earlier resigned in consequence of the resolution; or
> (c) himself resign his office.

10. The legislature is immune from dissolution by the executive.

No. The president can dissolve the legislature.

> Article 63
> (1) The President may at any time prorogue Parliament.
> (2) Subject to the provisions of this Constitution, the President may at any time dissolve Parliament.

11. Any executive initiative on legislation requires ratification or approval by the legislature before it takes effect; that is, the executive lacks decree power.

No. The president issues decrees that have the force of law.

12. Laws passed by the legislature are veto-proof or essentially veto-proof; that is, the executive lacks veto power, or has veto power but the veto can be overridden by a majority in the legislature.

No. A two-thirds majority vote is required to override a presidential veto. Even after such an override, the president can decide to dissolve the legislature rather than assent to the bill.

> Article 51
> (1) Subject to the provisions of section 52 and Schedule 4, the power of Parliament to make laws shall be exercised by Bills passed by the House of Assembly and the Senate and assented to by the President.
> (2) When a Bill is presented to the President for assent he shall, subject to the provisions of this section, within twenty-one days, either assent or withhold his assent.
> (3) Where this Constitution provides that a Bill of a specified description shall not be presented to the President for assent unless it is accompanied by a certificate, the President shall not assent to such Bill unless it is accompanied by the said certificate.
> (3a) Where the President withholds his assent to a Bill, the Bill shall be returned to the House of Assembly and, subject to the provisions of subsection (3b), the Bill shall not again be presented for assent.
> (3b) If, within six months after a Bill has been returned to the House of Assembly in terms of subsection (3a), the House of Assembly resolves upon a motion supported by the votes of not less than two-thirds of all the members of the House of Assembly that the Bill should again be presented to the President for assent, the Bill shall be so presented and, on such presentation, the President shall assent to the Bill within twenty-one days of the presentation, unless he sooner dissolves Parliament.

13. The legislature's laws are supreme and not subject to judicial review.

No. The Supreme Court can review the constitutionality of laws.

14. The legislature has the right to initiate bills in all policy jurisdictions; the executive lacks gatekeeping authority.

No. The legislature is prohibited from introducing legislation related to taxation, public expenditures, or government debt.

> Schedule Four
> (4) Except on the recommendation of a Vice-President, Minister or Deputy Minister, Parliament shall not –
> (a) proceed upon any Bill, including any amendment to a Bill, which, in the opinion of the President of the Senate or the Speaker, as the case may be, makes provision for any of the following matters –
> (i) imposing or increasing any tax;
> (ii) imposing or increasing any charge on the Consolidated Revenue Fund or other public funds of the State or varying any such charge otherwise than by reducing it;

(iii) compounding or remitting any debt due to the State or condoning any failure to collect taxes;

(iv) authorising the making or raising of any loan by the State;

(v) condoning unauthorised expenditure;

(b) proceed upon any motion, including any amendment to a motion, the effect of which, in the opinion of the President of the Senate or the Speaker, as the case may be, is that provision should be made for any of the matters specified in subparagraph (a); or

(c) receive any petition which, in the opinion of the President of the Senate or Speaker, as the case may be, requests that provision be made for any of the matters specified in subparagraph (a).

15. Expenditure of funds appropriated by the legislature is mandatory; the executive lacks the power to impound funds appropriated by the legislature.

No. The president can impound funds appropriated by the legislature.

16. The legislature controls the resources that finance its own internal operation and provide for the perquisites of its own members.

Yes. The legislature enjoys financial autonomy.

17. Members of the legislature are immune from arrest and/or criminal prosecution.

No. Legislators are subject to arrest, and legislators who oppose the president have regularly been subject to persecution.

Article 42

(1) Subject to the provisions of this section, in the event of a member of Parliament being convicted –

(a) within Zimbabwe of a criminal offence; or

(b) outside Zimbabwe of an offence, by whatever name called, which if committed within Zimbabwe would have been a criminal offence; and being sentenced by a court to death or imprisonment, by whatever name called, for a term of six months or more, such member shall cease forthwith to exercise his functions and to be entitled to any remuneration as a member and his seat shall become vacant at the expiration of thirty days from the date of such sentence.

18. All members of the legislature are elected; the executive lacks the power to appoint any members of the legislature.

No. The president appoints six of the sixty-six senators and twelve of the 150 members of the House of Assembly.

Article 34

(1) The Senate shall consist of sixty-six Senators, of whom –

(a) five shall be elected in each of the ten provinces by voters registered in the fifty senatorial constituencies referred to in subsection (4); and

(b) two shall be the President and the Deputy President of the Council of Chiefs; and

(c) eight shall be Chiefs representing each of the provinces, other than the metropolitan provinces, elected in accordance with the Electoral Law; and

(d) six shall be appointed by the President.

Article 38

(1) There shall be a House of Assembly which, subject to the provisions of section 76(3b), shall consist of one hundred and fifty members qualified in accordance with Schedule 3 for election or appointment to the House of Assembly, of whom –

(a) one hundred and twenty shall be elected by voters in the one hundred and twenty constituencies delimited in accordance with section 60; and

(b) ten shall be Provincial Governors; and

(c) eight shall be Chiefs representing each of the provinces, other than the metropolitan provinces, elected in accordance with the Electoral Law; and

(d) twelve shall be appointed by the President.

19. The legislature alone, without the involvement of any other agencies, can change the Constitution.

Yes. The legislature can change the constitution with a two-thirds majority vote in each house.

Article 52

(1) Parliament may amend, add to or repeal any of the provisions of this Constitution:

Provided that, except as provided in subsection (6), no law shall be deemed to amend, add to or repeal any provision of this Constitution unless it does so in express terms.

(2) A Constitutional Bill shall not be introduced into the Senate or the House of Assembly unless the text of the Bill has been published in the Gazette not less than thirty days before it is so introduced.

(3) A Constitutional Bill shall not be deemed to have been duly passed by Parliament unless, at the final vote thereon in the Senate and the House of Assembly, it received the affirmative votes of not less than two-thirds of the total membership of each House.

(4) If in the case of a Constitutional Bill which has been passed by the House of Assembly in accordance with subsection (3) but has not been passed by the Senate in accordance with that subsection within a period of one hundred and eighty days beginning on the day on which the Bill was first introduced into the Senate, the House of Assembly resolves after the expiration of that period by the affirmative votes of not less than two-thirds of its members that the Bill be presented to the President for assent in the form in which it was passed by the House of Assembly, except for minor changes required by the passage of time, and with such amendments, if any, as the Senate and the House of Assembly may have agreed, the Bill shall be deemed to have been duly passed in the form in which it is presented to the President.

(5) A Constitutional Bill shall not be submitted to the President for assent unless –

(a) it is accompanied by –
(i) a certificate from the President of the Senate that at the final vote thereon in the Senate the Bill received the affirmative votes of not less than two-thirds of the total membership of the Senate; and
(ii) a certificate from the Speaker that at the final vote thereon in the House of Assembly the Bill received the affirmative votes of not less than two-thirds of the total membership of the House of Assembly;
or
(b) it is accompanied by the certificate referred to in paragraph (a)(ii) and a further certificate from the Speaker stating that the Bill is a Bill to which the provisions of subsection (4) apply and that the Bill may lawfully be presented for assent by virtue of those provisions.
(6) An Act of Parliament that provides for a revision of the written law such as is referred to section 53(2) may make provision for –
(a) renumbering the provisions of this Constitution so as to reflect amendments that have been made thereto; and
(b) amending the provisions of this Constitution where it is necessary to do so as a consequence of any renumbering referred to in paragraph (a); and any such renumbering or amendment shall be valid as if it had been effected by means of an Act of Parliament passed in accordance with the provisions of this section.

20. The legislature's approval is necessary for the declaration of war.

No. The president can declare war without the legislature's approval.

Article 31H
(4) The President shall have power, subject to the provisions of this Constitution –
(d) to declare war and to make peace.

21. The legislature's approval is necessary to ratify treaties with foreign countries.

No. The president can conclude international treaties without the legislature's approval.

Article 31H
(4) The President shall have power, subject to the provisions of this Constitution –
(b) to enter into international conventions, treaties and agreements.

22. The legislature has the power to grant amnesty.

No. The president has the power to grant amnesty.

Article 31I
(1) The President may, subject to such lawful conditions as he may think fit to impose –
(a) grant a pardon to any person concerned in or convicted of a criminal offence against any law; or

(b) grant a respite, either indefinite or for a specified period, from the execution of any sentence for such an offence; or
(c) substitute a less severe punishment for that imposed by any sentence for such an offence; or
(d) suspend for a specified period or remit the whole or part of any sentence for such an offence or any penalty of forfeiture otherwise imposed on account of such an offence.

23. The legislature has the power of pardon.

No. The president has the power of pardon.

Article 31I
(1) The President may, subject to such lawful conditions as he may think fit to impose –
(a) grant a pardon to any person concerned in or convicted of a criminal offence against any law; or
(b) grant a respite, either indefinite or for a specified period, from the execution of any sentence for such an offence; or
(c) substitute a less severe punishment for that imposed by any sentence for such an offence; or
(d) suspend for a specified period or remit the whole or part of any sentence for such an offence or any penalty of forfeiture otherwise imposed on account of such an offence.

24. The legislature reviews and has the right to reject appointments to the judiciary; or the legislature itself appoints members of the judiciary.

No. The president makes judicial appointments, and the appointments do not require the legislature's approval.

Article 84
(1) The Chief Justice and other judges of the Supreme Court and the High Court shall be appointed by the President after consultation with the Judicial Service Commission.

25. The chairman of the central bank is appointed by the legislature.

No. The president appoints the governor of the Reserve Bank of Zimbabwe.

26. The legislature has a substantial voice in the operation of the state-owned media.

No. The legislature lacks a substantial voice in the operation of the public media.

27. The legislature is regularly in session.

Yes. The legislature regularly meets in ordinary session.

Article 62
(1) Subject to the provisions of subsection 2, the sessions of Parliament shall be held in such place and shall begin at such time as the President may, by proclamation in the Gazette, fix.

(2) There shall be a session of Parliament beginning in every calendar year so that a period of more than one hundred and eighty days shall not intervene between the last sitting of either House in any one session and the first sitting of Parliament in the next session.

28. Each legislator has a personal secretary.

No.

29. Each legislator has at least one non-secretarial staff member with policy expertise.

No.

30. Legislators are eligible for re-election without any restriction.

Yes. There are no restrictions on re-election.

31. A seat in the legislature is an attractive enough position that legislators are generally interested in and seek re-election.

Yes.

32. The re-election of incumbent legislators is common enough that at any given time the legislature contains a significant number of highly experienced members.

Yes. Re-election rates are sufficiently high to produce a significant number of highly experienced members.

3   Comprehensive Lists of Country Scores

Parliamentary Powers Index Scores by Country, in Alphabetical Order

COUNTRY	PPI
National Assembly of Afghanistan	0.38
Assembly of Albania	0.75
Parliament of Algeria	0.25
National Assembly of Angola	0.44
Argentine National Congress	0.50
Armenian National Assembly	0.56
Parliament of Australia	0.63
Austrian Parliament	0.72
Parliament of Azerbaijan	0.44
National Assembly of Bahrain	0.19
Bangladesh Parliament	0.59
National Assembly of Belarus	0.25
Federal Parliament of Belgium	0.75
National Assembly of Benin	0.56
National Assembly of Bhutan	0.22
Bolivian National Congress	0.44
Parliamentary Assembly of Bosnia and Herzegovina	0.63
National Assembly of Botswana	0.44
National Congress of Brazil	0.56
National Assembly of Bulgaria	0.78
National Assembly of Burkina Faso	0.53
Parliament of Burundi	0.41
National Assembly of Cambodia	0.59
National Assembly of Cameroon	0.25
Parliament of Canada	0.72
National Assembly of the Central African Republic	0.34
National Assembly of Chad	0.22
Congress of Chile	0.56
Chinese National People's Congress	0.34
Congress of Colombia	0.56
Assembly of Comoros	0.38
Parliament of Congo-Brazzaville (Republic of Congo)	0.38
National Assembly of Congo-Kinshasa (DRC)	0.25
Legislative Assembly of Costa Rica	0.53
National Assembly of Côte d'Ivoire	0.38
Parliament of Croatia	0.78

COUNTRY	PPI
National Assembly of People's Power of Cuba	0.28
House of Representatives of Cyprus	0.41
Parliament of the Czech Republic	0.81
Parliament of Denmark	0.78
National Congress of the Dominican Republic	0.41
National Congress of Ecuador	0.53
People's Assembly of Egypt	0.28
Legislative Assembly of El Salvador	0.59
National Assembly of Eritrea	0.25
Parliament of Estonia	0.75
Parliament of Ethiopia	0.50
Parliament of Fiji	0.63
Parliament of Finland	0.72
Parliament of France	0.56
Parliament of Gabon	0.44
National Assembly of The Gambia	0.31
Parliament of Georgia	0.59
Parliament of the Federal Republic of Germany	0.84
Parliament of Ghana	0.47
Parliament of Greece	0.81
Congress of Guatemala	0.50
National Assembly of Guinea	0.31
National People's Assembly of Guinea-Bissau	0.25
National Assembly of Guyana	0.38
National Assembly of Haiti	0.44
National Congress of Honduras	0.53
National Assembly of Hungary	0.75
Parliament of India	0.63
House of Representatives of Indonesia	0.56
Islamic Consultative Assembly of the Islamic Republic of Iran	0.44
Council of Representatives of Iraq	0.63
Parliament of Ireland	0.66
Parliament of Israel	0.75
Parliament of Italy	0.84
Parliament of Jamaica	0.63
National Diet of Japan	0.66
National Assembly of Jordan	0.22
Parliament of Kazakhstan	0.38

COUNTRY	PPI	COUNTRY	PPI
National Assembly of Kenya	0.31	Parliament of Romania	0.72
Supreme People's Assembly of the DPRK (North Korea)	0.13	Federal Assembly of the Russian Federation	0.44
National Assembly of the ROK (South Korea)	0.59	Parliament of Rwanda	0.47
		Consultative Council of Saudi Arabia	0.09
National Assembly of Kuwait	0.38	National Assembly of Senegal	0.44
Legislative Assembly of Kyrgyzstan	0.47	National Assembly of Serbia	0.69
National Assembly of Laos	0.28	Parliament of Sierra Leone	0.41
Parliament of Latvia	0.78	Parliament of Singapore	0.38
National Assembly of Lebanon	0.50	National Council of the Slovak Republic	0.72
Parliament of Lesotho	0.53	Parliament of Slovenia	0.75
National Assembly of Liberia	0.44	Transitional Federal Assembly of Somalia	0.00
General People's Congress of Libya	0.13	Parliament of South Africa	0.63
Parliament of Lithuania	0.78	The General Courts of Spain	0.72
Assembly of the Republic of Macedonia	0.81	Parliament of Sri Lanka	0.50
National Assembly of Madagascar	0.41	National Legislature of Sudan	0.22
National Assembly of Malawi	0.38	Parliament of Swaziland	0.25
Parliament of Malaysia	0.34	Parliament of Sweden	0.72
National Assembly of Mali	0.34	Federal Assembly of Switzerland	0.72
Parliament of Mauritania	0.31	People's Assembly of Syria	0.31
National Assembly of Mauritius	0.66	Legislative Yuan of Taiwan, Republic of China	0.59
Mexican Congress	0.44		
Parliament of Moldova	0.75	Supreme Assembly of Tajikistan	0.31
Great State Assembly of Mongolia	0.84	National Assembly of Tanzania	0.31
Parliament of Morocco	0.31	National Assembly of Thailand	0.59
Assembly of Mozambique	0.44	National Parliament of Timor-Leste	0.47
People's Assembly of Myanmar (Burma)	0.00	National Assembly of Togo	0.38
National Assembly of Namibia	0.50	Parliament of Trinidad and Tobago	0.53
Parliament of Nepal	0.44	National Parliament of Tunisia	0.28
States-General of the Netherlands	0.78	Turkish Grand National Assembly	0.78
Parliament of New Zealand	0.69	People's Council of Turkmenistan	0.06
National Assembly of Nicaragua	0.69	National Assembly of Uganda	0.44
National Assembly of Niger	0.50	Supreme Council of Ukraine	0.59
National Assembly of Nigeria	0.47	Federal National Council of the United Arab Emirates	0.06
Parliament of Norway	0.72		
Council of Oman	0.16	Parliament of the United Kingdom	0.78
Parliament of Pakistan	0.44	Congress of the United States of America	0.63
National Assembly of Panama	0.50		
National Parliament of Papua New Guinea	0.66	Uruguayan General Assembly	0.66
Congress of Paraguay	0.56	Supreme Assembly of Uzbekistan	0.28
Congress of Peru	0.66	National Assembly of Venezuela	0.53
Congress of the Philippines	0.56	National Assembly of Vietnam	0.34
Parliament of Poland	0.75	Parliament of Yemen	0.44
Assembly of Portugal	0.63	National Assembly of Zambia	0.28
Consultative Council of Qatar	0.22	Parliament of Zimbabwe	0.31

Parliamentary Powers Index Scores by Country, in Order of Scores

COUNTRY	PPI
Parliament of the Federal Republic of Germany	0.84
Parliament of Italy	0.84
Great State Assembly of Mongolia	0.84
Parliament of the Czech Republic	0.81
Parliament of Greece	0.81
Assembly of the Republic of Macedonia	0.81
National Assembly of Bulgaria	0.78
Parliament of Croatia	0.78
Parliament of Denmark	0.78
Parliament of Latvia	0.78
Parliament of Lithuania	0.78
States-General of the Netherlands	0.78
Turkish Grand National Assembly	0.78
Parliament of the United Kingdom	0.78
Assembly of Albania	0.75
Federal Parliament of Belgium	0.75
Parliament of Estonia	0.75
National Assembly of Hungary	0.75
Parliament of Israel	0.75
Parliament of Moldova	0.75
Parliament of Poland	0.75
Parliament of Slovenia	0.75
Austrian Parliament	0.72
Parliament of Canada	0.72
Parliament of Finland	0.72
Parliament of Norway	0.72
Parliament of Romania	0.72
National Council of the Slovak Republic	0.72
The General Courts of Spain	0.72
Parliament of Sweden	0.72
Federal Assembly of Switzerland	0.72
Parliament of New Zealand	0.69
National Assembly of Nicaragua	0.69
National Assembly of Serbia	0.69
Parliament of Ireland	0.66
National Diet of Japan	0.66
National Assembly of Mauritius	0.66
National Parliament of Papua New Guinea	0.66
Congress of Peru	0.66
Uruguayan General Assembly	0.66
Parliament of Australia	0.63
Parliamentary Assembly of Bosnia and Herzegovina	0.63
Parliament of Fiji	0.63
Parliament of India	0.63
Council of Representatives of Iraq	0.63
Parliament of Jamaica	0.63
Assembly of Portugal	0.63
Parliament of South Africa	0.63

COUNTRY	PPI
Congress of the United States of America	0.63
Bangladesh Parliament	0.59
National Assembly of Cambodia	0.59
Legislative Assembly of El Salvador	0.59
Parliament of Georgia	0.59
National Assembly of the ROK (South Korea)	0.59
Legislative Yuan of Taiwan, Republic of China	0.59
National Assembly of Thailand	0.59
Supreme Council of Ukraine	0.59
Armenian National Assembly	0.56
National Assembly of Benin	0.56
National Congress of Brazil	0.56
Congress of Chile	0.56
Congress of Colombia	0.56
Parliament of France	0.56
House of Representatives of Indonesia	0.56
Congress of Paraguay	0.56
Congress of the Philippines	0.56
National Assembly of Burkina Faso	0.53
Legislative Assembly of Costa Rica	0.53
National Congress of Ecuador	0.53
National Congress of Honduras	0.53
Parliament of Lesotho	0.53
Parliament of Trinidad and Tobago	0.53
National Assembly of Venezuela	0.53
Argentine National Congress	0.50
Parliament of Ethiopia	0.50
Congress of Guatemala	0.50
National Assembly of Lebanon	0.50
National Assembly of Namibia	0.50
National Assembly of Niger	0.50
National Assembly of Panama	0.50
Parliament of Sri Lanka	0.50
Parliament of Ghana	0.47
Legislative Assembly of Kyrgyzstan	0.47
National Assembly of Nigeria	0.47
Parliament of Rwanda	0.47
National Parliament of Timor-Leste	0.47
National Assembly of Angola	0.44
Parliament of Azerbaijan	0.44
Bolivian National Congress	0.44
National Assembly of Botswana	0.44
Parliament of Gabon	0.44
National Assembly of Haiti	0.44
Islamic Consultative Assembly of the Islamic Republic of Iran	0.44
National Assembly of Liberia	0.44
Mexican Congress	0.44
Assembly of Mozambique	0.44
Parliament of Nepal	0.44
Parliament of Pakistan	0.44

COUNTRY	PPI	COUNTRY	PPI
Federal Assembly of the Russian Federation	0.44	People's Assembly of Syria	0.31
		Supreme Assembly of Tajikistan	0.31
National Assembly of Senegal	0.44	National Assembly of Tanzania	0.31
National Assembly of Uganda	0.44	Parliament of Zimbabwe	0.31
Parliament of Yemen	0.44	National Assembly of People's Power of Cuba	0.28
Parliament of Burundi	0.41	People's Assembly of Egypt	0.28
House of Representatives of Cyprus	0.41	National Assembly of Laos	0.28
National Congress of the Dominican Republic	0.41	National Parliament of Tunisia	0.28
		Supreme Assembly of Uzbekistan	0.28
National Assembly of Madagascar	0.41	National Assembly of Zambia	0.28
Parliament of Sierra Leone	0.41	Parliament of Algeria	0.25
National Assembly of Afghanistan	0.38	National Assembly of Belarus	0.25
Assembly of Comoros	0.38	National Assembly of Cameroon	0.25
Parliament of Congo-Brazzaville (Republic of Congo)	0.38	National Assembly of Congo-Kinshasa (DRC)	0.25
		National Assembly of Eritrea	0.25
National Assembly of Côte d'Ivoire	0.38	National People's Assembly of Guinea-Bissau	0.25
National Assembly of Guyana	0.38	Parliament of Swaziland	0.25
Parliament of Kazakhstan	0.38	National Assembly of Bhutan	0.22
National Assembly of Kuwait	0.38	National Assembly of Chad	0.22
National Assembly of Malawi	0.38	National Assembly of Jordan	0.22
Parliament of Singapore	0.38	Consultative Council of Qatar	0.22
National Assembly of Togo	0.38	National Legislature of Sudan	0.22
National Assembly of the Central African Republic	0.34	National Assembly of Bahrain	0.19
		Council of Oman	0.16
Chinese National People's Congress	0.34	Supreme People's Assembly of the DPRK (North Korea)	0.13
Parliament of Malaysia	0.34		
National Assembly of Mali	0.34	General People's Congress of Libya	0.13
National Assembly of Vietnam	0.34	Consultative Council of Saudi Arabia	0.09
National Assembly of The Gambia	0.31	People's Council of Turkmenistan	0.06
National Assembly of Guinea	0.31	Federal National Council of the United Arab Emirates	0.06
National Assembly of Kenya	0.31		
Parliament of Mauritania	0.31	People's Assembly of Myanmar (Burma)	0.00
Parliament of Morocco	0.31	Transitional Federal Assembly of Somalia	0.00

4 List of Expert Consultants

Kees Aarts

Shain Abbasov

Jon Abbink

Abdulkhaleq Abdulla

Ron Abney

Andrés Mejía Acosta

Thomas Adelskov

Onek Adyanga

Osita George Afoaku

Julio Javier Aguayo

Q. K. Ahmad

Robert Akoko

Şener Aktürk

Sophia A. B. Akuffo

Achieng Akumu

Emmanuel Akwetey

Muthiah Alagappa

Awadh Al-Badi

Etannibi Alemika

Monique Alexis

Abdulrazak Al-Faris

Essa Al-Ghazali

Kaké Makanéra Al-Hassan

Intigam Aliyev

Taima Aljayoush

Ebtisam Al-Kitbi

Jaak Allik

Hind Al-Sheikh

Alison B. Alter

David Altman

Inge Amundsen

Leslie E. Anderson

Rudy B. Andeweg

Michele Penner Angrist

Milica Antić-Gaber

Hilary Appel

Gloria Ardaya

Esteban Areco

Charles K. Armstrong

Gorkhmaz Askerov

Nizam Assaf

Artur Atanesyan

Canan Atilgan

Daunis Auers

Hermenegildo Avelino

Nicholas Aylott

Vitus A. Azeem

Elisabete Azevedo

Rokia Ba

Greg Basue Babu-Kazadi

David Bach

H. Badjé

Aghi Bahi

Chris Baker

Richard Balme

Sanaullah Baloch

Lok Raj Baral

Naazneen Barma

Matthias Basedau

Francesco Battegazzorre

Rémy Bazenguissa-Ganga

Peter Beck

Abdallah Bedaida

Ahmad Behzad

Ana Maria Bejarano

Souhaïl Belhadj

David S. Bell

Kenneth Benoit

Saltanat Berdikeeva

Deryck M. Bernard

Desiree Bernard

Michael Bernhard

Harry Bhaskara

Stephen Bloom

Jonathan Boston

Igor Botan

Youcef Bouandel

Jean-Philippe Bras

John Bridge

Robin S. Brooks

Sylvain Brouard

Nathan J. Brown

Jason Brownlee

Kathleen Bruhn

Alessandro Bruno

Robert Buddan

L. Burma

Rustam Burnashev

Peter Burnell

Jennifer L. Butz

D. Byambajav

Jean-Pierre Cabestan

Joy Cadogan-Logie

Pietro Calogero

Mohamed Saliou Camara

Roderic A. Camp

David Campbell

Carles Campuzano

Giliberto Capano

Sheila Carapico

Giovanni Carbone

Guy Carcassonne

Dominic Cardy

John M. Carey

William Case

Ernesto Castaneda

Colin S. Cavell

Paul Chambers

Jonathan Chang

Robia Charles

Tun-jen Cheng

Arkady Cherepansky

Irina Chernykh

John Chesterman

Pach Ngoc Chien

Lazhar Chine

Blessings Chinsinga

Jamshed S. A. Choudhury

Yvonne T. Chua

Clive H. Church

John F. Clark

Terry D. Clark

Caty Clement

João Carlos Colaço

Dan Connell

Earl Conteh-Morgan

V. Coopoomootoo

Michael Coppedge

Sheryl Cowan

Philip Cowley

Noel Cox

Stuart Crampton

Frank Cranmer

Harold Crouch

Sally N. Cummings

Mary Cummins

Ruzica Dabić

Markoua Dadjo

Momodou N. Darboe

Paolo Dardanelli

Nestor Davilo

Adeed Dawisha

Brionne Dawson

Wondem Asres Degu

Juan del Aguila

Blanca Martin Delgado

Michael J. Denison

Donald Denoon

Sam Depauw

Kris Deschouwer

Sunanda Deshapriya

Scott W. Desposato

Sanket Dhruva

Malick Diakite

P. Nikiforos Diamandouros

Eduardo Díaz Reyna

Maria Socorro I. Diokno

Mamadou Diouf

Giuseppe Di Palma

Nadia Diuk

Ursula Dorfinger

Michael Dowdle

Ida-Denise Drameh

John Dugas

Annie Dzenga

Gerald M. Easter

Camille Edmond

Piret Ehin

Robert Elgie

Mohamed Abdellahi Mohamed
    Elhacen

Zachary Elkins

Jørgen Elklit

Silam El Yaghmouri

N. Enhbold

B. Enkhbat

Mátyás Eörsi

Bakhodirzhon Ergashev

Bakhtiyor Ergashev

Doğu Ergil

Hans J. Esderts

Navabeh Espahbodi

Flavio Dario Espinal

Abdoulaye Essy

Chris Fadzel

Yun Fan

Foukori Fati

Alain Faupin

Richard F. Fenno

Natalia Ferretti

Florin Fesnic

Jan Fidrmuc

Abdou Filali-Ansary

Rafael Filizzola

Max Fira

Alfred Fofie

Marco Fonseca

Joshua B. Forrest

Jon Fraenkel

Ana Freitas

Natalia Ajenjo Fresno

June Gachui

Alvaro Galvez

Mariam Gamal

Georgi Ganev

Venelin I. Ganev

Guillermo Garcia

Đorđe Gardašević

F. Gregory Gause

Daniel Gbondo

Sisay Gebre-Egziabher

Ömer Gençkaya

James Georgas

Richard Gerding

Angelos S. Gerontas

Pepijn Gerrits

Peter Gey

Bruce Gilley

Jane Rebecca Gingrich

Georgia Gionna

Brian Girvin

Marco Giuliani

Iris Glosemeyer

Martha Gning

Thomas B. Gold

Grigorii Golosov

Ch. Didier Gondola

Lameck Gondwe

Charles Gonthier

Maria Del Pilar Gonzalez Morales

Radu Gorincioi

Lawrence S. Graham

Rüdiger Graichen

Jefferson Morton Gray

Theocharis Grigoriadis

Jean-Germain Gros

Yonko Grozev

Anna M. Grzymała-Busse

Armando Marques
  Guedes

Carlos Guevara Mann

Ram Guragain

Luís Humberto Guzmán

Deepak Gyawali

Sten Hagberg

Magnus Hagevi

Mehrdad Haghayeghi

Samuel Haile

Ivlian Haindrava

Zuhra Halimova

Peter Hallahan

Lawrence Harding

Robert Harding

Erika Harris

Paul Harris

Ernest Harsch

Jonathan Hartlyn

Christof Hartmann

Zijad Hasić

Graham Hassall

Kathryn Hawley

Andrew Heard

John R. Heilbrunn

Daniel Hellinger

Gretchen Helmke

Shahnaz Hemmati

Michael Herb

Victor Hermosillo

Hartmut Hess

Gerti Hesseling

Allen Hicken

Ernst Hillebrand

Dragica Hinić

Jonas Hinnfors

Percy C. Hintzen

Hans Hirter

Robert Hislope

Jakob From Høeg

Barrie Hofmann

David Holiday

John Holm

Muhamad Nadratuzzaman
  Hosen

Mathurin Houngnikpo

Lidija Hristova

Eugene Huskey

Adem Huskić

Adnan Huskić

Christian Hütterer

Elda Hysenllari

Ari Hyytinen

Giuseppe Ieraci

Jānis Ikstens

Basil Ilangakoon

Altin Ilirjani

Ivars Indans

Christine Ingebritsen

Lidia Isamova

Mohammad Isaqzadeh

Jacqueline S. Ismael

Nicholas Jabko

Jakes Jacobs

Rob Jamieson

Krzysztof Jasiewicz

Maiah Jaskoski

Niraja Gopal Jayal

Nikola Jelić

Jadranka Jelinčić

E. G. H. Joffé

Mark P. Jones

Cédric Jourde

Benedict Jua

Mayke Kaag

Paul J. Kaiser

David C. Kang

Katerina Karakehagia

Georgi Karasimeonov

Sebastian Karcher

Kerim Can Kavakli

Jens Kayser

Solomon Kebede

Mari-Ann Kelam

Tunne Kelam

Marisa Kellam

Phil Kelly

Charles H. Kennedy

Apollonia Kerenge

Dimitris Keridis

Joseph Ketan

Abd al-Hadi Khalaf

Mona Khalaf

Mujeeb R. Khan

Nina Khatiskatsi

Sarmad Khawaja

Samuel S. Kim

Andreas Klein

Jacques Paul Klein

James R. Klein

Cassie Knight

Tim Knudsen

Qayyum Kochai

Thomas A. Koelble

Andrew Konitzer-Smirnov

Elahe Koolaee

Elena A. Korosteleva-Polglase

Neam Koy

Ellis S. Krauss

Amie Kreppel

Andrej Krickovic

Algis Krupavicius

Andrei Kunov

Kenji Kushida

Liisa Laakso

Mikko Lagerspetz

Damjan Lajh

Brij V. Lal

Moktar Lam

Bolívar Lamounier

Carl H. Landé

Nick Langton

Remzi Lani

Mong Hay Lao

Jody LaPorte

Peter Larmour

Adrienne LeBas

Gerardo Le Chevallier

Hong Yung Lee

Pei-Shan Lee

Nairobi Legis

Fabrice E. Lehoucq

David K. Leonard

Leonard Letsepe

Peter Lewis

Yury Likhtarovich

Seong-ho Lim

Fernando Limongi

Staffan I. Lindberg

Wolf Linder

Nicole Lindstrom

Johannes Lindvall

I-Chou Liu

Augustin Loada

Richard Lobban

Gerhard Loewenberg

Francis Loh

Timothy Longman

Hugo Lopez

Nehemías López Carrión

Laurence Louër

Claudiu Lucaci

Russell E. Lucas

Oscar Luengo

Alexander Lukashuk

Alvidas Lukosaitis

Thomas Lundberg

Pauline Jones Luong

Ellen Lust-Okar

Jimmy MacClure

Malcolm Mackerras

Jok Madut

Roberta Maffio

Pedro Magalhães

Nanfadima Magassouba

Abdeslam M. Maghraoui

Bruce A. Magnusson

José M. Magone

Gregory S. Mahler

Bettina Malka-Igelbusch

Darina Malovà

Fodé Mané

Christopher P. Manfredi

Carrie L. Manning

Zdenka Mansfeldová

Paul Christopher Manuel

Denis Marantz

Eleanor Marchant

Richard R. Marcus

Alexander Markarov

David R. Marples

Perry Mars

Michael Marsh

Desirèe Masi

Mikitaka Masuyama

Kuldeep Mathur

Peter Matijek

Khabele Matlosa

Mikko Mattila

Zibani Maundeni

Diane K. Mauzy

Demis Mavrellis

René Mayorga

Cédric Mayrargue

Maxime-Faustin Mbringa-
  Takama

Cynthia McClintock

Elizabeth McLeay

Edward McMahon

Alan McRobie

Brendan McSherry

Percy Medina

Andreas Mehler

Pratap Bhanu Mehta

Kirk Meighoo

Heiko Meinhardt

Albert P. Melone

Nimmith Men

Ivona Mendes

P. M. Karibe Mendy

Kidane Mengisteab

El Hadj Kassim Mensah

Immanuel Tatah Mentan

Sheku Mesali

Grigorij Mesežnikov

Sabine Mietzner

José Manuel Minjares Jimenez

Ahmed Mohamed

Amer K. Mohsen

Fatima Mojaddedi

José Molina

Ricardo Sosa Montás

Chelete Monyane

Jeremy Moon

Pete W. Moore

Maggy Morales

Erika Moreno

Bryn Morgan

Michael Morgan

Scott Morgenstern

Leonardo Morlino

Minion K. C. Morrison

Tor Arne Morskogen

Robert Mortimer

Homeira Moshirzadeh

Tamir Moustafa

Nancy Msibi

Aloys Muberanziza

Anne Mugisha

Rwekaza Mukandala

Bhaswar Mukhopadhyay

Pascal Musulay Mukonde

Leonard Mulenga

Mark Mullen

Wolfgang C. Müller

Alina Mungiu-Pippidi

Derwin Munroe

Gary Murphy

Michael Murphy

H. M. Mushala

Tamara Musić

Ana M. Mustapic

Adrian Muunga

Koen Muylle

David Myers

Benito Nacif

Zahara Nampewo

Faizullokhodzha Nasrulloev

Boris Navasardian

Patricio D. Navia

Boubacar N'Diaye

Daniel Neep

Gabriel Negretto

Michael Nelson

Nemanja Nenadić

François Ngolet

Naison Ngoma

Boubacar Niane

Richard G. Niemi

Louis-Marie Nindorera

Ghia Nodia

Akbar Noman

Charles Ntampaka

Artur Nura

Francis B. Nyamnjoh

Kevin J. O'Brien

Gideon Ochanda

Conor O'Dwyer

George Ola-Davies

Eoin O'Malley

Ziya Öniş

Joel M. Ostrow

Emanuele Ottolenghi

Olly Owen

Philip Oxhorn

Oyeleye Oyediran

Simón Pachano

Sari Pajula

Francisco Panizza

Danijel Pantić

Dennis Pantin

Dimitris G. Papadimitriou

Katia Papagianni

Vladimir Paramonov

Chan Wook Park

Andrew Parkin

Haslyn Parris

Jack D. Parson

David Patel

Andrius Pauga

David Payne

Peter Peetz

Eric Pelser

Rita Pemberton

T. J. Pempel

Jehan Perera

Orlando J. Pérez

Aníbal S. Pérez-Liñán

Robert Peri

Kenneth Perkins

Tim Pershing

Pete Peterson

Vladimir Petrović

Ana Petruseva

Pasuk Phongpaichit

Jon Pierre

Natalia Pisareva

Eduardo Pizarro

Grigore Pop-Eleches

Marina Popescu

Margaret Popkin

Natalia Postica

Rodger Potocki

Amit Prakash

Ralph R. Premdas

Robert M. Price

Geoffrey Pridham

Oleh Protsyk

James Putzel

Babak Rahimi

Saumura Rainsy

Lise Rakner

Dominique Rakotomalala

Shinasi A. Rama

Pai Ramachandra

Solofo Randrianja

Bjørn Erik Rasch

Sophoan Rath

Adrien M. Ratsimbaharison

Steven Ratuva

Tapio Raunio

Atiur Rehman

Megan Reif

Thomas F. Remington

Andrei Riabov

Juan Rial

Roberta L. Rice

José Luis Rivas Calero

R. H. O. Robbin-Coker

Jaime Rodríguez-Arana

Philip G. Roessler

Eelis Roikonen

Gérard Roland

Hilmar Rommetvedt

Mark Y. Rosenberg

Frances M. Rosenbluth

Guy Rossatanga-Rignault

Robert I. Rotberg

Sebastián Royo

Lars Rudebeck

Tito Rutaremara

Selwyn D. Ryan

Hawa Sisay Sabally

Alen Sabyrov

Ros Sagnelli

Sebastian M. Saiegh

Reinaldo Saily

Abdoulaye Saine

Rebecca Sako-John

Marwan Sakr

Alaksandar Salajka

Abdi Ismail Samatar

Peter R. Sampson

David Samuels

Richard J. Samuels

David J. Sanders

André de Oliveira Sango

Prakash Raj Sapkota

A. Tobias Schedlbauer

Eric Schickler

Vivien Ann Schmidt

Carsten Schneider

Gerald Schneider

Michael Schoiswohl

Peter J. Schraeder

Robert Schrire

Richard Schultz

Tobias Schulze-Cleven

Jillian Schwedler

Jason Seawright

Christophe Sebudandi

Nicole Seibel

Colette Selman

Jean-François Seznec

Masoud Shafigh

Michael Shafir

Nadia Shafiullah

Aqil Shah

Dina Sharipova

Robert Sharlet

Nicholas Shaxson

Nadim Shehadi

Samer Shehata

Nusrat Sheikh

Nadav Shelef

David H. Shinn

Charles R. Shipan

Hubert Sickinger

Rachel Sieder

Jelena Simjanović

Wendy M. Sinek

Anil Kumar Sinha

Abdulkader Sinno

Eduardo Sitoe

Asbjørn Skjæveland

Richard L. Sklar

Vanja Škorić

Kimberly Smiddy

Nicola Jo-Anne Smith

Susan M. Smith

Christian Soe

Otton Solís

Vladimir Solonari

Roger Southall

Regine Spector

Marc Spindler

Eva Stabell

Joshua Stacher

William Stanley

Aaron M. Stern

Ronald Bruce St. John

Leo Stollwitzer

Bruce Stone

G. J. C. Strydom

Anja Stuckert

Fuad Suleymanov

David Sullivan

Zaida Maria Sultanegy

L. Sumati

Yves Surel

Lars Svåsand

Diana Swain

Richard N. Swett

Marc Swyngedouw

Rein Taagepera

Alexander C. Tan

Ern Ser Tan

Kevin Tan

Moussa Michel Tapsoba

Harold Tarver

Nargess Tavassolian

Michelle M. Taylor-Robinson

Güneş Murat Tezcür

Deepak Thapa

Li-ann Thio

Michael Thurman

Goce Todoroski

Jurij Toplak

Bjarte Tørå

Arne Tostensen

Comi M. Toulabor

Linda Trudel

Valerie Tsanga

Dennis Tull

Aigul Turgunbaeva

Brian Turner

Karen Turner

Renata Uitz

Peter Ulram

Elizabeth Ungar

Rodrigo Uprimny

Jayadeva Uyangoda

Virgis Valentinavicius

Ellie Valentine

Jeff VanDenBerg

Diederik Vandewalle

Nicholas van de Walle

Jan Nico van Overbeeke

Karen van Rompaey

Alison Vasconez

Geronimo Velasco

Elysa Vieira

Kenneth Vigeant

Steven K. Vogel

Tuong Vu

Darren Wagner

Ian Walker

Vibeke Wang

Wei-fang Wang

Leonard Wantchekon

Roshanak Wardak

Colin Waugh

Lucan A. Way

Regina Wegemund

Richard F. Weisfelder

Jeffrey A. Weldon

Susanne Alice Wengle

Kurt Weyland

Erik Wibbels

Hasitha Wickremasinghe

Bruce M. Wilson

Susanna Wing

Jason Wittenberg

Raymond E. Wolfinger

Yu-Shan Wu

Dali L. Yang

Douglas A. Yates

Mossa Yattara

Sovandara Yin

Crawford Young

Reza Yousefian

Maureen Zamora

Rodrigo Zarazaga

María T. Zegada

Saloua Zerhouni

Darius Zeruolis

J. Nicholas Ziegler

Jakub Zielinski

Ricardo Israel Zipper

Eyal Zisser

Joel Zowa

Alan S. Zuckerman

SELECT BIBLIOGRAPHY

Aarts, Kees, Stuart Elaine MacDonald, and George Rabinowitz. "Issues and Party Competition in the Netherlands." *Comparative Political Studies* 32, 1 (February 1999): 63–99.

Abbink, Jon, and Gerti Hessling, eds. *Election Observation and Democratization in Africa*. New York: Palgrave Macmillan, 2000.

Acosta, Andrés Mejía. "Legislative Reelection in Ecuador." *Ecuador Debate* 62 (August 2004): 251–69.

Afoaku, Osita George. *Explaining the Failure of Democracy in the Democratic Republic of Congo: Autocracy and Dissent in an Ambivalent World*. Ceredigion, U.K.: Edwin Mellen, 2005.

Ágh, Attila. "Parliaments as Policy-Making Bodies in East Central Europe: The Case of Hungary." *International Political Science Review* 18, 4 (October 1997): 417–32.

Ahmed, Nizam. "From Monopoly to Competition: Party Politics in the Bangladesh Parliament, 1973–2001." *Pacific Affairs* 76, 1 (Spring 2003): 55–80.

Ahmed, Nizam. "Parliamentary Opposition in Bangladesh: A Study of Its Role in the Fifth Parliament." *Party Politics* 3, 2 (April 1997): 147–68.

Ahmed, Nizam. *The Parliament of Bangladesh*. Aldershot, U.K.: Ashgate, 2002.

Ahmed, Nizam. "Reforming the Parliament in Bangladesh: Structural Constraints and Political Dilemmas." *Commonwealth & Comparative Politics* 36, 1 (March 1998): 68–91.

Ahmed, Nizam, and Shahnaz Khan. "The Development of Parliamentary Oversight in Bangladesh: A Research Note." *Legislative Studies Quarterly* 20, 4 (November 1995): 573–83.

Ahn, Kyong Whan. "The Influence of American Constitutionalism on South Korea." *Southern Illinois Law Journal* 22 (Fall 1997): 71–115.

Akwetey, Emmanuel. *Trade Unions and Democratisation: A Comparative Study of Zambia and Ghana*. Stockholm: Department of Political Science, University of Stockholm, 1994.

Alagappa, Muthiah, ed. *Civil Society and Political Change in Asia*. Stanford, CA: Stanford University Press, 2004.

Alagappa, Muthiah. *Political Legitimacy in Southeast Asia: The Quest for Moral Authority*. Stanford, CA: Stanford University Press, 1995.

Alemán, Eduardo, and Thomas Schwartz. "Presidential Votes in Latin American Constitutions." *Journal of Theoretical Politics* 18, 1 (January 2006): 98–120.

Alemán, Eduardo, and George Tsebelis. "The Origins of Presidential Conditional Agenda-Setting Power in Latin America." *Latin American Research Review* 40, 2 (2005): 3–26.

Alen, André, ed. *Treatise on Belgian Constitutional Law*. Deventer, the Netherlands: Kluwer, 1992.

Al-Fahad, Abdulaziz H. "Ornamental Constitutionalism: The Saudi Basic Law of Governance." *Yale Journal of International Law* 30 (Summer 2005): 375–96.

Alnajjar, Ghanim. "The Challenges Facing Kuwaiti Democracy." *Middle East Journal* 54, 2 (Spring 2000): 242–58.

Alonso, Sonia, and Rubén Ruiz-Rufino. "Political Representation and Ethnic Conflict in New Democracies." *European Journal of Political Research* 46, 2 (March 2007): 237–67.

Alter, Alison B. "Minimizing the Risks of Delegation: Multiple Referral in the German Bundesrat." *American Journal of Political Science* 46, 2 (April 2002): 299–315.

Altman, David. "Popular Initiatives in Uruguay: Confidence Votes on Government or Political Loyalties?" *Electoral Studies* 21, 4 (December 2002): 617–30.

Ames, Barry. *The Deadlock of Democracy in Brazil: Interests, Identities, and Institutions in Comparative Perspective*. Ann Arbor: University of Michigan Press, 2001.

Ames, Barry, Aníbal S. Pérez-Liñán, and Mitchell A. Seligson. *Elites, instituciones y el público: Una nueva mirada a la democracia Boliviana*. La Paz: Universidad Católica Boliviana, 2004.

Amorim Neto, Octavio. "Agenda Power in Brazil's Camara dos Deputados, 1989–98." *World Politics* 55, 4 (July 2003): 550–78.

Amundsen, Inge, Cesaltina Abreu, and Laurinda Hoygaard. *Accountability on the Move: The Parliament of Angola*. Working Paper 11. Bergen, Norway: Chr. Michelsen Institute, 2005.

Anderson, Leslie E. "Postmaterialism from a Peasant Perspective: Political Motivation in Costa Rica and Nicaragua." *Comparative Political Studies* 23, 1 (April 1990): 80–113.

Anderson, Leslie E., and Lawrence C. Dodd. *Learning Democracy: Citizen Engagement and Electoral Choice in Nicaragua, 1990–2001.* Chicago: University of Chicago Press, 2005.

Andeweg, Rudy B. "Centrifugal Forces and Collective Decision-Making: The Case of the Dutch Cabinet." *European Journal of Political Research* 16, 2 (March 1988): 125–51.

Andeweg, Rudy B. "Executive-Legislative Relations in the Netherlands: Consecutive and Coexisting Patterns." *Legislative Studies Quarterly* 17, 2 (May 1992): 161–82.

Andeweg, Rudy B. "Ministers as Double Agents? The Delegation Process between Cabinet and Ministers." *European Journal of Political Research* 37, 3 (May 2000): 377–95.

Andeweg, Rudy B. "Parliamentary Democracy in the Netherlands." *Parliamentary Affairs* 57, 3 (July 2004): 568–80.

Andeweg, Rudy B., and J. J. A. Thomassen. "Modes of Political Representation: Toward a New Typology." *Legislative Studies Quarterly* 30, 4 (November 2005): 507–28.

Andrews, Josephine T., and Gabriella R. Montinola. "Veto Players and the Rule of Law in Emerging Democracies." *Comparative Political Studies* 37, 1 (February 2004): 55–87.

Angrist, Michele Penner. "The Expression of Political Dissent in the Middle East: Turkish Democratization and Authoritarian Continuity in Tunisia." *Comparative Studies in Society and History* 41, 4 (October 1999): 730–57.

Armijo, Leslie Elliot, Philippe Faucher, and Magdalena Dembinska. "Compared to What? Assessing Brazil's Political Institutions." *Comparative Political Studies* 39, 6 (August 2006): 759–86.

Armstrong, Charles K. *Korean Society: Civil Society, Democracy, and the State.* London: Routledge, 2002.

Arter, David. *Scandinavian Politics Today.* Manchester, U.K.: Manchester University Press, 1999.

Atkinson, Michael M., and Paul G. Thomas. "Studying the Canadian Parliament." *Legislative Studies Quarterly* 18, 3 (August 1993): 423–51.

Atwood, Roger. "Democratic Dictators: Authoritarian Politics in Peru from Leguia to Fujimori." *SAIS Review* 21, 2 (Summer–Fall 2001): 155–76.

Auers, Daunis. "European Elections in Eight New EU Member States." *Electoral Studies* 24, 4 (December 2005): 747–54.

Axelrod, Robert. "Building a Strong Legislature: The Western Experience." *PS: Political Science and Politics* 24, 3 (September 1991): 474–8.

Ayee, Joseph R. A. *Decentralization and Conflict: The Case of District Chief Executives and Members of Parliament in Ghana.* Accra: Friedrich Ebert Foundation, 1999.

Ayensu, K. B. *The Evolution of Parliament in Ghana.* Accra: Institute of Economic Affairs, 1999.

Aylott, Nicholas. "Let's Discuss This Later: Party Responses to Euro-Division in Scandinavia." *Party Politics* 8, 4 (July 2002): 441–61.

Aylott, Nicholas. *Swedish Social Democracy and European Integration: The People's Home on the Market.* Aldershot, U.K.: Ashgate, 1999.

Ayupova, Zaure. "The Republic of Kazakhstan: Six Years of Independent Development." *Tulsa Journal of Comparative and International Law* 6 (Fall 1998): 65–76.

Bahro, Horst, Bernhard H. Bayerlein, and Ernst Veser. "Duverger's Concept: Semi-Presidential Government Revisited." *European Journal of Political Research* 34, 6 (October 1998): 201–24.

Baldez, Lisa, and John M. Carey. "Presidential Agenda Control and Spending Policy: Lessons from Pinochet's Constitution." *American Journal of Political Science* 43, 1 (January 1999): 29–55.

Balme, Richard. *Les politiques du néo-régionalisme: Action collective régionale et globalisation.* Paris: Economica, 1996.

Banks, William C., and Edgar Alvarez. "The New Colombian Constitution: Democratic Victory or Popular Surrender?" *University of Miami Inter-American Law Review* 23, 1 (Fall 1991): 40–92.

Baral, Lok Raj, ed. *Election and Governance in Nepal.* New Delhi: Manohar Books, 2005.

Baral, Lok Raj. *Nepal: Problems of Governance.* Delhi: Konark, 1993.

Baral, Lok Raj. "Nepal in 2001: The Strained Monarchy." *Asian Survey* 42, 1 (January–February 2002): 198–202.

Baral, Lok Raj. "The 1994 Nepal Elections: Emerging Trends in Party Politics." *Asian Survey* 35, 5 (May 1995): 426–40.

Barker, Fiona, and Elizabeth McLeay. "How Much Change? An Analysis of the Initial Impact of Proportional Representation on the New Zealand Parliamentary Party System." *Party Politics* 6, 2 (April 2000): 131–54.

Barnes, James F. *Gabon: Beyond the Colonial Legacy.* Boulder, CO: Westview, 1992.

Barros, Robert. *Constitutionalism and Dictatorship: Pinochet, the Junta, and the 1980 Constitution.* Cambridge: Cambridge University Press, 2002.

Bartole, Sergio. "Organizing the Judiciary in Central and Eastern Europe." *East European Constitutional Review* 7, 1 (Winter 1998): 62–9.

Barton, Christopher P. "The Paradox of a Revolutionary Constitution: A Reading of the Nicaraguan Constitution." *Hastings International and Comparative Law Review* 12 (1988–9): 49–102.

Bauer, Gretchen, and Hannah E. Britton, eds. *Women in African Parliaments.* Boulder, CO: Lynne Rienner, 2006.

Baylis, Thomas A. "Presidents versus Prime Ministers: Shaping Executive Authority in Eastern Europe." *World Politics* 48, 3 (April 1996): 297–323.

Bazenguissa-Ganga, Rémy. "The Spread of Political Violence in Congo-Brazzaville." *African Affairs* 98, 390 (January 1999): 37–54.

Bazenguissa-Ganga, Rémy. *Les voies du politique au Congo: Essai de sociologie historique.* Paris: Karthala, 1997.

Beckett, Paul A., and Crawford Young, eds. *Dilemmas of Democracy in Nigeria.* Rochester, NY: University of Rochester Press, 1997.

Belge, Ceren. "Friends of the Court: The Republican Alliance and Selective Activism of the Constitutional Court of Turkey." *Law and Society Review* 40 (September 2006): 653–92.

Bell, David S. *French Politics Today.* Manchester, U.K.: Manchester University Press, 2002.

Bell, David S. "Parliamentary Democracy in France." *Parliamentary Affairs* 57, 3 (July 2004): 533–49.

Bell, David S., and Byron Criddle. "Presidentialism Restored: The French Elections of April–May and June 2002." *Parliamentary Affairs* 55, 4 (October 2002): 643–63.

Benoit, Kenneth. "Models of Electoral Change." *Electoral Studies* 23, 3 (September 2004): 363–89.

Benoit, Kenneth, and Jacqueline Hayden. "Institutional Change and Persistence: The Evolution of Poland's Electoral System, 1989–2001." *Journal of Politics* 66, 2 (May 2004): 396–427.

Benoit, Kenneth, and John W. Schiemann. "Institutional Choice in New Democracies: Bargaining over Hungary's 1989 Electoral Law." *Journal of Theoretical Politics* 13, 2 (April 2001): 153–82.

Berglund, Sten, Frank H. Aarebrot, Henri Vogt, and Georgi Karasimeonov, eds. *Challenges to Democracy: Eastern Europe Ten Years after the Collapse of Communism.* Northampton, MA: Edward Elgar, 2001.

Bernard, Deryck M. *A New Geography of Guyana.* Oxford: Macmillan Education, 1999.

Bernhard, Michael. "Civil Society after the First Transition: Dilemmas of Post-Communist Democratization in Poland and Beyond." *Communist and Post-Communist Studies* 29, 3 (September 1996): 309–30.

Bernhard, Michael. *Institutions and the Fate of Democracy: Germany and Poland in the Twentieth Century.* Pittsburgh, PA: University of Pittsburgh Press, 2005.

Berry, William D., Michael B. Berkman, and Stuart Schneiderman. "Legislative Professionalism and Incumbent Reelection: The Development of Institutional Boundaries." *American Political Science Review* 94, 4 (December 2000): 859–74.

Bhavna, Dave. "Kazakhstan's 2004 Parliamentary Elections: Managing Loyalty and Support for the Regime." *Problems of Post-Communism* 52, 1 (January–February 2005): 3–14.

Biberaj, Elez. *Albania in Transition: The Rocky Road to Democracy.* Boulder, CO: Westview, 1998.

Bingen, R. James, David Robinson, and John M. Staatz. *Democracy and Development in Mali.* East Lansing: Michigan State University Press, 2000.

Birch, Sarah, Frances Millard, Marina Popescu, and Kieran Williams. *Embodying Democracy: Electoral System Design in Post-Communist Europe.* Basingstoke, U.K.: Palgrave Macmillan, 2003.

Black, Duncan. *The Theory of Committees and Elections.* Cambridge: Cambridge University Press, 1958.

Blais, André, Louis Massicotte, and Agnieszka Dobrzynaska. "Direct Presidential Elections: A World Summary." *Electoral Studies* 16, 4 (December 1997): 441–55.

Blankart, Charles B., and Dennis C. Mueller. "The Advantages of Pure Forms of Parliamentary Democracy over Mixed Forms." *Public Choice* 121, 3–4 (December 2004): 431–52.

Blondel, Jean, and Ferdinand Muller-Rommel. *Cabinets in Eastern Europe.* New York: Palgrave Macmillan, 2001.

Bonora-Waisman, Camille. *France and the Algerian Conflict: Issues in Democracy and Political Stability, 1988–1995.* Aldershot, U.K.: Ashgate, 2003.

Boston, Jonathan, Stephen Church, and Tim Bale. "The Impact of Proportional Representation on Government Effectiveness: The New Zealand Experience." *Australian Journal of Public Administration* 62, 4 (December 2003): 7–22.

Boston, Jonathan, Paul Dalziel, and Susan St. John. *Redesigning the Welfare State in New Zealand: Problems, Policies, Prospects.* New York: Oxford, 1999.

Boston, Jonathan, Stephen Levine, Elizabeth McLeay, and Nigel S. Roberts. "Experimenting with Coalition Government: Preparing to Manage under Proportional Representation in New Zealand." *Journal of Commonwealth & Comparative Politics* 35, 3 (November 1997): 108–26.

Bouandel, Youcef. "Algeria's Presidential Election of April 2004: A Backward Step in the Democratisation Process or a Forward Step towards Stability?" *Third World Quarterly* 25, 8 (2004): 1525–40.

Bouandel, Youcef. "Political Parties and the Transition from Authoritarianism: The Case of Algeria." *Journal of Modern African Studies* 41, 1 (March 2003): 1–22.

Bouandel, Youcef, and Yahia H. Zoubir. "Algeria's Elections: The Prelude to Democratization." *Third World Quarterly* 19, 2 (June 1998): 177–90.

Brady, David W. *Critical Elections and Congressional Policy Making.* Stanford, CA: Stanford University Press, 1988.

Brand, D. J. "Constitutional Reform: The South African Experience." *Cumberland Law Review* 33 (2002–3): 1–14.

Bratton, Michael. "Formal versus Informal Institutions in Africa." *Journal of Democracy* 18, 3 (July 2007): 96–110.

Bratton, Michael, and Nicolas van de Walle. *Democratic Experiments in Africa: Regime Transitions in Comparative Perspective.* New York: Cambridge University Press, 1998.

Bräuninger, Thomas, and Thomas König. "The Checks and Balances of Party Federalism: German Federal Government in a Divided Legislature." *European Journal of Political Research* 36, 2 (October 1999): 207–34.

Bridge, John W. "Judicial Review in Mauritius and the Continuing Influence of English Law." *International and Comparative Law Quarterly* 46 (1997): 787–811.

Britton, Hannah E. "Coalition Building, Election Rules, and Party Politics: South African Women's Path to Parliament." *Africa Today* 49, 4 (Winter 2002): 33–67.

Brown, Ian Richard. "Clinging to Democracy: Assessing the Russian Legislative-Executive Relationship under Boris Yeltsin's Constitution." *Vanderbilt Journal of Transitional Law* 33 (May 2000): 645–91.

Brown, Nathan J. *Constitutions in a Nonconstitutional World: Arab Basic Laws and the Prospects for Accountable Government.* Albany: State University of New York Press, 2001.

Brown, Nathan J. "Regimes Reinventing Themselves: Constitutional Development in the Arab World." *International Sociology* 18, 1 (March 2003): 33–52.

Brownlee, Jason. " . . . And Yet They Persist: Explaining Survival and Transition in Neopatrimonial Regimes." *Studies in Comparative International Development* 37, 3 (Fall 2002): 35–63.

Brownlee, Jason. "The Decline of Pluralism in Mubarak's Egypt." *Journal of Democracy* 13, 4 (October 2002): 6–14.

Bruhn, Kathleen. *Taking on Goliath: The Emergence of a New Left Party and the Struggle for Democracy in Mexico.* University Park: Pennsylvania State University Press, 1996.

Brzezinski, Mark F. "Constitutional Heritage and Renewal: The Case of Poland." *Virginia Law Review* 77 (February 1991): 49–112.

Brzezinski, Mark F., and Leszek Garlicki. "Judicial Review in Post-Communist Poland: The Emergence of a Rechtsstaat?" *Stanford Journal of International Law* 31 (Winter 1995): 13–59.

Buddan, Robert. *Foundations of Caribbean Politics.* Kingston: Arawak, 2001.

Budge, Ian, and David H. McKay, eds. *Developing Democracy: Comparative Research in Honour of J. F. P. Blondel.* London: Sage, 1994.

Burnell, Peter, ed. *Democratization through the Looking Glass: Comparative Perspectives on Democratization.* Manchester, U.K.: University of Manchester Press, 2005.

Burnell, Peter. "Parliamentary Committees in Zambia's Third Republic: Partial Reforms, Unfinished Agenda." *Journal of Southern African Studies* 28, 2 (June 2002): 291–313.

Burnell, Peter. "Zambia's 2001 Elections." *Third World Quarterly* 23, 6 (December 2002): 1103–20.

Burnell, Peter, and Peter Calvert, eds. *Civil Society in Democratization.* London: Frank Cass, 2004.

Cabestan, Jean-Pierre. *L'administration chinoise après Mao: Les réformes de l'ère Deng Xiaopong et leurs limites.* Paris: Presses du CNRS, 1992.

Cabestan, Jean-Pierre. "China on the Way to Neoauthoritarianism, or the Revenge of Zhao Ziyang." *Revue d'études comparatives est-ouest* 23, 1 (March 1992): 5–27.

Cabestan, Jean-Pierre. *Le système politique de la Chine populaire.* Paris: Presses universitaires de France, 1994.

Caciagli, Mario, and Alan S. Zuckerman, eds. *Italian Politics: Emerging Themes and Institutional Responses.* Oxford: Berghahn Books, 2002.

Calvert, Randall L., and Richard F. Fenno. "Strategy and Sophisticated Voting in the Senate." *Journal of Politics* 56, 2 (May 1994): 349–76.

Calvo, Ernesto, and Maria Victoria Murillo. "Who Delivers? Partisan Clients in the Argentine Electoral Market." *American Journal of Political Science* 48, 4 (October 2004): 742–57.

Camara, Mohamed Saliou. *His Master's Voice: Mass Communication and Single-Party Politics in Guinea under Sékou Touré.* Trenton, NJ: Africa World Press, 2005.

Cameron, Maxwell A. "Latin American Autogolpes: Dangerous Undertows in the Third Wave of Democratization." *Third World Quarterly* 19, 2 (June 1998): 219–39.

Cameron, Maxwell A. "Self-Coups: Peru, Guatemala, and Russia." *Journal of Democracy* 9, 1 (January 1998): 125–39.

Camp, Roderic A. "Performing on the Mexican Democratic Stage: New Actors, New Scripts." *Latin American Research Review* 38, 2 (2003): 195–206.

Camp, Roderic A. *Politics in Mexico: The Decline of Authoritarianism.* New York: Oxford University Press, 1999.

Camp, Roderic A. *Politics in Mexico: The Democratic Transformation.* New York: Oxford University Press, 2002.

Carapico, Sheila. *Civil Society in the Yemen: The Political Economy of Activism in Modern Arabia.* Cambridge: Cambridge University Press, 1998.

Carcassone, Guy. *La Constitution.* Paris: Seuil, 2002.

Carcassonne, Guy. "France: *Conseil Constitutionnel* on the European Constitutional Treaty. Decision of 19 November 2004 2004–505 DC." *European Constitutional Law Review* 1, 2 (June 2005): 293–301.

Caress, Stanley M. "The Impact of Term Limits on Legislative Behavior: An Examination of a Transitional Legislature." *PS: Political Science and Politics* 29, 4 (December 1996): 671–6.

Carey, John M. "Competing Principals, Political Institutions, and Party Unity in Legislative Voting." *American Journal of Political Science* 51, 1 (January 2007): 92–107.

Carey, John M. "Discipline, Accountability, and Legislative Voting in Latin America." *Comparative Politics* 35, 2 (January 2003): 191–211.

Carey, John M. "Insurance for Good Losers and the Survival of Chile's Concertacion." *Latin American Politics & Society* 47, 2 (Summer 2005): 1–22.

Carey, John M. "The Reelection Debate in Latin America." *Latin American Politics & Society* 45, 1 (Spring 2003): 119–33.

Carey, John M. *Term Limits and Legislative Representation*. New York: Cambridge University Press, 1998.

Carey, John M. "Transparency versus Collective Action: Fujimori's Legacy and the Peruvian Congress." *Comparative Political Studies* 36, 9 (November 2003): 983–1006.

Carey, John M., Frantisek Formanek, and Ewa Karpowicz. "Legislative Autonomy in New Regimes: The Czech and Polish Cases." *Legislative Studies Quarterly* 24, 4 (November 1999): 569–603.

Carey, John M., Richard Niemi, and Lynda Powell. *Term Limits in the State Legislatures*. Ann Arbor: University of Michigan Press, 2000.

Carey, John M., and Matthew Soberg Shugart. *Executive Decree Authority*. New York: Cambridge University Press, 1998.

Case, William. "Malaysia's Resilient Pseudodemocracy." *Journal of Democracy* 12, 1 (January 2001): 43–57.

Case, William. "New Uncertainties for an Old Pseudo-Democracy: The Case of Malaysia." *Comparative Politics* 37, 1 (October 2004): 83–104.

Case, William. *Politics in Southeast Asia: Democracy or Less*. London: RoutledgeCurzon, 2003.

Case, William. "Singapore in 2002: Economic Lassitude and Threats to Security." *Asian Survey* 43, 1 (January–February 2003): 167–73.

Ceica, Ilona, and Ligita Vasermane. "Latvian Law Guide." *International Journal of Legal Information* 20 (Spring 2003): 31–45.

Chaisty, Paul. "Party Cohesion and Policy-Making in Russia." *Party Politics* 11, 3 (May 2005): 299–318.

Chaisty, Paul, and Petra Schleiter. "Productive but Not Valued: The Russian State Duma, 1994–2001." *Europe-Asia Studies* 54, 5 (July 2002): 701–24.

Chambers, Paul. "Evolving toward What? Parties, Factions, and Coalition Behavior in Thailand Today." *Journal of East Asian Studies* 5, 3 (September–December 2005): 495–520.

Chandler, Andrea. "Presidential Veto Power in Post-Communist Russia, 1994–1998." *Canadian Journal of Political Science* 34, 3 (September 2001): 487–516.

Charlick, Robert. *Niger: Personal Rule and Survival in the Sahel*. Boulder, CO: Westview, 1991.

Cheibub, José Antonio. *Presidentialism, Parliamentarism, and Democracy*. New York: Cambridge University Press, 2006.

Cheibub, José Antonio, and Fernando Limongi. "Democratic Institutions and Regime Survival: Parliamentary and Presidential Democracies Reconsidered." *Annual Review of Political Science* 5 (2002): 151–79.

Cheibub, José Antonio, Adam Przeworski, and Sebastian M. Saiegh. "Government Coalitions and Legislature Success under Presidentialism and Parliamentarism." *British Journal of Political Science* 34, 4 (October 2004): 565–87.

Cheng, Tun-jen. "Democratizing the Quasi-Leninist Regime in Taiwan." *World Politics* 41, 4 (July 1989): 471–99.

Cheng, Tun-jen, and Stephan Haggard, eds. *Political Change in Taiwan*. Boulder, CO: Lynne Rienner, 1991.

Cheng, Tun-jen, and Yi-shing Liao. "Taiwan in 1997: An Embattled Government in Search of New Opportunities." *Asian Survey* 38, 1 (January 1998): 53–63.

Chia, Ngam. *Political Power and Elections in Cameroon*. Bamenda, Cameroon: N.I.P. Publications, 1992.

Chibesakunda, Ng'ona Mwelwa. *The Parliament of Zambia*. Lusaka: National Assembly of Zambia, 2001.

Chirot, Daniel. "The Debacle in Côte d'Ivoire." *Journal of Democracy* 17, 2 (April 2006): 63–77.

Chodakiewicz, Marek Jan, John Radziłowski, and Dariusz Tołczyk, eds. *Poland's Transformation: A Work in Progress*. Charlottesville, VA: Leopolis Press, 2003.

Chua, Yvonne T. *Robbed: An Investigation of Corruption in Philippine Education*. Quezon City: Philippine Center for Investigative Journalism, 1999.

Church, Clive H. *The Politics and Government of Switzerland*. Basingstoke, U.K.: Palgrave Macmillan, 2004.

Clark, Andrew. "From Military Dictatorship to Democracy: The Democratization Process in Mali." *Journal of Third World Studies* 12, 1 (1995): 201–19.

Clark, John F. "The Neo-Colonial Context of the Democratic Experiment of Congo-Brazzaville." *African Affairs* 101, 403 (April 2002): 171–92.

Clark, John F., and David E. Gardinier, eds. *Political Reform in Francophone Africa*. Boulder, CO: Westview, 1997.

Clark, John F., and Bruce Magnusson. "Understanding Democratic Survival and Democratic Failure in Africa: Insights from the Divergent Democratic Experiments in Benin and Congo (Brazzaville)." *Comparative Studies in Society and History* 47, 3 (July 2005): 552–82.

Clark, Terry D. *Beyond Post-Communist Studies: Political Science and the New Democracies of Europe.* Armonk, NY: M. E. Sharpe, 2002.

Clark, Terry D. "Introduction: The Democratic Consolidation of Lithuania's State Institutions." *Journal of Baltic Studies* 32, 2 (Summer 2001): 125–40.

Clark, Terry D., and Nerijus Prekevičius. "Explaining the 2000 Lithuanian Parliamentary Elections: An Application of Contextual and New Institutional Approaches." *Slavic Review* 62, 3 (Fall 2003): 548–69.

Clark, Terry D., and Jill N. Wittrock. "Presidentialism and the Effect of Electoral Law in Postcommunist Systems: Regime Type Matters." *Comparative Political Studies* 38, 2 (March 2005): 171–88.

Clark, William A. "The Russian State Duma: 1993, 1995, and 1999." *Problems of Post-Communism* 46, 6 (November–December 1999): 3–11.

Colton, Timothy J. "Superpresidentialism and Russia's Backward State." *Post-Soviet Affairs* 11, 2 (April–June 1995): 144–8.

Conaghan, Catherine M. *Fujimori's Peru: Deception in the Public Sphere.* Pittsburgh, PA: University of Pittsburgh Press, 2005.

Conley, Richard S., and Amie Kreppel. "Toward a New Typology of Vetoes and Overrides." *Political Research Quarterly* 54, 4 (December 2001): 831–52.

Conteh-Morgan, Earl. *Democratization in Africa.* Westport, CT: Praeger, 1997.

Conteh-Morgan, Earl, and Mac Dixon-Fyle. *Sierra Leone at the End of the Twentieth Century: History, Politics, and Society.* New York: Peter Lang, 1999.

Coomaraswamy, Radhika, and Charmaine de los Reyes. "Rule by Emergency: Sri Lanka's Postcolonial Constitutional Experience." *International Journal of Constitutional Law* 2 (April 2004): 272–95.

Copeland, Gary W., and Samuel C. Patterson, eds. *Parliaments in the Modern World: Changing Institutions.* Ann Arbor: University of Michigan Press, 1994.

Coppedge, Michael. "Parties and Society in Mexico and Venezuela: Why Competition Matters." *Comparative Politics* 25, 3 (April 1993): 253–74.

Coppedge, Michael. *Strong Parties and Lame Ducks: Presidential Partyarchy and Factionalism in Venezuela.* Stanford, CA: Stanford University Press, 1994.

Corrales, Javier. *Presidents without Parties: The Politics of Economic Reform in Argentina and Venezuela in the 1990s.* University Park: Pennsylvania State University Press, 2002.

Cowley, Philip, ed. *Conscience and Parliament.* London: Frank Cass, 1998.

Cowley, Philip, and David Melhuish. "Peers' Careers: Ministers in the House of Lords, 1964–95." *Political Studies* 45, 1 (March 1997): 21–35.

Cowley, Philip, and Mark Stuart. "In Place of Strife? The PLP in Government, 1997–2001." *Political Studies* 51, 2 (June 2003): 315–31.

Cowley, Philip, and Mark Stuart. "Parliament: Hunting for Votes." *Parliamentary Affairs* 58, 2 (April 2005): 258–71.

Cowley, Philip, and Mark Stuart. "Parliament: More Revolts, More Reform." *Parliamentary Affairs* 56, 2 (April 2003): 188–204.

Cowley, Philip, and Mark Stuart. "Sodomy, Slaughter, Sunday Shopping and Seatbelts: Free Votes in the House of Commons, 1979 to 1996." *Party Politics* 3, 1 (January 1997): 119–30.

Cox, Gary W. *Making Votes Count: Strategic Coordination in the World's Electoral Systems.* Cambridge: Cambridge University Press, 1997.

Cox, Gary W., and Mathew D. McCubbins. *Legislative Leviathan: Party Government in the House.* Berkeley: University of California Press, 1993.

Cox, Gary W., and Scott Morgenstern. "Latin America's Proactive Presidents and Reactive Parliaments." *Comparative Politics* 33, 2 (January 2001): 171–89.

Cox, Gary W., and Frances M. Rosenbluth. "Factional Competition for the Party Endorsement: The Case of Japan's Liberal Democratic Party." *British Journal of Political Science* 26, 2 (April 1996): 259–69.

Cox, Gary W., Frances M. Rosenbluth, and Michael F. Thies. "Electoral Rules, Career Ambitions, and Party Structure: Comparing Factions in Japan's Upper and Lower Houses." *American Journal of Political Science* 44, 1 (January 2000): 115–22.

Crouch, Harold. *Government and Society in Malaysia.* Ithaca, NY: Cornell University Press, 1996.

Crowther, William E., and Irmina Matonyte. "Parliamentary Elites as a Democratic Thermometer: Estonia, Lithuania, and Moldova Compared." *Communist and Post-Communist Studies* 40, 3 (September 2007): 281–99.

Cruz Oliva, José A. *El Movimiento Ciudadano Hondureño y su relación con el Partido de Unificación Democrática: Una investigación de sociología política.* Tegucigalpa: Ediciones CIDEH, 1999.

Cummings, Sally N., ed. *Power and Change in Central Asia.* London: Routledge, 2001.

Cummings, Sally N., and Ole Nørgaard. "Conceptualizing State Capacity: Comparing Kazakhstan and Kyrgyzstan." *Political Studies* 52, 4 (December 2004): 685–708.

Curtis, Grant. *Cambodia Reborn? The Transition to Democracy and Development.* Washington, DC: Brookings Institution Press, 1998.

Cutler, Lloyd N., and Herman Schwartz. "Constitutional Reform in Czechoslovakia: E Duobus Unum?" *University of Chicago Law Review* 58 (Spring 1991): 511–53.

Dahl, Robert A. *Dilemmas of Pluralist Democracy.* New Haven, CT: Yale University Press, 1982.

Dardanelli, Paolo. *Between Two Unions.* Manchester, U.K.: Manchester University Press, 2006.

Dardanelli, Paolo. "The Parliamentary and Executive Elections in Switzerland, 2003." *Electoral Studies* 24, 1 (March 2005): 123–9.

Dawisha, Adeed. *Arab Nationalism in the Twentieth Century: From Triumph to Despair*. Princeton, NJ: Princeton University Press, 2005.

Dawisha, Adeed, and Larry Diamond. "Iraq's Year of Living Dangerously." *Journal of Democracy* 17, 2 (April 2006): 89–103.

Defeis, Elizabeth F. "Constitution Building in Armenia: A Nation Once Again." *Parker School Journal of East European Law* 2, 2 (1995): 153–200.

Della Sala, Vincent. "The Permanent Committees of the Italian Chamber of Deputies: Parliament at Work?" *Legislative Studies Quarterly* 18, 2 (May 1993): 157–83.

Denoon, Donald, Philippa Mein Smith, and Marivic Wyndham. *A History of Australia, New Zealand and the Pacific*. Oxford: Blackwell, 2000.

Derbyshire, J. Denis, and Ian Derbyshire. *Political Systems of the World*. New York: St. Martin's, 1996.

Deschouwer, Kris. "Political Parties in Multi-Layered Systems." *European Urban and Regional Studies* 10, 3 (July 2003): 213–26.

De Smith, S. A. "Mauritius: Constitutionalism in a Plural Society." *Modern Law Review* 31, 6 (November 1968): 601–22.

De Sousa Santos, Boaventura. "The Heterogeneous State and Legal Pluralism in Mozambique." *Law and Society Review* 40 (March 2006): 39–75.

Desposato, Scott W. "Legislative Politics in Authoritarian Brazil." *Legislative Studies Quarterly* 26, 2 (May 2001): 287–317.

Diamandouros, P. Nikiforos, and Richard Gunther. *Parties, Politics, and Democracy in the New Southern Europe*. Baltimore, MD: Johns Hopkins University Press, 2001.

Diamond, Larry. *Developing Democracy: Toward Consolidation*. Baltimore, MD: Johns Hopkins University Press, 1999.

Diamond, Larry, and Marc F. Plattner, eds. *Democratization in Africa*. Baltimore, MD: Johns Hopkins University Press, 1999.

Diaw, Moussa. 1998. "Elections et pouvoir tribal en Mauritanie." *Politique africaine* 71 (1998): 156–64.

Diescho, Joseph. *Government and Opposition in Post-Independence Namibia: Perceptions and Performance*. Windhoek: Konrad-Adenauer-Stiftung and Namibia Institute for Democracy, 1996.

Dingake, Oagile. *Key Aspects of the Constitutional Law of Botswana*. Gaborone: Pula Press, 2000.

Diokno, Maria Socorro I. *Human Rights Centered Development*. Honolulu: University of Hawaii Press, 2005.

Diop, Momar Coumba, and Mamadou Diouf. "Enjeux et contraintes politiques de la gestion municipale au Sénégal." *Canadian Journal of African Studies* 26, 1 (1992): 1–23.

Diouf, Mamadou. "L'échec du modèle démocratique du Sénégal, 1981–1993." *Afrika Spectrum* 29, 1 (1994): 47–64.

Di Palma, Giuseppe. "Founding Coalitions in Southern Europe: Legitimacy and Hegemony." *Government and Opposition* 15, 2 (1980): 162–89.

Di Palma, Giuseppe. "Institutional Rules and Legislative Outcomes in the Italian Parliament." *Legislative Studies Quarterly* 1, 2 (May 1976): 147–79.

Di Palma, Giuseppe. "Legitimation from the Top to Civil Society." *World Politics* 44, 1 (October 1991): 49–80.

Di Palma, Giuseppe. *Surviving without Governing: The Italian Parties in Parliament*. Berkeley: University of California Press, 1977.

Diuk, Nadia. "Ukraine: A Land in Between." *Journal of Democracy* 9, 3 (July 1998): 97–111.

Döring, Herbert. "Parliamentary Agenda Control and Legislative Outcomes in Western Europe." *Legislative Studies Quarterly* 26, 1 (February 2001): 145–65.

Döring, Herbert, ed. *Parliaments and Majority Rule in Western Europe*. New York: Palgrave Macmillan, 1995.

Dugan, John. *Structure and Agency in Explaining Democratization: Insights from the Colombian Case*. Bloomington: Indiana Center on Global Change and World Peace, 1994.

Duverger, Maurice. "A New Political System Model: Semi-Presidential Government." *European Journal of Political Research* 8, 1 (June 1980): 165–87.

Easter, Gerald M. "Preference for Presidentialism: Postcommunist Regime Change in Russia and the NIS." *World Politics* 49, 2 (January 1997): 184–211.

Eaton, Kent. "Parliamentarism and Presidentialism in the Policy Arena." *Comparative Politics* 32, 3 (October 2000): 355–76.

Eaton, Kent. "The Politics of Re-Centralization in Argentina and Brazil." *Latin American Research Review* 39, 1 (2004): 90–122.

Eboussi-Boulaga, Fabien. *Les conférences nationales en Afrique noire: Une affaire à suivre*. Paris: Karthala, 1993.

Edgar, Timothy H., and Michael D. Nicoleau. "Constitutional Governance in the Democratic Republic of the Congo: An Analysis of the Constitution Proposed by the Government of Laurent Kabila." *Texas International Law Journal* 35, 2 (Spring 2000): 207–37.

Edie, Carlene J. 2000. "Democracy in The Gambia: Past, Present and Prospect for the Future." *Africa Development* 25, 3/4 (2000): 161–98.

Ehin, Piret. "Determinants of Public Support for EU Membership: Data from the Baltic Countries." *European Journal of Political Research* 40, 1 (August 2001): 31–56.

Elgie, Robert. "The Classification of Democratic Regime Types: Conceptual Ambiguity and Contestable Assumptions." *European Journal of Political Research* 33, 2 (March 1998): 219–38.

Elgie, Robert. "Semi-Presidentialism: Concepts, Consequences and Contesting Explanations." *Political Studies Review* 2, 3 (2004): 314–30.

Elgie, Robert, ed. *Semi-Presidentialism in Europe.* Oxford: Oxford University Press, 1999.

El-Khawas, Mohamed A. "Democracy in Africa: Problems and Solutions." *Mediterranean Quarterly* 12, 3 (Summer 2001): 85–97.

Elklit, Jørgen, and N. S. Roberts. "A Category of Its Own? Four PR Two-Tier Compensatory Member Electoral Systems in 1994." *European Journal of Political Research* 30, 2 (September 1996): 217–40.

Engberg-Pederson, Lars. *Endangering Development: Politics, Projects, and Environment in Burkina Faso.* Westport, CT: Praeger, 2003.

Englebert, Pierre. *Burkina Faso: Unsteady Statehood in West Africa.* Boulder, CO: Westview, 1996.

Englebert, Pierre. *State Legitimacy and Development in Africa.* Boulder, CO: Lynne Rienner, 2000.

English, Linda, and James Guthrie. "Mandate, Independence, and Funding: Resolution of a Protracted Struggle between Parliament and the Executive over the Powers of the Australian Auditor-General." *Australian Journal of Public Administration* 59, 1 (March 2000): 98–114.

Ergil, Doğu. "The Kurdish Question in Turkey." *Journal of Democracy* 11, 3 (July 2000): 122–35.

Esaiasson, Peter, and Knut Heider, eds. *Beyond Westminster and Congress: The Nordic Experience.* Columbus: Ohio State University Press, 2000.

Esaiasson, Peter, and Sören Holmberg. *Representation from Above: Members of Parliament and Representative Democracy in Sweden.* Aldershot, U.K.: Dartmouth, 1996.

Escobar-Lemmon, Maria. "Political Support for Decentralization: An Analysis of the Colombian and Venezuelan Legislatures." *American Journal of Political Science* 47, 4 (October 2003): 683–97.

Fabbrini, Sergio. "Presidents, Parliaments, and Good Government." *Journal of Democracy* 6, 3 (July 1995): 128–38.

Fay, Claude. "La démocratie au Mali, ou le pouvoir en pâture." *Cahiers d'étude africaines* 35, 137 (1995): 19–53.

Fenno, Richard F. *Congress at the Grassroots: Representational Change in the South, 1970–1998.* Chapel Hill: University of North Carolina Press, 2000.

Fenno, Richard F. *Congressmen in Committees.* Boston: Little, Brown, 1973.

Fenno, Richard F. *The Power of the Purse: Appropriations Politics in Congress.* Boston: Little, Brown, 1966.

Ferejohn, John, and Charles R. Shipan. "Congressional Influence on Bureaucracy." *Journal of Law,* *Economics, and Organization* 6, Special Issue (1990): 1–20.

Ferreira Rubio, Delia, and Matteo Goretti. "Cuando el presidente gobierna solo: Menem y los decretos de necesidad y urgencia hasta la reforma constitucional (julio 1989–agosto 1994)." *Desarrollo Económico – Revista de Ciencias Sociales* 36, 141 (April–June 1996): 443–74.

Fidrmuc, Jan. "Economics of Voting in Postcommunist Countries." *Electoral Studies* 19, 2–3 (June–September 2000): 199–217.

Figueiredo, Argelina Cheibub, and Fernando Limongi. "Presidential Power, Legislative Organization, and Party Behavior in Brazil." *Comparative Politics* 32, 2 (January 2000): 151–70.

Filali-Ansary, Abdou. "Muslims and Democracy." *Journal of Democracy* 10, 3 (July 1999): 18–32.

Filali-Ansary, Abdou. *Par souci de clarté: A propos des sociétés musulmanes contemporaines.* Casablanca, Morocco: Editions le Fennec, 2001.

Fish, M. Steven. *Democracy Derailed in Russia: The Failure of Open Politics.* New York: Cambridge University Press, 2005.

Fish, M. Steven. "The End of Meciarism." *East European Constitutional Review* 8, 1–2 (Winter–Spring 1999): 47–55.

Fish, M. Steven. "Mongolia: Democracy without Prerequisites." *Journal of Democracy* 9, 3 (July 1998): 127–41.

Fish, M. Steven. "Stronger Legislatures, Stronger Democracy." *Journal of Democracy* 17, 1 (January 2006): 5–20.

Fitzgibbon, Russell H., ed. *The Constitutions of the Americas.* Chicago: University of Chicago Press, 1948.

Flinders, Matthew. "Shifting the Balance? Parliament, the Executive, and the British Constitution." *Political Studies* 50, 1 (March 2002): 23–42.

Fombad, Charles Manga. "Cameroon's Emergency Powers: A Recipe for (Un)constitutional Dictatorship?" *Journal of African Law* 48, 1 (2004): 62–81.

Fombad, Charles Manga. "The Separation of Powers and Constitutionalism in Africa: The Case of Botswana." *Boston College Third World Law Journal* 25, 2 (Spring 2005): 301–42.

Fomunyoh, Christopher. "Democratization in Fits and Starts." *Journal of Democracy* 12, 3 (July 2001): 37–50.

Fonseca, Marco. *Entre la comunidad y la república: Ensayos sobre ciudadanía y sociedad civil en Guatemala.* Guatemala: F & G Editores, 2004.

Ford, Christopher A. "The Indigenization of Constitutionalism in the Japanese Experience." *Case Western Reserve Journal of International Law* 28, 1 (Winter 1996): 3–62.

Forrest, Joshua B. "Ethnic State Political Relations in Postapartheid Namibia." *Journal of Commonwealth & Comparative Politics* 32, 3 (November 1994): 300–23.

Forrest, Joshua B. *Lineages of State Fragility: Rural Civil Society in Guinea-Bissau*. Athens: Ohio University Press, 2003.

Forrest, Joshua B. "A Promising Start: The Inauguration and Consolidation of Democracy in Namibia." *World Policy Journal* 9, 4 (Fall–Winter 1992): 739–53.

Forrest, Joshua B. *Subnationalism in Africa: Ethnicity, Alliances, and Politics*. Boulder, CO: Lynne Rienner, 2003.

Foweraker, Joe. "Institutional Design, Party Systems and Governability: Differentiating the Presidential Regimes of Latin America." *British Journal of Political Science* 28, 4 (October 1998): 651–76.

Fox, Donald T., and Anne Stetson. "The 1991 Constitutional Reform: Prospects for Democracy and the Rule of Law in Colombia." *Case Western Reserve Journal of International Law* 24, 2 (Spring 1992): 139–64.

Fox, Roddy, and Roger Southall. "The General Election in Lesotho, May 2002: Adapting to MMP." *Electoral Studies* 23, 3 (September 2004): 545–50.

Fraenkel, Jon, and Bernard Grofman. "Does the Alternative Vote Foster Moderation in Ethnically Divided Societies? The Case of Fiji." *Comparative Political Studies* 39, 5 (June 2006): 623–51.

Fraenkel, Jon, and Bernard Grofman. "A Neo-Downsian Model of the Alternative Vote as a Mechanism for Mitigating Ethnic Conflict in Plural Societies." *Public Choice* 121, 3–4 (October 2004): 487–506.

Frye, Timothy. "A Politics of Institutional Choice: Post-Communist Presidencies." *Comparative Political Studies* 30, 5 (October 1997): 523–52.

Fukuyama, Francis, Björn Dressel, and Boo-Seung Chang. "Challenge and Change in East Asia: Facing the Perils of Presidentialism?" *Journal of Democracy* 16, 2 (April 2005): 102–16.

Fumonyoh, Christopher. "Democratization in Fits and Starts." *Journal of Democracy* 12, 3 (July 2001): 37–50.

Gado, Boureïma. "Quel partenariat pour accompagner le renforcement du processus démocratique au Niger?" *Mondes et cultures* 62, 1/4 (2002): 400–23.

Gall, Gerald L. *The Canadian Legal System*. 3rd ed. Toronto: Carswell, 1990.

Gammeltoft-Hansen, Hans, Bernhard Gomard, and Allan Philip, eds. *Danish Law: A General Survey*. Copenhagen: G. E. C. Gads, 1982.

Ganev, Venelin I. "The Bulgarian Constitutional Court, 1991–1997: A Success Story in Context." *Europe-Asia Studies* 55, 4 (June 2003): 597–611.

Ganev, Venelin I. "Emergency Powers and the New East European Constitutions." *American Journal of Comparative Law* 45, 3 (Summer 1997): 585–612.

Ganev, Venelin I. "History, Politics, and the Constitution: Ethnic Conflict and Constitutional Adjudication in Postcommunist Bulgaria." *Slavic Review* 63, 1 (Spring 2004): 66–89.

Garreton, Manuel A. *Incomplete Democracy: Political Democratization in Chile and Latin America*. Chapel Hill: University of North Carolina Press, 2003.

Gasiorowski Mark J., and Timothy J. Power. "The Structural Determinants of Democratic Consolidation: Evidence from the Third World." *Comparative Political Studies* 31, 6 (December 1998): 740–71.

Gause, F. Gregory. *Oil Monarchies: Domestic and Security Challenges in the Arab Gulf States*. New York: Council on Foreign Relations Press, 1994.

Geddis, Andrew. "Gang Aft A-Gley: New Zealand's Attempt to Combat 'Party Hopping' by Elected Representatives." *Election Law Journal* 1, 4 (December 2002): 557–71.

Gehrke, William. "The Mozambique Crisis: A Case for United Nations Military Intervention." *Cornell International Law Journal* 24 (1991): 135–64.

Gellner, David N. "Nepal and Bhutan in 2006: A Year of Revolution." *Asian Survey* 47, 1 (January–February 2007): 80–6.

Ghufran, Nasreen. "Afghanistan in 2006: The Complications of Post-Conflict Transition." *Asian Survey* 47, 1 (January–February 2007): 87–98.

Gillen, Mark R. "The Malay Rulers' Loss of Immunity." *University of British Columbia Law Review* 29, 1 (1995): 163–97.

Gillen, Mark, and Ted L. McDorman. "The Removal of the Three Judges of the Supreme Court of Malaysia." *University of British Columbia Law Review* 25 (1991): 171–97.

Gilley, Bruce. *China's Democratic Future: How It Will Happen and Where It Will Lead*. New York: Columbia University Press, 2004.

Gilmour, John B., and Paul Rothstein. "Term Limitation in a Dynamic Model of Partisan Balance." *American Journal of Political Science* 38, 3 (August 1994): 770–96.

Ginsburg, Tom, and Gombosuren Ganzorig. "When Courts and Politics Collide: Mongolia's Constitutional Crisis." *Columbia Journal of Asian Law* 14 (Spring 2001): 309–26.

Girvin, Brian. "Consensus and Political Competition in the Irish Republic." *Parliamentary Affairs* 51, 1 (January 1998): 84–100.

Girvin, Brian. "Social Change and Political Culture in the Republic of Ireland." *Parliamentary Affairs* 46, 3 (July 1993): 380–98.

Girvin, Brian, and Gary Murphy, eds. *The Lemass Era: Politics and Society in the Ireland of Sean Lemass*. Dublin: University College Dublin Press, 2006.

Girvin, Brian, and Roland Sturm. *Politics and Society in Contemporary Ireland*. London: Gower, 1986.

Glosemeyer, Iris. *Liberalisierung und Demokratisierung in der Republik Jemen, 1990–1994: Einführung und Dokumente*. Hamburg: Deutsches Orient-Institut, 1995.

Goedde, Patricia. "Law 'of Our Own Style': The Evolution and Challenges of the North Korean Legal System." *Fordham International Law Journal* 27 (April 2004): 1265–88.

Goğanay, Ülkü. "The Turkish Parliament and Democracy." *Parliamentary Affairs* 60, 3 (July 2007): 388–408.

Gold, Thomas B. *State and Society in the Taiwan Miracle.* Armonk, NY: M. E. Sharpe, 1997.

Gold, Thomas B. "Tumultuous Times in Taiwan." *Issues and Studies* 40, 3–4 (September–December 2004): 418–27.

Gondola, Ch. Didier. *The History of Congo.* Westport, CT: Greenwood, 2002.

Good, Kenneth. "Authoritarian Liberalism: A Defining Characteristic of Botswana." *Journal of Contemporary African Studies* 14, 1 (January 1996): 29–52.

Graham, Lawrence S. "The Dilemmas of Managing Transitions in Weak States: The Case of Mozambique." *Public Administration and Development* 13, 4 (October 1993): 409–22.

Graham, Lawrence S. *The Portuguese Military and the State: Rethinking Transitions in Europe and Latin America.* Boulder, CO: Westview, 1993.

Graham, Lawrence S., and Douglas Wheeler. *In Search of Modern Portugal: The Revolution and Its Consequences.* Madison: University of Wisconsin Press, 1983.

Gros, Jean-Germain, ed. *Cameroon: Politics and Society in Critical Perspectives.* Lanham, MD: University Press of America, 2003.

Gros, Jean-Germain, ed. *Democratization in Late Twentieth-Century Africa: Coping with Uncertainty.* Westport, CT: Praeger, 1998.

Gros, Jean-Germain. "The Hard Lessons of Cameroon." *Journal of Democracy* 6, 3 (July 1995): 112–27.

Grosh, Barbara, and Rwekaza Mukandala, eds. *State-Owned Enterprises in Africa.* Boulder, CO: Lynne Rienner, 1994.

Grzymała-Busse, Anna M. "Political Competition and the Politicization of the State in East Central Europe." *Comparative Political Studies* 36, 10 (December 2003): 1123–47.

Grzymała-Busse, Anna M. *Redeeming the Communist Past: The Regeneration of Communist Parties in East Central Europe.* Cambridge: Cambridge University Press, 2002.

Grzymała-Busse, Anna M., and Pauline Jones Luong. "Reconceptualizing the State: Lessons from Post-Communism." *Politics and Society* 30, 4 (December 2002): 529–54.

Guevara Mann, Carlos. *Panamanian Militarism: A Historical Interpretation.* Athens: Ohio University Center for International Studies, 1996.

Guevara Mann, Carlos. "The Quality of Political Representation and the Size of Electoral Boundaries: A Comparison of Panamanian Assemblies of 1945 and 1999." *Revista de Ciencia Política* 24, 2 (2004): 94–115.

Gunn, Geoffrey C. "Laos in 2006: Changing of the Guard." *Asian Survey* 47, 1 (January–February 2007): 183–8.

Gunther, Richard, P. Nikiforos Diamandouros, and Hans-Jürgen Puhle. *The Politics of Democratic Consolidation: Southern Europe in Comparative Perspective.* Baltimore, MD: Johns Hopkins University Press, 1995.

Gustafson, Lindsey. "Kenya: The Struggle to Create a Democracy." *Brigham Young University Law Review* (1995): 647–70.

Gyandoh, Samuel O. "Interaction of the Judicial and Legislative Processes in Ghana since Independence." *Temple Law Quarterly* 56, 2 (1983): 351–404.

Gyimah-Boadi, E., ed. *Democratic Reform in Africa: The Quality of Progress.* Boulder, CO: Lynne Rienner, 2004.

Gyimah-Boadi, E. "The Rebirth of African Liberalism." *Journal of Democracy* 9, 2 (April 1998): 18–31.

Habachy, Saba. "A Study in Comparative Constitutional Law: Constitutional Government in Kuwait." *Columbia Journal of Transnational Law* 3 (1963–4): 116–26.

Hadenius, Axel, ed. *Decentralisation and Democratic Governance: Experiences from India, Bolivia and South Africa.* Stockholm: Almqvist & Wiksell, 2003.

Hadenius, Axel. *Institutions and Democratic Citizenship.* Oxford: Oxford University Press, 2001.

Hagberg, Sten. "Enough Is Enough: An Ethnography of the Struggle against Impunity in Burkina Faso." *Journal of Modern African Studies* 40, 2 (June 2002): 217–46.

Hagberg, Sten. *Poverty in Burkina Faso: Representations and Realities.* Uppsala, Sweden: Uppsala University Press, 2001.

Hagberg, Sten, and Alexis B. Tengan, eds. *Bonds and Boundaries in Northern Ghana and Southern Burkina Faso.* Uppsala, Sweden: Uppsala University Press, 2000.

Haggard, Stephan, and Matthew D. McCubbins, eds. *Presidents, Parliaments, and Policy.* New York: Cambridge University Press, 2001.

Haghayeghi, Mehrdad. "Changing Dynamics of Islamic Politics in Central Asia." *Muslim World* 92, 3–4 (Fall 2002): 315–31.

Haghayeghi, Mehrdad. "Politics and Ideology in the Islamic Republic of Iran." *Middle Eastern Studies* 29, 1 (January 1993): 36–52.

Hagopian, Frances, and Scott Mainwaring, eds. *The Third Wave of Democratization in Latin America: Advances and Setbacks.* New York: Cambridge University Press, 2005.

Hahn, Jeffrey W. *Democratization in Russia: The Development of Legislative Institutions.* Armonk, NY: M. E. Sharpe, 1996.

Haindrava, Ivlian. "Letter from Georgia: Looking beyond Shevardnadze." *Problems of Post-Communism* 50, 1 (January–February 2003): 22–8.

Hale, Henry E. "Regime Cycles: Democracy, Autocracy, and Revolution in Post-Soviet Eurasia." *World Politics* 58, 1 (October 2005): 133–65.

Haller, Walter. "The New Swiss Constitution: Foreign and International Influences." *International Journal of Legal Information* 30 (Summer 2002): 256–64.

Hammond, Thomas H., and Christopher K. Butler. "Some Complex Answers to the Simple Question 'Do Institutions Matter?' Policy Choice and Policy Change in Presidential and Parliamentary Systems." *Journal of Theoretical Politics* 15, 2 (2003): 145–200.

Hammond, Thomas H., and Gary J. Miller. "The Core of the Constitution." *American Political Science Review* 81, 4 (December 1987): 1155–74.

Haqqani, Husain. "History Repeats Itself in Pakistan." *Journal of Democracy* 17, 4 (October 2006): 110–24.

Harbeson, John, Donald Rothchild, and Naomi Chazan, eds. *Civil Society and the State in Africa.* Boulder, CO: Westview, 1994.

Harijanti, Susi Dwi, and Tim Lindsey. "Indonesia: General Elections Test the Amended Constitution and the New Constitutional Court." *International Journal of Constitutional Law* 4 (2006): 138–50.

Harris, Erika. *Nationalism and Democratization: Politics of Slovakia and Slovenia.* Aldershot, U.K.: Ashgate, 2002.

Harsch, Ernest. "Accumulators and Democrats: Challenging State Corruption in Africa." *Journal of Modern African Studies* 31, 1 (March 1993): 31–48.

Hartlyn, Jonathan. *The Struggle for Democratic Politics in the Dominican Republic.* Chapel Hill: University of North Carolina Press, 1998.

Hartmann, Christof. *Externe Faktoren im Demokratisierungsprozess: Eine vergleichende Untersuchung afrikanischer Länder.* Opladen, Germany: Leske and Budrich, 1999.

Hassall, Graham, and Cheryl Saunders. *Asia-Pacific Constitutional Systems.* Cambridge: Cambridge University Press, 2002.

Hayden, Robert M. *Blueprints for a House Divided: The Constitutional Logic of the Yugoslav Conflicts.* Ann Arbor: University of Michigan Press, 1999.

Hazan, Reuven Y. "Executive-Legislative Relations in an Era of Accelerated Reform: Reshaping Government in Israel." *Legislative Studies Quarterly* 22, 3 (August 1997): 329–50.

Heard, Andrew. *Canadian Constitutional Conventions: The Marriage of Law and Politics.* Toronto: Oxford University Press, 1991.

Heard, Andrew. "Constitutional Conventions and Parliament." *Canadian Parliamentary Review* 28, 2 (Summer 2005): 19–22.

Heard, Andrew, and Tim Swartz. "The Regional Veto Formula and Its Effects on Canada's Constitutional Amendment Process." *Canadian Journal of Political Science/Revue canadienne de science politique* 30, 2 (June 1997): 339–56.

Heilbrunn, John R. "Commerce, Politics, and Business Associations in Benin and Togo." *Comparative Politics* 29, 4 (July 1997): 473–92.

Heilbrunn, John R. "Social Origins of National Conferences in Benin and Togo." *Journal of Modern African Studies* 31, 2 (June 1993): 277–99.

Heller, William B. "Bicameralism and Budget Deficits: The Effect of Parliamentary Structure on Government Spending." *Legislative Studies Quarterly* 22, 4 (November 1997): 485–516.

Heller, William B., and Carol Mershon. "Party Switching in the Italian Chamber of Deputies, 1996–2001." *Journal of Politics* 67, 2 (May 2005): 536–59.

Hellinger, Daniel. "When 'No' Means 'Yes to Revolution': Electoral Politics in Bolivarian Venezuela." *Latin American Perspectives* 32, 3 (May 2005): 8–32.

Helmke, Gretchen. *Courts under Constraints: Judges, Generals, and Presidents in Argentina.* Cambridge: Cambridge University Press, 2004.

Helmke, Gretchen. "The Logic of Strategic Defection: Court-Executive Relations in Argentina under Dictatorship and Democracy." *American Political Science Review* 96, 2 (June 2002): 291–303.

Herb, Michael. *All in the Family: Absolutism, Revolution, and Democratic Prospects in the Middle Eastern Monarchies.* Albany: State University of New York Press, 1999.

Herb, Michael. "Emirs and Parliaments in the Gulf." *Journal of Democracy* 13, 4 (October 2002): 41–7.

Herb, Michael. "Princes and Parliaments in the Arab World." *Middle East Journal* 58, 3 (Summer 2004): 367–84.

Hesseling, Gerti. *Histoire politique du Sénégal: Institutions, droit et société.* Leiden, the Netherlands: Afrika-Studiecentrum, 1985.

Hibbing, John R. "Legislative Careers: Why and How We Should Study Them." *Legislative Studies Quarterly* 24, 2 (May 1999): 149–71.

Hibbing, John R., and Samuel C. Patterson. "A Democratic Legislature in the Making: The Historic Hungarian Elections of 1990." *Comparative Political Studies* 24, 2 (January 1992): 430–54.

Hicken, Allen, and Yuko Kasuya. "A Guide to the Constitutional Structures and Electoral Systems of East, South, and Southeast Asia." *Electoral Studies* 22, 1 (March 2003): 121–51.

Hicken, Allen, Shanker Satyanath, and Ernest Sergenti. "Political Institutions and Economic Performance: The Effects of Accountability and Obstacles to Policy Change." *American Journal of Political Science* 49, 4 (October 2005): 897–907.

Hickson, Jill E. "Using Law to Create National Identity: The Course to Democracy in Tajikistan." *Texas International Law Journal* 38 (Spring 2003): 347–79.

Hiebert, Janet L. "Interpreting the Bill of Rights: The Importance of Legislative Rights Review." *British Journal of Political Science* 35, 2 (April 2005): 235–55.

Hinnfors, Jonas. *Reinterpreting Social Democracy: A History of Stability in the British Labour Party and Swedish Social Democratic Party*. Manchester, U.K.: Manchester University Press, 2006.

Hinnfors, Jonas. "Still the Politics of Compromise? Agenda Setting Strategy in Sweden." *Scandinavian Political Studies* 20, 2 (June 1997): 159–77.

Hintzen, Percy C. "Bases of Elite Support for a Regime: Race, Ideology, and Clientelism as Bases for Leaders in Guyana and Trinidad." *Comparative Political Studies* 16, 3 (1983): 363–91.

Hintzen, Percy C. *The Costs of Regime Survival: Racial Mobilization, Elite Domination and Control of the State in Guyana and Trinidad*. Cambridge: Cambridge University Press, 1989.

Hintzen, Percy C. "Ethnicity, Class, and International Capitalist Penetration in Guyana and Trinidad." *Social and Economic Studies* 34, 3 (September 1985): 107–63.

Hitchner, R. Bruce. "From Dayton to Brussels: The Story behind the Constitutional and Governmental Reform Process in Bosnia and Herzegovina." *Fletcher Forum of World Affairs* 30, 1 (Winter 2006): 125–35.

Hix, Simon. "Backbenchers Learn to Fight Back: European Integration and Parliamentary Government." *West European Politics* 23, 4 (October 2000): 142–68.

Hofmeier, Rolf, and Andreas Mehler. *Afrika Jahrbuch 2001: Politik, Wirtschaft, und Gesellschaft in Afrika südlich der Sahara*. Opladen, Germany: Leske and Budrich, 2002.

Hogg, Peter W. "The New Canadian Constitution: Introduction." *American Journal of Comparative Law* 32, 2 (Spring 1984): 221–4.

Holiday, David. "El Salvador's 'Model' Democracy." *Current History* 104, 679 (February 2005): 77–82.

Holiday, David, and William Stanley. "Building the Peace: Lessons from El Salvador." *Journal of International Affairs* 42, 2 (1993): 415–38.

Holm, John, and Patrick Molutsi, eds. *Democracy in Botswana*. Gaborone: Macmillan, 1999.

Horowitz, Donald L. "Constitutional Courts: A Primer for Decision Makers." *Journal of Democracy* 17, 4 (October 2006): 125–37.

Hosen, Nadirsyah. "In Search of Islamic Constitutionalism." *American Journal of Islamic Social Sciences* 21, 2 (Spring 2004): 1–24.

Houngnikpo, Mathurin C. "Democratization in Africa: Double Standards in Benin and Togo." *Fletcher Forum of World Affairs* 25 (Summer 2001): 51–63.

Houngnikpo, Mathurin C. *Determinants of Democratization in Africa: A Comparative Study of Benin and Togo*. Lanham, MD: University Press of America, 2001.

Hovell, Devika, and George Williams. "A Tale of Two Systems: The Use of International Law in Constitutional Interpretation in Australia and South Africa." *Melbourne University Law Review* 29 (April 2005): 95–130.

Howard, Marc Morjé, and Philip G. Roessler. "Liberalizing Electoral Outcomes in Authoritarian Regimes." *American Journal of Political Science* 50, 2 (April 2006): 365–81.

Huber, John D. *Rationalizing Parliament: Legislative Institutions and Party Politics in France*. New York: Cambridge University Press, 1996.

Huber, John D. "The Vote of Confidence in Parliamentary Democracies." *American Political Science Review* 90, 2 (June 1996): 269–82.

Huber, John D., and Charles R. Shipan. *Deliberate Discretion? The Institutional Foundations of Bureaucratic Autonomy*. New York: Cambridge University Press, 2002.

Hunter, Wendy. *Eroding Military Influence in Brazil: Politicians against Soldiers*. Chapel Hill: University of North Carolina Press, 1997.

Husa, Jaakko. "Guarding the Constitutionality of Laws in the Nordic Countries: A Comparative Perspective." *American Journal of Comparative Law* 48 (Summer 2000): 345–81.

Huskey, Eugene. *Presidential Power in Russia*. Armonk, NY: M. E. Sharpe, 1999.

Hyden, Goran. "Top-Down Democratization in Tanzania." *Journal of Democracy* 10, 4 (October 1999): 142–55.

Ieraci, Giuseppe. *Le teorie delle coalizioni politiche*. Naples: Morano, 1994.

Ihonvbere, Julius Omozuanvbo, and John Mukum Mbaku, eds. *Political Liberalization and Democratization in Africa: Lessons from Country Experiences*. Westport, CT: Praeger, 2003.

Ikstens, Jānis. "Latvia." *European Journal of Political Research* 44, 7–8 (December 2005): 1077–85.

Ilchev, Ivan. *Bulgarian Parliament and Bulgarian Statehood*. Sofia: St. Kliment Ohridsky University Press, 2005.

Ilonszki, Gabriella. "Tradition and Innovation in the Development of Parliamentary Government in Hungary." *Journal of Theoretical Politics* 5, 2 (April 1993): 253–65.

Ingebritsen, Christine. *Scandinavia in World Politics*. Lanham, MD: Rowman and Littlefield, 2006.

Ingebritsen, Christine. "The Scandinavian Way and Its Legacy in Europe." *Scandinavian Studies* 74, 3 (Fall 2002): 255–64.

International Constitutional Law. "International Constitutional Law." Online at http://www.oefre.unibe.ch/law/icl/index.html. Site consulted 2006–7.

Ishida, Takeshi, and Ellis S. Krauss, eds. *Democracy in Japan*. Pittsburgh, PA: University of Pittsburgh Press, 1989.

Islam, Mahmudul. *Constitutional Law of Bangladesh.* Dhaka: Bangladesh Institute of Law and International Affairs, 1995.

Ismael, Jacqueline S. *Kuwait: Dependency and Class in a Rentier State.* Gainesville: University of Florida Press, 1993.

Jackson, Robert J., and Michael M. Atkinson. *The Canadian Legislative System: Politicians and Policymaking.* Toronto: Macmillan, 1980.

Jacobsohn, Gary Jeffrey. *Apple of Gold: Constitutionalism in Israel and the United States.* Princeton, NJ: Princeton University Press, 1994.

Jasiewicz, Krzysztof. "Dead Ends and New Beginnings: The Quest for a Procedural Republic in Poland." *Communist and Post-Communist Studies* 33, 1 (March 2000): 101–22.

Jasiewicz, Krzysztof. "Polish Politics on the Eve of the 1993 Elections: Toward Fragmentation or Pluralism." *Communist and Post-Communist Studies* 26, 4 (December 1993): 387–411.

Jayal, Niraja Gopal. *Democracy and the State: Welfare, Secularism and Development in Contemporary India.* New York: Oxford University Press, 1999.

Jayal, Niraja Gopal. *Democracy in India.* New York: Oxford University Press, 2001.

Jayal, Niraja Gopal, and Sudha Pai, eds. *Democratic Governance in India: Challenges of Poverty, Development and Identity.* London: Sage, 2001.

Jayal, Niraja Gopal, Amit Prakash, and Pradeep Sharma. *Local Governance in India: Decentralization and Beyond.* New York: Oxford University Press, 2006.

Jewell, Malcolm E., and Gerhard Loewenberg. "Editors' Introduction: Toward a New Model of Legislative Representation." *Legislative Studies Quarterly* 4, 4 (November 1979): 485–99.

Jewell, Malcolm E., Gerhard Loewenberg, and Samuel C. Patterson, eds. *Handbook of Legislative Research.* Cambridge, MA: Harvard University Press, 1985.

Joffé, E. G. H. "The Moroccan Nationalist Movement." *Journal of African History* 26, 4 (1985): 289–307.

Johnson, Carole, and Colin Talbot. "The UK Parliament and Performance: Challenging or Challenged?" *International Review of Administrative Studies* 73, 1 (March 2007): 113–31.

Jones, Mark P. *Electoral Laws and the Survival of Presidential Democracies.* Notre Dame, IN: University of Notre Dame Press, 1995.

Jones, Mark P. "Legislator Behavior and Executive-Legislative Relations in Latin America." *Latin American Research Review* 37, 3 (2002): 176–88.

Jones, Mark P., and Wonjae Hwang. "Party Government in Presidential Democracies: Extending Cartel Theory beyond the U.S. Congress." *American Journal of Political Science* 49, 2 (April 2005): 267–82.

Jones, Mark P., Sebastian M. Saiegh, Pablo T. Spiller, and Mariano Tommasi. "Amateur Legislatures – Professional Politicians: The Consequences of Party-Centered Electoral Rules in a Federal System." *American Journal of Political Science* 46, 3 (July 2002): 656–69.

Joseph, Richard. *Democracy and Prebendal Politics in Nigeria: The Rise and Fall of the Second Republic.* Cambridge: Cambridge University Press, 1987.

Juma, Laurence. "Ethnic Politics and the Constitutional Review Process in Kenya." *Tulsa Journal of Comparative and International Law* 9 (Spring 2002): 471–532.

Kaag, Mayke. *Usage foncier et dynamique sociale au Sénégal rural: L'histoire d'un bas-fond et de ses défricheurs.* Amsterdam: Rozenberg, 2001.

Kaiser, Paul J. "Power, Sovereignty, and International Observers: The Case of Zanzibar." *Africa Today* 46, 1 (Winter 1999): 29–46.

Kaiser, Paul J., and F. Wafula Okumu, eds. *Democratic Transitions in East Africa.* Aldershot, U.K.: Ashgate, 2004.

Kamal, Mustafa. *Bangladesh Constitution: Trends and Issues.* Dhaka: University of Dhaka Press, 1994.

Kang, David C. *Crony Capitalism: Corruption and Development in South Korea and the Philippines.* Cambridge: Cambridge University Press, 2002.

Kapur, Devesh, and Pratap Bhanu Mehta. *Public Institutions in India: Performance and Design.* New York: Oxford University Press, 2006.

Karasimeonov, Georgi. "The Legislature in Post-Communist Bulgaria." *Journal of Legislative Studies* 2, 1 (Spring 1996): 40–59.

Karasimeonov, Georgi. "Parliamentary Elections of 1994 and the Development of the Bulgarian Party System." *Party Politics* 1, 4 (October 1995): 579–87.

Karklins, Rasma. *Ethnopolitics and the Transition to Democracy: The Collapse of the USSR and Latvia.* Washington, DC: Woodrow Wilson Center Press, 1994.

Karklins, Rasma. *The System Made Me Do It: Corruption in Post-Communist Societies.* Armonk, NY: M. E. Sharpe, 2005.

Kasfir, Nelson. 1998. "Civil Society, the State and Democracy in Africa." *Commonwealth & Comparative Politics* 36, 2 (July 1998): 123–49.

Kennedy, Charles H. *Bureaucracy in Pakistan.* New York: Oxford University Press, 1988.

Khadka, Narayan. "Democracy and Development in Nepal: Prospects and Challenges." *Pacific Affairs* 66, 1 (Spring 1993): 44–71.

Khan, Mujeeb R. "Bosnia-Herzegovina and the Crisis of the Post–Cold War International System." *East European Politics and Societies* 9, 3 (Fall 1995): 459–98.

Kim, Dong-Hun, and Gerhard Loewenberg. "The Role of Parliamentary Committees in Coalition Governments: Keeping Tabs on Coalition Partners in the German Bundestag." *Comparative Political Studies* 38, 9 (November 2005): 1104–29.

Kim, Samuel S., ed. *Korea's Democratization.* New York: Cambridge University Press, 2003.

King, Dwight Y. "East Timor's Founding Elections and Emerging Party System." *Asian Survey* 43, 5 (September–October 2003): 745–57.

Kjekshus, Helge. "Parliament in a One-Party State: The Bunge of Tanzania, 1965–70." *Journal of Modern African Studies* 12, 1 (March 1974): 19–43.

Klesner, Joseph L. "Electoral Competition and the New Party System in Mexico." *Latin American Politics & Society* 47, 2 (Summer 2005): 103–42.

Kline, Harvey F. *State Building and Conflict Resolution in Colombia, 1986–1994.* Tuscaloosa: University of Alabama Press, 2001.

Koelble, Thomas A. *The Global Economy and Democracy in South Africa.* Piscataway, NJ: Rutgers University Press, 1999.

Kommers, Donald P. "German Constitutionalism: A Prolegomenon." *Emory Law Journal* 40 (Summer 1991): 837–73.

Konitzer-Smirnov, Andrew. "Serving Different Masters: Regional Executives and Accountability in Ukraine and Russia." *Europe-Asia Studies* 57, 1 (January 2005): 3–33.

Kopecky, Petr. *Parliaments in the Czech and Slovak Republics: Party Competition and Parliamentary Institutionalization.* Aldershot, U.K.: Ashgate, 2001.

Korosteleva, Elena A., Colin W. Lawson, and Rosalind J. Marsh, eds. *Contemporary Belarus: Between Dictatorship and Democracy.* London: Curzon Press, 2002.

Kotov, Anatoly K. "The Parliamentary Process in the Republic of Kazakhstan." *Widener Journal of Public Law* 8 (1999): 457–69.

Krašovec, Alenka, and Damjan Lajh. "The Slovene EU Accession Referendum: A Cat-and-Mouse Game." *West European Politics* 27, 4 (September 2004): 603–23.

Krauss, Ellis S., and Benjamin Nyblade. "'Presidentialization' in Japan? The Prime Minister, Media and Elections in Japan." *British Journal of Political Science* 35, 2 (April 2005): 357–68.

Krauss, Ellis S., and Robert Pekkanen. "Explaining Party Adaptation to Electoral Reform: The Discreet Charm of the LDP?" *Journal of Japanese Studies* 30, 1 (Winter 2004): 1–34.

Krehbiel, Keith. *Information and Legislative Organization.* Ann Arbor: University of Michigan Press, 1991.

Kreppel, Amie. *The European Parliament and Supranational Party System: A Study in Institutional Development.* Cambridge: Cambridge University Press, 2002.

Kreppel, Amie. "The Impact of Parties in Government on Legislative Output in Italy." *European Journal of Political Research* 33, 1 (April 1997): 327–50.

Kresak, Peter. "The Government Structure in the New Slovak Republic." *Tulsa Journal of Comparative and International Law* 4 (Fall 1996): 1–34.

Kriesi, Hanspeter. "The Federal Parliament: The Limits of Institutional Reform." *West European Politics* 24, 2 (April 2001): 59–76.

Krouwel, André. "Measuring Presidentialism and Parliamentarism: An Application to Central and East European Countries." *Acta Politica* 38, 4 (2003): 333–64.

Krouwel, André. "Otto Kirchheimer and the Catch-All Party." *West European Politics* 26, 2 (April 2003): 23–40.

Krupavicius, Algis. "Lithuania." *European Journal of Political Research* 44, 7–8 (December 2005): 1086–1101.

Krupavicius, Algis. "The Lithuanian Parliamentary Elections of 1996." *Electoral Studies* 16, 4 (December 1997): 541–9.

Krupavicius, Algis. "The Post-Communist Transition and Institutionalization of Lithuania's Parties." *Political Studies* 46, 3, Special Issue (1998): 465–91.

Kryvonos, Myroslava. "A Research Guide to Ukrainian Law." *International Journal of Legal Information* 31 (Spring 2003): 1–19.

Kufuor, Kofi Oteng. "Developments in the Resolution of the Liberian Conflict." *American University Journal of International Law and Policy* 10 (Fall 1994): 373–96.

Kufuor, Kofi Oteng. "The Ghanaian Council of State as a Constitutional Second Chamber." *International and Comparative Law Quarterly* 43 (October 1994): 934–45.

Kundsen, Tim, and Bo Rothstein. "State-Building in Scandinavia." *Comparative Politics* 26, 2 (January 1994): 203–20.

Kurczewski, Jacek. "Parliament and the Political Class in the Constitutional Reconstruction of Poland: Two Constitutions in One." *International Sociology* 18, 1 (March 2003): 162–80.

Kusovac, Zoran. "The Prospects for Change in Post-Tudjman Croatia." *East European Constitutional Review* 9, 3 (Summer 2000): 57–62.

Laakso, Liisa. "The Politics of International Election Observation: The Case of Zimbabwe in 2000." *Journal of Modern African Studies* 40, 3 (September 2002): 437–64.

Lagerspetz, Mikko. "Consolidation as Hegemonization: The Case of Estonia." *Journal of Baltic Studies* 32, 4 (Winter 2001): 402–20.

Lal, Brij V. *Another Way: The Politics of Constitutional Reform in Post-Coup Fiji.* Canberra: National Centre for Development Studies, Australian National University, 1998.

Lal, Brij V. *Broken Waves: A History of the Fiji Islands in the Twentieth Century*. Honolulu: University of Hawaii Press, 1992.

Lal, Brij V., and Peter Larmour, eds. *Electoral Systems in Divided Societies: The Fiji Constitution Review*. Canberra: National Centre for Development Studies, Australian National University, 1997.

Lamounier, Bolívar. "El modelo institucional de los años treinta y la presente crisis brasileña." *Desarrollo Económico – Revista de Ciencias Sociales* 32, 126 (July–September 1992): 185–98.

Landé, Carl H. "The Return of 'People Power' in the Philippines." *Journal of Democracy* 12, 2 (April 2001): 88–102.

Landé, Carl H., and Allan J. Cigler. "Competition and Turnover in Philippine Congressional Elections, 1907–1969." *Asian Survey* 19, 10 (1979): 977–1007.

Landé, Carl H., and Mickey Waxman. *Post-Marcos Politics: A Geographical and Statistical Analysis of the 1992 Presidential Election*. New York: St. Martin's, 1996.

Larmour, Peter. *Foreign Flowers: Institutional Transfer and Good Governance in the Pacific Islands*. Honolulu: University of Hawaii Press, 2005.

Larmour, Peter. "Public Choice in Melanesia: Community, Bureaucracy, and the Market in Land Management." *Public Administration and Development* 10, 1 (January–March 1990): 53–68.

Laver, Michael, and Norman Schofield. *Multiparty Government*. Ann Arbor: University of Michigan Press, 1998.

Laver, Michael, and Kenneth A. Shepsle, eds. *Making and Breaking Governments: Cabinets and Legislatures in Parliamentary Democracies*. New York: Cambridge University Press, 1996.

Lawson, Chappell H. "Fox's Mexico at Midterm." *Journal of Democracy* 15, 1 (January 2004): 139–53.

Lawson, Stephanie. *Tradition versus Democracy in the South Pacific: Fiji, Tonga and Western Samoa*. Cambridge: Cambridge University Press, 1997.

LeDuc, Lawrence, Richard G. Niemi, and Pippa Norris, eds. *Comparing Democracies: Elections and Voting in Global Perspective*. Thousand Oaks, CA: Sage, 1996.

Lee, Pei-Shan, and Yung-Ming Hsu. "Southern Politics? Regional Trajectories of Party Development in Taiwan." *Issues and Studies* 38, 2 (June 2002): 61–84.

Lee, Youngjae. "Law, Politics, and Impeachment: The Impeachment of Roh Moo-Hyun from a Comparative Constitutional Perspective." *American Journal of Comparative Law* 53 (Spring 2005): 403–32.

Lehoucq, Fabrice E. "Can Parties Police Themselves? Electoral Governance and Democratization." *International Political Science Review* 23, 1 (January 2002): 29–46.

Lehoucq, Fabrice E. "Costa Rica: Paradise in Doubt." *Journal of Democracy* 16, 3 (July 2005): 140–54.

Lehoucq, Fabrice E., and Ivan Molina. *Stuffing the Ballot Box: Fraud, Electoral Reform, and Democratization in Costa Rica*. Cambridge: Cambridge University Press, 2002.

Leonard, David K. *African Successes*. Berkeley: University of California Press, 1991.

Leonard, David K., and Scott Straus. *Africa's Stalled Development*. Boulder, CO: Lynne Rienner, 2003.

Leoni, Eduardo. "Ideologia, democracia e comportamento parlamentar: A Câmara dos Deputados (1991–1998)." *Dados* 45, 3 (2002): 361–86.

Leston-Bandeira, Christina. *From Legislation to Legitimation: The Role of the Portuguese Parliament*. London: Routledge, 2004.

Leston-Bandeira, Christina. "The Portuguese Parliament during the First Two Decades of Democracy." *West European Politics* 24, 1 (January 2001): 137–56.

Levine, Stephen, and Nigel S. Roberts. "From Lobby Fodder to Leadership: New Zealand Parliamentarians and Select Committees." *Political Science* 56, 2 (December 2004): 39–49.

Levitsky, Steven. "From Labor Politics to Machine Politics: The Transformation of Party-Union Linkages in Argentine Peronism, 1983–1999." *Latin American Research Review* 38, 3 (2003): 3–36.

Levitt, Jeremy I. "Illegal Peace? An Inquiry into the Legality of Power-Sharing with Warlords and Rebels in Africa." *Michigan Journal of International Law* 27 (Winter 2006): 495–577.

Lewis, Peter, ed. *Africa: Dilemmas of Development and Change*. Boulder, CO: Westview, 1998.

Lewis, Peter. "From Despair to Expectation." *Current History* 98, 628 (May 1999): 223–7.

Liao, Ta-chi. "How Does a Rubber Stamp Become a Roaring Lion? The Transformation of the Role of Taiwan's Legislative Yuan during the Process of Democratization, 1950–2000." *Issues and Studies* 41, 3 (September 2005): 31–79.

Liebert, Ulrike, and Maurizio Cotta, eds. *Parliament and Democratic Consolidation in Southern Europe: Greece, Italy, Portugal, Spain and Turkey*. London: Pinter, 1990.

Lijphart, Arend. *Democracy in Plural Societies*. New Haven, CT: Yale University Press, 1977.

Lijphart, Arend. *Parliamentary versus Presidential Government*. Oxford: Oxford University Press, 1992.

Lijphart, Arend. *Patterns of Democracy: Government Forms and Performance in Thirty-six Countries*. New Haven, CT: Yale University Press, 1999.

Lindberg, Staffan I. "Consequences of Electoral Systems in Africa: A Preliminary Inquiry." *Electoral Studies* 24, 1 (March 2005): 41–65.

Lindberg, Staffan I. *Democracy and Elections in Africa*. Baltimore, MD: Johns Hopkins University Press, 2006.

Lindberg, Staffan I. "Forms of States, Governance, and Regimes: Reconceptualizing the Prospects for Democratic Consolidation in Africa." *International Political Science Review* 22, 2 (April 2001): 173–99.

Lindberg, Staffan I., and Minion K. C. Morrison. "Exploring Voter Alignments in Africa: Core and Swing Voters in Ghana." *Journal of Modern African Studies* 43, 4 (December 2005): 565–86.

Linder, Wolf. *Swiss Democracy: Possible Solutions to Conflict in Multicultural Societies.* New York: St. Martin's, 1994.

Lindseth, Peter L. "The Paradox of Parliamentary Supremacy: Delegation, Democracy, and Dictatorship in Germany and France, 1920s–1950s." *Yale Law Journal* 113, 7 (May 2004): 1341–1418.

Lindvall, Johannes, and Joakim Sebring. "Policy Reform and the Decline of Corporatism in Sweden." *West European Politics* 28, 5 (November 2005): 1057–74.

Linz, Juan J., and Arturo Valenzuela, eds. *The Failure of Presidential Democracy.* Baltimore, MD: Johns Hopkins University Press, 1994.

Llanos, Mariana. "Council of Elders? The Senate and Its Members in the Southern Cone." *Latin American Research Review* 41, 1 (2006): 133–52.

Llanos, Mariana. *Privatization and Democracy in Argentina: An Analysis of President-Congress Relations.* New York: Palgrave Macmillan, 2002.

Lloyd, Angela M. "The Southern Sudan: A Compelling Case for Secession." *Columbia Journal of Transnational Law* 32 (1994): 419–54.

Loada, Augustin. 1995. "Les élections municipales du 12 février 1995 au Burkina Faso." *Politique africaine* 58 (1995): 135–42.

Loada, Augustin. 1999. "Réflexions sur la société civile en Afrique: Le Burkina Faso de l'après-Zongo." *Politique africaine* 76 (1999): 136–51.

Loewenberg, Gerhard. *Comparing Legislatures.* New York: Little, Brown, 1979.

Loewenberg, Gerhard, Peverill Squire, and D. Roderick Kiewiet, eds. *Legislatures: Comparative Perspectives on Representative Assemblies.* Ann Arbor: University of Michigan Press, 2002.

Loh, Francis Kok Wah, and Khoo Boo Teik. *Democracy in Malaysia: Discourses and Practices.* London: RoutledgeCurzon, 2001.

Londregan, John B. *Legislative Institutions and Ideology in Chile.* Cambridge: Cambridge University Press, 2002.

Longman, Timothy. *Proxy Targets: Civilians in the War in Burundi.* New York: Human Rights Watch, 1998.

Louis, Pierre A. "'Obscure Despotism' and Human Rights in Togo." *Columbia Human Rights Law Review* 23 (Winter 1991/1992): 133–65.

Lucas, Russell E. "Deliberalization in Jordan." *Journal of Democracy* 14, 1 (January 2003): 137–44.

Lucas, Russell E. *Institutions and the Politics of Survival in Jordan.* Albany: State University of New York Press, 2005.

Lucas, Russell E. "Monarchical Authoritarianism: Survival and Political Liberalization in a Middle Eastern Regime Type." *International Journal of Middle East Studies* 36, 1 (February 2004): 103–19.

Lucas, Russell E. "Press Laws as a Survival Strategy in Jordan, 1989–99." *Middle Eastern Studies* 39, 4 (October 2003): 81–98.

Ludwikowski, Rett R. "Constitution Making in the Countries of Former Soviet Dominance: Current Development." *Georgia Journal of International and Comparative Law* 23 (Summer 1993): 155–267.

Ludwikowski, Rett R. "'Mixed' Constitutions: Product of an East-Central European Constitutional Melting Pot." *Boston University International Law Journal* 16 (Spring 1998): 1–70.

Lukashuk, Alexander. "Yesterday as Tomorrow: Why It Works in Belarus." *East European Constitutional Review* 7, 3 (Summer 1998): 43–9.

Lukšič, Igor. "Corporatism Packaged in Pluralist Ideology: The Case of Slovenia." *Communist and Post-Communist Studies* 36, 4 (December 2003): 509–25.

Luna, Juan P., and Elizabeth J. Zechmeister. "Political Representation in Latin America: A Study of Elite-Mass Congruence in Nine Countries." *Comparative Political Studies* 38, 4 (May 2005): 388–416.

Luong, Pauline Jones. "After the Break-up: Institutional Design in Transitional States." *Comparative Political Studies* 33, 5 (June 2000): 563–92.

Luong, Pauline Jones. *Institutional Change and Political Continuity in Post-Soviet Central Asia: Power, Perceptions, and Pacts.* Cambridge: Cambridge University Press, 2002.

Lust-Okar, Ellen. *Structuring Conflict in the Arab World: Incumbents, Opponents, and Institutions.* New York: Cambridge University Press, 2005.

Lust-Okar, Ellen, and Amaney Ahmad Jamal. "Rulers and Rules: Reassessing the Influence of Regime Type on Electoral Law Formation." *Comparative Political Studies* 35, 3 (April 2002): 337–66.

Luther, Kurt Richard, and Kris Deschouwer, eds. *Party Elites in Divided Societies: Political Parties in Consociational Democracy.* London: Routledge, 1999.

Mackerras, Malcolm, and Ian McAllister. "Compulsory Voting, Party Stability, and Electoral Advantage in Australia." *Electoral Studies* 18, 2 (June 1999): 217–33.

Maddox, Robert L. *Constitutions of the World.* Washington, DC: Congressional Quarterly, 1995.

Magnusson, Bruce A. "Democratization and Domestic Insecurity: Navigating the Transition in Benin." *Comparative Politics* 33, 2 (January 2001): 473–92.

Maghraoui, Abdeslam M. "Depoliticization in Morocco." *Journal of Democracy* 13, 4 (October 2002): 24–32.

Maghraoui, Abdeslam M. "Monarchy and Political Reform in Morocco." *Journal of Democracy* 12, 1 (January 2001): 73–86.

Magone, José M., ed. *Regional Institutions and Governance in the European Union.* Westport, CT: Praeger, 2003.

Mahler, Gregory S. "Canadian Federalism and Constitutional Reform." *Journal of Commonwealth & Comparative Politics* 25, 2 (July 1987): 107–25.

Mahler, Gregory S. *Comparative Politics: An Institutional and Cross-National Approach.* 4th ed. Upper Saddle River, NJ: Prentice Hall, 2002.

Mahler, Gregory S. *The Knesset: Parliament in the Israeli Political System.* Madison, NJ: Fairleigh Dickinson University Press, 1981.

Mahler, Gregory S. *Politics and Government in Israel: The Maturation of a Modern State.* Lanham, MD: Rowman and Littlefield, 2004.

Mainwaring, Scott, and Aníbal S. Pérez-Liñán. "Party Discipline in the Brazilian Constitutional Congress." *Legislative Studies Quarterly* 22, 4 (November 1997): 453–83.

Mainwaring, Scott, and Matthew Soberg Shugart, eds. *Presidential Democracy in Latin America.* New York: Cambridge University Press, 1997.

Makumbe, John. "Is There a Civil Society in Africa?" *International Affairs* 74, 2 (1998): 305–17.

Malik, Yogendra K., Charles H. Kennedy, Robert C. Oberst, and Craig Baxter, eds. *Government and Politics in South Asia.* Boulder, CO: Westview, 2001.

Mallat, Chibli. "On the Specificity of Middle Eastern Constitutionalism." *Case Western Reserve Journal of International Law* 38 (2006): 13–57.

Malovà, Darina, and Tim Haughton. "Making Institutions in Central and Eastern Europe, and the Impact of Europe." *West European Politics* 25, 2 (April 2002): 101–20.

Mamadouh, Virginie, and Tapio Raunio. "The Committee System: Powers, Appointments, and Report Allocation." *Journal of Common Market Studies* 41, 2 (April 2003): 333–51.

Mandaza, Ibbo, and Arne Tostensen. *Southern Africa: In Search of a Common Future.* Gaborone: SADC, 1994.

Manfredi, Christopher P. "Institutional Design and the Politics of Constitutional Modification: Understanding Amendment Failure in the United States and Canada." *Law and Society Review* 31, 1 (1997): 111–36.

Manfredi, Christopher P. *Judicial Power and the Charter: Canada and the Paradox of Liberal Constitutionalism.* Don Mills, Ontario: Oxford University Press, 2005.

Manfredi, Christopher P., and Michael Lusztig. "Why Do Formal Amendments Fail? An Institutional Design Analysis." *World Politics* 50, 3 (April 1998): 377–400.

Manning, Carrie L. "Assessing African Party Systems after the Third Wave." *Party Politics* 11, 6 (November 2005): 707–27.

Manning, Carrie L. "Elite Habituation to Democracy in Mozambique: The View from Parliament, 1994–2000." *Journal of Commonwealth & Comparative Politics* 40, 1 (March 2002): 61–80.

Manning, Carrie L. *The Politics of Peace in Mozambique: Post-Conflict Democratization, 1992–2000.* Westport, CT: Praeger, 2002.

Manning, Carrie L., and Mijenko Antic. "The Limits of Electoral Engineering." *Journal of Democracy* 14, 3 (July 2003): 45–59.

Manow, Philip. "Electoral Rules and Legislative Turnover: Evidence from Germany's Mixed Electoral System." *West European Politics* 30, 1 (January 2007): 195–207.

Mansfeldova, Zdenka. "Executive-Legislative Relations in the Budgeting Process in the Czech Republic." *Czech Sociological Review* 41, 3 (June 2005): 443–59.

Manuel, Paul Christopher. *The Challenges of Democratic Consolidation in Portugal: Political, Economic, and Military Issues, 1976–1991.* Westport, CT: Praeger, 1996.

Manuel, Paul Christopher, and Anne Marie Cammisa. *Checks and Balances: How a Parliamentary System Could Change American Politics.* Boulder, CO: Westview, 1998.

Manzetti, Luigi. *Institutions, Parties, and Coalitions in Argentine Politics.* Pittsburgh, PA: University of Pittsburgh Press, 1993.

March, Michael, and Paul Mitchell, eds. *How Ireland Voted 1997.* Boulder, CO: Westview, 1999.

Marcus, Richard R., and Adrien M. Ratsimbaharison. "Political Parties in Madagascar: Neopatrimonial Tools or Democratic Institutions?" *Party Politics* 11, 4 (2005): 495–512.

Marcus, Richard R., and Paul Razafindrakoto. "Madagascar: A New Democracy?" *Current History* 102, 664 (May 2003): 215–21.

Marples, David R. *Belarus: A Denationalized Nation.* London: Routledge, 1999.

Marples, David R. "Europe's Last Dictatorship: The Roots and Perspectives of Authoritarianism in 'White Russia.'" *Europe-Asia Studies* 57, 6 (September 2005): 895–908.

Marples, David R. "The Prospects for Democracy in Belarus." *Problems of Post-Communism* 51, 1 (January–February 2004): 31–42.

Marples, David R., and Lyubov Pervushina. "Belarus: Lukashenko's Hunt for Red October." *Problems of Post-Communism* 52, 2 (March–April 2005): 19–28.

Mars, Perry. "Ethnic Politics, Mediation, and Conflict Resolution: The Guyana Experience." *Journal of Peace Research* 38, 3 (May 2001): 353–72.

Mars, Perry, and Alma H. Young, eds. *Caribbean Labor and Politics: Legacies of Cheddi Jagan and Michael Manley*. Detroit, MI: Wayne State University Press, 2004.

Marsh, Michael. "Testing the Second-Order Election Model after Four European Elections." *British Journal of Political Science* 28, 4 (October 1998): 591–607.

Martin, Elizabeth M. "An Informational Theory of the Legislative Veto." *Journal of Law, Economics, and Organization* 13, 2 (October 1997): 319–43.

Martin, Lanny W., and Randolph A. Stevenson. "Government Formation in Parliamentary Democracies." *American Journal of Political Science* 45, 1 (January 2001): 33–50.

Martin, Lanny W., and Georg Vanberg. "Coalition Policymaking and Legislative Review." *American Political Science Review* 99, 1 (February 2005): 93–106.

Masuyama, Mikitaka, and Benjamin Nyblade. "Japan: The Prime Minister and the Japanese Diet." *Journal of Legislative Studies* 10, 2–3 (Summer–Autumn 2004): 250–62.

Mathur, Kuldeep. *Development Policy and Administration*. London: Sage, 1999.

Mathur, Kuldeep. "The State and the Use of Coercive Power in India." *Asian Survey* 32, 4 (April 1992): 337–49.

Mathur, Kuldeep. *Top Policy Makers in India: Cabinet Ministers and Their Civil Service Advisors*. New Delhi: Concept Publishing, 1994.

Mathur, Kuldeep, and Niraja Gopal Jayal. *Drought, Policy, and Politics in India*. London: Sage, 1993.

Matland, Richard E., and Donley T. Studlar. "Determinants of Legislative Turnover: A Cross-National Analysis." *British Journal of Political Science* 34, 1 (2004): 87–108.

Matlosa, Khabele. "Democracy and Conflict in Post-Apartheid Southern Africa: Dilemmas of Social Change in Small States." *International Affairs* 74, 2 (April 1998): 319–37.

Matthews, Donald R., and Henry Valen. *Parliamentary Representation: The Case of the Norwegian Storting*. Columbus: Ohio State University Press, 1999.

Mattila, Mikko. "From Qualified Majority to Simple Majority: The Effects of the 1992 Change in the Finnish Constitution." *Scandinavian Political Studies* 20, 4 (November 1997): 317–31.

Mattila, Mikko, and Tapio Raunio. "Government Formation in the Nordic Countries: The Electoral Connection." *Scandinavian Political Studies* 25, 3 (September 2002): 259–80.

Maundeni, Zibani. "Mutual Criticism and State/Society Interaction in Botswana." *Journal of Modern African Studies* 42, 4 (December 2004): 619–36.

Maundeni, Zibani. "State Culture and Development in Botswana and Zimbabwe." *Journal of Modern African Studies* 40, 1 (March 2002): 105–32.

Mauzy, Diane K. "Singapore in 1995: Consolidating the Succession." *Asian Survey* 36, 2 (February 1996): 117–22.

Mauzy, Diane K. *Singapore Politics under the People's Action Party*. London: Routledge, 2002.

Mayer, Ann Elizabeth. "Conundrums of Constitutionalism: Islamic Monarchies in an Era of Transition." *UCLA Journal of Islamic and Near Eastern Law* 1 (Spring/Summer 2002): 183–228.

Mayer, Ann Elizabeth. "Moroccans – Citizens or Subjects? A People at the Crossroads." *New York University Journal of International Law and Politics* 26 (Fall 1993): 63–105.

Mayhew, David R. *Congress: The Electoral Connection*. New Haven, CT: Yale University Press, 1974.

Mayorga, Rene A. *Desmontaje de la Democracia Crítica de las propuestas de reforma política del Diálogo Nacional 2000 y las tendencias antisistémicas*. La Paz: Centro Boliviano de Estudios Multidisciplinarios, 2001.

Mazo, Eugene. "Post-Communist Paradox: How the Rise of Parliamentarism Coincided with the Demise of Pluralism in Moldova." Center on Democracy, Development, and the Rule of Law, Stanford University, working paper, August 2004.

Mbaku, John Mukum, and Joseph Takougang. *The Leadership Challenge in Africa: Cameroon under Paul Biya*. Trenton, NJ: Africa World Press, 2004.

Mbao, M. L. M. "Constitutional Government and Human Rights in Botswana." *Lesotho Law Journal* 6, 1 (1990): 179–97.

McCargo, Duncan. "Network Monarchy and Legitimacy Crises in Thailand." *Pacific Review* 18, 4 (December 2005): 499–519.

McCarty, Nolan M., and Keith T. Poole. "Veto Power and Legislation: An Empirical Analysis of Executive and Legislative Bargaining from 1961 to 1986." *Journal of Law, Economics, and Organization* 11, 2 (October 1995): 282–312.

McClintock, Cynthia. "Peru-Fujimori: A Caudillo Derails Democracy." *Current History* 92, 572 (March 1993): 112–19.

McClintock, Cynthia. *Revolutionary Movements in Latin America: El Salvador's FMLN and Peru's Shining Path*. Washington, DC: U.S. Institute of Peace, 1998.

McClintock, Cynthia. "An Unlikely Comeback in Peru." *Journal of Democracy* 17, 4 (October 2006): 95–109.

McCoy, Jennifer, Andres Serbin, and William C. Smith, eds. *Venezuelan Democracy under Stress*. Somerset, NJ: Transaction, 1995.

McDorman, Ted L. "The 1991 Constitution of Thailand." *Pacific Rim Law and Policy Journal* 3 (February 1995): 257–98.

McFaul, Michael, Nikolai Petrov, and Andrei Riabov. *Between Dictatorship and Democracy: Russian Post-Communist Political Reform.* Washington, DC: Carnegie Endowment for International Peace, 2004.

McLeay, Elizabeth. *The Cabinet and Political Power in New Zealand.* New York: Oxford University Press, 1995.

McPherson, Christina M. "Russia's 1993 Constitution: Rule of Law for Russia or Merely a Return to Autocracy?" *Hastings Constitutional Law Quarterly* 27 (Fall 1999): 155–80.

McRobie, Alan. "The New Zealand General Election of 1990." *Electoral Studies* 10, 2 (June 1991): 158–71.

McWhinney, Edward. "The New Canadian Constitution: The Constitutional Patriation Project, 1980–82." *American Journal of Comparative Law* 32, 2 (Spring 1984): 241–68.

Mehler, Andreas. *Kamerun in der Ära Biya: Bedingungen, erste Schritte und Blockaden einer demokratischen Transition.* Hamburg: Institut für Afrika-Kunde, 1993.

Mehler, Andreas, and Dennis Tull. "The Hidden Costs of Power-Sharing: Reproducing Insurgent Violence in Africa." *African Affairs* 104, 416 (July 2005): 375–98.

Meighoo, Kirk. *Politics in a Half-Made Society: Trinidad and Tobago, 1935–2001.* Princeton, NJ: M. Wiener, 2004.

Meinhardt, Heiko, and Nandini Patel. *Malawi's Process of Democratic Transition: An Analysis of Political Developments between 1990 and 2003.* Lilongwe: Konrad-Adenauer-Stiftung, 2003.

Melber, Henning, ed. *Limits to Liberation in Southern Africa: The Unfinished Business of Democratic Consolidation.* Cape Town: HSRC Press, 2003.

Melone, Albert P. "Bulgarian National Round-Table Talks and the Politics of Accommodation." *International Political Science Review* 15, 3 (July 1994): 257–73.

Melone, Albert P. *Creating Parliamentary Government: The Transition to Democracy in Bulgaria.* Columbus: Ohio State University Press, 1998.

Melone, Albert P. "Judicial Independence and Constitutional Politics in Bulgaria." *Judicature* 80, 6 (May–June 1997): 280–5.

Melone, Albert P. "The Struggle for Judicial Independence and the Transition toward Democracy in Bulgaria." *Communist and Post-Communist Studies* 29, 2 (June 1996): 231–43.

Mengisteab, Kidane. "New Approaches to State Building in Africa: The Case of Ethiopia's Ethnic-Based Federalism." *African Studies Review* 40, 3 (1997): 111–32.

Mengisteab, Kidane, and Cyril Daddieh, eds. *State Building and Democratization in Africa.* Westport, CT: Praeger, 1999.

Mengisteab, Kidane, and Okbazghi Yohannes. *Anatomy of an African Tragedy: Political, Economic, and Foreign Policy Crisis in Post-Independence Eritrea.* Trenton, NJ: Red Sea Press, 2005.

Mentan, Tatah. *Dilemmas of Weak States: Africa and Transnational Terrorism in the Twenty-first Century.* Aldershot, U.K.: Ashgate, 2004.

Mény, Yves, and Yves Surel, eds. *Democracies and the Populist Challenge.* New York: Palgrave Macmillan, 2002.

Meseznikov, Grigorii, Miroslav Kollar, and Tom Nicholson. *Slovakia 2002: A Global Report on the State of Society.* Bratislava: Institute for Public Affairs, 2003.

Metcalf, Lee Kendall. "Presidential Power in the Russian Constitution." *Journal of Transnational Law and Policy* 6 (Fall 1996): 125–42.

Metcalf, Michael, ed. *The Riksdag: A History of the Swedish Parliament.* London: Palgrave Macmillan, 1988.

Meyer, Steven A., and Shigeto Naka. "Legislative Influences in Japanese Budgetary Politics." *Public Choice* 94, 3–4 (March 1998): 267–88.

Mezey, Michael. *Comparative Legislatures.* Durham, NC: Duke University Press, 1979.

Miles, Lee. "Sweden: A Relevant or Redundant Parliament?" *Parliamentary Affairs* 50, 3 (July 1997): 423–37.

Milne, R. S., and Diane K. Mauzy. *Malaysian Politics under Mahathir.* London: Routledge, 1999.

Moe, Terry M., and Michael Caldwell. "The Institutional Foundations of Democratic Government: A Comparison of Presidential and Parliamentary Systems." *Journal of Institutional and Theoretical Economics* 150, 1 (1994): 171–95.

Molina, José. "The Electoral Effect of Underdevelopment: Government Turnover and Its Causes in Latin American, Caribbean and Industrialized Countries." *Electoral Studies* 20, 3 (September 2001): 427–46.

Molinar Horcasitas, Juan, and Jeffrey A. Weldon. "Elecciones de 1988 en México: Crisis del autoritarismo." *Revista Mexicana de Sociología,* 52, 4 (October–December 1990): 229–62.

Molinas, José, Aníbal S. Pérez-Liñán, and Sebastián Saiegh. "Political Institutions, Policymaking Processes, and Policy Outcomes in Paraguay, 1954–2003." *Revista de Ciencia Politica* 24, 2 (2004): 67–93.

Moon, Jeremy, and Anthony M. Sayers. "The Dynamics of Governmental Activity: A Long-Run Analysis of the Changing Scope and Profile of Australian Ministerial Portfolios." *Australian Journal of Political Science* 34, 2 (July 1999): 149–67.

Moore, Pete W. *Doing Business in the Middle East: Politics and Economic Crisis in Jordan and Kuwait.* Cambridge: Cambridge University Press, 2004.

Moore, Pete W. "What Makes Successful Business Lobbies? Business Associations and the Rentier State in Jordan and Kuwait." *Comparative Politics* 33, 2 (January 2001): 127–47.

Moraski, Bryon J., and Charles R. Shipan. "The Politics of Supreme Court Nominations: A Theory of Institutional Constraints and Choices." *American Journal of Political Science* 43, 4 (October 1999): 1069–95.

Moreno, Erika. "Whither the Colombian Two-Party System? An Assessment of Political Reforms and Their Limits." *Electoral Studies* 24, 3 (September 2005): 485–509.

Morgenstern, Scott. "Organized Factions and Disorganized Parties: Electoral Incentives in Uruguay." *Party Politics* 7, 2 (March 2001): 235–56.

Morgenstern, Scott. *Patterns of Legislative Politics: An Exploration of Roll Call Voting in the United States and Latin America's Southern Cone.* Cambridge: Cambridge University Press, 2003.

Morgenstern, Scott, and Benito Nacif, eds. *Legislative Politics in Latin America.* New York: Cambridge University Press, 2002.

Morlino, Leonardo. "Consolidation and Party Government in Southern Europe." *International Political Science Review* 16, 2 (April 1995): 145–67.

Morlino, Leonardo, and Marco Tarchi. "The Dissatisfied Society: The Roots of Political Change in Italy." *European Journal of Political Research* 30, 1 (July 1996): 41–63.

Morrison, Minion K. C. "Political Parties in Ghana through Four Republics: A Path to Democratic Consolidation." *Comparative Politics* 36, 4 (July 2004): 421–42.

Mortimer, Robert. "Bouteflika and Algeria's Path from Revolt to Reconciliation." *Current History* 99, 633 (January 2000): 10–15.

Mortimer, Robert. "Islamists, Soldiers, and Democrats: The Second Algerian War." *Middle East Journal* 50, 1 (Winter 1996): 18–39.

Moustafa, Tamir. "Law versus the State: The Judicialization of Politics in Egypt." *Law and Social Inquiry* 28, 4 (Fall 2003): 883–930.

Mphaisha, Chisepo J. J. "Retreat from Democracy in Post One-Party State Zambia." *Journal of Commonwealth & Comparative Politics* 34, 2 (1996): 65–84.

Mpundu, José. *Partis politiques.* Kinshasa: L'Epiphanie, 1991.

Msekwa, Pius. *Reflections on Tanzania's First Multi-Party Parliament, 1995–2000.* Dar es Salaam: Dar es Salaam University Press, 2000.

Mugisha, Anne. "Museveni's Machinations." *Journal of Democracy* 15, 2 (April 2004): 140–4.

Mukandala, Rwekaza. "Trends in Civil-Service Size and Income in Tanzania, 1967–1982." *Canadian Journal of African Studies* 17, 2 (1983): 253–63.

Muller, Pierre, and Yves Surel. *L'analyse des politiques publiques.* Paris: Montchrestien, 2000.

Müller, Wolfgang C. "The Austrian Election of October 1999: A Shift to the Right." *West European Politics* 23, 3 (July 2000): 191–200.

Müller, Wolfgang C. "Political Parties in Parliamentary Democracies: Making Delegation and Accountability Work." *European Journal of Political Research* 37, 3 (May 2000): 309–33.

Müller, Wolfgang C., and Franz Fallend. "Changing Patterns of Party Competition in Austria: From Multipolar to Bipolar System." *West European Politics* 27, 5 (November 2004): 801–35.

Müller, Wolfgang C., and Kaare Strøm, eds. *Coalition Governments in Western Europe.* Oxford: Oxford University Press, 2003.

Murphy, Richard W., and F. Gregory Gause. "Democracy and U.S. Policy in the Muslim Middle East." *Middle East Policy* 5, 1 (January 1997): 58–67.

Musolf, Lloyd D. *Malaysia's Parliamentary System: Representative Politics and Policymaking in a Divided Society.* Boulder, CO: Westview, 1979.

Mustapic, Ana M. "Oficialistas y diputados: Las relaciones Ejecutivo-Legislativo en la Argentina." *Desarrollo Económico – Revista de Ciencias Sociales* 39, 156 (January–March 2000): 571–95.

Mustapic, Ana M., and Matteo Goretti. "Gobierno y oposición en el Congreso: La práctica de la cohabilitación durante la presidencia de Alfonsín (1983–89)." *Desarrollo Económico – Revista de Ciencias Sociales* 32, 126 (July–September 1992): 251–69.

Mwalimu, Charles. "The Influence of Constitutions on the Development of a Nation's Law and Legal System: The Case of Zambia and Nigeria." *St. Louis University Public Law Review* 8 (1989): 157–88.

Mwalimu, Charles. "Police, State Security Forces and Constitutionalism of Human Rights in Zambia." *Georgia Journal of International and Comparative Law* 21 (1997): 217–43.

Mwenda, Andrew M. "Personalizing Power in Uganda." *Journal of Democracy* 18, 3 (July 2007): 23–37.

Nacif, Benito. "Las relaciones entre los poderes ejecutivo y legislativo en México tras el fin del presidencialismo." *Política y Gobierno* 11, 1 (2004): 9–41.

Nacif, Benito. "La rotación de cargos legislativos y la evolución del sistema de partidos en México." *Política y Gobierno* 4, 1 (1997): 115–46.

Nanakorn, Pinai. "Re-Making of the Constitution in Thailand." *Singapore Journal of International and Comparative Law* 6 (2002): 90–115.

Nardini, William J. "Passive Activism and the Limits of Judicial Self-Restraint: Lessons for America from the Italian Constitutional Court." *Seton Hall Law Review* 30 (1999): 1–63.

Nasong'o, Shadrack Wanjala. *Contending Political Paradigms in Africa: Rationality and the Politics of Democratization in Kenya and Zambia.* London: Taylor and Francis, 2005.

N'Diaye, Boubacar. "Mauritania's Stalled Democratization." *Journal of Democracy* 12, 3 (July 2001): 88–95.

N'Diaye, Boubacar, Abdoulaye Saine, and Mathurin Houngnikpo. *Not Yet Democracy: West Africa's Slow Farewell to Authoritarianism*. Durham, NC: Carolina Academic Press, 2005.

Ndulo, Muna. "The Democratization Process and Structural Adjustment in Africa." *Indiana Journal of Global Legal Studies* 10, 1 (Winter 2003): 315–68.

Negretto, Gabriel L. "Government Capacities and Policy Making by Decree in Latin America: The Cases of Brazil and Argentina." *Comparative Political Studies* 37, 5 (June 2004): 531–62.

Neher, Clark D. "Thailand in 1986: Prem, Parliament, and Political Pragmatism." *Asian Survey* 27, 2 (February 1987): 210–30.

Nichols, Thomas M. *The Russian Presidency: Society and Politics in the Second Russian Republic*. Basingstoke, U.K.: Macmillan, 2001.

Nielson, Daniel L., and Matthew Soberg Shugart. "Constitutional Change in Colombia: Policy Adjustment through Institutional Reform." *Comparative Political Studies* 32, 3 (May 1999): 313–41.

Niemi, Richard G., Simon Jackman, and Laura R. Winsky. "Candidacies and Competitiveness in Multimember Districts." *Legislative Studies Quarterly* 16, 1 (February 1991): 91–109.

Niemi, Richard G., and Herbert F. Weisberg. *Probability Models of Collective Decision Making*. Columbus, OH: Merrill, 1972.

Nobre, Augusto. "The Political Structure of the Federal Brazilian Republic under the Constitution of 1988." *University of Miami Inter-American Law Review* 21, 3 (Summer 1990): 551–88.

Nodia, Ghia. "The Democratic Path." *Journal of Democracy* 13, 3 (July 2002): 13–19.

Noorani, A. G. *Constitutional Questions in India: The President, Parliament, and the States*. New York: Oxford University Press, 2000.

Norton, Philip. *Legislatures*. Oxford: Oxford University Press, 2005.

Norton, Philip, ed. *Parliaments and Pressure Groups in Western Europe*. London: Frank Cass, 1999.

Noury, Abdul G., and Gérard Roland. "More Power to the European Parliament?" *Economic Policy* 35 (October 2002): 280–319.

Nousiainen, Jaakko. "From Semi-Presidentialism to Parliamentary Government: Political and Constitutional Developments in Finland." *Scandinavian Political Studies* 24, 2 (June 2001): 95–109.

Nyamnjoh, Francis B. *Africa's Media: Democracy and the Politics of Belonging*. London: Zed, 2005.

Oates, Sarah. "The 1999 Russian Parliamentary Elections." *Problems of Post-Communism* 47, 3 (May–June 2000): 3–14.

O'Brien, Kevin J. "Chinese People's Congresses and Legislative Embeddedness: Understanding Early Organizational Development." *Comparative Political Studies* 27, 1 (April 1994): 80–107.

O'Brien, Kevin J. "Hunting for Political Change." *China Journal* 41 (January 1999): 159–69.

O'Brien, Kevin J. *Reform without Liberalization: China's National People's Congress and the Politics of Institutional Change*. New York: Cambridge University Press, 1990.

O'Brien, Kevin J., and Laura M. Luehrmann. "Institutionalizing Chinese Legislatures: Trade-offs between Autonomy and Capacity." *Legislative Studies Quarterly* 23, 1 (February 1998): 91–108.

Oceana Law. "Constitutions of the Countries of the World." Online at http://www.oceanalaw.com. Site consulted 2006–7.

O'Donnell, Guillermo A. "Delegative Democracy." In Larry Diamond and Marc F. Plattner, eds., *The Global Resurgence of Democracy*. Baltimore, MD: Johns Hopkins University Press, 1996: 94–108.

O'Donnell, Guillermo A. "Democracy, Law, and Comparative Politics." *Studies in Comparative International Development* 36, 1 (Spring 2001): 7–36.

O'Dwyer, Conor. "Runaway State Building: How Political Parties Shape States in Postcommunist Eastern Europe." *World Politics* 56, 4 (July 2004): 520–53.

Oertel, Stéphane. *Governance Profile of Ethiopia*. Addis Ababa: United Nations Economic Commission for Africa, 2004.

Okere, B. Obinna. "Judicial Activism or Passivity in Interpreting the Nigerian Constitution." *International and Comparative Law Quarterly* 36 (1987): 788–816.

Okudaira, Yasuhiro. "Forty Years of the Constitution and Its Various Influences: Japanese, American, and European." *Law and Contemporary Problems* 53, 1 (Winter 1990): 17–49.

Olowu, Dele, and Adebayo Williams, eds. *Governance and Democratization in West Africa*. Lansing: Michigan State University Press, 1999.

Olson, David M. "New Wine in Old Institutions: Parliaments in Post-Communist Democracies." *Problems of Post-Communism* 46, 1 (January–February 1999): 15–23.

Olson, David M. "Paradoxes of Institutional Development: The New Democratic Parliaments of Central Europe." *International Political Science Review* 18, 4 (October 1997): 401–16.

Olson, David M., and William E. Crowther, eds. *Committees in Post-Communist Democratic Parliaments: Comparative Institutionalization*. Columbus: Ohio State University Press, 2002.

O'Malley, Eoin, and Michael March. "Ireland." *European Journal of Political Research* 44, 7–8 (December 2005): 1049–55.

Omitoogun, Wuyi, and Kenneth Onigu-Otite. *The National Conference as a Model for Democratic Transition: Benin and Nigeria*. Ibadan, Nigeria: IFRA/African Book Builders, 1996.

Öniş, Ziya. "Diverse but Converging Paths to European Union Membership: Poland and Turkey in Comparative Perspective." *East European Politics and Societies* 18, 3 (Summer 2004): 481–512.

Öniş, Ziya. "The Political Economy of Islamic Resurgence in Turkey: The Rise of the Welfare Party in Perspective." *Third World Quarterly* 18, 4 (September 1997): 743–66.

Öniş, Ziya. *State and Market: The Political Economy of Turkey in Comparative Perspective.* London: Milet, 1999.

Opello, Walter C. "Portugal's Parliament: An Organizational Analysis of Legislative Performance." *Legislative Studies Quarterly* 11, 3 (August 1986): 291–319.

Ortwein, Bernard Michael. "The Swedish Legal System: An Introduction." *Indiana International and Comparative Law Review* 13 (2003): 405–45.

Ostrow, Joel M. *Comparing Post-Soviet Legislatures: A Theory of Institutional Design and Political Conflict.* Columbus: Ohio State University Press, 2000.

Otayek, René. 1999. "La démocratie entre mobilisations identitaires et besoin d'etat: Y a-t-il une 'exception' africaine?" *Autrepart* 10 (1999): 5–22.

Ottaway, Marina S., Jillian Schwedler, Shibley Telhami, and Saad Eddin Ibrahim. "Democracy: Rising Tide or Mirage?" *Middle East Policy* 12, 2 (Summer 2005): 1–27.

Ottolenghi, Emanuele. "Choosing a Prime Minister: Executive-Legislative Relations in Israel in the 1990s." *Journal of Legislative Studies* 10, 2–3 (Summer–Autumn 2004): 263–77.

Ottolenghi, Emanuele. "Why Direct Election Failed in Israel." *Journal of Democracy* 12, 4 (October 2001): 109–22.

Oxhorn, Philip, Joseph S. Tulchin, and Andrew D. Selee, eds. *Decentralization, Democratic Governance, and Civil Society in Comparative Perspective: Africa, Asia, and Latin America.* Washington, DC: Woodrow Wilson Center Press, 2004.

Oyediran, Oyeleye, and Adigun Agbaje, eds. *Nigeria: Politics of Transition and Governance 1986–1996.* Lansing: Michigan State University Press, 1999.

Oyediran, Oyeleye, and Adigun Agbaje. "Two-Partyism and Democratic Transition in Nigeria." *Journal of Modern African Studies* 29, 2 (June 1991): 213–35.

Özbudun, Ergun. "Constitutional Debates on Parliamentary Inviolability in Turkey." *European Constitutional Law Review* 1, 2 (June 2005): 272–80.

Özbudun, Ergun. "Political Origins of the Turkish Constitutional Court and the Problem of Democratic Legitimacy." *European Public Law* 12, 2 (2006): 213–23.

Pachano, Simón. *Los diputados: Una élite política.* Quito: Corporación Editora Nacional, 1991.

Page, E. C. "The Civil Servant as Legislator: Law Making in British Administration." *Public Administration* 81, 4 (December 2003): 651–79.

Palmer, Geoffrey. "The New Zealand Constitution and the Power of Courts." *Transnational Law and Contemporary Problems* 15 (Spring 2006): 551–77.

Panizza, Francisco. "Late Institutionalisation and Early Modernisation: The Emergence of Uruguay's Liberal Democratic Political Order." *Journal of Latin American Studies* 29, 3 (October 1997): 667–91.

Panizza, Francisco, ed. *Populism and the Mirror of Democracy.* New York: W. W. Norton, 2005.

Pantin, Dennis, ed. *The Caribbean Economy: A Reader.* Kingston: Ian Randle, 2005.

Papadimitriou, Dimitris. *Romania and the European Union: From Marginalization to Membership?* London: Routledge, 2006.

Park, Chan Wook. "Constituency Representation in Korea: Sources and Consequences." *Legislative Studies Quarterly* 13, 2 (May 1988): 225–42.

Pasquino, Gianfranco. "The Government, the Opposition, and the President of the Republic under Berlusconi." *Journal of Modern Italian Studies* 8, 4 (December 2003): 485–99.

Pastukhov, Mikhail. "Presidential Abuse of Powers in Belarus." *Parker School Journal of East European Law* 4, 4 (1997): 479–98.

Patel, David Siddhartha. "Islam, Information, and Social Order: The Strategic Role of Religion in Muslim Societies." Ph.D. dissertation, Department of Political Science, Stanford University, 2007.

Patterson, Samuel C. "Understanding the British Parliament." *Political Studies* 37, 3 (September 1989): 449–62.

Patterson, Samuel C., and Anthony Mughan. *Senates: Bicameralism in the Contemporary World.* Columbus: Ohio State University Press, 1999.

Patzelt, Werner J. "Recruitment and Retention in Western Parliaments." *Legislative Studies Quarterly* 24, 2 (May 1999): 239–79.

Payne, Anthony. "Westminster Adapted: The Political Order of the Commonwealth Caribbean." In Jorge I. Dominguez, Robert A. Pastor, and R. DeLisle Worrell, eds., *Democracy in the Caribbean.* Baltimore, MD: Johns Hopkins University Press, 1993: 57–73.

Pei, Minxin. "Is China Democratizing?" *Foreign Affairs* 77, 1 (January–February 1998): 68–82.

Pempel, T. J. "The Dilemma of Parliamentary Opposition in Japan." *Polity* 8, 1 (1975): 63–79.

Pempel, T. J., ed. *Uncommon Democracies: The One Party Dominant Regimes.* Ithaca, NY: Cornell University Press, 1990.

Pepinsky, Thomas B. "Malaysia: Turnover without Change." *Journal of Democracy* 18, 1 (January 2007): 113–27.

Pereira, Carlos, and Bernardo Mueller. "A Theory of Executive Dominance of Congressional Politics: The

Committee System in the Brazilian Chamber of Deputies." *Journal of Legislative Studies* 10, 1 (Spring 2004): 9–49.

Pereira, Carlos, Timothy J. Power, and Lucio Rennó. "Under What Conditions Do Presidents Resort to Decree Power? Theory and Evidence from the Brazilian Case." *Journal of Politics* 67, 1 (February 2005): 178–200.

Pérez, Orlando J. "Democratic Legitimacy and Public Insecurity: Crime and Democracy in El Salvador and Guatemala." *Political Science Quarterly* 118, 4 (Winter 2003): 627–44.

Pérez, Orlando J. *Post-Invasion Panama: The Challenges of Democratization in the New World Order.* Lanham, MD: Lexington Books, 2000.

Pérez-Liñán, Aníbal S. "Democratization and Constitutional Crises in Presidential Regimes: Toward Congressional Supremacy?" *Comparative Political Studies* 38, 1 (February 2005): 51–74.

Pérez-Liñán, Aníbal S. "Power Struggles and Crisis in Governability: Moving towards a New Form of Autocratic Leadership?" *Latin American Research Review* 38, 3 (2003): 149–64.

Pérez-Liñán, Aníbal S. *Presidential Impeachment and the New Political Instability in Latin America.* New York: Cambridge University Press, 2007.

Perkins, Kenneth. *A History of Modern Tunisia.* Cambridge: Cambridge University Press, 2004.

Persson, Torsten, Gérard Roland, and Guido Tabellini. "Separation of Powers and Political Accountability." *Quarterly Journal of Economics* 112, 4 (November 1997): 1163–1202.

Peterson, Dave. "Burundi's Transition: A Beacon for Central Africa." *Journal of Democracy* 17, 1 (January 2006): 125–31.

Pettai, Vello, and Piret Ehin, eds. *Deciding on Europe: The EU Referendum in Estonia.* Tartu, Estonia: Tartu University Press, 2005.

Phongpaichit, Pasuk, and Chris Baker. "Challenge and Change in East Asia: 'Business Populism' in Thailand." *Journal of Democracy* 16, 2 (April 2005): 58–72.

Pierre, Jon. *Debating Governance: Authority, Steering, and Democracy.* New York: Oxford University Press, 2000.

Poguntke, Thomas, and Paul Webb, eds. *The Presidentialization of Politics: A Comparative Study of Modern Democracies.* Oxford: Oxford University Press, 2007.

Pohjolainen, Teuvo, and Jaakko Husa. "Prospects of Reforming the Finnish Constitution." *European Public Law* 3, 1 (1997): 45–56.

Popkin, Margaret. *Peace without Justice: Obstacles to Building the Rule of Law in El Salvador.* University Park: Pennsylvania State University Press, 2000.

Posner, Daniel N., and David J. Simon. "Economic Conditions and Incumbent Support in Africa's New Democracies: Evidence from Zambia." *Comparative Political Studies* 35, 3 (April 2002): 313–36.

Posusney, Marsha Pripstein, and Michele Penner Angrist, eds. *Authoritarianism in the Middle East: Regimes and Resistance.* Boulder, CO: Lynne Rienner, 2005.

Potocki, Rodger. "Dark Days in Belarus." *Journal of Democracy* 13, 4 (October 2002): 142–56.

Potter, Pitman B. "Curbing the Party: Peng Zhen and Chinese Legal Culture." *Problems of Post-Communism* 45, 3 (May–June 1998): 17–28.

Powell, G. Bingham. *Elections as Instruments of Democracy: Majoritarian and Proportional Visions.* New Haven, CT: Yale University Press, 2000.

Power, Timothy J., and Mark J. Gasiorowski. "Institutional Design and Democratic Consolidation in the Third World." *Comparative Political Studies* 30, 2 (April 1997): 123–55.

Premdas, Ralph R., and Bishnu Ragoonath. "Ethnicity, Elections and Democracy in Trinidad and Tobago: Analysing the 1995 and 1996 Elections." *Commonwealth & Comparative Politics* 36, 3 (November 1998): 30–53.

Prescott, Natalie. "Orange Revolution in Red, White, and Blue: U.S. Impact on the 2004 Ukrainian Election." *Duke Journal of Comparative and International Law* 16 (Winter 2006): 219–48.

Price, Robert M. *The Apartheid State in Crisis: Political Transformation of South Africa, 1975–1990.* New York: Oxford University Press, 1991.

Pridham, Geoffrey. "The European Union's Democratic Conditionality and Domestic Politics in Slovakia: The Meciar and Dzurinda Governments Compared." *Europe-Asia Studies* 54, 2 (March 2002): 203–27.

Pridham, Geoffrey. "The Slovak Parliamentary Election of September 2002: Its Systemic Importance." *Government and Opposition* 38, 3 (Summer 2003): 333–56.

Protsyk, Oleh. "Politics of Intraexecutive Conflict in Semipresidential Regimes in Eastern Europe." *East European Politics and Societies* 19, 2 (Spring 2005): 135–60.

Protsyk, Oleh. "Prime Ministers' Identity in Semi-Presidential Regimes: Constitutional Norms and Cabinet Formation Outcomes." *European Journal of Political Research* 44, 5 (August 2005): 721–48.

Protsyk, Oleh. "Troubled Semi-Presidentialism: Stability of the Constitutional System and Cabinet in Ukraine." *Europe-Asia Studies* 55, 7 (November 2003): 1077–95.

Przeworski, Adam, Michael Alvarez, José Antonio Cheibub, and Fernando Limongi. *Democracy and Development: Political Institutions and Well-Being in the Modern World, 1950–1990.* New York: Cambridge University Press, 2000.

Putzel, James. "Managing the Main Force: The Communist Party and the Peasantry in the Philippines." *Journal of Peasant Studies* 22, 4 (July 1995): 645–71.

Qodari, Muhammad. "Challenge and Change in East Asia: Indonesia's Quest for Accountable Governance." *Journal of Democracy* 16, 2 (April 2005): 73–87.

Quigley, John. "Perestroika African Style: One-Party Government and Human Rights in Tanzania." *Michigan Journal of International Law* 13 (Spring 1992): 611–52.

Radnitz, Scott. "What Really Happened in Kyrgyzstan?" *Journal of Democracy* 17, 2 (April 2006): 132–46.

Rakner, Lise. *Political and Economic Liberalisation in Zambia, 1991–2001.* Stockholm: Nordic Africa Institute, 2003.

Rakner, Lise, and Lars Svåsand. "From Dominant to Competitive Party System: The Zambian Experience, 1991–2001." *Party Politics* 10, 1 (January 2004): 49–68.

Rakner, Lise, and Lars Svåsand. "Maybe Free but Not Fair: Electoral Administration in Malawi, 1994–2004." Working Paper 5. Bergen, Norway: Chr. Michelsen Institute, 2005.

Rakner, Lise, Lars Svåsand, and Nixon S. Khembo. "Fissions and Fusions, Foes and Friends: Party System Restructuring in Malawi in the 2004 Elections." *Comparative Political Studies* 40, 9 (September 2007): 1112–37.

Ramkarran, Hari N. "Seeking a Democratic Path: Constitutional Reform in Guyana." *Georgia Journal of International and Comparative Law* 32, 3 (2004): 585–612.

Ramseyer, J. Mark, and Frances M. Rosenbluth. *Japan's Political Marketplace.* Cambridge, MA: Harvard University Press, 1993.

Randall, Vicky, and Lars Svåsand. "Party Institutionalization in New Democracies." *Party Politics* 8, 1 (January 2002): 5–29.

Rapaczynski, Andrzej. "Constitutional Politics in Poland: A Report on the Constitutional Committee of the Polish Parliament." *University of Chicago Law Review* 58 (Spring 1991): 595–631.

Rasch, Bjørn Erik. "Manipulation and Strategic Voting in the Norwegian Parliament." *Public Choice* 52, 1 (January 1987): 57–73.

Rasch, Bjørn Erik. "Parliamentary Floor Voting Procedures and Agenda Setting in Europe." *Legislative Studies Quarterly* 25, 1 (February 2000): 3–23.

Raunio, Tapio. "Always One Step Behind? National Legislatures and the European Union." *Government and Opposition* 34, 2 (Spring 1999): 180–202.

Raunio, Tapio. "The Changing Finnish Democracy: Stronger Parliamentary Accountability, Coalescing Political Parties and Weaker External Constraints." *Scandinavian Political Studies* 27, 2 (June 2004): 133–52.

Raunio, Tapio, and Simon Hix. "Backbenchers Learn to Fight Back: European Integration and Parliamentary Government." *West European Politics* 23, 4 (October 2000): 142–68.

Raunio, Tapio, and Teija Tiilikainen. *Finland in the European Union.* London: Frank Cass, 2003.

Rawlings, H. F. "The Malaysian Constitutional Crisis of 1983." *International and Comparative Law Quarterly* 35 (April 1986): 237–54.

Reich, Gary. "Executive Decree Authority in Brazil: How Reactive Legislators Influence Policy." *Legislative Studies Quarterly* 27, 1 (February 2002): 5–31.

Reilly, Benjamin. "Political Engineering in the Asia-Pacific." *Journal of Democracy* 18, 1 (January 2007): 58–72.

Reisinger, William M., Andrei Yu. Melville, Arthur H. Miller, and Vicki L. Hesli. "Mass and Elite Political Outlooks in Post-Soviet Russia: How Congruent?" *Political Research Quarterly* 49, 1 (March 1996): 77–101.

Rembe, Nasila S., and Evance Kalula, eds. *Constitutional Government and Human Rights in Africa.* Published by the *Lesotho Law Journal* 6 (1991).

Remington, Thomas F. "The Evolution of Executive-Legislative Relations in Russia since 1993." *Slavic Review* 59, 3 (Fall 2000): 499–520.

Remington, Thomas F. "Majorities without Mandates: The Russian Federation Council since 2000." *Europe-Asia Studies* 55, 5 (July 2003): 667–91.

Remington, Thomas F. *The Russian Parliament: Institutional Evolution in a Transitional Regime, 1989–1999.* New Haven, CT: Yale University Press, 2001.

Reynolds, Andrew, ed. *The Architecture of Democracy: Constitutional Design, Conflict Management, and Democracy.* New York: Oxford University Press, 2002: 81–103.

Reynolds, Thomas H., and Arturo A. Flores. *Foreign Law: Current Sources of Codes and Basic Legislation in Jurisdictions of the World.* Littleton, CO: Fred B. Rothman, 1989.

Reyntjens, Filip. "Constitution-Making in Situations of Extreme Crisis: The Case of Rwanda and Burundi." *Journal of African Law* 40, 2 (1996): 234–42.

Rial, Juan. "Transitions in Latin America on the Threshold of the 1990s." *International Social Science Journal* 43, 2 (May 1991): 285–300.

Rial, Juan, and Jaime Klaczko. "Historiographical and Historical Studies in Uruguay." *Latin America Research Review* 17, 3 (1982): 229–50.

Rice, Roberta, and Donna Lee Van Cott. "The Emergence and Performance of Indigenous Peoples' Parties in South America: A Subnational Statistical Analysis." *Comparative Political Studies* 39, 6 (August 2006): 709–32.

Richardson, John. *Paradise Poisoned: Learning about Conflict, Terrorism and Development from Sri Lanka's Civil Wars*. Kandy, Sri Lanka: International Centre for Ethnic Studies, 2005.

Ripley, Randall. *Congress: Process and Policy*. New York: W. W. Norton, 1983.

Robbins, John R., and Danica Fink-Hafner, eds. *Making a New Nation: The Formation of Slovenia*. Aldershot, U.K.: Dartmouth, 1997.

Roberts, Kenneth M., and Erik Wibbels. "Party Systems and Electoral Volatility in Latin America: A Test of Economic, Institutional, and Structural Explanations." *American Political Science Review* 93, 3 (September 1999): 575–90.

Roberts, Nigel S., Elizabeth McLeay, Stephen Levine, and Jonathan Boston, eds. *Electoral and Constitutional Change in New Zealand: An MMP Source Book*. Auckland: Dunmore Press, 1999.

Robinson, A. N. R. *The Mechanics of Independence: Patterns of Political and Economic Transformation in Trinidad and Tobago*. Kingston: University of the West Indies Press, 2001.

Robinson, Pearl T. "Niger: Anatomy of a Neo-Traditional Corporatist State." *Comparative Politics* 24, 1 (October 1991): 1–20.

Rodríguez-Arana, Jaime. *La administración única en el marco constitucional*. La Coruña, Spain: Fundación Instituto Gallego de Estudios Autonómicos y Comunitarios, 1993.

Roessler, Philip G. "Donor-Induced Democratization and the Privatization of State Violence in Kenya and Rwanda." *Comparative Politics* 37, 2 (January 2005): 207–27.

Rogers, James. "The Impact of Bicameralism on Legislative Production." *Legislative Studies Quarterly* 28, 4 (November 2003): 509–28.

Roggenband, Conny, and Rens Vliegenthart. "Divergent Framing: The Public Debate on Migration in the Dutch Parliament and the Media, 1995–2004." *West European Politics* 30, 3 (May 2007): 524–48.

Rogoff, Martin A. "A Comparison of Constitutionalism in France and the United States." *Maine Law Review* 49 (1997): 21–84.

Rohde, David W. *Parties and Leaders in the Postreform House*. Chicago: University of Chicago Press, 1991.

Rohrschneider, Robert. "Institutional Learning versus Value Diffusion: The Evolution of Democratic Values among Parliamentarians in Eastern and Western Germany." *Journal of Politics* 58, 2 (May 1996): 422–46.

Rohrschneider, Robert. "Pluralism, Conflict, and Legislative Elites in a United Germany." *Comparative Politics* 29, 1 (October 1996): 43–67.

Roland, Gérard. "Understanding Institutional Change: Fast-Moving and Slow-Moving Institutions." *Studies in Comparative International Development* 38, 4 (Winter 2004): 109–31.

Rommetvedt, Hilmar. *The Rise of the Norwegian Parliament*. London: Frank Cass, 2002.

Roper, Steven D. "Are All Semipresidential Regimes the Same? A Comparison of Premier-Presidential Regimes." *Comparative Politics* 34, 3 (April 2002): 253–72.

Rossatanga-Rignault, Guy. *L'état au Gabon: Histoire et institutions*. Libreville: Editions Raponda-Walker, 2000.

Rotberg, Robert I., ed. *Crafting the New Nigeria: Confronting the Challenges*. Boulder, CO: Lynne Rienner, 2004.

Rotberg, Robert I. *Ending Autocracy, Enabling Democracy: The Tribulations of Southern Africa, 1960–2000*. Washington, DC: Brookings Institution Press, 2002.

Rotberg, Robert I. "Strengthening Governance: Ranking Countries Would Help." *Washington Quarterly* 28, 1 (Winter 2005): 71–81.

Rothmayr, Christine. "Towards the Judicialisation of Swiss Politics?" *West European Politics* 24, 2 (April 2001): 77–94.

Roubaud, François. *Identités et transition democratique: L'exception Malgache?* Paris: Harmattan, 2000.

Royo, Sebastián. *From Social Democracy to Neoliberalism: The Consequences of Party Hegemony in Spain, 1982–1996*. Basingstoke, U.K.: Palgrave Macmillan, 2000.

Royo, Sebastián. "'A New Century of Corporatism?' Corporatism in Spain and Portugal." *West European Politics* 25, 3 (July 2002): 77–104.

Rudebeck, Lars. *On Democracy's Sustainability: Transition in Guinea-Bissau*. Stockholm: SIDA, 2001.

Rudebeck, Lars. "Political Mobilization for Development in Guinea-Bissau." *Journal of Modern African Studies* 10, 1 (1972): 1–18.

Rudebeck, Lars, Olle Törnquist, and Virgilio Rojas, eds. *Democratization in the Third World: Concrete Cases in Comparative and Theoretical Perspective*. New York: Palgrave Macmillan, 1998.

Russell, Meg. "What Are Second Chambers For?" *Parliamentary Affairs* 54, 3 (July 2001): 442–58.

Ryan, Curtis R., and Jillian Schwedler. "Return to Democratization or New Hybrid Regime? The 2003 Elections in Jordan." *Middle East Policy* 11, 2 (Summer 2004): 138–51.

Ryan, Selwyn D. *Deadlock: Ethnicity and Electoral Competition in Trinidad and Tobago, 1995–2002*. Mona, Jamaica: Sir Arthur Lewis Institute of Social and Economic Studies, 2003.

Ryan, Selwyn D. *Revolution and Reaction: A Study of Parties and Politics in Trinidad and Tobago, 1970–1981*. Mona, Jamaica: Institute of Social and Economic Research, University of the West Indies, 1989.

Ryssdal, Rolv. "The Relation between the Judiciary and the Legislative and Executive Branches of the Government of Norway." *North Dakota Law Review* 57 (1981): 527–39.

Saalfeld, Thomas. "Members of Parliament and Governments in Western Europe: Agency Relations and Problems of Oversight." *European Journal of Political Research* 37, 3 (May 2000): 353–76.

Sachs, Albie. "Constitutional Developments in South Africa." *New York University Journal of International Law and Politics* 28 (Summer 1996): 695–709.

Saiegh, Sebastian M. "Government Defeat: Coalitions, Responsiveness, and Legislative Success." Ph.D. dissertation, New York University, 2004.

Saif, Ahmed A. *A Legislature in Transition: The Yemeni Parliament*. Aldershot, U.K.: Ashgate, 2001.

Saine, Abdoulaye. "Post-Coup Politics in The Gambia." *Journal of Democracy* 13, 4 (October 2002): 167–72.

Sajó, András. *Limiting Government: An Introduction to Constitutionalism*. Budapest: Central European Press, 1999.

Sajó, András. "Reading the Invisible Constitution: Judicial Review in Hungary." *Oxford Journal of Legal Studies* 15, 2 (Summer 1995): 253–67.

Salih, M. A. Mohamed, ed. *African Parliaments: Between Governance and Government*. New York: Palgrave Macmillan, 2005.

Salzberger, Eli M., and Stefan Voigt. "On Constitutional Processes and the Delegation of Power, with Special Emphasis on Israel and Central and Eastern Europe." *Theoretical Inquiries in Law* 3 (January 2002): 207–63.

Samatar, Abdi Ismail. *An African Miracle*. Portsmouth, NH: Heinemann, 1999.

Samatar, Abdi Ismail, and Ahmed I. Samatar. *The African State: Reconsiderations*. Portsmouth, NH: Heinemann, 2002.

Samuels, David. "Ambition and Competition: Explaining Legislative Turnover in Brazil." *Legislative Studies Quarterly* 25, 3 (August 2000): 481–97.

Samuels, David. *Ambition, Federalism, and Legislative Politics in Brazil*. Cambridge: Cambridge University Press, 2003.

Samuels, David. "Presidentialized Parties: The Separation of Powers and Party Organization Behavior." *Comparative Political Studies* 35, 4 (May 2002): 461–86.

Samuels, Richard J. "Leadership and Political Change in Japan: The Case of the Second Rincho." *Journal of Japanese Studies* 29, 1 (Winter 2003): 1–31.

Sanchez-Moreno, Maria McFarland. "When a 'Constitution' Is a Constitution: Focus on Peru." *New York University Journal of International Law and Politics* 33 (Winter 2001): 561–616.

Santiso, Carlos, and Augustin Loada. "Explaining the Unexpected: Electoral Reform and Democratic Governance in Burkina Faso." *Journal of Modern African Studies* 41, 3 (September 2003): 395–419.

Sartori, Giovanni. *Comparative Constitutional Engineering: In Inquiry into Structures, Incentive and Outcomes*. London: Macmillan, 1997.

Savoie, Donald J. "The Rise of Court Government in Canada." *Canadian Journal of Political Science* 32, 4 (December 1999): 635–64.

Saxer, Carl J. "Generals and Presidents: Establishing Civilian and Democratic Control in South Korea." *Armed Forces and Society* 30, 3 (Spring 2004): 383–408.

Schamis, Hector E. "Argentina: Crisis and Democratic Consolidation." *Journal of Democracy* 13, 2 (April 2002): 81–94.

Schedler, Andreas, Larry Diamond, and Marc F. Plattner, eds. *The Self-Restraining State: Power and Accountability in New Democracies*. Boulder, CO: Lynne Rienner, 1999.

Schickler, Eric. *Disjointed Pluralism: Institutional Innovation and the Development of the U.S. Congress*. Princeton, NJ: Princeton University Press, 2001.

Schickler, Eric. "Institutional Change in the House of Representatives, 1867–1998: A Test of Partisan and Ideological Power Balance Models." *American Political Science Review* 94, 2 (June 2000): 269–88.

Schickler, Eric, Eric McGhee, and John Sides. "Remaking the House and Senate: Personal Power, Ideology, and the 1970s Reforms." *Legislative Studies Quarterly* 28, 3 (August 2003): 297–331.

Schmidt, Vivien Ann. *Democratizing France*. Cambridge: Cambridge University Press, 1991.

Schmidt, Vivien Ann. "Unblocking Society by Decree: The Impact of Governmental Decentralization in France." *Comparative Politics* 22, 4 (July 1990): 459–81.

Schneider, Gerald, Patricia A. Weitsman, and Thomas Bernauer, eds. *Towards a New Europe: Stops and Starts in Regional Integration*. Westport, CT: Praeger, 1995.

Schraeder, Peter J. *African Politics and Society: A Mosaic of Transformation*. Boston: Bedford/St. Martin's, 2003.

Schrire, Robert. "The President and the Executive." *Journal of Theoretical Politics* 8, 2 (April 1996): 159–75.

Schubert, Gunter. "Constitutional Politics in the Republic of China: The Rise of the Legislative Yuan." *Issues and Studies* 28, 3 (March 1992): 21–37.

Schwedler, Jillian. *Faith in Moderation: Islamist Parties in Jordan and Yemen*. New York: Cambridge University Press, 2006.

Schwedler, Jillian. "Yemen's Aborted Opening." *Journal of Democracy* 13, 4 (October 2002): 48–55.

Scott, Rena L. "Moving from Impunity to Accountability in Post-War Liberia: Possibilities, Cautions, and Challenges." *International Journal of Legal Information* 33 (Winter 2005): 345–417.

Shaffer, William R. *Politics, Parties, and Parliaments: Political Change in Norway*. Columbus: Ohio State University Press, 1998.

Shah, Aqil. "Democracy on Hold in Pakistan." *Journal of Democracy* 13, 1 (January 2002): 67–75.

Shapiro, Martin. "Judicial Delegation Doctrines: The United States, Britain, and France." *West European Politics* 25, 1 (January 2002): 173–99.

Sharif, Abdu H. "Weak Institutions and Democracy: The Case of the Yemeni Parliament, 1993–97." *Middle East Policy* 9, 1 (March 2002): 82–93.

Sharlet, Robert. "The Politics of Constitutional Amendment in Russia." *Post-Soviet Affairs* 13, 3 (July–September 1997): 197–227.

Sharlet, Robert. "Putin and the Politics of Law in Russia." *Post-Soviet Affairs* 17, 3 (July–September 2001): 195–234.

Sharlet, Robert. "Russian Constitutional Crisis: Law and Politics under Yeltsin." *Post-Soviet Affairs* 9, 4 (October–December 1993): 314–36.

Shaxson, Nicholas. "New Approaches to Volatility: Dealing with the 'Resource Curse' in Sub-Saharan Africa." *International Affairs* 81, 2 (March 2005): 311–24.

Shehadi, Nadim, and Dana Haffar-Mills, eds. *Lebanon: A History of Conflict*. London: I. B. Tauris, 1993.

Shevchenko, Iulia, and Grigorii V. Golosov. "Legislative Activism of Russian Duma Deputies, 1996–1999." *Europe-Asia Studies* 53, 2 (March 2001): 239–61.

Shinn, David H., and Thomas P. Ofcansky. *Historical Dictionary of Ethiopia*. Lanham, MD: Scarecrow Press, 2004.

Shipan, Charles R. *Designing Judicial Review: Interest Groups, Congress, and Communications Policy*. Ann Arbor: University of Michigan Press, 2000.

Shipan, Charles R. "The Legislative Design of Judicial Review: A Formal Analysis." *Journal of Theoretical Politics* 12, 3 (July 2000): 269–304.

Shipan, Charles R. "Regulatory Regimes, Agency Actions, and the Conditional Nature of Congressional Influence." *American Political Science Review* 98, 3 (August 2004): 467–80.

Shugart, Matthew Soberg. "The Inverse Relationship between Party Strength and Executive Strength: A Theory of Politicians' Constitutional Choices." *British Journal of Political Science* 28, 1 (January 1998): 1–29.

Shugart, Matthew Soberg, and John M. Carey. *Presidents and Assemblies: Constitutional Design and Electoral Dynamics*. Cambridge: Cambridge University Press, 1992.

Siaroff, Alan. "Comparative Presidencies: The Inadequacy of the Presidential, Semi-Presidential, and Parliamentary Distinction." *European Journal of Political Research* 42, 3 (May 2003): 287–312.

Siaroff, Alan. "Varieties of Parliamentarism in the Advanced Industrial Democracies." *International Political Science Review* 24, 4 (October 2003): 445–64.

Siavelis, Peter M. "Disconnected Fire Alarms and Ineffective Police Patrols: Legislative Oversight in Postauthoritarian Chile." *Journal of Interamerican Studies and World Affairs* 42, 1 (Spring 2000): 71–90.

Siavelis, Peter M. "Electoral System, Coalitional Disintegration, and the Future of Chile's Concertacion." *Latin American Research Review* 40, 1 (2005): 56–82.

Sieder, Rachel, ed. *Central America: Fragile Transition*. New York: Palgrave Macmillan, 1996.

Sieder, Rachel, ed. *Guatemala after the Peace Accords*. London: Institute of Latin American Studies, 1999.

Sieder, Rachel. "Honduras: The Politics of Exception and Military Reformism." *Journal of Latin American Studies* 27, 1 (February 1995): 99–127.

Sieder, Rachel, Alan Angell, and Line Schjolden, eds. *The Judicialization of Politics in Latin America*. New York: Palgrave Macmillan, 2005.

Sinclair, Barbara. *Legislators, Leaders, and Lawmaking: The U.S. House of Representatives in the Postreform Era*. Baltimore, MD: Johns Hopkins University Press, 1998.

Singh, Chandra Pal. "A Century of Constituency Delimitation in India." *Political Geography* 19, 4 (May 2000): 517–32.

Skjæveland, Asbjørn. "A Danish Party Cohesion Cycle." *Scandinavian Political Studies* 22, 2 (June 1999): 121–36.

Sklar, Richard L. *African Politics in Postimperial Times: The Essays of Richard L. Sklar*. Edited by Toyin Falola. Trenton, NJ: Africa World Press, 2001.

Sklar, Richard L. "Developmental Democracy." *Comparative Studies in Society and History* 29, 4 (October 1987): 686–714.

Smith, Benjamin B. "Life of the Party: The Origins of Regime Breakdown and Persistence under Single-Party Rule." *World Politics* 57, 3 (April 2005): 421–51.

Smith, Geoffrey, and Nelson W. Polsby. *British Government and Its Discontents*. New York: Basic Books, 1981.

Smith, Nicola Jo-Anne. *Showcasing Globalisation? The Political Economy of the Irish Republic*. Manchester, U.K.: Manchester University Press, 2006.

Smith, Peter H. *Democracy in Latin America: Political Change in Comparative Perspective*. New York: Oxford University Press, 2005.

Smith, Steven S., and Thomas F. Remington. *The Politics of Institutional Choice: The Formation of the Russian State Duma*. Princeton, NJ: Princeton University Press, 2001.

Smyth, Regina. "Building State Capacity from the Inside Out: Parties of Power and the Success of the President's Reform Agenda in Russia." *Politics and Society* 30, 4 (December 2002): 555–78.

Soe, Christian. *Comparative Politics*. New York: McGraw-Hill/Dushkin, 2005.

Solonari, Vladimir. "Narrative, Identity, State: History Teaching in Moldova." *East European Politics and Societies* 16, 2 (Spring 2002): 414–45.

Southall, Roger. "The Centralization and Fragmentation of South Africa's Dominant Party System." *African Affairs* 97 (389) (October 1998): 443–69.

Southall, Roger, ed. *Opposition and Democracy in South Africa*. London: Frank Cass, 2001.

Southall, Roger. "An Unlikely Success: South Africa and Lesotho's Election of 2002." *Journal of Modern African Studies* 41, 2 (June 2003): 269–96.

Southall, Roger, and Roddy Fox. "Lesotho's General Election of 1998: Rigged or Rigeur?" *Journal of Modern African Studies* 37, 4 (December 1999): 669–96.

Southall, Roger, and Henning Melber, eds. *Legacies of Power: Leadership Change and Former Presidents in African Politics*. Pretoria: Human Sciences Research Council, 2006.

Spasov, Georgi. "An Overview of the New Bulgarian Constitution." *Austrian Journal of Public and International Law* 44 (1992–3): 177–86.

Squire, Peverill. "Membership Turnover and the Efficient Processing of Legislation." *Legislative Studies Quarterly* 23, 1 (February 1998): 23–32.

Ssekandi, Francis M., and Cos Gitta. "Protection of Fundamental Rights in the Uganda Constitution." *Columbia Human Rights Law Review* 26 (Fall 1994): 191–213.

Stanley, William. *The Protection Racket State: Elite Politics, Military Extortion, and Civil War in El Salvador*. Philadelphia, PA: Temple University Press, 1996.

Stavrakis, Peter J. "Russia after the Elections: Democracy or Parliamentary Byzantium?" *Problems of Post-Communism* 43, 2 (March–April 1996): 13–20.

Stawrowski, Zbigniew. "The Constitutional Debate in Poland after 1989." In Marek Jan Chodakiewicz, John Radziłowski, and Dariusz Tołczyk, eds., *Poland's Transformation: A Work in Progress*. Charlottesville, VA: Leopolis Press, 2003: 77–88.

Stepan, Alfred, and Cindy Skach. "Constitutional Frameworks and Democratic Consolidation: Parliamentarianism versus Presidentialism." *World Politics* 46, 1 (October 1993): 1–22.

St. John, Ronald Bruce. *Libya and the United States: Two Centuries of Strife*. Philadelphia: University of Pennsylvania Press, 2002.

Stone, Bruce. "Bicameralism and Democracy: The Transformation of Australian State Upper Houses." *Australian Journal of Political Science* 37, 2 (July 2002): 267–81.

Stone, Bruce. "Changing Roles, Changing Rules: Procedural Development and Difference in Australian State Upper Houses." *Australian Journal of Political Science* 40, 1 (March 2005): 33–50.

Stone, Bruce. "Size and Executive-Legislative Relations in Australian Parliaments." *Australian Journal of Political Science* 33, 1 (March 1998): 37–55.

Stone-Sweet, Alec. "Constitutional Courts and Parliamentary Democracy." *West European Politics* 25, 1 (January 2002): 77–100.

Strøm, Kaare, Wolfgang C. Müller, and Torbjörn Bergman. *Delegation and Accountability in Parliamentary Democracies*. New York: Oxford University Press, 2004.

Strøm, Kaare, and Lars Svåsand, eds. *Challenges to Political Parties: The Case of Norway*. Ann Arbor: University of Michigan Press, 1997.

Suberu, R. T. "Can Nigeria's New Democracy Survive?" *Current History* 100, 646 (May 2001): 207–12.

Suksamran, Somboon. *Military Elite in Thai Politics: Brief Biographical Data on the Officers in the Thai Legislature*. Singapore: Institute for Southeast Asian Studies, 1984.

Swyngedouw, Marc. "The General Election in Belgium, May 2003." *Electoral Studies* 23, 3 (September 2004): 566–71.

Taagepera, Rein. "How Electoral Systems Matter for Democratization." *Democratization* 5, 3 (Autumn 1998): 68–91.

Taagepera, Rein, and Matthew Soberg Shugart. *Seats and Votes: The Effects and Determinants of Electoral Systems*. New Haven, CT: Yale University Press, 1989.

Takahashi, Kazuyuki. "Contemporary Democracy in a Parliamentary System." *Law and Contemporary Problems* 53, 1 (Winter 1990): 105–22.

Tan, Alexander C., Karl Ho, Kyung-Tae Kang, and Tsung-Chi Yu. "What If We Don't Party? Political Partisanship in Taiwan and Korea in the 1990s." *Journal of Asian and African Studies* 35, 1 (February 2000): 67–84.

Tan, Alexander C., and Jun-deh Wu. "The Presidential Election in Taiwan, March 2004." *Electoral Studies* 24, 3 (September 2005): 519–24.

Tan, Ern Ser. *Employing Organizations and the Dynamics of Social Mobility in Singapore*. Singapore: National University of Singapore, 1988.

Tan, Kevin. *The Singapore Legal System*. Singapore: Singapore University Press, 1999.

Tangri, Roger, and Andrew Mwenda. "Corruption and Cronyism in Uganda's Privatization in the 1990s." *African Affairs* 100, 398 (January 2001): 117–33.

Tanner, Murray Scot. *The Politics of Lawmaking in Post-Mao China: Institutions, Processes, and Democratic Prospects*. Oxford: Oxford University Press, 1999.

Tanner, Murray Scot, and Chen Ke. "Breaking the Vicious Cycles: The Emergence of China's National People's Congress." *Problems of Post-Communism* 45, 3 (May–June 1998): 29–47.

Taylor-Robinson, Michelle M., and Christopher Diaz. "Who Gets Legislation Passed in a Marginal Legislature and Is the Label *Marginal Legislature* Still Appropriate? A Study of the Honduran Congress." *Comparative Political Studies* 32, 5 (August 1999): 589–625.

Tessler, Mark, Carrie Konold, and Megan Reif. "Political Generations in Developing Countries: Evidence and Insights from Algeria." *Public Opinion Quarterly* 68, 2 (Summer 2004): 184–216.

Thapa, Deepak, and Bandita Sijapati. *A Kingdom under Siege: Nepal's Maoist Insurgency, 1996 to 2004*. London: Zed, 2005.

Thio, Li-ann. "Beyond the 'Four Walls' in an Age of Transnational Judicial Conversations: Civil Liberties, Rights Theories, and Constitutional Adjudication in Malaysia and Singapore." *Columbia Journal of Asian Law* 19 (Spring 2006): 428–518.

Thio, Li-ann. "Lex Rex or Rex Lex? Competing Conceptions of the Rule of Law in Singapore." *UCLA Pacific Basin Law Journal* 20 (Fall 2002): 1–76.

Thio, Li-ann. *Managing Babel: The International Legal Protection of Minorities in the Twentieth Century*. Leiden, the Netherlands: Martinus Nijhoff, 2005.

Thio, Li-ann. "The Right to Political Participation in Singapore: Tailor-Making a Westminster-Modelled Constitution to Fit the Imperatives of 'Asian' Democracy." *Singapore Journal of International and Comparative Law* 6 (2002): 181–243.

Thomas, Melissa A., and Oumar Sissokho. "Liaison Legislature: The Role of the National Assembly in Senegal." *Journal of Modern African Studies* 43, 1 (March 2005): 97–117.

Thompson, Leonard. *A History of South Africa*. New Haven, CT: Yale University Press, 1996.

Tien, Hung-mao, and Tun-jen Cheng. "Crafting Democratic Institutions in Taiwan." *China Journal* 37 (January 1997): 1–27.

Tikhinya, Valery. "The Legitimate Legislative Branch of the Republic of Belarus." *Parker School Journal of East European Law* 4, 3 (1997): 363–8.

Tostensen, Arne. "Election Observation as an Informal Means of Enforcing Political Rights." *Nordic Journal of Human Rights* 22, 3 (2004): 330–44.

Toulabor, Comi M. "Violence militaire, démocratisation et ethnicité au Togo." *Autrepart* 10 (1999): 105–15.

Treschsel, Alexander H., and Pascal Sciarini. "Direct Democracy in Switzerland: Do Elites Matter?" *European Journal of Political Research* 33, 1 (January 1998): 99–124.

Tripp, Aili Mari. "The Changing Face of Authoritarianism in Africa: The Case of Uganda." *Africa Today* 50, 3 (Spring 2004): 3–26.

Troxel, Tiffany A. *Parliamentary Power in Russia, 1994–2001: A New Era*. New York: Palgrave Macmillan, 2003.

Tsebelis, George. "Presidential Conditional Agenda Setting in Latin America." *World Politics* 57, 3 (April 2005): 396–420.

Tsebelis, George. *Veto Players: How Political Institutions Work*. Princeton, NJ: Princeton University Press, 2002.

Tsebelis, George, and Amie Kreppel. "The History of Conditional Agenda-Setting in European Institutions." *European Journal of Political Research* 33, 1 (January 1998): 41–71.

Tsebelis, George, and Jeanette Money. *Bicameralism*. New York: Cambridge University Press, 1997.

Tully, James. *Strange Multiplicities: Constitutionalism in an Age of Diversity*. Cambridge: Cambridge University Press, 1995.

Udagama, Deepika. "Taming of the Beast: Judicial Responses to State Violence in Sri Lanka." *Harvard Human Rights Journal* 11 (Spring 1998): 269–94.

Ugalde, Luis Carlos. *The Mexican Congress: Old Player, New Power*. Washington, DC: Center for Strategic and International Studies, 2000.

Uhr, John. *Deliberative Democracy in Australia: The Changing Place of Parliament*. Cambridge: Cambridge University Press, 1998.

Uitz, Renata. *Constitutions, Courts and History: Historical Narratives in Constitutional Adjudication*. Budapest: Central European University Press, 2005.

Uyangoda, Jayadeva. "Ethnic Conflict, Ethnic Imagination and Democratic Alternatives from Sri Lanka." *Futures* 37, 9 (November 2005): 959–88.

Valentinavicius, Virgis. "Lithuania: A Fragile Democracy on the Road to the West." *East European Constitutional Review* 11, 4–12, 1 (Fall 2002/Winter 2003): 111–15.

Vanberg, Georg. "Abstract Judicial Review, Legislative Bargaining, and Policy Compromise." *Journal of Theoretical Politics* 10, 3 (July 1998): 299–326.

Van Cott, Donna Lee. "Institutional Change and Ethnic Parties in South America." *Latin American Politics and Society* 45, 2 (Summer 2003): 1–39.

Vandewalle, Dirk. *Libya since Independence: Oil and State Building*. Ithaca, NY: Cornell University Press, 1998.

van de Walle, Nicolas. "Presidentialism and Clientelism in Africa's Emerging Party Systems." *Journal of Modern African Studies* 41, 2 (June 2003): 297–321.

van Koppen, Peter J. "The Dutch Supreme Court and Parliament: Political Decionmaking versus Nonpolitical Appointments." *Law and Society Review* 24, 3 (1990): 745–80.

Vengroff, Richard. "The Impact of Electoral System on the Transition to Democracy in Africa: The Case of Mali." *Electoral Studies* 13, 1 (March 1994): 29–37.

Venter, Denis. "Democracy and Multiparty Politics in Africa: Recent Elections in Zambia, Zimbabwe, and Lesotho." *Eastern Africa Social Science Research Review* 19, 1 (January 2003): 1–39.

Villalón, Leonardo, and Peter VonDoepp, eds. *The Fate of Africa's Democratic Experiments: Elites and Institutions*. Bloomington: Indiana University Press, 2005.

Villa-Vicencio, Charles. "Whither South Africa? Constitutionalism and Law-Making." *Emory Law Journal* 40 (Winter 1991): 141–62.

Vogel, Steven K. *Freer Markets, More Rules: Regulatory Reform in Advanced Industrial Countries*. Ithaca, NY: Cornell University Press, 1998.

von Beyme, Klaus. *The Legislator: German Parliament as a Centre of Political Decision-Making*. Aldershot, U.K.: Ashgate, 1998.

von Beyme, Klaus. *Parliamentary Democracy: Democratization, Destabilization, Reconsolidation 1789–1999.* Basingstoke, U.K.: Macmillan, 2000.

Vu, Tuong. "Workers and the Socialist State." *Communist and Post-Communist Studies* 38, 3 (September 2005): 329–56.

Walker, Edward W. "The New Russian Constitution and the Future of the Russian Federation." *Harriman Institute Forum* 5, 10 (June 1992).

Walker, Edward W. "Politics of Blame and Presidential Powers in Russia's New Constitution." *East European Constitutional Review* 2, 4 (Fall 1993/Winter 1994): 116–19.

Wang, T. Y., and I-Chou Liu. "Contending Identities in Taiwan: Implications for Cross-Strait Relations." *Asian Survey* 44, 4 (July–August 2004): 568–90.

Wantchekon, Leonard. "Clientelism and Voting Behavior: Evidence from a Field Experiment in Benin." *World Politics* 55, 3 (April 2003): 399–422.

Warhurt, John, and Malcolm Mackerras, eds. *Constitutional Politics.* Brisbane, Australia: University of Queensland Press, 2003.

Waugh, Colin M. *Paul Kagame and Rwanda: Power, Genocide, and the Rwandan Patriotic Front.* Jefferson, NC: McFarland, 2004.

Way, Lucan A. "Authoritarian State Building and the Sources of Regime Competitiveness in the Fourth Wave: The Cases of Belarus, Moldova, Russia, and Ukraine." *World Politics* 57, 2 (January 2005): 231–61.

Way, Lucan A. "Kuchma's Failed Authoritarianism." *Journal of Democracy* 16, 2 (April 2005): 131–45.

Way, Lucan A. "Rapacious Individualism and Political Competition in Ukraine, 1992–2004." *Communist and Post-Communist Studies* 38, 2 (June 2005): 191–205.

Way, Lucan A. "Weak States and Pluralism: The Case of Moldova." *East European Politics and Societies* 17, 3 (Summer 2003): 454–82.

Weaver, R. Kent, and Bert A. Rockman, eds. *Do Institutions Matter? Government Capabilities in the United States and Abroad.* Washington, DC: Brookings Institution Press, 1993.

Weber, Max. "Parliament and Government in a Reconstructed Germany." In Max Weber, *Economy and Society,* vol. 2. Berkeley: University of California Press, 1978: 1381–1469.

Wegemund, Regina. *Politisierte Ethnizität in Mauretanien und Senegal.* Hamburg: Institut für Afrika-Kunde, 1991.

Wehner, Joachim. "Budget Reform and Legislative Control in Sweden." *Journal of European Public Policy* 14, 2 (March 2007): 313–32.

Wehner, Joachim. "Parliament and the Power of the Purse: The Nigerian Constitution of 1999 in Comparative Perspective." *Journal of African Law* 46, 2 (2002): 216–31.

Weinrib, Lorraine Eisenstat. "Canada's Constitutional Revolution: From Legislative to Constitutional State." *Israel Law Review* 33, 1 (Winter 1999): 13–42.

Weinstein, Martin. *Uruguay: Democracy at the Crossroads.* Boulder, CO: Westview, 1988.

Weisman, Amy J. "Separation of Powers in Post-Communist Government: A Constitutional Case Study of the Russian Federation." *American University Journal of International Law and Policy* 10 (Summer 1995): 1365–98.

Weyland, Kurt. *The Politics of Market Reform in Fragile Democracies: Argentina, Brazil, Peru, and Venezuela.* Princeton, NJ: Princeton University Press, 2002.

White, Stephen. "Russia: Presidential Leadership under Yeltsin." In Ray Taras, ed., *Postcommunist Presidents.* Cambridge: Cambridge University Press, 1997: 38–66.

Whitmore, Sarah. *State Building in Ukraine: The Ukrainian Parliament, 1990–2003.* New York: RoutledgeCurzon, 2004.

Wiatr, Jerzy J. "Poland's Three Parliaments in the Era of Transition, 1989–1995." *International Political Science Review* 18, 4 (October 1997): 443–50.

Wibbels, Erik. *Federalism and the Market: Intergovernmental Conflict and Economic Reform in the Developing World.* New York: Cambridge University Press, 2005.

Williams, F. R. A. "Fundamental Rights and the Prospect for Democracy in Nigeria." *University of Pennsylvania Law Review* 115 (1966–7): 1073–90.

Wilson, Bruce M. *Costa Rica: Politics, Economics, and Democracy.* Boulder, CO: Lynne Rienner, 1998.

Wing, Susanna. "Questioning the State: Constitutionalism and the Malian *Éspace d'interpellation démocratique.*" *Democratization* 9, 2 (Summer 2002): 121–47.

Winterton, George. *Monarchy to Republic: Australian Republican Government.* Melbourne, Australia: Oxford University Press, 1994.

Wise, Michael B. "Nicaragua: Judicial Independence in a Time of Transition." *Willamette Law Review* 30 (Summer 1994): 519–79.

Wittenberg, Jason. *Crucibles of Political Loyalty: Church Institutions and Electoral Continuity in Hungary.* New York: Cambridge University Press, 2006.

Wolfinger, Raymond E. *Dynamics of American Politics.* Englewood Cliffs, NJ: Prentice-Hall, 1976.

Wolfinger, Raymond E., and Steven J. Rosenstone. *Who Votes?* New Haven, CT: Yale University Press, 1980.

Wolpe, Howard, and Steve McDonald. "Burundi's Transition: Training Leaders for Peace." *Journal of Democracy* 17, 1 (January 2006): 132–8.

Wu, Yu-Shan. "Comparing Third-Wave Democracies: East Central Europe and the ROC." *Issues and Studies* 37, 4 (July–August 2001): 1–37.

Wu, Yu-Shan. "The ROC's Semi-Presidentialism at Work: Unstable Compromise, Not Cohabitation."

Issues and Studies 36, 5 (September–October 2000): 1–40.

Wu, Yu-Shan. "Taiwan in 2000: Managing the Aftershocks from Power Transfer." *Asian Survey* 41, 1 (January–February 2001): 40–8.

Yacoubian, Mona. *Algeria's Struggle for Democracy.* New York: Council on Foreign Relations Press, 1997.

Yang, Dali L. *Calamity and Reform in China: State, Rural Society, and Institutional Change since the Great Leap Famine.* Stanford, CA: Stanford University Press, 1996.

Yang, Dali L. *Remaking the Chinese Leviathan: Market Transition and the Politics of Governance in China.* Stanford, CA: Stanford University Press, 2004.

Yates, Douglas A. *The Rentier State in Africa: Oil Rent Dependency and Neocolonialism in the Republic of Gabon.* Trenton, NJ: Africa World Press, 1996.

Yoon, Dae-Kyu. "The Constitution of North Korea: Its Changes and Implications." *Fordham International Law Journal* 27 (April 2004): 1289–1305.

Young, Crawford. *Ideology and Development in Africa.* New Haven, CT: Yale University Press, 1982.

Young, Crawford, and Thomas Turner. *The Rise and Decline of the Zairian State.* Madison: University of Wisconsin Press, 1985.

Zewde, Bahru, and Siegfried Pausewang, eds. *Ethiopia: The Challenge of Democracy from Below.* Somerset, NJ: Transaction, 2003.

Ziegler, J. Nicholas. *Governing Ideas: Strategies for Innovation in France and Germany.* Ithaca, NY: Cornell University Press, 2003.

Zielinski, Jakub. "The Polish Transition to Democracy: A Game-Theoretic Approach." *Archives européennes de sociologie* 36, 1 (1995): 135–58.

Zuckerman, Alan S. "New Approaches to Political Cleavage." *Comparative Political Studies* 15, 2 (1982): 131–44.

Zuckerman, Alan S. *The Politics of Faction: Christian Democratic Rule in Italy.* New Haven, CT: Yale University Press, 1979.

Zuckerman, Alan S., Michal Shamir, and Hanna Herzog. "The Political Bases of Activism in the Israeli Labor and Herut Parties." *Political Science Quarterly* 107, 2 (Summer 1992): 303–23.

INDEX

CPSIA information can be obtained at www.ICGtesting.com
Printed in the USA
267745BV00003B/2/P